POLISH
ENGLISH-POLISH
DICTIONARY

by

Iwo Cyprian Pogonowski

COMPLETE PHONETICS
POGONOWSKI'S SIMPLIFIED
PHONETIC NOTATION

HIPPOCRENE BOOKS
New York

Copyright© 1993, 1991, 1983, 1979
by Iwo Cyprian Pogonowski.
Fourth edition, Third printing, 1994.

For information, address:
HIPPOCRENE BOOKS, INC.
171 Madison Avenue
New York, NY 10016

Library of Congress Cataloging in Publication Data
Pogonowski, Iwo Cyprian, 1921-
  Dictionary, Polish-English, English-Polish
  1. Polish language-Dictionaries-English.
  2. English language-Dictionaries-Polish.
  I. Title
  PG6640.P54   491.8'5321   82-9211
                       AACR2
ISBN 0-7818-0085-4

Printed in the United States of America.

Contents

Also by Iwo Cyprian Pogonowski:

Jews in Poland: A Documentary History
0130   ISBN 0-7818-0116-8 $22.50 hc

Poland: A Historical Atlas
636   ISBN 0-7818-0117-6 $16.95 hc

**Polish-English/English-Polish Concise Dictionary
with Complete Phonetics**
0268   ISBN 0-7818-0133-8 $8.95 pb

Polish-English/English-Polish Standard Dictionary
0665   ISBN 0-87052-882-3 $22.50 hc

Polish-English/English-Polish Standard Dictionary
0207   ISBN 0-7818-0183-4 $16.95 pb

**Polish-English/English-Polish Standard Dictionary
Revised Edition (with Business Terms)**
298   ISBN 0-7818-0282-2 $18.95 pb

Polish Phrasebook and Dictionary
0192   ISBN 0-7818-0134-6 $9.95 pb

PRACTICAL

POLISH-ENGLISH

DICTIONARY

by

Iwo Cyprian Pogonowski

ABBREVIATIONS – SKRÓTY

a.	– attribute	– przydawka
adj.	– adjective	– przymiotnik
adj. f.	– adjective feminine	– przymiotnik żeński
adj. m.	– adjective masculine	– przymiotnik męski
adj. n.	– adjective neuter	– przymiotnik nijaki
adv.	– adverb	– przysłówek
am.	– American	– amerykański
chem.	– chemistry	– chemia
conj.	– conjunction	– spójnik
constr.	– construction	– budowa
etc.	– and so on	– i tak dalej
excl.	– exclamation	– wykrzyknik
expr.	– expression	– wyrażenie
f.	– substantive feminine	– rzeczownik żeński
gram.	– grammar	– gramatyka
hist.	– history	– historia
hyp.	– hyphen	– łącznik
indecl.	– indeclinable	– nieodmienny
inf.	– infinitive	– bezokolicznik
m.	– substantive musculine	– rzeczownik męski
m.in.	– among others	– między innymi
n.	– substantive neuter	– rzeczownik nijaki
num.	– numeral	– liczebnik
part.	– particle	– partykuła
pl.	– substantive plural	– rzeczownik liczba mnoga
poet.	– poetry	– poezja
polit.	– politics	– polityka
p.p.	– past participle	– imiesłów czasu przeszłego
prep.	– preposition	– przyimek
pron.	– pronoun	– zaimek
s.	– substantive	– rzeczownik
sb.	– somebody	– ktoś
slang	– slang	– gwara, żargon
v.	– verb	– czasownik
vulg.	– vulgarity	– ordynarność
wg	– according to	– według
W.W. II	– World War II	– druga wojna światowa
zob.	– see	– zobacz

A

a [a][as"a" in car] conj. and; or; but; then; at that time

a jakże! [a-yak-zhe] excl.: oh yes... ; yes indeed!

a to [a to] conj. and so

abażur [a-ba-zhoor] m. lamp shade; a device to screen light

abdykować [ab-di-ko-vaćh] v. abdicate, abdicate the throne

abecadło [a-be-tsa-dwo] n. A.B.C., alphabet; rudiment

abonament [a-bo-na-ment] m. subscription, season ticket

abonent [a-bo-nent] m. subscriber, holder of a season ticket; contract passenger

abonować [a-bo-no-vaćh] v. subscribe to a periodical etc.

absencja [ab-sen-tsya] f. absence, non-attendance

abstrakcja [ab-strak-tsya] f. abstraction; abstract

absurd [ab-soord] m. absurdity

aby [a-bi] conj. to; in order to, in order that, only to; that

ach! [akh] excl.: oh! ah!

aczkolwiek [ach-kol-vyek] conj. though; although, albeit

adapter [a-dap-ter] m. record player, adapter; pick-up

administracja [ad-mee-ńees-trats -ya] f. administration; (management); authorities

admirał [ad-mee-raw] m. admiral

adres [ad-res] m. address

adwokat [ad-vo-kat] m. lawyer

afera [a-fe-ra] f. swindle

aferzysta [a-fe-zhis-ta] m. swindler; confidence man

afisz [a-feesh] m. poster

afiszować [a-fee-sho-vaćh] v. advertise; flaunt; parade

agrafka [a-graf-ka] f. safety pin; hist.: buckle; brooch

agrest [ag-rest] m. gooseberry

aha! [akh-a!] excl.: oh yes...

akacja [a-kats-ya] f. acacia; locust tree; locust shrub

akcja [a-ktsya] f. action; share; plot; campaign; operation

AK [a-ka] f. Polish Home Army (W.W.II) (Armia Krajowa)

akowiec [a-kov-yets] m. soldier of the Polish Home Army (World War II)

aksamit [ak-sa-meet] m. velvet

akt kupna [akt koop-na] f. purchase deed; deed

akta [ak-ta] pl. documents; deeds; dossier; files; records

aktualny [ak-too-al-ni] m. timely; current; up to date; topical

akumulator [a-koo-moo-la-tor] m. battery; storage battery

akuszerka [a-koo-sher-ka] f. midwife; accoucheuse

akwarela [ak-va-re-la] f. a watercolor; painting in (with) watercolors; the watercolors

albo [a-lbo] conj. or; else

albowiem [al-bo-vyem] conj. for; as; since; because; on account of

ale [a-le] conj. however; but; still; yet; not at all; n. defect

aleja [a-le-ya] f. avenue; alley

ależ [a-lesh] conj. why (yes)

alfa [al-fa] f. alpha

alfabet [al-fa-bet] m. alphabet

alfons [al-fons] m. pimp; cadet

alimenty [a-lee-men-ti] pl. alimony for separated wife

alkohol [al-ko-khol] m. alcohol

alpejski [al-pey-skee] adj. m. Alpine; of the Alps

aluzja [a-looz-ya] f. hint; allusion; insinuation; dig

ałun [a-woon] m. alum

amant [a-mant] m. lover; beau

ambasada [am-ba-sa-da] f. embassy; ambassador and his staff; the embassy building

ambicja [am-beets-ya] f. ambition; aspiration; self esteem

ambona [am-bo-na] f. pulpit

Amerykanin [A-me-ri-ka-ńeen] m. American; man native of America

Amerykanka [A-me-ri-kan-ka] f.
American; American woman
amerykański [a-me-ri-kań-skee]
adj. m. American; of America
amnestia [am-nest-ya] f.
amnesty; act of pardon
amortyzacja [a-mor-ti-zats-ya] f.
depreciation; amortization
amory [a-mo-ri] pl. flirtation;
courting; love affairs
amperomierz [am-pe-ro-myesh]
m. ammeter; meter of
amperes; amperometer
amputować [am-poo-to-vaćh]
v. amputate; to cut off
amunicja [a-moo-ńee-tsya] f.
ammunition; munitions
analfabeta [a-nal-fa-be-ta] m.
illiterate; an ignorant
analiza [a-na-lee-za] f. analysis;
parsing; analysis of a sentence
analogia [a-na-log-ya] f. analogy;
parallelism; parallel; parity
ananas [a-na-nas] m. pineapple;
rascal; rogue; blighter
andrus [an-droos] m. rough kid
andrut [an-droot] m. wafer
anegdota [a-neg-do-ta] f.
anecdote; story; theme
aneksja [a-neks-ya] f.
annexation; rape of a country
anemia [a-ne-mya] f. anemia
angażować [an-ga-zho-vaćh] v.
engage; undertake; hire; bind
angielski [an-gyel-skee] adj. m.
English; English language
ani [a-ńee] conj. neither; nor;
not; not even; not as much; or
anielski [a-ńel-skee] adj. m.
angelic; cherubic; angelical
animusz [a-ńee-moosh] m.
courage; verve; vigor; zest
anioł [a-ńow] m. angel
aniżeli [a-ńee-zhe-lee] part.
rather; then; rather then
ankieta [an-ke-ta] f. poll; inquiry;
questionnaire; survey form
anons [a-nons] m. advertisement
(in a newspaper); ad
antybiotyki [an-ti-bee-yo-ti-kee]
pl. antibiotics
antyk [an-tik] m. antique
aparat [a-pa-rat] m. apparatus;

appliance; camera; gadget;
device; mechanism; machinery
apartament [a-par-ta-ment] m.
residence; suite of rooms
apel [a-pel] m. appeal; muster;
roll-call; roll; parade
apetyt [a-pe-tit] m. appetite
apostolski [a-pos-tol-skee] adj.
m. apostolic; missionary
aprobować [a-pro-bo-vaćh] v.
approve; endorse; sanction
aprowizacja [a-pro-vee-zats-ya] f.
food supply; provisions
apteczka [ap-tech-ka] f. first aid
kit; medicine chest
apteka [ap-te-ka] f. pharmacy
arbuz [ar-boos] m. watermelon
architekt [ar-khee-tekt] m.
architect
arcydzieło [ar-tsi-dźhe-wo] n.
masterpiece
arena [a-re-na] f. arena; stage
areszt [a-resht] m. arrest; jail
argument [ar-goo-ment] m.
argument; reason; contention
arkusz [ar-koosh] m. sheet
armata [ar-ma-ta] f. cannon
armator [ar-ma-tor] m. ship
owner; skipper; charterer
armia [ar-mya] f. army; array
arogancja [a-ro-gan-tsya] f.
arrogance; insolence; conceit
arteria [ar-ter-ya] f. artery
artretyzm [ar-tre-tizm] m.
arthritis; gout
artykuł [ar-ti-koow] m. article
artyleria [ar-ti-ler-ya] f. artillery;
gunnery; ordnance
artysta [ar-ti-sta] m. artist
arytmetyka [a-rit-me-ti-ka] f.
arithmetic
as [as] m. ace; A flat
asceta [as-stse-ta] m. ascetic
asekuracja [a-se-koo-ra-tsya] f.
insurance; assurance
aspiryna [as-pee-ri-na] f. aspirin
astma [ast-ma] f. asthma
asygnata [a-sig-na-ta] f. order (of
payment, early check
asymilować [a-si-mee-lo-vaćh]
v. assimilate; absorb; liken
asystować [a-sis-to-vaćh] v.
accompany; attend; court;

assist; escort; wait upon

atak [a-tak] m. attack; charge (fit); spasm; offensive

atlas [at-las] m. atlas

atleta [at-le-ta] m. athlete

atłas [at-was] m. satin

atmosfera [at-mos-fe-ra] f. atmosphere; air; climate; tone

atol [a-tol] m. atoll

atom [a-tom] m. atom

atomowy [a-to-mo-vi] adj. m. atomic; nuclear

atrakcja [a-trak-tsya] f. attraction; high light

atrament [a-tra-ment] m. ink

atut [a-toot] m. trump

audycja [aw-dits-ya] f. broadcast; program; pop

aukcja [awk-tsya] f. auction

autentyczny [aw-ten-tich-ni] adj. m. authentic; genuine

auto [aw-to] n. motor car

autor [aw-tor] m. author

autostrada [aw-to-stra-da] f. superhighway; freeway

awans [a-vans] m. promotion; advancement; preferment

awantura [a-van-too-ra] f. brawl; fuss; row; scandal

azot [a-zot] m. nitrogen

aż [ash] part. as much; up to; till; until; as far as; down to

ażeby [a-zhe-bi] conj. that; in order that; so that; to

ażurowy [a-zhoo-ro-vi] adj. m. lace-like; transparent

B

ba [ba] excl.: hey?; nay; indeed...; and even; what more; or rather; of course

baba [ba-ba] f. woman (old, simple); grandmother; ram

babiarz [bab-yash] m. lady chaser; ladies' man

babie lato [ba-bye la-to] n. Indian Summer

babka [bab-ka] f. grandmother; lass; chick; cake; flat hammer

babrać [bab-raćh] v. smear; stain; dabble; soil; fumble

bachor [ba-khor] m. kid; brat

baczność [bach-nośhćh] f. attention; watchfulness; care

bać się [baćh śhan] v. fear

badacz [ba-dach] m. researcher

badać [ba-daćh] v. investigate; examine; research; explore

badyl [ba-dil] m. steam; weed

badylarz [ba-di-lash] m. marketing gardener (slang)

bagatela [ba-ga-te-la] f. trifle; easy matter; a mere trifle

bagaż [ba-gash] m. luggage

bagażowy [ba-ga-zho-vi] m. porter; adj. m. baggage-; luggage-

bagnet [bag-net] m. bayonet

bagno [bag-no] m. swamp; fen; morass; marsh; bog; quagmire

bajka [bay-ka] f. fairy-tale; gossip; scandal; story; fable

bajoro [ba-yo-ro] n. muddy pool

bak [bak] m. gasoline tank; can; pl. side-whiskers; sideburns

bakterie [bak-ter-ye] pl. bacteria; germs; microbes

bal [bal] m. ball; bale; log

balet [ba-let] m. ballet

balia [bal-ya] f. wash tub

balkon [bal-kon] m. balcony

balustrada [ba-loos-tra-da] f. railing; hand rail; guard rail

bałagan [ba-wa-gan] m. mess; disorder; disarray; confusion

bałamucić [ba-wa-moo-ćheećh] v. lead astray; loiter; flirt; coax; seek to seduce

bałwan [baw-van] m. snowman; ass; breaking wave crest; blockhead; fool; nitwit; fetish; idol; lump; block; snow-mass

banał [ba-naw] m. stoke phrase; tag; banality; truism; triviality

banan [ba-nan] m. banana

banda [ban-da] f. band; gang

bandaż [ban-dash] m. bandage

bandera [ban-de-ra] f. flag

bandyta [ban-di-ta] m. bandit

bank [bank] m. bank; pool

bankiet [ban-ket] m. banquet
banknot [bank-not] m. banknote
bankrut [bank-root] m. bankrupt
baptysta [bap-tis-ta] m. baptist
bar [bar] m. bar; barium
barak [ba-rak] m. barrack
baran [ba-ran] m. ram; tup; idiot
baraszkować [ba-rash-ko-vaćh]
  v.frolic; gambol; romp; caper
barbarzyńca [bar-ba-zhiń-tsa]
  m. barbarian; savage; vandal
barczysty [bar-chis-ti] m. broad
  -shouldered; square built
bardziej [bar-dźhey] adv. more;
  (emphatic "bardzo"); worse
bardzo [bar-dzo] adv. very
bariera [bar-ye-ra] f. rail; barrier;
  hand rail; obstacle; dike; dyke
barki [bar-kee] pl. shoulders
barłóg [bar-woog] m. litter bed
barman [bar-man] m. barman
barszcz [barshch] m. beet soup
barwa [bar-va] f. color; hue
bary [ba-ri] pl. large shoulders;
  broad shoulders; parallel bars
barykada [ba-ri-ka-da] f.
  barricade; barrier; obstacle
baryłka [ba-riw-ka] f. barrel
basen [ba-sen] m. pool; tank
bastard [bas-tard] m. bastard
baśń [baśhń] f. fable; myth
bat [bat] m. whip; lash
bateria [ba-ter-ya] f. battery
bawełna [ba-vew-na] f. cotton
bawialnia [ba-vyal-ńa] f. sitting
  room; parlor; drawing room
bawić [ba-veećh] v. amuse;
  entertain; recreate; stay
bawidamek [ba-vee-da-mek] m.
  ladies' man; gallant
bawół [ba-voow] m. buffalo
baza [ba-za] f. base; basis
bazgrać [baz-graćh] v. scribble;
  scrawl; scratch; daub; splotch
bażant [ba-zhant] m. pheasant
bąbel [bown-bel] m. blister
bądź [bownćh] v. be this; conj.
  either-or; anyhow at any rate
bąk [bownk] m. horse fly;
  blunder; vulg. fart
bąkać [bown-kaćh] v. mumble;
  hint; mutter; hum; allude
bebechy [be-be-khi] pl. guts

beczka [bech-ka] f. barrel
bednarz [bed-nash] m. cooper
befsztyk [bef-shtik] m. beefsteak (broiled or fried)
beksa [bek-sa] f. cry baby
beletrystyka [be-le-tris-ti-ka] f.
  fiction; belles-lettres
belka [bel-ka] f. beam; bar
bełkot [bew-kot] m. mumbling
benzyna [ben-zi-na] f. gasoline
berbeć [ber-bećh] m. small kid;
  toddler; brat; dot
berek [be-rek] m. tag play
beret [be-ret] m. beret; cap
bestia [bes-tya] f. beast
besztać [besh-taćh] v. scold;
  rebuke; chide; rebuke: trounce
beton [be-ton] m. concrete
bety [be-ti] pl. bedding
bez [bes] prep. without
bez [bes] m. lilac
bez- [bes] prefix = suffix less
beza [be-za] f. meringue
bezbarwny [bez-barw-ni] adj. m.
  colorless; plain; drab; dull
bezbłędny [bez-bwand-ni] adj. m.
  faultless; correct; perfect
bezbolesny [bez-bo-les-ni] m.
  painless; without pain
bezbronny [bez-bron-ni] adj. m.
  defenseless; helpless; unarmed
bezcelowy [bez-tse-lo-vi] adj. m.
  aimless; pointless; useless
bezcenny [bez-tsen-ni] adj. m.
  priceless; invaluable; inestimable; beyond price
bezchmurny [bez-khmoo-rni] adj.
  m. cloudless; serene; clear
bezdomny [bez-dom-ni] adj. m.
  homeless; houseless; m.
  homeless person; outcast
bezdzietny [bez-dźhet-ni] adj. m.
  childless; without offspring
bezdźwięczny [bez-dźhvanch-
  -ni] adj. m. soundless; voiceless; sounded with the breath
bezecny [be-zets-ni] adj. m.
  wicked; infamous; ignominious
bezgotówkowy [bez-go-toov-ko-
  -vi] adj. m. without cash
bezgrzeszny [bez-gzhesh-ni] adj.
  m. sinless; innocent; chaste
bezkonkurencyjny [bez-kon-koo-

-ren-tsiy-ni] adj. m. unrivaled
bezkrwawy [bez-krva-vi] adj. m.
bloodless; free of bloodshed
bezkształtny [bez-kshtawt-ni]
adj.m. shapeless; formless
bezład [bez-wat] m. disorder
bezmiar [bez-myar] m.
immensity; boundlessness; no
end of; vastness; host; swarm
bezmyślność [bez-miśhl-
-nośhćh] f. thoughtlessness;
wantonness; inconsideration
beznadziejny [bez-na-dźhey-ni]
adj. m. hopeless; desperate
bez ogródek [bez o-groo-dek]
adv. bluntly; unequivocally
bezokolicznik [bez-o-ko-leech-
-ńeek] m. infinitive (mood)
bezowocny [bez-o-vots-ni] m.
fruitless; vain; unsuccessful
bezpieczeństwo [bez-pye-cheń-
-stvo] m. security; safety
bezpłatnie [bez-pwat-ńe] adv.
free of charge; gratuitously
bezpłciowy [bez-pwćho-vi] adj.
m. sexless; neutral; insipid
bezpodstawny [bez-pod-stav-ni]
adj. m. groundless; baseless
bezpośrednio [bez-po-śhred-
-ńo] adv. directly; personally
bezprawny [bez-prav-ni] adj. m.
lawless; illegal; illicit
bezprzedmiotowy [bez-pshed-
-myo-to-vi] adj. m. aimless
bezprzykładny [bez-pshi-kwad-ni]
adj. m. unprecedented
bezradny [bez-rad-ni] adj. m.
helpless; baffled; at a loss
bezręki [bez-ran-kee] adj. m.
armless; handless (cripple)
bezrobotny [bez-ro-bo-tni] adj. m.
unemployed; out of work
bezrolny [bez-rol-ni] adj. m.
landless; with no land
bezsenny [bez-sen-ni] adj. m.
sleepless; restless; wakeful
bezsens [bez-sens] m. nonsense
bezsilny [bez-śheel-ni] adj. m.
powerless; weak; helpless
bezskuteczny [bez-skoo-tech-ni]
adj. m. to no avail; futile;
ineffective; nugatory
bezsporny [bez-spor-ni] adj. m.

incontestable; undebatable
bezsprzeczny [bez-spshech-ni]
adj. m. indisputable; evident
bezstronność [bez-stron-
-nośhćh] f. impartiality;
fairness; open-mindedness
beztroski [bez-tros-kee] adj. m.
carefree; careless; jaunty
bezustanny [bez-oos-tan-ni] adj.
m. ceaseless; endless
bezużyteczny [bez-oo-zhi-tech-ni]
adj. m. useless; idle
bezwartościowy [bez-var-tośh-
-ćho-vi] adj. m. worthless
bezwarunkowy [bez-va-roon-ko-
-vi] adj. m. unconditional; utter
bezwładność [bez-vwad-
-nośhćh] f. inertia; torpor;
decline; palsy; inertness
bezwstydny [bez-vstid-ni] adj. m.
shameless; lewd; flagrant
bezwyznaniowy [bez-viz-na-ńo-
-vi] adj. m. nonsectarian
bezwzględny [bez-vzgland-ni]
adj. m. ruthless; despotic
bezzębny [bez-zanb-ni] adj. m.
toothless; edentate
bezzwłoczny [bez-zvwoch-ni] adj.
m. immediate; prompt
bezzwrotny [bez-zvrot-ni] adj. m.
not to be refunded
beż [besh] m. beige
bęben [ban-ben] m. drum; kid;
brat; barrel; cylinder; tumbler
bęcwał [bants-vaw] m.
nincompoop; dullard; chickle-
head; jolt-head; dolt
bękart [ban-kart] m. bastard
biadać [bya-daćh] v. moan
białaczka [bya-wach-ka] f.
leukemia; leukaemia
białko [byaw-ko] n. egg white;
protein; white of the eye
biały [bya-wi] adj. m. white
biba [bee-ba] f. drinking spree
biblia [beeb-lya] f. Bible
biblioteka [beeb-lyo-te-ka] f.
library; bookcase; book series
bibuła [bee-boo-wa] f. blotting
paper; illegal political
publication; literary trash
bicz [beech] m. whip; whiplash
bić [beećh] v. beat; defeat

biec [byets] v. run; trot; flow
bieda [bye-da] f. poverty; want;
    trouble; distress; evil days
biedny [byed-ni] adj. m. poor
bieg [byek] m. run; race; course
biegle [bye-gle] adv. fluently
biegun [bye-goon] m. pole;
    rocker; spindle; trunnion
biegunka [bye-goon-ka] f.
    diarrhea; dysentery
biel [byel] f. whiteness; white
bielizna [bye-leez-na] f. linen
bielmo [byel-mo] n. cataract
bierny [byer-ni] adj. m. passive
bieżący [bye-zhown-tsi] adj. m.
    current; flowing; running
bieżnia [byezh-ńa] f. runway;
    track; racecourse; tire tread
bigos [bee-gos] m. hashed
    meat and cabbage dish (tradi-
    tional Polish food)
bijatyka [bee-ya-ti-ka] f. fight;
    brawl; tussle; scrimmage
bila [bee-la] f. billiard ball
bilans [bee-lans] m. balance
    sheet; balance; rest;
    outcome; result
bilet [bee-let] m. note; ticket
biodro [byod-ro] n. hip; huckle
biszkopt [beesh-kopt] m. biscuit;
    sponge cake; cracker
bitny [beet-ni] adj. m. valiant
bitwa [beet-va] f. battle; fight
biuro [byoo-ro] n. office
biust [byoost] m. bust; breast
biustonosz [byoos-to-nosh] m.
    brassiere; bra; bust-bodice
biżuteria [bee-zhoo-ter-ya] f.
    jewelry; jewels
blacha [bla-kha] f. sheet metal;
    cook top; the range; tinware
blady [bla-di] adj. m. pale
blaga [bla-ga] f. lie; bluff
blankiet [blan-ket] m. blank
    form; printed form; blank
blask [blask] m. flush; luster
bliski [blees-kee] adj. m. near;
    imminent; near by; close
blizna [bleez-na] f. scar
bliźni [bleeźh-ńee] m. fellow
    man; fellow creature; twin;
    identical; neighbor
blokować [blo-ko-vać] v.

block; blockade; obstruct;
    stall; take up space; interlock
blondynka [blon-din-ka] f. blonde
    (girl); fair haired girl
bluzka [blooz-ka] f. blouse
bluźnić [blooźh-ńeeć] v.
    curse; blaspheme; talk non-
    sense; revile; profane
błahość [bwa-khośhćh] f.
    triviality; futility
błagać [bwa-gać] v. beseech
błazen [bwa-zen] m. clown;
    buffoon; fool; low comedian
błąd [bwownt] m. error; mistake;
    lapse; slip-up; fallacy; fault
błąkać się [bwown-kać śhan]
    v. wander; stray; roam; rove
błękit [bwan-kit] m. blue (color);
    azure; blue pigment; sky
błocić [bwo-ćheeć] v. get
    muddy; soil with mud; spatter
błogi [bwo-gee] adj. m. blissful;
    delightful; sweet; rapturous
błogosławić [bwo-go-swa-
    -veeć] v. bless; praise; exalt;
    thank; commend; glorify
błona [bwo-na] f. membrane;
    coat; film; tunic; velum; web
błonie [bwo-ńe] n. meadow;
    plain; public grassy land
błotnik [bwot-ńeek] m. (car)
    fender; mudguard; (front end
    fender) splash-board
błoto [bwo-to] n. mud; muck
błysk [bwisk] m. flash; flare
bo [bo] conj. because; for; or;
    as; since; or else; but then
bochenek [bo-khe-nek] m. loaf
bocian [bo-ćhan] m. stork
boczny [boch-ni] adj. m. lateral;
    side; collateral (line)
boczyć się [bo-chyćh śhan] v.
    sulk; be angry; look askance
bodaj [bo-day] part. may be;
    should be...; would be...
bodziec [bo-dźhets] m. stimulus
bogactwo [bo-gats-tvo] n. riches;
    wealth; means; fortune; plenty
bogaty [bo-ga-ti] adj. m. rich
bogobojny [bo-go-boy-ni] adj. m.
    pious; devout; church going
bohater [bo-kha-ter] m. hero
boisko [bo-ees-ko] n. stadium;

field; threshing floor; gridiron
bojaźń [bo-yaźhń] f. fear;
fright; anxiety; terror
boja [bo-ya] f. buoy; beacon
bojkot [boy-kot] m. boycott
bojownik [bo-yov-ńeek] m.
fighter; militant; champion
bok [bok] m. side; flank
boks [boks] m. boxing; stall
boleć [bo-lećh] v. pain; ache
bolesny [bo-les-ni] adj. m.
sore; painful; sad; woeful;
acute; dismal; agonizing
bomba [bom-ba] f. bomb; bomb
shell; a sensation; beer-mug
bombowiec [bom-bo-vyets] m.
bomber; bombing plane
borykać się [bo-ri-kaćh śhan]
v. cope; struggle; wrestle
bosak [bo-sak] m. boat hook
boso [bo-so] adv. barefoot
bosy [bo-si] adj. m. barefoot
bowiem [bo-vyem] conj. for;
because; since; as; hence
boży [bo-zhi] adj. m. God's
Bóg [book] m. God
bój [booy] m. fight; battle
ból [bool] m. pain; ache; sore
bór [boor] m. forest; wood
bóść [boośhćh] v. gore; sting
bóżnica [boozh-ńee-tsa] f.
synagogue; house of prayer
bractwo [brats-tvo] n. fraternity;
brotherhood; guild; sodality
brać [braćh] v. take; hold
brak [brak] m. lack; need; want;
scarcity; shortage; absence;
fault; privation; poverty
brama [bra-ma] f. gate; gateway;
front door; wicket; port
bransoletka [bran-so-let-ka] f.
bracelet; wristlet; bangle
brat [brat] m. brother; mate
bratać [bra-taćh] v. unite;
fraternize; chum up
bratanek [bra-ta-nek] m. nephew
bratanica [bra-ta-ńee-tsa] f.
niece (brother's daughter)
brednie [bred-ńe] n. nonsense
brew [brev] f. eyebrow
brewerie [bre-ver-ye] n. brawl
brezent [bre-zent] m. tarpaulin;
(waterproof) canvas

brnąć [brnownćh] v. wade
broczyć [bro-chićh] v. bleed
broda [bro-da] f. beard; chin
brodzić [bro-dźheećh] v. wade
broić [bro-eećh] v. make
mischief; frolic; romp; gambol
brom [brom] m. bromine
brona [bro-na] f. harrow
bronić [bro-ńeećh] v. defend;
protect; shield; interdict
bronz [brons] m. bronze
broń [broń] f. weapon; arms
broszka [brosh-ka] f. brooch
broszura [bro-shoo-ra] f.
pamphlet; folder; booklet
browar [bro-var] m. brewery
bród [brood] m. ford
brud [brood] m. dirt; filth
bruk [brook] m. pavement
brukiew [broo-kyev] f. turnip
brulion [brool-yon] m. rough
draft copy; notebook; exercise
book; preliminary draft
brunatny [broo-na-tni] adj. m.
brown; tawny; tan colored
brunetka [broo-net-ka] f.
brunette; dark-haired woman
brutal [broo-tal] m. brute
bruzda [brooz-da] f. furrow;
groove; deep wrinkle; streak
brwi [brvee] pl. eye brows
brykać [bri-kaćh] v. prance
bryła [bri-wa] f. lump; mass
bryzg [brizk] m. splash
bryzgać [briz-gaćh] v. splash
brzeg [bzhek] m. shore; margin
brzemię [bzhe-myan] n. burden
brzęk [bzhank] m. clink; chink;
rattle; ping; buzz; hum; drone
brzuch [bzhookh] m. belly;
abdomen; stomach; tummy;
guts; abdomen (of an insect)
brzydki [bzhid-kee] adj. m. ugly;
unsightly; hideous; foul
**brzydzić się [bzhi-dźheećh
śhan]** v. feel disgust; loathe;
abhor; detest; hold in disgust
brzytwa [bzhit-va] f. razor
buchać [boo-khaćh] v. squirt
bucik [boo-ćheek] m. shoe; boot
buda [boo-da] f. shed (stall)
budowa [boo-do-va] f.
construction; erection;

framework; structure
budowla [boo-**dov**-la] f. building
(large); edifice; house
budzić [boo-**dźheećh**] v. wake
up; awaken; rouse; stir; arise
budzik [boo-**dźheek**] m. alarm
clock; alarm
budżet [boo-jet] m. budget
bujać [boo-yaćh] v. rock; lie
bufor [boo-for] m. buffer
bułka [boow-ka] f. roll
(breakfast); bread roll; loaf
bunt [boont] m. mutiny
bura [boo-ra] f. reprimand
burak [boo-rak] m. beet
burda [boor-da] f. scuffle; row;
brawl; disturbance; wrangle;
rough neck; hoodlum
burmistrz [boor-meestsh] m.
mayor
bursztyn [boor-shtin] m. amber
burta [boor-ta] f. ship's side
bury [boo-ri] adj. m. dark gray
burza [boo-zha] f. tempest;
storm; wind storm; rain storm
burżuazja [boor-zhoo-az-ya] f.
bourgeoisie; middle class
busola [boo-so-la] f. compass
but [boot] m. boot; shoe; sabot
buta [boo-ta] f. arrogance
butelka [boo-tel-ka] f. bottle
butny [boot-ni] adj. m. arrogant;
insolent; overbearing
buzia [boo-źha] f. face; mouth
by [bi] conj. in order that;
(conditional) as if; at least
byczy [bi-chi] adj. m. 1. bull's;
2. very good; glorious
być [bićh] v. be; exist; live
bydlę [bid-lan] n. beast; brute
byle [bi-le] conj. in order to; so
as to; pron. any; slap-dash
były [bi-wi] adj. m. former
bynajmniej [bi-nay-mńey] adv.
by no means; not at all
bystrość [bis-trośhćh] f.
swiftness; shrewdness
byt [bit] m. existence
bytność [bit-nośhćh] f. stay
bywać [bi-vaćh] v. frequent
bywalec [bi-va-lets] m. patron
frequenter; man of the world
bzdura [bzdoo-ra] f. nonsense

bzik [bźheek] adj. m. crank;
loony; crazy; m. fad; craze
bzykać [bzi-kaćh] v. buzz

C

cackać się [tsats-kaćh śhan]
v. fondle; pamper; humor;
coddle; handle delicately
cacko [tsats-ko] n. jewel; trinket;
plaything; toy; beauty
cal [tsal] m. inch
całka [tsaw-ka] f. integral
całkiem [tsaw-kem] adv. quite;
entirely; completely; totally
całkowity [tsaw-ko-vee-ti]
adj. m. total; complete
cało [tsa-wo] adv. (in one piece)
safely; safe and sound
całować [tsa-wo-vaćh] v. kiss;
embrace; give a kiss
całus [tsa-woos] m. kiss
cap [tsap] m. billy goat
caber [tsown-ber] m. rump; fillet
cążki [tsownzh-kee] pl. small
tongs; pliers; pincers
ceber [tse-ber] m. bucket
cebula [tse-boo-la] f. onion
cech [tsekh] m. trade; guild
cecha [tse-kha] f. feature; mark;
characterize; calibrate
cedr [tsedr] m. cedar
cedzić [tse-dźheećh] v. strain;
filter; percolate; sip; trickle
cegielnia [tse-gel-ńa] f.
brickyard; brick factory
cegła [tseg-wa] f. brick
cel [tsel] m. purpose; aim
cela [tse-la] f. cell
celnik [tsel-ńeek] m. customs
inspector; customs officer
celować [tse-lo-vaćh] v. aim;
excel; exceed; be very good
celuloza [tse-loo-lo-za] f.
cellulose
cembrować [tsem-bro-vaćh] v.
case(well); timber (a shaft)
cement [tse-ment] m. cement

cena [tse-na] f. price; value
cenić [tse-ńeeć] v. value;
    rate; esteem; prize; evaluate
cennik [tsen-ńeek] m. price list;
    price catalogue; price-current
centnar [tsent-nar] m.
    hundredweight
centrala [tsen-tra-la] f. head
    office; main office; exchange
centrum [tsent-room] n. center
centryfuga [tsen-tri-foo-ga] f.
    centrifuge; separator
centymetr [tsen-ti-metr] m.
    centimeter
cep [tsep] m. flail; blockhead
cera [tse-ra] f. complexion; skin;
    mend; darn; darned place
ceramiczny [tse-ra-meech-ni] adj.
    m. ceramic; earthenware
cerata [tse-ra-ta] f. oilcloth
ceregiele [tse-re-ge-le] n. fuss;
    petty formalities; ceremony
certować się [tser-to-vaćh
    śhan] v. pretend; stand on
    ceremony; fuss; be ceremon-
    ious; pretend to decline
cewka [tsev-ka] f. spool
cągi [tsan-gee] pl. tongs; pliers;
    nippers; pincers; pipe-wrench
cątka [tsant-ka] f. dot
chałat [kha-wat] m. lab. coat
chałastra [kha-was-tra] f. mob
chałupa [kha-woo-pa] f. hut
cham [kham] m. roughneck; boor
charakter [kha-rak-ter] m.
    disposition; character; quality
charczeć [khar-chech] v.
    wheeze; snort; be hoarse
chata [kha-ta] f. hut; cabin
chcieć [khćhećh] v. want
chciwiec [khćhee-vyets] m.
    greedy man; grasping man
chełpić się [khew-peećh śhan]
    v. boast; brag; bluster; vaunt;
    swagger; glory; pride
chemia [khe-mya] f. chemistry
chemiczny [khe-meech-ni]
    adj. m. chemical
cherlak [kher-lak] m. weakling
chęć [khanćh] f. wish; desire
chądogi [khan-do-gee] adj. m.
    neat; clean; tidy; orderly
chichot [khee-khot] m. giggle;

laughter; chuckle; titter
chimera [khee-me-ra] f. whim
chinina [khee-ńee-na] f. quinine
chiński [kheeń-skee] adj. m.
    Chinese; of China
chirurg [khee-roorg] m. surgeon;
    sawbones (slang)
chlapać [khla-paćh] v. splash
chleb [khleb] m. bread
chlew [khlev] m. pigsty; pigpen
chlor [khlor] m. chlorine
chluba [khloo-ba] f. glory; pride
chlubić się [khloo-beećh śhan]
    v. boast; flatter oneself
chlusnąć [khloos-nownćh] v.
    splash; fling; spout; spurt
chłeptać [khwep-taćh] v. lap
    up; lap down; swill
chłodzić [khwo-dźeećh] v.
    cool; refresh; refrigerate
chłonąć [khwo-nownćh] v.
    absorb; devour; drink in;
    inhale; imbibe; take in
chłop [khwop] m. peasant; man
chłosta [khwos-ta] f. lashing
chłód [khwoot] m. cold;
    freshness; coolness; iciness;
    shiver; chilly atmosphere
chłystek [khwis-tek] m. squirt
chmara [khma-ra] f. swarm
chmiel [khmyel] m. hop; hops
chmura [khmoo-ra] f. cloud
chociaż [kho-ćhash] conj. albeit;
    even if; though, tho'; while
chociaż = choćby = chociażby
choć [khoćh] conj. at least
chodnik [khod-ńeek] m.
    sidewalk; pathway; stair
    carpet; foot-path; pavement
chodzić [kho-dźheećh] v. go;
    walk; move; creep; pace;
    attend; come; thread; stalk
choinka [kho-een-ka] f. fir
cholera [kho-le-ra] f. cholera;
    excl.: damn! hell! the devil!
cholewa [kho-le-va] f. boot
chorągiew [kho-rown-gev] f.
    flag; standard; ensign
choroba [kho-ro-ba] f. sickness
chory [kho-ri] adj. m. sick; ill;
    ailing; infirm; unwell
chować [kho-vaćh] v. hide
chód [khoot] m. gait; walk

chór [khoor] m. choir
chów [khoof] m. breeding
chrabąszcz [khra-<u>bown</u>shch] m. beetle; May-bug
chrapać [khra-paćh] v. snore
chroniczny [khro-ńeech-ni] adj. m. chronic; habitual
chronić [khro-ńeećh] v. shelter; protect; guard; shield; fence; give refuge; prevent
chropowaty [khro-po-va-ti] adj. m. rough; callous; coarse; harsh; uneven; rugged; harsh
chrust [khroost] m. kindling
chrupać [khroo-paćh] v. crunch
chrypka [khrip-ka] f. hoarseness; sore throat
Chrystus [khris-toos] m. Christ
chrzan [khzhan] m. horseradish
chrząstka [khzh<u>own</u>st-ka] f. cartilage; gristle; copula
chrząszcz [khsh<u>own</u>shch] m. May bug; beetle; cockchafer
chrzcić [khzhćheećh] v. baptize; christen; initiate
chrześcijanin [khshe-śhćhee--ya-ńeen] m. Christian
chrząst [khzh<u>an</u>st] m. clatter
chrzęścić [khzh<u>an</u>-śhćheećh] v. clank; jangle; grate; crunch
chuchać [khoo-khaćh] v. puff
chuchro [khookh-ro] m. weakling
chuć [khooćh] f. lust
chudnąć [khood-n<u>own</u>ćh] v. lose weight; grow thin; lose flesh; become thin; thin
chuligan [khoo-lee-gan] m. hoodlum; ruffian; roughneck
chustka [khoost-ka] f. handkerchief; kerchief; scarf
chwacki [khvats-kee] adj. m. brave; plucky; gallant; rakish
chwalić [khva-leećh] v. praise
chwała [kva-wa] f. praise; glory; splendor; pride of; a credit to
chwast [khvast] m. weed
chwiać [khvyaćh] v. waver
chwila [khvee-la] f. moment
chwycić [khvi-ćheećh] v. grasp; seize; get hold; grip
chwyt [khvit] m. grasp; grip
chyba [khi-ba] part. maybe
chybotać [khi-bo-taćh] v. rock

chybić [khi-beećh] v. miss
chylić [khi-leećh] v. bow
chyłkiem [khiw-<u>k</u>em] adv. stealthily; on the sly
chytry [khit-ri] adj. m. sly
chyży [khi-zhi] adj. m. swift
ci [ćhee] pron. these; they; part.: for you; well, well!
ciało [ćha-wo] n. body; substance; frame; anatomy; staff; aggregate; corpse; carcass
ciarki [ćhar-kee] pl. shudder
ciasnota [ćhas-no-ta] f. tightness; narrow-mindedness
ciastko [ćhast-ko] n. cake; pie
ciasto [ćhas-to] n. dough
ciąć [ćhownćh] v. cut; clip
ciągnąć [ćhowng-now<u>n</u>ćh] v. pull; draw; tag; lug; drag; haul; have in tow; trail;. obtain; pump; deduce; infer; suck; inhale; attract; stretch; expand; extend; continue; proceed; blow; sweep; run; tend; lean; dilate; wear on
ciągnik [ćhowng-ńeek] m. tractor; agrimotor; crawler
ciąża [ćhown-zha] f. pregnancy
ciążenie [ćhown-zhe-ńe] v. gravitation; tendency
cichaczem [ćhee-kha-chem] adv. stealthily; on the quiet
cichnąć [ćheekh-now<u>n</u>ćh] v. quiet down; subside; abate
cicho [ćhee-kho] adv. silently; noiselessly; softly; privately
cichy [ćhee-khi] adj. m. quiet; still; low; gentle; calm; serene
ciec [ćhets] v. leak; flow
ciecz [ćhech] f. liquid
ciekawy [ćhe-ka-vi] adj. m. cute; curious; interesting; prying; inquiring; inquisitive
cielak [ćhe-lak] m. calf
cielesny [ćhe-les-ni] adj. m. carnal; bodily; sexual
ciemię [ćhe-my<u>an</u>] n. crown of the head; septum of the skull
ciemiężenie [ćhe-my<u>an</u>-zhe-ńe] n. oppression; subjugation
ciemnia [ćhem-ńa] f. darkroom
ciemno [ćhem-no] adv. darkly
ciemny [ćhem-ni] adj. m. dark

cieniować [ćhe-ńo-vaćh] v.
shade; modulate; grade
cienisty [ćhe-ńees-ti] adj. m.
shady; shade giving
cienki [ćhen-kee] adj. m. thin
cień [ćheń] m. shade; shadow
cieplarnia [ćhep-lar-ńa] f.
greenhouse; hothouse; stove
ciepło [ćhep-wo] adv. warm
ciepławy [ćhep-wa-vi] adj. m.
lukewarm; tepid; not enthused
ciepły [ćhep-wi] adj. m. warm
cierń [ćherń] m. thorn; prickle
cierpiący [ćher-pyown-tsi]
adj. m. suffering; ailing; ill
cierpieć [ćher-pyećh] v. suffer;
anguish; be troubled; endure
cierpki [ćherp-kee] adj. m. tart;
acid; surly; acrid; sour; harsh
cierpliwość [ćher-plee-
-vośhćh] f. patience; endurance; forbearance
cierpliwy [ćher-plee-vi] adj. m.
enduring; patient; forbearing
cierpnąć [ćherp-nownćh] v.
grow numb; creep; go to sleep
ciesielstwo [ćhe-śhel-stvo] n.
carpentry (in construction)
cieszyć [ćhe-shićh] v. cheer
cieśla [ćheś-la] m. carpenter;
wood worker; shipwright;
wood construction worker
cietrzew [ćhe-tshev] m.
black-cock (male); black
grouse; grey hen (female)
cieśnina [ćheśh-ńee-na] f.
straits; narrows; sound; ravine
cięcie [ćhan-ćhe] n. cut; gash
cięciwa [ćhan-ćhee-va] f.
chord (in geometry); bow
string; string; subtense
cięgi [ćhan-gee] pl. lashing
cięty [ćhan-ti] adj. m. sharp-
tongued; biting; dogged; incisive; keen-witted; ready; tipsy
ciężar [ćhan-zhar] m. weight;
burden; gravity; onus; duty;
charge; task; encumbrance
ciężeć [ćhan-zhećh] v. grow
heavy; become heavy; be-
come a burden; encumber
ciężki [ćhanzh-kee] adj. m.
heavy; weighty; bulky;

oppressive; clumsy; dull; inapt
ciężko [ćhanzh-ko] adv. heavily
ciocia [ćho-ćha] f. auntie; aunt
cios [ćhos] m. blow; stroke; hit;
shock; ashlar; block; joint
cioteczny brat [ćho-tech-ni brat]
m. cousin
ciotka [ćhot-ka] f. aunt
ciosać [ćho-saćh] v. hew;
chop out; dress building stone
cis [ćhees] m. yew
cisawy [ćhee-sa-vi] adj. m.
chestnut (horse)
ciskać [ćhees-kaćh] v. fling;
cast; throw; hurl; sling; plunk;
let fly; fret; fume; storm; rage
cisnąć [ćhees-nownćh] v.
press; squeeze; bear; urge;
hurt; pinch; crowd; tighten
cisza [ćhee-sha] f. calm; silence
ciśnienie [ćheeśh-ńe-ńe] n.
pressure; blood pressure;
thrust; stress
ciuch [ćhookh] m. used clothing
ciułać [ćhoo-waćh] v. hoard
ciurkiem [ćhoor-kyem] adv. in a
trickle; with big drops
ciupa [ćhoo-pa] f. jail; clink
ciupasem [ćhoo-pa-sem] adv.
under convoy; (transport)
under an armed convoy
ciżba [ćheezh-ba] f. crowd
ckliwy [tsklee-vi] adj. m. qualmy;
sickly; faint; sloppy
clić [tsleećh] v. collect custom
duty; lay a custom duty
cło [tswo] n. customs
cmentarz [tsmen-tash] m.
cemetery; burial ground
cmokać [tsmo-kaćh] v. smack
cnota [tsno-ta] f. virtue
co [tso] pron. part. what; which
codzień [tso-dźheń] adv. daily
cofać się [tso-faćh śhan] v.
back up; retreat; regress;
retire; remove; withdraw
cokolwiek [tso-kol-vyek] pron.
anything; whatever; somewhat
comber [tsom-ber] m. saddle (of
mutton); rump; loin; haunch
coraz [tso-raz] adv. ever
coś [tsośh] pron. something
córka [tsoor-ka] f. daughter

cóż [tsoosh] pron. what then
cuchnąć [tsookh-nownćh] v.
  stink foul; smell foul
cucić [tsoo-ćheećh] v. revive
cud [tsoot] m. wonder; miracle
cudzołożyć [tsoo-dzo-wo-zhićh]
  v. commit adultery
codzoziemiec [tsoo-dzo-źhe-
  -myets] m. alien; foreigner
cudzy [tsoo-dzi] adj. m. someone
  else's; alien; foreign
cudzysłów [tsoo-dzi-swoof] m.
  quotation marks
cukier [tsoo-ker] m. sugar
cuma [tsoo-ma] f. mooring
cwał [tsvaw] m. full gallop
cwaniak [tsva-ńak] m. city
  slicker; sly dog; crafty guy
cwany [tsva-ni] adj. m. sly;
  cunning; crafty; artful
cyc [tsits] m. nipple (vulg.)
cyfra [tsif-ra] f. number
cygan [tsi-gan] m. gipsy; cheat;
  Gipsy; swindler; liar
cykl [tsikl] m. cycle
cylinder [tsi-leen-der] m. cylinder;
  barrel; (men's) top hat
cyna [tsi-na] f. tin
cynamon [tsi-na-mon] m.
  cinnamon; spice of laurel bark
cynober [tsi-no-ber] m. vermilion
cyngiel [tsin-gyel] m. trigger
cynik [tsi-ńeek] m. cynic
cynk [tsink] m. zinc; tutenag
cypel [tsi-pel] m. cape; tip
cyprys [tsi-pris] m. cypress
cyrk [tsirk] m. circus
cyrkiel [tsir-kel] m. compass
cysterna [tsis-ter-na] f. cistern;
  tank car; vat; storage tank
cytadela [tsi-ta-de-la] f. citadel;
  fortress; stronghold
cytata [tsi-ta-ta] f. quotation
cytryna [tsi-tri-na] f. lemon
cywil [tsi-veel] m. civilian
cyzelować [tsi-ze-lo-vaćh] v.
  engrave; carve; elaborate
czad [chat] m. carbon monoxide
czaić się [cha-eećh śhan] v.
  lie in wait; lurk; stalk; crouch
czajnik [chay-ńeek] m. tea-pot
czajka [chay-ka] f. gull
czako [cha-ko] f. shako

czapka [chap-ka] f. cap; pileus
czapla [chap-la] f. heron
czaprak [chap-rak] m. horse
  blanket; caparison; trappings
czar [char] m. spell; charm
czarno [char-no] adv. blackly
czart [chart] m. devil; deuce
czas [chas] m. time; duration
czaszka [chash-ka] f. skull
czaty [cha-ti] pl. watch; lookout;
  wait; ambush; outpost
cząstka [chownst-ka] f. particle
czcić [chćheećh] v. adore;
  worship; idolize; venerate
czcigodny [chćhee-god-ni]
  adj. m. honorable; revered;
  venerable
czcionka [chćhon-ka] f. type;
  character; letter in print
czczo [chcho] adv. empty
  (stomach); emptily; vainly; idly
czego [che-go] conj. why? what?
czek [chek] m. check (in
  banking); cheque
czekać [che-kaćh] v. wait;
  await; stand by; expect;
  waste time; be in store for
czekanie [che-ka-ńe] n. wait
czekan [che-kan] m. pickhammer
czekolada [che-ko-la-da] f.
  chocolate; slab of chocolate
czeladnik [che-lad-ńeek] m.
  apprentice; journeyman
czelność [chel-nośhćh] f.
  impudence; effrontery; nerve
czeluść [che-loośhćh] f.
  abyss; gulf; precipice; depths
czemu [che-moo] part. why? to
  what? what to? what for?
czepek [che-pek] m. bonnet;
  hood; night cap; caul; calyptra
czepiać się [chep-yaćh śhan]
  v. cling; hang on; peck at
czereda [che-re-da] f. gang;
  throng; crowd; swarm; pack
czerep [che-rep] m. shell; skull;
  fragment; splinter; shard
czereśnia [che-reśh-ńa] f.
  cherry; cherry tree; gean
czernić [cher-ńeećh] v.
  blacken; black; paint black
czerń [cherń] f. black color
czerpać [cher-paćh] v. scoop;

draw; ladle; derive (benefit)
czerstwy [chers-tvi] adj. m.
stale; robust (man); firm
czerw [cherv] m. worm; grub
czerwienić się [cher-vye-ńeeóh
śhąn] v. blush (redden)
czerwony [cher-vo-ni] adj. m.
red; scarlet; crimson; ruddy
czesać [che-saćh] v. comb;
brush; dress hair; do hair
czeski [ches-kee] adj. m. Czech
czesne [ches-ne] n. tuition
cześć [cheśhćh] f. honor;
cult; worship; respect;
adoration; reverence; good
name; greeting: hullo! cheerio!
często [chąns-to] adv. often
częstokroć [chąn-sto-króćh]
adv. often; repeatedly
częstość [chąns-tośhćh] f.
frequency; recurrence
częstotliwość [chąn-sto-tlee-
-vośhćh] f. frequency; recurrence; rapid occurrence
częstować [chąn-sto-vaćh] v.
treat to something; regale
częsty [chąns-ti] adj. m.
frequent; repeated often
częściowy [chąn-śhćho-vi]
adj. m. partial; fragmentary
część [chąnśhćh] f. part;
share; section; piece; quota
czkawka [chkav-ka] f. hiccups
człon [chwon] m. element;
segment; link; member; clause
członek [chwo-nek] m. limb;
member; man's sex organ
człowiek [chwo-vyek] m. man;
individual; chap; somebody
czmychnąć [chmikh-nownćh]
v. bolt; steal out; whisk away
czochrać [chokh-raćh] v. tousle;
ripple; hackle; scratch
czołg [chowg] m. tank (military);
reptile; crawler
czołgać [chow-gaćh] v. crawl
czoło [cho-wo] n. forehead
czop [chop] m. peg; plug; pin
czosnek [chos-nek] m. garlic
czterdzieści [chter-dźheśh-
-ćhee] num. forty
czternaście [chter-naśh-ćhe]
num. fourteen, 14

czteropiętrowy [chte-ro-pyąn-tro
-vi] adj. m. four stories high;
four storied (building)
cztery [chte-ri] num. four
czub [choop] m. tuft; crest
czucie [choo-ćhe] n. feeling;
smelling; sense perception
czuć [chooćh] v. feel; smell
czujka [chooy-ka] f. sentry
czułość [choo-wośhćh] f.
tenderness; affection; caress
czuły [choo-wi] adj. m. tender;
affectionate; sensitive; keen
czupurny [choo-poor-ni] adj. m.
pugnacious; boastful; defiant
czuwać [choo-vaćh] v. watch;
nurse; look-out; stay up; tend
czwartek [chvar-tek] m.
Thursday
czwarty [chvar-ti] num. fourth
czworobok [chvo-ro-bok] m.
quadrilateral; square; tetragon
czworokąt [chvo-ro-kownt] m.
quadrangle; quad; tetragon
czwórka [chvoor-ka] f. foursome;
crew of four; good mark
czy [chi] conj. if; whether
czychać [chi-khaćh] v. lurk
czyj [chiy] pron. whose
czyjś [chiyśh] pron.
somebody's; anybody's;
someone else's
czyli [chi-lee] conj. or; otherwise;
that is to say; in other words
czym...tym...[chim...tim] adv.
the sooner... the; the more
the...; the less... the...
czyn [chin] m. act; deed
czynsz [chinsh] m. rent
czynić [chi-ńeećh] v. do;
render; act; amount; cause
czyrak [chi-rak] m. boil; furuncle;
abscess; anbury; rising
czynnik [chin-ńeek] m. factor
czysto [chi-sto] adv. clean
czysty [chis-ti] adj. m. clean
czyszczenie [chish-che-ńe] n.
cleaning; brushing; diarrhoea
czyścić [chiśh-ćheećh] v.
clean; scour; brush; rub; purge
czyściec [chiśh-ćhets] m.
purgatory; woundwort
czytać [chi-taćh] v. read

czytelnia [chi-tel-ńa] f. reading room; lending library

czytelnik [chi-tel-ńeek] m. reader; reading individual

czytelny [chi-tel-ni] adj. m. legible; readable

czyż [chish] part. if; whether

ćma [ćhma] f. obscurity; swarm; night butterfly; night moth; darkness; dark night

ćmić [ćhmeećh] v. obscure; dim; darken; eclipse; smoke; sicken; blind; dazzle; glimmer

ćwiartka [ćhvyart-ka] f. one quarter; one fourth of a liter

ćwierć [ćhvyerćh] f. one fourth (of a liter etc.)

ćwiczenie [ćhvee-che-ńe] n. exercise; instruction; drill

ćwiek [ćhvyek] m. nail; stud

ćwikła [ćhveek-wa] f. red beet with horseradish (salad)

D

dach [dakh] m. roof; shelter

dać [daćh] v. give; pay; result

daktyl [dak-till] m. date

dal [dal] f. distance; remoteness; far away; aloof; distant

dalece [da-le-tse] adv. further; by far; so far; (so) much so

dalej [da-ley] moreover; further off; so on; later; further back

dalmierz [dal-myesh] m. range finder; telemeter

dalszy [dal-shi] adj. m. further; later; outlying; another

dama [da-ma] f. lady; partner

dana [da-na] adj. f. given (data)

danie [da-ńe] m. serving (of food); dish; course

danser [dan-ser] m.dancer

dane [da-ne] pl. data

dar [dar] m. gift; present

daremnie [da-rem-ńe] adv. in vain; without success

daremny [da-rem-ni] adj. m.

futile; vain; idle; ineffective

darmo [dar-mo] adv. free; gratuitously; to no avail

darować [da-ro-vaćh] v. give; forgive; overlook; spare

data [da-ta] f. date

datek [da-tek] n. small gift

dawać [da-vaćh] v. give (often)

dawno [dav-no] adv. long ago

dąb [downp] m. oak tree (wood)

dąć [downćh] v. blow; resound

dąsać się [down-saćh śhan] v. sulk; be in the pouts; mump

dążyć [down-zhićh] v. aspire; tend; aim; be bound; trend

dbać [dbaćh] v. care; set store

dach [dakh] m. breath; gust

decydować [de-tsi-do-vaćh] v. decide; resolve; determine

decyzja [de-tsis-ya] f. decision; ruling; resolve; resolution

defekt [de-fekt] m. defect; flaw;

delikatność [de-lee-kat-nośhćh] f. delicacy; gentleness; softness; subtleness; daintiness; tact; consideration; thoughtfulness; sensitiveness; frailness; nicety; fragility

defekt [de-fekt] m. defect; flaw; fault; damage; injury; reject

demaskować [de-mas-ko-vaćh] v. unmask; uncover; denounce

demokracja [de-mo-krats-ya] f. democracy; rule by the people

denerwować [de-ner-vo-vaćh] v. bother; make nervous; vex; irritate; upset; exasperate

dentysta [den-tis-ta] m. dentist

depesza [de-pe-sha] f. wire; telegram; cable; dispatch

deponować [de-po-no-vaćh] v. deposit; put in safe keeping

depozyt [de-po-zit] m. deposit

deptać [dep-taćh] v. trample (the soil); tread; pace up and down; stain; soil; muddy

derka [der-ka] f. rug; blanket

deseń [de-seń] m. pattern; design; decorative design

deska [des-ka] f. plank; board

desperacja [des-pe-rats-ya] f. desperation; despair

deszcz [deshch] m. rain

detal [de-tal] m. detail; trifling matter; retail trade

determinacja [de-ter-mee-nats-ya] f. determination; resoluteness

dewiza [de-vee-za] f. foreign money; motto; slogan; device

dębina [dan-bee-na] f. oak wood; oak bark; oak stand

dętka [dant-ka] f. pneumatic tire; tube; air chamber

diabeł [dya-bew] m. devil

dieta [dye-ta] f. diet; regimen

dla [dla] prep. for; to; towards

dlaczego [dla-che-go] prep. why; what for; why are you ...?

dlatego [dla-te-go] prep. because; this is why; and so

dławić [dwa-veećh] v. choke; squash; throttle; strangle

dłoń [dwoń] f. palm of the hand; hand; metacarpus; quart

dłubać [dwoo-baćh] v. groove; poke; pick one's teeth

dług [dwook] m. debt; obligation

długi [dwoo-gee] adj. m. long

długo [dwoo-go] adv. a long time; a long way; long before

dłuto [dwoo-to] n. chisel

dłutować [dwoo-to-vaćh] v. chisel; cut with chisel

dłużnik [dwoozh-ńeek] m. debtor; borrower; mortgager

dmuchać [dmoo-khaćh] v. blow

dniówka [dńoov-ka] f. day's work; work by day; time work

dno [dno] n. bottom; utterness

do [do] prep. to; into; up; till

doba [do-ba] f. 24 hours

dobić [do-beećh] v. deal a death blow; drive home (a point, etc.); reach (a shore)

dobierać [do-bye-raćh] v. match; take more; select

dobitny [do-beet-ni] adj. m. expressive; emphatic; distinct

doborowy [do-bo-ro-vi] adj. m. choice; select; picked

dobosz [do-bosh] m. drummer

dobór [do-boor] m. selection; assortment; choice

dobra [dob-ra] n. riches

dobranoc [do-bra-nots] (indecl.) good-night

dobrany [do-bra-ni] adj. m. matching; becoming; well-chosen; accordant

dobre [dob-re] adj. n. good

dobro [dob-ro] n. good; right

dobrobyt [do-bro-bit] m. well being; prosperity; welfare

dobroczynność [do-bro-chin-nośhćh] f. charity; works of mercy; philanthropy

dobroć [dob-roćh] f. kindness

dobroduszny [do-bro-doosh-ni] adj m. kindhearted; kindly

dobrodziej [do-bro-dźhey] m. benefactor; his reverence

dobrotliwy [do-bro-tlee-vi] adj. m. kind; good natured

dobrowolny [do-bro-vol-ni] adj. m. voluntary; gratuitous

dobry [dob-ri] adj. m. good; kind; right; hearty; retentive

dobrze [dob-zhe] adv. well; OK; rightly; properly; okay

dobudówka [do-boo-doov-ka] f. building extension

dobyć [do-bićh] v. pullout

dobytek [do-bi-tek] m. belongings; effects; livestock

doceniać [do-tse-ńach] v. duly appreciate; value; esteem

docent [do-tsent] m. associate professor; lecturer

dochodzenie [do-kho-dze-ńe] n. investigation; inquiry

dochodzić [do-kho-dźeećh] v. draw near; investigate; reach

dochód [do-khoot] m. income; revenue; profit; returns

dociąć [do-ćhownćh] c. sting; taunt; fit by cutting off

dociec [do-ćhets] v. find out

dociekać [do-ćhe-kaćh] v. search; investigate; find out

docierać [do-ćhye-raćh] v. draw near; reach; reduce friction; rub up; get at

docinek [do-ćhee-nek] m. taunt

doczekać [do-che-kaćh] v. wait; live to see; wait 'til

doczepiać [do-che-pyaćh] v. fix append; attach; hitch; link

doczesny [do-ches-ni] adj. m. temporal; worldly; mundane

dodać [do-daćh] v. add; sum up; join; affix; impart

dodatek [do-da-tek] m. supplement; addition; fixture; extra; appendage; bonus

dodatni [do-dat-ńee] adj. m. positive; advantageous; active

dodawanie [do-da-va-ńe] n. addition

dogadać się [do-ga-daćh śhan] v. scoff; jibe; gibe; flout; bicker; remark; come to terms; communicate well

dogadzać [do-ga-dzaćh] v. please; accommodate; satisfy

doglądać [do-glown-daćh] v. supervise; tend; oversee

dogmat [dog-mat] m. dogma

dogodny [do-god-ni] adj. m. convenient; suitable; handy

dogonić [do-go-ńeećh] v catch up; overtake; be in hot pursuit; be hot on the track

dogryzać [do-gri-zaćh] v. vex; tease; finish munching; disturb

doić [do-eećh] v. milk; fleece

dojarka [do-yar-ka] f. milk maid; milking machine

dojazd [do-yazt] m. access; drive; approach; means of transport; journey

dojechać [do-ye-khaćh] v. reach; arrive; approach; bang; hit; give a blow; jeer; peck

dojeżdżać [do-yezh-dzhaćh] v. commute; be coming; pull in

dojmujący [doy-moo-yown-tsi] adj. m. acute; piercing; sharp; keen; tormenting; stinging

dojrzały [doy-zha-wi] adj. m. ripe; mellow; mature; adult

dojrzeć [doy-zhećh] v. glimpse; notice; ripen; be ripen; mellow

dojście [doy-śhćhe] n. access; (avenue of) approach

dok [dok] m. dock

dokarmić [do-kar-meećh] v. nourish additionally

dokazać [do-ka-zaćh] v. prove; achieve; accomplish; do the trick; get by effort

dokazywać [do-ka-zi-vaćh] v. frolic; gambol; romp and play

dokąd [do-kownt] adv. where; till when? whither; where to? how far? till when? how long?

dokładać [do-kwa-daćh] v. add; throw in; say more; give more

dokładny [dok-wad-ni] adj. m. accurate; exact; precise

dokoła [do-ko-wa] adv. round; round about; all round

dokonać [do-ko-naćh] v. achieve; accomplish; carry out; fulfil; do; execute

dokończenie [do-koń-che-ńe] n. conclusion; completion; end

doktor [dok-tor] m. doctor

dokręcać [do-kran-tsaćh] v. tighten; screw tight; turn off

dokuczać [do-koo-chaćh] v. vex; annoy; nag; bully; sting; trouble; spite; worry; torment

dola [do-la] f. fortune; lot

dolar [do-lar] m. dollar

doliczyć [do-lee-chićh] v. count up; add; charge more; reckon

dolina [do-lee-na] f. valley; dale; glen; coomb; (slang) pocket

dolny [dol-ni] adj. m. lower

dołączyć [do-wown-chićh] v. add; join; enclose; affix; tack on; annex; accede; crop up

dołek [do-wek] m. dimple; pit

dom [dom] m. house; home

domagać się [do-ma-gaćh śhan] v. demand; claim; insist

domiar [do-myar] m. additional assessment; surtax; adv.: on top of it all; in addition

domniemany [do-mńe-ma-ni] adj. m. supposed; assumed; alleged; presumed

domostwo [do-mos-tvo] n. household; homestead; farmstead; family's home

domownik [do-mov-ńeek] m. in-mate; household member

domowy [do-mo-vi] adj. m. domestic; homemade; private

domysł [do-misw] m. guess

doniesienie [do-ńe-śhe-ńe] m. denunciation; report; news

doniosły [do-ńo-swi] adj. m. significant; far reaching

donosiciel [do-no-śhee-ćhel] m.

denunciator; informer
donośny [do-nośh-ni] adj. m.
resounding; ringing; loud
dookoła [do-o-ko-wa] adv. round;
round about; all around; all
around; right round
dopaść [do-paśhćh] v. run
up; overtake; reach at a run;
catch up; hunt down; seize
dopalać [do-pa-laćh] v.
after burn; finish burning; burn
out; finish smoking
dopasować [do-pa-so-vaćh] v.
fit; adapt; adjust; match; tone
dopatrywać [do-pa-tri-vaćh] v.
see to it; find out; keep an
eye; perceive; detect; watch
dopełnić [do-pew-ńeećh] v.
fulfil; fill up; complete; make
up; complement; supplement
dopędzić [do-pan-dźheećh] v.
catch up with; overtake; gain
on; drive (cattle to...)
dopiąć [do-pyownćh] v. attain;
buckle up; button up; obtain
dopiero [do-pye-ro] adv. only;
just; hardly; barely; not till
dopilnować [do-peel-no-vaćh]
v. see something done; make
sure; supervise; take care
dopisek [do-pee-sek] m.
postscript; foot note
dopłata [do-pwa-ta] f. extra
payment; surcharge; extra fare
dopływ [do-pwif] m. tributary
dopomagać [do-po-ma-gaćh] v.
help; be of assistance
dopominać się [do-po-mee-
-naćh śhan] v. put in a
claim; demand; call for
dopóki [do-poo-kee] conj. as
long; as far; while; until; till
dopóty [do-poo-ti] conj. till; until;
so far; up to here; as long as
dopraszać się [do-pra-shaćh
śhan] v. solicit; beg; insist
doprawdy [do-prav-di] adv. truly;
indeed; really; is that so?
doprawiać [do-pra-vyaćh] v.
add (to taste); replace
doprowadzić [do-pro-va-
-dźheećh] v. lead to; cause;
provoke; reduce; achieve;

convey; result; bring
dopust Boży [do-poost bo-zhi]
m. calamity; scourge; act of
God; decree of Providence
dopuszczać [do-poosh-chaćh]
v. admit; allow; permit; be
open; give access; be patient
dopytać się [do-pi-taćh śhan]
v. find out; inquire; question
dorabiać [do-ra-byaćh] v. make
additionally; replace; finish
doradca [do-rad-tsa] m. adviser;
counselor; guide; consultant
dorastać [do-ras-taćh] v.
mature; grow; grow up; reach
doraźnie [do-raźh-ńe] adv.
(immediately) on the spot
doręczyć [do-ran-chićh] v.
hand in; deliver; transmit
dorobek [do-ro-bek] m.
acquisition; rise to affluence
dorobkiewicz [do-rob-ke-veech]
m. upstart; parvenu; new rich
doroczny [do-roch-ni] adj. m.
yearly; annual; recurring yearly
dorodny [do-rod-ni] adj. m.
handsome; fine-looking;
shapely; good-looking
dorosły [do-ros-wi] adj. m. adult;
grown up; mature; grown
dorożka [do-rosh-ka] f. cab
dorównywać [do-roov-ni-vaćh]
v. match; equal; catch up with
dorsz [dorsh] m. cod (fish)
dorywczy [do-riv-chi] adj. m.
occasional; improvised; fitful;
off-and-on; hit-and-run
dorzecze [do-zhe-che] n. river
basin; drainage area
dorzeczny [do-zhech-ni] adj. m.
reasonable; sensible; efficient;
adequate; acceptable; logical
dorzucać [do-zhoo-tsaćh] v.
throw in; add; throw as far as
dosadny [do-sad-ni] adj. m.
forceful; expressive; crisp
dosiadać [do-śha-daćh] v.
mount (horse); bestride
dosięgać [do-śhan-gaćh] v.
reach; attain; catch up with
doskonalić [do-sko-na-leećh] v.
perfect; improve; cultivate
doskwierać [do-skvye-raćh] v.

pinch; gripe; trouble; worry

dosłowny [do-**swov**-ni] adj. m.
literal; verbal; textual

dosłyszeć [do-**swi**-shećh] v.
hear well; catch a sound

dostać [dos-**tać**h] v. obtain;
reach; take out

dostarczyć [do-**star**-chićh] v.
provide; supply; deliver

dostateczny [do-sta-**tech**-ni] adj.
m. sufficient; adequate

dostatek [do-**sta**-tek] m.
abundance; wealth; affluence

dostawca [do-**stav**-tsa] m.
supplier; provider

dostawa [do-**sta**-va] f. delivery

dostawać [do-sta-**vać**h] v.
reach; receive; be attended to

dostęp [dos-**tanp**] m. access

dostojnik [do-**stoy**-ńeek] m.
dignitary; notable of high rank

dostosować [do-sto-**so**-vaćh] v.
accommodate; subordinate; fit

dostroić [do-**stro**-eećh] v. tune
up; conform; adapt

dostrzec [dos-**tshets**] v. notice;
behold; perceive; spot; spy;
see

dostudzić [do-**stoo**-dźheećh] v.
cool off

dosyć [do-**sić**h] adv. enough;
plenty; sufficient

dosztukować [do-shtoo-**ko**-
-vaćh] v. piece on; eke out;
sew on; add on; patch with

dość [do**śćh**] adv. enough

dośrodkowy [do-**śhrod**-ko-vi]
adj. m. centripetal; concentric

doświadczyć [do-**śhvyad**-
-chićh] v. experience; sustain;
feel; undergo; suffer; scourge

dotarcie [do-**tar**-ćhe] n.
reaching; overcoming friction

dotąd [do-**townt**] adv. up till
now; here to fore; hitherto;
thus far; so far; yet; by then;
till then; still; not...as yet

dotkliwy [do-**tklee**-vi] adj. m.
painful; keen; intense; severe

dotknąć [dot-**known**ćh] v.
touch; finger; offend; hurt

dotknięcie [dot-**kńan**-ćhe] n.
touch; contact; feeling; stroke

dotrzeć [do-**tshe**ćh] v. reach;
overcome friction; rub up

dotrzymać [do-**tshi**-maćh] v.
keep; stick to one's
commitment; adhere; redeem

dotychczas [do-**tikh**-chas] adv.
up to now; hitherto; to date

dotyczyć [do-**ti**-chićh] v.
concern; relate; regard; affect

dotyk [do-**tik**] m. touch; feel

dowcip [dov-**ćh**eep] m. wit;
joke; jest; gag; quip; sally

dowiedzieć się [do-**vye**-dźhećh
śhan] v. get to know; learn

do widzenia [do vee-**dze**-ńa]
good bye; see you later

dowierzać [do-**vye**-zhaćh] v.
trust; have confidence in

dowieść [do-**vye**śhćh] v.
prove; bring; vindicate

dowieźć [do-**vye**źhćh] v. 1.
supply; 2. drive to

dowodzić [do-vo-**dźh**eećh] v.
conduct; keep proving

dowolnie [do-**vol**-ńe] adv. at
will; optionally; freely

dowolny [do-**vol**-ni] adj. m.
optional; any; whichever

dowód [do-**voot**] m. proof;
evidence; record; token

dowódca [do-**vood**-tsa] m.
commander

dowóz [do-**voos**] m. supply;
delivery

doza [do-**za**] f. dose

dozbroić [do-**zbro**-eećh] v.
rearm; supplement weapons

dozgonny [do-**zgon**-ni] adj. m.
lifelong; lasting till death

doznać [doz-**na**ćh] v. go
through; undergo; endure;
feel; suffer; experience

dozorca [do-**zor**-tsa] m.
caretaker; watchman; overseer

dozorować [do-zo-ro-**va**ćh] v.
oversee; supervise; attend

dozór [do-**zoor**] m. surveillance

dozwolić [do-zvo-**lee**ćh] v.
allow to happen; let happen

dożynki [do-**zhin**-kee] pl. harvest
festivities

dożywocie [do-zhee-**vo**-ćhe] n.
life estate; life pension

dół [doow] m. pit; bottom part
drab [drap] m. ruffian; scamp
drabina [dra-bee-na] f. ladder
dramat [dra-mat] m. drama
drań [drań] m. scoundrel;
  crumb; rotter; cad
drapacz [dra-pach] m. scraper
drapać [dra-pać] v. scratch
drapieżnik [dra-pyezh-ńeek] m.
  beast of prey; plunderer
drastyczny [dra-stich-ni] adj. m.
  drastic; rough; violent
dratwa [drat-va] f. pitched tread;
  shoemaker's twine
drażliwy [dra-zhlee-vi] adj. m.
  touchy; irritable; ticklish
drażnić [drazh-ńeeć] v. vex;
  tease; irritate; whet; annoy;
  jar; provoke; stimulate; gall
drąg [drownk] m. pole; bar
drążyć [drown-zhić] v. hollow
  out; bore; torment; fret; gnaw
drelich [dre-leekh] m. denim
dren [dren] m. drain (pipe)
dreptać [drep-tać] v. triptrot;
  toddle; totter; patter
dreszcz [dreshch] m. chill;
  shudder; thrill; flutter; shiver
dreszczowiec [dresh-cho-vyets]
  m. thriller (novel or movie)
drewno [drev-no] n. piece of
  wood; timber; log; xylem
dręczyć [dran-chić] v. torment
drętwieć [drant-vyeć] v. grow
  numb; grow stiff; stiffen
drgać [drgać] v. tremble;
  vibrate; quiver; throb; wobble
drobiazg [dro-byazk] m. trifle;
  detail; trinket; small fry
drobina [dro-bee-na] f. particle
drobne [drob-ne] pl. small
  change; petty cash; small coin
drobnica [drob-ńee-tsa] f. small
  goods; small size packages
drobnostka [drob-nost-ka] f.
  trifle; small mater; trinket
drobny [drob-ni] adj. m. small;
  tiny; trivial; petty; slight
droga [dro-ga] f. 1. road; 2.
  journey; 3. adj. f. dear
drogeria [dro-ger-ya] f. drugstore;
  drysaltery
drogi [dro-gee] adj. m. dear;

expensive; costly; beloved
drogowskaz [dro-gov-skas] m.
  road sign; signpost
drozd [drozt] m. thrush
drożdże [drozh-dzhe] pl. yeast
drożeć [dro-zheć] v. grow
  dear; rise in price; appreciate
drożyzna [dro-zhiz-na] f. high
  cost of living; high prices
drób [droop] pl.paltry
dróżka [droozh-ka] f. path
druciany [droo-ća-ni] adj. m. of
  wire; made out of wire
drugi [droo-gee] num. second ;
  other; the other one; latter
druh [drookh] m. buddy;
  companion; friend; boy scout
druk [drook] m. print; printing
drut [droot] m. wire
druzgotać [drooz-go-tać] v.
  smash; shatter; crush to
  pieces; pulverize; crush
drużba [droozh-ba] m. best man
drużyna [droo-zhi-na] f. team
drwal [drval] m. lumber jack
drwić [drveeć] v. mock; deride; sneer; scoff; jeer; jibe
drwiny [drvee-ni] pl. mockery
dryg [drik] m. knack; flair for
drzazga [dzhaz-ga] f. splinter
drzeć [dzheć] v. tear; pull
drzemka [dzhem-ka] f. nap
drzewo [dzhe-vo] n. tree
drzeworyt [dzhe-vo-rit] m.
  woodcut; wood engraving
drzwi [dzhvee] n. door
drżeć [drzheć] v. shiver;
  shake; tremble; quiver; quake
dubeltówka [doo-bel-toov-ka] f.
  double barrel gun; shotgun
duch [dookh] m. spirit; ghost;
  state of mind; intendment
duchowieństwo [doo-kho-vyeń-
  -stvo] pl. clergy; priesthood
dudek [doo-dek] m. 1. hoopoe;
  2. dupe; fool; dolt; booby
dudnić [dood-ńeeć] v.
  resound; rumble; roll; thump
dudy [doo-di] pl. bagpipe
dukat [doo-kat] m. ducat
dulka [dool-ka] f. oarlock
duma [doo-ma] f. pride; epic
dumać [doo-mać] v. meditate

dumny [doom-ni] adj. m. proud
dupa [doo-pa] f. ass (vulg.)
dur [door] m. typhoid fever
dureń [doo-reń] m. fool; ass
durzyć [doo-zhich] v. fool;
   infatuate; bewilder; dupe
dusić [doo-śheech] v. strangle
dusigrosz [doo-śhee-grosh] m.
   penny pincher; niggard;
   cheapskate; miser; skinflint
dusza [doo-sha] f. soul; psyche
dużo [doo-zho] adv. much; many
duży [doo-zhi] adj. m. big; large;
   great; fair-sized; pretty large
dwa [dva] num. two; 2
dwakroć [dva-kroch] num.
   twice; two times
dwanaście [dva-naśh-che]
   num. twelve; 12
dwieście [dvyeśh-che] num.
   two hundred; 200
dwoić [dvo-eech] v. double
dwojaczki [dvo-yach-kee] pl.
   twins; double pot
dwoje [dvo-ye] num. the two;
   two; in two; couple; two
   (fold); two (ways); 2
dworski [dvors-kee] adj. m.
   courtly; manorial; of court
dworzec [dvo-zhets] m. (rail)
   station; depot
dwókrotnie [dvoo-krot-ńe] adv.
   twice; twice over; two times
dwór [dvoor] m. country manor
dwunastka [dvoo-nast-ka] f.
   twelve; (team) of twelve
dwustronny [dvoo-stron-ni] adj.
   m. two-sided; bilateral
dyg [dik] m. curtsy; bob
dygnitarz [dig-ńee-tash] m.
   dignitary; high ranking man
dygotać [di-go-tach] v. tremble
dykta [dik-ta] f. plywood
dyktator [dik-ta-tor] m. dictator;
   absolute ruler; tyrant
dylemat [di-le-mat] m. dilemma;
   perplexity; fix
dym [dim] m. smoke; fumes
dymić [di-meech] v. smoke
dynamit [di-na-meet] m.
   dynamite; W.W.II German
   ersatz (artificial) bread
dyndać [din-dach] v. dangle

dynia [di-ńa] f. pumpkin
dyplom [di-plom] m. diploma
dyplomacja [di-plo-mats-ya] f.
   diplomacy; policy; tact
dyrekcja [di-rek-tsya] f.
   management; headquarters
dyrygent [di-ri-gent] m. orchestra
   conductor; orchestra leader
dyscyplina [di-sci-plee-na] f.
   discipline; branch; line
dysk [disk] m. disc; discus
dyskrecja [dis-kre-tsya] f.
   discretion; management
dyskusja [dis-koo-sya] f. discussion; debate; controversy
dysponować [dis-po-no-vach]
   v. dispose; control; order
dysputa [dis-poo-ta] f. dispute;
   debate; controversy
dystans [dis-tans] m. distance
dystyngowany [dis-tin-go-va-ni]
   adj. m. distinguished
dysza [di-sha] f. nozzle; blast
   pipe; snout; twyer
dyszeć [di-shech] v. gasp; pant
dywan [di-van] m. carpet; rug
dywidenda [di-vee-den-da] f.
   dividend; bonus
dywizja [di-veez-ya] f. division
dyżurny [di-zhoor-ni] adj. m. on
   call; on duty; orderly
dzban [dzban] m. jug; pitcher
dziać się [dźhach śhan] v.
   occur; happen; take place
dziadek [dźha-dek] m.
   grandfather
dział [dźhaw] m. section
działacz [dźha-wach] m. activist
   (in politics, religion etc.)
działać [dźha-wach] v. act;
   work; be active; be effective
działka [dźhaw-ka] f. parcel
działo [dźha-wo] n. cannon
dziarski [dźhars-kee] adj. m.
   brisk; lively; swinging; rakish
dziąsło [dźhown-swo] n. gum
dzicz [dźheech] pl. savages
dzida [dźee-da] f. spear; pike
dzieci [dźhe-chee] pl. children
dzieciństwo [dźhe-cheeń-
   -stvo] n. childhood; boyhood;
   infancy; babyhood
dziecko [dźhets-ko] n. child;

baby; trot; brat; kiddie; kid
dziedziczyć [dźhe-dźhee--chiĆh] v. inherit (property, features); come into (money)
dziedzina [dźhe-dźhee-na] f. realm; area; sphere; domain
dziedziniec [dźhe-dźhee-ńets] m. yard; court; backyard
dziegieć [dźhe-gyeĆh] m. tar
dzieje [dźhe-ye] pl. history
dziejowy [dźhe-yo-vi] adj. m. historical; historic
dziekan [dźhe-kan] m. dean
dzielić [dźhe-leeĆh] v. divide; share; split; distribute
dzielnica [dźhel-ńee-tsa] f. province; quarter; section
dzielny [dźhel-ni] adj. m. brave; resourceful; efficient
dzieło [dźhe-wo] n. achievement; work; composition; cause; result; outcome; doing
dziennik [dźhen-ńeek] m. daily news; daily; journal; diary
dzienny [dźhen-ni] m daily; diurnal; day's (pay, work, etc.)
dzień [dźheń] m. day; daylight
dzień dobry [dźheń dob-ri] exp. good morning; good day
dzierżawa [dźer-zha-va] f. lease; rental; holding; household
dzierżyć [dźher-zhiĆh] v. wield (power); hold tight; grip
dziesiątka [dźhe-śhownt-ka] f. ten; (team of) ten; 10
dziesięć [dźhe-śhanĆh] num. ten; 10
dziewczyna [dźhev-chi-na] f. girl; lass; wench; maid
dziewica [dźhe-vee-tsa] f. virgin; maiden
dziewięć [dźhe-vyanĆh] num. nine; 9
dziewiętnaście [dźhe-vyant--naśh-Ćhe] num. nineteen
dzięcioł [dźhan-Ćhow] m. woodpecker
dziękczynienie [dźhank-chi-ńe--ńe] n. thanksgiving
dziękować [dźhan-ko-vaĆh] v. thank; give thanks
dzik [dźheek] m. boar; tusker
dziobać [dźho-baĆh] v. peck

dziób [dźhoop] m. beak; bill
dzisiejszy [dźhee-śhey-shi] adj. m. today's; modern
dziś [dźheeśh] adv. today
dziupla [dźhoop-la] f. (tree) hollow; (tree) cavity
dziura [dźhoo-ra] f. hole
dziurawy [dźhoo-ra-vi] adj. m. leaky; full of holes
dziw [dźheef] m. wonder
dziwactwo [dźhee-vats-tvo] n. crank; fad; craze; peculiarity
dziwić [dźhee-veeĆh] v. astonish; surprise; wonder
dziwny [dźheev-ni] m. strange; odd; queer; peculiar; singular
dzwon [dzvon] m. bell; chime
dźwięczeć [dźhvyan-cheĆh] v. ring; sound; jingle; clang
dźwięk [dźhvyank] m. sound
dźwig [dźhveek] n. crane
dźwigać [dźhvee-gaĆh] v. lift; hoist; raise; heave; erect; carry; upheave; elevate; erect
dżdżysty [dzhdzhis-ti] adj. m. wet; rainy; drizzly (weather
dżem [dzhem] m. jam; fruit jam
dżet [dzhet] m. jet
dżinsy [dzheen-si] pl. blue jeans (pants); jeans
dżokej [dzho-key] m. jockey
dżudo [dzhoo-do] n. judo (sport)
dżuma [dzhoo-ma] f. plague
dżungla [dzhoon-gla] f. jungle

E

echo [ekho] n. echo; response
edukacja [e-doo-ka-tsya] f. education; formal schooling; instruction; teaching
efekt [e-fekt] m. effect
efektowny [e-fek-tov-ni] adj. m. showy; striking; attractive
efektywny [e-fek-tiv-ni] adj. m. efficient; effective; real
egida [e-gee-da] f. protection; auspices; protectorate

egoista [e-go-**ees**-ta] m. egotist
egoistyczny [e-go-ees-tich-ni]
  adj. m. selfish; self seeking
egzamin [eg-**za**-meen] m.
  examination; exam; standing a
  test; a set of questions
egzekucja [eg-ze-**kuts**-ya] f.
  execution; seizure; flogging
egzemplarz [eg-zem-**plazh**] m.
  copy (sample); specimen
egzystencja [eg-żis-ten-tsya] f.
  existence; livelihood
ekierka [e-ker-ka] f. set square;
  draftsman's triangle
ekipa [e-kee-pa] f. team; crew
ekonomia [e-ko-no-mya] f.
  economics; thrift; economy
ekran [ek-ran] m. screen; shield
ekspedient [eks-pe-dyent] m.
  salesperson; clerk; salesman
ekspedycja [eks-pe-**dits**-ya] f.
  dispatch; expedition; service
ekspert [eks-pert] m. expert
eksploatować [eks-plo-a-to-
  -vaćh] v. exploit; sweat;
  utilize (machines); operate
eksponat [eks-po-nat] m. exhibit
ekspozytura [eks-po-zi-**too**-ra] f.
  agency; branch office; branch
ekwipować [ek-vee-po-vaćh]
  v. equip; fit out; provide with
elaborat [e-la-bo-rat] m. study
  elaborate essay; dissertation
elastyczność [e-las-tich-
  -nośhćh] f. elasticity; resilience; flexibility; buoyancy
elegancja [e-le-gan-tsya] f.
  elegance; fashion; style
elektrociepłownia [e-lek-tro-
  -ćhep-**wov**-ńa] f. steam plant
elektryczność [e-lek-trich-
  -nośhćh] f. electricity
element [e-le-ment] m. element
elementarny [e-le-men-**tar**-ni] adj.
  m. fundamental; primary
elewator [e-le-**va**-tor] m.
  (grain) elevator; hoist
emalia [e-ma-lya] f. enamel
emeryt [e-me-rit] m. retired
  person; pensioner; pensionary
emigracja [e-mee-**grats**-ya] f.
  emigration; exile; emigrants
emisja [e-mees-ya] f. emission

emocja [e-mots-ya] f. thrill
entuzjazm [en-tooz-yazm] m.
  enthusiasm; rapture
energia [e-ner-gya] f. energy
energiczny [e-ner-geech-ni] adj.
  m. energetic; vigorous
epoka [e-po-ka] f. epoch
epitet [e-pee-tet] m. epithet
era [e-ra] f. era; epoch
erotyczny [e-ro-tich-ni] adj. m.
  erotic; sexual; amatory
eskadra [es-kad-ra] f. squadron;
  aerial fleet
eskorta [es-kor-ta] f. escort
estetyczny [es-te-tich-ni] adj. m.
  aesthetic; in good taste
etap [e-tap] m. stage (of
  development); halting place
etatowy [e-ta-to-vi] adj. m.
  permanent (job); full time
eter [e-ter] m. ether
etyczny [e-tich-ni] adj. m.
  ethical; moral (standard)
etykieta [e-ti-ke-ta] f. label;
  etiquette; formality; ceremonial; acceptable manners
ewakuacja [e-va-koo-ats-ya] f.
  evacuation; removal; emptying
ewangelia [e-van-gel-ya] f.
  gospel; gospel truth
ewangielik [e-van-ge-leek] m.
  protestant; Lutheran
ewentualność [e-ven-too-al-
  -nośhćh] f. possibility
ewentualnie [e-ven-too-al-ńe]
  adv. possibly; if need be
ewidencja [e-vee-den-tsya] f.
  records; lists; files; roll
ewolucja [e-vo-loo-tsya] f.
  evolution; development
ex- see eks-

F

fabryczny [fab-rich-ni] adj. m.
  manufactured; machine made
fabryka [fa-bri-ka] f. factory
fabuła [fa-boo-wa] f. fable; story

facet [fa-tset] m. guy
fachowiec [fa-kho-vyets] m.
expert; specialist; connoisseur
fajdać [fay-daćh] v. shit (vulg.)
fajans [fa-yans] f. earthenware
fajerka [fa-yer-ka] f. cook-top
unit; gas stove lid; burner
fajka [fay-ka] f. pipe (for
smoking); wild boar's tusk
fajtłapa [fay-twa-pa] m. all
thumbs guy (awkward, clumsy
man); dangling hand; crock
fakt [fakt] m. fact; reality
faktor [fak-tor] m. broker; agent;
factor (math.); intermediary
faktycznie [fak-tich-ńe] adv. in
fact; actually; indeed; truly
fala [fa-la] f. wave; tide; surge
falisty [fa-lees-ti] adj. m. wavy;
rolling; corrugated
falochron [fa-lokh-ron] m.
breakwater; pier; jetty; mole
falsyfikat [fal-si-fee-kat] m.
forgery; counterfeit; fake
fałd [fawt] m. fold (wrinkle)
fałsz [fawsh] m. falsehood
fałszować [faw-sho-vaćh] v.
falsify; fake; forge; sing flat
fama [fa-ma] f. fame; rumor
fanaberie [fa-na-be-rye] pl.
whims; fads; frills; ostentation
fanatyk [fa-na-tik] m. fanatic;
enthusiast; bigot; maniac
fanfaron [fan-fa-ron] m. braggart;
coxcomb; swaggerer
fantastyczny [fan-tas-tich-ni] adj.
m. fantastic; wild; odd
fantazja [fan-taz-ya] f. dash;
imagination; fiction; whim
fara [fa-ra] f. parish church
farba [far-ba] f. paint; dye color;
dyeing; oil color; ink; blood
farbować [far-bo-vaćh] v. dye
farsa [far-sa] f. farce; mockery
farsz [farsh] m. stuffing
fartuch [far-tookh] m. apron
fasola [fa-so-la] f. bean
fasonować [fa-so-no-vaćh] v.
fashion; shape; mold model
fastryga [fas-tri-ga] f. tack;
basting; baste; tacks
faszyzm [fa-shizm] m. fascism
fatalny [fa-tal-ni] adj. m. fatal; ill

-fated; awful; nasty; fateful
fatyga [fa-ti-ga] f. trouble;
fatigue; bother; pains
fatałaszki [fa-ta-wash-kee] pl.
knick-knacks; frippery; trinkets
febra [feb-ra] f. fever; the shakes
faworyzować [fa-vo-ri-zo-vaćh]
v. favor; play favorites
felczer [fel-cher] m. male nurse;
medical assistant
federacja [fe-de-rats-ya] f.
federation; union
feralny [fe-ral-ni] adj. m. unlucky;
ill-fated; hapless; disastrous
ferie [fe-rye] pl. holidays
ferma [fer-ma] f. farm; ranch
ferment [fer-ment] m. ferment
festyn [fes-tin] m. festival
fetor [fe-tor] m. stench; reek
figa [fee-ga] f. fig; nix
figiel [fee-gel] m. practical joke;
prank; trick; ill turn
figura [fee-goo-ra] f. figure;
shape; form; image; big wig
fikcja [feek-tsya] f. fiction
filar [fee-lar] m. pillar
filatelista [fee-la-te-lees-ta] m.
stamp-collector; philatelist
filc [feelts] m. felt
filia [fee-lya] f. branch (store);
branch-office; branch
filiżanka [fee-lee-zhan-ka] f. cup;
cupful; coffee-cup
film [feelm] m. film; picture
filolog [fee-lo-log] m. philologist;
linguist; linguistics teacher
filozof [fee-lo-zof] m. philosopher
filtr [feeltr] m. filter; strainer
filut [fee-loot] m. jester; rogue;
joker; fox; sly boots
finanse [fee-nan-se] pl. finances;
funds; money resources
finisz [fee-ńeesh] m. end (of a
run); the finish; finis; the end
fiołek [fyo-wek] m. violet
fiołkowy [fyow-ko-vi] adj. m.
purple; violet; of the violet
firanka [fee-ran-ka] f. curtain;
drapery; pl. hangings
firma [feer-ma] f. business; firm;
name of a firm; establishment
fisharmonia [fees-har-moń-ya] f.
philharmonic orchestra

fizjognomia [fees-yo-**gnom**-ya] f.
face; external aspect
fizjonomia [fees-yo-**nom**-ya] f.
face; physiognomy
fizjolog [feez-yo-log] m.
physiologist
fizyczny [fee-**zich**-ni] adj. m.
physical; bodily; manual
fizyk [**fee**-zik] m. physicist
flaczki [**flach**-kee] pl. tripe
flaga [**fla**-ga] f. banner; flag;
ensign; standard; signal
flaki [**fla**-kee] pl. bowels
flakon [**fla**-kon] m. vase
flanela [fla-**ne**-la] f. flannel
flaszka [**flash**-ka] f. bottle
flama [**fla**-ma] f. lady-love
flądra [**flown**-dra] f. flounder
flegma [**fleg**-ma] f. phlegm
flejtuch [**fley**-tookh] m. slut
flet [flet] m. flute
flirt [fleert] m. flirt
flisak [**flee**-sak] m. raft-man
flora [**flo**-ra] f. flora
floret [**flo**-ret] m. foil
flota [**flo**-ta] f. navy; fleet
fluksja [**flook**-sya] f. tooth
-infection; swelling
fluid [**floo**-eet] m. fluid
fochy [**fo**-khi] pl. blues; whims;
sulks; pouts; sudden fancy
foka [**fo**-ka] f. seal
folgować [fol-**go**-vaćh] v.
slacken; relax; indulge; abate
folklor [fol-klor] m. folklore
folusz [fo-**loosh**] m. fulling mill
folwark [**fol**-vark] m. farm
fonetyczny [fo-ne-**tich**-ni] adj.
phonetic; of speech sounds
fontanna [fon-**tan**-na] f. fountain;
spurt of water; waterworks
foremny [fo-**rem**-ni] adj. m.
shapely; handsome; regular;
symmetrical; well-proportioned
forma [**for**-ma] f. shape; mold
format [**for**-mat] m. size
formularz [for-**moo**-lazh] m.
(application) form; blank
formuła [for-**moo**-wa] f. formula
fornir [for-**ńeer**] m. veneer
forsa [**for**-sa] f. dough; chink;
bread; tin; a pot of money
forsować [for-**so**-vaćh] v.

force; strain; urge; exhort;
advocate; overcome; exert
fort [fort] m. fort; stronghold
forteca [for-te-**tsa**] f. fortress;
citadel; stronghold
fortel [for-tel] m. stratagem;
ruse; subterfuge; trick; device
fortepian [for-te-**pyan**] m. grand
piano; stringed keyboard
fortuna [for-**too**-na] f. fortune
fosa [**fo**-sa] f. moat; broad ditch
fosfat [**fos**-fat] m. phosphate
fosfor [**fos**-for] m. phosphorus
fotel [**fo**-tel] m. armchair
fotograf [**fo**-to-graf] m.
photographer
fotografia [fo-to-**gra**-fya] f
photograph; snap shot; picture
fracht [frakht] m. freight
fragment [**frag**-ment] m. frag-
 gment; episode; excerpt; scrap
frak [frak] m. evening formal
framuga [fra-moo-ga] f. recess
(structure); bay; embrasure
frant [frant] m. sly dog; knave
frasunek [fra-**soo**-nek] m. worry;
grief; sorrow; care; trouble
fraszka [**frash**-ka] f. trifle
frazes [**fra**-zes] m. platitude
frekwencja [frek-**ven**-tsya] f.
attendance; turnout; frequency
frędzla [**frandz**-la] f. fringe
fresk [fresk] m. fresco
front [front] m. front; face, etc.
froterować [fro-te-ro-vaćh] v.
rub; polish; wax (floors)
frunąć [froo-**nown**ćh] v. fly
away; fly about; flee
frymarczyć [fri-mar-chićh] v.
barter; trade; traffic
fryzjer [fri-**zyer**] m. barber;
hairdresser; beautician
fujara [foo-**ya**-ra] m. & f.
all thumbs; nincompoop; pan-
pipe; oaf; ninny; (muz.) pipe
fukać [foo-kaćh] v. scold; puff
fundacja [foon-da-**tsya**] f.
foundation; endowment
fundament [foon-da-**ment**] m.
foundation; substructure
fundusz [foon-doosh] m. fund
funkcja [foon-**ktsya**] f. function;
functions; office; duties

funt [foont] m. pound (weight)
fura [foo-ra] f. cart; wagon
furgon [foor-gon] m. truck; van
furia [foo-rya] f. fury; rage
furiat [foo-ryat] m. madman
furman [foor-man] m. carter
furora [foo-ro-ra] f. sensation
furtka [foort-ka] f. gate; door
fusy [foo-si] pl. lees; dregs
fuszer [foo-sher] m. bungler
futerał [foo-te-raw] m. (gun)
    case; holster; sheath; box
futro [foot-ro] n. fur (skin, coat)
futryna [foo-tri-na] f. door-frame;
    window-frame; opening-frame
futrzarz [foot-shash] m. furrier
fuzja [fooz-ya] f. fusion; merger;
    amalgamation; shotgun; rifle

G

gabardyna [ga-bar-di-na] f.
    gabardine; twilled cloth
gabinet [ga-bee-net] m. study;
    (ruling) cabinet; office
gablotka [gab-lot-ka] f. showcase
gad [gat] m. reptile; mean guy
gadać [ga-daćh] v. talk; yak;
    prattle; talk nonsense; chat
gaduła [ga-doo-wa] m. clapper
gaj [gay] m. grove
gala [ga-la] f. gala; festivity
galanteria [ga-lan-te-rya] f.
    gallantry; haberdashery
galareta [ga-la-re-ta] f. jelly
galeria [ga-le-rya] f. gallery
galimatias [ga-lee-ma-tyas] m.
    gibberish; hotchpotch; mess
galon [ga-lon] m. gallon
galop [ga-lop] m. gallop; run
galwaniczny [gal-va-ńeech-ni]
    adj. m. galvanic; volcanic
gałąź [ga-wownźh] f. branch
gałgan [gaw-gan] m. rag; rascal;
    good-for-nothing; scamp
gałganiarz [gaw-ga-ńazh] m.
    ragtagman; rag-picker; ragman
gałka [gaw-ka] f. knob; ball

gama [ga-ma] f. scale
gamoń [ga-moń] m. lout; oaf
ganek [ga-nek] m. balcony
gangrena [gan-gre-na] f.
    gangrene; depravity; cor-
    ruption; decay of tissue
ganić [ga-ńeećh] v. blame;
    criticize; rebuke; upbraid
gapa [ga-pa] f. oaf; stowaway
gapić się [ga-peećh śhan] v.
    gape; star-gaze; moon; stare
gapie [ga-pye] pl. gapers
garaż [ga-razh] m. garage
garb [garp] m. hunch; hump
garbarnia [gar-bar-ńa] f. tannery;
    tan-yard; tanning hides place
garbować [gar-bo-vaćh] v. tan
garbaty [gar-ba-ti] adj. m. hunch
    -backed; humpy; uneven; hilly
garbus [gar-boos] m. = garbaty
garbić [gar-beećh] v. stoop
garderoba [gar-de-ro-ba] f.
    wardrobe; dressing-room
gardło [gard-wo] n. throat
garłować [gard-wo-vaćh] v.
    talk big; clamor; cry for
gardłowy [gard-wo-vi] adj. m.
    guttural; punishable by death
gardzić [gar-dźheećh] v. de-
    spise; scorn; have in con-
    tempt; hold in contempt
gardziel [gar-dźhel] f. throat;
    fauces; choke; gorge; jaws
garnąć [gar-nownćh] v. gather
garncarz [garn-tsazh] m. potter
garnek [gar-nek] m. pot; potful
garnirować [gar-ńee-ro-vaćh]
    v. garnish; trim (a dres etc.)
garnitur [gar-ńee-toor] m. set;
    suite (clothes); assortment
garnizon [gar-ńee-zon] m.
    garrison; stationed troops
garnuszek [gar-noo-shek] m. cup
garstka [garst-ka] f. handful
garść [garśhćh] f. handful
gasić [ga-śheećh] v. expire;
    go out; die down; extinguish;
    quench; put out; eclipse
gasnąć [gas-nownćh] v.
    die down; go out; wane; fade
gaśnica [gaśh-ńee-tsa] f. fire
    -extinguisher
gastronomiczny [gas-tro-no

-meech-ni] adj. m. gastro-
nomic; of good cooking
gastryczny [gas-**trich**-ni] adj. m.
gastric; in or near the stomach
gatunek [ga-**too**-nek] m. kind;
quality; sort; class; species
gawęda [ga-**van**-da] f. chat
gawiedź [ga-**vyedźh**] f. mob;
rabble; populace; gaping
crowd; the common people
gawron [gav-ron] m. rook
gaz [gaz] m. gas; open throttle
gaza [ga-za] f. gauze
gazeciarz [ga-ze-ćhash] m. pa-
perboy; newsstand (kiosk)
gazeta [ga-ze-ta] f. newspaper
gazolina [ga-zo-lee-na] f.
gasoline; gasolene; petrol
gazomierz [ga-zo-myezh] m. gas
meter; gas gauge
gazownia [ga-zov-ńa] f.
gas plant; gas works
gaźnik [gaźh-ńeek] m. carbu-
rettor (for air-gasoline mixing)
gaża [ga-zha] f. wage; salary
gąbczasty [gownb-cha-sti] adj.
m. spongy; squashy; mushy
gąbka [gownb-ka] f. sponge
gąsienica [gown-śhe-ńee-tsa] f.
caterpillar; band; track
gąsior [gown-śhor] m. gander;
jar; demijohn; ridge tile
gaszcz [gownshch] m. thicket
gbur [gboor] m. rude; boor
gburowaty [gboo-ro-va-ti] adj. m.
boorish; rude; churlish; surly
gdakać [gda-kaćh] v. cackle;
yak; sound like a hen
gderać [gde-raćh] v. grumble
gdy [gdi] conj. when; as; that
gdyby [gdi-bi] conj. if
gdyż [gdizh] conj. for; because
gdzie [gdźhe] adv. conj. where
gdzie indziej [gdźhe een-dźhey]
elsewhere; somewhere else
gdziekolwiek [gdźhe-kol-vyek]
adv. anywhere; wherever
gdzieniegdzie [gdźhe-ńeg-
-dźhe] adv. here and there; in
places; at intervals
gdzieś [gdźheśh] adv. somewhere; (vulg. exp.: in my ass)
gejzer [gey-zer] m. geyser

gen [gen] m. gene
genealogia [ge-ne-a-lo-gya] f.
genealogy; origin; pedigree
generacja [ge-ne-rats-ya] f.
generation; production
generalny [ge-ne-ral-ni] adj. m.
general; widespread; full-scale
generał [ge-ne-raw] m. general
genetyczny [ge-ne-tich-ni] adj. m
genetic
geneza [ge-ne-za] f. origin;
genesis; birth; the beginning
genialny [ge-ńal-ni] adj. m.
ingenious; genial; great
geniusz [ge-ńyoosh] m. genius
geodezja [ge-o-dez-ya] f.
geodesy (grid of polygons)
geografia [ge-o-gra-fya] f.
geography; the physical traits
geologia [ge-o-lo-gya] f. geology
geometra [ge-o-met-ra] m.
surveyor; land surveyor
geometria [ge-o-met-rya] f.
geometry (of points, lines, etc)
georginia [ge-or-gee-ńa] f. dahlia
germański [ger-mań-skee]
adj. m. Germanic (languages)
gest [gest] m. gesture; motion
gestykulować [ges-ti-koo-lo-
-vaćh] v. gesticulate
getto [get-to] n. ghetto
gęba [gan-ba] f. mug; mouth;
puss; snout; muzzle; face; gob
gęgać [gan-gaćh] v. cackle
gęś [ganśh] f. goose
gęśl [ganśhl] f. lute
gęstość [gan-stośhćh] f. density; thickness; closeness
gęstwina [ganst-vee-na] f.
thicket; array; accumulation
giąć [gyownćh] v. bow; bend
gibki [geeb-kee] adj. m. pliant;
flexible; limber; supple
giełda [gew-da] f. stock
-exchange; money-market
giez [ges] m. gadfly; breeze
giętki [gant-kee]adj. m. flexible;
nimble; elastic; adaptable
gigant [gee-gant] m. giant
gilza [geel-za] f. (cartridge) case;
cartridge-shell; cigarette tube
gimnastyczny [geem-na-stich-ni]
adj. m. gymnastic; athletic

gimnazjum [geem-naz-yoom] n.
high-school; middle-school
ginąć [gee-nownćh] v. perish
ginekolog [gee-ne-ko-log] m.
gynecologist
gips [geeps] m. gypsum; plaster
gitara [gee-ta-ra] f. guitar
glazura [gla-zoo-ra] f. glaze
gleba [gle-ba] f. soil
glejt [gleyt] m. safe-conduct
ględzić [glan-dźheećh] v. talk
through one's hat; talk nonsense; twaddle; blather; prate
gliceryna [glee-tse-ri-na] f.
glycerin (soap. etc)
glin [gleen] m. aluminum
glina [glee-na] f. clay; loam
glista [glees-ta] f. earth-worm;
warm; ascaris; nema
glob [glop] m. globe; sphere
gładki [gwad-kee] adj. m. plain;
smooth; sleek; even; level;
glib; straight; lank; fluent
gładzić [gwa-dźheećh] v. level; smooth; sleek; (put to
death); mangle; stroke; press
głaskać [gwas-kaćh] v. caress;
fondle; stroke; pet; tickle
głaz [gwaz] m. boulder; rock
głąb [gwownp] f. depth; abyss
głąb [gwownp] f. stalk; fool
głębia [gwan-bya] f. depth;
deep; interior; intensity
głęboki [gwan-bo-kee] adj. m.
deep; distant; remote; intense
głębokość [gwan-bo-košhćh]
f. depth; profundity; keenness
głodny [gwod-ni] adj. m. hungry
głodować [gwo-do-vaćh] v.
starve; hunger; lay off food
głodzić [gwo-dźheećh] v. deprive, stint (of food); starve
(someone); underfeed
głos [gwos] m. voice; sound;
tone; toot; vote; opinion
głosować [gwo-so-vaćh] v.
vote; cast one's vote
głośnik [gwošh-ńeek] m.
loudspeaker; public-address
system; speaking trumpet
głośno [gwošh-no] adv. loud
głośny [gwošh-ni] adj. m. loud
głowa [gwo-va] f. head; chief

głowić się [gwo-veećh šhan]
v. beat one's brains out;
puzzle; rack one's brains
głód [gwoot] m. hunger; famine
głóg [gwook] m. hawthorn
główka [gwoov-ka] f. pinhead;
knob; tip; top; boss; heading
głównodowodzący [gwoov-no
-do-vo-dzown-tsi] m. com-
mander-in-chief (of an army)
główny [gwoov-ni] adj. m. main;
predominant; foremost; chief
głuchy [gwoo-khi] adj. m. deaf
głupi [gwoo-pee] adj. m. silly;
stupid; foolish; asinine
głupiec [gwoo-pyets] m.
addle-brain; fool; idiot; loony;
goof; numskull; addle-brain
głupota [gwoo-po-ta] f. stupidity;
imbecility; foolishness
głupstwo [gwoop-stvo] n. nonsense; trifle; blunder; mistake
głuszec [gwoo-shets] m. grouse
gmach [gmakh] m. large building
gmatwać [gmat-vaćh] v. mix
up; tangle; embroil; complicate; muddle; jumble; confuse
gmerać [gme-raćh] v. pry; poke
gmin [gmeen] m. populace
gmina [gmee-na] f. county;
parish; community; commune
gnat [gnat] m. bone (slang)
gnębić [gnan-beećh] v. oppress
gniady [gńa-di] adj. m. bay
(horse); dark brown horse
gniazdo [gńaz-do] n. nest
gnić [gńeećh] v. rot; decay
gnida [gńee-da] f. nit
gnieść [gńešhćh] v. squeeze
gniew [gńev] m. anger; wrath
gnieździć się [gńeźh-
-dźheećh šhan] v. nestle;
cluster; assemble; collect
gnilny [gńeel-ni] adj. m. putrid;
of rot; septic; putrefactive
gnoić [gno-eećh] v. putrefy
gnojówka [gno-yoov-ka] f. liquid
manure; manure pit; dunghill
gnój [gnooy] m. manure; dung;
stinker (vulg.); lousy bum
gnuśny [gnoošh-ni] adj. m.
sluggish; lazy; idle; listless
godło [god-wo] n. emblem

godność [god-nośhćh] f. dignity; name; pride; self-esteem;
self-respect; post; high rank
godny [god-ni] adj. m. worthy
gody [go-di] pl. nuptials; mating
godzić [go-dźheećh] v. reconcile; hire; square; engage; aim
godzien [go-dźhen] adj. m.
deserving; worthy
godzina [go-dźhee-na] f. hour
godziwy [go-dźhee-vi] adj. m.
proper; suitable; just; fair
goić [go-eećh] v. heal; cure
goleń [go-leń] m. shin-bone
golić [go-leećh] v. shave
golonka [go-lon-ka] f. pig's feet
dish; ham below the knee
gołąb [go-wownb] m. pigeon
gołoledź [go-wo-ledźh] f.
glazed frost; frozen; dew
gołosłowny [go-wo-swov-ni] adj.
m. unfounded; proofless; vain
goły [go-wi] adj. m. naked
gonić [go-ńeećh] v. chase;
hunt; pursue; track; run after
goniec [go-ńets] m. messenger
gonitwa [go-ńeet-va] f. chase
gont [gont] m. shingle
gorąco [go-rown-tso] n. heat
gorący [go-rown-tsi] adj. m. hot;
sultry; warm; hearty; lively
gorączka [go-rownch-ka] f. fever; shakes; excitement; heat;
temperature; heat; passion
gorczyca [gor-chi-tsa] f. white
mustard; charlock
gorętszy [go-rant-shi] adj. m.
hotter; fervent; more intense
gorliwiec [gor-lee-vyets] m.
zealot; ardent supporter
gorliwy [gor-lee-vi] adj. m.
zealous; keen; eager; devout
gorset [gor-set] m. girdle
gorszy [gor-shi] adj. m. worse
gorszyć [gor-shićh] v. demoralize; scandalize; shock; deprave; make improper; corrupt
gorycz [go-rich] f. bitterness
goryl [go-ril] m. gorilla
gorzałka [go-zhaw-ka] f. brandy
spirits; booze; spirit
gorzeć [go-zhećh] v. be ablaze
gorzej [go-zhey] adv. worse

gorzelnia [go-zhel-ńa] f. dis-
tillery; still; smell of booze
gorzki [gozh-kee] adj. m. bitter
gospoda [gos-po-da] f. inn
gospodarczy [gos-po-dar-chi] adj.
m. economic; farm; charring
gospodarka [gos-po-dar-ka] f.
economy; housekeeping; farming; husbandry; management
gospodarny [gos-po-dar-ni] adj.
m. economical; thrifty
gospodarstwo [gos-po-dar-stvo]
n. household; farm; property;
possession; holding
gospodarz [gos-po-dash] m.
landlord; landholder; host; farmer; manager; home-steward
gospodyni [gos-po-di-ńee] f.
landlady; hostess; manageress
gosposia [gos-po-śha] f.
housekeeper; maid; servant
gościć [gośh-ćheećh] v.
receive; entertain; treat; stay
at; to enjoy hospitality
gościna [gośh-ćhee-na] f.
visit; stay at sb. house
gościnność [gośh-ćheen-
-nośhćh] f. hospitality
gość [gośhćh] m. guest;
caller; visitor; customer
gościec [gośh-ćhets] m. gout;
arthritis; rheumatism
gotować [go-to-vaćh] v. cook;
boil; get ready; prepare
gotowość [go-to-vośhćh] f.
readiness; willingness
gotowy [go-to-vi] adj. m. ready;
done; complete; willing
gotówka [go-toov-ka] f. cash
gotyk [go-tik] m. Gothic
goździk [gożh-dźheek] m.
carnation; clove; lily-flower
góra [goo-ra] f. mountain
góral [goo-ral] m. mountaineer
górnictwo [goor-ńeets-tvo] n.
mining; mining industry
górnik [goor-ńeek] m. miner
górnolotny [goor-no-lot-ni]
adj. m. lofty; soaring; gaudy
górny [goor-ni] adj. m. upper
górować [goo-ro-vaćh] v.
prevail; excel; dominate; rise
górski [goor-skee] adj. m.

mountainous; mountain-
górzysty [goo-**zhis**-ti] adj. m.
hilly; mountainous
gówniarz [goov-**ńazh**] m. (vulg.)
shit-ass; whipster; squirt
gówno [goov-no] n. shit (vulg.)
gra [gra] f. game; sham; acting
grab [grab] m. hornbeam tree;
hardbeam tree
grabarz [gra-bazh] m. grave
-digger; sexton; burying beetle
grabić [gra-beech] v. rake;
plunder; rob; sack; rake up
grabie [gra-bye] n. rake
grabież [gra-byezh] f. plunder
graca [gra-tsa] f. rabbler; hoe
gracja [gra-tsya] f. grace
gracować [gra-tso-vach] v.
scrape; rake; mix mortar; hoe
gracz [grach] m. player; gambler;
crafty double-dealer; sly fox
grać [grach] v. play; act;
gamble; pretend; pulsate
grad [grad] m. hail; volley
grafika [gra-fee-ka] f. graphics;
arts; art of writing; engraving
gram [gram] m. gram
gramatyka [gra-ma-ti-ka] f.
grammar; grammar book
gramofon [gra-mo-fon] m. record
player (turntable); phonograph
gramolić się [gra-mo-leech
śhan] v. clamber; climb
granat [gra-nat] m. grenade
granatnik [gra-nat-ńeek] m.
mortar; howitzer
granatowy [gra-na-to-vi] adj. m.
navy blue; of grenades
granda [gran-da] f. swindle
graniastosłup [gra-ńa-sto-swoop]
m. prism (regular, right, etc.)
granica [gra-ńee-tsa] f. border; boundary; limit; frontier;
range; reach; confines; bounds
granit [gra-ńeet] m. granite
granulować [gra-noo-lo-vach] v.
granulate (form into grains)
grań [grań] f. mountain ridge;
crest; edge; razor's edge
grasować [gra-so-vach] v. ravage; roam; about; prowl; maraud; stalk; overrun; rove
grat [grat] m. run down furniture

(or man); crock; trash
gratis [gra-tees] adv. free of
charge; something given free
gratka [grat-ka] f. windfall
gratulacja [gra-too-lats-ya] f.
congratulations; felicitation
grawer [gra-ver] m. engraver
grawitacja [gra-vee-tats-ya] f.
gravitation (pull of gravity)
grdyka [grdi-ka] f. Adam's apple
grecki [grets-kee] adj. m. Greek
gremialnie [gre-myal-ńe] adv. in
-a-mass; collectively; altogether; in a group; one and all
grobla [grob-la] f. dike; dam
grobowiec [gro-bo-vyets] m.
tomb; sepulchre; family vault
grobowy [gro-bo-vi] adj. m.
grave; deathly; gloomy; dismal
groch [grokh] m. pea; pea plant
grom [grom] m. thunderclap
gromada [gro-ma-da] f. crowd;
throng; community; team
gromadzić [gro-ma-dźheech] v.
amass; hoard; gather; attract
gromić [gro-meech] v. storm;
rout; reprimand; defeat
grono [gro-no] n. bunch of
grapes; cluster; group; body of
people; company; circle
gronostaj [gro-no-stay] m. ermine
grosz [grosh] m. grosz; penny
groszek [gro-shek] m. green pea;
spotted pattern; (sweet) pea
grot [grot] m. dart; spike
grota [gro-ta] f. grotto; cave
groza [gro-za] f. dread; horror
grozić [gro-źheech] v. threaten
groźba [groźh-ba] f. threat
grób [groop] m. grave; tomb
gród [groot] m. (fortified) town
gródź [groodźh] m. f. bulkhead
grubiański [groo-byań-skee] adj.
m. rude; coarse; obscene
grubość [groo-boshch] f.
thickness; girth; size; grist
gruby [groo-bi] adj. m. thick; fat;
big; stout; large; low-pitched
gruchotać [groo-kho-tach] v.
shatter; batter; rattle; crash
gruczoł [groo-chow] m. gland
gruda [groo-da] f. lump; clod
grudzień [groo-dźheń] m.

(the month of) December
grunt [groont] m. ground; soil
grupa [groo-pa] f. group; class
grusza [groo-sha] f. pear-tree
gruz [groos] m. rubble; ruins
gruzeł [groo-zew] m. clot
gruzy [groo-zi] pl. debris
gruźlica [grooźh-lee-tsa] f. tuberculosis; consumption
gryka [gri-ka] f. buckwheat
grymas [gri-mas] m. grimace
grypa [gri-pa] f. flu; influenza
grysik [gri-śheek] m. grits
gryzoń [gri-zoń] m. rodent
gryźć [griźhćh] v. bite; gnaw; chew; prick; torment
grzać [gzhaćh] v. warm; fire; warm up; beat; shoot; thrash
grządka [gzhownd-ka] f. flower bed; patch; (hen-) roost
grząść [gzhownśhćh] v. wade; proceed with difficulty
grząski [gzhown-skee] adj. m. quaggy; slimy; slushy; miry
grzbiet [gzhbyet] m. back; spine; ridge; butt; edge; rib
grzebać [gzhe-baćh] v. bury; rummage; dig; rake up; fumble
grzebień [gzhe-byeń] m. comb; crest of a wave; teaser
grzech [gzhekh] m. sin; fault
grzechotka [gzhe-khot-ka] f. rattle; flapper; clapper
grzechotnik [gzhe-khot-ńeek] m. rattlesnake
grzeczność [gzhech-nośhćh] f. politeness; favor; attentions
grzęznąć [gzhanz-nownćh] v. get stuck; wade; flounder; sink in (a quagmire, mud)
grzmiący [gzhmyown-tsi] adj. m. thundering; thunderous; booming; fulminatory
grzmot [gzhmot] m. thunder; hag
grzyb [gzhip] m. mushroom; fungus; snuff; dry-rot
grzywa [gzhi-va] f. mane
grzywna [gzhiv-na] f. fine
gubernator [goo-ber-na-tor] m. governor (general)
gubić [goo-beećh] v. loose; ruin
gula [goo-la] f. knob; bump
gulasz [goo-lash] m. meat soup

gulgotać [gool-go-taćh] v. gurgle; bubble; mumble
guma [goo-ma] f. rubber
gumno [goom-no] n. barn (yard)
gust [goost] m. taste; palate
guz [goos] m. bump; tumor
guzdrać się [gooz-draćh śhan] v. dawdle; dally; waste time in trifling; trifle; delay; lag
gwałcić [gvaw-ćheećh] v. rape; violate; compel; coerce; force; outrage; transgress
gwałt [gvawt] m. rape; outrage
gwałtowny [gvaw-tov-ni] adj. m. outrageous; urgent; violent
gwar [gvar] m. hum; noise; buzz
gwara [gva-ra] f. dialect; slang; jargon; lingo; cant; patter; colloquial regional language
gwarancja [gva-ran-tsya] f. warranty; guarantee; pledge
gwardia [gvar-dya] f. guard
gwarny [gvar-ni] adj. m. noisy
gwarzyć [gva-zhićh] v. chat
gwiazda [gvyaz-da] f. star
gwint [gveent] m. thread (mech.)
gwintować [gveen-to-vaćh] v. cut thread; tap; rifle
gwizd [gveezt] m. whistle
gwoli [gvo-lee] conj. for the sake of; because of; in order to
gwóźdź [gvooźhćh] m. nail
gzyms [gzims] m. molding;

H

habit [kha-beet] m. monk's frock; habit; nun's frock
haczyk [kha-chik] m. small hook; barb; snag; catch
hafciarka [khaf-ćhar-ka] f. embroiderer
haft [khaft] m. embroidery
haftka [khaft-ka] f. clasp
hak [khak] m. hook; clamp; clasp; grapnel; upper-cut (box)
hala [kha-la] f. (sports)hall
halka [khal-ka] f. petticoat

halny wiatr [khal-ni **vyatr**] m.
 Tatra wind (foehn)
halucynacja [kha-loo-tsi-**nats**-ya]
 f. hallucination
hałas [kha-was] m. noise; din
hałasować [kha-wa-**so**-vaćh] v.
 make noise (racket); be noisy
hałastra [kha-**wast**-ra] f. mob;
 rabble; riff-raff; ragtag mob
hałaśliwy [kha-wa-**śhlee**-vi] adj.
 m. noisy; loud; rackety; rowdy
hamak [kha-mak] m. hammock
hamować [kha-mo-vaćh] v.
 apply brakes; restrain; hamper;
 curb; cramp; delay; retard
hamulec [kha-**moo**-lets] m. brake
hamulec ręczny [kha-**moo**-lets
 ranch-ni] m. hand brake
handel [khan-del] m. commerce
handlarz [khand-lash] m.
 merchant; shopkeeper; peddler
handlować [khand-lo-vaćh] v.
 trade; deal; be in business
hangar [khan-gar] m. hangar
haniebny [kha-**ńeb**-ni] adj. m.
 disgraceful; dirty; foul; vile
hańba [khań-ba] f. disgrace
hańbić [khań-beećh] v. disgrace; bring shame; dishonor
haracz [kha-rach] m. tribute
harcerstwo [khar-**tsers**-tvo] n.
 scouting; Boy Scouts
harcerz [khar-tsezh] m. boy
 scout
hardy [khar-di] adj. m. haughty
harfa [khar-fa] f. harp
harmider [khar-**mee**-der] m.
 hullabaloo; clatter; din; row
harmonia [khar-mo-ńa] f.
 harmony; accordion; harmo-
 nics; concord; chord
harować [kha-ro-vaćh] v. toil
harpun [khar-poon] m. harpoon
hart [khart] m. fortitude;
 hardness; sternness; temper;
 endurance; inflexibility; grit
hartować [khar-to-vaćh] v.
 temper; harden; anneal; season; inure; quench; toughen
hasać [kha-saćh] v. frisk; frolic;
 romp; gambol; dance; caper
hasło [khas-wo] m. password
haubica [khaw-**bee**-tsa] f.

 howitzer (a short cannon)
haust [khaust] m. gulp; swing
hazard [kha-zard] m. risk;
 hazard; the gaming table
heban [khe-ban] m. ebony
hebel [khe-bel] m. plane (tool)
hebrajski [kheb-**rays**-kee] adj. m.
 Hebrew (language); Hebraic
heca [khe-tsa] f. fun; fuss
hegemonia [khe-ge-mo-ńa] f.
 hegemony; dominance
hej [khey] excl.: hey! ho!
hejnał [khey-naw] m. trum-
 -pet call; bugle-call; reveille
hektar [khek-tar] m. hectare
hełm [khewm] m. helmet; dome
hemoroidy [khe-mo-roy-di] pl.
 piles; hemorrhoids
hen [khen] adv. far; away
herb [kherp] m. coat-of-arms
herbaciarnia [kher-ba-ćhar-ńa]
 f. tea-house; tea-room
herbata [kher-ba-ta] f. tea
herbatnik [kher-bat-ńeek] m.
 biscuit; small dry cake
heretyk [khe-**re**-tik] m. heretic
herezja [khe-rez-ya] f. heresy
hermetyczny [kher-me-tich-ni]
 adj. m. air-tight; hermetic
heroiczny [khe-ro-**eech**-ni] adj. m.
 heroic; daring and risky
heroizm [khe-ro-eezm] m.
 heroism (qualities and actions)
herszt [khersht] m. ringleader
het [khet] adv. far; away
hetman [khet-man] m. commander-in-chief; (chess) queen
hiacynt [khya-tsint] m. hyacinth
hiena [khee-**ye**-na] f. hyena
hierarchia [khye-rar-khya] f.
 hierarchy; order of ranks
hieroglif [khye-ro-gleef] m.
 hieroglyph; illegible writing
higiena [khee-**ge**-na] f. hygiene;
 sanitation; hygienics
hinduski [kheen-**doos**-kee]
 adj. m. Hindu
hiperbola [khee-per-bo-la] f.
 hyperbola; hyperbole
hipnotyczny [kheep-no-tich-ni]
 adj. m. hypnotic; mesmeric
hipochondryk [khee-po-**khon**-drik]
 m. hypochondriac

hipokryta [khee-po-kri-ta] m.
hypocrite; one who pretends
or dissembles; dissembler
hipopotam [khee-po-po-tam] m.
hippopotamus; hippo
hipoteka [khee-po-te-ka] f. title;
mortgage; records office
hipoteza [khee-po-te-za] f.
hypothesis; assumption
histeria [khee-ster-ya] f. hysteria;
outbreak of a hysterical fit
historia [khee-stor-ya] f. story;
history; affair; show; fuss
hiszpański [khee-shpań-skee]
adj. m. Spanish; of Spain
hitlerowiec [khee-tle-ro-vyets] m.
hitlerite; German Nazi
hodować [kho-do-vaćh] v. rear;
breed; rise; keep; nurse
hodowca [kho-dov-tsa] m.
breeder; grower; farmer; riser;
grower; cultivator
hojny [khoy-ni] adj. m. generous;
lavish; liberal; profuse; ample
hokej [kho-key] m. hockey
holenderski [kho-len-ders-kee]
adj. m. Dutch; of Holland
holować [kho-lo-vaćh] v. tow;
haul; drag; tug; truck
hołd [khowd] m. tribute
hołota [kho-wo-ta] f. riff-raff
honor [kho-nor] m. honor
honorarium [kho-no-rar-yoom] n.
fee; honorarium; charge
horda [khor-da] f. horde; throng
horendalny [kho-ren-dal-ni] adj.
m. awful; horrible; exorbitant
hormon [khor-mon] m. hormone
horoskop [kho-ros-kop] m.
horoscope; prophesy; prospect
horyzont [kho-ri-zont] m. horizon;
vistas; prospect; possibilities
hotel [kho-tel] m. hotel
hoży [kho-zhi] adj. m. brisk;
handsome; comely; fresh
hrabia [khra-bya] m. count
hrabina [khra-bee-na] f. countess
hrabianka [khra-byan-ka] f.
countess (miss)
hrabstwo [khrab-stvo] n. county
hreczka [khrech-ka] f. buckwheat
hreczkosiej [khrech-ko-śhey] m.
country bumpkin; clod-breaker

hubka [khoob-ka] f. tinder
huczeć [khoo-chećh] v. roar
hufnal [khoof-nal] m. horseshoe
nail; horseshoe fastener
huk [khook] m. bang; roar
hulać [khoo-laćh] v. carouse;
riot; make merry; run wild
hulajnoga [khoo-lay-no-ga] f.
scooter (without motor)
hulaka [khoo-la-ka] m. carouser;
debaucher; rioter; rake
hulanka [khoo-lan-ka] f. riot;
debauch; junket; carouse
hultaj [khool-tay] m. libertine;
rascal; good-for-nothing
humanista [khoo-ma-ńees-ta] m.
humanist; classical scholar
humanitarny [khoo-ma-ńee-tar-
-ni] m. humane; humanitarian
humor [khoo-mor] m. humor
hura [khoo-ra] hurrah! cheers!
long live! hurray
huragan [khoo-ra-gan] m.
hurricane; cyclone; storm
hurmem [khoor-mem] adv. in
swarms; in a mass; altogether
hurt [khoort] m. wholesale
humus [khoo-moos] m. humus
husarz [khoo-sash] m. Polish
winged-armor cavalryman;
light cavalryman (hist.)
huśtać [khoo-śhtaćh] v.
swing; rock; dandle; toss up
and down; see-saw; sway
huśtawka [khoośh-tav-ka] f.
swing; seesaw; swing boat
huta [khoo-ta] f. metal or glass
mill; smelting works
hutnik [khoot-ńeek] m. metal or
glass (man) worker; iron
master; metallurgist
hycel [khi-tsel] m. dogcatcher;
rascal; good for nothing
hydrant [khid-rant] m. hydrant
hydraulika [khid-raw-lee-ka] f.
hydraulics; plumbing
hymn [khimn] m. anthem; hymn

i [ee] conj. and; also; too
ichtiologia [eekh-tyo-log-ya] f.
ichthyology; zoology of fish
idea [ee-de-a] f. idea; aim
idealista [ee-de-a-lees-ta] m.
idealist; dreamer; visionary
idealny [ee-de-al-ni] adj. m. ideal;
perfect; visionary; sublime
identyczny [ee-den-tich-ni] adj.
m. identical; similar
ideologia [ee-de-o-log-ya] f.
ideology; doctrines; opinions
idiosynkrazja [ee-dyo-sin-kraz-ya]
f. idiosyncrasy; mannerism
idiota [ee-dyo-ta] m. idiot
idiotka [ee-dyot-ka] f. idiot
iglaste drzewo [eeg-las-te dzhe-
-vo] m. coniferous tree
iglica [eeg-lee-tsa] f. spire
igła [eeg-wa] f. needle
ignorancja [eeg-no-ran-tsya] f.
ignorance; lack of knowledge
igrać [eeg-rach] v. play; trifle
igrzysko [eeg-zhis-ko] n.
spectacle (games); contest
ikra [eek-ra] f. spawn; roe
ile [ee-le] adv. how much
ilekroć [ee-le-kroch] adv. every
time; whenever; when
iloczas [ee-lo-chas] m. quantity
(of a vowel or syllable)
iloczyn [ee-lo-chin] m.
(multiplication) product
iloraz [ee-lo-raz] m. (division)
quotient
ilościowy [ee-losh-cho-vi]
adj. m. quantitative; numerical
ilość [ee-loshch] f. quantity
iluminacja [ee-loo-mee-nats-ya] f.
illumination; floodlight
ilustracja [ee-loo-strats-ya] f.
illustration; figure; picture
iluzja [ee-looz-ya] f. illusion
ił [eew] m. loam; rich soil
im [eem] conj. the more...

imać [ee-mach] v. size upon
imadło [ee-mad-wo] n. (shope)
vice; chuck; holder; vise
imaginacja [ee-ma-gee-nats-ya] f.
imagination; empty fancy
imbir [eem-beer] m. ginger
imbryk [eem-brik] m. teapot
imieniny [ee-mye-nee-ni] n.
name-day; name-day party
imiennie [ee-myen-ńe] adv. by
name; personally; individually
imiennik [ee-myen-ńeek] m.
namesake
imiesłów [ee-mye-swoov] m.
participle
imię [ee-myan] n. name (given)
imigracja [ee-mee-grats-ya] f.
immigration; the immigrants
imigrant [ee-meeg-rant] m.
immigrant; foreign settler
imigrować [ee-mee-gro-vach] v.
immigrate; settle in a new
land; come into a new land
imitacja [ee-mee-tats-ya] f.
imitation; counterfeit; fake
imitować [ee-mee-to-vach] v.
imitate; mimic; simulate
impas [eem-pas] m. deadlock
imperialista [eem-pe-rya-lees-ta]
m. imperialist; empire builder
imperium [eem-pe-ryoom] n. empire; countries under one ruler
impertynent [eem-per-ti-nent] m.
an arrogant; pert, impertinent,
saucy, cheeky person
impet [eem-pet] m. impetus
imponować [eem-po-no-vach]
v. impress; impose on sb; inspire respect; dazzle
import [eem-port] m. import
impregnować [eem-pre-gno-
-vach] v. impregnate; make
waterproof; saturate; soak
impreza [eem-pre-za] f.
entertainment; spectacle;
show; stunt; meet; venture
improwizować [eem-pro-vee-zo-
-vach] v. improvise; extempo-
rize; arrange on the spot
impuls [eem-pools] m. impulse
inaczej [ee-na-chey] adv.
otherwise; differently; unlike
inauguracja [ee-naw-goo-rats-ya]

f. inauguration; opening
inaugurować [ee-naw-goo-ro-
-vaćh] v. inaugurate; initiate
in blanko [een blan-ko] adv. in
blank; blank check, document
incydent [een-tsi-dent]
m. incident; happening; event
indagacja [een-da-gats-ya] f.
investigation; questioning
indeks [een-deks] m. index
indemnizacja [een-dem-ńee-zats-
-ya] f. indemnity (for a loss)
indukcja [een-dook-tsya] f.
induction; reasoning leading to
a general conclusion
indyk [een-dik] m. turkey
indyczka [een-dich-ka] f. turkey
-hen; dish of turkey-hen
indywidualny [een-di-vee-doo-al-
-ni] adj. m. individual
inercja [ee-nerts-ya] f. inertia;
inaction; inertness
infekcja [een-fekts-ya] f.
infection; contamination
infiltracja [een-feel-trats-ya] f.
infiltration; penetration
inflacja [een-flats-ya] f. inflation
influenza [een-floo-en-za] f.
influenza; flu; grippe
informacja [een-for-mats-ya] f.
information; intelligence; news
informacyjny [een-for-ma-tsiy-ni]
adj. m. information (office)
informować [een-for-mo-vaćh]
v. inform; instruct; post up
ingerencja [een-ge-rents-ya] f.
interference; meddling
inhalacja [een-kha-lats-ya] f.
inhalation; breathing in
inicjał [ee-ńee-tsyaw] m. initial
(letter); ornate letter
inicjator [ee-ńee-tsya-tor] m.
originator; mover; founder
inicjatywa [ee-ńee-tsya-ti-va] f.
initiative; enterprise; lead
inkasować [een-ka-so-vaćh] v.
collect (money); get a blow
inklinacja [een-klee-nats-ya] f.
inclination; liking for; bias
inkwizycja [een-kvee-zits-ya] f.
inquisition; investigation
innowacja [een-no-vats-ya] f.
innovation; novelty

innowierca [een-no-vyer-tsa] m.
dissenter; heretic
inny [een-ni] adj. m. other;
different; another (one)
inscenizacja [een-stse-ńee-zats-
-ya] f. putting on stage
inspekcja [een-spek-tsya] f.
inspection; review; examination; parade; inspectorate
inspekty [een-spek-ti] n. hotbed;
glass covered frame
inspiracja [een-spee-rats-ya] f.
inspiration; breathing in
instalacja [een-sta-lats-ya] f.
installation; plumbing etc.
instalator [een-sta-la-tor] m.
plumber; fitter; electrician
instrukcja [een-struk-tsya] f.
instruction; order; training
instrument [een-stru-ment] m.
instrument; tool; deed; legal
instrument; appliance
instynkt [een-stinkt] m. instinct;
inborn aptitude; knack
instytucja [een-sti-too-tsya] f.
institution; establishment
insynuacja [een-si-noo-ats-ya] f.
insinuation; innuendo
integralny [een-te-gral-ni] adj. m.
integral; whole; entire
intelekt [een-te-lekt] m. intellect;
(high) intelligence; mind
intelektualista [een-te-lek-too-a-
-lees-ta] m. intellectual
inteligencja [een-te-lee-gents-ya]
f. intelligentsia; intelligence;
ability to learn, grasp, cope
inteligentny [een-te-lee-gent-ni]
adj. m. intelligent; clever; wise
intencja [een-ten-tsya] f.
intention; purpose; anything
intended; determination to act
intensywny [een-ten-siv-ni] adj.
m. intensive; strenuous
interes [een-te-res] m. interest;
business; store; matter
interesowny [een-te-re-sov-ni]
adj. m. selfish; greedy
interesujący [een-te-re-soo-yown-
-tsi] adj. m. interesting
internat [een-ter-nat] m. boarding
school (for boys or for girls)
interpretacja [een-ter-pre-tats-ya]

f. interpretation; explanation
interwencja [een-ter-ven-tsya] f.
  intervention; interference
intratny [een-trat-ni] adj. m.
  lucrative; profitable; paying
introligator [een-tro-lee-ga-tor] m.
  bookbinder; bookbinder's shop
intruz [een-troos] m. intruder
intryga [een-tri-ga] f. plot;
  intrigue; machination
intuicja [een-too-eets-ya] f.
  intuition; insight; feeling
intuicyjny [een-too-ee-tsiy-ni] m.
  adj. intuitive; subconscious
inwalida [een-va-lee-da] m.
  invalid; disabled (soldier)
inwazja [een-vaz-ya] f. invasion
inwencja [een-ven-tsya] f.
  inventiveness; invention
inwentarz [een-ven-tash] m.
  inventory; stock; list
inwestycja [een-ve-stits-ya] f.
  investment; capital outlay
inżynier [een-zhi-ńer] m.
  engineer; graduate engineer
inżynieria [een-zhi-ńer-ya] f.
  engineering (science)
ircha [eer-kha] f. suede-leather;
  chamois-leather; suede
irlandzki [eer-landz-kee] adj. Irish
irys [ee-ris] m. iris
ironia [ee-ro-ńya] f. irony
irygacja [ee-ri-gats-ya] f.
  irrigation; watering
irytacja [ee-ri-tats-ya] f. irritation;
  vexation; chafe; annoyance
iskać [ees-kaćh] v. seek lice;
  cleanse of vermin; delouse
iskra [ees-kra] f. spark; flash
istnieć [eest-ńećh] v. exist
istnienie [eest-ńe-ńe] n.
  existence; being; entity
istny [eest-ni] adj. m. real;
  veritable; downright; sheer
istota [ees-to-ta] f. being;
  essence; gist; sum; entity
istotny [ees-tot-ni] adj. m. real;
  substantial; vital; radical
istotnie [ees-tot-ńe] adv. indeed;
  truly; really; in fact; in reality
iście [eeśh-ćhe] adv. indeed;
  truly; really; in truth
iść [eeśhćh] v. go; walk

izba [eez-ba] f. room; chamber
izba handlowa [eez-ba khan-dlo-
  -va] f. Chamber of Commerce
izolacja [ee-zo-lats-ya] f.
  isolation; insulation; seal
izolator [ee-zo-la-tor] m.
  insulator; non-conductor
izolacyjna taśma [ee-zo-la-tsiy-
  -na taśh-ma] f. insulating
  tape; electrician's tape
izoterma [ee-zo-ter-ma] f.
  isotherm; line plotted to show
  an equal temperature
izotop [ee-zo-top] m. isotope
izraelicki [eez-ra-e-leets-kee] adj.
  m. Israeli; of Israel
izraelita [eez-ra-e-lee-ta] m.
  Israelite; citizen of Israel
iż [eesh] conj. that (literary)
iżby [eezh-bi] conj. m. in order
  that; in order to; lest

J

ja [ya] pron. I; (indecl.) self
jabłecznik [yab-wech-ńeek] m.
  apple cider; apple pie
jabłko [yab-ko] n. apple
jabłoń [yab-woń] f. apple tree
jacht [yakht] m. yacht
jachtklub [yakht-kloob] m. yacht
  club (for cruises, racing, etc.)
jad [yat] m. venom; poison
jadalnia [ya-dal-ńa] f.
  dining-room; mess; mess-hall
jadalny [ya-dal-ni] adj. m. eat-
  -able; edible; dining (room)
jadło [yad-wo] n. food; edibles
jadłodajnia [ya-dwo-day-ńa] f.
  restaurant; eating house
jadłospis [yad-wo-spees] m.
  menu; bill of fare
jaglana kasza [ya-gla-na ka-sha]
  f. millet-groat (porridge)
jaglica [yag-lee-tsa] f. trachoma;
  viral eye infection
jagnię [yag-ńan] n. lamb
jagoda [ya-go-da] f. berry

jajecznica [ya-yech-**ńee**-tsa] f. scrambled eggs
jajko [yay-ko] n. egg (small)
jajko na twardo [yay-ko na tvar--do] hard-boiled egg
jajko na miękko [yay-ko na my<u>an</u>k-ko] soft-boiled egg
jajnik [yay-ńeek] m. ovary
jajo [ya-yo] n. egg; ovum
jak [yak] adv. how; as; if; than
jakby [yak-bi] adv. as if; if
jak gdyby [yak-gdi-bi] adv. as if; seemingly; sort of; so to say
jaka [ya-ka] pron. f. what; which
jaki [ya-kee] pron. m. what; which one? that; some; like
jakie [ya-<u>ke</u>] pron. n. what; which=jaki (fem. & neuter)
jakiś [ya-keeśh] pron. some
jakkolwiek [yak-kol-vyek] conj. though; pron. somehow; anyhow; whichever; adv. somehow; anyhow; however
jako [ya-ko] adv. as; by way of
jako tako [ya-ko ta-ko] adv. so-so; tolerably well
jakoś [ya-kośh] adv. somehow
jakość [ya-kośhćh] f. quality
jakościowo [ya-kośh-ćho-vo] adv. m. qualitatively
jakże [yak-zhe] pron. how; sure; yes indeed; how can this be?
jałmużna [yaw-moozh-na] f. alms; charity; (endowment)
jałowcówka [ya-wov-tsoov-ka] f. gin; juniper-flavored vodka
jałowiec [ya-wo-vyets] m. juniper tree (Juniperus)
jałowieć [ya-wo-vyećh] v. grow-sterile; grow unproductive
jałowy [ya-wo-vi] adj. m. barren; sterile; arid; aseptic
jałówka [ya-woov-ka] f. heifer
jama [ya-ma] f. pit; hole; den; cavity; cave; burrow; hollow
jamnik [yam-ńeek] m. dachshund
jankes [yan-kes] m. Yankee
Japończyk [ya-poń-chik] m. Japanese; of Japan
japoński [ya-pońs-kee] adj. m. Japanese; of Japan
jar [yar] m. canyon; ravine

jarmark [yar-mark] m. fair
jarosz [ya-rosh] m. vegetarian
jarski [yar-skee] adj. m. vegetarian; meatless
jary [ya-ri] adj. robust; vigorous; hale; spring (wheat, rye, etc.)
jarząbiak [ya-zh<u>an</u>-byak] m. sorb brandy; rowan-berry vodka
jarzębina [ya-zh<u>an</u>-bee-na] f. sorb tree; rowan; rowan berry
jarzmo [yazh-mo] n. yoke
jarzyć [ya-zhićh] v. sparkle; glitter; glow; shimmer
jarzyna [ya-zhi-na] vegetable; dish of vegetables
jasełka [ya-sew-ka] pl. crib; Nativity play; creche
jasiek [ya-śhek] m. little pillow; bean; beans; bean dish
jaskinia [yas-kee-ńa] f. cave
jaskiniowiec [ya-skee-ńo-vyets] m. cave dweller; cave man
jaskółka [yas-koow-ka] f. swallow; martin; harbinger
jaskrawy [yas-kra-vi] adj. m. glowing; showy; vivid; bright; striking; glaring; extreme
jasno [yas-no] adv. clearly; brightly; cheerfully; plainly
jasny [yas-ni] adj. m. clear; bright; light; shining; noble
jasnowidz [yas-no-veets] m. clairvoyant person; crystal gazer; seer (of future events)
jastrząb [yas-tzh<u>own</u>p] m. falcon; hawk; goshawk
jaszczyk [yash-chik] m. muni--tions box; ammunition trailer
jaśmin [yaśh-meen] m. jasmine
jaśnieć [yaśh-ńećh] v. shine; sparkle; radiate; gleam; pale
jatka [yat-ka] f. shambles; butcher's shop; massacre
jatki [yat-kee] pl. shambles
jaw [yav] m. reality; v. expose
jawić [ya-vićh] v. appear; show
jawny [yav-ni] adj. m. evident; public; open; notorious; sheer
jawor [ya-vor] m. plane tree; maple tree; sycamore tree; sycamore wood (lumber)
jaz [yaz] m. weir; milldam
jazda [yaz-da] f. ride; driving

jaźń [yaźhń] f. ego; self; the
I; the inner man; psyche

jąć [yown̄ćh] v. seize; begin

jądro [yown-dro] n. nucleus;
testicle; kernel; core

jąkać [yown-kaćh] v. stutter

jątrzyć [yown-tshićh] v. irritate;
fester; vex; embitter; inflame

jechać [ye-khaćh] v. ride; drive

jeden [ye-den] num. one; some

jedenaście [ye-de-naśh-ćhe]
num. eleven; 11

jedlina [yed-lee-na] f. fir grove;
fir and spruce branches

jednać [yed-naćh] v. conciliate

jednak [yed-nak] conj. however;
yet; still; but; after all; though

jednaki [yed-na-kee] adj. m.
identical; similar; equal; alike

jedno- [yed-no] one-; uni-; single-

jednocześnie [yed-no-cheśh-
-ńe] adv. simultaneously; also

jednoczyć [yed-no-chićh] v.
unify; merge; join; unite

jednogłośnie [yed-no-gwośh-
-ńe] adv. unanimously; in a
chorus; with one voice, assent

jednokrotnie [yed-no-krot-ńe]
adv. one time; once (only)

jednostka [yed-nost-ka] f. unit;
individual; entity; measure;
digit; specimen; denomination

jedność [yed-nośhćh] f. unity

jedwab [yed-vap] m. silk

jedynaczka [ye-di-nach-ka] f.
an only daughter; only child

jedynak [ye-di-nak] m. only son

jedynie [ye-di-ńe] adv. only;
merely; solely; nothing but

jadyny [ye-di-ni] adj. m. the only
one; the sole; unique; dearest

jedzenie [ye-dze-ńe] n. meat;
food; victuals; feed; eats

jemioła [ye-myo-wa] f. mistletoe

jeleń [ye-leń] m. stag; deer

jelito [ye-lee-to] n. intestine;
bowel; gut; pl. entrails

jełczeć [yew-chećh] v. grow
rancid; become rancid

jeniec [ye-ńets] m. captive

jerzyna [ye-zhi-na] f. black berry

jasień [ye-śheń] f. autumn;
fall; the fall of the leaf

jesienny [ye-śhen-ni] adj. m.
autumnal; of autumn

jesion [ye-śhon] m. ash tree

jasionka [ye-śhon-ka] f. fall
overcoat; light overcoat

jesiotr [ye-śhotr] m. sturgeon

jestestwo [yes-tes-tvo] n. being;
nature; creature; existence

jeszcze [yesh-che] adv. still;
besides; more; yet; way back

jeść [yeśhćh] v. eat; feed sb

jeśli [yeśh-lee] conj. if

jezdnia [yezd-ńa] f. roadway

jezuita [ye-zoo-ee-ta] m. Jesuit;
member of Jesuit Order

jeździec [yeźh-dźhets] m.
horseman; rider; equestrian

jeż [yesh] m. porcupine

jeżdżenie [yezh-dzhe-ńe] n.
riding; driving; tyrannizing

jeżeli [ye-zhe-lee] conj. if

jeżyć się [ye-zhićh śhan] v.
bristle up; stand on end

jeżyna [ye-zhi-na] f. blackberry;
blackberry bush; bramble

jęczeć [yan-chećh] v. moan;
groan; wail; whine; complain

jęczmień [yanch-myeń] m.
barley; a cereal grass

jędrny [yandr-ni] adj. m. firm;
robust; strong; terse; pithy

jędza [yan-dza] f. witch; shrew

jęk [yank] m. groan; moan; wail

jęknąć [yank-nownćh] v. complain; moan; groan; whine;
grumble; wail; bellyache

język [yan-zik] m. tongue

jod [yod] m. iodine

jodła [yod-wa] f. fir tree; spruce

jodyna [yo-di-na] f. tincture of
iodine (antiseptic); iodine

jon [yon] m. ion

jowialny [yo-vyal-ni] adj. m.
jovial; debonair; genial

jubiler [yoo-bee-ler] m. jeweler
(store or profession)

jubileusz [yoo-bee-le-oosh] m.
jubilee; anniversary

jucht [yookht] m. Russian
leather; water-proof leather

juczny koń [yooch-ni koń]
adj. m. pack-horse; beast of
burden; carrying saddle-bags

judzić [yoo-dźheećh] v. instigate; incire; provoke; set on

juki [yoo-kee] pl. packsaddle

junak [yoo-nak] m. brave.
swaggerer; dashing fellow

jurysdykcja [yoo-ris-dik-tsya]
f.jurisdiction; legal authority

juta [yoo-ta] f. jute; jute plant

jutro [yoot-ro] adv. tomorrow

jutrzejszy [yoo-tshey-shi] adj. m.
tomorrow's; future

jutrzenka [yoo-tshen-ka] f. day
-break; morning star; dawn

już [yoozh] conj. already; at any
moment; by now; no more

jużci [yoozh-ćhee] conj. of
course; certainly; sure thing!

K

kabalarka [ka-ba-lar-ka] f. fortune
teller (by looking at cards)

kabała [ka-ba-wa] f. cabala

kabaret [ka-ba-ret] m. cabaret

kabel [ka-bel] m. cable

kabestan [ka-bes-tan] m.
capstan; winch; windlass

kabina [ka-bee-na] f. cabin

kabłąk [kab-wownk] m. bow;
hoop; bail; trigger-guard

kabotyn [ka-bo-tin] m. poser;
buffoon; second-rate actor

kabriolet [ka-bryo-let] m.
convertible car; gig

kabza [kab-za] f. purse

kac [kats] m. hangover

kacerz [ka-tsesh] m. heretic

kacet [ka-tset] m. Nazi-Ger-
man concentration camp

kaczka [kach-ka] f. duck

kadłub [kad-woop] m. trunk;
hull; fuselage; framework

kadra [ka-dra] f. staff; cadre

kadzić [ka-dźheećh] v.
incense; flatter; fart (vulg.)

kadzidło [ka-dźhee-dwo] n.
incense (at an altar); frank-
incense; (fragrance)

kadź [kadźh] f. tub; tubful

kafar [ka-far] m. pile driver

kafel [ka-fel] m. tile (ceramic)

kaftan [kaf-tan] m. jacket

kaftan bezpieczeństwa [kaf-tan
bez-pye-cheń-stva] m.
straight jacket; "waistcoat"

kaftanik [kaf-ta-ńeek] m. bodice;
vest; (baby's) jacket; caftan

kaganiec [ka-ga-ńets] m.
muzzle; gag; oil lamp; cresset;
torch of learning

kajać się [ka-yaćh śhan] v.
repent; confess with contrition

kajak [ka-yak] m. kayak; canoe

kajdany [kay-da-ni] pl. hand
-cuffs; shackles; chains; bonds

kajuta [ka-yoo-ta] f. ship-cabin

kajzerka [kay-zer-ka] f. fancy roll
of bread; kaiser roll

kakao [ka-ka-o] n. cocoa

kaktus [kak-toos] m. cactus

kalać [ka-laćh] v. pollute; foul
up; stain; sully; befoul

kalafior [ka-la-fyor] m.
cauliflower (a vegetable)

kalarepa [ka-la-re-pa] f. turnip
-cabbage; kohlrabi

kalectwo [ka-lets-tvo] n.
disability; lameness; inva-
lidism; cripplehood

kaleczyć [ka-le-chićh] v. cut;
wound; mutilate; hurt; injure;
lacerate; cripple; mangle

kalejdoskop [ka-ley-do-skop] m.
kaleidoscope; medley; miscellany; riot (of colors)

kaleka [ka-le-ka] m. f. cripple

kalendarz [ka-len-dash] m.
calendar; almanac

kalesony [ka-le-so-ni] pl.
underwear; drawers; shorts;
underpants; trunk drawers

kalina [ka-lee-na] f. guelder-rose;
cranberry shrub (tree)

kalka [kal-ka] f. carbon paper

kalkulacja [kal-koo-lats-ya] f.
calculation; computation

kalkulować [kal-koo-lo-vaćh] v.
calculate; compute; work out

kaloria [ka-lo-rya] f. calorie

kaloryfer [ka-lo-ri-fer] m. radiator;
steam heater; (water) heater

kalosz [ka-losh] m. rubber overshoe; galosh; rubber boot
kalumnia [ka-loom-ńa] f. calumny; slander; aspersion
kalwin [kal-veen] m. Calvinist
kał [kaw] m. excrement; stool
kałamarz [ka-wa-mash] m. ink -stand; ink pot; ink-well
kaluża [ka-woo-zha] f. puddle
kamelia [ka-me-lya] f. camellia
kameralna muzyka [ka-me-ral-na moo-zi-ka] chamber music
kamerdyner [ka-mer-di-ner] m. butler; valet (de chambre)
kamerton [ka-mer-ton] m. tuning- -fork ("U" shaped); pitch pipe
kamfora [kam-fo-ra] f. camphor
kamgarn [kam-garn] m. worsted
kamienica [ka-mye-ńee-tsa] f. apartment house; tenants
kamienieć [ka-mye-ńećh] v. petrify; turn into stone
kamieniołom [ka-mye-ńo-wom] f. quarry; stone pit
kamień [ka-myeń] m. stone
kamizelka [ka-mee-zel-ka] f. waistcoat; vest; camisole
kampania [kam-pa-ńa] f. campaign; drive (promotional)
kamrat [kam-rat] m. chum; pal
kamyk [ka-mik] m. pebble
kanadyjski [ka-na-diy-skee] adj. m. Canadian; of Canada
kanalia [ka-na-lya] f. scoundrel
kanalizacja [ka-na-lee-zats-ya] f. sewers; sanitation; drainage
kanał [ka-naw] m. channel; dike; (storm) sewer; duct; ditch; conduit; tube; gully; gutter
kanapa [ka-na-pa] f. sofa
kanapka [ka-nap-ka] f. sandwich; small size sofa; love seat
kanarek [ka-na-rek] m. canary
kancelaria [kan-tse-la-rya] f. office; chancellery; archives
kancerować [kan-tse-ro-vaćh] v. damage; mangle; lacerate; hack; tear jaggedly (roughly)
kanciarz [kan-ćhash] m. swindler; trickster; con man
kanciasty [kan-ćha-sti] adj. m. angular; awkward; stiff
kanclerz [kan-tslesh] m.
chancellor (chief of a go- vernment); church official
kandelabr [kan-de-labr] m. chandelier; street lamp
kandydat [kan-di-dat] m. candidate; applicant; aspirant
kangur [kan-goor] m. kangaroo
kanon [ka-non] m. canon (priest)
kanonierka [ka-no-ńer-ka] f. gunboat; patrol boat
kanonik [ka-no-ńeek] m. canon (priest); monsignor; prelate
kanonizować [ka-no-ńee-zo- -vaćh] v. canonize; glorify
kant [kant] m. edge; crease; swindle; trick; racket; chant
kantar [kan-tar] m. halter
kantor [kan-tor] m. exchange of- fice; counter; cantor (singer)
kantyna [kan-ti-na] f. canteen
kanwa [kan-va] f. canvas
kapa [ka-pa] f. bedspread; cover
kapać [ka-paćh] v. dribble; trickle; drip; fall drop by drop
kapela [ka-pe-la] f. band (of mu- musicians); (church) choir
kapelan [ka-pe-lan] m. chaplain (in armed forces, hospital)
kapelusz [ka-pe-loosh] m. hat
kapilarny [ka-pee-lar-ni] adj. m. capillary; of capillary tube
kapiszon [ka-pee-shon] m. hood
kapitalista [ka-pee-ta-lees-ta] m. capitalist; wealthy person
kapitalizm [ka-pee-ta-leezm] m. capitalism (private or state)
kapitał [ka-pee-taw] m. capital
kapitan [ka-pee-tan] m. captain
kapitulacja [ka-pee-too-lats-ya] f. surrender; capitulation; giving up to an enemy
kapitulować [ka-pee-too-lo- -vaćh] v. surrender; give up
kaplica [ka-plee-tsa] f. chapel
kapliczka [ka-pleech-ka] f. shrine (in a church); wayside shrine
kapłan [ka-pwan] m.priest
kapłon [ka-pwon] m. capon
kapota [ka-po-ta] f. long coat
kapral [kap-ral] m. corporal
kaprys [kap-ris] m. caprice; fad; whim; fancy; freak; vagary
kaptować [kap-to-vaćh] v. win

over; bring over; canvas
kaptur [kap-toor] m. hood
kapturowy sąd [kap-too-ro-vi **sownt**] kangaroo court
kapusta [ka-**poos**-ta] f. cabbage; a dish of cabbage
kapuś [ka-poośh] m. stool-pigeon; informer; police spy
kapuśniak [ka-**poośh**-ńak] m. cabbage soup; drizzle; mizzle
kara [ka-ra] f. penalty; fine; punishment; correction; chastisement; retribution; requital; a judgement; nuisance; pest
karabin [ka-ra-been] m. rifle
karać [ka-raćh] v. punish
karafka [ka-raf-ka] f. carafe; serving-bottle; (glass or metal) bottle; flagon; decanter
karakuły [ka-ra-koo-wi] pl. astrakhan sheep fur
karalny [ka-ral-ni] adj. m. punishable; deserving a fine
karaluch [ka-ra-lookh] m. cockroach; black beetle
karambol [ka-ram-bol] m. collision; cannon; carom
karaś [ka-raśh] m. crucian
karat [ka-rat] m. carat
karawaniarz [ka-ra-va-ńash] m. undertaker; coffin bearer
karb [karb] m. notch; score; crease; fold; nick; tally; curl
karbid [kar-beed] m. carbide
karbol [kar-bol] m. carbolic acid; phenol; (diluted) an antiseptic
karbować [kar-bo-vaćh] v. notch; curl; tally; crimp; fold
karbunkuł [kar-**boon**-koow] m. ulcer (under skin); carbuncle
karburator [kar-boo-ra-tor] m. carburetor (fuel mixing device)
karcer [kar-tser] m. prison; dark cell; detention (in a school)
karciarz [kar-ćhash] m. (cards) gambler; card player; gamester
karcić [kar-ćheećh] v. reproof; admonish; scold; castigate
karczemny [kar-chem-ni] adj. m. rude; vulgar; coarse
karczma [karch-ma] f. tavern
karczoch [kar-chokh] m. artichoke (thistle like plant)

karczować [kar-cho-vaćh] v. dig up (stumps); clear land
kardiografia [kar-dyo-**gra**-fya] f. (electro-) cardiography
kardynalny [kar-di-nal-ni] adj. m. fundamental; essential
kardynał [kar-di-naw] m. cardinal; prince (in the Catholic Church; elector of the pope)
karetka [ka-ret-ka] f. ambulance; (prison or mail) van; chaise
kariera [ka-rye-ra] f. career
kark [kark] m. neck; nape
karkołomny [kar-ko-**wom**-ni] adj. m. breakneck; neck-breaking
karłowaty [kar-wo-va-ti] adj. m. dwarfish; undersized
karamel [ka-ra-mel] m. caramel
karmić [kar-meećh] v. feed; nourish; nurse; suckle; nurture
karmin [kar-meen] m. carmine
karnawał [kar-na-vaw] m. carnival; period of feasting
karnie [kar-ńe] adv. penally; in perfect order (discipline)
karność [kar-nośhćh] f. discipline; orderly conduct
karny [kar-ni] adj. m. disciplined; penal (code, colony); punitive
karo [ka-ro] n. diamonds (in cards); square cut (bodice)
karoseria [ka-ro-**se**-rya] f. car (truck) body; enclosing frame
karp [karp] m. carp (fish)
karta [kar-ta] f. card; page; note; sheet; leaf; ticket; charter
kartel [kar-tel] m. (industrial) trust; cartel; combine; pool
kartofel [kar-to-fel] m. potato
kartoflanka [kar-to-flan-ka] f. m. potato soup; type of onion
kartograf [kar-to-graf] m. cartographer; map maker
karton [kar-ton] m. cardboard
kartoteka [kar-to-**te**-ka] f. card index; file
karuzela [ka-roo-**ze**-la] f. merry-go-round; carousel
kary koń [ka-ry koń] m. black horse
karygodny [ka-ri-**god**-ni] adj. m. unpardonable; guilty; gross
karykatura [ka-ri-ka-too-ra] f.

cartoon; caricature; parody
karykaturzysta [ka-ri-ka-too-**zhis-**
-ta] m. cartoonist
karzeł [ka-zhew] m. dwarf
kasa [ka-sa] f. cashier's desk;
cash register; ticket office
kasjer [kas-yer] m. cashier
kask [kask] m. helmet; tin hat
kaskada [kas-ka-da] f. cascade
kasować [ka-**so**-vaćh] v. cancel
kasta [kas-ta] f. caste
kastrować [kas-tro-vaćh] v.
castrate; geld; (sterilization)
kasyno [ka-si-no] n. casino; club;
mess-hall; mess-room
kasza [ka-sha] f. grits; groats;
cereals; gruel; porridge; mess
kaszel [ka-shel] m. cough
kaszkiet [kash-ket] m. cap
kasztan [kash-tan] m. chestnut
kat [kat] m. executioner
katafalk [ka-ta-falk] m. bier
kataklizm [ka-ta-kleezm] m.
cataclysm; disaster; calamity
katalizator [ka-ta-lee-**za**-tor] m.
catalyst; agent of catalysis
katalog [ka-ta-log] m. catalog
katar [ka-tar] m. head cold;
running nose; catarrh
katarakta [ka-ta-**rak**-ta] f.
cataract; opaque eye lens
kataryniarz [ka-ta-ri-ńash] m.
(street) organ grinder
katarynka [ka-ta-rin-ka] f. barrel
organ; street organ
katastrofa [ka-ta-**stro**-fa] f.
catastrophe; disaster; crash
katecheta [ka-te-khe-ta] m.
teacher of catechism
katedra [ka-te-dra] f. pulpit; univ.
dept. chair; cathedral
kategoria [ka-te-go-rya] f.
category; division; class
kategoryczny [ka-te-go-rich-ni]
adj. m. absolute; categorical
katoda [ka-to-da] f. cathode
katolicki [ka-to-leets-kee] adj. m.
Catholic; of the Cath. Church
katować [ka-to-vaćh] v.
torture; beat cruelly; hack
kaucja [kaw-tsya] f. bail; deposit;
security; recognizance
kauczuk [kaw-chook] m. India

natural rubber; caoutchouc
kaukaski [kaw-**kas**-kee] adj. m.
Caucasian; of Caucasus
kawa [ka-va] f. coffee
kawaler [ka-va-ler] m. bachelor;
suitor; beau; cavalier
kawaleria [ka-va-**le**-rya] f.
cavalry; young folks
kawalkada [ka-val-ka-da] f.
cavalcade (procession)
kawał [ka-vaw] m. piece; joke;
cheat; lump; funny business
kawałek [ka-**va**-wek] m. bit;
morsel; scrap; chunk
kawiarnia [ka-**vyar**-ńa] f. cafe
kawior [ka-vyor] m. caviar
kawka [kav-ka] f. jackdaw
kawon [ka-von] m. watermelon
kawowy [ka-vo-vi] adj. m. (of)
coffee; coffee-(plantation)
kazać [ka-zaćh] v. order; tell;
make sb. do sth; command
kazanie [ka-za-ńe] n. sermon
kazić [ka-żheećh] v. pollute;
corrupt; blemish; contaminate
kazirodztwo [ka-żhee-rodz-tvo]
n. incest
kaznodzieja [ka-zno-**dźhe**-ya] m.
preacher; evangelist
kaźń [kaźhń] f. execution
każdorazowy [kazh-do-ra-**zo**-vi]
adj. m. every time; each time;
every single (time)
każdy [kazh-di] pron. every;
each; respective; any; all
kącik [kown-ćheek] m. nook
kąkol [kown-kol] m. cockle;
corn cockle (in grainfield)
kąpać [kown-paćh] v. v. bathe;
bath; bask; soak; be steeped
kąpiel [kown-pyel] f. bath
kąpielisko [kown-pye-**lees**-ko] n.
resort; spa; public bath
kąsać [kown-saćh] v. bite
kąsek [kown-sek] m. bit; nip
kąt [kownt] m. corner; angle
kątomierz [kown-to-myesh] m.
protractor; dial-sight
kciuk [kćhook] m. thumb
kelner [kel-ner] m. waiter
kelnerka [kel-ner-ka] f. waitress;
bar maid; woman waiter
keson [ke-son] m. caisson

kędzierzawy [kan-dźhe-zha-vi] adj. m. curly; curled; fuzzy

kędzior [kan-dźhor] m. curl; lock (of hair); ringlet

kępa [kan-pa] f. cluster; holm; hurst; clump (of trees); tuft

kęs [kans] m. bit; mouthful

kibic [kee-beets] m. kibitzer

kibić [kee-beećh] f. figure of a person; waist; middle

kichać [kee-khaćh] v. sneeze

kiecka [kets-ka] f. frock; skirt; petticoat (inelegant)

kiedy [ke-di] conj. when; as; ever; how soon?; while; since

kiedy indziej [ke-di een-dźhey] some other time

kiedykolwiek [ke-di-kol-vyek] adv. whenever; at any time

kiedyś [ke-diśh] adv. someday; in the past; once; one day

kiedyż ? [ke-dish] adv. when then?; when on earth ?

kielich [ke-leekh] m. goblet; chalice; cup; cupful; glassful

kielnia [kel-ńa] f. trowel

kieł [kew] m. tusk; fang; canine tooth; cutting bit

kiełbasa [kew-ba-sa] f. sausage

kiełek [ke-wek] m. sprout

kiełkować [kew-ko-vaćh] v. sprout; germinate; spring up

kiełzać [kew-zaćh] v. bridle

kiep [kep] m. oaf; fool; gull

kiepski [kep-skee] adj. m. mean; bad; poor; second-rate

kier [ker] m. (cards) hearts

kierat [ke-rat] m. thrasher

kiermasz [ker-mash] m. fair

kierować [ke-ro-vaćh] v. steer; manage; run; show the way

kierownik [ke-rov-ńeek] m. manager; director; supervisor

kierunek [ke-roo-nek] m. direction; course; trend; line

kiesa [ke-sa] f. purse

kieszeń [ke-sheń] f. pocket

kij [keey] m. stick; cane; staff

kijanka [kee-yan-ka] f. tadpole

kikut [kee-koot] m. stump; stub

kilim [kee-leem] m. rug; carpet

kilka [keel-ka] num. a few; some

kilkakroć [keel-ka-króćh] adv. repeatedly; again and again

kilkakrotny [keel-ka-krot-ni] adj. m. repeated; recurring

kilkudniowy [keel-koo-dńo-vi] adj. m. of several days

kilkoro [keel-ko-ro] num. some; several; one or two; a number

kilof [kee-lof] m. pick; hack

kilogram [kee-lo-gram] m. kilogram = 2.2 pounds

kilometr [kee-lo-metr] m. kilometer = 3,280.8 feet

kiła [kee-wa] f. syphilis

kinetyka [kee-ne-ti-ka] f. kinematics; science of motion

kino [kee-no] n. cinema; movies

kiosk [kyosk] m. kiosk; booth

kipieć [kee-pyećh] v. boil

kisić [kee-śheećh] v. ferment

kisnąć [kees-nownćh] v. turn sour; ferment; pickle; fug

kisza [kee-sha] f. intestine

kiść [keeśhćh] f. bunch; wrist

kit [keet] m. putty; mastic

kiwać [kee-vaćh] v. v. rock; nod; wag; dangle; fool; dodge; jink; sway; swing; motion to

klacz [klach] f. mare

klajster [klay-ster] m. glue; paste; water base glue

klakson [klak-son] m. car horn

klamka [klam-ka] f. door knob

klamra [klam-ra] f. buckle; clasp; bracket; fastener; staple

klapa [kla-pa] f. lapel; valve

klapsy [klap-si] pl. spanking

klarować [kla-ro-vaćh] v. clarify; filter; clear; purify

klarnet [klar-net] m. clarinet

klasa [kla-sa] f. class; classroom; rank; order; division

klaskać [klas-kaćh] v. clap

klasowy [kla-so-vi] adj. m. class; of classes; class- (distinction)

klasyczny [kla-sich-ni] adj. m. classic; standard; conventional

klasyfikować [kla-si-fee-ko-vaćh] v. classify; sort; grade

klasztor [klash-tor] m. monastery; convent; cloister

klatka [klat-ka] f. cage; crate

klatka schodowa [klat-ka skho-do-va] f. staircase; stairway

klatka piersiowa [klat-ka pyer--śho-va] f. rib cage; chest
klauzula [klaw-zoo-la] f. clause; proviso; reservation
klawisz [kla-veesh] m. (piano) key; stool pigeon; jailer
kląć [klownćh] v. curse; swear
klątwa [klown-tva] f. curse; ban; excommunication; anathema
klecić [kle-ćheećh] v. botch
kleić [kle-eećh] v. glue; stick together; fudge; shape; size
kleik [kle-eek] m. gruel
klej [kley] m. glue; cement
klejnot [kley-not] m. jewel
klekotać [kle-ko-taćh] v. clatter; rattle; chatter; prate
kleks [klex] m. blot; ink-spot
klepać [kle-paćh] v. hammer; flatten; prattle; pat; blab; clap
klepka [klep-ka] f. stave
klepsydra [klep-sid-ra] f. hour-glass; obituary notice
kleptomania [klep-to-ma-ña] f. kleptomania; impulse to steal
kler [kler] m. clergy; priesthood
kleszcz [kleshch] m. tick
kleszcze [klesh-che] pl. pliers; tongs; claws; pincers; nippers
klękać [klan-kaćh] v. kneel down; bend the knee; kneel
klęska [klans-ka] f. defeat; disaster; calamity; repulse
klęsnąć [klans-nownćh] v. shrink; subside; go down
klient [klee-ent] m. customer
klika [klee-ka] f. clique
klimat [klee-mat] m. climate
klin [kleen] m. wedge; cotter
klinga [kleen-ga] f. (sword) blade; sabre-blade
kliniczny [klee-ñeech-ni] adj. m. clinical (diagnosis); clinic-
klinika [klee-ñee-ka] f. clinic
klisza [klee-sha] f. (photo) plate; printing plate; woodcut; cliche
klitka [kleet-ka] f. cubicle; cell
kloc [klots] m. log; block; chunk
klomb [klomp] m. flower bed
klon [klon] m. maple (tree)
klops [klops] m. meat loaf
klosz [klosh] m. glass cover; lamp shade; dish cover

klozet [klo-zet] m. toilet
klub [kloop] m. club; union
klucz [klooch] m. key; wrench
kluska [kloos-ka] f. boiled dough strip; dumpling; lump
kładka [kwad-ka] f. foot-bridge; gangway; gangplank; brow
kłaki [kwa-kee] pl. oakum; shaggy hair; matted hair
kłam [kwam] m. lie; falsehood
kłamać [kwa-maćh] v. lie
kłamca [kwam-tsa] m. liar
kłaniać się [kwa-ñaćh śhan] v. salute; bow; greet; worship
kłaść [kwaśhćh] v. lay; put down; place; set; deposit
kłąb [kwownp] m. clew; ball
kłąbek [kwown-bek] m. ball (of thread); hunk of yarn
kłębić się [kwan-beećh śhan] v. whirl; swirl; surge; billow
kłoda [kwo-da] f. log; clog
kłopot [kwo-pot] m. trouble
kłopotać [kwo-po-taćh] v. trouble; disturb; worry
kłopotliwy [kwo-pot-lee-vi] adj. m. troublesome; baffling
kłos [kwos] m. (corn) ear
kłócić [kwoo-ćheećh] v. stir; agitate; mix; disturb; quarrel
kłódka [kwood-ka] f. padlock
kłótliwy [kwoot-lee-vi] v. quarrelsome; cantankerous
kłótnia [kwoot-ña] f. quarrel
kłuć [kwooćh] v. stab; prick
kłus [kwoos] m. trot; jog trot
kłusownik [kwoo-sov-ñeek] m. poacher; trespassing hunter
kmieć [kmyećh] m. peasant
kminek [kmee-nek] m. cumin
knajpa [knay-pa] f. tavern
knebel [kne-bel] m. gag
knocić [kno-ćheećh] v. bungle
knot [knot] m. (candle) wick; fuse; kid; bad mark; bungle
knuć [knooćh] v. plot; scheme
koalicja [ko-a-lits-ya] f. coalition; temporary union (alliance)
kobiałka [ko-byaw-ka] f. wicker-basket; chip basket; pottle
kobieciarz [ko-bye-ćhash] m. lady chaser; lady's man
kobiecość [ko-bye-tsośhćh] f.

womanhood; feminity
kobiecy [ko-bye-tsi] adj. m.
  female; womanish; feminine
kobierzec [ko-bye-zhets] m.
  carpet; anything like a carpet
kobieta [ko-bye-ta] f. woman
kobyła [ko-bi-wa] f. mare
kobza [kob-za] f. bagpipe
koc [kots] m. blanket; coverlet
kochać [ko-khaćh] v. love
kochanie [ko-kha-ńe] n. love;
  darling; sweetheart; affection
kochany [ko-kha-ni] adj. m.
  beloved; loving; affectionate
kochliwy [kokh-lee-vi] adj. m.
  easily in love; amorous
koci [ko-ćhee] adj. m. catlike
kociak [ko-ćhak] m. kitty-cat;
  lassie; lass; pinup girl
kocioł [ko-ćhow] m. kettle;
  boiler; pot; encirclement
kocur [ko-tsoor] m. tomcat
koczować [ko-cho-vaćh] v.
  lead nomadic life; wander
  about; be encamped; bivouac
koczownik [ko-chov-ńeek] m.
  nomad; wanderer; vagrant
kodeks [ko-dex] m. (legal) code
koedukacja [ko-e-doo-kats-ya] f.
  coeducation (of both sexes)
koegzystencja [ko-eg-zis-ten-
  -tsya] f. coexistence
kofeina [ko-fe-ee-na] f. caffeine;
  alkaloid in coffee
kogut [ko-goot] m. cock; rooster
koić [ko-eećh] v. soothe
kojarzenie [ko-ya-zhe-ńe] n.
  matching; association; union
kojarzyć [ko-ya-zhićh] v. unite;
  bind; join; link; connect
kojący [ko-yown-tsi] adj. m.
  soothing; comforting; balmy
kojec [ko-yets] m. coop; pen
kokaina [ko-ka-ee-na] f. cocaine;
  an alkaloid addicting drug
kokarda [ko-kar-da] f. rosette;
  bow; slip-knot; true-love knot
kokietka [ko-ket-ka] f. flirt
kokietować [ko-ke-to-vaćh] v.
  flirt; court; woo; coquet
koklusz [kok-loosh] m. whooping
  cough; hooping cough
kokos [ko-kos] m. coconut

kokos [ko-kos] m. good
  business; a grand thing
kokoszka [ko-kosh-ka] f.
  brood hen; laying hen
koks [kox] m. coke; gas coke
koksownia [kok-sov-ńa] f.
  coking plant; cokery
kolaboracja [ko-la-bo-rats-ya] f.
  collaboration; collaborators
kolacja [ko-lats-ya] f. supper
kolano [ko-la-no] n. knee; bend
kolarstwo [ko-lar-stvo] n.
  cycling; bicycle sport
kolarz [ko-lash] m. cyclist
kolący [ko-lown-tsi] adj. m.
  prickly; thorny; spiked
kolba [kol-ba] f. (riffle) butt
kolczasty [kol-chas-ti] adj. m.
  barbed; thorny; spiny
kolczyk [kol-chik] m. earring;
  earmark; ear tag; eardrop
kolebka [ko-leb-ka] f. cradle
kolec [ko-lets] m. thorn
kolega [ko-le-ga] m. buddy;
  colleague; fellow worker
koleina [ko-le-ee-na] f. truck rut;
  wheel groove; wheel trace
kolej [ko-ley] f. railroad
kolejaka [ko-ley-ka] f. (waiting)
  line; narrow-gage railroad; turn
kolejno [ko-ley-no] adv. by turns;
  one after the other; in turns
kolejny [ko-ley-ni] adj. m. next;
  successive; following
kolekcja [ko-lek-tsya] f.
  collection; things collected
kolektywizacja [ko-le-kti-vee-zats-
  -ya] f. collectivization
koleżeństwo [ko-le-zheń-stvo]
  n. fellowship; comradeship
kolęda [ko-lan-da] f. Christmas
  carol; song of joy or praise
kolędować [ko-lan-do-vaćh] v.
  sing carols; wait a long time
koliber [ko-lee-ber] m. hum-
  -ming-bird; Trochilidae
kolia [ko-lya] f. necklace
kolidować [ko-lee-do-vaćh] v.
  collide; interfere; clash
koligacja [ko-lee-gats-ya] f.
  (family) relationship
kolisty [ko-lees-ti] adj. m.
  circular; round

kolizja [ko-lee-ya] f. collision;
clash; interference
kolka [kol-ka] f. colic
kolokwium [ko-lo-kvyoom] m.
oral examination; test
kolonia [ko-lo-ńa] f. colony
kolonista [ko-lo-ńees-ta] m.
settler; colonist; colonial
kolońska woda [ko-loń-ska vo-
-da] cologne water
kolor [ko-lor] m. color; tint; hue
koloryt [ko-lo-rit] m. coloring
kolosalny [ko-lo-sal-ni] adj. m.
colossal; vast; tremendous
kolportaż [kol-por-tash] m.
(paper) distribution
kolumna [ko-loom-na] f. column
kołatać [ko-wa-tać] v. knock;
rattle; beg; throb; bang
kołczan [kow-chan] m. quiver
kołdra [kow-dra] f. quilter-cover;
quilt; coverlet; eiderdown
kołek [ko-wek] m. peg; stake
kołnierz [kow-ńesh] m. collar
koło [ko-wo] n. wheel; circle
koło [ko-wo] prep. around; near;
about; by; in vicinity; close to
kołodziej [ko-wo-dźhey] m.
wheelwright; wheeler
kołowacizna [ko-wo-va-ćheez-
-na] f. dizziness; confusion
kołować [ko-wo-vać] v. stray;
revolve; confuse; circle; whirl;
be in a whirl; prevaricate
kołowrotek [ko-wo-vro-tek] m.
spinning-wheel; reel; winch
kołowrót [ko-wo-vroot] m. gin;
windlass; hoist; whip; turnpike; turnstile; large reel
kołowy ruch [ko-wo-vi rookh]
vehicular traffic; traffic
kołpak [kow-pak] m. pointed fur
cap; calpack; calpac
kołtun [kow-toon] m. hair snarl;
tangle; bigot; moron; Philistine
kołysać [ko-wi-sać] v. rock;
sway; toss to and fro; roll
kołysanka [ko-wi-san-ka] f.
lullaby; cradle song; berceuse
kołyska [ko-wis-ka] f. cradle
komar [ko-mar] m. mosquito
kombajn [kom-bayn] m. combine
kombinacja [kom-bee-nats-ya] f.

combination; union; scheme;
arrangement; (woman's) slip
kombinować [kom-bee-no-
vać] v. combine; speculate;
arrange; think; contrive
komedia [ko-me-dya] f. comedy
komenda [ko-men-da] f. word of
command; command; head-
quarters; an order
komentarz [ko-men-tash] m.
commentary; glossary; remark
kometa [ko-me-ta] f. comet
komfort [kom-fort] m. comfort
komiczny [ko-meech-ni] adj. m.
comic; amusing; funny; droll
komin [ko-meen] m. chimney
kominek [ko-mee-nek] m. fire
-place; hearth; open fire
kominiarz [ko-mee-ńash] m.
chimney-sweep
komis [ko-mees] m. (on)
commission sale; commission
shop; commission agent
komisariat [ko-mee-sa-ryat] m.
police station; commissariat
komisja [ko-mees-ya] f.
commission; board (of inquiry)
(standing) committee
komitet [ko-mee-tet] m.
committee; board
komitywa [ko-mee-ti-va] f.
intimacy; good friendly terms
komiwojażer [ko-mee-vo-ya-zher]
m. travelling salesman
komnata [kom-na-ta] f. chamber
komoda [ko-mo-da] f. chest of
drawers; low-boy; commode
komora [ko-mo-ra] f. chamber
komora celna [ko-mo-ra tsel-na]
f. customs office; custom
house (where duties are paid)
komorne [ko-mor-ne] n.
(apartment) rent; rental
komórka [ko-moor-ka] f. cell
kompan [kom-pan] m. chum; pal
kompania [kom-pa-ńya] f.
company; (stock, military)
company; society; pilgrimage
kompas [kom-pas] m. compass
kompensata [kom-pen-sa-ta] f.
compensation; indemnity
kompetentny [kom-pe-ten-tni]
adj. m. competent; qualified

kompleks [kom-plex] m.
complex (of buildings); group;
(inferiority) complex; whole
komplement [kom-ple-ment] m.
compliment; complement
komplet [kom-plet] m. complete
set; complete (full) group
kompozytor [kom-po-zi-tor] m.
composer (of music)
kompot [kom-pot] m. compote
kompres [kom-pres] m. compress
kompromis [kom-pro-mees] m.
compromise; accommodation
kompromitacja [kom-pro-mee-
-tats-ya] f. disgrace; loss of
face; shame; humiliation
komuna [ko-moo-na] f. commune
komunał [ko-moo-naw] m.
platitude; banality; trite
remark; commonplace
komunia [ko-moo-ńa] f. Communion (in Catholic church)
komunikacja [ko-moo-ńee-kats-
-ya] f. communication; contact
komunikat [ko-moo-ńee-kat] m.
bulletin; report; communique
komunikować [ko-moo-ńee-ko
-vaćh] v. inform; give news;
report; receive Communion
komunista [ko-moo-ńees-ta] m.
communist (party member)
konać [ko-naćh] v. agonize;
expire; be dying; die (with
greed, with laughter)
konar [ko-nar] m. limb; branch
koncentryczny [kon-tsen-trich-ni]
adj. m. concentric; converging
koncept [kon-tsept] m. concept;
idea; joke; plan; brain wave
koncert [kon-tsert] m. concert
koncesja [kon-tses-ya] f.
concession; conceding; right
to sell; licence; licence to do...
koniec [ko-ńets] m. end; finish
konkurencja [kon-koo-ren-tsya] f.
competition; rivalry; contest
konkurs [kon-koors] m. contest
konnica [kon-ńee-tsa] f. cavalry
konno [kon-no] adv. on horse
-back; sit astraddle; mounted
konny [kon-ni] adj. m. mounted
konopie [ko-no-pye] pl. hemp
konował [ko-no-vaw] m. farrier;

quack doctor; sawbones
konserwa [kon-ser-va] f.
preserve; conservatists
konserwatorium [kon-ser-va-tor-
-yoom] n. conservatory
konsola [kon-so-la] f. console
konspirować [kon-spee-ro-vaćh]
v. plot; conspire; keep secret
konstatować [kon-sta-to-vaćh]
v. state; ascertain; find
konsternacja [kon-ster-nats-ya] f.
consternation; dismay; shock
konstrukcja [kon-strook-tsya] f.
construction; design; plan
konstruować [kon-stroo-o-vaćh]
v. construct; build; make
konstytucja [kon-sti-toots-ya] f.
constitution; physique
konsulat [kon-soo-lat] m. consulate (office of a consul)
konsumować [kon-soo-mo-
-vaćh] v. consume; eat up;
drink up; use up; waste (fuel)
konsylium [kon-sil-yoom] n.
consultation (usually medical)
konszachty [kon-shakh-ti] pl. collusion; (underhand) scheming
kontakt [kon-takt] m. contact
kontaktować się [kon-tak-to-
-vaćh śhan] v. be in contact;
be in touch; communicate
konto [kon-to] n. account
kontrabanda [kon-tra-ban-da] f.
smuggled goods; contraband
kontrakt [kon-trakt] m. contract
enforceable by law
kontraktować [kon-trak-to-
-vaćh] v. contract (to supply);
hire; engage (an employee)
kontrast [kon-trast] m. contrast
(pointing the differences)
kontrastować [kon-tras-to-
-vaćh] v. contrast (with);
stand in contrast; stand out
kontratak [kontr-a-tak] m. count-
er-attack (opposing an attack)
kontrola [kon-tro-la] f. control;
checking; check up; inspection
kontrolny [kon-trol-ni] adj. m. of
inspection; of supervision
kontrolować [kon-tro-lo-vaćh]
v. control; check; verify
kontrpropozycja [kontr-pro-po-

-zits-ya] f. counter-proposal
kontrrewolucja [kontr-re-vo-
-loots-ya] f. counterrevolution
kontrowersja [kon-tro-**ver**-sya] f.
controversy; quarrel; dispute
kontuar [kon-**too**-ar] m. counter
kontur [kon-toor] m. outline
kontusz [kon-toosh] m. split
-sleeve Polish overcoat (of old)
kontuzja [kon-tooz-ya] f. shock
kontynent [kon-**ti**-nent] m.
continent; mainland; any main
land area of the earth
konwalia [kon-**va**-lya] f. lily of
the valley; convallaria
konwikt [kon-veekt] m. boarding
school (for boys or girls)
konwój [kon-vooy] m. convoy
konwulsja [kon-**vool**-sya] f.
convulsion; a fit; a spasm
koń [koń] m. horse; steed
koń mechaniczny [koń me-kha-
-**ńeech**-ni] m. mechanical
horsepower; horsepower
końcowy [koń-**tso**-vi] adj. m.
final; terminal; last; late
końcówka [koń-**tsoov**-ka] f.
ending; remainder; tail-piece
kończyć [koń-chiń] v. end;
finish; quit; be dying; stop
kończyna [koń-chi-na] f.
extremity; limb; member; leg
kooperacja [ko-o-pe-**rats**-ya] f.
cooperation; acting together
koordynacja [ko-or-di-**nats**-ya] f.
coordination (mental & phys.)
kopa [ko-pa] f. threescore (60);
pile; dozens; stack
kopa siana [ko-pa **śha**-na] f. hay
-stack; hayrick
kopać [ko-paćh] v. kick; dig
kopalnia [ko-pal-ńa] f. mine
koparka [ko-par-ka] f. excavator;
mechanical shovel; stripper
kopcić [kop-ćheećh] v. soot;
smoke; blacken with smoke
kopciuszek [kop-ćhoo-shek] m.
Cinderella; drudge; slavey
kopeć [ko-pećh] m. soot
koper [ko-per] m. dill; fennel
koperta [ko-per-ta] f. envelope;
quilt-case; (watch-)case
kopiasty [ko-**pyas**-ti] adj. m.

heaped; piled up; heaped
(plate); lying in a heap
kopiec [ko-pyets] m. mound;
barrow; heap; knoll; clamp
kopiować [ko-pyo-vaćh] v.
copy; reproduce; imitate
kopuła [ko-poo-wa] f. dome
kopyto [ko-pi-to] n. hoof
kora [ko-ra] f. bark; cortex
koral [ko-ral] m. coral (red)
korale [ko-ra-le] pl. bead
necklace; coral beads; gills
korba [kor-ba] f. crank; winch
kordon [kor-don] m. cordon
korek [ko-rek] m. cork; fuse;
stopper; traffic-jam; tie-up
korekta [ko-rek-ta] f. proof
korepetycja [ko-re-pe-**tits**-ya] f.
tutoring; private lesson
korespondencja [ko-res-pon-
-**dents**-ya] f. correspondence;
letters; mail; post
korespondent wojenny [ko-res-
-pon-dent vo-yen-ni] war
correspondent; war reporter
korkociąg [kor-ko-ćhowng] m.
corkscrew; tail-spin; twist
korniszon [kor-ńee-shon] m.
pickled cucumber; gherkin
korny [kor-ni] adj. m. humble
korona [ko-ro-na] f. crown
koronacja [ko-ro-**nats**-ya] f.
coronation; crowning
koronka [ko-ron-ka] f. lace
koronować [ko-ro-no-vaćh] v.
crown; be crowned
korowód [ko-ro-vood] m. procession; pageant; train; pl.
difficulties; exertions
korporacja [kor-po-**rats**-ya] f.
corporation; association; guild
korpulentny [kor-poo-lent-ni] adj.
m. fat; corpulent; obese; stout
korpus [kor-poos] m. body; staff;
(army) corps; all army officers
korsarz [kor-sash] m. pirate
kort tenisowy [kort te-ńee-**so**-vi]
tennis court
korupcja [ko-roop-tsya] f.
corruption; venality; bribery
korygować [ko-ri-go-vaćh] v.
correct; rectify; put right
korytarz [ko-ri-tash] m. corridor;

passage-way; lobby; tunnel
koryto [ko-ri-to] n. through; river
-bed; channel; chute; road-bed
korzec [ko-zhets] m. bushel
korzeń [ko-zheń] m. root; spice
korzyć [ko-zhićh] v. humble;
humiliate; prostrate; mortify
korzystać [ko-zhis-tać̇h] v.
profit; gain; enjoy a right
korzystny [ko-zhist-ni] adj. m.
profitable; favorable
korzyść [ko-zhiśhćh] f. profit
kos [kos] m. blackbird
kosa [ko-sa] f. scythe; tress
kosiarka [ko-śhar-ka] f. mower; mowing machine (time)
kosić [ko-śheećh] v. mow;
scythe; rake; sweep
kosmaty [kos-ma-ti] adj. m.
shaggy; hairy; fleecy
kosmetyczka [kos-me-tich-ka] f.
vanity bag; beautician
kosmetyk [kos-me-tik] m.
cosmetic; makeup (skin and
hair); cosmetic preparation
kosmiczny [kos-meech-ni] adj. m.
cosmic; outer space; vast
kosmopolita [kos-mo-po-lee-ta]
m. cosmopolite; cosmopolitan
kosmyk [kos-mik] m. wisp;
strand; tuft; flock (of hair)
kosodrzewina [ko-so-dzhe-vee-
-na] f. dwarf mountain pine
kosooki [ko-so-o-kee] adj. m.
with slanting eyes; with
scowling eyes; cross-eyed
kostium [kos-tyoom] m. suit;
dress; garb; tailor made suit
kostka [kost-ka] f. small bone;
ankle; knuckle; die; dice; lump
kostnica [kost-ńee-tsa] f.
morgue; mortuary; dead house
kostnieć [kost-ńećh] v. grow
stiff (numb); ossify; freeze
kosy [ko-si] adj. m. slanting
kosz [kosh] m. basket; grab-bag;
Tartar military camp
koszary [ko-sha-ri] pl. barracks
(military); caserns
koszenie [ko-she-ńe] n. mowing
koszerny [ko-sher-ni] adj. m.
kosher (clean or fit to eat)
koszmar [kosh-mar] m.

nightmare; frightening
experience (dream)
koszt [kosht] m. cost; price;
expense; charge; economic
costs; production cost etc.
kosztorys [ko-shto-ris] m.
estimate; cost calculation
kosztowny [kosh-tov-ni] adj. m.
expensive; costly; precious
koszula [ko-shoo-la] f. shirt
koszyk [ko-shik] f. small basket;
grab bag; hilt guard; basketful
koszykówka [ko-shi-koov-ka] f.
basketball
kościany [kośh-ća-ni] adj. m.
bone (handle etc.); osseous
kościec [kośh-ćhets] m.
skeleton; framework; frame
kościelny [kośh-ćhel-ni] adj.
m. of church; ecclesiastical;
m. sexton; sacristan
kościotrup [kośh-ćho-troop]
m. skeleton; thin man (vulg.)
kościół [kośh-ćhoow] m.
church; church organization
kościsty [kośh-ćhees-ti]
adj. m. bony; angular; raw-
boned; teleostean (fish)
kość [kośhćh] f. bone; spine
koślawić [kośh-la-veećh] v.
deform; distort; crook
koślawy [kośh-la-vi] adj. m.
crooked; lame; lopsided
kot [kot] m. cat; pussy cat; puss
kotara [ko-ta-ra] f. curtain
kotek [ko-tek] m. kitten; puss
kotlet [kot-let] m. cutlet
kotlina [kot-lee-na] f. dale
kotłować [kot-wo-vaćh] v.
whirl; seethe; surge; drive
crazy; bother; worry
kotłownia [kot-wov-ńa] f. boiler
room; boiler house; fire room
kotwica [kot-vee-tsa] f. anchor
kotwiczyć [kot-vee-chićh] v.
anchor; lie at anchor
kowadło [ko-va-dwo] n. anvil
kowal [ko-val] m. blacksmith
kowalny [ko-val-ni] adj. m.
malleable; ductile; forgeable
koza [ko-za] f. goat; jail
kozioł [ko-źhow] m. buck;
somersault; trestle; stack

koźlę [koźh-lan] n. kid; goatling
kożuch [ko-zhookh] m.
  sheepskin (coat); fur coat;
  coating on hot milk; film; hide
kół [koow] m. stake; post
kółko [koow-ko] m. small wheel;
  small circle; (soc.) circle
kpiarz [kpyash] m. scoffer
kpić [kpeećh] v. jeer; sneer
kpiny [kpee-ni] n. mockery; this
  is preposterous! (exp.)
kra [kra] f. ice flow; ice float
krach [krakh] m. crash; slump
kraciasty [kra-ćhas-ti] adj. m.
  chequered; grated; checkered
kradzież [kra-dźhesh] f. theft
kradziony [kra-dźho-ni] adj. m.
  stolen (object); robbed
kraina [kra-ee-na] f. land; region;
  province; country
kraj [kray] m. country; verge;
  edge; hem of a garment; land
krajać [kra-yaćh] v. cut; slice;
  carve; operate; hack; saw
krajobraz [kra-yo-bras] m.
  landscape; scenery painting
krajowy [kra-yo-vi] adj. m.
  native; nationally made
krajoznawczy [kra-yo-znav-chi]
  adj. m. hiking; touring
krakać [kra-kaćh] v. croak
kram [kram] m. booth; mess;
  trouble; stall; odds and ends
kramarz [kra-mash] m. huckster
kran [kran] m. tap; faucet
kraniec [kra-ńets] m. border;
  edge; end; extremity; margin
krańcowy [krań-tso-vi] adj. m.
  extreme; marginal; excessive
krasa [kra-sa] f. grace; beauty;
  loveliness; splendor
krasić [kra-śheećh] v. decorate
krasomówca [kra-so-moov-tsa]
  m. orator (very eloquent)
kraść [kraśhćh] v. steal; rob
kraśnieć [kraśh-ńećh] v.
  blush; grow beautiful; redden
krata [kra-ta] f. grate; grill
krater [kra-ter] m. crater
krawat [kra-vat] m. neck (tie)
krawcowa [krav-tso-va] f.
  seamstress; tailor's wife
krawędź [kra-vandźh] f. edge

krawężnik [kra-vanzh-ńeek] m.
  curb (stone); roof-hip
krawiec [kra-vyets] m. tailor
krąg [krownk] m. ring; vertebra;
  disk; range; circle; sphere
krążek [krown-zhek] m. small
  disk; potter's wheel; pulley
krążyć [krown-zhićh] v. rove;
  circulate; rotate; wander; stray
kreacja [kre-ats-ya] f. (dress)
  creation (of a theater part)
kreda [kre-da] f. chalk
kredens [kre-dens] m. china
  cabinet; cupboard; buffet
kredka [kred-ka] f. crayon;
  lipstick; chalk for writing
kredowy [kre-do-vi] adj. m.
  cretaceous; chalky; made of
  chalk; white like chalk
kredyt [kre-dit] m. credit
krem [krem] m. cream; custard
krematorium [kre-ma-to-ryoom]
  n. crematorium; crematory
kremowy [kre-mo-vi] adj. m.
  cream-colored; cream yellow
kreować [kre-o-vaćh] v. create;
  act; set up; institute; appoint
krepa [kre-pa] f. crepe
kres [kres] m. end; limit; term
kreska [kres-ka] f. dash (line);
  stroke; hatch; scar; accent
kreślić [kreśh-leećh] v. draw;
  trace; sketch; cross out
kret [kret] m. mole; schemer
kretowisko [kre-to-vees-ko] n.
  molehill (made by burrowing)
krew [krev] f. blood; race
krewetka [kre-vet-ka] f. shrimp
krewki [krev-kee] adj. m. rash;
  quick-tempered; impetuous
krewny [krev-ni] m. relative
kręcić [kran-ćheećh] v. twist;
  turn; shoot film; fuss; boss
kręcony [kran-tso-ni] adj. m.
  twisted; curled; winding; spiral
kręgle [kran-gle] n. bowling;
  (ninepins) game of bowling
kręgosłup [kran-go-swoop] m.
  spine; vertebral column; spinal
  column; backbone; willpower
kręgowiec [kran-go-vyets] m.
  vertebrate; animal with spine
krępować [kran-po-vaćh] v.

bind; embarrass; hamper; hinder; tie up; shackle; impede; fetter; peg down; cramp

krępy [kran-pi] adj. m. stocky; thickset; sturdy; short; squat

krętactwo [kran-tats-tvo] n. cheat; foul dealing; shuffle

krętacz [kran-tach] m. double -dealer; dodger; quibbler; cheat; crooked (lawyer etc.)

kręty [kran-ti] adj. m. curved; curly; winding; spiral; devious

krnąbrny [krnownb-rni] adj. m. stubborn; unruly; restive; insubordinate; balky; fractious

krochmal [krokh-mal] m. starch

krochmalić [krokh-ma-leech] v. starch; beat up; stiffen

krocie [kro-che] pl. thousands

kroczyć [kro-chich] v. stride

kroić [kro-eech] v. cut; slice

krok [krok] m. step; pace; march

krokiew [kro-kev] f. rafter

krokodyl [kro-ko-dil] m. crocodile; split flap (aviation)

kromka [krom-ka] f. slice

kronika [kro-ńee-ka] f. chronicle

kropić [kro-peech] v. sprinkle

kropka [krop-ka] f. dot; point

kropkować [krop-ko-vach] v. dot; speckle; spot

kropla [krop-la] f. drop

krosno [kros-no] n. loom

krosta [kros-ta] f. pimple

krotochwila [kro-to-khvee-la] f. joke; burlesque; farce

krowa [kro-va] cow; mine

krój [krooy] m. cut; fashion

król [krool] m. king; rabbit

królestwo [kroo-les-tvo] n. kingdom; the realms; sphere

królewicz [kroo-le-veech] m. crown prince; king's son

królewski [kroo-lev-skee] adj. m. royal; kingly; majestic; king's

królik [kroo-leek] m. rabbit

królikarnia [kroo-lee-kar-ńa] f. warren; rabbit warren

królowa [kroo-lo-va] f. queen

krótki [kroot-kee] adj. m. short; brief; terse; concise; curt

krótko [kroot-ko] adv. briefly; shortly; tersely; (hold) tightly

krtań [krtań] f. larynx

kruchy [kroo-khi] adj. m. brittle; frail; tender; crisp; crusty

krucjata [kroots-ya-ta] f. crusade; action for some cause

krucyfiks [kroo-tsi-feeks] m. crucifix; cross of Jesus

kruczek [kroo-chek] m. trick

kruczy [kroo-chi] adj. m. jet -black; raven's color

kruk [krook] m. raven

krupy [kroo-pi] pl. groats

kruszec [kroo-shets] m. (metal) ore; metal; gold; silver

kruszeć [kroo-shech] v. crumble; grow brittle; repent

kruszyć [kroo-shich] v. crush; crumb; destroy; shatter; disrupt; break into pieces

kruszyna [kroo-shi-na] f. crumb

krużganek [kroozh-ga-nek] m. portico; gallery; ambulatory

krwawica [krva-vee-tsa] f. hard won money; toil; labor

krwawić [krva-veech] v. bleed

krwawy [krva-vi] adj. m. bloody; bloodthirsty; bloodstained

krwiobieg [krvyo-byeg] m. blood circulation; circulation

krwisty [krvees-ti] adj. m. sanguineous; blood-red

krwotok [krvo-tok] m. hemorrhage; heavy bleeding

kryć [krich] v. hide; conceal; cover; roof over; shield; mask

kryjówka [kri-yoov-ka] f. hiding place; hide-out; cache

kryminalista [kri-mee-na-lees-ta] m. criminal; felon; criminologist

kryminał [kri-mee-naw] m. jail; prison; crime; felony; thriller

krynica [kri-ńee-tsa] f. spring

krystalizować [kris-ta-lee-zo-vach] v. crystallize; shape

kryształ [krish-taw] m. crystal

kryterium [kri-te-ryoom] n. criterion; touchstone; test

kryty [kri-ti] adj. m. covered

krytyczny [kri-tich-ni] adj. m. critical; decisive; crucial

krytyk [kri-tik] m. critic

krytyka [kri-ti-ka] f. criticism; review; censure; critique

kryzys [kri-zis] m. crisis
krzaczasty [kzha-chas-ti] adj. m.
bushy; shaggy (thick); beetle
krzak [kzhak] m. bush
krzątać [kzhown-tać] v. bustle
krzątanina [kzhown-ta-ńee-na] f.
bustle; comings and goings
krzem [kzhem] m. silicone
krzemień [kzhe-myeń] f. flint
krzepić [kzhe-peećh] v. brace
up; refresh; invigorate; fortify
krzepki [kzhep-kee] adj. vigorous;
lusty; robust; husky; sprightly
krzepnąć [kzhep-nownćh] v.
coagulate; gather strength; set
krzesać [kzhe-saćh] v. strike
fire (out of); strike sparks
krzesiwo [kzhe-śhee-vo] n.
tinder-box; flint (and steel)
krzesło [kzhes-wo] n. chair
krzew [kzhev] m. shrub
krzewić [kzhe-veećh] v. spread;
propagate; teach; graft
krzta [kzhta] f. whit; bit
krztusiec [kzhtoo-śhets] m.
whooping-cough
krztusić się [kzhtoo-śheećh
śhan] v. choke; stifle
krzyczeć [kzhi-chećh] v. shout;
cry; scream; yell; clamor
krzyk [kzhik] m. cry; scream;
shriek; yell; outcry; call
krzykacz [kzhi-kach] m. bawler;
crier; shouter; agitator
krzykliwy [kzhik-lee-vi] adj. m.
noisy; clamorous; loud; showy
krzywa [kzhi-va] f. curve
krzywda [kzhiv-da] f. harm; a
sense of wrong; wrong; injury
krzywdzący [kzhiv-dzown-tsi]
adj. m. harmful; injurious
krzywdzić [kzhiv-dźheećh] v.
harm; wrong; damage; be unfair (unjust); be prejudicial
krzywica [kzhi-vee-tsa] f. rickets;
rachitis; sweep (turning) saw
krzywić [kzhi-veećh] v. bend
krzywić się [kzhi-veećh śhan]
v. make faces; bend; warp
krzywo [kzhi-vo] adv. crooked
krzywy [kzhi-vi] adj. m. crooked;
skew; distorted; slanting
krzyż [kzhish] m. cross

krzyżować [kzhi-zho-vaćh] v.
cross; thwart; crucify
krzyżówka [kzhi-zhoov-ka] f.
crossword puzzle; hybrid
ksiądz [kśhownts] m. priest
książę [kśhown-zhan] m.
prince; duke; ruler of a duchy
książka [kśhownzh-ka] f. book
księga [kśhan-ga] f. register;
large book; volume; tome
księgarnia [kśhan-gar-ńa] f.
bookstore; books; book shop
księgarz [kśhan-gash] m.
bookseller; owner of a
bookstore
księgować [kśhan-go-vaćh] v.
keep books; enter in books
księgowy [kśhan-go-vi] m.
bookkeeper; accountant
księgozbiór [kśhan-go-zbyoor]
m. book collection; library
księstwo [kśhans-tvo] n. duchy
księżna [kśhan-zhna] f.
princess; wife of a prince
księży [kśhan-zhi] adj. m.
priestly; belonging to a priest
księżyc [kśhan-zhits] m. moon
kształcić [kshtaw-ćheećh] v.
educate; train; form; school
kształt [kshtawt] m. form;
shape; configuration; figure
kształtny [kshtawt-ni] adj. m.
shapely; neat; nicely made
kształtować [kshtaw-to-vaćh]
v. shape; form; mold; fashion
kto [kto] pron. who; all; those
kto bądź [kto bowndźh]
anybody; no one; just anyone
kto inny [kto een-ni] somebody
else; someone else
ktoś [ktośh] pron. somebody
którędy [ktoo-ran-di] adv. which
way; how to get there?
który [ktoo-ri] pron. who; which;
that; any; whichever; that
któż [ktoosh] pron. whichever
ku [koo] prep. towards; to
kubatura [koo-ba-too-ra] f.
(building) volume; cubature
kubek [koo-bek] m. cup; mug
kubeł [koo-bew] m. pail; bucket
kucharka [koo-khar-ka] f. cook
kucharz [koo-khash] m. cook

kuchenka gazowa [koo-khen-ka ga-zo-va] f. (gas) hot plate
kuchnia [kookh-ńa] f. kitchen; kitchen stove; cooking range
kucnąć [koots-nownćh] v. squat down; squat; crouch
kucyk [koo-tsik] m. small pony
kuć [kooćh] v. hammer; shoe a horse; forge; cram lessons; peck; pick; coin; whack
kudłaty [kood-wa-ti] adj. m. shaggy; hairy; hirsute
kudły [kood-wi] pl. shaggy hair
kufel [koo-fel] m. beer mug
kufer [koo-fer] m. trunk
kuglarz [koog-lash] m. juggler
kukiełkowy teatr [koo-kew-ko-vi te-atr] puppet-show
kukła [kook-wa] f. puppet
kukułka [koo-koow-ka] f. cuckoo bird; cuckoo clock
kukurydza [koo-koo-ri-dza] maize; corn; Indian corn
kula [koo-la] f. sphere; bullet crutch; ball; globe; shot
kulawy [koo-la-vi] adj. m. lame
kulbaczyć [kool-ba-chićh] v. saddle (a horse, a pony, etc.)
kuleć [koo-lećh] v. limp
kulić się [koo-leećh śhan] v. snuggle; crouch; cringe; nestle
kulinarny [koo-lee-nar-ni] adj. m. culinary; of cooking (cookery)
kulisy [koo-lee-si] pl. theater scenes; the inner facts; links
kulisty [koo-lees-ti] adj. m. spherical; ball-shaped; round
kulminacyjny [kool-mee-na-tsiy-ni] adj. m. culminating; final; climactic; of a turning point
kult [koolt] m. cult; worship
kultura [kool-too-ra] f. culture; good manners; cultivation
kuluar [koo-loo-ar] m. lobby
kułak [koo-wak] m. fist; punch
kum [koom] m. godfather; crony
kumoterstwo [koo-mo-ters-tvo] n. favoritism; log rolling
kumulacja [koo-moo-lats-ya] f. accumulation; merger; fusion
kuna [koo-na] f. marten
kundel [koon-del] m. mongrel
kunszt [koonsht] m. art; skill

kunsztowny [koon-shtov-ni] adj. m. artistic; artful; ingenious
kupa [koo-pa] f. heep; pile; lot; excrement; assemblage; set
kupczyć [koop-chićh] v. bargain; trade; influence peddling; traffic (in one's influence)
kupić [koo-peećh] v. buy
kupiec [koo-pyets] m. shopkeeper; merchant; dealer
kupno [koop-no] n. purchase
kupon [koo-pon] m. coupon
kur [koor] m. cock; cock crow
kura [koo-ra] f. hen; hen bird
kuracja [koo-rats-ya] f. cure
kuratorium [koo-ra-tor-yum] n. board of trustees (of schools)
kurcz [koorch] m. cramp; shrinking; twitching
kurczę [koor-chan] n. chicken
kurczyć [koor-chićh] v. shrink
kurek [koo-rek] m. tap; cock
kurier [koor-yer] m. courier
kurnik [koor-ńeek] m. chicken house; hen house; hen roost poultry house; hen cote
kuropatwa [koo-ro-pat-va] f. partridge (game bird)
kurować [koo-ro-vaćh] v. heal; cure; treat for an illness
kurs [koors] m. course; rate; fare
kursować [koor-so-vaćh] v. circulate; ferry; run; ply
kurtka [koor-tka] f. jacket
kurtyna [koor-ti-na] f. curtain
kurwa [koor-va] f. whore (vulg.)
kurz [koosh] m. dust
kurza ślepota [koo-zha śhle-po-ta] night blindness
kusić [koo-śheećh] v. tempt
kustosz [koos-tosh] m. curator; conservator
kusy [koo-si] adj. m. short; scanty; skimpy; meager
kusza [koo-sha] f. crossbow
kuśnierz [koośh-ńesh] m. furrier; fur dealer
kuter [koo-ter] m. cutter
kutwa [koot-va] f. miser
kuty [koo-ti] adj. m. forged; shod; cunning; sly; shrewd
kuzyn [koo-zin] m. cousin
kuźnia [kooźh-ńa] f. forge

kwadra [kvad-ra] f. quarter moon
kwadrans [kvad-rans] f. quarter of an hour; fifteen minutes
kwadrat [kvad-rat] m. square
kwakać [kva-kaćh] v. quack
kwalifikacja [kva-lee-fee-kats-ya] f. qualification; evaluation
kwalifikować [kva-lee-fee-ko-vaćh] v. qualify; class; appraise; describe; evaluate
kwapić się [kva-peećh śhan] v. be eager; be in a hurry
kwarantanna [kva-ran-tan-na] f. quarantine; period of isolation
kwarc [kvarts] m. quartz
kwarta [kvar-ta] f. quart
kwartalny [kvar-tal-ni] adj. m. quarterly; occurring quarterly
kwas [kvas] m. acid; pl. discord
kwasić [kva-śheećh] v. sour; ferment; embitter; be idle
kwaskowaty [kvas-ko-va-ti] adj. m. acrid; sourish; acidulous
kwasy [kva-si] pl. fusses; bad-blood; ill humor; dissent
kwaśny [kvaśh-ni] adj. m. sour
kwatera [kva-te-ra] f. quarters; lodging; living accommodation
kwaterka [kva-ter-ka] f. quarter of a liter; quarter liter bottle
kwesta [kves-ta] f. collection (for); passing the hat around
kwestia [kves-tya] f. question
kwestionariusz [kves-tyo-na-ryoosh] m. questionnaire
kwękać [kvan-kaćh] v. be for ever sickly (ailing); complain
kwiaciarka [kvya-ćhar-ka] f. florist; flower girl
kwiaciarnia [kvya-ćhar-ńa] f. flower shop; florist's
kwiat [kvyat] m. flower
kwiczeć [kvee-chećh] v. make a shrill cry; squeak; squeal
kwiczoł [kvee-chow] m. field-fare (Turdus pilavis)
kwiecień [kvye-ćheń] m. April
kwiecisty [kvye-ćhees-ti] adj. m. flowery; colorful; ornate
kwietnik [kvyet-ńeek] m. flower-bed; carpet bed
kwik [kveek] m. squeal; squeak
kwit [kveet] m. receipt

kwitnąć [kveet-nownćh] v. blossom; grow moldy; look healthy; thrive; prosper
kwitować [kvee-to-vaćh] v. give receipt; relinquish; forgo
kwoka [kvo-ka] f. sitting hen
kwota [kvo-ta] f. amount; amount (of money); allocation
kynologiczny związek [ki-no-lo-geech-ni zvyown-zek] kennel club; kennel association

L

labirynt [la-bee-rynt] m. labyrinth; maze
laborant [la-bo-rant] m. lab. technician. assistant chemist
laboratorium [la-bo-ra-tor-yoom] n. laboratory; lab
lać [laćh] v. pour; shed; (spill)
lada [la-da] part. any; whatever; the least; paltry; s. counter
lada kto [la-da kto] anybody
ladacznica [la-dach-ńee-tsa] f. harlot; prostitute; strumpet
laik [la-eek] m. layman
lak [lak] m. sealing wax
lakier [la-ker] m. varnish
lakmus [lak-moos] m. litmus
lakoniczny [la-ko-ńeech-ni] adj. m. terse; brief; curt; laconic stating much in few words
lakować [la-ko-vaćh] v. seal
lalka [lal-ka] f. doll; puppet
laktoza [lak-to-za] f. lactose
lament [la-ment] m. lament
lamować [la-mo-vaćh] v. trim; edge; border (with lace etc.)
lamówka [la-moov-ka] f. trim; border; edge; trimming; piping
lampa [lam-pa] f. lamp
lampart [lam-part] m. leopard
lampas [lam-pas] m. side stripe (on pants); lampas; stripe
lampion [lam-pyon] m. lampion
lamus [la-moos] m. storeroom
lanca [lan-tsa] f. lance; spear

lancet [lan-tset] m. lancet; fleam
landara [lan-da-ra] f. jalopy; old
  crate; rumble-tumble; jumbo
lanie [la-ńe] n. pouring; casting;
  beating; trashing; licking
lanolina [la-no-lee-na] f. lanolin;
  wool-fat (in ointments)
lansady [lap-sa-di] pl. prancing
  gait; skips; leaps; bounds
lansować [lan-so-vaćh] v. promote; launch; initiate; start
lapidarny [la-pee-dar-ni] adj. m.
  terse; concise; curt; crisp
lapis [la-pees] m. silver nitrate;
  lunar caustic
lapsus [lap-soos] m. lapse (slip)
laryngologia [la-rin-go-lo-gya] f.
  laryngology
las [las] m. wood; forest; thicket
lasek [la-sek] m. grove; copse
laska [las-ka] f. cane; stick
laskowy orzech [las-ko-vi o-
  -zhekh] m. hazelnut
lasować [la-so-vaćh] v. slake
lata [la-ta] pl. years
latać [la-taćh] v. fly; be running
latarka [la-tar-ka] f. flashlight;
  (electric) torch; small lamp
latarnia [la-tar-ńa] f. streetlight;
  lantern; beacon; lamppost
latarnia morska [la-tar-ńa mors-
  -ka] lighthouse; beacon
latarnik [la-tar-ńeek] m.
  lighthouse keeper; lamplighter
latawiec [la-ta-vyets] m. kite
lato [la-to] n. summer
latorośl [la-to-rośhl] f. shoot;
  offspring; scion; spring; sprout
laubzega [law-bze-ga] f. fretsaw;
  jigsaw; scroll saw
laufer [law-fer] m. runner (foot-
  man); (chess) bishop
laury [law-ri] pl. laurels
laureat [law-re-at] m. laureate;
  prize-winner; prizeman
lawa [la-va] f. volcanic lava
lawenda [la-ven-da] f. lavender;
  lavender water
laweta [la-ve-ta] f. gun carriage;
  heavy artillery gun base
lawina [la-vee-na] f. avalanche;
  shover (of words, rock, etc.)
lawirować [la-vee-ro-vaćh] v.

veer; tack; intrigue; shift
lazaret [la-za-ret] m. field
  hospital (for infections)
lazur [la-zoor] m. azure; sky blue;
  the blue; blue pigment
ląd [lownd] m. 1.land;
  2. mainland; 3. continent
lądować [lown-do-vaćh] v.
  land; disembark; go ashore;
  alight; save oneself
lecieć [le-ćhećh] v. fly; run;
  hurry; wing; drift; drop; fall
leciutko [le-ćhoot-ko] adv.
  barely touching; very lightly
leciwy [le-ćhee-vi] adj. m. up in
  years; advanced in years;
  aged; elderly
lecz [lech] conj. but; however
leczenie [le-che-ńe] n. healing;
  cure; treatment
lecznica [lech-ńee-tsa] f.
  hospital; clinic; nursing home
leczyć [le-chićh] v. heal; treat;
  nurse; practice medicine
ledwie [led-vye] adv. hardly; no
  sooner; scarcely; barely; almost; nearly; only just
ledwo że nie [led-vo zhe ńe]
  adv. almost; nearly; hardly
legacja [le-gats-ya] f. legation;
  legacy; bequest
legalizować [le-ga-lee-zo-vaćh]
  v. legalize; certify; attest
legalny [le-gal-ni] adj. m. legal;
  lawful; allowed by law
legat [le-gat] m. bequest; papal
  muncio; anything bequeathed
legawiec [le-ga-vyets] m. pointer;
  setter (a large hunting dog)
legenda [le-gen-da] f. legend
legendarny [le-gen-dar-ni] adj. m.
  legendary; fabulous; storied
legia [leg-ya] f.legion; multitude
legion [leg-yon] m. legion
legitymacja [le-gee-ti-mats-ya] f.
  i-d card; identification papers;
  membership card etc.; warrant
legitymować się [le-gee-ti-mo-
  -vaćh śhan] v. prove one's
  identity; identify oneself
legnąć [leg-nownćh] v. fall in
  battle; perish; lie down
legowisko [le-go-vees-ko] n.

berth; bedding; encampment;
den; pallet; lair; encampment
legumina [le-goo-mee-na] f.
dessert; sweet dish; legumin
lej [ley] m. crater; funnel
lejce [ley-tse] pl. reins
lejek [le-yek] m. small funnel
lek [lek] m. medicine; drug
lekarski [le-kars-kee] adj. m.
medical; medicinal; officinal
lekarz [le-kash] m. physician
lekceważący [lek-tse-va-zhown-
-tsi] adj. m. disrespectful
lekceważenie [lek-tse-va-zhe-ńe]
n. disdain; disrespect; scorn
lekceważyc [lek-tse-va-zhićh] v.
slight; scorn; neglect; disdain
lekcja [lek-tsya] f. lesson; class
lekki [lek-kee] adj. m. light; light
-hearted; graceful; slight
lekko [lek-ko] adv. easily; lightly
lekkoatletyka [lek-ko-at-le-ti-ka] f.
field & track sports; athletics
lekkomyślny [lek-ko-myśhl-ni]
adj. m. careless; thoughtless;
reckless; rash; fickle; hasty
lektura [lek-too-ra] f. reading
matter; reading list; reading
lemiesz [le-myesh] m. plough-
share; (shear) blade; vomer
lemoniada [le-mo-ńa-da] f.
lemonade; lemon squash
len [len] m. flax; linen
lenić się [le-ńeećh śhan] v.
be idle; be lazy; shed hair
lenieć [le-ńećh] v. shed hair;
slough (skin); moult(feathers)
leninizm [le-ńee-ńeezm] m.
Leninism; Lenin's system
lenistwo [le-ńeest-vo] n.
laziness; idleness; sloth;
sluggishness
leniwy [le-ńee-vi] adj. m. lazy
lennik [len-ńeek] m. vassal
pledging fealty to overlord
lenno [len-no] n. fief; feud
leń [leń] m. lazy-bones; idler;
lazy bum; sluggard
lep [lep] m. glue; flypaper
lepianka [le-pyan-ka] f. adobe;
mud hut; mud cabin
lepić [le-peećh] v. stick; glue
lepiej [le-pyey] adv. better;

rather; (feel) better
lepki [lep-kee] adj. m. sticky
lepszy [lep-shi] adj. m. better;
improved; superior; preferable
lesbijka [les-beey-ka] f. lesbian;
homosexual women
lesisty [le-śhees-ti] adj. m.
wooded; woody; forested
leszcz [leshch] m. bream
leszczyna [lesh-chi-na] f.
hazelnut tree; hazel grove
leśnictwo [leśh-ńeets-tvo] n.
forestry; forest-range
leśniczówka [leśh-ńee-choov-
ka] f. ranger's house
leśniczy [leśh-ńee-chi] m.
ranger; forest-ranger; forester
leśnik [leśh-ńeek] m. forester
leśny [leśh-ni] adj. m. of forest;
of forestry; forest-
letarg [le-tark] m. lethargy
letni [let-ńee] adj. m. lukewarm;
half-hearted; summer
letnik [let-ńeek] m. vacationer
letnisko [let-ńees-ko] n. summer
resort; summer vacation spot
lew [lev] m. lion; lady's man
lewa [le-va] f. left (side)
lewar [le-var] m. lever; jack
lewatywa [le-va-ti-va] f. enema
lewica [le-vee-tsa] f. the left
(polit.); left-hand side
lewo [le-vo] adv. to the left
lewy [le-vi] adj. m. left; false
leźć [leźhćh] v. crawl; creep-
along; climb; shuffle; lob
leżak [le-zhak] m. folding
(canvas) chair; deck-chair
leżeć [le-zhećh] v. lie; (fit)
lędźwie [landźh-vye] pl. loins
lęgnąć [lang-nownćh] v. hatch
lęk [lank] m. fear; anxiety; dread
lękać się [lan-kaćh śhan] v.
be afraid; dread; stand in awe
lękliwy [lank-lee-vi] adj. m. timid;
faint-hearted; apprehensive
lgnąć [lgnownćh] v. adhere;
sink; stick; be partial; feel
attracted; get stuck; cling
libacja [lee-bats-ya] f. drinking
party; drinking bout
liberalny [lee-be-ral-ni] adj. m.
liberal; broad-minded

liberał [lee-be-raw] m. liberal
libertyn [lee-ber-tin] m. libertine; free thinker; promiscuous man
lice [lee-tse] n. face; cheek; the right side; evidence (of guilt)
licencja [lee-tsen-tsya] f. license (permission to practice)
licho [lee-kho] adv. poorly; badly; indifferently; scantily
licho [lee-kho] n. evil; devil
lichota [lee-kho-ta] f. rubbish
lichtarz [leekh-tash] m. candlestick; candelabra
lichwa [leekh-va] f. usury
lichwiarz [leekh-vyash] m. usurer; loan shark; money lender (at high interest rate)
lichy [lee-khi] adj. m. shoddy; shabby; poor; mean; rotten; petty; miserable; inferior; paltry; flimsy; trivial; rotten
lico [lee-tso] n. face; cheek; surface; front; outer part
licować [lee-tso-vaćh] v. fit for...; comport; veneer; face
licytacja [lee-tsi-tats-ya] f. auction; bidding; the bid
licytować [lee-tsi-to-vaćh] v. auction; bid; offer; call
liczba [leech-ba] f. number; figure; integer; group; class
liczbowy [leech-bo-vi] adj. m. numerical; numeral
licznik [leech-ńeek] m. counter; numerator; gas meter; electric meter; etc.; taximeter; register
liczny [leech-ni] adj. m. numerous; large; abundant; plentiful; frequent
liczyć [lee-chićh] v. count; reckon; compute; calculate
liczydło [lee-chid-wo] n. abacus; counter; register
liga [lee-ga] f. league; alliance
lik [leek] m. lot; countless
lignia [leeg-ńa] f. lignin
likier [lee-ker] m. liquor
likwidacja [leek-vee-dats-ya] f. liquidation; closing down
likwidować [leek-vee-do-vaćh] v. liquidate; do away with
lila [lee-la] adj. m. (color) pale -violet; lily-; lilac (blue)

lilia [leel-ya] f. lily; nenuphar
liliowy [leel-yo-vi] adj. m. lilac (color); lily-; purple
liliput [lee-lee-poot] m. little dwarf; midget; pygmy
limfa [leem-fa] f. lymph
limit [lee-meet] m. limit
limuzyna [lee-moo-zi-na] f. limousine; pilot's enclosure
lin [leen] m. tench (fish)
lina [lee-na] f. line; rope
lincz [leench] m. lynch
linczować [leen-cho-vaćh] v. lynch; kill by mob action
lingwista [leen-gvees-ta] m. linguist (specialist)
linia [leeń-ya] f. line; lane
linijka [lee-ńeey-ka] f. ruler
liniować [lee-ńo-vaćh] v. rule; line (paper); rule paper
liniowy okret [lee-ńyo-vi ok-rant] liner (ship); battleship
linoleum [lee-no-le-oom] n. linoleum (floor covering)
linoskoczek [lee-no-sko-chek] m. tightrope artist; rope walker
linotyp [lee-no-tip] m. linotype (typesetting machine)
linowa kolejka [lee-no-va ko-ley--ka] cable car
lipa [lee-pa] f. 1. linden tree; 2. fake; cheat; fraud; trash
lipiec [lee-pyets] m. July
lira [lee-ra] f. lyre
liryczny [lee-rich-ni] adj. m. lyric (poetry etc.); lyrical (poet etc.)
liryka [lee-ri-ka] f. lyric poetry
lis [lees] m. fox; sly man
list [leest] m. letter; note
lista [lees-ta] f. list; roll; register; (attendance, time) record
listonosz [lees-to-nosh] m. postman
listopad [lees-to-pad] m. November
listownie [lees-tov-ńe] adv. by letter; by mail
listwa [lees-tva] f. trim
liszaj [lee-shay] m. herpes
liszka [leesh-ka] f. caterpillar; vixen; sly fox
liściasty [leeśh-ćhas-ti] adj. m. leafed; leafy; foliaceous

liść [leeśhćh] m. leaf; frond
litania [lee-ta-ńya] f. litany
litera [lee-te-ra] f. letter
literacki [lee-te-rats-kee] adj. m.
literary; of letters
literat [lee-te-rat] m. writer
literatura [lee-te-ra-too-ra] f.
literature; writings
litewski [lee-tevs-kee] adj. m.
Lithuanian; Lithuanian
language
litograf [lee-to-graf] m.
lithographer
litościwy [lee-tośh-ćhee-vi]
adj. m. merciful; pitying;
compassionate
litość [lee-tośhćh] f. pity;
mercy; compassion
litowac sie [lee-to-vaćh śhan]
v. have pity; feel pity
litr [leetr] m. liter
liturgia [lee-toor-gya] f. liturgy;
religious ritual
lity [lee-ti] adj. m. massive; solid;
cast; pure-; pure stand (trees)
lizać [lee-zaćh] v. lick; taste
lizol [lee-zol] m. lysol
lizus [lee-zoos] m. bootlicker
lniany [lńa-ni] adj. m. linen;
flaxen (thread); linseed (oil)
loch [lokh] m. dungeon; cellar
lodołamacz [lo-do-wa-mach] m.
icebreaker; ice shield
lodowaty [lo-do-va-ti] adj. m. icy;
ice-cold; chilling; frigid
lodowiec [lo-do-vyets] m. glacier;
mass of ice and snow
lodowisko [lo-do-vees-ko] n. ice
field; skating-rink; ice rink
lodownia [lo-dov-ńa] f. ice
-chamber; ice-cellar; icy cold
lodowy [lo-do-vi] adj. m. of ice
lodówka [lo-doov-ka] f. refrigerator; ice box; ice chest
lody [lo-di] pl. ice cream
logarytm [lo-ga-ritm] m. loga-
rithm; exponential expression
logiczny [lo-geech-ni] adj. m.
logical; consistent; sound
logik [lo-geek] m. logician; expert
in logic (cause and effect)
logika [lo-gee-ka] f. logic
lojalność [lo-yal-nośhćh] f.

loyalty; straightforwardness
lojalny [lo-yal-ni] adj. m. loyal;
staunch; low-abiding; true
lok [lok] m. curl; coil
lokaj [lo-kay] m. lackey
lokal [lo-kal] m. premises
lokalizować [lo-ka-lee-zo-vaćh]
v.localize; locate; range
lokalny [lo-kal-ni] adj. m. local;
regional; of a place
lokata [lo-ka-ta] f. investment
lokator [lo-ka-tor] m. tenant
lokomocja [lo-ko-mots-ya] f.
locomotion; communication
lokomotywa [lo-ko-mo-ti-va] f.
train engine; locomotive
lokować [lo-ko-vaćh] v. place
lombard [lom-bard] m. pawnshop
lont [lont] m. fuse; slow-match
lornetka [lor-net-ka] f. field
glasses; opera glasses
los [los] m. lot; fate; chance;
lottery ticket; destiny; hazard
losować [lo-so-vaćh] v. draw
lots; raffle; draw cuts
lot [lot] m. flight; speed
loteria [lo-ter-ya] f. lottery
lotnia [lot-ńa] f. hang glider
lotnictwo [lot-ńeets-tvo] n.
aviation; aeronautics; air force
lotnik [lot-ńeek] m. aviator
lotnisko [lot-ńees-ko] n. airport;
airfield; aerodrome
lotniskowiec [lot-ńees-ko-vyets]
m. aircraft carrier
lotny [lot-ni] adj. m. bright;
quick; swift; sharp; subtle
lotos [lo-tos] m. lotus
loża masońska [lo-zha ma-soń-
-ska] shriners' lodge
lód [loot] m. ice; pl. ice cream
lśniący [lśhńown-tsi] adj. m.
shining; bright; glossy; sleek
lśnić [lśhńeećh] v. glitter;
shine; gleam; glimmer; shimmer; glisten; sparkle
lub [loop] conj. or; or else
luba [loo-ba] f. sweetheart
lubić [loo-beećh] v. like; be
fond; enjoy; be partial
lubieżny [loo-byezh-ni] adj. m.
lustful; voluptuous; lewd
lubość [loo-bośhćh] f. delight

lubować się [loo-bo-vaćh śhan] v. take delight; find pleasure; relish; be fond (of)
lud [loot] m. people; nation
ludność [lood-nośhćh] f. population (of a given territory, city, country, etc.)
ludny [lood-ni] adj. m. populous; teeming; crowded
ludobójstwo [loo-do-booys-tvo] n. genocide; killing of a nation
ludowy [loo-do-vi] adj. m. populist; popular; country
ludożerca [loo-do-zher-tsa] m. cannibal; man-eater
ludzie [loo-dźhe] pl. people
ludzkość [loots-kośhćh] f. mankind; humaneness; humanity; human feelings; kindness
lufa [loo-fa] f. gunbarrel
luk [look] m. hatch; skylight
luka [loo-ka] f. gap; blank; break
lukier [loo-ker] m. sugar icing; frosting (on a cake)
lukratywny [loo-kra-tiv-ni] adj. m. lucrative; profitable
luksus [look-soos] m. luxury
lunatyk [loo-na-tik] m. 1. sleepwalker; 2. loony
lunąć [loo-nownćh] v. rain in torrents; slap; lash down in sheets; whack; fail; flunk
luneta [loo-ne-ta] field-glass; spy-glass; telescope; lunette
lupa [loo-pa] f. magnifying glass; jeweler's glass (loop); lens
lusterko [loos-ter-ko] n. hand glass; rear-view mirror (in a car); pocket looking-glass
lustro [loos-tro] n. mirror
lustrować [loo-stro-vaćh] v. inspect; review; check; audit
lut [loot] m. solder (brazing)
luteranin [loo-te-ra-ńeen] m. Lutheran (church member)
lutnia [loot-ńa] f. flute
lutować [loo-to-vaćh] v. solder
luty [loo-ti] m. February
luty [loo-ti] adj. m. bleak; grim; severe; m. February
luz [loos] m. clearance; play
luzak [loo-zak] m. loose; led horse; (replacement) horse

luzować [loo-zo-vaćh] v. replace; relieve; loosen; slacken; relay; ease off
luźny [loożh-ni] adj. m. loose
lwi [lvee] adj. m. lion's
lżej [lzhey] adv. lighter; easier; with less weight
lżenie [lzhe-ńe] n. abuse; insults; vituperation
lżyć [lzhićh] v. abuse; insult

Ł

łabędź [wa-bandźh] m. swan
łach [wakh] m. rang; clout
łacha [wa-kha] f. sandbank
łachman [wakh-man] m. rag
łachudra [wa-khood-ra] m. scoundrel; ragamuffin
łaciarz [wa-ćhash] m. patcher
łaciaty [wa-ćha-ti] adj. m. in patches; pinto (horse)
łacina [wa-ćhee-na] f. Latin
łaciński [wa-ćheeń-skee] adj. m. Latin; of Latin
ład [wad] m. order; orderliness
ładnie [wad-ńe] adv. nicely
ładnieć [wad-ńećh] v. grow pretty; grow (look) prettier
ładny [wad-ńi] adj. m. nice
ładować [wa-do-vaćh] v. load; charge (a battery); cram; fill
ładownica [wa-dov-ńee-tsa] f. cartridge pouch; charger
ładunek [wa-doo-nek] m. load; cargo; (electr.) charge; shipload; burden; freight; bulk
łagodność [wa-god-nośhćh] f. gentleness; kindliness; suavity
łagodny [wa-god-ni] adj. m. gentle; mild; soft; meek; easy
łagodzący [wa-go-dzown-tsi] adj. m. alleviating; extenuating
łagodzić [wa-go-dźheećh] v. soothe; relieve; alleviate; attenuate; mitigate; smooth
łajać [wa-yaćh] v. scold; chide
łajdactwo [way-dats-tvo] n.

mean trick; scoundrels; rabble
łajdak [way-dak] m. scoundrel;
rascal; villain; rogue; wretch
łajno [way-no] n. dung; shit
łaknąć [wak-<u>nown</u>ćh] v. hunger for; thirst for; crave for
łakocie [wa-ko-ćhe] pl. delicacies; sweets; tidbits; candy
łakomić się [wa-ko-meećh <u>śhan</u>] v. covet; lust; be tempted (by); be greedy (of)
łakomy [wa-ko-mi] adj. m. greedy; covetous; avid
łakomstwo [wa-koms-tvo] n. greed; gluttony; greediness
łamać [wa-maćh] v. break; crush; quarry; shatter; crack; snap; smash; fracture (a bone)
łamigłówka [wa-mee-gwoov-ka] f. riddle; puzzle; jigsaw puzzle
łamistrajk [wa-mee-strayk] m. scab; strikebreaker
łamliwy [wam-lee-vi] adj. m. fragile; frail; brittle; breakable
łan [wan] m. stand of wheat
łania [wa-ńa] f. hind; doe
łańcuch [wań-tsookh] m. chain; range; series; train; succession
łańcuchowa reakcja [wań-tsoo-kho-va re-ak-tsya] chain reaction (of nuclear fission)
łapa [wa-pa] f. paw; claw; arm
łapać [wa-paćh] v. catch; get hold (of); snatch; grasp; seize
łapanka [wa-pan-ka] f. roundup
łapcie [wap-ćhe] pl. bast sandals; moccasins
łapczywość [wap-chi-vośhćh] f. greed; greediness; avidity
łapczywy [wap-chi-vi] adj. m. greedy; money-grubbing; avid
łapka [wap-ka] f. (mouse) trap
łapówka [wa-poov-ka] f. bribe
łapserdak [wap-ser-dak] m. rogue; ragamuffin; scoundrel
łasica [wa-śhee-tsa] f. weasel
łasić się [wa-śheećh śhan] v. fawn; fawn on sb.; toady
łaska [was-ka] f. grace; clemency; favor; generosity; mercy; condescension; pity
łaskawy [was-ka-vi] adj. m. gracious; kind; generous

łaskotać [wa-sko-taćh] v. tickle; titillate; delight
łaskotliwy [wa-sko-tlee-vi] adj. m. ticklish; titillating
łasy [wa-si] adj. m. greedy
łaszczyć się [wash-chićh śhan] v. covet; lust
łata [wa-ta] f. patch
łatać [wa-taćh] v. patch up
łatanina [wa-ta-ńee-na] f. patch work; mending; bungled work
łatwo [wat-vo] adv. easily
łatwopalny [wa-tvo-pal-ni] adj. m. (easily) inflammable
łatwość [wat-vośhćh] n. easy; facility; aptitude; fluency
łatwowierny [wa-tvo-**vyer**-ni] adj. m. credulous; gullible
łatwy [wat-vi] adj. m. easy; simple; effortless; light
ława [wa-va] f. bench; footing
ławica [wa-vee-tsa] f. (fish) shoal; sandbank; shelf; layer
ławka [wav-ka] f. pew; bench
ławnik [wav-ńeek] m. juror; alderman; assessor
łazić [wa-źheećh] v. crawl; loiter; slouch about; creep
łazienka [wa-źhen-ka] f. bathroom; toilet; bath
łazik [wa-źheek] m. tramp; jeep
łaźnia [waźh-ńa] f. bath
łażący [wa-zhown-tsi] adj. m. dragging; crawling; scansorial
łączący [<u>wown</u>-**chown**-tsi] adj. m. uniting; joining; connecting
łącznica [<u>wown</u>-chńee-tsa] f. junction; (phone) switchboard
łącznie [**wownch**-ńe] adv. together; including; inclusive of; along with; jointly; conjointly
łącznik [**wownch**-ńeek] m. hyphen; liaison man; link; tie; bond; connecting rod; fastener
łączność [**wownch**-nośhćh] f. contact; communication; unity; signal service; connection; communion; liaison
łączny [**wownch**-ni] adj. m. joint; combined; total; global
łączyć [<u>wown</u>-chićh] v. join; unite; merge; link; bind; weld
łąka [<u>wown</u>-ka] f. meadow

łeb [wep] m. head; pate; top
lechtać [wekh-tać] v. tickle; flatter; titillate; lure
łąk [wank] m. saddlebow; syncline; arch; bow; pommel
łgać [wgać] v. lie; brag; boast
łgarstwo [wgar-stvo] n. lie
łgarz [wgash] liar; braggart
łkać [wkać] v. sob; weep
łobuz [wo-boos] m. rogue; rascal; scamp; scoundrel
łodyga [wo-di-ga] f. stem
łoić [wo-eeć] v. tallow; beat up; wallop; curry
łokieć [wo-kyeć] m. elbow
łom [wom] m. crowbar; scrap; junk; rubble; block chocolate
łomot [wo-mot] m. crash; crack
łono [wo-no] n. lap; bosom; womb; pubes
łopata [wo-pa-ta] f. spade
łopot [wo-pot] m. (sail) flutter
łoskot [wos-kot] m. clatter; bang; din; rumble; racket; boom; bluster (of a storm)
łosoś [wo-sośh] m. salmon
łoś [wośh] m. elk; moose
łotewski [wo-tev-skee] adj. m. Latvian; Latvian language
łotr [wotr] m. scoundrel; knave; rascal; rogue; thief
łowczy [wov-chi] adj. m. hunting; huntsman's; hunter's
łowić [wo-veeć] v. trap; fish; catch (sounds); hunt; chase
łowiectwo [wo-vyets-tvo] n. hunting; game shooting
łowy [wo-vi] pl. hunt; chase
łozina [wo-żhee-na] f. wicker; sallow; osier; osier-bed
łoże [wo-zhe] n. bed; cradle
łożyć [wo-zhić] v. spend
łożyska [wo-zhis-ko] n. (river) bed; (ball) bearing
łódka [wood-ka] f. small boat
łódź [woodźh] f. boat; craft
łój [wooy] m. tallow; suet
łów [woov] m. hunt; chase
łóżeczko [woo-zhech-ko] n. (child's) bed; small bed
łóżko [woozh-ko] n. bed; bunk
łubin [woo-been] m. lupin
łucznik [wooch-ńeek] m. archer

łuczywo [woo-chi-vo] n. resinous kindling; resinous chips
łudzący [woo-dzown-tsi] adj. m. delusive; deceptive; illusive
łudzić [woo-dźheećh] v. delude; deceive; give false hope; dangle hopes before someone
ług [woog] m. lye
ługować [woo-go-vać] v. leach; lixiviate
łuk [wook] m. bow; arch; bent; curve; vault; flying buttress
łuna [woo-na] f. glow (of light)
łup [woop] m. booty; spoils; plunder; loot; prey; quarry
łupać [woo-pać] v. cleave; split; ache; give shooting pain
łupek [woo-pek] m. slate; shale
łupić [woo-peećh] v. plunder
łupież [woo-pyesh] m. dandruff
łupieżca [woo-pyezh-tsa] m. plunderer; looter; pillager
łupina [woo-pee-na] f. husk; shell; peel; skin; hull; rind
łuska [woos-ka] f. scale; husk; shell; pod; flake; rind
łuskać [woos-kać] v. scale; husk; peel; pod; hull (rice)
łuszczyć [woosh-chićh] v. peel; pare; flake off; shell off
łuza [woo-za] f. billiard pocket
łydka [wit-ka] f. calf (leg-shank)
łyk [wik] m. gulp; sip; draft
łykać [wi-kać] v. swallow; gulp; sip; bolt; gorge; drink
łyko [wi-ko] n. bast; phloem
łykowaty [wi-ko-va-ti] adj. m. wiry; tough; fibrous
łypać [wi-pać] v. blink; wink
łysek [wi-sek] m. (bold head) bold; bold-faced animal
łysieć [wi-śhećh] v. become bold; grow bold; lose hair
łysina [wi-śhee-na] f. pate
łyskać [wis-kać] v. flash
łysy [wi-si] adj. m. bold
łyżeczka [wi-zhech-ka] f. teaspoon; dessert spoon; curette; small spoonful
łyżka [wizh-ka] f. spoon; spoonful; tablespoonful
łyżwa [wizh-va] f. skate
łyżwiarz [wizh-vyash] m. skater

łyżwowy [wizh-vo-vi] adj. of
skates; of a sledge runner
łza [wza] f. tear
łzawy [wza-vi] adj. m. tearful
łzowy kanał [wzo-vi ka-naw] tear
canal; tear duct

M

maca [ma-tsa] f. matzos
macać [ma-tsaćh] v. feel; try;
grope; finger; probe; cuddle
machać [ma-khaćh] v. wave;
whisk; swing; swish; lash;
wag; run; flap; brandish
macher [ma-kher] m. trickster
machina [ma-khee-na] f. (large)
machine; bureaucratic machine
machinacja [ma-khee-na-tsya] f.
machination; dodge; intrigue
machlojka [ma-khloy-ka] f.
swindle; defraudation
macica [ma-ćhee-tsa] f. uterus;
womb; screw nut; tap root
macierz [ma-ćhesh] f. mother
country; matrix; mother
macierzanka [ma-ćhe-zhan-ka] f.
thyme; wild thyme; mint
macierzyński [ma-ćhe-zhiń-
-skee] adj. m. maternal; mather's; motherly; like a mother
macierzyństwo [ma-ćhe-zhiń-
-stvo] n. maternity; motherhood; parenthood
macierzysty [ma-ćhe-zhi-sti] adj.
m. maternal; (parental)
maciora [ma-ćho-ra] f. sow
macka [mats-ka] f. tentacle;
feeler; antenna; horn; palp
macocha [ma-tso-kha] f.
stepmother; not as good as
(treating worse than) mother
maczać [ma-chaćh] v. dip in a
liquid; dip; soak
maczuga [ma-choo-ga] f. bat;
club; bludgeon; cudgel
magazyn [ma-ga-zin] m. store;
warehouse; repository; store

magazynier [ma-ga-zi-ńer] m.
warehouseman; storekeeper
magia [ma-gya] f. sorcery
magiczny [ma-geech-ni] adj. m.
magic; conjuring tricks
magister [ma-gees-ter] m. master
(diploma); chemist; apothecary
magisterium [ma-gees-ter-yum]
n. (university) master's degree
magistrat [ma-gees-trat] m. city
hall; municipal authorities
maglować [ma-glo-vaćh] v.
mangle; calender; bother;
crush; tire with; harp on
magnat [mag-nat] m. magnate
magnes [mag-nes] m. magnet
magnetofon [mag-ne-to-fon] m.
tape-recorder
magnetyczny [mag-ne-tich-ni]
adj. m. magnetic
magnetyzm [mag-ne-tizm] m.
magnetism; personal charm
magnez [mag-nes] m. mag-
nesium (metallic element)
magnezja [mag-nez-ya] f.
magnesia; magnesium
magnolia [mag-no-lya] f.
magnolia (bot. Magnolia)
mahometanin [ma-kho-me-ta-
-ńeen] m. Mohammedan;
Moslem; follower of Islam
mahoń [ma-khoń] m. mahogany
maić [ma-eećh] v. decorate
with green leaves (verdure)
maj [may] m. May; verdure
majaczyć [ma-ya-chićh] v.
rave; loom; be delirious
majątek [ma-yown-tek] m.
fortune; estate; property;
wealth; one's possessions
majdan [may-dan] m. parade
ground; open space; clearing;
personal junk; traps; chattels
majeranek [ma-ye-ra-nek] m.
marjoram; fragrant plant of
mint family used for cooking
majestat [ma-ye-stat] m.
majesty; kingship; stateliness
majętność [ma-yant-nośhćh]
f. wealth; fortune; property
majętny [ma-yant-ni] adj. m. well
to do; wealthy; affluent; rich
majonez [ma-yo-nes] m.

yonnaise; egg yoke dressing
major [ma-yor] m. major
majówka [ma-joov-ka] f.
Mayouting; picnic; junket
majster [may-ster] m. qualified
craftsman; boss; master (carpenter; baker, etc.); foreman
majstersztyk [may-ster-shtik] m.
masterpiece; greatest work
majstrować [may-stro-vaćh] v.
tinker; make (an object)
majtek [may-tek] m. deck hand
majtki [may-tkee] pl. panties
mak [mak] m. poppy seed
makaron [ma-ka-ron] m. macaroni; pasta in tubular form
makata [ma-ka-ta] f. tapestry
makler [mak-ler] m. broker
makolągwa [ma-ko-lowng-va] f.
linnet; young lass; lassie
makrela [ma-kre-la] f. mackerel
maksyma [mak-si-ma] f. axiom;
maxim; adage; rule of conduct
maksymalny [mak-si-mal-ni] adj.
m. maximum; top-:peak-;mostmakulatura [ma-koo-la-too-ra] f.
waste-paper; spoilage; rubbish
makuch [ma-kookh] m. oilcake
malaria [ma-lar-ya] f. malaria
malarstwo [ma-lar-stvo] n.
painting (art); house painting
malarz [ma-lash] m. painter
malec [ma-lets] m. youngster
maleć [ma-lećh] v. shrink;
dwindle; grow smaller; lessen
maleńki [ma-leń-kee] adj. m.
very small; tiny; insignificant
maleństwo [ma-leń-stvo] n. tiny
thing; little one; little mite
malina [ma-lee-na] f. raspberry
malować [ma-lo-vaćh] v. paint;
stain; color; make up; depict
malowidło [ma-lo-vid-wo] n.
painting; picture (painted)
malowniczy [ma-lov-ńee-chi]
adj. m. picturesque; vivid
maltretować [mal-tre-to-vaćh]
v. abuse; mistreat; ill treat
malwersacja [mal-ver-sats-ya] f.
embezzlement; peculation
mało [ma-wo] adv. little; few;
seldom; lack; not enough
małoduszny [ma-wo-doosh-ni]

adj. m. small-minded; narrowminded; cheap; fainthearted
małoletni [ma-wo-let-ńee]
adj. m. minor; under age;
juvenile; immature; young
małomówny [ma-wo-moov-ni]
adj. m. reticent; laconic;
taciturn; uncommunicative
małostkowy [ma-wo-stko-vi] adj.
m. fussy; mean; small-minded
małpa [maw-pa] f. ape; monkey
małpować [maw-po-vaćh] v.
ape; imitate poorly; trifle
mały [ma-wi] adj. m. little; small
size; low; modest; slight
małżeński [maw-zheń-skee]
adj. m. matrimonial; conjugal
małżeństwo [maw-zheń-stvo]
n. married couple; wedlock
małżonek [maw-zho-nek] m.
husband; spouse; consort;
mate; bedfellow; partner
małżonka [maw-zhon-ka] f. wife
mama [ma-ma] f. mamma; mather; mum; mummy; mama
mamałyga [ma-ma-wi-ga] f.
maize; gruel; hominy
mamić [ma-meećh] v. deceive;
delude; beguile; lure; tempt
mamidło [ma-mee-dwo] n.
illusion; delusion; lure; seduction; enticement; temptation
mamona [ma-mo-na] f. mammon
mamlać [mam-laćh] v. mumble
mamrotać [mam-ro-taćh] v.
mutter; mumble; gibber
mamut [ma-moot] m. mammoth
manatki [ma-nat-kee] pl. personal
belongings; traps; chattels
mandaryn [man-da-rin] m.
mandarin; Chinese dignitary
mandat [man-dat] m. mandate;
traffic ticket; fine
mandolina [man-do-lee-na] f.
mandolin with 8 to 10 strings
manekin [ma-ne-keen] m. mannequin; model of human body
manewr [ma-nevr] m. maneuver
manewrować [ma-ne-vro-vaćh]
v. manoeuver; steer; handle;
switch; shunt; plot; intrigue
maneż [ma-nesh] m. riding
school; horse-driven thrasher

mangan [man-gan] m.
manganese (used in alloys)
mania [ma-ńya] f. mania; fad
maniak [ma-ńyak] m. maniac;
crank; widely insane person
manicure [ma-ńee-keer] m.
manicure; trimming, polishing
doing, etc. one's fingernails
manić [ma-ńeećh] v. deceive;
tempt; delude; beguile; lure
maniera [ma-ńe-ra] f. manner
manierka [ma-ńer-ka] f. canteen
manifest [ma-ńee-fest] m.
manifesto; a public declaration
manifestacja [ma-ńee-fes-ta-
-tsya] f. manifestation; demonstration; ostentatious display
manifestować [ma-ńee-fes-to-
-vaćh] v. demonstrate; stage
a manifestation; display
manipulacja [ma-ńee-poo-lats-
-ya] f. manipulation; handling
manipulować [ma-ńee-poo-lo-
-vaćh] v. manipulate; handle;
tinker; manage artfully
mankiet [man-ket] m. cuff; turn
-up; wristband; ruffle
mankament [man-ka-ment] m.
defect; shortcoming; fault
manko [man-ko] n. (acc.)
shortage; allowance to cashier
for errors; cash shortage
manna [man-na] f. cream of
wheat; a godsend manna
manometr [ma-no-metr] m.
pressure gauge; steam gauge
manowce [ma-nov-tse] pl. mis-
guided direction; road less
area; wrong way
manufaktura [ma-noo-fak-too-ra]
f. fabric; manufacture; shop
manuskrypt [ma-noo-skript] m.
manuscript; (hand or typewritten) document, book, etc.
mańkuctwo [mań-koots-tvo] n.
left-handedness
mapa [ma-pa] f. map; chart
mara [ma-ra] f. ghost; apparition;
nightmare; dream; vision
marazm [ma-razm] m. torpor;
sluggishness; stagnation
marchew [mar-khev] f. carrot
marcepan [mar-tse-pan] m.

marzipan; marchpane
margaryna [mar-ga-ri-na] f.
margarine; marge (slang)
margines [mar-gee-nes] m.
margin; edge; border; minor
incidental, secondary) thing
mariaż [mar-yash] m. marriage
marionetka [ma-ryo-net-ka] f.
puppet; dummy; figurehead
marka [mar-ka] f. mark; brand;
stamp; trade mark; reputation
markotno [mar-kot-no] adv. sad;
in low spirits; in bad humor;
gloomily; sullenly; moodily
markotny [mar-kot-ni] adj. m.
peevish; moody; sullen; sad
marksistowski [mar-kśhee-
-stovs-kee] adj. m. Marxist
(socialist or communis)
marksizm [mar-kśheezm] m.
Marxism; Marxist believes
marmolada [mar-mo-la-da] f.
marmalade; jam; shambles
marmur [mar-moor] m. marble
marnieć [mar-ńećh] v. deteriorate; waste; decline; perish;
languish; fade; droop; pine
marność [mar-nośhćh] f.
futility; flimsiness; vanity
marnotrawny [mar-no-trav-ni]
adj. m. wasteful; prodigal
marnować [mar-no-vaćh] v. run
to waste; squander; spoil
marny [mar-ni] adj. m. poor;
meager; sorry; of no value
marsz [marsh] m. march; walk
marsz! [marsh] excl.: (command)
forward march! split! get out!
off you go! out! double!
marszałek [mar-sha-wek] m.
marshal; Polish Seym speaker
marszczyć [mar-shchićh] v.
wrinkle; frown; crease; ripple
marszruta [mar-shroo-ta] f. route;
itinerary; a record of a journey
martwica [mar-tvee-tsa] f.
necrosis; sinter; travertine
martwić [mar-tveećh] v. distress; grieve; vex; worry; sadden; afflict; (cause) trouble
martwy [mar-tvi] adj. m. dead
martyr [mar-tir] m. martyr
maruder [ma-roo-der] m.

marauder; straggler; loiterer
marudzić [ma-roo-dźheećh] v.
loiter; grumble; lag behind
mary [ma-ri] pl. mar; bier
marynarka [ma-ri-nar-ka] f.
jacket; sports coat; navy
marynarz [ma-ri-nash] m.
mariner; sailor; seaman
marynata [ma-ry-na-ta] f. pickle
marynować [ma-ri-no-vaćh] v.
pickle; marinade; side-track
marzec [ma-zhets] m. March
marzenie [ma-zhe-ńe] n. dream;
reverie; day dream; pensiveness; daydreaming
marznąć [marz-nownćh] v. be
frozen; freeze; freeze to death
marzyciel [ma-zhi-ćhel] m.
dreamer; fantast; visionary
marzyć [ma-zhićh] v. dream
masa [ma-sa] f. bulk; mass
masa perłowa [ma-sa per-wo-va]
f. mother of pearl
masakra [ma-sak-ra] f. massacre;
carnage; wholesale butchery
masakrować [ma-sa-kro-vaćh]
v. massacre; slaughter; butcher; mangle (a text); hack
masarnia [ma-sar-ńa] f. pork
-meat (pork butcher's) shop
masarz [ma-sash] m.
pork-butcher; pork meat
worker; pork sausage maker
masaż [ma-sash] m. massage
masażysta [ma-sa-zhis-ta] m.
masseur; rubber
maselniczka [ma-sel-ńeech-ka] f.
butter-dish; small churn
maska [mas-ka] f. mask; hood
maskować [mas-ko-vaćh] v.
disguise; mask; hide; screen
masło [mas-wo] n. butter
masoński [ma-soń-skee] adj. m.
masonic; freemason's
masować [ma-so-vaćh] v. give
a massage to; massage; rub
masowo [ma-so-vo] adv. wholesale; in a mass; in masses; in
great numbers (quantities)
masywność [ma-siv-nośhćh]
f. massiveness; solidity
masywny [ma-siv-ni] adj. m.
massive; solid; bulky; massy

maszerować [ma-she-ro-vaćh]
v. march; march on; keep
marching; advance steadily
maszkara [mash-ka-ra] f.
monster; scarecrow; eyesore
maszt [masht] m. mast; flagstaff
maszyna [ma-shi-na] f. machine
maszynka do golenia [ma-shin-
-ka do go-le-ńa] f. safety
razor; shaver
maszyneria [ma-shi-ner-ya] f.
machinery; mechanism
maszynista [ma-shi-ńees-ta] m.
railroad engineer; machinist
maszynistka [ma-shi-ńeest-ka] f.
typewriter typist; typist
maszynopis [ma-shi-no-pees] m.
typescript; typewritten copy
maść [maśhćh] f. ointment;
horse color; unguent; salve
maślanka [ma-śhlan-ka] f.
buttermilk; sour liquid; (a
product of churning butter)
mat [mat] m. flat color;
checkmate (one's opponent)
mata [ma-ta] f. mat; matting
matactwo [ma-tats-tvo] n. legal
trickery; fraudulence; deceit
matczyny [mat-chi-ni] adj. m.
maternal (love etc.); mother's
matematyczny [ma-te-ma-tich-ni]
adj. m. mathematical
matematyk [ma-te-ma-tik] m.
mathematician (also student)
matematyka [ma-te-ma-ti-ka] f.
mathematics; science of numbers, quantities, forms, etc.
materac [ma-te-rats] m. mattress
materia [ma-ter-ya] f. matter;
stuff; subject; point; puss;
cloth; any specified substance
materialista [ma-te-rya-lees-ta]
m. materialist; money grabber
materialistyczny [ma-te-rya-lee-
-stich-ni] adj. m. materialistic
(opposite to spiritual)
materiał [ma-te-ryaw] m.
material; substance; stuff;
cloth; fabric; assignment
matka [mat-ka] f. mother
matnia [mat-ńa] f. snare; trap
matowy [ma-to-vi] adj. m. flat
color; dull; lackluster

matrona [mat-ro-na] f. matron
matryca [mat-ri-tsa] f. matrix;
die; type; mold; stencil; swage
matrykuła [mat-ri-koo-wa] f.
register of university students
matrymonialny [ma-tri-mo-ńyal-
-ni] adj. m. matrimonial (a-
gency, office); marital
matura [ma-too-ra] f. final
high school examination
mauretański [maw-re-tań-skee]
adj. m. Moorish; of Moors
mazać [ma-zaćh] v. smear; defile; scribble; blot; stain; daub
mazgaj [maz-gay] m. crybaby
Mazur [ma-zoor] m. mazurka
rhythm; Mazurian
maź [maźh] f. grease; tallow
mącić [mown-ćheećh] v. blur;
ruffle; muddy; cloud; confuse
mączka [mownch-ka] f. fine
flour; powder; dust; starch
mądrość [mownd-rośhćh] f.
wisdom; intelligence; sagacity
mądry [mownd-ri] adj. m. sage
mąka [mown-ka] f. flour; meal
mąż [mownsh] m. husband; man
mąż stanu [mownsh sta-noo]
statesman; outstanding politician; outstanding diplomat
mdleć [mdlećh] v. faint; lose
consciousness; fail; weaken;
go off into a faint; droop; flag
mdlić [mdleećh] v. nauseate
mdłość [mdwośhćh] f. nau-
sea; fuzziness; indistinctness
mdło [mdwo] adv. dull;
nauseating; sickening; faintly
meble [meb-le] pl. furniture
macenas [me-tse-nas] m. lawyer
mech [mekh] m. moss; down
mechaniczny [me-kha-ńeech-ni]
adj. m. mechanical; automatic
mechanik [me-kha-ńeek] m.
mechanic; Jack of all trades
mechanika [me-kha-ńee-ka] f.
mechanics; (practical, political,
strategic etc.) mechanics
mechanizm [me-kha-ńeezm] m.
mechanism; gear; device
mecz [mech] m. sport match
meczet [me-chet] m. mosque
medal [me-dal] m. medal

mediacja [me-dya-tsya] f.
mediation; settling of differences between persons (nations)
meduza [me-doo-za] f. jellyfish
medycyna [me-di-tsi-na] f.
medicine; art of healing
medyczny [me-dich-ni] adj. m.
medical; medicinal
medyk [me-dik] m. medical
student; medic (physician)
medykament [me-di-ka-ment] m.
drug; medicine (hist. expr.)
medytacja [me-di-tats-ya] f.
meditation; thinking deeply
megafon [me-ga-fon] m.
loudspeaker; megaphone
megaloman [me-ga-lo-man] m.
megalomaniac; self appointed
boss; self-important person
melancholia [me-lan-kho-lya] f.
melancholy; the blues; dejection; despondency; low spirits
melasa [me-la-sa] f. molasses
meldować [mel-do-vaćh] v.
report; register; announce; inform; notify; give an account
meldunek [mel-doo-nek] m.
report; announcement; notification; registration
melioracja [me-lyo-rats-ya] f.
reclamation of land; drainage
melodia [me-lod-ya] f. melody
meloman [me-lo-man] m. music
lover; music enthusiast
melon [me-lon] m. melon
melonik [me-lo-ńeek] m. bowler
hat; derby; bowler; billycock
memoriał [me-mo-ryaw] m. memorial; minutes' journal;
written communication
menażeria [me-na-zher-ya] f.
menagerie; animal collection
menażka [me-nazh-ka] f. mess
kit; canteen; mess-tin; dixie
mennica [men-ńee-tsa] f. mint
menstruacja [men-stroo-ats-ya] f.
menstruation; menses; period
mentalność [men-tal-nośhćh]
f. mentality; way of thinking
menu [me-noo] m. menu; bill of
fare; list of foods served
mer [mer] m. mayor
merdać [mer-daćh] v. wag tail

merytoryczny [me-ri-to-**rich**-ni]
adj. m. of substance; essential
meszek [**me**-shek] m. down; nap
meta [**me**-ta] f. goal; hang-out
metafizyka [me-ta-**fee**-zi-ka] f.
metaphysics (speculative phil.)
metal [**me**-tal] m. metal
metalowy [me-ta-lo-vi] adj. m.
metallic (luster, sound etc.)
metalurgia [me-ta-**loor**-gya] f.
metallurgy; science of metals
metamorfoza [me-ta-mor-fo-za] f.
metamorphosis; a change
inform etc.; metamorphism
meteor [me-**te**-or] m. meteor
meteorologia [me-te-o-ro-lo-gya]
f. meteorology (weather etc.)
metoda [me-to-da] f. method;
system of doing or handling
metodyczny [me-to-**dich**-ni] adj.
m. methodical; systematic
metr [metr] m. meter; 39.97in.
metro [**met**-ro] n. subway
metropolia [me-tro-**pol**-ya] f.
metropolis; main large city
metryczny [met-**rich**-ni] adj. m.
metric; of metrical system
metryka [**met**-ri-ka] f. birth
-certificate; the public register
metys [**me**-tys] m. metis
mewa [**me**-va] f. sea-gull
mezalians [me-**za**-lyans] m.
misalliance; improper alliance
mezanin [me-**za**-ńeen] m. mez-
zanine (between two stories)
mączarnia [m<u>an</u>-**char**-ńa] f.
torture; torment; anguish; ago-
ny; tribulation; anxiety
mączennik [m<u>an</u>-**chen**-ńeek] m.
martyr; sufferer for faith etc.
mączyć [m<u>an</u>-chi**ch**] v. bother;
torment; oppress; tire; ex-
haust; trouble; torture; agonize
mądrek [m<u>an</u>-drek] m. smart
aleck; know-it-all; wiseacre
mądrzec [m<u>an</u>d-zhets] m. sage
mąka [m<u>an</u>-ka] f. fatigue; torment; pain; distress; nuisance;
suffering; anguish; vexation
mąski [m<u>an</u>-skee] adj. m. masculine; manly; man's; virile;
male; gentleman's; manlike
mąskość [m<u>an</u>-ko**ść**] f.

manhood; virility; manliness
mąstwo [m<u>an</u>-tvo] n. bravery;
courage; prowess; fortitude
mątny [m<u>an</u>t-ni] adj. m. turbid;
dull; dim; blurred; vague; fishy
mąty [m<u>an</u>-ti] pl. dregs; scum of
society; underworld; raffle
mążatka [m<u>an</u>-zhat-ka] f. married woman; femme covert
mążczyzna [m<u>an</u>zh-chiz-na] m.
man (on toilets: Gentleman)
mążnieć [m<u>an</u>zh-ńe**ch**] v.
grow manly; muster courage;
take heart; grow into a man
mążny [m<u>an</u>zh-ni] adj. m. brave
mglisty [mglees-ti] adj. m. foggy;
misty; dim; nebulous; vague
mgła [mgwa] f. fog; mist; cloud
mgławica [mgwa-vee-tsa] f.
nebula; cloud; hazy idea; haze
mgnienie [mgńe-ńe] n. blink;
twinkle; wink; flash; jiffy; trice
miał [myaw] m. dust; powder
miałki [myaw-kee] adj. m. fine
(sugar; sand etc.); powdered
miano [mya-no] n. name; designation; appellation (label)
mianować [mya-no-va**ch**] v.
appoint; promote; give a title
mianowicie [mya-no-**vee**-**ch**e]
adv. namely; to wit; that is ...
mianownik [mya-nov-ńeek] m.
denominator; nominative
miara [mya-ra] f. measure;
gauge; yard-stick; foot-rule;
amount; measuring rod; limit
miarkować [myar-ko-va**ch**] v.
guess; note; mitigate oneself
miarodajny [mya-ro-**day**-ni] adj.
m. authoritative; competent
miarowy [mya-ro-vi] adj. m.
rhythmic; steady; regular
miasteczko [mya-**stech**-ko] n.
borough; small country town
miasto [myas-to] n. town
miałczeć [myaw-che**ch**] v. mew
miazga [myaz-ga] f. pulp; squash
miażdżyć [myazh-dzhi**ch**] v.
crush; squash; smash; grind;
lacerate; reduce to a pulp
miąć [my<u>own</u>**ch**] v. crumple;
wrinkle; crease; rumple; crush
miąższ [my<u>own</u>sh] m. pulp;

flesh of fruit; pomace; squash
miech [myekh] m. bellows
miecz [myech] m. sword
mieć [myećh] v. have; hold;
run; own; keep; have to do
miednica [myed-ńee-tsa] f. hand
washtub; pelvis; wash basin
miedza [mye-dza] f. farm
boundary strip; bounds; balk
miedź [myedźh] f. copper
miedziak [mye-dźhak] m. copper
penny; copper coin
miedziany [mye-dźha-ni] adj. m.
of copper; coppery; of brass
miedzioryt [mye-dźho-rit] m.
copperplate engraving
miejsce [myeys-tse] n. place;
location; spot; room; space;
seat; employment; berth; point; scene; occupation; job
miejscowość [myey-stso-
-vośhćh] f. locality; place;
town; village; spot
miejscowy [myey-stso-vi] adj. m.
local; native; indigenous
miejski [myey-skee] adj. m. of
town; of city; urban
mielizna [mye-leez-na] f. shoal;
shallow water; sandbank
mielenie [mye-le-ńe] n. grinding;
milling; mincing; jabber;
prattling incoherently
mielony [mye-lo-ni] adj. m.
ground; milled; minced; pul-
verized; chewed up
mieniać [mye-ńaćh] v. change;
swap; exchange; convert
mienić [mye-ńeećh] v. call;
glitter; shimmer; change color; show a play of colors
mienić się [mye-ńeećh śhan]
v. change one's color; glitter
mienie [mye-ńe] n. property;
belongings; estate; effects
miernictwo [myer-ńeets-tvo] m.
surveying; land measuring
mierniczy [myer-ńee-chi] m.
surveyor; adj. m. geodetic
mierność [myer-nośhćh] f.
mediocrity; average range
miernota [myer-no-ta] average
intelligence; mediocrity
mierny [myer-ni] adj. m.

mediocre; mean; of moderate
means; moderate; indifferent
mierzeja [mye-zhe-ya] f. sand-bar
mierzić [myer-źheećh] v. be
disgusting; sicken; make (render) unbearable; disgust
mierznąć [myerz-nownćh] v.
become disgusting; pall on sb.
mierzwa [myezh-va] f. litter
mierzwić [myezh-veećh] v. manure a field; tousle; ruffle; mat
mierzyć [mye-zhićh] v. measure; judge; try on; aim; tend
towards; estimate; evaluate
miesiąc [mye-śhownts] m.
month; moon; lunar month
miesić [mye-śheećh] v.
massage; knead (dough, clay)
miesięcznie [mye-śhanch-ńe]
adv. monthly; every month
miesięcznik [mye-śhanch-ńeek]
m. monthly paper; monthly
mieszać [mye-shaćh] v. mix;
mingle; shuffle; confuse
mieszać się [mye-shaćh śhan]
v. meddle; become confused
mieszanina [mye-sha-ńee-na] f.
mixture; compound; medley
mieszanka [mye-shan-ka] f.
blend; mix; mixture; miscellany; composition; compound
mieszczanin [myesh-cha-ńeen]
m.burgher; townsman; citizen
mieszczaństwo [myesh-chań-
-stvo] n. middle class; towns
people; narrow-mindedness
mieszek [mye-shek] m. small
bellows; bag; money-bag
mieszkać [myesh-kaćh] v.
dwell; live; stay; have a flat;
lodge; reside; inhabit; abide
mieszkalny [myesh-kal-ni] adj. m.
inhabitable; habitable
mieszkanie [myesh-ka-ńe] n.
apartment; rooms; lodgings
mieszkaniec [myesh-ka-ńets] m.
inhabitant; lodger; resident
mieść [myeśhćh] v. sweep;
fling; hurl; blow (leaves etc.)
mieścić [myeśh-ćheećh] v.
contain; fit; hold; store; place
mieścina [myeśh-ćhee-na] f.
small town; out-of-the-way

miewać [mye-vaćh] v. have
occasionally; feel sometimes
miączak [myan-chak] m. mollusk
miądlić [myand-leećh] v.
bruise; hackle; crush; swingle;
scutch; hold forth; twaddle
miądzy [myan-dzi] prep.
between; among; in the midst
międzymorze [myan-dzi-mo-zhe]
n. isthmus; narrow strip of
land (with water on each side)
międzynarodowy [myan-dzi-na-
-ro-do-vi] adj. m. international
międzyplanetarny [myan-dzi-pla-
-ne-tar-ni] adj. m. inter-
planetary; of cosmic space
miąkczyć [myank-chićh] v.
soften; move; touch; palatalize
miąkisz [myank-keesh] m. pulp
miąkki [myank-kee] adj. m. soft;
flabby; limp; supple
miąkko [myank-ko] adv. softly;
gently; tenderly; limply; supply
miąkkość [myank-kośhćh] f.
softness; irresolution; pliancy
miąknąć [myank-nownćh] v.
soften up; relax; relent
miąsień [myan-śheń] m.
muscle; muscular strength
miąsisty [myan-śhees-ti] adj. m.
fleshy; meaty; pulpous
miąsiwo [myan-śhee-vo] n.
meat dish; dish of meat
miąso [myan-so] n. flesh; meat
miąsożerny [myan-so-zher-ni]
adj. m. carnivorous; meat-eat-
ing; insect-eating (as plants)
miąta [myan-ta] f. mint; trifle
miątosić [myan-to-śheećh] v.
crumble; knead; crush up
mig [meek] m. split second;
twinkle; sign language
migać [mee-gaćh] v. twinkle
migawka [mee-gav-ka] f. camera
shutter; news in brief
migdał [meeg-daw] m. almond;
tonsil; good and tasty thing
migi [mee-gee] pl. sign language;
speaking by (hand made) signs
migotać [mee-go-taćh] v. waver; twinkle; flicker; whisk;
flit; glimmer; shimmer; glitter
migracja [mee-grats-ya] f.

migration; migrating (of groups
of people, birds, etc.)
migrena [mee-gre-na] f. migraine;
sick headache; hemicrania
mijać [mee-yaćh] v. go past;
pass by; pass away; go by
mijać się z prawdą [mee-yaćh
śhan z prav-down] v. swerve
from the truth; to be untrue
mika [mee-ka] f. mica (mineral)
mikrob [mee-krob] m. microbe
mikrofon [mee-kro-fon] m.
microphone; transmitter
mikroskop [mee-kros-kop] m.
microscope
mikroskopijny [mee-kros-ko-peey-
-ni] adj. m. microscopic
mikstura [meek-stoo-ra] f.
mixture; concoction; medicine
mila [mee-la] f. mile
(1609.35 m.; 5,280 ft.;)
mila morska [mee-la mor-ska] f.
nautical mile (1853.2 m.)
milczący [meel-chown-tsi]
adj. m. silent; reticent; mum;
tacit; implicit; unspoken
milczeć [meel-chećh] v. be
silent; quit talking; be quiet
milczenie [meel-che-ńe] n.
silence; keeping still; stillness
milczkiem [meelch-kem] adv.
secretly; stealthily; on the sly
mile [mee-le] adv. pleasantly;
kindly; warmly; courteously
miliard [mee-lyard] m. thousand
million; billion (in America)
milicja [mee-leets-ya] f. militia;
police; constabulary
milicjant [mee-leets-yant] m.
policeman; constable
miligram [mee-lee-gram] m.
milligram; 1/1000 of a gram
milion [mee-lyon] m. million
milioner [mee-lyo-ner] m.
millionaire; a person owning at
least a million dollars (pounds)
milionowe miasto [mee-lyo-no-ve
myas-to] city of million people
militarny [mee-lee-tar-ni] adj. m.
military; fit for war (army)
militaryzować [mee-lee-ta-ri-zo-
-vaćh] v. militarize
milknąć [meel-knownćh] v.

abate; cease talking; die a-
way; calm down; be hushed
miło [mee-wo] adv. nicely;
pleasantly; agreeably
miło poznać [mee-wo poz-
-nać] exp. glad to meet; de-
lighted to meet; nice to meet
miłosierdzie [mee-wo-śher-
-dźhe] m. charity; mercy;
compassion; mercy
miłosierny [mee-wo-śher-ni] adj.
m. merciful; charitable
miłosny list [mee-wos-ni leest]
love letter
miłostka [mee-wost-ka] f. little
love affair
miłość [mee-wośhćh] f. love
miłośnik [mee-wośh-ńeek] m.
fancier; amateur; fan
miłować [mee-wo-vaćh] v. love
miły [mee-wi] adj. m. pleasant;
beloved; likable; nice; enjoy-
able; prepossessing; attractive
mimiczny [mee-meech-ni] adj. m.
mimic; imitative; make-believe
mimo [mee-mo] prep. in spite of;
notwithstanding; (al)though
mimo [mee-mo] adv. past; by
mimo woli [mee-mo vo-lee]
involuntarily; unintentional
mimo wszystko [mee-mo
vshist-ko] after all; in spite of
all; for all you may say
mimichodem [mee-mo-kho-dem]
adv. by the way; incidentally
mimowolny [mee-mo-vol-ni] adj.
m. involuntary; unintentional
mina [mee-na] f. facial
expression; look; appearance
mina [mee-na] f. mine; air
minaret [mee-na-ret] m. minaret
minąć [mee-nownćh] v. pass
by; go past; elapse; cease
mineralny [mee-ne-ral-ni] adj. m.
mineral; containing minerals
mineralogia [mee-ne-ra-lo-gya] f.
mineralogy
minerał [mee-ne-raw] m. mineral
minia [mee-ńya] f. minium; red
lead base; red lead
miniatura [mee-ńa-too-ra] f.
miniature; miniature copy
minimalny [mee-ńee-mal-ni] adj.

m. minimal; the least possible
minimum [mee-ńee-moom] n.
minimum; adv. at the very
least; at the lowest point
miniony [mee-ńo-ni] adj. m. by-
-gone; of long ago; olden
minister [mee-ńees-ter] m.
minister; cabinet member
ministerialny [mee-ńees-te-ryal-
-ni] adj. m. ministerial
ministerstwo [mee-ńees-ter-
-stvo] n. ministry; department
under a government minister
minorowy [mee-no-ro-vi] adj. m.
in minor key; low-spirited
minuta [mee-noo-ta] f. minute
minutowy [mee-noo-to-vi] adj. m.
of one minute
miodownik [myo-dov-ńeek] m.
gingerbread; bastard balm
miodowy miesiąc [myo-do-vi
mye-śhownts] honeymoon
miodosytnia [myo-do-sit-ńa] f.
mead bar; mead brewery
miot [myot] m. throw; cast;
littler; brood; animal birth;
fling; shooting party
miotacz [myo-tach] m. thrower
miotacz ognia [myo-tach og-ńa]
m. flamethrower
miotać [myo-taćh] v. throw;
fling; toss; hurl; stir; rave;
storm; sputter (abuse, curses)
miotła [myot-wa] f. broom
miód [myoot] m. honey; mead
mir [meer] m. esteem; respect
miriady [mee-rya-di] pl. myriads;
large numbers of persons etc.
mirra [meer-ra] f. myrrh
mirt [meert] m. myrtle
misa [mee-sa] f. platter; bowl
misja [mees-ya] f. mission
misjonarz [mees-yo-nash] m.
(religious) missionary
miska [mees-ka] f. dish; pan
misterny [mees-ter-ni] adj. m.
fine; delicate; subtle; clever
mistrz [meestsh] m. master;
maestro; champion; expert
mistrzostwo [mees-tzhos-tvo] m.
championship; mastery
mistrzowski ruch [mees-tzhov-
-skee rookh] master stroke

mistycyzm [mees-ti-tsizm] m.
mysticism; intuitive knowledge
mistyczny [mees-tich-ni] adj. m.
mystic; mystical; occult
mistyfikacja [mees-ti-fee-kats-ya]
f. mystification; hoax; catch
mistyfikować [mees-ti-fee-ko-
-vaćh] v. mystify; hoax; deceive; puzzle; perplex
mistyk [mees-tik] m. mystic
misyjny [mee-siy-ni] adj. m.
missionary; mission-
miś [meeśh] m. Teddy bear;
nylon fur coat or jacket
mit [meet] m. myth; mythology
mitologia [mee-to-lo-gya] f.
mythology; study of myths
mitologiczny [mee-to-lo-geech-ni]
adj. m. mythologic
mitra [meet-ra] f. mitre (hat)
mitręga [mee-tran-ga] f. delay;
waste of time; dawdler
mitrężyć [mee-tran-zhićh] v.
loiter; waste time; delay; lag
mityczny [mee-tich-ni] adj. m.
mythical; mythic; fictitious
mitygować [mee-ti-go-vaćh] v.
quiet; appease; check; restrain
mityng [mee-ting] m. (mass)
meeting; a mass gathering of
people; a coming together
mizantrop [mee-zan-trop] m.
misanthrope; hater of people
mizdrzyć się [meez-dzhićh
śhan] v. ogle; wheedle;
make eyes; cajole; coquet
mizerak [mee-ze-rak] m. poor
soul; weakling; poor devil
mizeria [mee-ze-rya] f. cucumber
salad; shabby possessions
mizerny [mee-zer-ni] adj. m.
meager; ill-looking; wretched;
paltry; haggard; poor; gaunt
mknąć [mknownćh] v. fleet;
rush; dash; speed; scurry; spin
mlaskać [mlas-kaćh] v. lap;
smack; make smacking noises
mlecz [mlech] m. marrow; milt
mleczarnia [mle-char-ńa] f.
dairy; creamery; milk bar
mleczny [mlech-ni] adj. m. milk;
milky; dairy; lactic; milk-white
mleć [mlećh] v. grind; mill

mleko [mle-ko] n. milk
młocarnia [mwo-tsar-ńa] f.
thresher; threshing-machine
młocka [mwots-ka] f. threshing
młoda [mwo-da] adj. f. young
młode [mwo-de] adj. pl. young;
n. pl. the young; litter
młodociany [mwo-do-ćha-ni]
adj. m. juvenile; youthful
młodość [mwo-dośhćh] f.
youth; early stage
młody [mwo-di] adj. m. young
młodzian [mwo-dźhan] m.
young man; lad; youth
młodzieniaszek [mwo-dźhe-ńa-
-shek] m. sprig; stripling; lad
młodzieniec [mwo-dźhe-ńets]
m. young man; lad; youth
młodzieńczy [mwo-dźheń-chi]
adj. m. youthful; immature
młodzież [mwo-dźhesh] f.
youth; young generation
młodzik [mwo-dźheek] m.
youngster; teenager; youngling
młokos [mwo-kos] m. kid
młot [mwot] m. sledge; hammer
młotek [mwo-tek] m. hammer;
tack-hammer; clapper
młócić [mwoo-ćheećh] v.
thresh (out); pommel; pound
młyn [mwin] m. mill; grinder
młynarz [mwi-nash] m. miller
młynek [mwi-nek] m. hand-
grinder; winnow mill; flay
młyński [mwiń-skee] adj. m.
mill-; of a mill
mnich [mńeekh] m. monk; friar
mniej [mńey] adv. less; fewer
mniej więcej [mńey vyan-tsey]
more or less; about; round
mniejsza o to [mńey-sha o to]
never mind that (exp.)
mniejszość [mńey-shośhćh]
f. minority; the lesser part
mniejszy [mńey-shi] adj. m.
smaller; lesser; less; minor
mniemać [mńe-maćh] v. suppose; deem; imagine; think;
consider; be of opinion
mniemanie [mńe-ma-ńe] n.
opinion; notion; conviction
mniszka [mńeesh-ka] f. nun
mnoga [mno-ga] num. plural

mnogi [mno-gee] adj. m.
numerous; of the plural
mnogość [mno-goshćh] f.
abundance; plurality; multitude
mnożenie [mno-zhe-ńe] n.
multiplication; increase; pro-
liferation; breeding
mnożyć [mno-zhićh] v. multiply
mnóstwo [mnoos-tvo] n. very
many; multitude; swarm; loads
mobilizacja [mo-bee-lee-zats-ya]
f. mobilization; call-up
mobilizować [mo-bee-lee-zo-
-vaćh] v. mobilize; call up
moc [mots] f. power; might;
great-deal; vigor; strength
mocarstwo [mo-tsar-stvo] n.
strong country; (world) power
mocarz [mo-tsash] m. strong
man; potentate; powerful man
mocny [mots-ni] adj. m. strong
mocować się [mo-tso-vaćh
śhan] v. wrestle; exert oneself; fight against (disease)
mocz [moch] m. urine
moczar [mo-char] m. bog; marsh
moczopędny [mo-cho-pand-ni]
adj. m. diuretic
moczowy [mo-cho-vi] adj. m.
uric; urinary; of urine
moczyć [mo-chićh] v. wet;
drench; steep; soak; urinate
moda [mo-da] f. fashion; style
model [mo-del] m. model; type
modelować [mo-de-lo-vaćh] v.
model; shape; mold; fashion
modernizować [mo-der-ńee-zo-
-vaćh] v. modernize; bring up
to date; make modern
modlić się [mod-leećh śhan] v.
pray; say one's prayer
modlitewnik [mod-lee-tev-ńeek]
m. prayer-book
modlitwa [mod-leet-va] f. prayer;
grace (at meal time)
modła [mod-wa] f. mold;
standard; fashion; model;
pattern; distinctive character
modniarka [mod-ńar-ka] f.
milliner; modiste; hat maker
modny [mod-ni] adj. m.
fashionable; in fashion; in
vogue; stylish; up to date

modry [mod-ri] adj. m. azure
-blue; deep blue; cerulean blue
modrzew [mod-zhev] m. larch
modulacja [mo-doo-lats-ya] f.
modulation; inflection
modulować [mo-doo-lo-vaćh] v.
modulate; inflect; regulate
modyfikacja [mo-di-fee-kats-ya]
f. modification; alteration
modyfikować [mo-di-fee-ko-
-vaćh] v. modify; alter; qualify; change partially
modystka [mo-dist-ka] f.modiste;
milliner; hat maker
mogący [mo-gown-tsi] adj. m.
able; capable; competent
mogiła [mo-gee-wa] f. tomb
mojżeszowy [moy-zhe-sho-vi]
adj. m. Mosaic; of Moses
mokka [mok-ka] f. natural
coffee; mocha; Mocha coffee
moknąć [mok-nownćh] v. get
wet; get soaked; drenched; be
soaked; be out in the rain
mokradło [mo-krad-wo] n. bog
mokry [mok-ri] adj. m. wet;
moist; watery; rainy; sweaty
molekularny [mo-le-koo-lar-ni]
adj. m. molecular; of molecule
molekuła [mo-le-koo-wa] f.
molecule (smallest particle)
molestować [mo-les-to-vaćh] v.
molest; annoy; vex; trouble
molo [mo-lo] n. pier; mole; jetty;
breakwater; quay
moment [mo-ment] m. moment
momentalny [mo-men-tal-ni] adj.
m. instantaneous; immediate
monarcha [mo-nar-kha] f.
monarch; sovereign; king
monarchista [mo-nar-khees-ta]
m. monarchist; royalist
moneta [mo-ne-ta] f. coin; chink
moneta brzęcząca [mo-ne-ta
bzhan-chown-tsa] cash; coins
mongolski [mon-gol-skee] adj. m.
Mongol; of Mongolia
monitor [mo-ńee-tor] m. monitor
monitować [mo-ńee-to-vaćh]
v. admonish; monitor; check
on (a person or timing)
monogram [mo-no-gram] m.
monogram; initials in a design

monokl [mo-nokl] m. eye-glass

monolog [mo-no-log] m.
monologue; soliloquy of one
actor; skit for one actor only

monopol [mo-no-pol] m.
monopoly; exclusive control

monoteizm [mo-no-te-eezm] m.
monotheism; belief in one god

monotonia [mo-no-to-ńya] f.
monotony; tiresome same-
ness; lack of variety;

monotonny [mo-no-ton-ni]
adj. m. monotonous; drab; dull

monstrualny [mon-stroo-al-ni]
adj. m. monstrous; horrible

monstrum [mon-stroom] n.
monster; monstrosity

montaż [mon-tash] m. mounting;
assembling; installation; set-up

monter [mon-ter] m. mechanic

montować [mon-to-vaćh] v.
install; put together; put up

monumentalny [mo-noo-men-tal-
-ni] adj. m. monumental

mops [mops] m. pug-dog

moralizator [mo-ra-lee-za-tor] m.
moralizer; moralist

moralizować [mo-ra-lee-zo-
vaćh] v. moralize; discuss
moral questions (tediously)

moralność [mo-ral-noshćh] f.
morals; morality; ethics

moralny [mo-ral-ni] adj. m.
moral; ethical; of good (sexual) conduct or character

morał [mo-raw] m. moral lesson

moratorium [mo-ra-to-ryoom] n.
moratorium; legalized delay

mord [mort] m. murder; unlawful killing; slaughter

morda [mor-da] f. snout; muzzle,
vulg.: mug; kisser; puss

morderca [mor-der-tsa] m.
murderer; assassin; cutthroat

morderczy [mor-der-chi] adj. m.
murderous; cutthroat; deadly

morderstwo [mor-der-stvo] n.
murder; assassination

mordęga [mor-dan-ga] f. toil;
drudge; moil; fag; strain

mordować [mor-do-vaćh] v.
kill; torment; harass; toil;
sweat; worry; assassinate

mordować się [mor-do-vaćh
śhan] v. kill oneself with
work; toil; sweat (over);
drudge; murder one another

morela [mo-re-la] f. apricot

morena [mo-re-na] f. moraine

morfina [mor-fee-na] f. morphine
(derivative of opium)

morfologia [mor-fo-lo-gya] f.
morphology; science of forms

morga [mor-ga] f. acre

morowy [mo-ro-vi] adj. m.
pestilential; clever; good
buddy; fine fellow; first-rate

mors [mors] m. walrus

morska choroba [mor-ska kho-ro-
-ba] seasickness; dizziness

morski [mor-skee] adj. m.
maritime; sea; nautical; naval

morwa [mor-va] f. mulberry

morze [mo-zhe] n. sea; ocean

morzyć [mo-zhićh] v. starve

mosiądz [mo-śhownts] m. brass

moskit [mos-keet] m. mosquito

most [most] m. bridge

mościć [mośh-ćheećh] v.
pad (a nest); make a bed of
straw; cushion (a seat etc.)

motać [mo-taćh] v. reel;
embroil; entangle; intrigue;
spool; involve in difficulty

motek [mo-tek] m. reel; ball

motłoch [mot-wokh] m. mob

motocykl [mo-to-tsikl] m.
motorcycle; motor bike

motor [mo-tor] m. motor; engine;
motive power; motor bike

motorówka [mo-to-roov-ka] f.
motorboat

motoryzacja [mo-to-ri-za-tsya] f.
motorization; mechanization

motoryzować [mo-to-ri-zo-vaćh]
v. motorize; mechanize

motyka [mo-ti-ka] f. hoe

motyl [mo-til] m. butterfly

motyw [mo-tiv] m. motif; motive

motywować [mo-ti-vo-vaćh] v.
give reasons; explain; justify

mowa [mo-va] f. speech; language; tongue; talk; address

mozaika [mo-zay-ka] f. mosaic

mozolić [mo-zo-leećh] v. toil;
take pains; exert oneself

mozolny [mo-zol-ni] adj. m.
 toilsome; strenuous arduous
mozół [mo-zoow] m. exertion
moździerz [moźh-dźhesh] m.
 mortar; mine thrower
może [mo-zhe] adv. perhaps;
 maybe; very likely; how a-
 bout? suppose...?
możliwość [mozh-lee-vośhćh]
 f. possibility; chance; con-
 tigency; capabilities; power
możliwości [mozh-lee-vośh-
 -ćhee] pl. scope; vistas;
 capabilities; chances; power
możliwy [mozh-lee-vi] adj.
 possible; fairly good; passable
można [mozh-na] v. imp. it is
 possible; one may; one can
możność [mozh-nośhćh] f.
 power; freedom to; free
 choice to; ability; opportunity
możny [mozh-ni] adj. m. potent;
 powerful; mighty; convincing
móc [moots] v. be free to; to
 be able; be capable of (doing)
mój [mooy] pron. my; mine
mól [mool] m. moth
mól książkowy [mool
 kśhownzh-ko-vi] bookworm
mór [moor] m. pestilence;
 epidemic; plague; pest
mórg [moorg] m. acre
mówca [moov-tsa] m. speaker
mówić [moo-veećh] v. speak;
 talk; say; tell; say things
mównica [moov-ńee-tsa] f.
 (pulpit); speaker's platform
mózg [moozg] m. brain; mind
mózgowy [mooz-go-vi] adj. m.
 cerebral; of the brain
mroczny [mroch-ni] adj. m.
 dusky; gloomy; obscure; dark
mrok [mrok] m. dusk; twilight
mrowić się [mro-veećh śhan]
 v. swarm; teem; be alive (with
 people, with insects etc.)
mrowie [mro-vye] n. swarm;
 tingle; gooseflesh; creeps
mrowisko [mro-vees-ko] n.
 anthill; ants' nest
mrozić [mro-źheećh] v. freeze;
 congeal; refrigerate; chill
mroźny [mroźh-ni] adj. m.

 frosty; icy; freezing
mrówka [mroov-ka] f. ant;
 emmet; pismire
mróz [mroos] m. frost; the cold
mruczeć [mroo-chećh] v.
 mumble; mutter; purr; murmur; grumble; growl; grunt
mrugać [mroo-gaćh] v. twinkle;
 blink; wink; flicker; flinch
mruk [mrook] m. mumbler; man
 of few words; growler
mrukliwy [mroo-klee-vi] adj. m.
 mumbling; sulky; gruff; taciturn; speaking indistinctly
mrużyć [mroo-zhićh] v. blink;
 wink; squint; half-shut (eyes)
mrzonka [mzhon-ka] f. illusion
msza [msha] f. mass (in church)
mszalny [mshal-ni] adj. m. for
 mass; of mass (in the church)
mszał [mshaw] m. missal
mściciel [mśhćhee-ćhel] m.
 avenger; retaliator
mścić [mśhćheećh] v. take
 vengeance; avenge; retaliate
mściwy [mśhćhee-vi] adj. m.
 vindictive; vengeful
mszczenie [mshche-ńe] n.
 vengeance; retaliation
mszyca [mshi-tsa] f. mite
mszysty [mshis-ti] adj. m. mossy
mucha [moo-kha] f. fly; trifle
mufka [moof-ka] f. muff
mularz [moo-lash] m. mason
mulat [moo-lat] m. mulatto
mulisty [moo-lees-ti] adj. m.
 muddy; oozy; slimy; sludgy
muł [moow] m. ooze; slime
muł [moow] m. mule
mumia [moo-mya] f. mummy
mundur [moon-door] m. uniform
municypalny [moo-ńee-tsi-pal-ni]
 adj. m. municipal
munsztuk [moon-shtook] m.
 (bridle) bit; mouthpiece
mur [moor] m. brick wall
murarz [moo-rash] m. bricklayer
murawa [moo-ra-va] f. lawn
murować [moo-ro-vaćh] v. lay
 bricks; build in brick (in stone)
murowany [moo-ro-va-ni] adj. m.
 of bricks; of stone; certain
murzyn [moo-zhin] m. negro

mus [moos] m. necessity;
   compulsion; constraint
mus [moos] m. froth; mousse
musieć [moo-śhećh] v. be ob-
   liged to; have to; be forced;
   must do; got to have it; want
muskać [moos-kaćh] v. touch
   lightly; skim; stroke
muskularny [moos-koo-lar-ni] adj.
   m. muscular; strong; hefty;
   sinewy; beefy; strong; brawny
muskuł [moos-koow] m. muscle
musować [moo-so-vaćh] foam;
   froth; bubble; fizz; sparkle
muszka [moosh-ka] f. fly;
   gunbead; face skin-spot; bow-
   tie; midge; dry-fly; patch (on
   the face); spot; gun sight
muszkat [moosh-kat] m. nutmeg
muszkiet [moosh-ket] m.
   musket; smooth bore firearm
muszla [moosh-la] f. shell; conch
musztarda [moosh-tar-da] f.
   mustard seasoning
musztra [moosh-tra] f. training;
   exercise; (military) drill
muślin [moośh-leen] m. muslin
mutacja [moo-ta-tsya] f.muta-
   tion; (voice) change; variation
muterka [moo-ter-ka] f. (bolt)
   nut; female screw
muza [moo-za] f. Muse
muzealny [moo-ze-al-ni] adj. m.
   of a museum; of museums
muzeum [moo-ze-oom] n.
   museum; exhibition building
muzułmanin [moo-zoow-ma-
   -ńeen] m. Moslem; Muslim;
   follower of Islam (Mussulman)
muzyczny [moo-zich-ni] adj. m.
   musical; set to music
muzyk [moo-zik] m. musician
muzyka [moo-zi-ka] f. music
muzykalność [moo-zi-kal-
   -nośhćh] f. ear for music
muzykalny [moo-zi-kal-ni] adj. m.
   having an ear for music
muzykant [moo-zi-kant] m. low
   class musician; bandsman
my [mi] pron. we; us
myć [mićh] v. wash
mycka [mits-ka] f. skull-cap
mydlarnia [mi-dlar-ńa] f.

soap store; soap works;
   perfumery
mydlarstwo [mi-dlar-stvo] n.
   soap-making; soap-boiling
mydlarz [mid-lash] m. soap-
   -maker; soap boiler
mydlić [mid-leećh] v. soap;
   froth; dress someone down
mydlić oczy [mid-leećh o-chi]
   pull wool over eyes
mydliny [mid-lee-ni] pl. soap
   -suds; lather
mydło [mid-wo] n. soap; soft
   soap; cake of soap
mylić [mi-leećh] v. mislead;
   misguide; confuse; deceive
mylny [mil-ni] adj. m. wrong
mysz [mish] f. mouse
myszkować [mish-ko-vaćh] v.
   covertly explore; trace scent
myśl [miśhl] f. thought; idea
myślący [mi-śhlown-tsi] adj. m.
   thoughtful; reflective
myśleć [miśh-lećh] v. think
myśliciel [miśh-lee-ćhel] m.
   thinker; one who thinks a lot
myśliwiec [miśh-lee-vyets] m.
   fighter plane; fighter pilot
myśliwy [miśh-lee-vi] m. hunter
myślnik [miśhl-ńeek] m. dash
   (mark); hyphen
myślowy [miśh-lo-vi] adj. m.
   mental; reflective; intellectual
myto [mi-to] n. toll; tollgate
mżyć [mzhićh] v. drizzle

N

na [na] prep. on; upon; at; for;
   by; in (NOTE : verbs with
   prefix na NOT INCLUDED
   HERE: CHECK WITHOUT THE
   PREFIX na")
nabawić się [na-ba-veećh
   śhan] v. bring upon oneself;
   incur; contract; catch (cold)
nabawić strachu [na-ba-veećh
   stra-khoo] v. frighten

nabiał [na-byaw] m. dairy
products including eggs
nabiegać się [na-bye-gaćh
śhan] v. have run a lot; exert
oneself; run about a great deal
nabić [na-beećh] v. load a
weapon; beat up (somebody);
whack; kill (a mass of); pack
nabiegły krwią [na-byeg-wi
krvy<u>own</u>] adj. m. bloodshot
nabierać [na-bye-raćh] v. take;
take in; tease; cheat; amass
nabijać [na-bee-yaćh] v. stud;
(repeatedly) load gun
nabijać się [na-bee-yaćh **śhan**]
v. make fun of (somebody)
nabożeństwo [na-bo-zheń-stvo]
n. church service
nabożny [na-bozh-ni] adj. m.
pious; religious; godly;
devoutly; devotional (hymn)
nabrać [nab-raćh] v. take; take
in; tease; cheat; gather; swell
nabój [na-booy] m. charge;
cartridge; round of ammunition
nabrzeże [na-bzhe-zhe] n. wharf;
embankment; landing pier
nabrzmiały [na-bzhmya-wi] adj.
m. swollen; distended
nabytek [na-bi-tek] m.
acquisition; purchase; new
recruit (new employee)
nabrzmiewać [na-bzhmye-vaćh]
v. swell; plump up; plump out
nabywać [na-bi-vaćh] v. buy;
acquire; obtain; gain; procure;
purchase; get; develop (habit)
nabywca [na-biv-tsa] m. buyer
nacechowany [na-tse-kho-**va**-ni]
adj. m. marked; characterized
nachodzić [na-kho-dźheećh] v.
intrude; (abstraction:) haunt
nachylać [na-khi-laćh] v. stoop;
bend; incline; lean; tilt; slant
nacięcie [na-ćhan-ćhe] n. cut;
incision; notch; nick; score;
indentation; scarification
naciągać [na-ćh<u>own</u>-gaćh] v.
stretch; draw; strain; pull
one's leg; take sb. in; infuse
naciek [na-ćhek] m. infiltration;
leak; swelling; (fluid) gathering
nacierać [na-ćhe-raćh] v. rub;

attack; harass; demand
nacinać [na-ćhee-naćh] v. cut
a great deal; notch; score;
nick; scarify; hoax; dupe
nacisk [na-ćheesk] m. pressure;
stress; accent; thrust; push
naciskać [na-ćhees-kaćh] v.
press; urge; bear on; push
nacjonalista [na-tsyo-na-**lees**-ta]
m. nationalist
nacjonalizacja [na-tsyo-na-lee-
-zats-ya] f. nationalization
nacjonalizm [na-tsyo-**na**-leezm]
m. nationalism
nacjonalizować [na-tsyo-na-lee-
-zo-vaćh] v. nationalize
naczekać się [na-che-kaćh
śhan] v. wait too long; tire of
waiting; wait indefinitely
na czczo [na chcho] adv. on an
empty stomach; unfed; fasting
naczelnik [na-chel-ńeek] m.
manager; chief; head; master
naczelny [na-chel-ni] adj. m.
chief; head; paramount; primate; principal; main; front
naczerpać [na-cher-paćh] v. dip
up; draw (fluid); scoop up
naczynie [na-chi-ńe] n. vessel
nad [nad] prep. over; above; on;
upon; beyond; at; of; for
nadajnik [na-**day**-ńeek] m.
transmitter; feeder
nadal [na-dal] adv. still; in future;
continue (to do); as before
nadaremnie [na-da-rem-ńe] adv.
in vain; unsuccessfully; to no
purpose; without result
nadaremny [na-da-rem-ni] adj. m.
fruitless; vain; unsuccessful
nadarzać się [na-da-zhaćh
śhan] v. happen; occur; turn
up; present itself; offer (of)
nadawać [na-da-vaćh] v. confer
bestow; grant; endow; christen; invest; vest; offer; cause
nadawca [na-dav-tsa] m. sender
nadąć [na-d<u>own</u>ćh] v. puff up
nadąsany [na-d<u>own</u>-**sa**-ni]
adj. m. sulky; sullen; stuffy
nadążać [na-d<u>own</u>-zhaćh] v.
keep up with; cope with; keep
pace; lag behind; follow

nadbałtycki [nad-baw-**tits**-kee] adj. m. on the Baltic; Baltic

nadbiec [nad-byets] v. come running up; hasten up; run up

nadbrzeże [nad-**bzhe**-zhe] n. shore; coast; littoral

nadbrzeżny [nad-**bzhezh**-ni] adj. m. coastal; sea-shore

nadbudowa [nad-boo-**do**-va] f. superstructure; added floor

nadbudować [nad-boo-**do**-vaćh] v. build on; add an upper floor

nadchodzić [nad-kho-**dźhee**ćh] v. approach; arrive; come; be forthcoming; be imminent

nadciągać [nad-**ćhown**-gaćh] v. draw near; be nearing; be imminent; be setting in; come

nadciśnienie [nad-ćhee-**śhńe**-ńe] n. hypertension

nadczłowiek [nad-**chwo**-vyek] m. superman; superhuman man

nadejście [na-dey-**śhćhe**] n. coming; arrival; oncoming

nadepnąć [na-dep-**nown**ćh] v. step on; tread on (crushing)

nader [na-der] adv. greatly; excessively; highly; most

nadesłać [na-de-**swa**ćh] v. send in; forward; remit (a sum)

nade wszystko [na-de **vshist**-ko] adv. above all (else)

nadęty [na-**dan**-ti] adj. m. puffed up; inflated; superior

nadgraniczny [nad-gra-**ńeech**-ni] adj. m. near-border; frontier-

nadjechać [nad-**ye**-khaćh] v. drive up; come up; arrive

nadlecieć [nad-le-**ćhe**ćh] v. fly in; arrive (drive up) in a hurry

nadleśniczy [nad-leśh-**ńee**-chi] m. chief ranger; forest inspector; head (chief) of rangers

nadliczbowy [nad-lich-**bo**-vi] adj. m. overtime; additional

nadludzki [nad-**loots**-kee] adj. m. superhuman; divine; terrific

nadmiar [nad-myar] m. excess

nadłamać [nad-**wa**-maćh] v. break slightly; cause a slight break; break off; fracture

nadmienić [nad-**mye**-ńeećh] v. mention; allude; hint; add

nadmierny [nad-**myer**-ni] adj. m. excessive; extravagant; undue

nadmorski [nad-**mors**-kee] adj. m. seaside-(resort); maritime

nadmuchać [nad-**moo**-khaćh] v. inflate; blow up with air

nadobny [na-**dob**-ni] adj. m. handsome; comely; pretty

nadobowiązkowy [nad-o-bo-**vyown**-sko-vi] adj. m. optional; elective; voluntary

na dół [na **doow**] adv. down; downstairs; downwards

nadpić [nad-peećh] v. take a sip; start overfilled drink

nadpłynąć [nad-pwi-**nown**ćh] v. sail in; swim in; enter

nadprodukcja [nad-pro-**doo**-ktsya] f. excess production

nadprogramowy [nad-pro-gra-**mo**-vi] adj. m. extra; additional

nadprzyrodzony [nad-pzhi-ro-**dzo**-ni] adj. m. supernatural

nadpsuty [nad-**psoo**-ti] adj. m. partly spoiled; impaired

nadrabiać [nad-ra-**bya**ćh] v. catch up with; make up; work ahead of schedule; compensate for (a deficiency); out do

nadruk [nad-rook] m. overprint

nadrzędny [nad-**zhand**-ni] adj. m. superior; primary; precedent

nadskakiwać [nad-ska-kee-**va**ćh] v. try to ingratiate oneself; curry favor (with)

nadsłuchiwać [nad-swoo-**khee**-vaćh] v. strain to listen

nadspodziewany [nad-spo-dźhe-**va**-ni] adj. m. unexpected

nadstawiać [nad-**sta**-vyaćh] v. expose; risk; hold out; cock

nadto [nad-to] adv. moreover; furthermore; nor; besides; too much; too many; amply

nadużycie [nad-oo-zhi-**ćhe**] n. abuse; excess; misuse

nadużywać [nad-oo-zhi-vaćh] v. abuse; take advantage; strain (relations); misuse

nadwaga [nad-va-ga] f. overweight; allowance of extra weight (in travel)

nadwartość [nad-**var**-tośhćh]

f. overvalue in economics
nadwątlić [nad-vownt-leećh] v.
weaken; impair; damage
nadwiślański [nad-vee-śhlań-
-skee] adj. m. on the Vistula
nadwodny [nad-vod-ni] adj. m.
near water; riverside; aquatic
nadwozie [nad-vo-źhe] n. car
-body; body of a car or truck
nadwyrążać [nad-vi-ran-zhaćh]
v. impair; strain; weaken
nadwyżka [nad-vizh-ka] f.
surplus; excess amount
nadymać [na-di-maćh] v. puff
up; inflate; swell out; fill out;
bulge; blow out; pump up; distend; bulge; put on airs
nadymić [na-di-meećh] v. fill
(a rooom) with smoke; make a
lot of smoke
nadzieja [na-dźhe-ya] f. hope
nadziemski [nad-źhem-skee]
adj. m. celestial; heavenly;
divine; super terrestrial
nadzienie [na-dźhe-ńe] n.
stuffing (of fowl, etc.) ; filling;
nadziewać [na-dźhe-vaćh] v.
stuff; pierce with; put on; fill
nadzorca [nad-zor-tsa] m.
overseer; superintendent;
supervisor (of work, workers)
nadzór [nad-zoor] m. supervision
nadzwyczaj [nad-zvi-chay] adv.
unusually; extremely; most
nadzwyczajny [nad-zvi-chay-ni]
adj. m. extraordinary; extreme
nafta [naf-ta] f. petroleum
naftalina [na-fta-lee-na] f.
naphthalene (moth repellent)
nagabywać [na-ga-bi-vaćh] v.
annoy; accost; trouble; molest
nagana [na-ga-na] f. blame
nagi [na-gee] adj. m. naked; in
buff; bare; nude; bald; empty
naginać [na-gee-naćh] v. bend
down; submit to; adapt; bow
nagle [nag-le] adv. suddenly
naglić [nag-leećh] v. urge
nagłość [nag-wośhćh] f.
urgency; suddenness; instancy
nagłówek [na-gwoo-vek] m.
heading; caption; title; headline; letter-head; headstall

nagły [nag-wi] adj. m. sudden;
urgent; instant; abrupt; pressing; unexpected; immediate
nagminny [nag-meen-ni] adj. m.
universal; usual; current;
general; epidemic; enzootic
nagniotek [nag-ńo-tek] m. (skin)
corn; callus (on the skin)
nagonka [na-gon-ka] f. campaign
against; hue and cry against
nagość [na-gośhćh] f. nudity
nagradzać [na-gra-dzaćh] v.
reward; give prize; recompense; indemnify; make up for
nagrobek [na-gro-bek] m. tomb
nagroda [na-gro-da] f. reward
nagrodzić [na-gro-dźeećh] v.
reward; requite; recompense
nagromadzić [na-gro-ma-
-dźeećh] v. accumulate; congregate; amass; heap up
nagrzewać [na-gzhe-vaćh] v.
warm up; heat up; preheat
naigrawać [na-ee-gra-vaćh] v.
mock; scoff; deride; ridicule
naiwny [na-eev-ni] adj. m. naive
najazd [na-yazd] m. invasion
najbardziej [nay-bar-dźhey] adv.
most (of all)
najechać [na-ye-khaćh] v.
overrun; invade; run into; ram;
crowd; run over; crush into
najedzony [na-ye-dzo-ni] adj. m.
full (of food); satiated
najem [na-yem] m. hire; renting
najemnik [na-yem-ńeek] m.
hireling; mercenary; free lance;
soldier of fortune; wage earner
najemny [na-yem-ni] adj. m.
venal; mercenary; hired labor
najeść się [na-yeśhćh śhan]
v. eat plenty of; eat a lot
najeźdźca [na-yeźhdźh-tsa]
m. invader; assailant; violator
najeżdżać [na-yezh-dzhaćh] v.
invade; run into; attack; ram
najeżony [na-ye-zho-ni] adj. m.
bristling; bristly; beset
najgorszy [nay-gor-shi] adj. m.
the worst; the worst of all
najgorzej [nay-go-zhey] adv.
worst of all; worst possible
najlepiej [nay-le-pyey] adv. best;

best of all
najlepszy [nay-**lep**-shi] adj. m.
  best; best of all; best possible
najmniej [nay-**mńey**] adv. least
najmniejszy [nay-**mńey**-shi] adj.
  m. least; smallest; least of all
najmować [nay-mo-**vaćh**] v.
  rent; hire; engage; lease
najpierw [nay-**pyerv**] adv. first of
  all; in the first place; at first
najście [nay-**śhćhe**] n. intrusion; inroad; invasion; incursion; irruption; encroachment
najść [nay**śhćh**] v. intrude; fill
najwięcej [nay-**vyan**-tsey] adv.
  most of all (worst of all)
największy [nay-**vyan**-kshi] adj.
  m. biggest; largest; extreme
najwyżej [nay-**vi**-zhey] adv.
  highest; at the very most
najwyższy [nay-**vizh**-shi] adj. m.
  highest; top; utmost; extreme
nakarmić [na-**kar**-meećh] v.
  feed (population); give food
nakaz [**na**-kaz] m. order; writ
nakazywać [na-ka-**zi**-vać] v.
  order; demand; command
nakleić [na-**kle**-eećh] v. stick
  on; paste up; mount; post
nakład [**na**-kwad] m. outlay
nakładać [na-**kwa**-daćh] v. lay
  on; put on; place; set; spread
nakładca [na-**kwad**-tsa] m.
  publisher (of printed work)
nakłaniać [na-**kwa**-ńaćh] v.
  persuade; induce; bring; get;
  urge; incite; incline; prevail
na koniec [na ko-**ńets**] adv.
  finally; at the (very) end
nakreślać [na-kre-**śhlaćh**] v.
  delineate; sketch; draft; write
nakręcać [na-**kran**-tsaćh] v.
  wind up; shoot (movie); turn;
  direct; set on; cheat; swindle
nakrętka [na-**krant**-ka] f. (screw)
  nut; female screw; jam nut
nakrycie [na-**kri**-ćhe] n. cover
nakrywać [na-**kri**-vaćh] v. cover
nakrywka [na-**kriv**-ka] f. lid
na kształt [na **kshtawt**] in form
  of...; in shape of; a kind of...
nalać [**na**-laćh] v. pour in; pour
  on (liquid only, no sand etc.)

nalegać [na-le-**gaćh**] v. insist
naleganie [na-le-ga-**ńe**] n.
  insistence; urgent demand
nalepiać [na-le-**pyaćh**] v. stick
  on; paste on; mount; glue on
nalepka [na-**lep**-ka] f. sticker
naleśnik [na-**leśh**-ńeek] m.
  pancake wrap around stuffing
nalewać [na-le-**vaćh**] v. pour in
należeć [na-le-**zhećh**] v. belong
należność [na-lezh-**nośhćh**] f.
  due; ration; charge; fee
należy [na-**le**-zhi] adj. m. due;
  owing; rightful; proper
należycie [na-le-zhi-**ćhe**] adv.
  properly; duly; suitably
należyty [na-le-**zhi**-ti] adj. m.
  proper; right; appropriate
nalot [**na**-lot] m. air raid; (skin)
  rush; coating; incursion; blitz
naładować [na-wa-do-**vaćh**] v.
  load; charge; cram; freight
nałogowiac [na-wo-go-**vyets**] m.
  addict; chain-smoker; drunkard
nałogowy [na-wo-**go**-vi] adj. m.
  addicted; inveterate; habitual
nałogowy pijak [na-wo-**go**-vi **pee-**
  -yak] alcoholic; drunkard
nałóg [**na**-woog] m. addiction
namacalny [na-ma-**tsal**-ni] adj.
  m. tangible; substantial
namaszczać [na-**mash**-chaćh]
  v. anoint; grease; smear
namaszczenie [na-mash-**che-ńe**]
  n. solemnity; anointing
namawiać [na-ma-**vyaćh**] v.
  persuade; prompt; urge; exhort; instigate; encourage
namazać [na-ma-**zaćh**] v. daub;
  anoint; scrawl (scribble)
namiastka [na-**myast**-ka] f.
  substitute; ersatz; stopgap
namiernik [na-**myer**-ńeek] m.
  direction finder; pelorus
namiestnik [na-**myest**-ńeek] m.
  regent; governor; viceroy
namiętność [na-**myant-**
  -nośhćh] f. passion; infa-
  tuation; fervor; keenness
namiętny [na-**myant**-ni] adj. m.
  passionate; keen; ardent; lusty
namiot [**na**-myot] m. tent; booth
namoczyć [na-mo-**chićh**] v.

wet; soak; steep; drench

namoknąć [na-mok-<u>nown</u>ćh] **v.**
get soaked; become saturated

namowa [na-mo-va] **f.** instigation; suggestion; persuasion

namulić [na-moo-leećh] **v.** slime up; silt up; mud up; ooze up

namydlić [na-mid-leećh] **v.** soap up; put soap lather on

namysł [na-misw] **m.** reflection

namyślać się [na-mi-śhlaćh śhan] **v.** ponder; reflect; think over; make up one's mind

nanosić [na-no-śheećh] **v.** bring; deposit; plot; track (mud); drift; mark (on a map)

na nowo [na no-vo] **adv.** anew

naocznie [na-och-ńe] **adv.** by eye; visually; clearly

naoczny świadek [na-och-ni śhvya-dek] eyewitness

na odwrót [na od-vroot] **adv.** inversely; the other way around; directly opposite

na ogół [na o-goow] **adv.** (in general) generally; on the whole; not specifically

na około [na o-ko-wo] **adv.** all around; about; right round

naokoło [na-o-ko-wo] **prep.** all around; about; on all sides

naoncza [na-on-chas] **adv.** at that time; then; in those days

naoliwić [na-o-lee-veećh] **v.** oil; lubricate; grease; make slippery or smooth; apply oil

na opak [na o-pak] **adv.** backward; perversely; the wrong way; upside-down

na ostatek [na o-sta-tek] **adv.** finally; in the end; at last

naostrzyć [na-ost-zhićh] **v.** sharpen up; become sharp

na oścież [na ośh-ćhesh] **adv.** wide open; opened all the way

na oślep [na ośh-lep] **adv.** blindly; full tilt; headlong

na ówczas [na oov-chas] **adv.** at that time; then; in those days

napad [na-pat] **m.** assault; fit; attempt; attack; outburst; invective; outbreak; onset

napadać [na-pa-daćh] **v.** assail

napar [na-par] **m.** infusion; brew; a beverage brewed

naparstek [na-par-stek] **m.** thimble; dram; thimble full

naparzyć [na-pa-zhićh] **v.** infuse; fight; beat up (badly)

napaskudzić [na-pas-koo-dźheećh] **v.** soil up; make a mess; dirty; foul; make trouble

napastliwy [na-past-lee-vi] **adj. m.** aggressive; malicious; bitter; quarrelsome

napastnik [na-past-ńeek] **m.** aggressor; assailant; forward, forward center (sport)

napastować [na-pas-to-vaćh] **v.** pester; attack; wax; molest; worry; assail; persecute

napaść [na-paśhćh] **f.** assault

napawać [na-pa-vaćh] **v.** fill up (with feelings, panic, wander)

napatrzyć się [na-pat-shićh śhan] **v.** see enough; have a good look; see a lot of

napełniać [na-pew-ńaćh] **v.** fill up; inspire; imbue; pervade

na pewno [na-pev-no] **adv.** surely; certainly; for sure; without fail; with assurance

napęd [na-<u>pand</u>] **m.** propulsion; drive; force; driving gear

napędowy [na-<u>pan</u>-do-vi] **adj. m.** motive; driving; impulsive

napędzać [na-<u>pan</u>-dzaćh] **v.** chase in; propel; round up; drift in; carry along; egg on

napić się [na-peećh śhan] **v.** have a drink; quench one's thirst; have to drink

napierać [na-pye-raćh] **v.** press forward; insist; advance

napięcie [na-<u>pyan</u>-ćhe] **n.** tension; strain; voltage; intensity; stress; stretch

napiętek [na-<u>pyan</u>-tek] **m.** heel

napiętnować [na-<u>pyant</u>-no-vaćh] **v.** brand; stigmatize; censure; condemn as being very bad; stamp

napięty [na-<u>pyan</u>-ti] **adj. m.** tense; taut; strained; tight

napinać [na-pee-naćh] **v.** strain

napis [na-pees] **m.** inscription

napitek [na-pee-tek] m. drink
napiwek [na-pee-vek] m. tip
napluć [na-plooćh] v. spit on
napływ [na-pwiv] m. influx
napływać [na-pwi-vaćh] v.
  inflow; flow in; flock; pour in
napływowy [na-pwi-vo-vi]
  adj. m. alluvial; immigrant;
  alien; extraneous; foreign
napoczynać [na-po-chi-naćh] v.
  start up; open; broach
napominać [na-po-mee-naćh] v.
  admonish; reprimand; rebuke
napomknąć [na-pom-knownćh]
  v. mention; hint at; allude to
napomnienie [na-po-mńe-ńe] n.
  admonition; reprimand; rebuke
na pomoc! [na po-mots] excl.:
  help! give help! please, help!
napotny [na-pot-ni] adj. m.
  perspiratory; diaphoretic
napotykać [na-po-ti-kaćh] v.
  run in; come across; be faced
  with; happen; be confronted
napowietrzny [na-po-vyetsh-ni]
  adj. m. aerial; overhead-
na powrót [na po-vroot] adv.
  return; again; on the way back
na pozór [na po-zoor] adv.
  apparently; on the face of it
napój [na-pooy] m. drink
na pół [na poow] adv. in half
napór [na-poor] m. pressure
naprawa [na-pra-va] f. repair;
  redress; renovation; reform
naprawdę [na-prav-dan] adv.
  indeed; really; truly; positively
naprawiać [na-pra-vyaćh] v.
  repair; fix; mend; rectify;
  reform; mend; set (put) right
naprędce [na-prand-tse] adv.
  hastily; in a hurry; slapdash
naprężenie [na-pran-zhe-ńe] n.
  tension; strain; tautness
naprężyć [na-pran-zhićh] v.
  tighten; stretch; strain
naprowadzać [na-pro-va-
  -dzaćh] v. lead in; direct to;
  point out to; advise; suggest
na próżno [na proozh-no] adv. in
  vain; uselessly; to no avail
naprzeciw [na-pzhe-ćheev] adv.
  opposite; vis-a-vis

naprzeć [na-pzhećh] press;
  urge; press hard; insist on
na przekór [na pzhe-koor] adv. in
  despite; just to spite
na przełaj [na pzhe-way] adv.
  shortcut (across obstacles)
na przemian [na pzhe-myan] adv.
  alternately; by turns
naprzód [na-pzhood] adv. in
  front; forwards; first; in the
  first place; forward; onward
na przykład [na pzhi-kwad] adv.
  for instance; for example
naprzykrzać się [na-pshik-
  shaćh śhan] v. bother; molest; pester; obtrude oneself
napuchnąć [na-poo-khnownćh]
  v. swell; become swollen
napuchły [na-poo-khwi] adj. m.
  swollen; bulging; distended
napuścić [na-poo-śhćheećh]
  v. set up; impregnate; let in
napuszony [na-poo-sho-ni] adj.
  m. puffed up; bristling; ruffled
napychać [na-pi-khaćh] v.
  stuff; cram; fill; pack; crowd;
  stow; line one's purse; gorge
narada [na-ra-da] f. consultation;
  council; conference; meeting
naradzać się [na-ra-dzhaćh
  śhan] v. consult on; confer
  with; deliberate; hold a council
naramiennik [na-ra-myen-ńeek]
  m . epaulet; shoulder-strap
narastać [na-ra-staćh] v. grow
  on; increase; accumulate; ac-
  crete; accrue (interest); gather
naraz [na-raz] adv. suddenly
na razie [na ra-źhe] adv. for the
  time being; for the present
narażać [na-ra-zhaćh] v. expose to danger; endanger
narciarstwo [nar-ćhars-tvo] n.
  skiing (sport); gliding on skis
narciarz [nar-ćhazh] m. skier
narcyz [nar-tsiz] m. narcissus
nareszcie [na-resh-ćhe] adv. at
  last; finally; at long last
naręcze [na-ran-che] n. armful
narkotyczny [nar-ko-tich-ni] adj.
  m. narcitic; causing numbness
narkotyk [nar-ko-tik] m. narcotic;
  drug for sleep and relief

narkoza [nar-ko-za] f. anesthesia; loss of sense of pain, touch
narobić [na-ro-beećh] v. mess up; cause nuisance; make a mess; cause a lot of (trouble)
narodowość [na-ro-do-vośhćh] f. nationality; national status (attachment)
narodowy [na-ro-do-vi] adj. m. national; of national character
narodzenie [na-ro-dzhe-ńe] n. birth; a being born; the beginning; Nativity; Christmas
narodzić się [na-ro-dźheećh śhan] v. be born; originate; a-rise; come into existence
narodziny [na-ro-dźhee-ni] pl. birth; origin; the beginning
narośl [na-rośhl] f. tumor; growth; excrescence; wart
narowisty [na-ro-vees-ti] adj. m. restive; vicious; skittish
narożnik [na-rozh-ńeek] m. corner; angle; cross-roads; gusset; quoin; corner brick
narożny [na-rozh-ni] adj. m. corner-; at the street corner
naród [na-root] m. nation; people; the nation; crowd
narów [na-roov] m. vice (restiveness); bad habit; fault
narta [nar-ta] f. ski; sleigh
naruszać [na-roo-shaćh] v. disturb; violate; injure; harm
naruszenie [na-roo-she-ńe] n. offense; disturbance; breach
narwany [nar-va-ni] adj. m. hot-headed; reckless; rash; fitful
narybek [na-ri-bek] m. small fry; coming generation
narząd [na-zhownt] m. organ
narzecze [na-zhe-che] n. (primitive) dialect
narzeczona [na-zhe-cho-na] f. fiancee; an engaged woman
narzeczony [na-zhe-cho-ni] m. fiance; an engaged man
narzekać [na-zhe-kaćh] v. complain; grumble; lament
narzekanie [na-zhe-ka-ńe] n. complaints; kick; bitching
narzędzie [na-zhan-dźhe] n. tool; utensil; implement

narzucać [na-zhoo-tsaćh] v. throw over; impose; shovel on
nasada [na-sa-da] f. base
nasenna pigułka [na-sen-na pee-goov-ka] f. sleeping pill
nasiadówka [na-sia-doov-ka] f. sitzbath; hip-bath
nasiąknąć [na-śhownk-nownćh] v. soak up; become saturated; imbibe; soak in
nasienie [na-śhe-ńe] n. seed; sperm; semen; posterity
nasilenie [na-śhee-le-ńe] n. intensification; intensity
naskórek [na-skoo-rek] m. outer skin; epidermis; cuticle
naskarżyć [na-skar-zhićh] v. denounce; lodge a complaint
nasłuchać się [na-swoo-khaćh śhan] v. hear plenty
nasłuchiwać [na-swoo-khee-vaćh] v. monitor (radio); listen; be on the watch for
nasmarować [na-sma-ro-vaćh] v. smear over; grease; oil; lubricate; rub with ointment
nastać [na-staćh] v. set in; enter; occur; come about
nastanie [na-sta-ńe] n. arrival; setting-in; advent; coming
nastarczyć [na-star-chićh] v. supply enough; keep pace with; cope with the demand
nastawać [na-sta-vaćh] v. insist; start service; be against
natawiać [na-sta-vyaćh] v. set up; set right; tune in; point
nastawienie [na-sta-vye-ńe] n. attitude; bias; disposition
następca [na-stanp-tsa] m. successor; heir (to the throne)
następnie [na-stanp-ńe] adv. next; then; subsequently
następny [na-stanp-ni] adj. m. next; the next; the following
następować [na-stan-po-vaćh] v. follow; tread; come after; ensue; step on; take place
następstwo [na-stanp-stvo] n. result; succession; upshot
następujący [na-stan-poo-yown-tsi] adj. m. the successive; the following; the next

nastraszyć [na-stra-shićh] v.
  frighten; intimidate; scare
nastręczać [na-stran-chaćh] v.
  afford; present; offer; procure
nastroić [na-stro-eećh] v.
  attune; tune up; dispose to
nastroszyć [na-stro-shićh] v.
  bristle up; perk up; heap up
nastrój [na-strooy] m. mood
nasturcja [na-stoor-tsya] f.
  nasturtium; lark-heel
nasuwać [na-soo-vaćh] v.
  shove up; draw over; afford;
  overthrust; offer possibilities
nasycać [na-si-tsaćh] v.
  satiate; satisfy; sate; saturate
nasycenie [na-si-tse-ńe] n.
  satiation; saturation; satisfaction; gratification
nasycony [na-si-tso-ni] adj. m.
  satiate; saturated; replete
nasyłać [na-si-waćh] v. send
  on (to pester, badger; kill)
nasyp [na-sip] m. embankment
nasypać [na-si-paćh] v. pour in;
  spread up (dry powder etc.)
nasz [nash] pron. our; ours
naszyć [na-shićh] v. sew on;
  trim (with fur, ribbons, etc.)
naszkicować [na-shkee-tso-
  vaćh] v. sketch; make a
  sketch of; draw up; outline
naszyjnik [na-shiy-ńeek] m.
  necklace; neck jewelry
naśladować [na-śhla-do-vaćh]
  v. imitate; mimic; reproduce
naśladowanie [na-śhla-do-va-
  -ńe] n. imitation; copy
naśladowca [na-śhla-dov-tsa]
  m. imitator
naśmiewać się [na-śhmye-
  -vaćh śhan] v. laugh at;
  deride; laugh to the full
naświetlać [na-śhvyet-laćh] v.
  explain; irradiate; expose
natarcie [na-tar-ćhe] n. 1.
  rubbing; 2. onslaught; attack;
  offensive; advance
natarczywość [na-tar-chi-
  -vośhćh] f. insistence; obtrusiveness; urgency; pressure
natarczywy [na-tar-chi-vi] adj.
  m. insistent; pressing; urgent

natchnąć [natkh-nownćh] v.
  inspire; infuse; penetrate
natchnienie [nat-khńe-ńe] n. inspiration; brain wave; impulse;
  afflation; happy thought
natenczas [na-ten-chas] adv.
  then; at that time; as
natężać [na-tan-zhaćh] v.
  strain; intensify; strengthen;
  exert; heighten; enhance
natężenie [na-tan-zhe-ńe] n.
  tension; strain; effort; pitch
natężony [na-tan-zho-ni] adj. m.
  intense; strained; concentrated
natknąć [nat-knownćh] v.
  come across; butt; stick; stud
natłoczony [na-two-cho-ni] adj.
  m. crowded; packed; huddled
natłoczyć [na-two-chićh] v.
  cram; pack; crowd; huddle
natłok [nat-wok] m. crowd;
  throng; pressure accumulation
natomiast [na-to-myast] adv.
  however; yet; on the contrary
natłuścić [na-twoo-
  -śhćheećh] v. oil; grease;
  lubricate; supply a lubricant
natrafić [na-tra-feećh] v.
  encounter; come across
natręctwo [na-tran-tstvo] n. in-
  trusiveness; obtrusiveness
natręt [na-trant] m. intruder
natrętni [na-tran-tni] adj. m.
  intrusive; bothersome
natrysk [na-trisk] m. shower
  -bath; shower; spraying
natrząsać się [na-tzhown-saćh
  śhan] v. scoff at; sneer at;
  poke fun; hold in derision
natrzeć [na-tzhećh] v. rub;
  attack; harass; scold; rate
natura [na-too-ra] f. nature
naturalizacja [na-too-ra-lee-za
  -tsya] f. naturalization
naturalizować [na-too-ra-lee-zo-
  -vaćh] v. naturalize
naturalny [na-too-ral-ni] adj. m.
  natural; true to life
natychmiast [na-tikh-myast] adv.
  at once; instantly; right away
natychmiastowy [na-tikh-myas-
  -to-vi] adj. m. instantaneous
nauczać [na-oo-chaćh] v.

teach; instruct; tutor; train
nauczanie [na-oo-cha-ńe] n.
teaching; instruction
nauczka [na-ooch-ka] f. (pointed)
lesson (unpleasant)
nauczyciel [na-oo-chi-ćhel] m.
teacher; instructor
nauczyć się [na-oo-chićh
śhan] v. learn; come to know
nauka [na-oo-ka] f. science; research work; learning; study;
teaching; knowledge; lesson
naukowiec [na-oo-ko-vyets] m.
scientist; scholar; researcher
naukowość [na-oo-ko-vośhćh]
f. erudition; scholarship; learning; scientific nature; erudition
naukowy [na-oo-ko-vi] adj. m.
scientific; scholarly; academic
naumyślnie [na-oo-miśhl-ńe]
adv. on purpose; of set purpose; deliberately; intentionally
nawa [na-va] f. nave; aisle
nawadniać [na-vad-ńaćh] v.
irrigate; saturate with water
nawalić [na-va-leećh] v. pile
up; fail; bungle; break down
nawał [na-vaw] m. no end of;
an overwhelming amount
nawała [na-va-wa] f.
overwhelming mass; swarms;
onslaught; enormous amount
nawałnica [na-vaw-ńee-tsa] f.
tempest; storm; hurricane
nawarstwienie [na-var-stvye-ńe]
n. stratification
nawarzyć [na-va-zhićh] v.
brew; cook; concoct; get in
trouble; cause trouble
nawet [na-vet] adv. even
nawet gdyby [na-vet gdi-bi] adv.
even if; even though; even
nawias [na-vyas] m. parenthesis
nawiasem [na-vya-sem] adv.
incidentally; by way of di-
gression; by the way
nawiasowy [na-vya-so-vi] adj. m.
parenthetical; incidental
nawiązać [na-vyown-zaćh] v.
tie to; refer to; enter in
nawiązanie [na-vyown-za-ńe] n.
connection; reference to
nawiedzać [na-vye-dzaćh] v.

visit; haunt; afflict; obsess
nawierzchnie [na-vyezh-khńa] f.
surface (finish); pavement
nawijać [na-vee-yaćh] v. wind
up; reel; roll up; spool; coil
nawlekać [na-vle-kaćh] v.
thread; string; slip on
nawodnienie [na-vod-ńe-ńe] n.
irrigation; saturation with
water; washing out (a cavity)
nawoływać [na-vo-wi-vaćh] v.
call; hail; exhort; urge; lure
nawozić [na-vo-źheećh] v.
fertilize; manure; truck; cart;
fill (a ditch); bring (gravel)
nawóz [na-vooz] m. manure;
dung; muck; fertilizer
na wpół [na vpoow] adv. half;
semi-; half-(finished, boiled)
nawracać [na-vra-tsaćh] v. turn
around; convert; turn back
nawrócenie [na-vroo-tse-ńe] n.
conversion; being converted
nawrót [na-vroot] m. return;
relapse; recurrence; set-back
na wskroś [na vskrośh] adv.
throughout; from end to end
nawyk [na-vik] m. habit; wont
nawykać [na-vi-kaćh] v.
accustom; fall into a habit
nawykły [na-vik-wi] adj. m.
accustomed; get used to...
na wylot [na vi-lot] adv. through
and through; right through
nawymyślać [na-vi-mi-śhlaćh]
v. revile; abuse; insult; invent
na wyrywki [na vi-riv-kee] adv.
at random; haphazardly
nawzajem [na-vza-yem] adv.
mutually; same to you
na wznak [na vznak] adv. on
one's back; supine
nazad [na-zat] adv. back (wards)
nazajutrz [na-za-yootsh] adv.
next morning; next day
nazbierać [naz-bye-raćh] v.
gather up; collect; assemble
nazbyt [naz-bit] adv. too much
na zewnątrz [na zev-nowntsh]
adv. out; outward; outside
naznaczyć [na-zna-chićh] v.
mark; fix; appoint; outline

nazwa [naz-va] f. designation; name; appellation; title

nazwisko [naz-vees-ko] n. family name; surname; reputation

nazywać [na-zi-vaćh] v. call; name; term; denominate; label; christen; give a name

nażarty [na-zhar-ti] adj. m. gorged; stuffed (greedily)

nażreć się [na-zhrećh śhan] v. gorge; stuff oneself (vulg.)

negacja [ne-gats-ya] f. negation; opposite of positive

negatyw [ne-ga-tiv] m. negative

negatywny [ne-ga-tiv-ni] adj. m. negative; saying "no"

negliż [ne-gleesh] m. undress; morning dress; dishabille

negocjacje [ne-go-tsya-tsye] pl. negotiations; settling a treaty

negować [ne-go-vaćh] v. deny

nekrolog [ne-kro-log] m. obituary notice; obituary

nektar [nek-tar] m. nectar

neofita [ne-o-fee-ta] m. convert; neophyte; proselyte

neologizm [ne-o-lo-geezm] m. neologism; new word; new meaning; new coined word

neon [ne-on] m. neon light

nepotyzm [ne-po-tizm] m. nepotism; favoritism shown to relatives in securing jobs, etc.

nerka [ner-ka] f. kidney

nerw [nerv] m. nerve; vigor; ardor; coolness in danger

nerwica [ner-vee-tsa] f. neurosis; nervous disturbance

nerwoból [ner-vo-bool] m. neuralgia; severe pain along a nerve; neuralgy

nerwowość [ner-vo-vośhćh] f. nervosity; irritability; fidgets

nerwowy [ner-vo-vi] adj. m. nervous (breakdown); made up of nerves; fearful; excitable

neseser [ne-se-ser] m. dressing case; make-up case

netto [net-to] adv. net (cost, price, profit, weight, result)

neutralizować [ne-oo-tra-lee-zo-vaćh] v. neutralize

neutralność [ne-oo-tral-

-nośhćh] f. neutrality; neutral status; impartiality

neutralny [ne-oo-tral-ni] adj. m. neutral; indifferent

neutron [ne-oo-tron] m. neutron

newralgia [ne-vral-gya] f. neuralgia; pain along a nerve

newroza [nev-ro-za] f. neurosis

nącić [nan-ćheećh] v. entice; court; allure; tempt; be seductive; be inviting; tantalize

nędza [nan-dza] f. misery

nędzarz [nan-dzash] m. destitute wretch; beggar; pauper

nędznik [nan-dźńeek] villain

nędzny [nandz-ni] adj. m. wretched; miserable; shabby; sorry; beggarly; abject; trashy

nąkać [nan-kaćh] v. molest; hurry; torment; harass; annoy; worry; gnaw; press hard

ni to ni owo [ńee to ńee o-vo] adv. neither this nor that

ni stąd ni zowąd [ńee stownt ńee zo-vownt] without any reason; suddenly; for no reason whatever; unexpectedly

niania [ńa-ńa] f. (baby's) nurse; nanny; dry nurse

niańczyć [ńań-chićh] v. nurse

niańka [ńań-ka] f. nurse

niby [ńee-bi] adv. as if; pretending; as it were; like; a sort of; as though; supposedly

nic [ńeets] pron. nothing at all; not a bit; nothing whatever

nic a nic [ńeets ah ńeets] expr.: nothing at all; nothing whatever; not a bit

nic nie szkodzi [ńeets ńe shko-dźhee] expr.: does not matter; do not mention it!

nic z tego [ńeets z te-go] expr.: no use; to no purpose; to no avail; no use for it

nici [ńee-ćhee] f. pl. 1. threads 2. nothing; nothing of it

nici będą z tego [ńee-ćhee ban-down s te-go] it will come to nothing; it will do no good

nicość [ńee-tsośhćh] f. nothingness; oblivion; nihility; nonentity; a mere nothing

nicpoń [ńeets-poń] m. good-for
-nothing; "nogoodnik"; scamp
niczego [ńee-che-go] pron. not
bad; quite good; ont unsightly
niczyj [ńee-chiy] adj. m. nobody's; no one's; ownerless
nić [ńeećh] f. thread
nie [ńe] part. no; not (any)
nie jeszcze [ńe yesh-che] not
yet; not for a long time
nieagresja [ńe-a-gre-sya] f.
nonaggression (treaty or pact)
nieaktualny [ńe-ak-too-al-ni] adj.
m. out of date; off the map;
no longer considered; stale
nieaktywny [ńe-ak-tiv-ni] adj. m.
niebaczny [ńe-bach-ni] adj. m.
imprudent; rush; inconsiderate
niebawem [ńe-ba-vem] adv. by
and by; before long; soon
niebezpieczeństwo [ńe-bez-pye-
-cheń-stvo] n. danger; peril
niebezpieczny [ńe-bez-pyech-ni]
adj. m. dangerous; risky;
tricky; unsafe; hazardous
niebiański [ńe-byań-skee]
adj. m. heavenly; divine
niebieskawy [ńe-bye-ska-vi] adj.
m. bluish; off blue
niebieski [ńe-byes-kee] adj. m.
blue; heavenly; of the sky
niebieskooki [ńe-byes-ko-o-kee]
adj. m. blue-eyed
niebiosa [ńe-byo-sa] pl.
Heavens; the visible sky
niebo [ńe-bo] n. sky
nieborak [ńe-bo-rak] m. poor
soul; poor devil
nieboszczyk [ńe-bosh-chik] m.
deceased; dead person
niebosiążny [ńe-bo-shanzh-ni]
adj. m. sky-high; towering
niebotyczny [ńe-bo-tich-ni] adj.
m. sky-high; sky reaching
nieboże [ńe-bo-zhe] n. poor
soul; poor thing; poor devil
nie byle jak [ńe bi-le yak]
expr.:not just any way; not
carelessly; unusually well
niebyły [ńe-bi-wi] adj. m. null
and void; non-existent
niebywale [ńe-bi-va-le] adv.
unusually; exceptionally

niebywały [ńe-bi-va-wi] adj. m.
unheard-of; unusual; uncommon; unparalleled; exceptional
niecały [ńe-tsa-wi] adj. m.
incomplete; defective; fragmentary; somewhat less than
niecenzuralny [ńe-tsen-zoo-ral-
-ni] adj. m. indecent; un-
printable; obscene; suggestive;
coarse; broad; ribald
niech [ńekh] part. let; suppose
niechcący [ńekh-tsown-tsi] adv.
unintentionally; unawares
niechęć [ńe-khańćh] f.
disinclination; aversion; ill-will
niechętny [ńe-khant-ni] adj. m.
unwilling; reluctant; averse
niechluj [ńe-khluy] m. grub;
sloppy; dirty; sloven; pig; slut
niechybny [ńe-khib-ni] adj. m.
without fail; certain; unerring
niechże [ńekh-zhe] part. let
niecić [ńe-ćheećh] v. kindle;
stir up; light (a fire)
nieciekawy [ńe-ćhe-ka-vi]
adj. m. blank; void of interest
niecierpliwić się [ńe-ćher-plee-
-veećh śhan] v. be impatient
niecierpliwy [ńe-ćher-plee-vi]
adj. m. impatient; restless
niecnota [ńets-no-ta] m. scamp;
rogue; rascal; roguery; infamy
niecny [ńets-ni] adj. m. vile
nieco [ńe-tso] adv. somewhat; a
little; a trifle; slightly
niecodzienny [ńe-tso-dźhen-ni]
adj. m. uncommon; unusual
nieczesany [ńe-che-sa-ni]
adj. m. unkempt; disorderly
nieczęsty [ńe-chan-sti] adj. m.
infrequent; not frequent
nieczuły [ńe-choo-wi] adj. m.
callous; heartless; insensible
nieczynny [ńe-chin-ni] adj. m.
inert; inactive; out of order
nieczysty [ńe-chis-ti] adj. m.
unclean; polluted; dirty; shady
nieczytelny [ńe-chi-tel-ni] adj. m.
illegible; cramped; crabbed
niedaleki [ńe-da-le-kee] adj. m.
near; not distant; at hand
niedaleko [ńe-da-le-ko] adv.
near; not far; a short way off

niedawno [ńe-**dav**-no] adv.
recently; not long ago; newly
niedbale [ńed-ba-le] adv. neg-
lectfully; carelessly; casually;
nonchalantly; heedlessly
niedbalstwo [ńed-**bal**-stvo] n.
negligence; laxity; care-
lessness; laxity; nonchalance
niedbały [ńed-ba-wi] adj. m.
negligent; untidy; lax; careless
niedługi [ńed-**woo**-gee] adj. m.
short; not long; brief; curt
niedługo [ńed-**woo**-go] adv.
soon; not long; before long;
by and by; a short time
niedobitki [ńe-do-**beet**-kee] pl.
survivors; routed soldiers
niedobór [ńe-do-boor] m. deficit;
shortage; scarcity; loss
niedobrany [ńe-do-**bra**-ni] adj. m.
ill-suited; ill-matched
niedobry [ńe-do-bri] adj. m. no
-good; bad; wicked; nasty
niedobrze [ńe-**dob**-zhe] adv. not
well; badly; wrong; improperly
nie doceniać [ńe do-tse-ńaćh]
v. underestimate; estimate too
low; set too low an estimate
niedociągnięcie [ńe-do-ćhown-
-gńan-́che] n. shortcoming
niedogodność [ńe-do-god-
-nośhćh] f. inconvenience;
drawback; lack of comfort
niedogodny [ńe-do-god-ni]
adj. m. inconvenient; undesirable; causing bother, etc.
niedogotowany [ńe-do-go-to-**va**-
-ni] adj. m. underdone; half-
cooked; half-raw
nie dojadać [ńe do-**ya**-daćh] v.
under-nourish; not eat enough
niedojda [ńe-**doy**-da] m. nitwit;
bungler; fumbler; lout
niedojrzały [ńe-doy-**zha**-wi] adj.
m. unripe; immature; under
age; green; raw; half-grown
niedokładny [ńe-do-**kwad**-ni] adj.
m. inaccurate; inexact
niedokończony [ńe-do-koń-**cho**-
-ni] adj. m. unfinished;
incomplete; uncompleted
niedokrwisty [ńe-do-**krvees**-ti]
adj. m. anemic; anaemic

niedola [ńe-do-la] f. adversity
niedołęga [ńe-do-**wan**-ga] m.
blunderer; cripple; duffer
niedołęstwo [ńe-do-**wans**-tvo] n.
inefficiency; clumsiness
niedomagać [ńe-do-ma-gaćh]
v. be unwell; be ailing
nie domknięty [ńe dom-**kńan**-ti]
adj. m. ajar; slightly open
niedomówienie [ńe-do-moo-**vye**-
-ńe] n. vague hint; insinuation
niedomyślny [ńe-do-**miśhl**-ni]
adj. m. slow thinking
niedopałek [ńe-do-**pa**-wek] m.
(cigarette) butt; stub; ember
niedopatrzenie [ńe-do-pa-**tshe**-
-ńe] n. oversight; neglect
niedopuszczalny [ńe-do-**poosh**-
-chal-ni] adj. m. inadmissible
niedorozwinięty [ńe-do-roz-vee-
-ńan-ti] adj. m. under-
developed; mentally retarded
niedorzeczność [ńe-do-**zhech**-
-nośhćh] f. (pure) nonsense
niedorzeczny [ńe-do-**zhech**-ni]
adj. m. absurd; ridiculous;
nonsensical; ludicrous
niedoskonały [ńe-do-sko-**na**-wi]
adj. m. imperfect; deficient
niedosłyszalny [ńe-do-swi-**shal**-
-ni] adj. m. inaudible
niedosmażony [ńe-do-sma-**zho**-
-ni] adj. m. underdone
nie dospać [ńe dos-paćh] v.
sleep too short time
niedostateczny [ńe-do-sta-**tech**-
-ni] adj. m. insufficient
niedostatek [ńe-do-**sta**-tek] m.
shortage; indigence; poverty
niedostępny [ńe-do-**stan**-pni]
adj. m. inaccessible; out of
reach; unattainable
niedostosowanie [ńe-do-sto-so-
-va-ńe] n. maladjustment
niedostrzegalny [ńe-do-stzhe-**gal**-
-ni] adj. m. imperceptible
niedościgły [ńe-do-**śhćheeg**-
-wi] adj. m. matchless; in-
imitable; peerless; unique
niedoświadczenie [ńe-do-
-śhvyad-**che**-ńe] n. inexperience; lack of experience
niedouczony [ńe-do-oo-**cho**-ni]

adj. m. half-educated
nie dowarzony [ńe do-va-zho-ni]
half-boiled; rough; immature
niedowiarek [ńe-do-vya-rek] m.
unbeliever; atheist; skeptic
niedowidzieć [ńe-do-vee-
-dźhećh] v. be short-sighted
nie dowierzać [ńe do-vye-
-zhaćh] v. distrust; disbelieve
niedowład [ńe-do-vwat] m.
paresis; partial paralysis
niedozwolony [ne-do-zvo-lo-ni]
adj. m. not allowed; illicit
niedrogi [ńe-dro-gee] adj. m.
cheap; inexpensive; low priced
nieduży [ńe-doo-zhi] adj. m.
small; little; not big; not tall
niedwuznaczny [ńe-dvoo-znach-
-ni] adj. m. unequivocal; clear
niedyskrecja [ńe-di-skrets-ya] f.
indiscretion; indelicacy
niedyspozycja [ńe-di-spo-zits-ya]
f. indisposition; ill-health
niedziela [ńe-dźhe-la] f. Sunday
niedźwiadek [ńe-dźhvya-dek]
m. bear cub; Teddy bear
niedźwiedzica [ńedźh-vye-
-dźhee-tsa] f. female bear
niedźwiedź [ńedźh-vyedźh]
m. bear; bearskin; clumsy man
nieelastyczny [ńe-e-la-stich-ni]
adj. m. inelastic
nieestetyczny [ńe-e-ste-tich-ni]
adj. m. unesthetic
nieetyczny [ńe-e-tich-ni] adj. m.
unethical; immoral
niefachowy [ńe-fa-kho-vi] adj.
m. incompetent; inexpert; unprofessional; amateurish
nieforemny [ńe-fo-rem-ni]
adj. m. shapeless; deformed
nieformalnie [ńe-for-mal-ńe]
adv. informally; illegally
niefortunny [ńe-for-toon-ni] adj.
m. unlucky; regrettable
niefrasobliwy [ńe-fra-so-blee-vi]
adj. m. care-free; jaunty
niegdyś [ńeg-diśh] adv.
formerly; once; at one time
niegodny [ńe-god-ni] adj. m.
unworthy; undignified; vile;
base; discreditable; shameful
niegodziwy [ńe-go-dźhee-vi]

adj. m. wicked; vile; base;
mean; foul; unscrupulous
niegościnny [ńe-go-śhćheen-
-ni] adj. m. inhospitable; desolate; forbidding; bleak
niegrzeczny [ne-gzhech-ni] adj.
m. rude; impolite; unkind; bad
niegustowny [ńe-goo-stov-ni]
adj. m. tasteless; in bad taste
niehigieniczny [ńe-khee-gye-
-ńeech-ni] adj. m. unsanitary
niehonorowy [ńe-kho-no-ro-vi]
adj. m. dishonorable; unfair
nieistotny [ńe-ee-stot-ni] adj. m.
inessential; immaterial
niejaki [ńe-ya-kee] adj. m. one;
certain; some; slight
niejasno [ńe-yas-no] adv. dimly;
vaguely; ambiguously; darkly;
obscurely; indistinctly
niejasny [ńe-yas-ni] adj. m. dim;
unclear; indistinct; vague; obscure; ambiguous; hazy; foggy
niejeden [ńe-ye-den] adj. m.
many a; quite a number
niejednokrotnie [ńe-yed-no-krot-
-ńe] adv. repeatedly; recur-
rently; more than once
nie karany [ńe ka-ra-ni] adj. m.
with a clean record; not
convicted before
niekiedy [ńe-ke-di] adv. now
and then; sometimes; at times
niekonsekwentny [ńe-kon-se-
-kvent-ni] adj. m. inconsistent
niekorzystny [ńe-ko-zhist-ni] adj.
m. disadvantageous
niekorzyść [ńe-ko-zhiśhćh] f.
disadvantage; detriment
niekształtny [ńe-kshtawt-ni] adj.
m. unshapely; formless
niektóry [ńe-ktoo-ri] adj. m.
some; one here and there
nieledwie [ńe-led-vye] adv. all
but; almost; practically
nielegalny [ńe-le-gal-ni] adj. m.
illegal; unlawful; illicit
nieletni [ńe-let-ńee] pl. under
age; juvenile; minor
nieliczny [ńe-leech-ni] adj. m.
not numerous; scarce; rare;
small; pl. some few; rare
nielitościwy [ńe-lee-to-

-śhćhee-vi] adj. m. unmerci-
ful; pitiless; ruthless
nielogiczny [ne-lo-**geech**-ni] adj.
m. illogical; nonsensical;
nieludzki [ńe-**loodz**-kee] adj. m.
inhuman; atrocious; ruthless
nieład [ńe-wad] m. disorder;
disarray; confusion; mess
nieładnie [ńe-**wad**-ńe] adv. not
nicely; unattractively; wrongly
niełaska [ńe-**was**-ka] f. disgrace;
disfavor; loss of respect
niemal [ńe-mal] adv. almost;
nearly; pretty nearly; well-nigh
niemało [ńe-ma-wo] adv. not a
few; pretty much; not a little
niemały [ńe-ma-wi] adj. m.
pretty big; fair-sized; goodly;
no mean; of considerable size
niemądry [ńe-**mown**-dri] adj. m.
unwise; ill-judged; silly; stupid
niemczyć [ńem-chićh] v.
Germanize (under pressure)
niemęski [ńe-**man**-skee] adj. m.
unmanly (without nerve, etc.)
niemiecki [ńe-**myets**-kee] adj. m.
German; German language
niemiły [ńe-**mee**-wi] adj. m.
unpleasant; unsightly; harsh;
surly; disagreeable; offensive
niemniej jednak [**ńem**-ńey yed-
-nak] nevertheless; all the
same; none the less; however
niemoc [ńe-mots] f. impotence
niemodny [ńe-**mod**-ni] adj. m.
outmoded; out of fashion
niemoralny [ńe-mo-**ral**-ni] adj. m.
immoral; dishonest; depraved
niemowa [ńe-mo-va] m. & f.
mute; dumb; speechless
niemowlę [ńe-mo-vlan] n. baby
niemożliwy [ńe-mo-**zhlee**-vi] adj.
m. impossible; unfeasible
niemrawy [ńe-mra-vi] adj. m.
sluggish; tardy; indolent
niemy [ńe-mi] adj. m. dumb
nienaganny [ńe-na-**gan**-ni]
adj. m. blameless; faultless
ninaruszalny [ńe-na-roo-**shal**-ni]
adj. m. inviolable; sacred
nienaruszony [ńe-na-roo-**sho**-ni]
adj. m. intact; undisturbed
nienasycony [ńe-na-si-co-ni] adj.

m. insatiable; voracious;
(chem. unsaturated)
nienaturalny [ńe-na-too-**ral**-ni]
adj. m. unnatural; insincere
nienawistny [ńe-na-**veest**-ni] adj.
m. hateful; full of hatred
nienawiść [ńe-na-**veeśhćh**] f.
hate; abomination; detestation
nie nazwany [ńe na-**zva**-ni] adj.
m. unnamed; not maned
nienormalny [ńe-nor-**mal**-ni] adj.
m. abnormal; insane
nieobecność [ńe-o-**bets**-
-nośhćh] f. absence; non-
attendance; truancy
nieobecny [ńe-o-**bets**-ni] adj. m.
absent; not present; not in
nieobeznany [ńe-o-bez-**na**-ni]
adj. m. uninformed; ignorant
nieobliczalny [ńe-o-blee-**chal**-ni]
adj. m. unreliable; incalculable;
irresponsible; unpredictable
nieobyczajny [ńe-o-bi-**chay**-ni]
adj. m. immoral; ill-mannered
nieoceniony [ńe-o-tse-**ńo**-ni]
adj. m. inestimable; priceless
nieoczekiwany [ńe-o-che-kee-**va**-
-ni] adj. m. unexpected
nieodłączny [ńe-o-**dwown**-chni]
adj. m. inseparable; inherent
nieodmienny [ńe-od-**myen**-ni]
adj. m. invariable; undeclinable
nieodparty [ńe-od-**par**-ti] adj. m.
irrefutable; compelling; cogent
nieodpowiedni [ńe-od-po-**vyed**-
-ńee] adj. m. inadequate; inappropriate; improper; wrong
nieodpowiedzialny [ńe-od-po-
-vye-dźhal-ni] adj. m. irresponsible; unpredictable
nieodstępny [ńe-od-**stanp**-ni]
adj. m. inseparable
nieodwołalny [ńe-od-vo-**wal**-ni]
adj. m. irrevocable; final;
irreversible; beyond recall
nieodzownie [ńe-od-**zov**-ńe]
adv. inevitably; absolutely
nieodzowny [ńe-od-**zov**-ni] adj.
m. indispensable; irrevocable
nieodżałowany [ńe-od-zha-wo-
-va-ni] adj. m. never enough
regretted; much regretted
nieoględny [ńe-o-**gland**-ni]

adj. m. inconsiderate; reckless; rash; heedless; too hasty

nieograniczony [ńe-o-gra-ńee--cho-ni] adj. m. infinite; boundless; unrestricted; unstinted; unlimited; indefinite; absolute

nieokiełzany [ńe-o-kew-za-ni] adj. m. unbridled; rampant; reinless; uncontrollable

nieokreślony [ńe-o-kre-śhlo-ni] adj. m. indefinite; undetermined; nondescript; uncertain

nieokrzesany [ńe-o-kzhe-sa-ni] adj. m. rude; crude; ill-mannered; coarse; uncouth

nieomal [ńe-o-mal] adv. almost; pretty nearly; practically

nieomylny [ńe-o-mil-ni] adj. m. infallible; unerring; sure

nieopatrzny [ńe-o-patsh-ni] adj. m. unguarded; inconsiderate

nieopisany [ńe-o-pee-sa-ni] adj. m. indescribable; excessive; extreme; inexpressible

nieopłacalny [ńe-o-pwa-tsal-ni] adj. m. unprofitable

nieopłacony [ńe-o-pwa-tso-ni] adj. m. unpaid; not paid for

nieopodal [ne-o-po-dal] adv. near by; close at hand; next door

nieorganiczny [ńe-or-ga-ńeech--ni] adj. m. inorganic (compound); inanimate

nieosobowy [ńe-o-so-bo-vi] adj. m. inpersonal; not personal

nieostrożny [ńe-o-strozh-ni] adj. m. careless; imprudent

nieoswojony [ńe-o-svo-yo-ni] adj. m. untamed; unfamiliar

nieoświecony [ńe-o-śhvye-tso--ni] adj. m. dark; ignorant

nieoznaczony [ńe-oz-na-cho-ni] adj. m. indefinite; unmarked

niepalący [ńe-pa-lown-tsi] adj. m. not smoking; non smoking; m. non-smoker

niepalność [ńe-pal-nośhćh] f. incombustibility

niepalny [ńe-pal-ni] adj. m. incombustible; uninflammable

niepamięć [ńe-pa-myanćh] f. oblivion; forgetfulness; unconsciousness; negligence

niepamiętny [ne-pa-myant-ni] adj. m. forgetful; immemorial

nieparlamentarny [ńe-par-la-men--tar-ni] adj. m. rough (language); using vulgar words

nieparzysty [ńe-pa-zhis-ti] adj. m. odd; uneven; unpaired

niepełnoletni [ńe-pew-no-let--ńee] adj. m. minor; underage

niepewność [ńe-pev-nośhćh] f. uncertainty; incertitude

niepewny [ńe-pev-ni] adj. m. uncertain; insecure; unsafe

niepisany [ńe-pee-sa-ni] adj. m. unwritten; not in writing

niepiśmienny [ńe-peeśh-myen--ni] adj. m. illiterate; unlettered

niepłacący [ńe-pwa-tsown-tsi] adj. m. non-paying

niepłodny [ńe-pwod-ni] adj. m. sterile; barren; infertile

niepłonny [ńe-pwon-ni] adj. m. well-founded; motivated

niepochlebny [ńe-po-khleb-ni] adj. m. unfavorable

niepocieszony [ńe-po-ćhe-sho--ni] adj. m. desolate

niepoczciwy [ńe-po-chćhee-vi] adj. m. wicked; unkind

niepoczytalny [ńe-po-chi-tal-ni] adj. m. irresponsible; insane

niepodejrzany [ńe-po-dey-zha-ni] adj. m. unsuspected

niepodległość [ńe-po-dleg--wośhćh] f. independence; sovereignty (of state, ruler)

niepodległy [ńe-po-dleg-wi] adj. m. independent; sovereign

niepodobieństwo [ńe-po-do--byeń-stvo] n. impossibility

niepodobna [ńe-po-dob-na] adv. it's impossible; there is no way; one cannot possibly

niepodobny [ńe-po-dob-ni] adj. m. (altogether) unlike; unlikely; (quite) dissimilar

niepodzielny [ńe-po-dźhel-ni] adj. m. indivisible; undivided

niepogoda [ńe-po-go-da] f. bad weather; foul weather

niepogwałcony [ńe-po-gvaw-tso--ni] adj. m. inviolate

niepohamowany [ńe-po-kha-mo-

-va-ni] adj. m. unrestrained
niepojętny [ńe-po-**yant**-ni]
adj. m. dull (man); stupid
niepojęty [ńe-po-**yan**-ti] adj. m.
inconceivable; incomprehensible; unimaginable; beyond
understanding
niepokalany [ńe-po-ka-**la**-ni] adj.
m. immaculate; faultless
niepokaźny [ńe-po-**kaźh**-ni]
adj. m. inconspicuous; modest; plain; shabby; wretched
niepokoić [ńe-po-ko-**eećh**] v.
disturb; trouble; annoy; pester
niepokonany [ńe-po-ko-**na**-ni]
adj. m. invincible; irresistible
niepokój [ńe-po-**kooy**] m. anxiety; unrest; trouble; agitation; concern; worry; disquiet
niepolityczny [ńe-po-lee-**tich**-ni]
adj. m. impolitical; inexpedient; improper; impolitic; nonpolitical; injudicious
niepomierny [ńe-po-**myer**-ni] adj.
m. excessive; extreme
niepomny [ńe-**pom**-ni] adj. m.
forgetful; oblivious
niepomyślny [ńe-po-**miśhl**-ni]
adj. m. adverse; unlucky
niepopłatny [ńe-po-**pwat**-ni] adj.
m. unprofitable; unrewarding
niepoprawny [ńe-po-**prav**-ni] adj.
m. incorrigible; incorrect
niepopularny [ńe-po-poo-**lar**-ni]
adj. m. unpopular
nieporadny [ńe-po-**rad**-ni] adj. m.
awkward; helpless; unskillful
nieporęczny [ne-po-**ranch**-ni] adj.
m. cumbersome; unhandy
nieporozumienie [ńe-po-ro-zoo-
-**mye**-ńe] n. misunderstanding
nieporównany [ńe-po-roov-**na**-ni]
adj. m. incomparable
nieporuszony [ńe-po-roo-**sho**-ni]
adj. m. immovable; firm
nieporządek [ńe-po-**zhown**-dek]
adj. m. disorder; mess
nieporządny [ńe-po-**zhownd**-ni]
adj. m. disorderly; untidy;
messy; slipshod; chaotic
nieposłuszeństwo [ńe-po-swoo-
-**sheń**-stvo] n. disobedience
nieposłuszny [ńe-po-**swoosh**-ni]

adj. m. disobedient; unruly
niepospolity [ńe-pos-po-**lee**-ti]
adj. m. uncommon; rare
niepostrzeżenie [ńe-po-stshe-
-**zhe**-ńe] adv. imperceptibly;
without being noticed
niepotrzebny [ńe-po-**tzheb**-ni]
adj. m. unnecessary; useless
niepowetowany [ńe-po-ve-to-
va-ni] adj. m. irreparable
niepowodzenie [ńe-po-vo-**dze**-
-ńe] n. failure; adversity
niepowołany [ńe-po-vo-**wa**-ni]
adj. m. uncalled for; incompetent; unfit; undesirable; wrong
niepowrotny [ńe-pov-**rot**-ni] adj.
m. irrevocable; irrecoverable;
beyond recall; irretrievable
niepowsrzymany [ńe-pov-stzhi-
-ma-ni] adj. m. irresistible
niepowszedni [ńe-pov-**shed**-ńee]
adj. m. uncommon; unusually
good; exceptional
niepowściągliwy [ńe-pov-
-śhćh<u>own</u>-**lee**-vi] adj. m.
intemperate; uncontrollable
niepozorny [ńe-po-**zor**-ni] adj. m.
inconspicuous; modest
niepożądany [ńe-po-zh<u>own</u>-**da**-
-ni] adj. m. undesirable; unwanted; objectionable
niepożyteczny [ńe-po-zhi-**tech**-
-ni] adj. m. useless; unprofitable; to no purpose
niepraktyczny [ńe-prak-**tich**-ni]
adj. m. impractical; unwieldy
niepraktykujący [ńe-prak-ti-koo-
-y<u>own</u>-tsi] adj. m. noncommunicant; retired (professional)
nieprawda [ńe-**prav**-da] f.
untruth; falsehood; lie; exp.:
impossible! isn't that so?
nieprawdopodobny [ńe-prav-do-
-po-**dob**-ni] adj. m. improbable
nieprawdziwy [ńe-prav-**dźhee**-
-vi] adj. m. untrue; false; bogus; faked; fictitious; unreal
nieprawidłowość [ńe-pra-vee-
-dwo-**vośhćh**] f. anomaly; irregularity; falsity; incorrectness; abnormality; faultiness
nieprawidłowy [ńe-pra-vee-
dwo-vi] adj. m. anomalous;

irregular; contrary to the rules
nieprawny [ńe-prav-ni] adj. m.
illegal; unlawful; invalid
nieprawomyślny [ńe-pra-vo-
-miśhl-ni] adj. m. unorthodox;
disloyal; unfaithful; not loyal
nieprawy [ńe-pra-vi] adj. m.
unrighteous; adulterous;
bastard; unlawful; illegitimate
nieproporcjonalny [ńe-pro-por-
-tsyo-nal-ni] adj. m. dispro-
portional; out of proportion
nieproszony [ńe-pro-sho-ni] adj.
m. uncalled for; self-invited;
unwelcome (guest)
nieprzebaczalny [ńe-pzhe-ba-
chal-ni] adj. m. unpardonable
nieprzebłagany [ńe-pzhe-bwa-
ga-ni] adj. m. implacable
nieprzebrany [ńe-pzhe-bra-ni]
adj. inexhaustible; countless
nieprzebyty [ńe-pzhe-bi-ti]
adj. m. impassable
nieprzejednany [ńe-pzhe-yed-na-
-ni] adj. m. irreconcilable; un-
compromising; implacable
nieprzejrzysty [ńe-pzhey-zhis-ti]
adj. m. not clear; opaque
nieprzekupny [ńe-pzhe-koop-ni]
adj. m. unbribable; incorrupt-
ible; refusing to take bribes
nieprzemakalny [ńe-pzhe-ma-kal-
-ni] adj. m. waterproof
nieprzeniknony [ńe-pzhe-ńeek-
-ńo-ni] adj. m. impenetrable;
impassable (area); inscrutable
nieprzepuszczalny [ńe-pzhe-
-poosh-chal-ni] adj. m.
impervious; impenetrable
nieprzerwany [ńe-pzher-va-ni]
adj. m. continuous; ceaseless
nieprześcigniony [ńe-pzheśh-
-ćheeg-ńo-ni] adj. m.
unsurpassable; unexcelled
nieprzewidziany [ńe-pzhe-vee-
-dźha-ni] adj. m. unforeseen
nieprzezorny [ńe-pzhe-zor-ni]
adj. m. improvident; unforsee-
ing; wanting of foresight
niprzeźroczysty [ńe-pzhe-źhro-
-chis-ti] adj. m. opaque
nieprzezwyciężony [ńe-pzhez-vi-
-ćhan-zho-ni] adj. m.

invincible; insurmountable
nieprzychylny [ńe-pzhi-khil-ni]
adj. m. unfriendly; prejudiced
nieprzydatny [ńe-pzhi-dat-ni] adj.
m. useless; unserviceable
nieprzygotowany [ńe-pzhi-go-to-
-va-ni] adj. m. unprepared
nieprzyjaciel [ńe-pzhi-ya-ćhel]
m. enemy; foe; ill-wisher
nieprzyjacielski [ńe-pzhi-ya-ćhel-
-skee] adj. m. enemy; hostile;
enemy's (tanks, guns, etc.)
nieprzyjazny [ńe-pzhi-yaz-ni] adj.
m. unfriendly; inimical
nieprzyjaźń [ńe-pzhi-yaźhń] f.
hostility; unfriendliness
nieprzyjemność [ńe-pzhi-yem-
-nośhćh] f. unpleasantness
nieprzyjemny [ńe-pzhi-yem-ni]
adj. m. unpleasant; disagee-
able; distasteful; annoying
nieprzystępny [ńe-pzhis-tanp-ni]
adj. m. inaccessible; grumpy
nieprzytomność [ńe-pzhi-tom-
-nośhćh] f. unconsciousness;
absentmindedness; senseless-
ness; foolishness
nieprzytomny [ńe-pzhi-tom-ni]
adj. m. unconscious; absent-
minded; frantic; mad; wild
nieprzyzwoitość [ńe-pzhi-zvo-
-ee-tośhćh] f. indecency
nieprzyzwoity [ńe-pzhi-zvo-ee-ti]
adj. m. indecent; obscene
nieprzyzwyczajony [ńe-pzhiz-vi-
-cha-yo-ni] adj. m. not
accustomed to; unaccustomed
niepunktualny [ńe-poon-ktoo-al-
-ni] adj. m. unpunctual; late
nierad [ńe-rad] adj. m. unwilling;
annoyed; adv. unwillingly
nieraz [ńe-raz] adv. often; again
and again; many a time
nierdzewny [ńe-rdzev-ni] adj. m.
rustproof; stainless; rustless
nierealny [ńe-re-al-ni] adj. m.
imaginary; unreal; unrealizable
nieregularność [ńe-re-goo-lar-
-nośhćh] f. irregularity
nieregularny [ńe-re-goo-lar-ni]
adj. m. irregular; erratic
nierelgijny [ńe-re-lee-geey-ni]
adj. m. not religious; profane;

impious; irreligious
nierogacizna [ńe-ro-ga-**ćheez**-
-na] f. pl. swines; hogs
nierozdzielny [ńe-roz-**dźhel**-ni]
adj. m. inseparable
nierozerwalny [ńe-ro-zer-**val**-ni]
adj. m. indissoluble
nierozgarnięty [ńe-roz-gar-**ńan**-
-ti] adj. m. dull; (dim-witted)
nieskuteczny [ńe-skoo-**tech**-ni]
adj. m. ineffective; futile
niesłabnący [ńe-swab-**nown**-tsi]
adj. m. unabated; unflagging
niesława [ńe-**swa**-va] f. infamy
niesławny [ńe-**swav**-ni] adj. m.
infamous; inglorious; disgraceful; having a bad reputation
niesłowny [ńe-**swov**-ni] adj. m.
unreliable; undependable
niesłuszność [ńe-**swoosh**-
-ność́h] f. injustice; unfair-
ness; groundlessness
nisłuszny [ńe-**swoosh**-ni] adj. m.
unjust; wrong; groundless
niesłychany [ńe-swi-**kha**-ni] adj.
m. unheard of; unprecedented
niesmaczny [ńe-**smach**-ni]
adj. m. tasteless; unsavory;
unseemly; unpalatable; coarse
niesmak [ńes-**mak**] m. bad
taste; disgust; repugnance;
nasty taste (in the mouth)
niesnaski [ńe-**snas**-kee] pl.
dissension; discord; quarrels
niespełna [ńe-**spew**-na] adv.
nearly; not all; not quite;
about; somewhat less than
niespodzianka [ńe-spo-**dźhan**-
-ka] f. surprise; surprise gift
niespodziewany [ńe-spo-dźhe-
-va-ni] adj. m. unexpected;
unlooked for; unforeseen
niespokojny [ńe-spo-**koy**-ni] adj.
m. restless; fussy; upset;
fretful; turbulent; ill at ease
niesporo [ńe-**spo**-ro] adv. slowly
nie sposób [ńe **spo**-soop] adv.
it's impossible; by no means
niespożyty [ńe-spo-**zhi**-ti]
adj. m. durable; indefatigable
niesprawiedliwość [ńe-spra-
-vye-dlee-**vość́h**] f. injustice
niesprawiedliwy [ńe-spra-vyed-

-lee-vi] adj. m. unjust; unfair
niesprawny [ńe-**sprav**-ni] adj. m.
ineffective; inefficient
nie sprzyjający [ńe spzhi-ya-
-**yown**-tsi] adj. m. adverse
niestały [ńe-**sta**-wi] adj. m.
unsteady; inconsistent; variable; fickle; unsteady; shifting
niestaranny [ńe-**sta**-ran-ni]
adj. m. careless; sloppy;
dowdy; neglectful; slapdash
niestateczny [ńe-**sta**-tech-ni] adj.
m. unstable; fickle; flighty
niestety [ńe-**ste**-ti] adv. alas;
unfortunately; exp.: I am sorry
niestosowny [ńe-sto-**sov**-ni] adj.
m. improper; unsuitable; unfit;
inappropriate; out of place
niestrawność [ńe-**strav**-
-ność́h] f. indigestion; dys-
pepsia; difficulty in digesting
niestrawny [ńe-**strav**-ni] adj. m.
indigestible; stodgy; dull
niestrudzony [ńe-stroo-**dzo**-ni]
adj. m. indefatigable; untiring
niestworzony [ńe-stvo-**zho**-ni]
adj. m. unreal; nonsense
niesumienny [ńe-soo-**myen**-ni]
adj. m. unscrupulous; uncon-
scientious; unreliable; careless
nieswojo [ńe-**svo**-yo] adv.
uneasily; strangely; qualmishly
nieswój [ńe-**svooy**] adj. m. ill at
ease; uncomfortable; seedy;
strange; off color
niesymetryczny [ńe-si-met-**rich**-
-ni] adj. m. asymmetrical
niesympatyczny [ńe-sim-pa-**tich**-
-ni] adj. m. unpleasant
nieszczególny [ńe-shche-**gool**-ni]
adj. m. mediocre; so-so
nieszczelny [ńe-**shchel**-ni]
adj. m. leaky; not shut tight
nieszczery [ńe-**shche**-ri] adj. m.
insincere; double dealing
nieszczęsny [ńe-**shchans**-ni] adj.
m. miserable; ill-fated
nieszczęście [ńe-**shchan**-
-ść́he] n. misfortune; disaster; adversity; bad luck
nieszczęśliwy [ńe-**shchan**-
-ść́hlee -vi] adj. m. unhappy;
ill-starred; luckless; wretched

nieszkodliwy [ńe-shko-dlee-vi] adj. m. harmless; not grave; inoffensive; innoxious

nieszlachcic [ńe-shlakh-ćheets] m. commoner (not a noble)

nieszpetny [ńe-shpet-ni] adj. m. fairly good-looking

nieszpory [ńe-shpo-ri] pl. vespers; evening prayers

nieścisły [ńe-śhćhees-wi] adj. m. inexact; inaccurate; faulty; imprecise; incoherent

nieściśliwy [ńe-śhćheeśh-lee- -vi] adj. m. incompressible

nieść [ńeśhćh] v. carry; bring; bear; lay; afford; drive; bear along; give as a sacrifice

nieślubny [ńe-śhloob-ni] adj. m. illegitimate; born out of wedlock; natural

nieśmiały [ńe-śhmya-wi] adj. m. coy; shy; timid; faint-hearted; bashful; sheepish

nieśmiertelny [ńe-śhmyer-tel- -ni] adj. m. immortal; ever-lasting; undying; imperishable

nieświadomy [ńe-śhvya-do-mi] adj. m. ignorant (of); unaware; unknowing (of); involuntary

nietakt [ńe-takt] m. lack of tact; slip; tactlessness; indelicacy

nietaktowny [ńe-tak-tov-ni] adj. m. tactless; indelicate

nietknięty [ńe-tkńan-ti] adj. m. intact; virgin; untouched

nietolerancja [ńe-to-le-ran-tsya] f. intolerance

nietoperz [ńe-to-pesh] m. bat

nietowarzyski [ńe-to-va-zhis-kee] adj. m. unsociable

nietrafny [ńe-traf-ni] adj. m. wrong; missing the mark

nietrzeźwy [ńe-tzheźh-vi] adj. m. drank; tipsy; unsound

nietutejszy [ńe-too-tey-shi] adj. m. stranger; non-resident

nietykalny [ńe-ti-kal-ni] adj. m. immune; inviolable

nie tyle [ńe ti-le] adv. not so much; not exactly; but; rather

nie tylko [ńe til-ko] adv. not only; anything but; not merely

nieubłagalny [ńe-oo-bwa-gal-ni] adj. m. implacable; irrevocable

nieuchronny [ńe-oo-khron-ni] adj. m. inevitable; inescapable

nieuchwytny [ńe-oo-khvit-ni] adj. m. elusive; evasive; inaud-ible; imperceptible

nieuctwo [ńe-oots-tvo] n. lack of education; ignorance

nieuczciwy [ńe-ooch-ćhee-vi] adj. m. dishonest; foul; unfair

nieuczynny [ńe-oo-chin-ni] adj. m. unobliging; disobliging

nieudolny [ńe-oo-dol-ni] adj. m. awkward; clumsy; decrepit

nieufny [ńe-oof-ni] adj. m. distrustful; suspicious

nieugaszony [ńe-oo-ga-sho-ni] adj. m. unextinguished; unquenchable; unsuppressible

nieugięty [ńe-oo-gyan-ti] adj. m. inflexible; unyielding

nieuk [ńe-ook] m. know-nothing

nieukojony [ńe-oo-ko-yo-ni] adj. m. inconsolable (grief, etc.)

nieuleczalny [ńe-oo-le-chal-ni] adj. m. incurable

nieumiarkowany [ńe-oo-myar-ko- -va-ni] adj. m. intemperate

nieumiejętny [ńe-oo-mye-yant- -ni] adj. m. inexpert; unskilled

nieumyślny [ńe-oo-miśhl-ni] adj. m. unintentional

nieunikniony [ńe-oo-ńeek-ńo-ni] adj. m. unavoidable; inevitable

nieuprzedzony [ńe-oo-pzhe-dzo- -ni] adj. m. unbiased; not forewarned; not prejudiced

nieuprzejmy [ńe-oo-pzhey-mi] adj. m. impolite; discourteous; unkind; lacking compassion

nieurodzaj [ńe-oo-ro-dzay] m. bad harvest; bad crops; scarcity (of crops, etc.)

nieusprawiedliwiony [ńe-oo- -spra-vye-dlee-vyo-ni] adj. m. unexcused; unjustified

nieustanny [ńe-oos-tan-ni] adj. m. constant; perpetual; un-ceasing; continual; incessant

nieustraszony [ńe-oos-tra-sho-ni] adj. m. fearless; intrepid

nieusuwalny [ńe-oo-soo-val-ni] adj. m. immovable (object);

irremovable (from office)
nie uszkodzony [**ńe** oosh-ko-dzo-
-ni] adj. m. unhurt; not hurt
undamaged; not damaged
nieuwaga [ńe-oo-**va**-ga] f.
inattention; absentmindedness
nieuważny [ńe-oo-**vazh**-ni]
adj. m. inattentive; careless
nieuzasadniony [ńe-oo-za-sad-
-ńo-ni] adj. m. unfounded;
unjustified; groundless
nieuzbrojony [ńe-ooz-bro-**yo**-ni]
adj. m. unarmed; disarmed
nieużyteczny [ńe-oo-zhi-**tech**-ni]
adj. m. useless; superfluous
nieużyty [ńe-oo-**zhi**-ti] adj. m.
unused; not worn; uncoope-
rative; disobliging
niewart [**ńe**-vart] adj. m. not
worth; unworthy (of reward,
praise, etc.); not deserving
nie warto [ńe **var**-to] adv. not
worth (talking about it); not
worthwhile (considering it)
niważny [ńe-**vazh**-ni] adj. m.
invalid; trivial; null and void
niewątpliwy [ńe-vownt-**plee**-vi]
adj. m. sure; doubtless
niewczesny [ńe-**vches**-ni]
adj. m. untimely; late; ill-
timed; inopportune; premature
niewdzięczny [ńe-vdźhanch-ni]
adj. m. ungrateful; thankless
niewesoły [ńe-ve-**so**-wi] adj. m.
sad; joyless; pretty bad
niewiadomy [ńe-vya-**do**-mi] adj.
m. unknown (direction, origin,
quantity, reason, etc.)
niewiara [ńe-**vya**-ra] f. disbelief
(in); mistrust (of); unbelief
niewiasta [ńe-**vyas**-ta] f. woman
niewidomy [ńe-vee-**do**-mi]
adj. m. blind; lacking insight
niewidzialny [ńe-vee-dźhal-ni]
adj. m. invisible; obscure
niewiedza [ńe-**vye**-dza] f.
ignorance (of); unawareness
niewiela [ńe-**vye**-le] adv. not
much; not many; little; few
niewielki [ńe-**vyel**-kee] adj. m.
small; little; unimportant
niewierny [ńe-**vyer**-ni] adj. m.
disloyal; infidel; unfaithful

niewieści [ńe-**vyeśh**-ćhee]
adj. m. womanly; feminine
niewinność [ńe-**veen**-
-nośhćh] f. innocence; purity; chastity; unsophistication
niewinny [ńe-**veen**-ni] adj. m.
not guilty; innocent; harmless
niewłaściwy [ńe-vwaśh-ćhee-
-vi] adj. m. improper; unsuitable; wrong; inappropriate
niewola [ńe-**vo**-la] f. captivity;
bondage; servitude; slavery
niewolić [ńe-vo-leećh] v.
enslave; compel; oppress
niewolnica [ńe-vol-**ńee**-tsa] f.
slave; serf; prisoner of war
niewolnik [ńe-**vol**-ńeek] m.
slave; serf; prisoner of war
nie wolno [ńe vol-no] v. not allowed; not permitted
niewód [ńe-**voot**] m. dragnet
niewprawny [ńe-**vprav**-ni]
adj. m. unversed; unskilled; inexpert; incompetent; clumsy;
awkward; inefficient
niewspółmierny [ńe-vspoow-
-**myer**-ni] adj. m. incommen-
surable; out of proportion
nie wtajemniczony [ńe vta-yem-
-ńee-cho-ni] adj. m. uninitiated; uninformed; not privy
niewyczerpany [ńe-vi-cher-**pa**-ni]
adj. m. inexhaustible
niewygoda [ńe-vi-**go**-da] f.
discomfort; trouble; hardship
niwygodny [ńe-vi-**god**-ni] adj. m.
uncomfortable; awkward
niewykonalny [ńe-vi-ko-**nal**-ni]
adj. m. unfeasible; unworkable
niewykształcony [ńe-vi-kshtaw-
-tso-ni] adj. m. uneducated
niewymierny [ńe-vi-**myer**-ni] adj.
m. irrational; surd
niewymowny [ńe-vi-**mov**-ni] adj.
m. unspeakable; inexpressible
niewymuszony [ńe-vi-moo-**sho**-
-ni] adj. m. unconstrained;
voluntary; natural; unaffected
niewymyślny [ńe-vi-**miśhl**-ni]
adj. m. unsophisticated; plain
niewypał [ńe-**vi**-paw] m. dud
niewypłacalny [ńe-vi-pwa-**tsal**-
-ni] adj. m. insolvent

niewypowiedziany [ńe-vi-po-vye-
-dźha-ni] adj. m. untold
niewyraźnie [ńe-vi-raźh-ńe]
adv. indistinctly; seedily
niewyraźny [ńe-vi-raźh-ni]
adj. m. queer; indistinct
niewyrobiony [ńe-vi-ro-byo-ni]
adj. m. raw; inexperienced
niewyrozumiały [ńe-vi-ro-zoo-
-mya-wi] adj. m. intolerant
niewysłowiony [ńe-vi-swo-vyo-
-ni] adj. m. ineffable
niewyspany [ńe-vis-pa-ni]
adj. m. sleepy (not enough
sleep); heavy with sleep
niewystarczający [ńe-vis-tar-
-cha-yown-tsi] adj. m.
insufficient; inadequate
niewystawny [ńe-vis-tav-ni] adj.
m. frugal; modest; simple
niewytłumaczony [ńe-vi-twoo-
-ma-cho-ni] adj. m. inexplicable; incomprehensible
niewytrwały [ńe-vi-trva-wi]
adj. m. not persistent
niewytrzymały [ńe-vi-tzhi-ma-wi]
adj. m. not enduring
niewzruszony [ńe-vzroo-sho-ni]
adj. m. unmoved; rigid
niezachwiany [ńe-za-khvya-ni]
adj. m. unshaken; undeterred
niezadowolenie [ńe-za-do-vo-le-
-ńe] n. discontent; displeasure
niezadowolony [ńe-za-do-vo-lo-
-ni] adj. m. dissatisfied; displeased (with); unsatisfied
niezakłócony [ńe-za-kwoo-tso-ni]
adj. m. undisturbed; unmarred
niezależnośćh [ńe-za-lezh
-nośćh] n. independence;
self-sufficiency; detachment
niezależny [ńe-za-lezh-ni]
adj. m. independent; self-
contained; self-sufficient
niezamężna [ńe-za-manzh-na]
adj. f. unmarried; single
niezamożny [ńe-za-mozh-ni] adj.
m.poor; indigent; unpropertied
niezapominajka [ńe-za-po-mee-
-nay-ka] f. forget-me-not
nizapomniany [ńe-za-pom-ńa-ni]
adj. m. not-to-be-forgotten;
unforgettable; memorable

niezaprzeczalny [ńe-za-pzhe-
chal-ni] adj. m. undeniable
niezaradny [ńe-za-rad-ni] adj. m.
helpless; shiftless
niezasłużony [ńe-za-swoo-zho-
-ni] adj. m. undeserved
niezawisły [ńe-za-vees-wi]
adj. m. independent; self-reliant; self-governing; free
niezawodnie [ńe-za-vod-ńe]
adv. surely; without fail;
infallibly; unfailingly
niezawodny [ńe-za-vod-ni]
adj. m. sure; never failing;
safe; unerring; steadfast
niezbadany [ńe-zba-da-ni]
adj. m. unexplorable; in-
scrutable; unfathomable
niezbędny [ńe-zband-ni] adj. m.
indispensable; essential
niezbity [ńe-zbee-ti] adj. m.
irrefutable; incontrovertible
niezbyt [ńe-zbit] adv. not very
(much); none too; not too
niezdarny [ńe-zdar-ni] adj. m.
clumsy; awkward; bungled
niezdatny [ńe-zdat-ni] adj. m.
unfit (for use); unqualified (for
doing); unserviceable
niezdecydowany [ńe-zde-tsi-do-
-va-ni] adj. m. undecided
niezdolnośćh [ńe-zdol-nośćh]
f. inability; unfitness
niezdolny [ńe-zdol-ni] adj. m.
incapable; unable; unfit; dull
niezdrowy [ńe-zdro-vi] adj. m.
unhealthy; unwell; ill; sickly
niezdyscyplinowany [ńe-zdis-tsi-
-plee-no-va-ni] adj. m.
undisciplined; unruly
niezgłębiony [ńe-zgwan-byo-ni]
adj. m. inscrutable; abyssal
niezgoda [ńe-zgo-da] f. discord;
disagreement; dissension
niezgodnośćh [ńe-zgod-
-nośćh] f. inconsistency; in-
compatibility; disagreement
niezgodny [ńe-zgod-ni] adj. m.
discordant; incompatible
niezgrabny [ńe-zgrab-ni] adj. m.
unhandy; clumsy; shapeless
nieziszczalny [ńe-zeesh-chal-ni]
adj. m. unattainable

niezliczony [ńe-zlee-cho-ni] adj.
m. uncountable; countless
niezłomny [ńe-zwom-ni] adj. m.
inflexible; firm; steadfast
niezmącony [ńe-zmown-tso-ni]
adj. m. unruffled; undisturbed
niezmienny [ńe-zmyen-ni]
adj. m. invariable; constant;
fixed; unchanging; permanent
niezmierny [ńe-zmyer-ni] adj. m.
immense; vast; boundless
niezmordowany [ńe-zmor-do-va-
-ni] adj. m. indefatigable;
tireless; untiring; unflagging
nieznaczny [ńe-znach-ni] adj. m.
trivial; insignificant
nieznajomość [ńe-zna-yo-
-mośhćh] f. ignorance; unawareness; unacquaintance
nieznajomy [ńe-zna-yo-mi]
adj. m. unknown (people);
strange; m. stranger
nieznany [ńe-zna-ni] adj. m.
unknown; unfamiliar; obscure
nieznośny [ńe-znośh-ni]
adj. m. unbearable; annoying;
nasty; pesky; intolerable
niezręczny [ńe-zranch-ni] adj. m.
awkward; clumsy; tactless
niezrozumiały [ńe-zro-zoo-mya-
-wi] adj. m. unintelligible
niezrównany [ńe-zroov-na-ni]
adj. m. matchless; incomparable; peerless; unique; grand;
beyond compare; unrivalled
niezwłoczny [ńe-zvwoch-ni] adj.
m. instant; prompt; immediate
niezwyciężony [ńe-zvi-ćhan-
-zho-ni] adj. m. invincible
niezwykły [ńe-zvik-wi] adj. m.
unusual; extreme; rare; odd
nieżonaty [ńe-zho-na-ti] adj. m.
unmarried; single; bachelor
nieżyczliwy [ńe-zhich-lee-vi] adj.
m. unfriendly; ill-disposed
nieżyt [ńe-zhit] m. inflammation;
catarrh; hay fever; colitis
nieżywy [ńe-zhi-vi] adj. m.
dead; lifeless; inanimate
nigdy [ńeeg-di] adv. never
nigdzie [ńeeg-dźhe] adv.
nowhere; anywhere (after
negation)

nijaki [ńee-ya-kee] adj. m. none;
neuter (gender); indistinct
nikczemnik [ńeek-chem-ńeek]
m. villain; scoundrel; wretch
nikczemny [ńeek-chem-ni] adj.
m. vile; abject; despicable;
base; shabby; mean; dirty
nikiel [ńee-kel] m. nickel
nikły [ńeek-wi] adj. m. scanty
niknąć [ńeek-nownćh] v. vanish; dwindle; waste away
nikotyna [ńee-ko-ti-na] f.
nicotine; poisonous tobacco
extract causing nicotinism
nikt [ńeekt] pron. nobody
nim [ńeem] conj. before; till
nimb [ńeemp] m. halo; aureole
niniejszy [ńee-ńey-shi] adj. m.
this; present; the present
niski [ńees-kee] adj. m. low
nisko [ńees-ko] adv. low
nisza [ńee-sha] f. niche; recess
niszczący [ńeesh-chown-tsi] adj.
m. destructive; disruptive
niszczeć [ńeesh-chećh] v.
waste away; deteriorate; get
wasted; decay; go to ruin
niszczyciel [ńeesh-chi-ćhel] m.
devastator; destroyer; waster
niszczyć [ńeesh-chićh] v.
destroy; spoil; ruin; wreck;
damage; demolish; lay waste
nit [ńeet] m. rivet
nitke [ńeet-ka] f. thread
nitować [ńee-to-vaćh] v. rivet
niwa [ńee-va] f. field; soil
niweczyć [ńee-ve-chićh] v.
destroy; annihilate; lay waste
niwelacja [ńee-ve-lats-ya] f.
leveling; survey; surveying
nivelować [ńee-ve-lo-vaćh] v.
make level; demolish; survey
nizina [ńee-źhee-na] f. lowland
niż [ńeezh] m. lowland; depression; atmospheric low; low
niż [ńeesh] conj. than
niżej [ńee-zhey] adv. lower;
below; down; further down
niższość [ńeesh-shośhćh] f.
inferiority (complex etc.)
niższy [ńeezh-shi] adj. m. lower;
inferior; shorter; subordinate
no [no] part. why; well; now;

then; just; there; there now!
noc [nots] f. night
nocleg [nots-leg] m. place to sleep; night's lodging
nocny [nots-ni] adj. m. nocturnal; night-
nocować [no-tso-vaćh] v. spend night; stay (accommodation) overnight; sleep
noga [no-ga] f. leg; foot
nogawica [no-ga-vee-tsa] f. legging; trouser leg
nomenklatura [no-men-kla-too-ra] f. nomenclature; terminology
nominacja [no-mee-nats-ya] f. appointment; nomination
nominalny [no-mee-nal-ni] adj. m. nominal; (face) value
nonsens [non-sens] m. nonsense
nora [no-ra] f. burrow; den
norma [nor-ma] f. standard; norm; rule; general principle
normalizacja [nor-ma-lee-zats-ya] f. normalization; standard
normalizować [nor-ma-lee-zo-vaćh] v. normalize (metal); standardize; make standard
normalny [nor-mal-ni] adj. m. normal; standard; ordinary
normować [nor-mo-vaćh] v. regulate; standardize; make standard or uniform; normalize
nos [nos] m. nose; snout
nosić [no-śheećh] v. carry; wear; bear; have about one
nosorożec [no-so-ro-zhets] m. rhinoceros (with horn)
nostalgia [nos-tal-gya] f. nostalgia; homesickness
nosze [no-she] pl. stretchers
nota [no-ta] f. note; grade
notariusz [no-tar-yoosh] m. notary public
notatka [no-tat-ka] f. note
notatnik [no-tat-ńeek] m. notebook; diary; notes
notes [no-tes] m. pocket notebook; small notebook
notoryczny [no-to-rich-ni] adj. m. notorious; flagrant; arrant
notować [no-to-vaćh] v. make notes; take notes; write down
notowanie [no-to-va-ńe] n.

quotation; record (of facts)
nowela [no-ve-la] f. short story; amendment (to a constitution)
nowelista [no-ve-lees-ta] m. short story writer
nowicjat [no-vee-tsyat] m. novitiate; novitiate
nowicjusz [no-veets-yoosh] novice; beginner; freshman
nowina [no-vee-na] f. news
nowinka [no-veen-ka] f. fad
nowiutki [no-vyoot-kee] adj. m. brand-new; spick-and-span
nowoczesny [no-vo-ches-ni] adj. m. modern; up to date; present day; newest; progressive
noworoczny [no-vo-roch-ni] adj. m. New Year's; of New Year
nowość [no-voshćh] f. novelty; newness; strangeness;
nowotwór [no-vo-tvoor] m. tumor; newly-coined word
nowożytny [no-vo-zhit-ni] adj. m. (of) modern (period)
nowy [no-vi] adj. m. new
nozdrze [noz-dzhe] n. nostril
nożownik [no-zhov-ńeek] m. knifer; cutthroat; gangster
nożyce [no-zhi-tse] pl. shears; clippers; large shears
nożyczki [no-zhich-kee] pl. scissors; small scissors
nożyk [no-zhik] m. pocketknife
nów [noov] m. new moon
nóż [noosh] m. knife; cutter
nucić [noo-ćheećh] v. hum
nuda [noo-da] f. boredom;
nudności [nood-nośh-ćhee] pl. nausea; impulse to vomit
nudny [nood-ni] adj. m. boring; nauseating; dull; sickening
nudysta [noo-dis-ta] m. nudist
nudziarz [noo-dźhash] m. bore
nudzić [noo-dźheećh] v. bore
numer [noo-mer] m. number
numerować [noo-me-ro-vaćh] v. number; give a number to
numerowy [noo-me-ro-vi] m. porter; bell-boy; hotel waiter
numizmatyka [noo-meez-ma-ti-ka] f. numismatics; study (or collection) of coins, medals
nuncjusz [noon-tsyoosh] m.

nuncio; papal ambassador
nurek [noo-rek] m. diver
nurkować [noor-ko-vaćh] v.
  dive; plunge; duck; nose-dive
nurt [noort] m. current (flowing);
  stream; trend; wake
nurtować [noor-to-vaćh] v.
  fret; penetrate; pervade; ferment in; rankle; pray on
nurzać [noo-zhaćh] v. dip;
  welter in; plunge into; wallow
  in; immerse in; steep into
nuta [noo-ta] f. (sound) note
nuty [noo-ti] pl. written music;
  printed music; music score
nuż [noozh] adv. if; and if
nużący [noo-zhown-tsi] adj. m.
  tiring; tiresome; wearisome
nużyć [noo-zhićh] v. tire;
  weary; make tired; oppress
nygus [ni-goos] m. lazybones
nygusować [ni-goo-so-vaćh] v.
  lounge about; loiter; loaf
nylon [ni-lon] m. nylon
nyża [ni-zha] f. niche; alcove

O

o [o] prep. of; for; at; by; about;
  against; with; to; over; oh!
oaza [o-a-za] f. oasis
oba [o-ba] pron. both
obabrać [o-ba-braćh] v. besmear; smear over; make dirty
obaj [o-bay] pron. both
obalenie [o-ba-le-ńe] n.
  overthrow; subversion; refutation; reversal; abolition
obalić [o-ba-leećh] v.
  overthrow; knock down; fell;
  refute; throw down; subvert
obarczyć [o-bar-chićh] v.
  encumber; saddle; load; weigh
  down; burden; saddle (with)
obarzanek [o-ba-zha-nek] m.
  round cracknel (torus shaped)
obawa [o-ba-va] f. fear;
  apprehension; phobia; anxiety

obawiać się [o-ba-vyaćh śhan]
  v. be anxious; fear; dread
obcas [ob-tsas] m. heel
obcążki [ob-tsownzh-kee] pl.
  (small) tongs; pincers; pliers
obcesowo [ob-tse-so-vo] adv.
  headlong; outright; abruptly
obcęgi [ob-tsan-gee] pl. tongs
obchodzić [ob-kho-dźheećh] v.
  go around; evade; elude;
  celebrate; inspect; by-pass
obchód [ob-khoot] m. (daily)
  beat; celebration; circuit
obciągać [ob-ćhown-gaćh] v.
  pull down; cover; pull tight
obciążać [ob-ćhown-zhaćh] v.
  burden; charge (account)
obcierać [ob-ćhe-raćh] v. wipe
obcinać [ob-ćhee-naćh] v. cut
  off; clip; crop; chop off
obcisły [ob-ćhees-wi] adj. m.
  tight; close fitting; clinging
obcokrajowiec [ob-tso-kra-yo-
  -vyets] m. foreigner; alien
obcokrajowy [ob-tso-kra-yo-vi]
  adj. m. foreign; alien
obcować [ob-tso-vaćh] v. associate; mix with; have sex
obcowanie [ob-tso-va-ńe] n.
  intercourse; association
obcy [ob-tsi] adj. m. strange;
  foreign; unfamiliar; unrelated
obczyzna [ob-chiz-na] f. foreign
  country; exile; foreign land
obdarować [ob-da-ro-vaćh] v.
  bestow; lavish gifts on...
obdarty [ob-dar-ti] adj. m.
  ragged; in rags; tattered
obdarzyć [ob-da-zhićh] v.
  bestow; lavish gifts on...
obdzielić [ob-dźhe-leećh] v.
  divide; distribute; deal; endow
obdzierać [ob-dźhe-raćh] v. rip
  off; skin off; strip; fleece
obecnie [o-bets-ńe] adv. at
  present; just now; to-day
obecność [o-bets-nośhćh] f.
  presence (in); attendance (at)
obejmować [o-bey-mo-vaćh] v.
  embrace; enfold; span; enfold;
  include; take over; take in;
  hug; grasp; clasp; encircle
obejrzeć [o-bey-zhećh] v.

inspect; glance at; see
obejście [o-bey-śhće] n. by
-pass; farmyard; manner
obejść [o-beyśhćh] v. go a-
round; by-pass; affect
obelga [o-bel-ga] f. (open) insult;
affront; invective; pl. abuse
obelżywy [o-bel-zhi-vi] adj. m.
insulting; abusive; opprobrious
oberwać [o-ber-vaćh] v. tear
off; cop it; pluck; get a nock
oberża [o-ber-zha] f. inn; tavern
oberżysta [o-ber-zhis-ta] m.
innkeeper; owner of an inn
oberżnąć [o-ber-zhn<u>own</u>ćh] v.
cut off; trim; clip; edge; cheat
obeschnąć [o-bes-khn<u>own</u>ćh]
v. dry up; get dry; dry
obetrzeć [o-bet-zhećh] v. wipe
out; dust; rub sore; skin
obezwładnić [o-bez-vwad-
-ńeećh] v. overpower; subdue; disable; make helpless
obeznany [o-bez-na-ni] adj. m.
familiar (with); acquainted
(with); conversant (with)
obfitość [ob-fee-tośhćh] f.
plenty; abundance; profusion
obfity [ob-fee-ti] adj. m.
abundant; ample; profuse; liberal; plentiful; abounding in
obgadywać [ob-ga-di-vaćh] v.
talk ill; talk over; crab
obgryzać [ob-gri-zaćh] v. nibble
bare; gnaw; pick a bone; bite
obiad [o-byat] m. dinner
obicie [o-bee-ćhe] n. upholstery;
(door) padding; chip; beating;
bruise; drubbing
obiecywać [o-bye-tsi-vaćh] v.
promise; look forward to
obieg [o-byek] m. circulation
obiegać [o-bye-gaćh] v. run
around; circulate; revolve;
skirt; make the round; orbit
obiekcja [o-byek-tsya] f.
objection; demur; hesitation
obiekt [o-byekt] m. object;
subject; building; target
obiektyw [o-byek-tiv] m. object
-lens; object-glass; objective
obiektywny [o-byek-tiv-ni]
adj. m. objective; impartial

obierać [o-bye-raćh] v. choose;
elect; peel; pick; strip; adopt
obierzyny [o-bye-zhi-ni] pl.
peelings; parings; offals
obieralny [o-bye-ral-ni] adj. m.
elective; eligible
obietnica [o-byet-ńee-tsa] f.
promise; engagement
obijać [o-bee-yaćh] v. chip;
hoop; loaf; hurt; injure
objadać się [ob-ya-daćh śh<u>an</u>]
v. gorge; overeat; cram; gnaw
objaśniać [ob-yaśh-ńaćh] v.
explain; make clear; gloss
objaw [ob-yav] m. symptom
objawić [ob-ya-veećh] v. reveal
objazd [ob-yazt] m. tour; circuit;
detour; diversion; bypass
objąć [ob-y<u>own</u>ćh] v. embrace;
assume; grasp; encompass;
enfold; hug; span; take over
objeżdżać [ob-yezh-dzhaćh] v.
ride; around; break in a horse
objętość [ob-y<u>an</u>-tośhćh] f.
volume; bulk; capacity; size;
measurement; content
obkładać [ob-kwa-daćh] v. cover (up); wrap; line (a pipe);
impose; hit; buffet; deal blows
oblegać [ob-le-gaćh] v. besiege
oblać [ob-laćh] v. pour on
(water); spill; drench; fail
oblekać [ob-le-kaćh] v. clothe;
put on; cover; encase; don
oblepiać [ob-le-pyaćh] v. paste
over; stick; post; plaster over
oblewać [ob-le-vaćh] v. pour
on; drench; bathe; sprinkle;
wash; spill; celebrate; fail
oblężenie [ob-l<u>an</u>-zhe-ńe] m.
siege; state of siege
obliczać [ob-lee-chaćh] v.
count; reckon; figure out; calculate; estimate; design; mean
oblicze [ob-lee-che] n. face
obliczenie [ob-lee-che-ńe] n.
calculation; evaluation; count
obligacja [ob-lee-gats-ya] f.
obligation; bond; share
oblizać [ob-lee-zaćh] v. lick
obładować [ob-wa-do-vaćh] v.
load down; heap; burden
obława [ob-wa-va] f. roundup;

posse; man hunt; chase; raid
obłąkany [ob-w<u>ow</u>n-ka-ni]
adj. m. insane; loony; madman
obłęd [ob-w<u>a</u>nt] m. insanity
obłędny [ob-w<u>a</u>nd-ni] adj. m.
mad; wild; insane; crazy
obłok [ob-wok] m. cloud
obłowić się [ob-wo-veećh
<u>śhan</u>] v. pick up a lot; make
a pile; fill (line) one's pockets
obłożnie [ob-wozh-ńe] adv. bed
-ridden; severely (ill)
obłożyć [ob-wo-zhićh] v. cover up; wrap; line; impose; hit;
buffet; seize; put dues on
obłuda [ob-woo-da] f. hypocrisy
obłudnik [ob-wood-ńeek] m.
hypocrite; snuffler; dissembler
obłudny [ob-wood-ni] adj. m.
hypocritical; false; canting
obłupać [ob-woo-paćh] v. shell;
peel; bark; flay; skin; fleece
obłuszczać [ob-woosh-chaćh]
v. scale; shell; husk; flay; skin
obły [ob-wi] adj. m. oval;
tapering; cylindrical
obmacać [ob-ma-tsaćh] v. feel
about; explore with fingers;
palpate; handle (a fabric etc.)
obmawiać [ob-ma-vyaćh] v.
slander; gossip; speak ill
obmierznąć [ob-myerz-n<u>own</u>ćh]
v. get sick of (something)
obmowa [ob-mo-va] f. slander;
detraction; backbiting
obmurować [ob-moo-ro-vaćh]
v. brick in; brick veneer
obmyślać [ob-miśh-laćh] v.
design; contrive; reflect
obmywać [ob-mi-vaćh] v. wash
-up; sponge down; give a
wash; wash the dirt off
obnażać [ob-na-zhaćh] v.
denude; bare; unclothe; strip
off clothes; uncover; lay bare
obniżać [ob-ńee-zhaćh] v.
lower; sink; drop; abate; level
down; draw down; reduce
obniżenie [ob-ńee-zhe-ńe] n.
decrease; reduction; lowering
obniżka [ob-ńeezh-ka] f.
reduction; depreciation; drop;
fall; diminution; decrease

obojczyk [o-boy-chik] m. collar
bone; clavicle; amice; gorget
obnosić [ob-no-śheećh] v.
take around; flaunt; parade
obojętnie [o-bo-y<u>a</u>nt-ńe] adv.
indifferently; slang: no matter
obojętność [o-bo-y<u>a</u>nt-
-nośhćh] f. indifference; in-
sensibility; neutrality
obojętny [o-bo-y<u>a</u>nt-ni] adj. m.
indifferent; neutral
obok [o-bok] adv. prep. beside;
next; about; close by; by;
close; next door; alongside
obopólny [o-bo-pool-ni] adj. m.
common; mutual; reciprocal
obora [o-bo-ra] f. cow barn
obosieczny [o-bo-śhech-ni] adj.
m. two-edged; double edged
obowiązek [o-bo-vy<u>ow</u>n-zek] m.
duty; obligation; responsibility
obowiązkowy [o-bo-vy<u>own</u>z-ko-
-vi] adj. m. dutiful; compulsory
obowiązany [o-bo-vy<u>own</u>-za-ni]
adj. m. obligated; compelled
obowiązujący [o-bo-vy<u>own</u>-zoo-
-y<u>own</u>-tsi] adj. m. obligatory
obowiązywać [o-bo-vy<u>own</u>-zi-
-vaćh] v. be in force (law
etc.); bind; compel; oblige
obozować [o-bo-zo-vaćh] v.
camp; camp out; tent; tent it;
(lie) encamp(ed); bivouac
obój [o-booy] m. oboe; (horn)
obóz [o-boos] m. camp
obrabiać [o-bra-byaćh] v.
machine (metal, wood etc.);
work-over; fashion; shape; till;
hem; stitch; gosip; rifle; beat
obrabiarka [o-bra-byar-ka] f.
machine tool; lathe
obrabować [ob-ra-bo-vaćh] v.
rob (a train); strip of money
obracać [ob-ra-tsaćh] v. turn
-over; turn into; rotate; crank
obrachować [ob-ra-kho-vaćh]
v. compute; figure out; calculate; count; reckon; estimate
obrachunek [ob-ra-khoo-nek] m.
settlement; bill; "day of
reckoning"; count; reckoning
obrada [ob-ra-da] f. conference
obradować [ob-ra-do-vaćh] v.

confer; deliberate; debate; sit
obradzać [ob-ra-dzáć] v. bear
crops; yield a crop; be plentiful; yield an abundant crop
obramować [ob-ra-mo-váć] v.
frame; encircle; encase; hem; edge (a garment); border
obrastać [ob-ras-táć] v. over-grow; grow; grow all over
obraz [ob-raz] m. picture; image; painting; drawing; likeness
obraza [ob-ra-za] f. affront; offense; insult; outrage; feeling of offence; transgression
obrazek [ob-ra-zek] m. illustration; small picture
obrazić [ob-ra-źheéć] v. offend; affront; insult; sting
obrazowy [ob-ra-zo-vi] adj. m. pictorial; picturesque; vivid
obrażenie [ob-ra-zhe-ńe] n. offense (s); injury; insults
obraźliwy [ob-raźh-lee-vi] adj. m. offensive; touchy; resentful; abusive; insulting
obrażać [ob-ra-zháć] v. offend; (repeatedly) insult; affront; transgress (against)
obrąb [ob-rownb] m. cutoff
obrąbek [ob-rown-bek] m. hem
obrączka [ob-rownch-ka] f. ring
obręb [ob-ranb] m. compass; area; reach; extent; precincts
obrębiać [ob-ran-byáć] v. hem
obręcz [ob-ranch] f. hoop; tire; rim; band; girdle; ring; circle
obrobić [ob-ro-beéć] v. machine; fashion; shape; till; hem
obrok [ob-rok] m. feed; fodder
obrona [o-bro-na] f. defense
obronność [ob-ron-noshćh] f. defense capability; defenses
obronny [ob-ron-ni] adj. m. defensive; fortified; protective
obrońca [ob-roń-tsa] f. defender guard; barrister; advocate (of a cause); counsel for
obrośnięty [ob-roś-ńan-ti] adj. m. overgrown; unshaven
obrotny [ob-rot-ni] adj. m. active; skillful; nimble; agile; shrewd
obrotowy [ob-ro-to-vi] adj. m. turnover (tax); rotary; rota-

tive; revolving; circulating
obroża [ob-ro-zha] f.(dog) collar; neck band; a circular band
obrócić [ob-roo-ćheéć] v. rotate; revolve; turn; go
obrót [ob-root] m. turn; turn-over; revolution; slew; sales
obrus [ob-roos] m .tablecloth
obruszać [ob-roo-sháć] v. loosen up; irritate; bring down
obrywać [ob-ri-váć] v. tear off; tear away; pluck; wrench off; curtail; get (spanking)
obryzgiwać [ob-riz-gee-váć] v. splash; spatter (with mud)
obrząd [ob-zhant] m. rite; ceremony; custom; dispensation
obrzęk [ob-zhank] m. swelling
obrzękły [ob-zhank-wi] adj. m. swollen; tumid; bulged
obrzmiały [obzh-mya-wi] adj. m. swollen; tumid; bulged
obrzucać [ob-zhoo-tsáć] v. throw upon; hurl; pelt; fell
obrzydliwy [ob-zhid-lee-vi] adj. m. revolting; disgusting
obrzydzenie [ob-zhi-dze-ńe] n. aversion; nausea; disgust
obrzynać [ob-zhi-náć] v. clip; cut; cut off; edge; trim; cheat
obsada [ob-sa-da] f. cast; crew; garrison; staff; mounting
obsadka [ob-sad-ka] f. penholder; small mounting
obsadzać [ob-sa-dzáć] v. plant; staff; set; fix; occupy; stock; border; line; mount; fill
obserwacja [ob-ser-vats-ya] f. observation; remark
obserwator [ob-ser-va-tor] m. observer; look out man; witness; viewer (of something)
obserwatorium [ob-ser-va-tor-yoom] m. observatory
obserwować [ob-ser-vo-váć] v. watch; observe; take stock
obsługa [ob-swoo-ga] f. attendance; service; staff
obsługiwać [ob-swoo-gee-váć] v. wait-upon; service
obstalować [ob-sta-lo-váć] v. order (a suit of clothes etc.)
obstalunek [ob-sta-loo-nek] m.

order; a request to supply
obstawać [ob-**sta**-vaćh] v.
insist on; hold to; stand by;
persist in; abide by; stick to
obstąpić [ob-s<u>town</u>-peećh] v.
surround; form a circle; cluster
obstrzał [ob-stzhaw] m. gun-fire;
scope of fire; firing
obstrukcja [ob-strook-tsya] f.
obstruction; constipation
obsuwać [ob-**soo**-vaćh] v. slide
down; creep; lower; bring
down; push down; give way
obsuwisko [ob-soo-**vees**-ko] n.
landslide; mud slide
obsychać [ob-**si**-khaćh] v. dry
up; get parched; run dry; go
dry; get dry; become dry
obsyłać [ob-**si**-waćh] v. send
around (messengers etc.)
obsypywać [ob-si-pi-vaćh] v.
strew; sprinkle; shower; heap
obszar [ob-shar] m. area; range
obszarnik [ob-**shar**-ńeek] m.
landowner; large scale farmer
obszerny [ob-**sher**-ni] adj. m.
spacious; extensive; vast;
broad; wide; roomy; ample
obsztorcować [ob-shtor-tso-
-vaćh] v. snub; give hard time
obszukać [ob-shoo-kaćh] v.
search; ransack; make a thorough search; plunder; pillage
obszyć [ob-shićh] v. sew
around; hem; trim; mend
obuch [/o-bookh] m. back of an
axe; sledge; head of an axe
obudzić [o-boo-**dźhee**ćh] v.
wake up; awaken; excite; stir
up; rouse from sleep; arise
obumarły [o-boo-**mar**-wi] adj. m.
deadened; half dead; decaying
obumierać [o-boo-**mye**-raćh] v.
wither; atrophy; decay; shrink
oburącz [o-boo-**rownch**] adv.
with both hands (arms)
oburzać [o-boo-zhaćh] v.
revolt; shock; rouse (provoke)
indignation; be revolting; be
disgusting; be outrageous
oburzony [o-boo-**zho**-ni] adj. m.
indignant (at); resentful (of)
obustronny [o-boo-**stron**-ni] adj.

m. bilateral; mutual; reciprocal
obuwie [o-boo-vye] n. footwear
obwarowywać [ob-va-ro-vi-
-vaćh] v. fortify (a town); en-
trench (a position); secure
obwąchiwać [ob-v<u>own</u>-khee-
-vaćh] v. sniff around; smell
around; sniff at; smell at
obwiązywać [ob-vy<u>own</u>-zi-
-vaćh] v. bind up; bandage;
tie around something
obwieszczać [ob-**vyesh**-chaćh]
v. announce; proclaim; notify
obwieszczenie [ob-vyesh-**che**-
-ńe] n. proclamation; notice
obwiniać [ob-vee-**ńaćh**] v.
accuse of; charge with
obwisać [ob-**vee**-saćh] v. sag;
droop; hang loosely; flag
obwodowy [ob-vo-do-vi] adj. m.
circumferential; district
obwoluta [ob-vo-loo-ta] f.
wrapper; book-jacket; file
(cardboard) cover; frame
obwołać [ob-vo-waćh] v.
acclaim; proclaim; call names
obwód [ob-voot] m. perimeter
oby [o-bi] part. may...; may you
obycie [o-bi-ćhe] n. good
manners; experience; good
breeding; familiarity (with)
obyczaj [o-bi-chay] m. custom
obyczajność [o-bi-**chay**-
-nośhćh] f. decency; good
conduct; morality; morals
obyczajny [o-bi-chay-ni] adj. m.
decent; of moral conduct
obydwaj [o-bi-dvay] num. both
obyty [o-bi-ti] adj. m. familiar;
easy mannered; polished
obywać się [o-bi-vaćh **śhan**]
v. do without; dispense with
obywatel [o-bi-va-tel] m. citizen;
squire; inhabitant; freeman
obywatelka [o-bi-va-**tel**-ka] f.
(female) citizen; inhabitant
obywatelstwo [o-bi-va-**tel**-stvo]
m. citizenship; nationality
obznajomić [ob-zna-yo-**meećh**]
v. familiarize; acquaint; inform
obżarstwo [ob-zhar-stvo] n.
gluttony; stuffing oneself
ocaleć [o-**tsa**-lećh] v. survive

(danger); rescue; save

ocalenie [o-tsa-le-ńe] n. rescue; salvation; escape; rescuing

ocalić [o-tsa-leech] v. rescue

ocean [o-tse-an] m. ocean

ocena [o-tse-na] f. grade; estimate; appraisal; criticism

ocet [o-tset] m. vinegar

och! [okh!] excl. oh!

ochędożyć [o-khan-do-zhich] v. clean; put in order; tidy up

ochlapać [o-khla-paćh] v. splash; splatter (with mud)

ochładzać [o-khwa-dzaćh] v. cool; chill; refresh

ochłap [o-khwap] m. offal; trash; scrap of meat; offal; remnant

ochłonąć [o-khwo-nownch] v. calm down; get cooler; cool

ochoczo [o-kho-cho] adv. eagerly; cheerfully; gladly; gaily; willingly; readily; with zest

ochota [o-kho-ta] f. eagerness; forwardness; willingness

ochotnik [o-khot-ńeek] n. volunteer; serving of free will

ochraniać [o-khra-ńaćh] v. protect; preserve; shield

ochrona [o-khro-na] f. (shelter) protection; conservation

ochronny [o-khron-ni] adj. m. protective; preventive

ochrypły [o-khrip-wi] adj. m. hoarse; husky; raucous

ochrypnąć [o-khrip-nownch] v. hoarsen; grow hoarse

ochrzcić [okh-zhćheech] v. baptize; christen; name; dub

ociągać się [o-chown-gaćh śhan] v. linger; delay; put off

ociec [o-ćhets] v. drain; drip

ociekać [o-ćhe-kaćh] v. drain; drip; stream; overflow; dry

ociemniały [o-ćhem-ńa-wi] adj. m. blind; blind man

ocieniać [o-ćhe-ńaćh] v. shade over; protect from the sun; overshadow; shade

ocieplać [o-ćhe-plaćh] v. warm up; make warmer; get warm

ocierać [o-ćhe-raćh] v. wipe off; rub sore; gall; abrade

ociężały [o-ćhan-zha-wi] adj. m.

inert; (lazy) heavy; tardy; dull; ponderous; languid; bovine

ociosać [o-ćho-saćh] v. hew

ocknąć się [ots-knownch śhan] v. wake up (from a nap, meditation, etc,-.); awake

oclić [ots-leećh] v. assess custom; collect duty; levy duty (for); pay duty (for)

oczarować [o-cha-ro-vaćh] v. charm; enchant; fascinate; ravish; cast a spell; bewitch

oczekiwać [o-che-kee-vaćh] v. wait for; await; expect; hope

oczekiwanie [o-che-kee-va-ńe] n. expectation; prospect

oczerniać [o-cher-ńaćh] v. slander; malign; defame; vilify

oczko [och-ko] n. (needle) eyelet; little eye; mesh; stitch

oczny [och-ni] adj. m. optic

oczyszczać [o-chish-chaćh] v. clean; purify; dust; clear

oczytany [o-chi-ta-ni] adj. m. well-read; of wide reading

oczywisty [o-chi-vees-ti] adj. m. obvious; self-evident; plain

oczywiście [o-chi-veeśh-ćhe] adv. obviously; of course

od [od] prep. from; off; of; for; since; out of; with; per; by (the line); then (idiomatic)

odbarwić [od-bar-veećh] v. bleach; decolonize

odbicie [od-bee-ćhe] n. reflection; bounce; ricochet; beating back; deflection; repercussion; reflex; reverberation; repulse

odbić [od-beećh] v. bounce back; rescue; recover; reflect; print; divert; deflect; detach

odbiegać [od-bye-gaćh] v. desert; deviate; stray; digress

odbijać [od-bee-yaćh] v. reflect; print; put off; fend off; stand out; leave a trace; kick

odbiorca [od-byor-tsa] m. receiver; customer; addressee

odbiornik [od-byor-ńeek] m. (radio) receiver; collector

odbiór [od-byoor] m. receipt; reception; (money) collection

odbitka [od-beet-ka] f. copy;

reprint; impression; proof; slip
odblask [od-blask] m. reflection of light; gleam; irradiation
odbudowa [od-boo-do-va] f. reconstruction; restoration
odbudować [od-boo-do-vaćh] v. rebuild; restore; reconstruct
odbyt [od-bit] m. 1. sale, 2. anus; end of alimentary tract
odbywać [od-bi-vaćh] v. do; perform; be in progress
odcedzić [od-tse-dźheećh] v. strain; strain out; drain away
odchodzić [od-kho-dźheećh] v. go away; leave; walk off; split; sail; retire; withdraw
odchudzać [od-khoo-dzaćh] v. reduce (weight); slim; make slimmer; slenderize
odchylać [od-khi-laćh] v. deflect; slant; slope; bend back; deviate; half-open
odchylenie [od-khi-le-ńe] n. deviation; declination; deflection (of rays); variation
odciągać [od-ćhown-gaćh] v. draw aside; retract; divert; delay; pull back; withdraw
odciążać [od-ćhown-zhaćh] v. relieve; unburden; lighten; ease; take the strain off
odcień [od-ćheń] m. shade (of difference); tint; undertone; tinge; hue; cast; (semi) tone
odcierpieć [od-ćher-pyećh] v. suffer for; expiate; atone
odcinać [od-ćhee-naćh] v. cut off; sever; amputate; detach
odcinek [od-ćhee-nek] m. sector; segment; space; portion; period; fragment; passage
odcisk [od-ćheesk] m. imprint; skin-corn; stamp; trace; impression; squeeze; mark
odcyfrować [od-tsif-ro-vaćh] v. decipher; make out; decode
odczekać [od-che-kaćh] v. wait out; wait for the right moment
odczepić [od-che-peećh] v. detach; unhook; get rid; disconnect; unhitch; unfasten
odczuć [od-chooćh] v. feel; notice; resent; smart from

odczyn [od-chin] m. (chem.) reaction; chemical change
odczynnik [od-chin-ńeek] m. reagent; reacting substance
odczyt [od-chit] m. lecture
odczytać [od-chi-taćh] v. read over; take the reading; call
oddać [od-daćh] v. give back; pay back; render; deliver
oddalać [od-da-laćh] v. remove; send away; drive away
oddalony [od-da-lo-ni] adj. m. distant; remote; far away
oddany [od-da-ni] adj. m. given up; devoted; loving; intent
oddawać [od-da-vaćh] v. give back; pay back; return; repay
od dawna [od dav-na] since a long time; long since
oddech [od-dekh] m. breath
oddychać [od-di-khaćh] v. breathe; take breath; respire
oddział [od-dźhaw] m. division; section; ward; branch; detail
oddziaływać [od-dźha-wi-vaćh] v. influence; affect
oddzielać [od-dźhe-laćh] v. separate; divorce; split
oddzielny [od-dźhel-ni] adj. m. separate; individual; discrete
oddzierać [od-dźhe-raćh] v. tear off; pull off; pull away
oddźwięk [od-dźhvyank] m. echo; resonance; repercussion
odebrać [o-de-braćh] v. take away from; receive; withdraw; take back; regain; deprive of
odechcieć się [o-dekh-ćhećh śhan] v. lose interest; cease liking; be sick of (it, etc.)
odegnać [o-deg-naćh] v. chase away; drive away; drive off
odegrać się [o-de-graćh śhan] v. win back; recover; take revenge; retrieve; recoup losses
odejmować [o-dey-mo-vaćh] v. subtract; deduct; take away; diminish; withdraw; deprive
odejście [o-dey-śhćhe] n. departure; withdrawal; divergence; deviation (from a line)
odejść [o-deyśhćh] v. depart; go away; leave; abandon

odemknąć [o-dem-knownćh] v.
open; half open (a door, window, etc.); set ajar; unbolt

odepchnąć [o-dep-khnownćh]
v. shove away; beat back; elbow aside; drive back; spurn

odeprzeć [o-dep-zhećh] v.
repel; repulse; fight off; retort

oderwać [o-der-vaćh] v. tear
off; break off; detach; sever

odesłać [o-des-waćh] v. send
back; return; refer; direct

odetchnąć [o-det-khnownćh] v.
breathe (freely); respire

odetkać [o-det-kaćh] v. unstop;
uncork; unchoke; fall out

odezwa [o-dez-va] f. proclamation (to the nation); appeal;
urgent request (to the people)

odgadywać [od-ga-di-vaćh] v.
guess; surmise; solve a riddle

odgałęziać [od-ga-wan-źhaćh]
v. branch away; fork off; ramify; branch out; branch off

odganiać [od-ga-ńaćh] v.
chase away; drive off; dismiss

odgarniać [od-gar-ńaćh] v.
shove away; rake aside; push
aside; clear (the snow, etc.)

odginać [od-gee-naćh] unbend;
fold back; straighten curve

odgłos [od-gwos] m. echo;
resonance; sound; noise; thud

odgniatać [od-gńa-taćh] v.
bruise; wrinkle (the dress,
etc.); crease (the skin, etc.)

odgradzać się [od-gra-dzaćh
śhan] fence off; screen off;
separate; shut oneself off

odgrażać się [od-gra-zhaćh
śhan] v. talk big; threaten

odgrodzić [od-gro-dźheećh] v.
divide off; fence off; shut off

odgruzować [od-groo-zo-vaćh]
v. clear off rubbish from a
space; remove the rubble

odgrywać [od-gri-vaćh] v. play
off; perform; act; make believe; pretend; sham; recover

odgryzać [od-gri-zaćh] v. bite
off; snap off; gnaw off

odgrzebywać [od-gzhe-bi-vaćh]
v. dig up; rake up; unearth;
turn up; clear (the rubble)

odgrzewać [od-gzhe-vaćh] v.
rewarm; rehash (an old story);
warm up (food, soup, etc.)

odjazd [od-yazt] m. departure

odjeżdżać [od-yezh-dzhaćh] v.
depart; be off; abandon; start

odjęcie [od-yan-ćhe] n. amputation; deduction; withdrawal; subtraction; weaning

odkazić [od-ka-źheećh] v.
disinfect; sterilize

odkażać [od-ka-zhaćh] v.
disinfect (repeatedly); sterilize

odkażenie [od-ka-zhe-ńe] n.
disinfection; sterilization

odkąd [od-kownt] adv. since;
since when?; ever since; from

odkleić [od-kle-eećh] v. unglue;
unstick; detach; ungum

odkładać [od-kwa-daćh] v. put
aside; save; put back; put off

odkłonić się [od-kwo-ńeećh
śhan] v. greet back

odkopać [od-ko-paćh] v. dig up

odkorkować [od-kor-ko-vaćh]
v. uncork; unjam (the traffic)

odkręcić [od-kran-ćheećh] v.
unscrew; turn around

odkroić [od-kro-eećh] v. cut
off; carve off; slice off

odkryć [od-krićh] v. discover;
uncover; lay bare; expose; dig
up; unearth; notice; reveal

odkrycie [od-kri-ćhe] n.
discovery; exploration (of the
unknown); exposure; (a) find

odkupić [od-koo-peećh] v. repurchase; redeem; buy back;
replace; compensate; ransom

odkupienie [od-koo-pye-ńe] n.
redemption; repurchase

odkurzacz [od-koo-zhach] m.
vacuum cleaner; dust exhauster; carpet sweeper; sl. vac

odkuwać się [od-koo-vaćh
śhan] v. recoup losses; make
money (out of); make up (for)

odlać [od-laćh] v. pour off

odlatywać [od-la-ti-vaćh] v. fly
away; fly off; take off

odległość [od-leg-wośhćh] f.
distance; remoteness; interval

odległy [od-leg-wi] adj. m.
distant; remote; far away;
long ago; far removed

odlepiać [od-le-pyać] v.
unglue; unstick; detach (a
stamp, etc.); ungum

odlew [od-lef] m. cast; pour

odlewać [od-le-vać] v. pour
off; cast; mould; pour out

odlewacz [od-le-vach] m. founder

odlewnia [od-lev-ńa] f. foundry

odliczać [od-lee-chać] v.
deduct; count off; reckon off;
allow (for sale's tax, etc.)

odliczenie [od-lee-che-ńe] n.
deduction; allowance

odlot [od-lot] m. departure (by
plane); take-off; start

odludek [od-loo-dek] m. recluse

odludny [od-lood-ni] adj. m.
solitary; lonely; secluded

odłam [od-wam] m. fraction

odłamać [od-wa-mać] break
off; sever; snap off

odłamek [od-wa-mek] m. chip;
splinter; fragment; chip; stub

odłazić [od-wa-źheeć] v.
crawl away; get unstuck;
come off (the shoe, etc.)

odłączyć [od-wown-chíć] v.
sever; disconnect; separate

odłożyć [od-wo-zhíć] v. set
aside; put off; put back

odłóg [od-wook] m. fallow

odłupać [od-woo-pać] v. split
off; chip off; break off

**odma płucna [od-ma pwoots-na]
f.** pneumothorax; pneumatosis

**odmarznąć [od-marz-nownć]
v.** thaw (the snow, etc.); melt;
get warm; unfreeze

odmawiać [od-ma-vyać] v.
refuse; say prayers; decline
(an offer, etc.); recite

**odmeldować [od-mel-do-vać]
v.** take a formal leave

odmęt [od-mant] m. chaotic
whirlpool; confusion; depths

odmiana [od-mya-na] f. change;
alteration; modification

odmieniać [od-mye-ńać] v.
change; alter; decline; conjugate (a verb); modify

odmienny [od-myen-ni] adj. m.
mutable; different; unlike

odmierzać [od-mye-zhać] v.
measure off; mark off

**odmłodzić [od-mwo-dźheeć]
v.** rejuvenate; make (look)
younger; infuse new blood

odmowa [od-mo-va] f. refusal to
do; denial; saying "no"

odmówić [od-moo-veeć] v.
refuse; say prayers; say "no"

odmrozić [od-mro-źheeć] v.
get frostbite; get frozen; thaw

odmrożenie [od-mro-zhe-ńe] n.
frostbite; kibe; chilblain

**odmruknąć [od-mrook-nownć]
v.** mutter back; grunt out

odnająć [od-na-yownć] v.
sublet (rent) a room (from)

odnawiać [od-na-vyać] v.
renew; renovate; restore; recondition; reform; resume

odnajdywać [od-nay-di-vać] v.
recover; find; discover

od niechcenia [od ńe-khtse-ńa]
adv. carelessly; willy-nilly

odniemczać [od-ńem-chać] v.
remove German influence; de-
Germanize (language etc.)

odniesienie [od-ńe-śhe-ńe] n.
carrying back; reference (line)

odnieść [od-ńeśhć] v. bring
back; take back; sustain

odnoga [od-no-ga] f. spur;
branch; offshoot; river pass

odnosić [od-no-śheeć] v.
take back; carry back; bring
back (repeatedly); refer (to)

odnośnie [od-nośh-ńe] prep.
concerning; in comparison

odnośnik [od-nośh-ńeek] m.
reference; footnote (in a text)

odnośny [od-nośh-ni] adj. m.
relative; respective; proper

odnotować [od-no-to-vać] v.
check off; note down; state

odnowa [od-no-va] f. renewal;
restoration; regeneration

odnowić [od-no-veeć] v.
renew; renovate; reform; revive; restore; condition; do up

odosobnić [o-do-sob-ńeeć] v.
isolate; confine; stand alone

odosobnienie [o-do-sob-ńe-ńe]
n. isolation; privacy; seclusion

odór [o-door] m. reek; smell

odpad [od-pad] m. refuse; drop
-out; waste; muck; scraps

odpadać [od-pa-daćh] v. drop
off; come off; fall off; peel off

odpadki [od-pad-kee] pl. waste

odparcie [od-par-ćhe] n.
repulsion; rejection; refutation

odparować [od-pa-ro-vaćh] v.
parry; repel; evaporate

odparzenie [od-pa-zhe-ńe] n.
gall; scald; chafe (skin)

odparzyć [od-pa-zhićh] v.
blister; chafe one's skin

odpędzać [od-pan-dzaćh] v.
chase away; repel; expel; keep
back (away, off); banish

odpiąć [od-pyownćh] v.
unfasten; unbuckle; unclasp

odpieczętować [od-pye-chan-to-
-vaćh] v. unseal; open (a
letter); break the seal (of)

odpinać [od-pee-naćh] v. unbutton; disconnect; undo; detach; unclasp; unbuckle

odpierać [od-pye-raćh] v. repel;
refute; force back; disprove

odpiłować [od-pee-wo-vaćh] v.
saw off; file off; cut off

odpis [od-pees] m. copy

odpisać [od-pee-saćh] v. copy;
write back; answer; deduct

odpłacić [od-pwa-ćheećh] v.
repay; reciprocate; get back at

odpłata [od-pwa-ta] f. reim-
bursement; retribution; repayment; retaliation; recompense

odpłynąć [od-pwi-nownćh] v.
float away; sail away; swim
away; put to sea; row away

odpływ [od-pwif] m. low tide;
ebb; outflow; drainage; spout

odpoczynek [od-po-chi-nek] m.
rest; repose; relax from work

odpoczywać [od-po-chi-vaćh]
v. rest; have a rest; take a
rest; repose (on a sofa, etc.)

odpokutować [od-po-koo-to-
-vaćh] v. expiate; atone; pay
dearly; suffer a penalty (for)

odporność [od-por-nośhćh] f.

immunity; (power of) resistance; hardiness (of plants)

odpowiadać [od-po-vya-daćh]
v. answer to; correspond to

odpowiedni [od-po-vyed-ńee]
adj. m. respective; adequate;
suitable; fit; right; due; opportune; competent (official)

odpowiedzialność [od-po-vye-
-dźhal-nośhćh] f. respon-
sibility; liability; civil liability;
accountability (personal, etc.)

odpowiedzialny [od-po-vye-
-dźhal-ni] adj. m. responsible;
liable; accountable; trustworthy; reliable; sl. spanking

odpór [od-poor] m. opposition;
resistance; making a stand

odprasować [od-pra-so-vaćh] v.
press; iron; press out; express

odprawa [od-pra-va] f. dispatch;
rebuff; briefing; debriefing

odprawiać [od-pra-vyaćh] v.
dispatch; dismiss; celebrate
(mass); order away; rebuff;
send away; pay off; discharge

odprężać [od-pran-zhaćh] v.
relax; slacken; let down; recoil

odprężenie [od-pran-zhe-ńe] m.
relaxation; easing of tension;
detente; slackening

odprowadzać [od-pro-va-dzaćh]
v. divert; drain off; escort

odpruwać [od-proo-vaćh] v. rip
off (buttons); rip away

odpust [od-poost] m. indulgence

odpuszczenie [od-poosh-che-ńe]
n. forgiveness; remission

odpychać [od-pi-khaćh] v. repel

odpychanie [od-pi-kha-ńe] n.
repulsion; repelling

odra [od-ra] f. measles; pl.
rubeola (high fever & skin
eruption, usually of children)

odrabiać [od-ra-byaćh] v. work
off; work out; get done; undo

odraczać [od-ra-chaćh] v. put
off; postpone; defer; delay

odradzać [od-ra-dzaćh] v.
advise against; regenerate;
revive; infuse new life (into)

odrapać [od-ra-paćh] v.
scratch; dilapidate; scrape off

odrastać [od-ras-tać] v. grow
back; sprout again; shoot
again; grow again; sucker
odraza [od-ra-za] f. aversion
odrazu [od-ra-zoo] adv. at once
odrażający [od-ra-zha-yown-tsi]
adj. m. repulsive; hideous
odrąbać [od-rown-bać] v.
chop off; hew away; cut off
odrębność [od-ranb-nośhćh]
n. distinction; individuality
odrębny [od-ranb-ni] adj. m.
distinct; individual; separate
odręczny [od-ranch-ni] adj. m.
freehand; personal; longhand
odrętwiały [od-rant-vya-wi] adj.
m. numbed; torpid; stiff
odrobić [od-ro-beećh] v. work
off; work out; get done; do
odrobina [od-ro-bee-na] f. small
bit; particle; shred; a dash
odroczenie [od-ro-che-ńe] n.
adjournment; postponement
odroczyć [od-ro-chićh] v. put
off; delay; defer; postpone
odrodzenie [od-ro-dze-ńe] m.
rebirth; renaissance
odrodzić [od-ro-dźheećh] v.
regenerate; renew; revive
odróżniać [od-roozh-ńaćh] v.
distinguish; differentiate
odróżniać się [od-roozh-ńaćh
śhan] v. differ; be different
odruch [od-rookh] m. reflex
odrywać [od-ri-vaćh] v. tear
off; sever; separate; break off
odrzeć [od-zhećh] v. reply
odrzucać [od-zhoo-tsaćh] v.
reject; repulse; cast away
odrzutowiec [od-zhoo-to-vyets]
m. jet-propelled plane; jet
odrzwia [odzh-vya] pl. door
-frame; mine prop set
odrzynać [od-zhi-naćh] v. cut
off; cut away; detach; sever
odsądzać [od-sown-dzaćh] v.
deny (talent); deprive of merit;
refuse to acknowledge
odsetka [od-set-ka] f. interest
point; percentage; proportion
odsiadywać [od-śha-di-vaćh]
v. sit out; serve (sentence)
odsiecz [od-śhech] f. rescue (of

besieged fortress, etc.)
odskoczyć [od-sko-chićh] v.
jump off; spring back; dart
away; make a leap aside
odsłonić [od-swo-ńeećh] v.
unveil; expose; display; show
odsprzedać [od-spshe-daćh] v.
resell; sale at second hand
odsprzedaż [od-spshe-dash] f.
resale; sale at second hand
odstawać [od-sta-vaćh] v. hang
loose; not fit; come off
odstawić [od-sta-veećh] v. put
aside; deliver; play (dumb)
odstąpić [od-stown-peećh] v.
step back; secede; cede
odstęp [od-stanp] m. margin;
space; interval; lapse (of time)
odstępca [od-stanp-tsa] m.
renegade; deserter; turncoat
odstępne [od-stanp-ne] n.·
payment for giving up a lease
odstraszyć [od-stra-shićh] v.
deter; frighten away; scare
odstręczyć [od-stran-chićh] v.
dissuade; turn away; repel;
deter; be repulsive; frighten
odstrzał [od-stshaw] m. shooting
off; firing (game, mine)
odsunąć [od-soo-nownćh] v.
push away; shove away; put
away; brush aside; remove
odsyłacz [od-si-wach] m.
reference mark; footnote mark
odsyłać [od-si-waćh] v. send
back; refer; return; direct
odsypać [od-si-paćh] v. pour
off (not liquid); alluviate
odsypiać [od-si-pyaćh] v. catch
up on sleep; sleep off
odszkodowanie [od-shko-do-va-
-ńe] n. indemnity; compensation; (war) damages; award
odszukać [od-shoo-kaćh] v.
retrieve; run down; seek out;
find; detect (a leak, etc.)
odśrodkowy [od-śhrod-ko-vi]
adj. m. centrifugal
odświeżyć [od-śhvye-zhićh]
v. refresh; recondition; restore
odświętny [od-śhvyant-ni]
adj. m. festive; ceremonial;
showy; one's Sunday best

odtąd [od-townt] adv. hence
-forth; from now on; from
here; thereafter; since then
odtłuścić [od-twoośh-
-ćheećh] v. degrease; reduce
weight; extract the fat; scour
odtrącać [od-trown-tsaćh] v.
repel; jostle; knock off; deduct
(charges); thrust aside; spurn
odtrutka [od-troot-ka] f. antidote
against poison; counterpoison
odtwarzać [od-tva-zhaćh]
v. reproduce; reconstitute
odtwórca [od-tvoor-tsa] m. ren-
derer; reproducer; performer
oduczać [o-doo-chaćh] v. dis-
accustom; unteach; unlearn;
break (cure, correct) a habit
odurzać [o-doo-zhaćh] v. stun;
make dopey; stupefy; daze;
dizzy; intoxicate; fuddle
odurzenie [o-doo-zhe-ńe] n.
stupor; giddiness; intoxication
odwadniać [od-vad-ńaćh] v.
drain; dehydrate; desiccate
odwaga [od-va-ga] f. courage
odwalić [od-va-leećh] v. push
away; beat it; copy; get over
with; roll aside; remove; sham
odwar [od-var] m. decoction
odważnik [od-vazh-ńeek] m.
scale-weight; (pound) weight
odważny [od-vazh-ni] adj. m.
brave; courageous; bold
(man); daring; plucky; spunky
odważyć [od-va-zhićh] v.
weigh; weigh out; consider
odważyć się [od-va-zhićh
śhan] v. dare; have the
courage (the pluck); risk
odwdzięczyć się [od-vdźhan-
-chićh śhan] v. repay (with
gratitude); return; requite
odwet [od-vet] m. retaliation;
retort; revenge; requital
odwiązać [od-vyown-zaćh] v.
untie; unfasten; unbuckle;
undo; unbend (a wire, etc.)
odwieczny [od-vyech-ni] adj. m.
eternal; immemorial; age long
odwiedzać [od-vye-dzaćh] v.
visit; call on; pay a visit; pay a
call; come and see; frequent

odwiedziny [od-vye-dźhee-ni] n.
visit; call; coming to see
odwijać [od-vee-yaćh] v.
unwrap; draw back one's fist
odwilż [od-veelzh] f. thaw
odwlekać [od-vle-kaćh] v. put
off; postpone; delay; drag
away; haul aside; defer
odwodnić [od-vod-ńeećh] v.
drain; desiccate; dehydrate
odwodzić [od-vo-dźheećh] v.
draw off; draw aside; dissuade; abduct; cock (a gun)
odwołać [od-vo-waćh] v. take
back; appeal; refer; recall
odwołanie [od-vo-wa-ńe] n.
recall; appeal; repeal; can-
cellation; withdrawal; revo-
cation; annulment; removal
odwozić [od-vo-źheećh] v.
take back (by car); drive back
odwód [od-voot] m. reserve
odwracać [od-vra-tsaćh] v.
reverse; turn around; invert
odwrotny [od-vrot-ni] adj. m.
reverse; opposite; converse
odwrót [od-vroot] m. retreat;
reverse (side); withdrawal
odwykać [od-vi-kaćh] v. break
a habit; loose a habit
odwzajemniać [od-vza-yem-
-ńaćh] v. reciprocate (a
feeling, etc,); repay; return
odyniec [o-di-ńets] m. boar
odzew [od-zev] m. echo; reply
odziedziczyć [o-dźhe-dźhee-
-chićh] v. inherit; succeed
odzienie [o-dźhe-ńe] n. clothing
odzież [o-dźhesh] f. clothes
odznaczać [od-zna-chaćh] v.
distinguish; decorate; mark off
odznaczenie [od-zna-che-ńe] n.
distinction; award; decoration
odznaka [od-zna-ka] f. badge
odzwierciedlać [od-zvyer-će-
-dlaćh] v. reflect (something)
odzwyczajać [od-zvi-cha-yaćh]
v. break (cure, correct) a
habit; make loose a habit
odzyskać [od-zis-kaćh] v.
retrieve; regain; recover; win
back; resume possession
odzywać się [od-zi-vaćh śhan]

v. speak up; drop a line; respond; address; pass a word

odźwierny [o-dźhvyer-ni] m.
doorman; janitor; caretaker

odżyć [od-zhićh] v. come back to life; be reborn; reappear

odżywczy [od-zhiv-chi] adj. m.
nutritious; nourishing; alimentary; nutritive; refreshing

odżywiać [od-zhi-vyaćh] v.
nourish; feed; supply a person with (food) nourishment

odżywienie [od-zhi-vye-ńe] n.
food; nourishment; diet

ofensywa [o-fen-si-va] f.
offensive; push; attack

oferma [o-fer-ma] f. sad sack

oferta [o-fer-ta] f. offer

ofiara [o-fya-ra] f. victim;
offering; sacrifice; dupe

oficer [o-fee-tser] m. (military)
officer (in the army)

oficjalny [o-feets-yal-ni] adj. m.
official; formal; reserved

oficyna [o-fee-tsi-na] f.
back house; printing shop;
annex; outbuilding

ofuknąć [o-fook-nownćh] v.
rebuke (severely or formally);
reprimand; trounce; rate

ogar [o-gar] m. bloodhound

ogarek [o-ga-rek] m. candle-end;
stump; stub; cigarette end

ogarniać [o-gar-ńaćh] v. seize;
comprehend; take in; grasp

ogień [o-gyeń] m. fire; flame

ogier [o-gyer] m. stallion

oglądać [o-glown-daćh] v.
inspect; consider; see

oględny [o-gland-ni] adj. m.
circumspect; moderate; cautious; gentle (words, etc.)

ogłada [o-gwa-da] f. good
manners (delicacy and elegance); refinement; urbanity

ogłaszać [o-gwa-shaćh] v.
advertise; declare; publish

ogłuchnąć [o-gwookh-nownćh]
v. become deaf; be hushed

ogłupieć [o-gwoo-pyećh] v.
become stupid; grow silly

ognie sztuczne [o-gńe shtooch-
-ne] pl. fireworks

ogniotrwały [o-gńo-**trva**-wi] adj.
m. fireproof; incombustible

ognisko [og-ńees-ko] n. hearth;
focus; camp fire; fire place

ognisty [og-ńees-ti] adj. m.
fiery; flaming; passionate

ogniwo [o-gńee-vo] n. link

ogolić [o-go-leećh] v. shave

ogon [o-gon] m. tail; trail; scut

ogonek [o-go-nek] m. waiting
line; queue; diacritical mark

ogorzały [o-go-zha-wi] adj. m.
sunburnt; tanned; weather
beaten (man, car, etc,); tawny

ogólnie [o-gool-ńe] adv.
generally; as a rule; universally

ogólny [o-gool-ni] adj. m.
general; prevailing; global; total; universal; common (room)

ogół [o-goow] m. people; public

ogółem [o-goo-wem] adv. on the
whole; as a whole; altogether

ogórek [o-goo-rek] m. cucumber

ogórkowy sezon [o-goor-ko-vi se-
-zon] slack time (season)

ograbić [o-gra-beećh] v. rob

ograniczony [o-gra-ńee-cho-ni]
adj. m. narrow-minded; limited

ogrodnik [o-grod-ńeek] m.
gardener; horticulturist

ogrodzić [o-gro-dźheećh] v.
fence in (one's farm, property,
etc.); enclose; wall in; rail in;

ogromny [o-grom-ni] adj. m.
huge; tremendous; colossal

ogród [o-groot] m. garden

ogryzać [o-gri-zaćh] v. gnaw
away; nimble at; pick (a bone)

ogrzewać [o-gzhe-vaćh] v. heat

ohydny [o-khid-ni] adj. m.
hideous; ghastly; abominable;
vile; offensive; filthy; horrid

o ile [o ee-le] conj. as far as

ojciec [oy-ćhets] m. father

ojciec chrzestny [oy-ćhets
khzhest-ni] godfather

ojczym [oy-chim] m. stepfather

ojczysty język [oy-chis-ti **yan**-zik]
native tongue; mother tongue

ojczyzna [oy-chiz-na] f. native
country (land, soil); motherland; homeland; fatherland

okaleczyć [o-ka-le-chićh] v.

maim; cripple; lame; mutilate
oka mgnienie [o-ka mgńe-ńe] n.
eye blink; split second
okap [o-kap] m. eaves; overlap
okaz [o-kas] m. specimen; type
okazać [o-ka-zaćh] v. show;
demonstrate; evidence; exhibit
okazały [o-ka-za-wi] adj. m.
magnificent; stately; grand
okaziciel [o-ka-źhee-ćhel] m.
bearer (of a check etc.)
okazja [o-ka-zya] f. opportunity
okazyjny [o-ka-ziy-ni] adj. m.
occasional; opportune (buy);
chance (acquaintance, etc.)
okazywać [o-ka-zi-vaćh] v.
demonstrate; show (one's
passport); manifest; display
oklaski [o-klas-kee] pl. applause;
clapping; acclamation
oklaskiwać [o-klas-kee-vaćh] v.
applaud; clap (one's hands)
okleić [o-kle-eećh] v. paste-
-over; stick over; smear over
oklepany [o-kle-pa-ni] adj. m.
commonplace; (well) worn
okład [o-kwat] m. compress;
hot pad; lining; wrapping
okładka [o-kwad-ka] f. (book)
cover; book binding
okłamać [o-kwa-maćh] v.
deceive; tell a lie; delude
okno [o-kno] n. window
oko [o-ko] n. eye; eye sight
okolica [o-ko-lee-tsa] f. region;
surroundings; vicinity
okoliczność [o-ko-leech-
-nośćh] f. circumstance;
fact; occasion
około [o-ko-wo] prep. near;
about; more or less; on; or
okoń [o-koń] m. perch; bass
okop [o-kop] m. trench
okopcić [o-kop-ćheećh] v.
soot; blacken with smoke
okopcony [o-kop-tso-ni] adj. m.
sooty; blackened with soot
okostna [o-kost-na] f.
periosteum; (very sensitive)
lining of the bones
okólnik [o-kool-ńeek] m. circular
(letter); corral; poultry yard
okpić [o-kpeećh] v. pull wool

over eyes; deceive; cheat; gull
okradać [o-kra-daćh] v. pick
-pocket; burglarize; rob
okrakiem [o-kra-kem] adv.
astraddle; with legs wide apart
okrasa [o-kra-sa] f. fat;
ornament; embellishment; flavoring; seasoning; gravy; lard
okrasić [o-kra-śheećh] v.
adorn; season; add a
condiment; embellish a dish
okratować [o-kra-to-vaćh] v.
grate; bar (a window)
okratowanie [o-kra-to-va-ńe] m.
grating; railings; bars
okrąg [o-krownk] m. district
okrągły [o-krown-gwi] adj. m.
round; spherical; full (month,
hour, etc.); well-mannered
okrążać [o-krown-zhaćh] v.
encircle; circle; revolve; detour
okres [o-kres] m. period; phase
określać [o-kreśh-laćh] v.
define; qualify; fix; appoint
okręcać [o-kran-tsaćh] v. coil
around; wrap; turn around
okręt [o-krant] m. ship; boat
okrężny [o-kranzh-ni] adj. m.
roundabout; indirect; devious
(ways); circuitous; circular;
travelling-peddlar's (trader)
okropność [o-krop-nośćh] f.
horror; atrocity; outrage
okropny [o-krop-ni] adj. m.
horrible; fearful; awful; extreme; ghastly; atrocious
okruch [o-krookh] m. crumb
okrucieństwo [o-kroo-ćheń-
-stvo] n. cruelty; atrocities
okrutny [o-kroot-ni] adj. m. cruel;
savage; excessive; sore
okrycie [o-kri-ćhe] n. covering;
wrap; garment; overcoat
okrywać [o-kri-vaćh] v. cover
okrzyczany [o-kzhi-cha-ni]
adj. m. notorious; famous;
renowned; far-famed (person)
okrzyk [o-kzhik] m. outcry
okrzyknąć [o-kzhik-nownćh] v.
proclaim; declare; brand
oktawa [o-kta-va] f. octave
okucie [o-koo-ćhe] n. hardware;
ferrule; fitting; fixtures

okuć [o-kooćh] v. shoe a
   horse; hackle; fit a lock and
   hinges; fix metal fittings
okularnik [o-koo-lar-ńeek] m.
   cobra; poisonous snake of
   Asia (Naja naja)
okulary [o-koo-la-ri] pl.
   eyeglasses; eyepiece
okulista [o-koo-lees-ta] m. eye
   doctor; eye surgeon; oculist
okultyzm [o-kool-tizm] m.
   occultism; hidden knowledge
okup [o-koop] m. ransom
okupacja [o-koo-pats-ya] f.
   occupation; occupancy
okupować [o-koo-po-vaćh] v.
   occupy; invade a territory
okupywać [o-koo-pi-vaćh] v.
   pay ransom; pay dearly; buy;
   compensate; redeem; atone
olbrzym [ol-bzhim] m. giant
olbrzymi [ol-bzhi-mee] adj. m.
   gigantic; huge; colossal; excessive; tremendous; untold
olcha [ol-kha] f. alder tree
oleander [o-le-an-der] m.
   oleander (an evergreen shrub)
olej [o-ley] m. oil; oil paint
olej lniany [o-ley lńa-ni] m.
   linseed-oil (from flaxseed)
oligarchia [o-lee-gar-khya] m.
   oligarchy; the ruling persons
oliwa [o-lee-va] f. olive; oil
oliwić [o-lee-veećh] v. oil
oliwka [o-leev-ka] f. olive-tree
olszyna [ol-shi-na] f. alder-tree
   stand (forest); alder wood
olśniewać [ol-śhńe-vaćh] v.
   dazzle; ravish; enchant
ołów [o-woof] m. lead; lead shot
ołówek [o-woo-vek] m. lead
   pencil; drawing in pencil
ołtarz [ow-tash] m. altar
omackiem [o-mats-kem] adv.
   gropingly; blindfold
omal [o-mal] adv. nearly
omamić [o-ma-meećh] v.
   deceive; beguile; delude
omaścić [o-maśh-ćheećh] v.
   add fat; add butter (on bread
   etc.); flavor (a dish)
omawiać [o-ma-vyaćh] v.
   discuss (a subject, etc.)

omdlały [om-dla-wi] adj. m.
   fainted; faint; languid
omdleć [om-dlećh] v. faint
omen [o-men] m. omen
omieszkać [o-myesh-kaćh] v.
   fail; omit; neglect (to do)
omijać [o-mee-yaćh] v. pass
omlet [om-let] m. omelet
omłócić [om-woo-ćheećh] v.
   thrash out; give a thrashing
omotać [o-mo-taćh] v. entangle
omówić [o-moo-veećh] v.
   discuss (pending matters)
omylić [o-mi-leećh] v. mislead
omylny [o-mil-ni] adj. m. fallible;
   misleading; deceitful
omyłka [o-miw-ka] f. error
on [on] pron. he; this (man)
ona [o-na] pron. she
ondulacja [on-doo-lats-ya]
   f. (hair) wave; (permanent
   hair) wave; wave in the hair
ondulacja trwała [on-doo-lats-ya
   trva-wa] permanent (wave)
onegdaj [o-neg-day] adv. the
   other day; two days ago
ongiś [on-geeśh] adv. (arch) at
   one time; once upon a time
oni [o-ńee] pron. m. pl. they
oniemiały [o-ńe-mya-wi] adj. m.
   mute; dumb; speechless
onieśmielać [o-ńe-śhmye-
   -laćh] v. intimidate; browbeat;
   cow; overawe; abash
ono [o-no] pron. it
opactwo [o-pats-tvo] n. abbey
opaczny [o-pach-ni] adj. m.
   wrong; mistaken; improper
opad [o-pat] m. (rain) fall
opadać [o-pa-daćh] v. subside
(na) opak [na o-pak] adv. upside
   down; reverse; wrong way
opakowanie [o-pa-ko-va-ńe] n.
   wrapping; packing; wrappage
opal [o-pal] m. opal
opalać się [o-pa-laćh śhan] v.
   suntan; tan; bronze; lie (bask)
   in the sun; get sunburnt
opalanie [o-pa-la-ńe] n. heating
   (house etc.); fire marking
opalenizna [o-pa-le-ńeez-na] f.
   suntan; tan; scorched remains
opał [o-paw] m. fuel for heating

opamiętać [o-pa-my<u>an</u>-taćh] v. sober up; bring to reason

opanować [o-pa-no-vaćh] v. master; conquer; seize; learn

opanowany [o-pa-no-**va**-ni] adj. m. cool-headed (person); composed; calm; self-possessed

opary [o-**pa**-ri] pl. fumes

oparcie [o-par-ćhe] n. support

oparzyć [o-pa-zhićh] v. scald

opasać [o-pa-saćh] v. belt; girdle; grid; encircle; surround

opaska [o-pas-ka] f. band

opasły [o-pas-wi] adj. m. obese

opaść [o-paśhćh] v. drop; sink; hang loose; settle; collapse; slump; fall away

opatentować [o-pa-ten-to-vaćh] v. patent; take out a patent

opatrunek [o-pa-troo-nek] m. dressing; bandage; field dressing (of a wound, etc,)

opatrywać [o-pa-tri-vaćh] v. fix; dress; provide; prepare

opera [o-pe-ra] f. opera; opera house; no end of a joke

operacja [o-pe-rats-ya] f. surgery; operation; action; process

operować [o-pe-ro-vaćh] v. operate (on a person); manipulate; act; handle; use; run carry on (financial operations)

opętanie [o-p<u>an</u>-ta-ńe] n. obsession (demonical, etc.)

opieczętować [o-pye-ch<u>an</u>-to -vaćh] v. seal up; seal

opieka [o-pye-ka] f. care

opiekować [o-pye-ko-vaćh] v. take care of; care for; have charge of; nurse (a patient)

opiekun [o-pye-koon] m. guardian; curator; foster-parent; curator; warden

opierać się [o-pye-raćh śh<u>an</u>] v. lean; base; relay; rest; defy

opieszały [o-pye-sha-wi] adj. m. slow; tardy; lazy; inert

opinia [o-pee-ńya] f. opinion; view; reputation; sentiment

opis [o-pees] m. description

oplątać [o-pl<u>own</u>-taćh] v. ensnare; entangle; entwine

opluwać [o-ploo-vaćh] v. spit on; spit at; slander; defame

opłacać [o-pwa-tsaćh] v. pay; bribe; cover the cost; reward

opłakany [o-pwa-ka-ni] adj. m. deplorable; sad; pitiful

opłakiwać [o-pwa-kee-vaćh] v. lament; deplore; mourn

opłata [o-pwa-ta] f. fee

opłatek [o-pwa-tek] m. wafer

opłucna [o-pwoots-na] f. pleura; membrane around the lungs

opłukiwać [o-pwoo-kee-vaćh] v. rinse; wash with water

opływać [o-pwi-vaćh] v. sail around; abound; encircle; roll

opływowy [o-pwi-vo-vi] adj. m. streamlined; streamline

opodal [o-po-dal] adv. near by

opodatkować [o-po-dat-ko -vaćh] v. tax; impose a tax

opona [o-po-na] f. tire

oponować [o-po-no-vaćh] v. oppose; take exception

opornie [o-por-ńe] adv. with difficulty; arduously

oporny [o-por-ni] adj. m. balky; recalcitrant; refractory

opowiadać [o-po-vya-daćh] v. tell-tale; relate; record

opozycja [o-po-zits-ya] f. opposition; resistance

opór [o-poor] m. resistance

opóźniać [o-poożh-ńaćh] v. delay; retard; slow down; defer; hold back; detain

opóźnienie [o-poożh-ńe-ńe] n. delay; deferment; tardiness

opracować [o-pra-tso-vaćh] v. work up; elaborate; compile

oprawa [o-pra-va] f. frame; binding; framework; handle

oprawca [o-prav-tsa] m. skinner; executioner; torturer; assassin

opresja [o-pres-ya] f. oppression

oprocentowanie [o-pro-tsen-to- -va-ńe] n. interest (on money)

oprowadzać [o-pro-va-dzaćh] v. show around; act as a guide

oprócz [o-prooch] prep. except; besides; apart from; but; save

opróżniać [o-proozh-ńaćh] v. empty; clear; evacuate; unload

opryskliwy [o-pris-klee-vi] adj. m.

peevish; gruff; harsh
opryszek [o-**pri**-shek] m.
  hoodlum; hooligan; rowdy
  (man); rough-neck; gangster
oprzeć [o-**pzheć**] v. lean on;
  base; rest; prop up; resist;
  become inflamed; inflame
oprzytomnieć [o-pzhi-tom-
  -**ńeć**] v. recover; collect
  oneself; regain consciousness
optyk [op-tik] m. optician
optymista [op-ti-**mees**-ta] m.
  optimist; one of cheerful
  views that good prevails
opublikować [o-poo-blee-ko-
  -vać] v. publish; make public
opuchły [o-pookh-wi] adj. m.
  swollen; dilated; distended
opuchlina [o-pookh-lee-na] f.
  swelling; dilatation
opuszczać [o-poosh-chać] v.
  leave; omit; abandon; lower;
  let down; lower (a price)
opustoszały [o-poos-to-sha-wi]
  adj. m. deserted; desolate;
  empty; abandoned; vacant
opuszczenie [o-poosh-che-ńe] n.
  omission; lowering; reduction
orać [o-rać] v. till; plough
oranżeria [o-ran-zher-ya] f.
  greenhouse; hothouse
oraz [o-ras] conj. as well as
orbita [or-bee-ta] f. orbit
order [or-der] m. decoration;
  order (for service rendered)
ordynarny [or-di-nar-ni] adj. m.
  gross; coarse; vulgar; trashy;
  uncouth; unrefined; boorish
orędzie [o-ran-dźhe] n. (official)
  message; proclamation
oręż [o-ransh] m. weapon
organiczny [or-ga-ńeech-ni] adj.
  m. organic; constitutional
organista [or-ga-ńees-ta] m.
  organist; organ player
organizacja [or-ga-ńee-zats-ya] f.
  organization; organized group
organizm [or-ga-ńeezm] m.
  organism; any living thing
orgia [or-gya] f. orgy
orka [or-ka] f. tillage
orkiestra [or-kes-tra] f.
  orchestra; orchestra pit

orny [or-ni] adj. m. arable
orszak [or-shak] m. retinue
ortodoksja [or-to-doks-ya] f.
  orthodoxy; conventionality
ortografia [or-to-gra-fya] f.
  orthography; correct spelling
oryginalny [o-ri-gee-nal-ni]
  adj. m. original; inventive; new
orzech [o-zhekh] m. nut; walnut
orzeczenie [o-zhe-che-ńe] m.
  decision; sentence; ruling
orzeł [o-zhew] m. eagle; genius
orzeźwiać [o-zheźh-vyać] v.
  refresh; brace up; invigorate
osa [o-sa] f. wasp; vixen; shrew
osad [o-sat] m. sediment; dregs
osada [o-sa-da] f. settlement
osadnik [o-sad-ńeek] m. settler
osadzać [o-sa-dzać] v. plant;
  seat; settle; place; fix; steady
osamotnienie [o-sa-mot-ńe-ńe]
  n. isolation; loneliness
osądzać [o-sown-dzać] v.
  sentence; judge; prejudge
oschły [oskh-wi] adj. m. arid;
  dry; cold; stiff; stand-offish
osełka [o-sew-ka] f. whetstone
oset [o-set] m. thistle; teasel
osiadać [o-śha-dać] v. settle;
  subside; make a settlement
osiągnąć [o-śhowng-nownć]
  v. attain; achieve; gain; reach
osiedlać [o-śhed-lać] v.
  settle; make a settlement
osiem [o-śhem] num. eight; 8
osiemdziesiąt [o-śhem-dźhe-
  -śhownt] num. eighty; 80
osiemnaście [o-śhem-naśh-
  -ćhe] num. eighteen; 18
osiemset [o-śhem-set] num.
  eight hundred; 800
osierocić [o-śhe-ro-ćheećh] v.
  orphaned (a child); desert
osika [o-śhee-ka] f. aspen
osikać [o-śhee-kaćh] v.
  sprinkle; piss on (vulg.)
osiodłać [o-śhod-waćh] v.
  saddle; reduce to subjugation
osioł [o-śhow] m. donkey; ass
oskarżać [os-kar-zhaćh] v.
  accuse; charge with; indict
oskrzela [os-kshe-la] pl. n.
  bronchia; two main branches

of the windpipe
oskrzydlać [os-kshid-laćh] v.
outflank; go beyond; cut off
oskubać [os-koo-baćh] v.
fleece; feather; pluck (a fowl,
etc.); skin; soak (somebody)
osłabiać [o-swa-byaćh] v. impair; weaken; reduce; lessen;
diminish; attenuate; abate
osłabienie [o-swa-bye-ńe] n.
weakness; diminution; debili-
tation; mitigation; abatement
osłona [o-swo-na] f. shield;
cover; protection; defense
osładzać [o-swa-dzaćh] v.
sweeten; put sugar; cheer up
osłupiały [o-swoo-pya-wi] adj. m.
amazed; aghast; astounded
osmarować [o-sma-ro-vaćh] v.
besmear; libel; run down; soil
osoba [o-so-ba] f. person
osobisty [o-so-bees-ti] adj. m.
personal; private; particular
osobiście [o-so-beeśh-ćhe]
adv. personally; in person
osobnik [o-sob-ńeek] m.
individual; specimen; person
osobny [o-sob-ni] adj. m.
separate; private; individual
osobowość [o-so-bo-vośhćh]
f. personality; individuality
osowiały [o-so-vya-wi] adj. m.
depressed; dejected; glum;
mopish; chap-fallen (person)
ospa [os-pa] f. smallpox
ospały [os-pa-wi] adj. m.
drowsy; sleepy; sluggish; dull
ostatecznie [o-sta-tech-ńe] adv.
finally; after all; at last
ostateczny [os-ta-tech-ni]
adj. m. final; ultimate; decisive; eventual; extreme
ostatek [o-sta-tek] m. reminder;
rest; remains; scrap; leavings
ostatni [o-stat-ńe] adj. m. last;
late; end; closing; parting
ostatnio [o-sta-tńo] adv. of late;
lately; not long ago; recently
ostoja [o-sto-ya] f. mainstay
ostroga [o-stro-ga] f. spur
ostrokątny [o-stro-kownt-ni] adj.
m. sharp-angled (object)
ostrożność [o-strozh-no śhćh]

f. caution; prudence; care
ostrożny [o-strozh-ni] adj. m.
careful; prudent; cautious;
wary; circumspect; discreet
ostry [o-stri] adj. m. sharp
ostryga [o-stri-ga] f. oyster
ostrze [o-stshe] n. cutting edge;
spike; blade; point; prong
ostrzegać [o-stshe-gaćh] v.
warn of; warn against; admonish; put on guard; advise
ostrzeliwać [o-stshe-lee-vaćh]
v. shoot at; strafe; fire at;
accustom to gun fire
ostrzeżenie [o-stshe-zhe-ńe] n.
warning; danger sign; notice
ostrzyć [o-stshićh] v. sharpen;
whet; grind; put an edge
ostrzygać [o-stshi-gaćh] v. cut
(hair); shear sheep; trim
ostudzać [o-stoo-dzaćh] v. cool
ostygać [o-sti-gaćh] v. cool
down; chill; cool off; abate
osuszać [o-soo-shaćh] v. dry;
drain; dehumidify; wipe; mop
oswobodzić [o-svo-bo-
-dźheećh] v. free; liberate;
rescue; rid of; set free
oswoić [o-svo-eećh] v. tame;
familiarize; domesticate
oszacować [o-sha-tso-vaćh] v.
evaluate; estimate; appraise
oszczep [osh-chep] m. javelin
oszczerstwo [osh-cher-stvo] n.
calumny; libel; defamation
oszczędności [osh-chand-nośh
-ćhee] pl. savings (money)
oszklenie [osh-kle-ńe] n. glazing
(of windows); window panes
oszołomić [o-sho-wo-meećh] v.
stun, daze; stupefy; bewilder
oszpecić [o-shpe-ćheećh] v.
deface; disfigure; deform; mar
oszukać [o-shoo-kaćh] v. cheat
oszust [o-shoost] m. cheater
oś [ośh] f. axle (axis)
ościenny [ośh-ćhen-ni] adj. m.
bordering; adjoining; adjacent
ość [ośhćh] f. (fish) bone
oślepiać [o-śhle-pyaćh] v.
blind; dazzle; strike blind
ośmieszać [o-śhmye-shaćh]
v. ridicule; deride; make fun of

ośrodek [o-**śhro**-dek] m. center
oświadczenie [o-śhviad-che--ńe] n. declaration; assertion; pronouncement
oświadczyny [o-śhvyad-chi-ni] pl. marriage proposal
oświata [o-**śhvia**-ta] f. education; learning
oświecać [o-**śhvye**-tsaćh] v. light up; enlighten; educate
oświetlenie [o-śviet-le-ńe] n. lighting; light; illumination
otaczać [o-ta-chaćh] v. surround; enclose; turn on a lathe; embrace; encircle
otchłań [ot-khwań] f. abyss
otępienie [o-<u>tan</u>-pye-ńe] n. dullness; stupor; stupefaction
oto [o-to] part. here; there
otoczenie [o-to-che-ńe] n. environment; setting; neighborhood; (one's) associates
otoczyć [o-to-chićh] v. surround; enclose; turn on a lathe; embrace; encircle
otomana [o-to-ma-na] f. couch
otóż [o-toosh] conj. now
otruć [o-trooćh] v. poison
otrucie [o-troo-ćhe] n. poisoning
otrzaskać [o-tzhas-kaćh] v. acquaint with; accustom to
otrząsać [o-tzh<u>own</u>-saćh] v. shake loose; shudder; strew
otrzewna [o-tzhev-na] f. peritoneum; lining of abdomen
otrzeźwieć [o-tzheźh-vyećh] v. sober up; be disillusioned; brisk up; bring around (back)
otrzymać [o-tzhi-maćh] v. receive; get; be given; acquire
otulić [o-too-leećh] v. tuck in; wrap; wrap up; shroud; envelop; enfold with; lag with
otwarcie [o-tvar-ćhe] adv. 1. openly; frankly; in plain words; outright; 2. n. opening
otwarty [o-tvar-ti] adj. m. open; frank; overt; professed
otwierać [o-tvye-raćh] v. open
otwór [ot-voor] m. opening
otyły [o-ti-wi] adj. m. obęse
owa [o-va] f. pron. that
owad [o-vad] m. insect

owal [o-val] m. oval
owca [ov-tsa] f. sheep
owczarek [ov-cha-rek] m. sheep-dog
owczarnia [ov-char-ńa] f. sheep-fold; fold
owdowiały [ov-do-vya-wi] adj. m. widowed; a man who lost wife and did not remarry
owe [o-ve] pl. f. pron. that
owacja [o-vats-ya] f. ovation
owies [o-vyes] m. oats
owi [o-vee] pl. m. pron. that
owiewać [o-vye-vaćh] v. blow upon; sweep over; encompass; inspire; enwrap
owijać [o-vee-yaćh] v. wrap up
owłosiony [o-vwo-**śho**-ni] adj. m. hairy; hirsute; pilose (man); shaggy (animal)
owo [o-vo] n. pron. that; that thing; the said (thing)
owoc [o-vots] m. fruit; fruitage
owrzodzenie [o-vzho-dze-ńe] n. ulceration; sore; sores
owsianka [ov-śhan-ka] f. oatmeal; kasha; porridge
owszem [ov-shem] part. yes; certainly; on the contrary
ozdabiać [oz-da-byaćh] v. decorate; adorn; trim; garnish
ozdoba [oz-do-ba] f. decoration
oziębiać [o-źhan-byaćh] v. cool off; chill; cool down; damp (spirits); refrigerate
oziębły [o-źhanb-wi] adj. m. frigid; cold; reserved; dry
oznaczać [o-zna-chaćh] v. mark; signify; indicate; fix; spell out; denote; determine
oznajmiać [o-znay-myaćh] v. announce; inform; notify; state (one's opinion, etc.)
oznaka [o-zna-ka] f. sign; symptom; badge; mark; token
ozór [o-zoor] m. (bull's) tongue; gossiping tongue; (ox) tongue
ożenić [o-zhe-ńeećh] v. marry
ożywiać [o-zhi-vyaćh] v. bring to life; animate; brisk up
ożywienie [o-zhi-vye-ńe] n. animation; liveliness; stir
ożywiony [o-zhi-vyo-ni] adj. m.

animated; lively; brisk

Ó

ósemka [oo-sem-ka] f. eight; 8
ósma godzina [oos-ma go--dźhee-na] eight o'clock
ósmak [oos-mak] m. eighth grader; eighth grade pupil
ów [oof] m. pron. that
ówczesny [oov-ches-ni] adj. m. the then; of those days
ówdzie [oov-dźhe] adv. elsewhere; there

P

pa ! [pa] excl.: bye-bye !
pacha [pa-kha] f. armpit
pachnąć [pakh-nownćh] v. smell (good); have a fragrance
pacholek [pa-kho-wek] m. boy; page; servant; menial; flunky
pachwina [pakh-vee-na] f. groin
pacierz [pa-ćhesh] m. prayer
pacierzowy stos [pa-ćhe-zho-vi stos] m. spinal column; spine
paciorki [pa-ćhor-kee] pl. string of beads; short prayer
pacjent [pa-tsyent] m. patient
pacyfista [pa-tsi-fees-ta] m. pacifist; believer in peace
pacyfizm [pa-tsi-feezm] m. pacifism; ideology of peace
paczka [pach-ka] f. parcel
paczyć [pa-chićh] v. warp
padać [pa-daćh] v. fall down
padalec [pa-da-lets] m. blind -worm; slow warm
padlina [pa-dlee-na] f. carrion
pagórek [pa-goo-rek] m. hill
pająk [pa-yownk] m. spider
pajęczyna [pa-yan-chi-na] f. cobweb; spider's web;

gossamer
paka [pa-ka] f. crate; lock-up
pakować [pa-ko-vaćh] v. pack; cram; wrap; pack off; pack up
pakunek [pa-koo-nek] m. baggage; package; parcel; bundle
pal [pal] m. pile; stake; picket
palący [pa-lown-tsi] m. smoker
palec [pa-lets] m. finger; toe
palenie [pa-le-ńe] n. smoking
palenisko [pa-le-ńees-ko] n. hearth; fireplace; grate
paleta [pa-le-ta] f. palette
palić [pa-leećh] v. burn; smoke cigarette; heat; scorch; shoot
paliwo [pa-lee-vo] n. fuel
palma [pal-ma] f. palm tree
palnik [pal-ńeek] m. burner
palto [pal-to] m. overcoat
pałac [pa-wats] m. palace
pałka [paw-ka] f. stick; club
pamflet [pam-flet] m. pamphlet
pamiątka [pa-myownt-ka] f. souvenir; keepsake; token of remembrance; reminder; relic
pamięć [pa-myanćh] f. memory
pamiętać [pa-myan-taćh] v. remember; recall; be careful
pamiętnik [pa-myant-ńeek] m. diary; memoirs; album
pan [pan] m. lord; master; mister; you; gentleman; squire
pan młody [pan mwo-di] m. bride groom; groom
pani [pa-ńee] f. lady; you; madam; mistress (in school)
panika [pa-ńee-ka] f. panic; scare; an unreasoning fear
panna [pan-na] f. miss; girl; lass
panna młoda [pan-na mwo-da] f. bride (about to be married)
panoszyć się [pa-no-shićh śhan] v. domineer; boss; run the show; lord it; be rife
panować [pa-no-vaćh] v. rule (a nation); reign (supreme); be master of; command; control; dominate (over a people); prevail; be rife; predominate
panteizm [pan-te-eezm] m. pantheism; the doctrine that the entire universe is God
pantera [pan-te-ra] f. panther

pantoflarz [pan-to-flash] m.
  henpecked (subdued) husband
pantofel [pan-to-fel] m. slipper;
  light shoe; light low shoe
pantomima [pan-to-mee-ma] f.
  pantomime; a drama of action
  and gestures -- no words
panujący [pa-noo-yown-tsi] adj.
  m. prevailing; ruling
pański [pańs-kee] adj. m.
  lord's; your's; lordly
państwo [państ-vo] n. state;
  nation; married couple
papa [pa-pa] f. felt paper
papier [pa-pyer] m. paper
papieros [pa-pye-ros] m.
  cigarette; a small cigar
papieski [pa-pyes-kee] adj. m.
  papal; of the Pope
papież [pa-pyesh] m. pope
papka [pap-ka] f. pulp; mash;
  pap; gruel; paste; slurry
paplać [pap-laćh] v. prattle
paproć [pa-proćh] f. fern
papryka [pa-pri-ka] f. red-pepper;
  paprica; paprika
papuga [pa-poo-ga] f. parrot
para [pa-ra] f. 1. couple; 2.
  steam; the power of steam
  under pressure; vigor; energy
parabola [pa-ra-bo-la] f. parabola
parada [pa-ra-da] f. parade
paradoks [pa-ra-doks] m.
  paradox; apparent self-con-
  tradictory statement
parafia [pa-ra-fya] f. parish
parafina [pa-ra-fee-na] f. paraffin
  (waxy petroleum in candles)
paragraf [pa-ra-graf] m.
  paragraph (a distinct section)
paraliż [pa-ra-leesh] m. paralysis;
  crippling of activities
parametr [pa-ra-metr] m.
  parameter; element of an orbit
parapet [pa-ra-pet] m. window
  -sill; stool; rail; breastwork
parasol [pa-ra-sol] m. umbrella
parawan [pa-ra-van] m. screen
parcelować [par-tse-lo-vaćh] v.
  parcel out (land); cut up
parcie [par-ćhe] n. thrust
park [park] m. park (wooded)
parkan [par-kan] m. fence; net;
  hoarding (hiding)
parlament [par-la-ment] m.
  parliament; national legislative body (council)
parny [par-ni] adj. m. sultry
parobek [pa-ro-bek] m. farm
  -hand; plough man; rustic
parodia [pa-ro-dya] f. parody
parokrotnie [pa-ro-krot-ńe] adv.
  repeatedly; a couple of times
parostatek [pa-ro-sta-tek] m.
  steamboat; steamer; steamship (driven by steam power)
parować [pa-ro-vaćh] v. 1.
  evaporate; vaporize; cook by
  steam; 2. parry (a blow)
parowiec [pa-ro-vyets] m.
  steamboat; steamer; steamship (driven by steam power)
parowóz [pa-ro-voos] m. steam
  locomotive; railroad engine
parów [pa-roov] m. ravine
parówki [pa-roov-kee] pl. hot
  dogs; sausages; frankfurters
parszywy [par-shi-vi] adj. m.
  mangy; scabby; lousy; horrid
partacki [par-tats-kee] adj. m.
  bungled up; botched; fudged
partacz [par-tach] m. bungler
parter [par-ter] m. ground floor;
  first floor; parterre
partia [par-tya] f. party; card
  game; political party; game
partner [part-ner] m. partner
partyjny [par-tiy-ni] adj. m. party
  -(member); party member
partykuła [par-ti-koo-wa] f.
  particle; tiny fragment
partyzantka [par-ti-zant-ka] f.
  guerrilla; partisan war
parytet [pa-ri-tet] m. parity
parzyć [pa-zhićh] v. scald;
  steam; burn; percolate; couple
parzysty numer [pa-zhis-ti noo-
  -mer] m. even number
pas [pas] m. belt; traffic lane
pasat [pa-sat] m. trade wind
pasażer [pa-sa-zher] m.
  passenger; chap; fellow; liner
pasek [pa-sek] m. belt; band
pasieka [pa-śhe-ka] f. apiary
pasierb [pa-śherb] m. stepson
pasierbica [pa-śher-bee-tsa] f.

stepdaughter
pasja [pas-ya] f. passion
paskarz [pas-kazh] m. profiteer
pasmo [pas-mo] n. streak; tract;
range; traffic lane
pasożyt [pa-so-zhit] m. parasite;
sponger (living as a parasite)
pasta [pas-ta] f. paste
pasterka [pas-ter-ka] f. midnight
mass; shepherdess
pasterz [pas-tesh] m. shepherd
pastwa [pas-tva] f. prey
pastwisko [pas-tvees-ko] n.
pasture; grass land; pasturage
pastylka [pas-til-ka] f. tablet
pasywny [pa-siv-ni] adj. m.
passive; acted upon; inactive
pasza [pa-sha] f. fodder
paszcza [pash-cha] f. jaw
paszport [pash-port] m. passport;
certificate of identity
paść [pashćh] v. fall down;
graze; tend cattle; feed
patelnia [pa-tel-ńa] f. frying pan
patent [pa-tent] m. patent
patetyczny [pa-te-tich-ni] adj. m.
pathetic; pompous; turgid
patolog [pa-to-lok] m.
pathologist; specialist in
pathology (of abnormalities)
patriarcha [pa-tryar-kha] m.
patriarch; high ranking bishop
patriota [pa-tryo-ta] m. patriot
patron [pa-tron] m. sponsor;
stencil; pattern; protector
patronat [pa-tro-nat] m.
patronage; power to grant
favors, support, etc.
patroszyć [pa-tro-shićh] v.
disembowel; gut; draw fowl
patrzeć [pa-tshećh] v. look at;
look on; stare at; see in retrospect; glare at; watch
patyk [pa-tik] m. stick
patyna [pa-ti-na] f. patina
pauza [paw-za] f. pause
paw [pav] m. peacock
paznokieć [paz-no-kyećh] m.
(finger) nail; toe nail
pazur [pa-zoor] m. claw
paź [pażh] m. page
październik [pażh-dźher-ńeek]
m. October

pączek [pown-chek] m. bud
pąsowy [pown-so-vi] adj. m. red;
crimson; bright red; poppy red
pchać [pkhaćh] v. push; thrust;
shove; impel; propel; urge;
egg on; drive; cram; stuff; dispatch; send; rush
pchła [pkhwa] f. flea
pchnięcie [pkhńan-ćhe] n.
push; thrust; jostle; shove
pech [pekh] m. bad luck
pechowiec [pe-kho-vyets] m.
unlucky fellow; luckless chap
pedagog [pe-da-gok] m.
pedagogue; educator
pedał [pe-daw] m. 1. pedal; 2.
gay; homosexual; pansy boy
pedant [pe-dant] m. pedant
pejcz [peych] m. horsewhip
pejzaż [pey-zash] m. landscape
peleryna [pe-le-ri-na] f. cape
pelikan [pe-lee-kan] m. pelican
pełnia [pew-ńa] f. fullness
pełnić [pew-ńeećh] v. fulfill
pełno [pew-no] adv. plenty
pełnoletni [pew-no-let-ńee] adj.
m. adult; of age; mature
pełnomocnictwo [pew-no-mo-
-tsńeets-tvo] n. power of
attorney; full powers (legal)
pełny [pew-ni] adj. m. full
pełzać [pew-zaćh] v. creep;
crawl; fawn; drag; cringe
penicylina [pe-ńee-tsi-lee-na] f.
penicillin (antibiotic)
pensja [pens-ya] f. salary;
pension; allowance; wages
pensjonat [pen-syo-nat] m.
boarding house; pension
perfidny [per-feed-ni] adj. m.
perfidious; double dealing
perfumy [per-foo-mi] pl. scent;
perfume; perfumes
pergamin [per-ga-meen] m.
parchment; sheep skin
period [pe-ryod] m. period
perkal [per-kal] m. calico
perła [per-wa] f. pearl
peron [pe-ron] m. train-platform
perski [pers-kee] adj. m. Persian;
Iranian; of Iran
personalny [per-so-nal-ni] adj. m.
personal; personnel officer

personel [per-so-nel] m. staff;
personnel; employees
perpektywa [per-spe-kti-va] f.
perspective; vista; sense of
proportion; view; outlook
perswazja [per-sva-zya] f.
persuasion; power of per-
suading; arguments
pertraktacja [per-tra-kta-tsya] f.
negotiation; parley
peruka [pe-roo-ka] f. wig
peruwiański [pe-roo-vyań-skee]
adj. m. Peruvian; of Peru
peryskop [pe-ris-kop] m.
periscope (optical instr.)
pestka [pest-ka] f. kernel; pip;
drupe; stone; trifle
pesymista [pe-si-mees-ta] m.
pessimist expecting the worst
petent [pe-tent] m. petitioner
pewien [pe-vyen] adj. m. certain;
one; a; an; some; sure
pewnik [pev-ńeek] m. axiom
pewniak [pev-ńak] m. cinch;
surefooted man; certainty
pewny [pev-ni] adj. m. sure;
secure; dependable; safe
pęcak [pan-tsak] m. peeled
barley; hulled barley
pęcherz [pan-khesh] m. bladder
pęcznieć [panch-ńećh] v.
swell; heave; bulge; bilge
pęd [pand] m. rush; dash; run;
speed; impetus; urge; shoot;
sprout; onward rush; scud
pędzel [pan-dzel] m. (paint)
brush; tuft of hair
pędzić [pan-dźheećh] v. drive;
run; lead; distill; hurry
pęk [pank] m. bunch
pękać [pan-kaćh] v. burst;
split; crack; go off; flaw;
snap; cleave; rift; break
pępek [pan-pek] m. navel
pętać [pan-taćh] v. shackle;
hobble; knock about; clog
pętak [pan-tak] m. squirt
pętelka [pan-tel-ka] f. loop;
small noose; small knot
piać [pyaćh] v. crow; sing
piana [pya-na] f. foam
pianino [pya-ńee-no] n. piano
piasek [pya-sek] m. sand

piasta [pyas-ta] f. hub; nave
piastować [pya-sto-vaćh] v.
nurse; tend; hold (an office)
piąć się [pyownćh śhan] v.
climb up; rise; creep; aspire
piątek [pyown-tek] m. Friday
piątka [pyown-ka] f. five; 5
piąty [pyown-ti] num. fifth; 5th
picie [pee-će] n. drinking
pić [peećh] v. drink; booze
picuś [pee-tsoośh] m. dandy
piec [pyets] m. stove; oven;
furnace; kitchen stove; kiln
piec [pyets] v. bake; roast; burn;
scorch; sting; smart
piechota [pye-kho-ta] f. infantry;
a variety of beans
piechotą [pye-kho-town] adv. on
foot; (go) on foot
piecza [pye-cha] f. care; charge
pieczarka [pye-char-ka] f.
meadow mushroom
pieczątka [pye-chownt-ka] f.
seal; stamp; signet
pieczeń wołowa [pye-cheń vo-
-wo-va] f. roast beef
pieczyste [pye-chi-ste] f. roast
meat; meat course; joint; roast
pieczywo [pye-chi-vo] n. bakery
-goods; bread; baking
pieg [pyek] m. freckle; ephelis
piegowaty [pye-go-va-ti] adj. m.
freckled (with brownish spots)
piekarnia [pye-kar-ńa] f. bakery;
baker's shop; baked goods
piekarz [pye-kash] m. baker
piekielny [pye-kel-ni] adj. m.
infernal; of hell; hellish
piekło [pye-kwo] n. hell
pielęgniarka [pye-lan-gńar-ka] f.
nurse; hospital nurse
pielęgnować [pye-lan-gno-vaćh]
v. nurse; tend; care; cultivate
pielgrzym [pyel-gzhim] m.
pilgrim; wanderer to a holy
place (often in a group)
pielucha [pye-loo-kha] f. diaper;
baby's napkin; napkin
pieniądz [pye-ńownts] m.
money; coin; currency; funds
pienić [pye-ńeećh] v. foam;
sparkle; cover with foam
pieniężny [pye-ńanzh-ni] adj. m.

monetary; pecuniary; moneyed

pień [pyeń] m. trunk; stem;
stump; snag; stock; root

pieprz [pyepsh] m. pepper

pierdzieć [pyer-dźhećh] v. fart
(vulg); stink up; shit

pietdzioch [pyer-dźhokh] m. old
fart (vulg.); old stinker

piernat [pyer-nat] m. feather-bed

piernik [pyer-ńeek] m. 1. ginger
bread; 2. an old fogey; duffer

pierś [pyerśh] f. breast; chest

pierścień [pyerśh-ćheń] m.
ring; collar; circle; hoop

pierścionek [pyer-śhćho-nek]
m. ring; engagement ring

pierwej [pyer-vey] adv. of first;
sooner; before; first

pierwiastek [pyer-vya-stek] m.
root; element; radical

pierworodny [pyer-vo-rod-ni] adj.
m. firstborn (son or daughter)

pierwotny [pyer-vot-ni] adj. m.
primitive; primary; original

pierwszeństwo [pyerv-sheń-
-stvo] n. priority; precedence

pierwszy [pyerv-shi] num. first

pierzchać [pyezh-khaćh] v. run
away; fly; flee; disperse;
scatter; take flight; vanish

pierze [pye-zhe] n. feathers

pierzyna [pye-zhi-na] f.
featherbed; eider down; quilt

pies [pyes] m. 1. dog; 2. cur

piesko [pyes-ko] adv. badly

pieszczota [pyesh-cho-ta] f.
caress; endearment

pieszo [pye-sho] adv. on foot

pieścić [pyeśh-ćheećh] v.
fondle; caress; pet; hug;
babble; handle lovingly

pieśń [pyeśhń] f. song

pietruszka [pye-troosh-ka] f.
parsley (used for garnishing)

pięciobój [pyan-ćho-booy] m.
pentathlon (of five events)

pięcioletni [pyan-ćho-let-ńee]
adj. m. five years old

pięć [pyanćh] num. five; 5

piędź [pyandźh] f. palm. span

pięćdziesiąt [pyanćh-dźhe-
-śhownt] num. fifty; 50

pięćset [pyanćh-set] num.

five hundred; 500

piękność [pyank-nośhćh] f.
beauty; good looks; loveliness

piękny [pyank-ni] adj. m.
beautiful; lovely; fine; handsome; good-looking; pretty

pięściarz [pyanśh-ćhash] m.
boxer; prize-fighter

pięść [pyanśhćh] f. fist

pięściarstwo [pyanśh-ćhar-
-stvo] n. box; boxing; pugilism

pięta [pyan-ta] f. heel

piętnastoletni [pyan-tna-sto-let-
-ńee] adj. m. fifteen years old

piętnasty [pyant-nas-ti] num.
fifteenth; 15th

piętnaście [pyant-naśh-ćhe]
num. fifteen; 15

piętno [pyant-no] n. mark;
stigma; brand; stamp; impress

piętro [pyant-ro] n. story; floor;

piętrzyć [pyant-shićh] v. pile
up; bank up; heap; accumulate; rise; tower; be heaped
high (with crates, boxes, etc.)

pigułka [pee-goow-ka] f. pill

pijak [pee-yak] m. drunk

pijany [pee-ya-ni] adj. m. drunk;
tipsy; intoxicated; elated

pijawka [pee-yav-ka] f. leech

pikantny [pee-kant-ni] adj. m.
spicy; piquant; pungent; sharp

piknik [peek-ńeek] m. picnic

pilnik [peel-ńeek] m. file

pilność [peel-nośhćh] f.
diligence; urgency; industry;
care; assiduity; urgency

pilny [peel-ni] adj. m. diligent;
urgent; industrious; careful

pilot [pee-lot] m. pilot

pilśń [peelśhń] f. felt

piła [pee-wa] f. saw; bore

piłka [peew-ka] f. ball; handsaw;
football; socker; shot

piłować [pee-wo-vaćh] v. saw;
bore (a person); rasp on...

pingwin [peen-gveen] m. penguin

piołunówka [pyo-woo-noov-ka] f.
absinth flavored liqueur

pion [pyon] m. plumb (line)

pionek [pyo-nek] m. pawn

pionier [pyo-ńer] m. pioneer

pionowy [pyo-no-vi] adj. m.

vertical; upright; plumb
piorun [pyo-roon] m. thunderbolt;
lightning shaft; lightning
piorunochron [pyo-roo-no-khron]
m. lightning-rod (conductor)
piosenka [pyo-sen-ka] f. song
piórko [pyoor-ko] n. (small)
feather; pen; plume
pióro [pyoo-ro] n. feather; pen
piramida [pee-ra-mee-da] f.
pyramid (polygonal figure)
pirat [pee-rat] m. pirate
pirotechnika [pee-ro-tekh-ńee-ka]
f. pyrotechnics (display)
pisać [pee-saćh] v. write
pisarz [pee-sash] m. writer
pisemnie [pee-sem-ńe] adv. in
writing; in black and white
pisk [peesk] m. squeal; squeak
piskliwy [pees-klee-vi] adj. m.
shrill; squeaky; thin; strident;
piping; high-pitched
piskle [pees-kle] n. chicken;
nestling; squealer
piskorz [pees-kosh] m. (long) eel
pismo [pees-mo] n. writing;
letter; newspaper; scripture;
alphabet; type; print
pisownia [pee-sov-ńa] f.
spelling; orthography
pistolet [pee-sto-let] m. pistol;
handgun; gun; spray gun
pisuar [pee-soo-ar] m. urinal
piszczeć [peesh-chećh] v. 1.
creak; squeak; screech; make
high-pitched sounds; 2. claim
piszczel [peesh-chel] m.
shinbone; tibia; blow pipe
piśmiennictwo [peeśh-myen-
-ńeets-tvo] n. literature
piśmiennie [peeśh-myen-ńe]
adv. in writing; in black and
white (written on paper)
piwiarnia [pee-vyar-ńa] f. beer
hall; beer house; saloon
piwnica [peev-ńee-tsa] f. cellar;
basement; coal cellar
piwny [peev-ni] adj. m. brown
(color); hasel; beer-
piwo [pee-vo] n. beer
piwonia [pee-vo-nya] f. peony
piwowar [pee-vo-var] m. brewer
piżama [pee-zha-ma] f. pajamas

plac [plats] m. square; area;
ground; building site; field
plac boju [plats bo-yoo] m. battle
field; field of battle; the field
placek [pla-tsek] m. cake; pie
placówka [pla-tsoov-ka] f.
sentry; post; outpost; agency
plaga [pla-ga] f. plague
plagiator [pla-gya-tor] m.
plagiarist (male)
plakat [pla-kat] m. poster
plama [pla-ma] f. blot; stain
plamić [pla-meećh] v. blot;
stain; soil; tarnish; defile
plan [plan] m. plan; design; map
planeta [pla-ne-ta] f. planet
planować [pla-no-vaćh] v. plan
planowo [pla-no-vo] adv.
according to (a fixed) plan;
systematically; methodically
plantacja [plan-ta-tsya] f.
(sugar, etc.) plantation
plaster [plas-ter] m. plaster;
patch; tape; adhesive; slice
plastyczne sztuki [plas-tich-ne
shtoo-kee] fine arts
plastyczny [plas-tich-ni] adj. m.
plastic; artistic; vivid
plastyk [plas-tik] m. artist;
plastic (substance)
platerować [pla-te-ro-vaćh] v.
plate (with na other metal)
platforma [plat-for-ma] f.
platform; truck; lorry; shelf
platoniczny [pla-to-ńeech-ni] adj.
m. Platonic; unsubstantial
platyna [pla-ti-na] f. platinum
plazma [plaz-ma] f. plasma
plaża [pla-zha] f. beach
plażować [pla-zho-vaćh] v. sun
bathe; lie on the beach
plądrować [plown-dro-vaćh] v.
plunder; ransack; ravage; loot
pląsy [plown-si] pl. dance
plątać [plown-taćh] v. entangle
plebania [ple-ba-ńya] f. rectory
plebiscyt [ple-bees-tsit] m.
plebiscite; people's direct vote
plecak [ple-tsak] m. rucksack;
backpack; (soldier's) knapsack
plecionka [ple-ćhon-ka] f. plaid
braid; wattle; basket work
plecy [ple-tsi] pl. back; backing

pleć [plećh] v. weed (a garden)
plemienny [ple-myen-ni] adj. m. tribal; of a tribe
plemię [ple-my<u>an</u>] n. tribe
plemnik [plem-ńeek] m. sperm
plenum [ple-noom] n. plenary session; plenary assembly
pleść [pleśhćh] v. twist; blab; weave; interlace; talk nonsense; blab; jabber; tangle
pleśnieć [pleśh-ńećh] v. mold; go mouldy; mildew
pletwa [plet-va] f. fin; dovetail
plewić [ple-veećh] v. weed
plik [pleek] m. bundle; sheaf
plisa [plee-sa] f. pleat
plomba [plom-ba] f. lead seal; tooth filling; stopping
plon [plon] m. crop; yield
plotka [plot-ka] f. gossip; rumor; piece of gossip; pl. tales
pluć [plooćh] v. spit; abuse
plugawy [ploo-ga-vi] adj. m. filthy; squalid; foul; obscene
plus [ploos] m. plus; asset
plusk [ploosk] m. splash
pluskać [ploos-kaćh] v. splash
pluskiewka [ploos-kev-ka] f. thumbtack; drawing pin
pluskwa [ploos-kva] f. bedbug
plusz [ploosh] m. plush
plutokracja [ploo-to-kra-tsya] f. plutocracy (of the wealthy)
pluton [ploo-ton] m. platoon
plwocina [plvo-ćhee-na] f. spittle; expectoration; spit
płaca [pwa-tsa] f. wage; salary
płachta [pwakh-ta] f. sheet
płacić [pwa-ćheećh] v. pay
płacz [pwach] m. cry; weep
płakać [pwa-kaćh] v. cry; weep
płaski [pwas-kee] adj. m. flat
płaskorzeźba [pwa-sko-zheźh--ba] f. low relief; bas-relief
płaskowyż [pwa-sko-vish] m. high plateau; high table land
płaszcz [pwashch] m. overcoat
płaszczyć [pwash-chićh] v. flatten; become flat; fall flat
płaszczyzna [pwash-chiz-na] f. plane; surface; area; sheet (of water, etc.); plain; expanse
płat [pwat] m. slice; lobe

płatać [pwa-taćh] v. cut; play (tricks); slice; split; fell
płatek [pwa-tek] m. flake
płatność [pwat-nośhćh] f. payment; remittance; bill
pławić [pwa-veećh] v. float; wallow; duck; drown; soak
płaz [pwas] m. 1. reptile
płaz [pwas] m. 2. flat of a sabre
płciowy [pwćho-vi] adj. m. sexual; genital; sex-(urge etc.)
płeć [pwećh] f.sex; complexion
płetwa [pwet-va] f. (swim-) fin
płochliwy [pwo-khlee-vi] adj. m. timid; shy; skittish; scared
płochy [pwo-khi] adj. m. frivolous; shy; timid; fickle
płodny [pwod-ni] adj. m. fertile; productive; prolific; fruitful
płodzić [pwo-dźheećh] v. beget; procreate; sire; breed
płomień [pwo-myeń] m. flame
płonąć [pwo-n<u>own</u>ćh] v. be on fire; blaze; be inflamed; glow
płonny [pwon-ni] adj. m. sterile; useless; vain; of no avail
płoszyć [pwo-shićh] v. frighten
płot [pwot] m. fence; hoarding
płowieć [pwo-vyećh] v. fade
płowy [pwo-vi] adj. m. flaxen; fair; buff; fallow; fawn
płód [pwoot] m. fetus; fruit
płócienny [pwoo-ćhen-ni] adj. m. linen (sheets, etc.); canvas-(sail, shoes etc.)
płótno [pwoot-no] n. linen; canvas; cloth; scrim; painting
płuco [pwoo-tso] n. lung
płucny [pwoots-ni] adj. m. pulmonary; of the lungs
pług [pwook] m. plough; plow
płukać [pwoo-kaćh] v. rinse; wash; gargle one's throat
płyn [pwin] m. liquid; fluid
płynąć [pwi-n<u>own</u>ćh] v. flow; swim; sail; drift; go by; come
płynny [pwin-ni] adj. m. liquid; fluent; fluid; smooth; graceful
płyta [pwi-ta] f. plate; slab; disk; sheet; board; (musical) record
płyta gramofonowa [pwi-ta gra--mo-fo-no-va] f. (musical) record; (gramophone) disk

płytki [pwit-kee] adj. m. shallow;
flat; trivial; pointless

pływać [pwi-vaćh] v. 1. swim;
float; navigate; be afloat; sail
2. quibble; be evasive

pływak [pwi-vak] m. swimmer;
float; quibbler; buoy

pniak [pńak] m. stump; trunk

po [po] prep. after; to; up to; till;
upon; for; at; in; up; of; next;
along; about; over; past;
behind; as far as; how (much)

pobicie [po-bee-ćhe] n. battery

pobić [po-beećh] v. beat up;
defeat; beat in; thrash; spank

pobielać [po-bye-laćh] v.
whiten; tin; make white; paint
white; whitewash; grow white

pobierać [po-bye-raćh] v. take;
collect; receive; get; draw (rations, etc.); charge; derive

pobliski [po-blees-kee] adj. m.
nearby; neighboring (inn, etc.)

pobłażać [po-bwa-zhaćh] v.
indulge; forbear; be tolerant

pobłażliwy [po-bwa-zhlee-vi] adj.
m. lenient; forgiving; tolerant

poboczny [po-boch-ni] adj. m.
lateral; secondary; accessory

poborca [po-bor-tsa] m. (tax)
(tax) collector; tax gatherer

poborowy [po-bo-ro-vi] adj. m.
recruit; recruiting (board)

pobory [po-bo-ri] pl. salary

pobrać [po-braćh] v. receive;
collect; get; draw; gather

pobudka [po-boot-ka] f.
incentive; motive; reveille

pobudliwy [po-boo-dlee-vi] adj.
m. excitable; ebullient

pobyt [po-bit] m. stay; visit

pocałować [po-tsa-wo-vaćh] v.
give a kiss; kiss (good-bye)

pocałunek [po-tsa-woo-nek] m.
kiss; caress with the lips

pochlebiać [po-khle-byaćh] v.
flatter; adulate; expect; fawn

pochlebny [po-khleb-ni] adj. m.
flattering; complimentary

pochłaniać [po-khwa-ńaćh] v.
absorb; swallow up; engulf

pochmurny [po-khmoor-ni] adj.
m. gloomy; cloudy; overcast

pochodnia [po-khod-ńa] f. torch

pochodny [po-khod-ni] adj. m.
derivative; derived

pochodzenie [po-kho-dze-ńe] n.
origin; descant; source

pochopny [po-khop-ni] adj. m.
hasty; eager; rush; ready

pochować [po-kho-vaćh] v.
bury; hide; conceal; put away

pochód [po-khoot] m. march;
procession; parade; progress

pochwa [pokh-va] f. vagina;
sheath (of a sword); scabbard

pochwała [pokh-va-wa] f. praise;
eulogy; approval; applause

pochylić [po-khi-leećh] v.
incline; slope; slant; droop

pochyły [po-khi-wi] adj. m.
inclined; stooped; sloping; out
of the vertical; oblique

pociąć [po-ćhownćh] v. cut
up into pieces; slash; sting;
saw up; furrow; intersect

pociąg [po-ćhownk] m. train;
affinity; inclination

pociągać [po-ćhown-gaćh] v.
pull; draw; attract; tug; coat

pociągnięcie [po-ćhowng-ńan-
-ćhe] n. pull; move; stroke;
pluck; a tug; a swig (at)

po cichu [po ćhee-khoo] adv.
secretly; silently; softly

pocić [po-ćheećh] v. sweat

pociecha [po-ćhe-kha] f.
comfort; joy; solace; satisfaction; consolation; offspring

po ciemku [po ćhem-koo] adv.
in the dark; while in the dark

pocierać [po-ćhe-raćh] v. rub

pocieszać [po-ćhe-shaćh] v.
console; comfort; cheer up;
solace; bring consolation

pocieszenie [po-ćhe-she-ńe] n.
consolation; comfort; solace

pocieszny [po-ćhesh-ni] adj. m.
funny; amusing; droll; comic

pocisk [po-ćheesk] m. missile;
(gun, etc,) bullet; projectile

po co ? [po tso] what for ?

począć [po-chownćh] v. begin;
conceive; become pregnant

początek [po-chown-tek] m.
beginning; start; outset; fore-

part; early stage; outset
początkujący [po-ch<u>ow</u>n-tkoo-
-y<u>ow</u>n-tsi] adj. m. beginner
poczciwy [poch-ćhee-vi] adj. m.
good-hearted; friendly; kindly
poczekać [po-che-kaćh] v. wait
poczekalnia [po-che-kal-ńa] f.
waiting room; waiting hall
poczęstować [po-ch<u>an</u>-**sto**-
-vaćh] v. treat to; entertain;
serve (food); regale (with)
poczęstunek [po-ch<u>an</u>-**stoo**-nek]
m. treat; drinks; entertainment
poczta [poch-ta] f. post; mail
pocztówka [poch-**toov**-ka] f.
postcard; picture postcard
poczucie [po-choo-ćhe] n.
feeling; sense; consciousness
poczwórny [po-ch**voor**-ni] adj. m.
fourfold; four times as large,
as tall; as long, as big
poczynać [po-chi-naćh] v.
begin (aggressively); conceive
poczytalny [po-chi-tal-ni] adj. m.
accountable; sane; responsible
poczytny [po-chit-ni] adj. m.
popular (book); widely read
pod [pod] prep. under; below;
towards; on in underneath
podać [po-daćh] v. give; hand;
pass; serve; shake (hand)
podanie [po-da-ńe] n.
application; request; legend
podarek [po-da-rek] m. gift
podarty [po-dar-ti] adj. m. torn
podatek [po-da-tek] m. tax; duty
podatnik [po-dat-ńeek] m. tax-
-payer; rate payer
podaż [po-dash] f. supply
podążać [po-d<u>ow</u>n-zhaćh] v.
make for; draw to; make
one's way (towards a place)
podbicie [pod-bee-ćhe] n.
conquest; instep; lining; ceiling
podbiec [pod-byets] v. run up
podbiegunowy [pod-bye-goo-no-
-vi] adj. m. polar; near pole
podbój [pod-booy] m. conquest
podbudowa [pod-boo-do-va] f.
substructure; base course
podbródek [pod-broo-dek] m.
chin; bib; feeder
podburzać [pod-boo-zhaćh] v.

stir up; incite to revolt
podchmielony [pod-khmye-lo-ni]
adj. m. tipsy; in drink
podchodzić [pod-kho-dźheećh]
v. approach; assume an attitude; walk up; step up; climb;
treat; seep; steel up; outwit
podchwycić [pod-khvi-ćheećh]
v. catch up; snatch up; spot
podchwytliwy [pod-khvi-tlee-vi]
adj. m. captious (question)
podciągać [pod-ćh<u>ow</u>n-gaćh]
v. draw up; pull up; improve;
raise; elevate; include; class
podczas [pod-chas] prep. during;
while; when; whereas
podczerwony [pod-cher-vo-ni]
adj. m. infrared
poddać [pod-daćh] v.
surrender; suggest; submit;
expose; subject; bare a hand
pod dostatkiem [pod do-**stat**-
-kem] adv. plenty; enough
podejmować [po-dey-mo-vaćh]
v. take up; entertain; pick up
podejrzany [po-dey-zha-ni] adj.
m. suspect; suspicious; shady
podejrzliwy [po-dey-zhlee-vi] adj.
m. suspicious; distrustful
podeptać [po-dep-taćh] v.
tramp (under foot); bustle
(about a purchase, etc.)
poderwać [po-der-vaćh] v. jerk
up; pick up; weaken; rouse
podeszwa [po-desh-fa] f. sole
podginać [pod-gee-naćh] v.
tuck up (one's shirt, etc.);
cock; turn up; bend (a knee)
podglądać [pod-gl<u>ow</u>n-daćh] v.
(play a) spy; peep; pry; snoop
podgórski [pod-goor-skee]
adj. m. foot-hill; piedmont
podjechać [pod-ye-khaćh] v.
drive up; ride up hill; come up
podgrzewać [pod-gzhe-vaćh] v.
warm up (some food); heat up
podjudzać [pod-yoo-dzaćh] v.
stir up; incite (to evil)
podkasać [pod-ka-saćh] v. tuck
up; turn up (sleeves); rise
podkład [pod-kwat] m. base;
railroad tie; undercurrent; bedding; groundwork; foundation

podkładać [pod-**kwa**-daćh] v.
lay under; put under; plant as
evidence; underlay; set (fire)
podkop [pod-**kop**] m. mine; sap
podkowa [pod-**ko**-va] f. horse
-shoe; semicircle
podkradać [pod-**kra**-daćh] v.
thieve; pilfer; creep up
podkreślać [pod-**kre**-śhlaćh]
v. stress; underline (an error);
emphasize; accentuate; insist
podkuwać [pod-**koo**-vaćh] v.
shoe (horse); hobnail a shoe;
cram (for an examination)
podlegać [pod-**le**-gaćh] v. be
subject; be liable; succumb;
undergo; be submitted to
podległość [pod-**le**-gwośhćh]
f. dependence; subjection;
subordination; submission
podlewać [pod-**le**-vaćh] v.
water (flowers); baste
podlizywać się [pod-lee-zi-vaćh
śh**an**] v. suck up to; make up
to somebody; toady somebody
podlotek [pod-**lo**-tek] m.
fledgling (girl); flapper (girl);
girl in her teens
podłoga [pod-**wo**-ga] f. floor
podłość [pod-**wo**śhćh] f. dirty trick; meanness; baseness
podług [pod-**wook**] prep.:
according to; in conformity
with; after (masters, etc.)
podłużny [pod-**woozh**-ni] adj. m.
oblong; longitudinal; elongated
podły [pod-**wi**] adj. m. mean
podmiejski [pod-**myeys**-kee] adj.
m. suburban; of the suburbs
podminować [pod-mee-**no**-
-vaćh] v. undermine; sap
podmiot [pod-**myot**] m. subject
podmuch [pod-**mookh**] m. gust;
blow; puff; waft; breath; blast
podmywać [pod-mi-vaćh] v.
wash under; sap; undermine;
wash away; wash up
podniebienie [pod-ńe-bye-ńe] n.
palate; roof of the mouth
podniecać [pod-**ńe**-tsaćh] v.
flurry excite; agitate; rouse;
egg on; fluster; rouse; stir up
podnieść [pod-ńeśhćh] v.

lift; hoist (a flag); rise; elevate;
rear; increase (wages, etc,)
podnieta [pod-**ńe**-ta] f. stimulus;
impulse; spur; stimulant
podniosły [pod-**ńo**-swi] adj. m.
sublime; elevated; lofty
podnosić [pod-no-**śhee**ćh] v.
hoist; raise (a question); lift;
take up; elevate; increase; rear
podnóżek [pod-**noo**-zhek]
footstool; ottoman; leg rest
podobać się [po-do-baćh
śh**an**] v. please; be attractive;
take sombody's fancy; enjoy
podobny [po-**dob**-ni] adj. m.
similar; like; congenial
podoficer [pod-o-**fee**-tser] m.
noncommissioned officer
podołać [po-do-waćh] v. be up
to; cope; manage; be equal to
podomka [po-**dom**-ka] f.
houserobe; dressing gown
podówczas [pod-**oof**-chas] adv.
at that time; at the time; then
podpadać [pod-**pa**-daćh] v. be
spotted; fall under a category
podpalenie [pod-pa-le-ńe] n.
arson; setting of fire
podpatrzyć [pod-**pa**-tshićh] v.
spy; peep; find out; pry
podpierać [pod-**pye**-raćh] v.
prop up; support; bolster
podpinać [pod-pee-naćh] v. pin;
buckle up; strap; fasten; gird
podpis [pod-**pees**] m. signature
podpływać [pod-**pwi**-vaćh] v.
swim up; sail up; row up
podpora [pod-**po**-ra] f. prop
podporucznik [pod-po-**rooch**-
-ńeek] m. second lieutenant
podporządkować [pod-po-
-**zhownd**-ko-vaćh] v. subordinate; submit; conform
podprowadzić [pod-pro-**va**-
-dźheećh] v. bring near
podpułkownik [pod-poow-**kov**-
-ńeek] m. lieutenant colonel
podrażnić [pod-**razh**-ńeećh] v.
displease; irritate; vex; gall
podręcznik [pod-**ranch**-ńeek] m.
handbook; textbook; manual
podrożeć [pod-ro-zhećh] v. go
up; grow dear; rise in price

podróż [pod-roosh] f. travel;
voyage; journey; passage
podróżnik [pod-roozh-ńeek] m.
traveler; voyager; wayfarer
po drugie [po droo-ge] adv. in
the second place; second
podrzeć [pod-zheć] v. tear up
podrzędny [pod-zhand-ni] adj. m.
subordinate; secondary
podsądny [pod-sownd-ni] m.
defendant; the person sued
podskakiwać [pod-ska-kee-
-vać] v. leap; jump up; hop;
skip; frisk; bounce; soar; jolt
podsłuch [pod-swookh] m.
eavesdropping; wire tapping;
listening in (on the phone)
podstawa [pod-sta-va] f. base;
basis; footing; mount; rest;
foundation; principle
podstawić [pod-sta-veeć] v.
substitute; put under; bring
round; place under; push to
podstęp [pod-stanp] m. trick;
ruse; guile; piece of deceit;
stratagem; cunning devices
podstępny [pod-stanp-ni] adj. m.
deceitful; tricky; crafty;
insidious; scheming; guileful
podstrzygać [pod-stshi-gać] v.
trim the hair; shorten the hair
podsuwać [pod-soo-vać] v.
push near; plant; suggest; slip
under; move to; prompt with
(an answer); offer (an opinion)
podsycać [pod-si-tsać] v.
foment; feed; fan (a quarrel)
podsypywać [pod-si-pi-vać] v.
pour (sand etc.); strew;
sprinkle (with sugar, etc.)
podszept [pod-shept] m.
suggestion; prompting; insinuation; instigation
podszeptywać [pod-shep-ti-
-vać] v. prompt; suggest;
hint; insinuate; whisper into
somebody's ear; instigate
podszewka [pod-shev-ka] f.
lining; inside information
podświadomy [pod-śhvya-do-
-mi] adj. m. subconscious
podupadać [pod-oo-pa-dać] v.
decline; deteriorate; fall into

decay; fall into poverty
poduszka [po-doosh-ka] f. pillow;
pad; cushion; ball (of the
thumb); cushion pad; finger tip
podwajać [pod-va-yać] v.
double; duplicate; increase
twofold; reduplicate
podważyć [pod-va-zhić] v.
lever up; pry up; shake (an
opinion); prize a lid open
podwiązka [pod-vyownz-ka] f.
garter; suspender; ligature
podwieczorek [pod-vye-cho-rek]
m. afternoon tea (snack)
podwieźć [pod-vyeźhćh] v.
give a ride; give a lift (in one's
car); bring to doorstep; provide with; supply (groceries)
podwładny [pod-vwad-ni] adj. m.
subordinate (to somebody);
inferior; m.subordinate
podwodna łódź [pod-vod-na
woodźh] f. submarine
podwoić [pod-vo-eećh] v.
double; increase twofold; duplicate; reduplicate
podwozie [pod-vo-źhe] n.
chassis; under-carriage
podwórko [pod-voor-ko] n.
backyard; farmyard; court;
courtyard; barnyard
podwyżka [pod-vish-ka] f. raise
podzelować [pod-ze-lo-vać] v.
resole (shoes; boots; foot)
podziać [po-dźhać] v. loose;
put somewhere; mislay
podział [po-dźhaw] m. division
podziałka [po-dźhaw-ka] f.
scale; graduation; division
podzielać [po-dźhe-lać] v.
share; participate; concur
podzielić [po-dźhe-leećh] v.
divide (into parts)
podzielny [po-dźhel-ni] adj. m.
divisible (easily)
podziemie [po-źhe-mye] n.
basement; underworld
podziemny [po-źhem-ni]
adj. m. underground; secret
podziękować [po-dźhan-ko-
-vać] v. thank; decline with
thanks (for something)
podziewać [po-dźhe-vać] v.

loose; mislay; leave
somewhere; put somewhere
podziw [po-dźheef] m. admiration; wander; an admiration
podzwrotnikowy [pod-zvrot-ńee--ko-vi] adj. m. tropical
podżegacz [pod-zhe-gach] m. instigator; warmonger; abettor
poemat [po-e-mat] m. poem
poeta [po-e-ta] m. poet
poetka [po-et-ka] f. poet
poezja [po-e-zya] f. poetry
pogadanka [po-ga-dan-ka] f. talk; chat; chatty (talk) lecture
poganiać [po-ga-ńaćh] v. drive; egg on; urge on; prod on; hustle; urge forwards
poganin [po-ga-ńeen] m. pagan
pogarda [po-gar-da] f. contempt
pogarszać [po-gar-shaćh] v. make worse; aggravate; worsen; deteriorate; grow worse
pogawędka [po-ga-vand-ka] f. chat; chit-chat; chatty talk
pogląd [po-glownd] m. opinion
pogłębiać [po-gwan-byaćh] v. deepen; dig deeper; dredge
pogłoska [po-gwos-ka] f. rumor
pogniewać się [po-gńe-vaćh śhan] v. get angry; be angry
pogoda [po-go-da] f. weather; cheerfulness; fine weather
pogodny [po-god-ni] adj. m. serene; cheerful; sunny
pogodzić [po-go-dźheećh] v. reconcile; square (things)
pogoń [po-goń] f. pursuit; chase; hunt; quest; pursuers
pogorszenie [po-gor-she-ńe] n. worsening; deterioration
pogorszyć [po-gor-shićh] v. make worse; aggravate
pogorzelisko [po-go-zhe-lees-ko] n. after fire ruins
pogotowie [po-go-to-vye] n. ambulance service; readiness
pogranicze [po-gra-ńee-che] n. borderland; border line
pogrom [po-grom] m. rout; pogrom; crushing defeat
pogromca [po-grom-tsa] m. (animal) tamer; conqueror
pogróżka [po-groosh-ka] f.

threat; threatening expression
pogrzeb [po-gzhep] m. funeral
pogrzebacz [po-gzhe-bach] m. poker (for stirring a fire)
pogwałcić [po-gvav-ćheećh] v. violate; outrage; transgress
poić [po-eećh] v. water; ply
pojawić się [po-ya-veećh śhan] v. appear; emerge; become visible; occur; arise
pojazd [po-yazt] m. car; vehicle
pojąć [po-yownćh] v. grasp; marry; comprehend; understand; conceive; imagine
pojechać [po-ye-khaćh] v. go; leave; take (train; boat etc.)
pojednać [po-yed-naćh] v. reconcile (two or more parties)
pojednawczy [po-yed-nav-chi] adj. m. conciliatory
pojedynczy [po-ye-din-chi] adj. m. single; individual; one-fold; single-entry (books)
pojedynek [po-ye-di-nek] m. duel; encounter; single combat
pojemnik [po-yem-ńeek] m. container; vessel; receptacle
pojemność [po-yem-nośhćh] f. capacity; cubic content
pojezierze [po-ye-źhe-zhe] n. lake land; lake district
pojęcie [po-yan-ćhe] n. notion; idea; concept; comprehension
pojętny [po-yant-ni] adj. m. intelligent; sharp; teachable
pojmować [poy-mo-vaćh] v. comprehend; conceive; grasp; imagine; understand
pojutrze [po-yoot-zhe] adv. the day after tomorrow
pokarm [po-karm] m. food; feed
pokaz [po-kas] m. display; shaw
pokazywać [po-ka-zi-vaćh] v. show; point; exhibit; let see
pokaźny [po-kaźh-ni] adj. m. respectable; appreciable
pokład [po-kwat] m. deck; layer
pokątny [po-kownt-ni] adj. m. underhanded; secret; illegal
pokłon [po-kwon] m. bow before (sb); homage; greeting
pokłócić się [po-kwoo-ćheećh śhan] v. fall out with; quarrel

pokochać [po-ko-khaćh] v. fall in love; become fond of
pokoik [po-ko-eek] m. little room; little cozy room
pokojówka [po-ko-yoof-ka] f. housemaid; chamber maid
pokolenie [po-ko-le-ńe] n. generation; about 30 years
pokonać [po-ko-naćh] v. defeat (an army); conquer; subdue
pokorny [po-kor-ni] adj. m. humble; meek; submissive
pokost [po-kost] m. varnish
pokrajać [po-kra-yaćh] v. cut up; carve up; slice; slash
pokój [po-kooy] m. room; peace
pokrapiać [po-kra-pyaćh] v. sprinkle; wash down (a meal)
pokrewieństwo [po-kre-vyeń-stvo] n. kinship; kindred; relation; relationship; affinity
pokrewny [po-krev-ni] adj. m. related; kindred; akin; cognate
pokrótce [po-kroot-tse] adv. in short; in brief; concisely
pokrycie [po-kri-ćhe] n. cover
pokryć [po-krićh] v. cover
po kryjomu [po kri-yo-moo] adv. secretly; on the sly; in secret
pokrywa [po-kri-va] f. lid
pokrywać [po-kri-vaćh] v. cover; upholster; serve (mare)
pokrzepić [po-kzhe-peećh] v. invigorate; refresh; fortify
pokrzywa [po-kzhee-va] f. nettle
pokrzyżować [po-kzhi-zho-vaćh] v. cross up; confound; tangle; put crosswise; thwart
pokup [po-koop] m. demand
pokupny [po-koop-ni] adj. m. in demand; sellable; salable
pokusa [po-koo-sa] f. temptation
pokuta [po-koo-ta] f. penance
pokwitować [po-kvee-to-vaćh] v. receipt; acknowledge receipt (of a sum, etc.)
pokwitowanie [po-kvee-to-va-ńe] n. receipt; written receipt
polać [po-laćh] v. (liquid) pour; pour over; flow; shed; gusher
Polak [po-lak] m. Polonian; Pole; Polonius (as in Hamlet)
polana [po-la-na] f. glade

polano [po-la-no] n. billet; log
polarny [po-lar-ni] adj. m. polar; of the polar (axis, direction)
pole [po-le] n. field; area
polec [po-lets] v. fall; be killed (in battle); bite the dust; die
polecać [po-le-tsaćh] v. recommend; commend; instruct; order; enjoin; tell (to do)
polegać [po-le-gaćh] v. rely
polemika [po-le-mee-ka] f. polemics; controversy
polepszać [po-lep-shaćh] v. improve; ameliorate; mend; get better; grow better
polerować [po-le-ro-vaćh] v. polish; furbish; burnish; refine
polewać [po-le-vaćh] v. water; glaze; enamel; ice (cakes)
polewka [po-lev-ka] f. broth
polędwica [po-land-vee-tsa] f. sirloin; loin; fillet (of beef)
policja [po-leets-ya] f. police
policzek [po-lee-chek] m. cheek
politechnika [po-lee-tekh-ńee-ka] f. polytechnic institute; technical university or college
politowanie [po-lee-to-va-ńe] n. pity; compassion; sympathy
polityk [po-lee-tik] m. politician experienced in government
polka [pol-ka] f. polka (dance)
polka [pol-ka] f. Polish girl; Polish women; Pole; Polish lady
polny [pol-ni] adj. m. field
polon [po-lon] m. polonium
polonez [po-lo-nez] m. polonaise
Polonia [po-lo-ńa] f. Polish colony; Polish emigrants
Polonus [po-lo-noos] m. Pole of old; typical Pole of the past
polot [po-lot] m. elan; imaginativeness; loftiness
polować [po-lo-vaćh] v. hunt
polski [pol-skee] adj. m. Polish; Polish language
polskość [pol-skośhćh] f. Polish character; traits, etc.
polszczyć [polsh-chićh] v. Polonize; invest with Polish traits, culture, language, etc.
polszczyzna [pol-shchiz-na] f. Polish language; Polish traits

polubić [po-**loo**-beećh] v. get to like; become fond of; take a fancy to; take a liking to
polubownie [po-loo-**bov**-ńe] adv. amicably; by compromise
połamać [po-**wa**-maćh] v. break
połączenie [po-**wown-che**-ńe] n. connection; linkage; contact
połknąć [pow-kn**ownćh**] v. swallow; gulp down; drink down; gulp bach (tears, etc.)
połowa [po-**wo**-va] f. half
położenie [po-wo-**zhe**-ńe] n. position; situation; site
położna [po-**wozh**-na] f. midwife
położnica [po-wozh-**ńee**-tsa] f. woman lying-in (in childbed)
położyć [po-**wo**-zhićh] v. lay down; place; deposit; fell; ruin
połóg [po-**wook**] m. childbirth
połów ryb [po-**woov** rib] fish catch; fishing; fish haul
południe [po-**wood**-ńe] n. noon; south; midday; the South
południk [po-**wood-ńeek**] m. meridian; the line of longitude
południowo-wschodni [po-wood--ńo-vo vskhod-ńee] adj. m. south-east; of south-east
południowo-zachodni [po-wood--ńo-vo za-khod-ńee] adj. m. south-west; of south west
południowy [po-wood-ńo-vi] adj. m. south; midday; southerly
połykać [po-**wi**-kaćh] v. swallow; gulp down; bolt
połysk [po-**wisk**] m. glitter; gloss; luster; sheen; sparkle
pomadka [po-**mad**-ka] f. lipstick
pomagać [po-ma-gaćh] v. help
pomaleńku [po-ma-leń-koo] adv. little by little; very slowly
pomału [po-ma-woo] adv. little by little; slowly; leisurely
pomarańcza [po-ma-rań-cha] f. orange; orange tree
pomarszczony [po-mar-**shcho**-ni] adj. m. wrinkled; creased
pomazać [po-**ma-**zaćh] v. smear-over; anoint; soil; scrawl; spread (butter, etc.)
pomawiać [po-ma-vyaćh] v. accuse; impute; charge with

pomiar [po-myar] m. measurement; survey; surveying; mensuration; measurements
pomiatać [po-mya-taćh] v. push around; spurn; hold in contempt; ill-treat; sweep
pomidor [po-mee-dor] m. tomato
pomieszać [po-mye-shaćh] v. mix up; mingle; blend; stir; tangle; muddle up; embroil; mistake; jumble up; drive mad
pomieszanie zmysłów [po-mye--sha-ńe zmis-woov] insanity; madness; mental derangement
pomieszczać [po-**myesh**-chaćh] v.admit;contain; accommodate
pomiędzy [po-my**an**-dzi] prep. between; among; in the midst
pomijać [po-mee-yaćh] v. pass over; omit; overlook; leave out
pomimo [po-mee-mo] prep. in spite of; notwithstanding
pomnażać [po-mna-zhaćh] v. multiply; increase; intensify
pomniejszać [po-mńey-shaćh] v. diminish; lessen; reduce; dwarf; belittle; minimize
pomnik [pom-ńeek] m. monument (to a great man, etc,)
pomoc [po-mots] f. help; aid
pomocnik [po-mots-ńeek] m. helper; assistant; helpmate; (an) aid; one who assists
pomocny [po-mots-ni] adj. m. helpful in; instrumental in
pomorski [po-mors-kee] adj. m. Pomeranian; of Pomerania
pomost [po-most] m. platform
pomóc [po-moots] v. help; assist
pompa [pom-pa] f. pump; pomp
pompować [pom-po-vaćh] v. pump; blow up (inflate a tire)
pomsta [pom-sta] f. vengeance
pomruk [pom-rook] m. murmur; grumble; growl; purr; rumble
pomstować [pom-sto-vaćh] v. curse; swear; revile; vituperate
pomyje [po-mi-ye] pl. dishwater; hog-wash; swill; lap; slops
pomylić [po-mi-leećh] v. confound; mistake (facts); be mistaken; mislead; misinform
pomyłka [po-**miw**-ka] f. error

pomysł [po-misw] m. idea
pomyślność [po-miśhl-
-nośhćh] f. prosperity; success; happiness; welfare
pomyślny [po-miśhl-ni] adj. m.
successful; favorable; good
pomywaczka [po-mi-vach-ka] f.
dishwasher; scullery maid
ponad [po-nat] prep. above;
over; beyond; upwards of;
super-; more than; over and
above; besides; apart from
ponadto [po-nad-to] prep.
moreover; besides; over and
above; furthermore; also
ponaglać [po-na-glaćh] v. rush;
urge; remind; press; urge on
ponaglenie [po-na-gle-ńe] n.
reminder; pressure; urging
ponawiać [po-na-vyaćh] v.
renew (efforts); reiterate
ponętny [po-nant-ni] adj. m.
seductive; attractive; alluring
poniechać [po-ńe-khaćh] v.
give up; relinquish; renounce;
forsake; desist; forbear; drop
poniedziałek [po-ńe-dźha-wek]
m. Monday (week's 2nd day)
poniekąd [po-ńe-kownt] adv.
partly; in a way; in a sense
ponieść [po-ńeśhćh] v. sustain; carry; bear; suffer; incur;
push; take; overcome; bolt
ponieważ [po-ńe-vash] conj.
because; as; since; for
poniewczasie [po-ńe-vcha-śhe]
adv. too late; after the event
poniewierać [po-ńe-vye-raćh]
v. kick around; slight; hold in
contempt; ill-treat; mishandle
poniżej [po-ńee-zhey] adv.
below; beneath; hereunder;
under; lower down; less than
poniżyć [po-ńee-zhićh] v.
degrade; humble; tread down
ponosić [po-no-śheećh] v.
bear; carry (away); suffer; incur; bolt (a rider); push; carry
ponowić [po-no-veećh] v. renew; reiterate (demands, etc.)
ponownie [po-nov-ńe] adv.
anew; again; afresh; a second
time; another time; re-(do)

ponowny [po-nov-ni] adj. m.
repeated; renewed; reiterated
ponton [pon-ton] m. pontoon
ponury [po-noo-ri] adj. m.
gloomy dismal; sullen; dreary
pończocha [poń-cho-kha] f.
stocking; piece of hosiery
popadać [po-pa-daćh] v. fall in
poparcie [po-par-ćhe] n.
support; backing; promotion;
push; advancement; advocacy
popaść [po-paśhćh] v. fall in
popatrzeć [po-pa-tshećh] v.
look awhile (at); glance; see
popchnąć [pop-khnownćh] v.
push; shove up (down, along);
hassle; jostle; steer; direct
popelina [po-pe-lee-na] f. poplin
popełniać [po-pew-ńaćh] v.
commit (an error, crime, etc.);
perpetrate (crime, murder)
popęd [po-pant] m. impulse
popędliwy [po-pan-dlee-vi] adj.
m. impetuous; rush; hot headed; irritable; impulsive
popędzać [po-pan-dzaćh] v.
drive on; urge; push on; prod;
spur; goad; hustle on; hurry
popielaty [po-pye-la-ti] adj. m.
charcoal-grey; ashen; gray
popielec [po-pye-lets] m. Ash
Wednesday (1st day of Lent)
popielniczka [po-pyel-ńeech-ka]
f. ash-tray; ash pan
popierać [po-pye-raćh] v.
support; back; promote; favor;
uphold; give one's backing to
popiersie [po-pyer-śhe] n. bust
popić [po-peećh] v. rinse down
popiół [po-pyoow] m. ashes;
ash; cinders; slag
popis [po-pees] m. show; parade
popisywać się [po-pee-si-vaćh
śhan] v. show off; flaunt; parade; make a show (of wit)
popleczmik [po-plech-ńeek] m.
backer; upholder; partisan
popłatny [po-pwat-ni] adj. m.
profitable ; lucrative
popłoch [po-pwokh] m. panic
popołudnie [po-po-wood-ńe] n.
afternoon; after 12 at noon
po południu [po po-wood-ńu] in

(during) the afternoon
poprawa [po-pra-va] f.
 improvement; change for the
 better; (signs of) recovery
poprawka [po-prav-ka] f.
 correction; amendment; alteration; (final) rectification
poprawny [po-prav-ni] adj. m.
 correct; faultless; proper
po prostu [po pros-too] adv.
 simply; openly; candidly; un-
 ceremoniously; in plain words
poprzeczka [po-pshech-ka] f.
 crossbar; crossbeam; the bar
poprzedni [po-pshed-ńee]
 adj. m. previous; preceding;
 former; foregoing; anterior
poprzedzać [po-pshe-dzaćh] v.
 precede; prelude; go before
poprzestać [po-pshes-taćh] v.
 settle for; be satisfied
popularny [po-poo-lar-ni] adj. m.
 popular; prevalent; in vogue
popychać [po-pi-khaćh] v.
 push (along, up, down, aside);
 shove; ill treat; hustle; jostle;
popychadło [po-pi-khad-wo] n.
 (a slow) drudge; scapegrace
popyt [po-pit] m. demand
pora [po-ra] f. time; season
porachunek [po-ra-khoo-nek] m.
 reckoning; a bone to pick
porada [po-ra-da] f. advice
poradnia [po-rad-ńa] f.
 information bureau; (also) dis-
 pensary, clinic etc.
poradnik [po-rad-ńeek] m. guide;
 handbook; reference book
poradzić [po-ra-dźheećh] v.
 advise to do; cope with; help
poranek [po-ra-nek] m. morning
porastać [po-ras-taćh] v.
 overgrow; grow; become overgrown with; cover; sprout
poratować [po-ra-to-vaćh] v.
 help in distress; recuperate
porażenie [po-ra-zhe-ńe] n.
 stroke; shock; paralysis
porażka [po-razh-ka] f. defeat;
 set back; reverse; a beating
porcelana [por-tse-la-na] f. china;
 porcelain; crockery; dishes
porcja [por-tsya] f. portion

poręcz [po-ranch] f. banister
poręczenie [po-ran-che-ńe] n.
 guarantee; bail; warranty;
 pledge to guarantee for
poręka [po-ran-ka] f. guaranty;
 pledge; sponsorship; surety
poronić [po-ro-ńeećh] v. abort;
 miscarry; have a miscarriage
porost [po-rost] m. growth
porowaty [po-ro-va-ti] adj. m.
 porous; full of pores
porozdawać [po-roz-da-vaćh] v.
 give away; pass around
porozumianie [po-ro-zoo-mye-ńe]
 n. understanding; agreement
poród [po-root] m. child delivery;
 childbirth; parturition
porównać [po-roov-naćh] v.
 compare; draw a comparison;
 liken; parallel (two items)
porównanie [po-roov-na-ńe] n.
 comparison; equalization
poróżnić [po-roozh-ńeećh] v.
 disunite; divide; embroil
port [port] m. port; harbor
portfel [port-fel] m. wallet
portier [por-tyer] m. doorman
portki [port-kee] pl. pants (vulg.);
 breeches; (sloppy) trousers
portmonetka [port-mo-net-ka] f.
 purse; billfold; wallet
porto [por-to] n. postage
portret [por-tret] m. portrait
portugalski [por-too-gals-kee] adj.
 m. Portuguese; of Portugal
poruczać [po-roo-chaćh] v.
 entrust; charge with
porucznik [po-rooch-ńeek] m.
 Lieutenant; Flying Officer
poruszać [po-roo-shaćh] v.
 move; touch; sway; set in motion; keep in motion; wag
poruszenie [po-roo-she-ńe] n.
 agitation; movement; stir; disturbance; touch; commotion
poryw [po-riv] m. impulse;
 rapture; gust; onrush; elation
porywać [po-ri-vaćh] v. snatch;
 carry off; whisk away; grab;
 thrill; snap up; sweep away
porywacz [po-ri-vach] m.
 kidnaper; abductor; ravisher
porywczy [po-riv-chi] adj. m.

rash; irritable; impetuous; hasty; impulsive; hot-tempered

porządek [po-zhown-dek] m. order; tidiness; regularity; system; arrangement; sequence

porządny [po-zhownd-ni] adj. m. neat; decent; accurate; reliable

porzucać [po-zhoo-tsaćh] v. abandon; desert; forsake; jilt; leave; cast away; give up

porzucić [po-zhoo-ćheećh] v. abandon; give up; cast away

posada [po-sa-da] f. employment

posadzka [po-sadz-ka] f. parquet floor; tile (marble) floor

posąg [po-sowng] m. statue

poselstwo [po-sels-tvo] n. legation; deputation; envoys

poseł [po-sew] m. envoy; congressman; deputy; legate

posępny [po-sanp-ni] adj. m. gloomy; dismal; dreary; dark

posiadacz [po-śha-dach] m. bearer; holder; possessor; owner (of properties, etc.)

posiadać [po-śha-daćh] v. hold; own; possess; acquire; dominate; be in possession

posiadłość [po-śhad-wośhćh] f. estate; property; dominion

posiedzenie [po-śhe-dze-ńe] n. session; conference; meeting

posilać [po-śhee-laćh] v. refresh; nourish; feed

posiłek [po-śhee-wek] m. meal; refreshment; reinforcement

posłać [po-swaćh] v. send; make a bed; dispatch somewhere; dispatch; forward

posłanie [po-swa-ńe] n. bed; bedding; message; dispatch

posłaniec [po-swa-ńets] m. messenger; commissioner

posłuchać [po-swoo-khaćh] v. listen; obey; take advice

posługa [po-swoo-ga] f. service

posługacz [po-swoo-gach] m. servant; orderly (in a hospital); attendant; commissioner

posłuszny [po-swoosh-ni] adj. m. obedient; submissive; docile

pospolity [pos-po-lee-ti] adj. m. vulgar; common; ordinary; commonplace; everyday

posrebrzać [po-sreb-zhaćh] v. silver (plate); silver foil

post [post] m. fast; fast day

postać [po-staćh] v. form; human shape; personage

postanowić [po-sta-no-veećh] v. decide; enact; resolve; determine; make up one's mind

postanowienie [po-sta-no-vye-ńe] n. decision; resolve; provision (of the law); resolution

postarać się [po-sta-raćh śhan] v. procure; obtain; get; try (one's best); find; attempt

postawa [po-sta-va] f. attitude; posture; pose; bearing; stature; demeanor; mien; position

postawny [po-stav-ni] adj. m. portly; handsome; well made

postawić [po-sta-veećh] v. set up; put up; put on; bet; raise; erect; build; stake

postąpić [po-stown-peećh] v. proceed; act; deal; follow; advance; progress; treat; behave

posterunek [po-ste-roo-nek] m. outpost; sentry; police station

postęp [po-stanp] m. progress; advance; march; headway

postępowanie [po-stan-po-va-ńe] n. behavior; advance; conduct; (legal) procedure

postojowe [po-sto-yo-ve] n. demurrage; adj. n. parking

postój [pos-tooy] m. halt; stop; stand; parking; stopping place

postrach [po-strakh] m. terror; dread; scare; fright; bugaboo

postrzał [po-stshaw] m. gunshot; wound; (gun) shot; rifle shot; rifle shot wound; lumbago

postrzelony [po-stshe-lo-ni] adj. m. wounded; crazy; cracked

postulat [po-stoo-lat] m. demand; claim; requirement

postument [po-stoo-ment] m. pedestal (of a statue); socle

posucha [po-soo-kha] f. drought

posuw [po-soov] m. feed (of a drill); feed of a lathe

posuwać [po-soo-vaćh] v. move; shove; push on; carry;

dash; speed; shift; advance
posyłać [po-si-waćh] v. send
over; send to; dispatch
posyłka [po-siw-ka] f. errand
posypywać [po-si-pi-vaćh] v.
dust; pour; sprinkle (dry)
poszanowanie [po-sha-no-va-ńe]
n. respect; observance (of a
law); esteem; good opinion
poszarpać [po-shar-paćh] v.
maul; tear up; jag up; mangle;
rend; rough up; pull about
poszczególny [po-shche-gool-ni]
adj. m. individual
poszerzać [po-she-zhaćh] v.
widen; broaden; extend; ream;
spread; open out; let out
poszewka [po-shev-ka] f. pillow
case; pillow slip
poszkodowany [po-shko-do-va-ni]
adj. m. victim; sufferer
poszlaka [po-shla-ka] f. trace;
circumstantial evidence; sign
poszukiwać [po-shoo-kee-vaćh]
v. search; look for; inquire;
seek; claim; be in want of
poszukiwanie [po-shoo-kee-va-
-ńe] n. search; quest; research; investigation; inquiry
pościć [pośh-ćheećh] v. fast
pościel [pośh-ćhel] f. bedclothes sheets and blankets
pościg [pośh-ćheeg] m. chase;
pursuit (of a criminal, etc.)
pośladek [po-śhla-dek] m.
buttock; rump; bum
poślizgnąć się [po-śhleez-
-nownćh śhan] v. slip; make
a slip; lose footing, etc.
poślubić [po-śhloo-beećh] v.
marry; take in marriage
pośmiertny [po-śhmyert-ni] adj.
m. posthumous (child; works,
obituary notice, etc.)
pośmiewisko [pośh-mye-vees-
-ko] n. laughingstock; butt of
ridicule; object of ridicule
pośpiech [pośh-pyekh] m.
haste; hurry; dispatch
pośredni [po-śhred-ńee]
adj. m. intermediate; indirect
pośrednik [po-śhred-ńeek] m.
go-between; intermediary

pośredniczyć [po-śhred-ńee-
-chićh] v. mediate; be a go-
between; run a sales' agency
pośród [po-śhroot] prep. in
the midst of; among; amid(st)
poświadczać [po-śhvyad-
-chaćh] v. attest; certify; au-
thenticate; testify; witness
poświadczenie [po-śhvyad-
-che-ńe] n. certificate; attestation; certification of
poświęcać [po-śhvyan-tsaćh]
v. sacrifice; sanctify
poświęcenie [po-śhvyan-tse-
-ńe] n. devotion; sacrifice
pot [pot] m. sweat; perspiration
potajemny [po-ta-yem-ni] adj. m.
secret; clandestine; underhand
potakiwać [po-ta-kee-vaćh] v.
assent; agree; acquiesce
potas [po-tas] m. potassium
potaż [po-tash] m. potash
potąd [po-townt] adv. up to
here; up to this place
potem [po-tem] adv. after;
afterwards; then; later on
potencjalny [po-ten-tsyal-ni] adj.
m. potential; virtual
potęga [po-tan-ga] f. power;
might; force; impressiveness
potęgować [po-tan-go-vaćh] v.
intensify; raise to a power
potępiać [po-tan-pyaćh] v.
damn; run down; condemn
potępienie [po-tan-pye-ńe] n.
damnation; disapproval; blame
potężny [po-tanzh-ni] adj. m.
mighty; tremendous; powerful
potknąć się [pot-knownćh
śhan] v. slip on; trip over;
stumble against; make a slip
potknięcie [pot-kńan-ćhe] v.
slip; stumble; trip; a lapse
potoczny [po-toch-ni] adj. m.
current; common; everyday;
daily; of frequent occurrence
potok [po-tok] m. stream; brook
potomek [po-to-mek] m.
descendant; offspring; scion
potomność [po-tom-nośhćh]
f. posterity; future generations
potomstwo [po-tom-stvo] pl.
issue; progeny; offspring;

breed of animals; young
potop [po-top] m. deluge; flood
potrafić [po-tra-feećh] v. know
how to do; manage to do; be
able to do; be capable to do
potrawa [po-tra-va] f. dish
potrawka [po-traf-ka] f.
fricassee; ragout
potrącić [po-trown-ćheećh] v.
knock; deduct; poke; push;
jostle; nudge; touch upon
po trochu [po tro-khoo] little by
little; gradually; by driblets
potrójny [po-trooy-ni] adj. m.
triple; triplicate; treble
potrask [po-tshask] m. trap
potrząsać [po-tshown-saćh] v.
shake; brandish; agitate; strew
potrzeba [po-tzhe-ba] f. need;
want; call for; emergency; extremity; necessity; evacuation
potrzebny [po-tsheb-ni] adj. m.
necessary; needed; wanted
potulny [po-tool-ni] adj. m.
docile; submissive; humble;
meek; easy to discipline
poturbować [po-toor-bo-vaćh]
v. manhandle; rough up; beat;
maul; batter; knock about; ill-
treat; give a rough handling
potwarz [po-tvash] f. slander;
calumny; libel (against)
potwierdzać [po-tvyer-dzaćh] v.
confirm; attest; corroborate
potwór [po-tvoor] m. monster
potykać się [po-ti-kaćh śhan]
v. stumble; skirmish; joust
potylica [po-ti-lee-tsa] f. occiput;
back part of the skull
pouczać [po-oo-chaćh] v.
instruct; teach; give instructions; tutor; brief; admonish
pouczenie [po-oo-che-ńe] n.
instruction; giving instructions
poufalić się [po-oo-fa-leećh
śhan] v. take liberties; hob-
nob (with); be familiar (with)
poufały [po-oo-fa-wi] adj. m.
intimate; unceremonious; free
with; too familiar; mately;
hobnobbing with (somebody)
poufny [po-oof-ni] adj. m.
confidential; private; secret

powab [po-vap] m. charm; attraction; lure; seduction; loveliness; grace; attractiveness
powabny [po-vab-ni] adj. m.
attractive; charming; alluring
powaga [po-va-ga] f. gravity;
seriousness; dignity; prestige
powalać [po-va-laćh] v. soil;
dirty; overthrow; kill; slay
powalić [po-va-leećh] v. knock
down; floor (an adversary);
overthrow; kill; slay; fell
powała [po-va-wa] f. ceiling
poważać [po-va-zhaćh] v.
respect; esteem; have regard
poważny [po-vazh-ni] adj. m.
earnest; grave; dignified; serious; solemn; business-like
powątpiewać [po-vownt-pye-
-vaćh] v. doubt; have doubts
about; be dubious about
powetować [po-ve-to-vaćh] v.
make up for a loss; indemnify
oneself for; retrieve; repair
powiadać [po-vya-daćh] v. say;
tell; speak; (a legend, a rumor, etc.) has it that...
powiadomić [po-vya-do-meećh]
v. inform; notify; let know
powiastka [po-vyast-ka] f. tale
powiat [po-vyat] m. county;
district; district authorities
powicie [po-vee-ćhe] n.
swaddling (child) clothes
powidła [po-veed-wa] pl. jam;
marmalade; (plum) jam
powiedzieć [po-vye-dźhećh] v.
say to; tell; intend to say;
express; declare; make known
powieka [po-vye-ka] f. eyelid
powielacz [po-vye-lach] m.
mimeograph for making copies
powiernica [po-vyer-ńee-tsa] f.
confidante; trusted friend
powierzać [po-vye-zhaćh] v.
confide; charge with a task
powierzchnia [po-vyezh-khńa] f.
surface; plane; area; acreage
powiesić [po-vye-śheećh] v.
hang (a person, picture, etc.);
suspend; hung up; ring off
powieść [po-vyeśhćh] f.
novel; v. lead somebody

powieść się [po-vyeśhćh
śhan] v. succeed; be successful; come off
powietrze [po-vyet-zhe] n. air
powiew [po-vyef] m. breeze
powiększać [po-vyank-shaćh]
v. enlarge; augment; extend;
add; magnify; aggrandize
powiększenie [po-vyank-she-ńe]
n. enlargement; magnification
powijaki [po-vee-ya-kee] pl.
swathing; initial stage
powikłać [po-**vee**-kwaćh] v.
complicate; embroil; confuse
powinność [po-veen-nośhćh]
f. duty; obligation
powinowaty [po-vee-no-**va**-ti]
adj. m. related; akin
powitać [po-vee-taćh] v.
welcome; salute; bid welcome
powlekać [po-vle-kaćh] v.
cover; drag; coat; smear;
spread; put on bed-linen
powłoczka [po-vwoch-ka] f.
pillowcase; envelope; covering
powłoka [po-vwo-ka] f. (paint)
coat; covering; envelope; shell
powłóczysty [po-vwoo-chis-ti]
adj. m. trailing; enticing
powodować [po-vo-do-vaćh] v.
cause; bring about; touch off;
effect; induce; give occasion
powodzenie [po-vo-dze-ńe] n.
success; well-being; prosperity
powodzić się [po-**vo**-dźheećh
śhan] v. fare (well, ill); be
well off; be prospering
powojenny [po-vo-yen-ni] adj. m.
post-war; after-war
powoli [po-**vo**-lee] adv. slow
powolny [po-**vol**-ni] adj. m. slow;
tardy; leisurely; gradual
powołanie [po-vo-wa-ńe] n.
vocation; call; appointment;
quotation; reference; plea of
powonienie [po-vo-ńe-ńe] n.
sense of smell; smell
powód [po-voot] m. cause;
reason; ground; motive; rise;
provocation; the plaintiff
powódź [po-voodźh] f. flood
powój [po-vooy] m. bindweed
powóz [po-voos] m. carriage

powracać [po-**vra**-tsaćh] v.
return; come back; resume; recover; ride back; drive back
powrotny [po-**vrot**-ni] adj. m.
return; return (ticket)
powrót [po-vroot] m. return
powróz [po-vroos] m. rope
powstanie [po-vsta-ńe] n. rising
(to honor); uprising; revolt;
rebellion origin; rise; birth
powstaniec [po-**vsta**-ńets] m.
insurgent; rebel (soldier)
powstawać [po-vsta-vaćh] v.
rise up; stan up; revolt
powstrzymać [po-vstzhi-maćh]
v. restrain; refrain; hold back
powszechny [po-vshekh-ni] adj.
m. universal; general; public
powszedni [po-vshed-ńee]
adj. m. everyday; common-
place; daily; ordinary; common
powściągliwość [pov-
-śhćhowng-lee-vośhćh] f.
abstinence; temperance; moderation; restraint; reserve
powściągliwy [po-vśhćhown-
-glee-vi] adj. m. reserved;
abstinent; moderate; reticent;
temperate; self-restrained
powtarzać [po-vta-zhaćh] v.
say again; go over; repeat;
reproduce; reiterate; retell
po wtóre [po vtoo-re] adv.
secondly; in the second place;
in the second group; then
powtórnie [po-vtoor-ńe] adv.
anew; again; a second time
powtórny [po-vtoor-ni] adj. m.
repeated; renewed; second-
powyżej [po-vi-zhey] adv. above;
here in before; higher up; over
powziąć [po-vźhownćh] v.
take up; form; decide; conceive (a plan, suspicion, etc.)
poza [po-za] f. pose; attitude;
posture; affection; sham
poza [po-za] prep. beyond;
besides; except; apart; outside; apart from; past; extra-
pozagrobowy [po-za-gro-bo-vi]
adj. m. of beyond the grave;
from the hereafter; from beyond the grave; of the beyond

pozbawiać [po-zba-vyaćh] v.
deprive; dispossess of; take
away; divest; strip; remove
pozbyć się [poz-bićh śhan] v.
rid oneself; get rid; shake off
pozdrawiać [po-zdra-vyaćh] v.
greet; send one's greetings
pozew [po-zef] m. summons; order to came; writ; citation
poziom [po-źhom] m. level
poziomka [po-źhom-ka] f. wild
strawberry (fruit or plant)
poziomy [po-źho-mi] adj. m.
horizontal; level; uninspired
pozłota [po-zwo-ta] gilding
poznać [po-znaćh] v. get to
know; come to know; recognize; taste; acquaint; see
poznajomić [po-zna-yo-meećh]
v. acquaint; introduce
poznanie [po-zna-ńe] n.
cognition; acquaintance;
learning; study; knowledge
pozornie [po-zor-ńe] adv.
apparently; on the surface
pozostać [po-zos-taćh] v.
remain; stay behind; continue
pozostały [po-zo-sta-wi] adj. m.
remaining; residual; left
pozostawiać [po-zo-sta-vyaćh]
v. leave (behind); bequeath
pozór [po-zoor] m. appearance;
pretext; sham; look; mask;
cloak; face; show; semblance
pozwać [po-zvaćh] v. summon
pozwalać [po-zva-laćh] v. let;
allow; permit; tolerate; suffer
pozwany [po-zva-ni] m.
defendant; person sued or accused in a court of law, etc.
pozwolenie [po-zvo-le-ńe] n.
permission; consent; permit
pozycja [po-zits-ya] f. position;
item; status; posture; place
pozyskać [po-zis-kaćh] v. gain;
win over (to); gain good will
pozytywny [po-zi-tiv-ni] adj. m.
positive; affirmative; favorable
pozywać [po-zi-vaćh] v. sue;
cite; summon; cite (to court)
pożałować [po-zha-wo-vaćh] v.
repent; regret; take pity
pożar [po-zhar] m. fire (woods,

buildings); conflagration
pożądać [po-zhown-daćh] v.
desire; covet; lust after
pożądany [po-zhown-da-ni] adj.
m. desirable; welcome; desired
pożądliwy [po-zhown-dlee-vi]
adj. m. greedy; covetous; lascivious; lewd; lustful; leer
pożegnać [po-zheg-naćh] v. bid
goodbye; see off; dismiss
pożerać [po-zhe-raćh] v. devour; glut; gorge (one's food)
pożoga [po-zho-ga] f. fire;
conflagration; ravages (of war)
pożółknąć [po-zhoow-
-knownćh] v. grow yellow;
turn yellow; become yellow
pożycie [po-zhi-ćhe] n.
intercourse; conjugal life
pożyczka [po-zhich-ka] f. loan
pożyteczny [po-zhi-tech-ni] adj.
m. useful; profitable
pożytek [po-zhi-tek] m. use;
advantage; usefulness; benefit
pożywić [po-zhi-veećh] v. feed;
nourish; refresh; give food
pożywny [po-zhiv-ni] adj. m.
nutritious; nourishing
pójść [pooyśhćh] v. go; go
(home, school) away; go up...;
leave; fly; drift; pan out
póki [poo-kee] conj. till; until; as
long as; while; when; before
pół [poow] num. half; semi-;
demi; a one half; mid (way); in
mid course; half-way; hemi-
półbucik [poow-boo-ćheek] m.
half boot; low shoe
półgłosem [poow-gwo-sem] adv.
in a low voice; in an undertone; under one's breath
półgłówek [poow-gwoo-vek] m.
half-wit; fool; simpleton; dolt
półka [poow-ka] f. shelf; ledge
półkole [poow-ko-le] n. semi
-circle; half-circle; hemicycle
półksiężyc [poow-kśhan-zhits]
m. half-moon; crescent; the
Crescent of Islam; Islam
półkula [poow-koo-la] f. hemi-
-sphere; half of a sphere
półmisek [poow-mee-sek] m.
charger dish; (serving) dish

półnagi [poow-na-gee] adj. m.
half naked; half dressed
północ [poow-nots] f. midnight;
north; North; the North
północno-wschodni [poow-nots-
-no vskhod-ńee] northeast
północno-zachodni [poow-nots-
-no za-khod-ńee] northwest
północny [poow-nots-ni] adj. m.
north; Northern; Northerly
półroczny [poow-roch-ni] adj. m.
half-yearly; semi-annual
półświatek [poow-śhvya-tek]
m. love industry; demimonde
półtora [poow-to-ra] num. one
and half; a (day etc.) and half
półurzędowy [poow-oo-zhan-do-
-vi] adj. m. semi-official
półwysep [poow-vi-sep] m.
peninsula; almost an island
póty [poo-ti] conj. as long
później [pooźh-ńey] adv. later
on; afterwards; at a later date
późno [pooźh-no] adv. late;
well on; tardily; late-
późny [pooźh-ni] adj. m. late
prababka [pra-bab-ka] great
grandmother; ancestor
praca [pra-tsa] f. work; job
pracodawca [pra-tso-dav-tsa] m.
employer; adj. m. (man) em-
ploying people for wages
pracowity [pra-tso-vee-ti] adj. m.
industrious; hard-working
pracownik [pra-tsov-ńeek] m.
worker;employee;clerk;official
praczka [prach-ka] f. wash-
(washer)woman; laundress
prać [prać] v. wash clothes;
launder; thrash; strike; beat up
pradziad [pra-dźhat] m. great
grandfather; ancestor
pragnąć [prag-nownć] v. be
thirsty; desire; wish; long for
pragnienie [prag-ńe-ńe] n. wish;
thirst; desire; lust for
praktyczny [prak-tich-ni] adj. m.
practical; sensible; expedient
praktyka [prak-ti-ka] f. practice;
usage; apprenticeship
praktykować [prak-ti-ko-vać]
v. practice; be in training
pralka [pral-ka] f. washing

machine; washer; wash board
pralnia [pral-ńa] f. laundry
pranie [pra-ńe] n. washing
praojciec [pra-oy-ćhets] m.
forefather; ancestor
prasa [pra-sa] f. press; print
prasować [pra-so-vać] v. iron
(linen etc.); press; print
prawda [prav-da] f. truth
prawdomówność [prav-do-
-moov-nośhćh] f. veracity;
truthfulness; truth of words
prawdopodobny [prav-do-po-dob-
-ni] adj. m. probable; likely
prawdziwie [prav-dźhee-vye]
adv. truly; genuinely; indeed
prawdziwy [prav-dźhee-vi] adj.
m. true; real; authentic
prawica [pra-vee-tsa] f. the
Right; right hand; right wing
prawić [pra-veećh] v. talk; say
prawidło [pra-veed-wo] n. rule;
boot tree; law; centering
prawidłowy [pra-vee-dwo-vi] adj.
m. regular; correct; proper
prawie [pra-vye] adv. almost;
nearly; practically; all but
prawnik [prav-ńeek] m. lawyer
prawnuczka [prav-nooch-ka] f.
great granddaughter
prawnuk [prav-nook] m. great
grandson (grandson's son)
prawny [prav-ni] adj. m. legal;
lawful; legitimate; rightful
prawo [pra-vo] adv. right; law
prawo [pra-vo] n. law; (driving)
license; statute; claim
prawodawca [pra-vo-dav-tsa] m.
legislator; lawmaker; lawgiver
prawodawstwo [pra-vo-dav-stvo]
n. legislation; legislature
prawomocny [pra-vo-mots-ni]
adj. m. legal; valid
prawosławny [pra-vo-swav-ni]
adj. m. (also m.) Orthodox
prawość [pra-vośhćh] f.
honesty; integrity; rectitude;
righteousness; uprightness
prawować się [pra-vo-vać
śhan] v. litigate a cause; sue
for; be engaged in a lawsuit;
be at law with somebody
prawowity [pra-vo-vee-ti] adj. m.

legal (heir apparent, heir, etc.)
prawy [pra-vi] adj. m. honest;
right; right hand-; upright; lawful; right (wheel, hand, side)
prażyć [pra-zhićh] v. grill; roast
burn; keep heavy gunfire on
prąd [prownd] m. current; flow
stream; air flow; tendency;
trend; movement (air, water)
prądnica [prownd-ńee-tsa] f.
electric generator; dynamo
prąd stały [prownd sta-wi] m.
direct (electric) current
prąd zmienny [prownd zmyen-ni]
m. alternating (electric) current
prążek [prown-zhek] m. stripe
precyzja [pre-tsi-zya] f. precision;
accuracy; definiteness
precyzować [pre-tsi-zo-vaćh] v.
define; state precisely; define
precz! [prech] adv. go away; do
away with; down (off) with
prefabrykować [pre-fa-bri-ko-;
-vaćh] v. prefabricate
prefiks [pre-feeks] m. prefix
prelegent [pre-le-gent] m.
lecturer (presenting a lecture)
prelekcja [pre-lek-tsya] f. lecture
(informative talk); talk
preliminarz [pre-lee-mee-nash] m.
estimate of a budget, etc.
premedytacja [pre-me-di-tats-ya]
f. premeditation
premia [pre-mya] f. premium;
bonus; bounty; prize; gift
premier [pre-myer] m. prime
minister of a country; premier
premiera [pre-mye-ra] f. first
night show; first night
prenumerata [pre-noo-me-ra-ta] f.
subscription (to a paper etc.)
preparat [pre-pa-rat] m.
preparation; concoction; specimen (also for scientific use)
prerogatywa [pre-ro-ga-ti-va] f.
privilege; prerogative (power)
presja [pres-ya] f. pressure
prestiż [pres-teesh] m. prestige;
high esteem (influence power)
pretekst [pre-tekst] m. pretext;
excuse; false reason or motive
pretensja [pre-ten-sya] f. claim;
grudge; debt; pretentiousness

prezerwatywa [pre-zer-va-ti-va] f.
contraceptive sheath; condom
prezent [pre-zent] m. gift
prezes [pre-zes] m. chairman
prezydent [pre-zi-dent] m.
president; mayor; Lord Mayor
pręcik [pran-ćheek] m. (small)
stick; stamen; rod; graphite
prędki [prand-kee] adj. m. swift;
quick; rapid; fast; prompt; immediate; hasty; instant; nimble
prędko [prand-ko] adv. quickly;
fast; soon; at once; rapidly
prędkość [prand-kośhćh] f.
speed; swiftness; velocity; im-
petuosity; impulsiveness
prędzej [pran-dzey] adv. quicker;
sooner; rather; with all haste
pręga [pran-ga] f. stripe; wale
pręgierz [pran-gesh] m. pillory
pręgowaty [pran-go-va-ti] adj. m.
striped; with stripes (wales)
pręt [prant] m. rod; bar; pole;
switch; stick; wand; twig;
perch; (gauging-) rod; stave
prężność [pranzh-nośhćh] f.
resilience; elasticity; energy
prężny [pranzh-ni] adj. m.
elastic; resilient; supple
prężyć [pran-zhićh] v. strain
probierczy kamień [pro-byer-chi
ka-myeń] m. touchstone
problem [pro-blem] m. problem
probostwo [pro-bos-tvo] n.
parsonage; parish; rectory
proboszcz [pro-boshch] m.
pastor; parish priest; parson
probówka [pro-boof-ka] f. test
-tube; (laboratory) test glass
proca [pro-tsa] f. sling; catapult
proceder [pro-tse-der] m. trade;
(shady) dealings; a plot
procedura [pro-tse-doo-ra] f.
procedure; legal practice
procent [pro-tsent] m.
percentage; interest on money
procentować się [pro-tsen-to-
-vaćh śhan] v. bring interest
proces [pro-tses] m. lawsuit
procesja [pro-tses-ya] f.
procession; (marching, pro-
ceeding) moving as in parade
procesować [pro-tse-so-vaćh]

v. sue; be engaged in a litigation; litigate a cause (with)
proch [prokh] m. powder; dust
proch strzelniczy [prokh stzhel--ńee-chi] m. gunpowder
producent [pro-doo-tsent] m. producer; manufacturer; maker
produkcja [pro-dook-tsya] f. production; (factory, literary) output; produce; performance
produkować [pro-doo-ko-vaćh] v. produce; grow; generate; manufacture; turn out; stage
produkt [pro-dookt] m. product
profanować [pro-fa-no-vaćh] v. profane; desecrate; despoil
profesor [pro-fe-sor] m. (university) professor; teacher
profil [pro-feel] m. profile
profilaktyczny [pro-fee-lak-tich-ni] adj. m. prophylactic
prognoza [prog-no-za] f. prognosis; forcast (of weather)
program [pro-gram] m. program; plan; agenda (of a meeting)
progresja [pro-gres-ya] f. progression; sequence
prohibicja [pro-khee-beets-ya] f. prohibition; forbidden
projekcja [pro-yek-tsya] f. projection (on a screen etc.)
projekt [pro-yekt] m. project
projektować [pro-yek-to-vaćh] v. design; plan; lay out; draft
proklamować [pro-kla-mo-vaćh] v. proclaim; announce officially; announce to be
prokurator [pro-koo-ra-tor] m. public prosecutor
proletariat [pro-le-ta-ryat] proletariat; working class
prolog [pro-log] m. prologue
prolongować [pro-lon-go-vaćh] v. prolong; extend; renew
prom [prom] m. ferry (boat)
promienieć [pro-mye-ńećh] v. radiate; beam (with joy etc.)
promieniotwórczy [pro-mye-ńo--tvoor-chi] adj. m. radioactive (matter; isotopes etc.)
promieniować [pro-mye-ńo--vaćh] v. radiate (heat, light); beam; glow; brim over (with)

promienisty [pro-mye-ńees-ti] adj. m. radial; radiant; radiate
promienny [pro-myen-ni] adj. m. radiant; beaming; bright
promień [pro-myeń] adj. m. ray beam; gleam; radius; fin ray
promocja [pro-mots-ya] f. promotion; conferment of a university (doctoral) degree
propaganda [pro-pa-gan-da] f. propaganda; publicity; popularization; information; boosting
propagować [pro-pa-go-vaćh] v. propagate; publicize; boost
proponować [pro-po-no-vaćh] v. propose; put forwards; suggest; submit (a plan); offer
proporcja [pro-por-tsya] f. proportion; ratio; relation
proporcjonalny [pro-por-tsyo-nal--ni] adj. m. proportional
proporzec [pro-po-zhets] m. pennon; banner; streamer; pennant; (stem) jack
propozycja [pro-po-zits-ya] f. proposal; offer; suggestion
proroctwo [pro-rots-tvo] n. prophecy; prediction (future)
prorok [pro-rok] m. prophet
prosić [pro-śheećh] v. beg; pray; ask; invite; request
prosię [pro-śhan] n. young pig
proso [pro-so] n. millet
prospekt [pro-spekt] m. prospect; folder; view; panorama; outlook; anticipation
prosperować [pro-spe-ro-vaćh] v. prosper; be prosperous; be doing well; thrive; succeed
prostacki [pro-stats-kee] adj. m. boorish; rude; vulgar; coarse
prostak [pros-tak] m. boor; gull
prostata [pro-sta-ta] f. prostate (gland at the male bladder)
prosto [pros-to] adv. straight; right; upright; simply; candidly
prostoduszny [pro-sto-doosh-ni] adj. m. simple-hearted; naive
prostokąt [pro-sto-kownt] m. rectangle (four-sided plane figure with four right angles)
prostolinijny [pro-sto-lee-ńeey-ni] adj. m. straightforward

prostopadła [pro-sto-**pad**-wa] f.
perpendicular; normal; sheer
prostota [pro-**sto**-ta] f. simplicity;
neatness; boorishness
prostować [pro-**sto**-vaćh] v.
straighten; correct; revise
prosty [**pros**-ti] adj. m. straight;
direct simple; vulgar; plain
prostytucja [pro-sti-too-tsya] f.
prostitution; streetwalking
prostytutka [pro-sti-**toot**-ka] f.
prostitute; streetwalker
proszek [pro-shek] m. powder
(for baking etc.); wafer
proszę [pro-**shan**] please
prośba [**prośh**-ba] f. request;
demand; petition; application
proszkować [prosh-ko-vaćh] v.
pulverize; grind to powder
protegowany [pro-te-go-**va**-ni]
adj. m. protege (helped, etc.)
protekcja [pro-**tek**-tsya] f. pull;
patronage; backing; influence;
push; a person that protects
protest [pro-test] m. protest
protestant [pro-**te**-stant] m.
Protestant; evangelical
protestantyzm [pro-te-stan-tizm]
m. Protestantism
proteza [pro-te-za] f. artificial
limb, tooth, or denture, etc.
protokół [pro-to-koow] m.
record; protocol; minutes; official record; formal record
prototyp [pro-to-tip] m.
prototype; archetype; proto-
plast; proterotype; model
prowadzenie [pro-va-dze-**ńe**] n.
management; conduct; leadership; directing; prosecution
prowadzić [pro-va-**dźheećh**] v.
steer; lead; conduct; guide;
keep; live; carry on (a conversation); show the way; escort;
run; manage (an institution)
prowadzić auto [pro-va-
-**dźheećh** aw-to] **drive a car**
prowiant [pro-vyant] m.
provisions; eatables; rations
prowincjonalny [pro-veen-tsyo-
-nal-ni] adj. m. provincial
prowizja [pro-**veez**-ya] f.
commission; percentage; pro-

vision; brokerage
prowizoryczny [pro-vee-zo-**rich**-
-ni] adj. m. provisional
prowodyr [pro-**vo**-dir] m.
ringleader; gang leader
prowokacja [pro-vo-**kats**-ya] f.
provocation; stirring trouble
proza [pro-za] f. prose; dullness
próba [proo-ba] f. trial; test;
proof; ordeal; acid test; try; go
próbka [**proob**-ka] f. sample
próbny [**proob**-ni] adj. m. ex-
perimental; tentative; test-
próbować [proo-bo-vaćh] v.
try; test; taste; put to the
test; make an attempt; offer
próchnica [prookh-**ńee**-tsa] f.
molder; (tooth) decay; humus
próchno [prookh-no] n. rotten
wood; mould; rot; wood dust
prócz [prooch]prep.save; except;
besides; apart from; moreover
próg [proog] m. threshold
prószyć [proo-shićh] v. sift;
flake; make dust; sprinkle
(dust, snow); spray (powder)
próżnia [proozh-**ńa**] f. vacuum
próżniaczy [proozh-**ńa**-chi]
adj. m. lazy; idle; inactive;
leisure; work-shy; sluggish
próżniak [proozh-**ńak**] m. idler
próżno [proozh-no] adv. vainly;
empty-; in vain; to no avail
próżność [proozh-**nośhćh**] f.
vanity; false pride; futility
próżny [proozh-ni] adj. m. 1.
empty; void; 2. vain; futile
pruć [prooćh] v. rip; unsew
pruski [proos-kee] adj. m.
Prussian; of Prussia
prychać [pri-khaćh] v. snort
prycza [pri-cha] f. plank-bed
pryk stary [prik sta-ri] m. old
goat; old duffer; old codger
prym [prim] m. lead; first place;
superiority; the lead
prymas [pri-mas] m. primate
prymka [prim-ka] f. chewing
tobacco (a plug of)
pryskać [pris-kaćh] v. splash;
spray; splatter; sputter; fly;
clear out; bolt; scamper away;
burst; hop it; dissolve; vanish

pryszcz [prishch] m. pimple
prysznic [prish-ńeets] m. shower bath; shower (fixture)
prywatny [pri-vat-ni] adj. m. private; personal; confidential
pryzmat [priz-mat] m. prism
prządka [pshownd-ka] f. spinner
prząść [pshownśhćh] v. spin
przebaczać [pshe-ba-chaćh] v. forgive; pardon; condone
przebaczenie [pshe-ba-che-ńe] n. pardon; forgiveness; remittal (of sins); absolution
przebąkiwać [pshe-bown-kee-vaćh] v. mutter; hint (that); allude to something; mention
przebić [pshe-beećh] v. pierce; perforate; puncture; stab; dig; recoin; transfix; bore; punch
przebieg [pshe-byek] m. course; run; progress; process; milage
przebiegać [pshe-bye-gaćh] v. run cross; take place; proceed
przebiegły [pshe-byeg-wi] adj. m. cunning; sly; wily; crafty
przebierać [pshe-bye-raćh] v. choose; sort; change clothes; sift; disguise; manipulate
przebijać [pshe-bee-yaćh] v. pierce; puncture; stab; reveal; show through; make visible
przebłysk [pshe-bwisk] m. glimpse; ray; flash; sparkle; glimmer; stroke of (genius)
przebłyskiwać [pshe-bwi-skee-vaćh] v. gleam; shine; flash
przeboleć [pshe-bo-lećh] get over; put up with; get over it
przebój [pshe-booy] m. hit; success; breakthrough; clou
przebranie [pshe-bra-ńe] n. disguise; being disguised
przebrnąć [psheb-rnownćh] v. muddle through; wade through
przebrzmiały [psheb-zhmya-wi] adj. m. overblown; has-been
przebudowa [pshe-boo-do-va] f. remodeling; rebuilding
przebudzić [pshe-boo-dźheećh] v. wake up; awake; rouse; revive; awaken; make active
przebyć [pshe-bićh] v. be over through; surmount; ride out
storm; travel; cross; pass; dwell; cover distance (space)
przebywać [pshe-bi-vaćh] v. stay; reside; dwell; inhabit
przecedzać [pshe-tse-dzaćh] v. filter; strain through a sieve
przeceniać [pshe-tse-ńaćh] v. overrate; lower the price
przechadzka [pshe-khadz-ka] f. walk; stroll; tour; airing
przechadzać się [pshe-kha-dzaćh śhan] v. take a walk; stroll; go for a walk; saunter
przechodzić [pshe-kho-dźheećh] v. pass (through)
przechodzień [pshe-kho-dźheń] m. passerby; pedestrian
przechowanie [pshe-kho-va-ńe] n. safekeeping; storage
przechowywać [pshe-kho-vi-vaćh] v. store; preserve; harbore; keep; retain; shelter
przechrzcić [pshekh-shćheećh] v. convert; change name
przechwalać [pshe-khva-laćh] v. talk big; overpraise; extol; puff; give exaggerated praise
przechwycić [pshe-khvi-ćheećh] v. intercept; seize
przechylić [pshe-khi-leećh] v. tilt; lean; tip; incline
przechytrzyć [pshe-khit-zhićh] v. outwit; overreach; outsmart
przeciąć [pshe-ćhownćh] v. cut; cross; intersect; slice; cleave; cut across; bisect
przeciąg [pshe-ćhowng] m. draught; span; spell; time lapse; space (stretch) of time
przeciągać [pshe-ćhown-gaćh] v. draw; drag; delay; stretch
przeciążać [pshe-ćhown-zhaćh] v. overload; overburden; overwork; congest
przecie [pshe-ćhe] conj. yet; of course but; after all; still
przeciekać [pshe-ćhe-kaćh] v. leak; ooze; drain; percolate
przecierać [pshe-ćhe-raćh] v. rub; wipe clear; threadbare; fret; polish (shoes); clear up
przecierpieć [pshe-ćher-pyećh] v. endure; bear; suffer

przecież [pshe-ćhesh] conj. yet; still; after all; now; though

przeciętny [pshe-ćhant-ni] adj. m. average; ordinary; indifferent; mediocre; common

przecinać [pshe-ćhee-naćh] v. cut; intersect; slice; cleave

przecinek [pshe-ćhee-nek] m. comma (mark of punctuation)

przeciskać się [pshe-ćhees-kaćh śhan] v. squeeze (press) through; push through; elbow one's way through

przeciw [pshe-ćheev] prep. against; versus; contrary to

przeciwko [pshe-ćheev-ko] prep. against; contrary; versus

przeciwdziałać [pshe-ćheev-dźha-waćh] v. counteract

przeciwległy [pshe-ćheev-leg-wi] adj. m. opposite; contrary

przciwlotniczy [pshe-ćheev-lot-ńee-chi] adj. m. antiaircraft (artillery, defence etc.)

przeciwnie [pshe-ćheev-ńe] adv. on the contrary; reverse

przeciwnik [pshe-ćheev-ńeek] m. opponent; adversary; enemy; foe; antagonist

przeciwność [pshe-ćheev-nośhćh] f. adversity; setback; reverse (of fortune)

przeciwstawiać [pshe-ćheev-sta-vyaćh] v. oppose; set against; contrast; resist; defy

przeciwwaga [pshe-ćheev-va-ga] f. counterweight; balance weight; counterbalance

przecudny [pshe-tsood-ni] adj. m. most wonderful; just simply marvelous; most admirable

przeczący [pshe-chown-tsi] adj. m. negative; contradictory

przeczenie [pshe-che-ńe] n. negation; negative (answer); denial; answer in the negative

przecznica [pshech-ńee-tsa] f. side-street; cross street

przeczucie [pshe-choo-ćhe] n. foreboding; presentiment

przeczulony [pshe-choo-lo-ni] adj. m. high-strung; oversensitive; touchy; easily irritated

przeczyć [pshe-chićh] v. deny; belie; negate; contradict

przeczyszczać [pshe-chish-chaćh] v. purge; cleanse; scour; wipe; purge; clean out

przeczytać [pshe-chi-taćh] v. read through; peruse; read over again; re-read

przeć [pshećh] v. insist on; urge; press on; push; exert pressure; impel; drive; insist; bear down; urge; impel; strive

przed [pshet] prep. before; in front of; ahead of; previous to; from; since; ago; against

przedajny [pshe-day-ni] adj. m. venal; open to bribery

przedawnienie [pshe-dav-ńe-ńe] n. expiration of validity

przedawniony [pshe-dav-ńo-ni] adj. m. of expired validity

przeddzień [pshed-dźheń] m. on the eve; the day before

przede wszystkim [pshe-de vshist-keem] adv. above all; first and foremost; first of all; in the first place; to start with

przedhistoryczny [pshed-khee-sto-rich-ni] adj. m. prehistoric; before the recorded history

przedimek [pshed-ee-mek] m. article (in grammar)

przedkładać [pshed-kwa-daćh] v. submit; refer; propose; present; give priority

przedłużać [pshe-dwoo-zhaćh] v. lengthen; prolong; extend

przedmieście [pshed-myeśh-ćhe] n. suburb; a district on the outskirts of a city

przedmiot [pshed-myot] m. object; subject; subject matter

przedmiotowy [pshed-myo-to-vi] adj. m. objective; at issue

przedmowa [pshed-mo-va] f. preface; foreword; introduction (a preliminary section)

przedmówca [pshed-moov-tsa] m. previous speaker

przedni [pshed-ńee] adj. m. leading; front (seat, tooth); forward; choice; fine; foremost; superior; high-quality

przedostać się [pshe-do-stańć śhan] v. penetrate; get in; (pass, work, force) through

przedostatni [pshe-do-stat-ńee] adj. m. last but one

przedpłata [pshed-pwa-ta] f. advance payment; subscription

przedpokój [pshed-po-kooy] m. (waiting-room) lobby; antechamber; anteroom; entry hall

przedpole [pshed-po-le] n. foreground; foreland

przedpołudnie [pshed-po-wood-ńe] n. morning; forenoon

przdpotopowy [pshed-po-to-po-vi] adj. m. fossil; fossilized; obsolete; antediluvian

przedramię [pshed-ra-myan] n. forearm; antebrachium

przedrostek [pshed-ros-tek] m. prefix (in grammar)

przedruk [pshe-drook] m. reprint; reimpression; impression

przedrzeć [pshed-zheńć] v. tear up; tear through; rend; break through; penetrate; burst

przedrzeźniać [pshed-zheźh-ńáćh] v. ape; mimic; mock; take off; imitate like an ape

przedsiębiorca [pshed-śhan-byor-tsa] m. contractor; businessman; entrepreneur

przedsiębiorstwo [pshed-śhan-byor-stvo] n. business; concern; enterprise; firm

przedsiębrać [pshed-śhan-braćh] v. undertake; embark on (upon); enter upon (on)

przedsionek [pshed-śho-nek] m. lobby; vestibule; porch; auricle

przedsmak [pshed-smak] m. foretaste; earnest (of future events, what is to come)

przedstawić [pshed-sta-veećh] v. present; represent; introduce to; recommend; imagine

przedstawiciel [pshed-sta-vee-ćhel] m. representative

przedstawicielstwo [pshed-sta-vee-ćhel-stvo] n. agency

przedstawienie [pshed-sta-vye-ńe] n. performance; show; version; play; introduction

przedszkole [pshed-shko-le] n. kindergarten; nursery school

przedświt [pshed-śhveet] m. predawn; daybreak; harbinger

przedtem [pshed-tem] adv. before; beforehand; before that; before then; formerly; in advance; before now; earlier

przedterminowy [pshed-ter-mee-no-vi] adj. m. advance; premature; done ahead of time

przedwczesny [pshed-vches-ni] adj. m. premature; untimely

przedwczoraj [pshed-vcho-ray] adv. the day before yesterday

przedwieczny [pshed-vyech-ni] adj. m. eternal; primeval; ancient; secular; everlasting

przedwiośnie [pshed-vyośh-ńe] n. early spring (springtime)

przedwojenny [pshed-vo-yen-ni] adj. m. prewar; before the war

przedział [pshe-dźhaw] m. partition; compartment; section; interstice; parting

przedzielić [pshe-dźhe-leećh] v. divide; part; separate

przedzierać [pshe-dźhe-raćh] v. tear down; tear up; rend

przedziurawić [pshe-dźhoo-ra-veećh] v. perforate; make a puncture; riddle; pierce; make a hole (holes); poke a hole

przedziwny [pshe-dźheev-ni] adj. m. prodigious; admirable; quite (very) odd; strange

przeforsować [pshe-for-so-vaćh] v. ram through; force through; overstrain

przegapić [pshe-ga-peećh] v. let slip; over look; miss

przeginać [pshe-gee-naćh] v. bend (over); turn up; turn down; incline; inflect; bow

przegląd [pshe-glownd] m. review; inspection; survey

przegłosować [pshe-gwo-so-vaćh] v. outvote; take a vote

przegonić [pshe-go-ńeećh] v. overtake; drive out; drive through; drive away; rush past

przegotować [pshe-go-to-vaćh] v. boil; overcook; over boil

przegrać [pshe-grać] v. lose (war, game, battle, lawsuit, fortune, etc.); gamble away

przegradzać [pshe-gra-dzać] v. partition; divide; separate

przegrana [pshe-gra-na] f. defeat; loss; beating; licking

przegryzać [pshe-gri-zać] v. bite through; bite in two

przegroda [pshe-gro-da] f. partition; division; stall; cell

przegub [pshe-goob] m. wrist; ball-and-socket joint

przeholować [pshe-kho-lo-vać] v. overshoot; rush into excess

przeistoczyć [pshe-ee-sto--chić] v. transform; remold; convert (turn) into; refashion

przejaśnienie [pshe-yaśh-ńe--ńe] n. clearing up; bright interval; break in the clouds

przejaw [pshe-yav] m. symptom; sign; indication; manifestation

przejawiać [pshe-ya-vyać] v. reveal; display; manifest; evidence; show (satisfaction etc.)

przejazd [pshe-yazt] m. crossing; passage; thoroughfare; journey

przejąć [pshe-yownć] v. take over; seize; adopt; master; succeed; perturb; make fret

przejechać [pshe-ye-khać] v. pass; ride; cross; run over

przejęty [pshe-yan-ti] adj. m. impressed; upset; deeply stirred; perturbed; wrapped up

przejmować [pshey-mo-vać] v. take over; seize; penetrate

przejrzeć [pshey-zheć] v. see through; recover sight; revise

przejrzysty [pshey-zhis-ti] adj. m. transparent; clear; sheer

przejście [pshey-śhćhe] n. pass; transition; conversion; roadway; alley; aisle; ordeal

przejściowo [pshey-śhćho-vo] adv. temporarily; provisionally

przejść [psheyśhćh] v. pass; cross; experience; go across

przekaz [pshe-kas] m. transfer; money order; remittance

przekazywać [pshe-ka-zi-vać] v. transfer; pass on; send on;

transmit; deliver; direct

przekaźnik [pshe-każh-ńeek] m. relay; repeater; transmitter

przekąsem [pshe-kown-sem] adv. ironically; mockingly; contemptuously; sneeringly

przekąska [pshe-kown-ska] f. snack; refreshment

przekątna [pshe-kownt-na] f. diagonal (line)

przekleństwo [pshe-kleń-stvo] n. curse; profanity; damnation

przekład [pshe-kwat] m. translation; rendering; rearrangement; transposition

przekładać [pshe-kwa-dać] v. shift; transfer; prefer; move; translate; reach; put between

przekładnia [pshe-kwad-ńa] f. gearbox; clutch; transposition

przekłuć [pshe-kwooćh] v. prick (a bubble); pierce; puncture (a tire); perforate

przekonać [pshe-ko-nać] v. convince; persuade; bring round; reason with; urge; talk

przekonanie [pshe-ko-na-ńe] n. conviction; persuasion; opinion

przekop [pshe-kop] m. trench; ditch; tunnel; cutting; piercing

przekopać [pshe-ko-pać] v. dig-through; turn over; excavate; cut (a passage, ditch)

przekora [pshe-ko-ra] f. spite

przekraczać [pshe-kra-chać] v. overstep; cross; surpass

przekradać się [pshe-kra-dać śhan] v. steal through

przekreślić [pshe-kreśh-leećh] v. cross out; delete; annul

przekręcić [pshe-kran-ćheećh] v. twist; distort (a statement)

przekroczenie [pshe-kro-che-ńe] n. crossing; offence; transgression; sin (against)

przekroczyć [pshe-kro-chićh] v. cross; trespass; exceed; offend; violate; transgress (the law); step over; overstep

przekroić [pshe-kro-eećh] v. cut

przekrój [pshe-krooy] m. cross section; profile; review

przekrwienie [pshe-krvye-ńe] n.

hyperemia; congestion
przekształcić [pshe-kshtaw--ćheećh] v. transform
przekupić [pshe-koo-peećh] v. bribe; buy over; corrupt
przekupka [pshe-koop-ka] f. huckstress; vendor; wrangler
przekupny [pshe-koop-ni] adj. m. venal; bribable; corruptible
przekupstwo [pshe-koop-stvo] n. bribery; graft; corruption
przekwitać [pshe-kvee-taćh] v. wither; fade; decay; shed blossom; come out of bloom
przelatywać [pshe-la-ti-vaćh] v. fly through; cross; run; pass
przelew [pshe-lef] m. transfusion; transfer; overflow
przelewać [pshe-le-vaćh] v. overfill; transfer; shed
przelękły [pshe-lank-wi] adj. m. frightened; intimidated
przelęknąć [pshe-lank-nownćh] v. frighten; scare; terrify
przelicytować [pshe-lee-tsi-to--vaćh] v. outbid (one another)
przeliczyć [pshe-lee-chićh] v. miscalculate; count over
przelot [pshe-lot] m. overflight; flight; passage; transit by air
przelotny [pshe-lot-ni] adj. m. fleeting; passing; transient
przeludnienie [pshe-lood-ńe-ńe] n. overpopulation; congestion
przeładować [pshe-wa-do-vaćh] v. overload; transship; reload
przeładunek [pshe-wa-doo-nek] m. load transfer; reloading
przełamać [pshe-wa-maćh] v. break through; break in two
przełazić [pshe-wa-źheećh] v. climb over; creep across
przełącznik [pshe-wownch-ńeek] m. switch; shift; commutator
przełęcz [pshe-wanch] f. pass; saddle; mountain pass
przełknąć [pshew-known´ćh] v. swallow; swallow down
przełom [pshe-wom] m. break-through; turning point; gorge
przełożony [pshe-wo-zho-ni] m. principal; superior; chief
przełożyć [pshe-wo-zhićh] v.

transfer; prefer; shift; reach
przełyk [pshe-wik] m. gullet; esophagus; oesophagus; throat
przemakać [pshe-ma-kaćh] v. ooze; get wet; be permeable
przemarsz [pshe-marsh] m. marching past; march of troops; passage of troops
przemarznąć [pshe-mar--znownćh] v. be chilled to the marrow; be (get) frozen stiff;
przemawiać [pshe-ma-vyaćh] v. speak; harangue; address
przemądrzały [pshe-mownd-zha--wi] adj. m. too smart; wise guy; smart; pert; too clever
przemęczać [pshe-man-chaćh] v. overstrain; overwork; spend
przemęczenie [pshe-man-che-ńe] n. strain; overwork; tiredness
przemiał [pshe-myaw] m. grinding (of grain); milling (of grain); meal; grist; shoal
przemiana [pshe-mya-na] f. change; transformation; alteration; conversion; mutation
przemianować [pshe-mya-no--vaćh] v. rename; change name; give an other name
przemienić [pshe-mye-ńeećh] v. change; transform; alter; turn; convert; transmute into
przemieścić [pshe-myeśh--ćheećh] v. displace; dislocate; shift; trans-locate
przemijać [pshe-mee-yaćh] v. go by; be over; pass; cease
przemilczeć [pshe-meel-chećh] v. keep secret; leave unsaid
przemoc [pshe-mots] f. force; violence; constraint; compulsion; (act of force) violence
przemoczyć [pshe-mo-chićh] v. soak; drench; wet; seep; sop
przemoknąć [pshe-mok--nownćh] v. be soaked; get wet; soak through to the skin
przemowa [pshe-mo-va] f. (long) speech; oration; for- mal address; harangue; tirade
przemóc [pshe-moots] v. overcome; conquer; defeat; master; prevail; predominate

przemówić [pshe-moo-veećh]
v. speak up; make a mistake
(speaking); recover speech
przemówienie [pshe-moo-vye-
-ńe] n. speech; oration
przemycać [pshe-mi-tsaćh] v.
smuggle (into a country, etc.)
przemyć [pshe-mićh] v. rinse;
scrub; wash off (the dirt); give
a wash; lavage; flush; rinse
przemysł [pshe-misw] m.
industry; trade; ingenuity
przemysłowy [pshe-mi-swo-vi]
adj. m. industrial; factory
(workers); manufacturing
przemyśliwać [pshe-mi-śhlee-
-vaćh] v. ponder; think over
przemyślny [pshe-miśhl-ni] adj.
m. ingenious; clever; cunning
przemyt [pshe-mit] m. smuggling
przemytnik [pshe-mit-ńeek] m.
smuggler; contrabandist
przemywać [pshe-mi-vaćh] v.
rinse; wash; scrub; lavage;
flush; give a wash (scrub etc.)
przenieść [pshe-ńeśhćh] v.
transfer; surpass; carry over;
remove; convey; move (to);
retrace; exceed; overshoot
przenigdy [pshe-ńeeg-di] adv.
nevermore; never again
przenikać [pshe-ńee-kaćh] v.
penetrate; pierce; permeate
przenikliwy [pshe-ńee-klee-vi]
adj. m. penetrating; acute;
sharp; piercing; keen; shrewd
przenocować [pshe-no-tso-
-vaćh] v. pass the night; put
up for the night; sleep
przenośnia [pshe-nośh-ńa] f.
metaphor; figure of speech
przenośny [pshe-nośh-ni]
adj. m. portable; mobile; transferable; metaphorical
przeobrażać [pshe-o-bra-zhaćh]
v. transform; modify; change
przeoczenie [pshe-o-che-ńe] n.
oversight; omission
przeoczyć [pshe-o-chićh] v.
overlook; leave out; omit
przepadać [pshe-pa-daćh] v. be
lost; be extremely fond; vanish; disappear; perish; fail

przepalić [pshe-pa-leećh] v.
burn through; overheat; fire in
a stove occasionally; scorch
przepasać [pshe-pa-saćh] v.
gird; belt; tie; overfeed
przepaska [pshe-pas-ka] f. band
przepaść [pshe-paśhćh] v.
abyss; precipice; chasm; gulf
przepchać [pshep-khaćh] v.
push through; pass through;
clean out; swab (a pipe)
przepełniać [pshe-pew-ńaćh]
v. overfill; cram; over cram
przepełnienie [pshe-pew-ńe-ńe]
n. overfill; crowd; excess
przepędzać [pshe-pan-dzaćh] v.
drive away; spend; distill; stay
przepić [pshe-peećh] v. spend
on drinking; drink away;
waste money on drinking
przepierać [pshe-pye-raćh] v.
launder; wash clothes
przepierzenie [pshe-pye-zhe-ńe]
n. partition (wall etc.)
przepiękny [pshe-pyank-ni] adj.
m. very beautiful; gorgeous
przepiłować [pshe-pee-wo-
-vaćh] v. saw through; file
through; saw off; file away
przepiórka [pshe-pyoor-ka] f.
quail (migratory game bird)
przepis [pshe-pees] m. regulation
przepis [pshe-pees] m. recipe
przepisać [pshe-pee-saćh] v.
prescribe; write over again
przepisać [pshe-pee-saćh] v.
copy; transfer (property)
przepłacać [pshe-pwa-tsaćh] v.
overpay; pay too much; bribe
przepłukać [pshe-pwoo-kaćh]
v. rinse; gargle; scour; wash
przepłynąć [pshe-pwi-nownćh]
v. swim across; row across
przepływać [pshe-pwi-vaćh] v.
flow; float across; swim
across; row across; sail across
przepocić [pshe-po-ćheećh] v.
sweat through; sweat (a shirt)
przepoić [pshe-po-eećh] v.
impregnate; saturate; fill
przepona [pshe-po-na] f.
diaphragm; midriff; stiffener
przepowiadać [pshe-po-vya-

-dać] v. predict; foretell;
prophesy; repeat one's lesson;
foretell future events; divine
przepracować się [pshe-pra-tso-
-vaćh **śhan**] v. overwork
(oneself); overtrain oneself
przepraszać [pshe-pra-shaćh] v.
apologize; excuse oneself
przeprawa [pshe-pra-va] f.
passage; crossing; journey
przeprawa [pshe-pra-va] f. fight;
incident; scene; row
przeprawiać [pshe-pra-vyaćh]
v. cross over; carry across
przeproszenie [pshe-pro-she-ńe]
n. apology; apologies
przeprowadzać [pshe-pro-va-
-dzaćh] v. convey; lead;
conduct; escort; see across
przeprowadzka [pshep-ro-vadz-
-ka] f. moving (from a house)
przepuklina [pshe-poo-klee-na] f.
hernia (protrusion); rupture
przepustka [pshe-poost-ka] f.
pass; permit; liberty; sluice
przepuszczać [pshe-poosh-
-chaćh] v. let pass; promote;
leak; miss; let slip; waste;
squander away; be pervious
przepuszczalność [pshe-poosh-
-chal-nośhćh] f. permeability
przepych [pshe-pikh] m. luxury;
pageantry; splendor; ostentation; magnificence; glamor
przepychać [pshe-pi-khaćh] v.
push through; force through
przepytywać [pshe-pi-ti-vaćh]
v. examine; inquire; question
przerabiać [pshe-ra-byaćh] v.
do over; revise; remodel; alter
przerachować [pshe-ra-kho-
-vaćh] v. miscalculate; count
over again; re-count; convert
przeradzać się [pshe-ra-dzaćh
śhan] v. change (into)
przerastać [pshe-ras-taćh] v.
outgrow; rise above; surpass
przerazić [pshe-ra-źheećh] v.
terrify; appall; consternation
przeraźliwy [pshe-raźh-lee-vi]
adj. m. appalling; terrifying
shrill; awesome; acute; sharp
przerażenie [pshe-ra-zhe-ńe] n.

terror; horror; dread; dismay
przerażony [pshe-ra-zho-ni] adj.
m. horror stricken; terrified
przeróbka [pshe-roob-ka] f.
revision; reshaping; alteration
przerwa [psher-va] f. pause;
break; recess; interval
przerys [pshe-ris] m. tracing
przerysować [pshe-ri-so-vaćh]
v. trace; copy; retrace
przerwać [psher-vaćh] v.
interrupt; pause; cut-off
przerzedzić [pshe-zhe-
-dźheećh] v. thin out;
decimate (a population)
przerzucić [pshe-zhoo-ćheećh]
v. throw over; shift; move;
flip; browse; transfer
przerzynać [pshe-zhi-naćh] v.
cut through; cut in two
przesada [pshe-sa-da] f.
exaggeration; overstatement
przesadzać [pshe-sa-dzaćh] v.
exaggerate; jump (leap) over
przesadzać [pshe-sa-dzaćh] v.
transplant; bed out seedlings
przesalać [pshe-sa-laćh] v.
oversalt; put too much salt
przesąd [pshe-sownt] m.
prejudice; superstition; fallacy
przesądny [pshe-sownd-ni] adj.
m. superstitious; prejudiced
przesiadać się [pshe-śha-daćh
śhan] v. change (places, bus,
train); move to another seat
przesiedlać [pshe-śhed-laćh] v.
displace; migrate; transplant
przesiewać [pshe-śhe-vaćh] v.
sift; sieve; screen out; riddle
przesilać się [pshe-śhee-laćh
śhan] v. subside; get over;
culminate; overcome; over-
strain; rich high point
przesilenie [pshe-śhee-le-ńe] n.
crisis; turning point
przeskoczyć [pshes-ko-chićh]
v. jump over; vault; outstrip;
skip; leap across (a ditch etc.)
przesłać [pshes-waćh] v. send
przesłać [pshes-waćh] v. make
a bed over; rearrange a bed
przesłaniać [pshe-swa-ńaćh] v.
screen off; veil; cover; hide;

shade; conceal; dim (lights)
przesłanka [pshe-**swan**-ka] f.
premise; prerequisite;(necessary) condition; reason; datum
przesłuchiwać [pshes-woo-khee-
-vaćh] v. interrogate; hear;
examine; question (witnesses)
przesmyk [pshes-mik] m. strait
przesolony [pshe-so-lo-ni] adj. m.
oversalted; with excess salt
przespać [pshes-paćh] v. sleep
over; fail to wake up for
przestać [pshes-taćh] v. cease
przestanek [pshes-ta-nek] m.
pause; rest; stop; (bus) stop
przestankowaćh [pshes-tan-ko-
-vaćh] v. punctuate (written
matter; text; letter, etc.)
przestarzały [pshe-sta-zha-wi]
adj. m. obsolete; time worn
przestawać [pshe-**sta**-vaćh] v.
stop; cut out; break off
przestawać [pshe-**sta**-vaćh] v.
associate; hobnob; keep
company; stand (some time)
przestawiać [pshe-sta-vyaćh] v.
displace; transpose; shift
przestąpić [pshe-**stown**-peećh]
v. step over; transgress; cross
przestępca [pshe-**stanp**-tsa] m.
criminal; felon; law breaker
przestępny [pshe-**stanp**-ni] adj.
m. leap (year); felonious
przestępstwo [pshe-**stanp**-stvo]
n. offense; crime; transgression; misdemeanor; felony
przestrach [pshe-strakh] m.
fright; alarm; fear; terror
przestraszyć [pshe-stra-shićh]
v. scare; startle; alarm
przestroga [pshe-stro-ga] f.
warning; admonition; caution
przestronny [pshe-stron-ni] adj.
m. spacious; roomy; vast
przestrzegać [pshe-stshe-gaćh]
v. observe (rules); caution
przestrzelić [pshe-stshe-leećh]
v. shoot through; shoot down
przestrzenny [pshe-stshen-ni]
adj. m. spatial; roomy; vast
przestrzeń [pshe-stsheń] f.
space; outer space; room
przestworze [pshe-**stvo**-zhe] n.

expanse; infinity; space
przesunięcie [pshe-soo-**ńan**-
-ćhe] n. shift; transfer;
displacement; reshuffle (of)
przesuwać [pshe-**soo**-vaćh] v.
move; shift; shove; transfer
przesycać [pshe-si-tsaćh] v.
saturate; glut; impregnate
przesyłać [pshe-si-waćh] v.
send; dispatch; forward
przesyłka [pshe-siw-ka] f.
shipment; mail; parcel
przesypiać [pshe-si-pyaćh] v.
oversleep; sleep away
przesyt [pshe-sit] m. glut
przeszczep [pshe-shchep] m.
transplant; graft; grafting
przeszkadzać [pshe-shka-dzaćh]
v. hinder; trouble; prevent
przeszkoda [pshe-shko-da] f.
obstacle; hitch; obstruction
przeszkolenie [pshe-shko-le-ńe]
n. training; instruction course
przeszło [pshesh-wo] adv. more
than; over (an amount); last
przeszłość [pshesh-wośćh]
f. past; record; antecedents
przeszukać [pshe-shoo-kaćh] v.
search over; ransack; scour
przeszyć [pshe-shićh] v. sew
-through; pierce; gore; quilt
prześcieradło [pshe-śhćhe-ra-
-dwo] n. bedsheet; sheet
prześcignąć [pshe-śhćheeg-
-**nown**ćh] v. outdistance;
outdo; outstrip; overtake; excel; surpass; exceed; out-rival
prześladować [pshe-śhla-do-
-vaćh] v. persecute; harass;
haunt; pester; molest; worry
prześladowanie [pshe-śhla-do-
-va-ńe] n. persecution; oppression; obsession; molesting
prześliczny [pshe-śhleech-ni]
adj. m. most beautiful; lovely
prześliznąć [pshe-śhleez-
-**nown**ćh] v. slip through;
glide past; sneak through
przeświadczenie [pshe-śhvyad-
-che-ńe] n. conviction; persuasion; certitude; confidence
prześwietlać [pshe-śhvyet-
-laćh] v. shine through;

fluoroscope (through)
przetak [pshe-tak] m. riddle
przetaczać [pshe-ta-chaćh] v.
1. roll; wheel; pour; decant
przetaczać [pshe-ta-chaćh] v.
2. transfuse (blood)
przetapiać [pshe-ta-pyaćh] v.
recast; smelt (metals); melt
przetarg [pshe-tark] m. auction
przetarty [pshe-tar-ti] adj. m.
threadbare; rubbed through
przetłumaczyć [pshe-twoo-ma-
-chićh] v. translate; explain
przeto [pshe-to] conj. therefore;
accordingly; consequently
przetrawić [pshe-tra-veećh] v.
digest; ruminate; etch; corrode
przetrwać [pshe-trvaćh] v.
survive; outlast; remain; keep
przetrwonić [pshe-trvo-ńeećh]
v. squander; waste away; fritter away (money, fortune etc.)
przetrząsnąć [pshe-tshowns-
-nowńćh] v. search (shake
through); ransack; comb out
przetrzymać [pshe-tshi-maćh]
v. endure; outdo; keep waiting
przetwarzać [pshe-tva-zhaćh]
v. remake; manufacture
przetwórnia [pshe-tvoor-ńa] f.
factory; processing plant
przewaga [pshe-va-ga] f.
predominance; overbalance;
lead; superiority; majority
przeważać [pshe-va-zhaćh] v.
outweigh; prevail; over-
balance; predominate
przeważający [pshe-va-zha-
-yown-tsi] adj. m. prevailing;
superior; predominant
przeważnie [pshe-vazh-ńe] adv.
mainly; mostly; chiefly; largely
przewiązać [pshe-vyown-zaćh]
v. bind up; change dressing
przewidywać [pshe-vee-di-
-vaćh] v. anticipate; foresee
przewiercić [pshe-vyer-ćheećh]
v. drill through (pierce)
przewiesić [pshe-vye-śheećh]
v. sling over; hang over;
rehang (pictures, etc.)
przewietrzyć [pshe-vyet-shićh]
v. ventilate; be aerated

przewiew [pshe-vyev] m. gust
of wind; draught; breeze;
breath of (fresh) air; whiff
przewiezienie [pshe-vye-źhe-ńe]
n. transport; transportation;
carriage; conveyance; move
przewijać [pshe-vee-yaćh] v.
wrap up; change dressing
przewinienie [pshe-vee-ńe-ńe]
n. offence; delinquency
przewlekły [pshe-vlek-wi] adj. m.
protracted; lingering; lasting
przewodni [pshe-vod-ńee]
adj. m. leading; guiding (light,
principle, notion etc.)
przewodniczący [pshe-vod-ńee-
-chown-tsi] m. chairman
przewodnik [pshe-vod-ńeek] m.
guide; conductor; leader
przewodzić [pshe-vo-dźheećh]
v. head; command (a unit);
lead (a group); conduct; carry
przewozić [pshe-vo-źheećh] v.
convey; transport; cart across
przewoźnik [pshe-voźh-ńeek]
m. ferryman; carter; carrier
przewód [pshe-voot] m. conduit;
channel; wire; procedure
przewóz [pshe-voos] m.
transport; freight; cartage
przewracać [pshe-vra-tsaćh] v.
overturn; turn over; upset;
toss; topple; invert; reverse
przewrotność [pshe-vrot-
-nośhćh] f. perversity; per-
fidy; deceit; perverseness
przewrót [pshe-vroot] m.
revolution; upheaval; coup
przewyższać [pshe-vizh-shaćh]
v. out do; exceed; surpass
przez [pshes] prep. across; over
(the fence); through; during;
within; in; on the other side
przeziębić się [pshe-źhan-
-beećh śhan] v. catch cold;
become cold; grow cold
przezimować [pshe-źhee-mo-
-vaćh] v. winter; hibernate
przeznaczać [pshez-na-chaćh]
v. intend; earmark; mean;
destine; assign; allocate;
design; appropriate (for)
przeznaczenie [pshez-na-che-ńe]

n. destiny; purpose; fate
przezorność [pshe-zor-
-nośhćh] f. caution; pru-
dence; foresight; cautiousness
przeźrocze [psheźh-ro-che] n.
transparency; slide; open work
przeźroczysty [pshe-źhro-chis-
-ti] adj. m. transparent
przezwisko [pshez-vees-ko] n.
1. nickname; surname
przezwisko [pshez-vees-ko] n.
2. abusive (bad) name
przezwyciężać [pshe-zvi-ćhan-
-zhaćh] v. overcome; conquer
przezywać [pshe-zi-vaćh] v.
revile; abuse; call names
przeżegnać się [pshe-zheg-
-naćh śhan] v. cross oneself
przeżuwać [pshe-zhoo-vaćh] v.
chew; masticate; ponder over
przeżycie [pshe-zhi-ćhe] n. (bad,
good) experience; survival
przeżyć [pshe-zhićh] v.
survive; live through; outlive
przeżytek [pshe-zhi-tek] m. relic
of the past; old timer
przędza [pshan-dza] f. yarn
przędzalnia [pshan-dzal-ńa] f.
spinning mill; spinning room
przęsło [pshans-wo] n. (bridge)
bay; (stair) flight; span
przodek [psho-dek] m. ancestor
przodek [psho-dek] m. front;
heading; end; top
przodować [psho-do-vaćh] v.
lead; excel; be the best
przodownictwo [psho-dov-ńeets-
-tvo] n. leadership; hegemony
przodownik [psho-dov-ńeek] m.
leader; foreman (head of a
group); police inspector
przód [pshoot] front; ahead; bow
przy [pshi] prep. by; at; nearby;
with; on; about; close; beside
przybić [pshi-beećh] v. nail
down; fasten; fix; dishearten
przybiec [pshi-byets] v. run up;
hasten; come up running
przybierać [pshi-bye-raćh] v.
dress up; put on; adopt; adorn
przybliżać [pshi-blee-zhaćh] v.
bring near; draw near; magnify
przybliżony [pshi-blee-zho-ni] adj.

m. approximate; very near
przyboczny [pshi-boch-ni] adj. m.
side (kick); personal (aide);
body (guard); adjutant (officer)
przybory [pshi-bo-ri] pl.
accessories; outfit; tools; fittings; tackle; (toilet) articles
przybór [pshi-boor] m. rise (of a
river); flood (rising waters)
przybrać [pshi-braćh] v. adorn;
put on; assume; adopt; rise;
grow; increase; swell (a river)
przybrzeżny [pshi-bzhezh-ni] adj.
m. coastal; riverside; inshore
przybudówka [pshi-boo-doov-ka]
f. annex; addition (to a building); penthouse; lean to
przybycie [pshi-bi-ćhe] n. arrival;
gain; growth; accession
przybysz [pshi-bish] m. newcomer; new arrival; stranger
przybytek [pshi-bi-tek] m.
increase; sanctuary; repository
przybywać [pshi-bi-vaćh] v.
arrive; come; reach; attain
przybywać [pshi-bi-vaćh] v.
increase; rise; attain; reach
przychodnia [pshi-khod-ńa] f.
outpatient clinic; ambulatory
przychodzić [pshi-kho-
-dźheećh] v. come over, a-
round, along, to, again; turn
up; arrive; be first at; follow
przychód [pshi-khoot] m.
income; profit; takings; proceeds; receipts; receipt (book)
przychylać [pshi-khi-laćh] v.
incline; comply; bend; stoop
przychylny [pshi-khil-ni] adj. m.
favorable; kind; friendly
przyciągać [pshi-ćhown-gaćh]
v. attract; draw near; appeal;
lure; entice; come; arrive
przyciąganie ziemskie [pshi-
-ćhown-ga-ńe źhem-ske]
gravitation; gravitational pull
przyciemniać [pshi-ćhem-
-ńaćh] v. dim; darken; shade;
black out; obscure; subdue
przycinać [pshi-ćhee-naćh] v.
1. cut off; shorten; clip; trim
przycinać [pshi-ćhee-naćh] v.
2. make fun of; sting; peck at

przycisk [pshi-ćheesk] m.
1. pressure; stress; squeeze
przycisk [pshi-ćheesk] m.
2. accent; emphasis; stress
przycisk [pshi-ćheesk] m.
3. weight; (paper-weight, etc.)
przyciskać [pshi-ćhees-kaćh]
v. press; keep down; squeeze
przycupnąć [pshi-tsoop-
-nownćh] v. squat down; lie
in wait; crouch; cower; lurk
przyczaić się [pshi-cha-eećh
śhan] v. lurk; sulk; ambush;
lie in ambush; hide; be hidden
przyczepić [pshi-che-peećh] v.
attach; fasten; link; fix; pin;
hook; charge with an offense
przyczepić się [pshi-che-peećh
śhan] v. cling; pick a quarrel;
find fault; hold tight; attach
przyczepka [pshi-chep-ka] f.
trailer; exp.: on top of it all
przyczółek [pshi-choo-wek] m.
abutment; bridgehead; beachhead; fronton; frontal; pedi-
ment (an ornamental gable)
przyczyna [pshi-chi-na] f. cause;
reason; ground; intersection
przyrzyczynek [pshi-chi-nek] m.
contribution (to science etc.)
przyczyniać [pshi-chi-ńaćh] v.
add; add to; contribute
przyczynowość [pshi-chi-no-
-vośhćh] f. causation; cau-
sality; a causing
przyćmiewać [pshi-ćhmye-
-vaćh] v. dim; tarnish; obscure; outshine; overshadow;
darken; eclipse; cloud over
przydać [pshi-daćh] v. add;
append; lend; add weight
przydatny [pshi-dat-ni] adj. m.
useful; helpful; serviceable
przydawka [pshi-dav-ka] f.
attribute (gram.); qualifier
przydeptać [pshi-dep-taćh] v.
thread upon; step on (upon)
przydługi [pshi-dwoo-gee] adj. m.
lengthy; somewhat too long
przydomek [pshi-do-mek] m. by
-name; surname; nickname
przydreptać [pshi-drep-taćh] v.
trip along; come tripping

przydrożny [pshi-drozh-ni]
adj. m. roadside (shrine etc.)
przydusić [pshi-doo-śheećh] v.
throttle; smother; press down
przydybać [pshi-di-baćh] v.
overtake; take unawares; nab
przydymać [pshi-di-maćh] v.
foot it along; run up (slang)
przydymiony [pshi-di-myo-ni] adj.
m. smoky (food); tinted (glass)
przydział [pshi-dźhaw] m.
allotment; ration; allowance
przydzielać [pshi-dźhe-laćh] v.
assign; allocate; allot
przyganiać [pshi-ga-ńaćh] v.
blame; find fault with;
criticize; rebuke; reprimand
przygarnąć [pshi-gar-nownćh]
v. take up; adopt; hug; grasp;
clasp; gather; press; shelter
przygasać [pshi-ga-saćh] v.
dim; subside; abate; go out;
die down; diminish; subside
przyglądać się [pshi-glown-
-daćh śhan] v. observe; look
on; scan; see; watch; survey
przygnać [pshi-gnaćh] v. drive
near; bring; run up; hasten
przygnębiać [pshi-gnan-byaćh]
v. depress; deject; dishearten
przygnębienie [pshi-gnan-bye-
-ńe] n. depression; low spirits
przygniatać [pshi-gńa-taćh] v.
crush; overwhelm; oppress;
burden; press down; squeeze;
pinch; bow down; weigh on
przygoda [pshi-go-da] f.
adventure; accident; experience (pleasant, unpleasant)
przygodny [pshi-god-ni] adj. m.
occasional; casual; accidental
przygotować [pshi-go-to-vaćh]
v. prepare; get ready; worn;
fit; coach; train; make ready;
pack up; turn on (the bath)
przygotowanie [pshi-go-to-va-
-ńe] n. preparation; getting
ready; pl. arrangements, etc.
przygotowawczy [pshi-go-to-vav-
-chi] adj. m. preparatory; initial
przygrywać [pshi-gri-vaćh] v.
1. play the accompaniment
przygrywać [pshi-gri-vaćh] v.

2. play (music for pleasure)
przygrzewać [pshi-gzhe-vaćh]
v. warm up; heat up; swelter
przygwoździć [pshi-gvo-
-źhdźheećh] v. nail down;
pin down; fasten permanently
przyimek [pshi-ee-mek] m.
preposition (relation word)
przyjaciel [pshi-ya-ćhel] m.
friend; good friend; close
friend; intimate friend
przyjaciółka [pshi-ya-ćhoow-ka]
f. girl friend; close friend
przyjazd [pshi-yazt] m. arrival;
scheduled time of arrival
przyjazny [pshi-yaz-ni] adj. m.
friendly; amicable; kindly
przyjaźń [pshi-yaźhń] m.
friendship; friendly relations;
amity; kindest regards etc.
przyjaźnić się [pshi-yaźh-
-ńeećh śhan] v. be friends,
on friendly terms; pal; chum
przyjechać [pshi-ye-khaćh] v.
come (over); arrive; come
przyjemność [pshi-yem-
-nośhćh] f. pleasure; (keen)
enjoyment; gusto; zest;
przyjemny [pshi-yem-ni] adj. m.
pleasant; attractive; nice; cosy
przyjezdny [pshi-yezd-ni] m.
stranger; sightseer; visitor
przyjeżdżać [pshi-yezh-dzhaćh]
v. arrive (by transportation)
przyjęcie [pshi-yan-ćhe] n.
admission; adoption; reception
przyjęty [pshi-yan-ti] adj. m.
customary; acceptable
przyjmować [pshiy-mo-vaćh] v.
receive; accept; entertain
przyjście [pshiyśh-ćhe] n.
arrival; coming; advent
przyjść [pshiyśhćh] v. come
-over; come along; come in
(around); arrive; turn up
przykazać [pshi-ka-zaćh] v.
order; tell; enjoin to do
przykazanie [pshi-ka-za-ńe] n.
commandment; injunction
przyklasnąć [pshi-klas-nownćh]
v. applaud; commend; praise
przykleić [pshi-kle-eećh] v.
stick; glue; paste; stick on

(stamp, sticker, label, etc.)
przyklękać [pshi-klan-kaćh] v.
genuflect; bend the knee
przykład [pshi-kwat] m. example;
instance; pattern; sample
przykładać [pshi-kwa-daćh] v.
apply; affix; lend a hand
przykładać [pshi-kwa-daćh] v.
beat up with; apply a force
przykładny [pshi-kwad-ni] adj. m.
exemplary; well fitting
przykrajać [pshi-kra-yaćh] v.
cut off length; cut to fit; cut
out (a cloth, garments etc.)
przykrawać [pshi-kra-vaćh] v.
cut out (a cloth, garments,
etc.); cut off (the length)
przykręcać [pshi-kran-tsaćh] v.
1. screw on; screw down
przykręcać [pshi-kran-tsaćh] v.
2. turn (off, on) tight
przykrość [pshi-krośhćh] f.
annoyance; irritation; vexation
przykry [pshi-kri] adj. m.
disagreeable; painful; nasty;
bad; unpleasant; annoying
przykrywać [pshi-kri-vaćh] v.
cover; roof over; put on a cap
przykrywka [pshi-kriv-ka] f. lid;
(under the) cover (of love etc.)
przykrzyć się [pshi-kshićh
śhan] v. be bored; having nothing to do; pall on; be weary;
bore; yearn; become tedious
przykucnąć [pshi-koots-
-nownćh] v. squat down; sit
down (low); crouch; squat
przykuć [pshi-kooćh] v.
chain; grip; hammer on; rivet;
attach with chains, etc.
przykuć [pshi-kooćh] v. arrest
(attention); chain; grip; rivet;
fascinate; hold spellbound
przylatywać [pshi-la-ti-vaćh] v.
fly in; fly into (a room)
przylądek [pshi-lown-dek] m.
cape; tip of land; headland
przylecieć [pshi-le-ćhećh] v.
fly in; arrive; come running
przylegać [pshi-le-gaćh] v. fit;
cling; adhere; lie close
przylegać [pshi-le-gaćh] v.
adjoin; abut; be contiguous

przyległy [pshi-leg-wi] adj. m.
adjacent; adjoining; contiguous
przylepić [pshi-le-peećh] v.
stick; glue on; stick to; post
przylepiec [pshi-le-pyets] m.
adhesive tape; court plaster
przylgnąć [pshil-gnownćh] v.
stick; cling; adhere; nestle up
przylot [pshi-lot] m. plane arrival
przylutować [pshi-loo-to-vaćh]
v. solder on; sweat on
przyłączać [pshi-wown-chaćh]
v. annex (to); join (with); add;
connect; attach; incorporate
przyłączenie [pshi-wown-che-
-ńe] n. annexation; incorporation; connection; addition
przyłbica [pshiw-bee-tsa] f. visor;
beaver; welder's helmet
przymawiać [pshi-ma-vyaćh] v.
criticize; rebuke; pinprick;
nettle; nag; allude to; hint
przymawiać się [pshi-ma-vyaćh
śhan] v. hint around for
przymiarka [pshi-myar-ka] f.
fitting on; trying on clothes
przymierać [pshi-mye-raćh] v.
starve; be half dead; be dying
przymierzać [pshi-mye-zhaćh]
v. try on; set to; apply to
przymierze [pshi-mye-zhe] n.
alliance; covenant; Testament; (Ark of the) Covenant
przymierzyć [pshi-mye-zhićh] v.
try on; set on; apply to
przymieszka [pshi-myesh-ka] f.
admixture; addition; modicum;
dash (of salt, spirits, etc.)
przymiot [pshi-myot] m. (man's)
quality; trait; attribute
przymiotnik [pshi-myot-ńeek] m.
adjective (grammar)
przymknięty [pshim-kńan-ti] adj.
m. half-closed; shut up
przymocować [pshi-mo-tso-
-vaćh] v. fasten down; fix to;
secure to; attach; make fast
przymówka [pshi-moov-ka] f.
gibe; hint; allusion; scoff; jeer
przymrozek [pshi-mro-zek] m.
slight frost; ground frost
przymrużyć oczy [pshi-mroo-
-zhićh o-chi] blink; narrow

(half-close) one's eyes; wink
przymus [pshi-moos] m.
compulsion; constraint; pressure; coercion; duress
przymusić [pshi-moo-śheećh]
v. compel; force(into a decision, etc.); oblige; coerce
przymusowy [pshi-moo-so-vi]
adj. m. obligatory; coercive
(measures, etc.); forced
przynaglać [pshi-na-glaćh] v.
urge; haste; push on; hustle;
spur on; impel; hurry
przynajmniej [pshi-nay-mńey]
adv. at least; at any rate; anyway; in the smallest degree
przynależeć [pshi-na-le-zhećh]
v. belong; be a member (of a
party); be affiliated with
przynależność [pshi-na-lezh-
-nośhćh] v. (nationality)
membership; affiliation; (national) status; pl. pertinents
przynależny [pshi-na-lezh-ni] adj.
m. belonging; appurtenant
przynęta [pshi-nan-ta] f. bait;
lure; enticement; lure; decoy
przynosić [pshi-no-śheećh] v.
1. bring (up, down etc.); fetch
przynosić [pshi-no-śheećh] v.
2. bear; yield; bring (profit,
honor, ill luck, news); afford;
przyobiecać [pshi-o-bye-tsaćh]
v. promise; give a promise
przyobiecywać [pshi-o-bye-tsi-
-vaćh] v. promise; give a
promise (to do or not to do)
przypadać [pshi-pa-daćh] v. be
due; fall; come; happen; take
przypadek [pshi-pa-dek] m.
event; chance; case; incident
przypadkiem [pshi-pad-kem]
adv. by chance; accidentally
przypadkowo [pshi-pad-ko-vo]
adv. accidentally; by chance;
unintentionally; by accident
przypadłość [pshi-pad-
-wośhćh] f. affliction; indisposition; ailment; disease
przypalić [pshi-pa-leećh] v.
singe; burn(the food, milk)
smoke; scorch; sear; light up
przypasać [pshi-pa-saćh] v.

attach (to belt); grid on

przypatrywać się [pshi-pa-**tri**- -vaćh **śh**an] v. observe; look at (this or that); contemplate; have a look at this (or that)

przypatrzyć się [pshi-pa-tshićh **śh**an] v. observe; look at; see (in detail); contemplate

przypędzać [pshi-pan-dzaćh] v. 1. come in haste; run up (to)

przypędzać [pshi-pan-dzaćh] v. 2. drive up; drive (cattle)

przypiąć [pshi-pyownćh] v. pin; fasten; attach; buckle; pin on

przypieczętować [pshi-pye- -chan-to-vaćh] v. seal up; set one's seal to papers; confirm

przypisek [pshi-pee-sek] m. note; postscript; added note

przypisywać [pshi-pee-si-vaćh] v. ascribe; attribute; credit

przypłacać [pshi-pwa-tsaćh] v. pay (with life, health, pro- perty, etc.); pay (very dearly)

przypłynąć [pshi-pwi-nownćh] v. arrive sailing or swimming; come to shore; swim up; sail up; row up; come; arrive

przypływ [pshi-pwif] m. high tide; inflow; influx; high water

przypodobać się [pshi-po-do- -baćh śhan] v. get into good graces of; endear oneself to

przypominać [pshi-po-mee- -naćh] v. remind; recollect; resemble; recall(to mind)

przypomnienie [pshi-pom-ńe-ńe] n. reminder; memento; sou- venir; a cause to remember

przypowieść [pshi-po- -vyeśhćh] f. tale; parable (a simple moral lesson); allegory

przyprawa [pshi-pra-va] f. seasonings; spice (relish, pe- per, etc,); sauce; condiment

przyprawiać [pshi-pra-vyaćh] v. 1. season; flavor; spice

przyprawiać [pshi-pra-vyaćh] v. 2. cause a loss; fasten; put on

przyprowadzać [psi-pro-va- -dzaćh] v. bring along; fetch

przypuszczać [pshi-poosh- -chaćh] v. suppose; let ap-

proach; admit; let enter

przypuszczalnie [pshi-poosh-**chal**- -ńe] adv. supposedly; likely

przypuszczalny [pshi-poosh-**chal**- -ni] adj. m. supposed

przypuszczenie [pshi-poosh-**che**- -ńe] n. guess; supposition

przyroda [pshi-ro-da] f. nature

przyrodni brat [pshi-**rod**-ńee brat] half brother

przyrodnia siostra [pshi-**rod**-ńa śhos-tra] half sister

przyrodnik [pshi-rod-ńeek] m. naturalist; natural historian

przyrodzony [pshi-ro-dzo-ni] adj. m. innate; natural; inborn

przyrost naturalny [**pshi**-rost na- -too-ral-ni] birthrate

przyrostek [pshi-**ros**-tek] m. suffix (grammatical term)

przyrząd [pshi-zhownt] m. instrument; tool; appliance; device; gadget; contraption

przyrządzać [pshi-zhown- -dzaćh] v. make ready; pre- pare; cook; get ready; dress

przyrzeczenie [pshi-zhe-che-ńe] n. promise; plighted word

przyrzekać [pshi-zhe-kaćh] v. promise to do (something)

przysadka [pshi-sad-ka] f. pituitary gland; stipule

przysądzać [pshi-**sown**-dzaćh] v. award; adjudge; allocate

przysiad [pshi-śhat] m. squat

przysiadać [pshi-śha-daćh] v. sit down; crouch; sit up

przysięga [pshi-śhan-ga] f. oath; sworn attestation (in a court)

przysięgać [pshi-śhan-gaćh] v. swear to do; take an oath

przysięgły [pshi-śhang-wi] adj. m. sworn (jury man)

przysłać [pshi-swaćh] v. send in; send along; send up

przysłaniać [pshi-swa-ńaćh] v. shade; vail; cover up; screen

przysłona [pshi-swo-na] f. veil; shade; screen; diaphragm; stop; curtain to conceal

przysłowie [pshi-swo-vye] n. proverb; byword

przysłówek [pshi-swoo-vek] m.

adverb (grammatical term)
przysłuchiwać się [pshi-swoo-
-khee-vaćh śhan] v. listen to
przysługa [pshi-swoo-ga] f.
service; good turn; favor;
kindness; a good deed
przysługiwać [pshi-swoo-gee-
-vaćh] v. to have right to; be
vested in; be entitled to
przysłużyć się [pshi-swoo-
-zhićh śhan] v. render
service; do (be of) service to
przysmak [pshi-smak] m. tid-
-bit; delicacy; choice morsel
przysmażyć [pshi-sma-zhićh] v.
roast; fry a little; brown; devil
przysparzać [pshi-spa-zhaćh] v.
1. increase; add to; enlarge
przysparzać [pshi-spa-zhaćh] v.
2. cause (trouble); bring (add)
unpleasantness (misery, etc.)
przyśpieszać [pshi-śhpye-
-shaćh] v. accelerate; urge;
speed up; hasten; rush; hurry
przyśpieszenie [pshi-śhpye-she-
-ńe] n. acceleration (of gravity); speeding up; activation
przysposabiać [pshi-spo-sa-
-byaćh] v. prepare; adapt; a-
dopt; fit; qualify; train
przystać [pshis-taćh] v. join;
comply; cohere; fit together;
befit; be suitable; consent
przystanąć [pshi-sta-nownćh]
v. stop; pause; halt
przystanek [pshi-sta-nek] m.
stop; station; bus stop etc.
przystań [pshi-stań] f. small
(boat) harbor (inland); port
przystawać [pshi-sta-vaćh] v.
fit; enlist; coincide; halt
przystawiać [pshi-sta-vyaćh] v.
place near; set against; put
przystawka [pshi-stav-ka] f. side
dish; hors-d'oeuvre
przystęp [pshi-stanp] m. access
przystępny [pshi-stanp-ni]
1. adj. m. accessible; easy to
approach; affable
przystępny [pshi-stanp-ni]
2. adj. m. intelligible; clear; lucid; plain; straightforward;
moderate (conditions, prices)

przystojny [pshi-stoy-ni] adj. m.
handsome; decent; suitable
przystosować [pshi-sto-so-
-vaćh] v. adjust; fit; accommodate; adapt; conform
przystrajać [pshi-stra-yaćh] v.
decorate; adorn; dress; trim
przysunąć [pshi-soo-nownćh]
v. move near; push nearer
przyswajać [pshi-sva-yaćh] v.
acquire (a knowledge); assimilate; adopt; familiarize with
przysyłać [pshi-si-waćh] v.
send; send along; send up
przysypać [pshi-si-paćh] v.
cover (with earth; snow, etc.)
przyszłość [pshish-wośhćh] f.
the future; days to come
przyszyć [pshi-shićh] v. sew on
przyszykować [pshi-shi-ko-
-vaćh] v. prepare; make ready
przyśnić się [pshiśh-ńeećh
śhan] v. appear in a dream
przyśrubować [pshi-śhroo-bo-
-vaćh] v. screw on; screw
down; fasten with a screw
przyświadczyć [pshi-śhvyad-
-chićh] v. agree with; attest
przytaczać [pshi-ta-chaćh] v.
quote; cite; wheel up; bring
up; roll up; mention; allege
przytakiwać [pshi-ta-kee-vaćh]
v. say yes; assent; acquiesce
przytępić [pshi-tan-peećh] v.
dull; blunt somewhat; dim;
befog (memory etc.); deaden
przytępienie [pshi-tan-pye-ńe] n.
dullness; bluntness; dimness
przytknąć [pshit-knownćh] v.
place touching; set to; apply
to; join; meet; abut; border
przytłaczać [pshi-twa-chaćh] v.
overwhelm; press to earth;
crush to earth; weigh down
przytłumić [pshi-twoo-meećh]
v. damp; deaden; stifle; subdue (a passion); dim; muffle
przytoczyć [pshi-to-chićh] v.
quote; cite; roll up; bring up
przytomnie [pshi-tom-ńe] adv.
with presence; of mind; lucidly
przytomność [pshi-tom-
-nośhćh] f. consciousness;

(one's) senses; lucid intervals
przytomny [pshi-tom-ni] adj. m.
  conscious; quick-witted
przytrafiać się [pshi-tra-fyaćh
  śhan] v. happen; occur; befall
przytrzymać [pshi-tshi-maćh] v.
  hold; detain; keep in place; arrest; hold back; apprehend
przytulić [pshi-too-leećh] v.
  snuggle; cuddle; hug; fold
przytułek [pshi-too-wek] m.
  shelter; alms-house; poor
  house; (place of) refuge
przytwierdzić [pshi-tvyer-
  -dźheećh] v. fasten; fix; affix; attach to; acquiesce in
przytyk [pshi-tik] m. dig; allusion;
  hint at; reference to; junction
przytykać [pshi-ti-kaćh] v. 1. a-
  but; meet; join to; adjoin to
przytykać [pshi-ti-kaćh] v. 2.
  set; be contiguous to; border
przy tym [pshi tim] adv. besides
przyuczać [pshi-oo-chaćh] v.
  train; accustom an animal
przywabiać [pshi-va-byaćh] v.
  decoy; lure (with a bait)
przywara [pshi-va-ra] f. vice;
  fault; defect; shortcoming
przywiązać [pshi-vyown-zaćh]
  v. bind; tie; attach; hitch;
  lash; fasten; connect; endear
przywdziewać [pshi-vdźhe-
  vaćh] v. put on (clothes)
przywidzenie [pshi-vee-dze-ńe]
  n. illusion; delusion; phantasm
przywieźć [pshi-vyeśhćh] v.
  import; bring; drive up; recall
przywilej [pshi-vee-ley] m.
  privilege; prerogative; a special right or favor granted
przywitać [pshi-vee-taćh] v.
  welcome; greet; bid (each
  other) good morning
przywłaszczać [pshi-vwash-
  -chaćh] v. usurp; appropriate
przywodzić [pshi-vo-dźheećh]
  v. lead; bring about (back) the
  (realization of); remind; recall
przywłaszczenie [pshi-vwa-
  -shche-ńe] n. appropriation;
  usurpation (of rights etc.)
przywołać [pshi-vo-waćh] v.

summon; call in; signal; sign
przywozić [pshi-vo-źheećh] v.
  bring (by car); import; deliver
przywódca [pshi-vood-tsa] m.
  leader; ringleader; chieftain
przywóz [pshi-voos] m. import;
  delivery; transport; carriage
przywracać [pshi-vra-tsaćh] v.
  restore; bring back; reappoint
przywrócenie [pshi-vroo-tse-ńe]
  n. restoration; reinstatement
przywyknąć [pshi-vi-knownćh]
  v. get accustomed; get used
przyznać [pshi-znaćh] v. admit; award; allow; grant; acknowledge; recognize; concede
przyzwalać [pshi-zva-laćh] v.
  consent; approve; agree; concede; acquiesce in; assent to
przyzwoitość [pshi-zvo-ee-
  -tośhćh] f. decency; propriety; decorum; ordinary decency
przyzwoity [pshi-zvo-ee-ti] adj.
  m. decent; proper; seemly; becoming; suitable; appropriate
przyzwolenie [pshi-zvo-le-ńe] n.
  consent; acquiescence; assent
przyzwyczajać [pshi-zvi-cha-
  -yaćh] v. accustom; habituate
przyzwyczajenie [pshi-zvi-cha-ye-
  -ńe] n. habit; custom
przyzywać [pshi-zi-vaćh] v.
  call in; call sb.; beckon; sign
psalm [psalm] m. psalm
pseudonim [psew-do-ńeem] m.
  pen name; fictitious name
psiarnia [pśhar-ńa] f. kennel
psie pieniądze [pśhe pye-nown-
  -dze] dirt cheap; dog cheap
psikus [pśhee-koos] m. prank
psota [pso-ta] f. prank; mischief;
  practical joke; (nasty) trick
psotnik [psot-ńeek] m. prank-
  ster; practical joker; jester;
  scamp; roguish kid; tomboy
pstrąg [pstrowng] m. trout; kelt
pstry [pstri] adj. m. mottled;
  speckled; spotted; colorful
pstry [pstri] adj. m. gaudy;
  showy in bad taste; freaked
psuć [psooćh] v. spoil; decay;
  waste; corrupt; deprave; damage; put out of order; mess

up; throw out of gear; injure
psychiatra [psi-**khyat**-ra] m.
psychiatrist; shrink; alienist
psychiczny [psi-**kheech**-ni] adj.
m. mental (state, disease)
psycholog [psi-**kho**-lok] m.
psychologist; behaviorist dealing with mental processes
pszczelarstwo [pshche-lar-stvo]
n. beekeeping; apiculture
pszczelarz [**pshche**-lash] m.
beekeeper; apiarist
pszczoła [**pshcho**-wa] f. bee
pszenica [pshe-**ńee**-tsa] f. wheat
ptactwo [**ptats**-tvo] pl. fowl;
birds; the species of birds
ptak [ptak] m. bird; fowl
ptaszek [**pta**-shek] m. little bird;
small bird; confidence man
publicysta [poo-blee-**tsis**-ta] m.
columnist; journalist
publiczność [poo-**bleech**-
-**nośhćh**] pl. public; community; audience; the house
publikacja [poo-blee-**kats**-ya] f.
publication; something publish-
ed (as a periodical, book, etc.)
puch [pookh] m. down; fluff
puchacz [**poo**-khach] m. eagle
owl (night bird of prey)
puchar [**poo**-khar] m. cup; bowl
puchlina wodna [pookh-lee-na
vod-na] f. dropsy; hydropsy
puchnąć [**pookh**-nownćh] v.
swell; (sport) flag
puchowy [poo-**kho**-vi] adj. m.
downy; fluffy; eiderdown
pucołowaty [poo-tso-wo-va-ti]
adj. m. chubby (-cheeked)
pucz [pooch] m. Putsch
pudełko [poo-**dew**-ko] n. (small)
box; tin; can; hand box
puder [**poo**-der] m. powder
puderniczka [poo-der-**ńeech**-ka]
f. powder box; compact; puff
box; a small cosmetic case
pukać [**poo**-kaćh] v. knock; rap
pugilares [poo-gee-la-res] m.
billfold; pocket book; wallet
pukiel [**poo**-kyel] m. curl; lock
pula [**poo**-la] f. pool; kitty
pularda [poo-**lar**-da] f. poularde;
fattened boiler (chicken)

pulchny [**pool**-khni] adj. m.
plump; mellow; loose; spongy
pulower [poo-**lo**-ver] m. pull-over
pulpit [**pool**-peet] m. desk;
lectern; shelf; book rest
puls [pools] m. pulse; vibration
pulsować [pool-**so**-vaćh] v.
pulsate; palpitate; throb;
vibrate; beat rhythmically
pułap [**poo**-wap] m. ceiling
pułapka [poo-**wap**-ka] f. trap
pułk [poowk] m. regiment; group
pułkownik [poow-**kov**-ńeek] m.
colonel; group captain
pumeks [**poo**-meks] m. pumice
punkt [poonkt] m. point; mark
punktualny [poon-ktoo-al-ni] adj.
m. punctual; exact; prompt
pupa [**poo**-pa] f. behind;
buttocks; bottom; an ass
pupil [**poo**-peel] m. ward; pupil;
favorite; pet (like a pet)
purchawka [poor-**khav**-ka] f. puff
-ball (lycoperdon)
purchawka [poor-**khav**-ka] f.
grumpy fellow
purpura [poor-**poo**-ra] f. purple
purytanin [poo-ri-**ta**-ńeen] m.
Puritan; man of strict religion
pustelnia [poos-**tel**-ńa] f.
hermitage; solitary secluded
place; secluded retreat
pustelnik [poo-**stel**-ńeek] m.
hermit; (secluded) recluse
pustka [**poost**-ka] f. solitude;
empty (place); emptiness; void
pustkowie [poost-**ko**-vye] n.
deserted place; desert; solitude; barren desolation
pustoszyć [poos-to-**shićh**] v.
devastate; ravage; lay waste;
overrun; override; ruin
pusty [**poos**-ti] adj. m. empty
pustynia [poos-ti-ńa] f. desert
puszcza [**poosh**-cha] f. primeval
forest; wilderness
puszczać [**poosh**-chaćh] v. let
go; let fall; set afloat; free;
fade; drop; let out; emit; start;
release; relinquish (a hold)
puszczać się [poosh-**chaćh**
śhan] v. draw apart; dart after; let go; be a permissive

girl; go to bed with; set out

puszek [poo-shek] m. down

puszka blaszana [poosh-ka bla-sha-na] tin can; tin box

puszysty [poo-shis-ti] adj. m. downy; fluffy (snow); flossy; flaky (snow); nappy (carpet)

puścić [poośh-ćheećh] v. let go; let free; release; let fall

puzon [poo-zon] m. trombone (one octave below trumpet)

pycha [pi-kha] f. 1. pride; conceit; haughtiness

pycha [pi-kha] f. 2. excellent tid-bit; fine stuff

pykać [pi-kaćh] v. puff; pop

pylić [pi-leećh] v. dust; be dusty; rise dust; pollen

pył [piw] m. dust; powder

pyskować [pis-ko-vaćh] v. be saucy; bark; bawl

pysk [pisk] m. muffle; snout; mug; muzzle; phiz; rowdyism

pyskaty [pis-ka-ti] adj. m. foulmouthed; saucy; pert; bawling (quarrelsome)

pyszałek [pi-sha-wek] m. boaster; braggart; coxcomb

pysznić się [pish-ńeećh śhan] v. swagger; prance; swank; strut; put on airs; flaunt

pysznie [pish-ńe] adv. proudly; admirably; in grand fashion

pytać [pi-taćh] v. ask; inquire; question; interrogate

pytanie [pi-ta-ńe] n. question; inquiry; query; interrogation

pytel [pi-tel] m. bolter

pytlować [pit-lo-vaćh] v. sift; bolt (flour); be a chatterbox

pyton [pi-ton] m. python

pyza [pi-za] f. dumpling

pyzaty [pi-za-ti] adj. m. chubby; full-cheeked; full-moon face

R

rab [rab] m. slave; servant

rabarbar [ra-bar-bar] m. rhubarb

rabat [ra-bat] m. discount; rebate; reduction (in price)

rabin [ra-been] m. rabbi

rabować [ra-bo-vaćh] v. rob; maraud; plunder; pirate; take by force; steal; pirate

rabunek [ra-boo-nek] m. robbery; plunder; holdup; depredation

rabuś [ra-boośh] m. robber; plunderer; pillager; holdup man

rachityczny [ra-khee-tich-ni] adj. m. rickety; rachitic

rachmistrz [rakh-meestsh] m. (public) accountant; calculator

rachować [ra-kho-vaćh] v. calculate; count; reckon; compute; rely; estimate; suppose

rachunek [ra-khoo-nek] m. bill to be paid or settled; account; calculation; sum; addition

rachunkowość [ra-khoon-ko-vośhćh] f. book-keeping

racica [ra-ćhee-tsa] f. cloven hoof; cow hoof; split hoof

racja [ra-tsya] f. reason; right; ration; propriety; correctness

racjonalizować [ra-tsyo-na-lee-zo-vaćh] v. rationalize (food, etc.); improve (a process)

racjonalny [ra-tsyo-nal-ni] adj. m. rational; reasonable; sensible

raczej [ra-chey] adv. rather; sooner (than); rather than

raczkować [rach-ko-vaćh] v. go on all fours; crawl on all four

raczyć [ra-chićh] v. treat to; condescend; deign; stoop to do; treat; be pleased to do

rad [rad] adj. m. pleased; glad

rad [rad] m. radium

rada [ra-da] f. advice; counsel

radar [ra-dar] m. radar

radca [rad-tsa] m. advisor; counselor; legal advisor

radcostwo [rad-tsos-tvo] n. councillorship; post of a (legal) advisor (councillor)

radio [ra-dyo] n. radio; wireless; broadcasting (system)

radiofonia [ra-dyo-fo-ńya] f. broadcasting; radiotelephony

radioaktywny [ra-dyo-ak-tiv-ni]

adj. m. radioactive
radiostacja [ra-dyo-**stats**-ya] f.
radio station
radiodepesza [ra-dyo-de-pe-sha]
f. radio telegram
radioterapia [ra-dyo-te-ra-pya] f.
radiotherapy; X-ray teraphy
radny [rad-ni] m. alderman
radosny [ra-**dos**-ni] adj. m. gay;
glad; festive (day etc.)
radość [ra-dośhćh] f. joy;
gladness; delight; merriment;
glee; feeling of happiness
radykalny [ra-di-kal-ni] adj. m.
radical; man of radical views
radykał [ra-di-kaw] m. radical
radzić [ra-dźheećh] v.
deliberate; suggest; give an
advice; (give, hold) counsel
radziecki [ra-**dźhets**-kee] adj. m.
Soviet; of Soviet Union
(should use "**sowiecki**")
rafa [ra-fa] f. reef; rim; ripple
rafineria [ra-fee-ne-rya] f.
refinery; refining works
rafinować [ra-fee-no-vaćh] v.
refine; purify; distill
raid [rayd]m. sport rally (race)
raj [ray] m. paradise; heaven
rak [rak] m. crayfish; cancer
rakieta [ra-**kye**-ta] f. rocket; flare
rakieta [ra-**kye**-ta] f. (tennis)
racket; a light bat for tennis
rama [ra-ma] f. frame; scheme;
case; stretcher (for oil canvas)
ramię [ra-my<u>an</u>] n. shoulder
ramowy [ra-mo-vi] adj. m. frame
rampa [ram-pa] f. ramp; loading
platform; bar; barrier; float
rana [ra-na] f. wound; injury;
sore; hurt (to man, plant etc.)
randka [rand-ka] f. date
ranek [ra-nek] m. morning; day
-break; break of day
ranga [ran-ga] f. rank; standing
ranić [ra-ńeećh] v. wound;
hurt; inflict a wound; maul
ranny [ran-ni] adj. m. 1. wound-
-ed, injured person; casualty
ranny [ran-ni] adj. m. morning;
early morning (hours, time)
rano [ra-no] adv. early
rano [ra-no] adv. morning;

forenoon; too early
rapier [ra-pyer] m. rapier
raport [ra-port] m. report;
account; statement; log
raptem [rap-tem] adv. suddenly;
abruptly; no more than; all in
all; all of a sudden
raptowny [rap-tov-ni] adj. m.
abrupt; sudden; impulsive; unexpected; heady; impetuous
rasa [ra-sa] f. race; stock; breed;
(plant) variety; blood
rasizm [ra-śheezm] m. racism
rasowy [ra-**so**-vi] adj. m. racial;
thoroughbred; purebred; racy
raszpla [rash-pla] f. rasp
rata [ra-ta] f. instalment
(payment); part payment (plan)
ratować [ra-to-vaćh] v. rescue
(from drowning); save; deliver
(from danger, predicament)
ratownictwo [ra-tov-ńeets-tvo]
n. life saving (system)
ratownik [ra-tov-ńeek] m. life
-guard; rescuer; life saver
ratunek [ra-too-nek] m. rescue;
salvation; help; assistance; the
last resort; deliverance
ratunkowy pas [ra-toon-ko-vi
pas] m. life belt; life jacket
ratusz [ra-toosh] m. city hall
ratyfikacja [ra-ti-fee-kats-ya] f.
ratification; validation
raut [rawt] m. evening party
raz [ras] m. 1. one time
raz [ras] m. 2. blow; stroke
raz [ras] adv. 3. once; at one
time; at last; time being
razem [ra-zem] adv. together
razić [ra-źheećh] v. 1. strike
razić [ra-źheećh] v. 2. offend
razić [ra-źheećh] v. 3. dazzle;
shock; hit
razowy [ra-zo-vi] adj. m. brown
(bread); whole meal (bread)
razowiec [ra-zo-vyets] m. brown
bread; whole meal bread
rażący [ra-zhown-tsi] adj. m.
1. glaring; gaudy; blinding
rażący [ra-zhown-tsi] adj. m.
2. flagrant; rank; gross
raźnie [ra-źhńe] adv.
cheerfully; briskly; at a lively

pace; safely; securely

rąb [rownb] m. rim; pane;
clearing of a forest

rąbać [rown-baćh] v. chop;
hew; fell (trees); hack out ice

rąbać [rown-baćh] v. say truth
to somebody's face; slash

rączka [rownch-ka] f. handle;
small hand; handgrip; holder

rączy [rown-chi] adj. m. swift

rdza [rdza] f. rust; mildew; blight

rdzenny [rdzen-ni] adj. m.
essential; original; specific

rdzeń [rdzeń] m. core; pith;
marrow; gist; essence; log

rdzoodporny [rdzo-od-por-ni] adj.
m. rust-proof; stainless

rdzewieć [rdze-vyećh] v.
corrode; rust; get rusty; gather rust; get the color of rust

reagować [re-a-go-vaćh] v.
react; respond; be susceptible

reakcja [re-ak-tsya] f. reaction

reakcjonista [re-ak-tsyo-ńees-ta]
m. reactionary

reakcyjny [re-ak-tsiy-ni] adj. m.
reactionary; retrograde

reaktywować [re-ak-ti-vo-vaćh]
v. start (make active) again

reaktywować [re-ak-ti-vo-vaćh]
v. reactivate; bring back to life
(military duty); recall

realia [re-al-ya] pl. realia; realities

realista [re-a-lees-ta] m. realist;
advocate of realism

realizm [re-a-leezm] m. realism
facing facts; being practical

realizować [re-a-lee-zo-vaćh] v.
actualize; realize; cash (assets)

realność [re-al-nośhćh] f. real
estate; land including buildings

realność [re-al-nośhćh] f.
reality; the real (fact)

realny [re-al-ni] adj. m. real;
concrete; actual; genuine; true

rebelia [re-be-lya] f. rebellion;
uprising against government

recenzent [re-tsen-zent] m. critic;
reviewer (of books, plays)

recenzja [re-tsen-zya] f. review
(of books, plays, etc.)

recepcja [re-tsep-tsya] f.
reception (desk, office); formal

social function

recepis [re-tse-pees] m. receipt;
recipe; written receipt

recepta [re-tsep-ta] f.
prescription; doctor's order

rechot [re-khot] m. shrieking;
laughter; croak (of frogs)

recydywista [re-tsi-di-vees-ta] m.
recidivist; old offender

recytować [re-tsi-to-vaćh] v.
recite; give a recitation

redagować [re-da-go-vaćh] v.
edit; draw up; formulate; draft

redakcja [re-dak-tsya] f. editing

redakcja [re-dak-tsya] f. editor's
office; editorial stuff

redaktor [re-dak-tor] m. editor

redukcja [re-dook-tsya] f.
reduction (in size, price, etc.)

redukować [re-doo-ko-vaćh] v.
reduce; lay off; cut down

referat [re-fe-rat] m. report

referencja [re-fe-ren-tsya] f.
reference; testimonial

referent [re-fe-rent] m. clerk

refleks [re-fleks] m. reflex

refleksja [re-fleks-ya] f.
reflection; thought; cogitation

reflektor [re-flek-tor] m. reflector;
searchlight; headlight

reflektować [re-flek-to-vaćh] v.
1. apply for; want; make a bid

reflektować [re-flek-to-vaćh] v.
2. reflect; bring (listen) to
reason; moderate; restrain

reforma [re-for-ma] f. reform

reformacja [re-for-mats-ya] f.
reformation; Reformation

reformować [re-for-mo-vaćh] v.
reform; reorganize

regaty [re-ga-ti] pl. boat race

regencja [re-gen-tsya] f. regency;
regency style (in furniture)

regionalny [re-gyo-nal-ni] adj. m.
regional; local

regulacja [re-goo-lats-ya] f.
regulation; control; regulator

regularny [re-goo-lar-ni] adj. m.
regular; even; systematic

regulować [re-goo-lo-vaćh] v.
1. regulate; control; set (time)

regulować [re-goo-lo-vaćh] v.
2. settle; adjust; regularize

reguła [re-goo-wa] f. rule; law
rehabilitować [re-kha-bee-lee-to-
-vaćh] v. rehabilitate
reja [re-ya] f. yardarm
rejent [re-yent] m. notary public;
notary's office; regent
rejestr [re-yestr] m. register; file;
index; roll; register mark
rejestracja [re-yes-trats-ya] f.
registration; licensing
rejestrować [re-yes-tro-vaćh] v.
register; enroll; record
rejon [re-yon] m. region
rejwach [rey-vakh] m. uproar;
hullabaloo; row; hurly-burly
rekin [re-keen] m. shark
reklama [re-kla-ma] f.
advertising; publicity (commercial, political, etc.)
reklamacja [re-kla-mats-ya] f.
complaint; demand for compensation, damages, etc.
reklamować [re-kla-mo-vaćh] v.
complain; make formal charge
reklamować [re-kla-mo-vaćh] v.
advertise; make publicity
rekolekcje [re-ko-lek-tsye] pl.
retreat; period of contemplation (in a quiet place)
rekomendacja [re-ko-men-dats-
-ya] f. recommendation;
(personal, etc.) reference
rekompensata [re-kom-pen-sa-ta]
f. compensation; recompense
rekonwalescent [re-kon-va-les-
-tsent] m. convalescent
rekord [re-kord] m. (sports)
record; (world) record
rekordzista [re-kor-dźhees-ta] m.
record holder; champion
rekreacja [re-kre-ats-ya] f.
recreation; amusement
rekrut [re-kroot] m. recruit;
conscript; recently enlisted
man; sl. rookie; rooky
rekrutować [re-kroo-to-vaćh] v.
recruit; enlist (new people)
rektor [rek-tor] m. university
president; university head
rektyfikować [re-kti-fee-ko-
-vaćh] v. rectify; correct; put
right; purify; convert current
rekwizycja [re-kvee-zits-ya] f.

requisition; seizure
relacja [re-lats-ya] f. report
relacja [re-lats-ya] f. rate; relation
relatywizm [re-la-ti-veezm] m.
relativity; relativism
relegacja [re-le-gats-ya] f.
expulsion; relegation; exile
religia [re-lee-gya] f. religion
religijny [re-lee-geey-ni] adj. m.
religious; godly; sacred
relikwia [re-leek-vya] f. relic
remanent [re-ma-nent] m.
remainder; inventory; stock
remis [re-mees] m. (sport) draw
remiza [re-mee-za] f. engine
-shed; engine-house; depot;
barn; coach-house; fire-station
remont [re-mont] m. 1. repair(s)
remont [re-mont] m. 2. (horse)
remount; replacement horse
remontować [re-mon-to-vaćh]
v. repair; recondition; overhaul
renumeracja [re-noo-me-rats-ya]
f. re-enumeration; recount
ren [ren] m. reindeer; caribou
renegat [re-ne-gat] m. renegade
renifer [re-ńee-fer] m. reindeer;
(domesticated) arctic deer
renoma [re-no-ma] f. renown
renta [ren-ta] f. rent; fixed
income; annuity; pension
rentowność [ren-tov-nośhćh]
f. profitability; earning capacity; financial feasibility
rentgenolog [rent-ge-no-lok] m.
radiologist; roentgenologist
rentowny [ren-tov-ni] adj. m.
profitable; remunerative
reorganizacja [re-or-ga-ńee-zats-
-ya] f. reorganization
reperacja [re-pe-rats-ya] f. repair
reperacja [re-pe-rats-ya] f.
reparation; war reparation
repatriacja [re-pat-ryats-ya] f.
repatriation (home, etc.)
reperować [re-pe-ro-vaćh] v.
mend; repair; fix; set right
repertuar [re-per-too-ar] m.
repertory; repertoire
repetycja [re-pe-tits-ya] f.
repetition (of a lesson etc.)
replika [re-plee-ka] 1. f. replica;
2. f. rebuttal; 3. f. (theatre)

replikować   163   ręczyć

cue; retort; rejoinder
replikować [re-plee-**ko**-vaćh] v.
  answer back; rejoin; retort
reportaż [re-**por**-tash] m. account
reportaż [re-**por**-tash] m. report-
  ing; commentary; coverage (of
  an event, news report, etc.)
represja [re-**pre**-sya] f. reprisal;
  repressive measures, etc.
reprezentacja [re-pre-zen-**tats**-ya]
  f. representation; dignity
reprezentant [re-pre-**zen**-tant] m.
  representative (typical)
reprezentować [re-pre-zen-**to**-
  -vaćh] v. represent; display
reprodukcja [re-pro-**dook**-tsya] f.
  reproduction; copy; replica
republika [re-**poo**-blee-ka] f.
  republic (based on elections)
republikański [re-poo-blee-**kań**-
  -skee] adj. m. republican
reputacja [re-poo-**tats**-ya] f.
  reputation; (character)
resor [re-sor] m. (car) spring
resort [re-sort] m. 1. agency
resort [re-sort] m. 2. competence; scope; province
respekt [res-pekt] m. respect
restauracja [res-taw-**rats**-ya] f.
  1. restaurant; diner
restauracja [res-taw-**rats**-ya] f.
  2. restoration (of objects of
  art, historic buildings, etc.)
restrykcja [res-**trik**-tsya] f.
  restriction; reservation
restytucja [res-ti-**toots**-ya] f.
  restitution; restoration
reszta [**resh**-ta] f. rest; reminder;
  change; residue; the rest
retoryka [re-to-**ri**-ka] f. rhetoric;
  manual (text) of rhetorics
retusz [re-toosh] m. retouch
retuszować [re-too-**sho**-vaćh] v.
  touch up; retouch
reumatyczny [rew-ma-**tich**-ni]
  adj. m. rheumatic
reumatyzm [rew-ma-tizm] m.
  rheumatism (pain in the joints)
rewanż [re-vansh] m. 1. rematch
rewanż [re-vansh] m. 2. re-
  -venge; recompense; etc.
rewelacja [re-ve-**lats**-ya] f.
  revelation; striking disclosure

rewers [re-vers] m. 1. receipt
rewers [re-vers] m. 2. reverse
  (side of a coin, etc.)
rewia [re-vya] f. parade
rewia [re-vya] f. (theatre) revue
rewidować [re-vee-**do**-vaćh] v.
  revise; reconsider; review
rewidować [re-vee-**do**-vaćh] v.
  house-search; make a search
rewidować [re-vee-**do**-vaćh] v.
  audit (accounts); inspect
rewizja [re-**veez**-ya] f. revision;
  search; audit; inspection; re-
  trial; (customs) examination
rewizjonizm [re-veez-**yo**-ńeezm]
  m. revisionism (change)
rewizyta [re-vee-**zi**-ta] f. return
  (somebody's) visit
rewolucja [re-vo-**loots**-ya] f.
  revolution; complete change
rewolucyjny [re-vo-loo-**tsiy**-ni]
  adj. m. revolutionary
rewolwer [re-**vol**-ver] m.
  revolver; hand gun (with revolving cylinder)
rezerwa [re-**zer**-va] f. reserve
rezerwat [re-**zer**-vat] m.
  reservation; game preserve
rezerwować [re-zer-**vo**-vaćh] v.
  reserve; set aside; book
rezerwuar [re-zer-**voo**-ar] m.
  reservoir; (storage) tank
rezolutny [re-zo-**loot**-ni] adj. m.
  resolute; determined; game
rezonans [re-**zo**-nans] m.
  resonance (intensifying vibrations, often destructive)
rezultat [re-**zool**-tat] m. result;
  effect; numerical answer
rezydencja [re-zi-**den**-tsya] f.
  residence; dwelling place
rezydent [re-**zi**-dent] m. resident
  (permanent, not a transient)
rezygnacja [re-zig-**nats**-ya] f. f.
  resignation; patient submission
reżim [re-zheem] m. regime
reżyser [re-**zhi**-ser] m. stage
  manager; (film) director
ręcznie [**ranch**-ńe] adv. by hand
ręcznik [**ranch**-ńeek] m. towel
ręczny [**ranch**-ni] adj. m. manual;
  hand made; wrist (watch)
ręczyć [**ran**-chićh] v. guarantee

ręka [ran-ka] f. hand; arm; touch
rękaw [ran-kav] m. sleeve
rękawica [ran-ka-vee-tsa] f.
  mitten; gauntlet; mitt; glove
rękawiczka [ran-ka-veech-ka] f.
  glove (fur lined, velvet, etc.)
rękodzielnik [ran-ko-dźhel-ńeek]
  m. craftsman; handicraftsman
rękojeść [ran-ko-yeśhćh] f.
  hilt; handle; handgrip; helve
rękojmia [ran-koy-mya] f.
  guarantee; pledge (to replace);
  gage (security); warranty
rękopis [ran-ko-pees] m.
  manuscript; script; MS
robactwo [ro-bats-tvo] n. vermin
robak [ro-bak] m. worm; beetle;
  grub; maggot; anxiety; worry
rober [ro-ber] m. (bridge) rubber
  (in a card game of bridge)
robić [ro-beećh] v. make; do;
  act; work; become; get; feel;
  turn; knit; raise (an alarm)
robociarz [ro-bo-ćhash] m.
  common laborer (slang);
  mechanic; working man
robocizna [ro-bo-ćheez-na] f.
  wages; cost of labor; labor
roboczogodzina [ro-bo-cho-go-
  -dźhee-na] f. man-hour
robot [ro-bot] m. robot
robota [ro-bo-ta] f. work; job
robotnica [ro-bot-ńee-tsa] f.
  workwoman; operative; factory girl; female farmhand
robotnik [ro-bot-ńeek] m.
  worker; operative; mechanic
robótki [ro-boot-kee] pl.
  needlework; fancy work
rocznica [roch-ńee-tsa] f.
  anniversary
rocznie [roch-ńe] adv. yearly
rocznik [roch-ńeek] m. annual;
  yearbook; annual set (volume,
  edition, etc.); age group
roczny [roch-ni] adj. m. annual;
  one year's (duration etc.)
rodak [ro-dak] m. compatriot
rodowity [ro-do-vee-ti] adj. m.
  native; by birth; true-born
rodowód [ro-do-voot] m.
  genealogy; origin; pedigree;
  descent; lineage; filiation

rodzaj [ro-dzay] m. kind; sort;
  gender; type; race; manner; a-
  spect; nature; type; genre
rodzajnik [ro-dzay-ńeek] m.
  article (definite od indefinite)
rodzeństwo [ro-dzeń-stvo] n.
  siblings; brothers and sisters
rodzice [ro-dźhee-tse] pl.
  parents; father and mother
rodzić [ro-dźheećh] v. bear;
  procreate breed; yield (crops)
rodzina [ro-dźhee-na] f. family
rodzinny [ro-dźheen-ni] adj. m.
  family; native; home (life etc.)
rodzynek [ro-dzi-nek] m. raisin;
  currant; plum (for cakes)
rogacz [ro-gach] m. stag
rogacz [ro-gach] m. cuckold;
  deer; stag; deceived husband
rogatka [ro-gat-ka] f. toll-gate;
  toll-bar; toll-booth; turnpike
rogaty [ro-ga-ti] adj. m. horned;
  haughty; deceived (husband)
rogatywka [ro-ga-tiv-ka] f. four
  -corned cap (Polish style)
rogowacieć [ro-go-va-ćhećh]
  v. grow horny; become horny;
  grow (become) corneous
rogowaty [ro-go-va-ti] adj. m.
  corneous; horny; keratose
rogówka [ro-goov-ka] f. cornea
rogóżka [ro-goozh-ka] f. (door)
  mat (flat, woven of straw)
roić [ro-yeećh] v. 1. dream;
  imagine or fancy (all sorts of
  things, very many things)
roić [ro-yeećh] v. swarm; teem;
  run; be alive with; crawl
rojalista [ro-ya-lees-ta] m.
  royalist; supporter of the king
rojny [roy-ni] adj. m. teeming;
  swarming (crowds etc.)
rojowisko [ro-yo-vees-ko] n. hive;
  swarm; gathering place
rok [rok] m. year; a twelvemonth
rok przestąpny [rok pzhe-stanp-
  -ni] leap year (bissextile)
rokować [ro-ko-vaćh] v. 1. negotiate; augur (ill, well)
rokować [ro-ko-vaćh] v. 2. expect; promise oneself; hope
rokowania [ro-ko-va-ńa] 1. pl.
  negotiations 2. pl. prognosis

rola [ro-la] 1. f. arable land
2. f. (theatre) part; scroll;
weight; (political, etc.) role
rolka [rol-ka] f. roll; spool; reel;
runner; pulley; castor; trolley
rolnictwo [rol-ńeets-tvo] n.
agriculture; farming; animal
husbandry; land cultivation
rolnik [rol-ńeek] m. farmer
romans [ro-mans] 1. m. novel
of love, adventure, etc.
2. love affair; liaison
romantyczny [ro-man-tich-ni] adj.
m. romantic; full of romance
romantyk [ro-man-tik] m. romantic; not practical; visionary;
suited for (full of) romance
romantyzm [ro-man-tizm] m.
romanticism (literary style)
romański [ro-mań-skee] adj. m.
Romance; Romanesque
romb [romb] m. rhomb; diamond
rondel [ron-del] m. stew-pan
rondo [ron-do] n. brim; circular
plaza; traffic circle; circus
ronić [ro-ńeeć] v. 1. shed
ronić [ro-ńeeć] v. 2. miscarry; drop; cast; emit; moult
ropa [ro-pa] f. 1. puss
ropa [ro-pa] f. 2. crude oil; rock
oil; naphtha; petroleum
ropieć [ro-pyeć] v. fester;
have oozing sore; suppurate
ropień [ro-pyeń] m. abscess
ropny [rop-ni] adj. m. purulent;
oil fired; oil- (derrick etc.)
ropucha [ro-poo-kha] f. toad
rosa [ro-sa] f. dew
rosły [ros-wi] adj. m. tall; big
frame; stalwart; strong; sturdy
rosnąć [ros-nownć h] v. grow
rosół [ro-soow] m. broth;
bouillon; clear soup; pickle
rostbef [rost-bef] m. roast-beef;
baked beef; (beef or ox) rump
rosyjski [ro-siy-skee] adj. m.
Russian; of Russia
roszczenie [rosh-che-ńe] n.
claim; pretension; pretence
rościć [roś-ćheeć h] v. claim
roślina [roś-lee-na] f. plant;
vegetable; living plant
roślinność [roś-leen-

-nośćh] f. flora; vegetation
rowek [ro-vek] m. (small)
channel; groove; (small) gutter; rut; furrow
rower [ro-ver] n. bike; cycle
rowerzysta [ro-ve-zhis-ta] m.
cyclist; a cycle rider
rozbawiony [roz-ba-vyo-ni] adj.
m. merry; amused; in high
spirits; in festive mood
rozbestwić [roz-best-veećh] v.
enrage; turn into a wild beast
rozbicie [roz-bee-ćhe] n. break;
wreck; jumble; defeat; rout;
hurt; smash; breakage; failure
rozbić [roz-beećh] v. smash;
defeat; wreck; shatter; disrupt
rozbiegać się [roz-bye-gaćh
śhan] v. scatter; run in all directions; swarm; take off; bolt
rozbierać [roz-bye-raćh] v.
undress (somebody); strip; dismount; seize; analyze; divide
rozbieżny [roz-byezh-ni] adj. m.
divergent; different; discordant
rozbijać [roz-bee-yaćh] v. break
up; rout; crush; bluster; storm
rozbiór [roz-byoor] m. analysis
rozbiór [roz-byoor] m.
dismemberment; partition
rozbiórka [roz-byoor-ka] f.
demolition; taking to pieces
rozbitek [roz-bee-tek] m. ship
-wrecked person; castaway;
wreck; down-and-out; waif
rozbój [roz-booy] m. robbery;
piracy; banditry; high-jacking
rozbójnik [roz-booy-ńeek] m.
bandit; robber; cutthroat; hi-
jacker; brigand; highwayman
rozbrajać [roz-bra-yaćh] v.
disarm (a person, a country, a
mine, etc.); dismantle (a ship);
appease; pacify
rozbrat [roz-brat] m. split;
dis-union; gap between two
things; break with somebody
rozbrojenie [roz-bro-ye-ńe] n.
disarmament; reduction of
arms; discharge (a battery)
rozbrojeniowy [roz-bro-ye-ńo-vi]
adj. m. disarmament
rozbrzmiewać [roz-bzhmye-

-vać] v. resound; ring out; re
(echo); sound with (applause)
rozbudowa [roz-boo-do-va] f.
build up; extension; expansion
rozbudować [roz-boo-do-vać]
v. extend; enlarge; expand;
develop; increase in size etc.
rozbudzić [roz-boo-dźheećh] v.
rouse up; wake up; excite; stir
rozchmurzyć [roz-khmoo-zhićh]
v. clear up; brighten up
rozchodzić [roz-kho-dźheećh]
v. 1. stretch, wear (shoes)
rozchodzić [roz-kho-dźheećh]
v. 2. spread come apart
rozchodzić [roz-kho-dźheećh]
v. 3. get into the swing of
walking, marching, etc.
rozchód [roz-khoot] m.
expenditure; expenses etc.
rozchwytać [roz-khvi-tać] v.
snatch up; scramble for;
sweep off; snatch away
rozchylać [roz-khi-lać] v.
open; force apart; spread
rozciągać [roz-ćhown-gać] v.
stretch; extend; widen; expand; distend; dilate; spread
rozcieńczyć [roz-ćheń-chićh]
v. thin (down); dilute; rarefy;
attenuate; weaken with water
rozcierać [roz-ćhe-rać] v. rub;
grind; crush; spread (ointment)
rozcinać [roz-ćhee-nać] v. cut
up (open); dissect; rip open
rozczarować [roz-cha-ro-vać]
v. disappoint disenchant
rozczesać [roz-che-sać] v.
comb down; brush out (hair)
rozczłonkować [roz-chwon-ko-
-vać] v. dismember; divide
up; break up; partition
rozczulić [roz-choo-leećh] v.
move; touch; affect; stir
(feelings, the heart, soul etc.)
rozczyn [roz-chin] m. solution
(chem.); leaven (yeast)
rozdać [roz-dać] v. distribute;
give away; deal out; dispense
rozdarcie [roz-dar-ćhe] n. tear
rozdarcie [roz-dar-ćhe] n.
disruption; (internal) split
rozdeptać [roz-dep-tać]

v. trample (crush, grind) under
foot; tread on (out of shape)
rozdęcie [roz-dan-ćhe] n.
swelling; inflation; expansion
rozdmuchać [roz-dmoo-khać]
v. fan; inflate; blow about;
amplify; scatter; dishevel hair
rozdrapać [roz-dra-pać] v.
1. scratch (a pimple, etc.)
rozdrapać [roz-dra-pać] v.
2. snatch up; scramble for
rozdrażnić [roz-drazh-ńeećh] v.
irritate; exasperate; vex
rozdrobnić [roz-drob-ńeećh] v.
split up; divide; crumble; morsel; fritter down; granulate
rozdroże [roz-dro-zhe] n.
crossroads; parting of the
ways; condition of doubt etc.
rozdwoić [roz-dvo-eećh] v.
split; cleave; divide in two
rozdymać [roz-di-mać] v.
inflate; swell; expand; puff out
rozdział [roz-dźhaw] m.
distribution; disunion; parting
(hair); dispensation; chapter
rozdzielać [roz-dźhe-lać] v.
divide; distribute; set at odds
rozdzierać [roz-dźhe-rać] v.
tear up; tear asunder; rend;
pierce; rip open; break (heart)
rozdźwięk [roz-dźhvyank] m.
discord; dissonance; clash
rozebrać [ro-zeb-rać] v.
undress; analyze; take apart
rozedma [ro-zed-ma] f.
emphysema (distended lungs
deprived of elasticity)
rozejm [ro-zeym] m. truce
rozejrzeć się [ro-zey-zhećh
śhan] v. look around
rozejść się [ro-zeyśhćh
śhan] v. split; part; separate
rozerwać się [ro-zer-vać
śhan] v. divert oneself; get
torn; burst; come apart; snap
rozgałęzić [roz-ga-wan-
-źheećh] v. branch out; fork
off (out); branch off; ramify
rozgałęzienie [roz-ga-wan-źhe-
-ńe] n. branching; ramification
rozgardiasz [roz-gard-yash] m.
bustle; chaos; confusion

rozgarnąć [roz-gar-n<u>own</u>ćh] v.
rake aside; part; brush apart
rozgarnięty [roz-gar-<u>ńan</u>-ti] adj.
m. bright; clever; sharp
rozglądać się [roz-gl<u>own</u>-daćh
śhan] v. look around; look for
rozgłaszać [roz-gwa-shaćh] v.
make known ; broadcast
rozgłos [roz-gwos] m. publicity;
fame; renown; repute; notorie-
ty; publication; promulgation
rozgłośnia [roz-gwośh-ńa] f.
broadcasting station
rozgmatwać [roz-gmat-vaćh] v.
disentangle; extricate
rozgnieść [roz-gńeśhćh] v.
flatten; squash (once)
rozgniatać [roz-gńa-taćh] v.
squash; flatten (often)
rozgniewać [roz-gńe-vaćh] v.
anger; vex; irritate
rozgoryczenie [roz-go-ri-che-ńe]
n. bitterness; exasperation
rozgoryczyć [roz-go-ri-chićh] v.
embitter; exacerbate; disgust
rozgotować [roz-go-to-vaćh] v.
cook to a pulp; cook to rags
rozgraniczyć [roz-gra-ńee-
-chićh] v. delimit; mark the
boundaries; demarcate; divide
rozgromić [roz-gro-meećh] v.
rout (the enemy); crush (an
army); put to the flight
rozgrywać [roz-gri-vaćh] v. play
one's game; put through a policy etc.; fight (a battle)
rozgryźć [roz-griźhćh] v. bite
through; bite in two; crack
(nuts, etc.); crush (a pill)
rozgrzać [roz-gzhaćh] v. warm
up; heat up; get hot; rouse
rozgrzebać [roz-gzhe-baćh] v.
dig up; rake up; scatter
rozgrzeszyć [roz-gzhe-shićh] v.
absolve (of sins); forgive
rozgrzewać [roz-gzhe-vaćh] v.
warm up; rouse; stimulate
rozhukany [roz-khoo-ka-ni] adj.
m. wild; unruly; riotous
rozhuśtać [roz-khoośh-taćh]
v. set swinging; set rocking
roziskrzyć [roz-ees-kzhićh] v.
start sparkle; make sparkle

rozjaśnić [roz-yaśh-ńeećh] v.
brighten; clear up; clarify
rozjątrzyć [roz-y<u>own</u>t-zhićh] v.
exasperate; irritate; chafe
rozjemca [roz-yem-tsa] m.
referee; arbiter; umpire
rozjeżdżać się [roz-yezh-
-dzhaćh **śhan**] v. disperse;
part; be for ever travelling
rozjuszyć [roz-yoo-shićh] v.
enrage; infuriate; exasperate
rozkapryszony [roz-ka-pri-**sho**-ni]
adj. m. whimsical; fitful
rozkaz [roz-kas] m. order
rozkiełznąć [roz-**kew**-
-zn<u>own</u>ćh] v. unbridle; unchain; let (make) loose
rozkleić [roz-kle-eećh] v. 1.
unglue; unstick; weaken, etc.
rozkleić [roz-kle-eećh] v. 2.
post up (posters, notices, etc.)
rozkład [roz-kwat] m. dissolution;
decay; disposition; timetable;
train schedule; breakdown
rozkładać [roz-**kwa**-daćh] v.
decompose; spread; display;
stagger (hours); lay out; distribute; arrange; dispose
rozkołysać [roz-ko-**wi**-saćh] v.
set rocking; set swinging;
agitate; swing with great force
rozkopywać [roz-ko-pi-vaćh] v.
dig up; rip up; kick apart;
tumble; make excavations
rozkosz [roz-kosh] f. delight
rozkrajać [roz-kra-yaćh] v. cut
up; carve; slice; divide
rozkręcić [roz-**kran**-ćheećh] v.
unscrew; un-reel; take to
pieces; loosen a screw; uncurl
rozkruszyć [roz-kroo-shićh] v.
crush up; grind; disintegrate
rozkrzewić [roz-**kzhe**-veećh] v.
propagate; increase; diffuse
rozkuć [roz-koočh] v.
unshackle; unshod (a horse);
unchain, un-fetter (a convict,
etc.); hammer out (a metal);
rozkulbaczyć [roz-kool-**ba**-
-chićh] v. unsaddle (a horse)
rozkupić [roz-koo-peećh] v. buy
up; buy everything; buy all
rozkwit [roz-kveet] m. bloom

rozkwitać [roz-**kvee**-tać] v.
burst into flower; bloom; o-
pen; blossom; beam; light up
rozlatywać się [roz-la-**ti**-vać
śhan] v. fly away; break up;
scatter; disperse; run away;
scamper away; burst asunder
rozlazły [roz-**laz**-wi] adj. m. slack;
loose; spread out; sloppy
rozległy [roz-**leg**-wi] adj. m.
spacious; vast; wide; far-
flung; extensive (knowledge)
rozleniwiać [roz-le-**ńee**-vyać]
v. make lazy; induce to laziness; induce to sloth
rozlepić [roz-**le**-peeć] v. post;
put up; paste up; stick; unstick (sheets of paper, etc.)
rozlew [roz-lev] m. flood
rozlew krwi [roz-lev krvee] m.
bloodshed; killing; slaughter
rozlewać [roz-le-vać] v. spill;
slop; splash; shed; diffuse;
pour (out); ladle out (soup)
rozliczenie [roz-lee-**che**-ńe] n.
settling; reckoning; settlement
rozliczny [roz-**leech**-ni] adj. m.
manifold; diverse; numerous
rozliczyć [roz-lee-**chiсh**] v.
settle up (accounts); calculate
rozlokować [roz-lo-ko-vać] v.
put up; make at home; quarter
rozlosować [roz-lo-**so**-vać] v.
allot; distribute by lot
rozluźnić [roz-**looźh**-ńeećh]
v. slacken; relax; unfasten
rozluźnienie [roz-looźh-ńe-ńe]
n. loosening; laxity; slackness
rozładować [roz-wa-do-vać] v.
unload; discharge (a battery)
rozłam [roz-wam] m. breach;
split; break; division; dissent
rozłamać [roz-**wa**-mać] v.
break (in two); split
rozłazić się [roz-**wa**-źheećh
śhan] v. fall apart; disperse
rozłączenie [roz-**wown**-che-ńe]
n. separation; dis-junction
rozłączyć [roz-**wown**-chiсh] v.
disconnect; sever; uncouple
rozłąka [roz-**wown**-ka] f.
separation (of people)
rozłożyć [roz-**wo**-zhiсh] v.

spread; lay out; disassemble
rozłupać [roz-**woo**-pać] v.
split; cleave; rift; slit (logs);
crack (nuts, heads, etc.); rive
rozmach [roz-makh] m. impetus;
dash; verve; grand style; momentum; force; swing; vigor;
spirit; kick; (swinging) blow
rozmaitości [roz-ma-ee-**tośh**-
-ćhee] pl. miscellany; vaude-
ville theater; variety theater
rozmaity [roz-ma-ee-ti] adj. m.
varied; miscellaneous; diverse
rozmaryn [roz-ma-rin] m.
rosemary (Rosmarinus)
rozmarzenie [roz-ma-**zhe**-ńe] n.
daydream; dreaminess; reverie
rozmawiać [roz-ma-vyać] v.
converse; talk; speak with
rozmazać [roz-ma-zać] v. blur;
smear; daub; let out (a secret)
rozmiar [roz-myar] m. dimension;
size; proportion; scale
rozmienić [roz-**mye**-ńeećh] v.
change (money, bank-note,
etc.); get the change
rozmieszczać [roz-**myesh**-
-chać] v. arrange; dispose;
place; put; assign places
rozmieszczenie [roz-myesh-**che**-
-ńe] n. distribution; layout
rozmiękczyć [roz-my**ank**-chiсh]
v. soften (clay, a man, etc.);
soak; steep; make soft
rozmięknąć [roz-my**ank**-
-n**own**ćh] v. become soft; get
soaked; get drenched; sop
rozmijać się [roz-mee-yać
śhan] v. miss; swerve from;
pass; fail to (meet, notice)
rozmiłować się [roz-mee-**wo**-
-vać **śhan**] v. take a liking
to; develop a love for
rozminąć się [roz-mee-n**own**ćh
śhan] v. miss (on road); pass
each other; fail to meet
rozmnażać [roz-mna-zhać] v.
breed; multiply; propagate;
increase in numbers; augment
rozmoczyć [roz-mo-chiсh] v.
soak; steep; wet thoroughly;
sodden; make (very) soggy
rozmoknąć [roz-mo-kn**own**ćh]

v. become soaked; get soggy
rozmowa [roz-mo-va] f.
conversation; talk; discourse
rozmowny [roz-mov-ni] adj. m.
communicative; talkative
rozmówca [roz-moov-tsa] m.
interlocutor (in conversation)
rozmówić się [roz-moo-veech
śhan] v. talk over; make oneself understood; speak with
rozmysł [roz-misw] m. intent;
premeditation; consideration;
intention; purpose; design
rozmyślać [roz-miśh-lach] v.
meditate; ponder how to do
rozmyślanie [roz-miśh-la-ńe] n.
meditation; contemplation
rozmyślić się [roz-miśh-leech
śhan] v. change one's mind
rozmyślny [roz-miśhl-ni] adj. m.
deliberate; intentional; wilful
roznamiętnić [roz-na-myant-
-ńeech] v. impassion; excite
rozniecić [roz-ńe-ćheech] v.
inflame; enkindle a fire; inspire
roznosić [roz-no-śheech] v.
carry (take) around; serve; deliver; rout; distribute; smash
rozochocić [roz-o-kho-ćheech]
v. make merry; animate
rozogniać się [roz-og-ńach
śhan] v. inflame; become excited; flare up; flush
rozpacz [roz-pach] f. despair;
distress; (utter) desperation
rozpad [roz-pat] m. decay; break
up; collapse; disintegration
rozpakować [roz-pa-ko-vach] v.
unpack (one's luggage); unwrap (a parcel, a package)
rozpalić [roz-pa-leech] v. fire
up; ignite; start a fire; set
ablaze; light (a cigarette)
rozpamiętywać [roz-pa-myan-ti-
-vach] v. contemplate; reflect
upon; ponder over; recollect
rozpaplać [roz-pa-plach] v. blab
out; divulge; babble out
rozpasany [roz-pa-sa-ni] adj. m.
unbridled; dissolute; licentious
rozpatrywać [roz-pa-tri-vach] v.
consider; act upon; examine
rozpęd [roz-pant] m. impetus;

dash; momentum; taking a run
rozpędzać [roz-pan-dzach] v.
pick up speed; scatter; disperse; dispel; dissipate; give
an impetus; accelerate
rozpętać [roz-pan-tach] v.
unshackle; unleash; let loose
rozpiąć [roz-pyownch] v.
unbuckle; undo; stretch (sail)
rozpieczątować [roz-pye-chan-
-to-vach] v. unseal; open
rozpierać [roz-pye-rach] v.
expand; extend; push aside
rozpierzchnąć się [roz-pyezh-
-khnownch śhan] v. scatter
rozpieszczać [roz-pyesh-chach]
v. pamper; spoil; coddle up
rozpiątość [roz-pyan-tośhch]
f. span; spread; range; stretch
rozpinać [roz-pee-nach] v.
unbutton; unbuckle; stretch;
spread (sails, nets, etc.)
rozplątać [roz-plown-tach] v.
untangle; untie (a knot); unravel (a plot); disentangle
rozpleść [roz-pleśhch] v.
unbraid; un-twine (a cord); un-
plait (hair); unravel; unclasp
rozpłakać się [roz-pwa-kach
śhan] v. burst into tears;
start weeping; become tearful
rozpłaszczyć [roz-pwash-chich]
v. flatten out; flat (metal)
rozpłatać [roz-pwa-tach] v. slit;
split; split into two
rozpłodowy [roz-pwo-do-vi] adj.
m. (for) breeding; breeding-
rozpłodzić [roz-pwo-dźheech]
v. propagate; cause reproduction (of a specie, clan, etc.)
rozpłód [roz-pwoot] m.
propagation; reproduction
rozpływać się [roz-pwi-vach
śhan] v. melt away; out-
break; dissolve; flow; spread
rozpoczęcie [roz-po-chan-ćhe] n.
start; outbreak; beginning;
commencement; lead-off
rozpoczynać [roz-po-chi-nach]
v. begin; start going; open;
initiate; launch; embark upon
rozpogodzić się [roz-po-go-
-dźheech śhan] v. clear up;

brighten up; cheer up
rozporek [roz-po-rek] m. fly; slit
rozporządzać [roz-po-zhown-
-dzáćh] v. dispose; decree;
order; control; command
rozpościerać [roz-pośh-ćhe-
-raćh] v. unfurl; spread out;
expand; stretch; fling out
rozpowiadać [roz-po-vya-daćh]
v. tell tales (left and right);
divulge; talk (at length) about
rozpowszechniać [roz-pov-
-shekh-ńaćh] v. widespread;
diffuse; disseminate; propagate; spread (around, all over)
rozpowszechnienie [roz-pov-
-shekh-ńe-ńe] n. propagation;
spread; diffusion; prevalence
rozpoznać [roz-poz-naćh] v.
recognize; spot; diagnose
rozpoznanie [roz-poz-na-ńe] n.
diagnosis; identification;
reconnaissance; recognition
rozpoznawczy [roz-poz-nav-chi]
adj. m. diagnostic; distinctive
rozpraszać [roz-pra-shaćh] v.
scatter; dispel; distract; disperse; dissipate; make vanish
rozprawa [roz-pra-va] f. trial;
showdown; dissertation; debate; court trial (hearing)
rozprawiać [roz-pra-vyaćh] v.
debate; argue; dispute; reason; talk at length; discuss
rozprawić się [roz-pra-veećh
śhaṉ] v. settle matters; fight
out; dispose of; floor
rozprężyć [roz-praṉ-zhićh] v.
distend; expand; dilate; resile;
deprive of elasticity; relax
rozprostować [roz-pros-to-vaćh]
v. straighten; unbend; stretch
(legs, etc.); smooth out
rozproszyć [roz-pro-shićh] v.
disperse; scatter; dispel; distract; diffuse (light); spread
rozprowadzić [roz-pro-va-
-dźheećh] v. spread; retail;
distribute; dilute; convey; thin
down; attenuate; smear
rozpruć [roz-prooćh] v. rip up;
open; un-sew; unravel; rip
open; unstitch; unpick; slit

rozprzedać [roz-pzhe-daćh] v.
sell out; sell (successively)
rozprzedaż [roz-pzhe-dash] f.
sale; complete sale; retailing
rozprzestrzenić [roz-pzhe-stshe-
-ńeećh] v. spread; propagate
rozprzęgać [roz-pzhaṉ-gaćh] v.
1. unhitch; unharness (horses)
rozprzęgać [roz-pzhaṉ-gaćh] v.
2. disorganize; dislocate
rozprzężenie [roz-pzhaṉ-zhe-ńe]
n. anarchy; demoralization
rozpusta [roz-poos-ta] f.
debauch; riot; licentiousness
rozpustnica [roz-poost-ńee-tsa]
f. rake; rip; libertine;
debauchee; profligate
rozpustnik [roz-poost-ńeek] m.
rake; rip; libertine; debauchee;
profligate; reprobate
rozpuszczać [roz-poosh-chaćh]
v. dissolve; dismiss; let go;
disband; dilute; thaw; melt;
defrost; unfreeze; extend
rozpuszczalnik [roz-poosh-chal-
-ńeek] m. solvent; dis-solvent
rozpuszczalny [roz-poosh-chal-ni]
adj. m. soluble; dissolvable
rozpychać się [roz-pi-khaćh
śhaṉ] v. shove aside; jostle
one's way; elbow one's way;
push one's way though
rozpylacz [roz-pi-lach] m.
sprayer; nozzle; atomizer
rozpylać [roz-pi-laćh] v. spray;
pulverize; atomize
rozpytywać [roz-pi-ti-vaćh] v.
ask for; inquire around; ask all
sorts of questions
rozrachować [roz-ra-kho-vaćh]
v. settle accounts; calculate
rozrachunek [roz-ra-khoo-nek] m.
squaring up accounts
rozradzać się [roz-ra-dzaćh
śhaṉ] v. breed; propagate
rozrastać się [roz-ras-taćh
śhaṉ] v. grow larger (stronger); increase; develop; expand
rozrąbać [roz-rown-baćh] v. cut
asunder; hew apart; chop up
rozrobić [roz-ro-beećh] v. stir
up; dilute; scheme; intrigue;
make trouble; kick up a row

rozrodczość [roz-**rod**-
-chośhćh] f. reproduction;
reproductiveness; generation
rozróżniać [roz-roozh-ńaćh] v.
distinguish; tell apart; discern
rozruchy [roz-roo-khi] pl. riots;
disturbances; violent disorders
rozruszać [roz-roo-shaćh] v.
start up; stir up; put in motion; set in motion; animate
rozrywać [roz-ri-vaćh] v. burst;
disrupt; tear open; entertain
rozrywka [roz-riv-ka] f.
amusement; recreation; entertainment; pastime; diversion
rozrządnica [roz-zhownd-ńee-
-tsa] f. control panel
rozrzedzić [roz-zhe-dźheećh] v.
dilute; rarefy; thin down
(paint, a soup, etc.); weaken
rozrzewnić [roz-zhev-ńeećh] v.
move; touch (pathetically); affect; stir (the soul, the heart)
rozrzucać [roz-zhoo-tsaćh] v.
scatter; squander; distribute
rozrzutność [roz-zhoot-
-nośhćh] f. extravagance;
wastefulness; lavishness
rozrzutny [roz-zhoot-ni] adj. m.
wasteful; extravagant; thriftless; squandering; prodigal;
spendthrift; lavish
rozsada [roz-sa-da] f. seedling;
seedlings (grown from seeds)
rozsadzać [roz-sa-dzaćh] v.
space-out; place; seat separately; blow up; explode; split
rozsądek [roz-**sown**-dek] m.
good sense; discretion; intellect; reason; judgement; sense
rozsądny [roz-**sownd**-ni] adj. m.
sensible; reasonable;
advisable; sound; judicious
rozsiadać się [roz-śha-daćh
śhan] v. sit stretched; sprawl
round; settle comfortably
rozsiekać [roz-śhe-kaćh] v. cut
up; slash asunder; hack up
rozsiewać [roz-śhe-vaćh] v.
saw; disseminate; spread; diffuse; shed; propagate (gossip)
rozsiodłać [roz-śhod-waćh] v.
unsaddle; take the saddle off

rozsławiać [roz-**swa**-vyaćh] v.
glorify; make famous; extol
rozstać się [roz-staćh **śhan**] v.
part; give up; part with
rozstanie [roz-sta-ńe] n. parting
1. separation; 2. leave-taking
rozstawać się [roz-sta-vaćh
śhan] v. part with; give up
rozstawiać [roz-sta-vyaćh] v.
disperse; place apart; space;
spread; put at intervals
rozstąpić się [roz-**stown**-peećh
śhan] v. step aside; come
apart; draw aside (apart); split
rozstęp [roz-stanp] m. gap;
space; slit; interval; heave
rozstroić [roz-stro-eećh] v. put
out of tune; upset; disarray;
derange; disorder; un-tune
rozstrój [roz-strooy] m. upset;
disorder; confusion; derangement; (nervous) breakdown
rozstrzelać [roz-stzhe-laćh] v.
1. scatter; distract (attention)
rozstrzelać [roz-stzhe-laćh] v.
2. execute by shooting; put
before a firing squad
rozstrzygać [roz-**stzhi**-gaćh] v.
try out; decide; fight out; determine; judge; arbitrate; settle
rozstrzygnięcie [roz-stzhig-**ńan**-
-će] f. decision; settlement
rozsuwać [roz-soo-vaćh] v.
part; draw aside; separate; expand; spread; part; extend
rozsyłać [roz-si-waćh] v.
distribute; circulate; send out
rozsypać [roz-si-paćh] v.
disperse (a granular sub-
stance); spill; scatter; spread
rozszarpać [roz-**shar**-paćh] v.
tear up; claw; disjoin; mangle
rozszczepiać [roz-shche-pyaćh]
v. split; cleave; fissure
rozszczepienie [roz-shche-**pye**-
-ńe] n. split; diffraction
rozszerzać [roz-she-zhaćh] v.
widen; broaden; enlarge; expand; spread out; extend; dilate; open; propagate; spread
rozszerzenie [roz-she-**zhe**-ńe] n.
enlargement; dilation
rozsznurować [roz-shnoo-**ro**-

-vać] v. unlace; loosen the lace; come (become) unlaced

rozszyfrować [roz-shif-ro-vać] v. decode; break the code

rozścielać [roz-śhćhe-lać] v. spread (out); make the bed

rozśmieszać [roz-śhmye--shać] v. amuse; make laugh; be amusing; be funny

rozświecić [roz-śhvye--ćhećh] v. light up; throw light on; shine on; brighten up

roztaczać [roz-ta-chać] v. roll out; spread; unfold; display; bore; take under (protection)

roztajać [roz-ta-yać] v. thaw

roztapiać [roz-ta-pyać] v. melt; smelt (metal); thaw (ice)

roztargać [roz-tar-gać] v. tear to pieces; ruffle; dishevel

roztargniony [roz-tar-gńo-ni] adj. m. absentminded; distracted; scatterbrained; far-away

rozterka [roz-ter-ka] f. tearing between; dissension; suspense

roztkliwiać [roz-tklee-vyać] v. feel for; touch; move; stir

roztłuc [roz-twoots] v. smash up

roztopy [roz-to-pi] pl. thaw

roztratować [roz-tra-to-vać] v. run over; trample; tread under foot; trample to death

roztrąbić [roz-trown-beećh] v. broadcast; blaze abroad

roztrącić [roz-trown-ćheećh] v. push aside; elbow; part; jostle

rozstropność [roz-strop--nośhćh] f. prudence; circumspection; thoughtfulness

rozstropny [roz-strop-ni] adj. m. wise; cautious; circumspect; politic; sensible; cautious; well-advised; discriminating

roztrwonić [roz-trvo-ńeećh] v. squander (a fortune, money)

roztrzaskać [roz-tzhas-kać] v. smash; shatter; crash; dash; break (to pieces with a noise)

roztrzepanie [roz-tzhe-pa-ńe] n. scatterbrain; fickleness

roztrzepany [roz-tzhe-pa-ni] adj. m. scatterbrain; giddy

roztwór [roz-tvoor] m. (chem.)

solution (colloidal, molal, etc.)

roztyć się [roz-tićh śhan] v. grow (very) fat; become fat

rozum [ro-zoom] m. mind; reason; intellect; understanding; wit; senses; judgment; brains; intelligence; senses; judiciousness; wits

rozumieć [ro-zoo-myećh] v. understand; get; perceive

rozumny [ro-zoom-ni] adj. m. rational; reasonable; wise

rozumować [ro-zoo-mo-vać] v. reason (out); argue (about)

rozwaga [roz-va-ga] f. deliberation; thoughtfulness; prudence; reflection; caution

rozwalać [roz-va-lać] v. shatter; demolish; smash; pull down (building, etc.); sprawl

rozwarty kąt [roz-var-ti kownt] m. obtuse angle

rozważać [roz-va-zhać] v. 1. weigh out (quantities of...)

rozważać [roz-va-zhać] v. 2. consider; ponder; meditate

rozweselić [roz-ve-se-leećh] v. cheer up; put in good humor

rozwiać [roz-vyać] v. blow away; scatter; disperse; dispel

rozwiązać [roz-vyown-zać] v. untie; solve; undo; dissolve; loosen; unbind; unravel; undo

rozwiązanie [roz-vyown-za-ńe] n. solution; way out; (child) delivery; realization; execution

rozwiązły [roz-vyownz-wi] adj. m. fast; dissolute; debauched; licentious; profligate

rozwidniać [roz-veed-ńać] v. dawn; be lit up; become lit up

rozwiedziona [roz-vye-dźho-na] adj. f. divorcee (a woman)

rozwiedziony [roz-vye-dźho-ni] adj. m. divorced (a man)

rozwierać [roz-vye-rać] v. open wide; fling (wide) open

rozwieszać [roz-vye-shać] v. hang about; stretch; spread out; hung up (here and there)

rozwieść się [roz-vyeśhćh śhan] v. divorce; dwell upon

rozwijać [roz-vee-yać] v.

unwrap; unfold; develop; unroll; un-reel; spread; deploy
rozwikłać [roz-**veek**-waćh] v.
disentangle; unravel; clear up
rozwikłanie [roz-veek-**wa**-ńe] n.
unraveling; disentanglement
rozwlekać [roz-**vle**-kaćh] v.
drag out; protract; spread
rozwlekły [roz-**vlek**-wi] adj. m.
verbose; lengthy; long-spun
rozwodnić [roz-vod-**ńeećh**] v.
dilute; water down; weaken
rozwodnik [roz-vod-**ńeek**] m.
divorced man; divorcee
rozwodowy [roz-vo-do-vi] adj. m.
divorce (proceedings etc.)
rozwodzić [roz-vo-**dźheećh**] v.
divorce (a married couple)
rozwojowy [roz-vo-yo-vi] adj. m.
evolutional; developmental
rozwolnienie [roz-vol-ńe-ńe] n.
diarrhea; lax bowels; open
bowels; too frequent bowels
rozwozić [roz-vo-**źheećh**] v.
transport; deliver (mail etc.)
rozwód [roz-vood] m. divorce
rozwódka [roz-vood-ka] f.
divorcee; divorced woman
rozwój [roz-vooy] m.
development; evolution; extension; progress; (up)growth
rozwścieczony [roz-vśhćhe-
-cho-ni] adj. m. enraged;
furious; mad with rage; rabid
rozwydrzony [roz-vid-zho-ni] adj.
m. rampant; wild; lawless
rozzłościć [roz-**zwośh**-
-ćheećh] v. irritate; provoke;
make angry; vex; anger
rozżalenie [roz-zha-le-ńe] n.
grudge; resentment; bitterness
rozżarzyć [roz-zha-zhićh] v.
inflame; set on fire; fire
rożek [ro-zhek] m. small horn;
croissant; small corner
rożen [ro-zhen] m. roasting spit
ród [rood] m. clan; breed; family;
stock; race; origin; line
róg [roog] m. horn; corner; ant-
ler; bugle; corner kick (sport);
pl. woman's marital infidelity
rój [rooy] m. swarm; hive; bevy;
cluster; colony; galaxy

róść [roośhćh] v. grow; age;
go up; shoot up; spring up
rów [roov] vm. ditch; trench;
trough; drainage ditch
rówieśnik [roo-vyeśh-ńeek] m.
peer of the same age; contemporary (man); equal (age)
równać [roov-naćh] v. equalize;
level; make even; smooth out
równanie [roov-na-ńe] n.
equation; equalization; comparison; making equal
równia [roov-ńa] f. plane; level
równie [roov-ńe] adv. equally
również [roov-ńesh] conj. also;
too; likewise; as well
równik [roov-ńeek] m. equator
równina [roov-ńee-na] f. plain;
flat country; level landscape
równo [roov-no] adv. even;
flat; level; straight; equi-
równoboczny [roov-no-**boch**-ni]
adj. m. equilateral
równoczesny [roov-no-**ches**-ni]
adj. m. simultaneous
równoległobok [roov-no-leg-**wo**-
-bok] m. parallelogram
równoległy [roov-no-**leg**-vi] adj.
m. parallel to; collateral
równoleżnik [roov-no-lezh-ńeek]
m. parallel (of latitude)
równomierny [roov-no-**myer**-ni]
adj. m. even; uniform; steady
równoramienny [roov-no-ra-
-myen-ni] adj. m. isosceles
(triangle); of equal sides
równorzędny [roov-no-zhand-ni]
adj. m. equal rank; equivalent
róvność [roov-nośhćh] f.
equality; parity; identity
równouprawnienie [roov-no-oo-
-prav-ńe-ńe] n. equality of
rights (of women, men, etc.)
równowaga [roov-no-**va**-ga] f.
equilibrium; balance; poise
równowartościowy [roov-no-
-var-tośh-ćho-vi] adj. m.
equivalent; equipollent
równoważny [roov-no-**vazh**-ni]
adj. m. equivalent; equipollent; equiponderant
równoważyć [roov-no-**va**-zhićh]
v. balance; equalize; even up

równoznaczny [roov-no-znach-ni]
adj. m. synonymous; tanta-
mount; amounting to (a denial)
rózga [rooz-ga] f. switch; cane
róż [roozh] m. rouge; pink
róża [roo-zha] f. rose
różaniec [roo-zha-ńets] m.
(praying with a) rosary; beads
różdżka [roozhdzh-ka] f.
dowsing rod; twig; diving rod;
magic wand; fairy's wand
różnica [roozh-ńee-tsa] f.
difference; disparity; dissimi-
larity; result of subtraction
różniczka [roozh-ńeech-ka] f.
differential; small difference
różnić się [roozh-ńeećh śhan]
v. differ; be at variance
różnobarwny [roozh-no-barv-ni]
adj. m. many colored; motley
różnojęzyczny [roozh-no-yan-
-zich-ni] adj. m. many-tongued
różnolity [roozh-no-lee-ti] adj. m.
diverse; varied; heterogenous
różnorodny [roozh-no-rod-ni] adj.
m. heterogenous; various
różnoznaczny [roozh-no-znach-ni]
adj. m. ambiguous; vague
różny [roozh-ni] adj. m. different;
miscellaneous; sundry; varied
różowy [roo-zho-vi] adj. m. pink;
rosy; ruddy; rose color
rtęciowy [rtan-ćho-vi] adj. m.
mercuric (compounds etc.)
rtęć [rtanćh] f. mercury
rubaszny [roo-bash-ni] adj. m.
coarse; ill-mannered; gruff
rubin [roo-been] m. ruby (red)
rubryka [roo-bri-ka] f. space;
column; blank space; rubric
ruch [rookh] m. move; movement; traffic; motion; gesture;
circulation; agitation; rush
ruchawka [roo-khaw-ka] f. riot
ruchliwy [rookh-lee-vi] adj. m.
busy; mobile; agile; active
ruchomości [roo-kho-mośh-
-ćhee] pl. movables (personal
property); belongings; chattels
personal effects; one's things
ruchomy [roo-kho-mi] adj. m.
mobile; moving; shifting; flexible; floating;dis-placeable

ruczaj [roo-chay] m. brook
ruda [roo-da] f. ore (metallic)
rudera [roo-de-ra] f. run-down
house; shanty; ruin; hovel
rudy [roo-di] adj. m. red (haired);
russet; ginger; foxy; ruddy
rufa [roo-fa] f. stern; poop
rugować [roo-go-vaćh] v. eject;
oust; evict; eliminate; displace
ruina [roo-ee-na] f. ruin; wreck
ruja [roo-ya] f. heat; rut
rujnować [rooy-no-vaćh] v.
ruin; undo; destroy; wreck
ruleta [roo-le-ta] f. roulette
rulon [roo-lon] m. roll; rouleau
rum [room] m. rum (drink)
rumak [roo-mak] m. charger;
steed; palfrey; courser
rumianek [roo-mya-nek] m.
camomile; chamomile (tea)
rumiany [roo-mya-ni] adj. m.
rosy; ruddy; browned; florid
rumienić [roo-mye-ńeećh] v.
blush; brown; redden; color
rumieniec [roo-mye-ńets] m.
blush; ruddiness; floridity
rumor [roo-mor] m. racket;
uproar; rumble; clatter; din
rumowisko [roo-mo-vees-ko] n.
debris; rubble; brash
rumuński [roo-mooń-skee]
adj. m. Rumanian; of Rumania
runąć [roo-nownćh] v. fall
down; collapse; crash; swoop;
come down; topple; resound
runda [roon-da] f. bout; round;
lap; fall (in wrestling)
runo [roo-no] n. fleece; nap
rupiecie [roo-pye-ćhe] pl.
rubbish; rash; junk; stuff;
oddments; odds and ends
ruptura [roop-too-ra] f. hernia
rura [roo-ra] f. tube; pipe
rurka [roor-ka] f. small pipe
rurociąg [roo-ro-ćhowng] m.
pipeline; run of pipes; piping
rusałka [roo-saw-ka] f. undine;
naiad; water nymph; vanessa
ruszać [roo-shaćh] v. move;
stir; start; take away; withdraw; touch; tamper; remove
rusznikarz [roosh-ńee-kash] m.
gunsmith (man or shop)

rusztowanie [roosh-to-**va**-ńe] n.
scaffold; cradle (hanging)
rutyna [roo-**ti**-na] f. routine
rutynowany [roo-ti-no-**va**-ni] adj.
m. experienced; competent
rwać [rvaćh] v. pluck; tear; pull
out; pull up; rush; burst
rwący [**rvown**-tsi] adj. m. rapid;
racking (pain); swift flowing
rwetes [rve-tes] m. bustle; ado;
racket; turmoil; agitation; stir
ryba [**ri**-ba] f. fish; the Fish
rybak [**ri**-bak] m. fisherman
rybny staw [rib-ni **stav**] fish pond
(artificially made pond)
rybołóstwo [ri-bo-**woos**-tvo] n.
fishery; fishing industry
rycerski [ri-tser-skee] adj. m.
chivalrous; courteous; gallant
rycerz [ri-tsesh] m. knight
rychło [rikh-wo] adv. soon;
quickly; early; soon after
rychły [rikh-wi] adj. m. speedy;
early; prompt; approaching
rycina [ri-ćhee-na] f. engraving;
illustration; cartoon; drawing;
plate; figure; picture
rycynus [ri-tsi-noos] m. castor
oil; castor oil plant
ryczałt [ri-chawt] m. lump sum;
global sum; the lump
ryczeć [ri-chećh] v. roar; moo;
bellow; low; growl; bray; (elephant) trumpet; hoot; yell
ryć [rićh] v. dig; root; engrave;
carve; excavate; burrow; incise; plough; tunnel; inscribe
rydel [ri-del] m. spade; spud
rydwan [rid-van] m. chariot
rygiel [ri-gel] m. bolt; bar; lock
rygor [ri-gor] m. rigor; severity;
discipline; penalty; strictness
ryj [riy] m. snout; phiz; mug
ryk [rik] m. roar; moo; low; yell
rylec [ri-lets] m. burin; graver;
chisel; etching needle; dry
point; (cyclostyle) pen
rym [rim] m. 1. rhyme; 2. bang!
rymarz [ri-mash] m. saddler
rymować [ri-mo-vaćh] v. rhyme
rynek [ri-nek] m. market (square)
rynna [rin-na] f. gutter; chute
rynsztok [rin-shtok] m. sewer

rynsztunek [rin-**shtoo**-nek] m.
armor; armature; outfit; kit
rys [ris] m. feature; trait
rysa [ri-sa] f. crack; flow;
fissure; scratch; rift; crevice;
chink; cranny; a partial break
rysopis [ri-**so**-pees] m.
description (of a person for a
passport, military service, etc.)
rysować [ri-**so**-vaćh] v. draw;
design; sketch; draft; trace;
pencil; describe; delineate; line
rysownica [ri-sov-**ńee**-tsa] f.
drawing board; drafting table
rysownik [ri-**sov**-ńeek] m.
draftsman; illustrator; designer
rysunek [ri-**soo**-nek] m. sketch;
drawing; draft; outline; deline-
ation; draftsmanship; cartoon
rysunkowy [ri-soon-**ko**-vi] adj. m.
tracing; drawing (board, block,
etc.); cartoon (film); drawn
ryś [riśh] m. lynx
rytm [ritm] m. rhythm; cadence
rytmiczny [rit-**meech**-ni] adj. m.
rhythmic; regular; measured
rytownictwo [rit-ov-**ńeets**-tvo] n.
engraving (trade); dye sinking
rytownik [ri-tov-**ńeek**] m.
engraver; master dye sinker
rytuał [ri-too-aw] m. ritual
rywal [ri-val] m. rival; contestant
rywalizacja [ri-va-lee-**zats**-ya] f.
rivalry; competition; emulation
ryza [ri-za] f. ream; restraint
ryzyko [ri-zi-ko] n. risk; venture
ryzykować [ri-zi-ko-vaćh] v.
risk; venture; gamble; hazard
ryzykowny [ri-zi-**kov**-ni] adj. m.
risky; hazardous; venturesome
ryż [rizh] m. rice; rice paddy
ryży [ri-zhi] adj. m. red (haired);
russet; ginger; foxy (person);
red-brown; ginger-haired
rzadki [zhad-kee] adj. m. rare;
thin; watery; weak; loose
rzadko [zhad-ko] adv. seldom;
thinly; rarely; far apart; exceptionally; sparsely
rzadkość [zhad-kośhćh] f. rarity; sparseness; curiosity; curio; rareness; thinness
rząd [zhownt] m. row; rank; file;

line up; government; rule
rządca [zhownd-tsa] m.
administrator; land steward
rządowy [zhown-do-vi] adj. m.
governmental; government-;
state-(schools, administration)
rządzić [zhown-dźheećh] v.
rule over; govern; control; direct; be in power; run; boss
rzec [zhets] v. say; utter
rzecz [zhech] m. thing; matter;
act; stuff; deal; work; subject;
theme; object; business; concern; point; purpose; question
rzeczka [zhech-ka] f. small river;
river; brook; (small) stream
rzecznik [zhech-ńeek] m.
spokesman; attorney; patent
agent; intercessor; advocate
rzeczownik [zhe-chov-ńeek] m.
noun; substantive (grammar)
rzeczowo [zhe-cho-vo] adv.
factually; terse; business like;
to the point; objectively
rzeczoznawca [zhe-cho-znav-tsa]
m. expert; specialist (authority
in a special field)
rzeczpospolita [zhech-pos-po-lee-
-ta] f. republic; commonwealth
rzeczywistość [zhe-chi-vees-
-tośhćh] f. reality; actuality
rzeczywisty [zhe-chi-vees-ti] adj.
m. real; actual; virtual
rzednieć [zhed-ńećh] v. grow
thin; become rare; scatter;
thin; become scarce; disperse
rzeka [zhe-ka] f. river; stream
rzekomo [zhe-ko-mo] adv. would
be; allegedly; supposedly; by
all accounts; pretendedly
rzekomy [zhe-ko-mi] adj. m.
make believe; reputed; supposed; sham; alleged; imaginary; so called; would be
rzemień [zhe-myeń] m. leather
strap; leather bond; leather
belt; thong; shoulder strap
rzemieślniczy [zhe-myeśhl-ńee-
-chi] adj. m. trade; craft-
rzemieślnik [zhe-myeśhl-ńeek]
m. artisan; craftsman; mechanic; tradesman
rzemiosło [zhe-myos-wo] n.

(handi) craft; craft; trade; job;
business; craftsmanship
rzemyk [zhe-mik] m. thong;
leather strap; chin strap
rzepa [zhe-pa] f. turnip
rzepak [zhe-pak] m. rape-seed
rzesza [zhe-sha] f. crowd; Reich
throng; multitude; mass(es)
rzeszoto [zhe-sho-to] n. sieve
rześki [zheśh-kee] adj. m.
lively; brisk; spry; fresh
rześkość [zheśh-kośhćh] f.
vigor; sprightliness; briskness
rzetelny [zhe-tel-ni] adj. m.
honest; upright; fair; real;
straightforward; just; reliable
rzewny [zhev-ni] adj. m. wistful
moving; touching; mournful
rzezać [zhe-zaćh] v. slaughter;
castrate; circumcise (ritually)
rzezimieszek [zhe-źhee-mye-
-shek] m. cutpurse; thief; pickpocket; cutthroat; criminal
rzeź [zheźh] f. carnage; massacre; slaughter; shambles;
carnage; butchering (people)
rzeźba [zheźh-ba] f. sculpture
rzeźbiarstwo [zheźh-byar-stvo]
n. sculpture; sculpturing
rzeźbiarz [zheźh-byash] m.
sculptor (a creating artist)
rzeźbić [zheźh-beećh] v.
carve; cut; sculpture; weather
(the earth, mountains, etc.)
rzeźnia [zheźh-ńa] f. slaughter
-house; knackery (for horses)
rzeźnik [zheźh-ńeek] m.
butcher; brutal killer
rzeźwić [zheźh-veećh] v. refresh; cool; invigorate; sober
rzeźwość [zheźh-vośhćh] f.
agility; briskness; sprightliness
rzeźwy [zheźh-vi] adj. m. agile;
brisk; smart; spry; lively; refreshing; bracing; crisp (air)
rzeżączka [zhe-zhownch-ka] f.
gonorrhea (a venereal disease)
rzędem [zhan-dem] adv. in a row
rzędna [zhand-na] f. ordinate
rzępolić [zhan-po-leećh] v.
scrape (on fiddle); rasp (on the
fiddle, violin, etc.); fiddle
rzęsa [zhan-sa] f. eyelash

rzęsisty [zhan-**shees**-ti] adj. m.
profuse; heavy; abundant; copious; perky; warm (applause)
rzęzić [zhan-źheećh] v. death
rattle; ruckle (in sickness)
rznąć [zhnownćh] v. cut;
carve; butcher; saw; slaughter; vulg.: screw; have sex
rzodkiew [zhod-kyev] f. radish
rzodkiewka [zhod-kyev-ka] f.
radish (the pungent root)
rzucać [zhoo-tsaćh] v. throw;
fling; pitch; dash; hurl; toss;
chuck at; lay down; leave
rzucić [zhoo-ćheećh] v. throw;
cast; plunge; dash; pitch; fling
rzut [zhoot] m. throw; cast;
projection; view; sketch
rzutki [zhoot-kee] adj. m. brisk;
lively; enterprising; active
rzutkość [zhoot-koshćh] f.
briskness; initiative
rzyć [zhićh] v. f. (vulg.) ass
rzygać [zhi-gaćh] v. vomit;
belch out; spew; eject; emit
rzymski [zhim-skee] adj. m.
Roman; of Rome (church, rite)
rżeć [rzhećh] v. whinny; neigh
rżnąć [rzhnownćh] v. cut;
saw; engrave; carve; butcher;
bang; play cards; do with
zest; (vulg.) screw; have sex;
rżnięcie [rzhńan-ćhe] n. colic;
bellyache; (slang) beating
rżysko [rzhis-ko] n. stubble-field;
rye field; short, bristly growth

S

sabat [sa-bat] m. Sabbath
sabotaż [sa-bo-tash] m.
sabotage; act of sabotage
sacharyna [sa-kha-ri-na] f.
saccharin (a sugar substitute)
sad [sad] m. orchard
sadło [sad-wo] n. lard; suet
sadowić [sa-do-veećh] v. place;

show to a seat; seat
sadownik [sa-dov-ńeek] m. fruit
-grower; fruit farmer; orchard-
ist; orchard-man (owner)
sadyba [sa-di-ba] f. dwelling-
house; human habitation;
home; abode; hamlet; village
sadysta [sa-dis-ta] m. sadist
sadza [sa-dza] f. soot; black
sadzać [sa-dzaćh] v. show to a
seat; seat; make sit down
sadzawka [sa-dzav-ka] f. pool
sadzić [sa-dźheećh] v. plant
(seedlings, etc.); set; run;
grow; speed; stud (decorate)
sadzonka [sa-dzon-ka] f.
seedling; quick-set; cutling
sadzone jajka [sa-dzo-ne yay-ka]
s. fried eggs sunny side up
safanduła [sa-fan-doo-wa] f.
bungler; yes-man; oaf; muff;
duffer; clumsy spoiler
safian [sa-fyan] m. morocco
(leather); saffian (leather)
sagan [sa-gan] m. kettle; pot
sak [sak] m. dip-net; sack
sakrament [sa-kra-ment] m.
sacrament (of matrimony etc.)
sakwa [sak-fa] f. wallet; purse
money-bag; travelling bag;
feed bag; (horse's) nose bag
sala [sa-la] f. hall; room
sala [sa-la] f. audience (in a hall)
salaterka [sa-la-ter-ka] f. salad
bowl; vegetable dish
salceson [sal-tse-son] m. head
-cheese; (mock) brawn
saletra [sa-let-ra] f. niter;
saltpeter; potassium nitrate
salina [sa-lee-na] f. salt-works;
saline; salt mine
salmiak [sal-myak] m. ammonium
chloride; sal-ammoniac
salon [sa-lon] m. drawing-room
salonka [sa-lon-ka] f. club car
(railroad); parlor car
salutować [sa-loo-to-vaćh] v.
salute; dip the flag
salwa [sal-va] f. volley; salvo
sałata [sa-wa-ta] f. lettuce; salad
sam [sam] adj. m. alone; oneself; myself; yourself; nothing
but; very; right; mere

samica [sa-mee-tsa] f. female
samiec [sa-myets] m. male
samobójca [sa-mo-booy-tsa]
m.suicide; suicidal man
samobójczy [sa-mo-booy-chi] adj.
m. suicidal; leading to suicide
samobójstwo [sa-mo-booy-stvo]
n. suicide; act of killing
oneself, committing suicide
samochód [sa-mo-khood] m.
mobile; car; motor car
samochwał [sa-mo-khvaw] m.
braggart; boaster; blow hard
samodział [sa-mo-dźhaw] m.
homespun (cloth)
samodzielność [sa-mo-dźhel-
-nośhćh] f. independence
samodzielny [sa-mo-dźhel-ni]
adj. m. self-reliant; independent; self-contained
samogłoska [sa-mo-gwos-ka] f.
vowel; vocal (speech sound)
samogon [sa-mo-gon] m.
moonshine (unlawfully made)
samoistny [sa-mo-eest-ni] adj. m.
independent; autonomous
samokrytyka [sa-mo-kri-ti-ka] f.
self-criticism; self-accusation
samokształcenie [sa-mo-kshtaw-
-tse-ńe] n. self-education
samolot [sa-mo-lot] m. airplane
samolub [sa-mo-loob] m. egoist
samolubstwo [sa-mo-loob-stvo]
n. selfishness; egoism
samolubny [sa-mo-loob-ni] adj.
m. selfish; self-seeking;
egoistic; conceited
samoobrona [sa-mo-o-bro-na] f.
self-defense
samopas [sa-mo-pas] adv. alone;
by oneself; loosely; unheeded
samopoczucie [sa-mo-po-choo-
-ćhe] n. frame of mind; self-
consciousness; feeling (good)
samopomoc [sa-mo-po-mots] f.
self-help; mutual aid (society)
samorodek [sa-mo-ro-dek] m.
(gold) nugget of native gold
samorodny [sa-mo-rod-ni] adj. m.
autogenous; natural; virgin
samorząd [sa-mo-zhownt] m.
autonomy; self-government
samotnik [sa-mot-ńeek] m.

recluse; hermit; solitary; rogue
samostanowienie [sa-mo-sta-no-
-vye-ńe] n. self-determination
samotność [sa-mot-nośhćh] f.
solitude; loneliness; retirement
samouctwo [sa-mo-oots-tvo] n.
self-education; self instruction
samouczek [sa-mo-oo-chek] m.
handbook (for self-instruction)
samouk [sa-mo-ook] m. self
-taught (man, person, etc.)
samowładczy [sa-mo-vwad-chi]
adj. m. autocratic; arbitrary
samowola [sa-mo-vo-la] f.
license (arbitrariness); law-
lessness (abuse of freedom)
samowystarczalny [sa-mo-vis-tar-
-chal-ni] adj. m. self-sufficient;
self contained; unsubsidized
samozachowawczy instynkt [sa-
-mo-za-kho-vav-chi een-stinkt]
m. self-preservation instinct
samozapalenie się [sa-mo-za-pa-
-le-ńe śhan] n. spontaneous
combustion; self ignition
samozwaniec [sa-mo-zva-ńets]
m. usurper; pretender
sanatorium [sa-na-tor-yoom] m.
sanitorium; sanatorium
sandacz [san-dach] m. perch-
-pike (a fresh water fish)
sandał [san-daw] m. sandal
sanie [sa-ńe] pl. sleigh; sledge
sanitariuszka [sa-ńee-tar-yoosh-
-ka] f. nurse (military, etc.)
sanitarny [sa-ńee-tar-ni] adj. m.
sanitary; of sanitation; health-
sankcja [sank-tsya] f. sanction
(international, etc.); approval
sankcjonować [sank-tsyo-no-
-vaćh] v. sanction; authorize
sanki [san-kee] pl. sled; sleigh
sanskryt [san-skrit] m. Sanskrit;
Sanscrit; old Aryan language
sapać [sa-paćh] v. gasp; pant;
heave; snort; puff and blow;
chug; breathe heavily; wheeze
saper [sa-per] m. combat engineer; sapper; army engineer
sardynka [sar-din-ka] f. sardine
sarkać [sar-kaćh] v. grumble
at (against); complain about
(at); snort out (an order etc.)

sarkastyczny [sar-kas-tich-ni] adj.
m. sarcastic (smile etc.)
sarna [sar-na] f. roe deer
sarnia skóra [sar-ńa skoo-ra] f.
buckskin; roe deer's hide
satelita [sa-te-lee-ta] f. satellite;
attendant; planet pinion
satyna [sa-ti-na] f. satin
satyra [sa-ti-ra] f. satire
satysfakcja [sa-tis-fak-tsya] f.
satisfaction; compensation
sączyć się [sown-chićh śhan]
v. drip; trickle; distill; sift;
ooze out; seep; percolate
sąd [sownd] m. judgment; court
sądownictwo [sown-dov-ńeets-
-tvo] n. judicature; jurisdiction
sądowy [sown-do-vi] adj. m.
judicial; of court; judiciary
sądzić [sown-dźheećh] v. try;
judge; think; believe; expect;
guess; pass judgement; doom
sąg [sowng] m. cord (of wood)
sąsiad [sown-śhad] m. neighbor
sąsiadka [sown-śhad-ka] f.
neighbor; lady next door
sąsiedni [sown-śhed-ńee]
adj. m. adjacent; neighboring
sąsiedztwo [sown-śhedz-tvo] n.
neighborhood; nearness; proxi-
mity; vicinity; environs
sążeń [sown-zheń] m. fathom;
cord; approximately six feet
scalić [stsa-leećh] v. integrate
scedzić [stse-dźheećh] v.
strain off; decant (a liquid);
pour off (a liquid)
scena [stse-na] f. scene; stage
scenariusz [stse-nar-yoosh] m.
scenario; script; screenplay
sceneria [stse-ner-ya] f. scenery;
stage decorations; backdrops
sceptyczny [stsep-tich-ni] adj. m.
skeptic; skeptical (smile etc.)
sceptyk [stsep-tik] m. skeptic
schab [skhab] m. pork chop
schadzka [skhadz-ka] f. date
scheda [skhe-da] f. inheritance;
inheritance; heirloom
schemat [skhe-mat] m. scheme;
plan; draft; outline; diagram
schematyczny [skhe-ma-tich-ni]
adj. m. schematic (drafting...)

schizma [skheez-ma] f. schism
schlebiać [skhle-byaćh] v.
flatter; wheedle; adulate; gratify somebody's whims, fancies
schludny [skhlood-ni] adj. m.
neat; clean; trim; slick; tidy
schnąć [skhnownćh] v. dry;
dry up; wane; waste; parch;
wither; become dry; go dry
schodki [skhod-kee] pl. steps
(small); small stairs
schodowa klatka [skho-do-va
klat-ka] staircase
schody [skho-di] pl. stairs
schodzić [skho-dźheećh] v.
get down; go down stairs;
step down; come (walk) down
scholastyka [skho-las-ti-ka] f.
scholasticism; Scholasticism
schorowany [skho-ro-va-ni] adj.
m. invalid; ailing; ill; sick
schować [skho-vaćh] v. hide;
pocket; conceal; put away;
tuck away; save (for future)
schowek [skho-vek] m. closet;
safe; hiding place; recess
schód [skhood] m. stair; step
schron [skhron] m. shelter;
pillbox; air raid shelter etc.
schronić się [skhro-ńeećh
śhan] v. take refuge; take
cover; find shelter (from the
cold, the rain, etc.);
schronisko [skhro-ńees-ko] n.
shelter; hiding place; refuge
schudnięcie [skhood-ńan-ćhe]
n. loss of fat; loss of weight;
slimming down; slimming
schwycić [skhvi-ćheećh] v.
seize; catch hold of; grasp
schylać [skhi-laćh] v. bend;
bow; incline; stoop down
schyłek [skhi-wek] m. decline
scyzoryk [stsi-zo-rik] m. pocket
knife; clasp knife; pen knife
seans [se-ans] m. seance; sitting; showing; performance
secesja [se-tses-ya] f. secession;
Secession style (architecture)
sedes [se-des] m. toilet seat
sedno [sed-no] n. crux; core;
gist; essence (of the matter)
sejm [seym] m. Polish parliament

(bicameral since 1493)

sekcja [sek-tsya] f. dissection; section; cross-section; division

sekret [se-kret] m. secret

sekretarz [se-kre-tash] m. secretary; reporter; minuter

seksualny [se-ksoo-al-ni] adj. m. sexual; sex- (appeal, urge)

sekta [sek-ta] f. sect

sektor [sek-tor] m. sector

sekunda [se-koon-da] f. second

sekundnik [se-koond-ńeek] m. second-hand (of a watch)

sekutnica [se-koot-ńee-tsa] f. shrew; scold; vixen

seledynowy [se-le-di-no-vi] adj. m. aquamarine; willow green

selekcja [se-lek-tsya] f. selection (by elimination, natural, etc.)

seler [se-ler] m. celery

semafor [se-ma-for] m. semaphore (signaling system)

semicki [se-meets-kee] adj. m. Semitic (character etc.)

seminarium [se-mee-nar-yoom] n. seminar; seminary; training school (doing research)

sen [sen] m. sleep; slumber; dormancy; torpidity; dream

senat [se-nat] m. senate (in Poland evolved from royal council in XV c.); Upper House of the parliament

senator [se-na-tor] m. senator

senior [se-ńyor] m. senior

senny [sen-ni] adj. m. sleepy

sens [sens] m. sense; significance; meaning; point

sensacja [sen-sats-ya] f. sensation; a hit; making a hit

sensacyjny [sen-sa-tsiy-ni] adj. m. sensational; exciting

sentencja [sen-tents-ya] f. maxim; dictum; pronouncement; concise rule of conduct

sentyment [sen-ti-ment] m. sentiment; partiality; fondness; opinions and feelings combined

separacja [se-pa-rats-ya] f. separation (from bed and board); isolation (in general)

separatka [se-pa-rat-ka] f. private-room; solitary cell

separować [se-pa-ro-vaćh] v. separate (a couple); isolate

seplenić [se-ple-ńeećh] v. lisp; have a lisp; speak with lisp

ser [ser] m. (cottage etc.) cheese

serce [ser-tse] n. heart; kindness

sercowy [ser-tso-vi] adj. m. cardiac; love- (affair, secret, etc.); heart (attack, disease)

serdak [ser-dak] m. sleeveless (furred traditional) waistcoat

serdeczność [ser-dech-ńośhćh] f. cordiality; heartiness; caresses; warmth; love

serdeczny [ser-dech-ni] adj. m. hearty; cordial; sincere

serdelek [ser-de-lek] m. small sausage (specially smoked)

serenada [se-re-na-da] f. serenade (music and song at night under lady's window)

seria [ser-ya] f. series; chain; set; train (of events etc.)

serio [ser-yo] adv. seriously

sernik [ser-ńeek] m. cheesecake; (biology) casein

serwatka [ser-vat-ka] f. whey

serweta [ser-ve-ta] f. (small) table cloth; doily; serviette

serwetka [ser-vet-ka] f. napkin

serwilizm [ser-vee-leezm] m. servility; humbly submission

serwis [ser-vees] m. dinner set; service (tennis); turn of serving; set; tea-service etc.

serwować [ser-vo-vaćh] v. serve; do services; aid; help

seryjny [se-riy-ni] adj. m. serial; consecutive; repetitive (work)

sesja [ses-ya] f. session; sitting

setka [set-ka] f. hundred, 100

setny [set-ni] adj. m. hundredth

sezon [se-zon] m. season

sędzia [san-dźha] m. judge; referee; magistrate; umpire

sędziwy [san-dźhee-vi] adj. m. aged; old; grey headed; hoary; ancient; of great antiquity

sęk [sank] m. knot; knag; knar

sękaty [san-ka-ti] adj. m. knotty; knaggy; gnarly; nodose; rugged; obstinate; self-willed

sęp [sanp] m. vulture

sfera [sfe-ra] f. sphere; zone atmosphere; area; domain; orb
sferyczny [sfe-rich-ni] adj. m. spherical (geometry, triangle)
sfinks [sfeenks] m. sphinx
sfora [sfo-ra] f. pack of dogs
siać [śhaćh] v. sow (corn); sift; loose; drop; spread; pour
siadać [śha-daćh] v. sit down; take a seat; get stranded; go flat; squat down; go aground
siano [śha-no] n. hay
sianokosy [śha-no-ko-si] pl. hay-making; hay cutting
siarczan [śhar-chan] m. sulfate
siarka [śhar-ka] f. sulfur
siarkowy [śhar-ko-vi] adj. m. sulfuric (acid etc.)
slatka [śhat-ka] f. net; screen
siatkówka [śhat-koov-ka] f. retina (anatomy); volley-ball
siąść [śhownéhćh] v. sit down; take a seat (a chair)
sidło [śheed-wo] n. snare; trap
siebie [śhe-bye] pron. (for) self; oneself; one; each other
siec [śhets] v. cut; mow; whip
sieczka [śhech-ka] f. chop straw; chaff; (empty) head
sieczna [śhech-na] f. secant
sieczna broń [śhech-na broń] f. cutting weapons
sieć [śhećh] f. net; network; grid; fishing net; trap; snare; web; ramification (of a plot); system; network; grid; mains
siedem [śhe-dem] num. seven
siedemdziesiąt [śhe-dem-dźhe- -śhownt] num. seventy; 70
siedemdziesiąty [śhe-dem- -dźhe-śhown-ti] num. seventieth; 70th
siedemnasty [śhe-dem-nas-ti] num. seventeenth; 17th
siedemnaście [śhe-dem-naśh- -ćhe] num. seventeen; 17
siedemset [śhe-dem-set] num. seven hundred; 700
siedlisko [śhed-lees-ko] n. seat; abode; habitation; hotbed (of sedition, etc.); nest; habitat
siedmiokrotny [śhed-myo-krot- -ni] adj. m. seven-fold

siedmioletni [śhed-myo-let-ńee] adj. m. seven year (old, etc.)
siedzący [śhe-dzown-tsi] adj. m. sitting (posture); sedentary
siedzenie [śhe-dze-ńe] n. seat; (person's) bottom; behind
siedziba [śhe-dźhee-ba] f. seat; abode; habitat (of an animal); seat (of government, etc.)
siedzieć [śhe-dźhećh] v. sit (stay); be perched; be settled
siejba [śhey-ba] f. sowing; sowing time; sowing season
siekacz [śhe-kach] m. incisor; chopping knife; chopper
siekanina [śhe-ka-ńee-na] f. hash; chopping up; cutting up
siekiera [śhe-kye-ra] f. hatchet; small axe; small hatchet
sielanka [śhe-lan-ka] f. idyll
sielankowy [śhe-lan-ko-vi] adj. m. idyllic; pastoral; rural; bucolic; of a pastoral life
sielski [śhel-skee] adj. m. rural; idyllic; pastoral; rural
siemię [śhe-myan] n. bird seed
siennik [śhen-ńeek] m. straw -mattress; pallet; paillasse
sień [śheń] f. hallway; corridor; vestibule; entrance hall (of a manorial residence)
siepacz [śhe-pach] m. (rough) henchman; hired assassin
sierota [śhe-ro-ta] f. m. orphan; lonesome person; poor fellow
sierp [śherp] m. sickle
sierpień [śher-pyeń] m. August
sierść [śherśhćh] f. hair (coat); fur; game beasts
sierżant [śher-zhant] m. sergeant (military rank)
siew [śhev] m. sowing; seeds
siewca [śhev-tsa] m. sower
siewnik [śhev-ńeek] m. seeder; sowing-machine (for wheat)
się [śhan] pron. self (oneself, myself, etc.; of itself, by itself, one, you); each other
sięgać [śhan-gaćh] v. reach
sikać [śhe-kaćh] v. squirt; spout; gush; piss (vulg.)
sikawka [śhee-kav-ka] f. fire hose; squirt; fire engine

sikora [śhee-ko-ra] f. titmouse
siksa [śheek-sa] f. hussy of low
morals; small girl piddler
silnik [śheel-ńeek] m. motor
silnik spalinowy [śheel-ńeek
spa-lee-no-vi] combustion
engine (oil or gas fuel)
silny [śheel-ni] adj. m. strong;
powerful; mighty; hefty; lusty;
sturdy; stiff; robust; nasty
silos [see-los] m. silo; (store) pit
siła [śhee-wa] f. force; might;
strength; power; energy; vigor
siła [śhee-wa] f. many; much
siłacz [śhee-wach] m. strong-
man; athlete; weight lifter
siłownia [śhee-wov-ńa] f.
power plant; power station;
power house; electricity works
sinawy [śhee-na-vi] adj. m.
bluish; somewhat blue
siniak [śhee-ńak] m. bruise
sinus [see-noos] m. sine of an
angle (trigonometric function)
siny [śhee-ni] adj. m. livid; blue;
purple; blue in the face
siodełko [śho-dew-ko] n. bicycle
seat; small (pony) saddle
siodlarz [śhod-lash] m. saddler
siodłać [śhod-waćh] v. saddle
siodło [śhod-wo] n. saddle
sioło [śho-wo] n. hamlet; village
siostra [śhos-tra] f. sister
siostrzenica [śhos-tshe-ńee-tsa]
f. niece
siostrzeniec [śhos-tshe-ńets] m.
nephew
siostrzyczka [śhos-tshich-ka] f.
little sister
siódemka [śhoo-dem-ka] f.
seven; 7
siódmy [śhood-mi] num.
seventh; 7th
sito [śhee-to] n. sieve; strainer
sitowie [śhee-to-vye] n. bulrush
siusiać [śhoo-śhaćh] v. tinkle;
urinate; piss; pee; piddle
siwek [śhee-vek] m. gray horse
siwieć [śhee-vyećh] v. grow
gray; become gray-haired
siwucha [śhee-voo-kha] f. low
grade vodka; rot gut
siwy [śhee-vi] adj. m. gray;

blue; grizzly; gray-haired;
hoary; darkish; dreary
skafander [ska-fan-der] m. diving
suit; pressure suit; wind jacket
skakać [ska-kaćh] v. jump;
spring; bounce; leap; pop;
skip; dive; gambol; plunge
skakanka [ska-kan-ka] f. jumping
rope; skipping rope
skala [ska-la] f. scale; extent
skaleczenie [ska-le-che-ńe] n.
cut; injury; hurt; wound
skaleczyć [ska-le-chićh] v. hurt;
injure; cut; prick; wound
skalisty [ska-lees-ti] adj. m.
rocky (mountain, etc.)
skalp [skalp] m. scalp
skała [ska-wa] f. rock; stone
skamieniały [ska-mye-ńa-wi] adj.
m. petrified; fossil-; stone-
skamienieć [ska-mye-ńećh] v.
become petrified; turn into
stone; turn into rock
skandal [skan-dal] m. scandal
skarb [skarb] m. treasure;
treasury; riches; beloved
person; darling; love; hoard
skarbiec [skar-byets] m.
treasury; strong room; safe
deposit box; treasure-house
skarbnik [skarb-ńeek] m.
treasurer; cashier; paymaster
skarbonka [skar-bon-ka] f. piggy
bank; money box; poor box
skarcić [skar-ćheećh] v.
admonish; rebuke; reprimand;
scold; un-braid; rate
skarga [skar-ga] f. complaint;
suit; claim; charge; grievance
skarłowaciały [skar-wo-va-ćha-
-wi] adj. m. stunted; dwarfish
skarpa [skar-pa] f. scarp;
buttress; slope; escarpment
skarpetka [skar-pet-ka] f. sock; a
short stocking
skarżyć [skar-zhićh] v. sue;
denounce; complain; tell tales
skarżypyta [skar-zhi-pi-ta] m.
squealer; informer; telltale
skaza [ska-za] f. tarnish; brab;
blot; flaw; spot; speck
skazać [ska-zaćh] v. condemn;
sentence; pass judgement;

pass sentence; doom (to)

skazaniec [ska-za-ńets] m.
condemned man (to death)

skazić [ska-źheećh] v. spoil;
corrupt; adulterate; pollute

skąd [skownd] adv. from where;
since when; where from?

skądinąd [skownd-ee-nownt]
adv. otherwise; on the other
hand; from somewhere else

skąpić [skown-peećh] v.
skimp; stint; begrudge (food,
money, hospitality, etc.)

skąpiec [skown-pyets] m. miser

skąpstwo [skownp-stvo] n.
parsimony; avarice; stinginess

skąpy [skown-pi] adj. m. stingy;
scanty; meager; avaricious;
niggardly; miserly; mean

skiba [skee-ba] f. clod

skinąć [skee-nownćh] v. signal;
motion; nod; bow (one's head)

skinienie [skee-ńe-ńe] n. nod;
bow; sign; gesture; motion

sklejać [skle-yaćh] v. glue
together; stick; paste; patch

sklejka [skley-ka] f. plywood

sklep [sklep] m. store; shop

sklepienie [skle-pye-ńe] n. vault;
vaulting; dome; canopy

sklepikarz [skle-pee-kash] m.
shopkeeper; tradesman

sklepowa [skle-po-va] f.
saleslady; saleswoman

skleroza [skle-ro-za] f. sclerosis;
hardening of body tissues

skład [skwat] m. composition;
warehouse; store; framework

składać [skwa-daćh] v. make
up; compose; piece; fold; set
together; assemble; deposit

składacz [skwa-dach] m. type
-setter; compositor

składany [skwa-da-ni] adj. m.
compound; folding; collapsible;
miscellaneous; plicate (leaf)

składka [skwad-ka] f.
contribution; membership fee

składnia [skwad-ńa] f. syntax

składnica [skwad-ńee-tsa] f.
depository; warehouse; depot

składnik [skwad-ńeek] m.
ingredient; component; con-

stituent; element

składowe [skwa-do-ve] n. warehouse fee; storage charges

skłamać [skwa-maćh] v. tell a
lie; tell an untruth; lie

skłaniać [skwa-ńaćh] v. bend;
lean; incline; induce; impel;
dispose; prompt; determine to
do; bow down; defer to; rest

skłon [skwon] m. slope; bow

skłonność [skwon-nośhćh] f.
inclination to do; tendency to
do; disposition; proneness to

skłonny [skwon-ni] adj. m.
disposed; inclined; prone; apt

skłócić [skwoo-ćheećh] v. stir
up; agitate; cause to disagree

sknera [skne-ra] m. f. miser

skobel [sko-bel] m. staple

skoczek [sko-chek] m. jumper

skocznia [skoch-ńa] f. ski-jump
(rump); take off ramp

skoczny [skoch-ni] adj. m. brisk;
lively; vivacious; saltatory

skoczyć [sko-chićh] v. leap;
jump; make a dash; hurry

skojarzenie [sko-ya-zhe-ńe] n.
association; union; conjunction

skok [skok] m. jump; leap; hop

skok tłoka [skok two-ka] m.
piston stroke (the length of)

skołatany [sko-wa-ta-ni] adj. m.
worn; battered; shattered

skołować [sko-wo-vaćh] v.
confound; muddle; exhaust

skomleć [skom-lećh] v. whine

skomplikowany [skom-plee-ko-
-va-ni] adj. m. complex; intricate; full of details

skonać [sko-naćh] v. expire;
die; pass away; stop living

skończyć [skoń-chićh] v.
finish; end; stop; have done

skoro [sko-ro] conj. after; at;
since; as; soon; if; once; as
soon as; now that; seeing that

skoro [sko-ro] adv. very soon; by
and by; quickly; as soon as

skoroszyt [sko-ro-shit] m. folder;
letter file; folder with letters

skorowidz [sko-ro-veetz] m.
index; indexed note book

skorpion [skor-pyon] m.

scorpion with poisonous sting

skorupa [sko-roo-pa] f. crust; shell; incrustation; carapace

skory [sko-ri] adj. m. quick; eager; prompt (to act); swift

skostniały [skost-ńa-wi] adj. m. ossified; numb; stiff; fossilized

skośny [skośh-ni] adj. m. slanting; oblique; inclined

skotłować [skot-wo-vaćh] v. whirl; bewilder; agitate; swirl; seethe; bother; drive crazy

skowronek [sko-vro-nek] m. lark; skylark (old-world songbird)

skowyczeć [sko-vi-chech] v. yelp; whine; squeal; whimper; whine with high-pitched sound

skowyt [sko-vit] m. yelp; squeal

skóra [skoo-ra] f. skin; hide; leather; coat; pelt; fell

skórka [skoor-ka] f. skin; peel; crust; cuticle; agnail; pelt; fur

skórny [skoor-ni] adj. m. cutaneous; dermal; skin-(disease department, etc.)

skórzany [skoo-zha-ni] adj. m. leather made; leathery; leather-(gloves, shoes, etc.)

skra [skra] f. spark (poetic)

skracać [skra-tsaćh] v. shorten; cut down; lessen; abridge

skradać się [skra-daćh śhan] v. steal up; creep up; advance stealthily; slink; sneak up

skraj [skray] m. border; edge; brink; margin; fringe; rand; outskirts; border; periphery

skrajać [skra-yaćh] v. cut off; cut (cloth); cut up (to pieces)

skrajność [skray-nośhćh] f. extremism; (the) extreme

skrajny [skray-ni] adj. m. extreme; intense; utmost; ultra; utter; radical; abject; dire

skrapiać [skra-pyaćh] v. damp; sprinkle; moisten; water

skraplać [skrap-laćh] v. liquefy; condense; precipitate

skrawek [skra-vek] m. shred; snip; strip; patch; chip; fragment; patch; pl. parings

skreślić [skreśh-leećh] v. sketch; cancel; jot down;

delete; erase; depict; note

skręcać [skran-tsaćh] v. twist; turn off; break (neck); strand

skrępować [skran-po-vaćh] v. tie up; restrict; embarrass; impede; cramp; hinder; cumber

skręt [skrant] m. twist; twisting; turn; torsion; veer; winding

skrobaczka [skro-bach-ka] f. rasp; scrapper; foot scrapper

skrobać [skro-baćh] v. scrape; rasp; scratch; scale (fish); tread on; stab; spear; scribble

skromny [skrom-ni] adj. m. coy; modest; simple; lowly; chaste; unassuming; scant; frugal

skroń [skroń] f. temple

skropić [skro-peećh] v. liquefy; sprinkle; water; moisten; damp

skrócić [skroo-ćheećh] v. abbreviate; shorten; cut down; curtail; lessen; abridge

skrót [skroot] m. abbreviation

skrucha [skroo-kha] f. contrition; repentance; compunction

skrupulatny [skroo-poo-lat-ni] adj. m. scrupulous; precise; exact; conscientious

skrupuł [skroo-poow] m. scruple

skruszyć [skroo-shićh] v. crumble; crush; bring to repentance; break down

skrycie [skri-ćhe] adv. secretly

skryć [skrićh] v. hide; obscure

skrypt [skript] m. script; mimeographed lecture; I.O.U.

skrytka pocztowa [skrit-ka poch--to-va] post office box

skrytość [skri-tośhćh] f. secrecy; secretiveness

skryty [skri-ti] adj. m. underhanded; secret; reticent

skrzek [skshek] m. scream; croak; frog-spawn; screeching

skrzep [skshep] m. clot; coagulation (of blood); grume

skrzepnąć [skshep-nownćh] v. clot; coagulate; set; freeze; solidify; congeal; stiffen; acquire new vigor; harden

skrzątnie [skshant-ńe] adv. sedulously; diligently; busily

skrzątny [skshant-ni] adj. m.

industrious; busy; diligent
skrzydlaty [skshi-dla-ti] adj. m.
winged; wing shaped
skrzydło [skshid-wo] n. wing of
(bird, plane, insect); leaf; brim;
(fan) arm; extension; flank
skrzynia [skshi-ńa] f. chest; bin;
box; hutch; case; crate; coffer
skrzynka [skshin-ka] f. box;
chest; (gear) case; coffer
skrzynka biegów [skshin-ka bye-
-goov] f. gearbox; gear case
skrzypce [skship-tse] n. violin;
fiddle; person playing fiddle
skrzypek [skshi-pek] m. violinist;
violin player; fiddler
skrzypieć [skshi-pyećh] v.
crunch; creak; screech; grind;
squeak; gride; scratch; gride
skrzywiać [skshi-vyaćh] v.
bend; distort (facts); twist;
contort; put awry; make faces
skrzyżowanie dróg [skshi-zho-va-
-ńe droog] pl. f. cross-roads;
crossing; intersection
skrzyżowany [skshi-zho-va-ni]
adj. m. crossbred
skubać [skoo-baćh] v. nibble;
pluck; pick; fleece; graze;
tease; pinch; nibble; browse
skuć [skooćh] v. shackle; chain
skulić [skoo-leećh] v. curl up;
cuddle up; squat; lie low;
crouch; bend one's shoulders
skup [skoop] m. purchasing
center (of farm products, etc.)
skupiać [skoo-pyaćh] v. concentrate; bring together; gather; collect; rally; cluster
skupienie [skoo-pye-ńe] n.
concentration; focussing; compression; conglomeration
skupiony [skoo-pyo-ni] adj. m.
collected; concentrated; dense
skupować [skoo-po-vaćh] v.
buy; buy up; keep buying; buy
out; purchase (a lot)
skurcz [skoorch] m. cramp;
shrinking; spasm; twitch;
systole; contraction
skurczyć [skoor-chićh] v. draw
in; shrink; contract; lessen;
diminish; retract; reduce

skuteczność [skoo-tech-
-nośhćh] f. efficiency; efficacy; good result, results
skutecznie [skoo-tech-ńe] adv.
with good result; effectively
skuteczny [skoo-tech-ni] adj. m.
effective; efficient; operative
skutek [skoo-tek] m. effect;
result; outcome; consequence
skuter [skoo-ter] m. motor-
-scooter; scooter
skutkować [skoot-ko-vaćh] v.
have effect; work; operate
skwapliwy [skvap-lee-vi] adj. m.
eager; willing; ready
skwar [skvar] m. scorching heat
skwarek [skva-rek] m. crackling
skwaśniały [skvaśh-ńa-wi] adj.
m. sour; turned sour; glum
skwer [skver] m. square
słabiutki [swa-byoot-kee] adj. m.
very weak (in diminutive)
słabnąć [swab-nownćh] v.
weaken; grow feeble; decline;
diminish; grow weaker; abate
słabość [swa-bośhćh] f. infirmity; weakness; illness; debility; fragility; impotence
słabowity [swa-bo-vee-ti] adj. m.
weakly; feeble; fragile; puny
słaby [swa-bi] adj. m. weak;
frail; feeble; infirm; faint;
flimsy; poor; lacking character
słać [swaćh] v. send; make
bed; spread (a table cloth etc.)
słaniać się [swa-ńaćh śhan]
v. totter; stagger; lurch; reel
sława [swa-va] f. glory; renown;
fame; celebrity; reputation; repute; good (ill) name; celebrity
sławetny [swa-vet-ni] adj. m.
notorious; famous; ill famous
sławić [swa-veećh] v. praise;
celebrate; glorify; laud; blazon
sławny [swav-ni] adj. m. famous; glorious; celebrated; illustrious; well-known; of note
słodkawy [swod-ka-vi] adj. m.
sweetish; slightly sweet
słodki [swod-kee] adj. m. sweet
słodycze [swo-di-che] pl. sweets
słodzić [swo-dźheećh] v. sugar; sweeten; put some sugar

słoik [swo-eek] m. jar; gallipot; glass; pot; little jar

słojowaty [swo-yo-**va**-ti] adj. m. grained; veined; showing grain

słoma [swo-ma] f. straw

słomianka [swo-myan-ka] f. straw mat; doormat of straw; basket of plaited straw

słomiany wdowiec [swo-**mya**-ni vdo-vyets] m. grass widower

słomka [swom-ka] f. small straw

słonecznik [swo-nech-ńeek] m. sunflower (daisy-like flower)

słoneczny [swo-nech-ni] adj. m. sunny; solar (system, year, etc.); sun-(bath, rays, spots)

słonina [swo-ńee-na] f. lard

słoniowa kość [swo-ńo-va kośhćh] f. ivory (tusk)

słonka [swon-ka] f. wood-cock

słony [swo-ni] adj. m. salty

słoń [swoń] m. elephant

słońce [swoń-tse] n. sun; sunlight (self-luminous)

słota [swo-ta] f. foul weather

słotny dzień [swot-ni dźheń] m. rainy day; bad weather day

słowacki [swo-**vats**-kee] adj. m. Slovak; Slovakian: of Slovakia

słowianin [swo-vya-ńeen] m. Slav (of the Slavic group)

słowiański [swo-vyań-skee] adj. m. Slav; Slavonic; of Slavdom

słowik [swo-veek] m. nightingale; good singer

słownictwo [swov-ńeets-tvo] n. vocabulary; list of words

słownik [swov-ńeek] m. dictionary; vocabulary; language (word listing book)

słowny [swov-ni] adj. m. verbal; reliable; dependable (man)

słowo [swo-vo] n. word

słoworód [swo-vo-rood] m. etymology; origin of words

słowotwórstwo [swo-vo-tvoor--stvo] n. word formation

słód [swood] m. malt; grist

słój [swooy] m. jar; (annual tree) ring; pot; vain; grain

słówko [swoov-ko] n. (little or sweet) word; nice word

słuch [swookh] m. hearing

słuchacz [**swoo**-khach] m. listener; (university) student; hearer; auditor; pl. audience

słuchać [swoo-khaćh] v. hear; obey; listen; obey orders

słuchawka [swoo-**khav**-ka] f. (tel.) receiver; earphone

słuchowisko [swoo-kho-**vees**-ko] n. radio-(drama, play, comedy, etc.); broadcast drama

słuchy [swoo-khi] pl. rumors; (animal) ears; uncertain news

sługa [swoo-ga] f. servant

słup [swoop] m. pillar; column; post; pole; pylon; landmark

słupek [swoo-pek] m. pillaret; small post; stake; stud; rail

słuszność [swoosh-nośhćh] f. rightness; equity; rightfulness; legitimacy; aptness; justice

słuszny [swoosh-ni] adj. m. just; fair; right; pertinent; apt

służalczy [swoo-zhal-chi] adj. m. servile; cringing; subservient

służąca [swoo-zh**own**-tsa] f. maid; servant; cleaning woman; domestic woman servant

służący [swoo-zh**own**-tsi] m. servant; manservant; domestic

służba [swoozh-ba] pl. service

służbowy [swoozh-bo-vi] adj. m. official; business (trip etc.)

służyć [swoo-zhićh] v. serve

słychać [swi-khaćh] v. people say; one hears; be heard

słynąć [swi-**nown**ćh] v. be famed (renowned, celebrated)

słynny [swin-ni] adj. m. famous

słyszalny [swi-shal-ni] adj. m. audible; within hearing range

słyszeć [swi-shećh] v. hear

smacznego! [smach-ne-go] exp. (have a) good apatite!

smaczny [smach-ni] adj. m. **tasty**

smagać [sma-gaćh] v. lash; whip; flog; swish; slash

smagły [smag-wi] adj. m. swarthy; dark-complexioned

smak [smak] m. taste; relish; savor; palate; liking; appetite

smakołyk [sma-ko-wik] m. tidbit; delicacy; dainty; choice morsel

smakować [sma-**ko**-vaćh] v.

taste; relish; delight (in)
smakowity [sma-ko-**vee**-ti] adj.
  m. savory; appetizing; tasty
smalec [sma-lets] m. lard; fat
smar [smar] m. grease; lubricant
smarkać [smar-kaćh] v. blow
  one's nose; wipe one's nose
smarkacz [smar-kach] m. squirt;
  snot; whippersnapper; raw lad
smarkaty [smar-ka-ti] adj. m.
  snotty; callow; raw; nasty
smarować [sma-ro-vaćh] v.
  smear; oil; lubricate; grease
smarowidło [sma-ro-**veed**-wo] n.
  grease; lubricant; ointment
smażyć [sma-zhićh] v. fry;
  scorch; bake in the sun
smętny [sman-tni] adj. m.
  melancholy; blue; doleful
smoczek [smo-chek] m. nipple;
  pacifier; dummy; comforter
smok [smok] m. dragon; cowl
smoking [smo-king] m. dinner
  jacket; tuxedo; formal jacket
smolny [smol-ni] adj. m.
  resinous; pitchy; tarry
smoła [smo-wa] f. pitch; tar
smrodliwy [smrod-**lee**-vi] adj. m.
  rank; stinky; smelly; foul
smród [smroot] m. stench; fetor
smucić [smoo-ćheećh] v. sadden; grieve; afflict; distress
smukły [smook-wi] adj. m.
  slender; slim; willowy; gracile
smutek [smoo-tek] m. sorrow;
  sadness; grief; mournfulness
smutny [smoot-ni] adj. m. sad
smycz [smich] f. leash; dog lead
smyczek [smi-chek] m. (violin)
  bow; fiddle stick; pl. strings
smyk [smik] m. whippersnapper;
  brat; kid; small (lively) boy
snop [snop] m. sheaf; bunch
snop światła [snop shvyat-wa]
  light beam; light shaft
snuć [snoośh] v. spin; reel off
snycerz [sni-tsesh] m. sculptor
sobek [so-bek] m. egoist
sobota [so-bo-ta] f. Saturday
sobowtór [so-bov-toor] m.
  double; second (other) self
soból [so-bool] m. sable (fur)
sobór [so-boor] m. synod

socjalista [so-tsya-**lees**-ta] m.
  socialist (a believer)
socjalizacja [so-tsya-lee-**zats**-ya]
  f. socialization (nationalization)
socjalizm [so-**tsya**-leezm] m.
  socialism (state control etc.)
socjologia [so-tsyo-lo-gya] f.
  sociolog; social science
soczewica [so-che-**vee**-tsa] f.
  lentil; lentils (pottage)
soczewka [so-**chev**-ka] f. lens
soczysty [so-**chis**-ti] adj. m.
  juicy; sappy; mellow; coarse
soda [so-da] f. soda
sodowa woda [so-**do**-va **vo**-da] f.
  soda water (with sodium)
sofa [so-fa] f. lounge; sofa
sofistyczny [so-fees-**tich**-ni] adj.
  m. sophistical; captious
sojusz [so-yoosh] m. alliance
sojusznik [so-**yoosh**-ńeek] m.
  ally; associate joined for a
  common and specific purpose
sok [sok] m. sap; juice
sokół [so-koow] m. falcon
solanka [so-lan-ka] f. salt spring;
  salted bread roll; brine
solić [so-leećh] v. salt; add salt
solidarność [so-lee-**dar**-
  -noshćh] f. solidarity
Solidarność [so-lee-**dar**-
  -noshćh] s. Solidarity Labor
  Union formed in Poland (1980)
solidarny [so-lee-dar-ni] adj. m.
  solidary; sympathetic
solidny [so-**leed**-ni] adj. m. solid;
  firm; sound; reliable; safe
solista [so-**lees**-ta] f. soloist
soliter [so-lee-ter] m. tapeworm
  (parasite in the intestines); solitary tree; solitaire (gem)
solniczka [sol-**ńeech**-ka] f.
  salt-shaker; saltcellar
solo [so-lo] adv. solo
solny [sol-ni] adj. m. saline
solony [so-lo-ni] adj. m. salted;
  corned (beef); salt cured
sołtys [sow-tis] m. village head
  (officer below wójt)
sonata [so-na-ta] f. sonata
sonda [son-da] f. probe; feeler;
  sonde; searcher; explorer; plummet; lead; sounding balloon

sonet [so-net] m. sonnet
sopel [so-pel] m. icicle
sopran [sop-ran] m. soprano
sortować [sor-to-vaćh] v. sort
sos [sos] m. gravy; sauce
sosna [sos-na] f. pine (tree)
sośnina [sośh-ńee-na] f. pine
-wood; pine tree; pine branches; pine (boards) lumber
sowa [so-va] f. owl (bird)
sowiecki [so-vyets-kee] adj. m.
of Soviet Union; of the USSR
sowity [so-vee-ti] adj. m. lavish;
ample; abundant; plentiful
sód [sood] m. sodium (element)
sól [sool] f. salt (mineral)
spacerować [spa-tse-ro-vaćh]
v. walk; stroll; walk about
spacja [spats-ya] f. (print) space
spaczać [spa-chaćh] v. warp;
pervert; twist; distort
spaczenie [spa-che-ńe] n.
distortion; perversion; warp
spać [spaćh] v. sleep; slumber
spad [spat] m. slope; drop
spadać [spa-daćh] v. fall; drop
spadek [spa-dek] v. fall;
inheritance; downfall; slope;
dip; drop; decline; down grade
spadkobierca [spad-ko-byer-tsa]
f. heir; inheritor; successor
spadochron [spa-do-khron] m.
parachute (statichute, etc.)
spadzisty [spa-dźhees-ti] adj. m.
steep; sloping; precipitous
spajać [spa-yaćh] v. weld;
solder; link; joint; unite; bond
spalenizna [spa-le-ńeez-na] f.
(smell of) burning (smoke)
spalić [spa-leećh] v. burn out
spalony [spa-lo-ni] adj. m. parched; (sport) offside; burned up
sparzyć [spa-zhićh] v. burn;
sting; scald; blister; scorch
spasły [spas-wi] adj. m. fat
spaść [spaśhćh] v. fall; fatten
spawacz [spa-vach] m. welder
spawać [spa-vaćh] v. weld;
solder (pipes etc.); weld metal
spawanie [spa-va-ńe] n. welding
(of metals, structures, etc.)
spazm [spazm] m. spasm; convulsion; convulsive sobbing

spec [spets] m. specialist;
expert; craftsman; dab hand;
dab; sharp-(shooter, etc.))
specjalizacja [spe-tsya-lee-zats-
-ya] f. specialization; major
specjalność [spe-tsyal-
-nośhćh] f. specialty; peculiarity; specialty; special-
specjalny [spe-tsyal-ni] adj. m.
special; express; particular
specyficzny [spe-tsi-feech-ni] adj.
m. specific; peculiar; concrete
spedytor [spe-di-tor] m. shipping
agent; forwarding agent
spekulacja [spe-koo-lats-ya] f.
speculation; (business) venture
spekulant [spe-koo-lant] m.
profiteer; speculator; gambler
spekulować [spe-koo-lo-vaćh]
v. speculate; profiteer; gamble
spelunka [spe-loon-ka] f. joint
spełniać [spew-ńaćh] v. perform; fulfill; comply with; accomplish; answer; satisfy; do
spędzać [span-dzaćh] v. round
up (cattle); spend (time); a-
bort; drive away; gather; pass
(time); gather; bring together
spichlerz [speekh-lesh] m.
granary (storage of grain)
spiczasty [spee-chas-ti] adj. m.
pointed (sharply); peaked; acu-
minate; tapering; sharp
spiec [spyets] v. burn; scorch;
sun-blister; blush; parch; singe
spieniężyć [spye-ńan-zhićh] v.
cash (checks); sell (property)
spieniony [spye-ńo-ni] adj. m.
foamy; foaming; (horse, etc.)
covered with foam
spierać się [spye-raćh śhan] v.
argue; contend; quarrel; dispute; come off in the wash
spieszny [spyesh-ni] adj. m.
hasty; quick; hurried
spieszyć się [spye-shićh śhan]
v. hurry; dismount; be eager
spięcie [spyan-ćhe] n. buckle;
short circuit; collision; clash
spiętrzyć [spyan-tshićh] v. pile
up; heap up; bank up; dam up
spiker [spee-ker] m. (radio)
announcer; speaker

spinacz [spee-nach] m. fastener
spinać [spee-naćh] v. fasten;
pin up; clasp; spur (horse)
spinka [speen-ka] f. clasp
spirala [spee-ra-la] f. spiral; coil;
volute; helix; spiral glide
spiralny [spee-ral-ni] adj. m.
spiral; helical; involuted
spirytus [spee-ri-toos] m. spirits;
alcohol; rectified (proof) spirit
spis [spees] m. list; register;
inventory; record; roll; census
spis rzeczy [spees zhe-chi] table
(list, etc.) of contents
spisać [spee-saćh] v. record;
write down; make a list (of);
acquit oneself (well...)
spisek [spee-sek] f. plot
conspiracy; hatching a plot
spiskowiec [spees-ko-vyets] m.
conspirator; (secret) plotter
spiż [speezh] m. brass; bronze
spiżarnia [spee-zhar-ńa] f.
pantry; buttery; cupboard
spiżowy [spee-zho-vi] adj. m.
brass; bronze; booming (voice)
splatać [spla-taćh] v. braid;
interlace; interlock; plait
splątać [splown-taćh] v. snarl
up; mat; ravel; confuse; in-
terweave; interlace; muddle up
spleśniały [spleśh-ńa-wi]
adj. m. moldy; musty; mouldy;
mildewy; covered with fungus
splot [splot] m. twine; twist;
coil; tangle; plait coincidence
splunąć [sploo-nownćh] v. spit
spluwaczka [sploo-vach-ka] f.
spittoon; cuspidor
spłacić [spwa-ćheećh] v. pay
off; repay (a debt, a creditor)
spłaszczyć [spwash-chićh] v.
flatten out; humble (another)
spłata [spwa-ta] f. refund;
instalment payment; amortization; repayment; part payment
spłatać figla [spwa-taćh feeg-
-la] v. play a trick; play a joke
spław [spwav] m. rafting; river (flotilla) trade; floating
spławiać [spwa-vyaćh] v. float;
get rid; shunt; raft (timber);
participate in the river trade

spławik [spwa-veek] m. (fishing)
float (dipping when fish bites)
spławny [spwav-ni] adj. m. navigable (river, waterway, etc.)
spłodzi⌐ [spwo-dźheećh] v.
beget; generate; put out; produce; be delivered; cause
spłonąć [spwo-nownćh] v.
burn down; go up in flames;
be consumed by fire; redden
spłonka [spwon-ka] f. percussion
cap; primer; detonator
spłoszyć [spwo-shićh] v. scare
away; frighten; startle; flush
spłowiały [spwo-vya-wi] adj. m.
faded (appearance); discolored
spłukać [spwoo-kaćh] v. rinse;
flush; swill out; wash away
spływać [spwi-vaćh] v. flow
(down); drift (with the current,
down-stream); float (with the
current); be streaming (with)
spochmurnieć [spo-khmoor-
-ńećh] v. grow cloudy, gloomy; cloud over; grow sullen
spocić się [spo-ćheećh śhan]
v. sweat; become sweaty; be
in perspiration; perspire
spoczynek [spo-chi-nek] m. rest
spoczywać [spo-chi-vaćh] v.
sit; rest; lie down; be at rest;
rest on; sit down; lie; be at
spod [spod] prep. from under
spodek [spo-dek] m. saucer
spodenki [spo-den-kee] pl. knee
-pants; shorts; knickers
spodlić [spod-leećh] v. debase;
degrade; disgrace; demean
spodnie [spod-ńe] pl. trousers;
pants; slacks; breeches
spodobać się [spo-do-baćh
śhan] v. take a liking; take a
fancy; feel inclined (like)
spodziewać się [spo-dźhe-
-vaćh śhan] v. expect; hope
for; think that it will happen
spoglądać [spo-glown-daćh] v.
look out; look at; contemplate
spoić [spo-eećh] v. make
drunk; weld; ply with liquor
spoistość [spo-ees-tośhćh] f.
cohesion; compactness; density; tenacity; closeness; unity

spoisty [spo-**ees**-ti] adj. m.
compact; cohesive; dense; tenacious; closely packed; terse
spojenie [spo-**ye**-ńe] n. weld;
joint; public symphysis
spojówka [spo-**yoov**-ka] f.
conjunctiva (eyelid membrane)
spojrzeć [**spoy**-zhećh] v. look;
glance at; gaze at; view
spojrzenie [spoy-**zhe**-ńe] n.
glance; look; gaze; peep
spokojny [spo-**koy**-ni] adj. m.
quiet; calm; peaceful; still
spokój [**spo**-kooy] m. peace;
calm; quiet; serenity; placidity
spokrewniony [spo-krev-**ńo**-ni]
adj. m. related to; related
spoliczkować [spo-leech-ko-
-**vaćh**] v. slap in the face
społeczeństwo [spo-we-**cheń**-
-stvo] n. society; public;
community; the public; people
społeczny [spo-**wech**-ni] adj. m.
social (evil, psychology, etc.);
public; welfare; collective
społem [**spo**-wem] adv. together
in common; jointly; unitedly
spomiędzy [spo-**myan**-dzi] prep.
from among; from the midst
sponad [**spo**-nat] prep. from
above; from over (the top)
sponiewierać [spo-ńe-**vye**-raćh]
v. abuse; ill-treat; maltreat;
revile; batter; put in distress
spontaniczny [spon-ta-**ńeech**-ni]
adj. m. spontaneous; voluntary
sporadyczny [spo-ra-**dich**-ni] adj.
m. sporadic; occasional; stray
sporny [**spor**-ni] adj. m.
controversial; debatable; questionable; contestable; litigious
sporo [**spo**-ro] adv. good deal; a
lot of; briskly; quite a few
sport [**sport**] m. sport; athletics
sportowiec [spor-to-**vyets**] m.
sportsman; athlete; sporting
man (acting sportsmanlike)
spory [**spo**-ri] adj. m. pretty big;
fast; useful; considerable; fair
sporządzać [spo-**zhown**-dzaćh]
v. make up; draw up; make
out; prepare; write out
sposobić [spo-**so**-beećh] v.

prepare; make ready (colloquial exp.); make up for
sposobność [spo-**sob**-nośhćh]
f. opportunity to do; occasion
(much scope); chance for
sposobny [spo-**sob**-ni] adj. m.
convenient; capable; able
sposób [**spo**-soop] m. means;
way; manner; fashion; method
spostrzegać [spos-**tshe**-gaćh] v.
notice; perceive; observe; spot
spostrzegawczy [spos-tshe-**gav**-
-chi] adj. m. quick to notice;
keen; observant; perceptive
spostrzeżenie [spos-tshe-**zhe**-ńe]
n. observation; awareness; realization; remark; perception
spośród [**spośh**-rood] prep.
from among; from the midst
spotęgować [spo-**tan**-go-vaćh]
v. intensify; increase; intensify; strengthen; enhance
spotkać [**spot**-kaćh] v. come
across; meet; run across; befall; come across; happen; find
spotkanie [spot-**ka**-ńe] n.
meeting; date; encounter
spotwarzać [spo-**tva**-zhaćh] v.
calumniate; defame; slander
spoufalać się [spo-oo-**fa**-laćh
śhan] v. become intimate
spowiadać [spo-**vya**-daćh] v.
confess; listen to confession
spowiednik [spo-**vyed**-ńeek] m.
confessor; father confessor
spowiedź [**spo**-vyedźh] f.
confession; confided secrets
spowijać [spo-**vee**-yaćh] v.
swathe; wrap; shroud; cover
spowodować [spo-vo-**do**-vaćh]
v. cause; induce; set off
spoza [**spo**-za] prep. from
behind; from beyond; from
outside; from across
spozierać [spo-**źhe**-raćh] v.
glance at; look; gaze at
spożycie [spo-**zhi**-ćhe] n.
consumption; intake (food, calories, fluids, etc.)
spożywać [spo-**zhi**-vaćh] v.
consume; eat; drink; have a
meal; take (partake of) a meal
spożywca [spo-**zhiv**-tsa] m.

consumer (of food, etc.)
spożywcze artykuły [spo-zhiv--che ar-ti-koo-wi] pl. n.
groceries; food products
spód [spoot] m. bottom; foot
spódnica [spood-ńee-tsa] f.
skirt; petticoat; apron strings
spójnia [spooy-ńa] f. bond; link;
union; tie; glue; junction
spójnik [spooy-ńeek] m.
conjunction (grammar)
spółdzielczość [spoow-dźhel--chośhćh] f. cooperation
spółdzielnia [spoow-dźhel-ńa] f.
coop; cooperative (society)
spółgłoska [spoow-gwos-ka] f.
consonant (grammar)
spółka [spoow-ka] f. partnership;
(joint stock) company; society
spór [spoor] m. strife; dispute
spóźniać się [spooźh-ńaćh
śhan] v. be late; be slow; be
behind time; be delayed; lose
spóźnienie [spooźh-ńe-ńe] n.
delay; late coming; late arrival
spóźniony [spooźh-ńo-ni]
adj. m. late; delayed; belated;
tardy (excuses etc.); backward
spracować się [spra-tso-vaćh
śhan] v. be tired; be ex-
hausted; have worked hard
spracowany [spra-tso-va-ni] adj.
m. overworked; exhausted;
tired out (by too much work)
spragniony [sprag-ńo-ni] adj. m.
thirsty; thirsting for
sprawa [spra-va] f. affair;
matter; cause; case; question;
job; business; deal; action
sprawca [sprav-tsa] f. doer;
author; culprit; originator
sprawdzić [sprav-dźheećh] v.
verify; examine; test; check
sprawdzian [sprav-dźhan] m.
test; gauge; criterion; template
sprawiać [spra-vyaćh] v.
cause; bring to pass; occasion; afford; bring about; give
sprawiedliwość [spra-vyed-lee--vośhćh] f. justice; equity
sprawiedliwy [spra-vyed-lee-vi]
adj. m. just; righteous; fair
sprawka [sprav-ka] f. doing;

trick; small offense; prank
sprawność [sprav-nośhćh] f.
efficiency; dispatch; skill
sprawny [sprav-ni] adj. m. able;
efficient; deft; dexterous
sprawować [spra-vo-vaćh] v.
perform; discharge; hold;
exercise; fulfil (duties etc.)
sprawowanie [spra-vo-va-ńe] n.
conduct; behavior; performance; discharge (of duties)
sprawozdanie [spra-voz-da-ńe]
n. report; account; statement
sprawozdawca [spra-voz-dav-tsa]
m. reviewer; reporter
sprawunek [spra-voo-nek] m.
purchase (made while shopping); pl. shopping
sprężać [spran-zhaćh] v.
compress; tense; pre-stress
sprężarka [spran-zhar-ka] f.
compressor; air compressor
sprężenie [spran-zhe-ńe] n.
compression; prestress; pretension (of concrete, etc.)
sprężyna [spran-zhi-na] f. spring;
mainspring; impulse; incentive
sprężystość [spran-zhis--tośhćh] f. elasticity; energy;
resilience; buoyancy; firmness
sprężysty [spran-zhis-ti] adj. m.
elastic; springy; energetic
sprostować [spros-to-vaćh] v.
rectify; correct; right
sprostowanie [spros-to-va-ńe] n.
rectification; correction
sproszkować [sprosh-ko-vaćh]
v. pulverize; levigate; triturate
sprośny [sprośh-ni] adj. m.
obscene; lewd; foul (language)
sprowadzać [spro-va-dzaćh] v.
bring; import; fetch; call in
spróchniały [sprookh-ńa-wi] adj.
m. rotten; decayed; moulded
spróchnieć [sprookh-ńećh] v.
rot (wood, etc.); decay
(teeth); moulder; grow carious
spryciarz [spri-ćhash] m.
dodger; trickster; sly-boots
spryskać [spris-kaćh] v. splash
spryt [sprit] m. shrewdness;
cunning; gumption; knack
sprytny [sprit-ni] adj. m. tricky;

clever; cunning; cute

sprzączka [spshownch-ka] f.
buckle; clasp; fastening

sprzątaczka [spshown-tach-ka] f.
cleaning woman; charwoman

sprzątać [spshown-taćh] v.
tidy up; clean up (the mess,
etc.); clear up; pitch up; take
away; snatch away; remove

sprzątanie [spshown-ta-ńe] n.
clearing; tidying up; housework; house (office) cleaning

sprzeciw [spshe-ćheev] m.
objection; opposition; resistance; objection; demur

**sprzeciwiać się [spshe-ćhee-
-vyaćh śhan] v.** object;
oppose; stand against; resist

**sprzeczać się [spshe-chaćh
śhan] v.** fight; argue; dispute
(about); squabble; quarrel (a-
bout parking, etc.); contend

sprzeczka [spshech-ka] f.
quarrel; squabble; altercation;
tiff; flare-up; dispute

**sprzeczność [spshech-
-nośhćh] f.** contradiction;
discrepancy; inconsistency

sprzeczny [spshech-ni] adj. m.
contradictory; incompatible

sprzedać [spshe-daćh] v.
dispose of; sell; trade away

sprzedajny [spshe-day-ni] adj. m.
venal; corrupt; corruptible

sprzedawca [spshe-dav-tsa] m.
salesman; shopkeeper; dealer

**sprzedawczyni [spshe-dav-chi-
-ńee] f.** saleslady; saleswoman; vendor; seller

sprzedaż [spshe-dash] f. sale

**sprzedaż detaliczna [spshe-dash
de-ta-leech-na] f.** retail; sale at
retail prices (in retail stores)

**sprzedaż hurtowa [spshe-dash
khoor-to-va] f.** wholesale

**sprzeniewierzenie [spshe-ńe-vye-
-zhe-ńe] n.** embezzlement

sprzęgać [spshan-gaćh] v.
couple; tie; link; team up
(horses); connect (wagons)

sprzęgło [spshan-gwo] n. clutch;
coupling; coupler; attachment

sprzęt [spshant] m. implement;

furniture; accessories; utensils; tackle; outfit; chattels

sprzyjać [spshi-yaćh] v. favor;
be friendly; promote; further

sprzykrzyć [spshik-shićh] v. get
sick of; get fed up with

**sprzymierzeniec [spshi-mye-zhe-
-ńets] m.** ally; confederate

**sprzymierzony [spshi-mye-zho-ni]
adj. m.** allied; confederated

**sprzysiągać się [spshi-śhan-
-gaćh śhan] v.** conspire; plot

**sprzysiążenie [spshi-śhan-zhe-
-ńe] n.** plot; conspiracy

spuchnąć [spookh-nownćh] v.
swell; bulge; curve out

spulchniać [spoolkh-ńaćh] v.
fluff up; loosen; cultivate (soil)

spust [spoost] m. release; catch;
slip; trigger; appetite; drain

**spustoszenie [spoos-to-she-ńe]
n.** devastation; ravage; ruin

spustoszyć [spoos-to-shićh] v.
devastate; ravage; make havoc (of a country); lay waste

spuszczać [spoosh-chaćh] v.
let down; drop; droop; lower;
drain; let fall; throw down; roll
down; put down; let loose

spuścizna [spoośh-ćheez-na] f.
inheritance; legacy; heritage

spychacz [spi-khach] m.
bulldozer; stripper

spychać [spi-khaćh] v. push
down; relegate; drive away

spytać się [spi-taćh śhan] v.
ask; ask a question

srać [sraćh] v. shit (vulg.)

srebrnik [srebr-ńeek] m. silver
-coin; silversmith

srebrny [srebr-ni] adj. m. silver

srebro [sreb-ro] n. silver

srebrzyć [sreb-zhićh] v. sil-
verplate; wash with silver

srebrzysty [sreb-zhis-ti] adj. m.
silvery (glow, color, etc.)

srogi [sro-gee] adj. m. fierce;
cruel; severe; strict; grim

sroka [sro-ka] f. magpie

srokaty [sro-ka-ti] adj. m. piebald
(horse); with patches

srom [srom] m. disgrace; vulva

sromota [sro-mo-ta] f. shame;

ignominy; disgrace
sromotny [sro-mot-ni] adj. m.
  shameful; disgraceful; infamous; disreputable (act, deed)
srożyć [sro-zhić] v. rage;
  torment; storm; oppress; be
  (look) severe; harass; be rife
ssać [ssać] v. suck; exploit
ssak [ssak] m. mammal;
  mammalian (milk sucking)
ssawka [ssav-ka] f. sucker
ssąca pompa [ssown-tsa pom-
  -pa] f. suction pump
stabilizować [sta-bee-lee-zo-
  -vać] v. stabilize; fix
stacja [stats-ya] f. station
stacja benzynowa [stats-ya ben-
  -zi-no-va] f. filling or service
  station; gas station
stacjonować [sta-tsyo-no-vać]
  v. be stationed; be in garrison
staczać [sta-chać] v. roll
  down; fight (a battle, etc.)
staczać się [sta-chać śhan]
  v. roll down; go from bad to
  worse; be on the down grade
stać [stać] v. stand; be
  stopped; farewell; ill-afford;
  rise; be at a station; stagnate
stać się [stać śhan] v.
  become; grow; occur; happen
stadion [sta-dyon] m. stadium
stadło [sta-dwo] n. couple
stadnina [stad-ńee-na] f. stud
stado [sta-do] n. flock; herd
stagnacja [stag-nats-ya] f.
  stagnation; recession; stag-
  nancy; depression; at low ebb
stajnia [stay-ńa] f. stable
stal [stal] f. steel
stale [sta-le] adv. constantly;
  always; for ever; incessantly
stalownia [sta-lov-ńa] f. steel
  -mill; steel plant; steel works
stalowy [sta-lo-vi] adj. m. steel;
  steely; steel gray
stała [sta-wa] f. constant
stałość [sta-wośhć] f.
  stability; firmness; steadiness
stały [sta-wi] adj. m. stable;
  permanent; solid; fixed; firm
stamtąd [stam-townt] prep.
  from there; from over there;

out of it;
stan [stan] m. state; status;
  condition; order; estate; class
stanąć [sta-nownć] v. stand
  up; stop at; put up; rise; set
  foot; get on one's feet, etc.
standaryzować [stan-da-ri-zo-
  -vać] v. standardize
stanik [sta-ńeek] m. bodice; bra;
  brassiere; waste; corsage
staniol [sta-ńol] m. tin foil
stanowczość [sta-nov-
  -chośhć] f. determination;
  finality; assertiveness; fixity
stanowczy [sta-nov-chi] adj. m.
  final; positive; decided; firm
stanowić [sta-no-veeć] v.
  establish; determine; constitute; decide; proclaim
stanowisko [sta-no-vees-ko] n.
  position; post; status; stand;
  rank; appointment; attitude
starać się [sta-rać śhan] v.
  take care; try one's best
staranie [sta-ra-ńe] n. care;
  endeavor; exertion; pains
staranny [sta-ran-ni] adj. m.
  careful; accurate; nice; exact
starcie [star-će] n. clash;
  collision; friction; squabble
starczy [star-chi] adj. m. senile;
starczy [star-chi] v. it is enough
starczyć [star-chić] v. suffice
starodawny [sta-ro-dav-ni] adj.
  m. old time; ancient; antique
staromodny [sta-ro-mod-ni] adj.
  m. old fashioned; outmoded
starosta [sta-ros-ta] m. country
  -head; wedding host; foreman
starość [sta-rośhć] f. old
  age; very old age; antiquity
staroświecki [sta-ro-śhvyets-
  -kee] adj. m. old fashioned
starożytność [sta-ro-zhit-
  -nośhć] f. antiquity; ancient times (period, epoch)
starożytny [sta-ro-zhit-ni] adj. m.
  ancient; antique; old world
starszeństwo [star-sheń-stvo]
  n. seniority; superiority
starszy [star-shi] adj. m. older;
  elder; superior (officer)
starszyzna [star-shiz-na] f. the

elders; the seniors; the chiefs
start [start] m. take-off; start
startować [star-to-vaćh] v.
start; take off; make a start
staruszek [sta-roo-shek] m. old
fellow; old man, gentleman
stary [sta-ri] adj. m. old; old-
-looking; former; stale
starzec [sta-zhets] m. old man
starzeć się [sta-zhećh śhan] v.
grow old; age; grow stale; go
bad; be sensecent (food)
stateczny [sta-tech-ni] adj. m.
stable; buoyant; staid
statek [sta-tek] m. ship; craft;
vessel; boat; steamship
statki [stat-kee] pl. kitchen pots
and pans; kitchen utensils
statua [sta-too-a] f. statue
statut [sta-toot] m. statute
statyka [sta-ti-ka] f. statics
statysta [sta-tis-ta] m.
supernumerary (actor with a
nonspeaking part); dummy
statystyczny [sta-tis-tich-ni] adj.
m. statistical; statistic
statystyka [sta-tis-ti-ka] f.
statistics; returns
statyw [sta-tiv] m. stand;
(camera) support; tripod
staw [stav] m. pond; joint
stawać się [sta-vaćh śhan] v.
become; grow (scarce, big)
stawiać [sta-vyaćh] v. place;
erect; put; stand; offer; lay
down; post; station; put upright; give (grades); defy; rise;
set (sail); move (a resolution)
stawka [stav-ka] f. stake
stąd [stownt] prep. from here;
away; therefore; that is why
stągiew [stown-gev] f. vat
stąpać [stown-paćh] v. pace;
tramp; tread (softly); plod
along; lumber along; strut
stchórzyć [stkhoo-zhićh] v.
show fear; shrink with fright
stearyna [ste-a-ri-na] f. stearin
stek [stek] m. 1.steak; 2. pile of
(lies, insults, etc.); 2. pack of
(insults); shower of abuse
stelmach [stel-makh] m.
cart-wright; wheelwright

stempel [stem-pel] m. stamp;
prop; ramrod; punch; die
stemplowany [stem-plo-va-ni]
adj. m. cancelled; used
stenograf [ste-no-graf] m.
stenographer; shorthand writer
stenografia [ste-no-gra-fya] f.
shorthand; stenography
stenotypistka [ste-no-ti-peest-ka]
f. stenotypist; steno
step [step] m. steppe
ster [ster] m. helm; rudder
sterczeć [ster-chećh] v. stand
out; stick out; tower; bulge
stereoskop [ste-re-os-kop] m.
stereoscope (two eyepieces)
stereotypowy [ste-re-o-ti-po-vi]
adj. m. stereotyped (notion)
sternik [ster-ńeek] m. pilot
sterować [ste-ro-vaćh] v. steer
sterta [ster-ta] f. stack; rick
stebnować [steb-no-vaćh] v.
stitch; quilt; backstitch
stęchlizna [stan-khleez-na] f.
fusty smell; musty smell
stęchły [stankh-wi] adj. m.
musty; stale; foul; fusty; no
longer fresh
stękać [stan-kaćh] v. moan;
groan; utter a groan; complain
stępić [stan-peećh] v. blunt;
dull; take the edge off
stępienie [stan-pye-ńe] n.
dullness (of knife, mind, etc.)
stęskniony [stan-skńo-ni]
adj. m. sick for; yearning for;
hankering for; nostalgic
stężały [stan-zha-wi] adj. m.
hardened; stiff; concentrated;
solidified; coagulated
stężeć [stan-zhećh] v. harden;
stiffen; coagulate; concentrate
stężenie [stan-zhe-ńe] n.
concentration; strength (of a
solution, etc.); rigor (mortis)
stłoczyć [stwo-chićh] v. cram;
compress; jam; squeeze; pack;
pile up; crowd things together
stłuc [stwoots] v. smash; break;
bruise; shatter; injure; beat up
stłuczenie [stwoo-che-ńe] n.
bruise; break; contusion; injury
stłumiać [stwoo-myaćh] v.

dampen; muffle; deaden; dull;
suppress; stifle; restrain
sto [sto] num. hundred; 100
stocznia [stoch-ńa] f. shipyard
stodoła [sto-do-wa] f. barn
stoik [sto-eek] m. Stoic
stoisko [sto-ees-ko] n. stand
stojak [sto-yak] m. stand
stojący [sto-yown-tsi] adj. m.
standing; stagnant; erect;
upright; stan-up (collar, etc.)
stok [stok] m. slope; hillside
stokroć [sto-kroch] adv.
hundred times; hundredfold
stokrotka [sto-krot-ka] f. daisy
stokrotny [sto-krot-ni] adj. m.
hundredfold repeated
stolarnia [sto-lar-ńa] f. joiner's
shop; carpenter's shop
stolarz [sto-lash] m. cabinet
maker; joiner; carpenter
stolec [sto-lets] m. stool; faeces;
excrement; bowel movement
stolica [sto-lee-tsa] f. capital (of
a country, state, island, etc.)
stolik [sto-leek] m. small table;
nice little (card, etc.) table
stolnica [stol-ńee-tsa] f. molding
board; paste board (kitchen)
stołeczny [sto-wech-ni] adj. m.
metropolitan (taxes, etc.);
capital (city); of capital (city)
stołek [sto-wek] m. small stool
stołować [sto-wo-vach] v.
board; serve meals to lodgers
stołownik [sto-wov-ńeek] m.
boarder (provided with meals)
stołówka [sto-woov-ka] f. mess
(dining) hall; mess; canteen
stonka [ston-ka] f. potato beetle;
potato bug; Colorado beetle
stonoga [sto-no-ga] f. centipede;
(warm-like) wood louse
stop [stop] m. (metal) alloy;
melt; traffic sign; stop; halt
stopa [sto-pa] f. foot; standard
stopa procentowa [sto-pa pro-
-tsen-to-va] f. interest rate
stopa życiowa [sto-pa zhi-cho-
-va] f. living standard
stoper [sto-per] m. stopwatch
stopić [sto-peech] v. melt
stopień [sto-pyeń] m. (stair)

step; degree; grade; extent
stopniały [stop-ńa-wi] adj. m.
molten away; dwindled; soft-
ened; shrunk; unfrozen
stopnieć [stop-ńech] v. melt
down; melt away; shrink; soft-
en; dwindle; become smaller
stopniowo [stop-ńo-vo] adv.
gradually; little by little
stopniowy [stop-ńo-vi] adj. m.
gradual; progressive
stora [sto-ra] f. shade; blind
storczyk [stor-chik] m. orchid
stos [stos] m. (wood) pile
stos atomowy [stos a-to-mo-vi]
m. atomic pile; atomic reactor
stosować [sto-so-vach] v. use
stosownie [sto-sov-ńe] adv.
accordingly; in compliance
stosowny [sto-sov-ni] adj. m.
proper; convenient; opportune
stosunek [sto-soo-nek] m. rate;
relation; proportion; attitude
stosunek płciowy [sto-soo-nek
pwcho-vi] m. sexual relations;
sexual intercourse; sex
stosunki handlowe [sto-soon-kee
khand-lo-ve] pl. trade
relations; commercial relations
stosunkowy [sto-soon-ko-vi] adj.
m. relative; proportional
stowarzyszenie [sto-va-zhi-she-
-ńe] n. association; club
stożek [sto-zhek] m. cone
stożkowaty [stozh-ko-va-ti] adj.
m. conical; cone shaped
stóg [stook] m. stack (rick)
stół [stoow] m. table; fare
stracenie [stra-tse-ńe] n.
execution; loss; doom
straceniec [stra-tse-ńets] m.
desperado; madcap (man)
strach [strakh] m. fear; fright
stracić [stra-cheech] v. lose;
execute (a man); shed (teeth
etc.); sustain a loss
stragan [stra-gan] m. booth;
stand; (market) stall
straganiarz [stra-ga-ńash] m.
stand owner; stall holder
strajkować [stray-ko-vach] v.
go on strike; strike; be out
strapić [stra-peech] v. sadden;

pain; distress; afflict; grieve;
worry; inflict pain, distress

strapienie [stra-pye-ńe] n.
worry; distress; heartbreak

strapiony [stra-pyo-ni] adj. m.
worried; dejected; distressed

straszak [stra-shak] m. noisy toy
pistol; scarecrow; bugbear

straszliwy [strash-lee-vi] adj. m.
horrible; fearsome; awful

straszny [strash-ni] adj. m.
awful; terrible; awesome; ee-
rie; gruesome; dreadful; frightful; terrific; horrible

straszyć [stra-shiĆh] v.
frighten; haunt; threaten; bluff

straszydło [stra-shid-wo] n.
scarecrow; (unsightly) fright

strata [stra-ta] f. loss

strateg [stra-teg] m. strategist

strategia [stra-teg-ya] f. strategy

strategiczny [stra-te-geech-ni]
adj. m. strategic; of strategy

strategik [stra-te-geek] m.
strategist (using stratagems)

stratny [strat-ni] adj. m. one that
lost something; being the loser

stratować [stra-to-vaĆh] v.
trample; tread under foot

strawa [stra-va] f. food; meal

strawić [stra-veeĆh] v. digest;
consume; bear; stomach; sap;
stand; ruin; destroy; etch

strawna [strav-na] adj. f.
digestible; palatable (food)

strawne [strav-ne] n. food ration
(in the army etc.); adj. n.
digestible; palatable (food)

strawny [strav-ni] adj. m.
digestible; palatable (food)

straż [strash] f. guard; watch;
safe custody; strict guard;
escort; convoy; (van-) guard

straż pożarna [strash po-zhar-na]
f. fire brigade; fire department

straż przednia [strash pshed-ńa]
f. vanguard; advance guard

straż tylna [strash til-na] f.
rear-guard; rear guard

strażak [stra-zhak] m. fireman

strażnica [strazh-ńee-tsa] f.
guardhouse; watchtower

strażnik [strazh-ńeek] m. guard;

watchman; sentry

strącić [strown-ĆheeĆh] v.
knock off (apples); throw, hurl
down; down; deduct

strączek [strown-chek] m.
(small) pod; hull; husk; legume

strąk [strownk] m. pod; hull;
husk; legume pod or seed

strefa [stre-fa] f. zone; area

stres [stres] m. stress

streszczać [stresh-chaĆh] v.
sum up; summarize; boil
down; condense; abbreviate

streszczenie [stresh-che-ńe] n.
resume; summary; digest

stręczyciel [stran-chi-Ćhel] m.
pimp; procurer; broker

stręczyć [stran-chiĆh] v.
procure (women); recommend

stroczyć [stro-chiĆh] v. strap

strofa [stro-fa] f. strophe

strofować [stro-fo-vaĆh] v.
reprimand; admonish; scold;
chide; sermonize; reprimand

stroić [stro-eeĆh] v. dress up;
tune up; make fun; trim; add
beauty; adorn; arrange; mock

strojnie [stroy-ńe] adv.
beautifully (richly) dressed

strojny [stroy-ni] adj. m. dressed
up; elegant; smart; spruce

stromo [stro-mo] adv. steeply;
abruptly; precipitously; sheer

stromy [stro-mi] adj. m. steep

strona [stro-na] f. page; side;
region; aspect; part; party

stronić [stro-ńeeĆh] v. avoid;
shun; keep oneself away

stronnictwo [stron-ńeets-tvo] n.
party (political)

stronniczy [stron-ńee-chi]
adj. m. partial; biased; unfair

stronnik [stron-ńeek] m.
partisan; supporter; follower;
henchman; backer; adherent

strop [strop] m. (room) ceiling;
(house) roof; (sailing) sling

stropić [stro-peeĆh] v.
discourage; confound; abash;
put out of countenance

stroskany [stros-ka-ni] adj. m.
worried; sorrowful; dejected

strój [strooy] m. attire; dress

stróż [stroosh] m. watchman
stróżka [stroozh-ka] f. (woman)
  caretaker; wife of a caretaker
struchlały [strookh-la-wi] v.
  terrified; paralysed with fear
strucie [stroo-che] n. food
  poisoning; dejection (feeling)
struć [strooćh] v. poison;
  depress; deject; dishearten;
  embitter (another person)
strudzony [stroo-dzo-ni] adj. m.
  weary; tired; exhausted
strug [strook] m. plane (wood
  working tool used to smooth)
struga [stroo-ga] f. stream;
  creek; trickle; flow in streams
strugać [stroo-gaćh] v. whittle;
  scrape; carve; cut out
struktura [strook-too-ra] f.
  structure; texture; framework
strumień [stroo-myeń] m.
  stream; flow; flux; jet; torrents
strumyk [stroo-mik] m. brook;
  creek; streamlet
struna [stroo-na] f. string; chord;
  note; wire; (metal) wire; cord
**struna głosowa [stroo-na gwo-
-so-va]** f. vocal cord
strup [stroop] m. scab; crust
strupieć [stroo-pyećh] v. to be
  a dead body; form a scab
strupieszały [stroo-pye-sha-wi]
  adj. m. decrepit; worn out
strupieszeć [stroo-pye-shećh]
  v. grow decrepit; become
  obsolete; become antiquated
strupowaty [stroo-po-va-ti] adj.
  m. scabby; having many scabs
struty [stroo-ti] adj. m. dejected;
  crestfallen; poisoned
struś [strooćh] m. ostrich
strwonić [strvo-ńeećh] v.
  squander away (a fortune etc.)
strych [strikh] m. attic
strychnina [strikh-ńee-na] f.
  strychnine (poisonous alkaloid)
stryczek [stri-chek] m. (hanging)
  rope; noose; the halter
stryj [striy] m. uncle
stryjeczny brat [stri-yech-ni brat]
  m. cousin; uncle's son
strzał [stshaw] m. shot
strzała [stsha-wa] f. arrow

strzaskać [stshas-kaćh] v.
  smash to pieces; shatter
strząsać [stshown-saćh] v.
  shake off; shake down; flick
  off (ash); brush away; shake
strzec [stshets] v. guard; watch;
  keep an eye on; protect; keep
strzelać [stshe-laćh] v. shoot;
  fire; slap; score; blunder
strzelanie [stshe-la-ńe] n.
  shooting (practice); gunfire
strzelanina [stshe-la-ńee-na] f.
  gunfire; shots; gunplay
strzelba [stshel-ba] f. shotgun
strzelec [stshe-lets] m. shooter;
  rifleman; sniper; gunner;
  scorer; fusilier; marksman
strzelnica [stshel-ńee-tsa] f.
  shooting range; rifle range
**strzelniczy proch [stshel-ńee-chi
prokh]** m. gunpowder
strzemienne [stshe-myen-ne] n.
  parting drink; stirrup cup
strzemię [stshe-myan] n. stirrup
strzepać [stshe-paćh] v. brush
  off; flick off; shake off (away)
strząp [stshanp] m. shred; tatter
strzępek [stshan-pek] m. shred;
  (small) fragment; (small) scrap
strzępić [stshan-peećh] v.
  shred; reduce to shreds; fray
**strzępić się [strzan-peećh
śhan]** v. be reduced to shreds
**strzępić język [stshan-peećh
yan-zik]** v. wag one's tongue;
  waste breath; talk nonsense
strzyc [stshits] v. cut; clip;
  shear; mow; trim; graze
**strzyc uszami [stshits oo-sha-
-mee]** v. prick up ears
strzykać [stshi-kaćh] v. squirt;
  spray; inject; ache
strzykawka [stshi-kav-ka] f.
  syringe; hypodermic syringe
strzyżenie [stshi-zhe-ńe] n.
  (hair) cut; sheep shearing
strzyżony [stshi-zho-ni] adj. m.
  cropped; cut; clipped
student [stoo-dent] m. student
studenteria [stoo-den-ter-ya] pl.
  students; student folks
studia [stoo-dya] pl. university
  studies; university research

studio [stoo-dyo] n. atelier; (film, artist's, etc.) studio
studiować [stoo-dyo-vaćh] v. study; investigate; peer
studium [stoo-dyoom] n. investigation; university studies
studnia [stood-ńa] f. well
studzić [stoo-dźheećh] v. cool down (one's tea, coffee, etc.)
studzienny [stoo-dźhen-ni] adj. m. well- (shaft, water, etc.)
stuk [stook] m. knock; clutter
stukać [stoo-kaćh] v. knock; tap; hit; rap; patter; rattle; drum; clatter; clink (glasses)
stulecie [stoo-le-ćhe] n. century; an age; hundred years
stuletni [stoo-let-ńee] adj. m. hundred years old; age old
stulić [stoo-leećh] v. press tight; close up; coil up
stuszować [stoo-sho-vaćh] v. touch up (photo); tone down
stutonowy [stoo-to-no-vi] adj. weighing one hundred ton
stwardnieć [stvard-ńećh] v. harden; stiffen; grow callous
stwardniały [stvard-ńa-wi] adj. m. hardened; hard-set; grown hard; hard; sclerotic
stwardnienie [stvard-ńe-ńe] n. hardening; callosity (of skin)
stwierdzać [stvyer-dzaćh] v. state; find out; confirm
stwierdzenie [stvyer-dze-ńe] n. statement; ascertainment
stworzenie [stvo-zhe-ńe] n. creature; formation; creation
stworzyciel [stvo-zhi-ćhel] m. creator; maker (of the world)
stworzyć [stvo-zhićh] v. create; produce; set up; compose
stwór [stvoor] m. monster
Stwórca [stvoor-tsa] f. Creator (of the universe, etc.) Maker
styczeń [sti-cheń] m. January
styczna [stich-na] f. tangent; adj. f. adjacent (wall, side, etc.)
styczność [stich-nośhćh] f. contact; tangency; adjacency
styczny [stich-ni] adj. m. adjacent; contiguous
stygmat [stig-mat] m. stigma

stygnąć [stig-nownćh] v. cool down; cool off; be cooling off
styk [stik] m. contact; butt
stykać się [sti-kaćh śhan] v. contact; touch; adjoint; meet
stykowy [sti-ko-vi] adj. m. contact (effect, print, etc.)
styl [stil] m. style; fashion; order
stylisko [sti-lees-ko] n. helve; shaft; handle (of a spade etc.)
stylista [sti-lees-ta] m. stylist
stylistyka [sti-lees-ti-ka] f. art of composition; syntax; stylistics
stylizacja [sti-lee-zats-ya] f. stylization (in art, etc.); mode of expression (in writing, etc.)
stylizować [sti-lee-zo-vaćh] v. adapt to a certain style; conform to a style (mode); stylize
stylowy [sti-lo-vi] adj. m. stylish; (forms) of style; in a style
stypa [sti-pa] f. wake; funny confusion; funeral banquet
stypendium [sti-pend-yoom] n. scholarship; stipend; grant
subiekcja [soob-yek-tsya] f. inconvenience (of a delay)
subiektywny [soo-byek-tiv-ni] adj. m. subjective
sublokator [soob-lo-ka-tor] m. lodger; subtenant
subordynacja [soo-bor-di-nats-ya] f. subordination
subskrypcja [soob-skrip-tsya] f. subscription; a subscribing
substancja [soob-stan-tsya] f. substance; (physical) matter
subsydiować [soob-sid-yo-vaćh] v. subsidize
subtelność [soob-tel-nośhćh] f. subtlety; niceness; delicacy
subtelny [soob-tel-ni] adj. m. subtle; nice; fine; refined
subwencja [soob-ven-tsya] f. subsidy; grant in aid
suchar [soo-khar] m. dry-bread ration; cracker; biscuit
sucharek [soo-kha-rek] m. cracker; (a dry) biscuit
sucho [soo-kho] adv. dryly; uninterestingly; dry weather
suchość [soo-khośhćh] f. dryness; abruptness

suchotnik [soo-khot-ńeek] m.
consumptive (patient)
suchoty [soo-kho-ti] pl.
consumption; phthisis
suchy [soo-khi] adj. m. dry;
withered; lean; uninteresting
sudecki [soo-dets-kee] adj. m. of
Sudeten, Sudetic Mountains
sufit [soo-feet] m. ceiling
suflować [soof-lo-vaćh] v.
prompt (an actor on stage)
sugerować [soo-ge-ro-vaćh] v.
suggest; allude; hint
sugestia [soo-ges-tya] f.
suggestion; motion; proposal
sugestywny [soo-ges-tiv-ni] adj.
m. suggestive (speech etc.)
suka [soo-ka] f. bitch
sukces [sook-tses] m. success
sukcesja [sook-tses-ya] f.
succession; inheritance; devo-
lution; the act of succeeding
sukcesor [sook-tse-sor] m. heir
sukcesorka [sook-tse-sor-ka] f.
heiress (of an inheritance)
sukienka [soo-kyen-ka] f. dress
sukiennice [soo-kyen-ńee-tse] n.
weaver's or draper's market
hall; clothier's hall
sukiennik [soo-kyen-ńeek] m.
draper; clothier (dealer)
suknia [sook-ńa] f. gown; dress
sukno [sook-no] n. woolen cloth
sułtan [soow-tan] m. sultan
sum [soom] m. catfish
suma [soo-ma] f. sum; total;
high mass; entirety; whole
sumaryczny [soo-ma-rich-ni] adj.
m. summary; total; global
sumienie [soo-mye-ńe] n.
conscience (clear, guilty etc.)
sumienny [soo-myen-ni] adj. m.
conscientious; scrupulous
sumować [soo-mo-vaćh] v.
sum up; add up; reckon
sunąć [soo-nownćh] v. glide;
push; move; skim along
supeł [soo-pew] m. knot
supernowoczesny [soo-per-no-
-vo-ches-ni] adj. m. ul-
tramodern; the most modern
supersam [soo-per-sam] m.
supermarket (of groceries)

surdut [soor-doot] m. frock;
coat; overcoat; long jacket
surogat [soo-ro-gat] m.
surrogate; substitute for
surowica [soo-ro-vee-tsa] f.
serum (any animal fluid)
surowiec [soo-ro-vyets] m. raw
material; staple; rawhide
surowo [soo-ro-vo] adv.
severely; strictly; sternly;
harshly; austerely; in the raw
surowość [soo-ro-voshćh] f.
severity; crudeness; rigor
surowy [soo-ro-vi] adj. m.
severe; raw; coarse; harsh
surówka [soo-roov-ka] f. pig
iron; fruit salad; raw hide
susza [soo-sha] f. drought;
dryness; (very) dry weather
suszarka [soo-shar-ka] f. (hair,
clothes) dryer; desiccator
suszarnia [soo-shar-ńa] f. drying
shed; drying plant; kiln
suszka [soosh-ka] f. blotter
suszyć [soo-shićh] v. dry
sutanna [soo-tan-na] f. cassock
sutener [soo-te-ner] m. cadet;
soutener; bully; ponce
suterena [soo-te-re-na] f.
basement (below the ground)
sutka [soot-ka] f. nipple
suty [soo-ti] adj. m. copious;
abundant; lavish; plentiful; rich
suwać [soo-vaćh] v. shove
suwak [soo-vak] m. slide rule
swada [sva-da] f. eloquence
swar [svar] m. squabble; quarrel;
rife; dissension; contention
swarliwy [svar-lee-vi] adj. m.
quarrelsome; cantankerous
swastyka [svas-ti-ka] f.
swastica; swastika (emblem)
swat [svat] m. matchmaker
swatać [sva-taćh] v. match-
make; want to match (with)
swaty [sva-ti] n. matchmaking
swawola [sva-vo-la] f. anarchy
swawolny [sva-vol-ni] adj. m.
unruly; playful; frolicsome;
wilful; immoral; dissolute
swąd [svownt] m. reek; stench
sweter [sve-ter] m. sweater
swędzenie [svan-dze-ńe] n. itch;

an itch; tingle (int he skin)
swędzić [svan-dźheećh] v.
   itch; itch to do something
swoboda [svo-bo-da] f. freedom;
   ease; latitude; liberty
swoboda działania [svo-bo-da
   dźha-**wa-**ńa] f. freedom to
   act; discretion; be free to do
swobodny [svo-bod-ni] adj. m.
   free; easy; at liberty; loose;
   lax; unconstrained; at large
swoisty [svo-**ees-**ti] adj. m.
   specific; characteristic
swojski [**svoy-**skee] adj. m.
   homely; familiar; friendly;
   tame; (well) domesticated
sworzeń [svo-zheń] m. carriage
   bolt; lug bolt; cotter; pin
swój [svooy] pron. his; hers; my;
   its; our; your; their; one's own
swój człowiek [svooy chwo-
   -vyek] m. trustworthy man
sybaryta [si-ba-ri-ta] m. Sybarite;
   sybarite; voluptuary
syberyjski [si-be-riy-skee] adj. m.
   Siberian; of Siberia
sycić [si-ćheećh] v. satiate
syczeć [si-chećh] v. hiss
syfon [si-fon] m. siphon
sygnalizować [sig-na-lee-zo-
   -vaćh] v. signalize; signal
sygnał [sig-naw] m. signal
sygnatura [sig-na-too-ra] f.
   (official) signature
sygnet [sig-net] m. signet; seal
   ring; imprint; colophon
syk [sik] m. hiss; sizzle; fizzle
sylaba [si-la-ba] f. syllable
sylogizm [si-lo-geezm] m.
   syllogism (form of reasoning)
sylweta [sil-**ve-**ta] f. silhouette;
   outline; profile; figure
symbioza [sim-byo-za] f.
   symbiosis; living together
symbol [**sim-**bol] m. symbol
symboliczny [sim-bo-leech-ni]
   adj. m. symbolic; symbolical
symbolizować [sim-bo-lee-zo-
   -vaćh] v. symbolize; stand for
symetria [si-metr-ya] f. symmetry
symetryczny [si-me-trich-ni] adj.
   m. symmetrical
symfonia [sim-**foń-**ya] f.

symphony (of sounds, colors)
symfoniczny [sim-fo-ńeech-ni]
   adj. m. symphonic (orchestra)
sympatia [sim-pat-ya] f. liking
sympatyczny [sim-pa-tich-ni] adj.
   m. congenial; attractive
sympatyk [sim-pa-tik] m. well
   -wisher; sympathizer
sympatyzować [sim-pa-ti-**zo-**
   -vaćh] v. like; go along; feel
   with; share the feelings, ideas
symptom [simp-tom] m. symptom (of a particular disease)
symulacja [si-moo-lats-ya] f.
   simulation; make believe;
   sham; false appearance
symulować [si-moo-lo-vaćh] v.
   simulate; feign; pretend; affect
syn [sin] m. son; (a descendant)
synagoga [si-na-go-ga] f. synagogue (Jews' worship place)
syndykat [sin-di-kat] m.
   syndicate; syndicate; labor
   union; (criminal) organization
synek [si-nek] m. sonny (boy)
synekura [si-ne-koo-ra] .f
   sinecure; cosy job; fat job
synod [si-nod] m. synod; council
synonim [si-no-ńeem] m. synonym (word of same meaning)
synowa [si-no-va] f. daughter-in-
   -law (the wife of a son)
synowiec [si-no-vyets] m.
   nephew (son of a relative)
syntetyczny [sin-te-tich-ni] adj.
   m. synthetic; artificial
synteza [sin-te-za] f. synthesis
sypać [si-paćh] v. strew; pour;
   scatter (dry matter); shower
   (blows, etc.); betray secrets
sypialnia [si-pyal-ńa] f. bedroom;
   bedroom furniture suite
sypki [sip-kee] adj. m. loose
   (rocks); granular (substance);
   friable; dry (goods, etc.)
sypki towar [sip-kee to-var] m.
   granular goods; dry goods
syrena [si-**re-**na] f. siren;
   mermaid; hooter; the emblem
   of Warsaw, capital of Poland
syrop [si-rop] m. syrup
syryjski [si-riy-skee] adj. m.
   Syrian; of Syria

system [sis-tem] m. system
systematyczny [sis-te-ma-tich-ni]
adj. m. systematic; neat
syt [sit] m. satiate; full
sytny [sit-ni] adj. m. filling up;
nourishing; satiating
sytuacja [si-too-ats-ya] f.
situation; circumstances; position; things; state of affairs
sytuować [si-too-o-vaćh] v.
situate; locate; position
sytuowany [si-too-o-va-ni]
adj. m. situated; placed; located; conditioned; (well) off
syty [si-ti] adj. m. satiate; dilled
up; well-fed; nourishing
szabla [shab-la] f. sabre
szablon [shab-lon] m. stencil;
pattern; model; stereotype
szablonowy [sha-blo-no-vi] adj.
m. routine; stereotype
szach-mat [shakh-mat] m. check
-mate (in the chess game)
szachista [sha-khees-ta] m.
chess player (man)
szachować [sha-kho-vaćh] v.
check (in the chess game)
szachownica [sha-khov-ńee-tsa]
f. chessboard; checker board
szachraj [shakh-ray] m. cheat
szachrować [shakh-ro-vaćh] v.
cheat; swindle; jockey
szachy [sha-khi] pl. chess
szacować [sha-tso-vaćh] v.
evaluate; estimate; size up
szacunek [sha-tsoo-nek] m.
1. valuation; assessment
szacunek [sha-tsoo-nek] m.
2. respect; esteem; deference
szafa [sha-fa] f. chest; wardrobe;
bookcase; cupboard
szafir [sha-feer] m. sapphire
szafka nocna [shaf-ka nots-na] f.
night table; bedside table
szafot [sha-fot] m. (execution)
scaffold; execution block
szafować [sha-fo-vaćh] v.
lavish; squander; be liberal
szafran [shaf-ran] m. saffron
ka [shay-ka] f. gang
szakal [sha-kal] m. jackal
szal [shal] m. shawl; scarf
szala [sha-la] f. scale

szalbierstwo [shal-byer-stvo] n.
swindle; fraud; imposition
szalbierz [shal-byesh] m. fraud;
swindler; quack; impostor
szaleć [sha-lećh] v. rage; rave
szalenie [sha-le-ńe] adv. madly;
terribly; awfully; like mad
szaleniec [sha-le-ńets] m.
madman; daredevil; desperado
szaleńczy [sha-leń-chi] adj. m.
frantic; mad; insane; reckless
szaleństwo [sha-leń-stvo] n.
fury; madness; craze; frenzy
szalik [sha-leek] m. scarf
szalony [sha-lo-ni] adj. m. mad
szał [shaw] m. rage; fury; frenzy
szałas [sha-was] m. tent; shanty;
shed; shelter; chalet; hut
szamotać się [sha-mo-taćh
śhan] v. scuffle; struggle;
tussle; jerk; pull about
szampan [sham-pan] m. champagne (of Champagne, France)
szaniec [sha-ńets] m. bastion
szanować [sha-no-vaćh] v.
respect (person, tradition)
honor; have regard; esteem
szanowny [sha-nov-ni] adj. m.
honorable; worthy; dear (sir)
szansa [shan-sa] f. chance
szantaż [shan-tash] m.
blackmail; extortion
szantażować [shan-ta-zho-
-vaćh] v. blackmail; make
squeal; extort (money, etc.)
szantażysta [shan-ta-zhis-ta] m.
blackmailer; extortioner
szarak [sha-rak] m. hare; average
man of the street; yeoman
szarańcza [sha-rań-cha] f.
locust; swarm of locust;
swarm of any flying insects
szarfa [shar-fa] f. scarf; sash
szargać [shar-gaćh] v.
besmear; foul up; slander;
tarnish; slur (a reputation)
szarlatan [shar-la-tan] m.
confidence man; charlatan
szarotka [sha-rot-ka] f. edelweiss
szarość [sha-rośhćh] f.
greyness; drabness; dullness;
duskiness; gray tint (color)
szarpać [shar-paćh] v. jerk;

pull; tear; tousle; knock about;
assail; prey; impair; slander
szaruga [sha-roo-ga] f. gray, foul
(bad) weather; gray skies
szary [sha-ri] adj. m. gray; drab
szarzeć [sha-zhećh] v. loom;
gray; grow dusky; show gray
szarzyzna [sha-zhiz-na] f.
grayness; drabness; duskiness
szarża [shar-zha] f. (cavalry)
charge; (military) rank; officer
szarżować [shar-zho-vaćh] v.
charge (recklessly); overact
szastać [shas-taćh] v. squander
szata [sha-ta] f. garment; gown
szatan [sha-tan] m. satan; devil;
a very strong coffee drink
szatański [sha-tań-skee] adj. m.
devilish; infernal; satanic
szatkować [shat-ko-vaćh] v.
cut; chop; shred; slice
szatnia [shat-ńa] f. locker room;
coat-room; a large coat closet
szatynka [sha-tin-ka] f. dark
-blond girl; auburn haired
(woman, girl, lady, etc.)
szczać [shchaćh] v. piss (vulg.)
szczapa [shcha-pa] f. split log;
splint; chip; sliver; thin man
szczaw [shchav] m. sorrel
szczątek [shchown-tek] m.
remnant; vestige; fragment
szczebel [shche-bel] m. (ladder)
rung; spoke; grade; round
szczebiot [shche-byot] m.
chatter; chirp (of birds); lisp;
prattle; chirrup; warble; babble
szczebiotać [shche-byo-taćh] v.
chirrup; chirp; chatter; bable
szczebiotanie [shche-byo-ta-ńe]
n. chatter; prattle; chirp; lisp
(of children); warble; chirrup
szczecina [shche-ćhee-na] f.
bristle (of hogs); stubble beard
szczególnie [shche-gool-ńe] adv.
particularly; in particular;
especially; principally; chiefly;
above all; peculiarly; singularly
szczególność [shche-gool-
-nośćh] f. peculiarity; singularity; specific character
szczególny [shche-gool-ni] adj.
m. peculiar; special; specific

szczegół [shche-goow] m. detail
szczgółowo [shche-goo-**wo**-vo]
adv. in detail; in full; with full
particulars; closely; narrowly
szczegółowość [shche-goo-**wo**-
-vośćh] f. minuteness of
detail; full particulars; in full
szczegółowy [shche-goo-**wo**-vi]
adj. m. detailed; minute;
thorough; lengthy (document)
szczekać [shche-kaćh] v. bark
szczekanie [shche-ka-ńe] n. bark
szczekotanie [shche-ko-**ta**-ńe] n.
rattle; sharp short sounds
szczelina [shche-lee-na] f. slot;
crevice; cleft; slit; rift; crack
szczelny [shchel-ni] adj. m.
(water, air, etc.) tight
szczeniak [shche-ńak] m. puppy;
kid; pup; young dog; bad boy
szczep [shchep] m. graft; tribe;
seedling (grown from a seed)
szczepić [shche-peećh] v.
graft; vaccinate; inoculate
szczepienie [shche-**pye**-ńe] n.
grafting; vaccination
szczepionka [shche-**pyon**-ka] f.
vaccine (for a specific disease)
szczerba [shcher-ba] f. jag;
notch; gap; nick; chip; dent
szczerbaty [shcher-ba-ti] adj. m.
gap-toothed; jagged; notched
szczerbić [shcher-beećh] v. jag
szczerość [shche-rośćh] f.
sincerity; open-heartedness
szczerozłoty [shche-ro-**zwo**-ti]
adj. m. of pure gold; golden
szczery [shche-ri] adj. m.
sincere; frank; candid
szcządzić [shchan-dźheećh] v.
spare; economize; grudge; be
sparing (in giving, using); stint
szczęk [shchank] m. clink; clash;
clang; rattle; ringing sound
szczęka [shchan-ka] f. jaw;
mandible; clamp; denture plate
szczękać [shchan-kaćh] v.
clink; clang; jangle; rattle
szczęścić się [shchanśh-
-ćheećh **śhan**] v. be thriving; have a good luck
szczęście [shchanśh-ćhe] n.
happiness; good luck; success

szczęśliwy [shchan-śhlee-vi]
adj. m. happy; lucky; successful; thriving; prosperous; joyful

szczodrość [shchod-rośhćh]
f. generosity; open-handed-
ness; munificence

szczodry [shchod-ri] adj. m.
generous; abundant; ample

szczoteczka [shcho-tech-ka] f.
small brush; toothbrush

szczotka [shchot-ka] f. brush

szczotkarski [shchot-kar-skee]
adj. m. brush; brush maker's

szczotkować [shchot-ko-vaćh]
v. brush down; brush (a coat,
etc.); polish (floors, etc.)

szczuć [shchooćh] v. hiss; bait;
embitter against; set dogs on

szczudło [shchood-wo] n. stilt;
crutch; pole with a footrest

szczupak [shchoo-pak] m. pike

szczupleć [shchoo-plećh] v.
slim down; reduce; diminish

szczupłość [shchoo-wośhćh]
f. slimness; scantiness

szczupły [shchoop-wi] adj. m.
slim; slender; thin; lean

szczur [shchoor] m. rat

szczwany [shchva-ni] adj. m. sly;
cunning; crafty; slyly deceitful

szczycić się [shchi-ćheećh
śhan] v. boast; take pride; be
(very) proud of; take glory in

szczypać [shchi-paćh] v. pinch;
tweak; squeeze; nip; sting

szczypce [shchip-tse] pl. tongs;
pliers; pincers; clippers

szczypczyki [shchip-chi-kee] pl.
tweezers; forceps; small tongs

szczypiorek [shchi-pyo-rek] m.
chive (used for flavoring)

szczypta [shchip-ta] f. pinch

szczyt [shchit] m. top; summit;
peak; apex; climax; vortex

szczytnie [shchit-ńe] adv.
laudably; commendably; loftily

szczytny [shchit-ni] adj. m. lofty;
sublime; commendable; proud

szczytowy [shchi-to-vi] adj. m.
peak; culminating; uppermost;
top; climactic; supreme; gable-

szef [shef] m. boss; chief

szefostwo [she-fost-vo] n.

management (of a business);
leadership; post of a chief

szejk [sheyk] m. sheik

szelest [she-lest] m. rustle

szeleścić [she-leśh-ćheećh]
v. rustle; whisper (in the wind)

szelka [shel-ka] f. strap; belt

szelki [shel-kee] pl. suspenders;
(pair of) straps; belts; braces

szelma [shel-ma] f. rogue;
scoundrel; wretch; knave

szelmostwo [shel-mos-tvo] n.
piece of roguery; rascally trick

szemrać [shem-raćh] v.
murmur; grumble; prattle;
whisper; ripple; mutter; repine

szept [shept] m. whisper

szeptać [shep-taćh] v. whisper

szepnąć [shep-nownćh] v.
whisper; murmur; conspire;
scheme; prompt a thought to

szereg [she-rek] m. row; file;
series; range; chain (of events)

szeregować [she-re-go-vaćh] v.
rank; classify; arrange

szeregowy [she-re-go-vi] adj. m.
1. series (mathematical)

szeregowy [she-re-go-vi] m.
2. soldier in the ranks

szermierka [sher-myer-ka] f.
fencing; swordsmanship; fight

szermierz [sher-myesh] m. fencer

szeroki [she-ro-kee] adj. m. wide
range; broad; ample; extensive

szeroko [she-ro-ko] adv. widely;
broadly; wide; far and wide

szerokość [she-ro-kośhćh] f.
width; latitude; breath

szerokotorowa kolej [she-ro-ko-
-to-ro-va ko-ley] f. wide gauge
railroad (mainly Russian)

szerszeń [sher-sheń] m. hornet;
large yellow and black wasp

szerzenie [she-zhe-ńe] n. spread;
propagation; dissemination

szerzyć [she-zhićh] v. spread;
propagate; promulgate; disseminate; pervade; radiate

szesnastka [shes-nast-ka] f. the
figure sixteen; 16

szesnastoletni [shes-nas-to-let-
-ńee] adj. m. sixteen-year-old

szesnastowieczny [shes-nas-to-

-vyech-ni] adj. m. sixteenth-century; of the 16th century

szesnasty [shes-**nas**-ti] num. sixteenth; 16th

szesnaście [shes-**naśh**-ćhe] num. sixteen; 16

sześcian [**sheśh**-ćhan] m. cube (number's third power)

sześcienny [sheśh-**ćhen**-ni] adj. m. cubic (third power)

sześciobok [sheśh-ćho-bok] m. hexagon; hexahedron

sześciokrotny [sheśh-ćho-**krot**--ni] adj. m. six-fold

sześciolatek [sheśh-ćho-la-tek] m. boy of six; six year old

sześcioro [śheśh-ćho-ro] num. six (children)

sześć [śheśhćh] num. six; 6

sześdziesiąt [sheśhćh-**dźhe**--śhownt] num. sixty; 60

sześdziesiąty [sheśhćh-**dźhe**--śhown-ti] adj. m. sixtieth

sześdziesięcioletni [sheśh--dźhe-śhan-ćho-let-ńee] adj. m. sixty years old; of sixty (60) years' duration

sześćset [sheśhćh-set] num. six hundred; 600

szew [shev] m. seam; stitch; juncture; raphe; suture

szewc [shevts] m. shoemaker; boot-maker; (mending) cobbler

szewstwo [shev-stvo] n. shoe-making; shoe-making trade

szkalować [shka-lo-vaćh] v. slander; defame; calumniate

szkapa [shka-pa] f. screw; jade, a worthless horse; crock

szkarada [shka-ra-da] f. eyesore; an abomination; fright

szkaradny [shka-rad-ni] adj. m. hideous; ugly; abominable; nasty; repulsive; revolting

szkarlatyna [shkar-la-ti-na] f. scarlet fever; scarlatina

szkarłat [shkar-wat] m. scarlet

szkarłatny [shkar-wat-ni] adj. m. scarlet; crimson; purple

szkatuła [shka-too-wa] f. box; casket; financial means; funds

szkic [shkeets] m. outline; sketch; essay; study; tracing

szkicować [shkee-tso-vaćh] v. sketch; outline; draw up; design; trace; pencil; chalk out

szkicownik [shkee-tsov-ńeek] m. sketch pad; sketchbook

szkielet [shke-let] m. skeleton; framework; shell; carcass

szkiełko [shkew-ko] n. small glass; pane; slide; crystal

szkiełko od zegarka [shkew-ko od ze-gar-ka] n. watch-glass

szklanka [shklan-ka] f. (drinking) glass; glassful (of water etc.)

szklany [shkla-ni] adj. m. glass; glassy (eye, etc.); vitreous

szklarz [shklash] m. glazier

szklić [shkleećh] v. glaze; brag

szkisty [shklees-ti] adj. m. glassy; glazy; vitreous; hyaline

szkliwo [shklee-vo] n. enamel; glaze; (desert) varnish

szkło [shkwo] n. glass; pane

szkocki [shkots-kee] adj. m. Scottish; of Scotland

szkoda [shko-da] f. damage; harm; detriment; mischief; injury; hurt; exp.: that's too bad! what a pity! what a shame! how annoying!

szkodliwy [shkod-lee-vi] adj. m. harmful; detrimental; damaging; destructive; pernicious

szkodnik [shkod-ńeek] m. wrong-doer; pest; nuisance

szkodzić [shko-dźheećh] v. do harm; injure; be harmful; cause damage; disagree with

szkolenie [shko-le-ńe] n. training; instruction; schooling

szkolić [shko-leećh] v. school; train; give instruction; instruct

szkolnictwo [shkol-ńeets-tvo] n. school system; education

szkolny [shkol-ni] adj. m. school; scholastic; of school; school-

szkoła [shko-wa] f. school

szkop [shkop] m. Kraut; Hun (vulg.); (an invading) German

szkopuł [shko-poow] m. obstacle

szkorbut [shkor-boot] m. scurvy

szkuner [shkoo-ner] m. schooner

szkwał [shkvaw] m. squall; flaw

szlaban [shla-ban] m. tollgate;

barrier; train crossing barrier

szlachcic [shlakh-ćheets] m.
squire; nobleman; gentleman

szlachecki [shla-khets-kee] adj.
m. noble; gentle; gentleman's

szlachetny [shla-khet-ni] adj. m.
noble; noble-minded; elegant

szlachta [shlakh-ta] f. gentry

szlachtować [shlakh-to-vaćh] v.
slaughter; brutal killing

szlafrok [shlaf-rok] m.
house-robe; woman's wrapper
(at home); dressing gown

szlak [shlak] m. trail; track;
border; (trade) route; band;
selvage; (animal) scent

szlam [shlam] m. slime; ooze; slit

szlem [shlem] m. big slam
(in bridge, a card game)

szlemik [shle-meek] m. little slam
(in bridge, a card game)

szlifa [shlee-fa] f. epaulettes

szlifierka [shlee-fyer-ka] f.
grinding machine; grinder

szlifierz [shlee-fyesh] m. polisher;
(diamond, etc.) cutter; grinder

szlifować [shlee-fo-vaćh] v.
polish; burnish; cut (diamonds)

szlify [shlee-fi] pl. epaulets

szlochać [shlo-khaćh] v. sob

szmaciany [shma-ćha-ni] adj. m.
rag (doll); made out of rags

szmaragd [shma-ragd] m.
emerald; emerald green color

szmat [shmat] m. large piece;
long way; a good bit; expanse

szmata [shma-ta] f. clout; rag

szmatławiec [shma-twa-vyets]
m. shabby newspaper; smear
sheet; rag; cheep tabloid

szmelc [shmelts] m. scrap; junk;
rubbish; scrap-heap (of metal)

szmer [shmer] m. murmur; rustle

szmerać [shme-raćh] v.
murmur; whisper (of trees)

szmergiel [shmer-gel] m. emery

szminka [shmeen-ka] f. lipstick;
paint; rouge; make up

szmira [shmee-ra] f. literary
garbage; trash; muck

szmirowaty [shmee-ro-va-ti] adj.
m. trashy (literature, paper)

szmonces [shmon-tses] m.

Jewish quip or joke; nonsense
(slang); sarcastic remark

szmugiel [shmoo-gel] m.
smuggle; smuggling; contraband; smuggled goods

szmuglować [shmoo-glo-vaćh]
v. smuggle (goods, etc.)

szmuklerstwo [shmook-ler-stvo]
n. haberdashery (ties, shirts)

szmuklerz [shmook-lesh] m.
haberdasher (men's apparel)

sznur [shnoor] m. rope; cord;
line; twine; twist; raft

sznurek [shnoo-rek] m. string

sznurować [shnoo-ro-vaćh] v.
lace up; lace; tie; purse

sznurowadło [shnoo-ro-vad-wo]
n. shoe lace; lace; shoe string

sznurowany [shnoo-ro-va-ni] adj.
m. laced (shoes, etc.)

sznycel po wiedeńsku [shni-tsel
po vye-deń-skoo] m. Wiener
cutlet; veal cutlet (minced)

szofer [sho-fer] m. chauffeur;
driver; (bus) driver; (truck)
driver; (lorry) driver

szopa [sho-pa] f. shed; lark; fun;
thatch (hairdo) (slang)

szopka [shop-ka] f. puppet
show; little shed; lark; fun;
farce; home-made Christ's crib

szorować [sho-ro-vaćh] v. rub;
scour; scrub; wash; grate; run

szorstki [shorst-kee] adj. m.
coarse; rough; crude; harsh

szorstko [shorst-ko] adv.
roughly; coarsely; bluntly;
crudely; curtly; rudely

szorstkość [shorst-košhćh] f.
roughness; harshness; bluntness; rudeness; crudeness

szosa [sho-sa] f. highway; road

szowinizm [sho-vee-ńeezm] m.
chauvinism; jingoism

szóstka [shoost-ka] f. the figure
six; 6

szósty [shoos-ti] adj. m. num.
sixth; 6th

szpachelka [shpa-khel-ka] f.
small spatula; small putty-
knife; stopping knife

szpachla [shpakh-la] f. spatula;
putty-knife; palette knife

szpachlówka [shpakh-loov-ka] f.
filler; putty; caulking
compound; painter's putty

szpada [shpa-da] f. sword; epee
(fencing sword like a foil)

szpadel [shpa-del] m. spade

szpagat [shpa-gat] m. string;
(ballet) split; cord; twine; twist

szpaler [shpa-ler] m. double
(tree) row; double lane of
people; hedge; two rows of
people (one on each side)

szpalta [shpal-ta] f. (newspaper,
magazine, etc.) column; (printer's) slip; (tanner's) split

szpara [shpa-ra] f. gap; slot; rift;
chink; crack; slit; crevice;
cranny; interstice

szparag [shpa-rak] m. asparagus

szpareczka [shpa-rech-ka] f.
narrow chink; small crack

szpargał [shpar-gaw] m. scrap
paper; scrap of paper

szpatułka [shpa-toow-ka] f.
spatula; tongue-depressor

szpecić [shpe-ćheećh] v.
disfigure; make ugly; mar
beauty; blemish; impair

szperacz [shpe-rach] m. ferreter;
(military) scout; sniper; rum-
mager; searcher (in archives)

szperać [shpe-raćh] v. forage;
burrow; poke about; search (in
books; archives, etc.)

szpetnie [shpet-ńe] adv. in an
ugly fashion; uglily; badly;
shabbily; basely; odiously

szpetny [shpet-ni] adj. m. ugly;
unsightly; shabby; base; vile

szpetota [shpe-to-ta] f. ugliness;
unsightliness; shabbiness

szpic [shpeets] m. spike; peak;
(sharp) point; Pomeranian dog
(Scandinavian Samoyed)

szpica [shpee-tsa] f. picket; head
of an advance military guard

szpicel [shpee-tsel] m. stool
pigeon; informer; sl. nark;
plain-clothes man; spy

szpiczasty [shpee-chas-ti] adj. m.
pointed; tapering (sharply)

szpieg [shpyeg] m. spy; sleuth

szpiegostwo [shpye-gos-tvo] n.

espionage; spying; intelligence

szpiegować [shpye-go-vaćh] v.
spy upon; shadow somebody;
watch somebody; eavesdrop

szpik [shpeek] m. marrow;
medulla; (fatty) bone marrow

szpikować [shpee-ko-vaćh] v.
stuff (with information); lard
(meat etc.); run through

szpilka [shpeel-ka] f. pin (small)

szpilkowy [shpeel-ko-vi] adj. m.
conifer (tree); pegged (soles)

szpikulec [shpee-koo-lets] m.
sharp pin; larding pin; skewer;
spit; (ice) pick

szpila [shpee-la] f. bodkin

szpilka [shpeel-ka] f. pin

szpilkowaty [shpeel-ko-va-ti] adj.
m. needle-like; sharply pointed

szpinak [shpee-nak] m. spinach

szpital [shpee-tal] m. hospital

szpon [shpon] m. claw; talon
pl. (evil, etc.) clutches

szponder [shpon-der] m. flank
(meat); sirloin

szprotka [shprot-ka] f. sprat

szpryca [shpri-tsa] f. syringe

szprycha [shpri-kha] f. spoke

szprycować [shpri-tso-vaćh] v.
sprinkle; syringe

szpula [shpoo-la] f. spool; reel
(for wire, film, etc.); coil

szpulka [shpool-ka] f. bobbin

szpunt [shpoont] m. plug;
stopper; bung; peg; (cabinet
maker's) tongue; feather

szpuntować [shpoon-to-vaćh]
v. bung (barrel); plug; peg

szrama [shra-ma] f. scar; slash

szranki [shran-kee] pl. lists;
bounds; reins; tilt (tournament) yard; barriers; leash

szreń [shreń] f. neve; frost

szron [shron] m. hoar frost; rime;
coat of rime; very light frost

sztab [shtab] m. staff;
headquarters; (General) Staff

sztaba [shta-ba] f. bar; (gold)
ingot; ingot (of silver)

sztabowy [shta-bo-vi] adj. m.
staff (officer, plan, etc.)

sztachety [shta-khe-ti] pl.
(picket) fence; railing

sztafeta [shta-fe-ta] f. relay (race); (military, etc.) courier
sztaluga [shta-loo-ga] f. easel
sztama [shta-ma] f. good understanding (sl.); stay friends
sztanca [shtan-tsa] f. die; stamp; punch (used with a die)
sztandar [shtan-dar] m. banner; (national) flag; infantry colors
sztanga [shtan-ga] f. iron bar; bar-bells; weight-lifting bar
sztangista [shtan-gees-ta] m. weight-lifter (sportsman)
sztokfisz [shtok-feesh] m. stock -fish; cod; codfish
sztolnia [shtol-ńa] f. gallery
sztora [shto-ra] f. blind
sztorm [shtorm] m. gale; storm
sztos [shtos] m. blow; stroke; sexual connection (vulg.)
sztuba [shtoo-ba] f. sl. school
sztubak [shtoo-bak] m. school kid; grade school pupil
sztucer [shtoo-tser] m. rifle (gun); sporting rifle
sztuciec [shtoo-ćhets] m. fork
sztuczka [shtooch-ka] f. trick; small piece; dodge; manoeuvre
sztuczne tworzywo [shtoo-chne tvo-zhi-vo] n. plastic
sztuczny [shtooch-ni] adj. m. artificial; sham; false; immitation
sztućce [shtooćh-tse] pl. (table) silver; knife, fork, and spoons
sztuka [shtoo-ka] f. art; piece; head of cattle; (stage) play; stunt; craft; art (of war); unit
sztukateria [shtoo-ka-ter-ya] f. stucco work; stucco
sztukować [shtoo-ko-vaćh] v. piece; patch up; eke out (a living); lengthen (dress, etc.)
szturchać [shtoor-khaćh] v. poke; dig; prod; jab; push; jostle; knuckle; knock about
szturm [shtoorm] m. attack; storm; assault; onslaught
szturmować [shtoor-mo-vaćh] v. storm; attack; assault; harass; molest; beset
sztych [shtikh] m. stab; engraving; etching; woodcut;

spade thrust (in fencing, etc.)
sztyft [shtift] m. tag; pin; peg; prong; fang; needle
sztylet [shti-let] m. stiletto; dagger; poniard; bodkin; spike
sztywnieć [shtiv-ńéćh] v. stiffen; grow stiff; become stiff; grow (become) rigid
sztywno [shtiv-no] adv. stiffly
sztywny [shtiv-ni] adj. m. stiff; rigid; inflexible; unbending; fixed; stark; puffed up; offish
szubienica [shoo-bye-ńee-tsa] f. gallows (for hanging men)
szubrawiec [shoo-bra-vyets] m. scoundrel; rascal; rogue
szubrawstwo [shoob-rav-stvo] n. villainy; rascally trick; rabble
szufelka [shoo-fel-ka] f. scoop; small shovel; small scoop
szufla [shoof-la] f. shovel
szuflada [shoo-fla-da] f. drawer; shunting; shelving
szuja [shoo-ya] f. scoundrel; rascal; rogue; confidence man
szukać [shoo-kaćh] v. look for; seek; search; cast about for; be bent on; be out for
szukanie [shoo-ka-ńe] n. search; quest; a probing; a seeking
szuler [shoo-ler] m. gambler; card-cheat; cheat; sharp
szulernia [shoo-ler-ńa] f. gambling den; gambling house
szum [shoom] m. (wind) noise; hum; roar; uproar; murmur; scum; spatter; frost
szumieć [shoo-myećh] v. buzz; roar; froth; hum; rustle; fizz; sparkle; revel; carouse
szumnie [shoom-ńe] adv. noisily; boisterously; uproariously; with pump
szumny [shoom-ni] adj. m. roaring; noisy; boisterous; humming; buzzing; frothy; high sounding; bombastic; pompous; uproarious; sonorous
szumowiny [shoo-mo-vee-ni] pl. scum; scum, dregs, lees of society; scum of society
szurać [shoo-raćh] v. scrape; shuffle; rasp; kick up a row;

bluster
szurgać [shoor-gaćh] v. shuffle
noisily; scrape one's foot on
the floor; pick up a trouble
szus [shoos] m. freak; ski run
straight down
szuter [shoo-ter] m. gravel;
broken stone
szuwary [shoo-va-ri] pl. rushes in
wet lands
szwab [shvab] m. roach;
cockroach; Hun; detested
German invader
szwabić [shva-beećh] v. cheat;
swindle
szwaczka [shvach-ka] f.
seamstress; needle woman
szwadron [shvad-ron] m.
squadron; (cavalry) squadron;
troop
szwagier [shva-ger] m. brother-in
-law
szwagierka [shva-ger-ka] f. sister
-in-law
szwagrostwo [shvag-rost-vo] pl.
brother-in-law and wife
szwagrowa [shvag-ro-va] f. wife
of brother-in-law
szwajcar [shvay-tsar] m.
doorman
Szwajcar [shvay-tsar] m. Swiss
szwajcarski [shvay-tsar-skee] adj.
m. Swiss; of Switzerland
szwajcować [shvay-tso-vaćh]
v. weld
szwalnia [shval-ńa] f. underwear
factory; tailoring shop
szwank [shvank] m. injury, loss
szwankować [shvan-ko-vaćh]
v. be faulty; be deficient; be
defective; be out of order
szwarc [shvarts] m. smuggling;
contraband (slang)
szwarcować [shvar-tso-vaćh]
v. smuggle in; smuggle out;
steal in; steal out; dodge the
customs officials; gate-crush
szwargot [shvar-got] m.
gibberish; jabber; lingo
szwargotać [shvar-go-taćh] v.
gibber; jabber
szwedzki [shvedz-kee] adj. m.
Swedish; of Sweden

szwejsować = szwajcować (to
weld)
**szwendać się [shven-daćh
śhan]** v. loiter; hang about;
lop about; gad about
szwindel [shveen-del] m.
swindle; trickery; hanky-
panky; shenanigan
szwindlarz [shveend-lash] m.
swindler; crook; trickster
szwoleżer [shvo-le-zher] m. light
-cavalryman
szyb [shib] m. shaft; (oil) well;
pit; coal shaft; groove; stack
szyba [shi-ba] f. (glass) pane;
wind-shield; sheet of water
szybciej [shib-ćhey] adv. hurry
up! jump to it!
szybka [shib-ka] f. small glass
panel; piece of glass
szybki [shib-kee] adj. m. quick;
fast; prompt; rapid; sharp
(walk); smart (pace)
szybko [shib-ko] adv. quickly;
fast; promptly; swiftly; rapidly;
speedily; apace; hurry up!
**szybkodziałający [shib-ko-dźha
-wa-yown-tsi]** adj. quick-acting
szybkostrzelny [shib-ko-stshel-ni]
adj. rapid-firing
szybkość [shib-kośhćh] f.
speed; rate; velocity; rapidity;
fastness; quickness
szybować [shi-bo-vaćh] v.
glide; soar; tower; sail; plane
szybowiec [shi-bo-vyets] m.
glider (motor-less)
**sztychta nocna [shtikh-ta nots-
-na]** f. night shift
szycie [shi-ćhe] n. sewing
szyć [shićh] v. sew; sew up
szydełko [shi-dew-ko] n. crochet
-needle; crochet hook
szydełkować [shi-dew-ko-vaćh]
v. make by crochet; crochet
szyderca [shi-der-tsa] m. scoffer;
giber; railer
szderczo [shi-der-cho] adv.
scoffingly; sneeringly; jeeringly
szyderczy [shi-der-chi] adj. m.
scoffing; sarcastic; derisive;
sneering; jeering; railing
szyderstwo [shi-der-stvo] n.

scoff; jeer; sneer; gibe;
derision; flout; raillery

szydło [shid-wo] n. awl; pricker

szydzić [shi-dźheéń] v. scoff
at; sneer at; jeer at; gibe at;
flout at; rail at; deride

szyfr [shifr] m. code; cipher

szyfrant [shif-rant] m.
cryptographer; coder

szyja [shi-ya] f. neck; bottleneck;
gullet; throat

szyk [shik] m. order; elegance;
(battle) array; formation

szykana [shi-ka-na] f. chicanery;
vexation; difficulties; petty
annoyances; (great) style

szykanować [shi-ka-no-vaćh] v.
vex; chicane; annoy; nag; pick
at; worry; persecute

szykować [shi-ko-vaćh] v.
make ready; prepare; get
ready; array; marshal

szykować się [shi-ko-vaćh
śhan] v. get ready; be in
prospect; prepare

szykownie [shi-kov-ńe] adv. in
style; smartly; elegantly;
fashionably; with elegance

szykowność [shi-kov-nośhćh]
f. elegance; smartness; style;
chic; recent fashion

szykowny [shi-kov-ni] adj. m.
smart; elegant; fashionable;
classy; dressy; chic

szyld [shild] m. sign-board; shop
sign; facia

szyldwach [shild-vakh] m.
sentry; military guard

szyling [shi-leeng] m. shilling

szympans [shim-pans] m.
chimpanzee

szympansica [shim-pan-śhee-
-tsa] f. female chimpanzee

szyna [shi-na] f. rail; slide-bar;
splint; pl. track, see: szyny

szynel [shi-nel] m. military
overcoat; greatcoat

szynk [shink] m. bar; saloon; pub

szynka [shin-ka] f. ham

szynkarka [shin-kar-ka] f.
barmaid

szynkarz [shin-kash] m. barman

szyny [shi-ni] pl. (railroad) track

szyper [shi-per] m. skipper

szypuła [shi-poo-wa] f. stalk;
stem; peduncle

szypułka [shi-poow-ka] f. small
stalk; stem; shank

szyszak [shi-shak] m. helmet

szyszka [shish-ka] f. (tree) cone;
strobile; bigwig; top-dog

szyzma [shiz-ma] f. schism

Ś

ściana [śhćha-na] f. wall

ścianka [śhćhan-ka] f.
partition; bulkhead; small wall

ściągać [śhćhown-gaćh] v.
draw down or together; cheat
in class; assemble; collect
(taxes, debts, etc.)

ściągaczka [śhćhown-gach-ka]
f. cheat note; crib

ścieg [śhćhek] m. stitch

ściec [śhćhets] v. drain off;
run off; trickle down; drip

ściek [śhćhek] m. sewer;
gutter; sink; sewage; drain;
gully; sullage

ściekać [śhćhe-kaćh] v.
drain off; flow down; trickle
down; drip; gutter

ściemniać [śhćhem-ńaćh] v.
darken; dim; obscure; dim the
lights; turn down the lights

ścienny [śhćhen-ni] adj. m.
mural (painting); wall (map
clock, calendar etc.)

ścierać [śhćhe-raćh] v. rub
off; grind down; wear off

ścierka [śhćher-ka] f. duster;
rug; kitchen towel; clout

ściernisko [śhćher-ńees-ko] n.
stubble field; stubble

ścierń [śhćherń] m. stubble

ścierpły [śhćherp-wi] adj. m.
numb; gone to sleep

ścierwo [śhćher-vo] n. carrion

ścieśniać [śhćheśh-ńaćh]
v. cramp; tighten; narrow;

restrict; close; confine

ścieżka [śhćhezh-ka] f. trail;
pass; (foot) pass; alley

ścięcie [śhćhan-ćhe] n.
beheading; cutting off;
truncation; coagulation

ścięgno [śhćhang-no] n.
tendon; sinew

ścięty [śhćhan-ti] adj.
m. truncated; cut off;
beheaded; coagulated

ścigacz [śhćhee-gach] m.
torpedo boat; motor gun boat

ścigać [śhćhee-gaćh] v.
chase; pursue; run after; hunt
for; prosecute

ścinać [śhćhee-naćh] v. cut
off; cut down; fell (tree); clip;
clot; shear; remove; behead

ścinać się [śhćhee-naćh
śhan] v. coagulate; congeal;
fix; clot; fail (an examination)

ściółka [śhćhoow-ka] f. litter
bed; litter bedding; barn litter

ścisk [śhćheesk] m. throng;
press; crowd; squeeze; crush;
clamp; cleat; hand-screw

ściskać [śhćhees-kaćh] v.
compress; shake (hand); hug;
squeeze; press; clench; pack

ścisłość [śhćhees-wośhćh]
f. exactness; accuracy; compactness; density; reliability;
cohesion; strictness; fidelity

ścisły [śhćhees-wi] adj. m.
exact; precise; compact;
accurate; dense; close-knit

ściśle [śhćheeśh-le] adv.
exactly; tightly; compactly

ślad [śhlat] m. trace; track;
(foot) print; footstep

ślamazara [śhla-ma-za-ra] f.
sluggard; slow headed person

ślamazarny [śhla-ma-zar-ni] adj.
m. sluggish; listless

śląski [śhlown-skee] adj. m.
Silesian; of Silesia

śledczy [śhled-chi] adj. m.
inquisitional; of inquiry

śledzić [śhle-dźheećh] v.
spy; watch; investigate;
observe; shadow; follow

śledziona [śhle-dźho-na] f.

spleen; milt

śledziowy [śhle-dźho-vi]
adj. m. herring (oil, salad, etc.)

śledztwo [śhledz-tvo] n.
investigation; inquest; inquiry

śledź [śhledźh] m. herring

ślepie [śhle-pye] n. (animal's)
eye; eye; lights

ślepnąć [śhlep-nownćh] v. go
blind; loose one's eyesight

ślepa ulica [śhle-pa oo-lee-tsa]
s. dead-end street

ślepota [śhle-po-ta] f.
blindness; cecity; lack of
foresight

ślepy [śhle-pi] adj. m. blind

ślęczeć [śhlan-chećh] v. drag
study or reading; drudge; pore
(over a book); plod; slog
away; boggle; grind

śliczny [śhleech-ni] adj. m.
pretty; lovely; dandy

ślimacznica [śhlee-mach-ńee-
-tsa] f. road access ramp;
helix; warm-wheel; scroll

ślimak [śhlee-mak] m. snail

ślina [śhlee-na] f. saliva

śliniak [śhlee-ńak] m. bib

śliski [śhlees-kee] adj. m.
slippery; slimy; scabrous

śliwa [śhlee-va] f. plum tree

śliwka [śhleev-ka] m. plum

śliwowica [śhlee-vo-vee-tsa] f.
plum brandy; plum vodka

ślizgacz [śhleez-gach] m. speed
-boat; gliding boat

ślizgać się [śhleez-gaćh
śhan] v. slide; glide; slip;
skid; skate (on ice)

ślizgawka [śhleez-gav-ka] f.
skating rink; kid's slide

ślizgowiec [śhleez-go-vyets] m.
hydrofoil; gliding boat; speed
boat

ślub [śhloop] m. wedding; vow

ślubna obrączka [śhloob-na o-
-brownch-ka] f. wedding ring

ślubny [śhloob-ni] adj. m.
nuptial; wedding-(ring);
legitimate (son)

ślubować [śhloo-bo-vaćh] v.
vow; take an oath; pledge

ślusarz [śhloo-sash] m. lock

-smith; ironworker; metal worker

śluz [śhloos] m. slime; phlegm

śluza [śhloo-za] f. sluice

śmiać się [śhmyaćh śhan] v. laugh; laugh at; chuckle; scoff at; make sport of

śmiałek [śhmya-wek] m. daredevil; mad cap

śmiałość [śhmya-wośhćh] f. boldness; courage; bravery; daring; guts; pluck; audacity

śmiały [śhmya-wi] adj. m. bold

śmiech [śhmyekh] m. laughter

śmieci [śhmye-ćhee] pl. rubbish; garbage; rag; shred; scrap of paper; refuse

śmiecić [śhmye-ćheećh] v. litter; throw litter about

śmiecie [śhmye-ćhe] pl. rubbish; garbage; rag; shred; scrap; refuse; sweepings

śmieć [śhmyećh] m. litter; rag; scrap; shred

śmiercionośny [śhmyer-ćho-nośh-ni] adj. m. lethal; deadly; murderous

śmierć [śhmyerćh] f. death

śmierdzieć [śhmyer-dźhećh] v. stink; smell; reek (of vodka, nicotine, carrion)

śmiertelnik [śhmyer-tel-ńeek] m. mortal man; mortal

śmiertelność [śhmyer-tel-nośhćh] f. mortality; deadliness; death rate

śmiertelny [śhmyer-tel-ni] adj. m. mortal; deadly; death-(throes, blow, rattle); fatal

śmieszność [śhmyesh-nośhćh] f. comic trait; the ridiculous; drollery

śmieszny [śhmyesh-ni] adj. m. funny; ridiculous; comic; absurd; amusing; droll

śmieszyć [śhmye-shićh] v. make (people) laugh; cause laughter; amuse

śmietana [śhmye-ta-na] f. sour cream; clotted cream

śmietanka [śhmye-tan-ka] f. cream; flower (of society etc.)

śmietnik [śhmyet-ńeek] m.

garbage can; garbage dump

śmiga [śhmee-ga] f. (windmill) sail

śmigło [śhmeeg-wo] n. propeller; adv. swiftly; nimbly

śmigłowiec [śhmee-**gwo**-vyets] m. helicopter

śniadanie [śhńa-**da**-ńe] n. breakfast; luncheon

śniady [śhńa-di] adj. m. swarthy; sun-tanned; dusky; tawny; dark-skinned

śnić [śhńeećh] v. dream (about something); have a dream; dream that

śniedź [śhńedźh] f. verdigris

śnieg [śhńek] m. snow; snow-scape

śniegowce [śhńe-gov-tse] pl. snow boots; overshoes; galoshes

śnieg pada [śhńek pa-da] exp. it snows

śnieżka [śhńezh-ka] f. snowball; Snow White

śnieżnobiały [śhńezh-no-**bya**-wi] adj. m. snow-white

śnieżny [śhńezh-ni] adj. m. snowy; snow white; snow-

śnieżyca [śhńe-zhi-tsa] f. snow -storm; blizzard

śpiący [śhp**yown**-tsi] adj. m. sleepy; drowsy; slumberous

śpiączka [śhp**yown**ch-ka] f. sleeping sickness

śpieszyć się [śhpye-shićh śhan] v. hurry; hasten; be in a hurry; make haste; be fast

śpiew [śhpyev] m. song; singing; singing lesson

śpiewaczka [śhpye-vach-ka] f. singer (girl or woman)

śpiewać [śhpye-vaćh] v. sing

śpiewak [śhpye-vak] m. singer

śpiewnik [śhpye-ńeek] m. songbook; hymn-book

śpiewny [śhpyev-ni] adj. m. melodious; singsong- (accent)

śpioch [śhpyokh] m. sleepy head; lie-abed; slug-abed

śpiwór [śhpee-voor] m. sleeping bag

średni [śhred-ńee] adj. m.

average; medium; mean; intermediary; middle; mediocre

średnica [śhred-ńee-tsa] f.
diameter; bore; middle register

średnik [śhred-ńeek] m.
semicolon

średnio [śhred-ńo] adv.
average; medium-; fairly well

średniowiecze [śhred-ńo-vye-
-che] n. Middle Ages

średniowieczny [śhred-ńo-
-vyech-ni] adj. m. medieval

środa [śhro-da] f. Wednesday

środek [śhro-dek] m. center;
middle; measures; means;
remedy; interior; midst; inside;
agent; medium; device

środkowy [śhrod-ko-vi] adj. m.
central; center- (line); middle

środowisko [śhro-do-vees-ko]
n. surroundings; environment;
habitat; range; (chem.)
medium

śródmieście [śhrood-myeśh-
-ćhe] n. city center; center of
town; down town area

Śródziemne Morze [śhrood-
-źhem-ne mo-zhe] n.
Mediterranean sea;
Mediterranean

śruba [śhroo-ba] f. screw

śrubokręt [śhroo-bo-krant] m.
screwdriver; turn-screw

śrut [śhroot] m. (lead) shot

świadczenie [śhvyad-che-ńe]
n. benefit; charge; testimony

świadczyć [śhvyad-chićh] v.
witness; attest; bear witness

świadectwo [śhvya-dets-tvo] n.
certificate; bill of health

świadek naoczny [śhvya-dek
na-och-ni] m. exp.: an
eyewitness

świadomość [śhvya-do-
-mośhćh] f. consciousness;
awareness; notice (of sth)

świadomy [śhvya-do-mi]
adj. m. conscious; aware;
wilful; cognizant; voluntary

świat [śhvyat] m. world

światło [śhvyat-wo] n. light

światłomierz [śhvya-two-
-myesh] m. light meter

photometer

światopogląd [śhvya-to-po-
-glownt] m. ideology; outlook
on life; philosophy of life

światowy [śhvya-to-vi] adj. m.
world; worldly; global; society-

świąteczny [śhvyown-tech-ni]
adj. m. festive; holiday
(mood); solemn

świątynia [śhvyown-ti-ńa] f.
temple; place of worship

świder [śhvee-der] m. drill;
auger; bore; borer; perforator

świdrować [śhvee-dro-vaćh]
v. drill; bore; perforate; pierce

świeca [śhvye-tsa] f. candle

świecić [śhvye-ćheećh] v.
light up; shine; glitter; sparkle

świecki [śhvyets-kee] adj. m.
secular; mundane; laic; lay

świecki ksiądz [śhvyets-kee
kśhownts] m. secular priest

świeczka [śhvyech-ka] f.
(small) candle

świecznik [śhvyech-ńeek] m.
chandelier; candlestick

świergot [śhvyer-got] m.
twitter; chirp; warble; chirrup;
tweet; short and shrill tone

świergotać [śhvyer-go-taćh]
v. chirp; chirrup; warble;
tweet; sound like a bird

świerk [śhvyerk] m. fir tree

świerkowy [śhvyer-ko-vi]
adj. m. fir; spruce; of spruce

świerszcz [śhvyershch] m.
cricket; grasshopper

świerzb [śhvyezhb] m. scabies

świerzbieć [śhvyezh-byećh]
v. itch; be itching

świetlica [śhvyet-lee-tsa] f.
reading hall; community center

świetlik [śhvyet-leek] m.
firebug; glow worm; skylight;
firefly; glowing beetle

świetlny [śhvyetl-ni] adj. m.
lighting (gas etc.)

świetność [śhvyet-nośhćh]
f. splendor; magnificence;
glamor; luster

świetny [śhvyet-ni] adj. m.
splendid; excellent; first rate

świeżo [śhvye-zho] adv. fresh

świeży [śhvye-zhi] adj. m.
fresh; new; recent; fresh; raw;
ruddy; brisk; crisp; breezy

święcenie [śhvyan-tse-ńe] n.
celebration; blessing;
observance; consecration

święcić [śhvyan-ćheećh] v.
celebrate; keep a holiday;
bless; observe; ordain

święcone [śhvyan-tso-ne] n.
Easter blessed food (Polish
style traditionally displayed)

święta [śhvyan-ta] pl. holiday

święto [śhvyan-to] n. holiday

świętokradztwo [śhvyan-to-
-krads-tvo] n. sacrilege

świętoszek [śhvyan-to-shek]
m. bigot; sanctimonious
hypocrite

świętość [śhvyan-tośhćh] f.
sanctity; holiness; sainthood

święty [śhvyan-ti] adj. m.
saint; holy; saintly; pious;
sacred; sacrosanct; inviolate

świnia [śhvee-ńa] f. swine;
hog; pig; exp.: dirty pig

świnić [śhvee-ńeećh] v.
make a mess; litter up; play
dirty or shabby tricks

świnka morska [śhveen-ka
mors-ka] f. guinea pig; cavy

świństwo [śhveeńs-tvo] n.
dirty deed; meanness; nasty
stuff; dross

świsnąć [śhvees-nownćh] v.
whistle; pilfer; bolt

świst [śhveest] m. whistle
sound; bullet sound

świstak [śhvees-tak] m.
ground hog; woodchuck

świstawka [śhvees-tav-ka] f.
whistle

świstek [śhvees-tek] m. scrap
of paper; slip of paper

świt [śhveet] m. daybreak;
dawn; sunrise; break of day

świtać [śhvee-taćh] v. dawn
(upon); rise (of sun or moon)

świtezianka [śhvee-te-źhan-ka]
f. water-nymph

T

tabaka [ta-ba-ka] f. snuff

tabakierka [ta-ba-ker-ka] f.
snuff box

tabela [ta-be-la] f. table; index;
list; tabulated figures

tabletka [tab-let-ka] f.
tablet; pill (aspirin etc.)

tablica [tab-lee-tsa] f.
blackboard; switchboard; slab;
signboard; bulletin-board

tablica rozdzielcza [tab-lee-tsa
roz-dźhel-cha] f. switchboard

tabliczka mnożenia [tab-leech-ka
mno-zhe-ńa] f. multiplication
table

tabor kolejowy [ta-bor ko-le-yo-
-vi] m. rolling stock (r.r.)

taboret [ta-bo-ret] m. taboret

tabu [ta-boo] n. taboo

tabun [ta-boon] m. horse herd

taca [ta-tsa] f. tray; salver

taczki [tach-kee] pl. wheelbarrow

tafla [taf-la] f. plate; slab

taić [ta-eećh] v. hide; conceal

tajać [ta-yaćh] v. thaw; melt

tajemnica [ta-yem-ńee-tsa] f.
secret; mystery; secrecy

tajemniczy [ts-yem-ńee-chi] adj.
m. mysterious; inscrutable;
weird; uncanny; secret

tajny [tay-ni] adj. m. secret

tak [tak] part. yes; adv. thus; as;
indecl.: like this; so

tak czy tak [tak chi tak] exp.
anyhow; either way; in any
case; one way or the other

taki [ta-kee] adj. m. such

taki sam [ta-kee sam] adj. m.
identical; similar

takielunek [ta-ke-loo-nek] m.
rig; rigging; tackle

taksa [tak-sa] f. tariff; rate

taksacja [tak-sa-tsya] f. tax
-appraisal

taksować [tak-so-vaćh] v.

estimate; rate; appraise; value
taksówka [tak-**soov**-ka] f. taxi
takt [takt] m. tact; stroke
taktowny [tak-tov-ni] adj. m.
  tactful; considerate
taktyczny [tak-tich-ni] adj. m.
  tactical; political
taktyka [tak-ti-ka] f. tactics
także [tak-zhe] adv. also; too; as
  well; likewise; alike
talent [ta-lent] m. talent
talerz [ta-lesh] m. (food) plate;
  plateful; disk; planting scalp
talerzyk [ta-le-zhik] m. small
  plate; ski-stick disk; scale
talia [ta-lya] f. waist; card deck;
  pack of cards; tackle; middle
talk [talk] m. talcum; talc
talon [ta-lon] m. coupon
tam [tam] adv. there; yonder
tama [ta-ma] f. dam; dike
tamować [ta-mo-vaćh] v. dam
  up; block; check; stem; clog
tamtejszy [tam-tey-shi] adj. m.
  from there; living there
tamten [tam-ten] pron. that
tamtędy [tam-tan-di] adv. that
  way; the other way
tamże [tam-zhe] adv. there in; in
  the same place; at which
  place; (by the same author)
tancerka [tan-tser-ka] f. dancer;
  ballet-dancer; partner
tancerz [tan-tsesh] m. dancer
tandeta [tan-de-ta] f. trashy
  products; shoddy goods
taneczny [ta-nech-ni] adj. m.
  dancing-(school, master, hall);
  dance-(step; music etc.)
tangens [tan-gens] m. tangent
tani [ta-ńee] adj. m. cheap
taniec [ta-ńets] m. dance
tanieć [ta-ńećh] v. get
  cheaper; cheapen; grow
  cheaper; fall in price
taniość [ta-ńośhćh] f.
  cheapness; low prices
tańczyć [tań-chićh] v. dance
tankowiec [tan-ko-vyets] m.
  tanker (ship)
tapczan [tap-chan] m. couch;
  convertible bed
tapeta [ta-pe-ta] f. wallpaper

tapicer [ta-pee-tser] m.
  upholsterer; upholsterer's shop
taran [ta-ran] m. battering ram
tarapaty [ta-ra-pa-ti] pl. trouble;
  predicament; sad fix
taras [ta-ras] m. terrace
tarasować [ta-ra-so-vaćh] v.
  block; stand in the way
tarcica [tar-ćhee-tsa] f. plank;
  deal; sawn board
tarcie [tar-ćhe] n. friction;
  frictional resistance
tarcza [tar-cha] f. shield; disk
tarczowa piła [tar-cho-va pee-
  -wa] f. circular saw
tarczyca [tar-chi-tsa] f. thyroid
  gland
targ [tark] m. country market
targować [tar-go-vaćh] v. sell;
  bargain; trade; haggle; deal
tarka [tar-ka] f. rasp; grater
tartak [tar-tak] m. sawmill
taryfa [ta-ri-fa] f. tariff
tarzać się [ta-zhaćh śhan] v.
  wallow; welter; roll (in mud)
tasak [ta-sak] m. chopper;
  broad blade cleaver
tasiemiec [ta-śhe-myets] m.
  tapeworm; cestoid; taenia
tasiemka [ta-śhem-ka] f. ribbon;
  tape; narrow strip
tasować [ta-so-vaćh] v. shuffle
taśma [taśh-ma] f. band; tape
taśma ruchoma [taśh-ma roo-
  -kho-ma] f. belt conveyor
tatarka [ta-tar-ka] f. buckwheat
taternik [ta-ter-ńeek] m.
  mountain climber; alpinist
tatuować [ta-too-o-vaćh] v.
  tattoo; make a tattoo mark
tatuś [ta-toośh] m. daddy; dad
tchawica [tkha-vee-tsa] f.
  trachea; windpipe
tchnąć [tkhnownćh] v. inspire
tchnienie [tkhńe-ńe] n. breath
tchórz [tkhoosh] m. skunk;
  coward; craven; poltroon; funk
tchórzliwy [tkhoo-zhlee-vi] adj.
  m. cowardly; chicken-hearted
tchórzostwo [tkhoo-zhost-vo] n.
  cowardice; lack of courage
teatr [te-atr] m. theatre; the
  stage

teatralny [te-a-tral-ni] adj. m.
theatrical; scenic; stage-

techniczny [tekh-ńeech-ni] adj.
m. technical (terms, school,
staff); technological (progress)

technik [tekh-ńeek] m.
technician; engineer; mechanic

technika [tekh-ńee-ka] f.
technique; engineering;
technology

technologia [tekh-no-lo-gya] f.
technology; production
engineering; technique

teczka [tech-ka] f. briefcase;
folder; portfolio; jacket; binder

tegoroczny [te-go-roch-ni]
adj. m. this year's

teka [te-ka] f. (large) briefcase;
portfolio; file; folder; case

tekst [tekst] m. text; wording

tekstylny [tek-stil-ni] adj. m.
textile; textile-; draper;
clothier-

tektura [tek-too-ra] f. cardboard;
pasteboard (corrugated)

telefon [te-le-fon] m. telephone;
phone; phone receiver

telefonistka [te-le-fo-ńeest-ka] f.
telephone operator

telefonować [te-le-fo-no-vaćh]
v. ring up; telephone; call up

telegraf [te-le-graf] m. telegraph;
telegraph office

telegraficzny [te-le-gra-feech-ni]
adj. m. telegraphic

telegrafować [te-le-gra-fo-vaćh]
v. cable; wire; telegraph

telegram [te-le-gram] m.
telegram; cable; wire;
cablegram

telepatia [te-le-pa-tya] f.
telepathy; tough transference

teleskop [te-le-skop] m.
telescope; telescopic spring

teleskopowy [te-le-sko-po-vi] adj.
m. telescopic

telewizja [te-le-veez-ya] f.
television; TV

telewizor [te-le-vee-zor] m.
television set; TV set

temat [te-mat] m. subject

temblak [tem-blak] m. sling

temperament [tem-pe-ra-ment]
m. temper; nature; mettle

temperatura [tem-pe-ra-too-ra] f.
temperature; fever

temperować [tem-pe-ro-vaćh]
v. temper; sharpen; mitigate

tamperówka [tem-pe-roov-ka] f.
pencil sharpener

tempo [tem-po] n. rate; tempo

temu [te-moo] adv. ago

ten; ta; to [ten, ta, to] m.f.n.
pron. this; this one

ten sam [ten sam] pron. the
same (man, pencil, etc.)

tendencja [ten-den-tsya] f.
tendency; inclination; drift;
trend; bias; proclivity

tendencyjny [ten-den-tsiy-ni] adj.
m. biased; tendentious

tenis [te-ńees] m. tennis

tenor [te-nor] m. tenor (voice)

tenuta [te-noo-ta] f. land holding;
rent; tenure; lease

tenże [ten-zhe] m. pron. the
same (individual etc.)

teolog [te-o-lok] m. theologian

teologia [te-o-lo-gya] f. theology;
Faculty of Theology

teoretyczny [te-o-re-tich-ni] adj.
m. theoretical; speculative

teoretyk [te-o-re-tyk] m.
theoretician; theorist

teoria [te-o-rya] f. theory

terapia [te-ra-pya] f.
therapeutics; therapy

teraz [te-ras] adv. now;
nowadays; at present

teraźniejszość [te-raźh-ńey-
-shośhćh] f. present (time)

teraźniejszy kurs [te-raźh-ńey-
-shi koors] m. present rate

teren [te-ren] m. terrain

terenowy samochód [te-re-no-vi
sa-mo-khood] m. cross-
country car (four wheel drive)

terkotać [ter-ko-taćh] v. rattle;
clatter; chatter (away)

termin [ter-meen] m. term;
expression; apprenticeship;
time limit; fixed date

termin ostateczny [ter-meen o-
-sta-tech-ni] m. deadline

terminator [ter-mee-na-tor] m.
apprentice; terminator

terminarz [ter-mee-nash] m.
 appointment calendar; agenda
terminologia [ter-mee-no-lo-gya]
 f. terminology; nomenclature
terminowo [ter-mee-no-vo] adv.
 on time; in due time;
 punctually; promptly
termit [ter-meet] m. termite
termometr [ter-mo-metr] m.
 thermometer
termos [ter-mos] m. thermos
 -bottle; vacuum bottle (flask)
terpentyna [ter-pen-ti-na] f.
 turpentine (oil)
terror [ter-ror] m. terror
terroryzować [ter-ro-ri-zo-vaćh]
 v. terrorize; bully
terytorialny [te-ry-tor-yal-ni] adj.
 m. territorial
terytorium [te-ri-tor-yoom] n.
 territory
testament [te-sta-ment] m.
 testament; (last) will
teściowa [teśh-ćho-va] f.
 mother-in-law
teść [teśhćh] m. father-in-law
teza [te-za] f. thesis; argument
też [tesh] adv. also; too;
 likewise; as well
tęchnąć [tankh-nownćh] v. get
 musty; grow mouldy; reduce
 swelling; become reduced
tęcza [tan-cha] f. rainbow
tęczówka [tan-choov-ka] f. iris
tędy [tan-di] adv. this way
tęgi [tan-gee] adj. m. stout;
 strong; solid; fat; big; portly
tęgo [tan-go] adv. stoutly; ably;
 amply; mightily; powerfully
tępak [tan-pak] m. dullard
tępić [tan-peećh] v. dull; blunt;
 destroy; combat; exterminate;
 oppose; fight; persecute
tępota [tan-po-ta] f. dullness;
 stupidity; obtuseness; stolidity
tępy [tan-pi] adj. m. dull; point
 less; slow-witted; stolid
tęsknić [tansk-ńeećh] v. long
 (for); yearn; be nostalgic
tęsknota [tans-kno-ta] f. longing;
 hankering; nostalgia
tęskny [tansk-ni] adj. m.
 melancholy; wistful; longing;

yearning; lingering;sad
tętent [tan-tent] m. hoof beat
tętnica [tan-tńee-tsa] f. artery
tętnić [tant-ńeećh] v. pulsate
tętno [tant-no] n. pulse rate;
 heartbeats; vibrations
tężec [tan-zhets] m. tetanus
tężeć [tan-zhećh] v. stiffen;
 solidify; set; clot; curdle;
 coagulate; grow stronger;
 acquire strength and vigor
tężyzna [tan-zhiz-na] f. vigor
tkacki [tkats-kee] adj. m. textile;
 weaver's; of textiles
tkactwo [tkats-tvo] n. weaving
tkacz [tkach] m. weaver (man)
tkać [tkaćh] v. weave; poke
tkanina [tka-ńee-na] f. fabric
tkanka [tkan-ka] f. tissue
tkliwość [tklee-vośhćh] f.
 tenderness; love; affection
tkliwy [tklee-vi] adj. m. tender;
 loving; affectionate; sensitive
tknąć [tknownćh] v. touch;
 strike; size; affect
tkwić [tkveećh] v. stick; stay
tleć [tlećh] v. smoulder
tlen [tlen] m. oxygen
tlenek [tle-nek] m. oxide
tlić się [tleećh śhan] v.
 smoulder; glow; burn lightly
tło [two] n. background
tłocznia [twoch-ńa] f. press
tłoczyć [two-chićh] v. press;
 crowd; print; stamp; crush
tłok [twok] m. piston; crowd
tłuc [twoots] v. pound; hammer;
 batter; smash; shatter
tłuczek [twoo-chek] m. pestle
tłuczeń [twoo-cheń] m.
 macadam; broken stone; road
 gravel; break-stone
tłum [twoom] m. crowd; mob;
 host; throng; multitude
tłumacz [twoo-mach] m.
 interpreter; translator
tłumaczenie [twoo-ma-che-ńe]
 n. translation; explanation;
 interpretation; excuse
tłumaczyć [twoo-ma-chićh] v.
 translate; interpret; justify
tłumić [twoo-meećh] v. muffle;
 put down; dampen; suppress;

stifle; stamp out; deaden
tłumik [twoo-meek] m. muffler
tłumny [twoom-ni] adj. m.
 crowded; numerous; populous
tłumok [twoo-mok] m. bundle
tłusty [twoos-ti] adj. m. obese;
 fat (meat; pig etc.); rich; oily;
 greasy; corpulent; fatty
tłuszcz [twooshch] m. fat;
 grease
tłuszcza [twoosh-cha] f. mob
tłuścić [twoośh-ćheećh]
 grease; smear with grease
to [to] pron it; this; that; so
toaleta [to-a-le-ta] f. toilet;
 dress; dressing table
toaletowe przybory [to-a-le-to-ve
 pzhi-bo-ri] pl. toilet-articles;
 cosmetics
toast [to-ast] m. toast
tobół [to-boow] m. pack; bundle
toczony [to-cho-ni] adj. m.
 turned; shaped; rounded
toczyć [to-chićh] v. roll;
 machine; wage (war); wheel;
 carry on; shape; fester
toga [to-ga] f. gown; Roman
 toga
tok [tak] m. course; progress
tokarka [to-kar-ka] f. lathe
tokarnia [to-kar-ńa] f. lathe
tokarz [to-kash] m. machinist;
 turner; lathe operator
tokować [to-ko-vaćh] v. toot
tolerancja [to-le-rants-ya] f.
 tolerance; broad-mindedness
tolerować [to-le-ro-vaćh] v.
 tolerate; suffer; stand for
tom [tom] m. volume
ton [ton] m. sound; tone; note
tona [to-na] f. ton (metric etc.)
tonacja [to-na-tsya] f. pitch; key;
 mode; tone; tonal character
tonaż [to-nash] m. tonnage
tonąć [to-nownćh] v. drown
toń [toń] f. deep (water); flood;
 deep sea; depth of water
topaz [to-pas] m. topaz
topić [to-peećh] v. drown;
 thaw; melt down; smelt
 (metals); sink; flux
topiel [to-pyel] f. abyss; gulf
topliwy [to-plee-vi] adj. m.

meltable; fusible; liquescent
topnieć [top-ńećh] v. melt
topografia [to-po-gra-fya] f.
 topography; lay of the land
topola [to-po-la] f. poplar
toporek [to-po-rek] m. hatchet
topór [to-poor] m. (big) hatchet;
 axe; battle axe
tor [tor] m. track; lane; path
tor kolejowy [tor ko-le-yo-vi] m.
 rail-track; railroad track
torba [tor-ba] f. bag; bagful
torcik [tor-ćheek] m. small layer
 cake
torebka [to-reb-ka] f. (hand) bag;
 purse; small bag (or pouch)
torf [torf] m. peat
torfowisko [tor-fo-vees-ko] n.
 peat bog; turbary
torować [to-ro-vaćh] v. clear;
 pave; clear a path; show the
 way; pave the way for
torpeda [tor-pe-da] f. torpedo;
 motor driven rail car
torpedować [tor-pe-do-vaćh] v.
 torpedo; scuttle; obstruct
torpedowiec [tor-pe-do-vyets] m.
 torpedo boat
tors [tors] m. torso
tort [tort] m. tort (multi-layer)
 fancy cake
tortura [tor-too-ra] f. torture
torturować [tor-too-ro-vaćh] v.
 torture; torment; put to torture
totalny [to-tal-ni] adj. m.
 totalitarian; total; entire
towar [to-var] m. merchandise
towarowy dom [to-va-ro-vi dom]
 m. department store
towarzyski [to-va-zhis-kee] adj.
 m. sociable; social
towarzystwo [to-va-zhist-vo] n.
 company; society; companionship; entourage
towarzysz [to-va-zhish] m.
 companion; pal; associate;
 comrade; chum; mate
towarzyszka [to-va-zhish-ka] f.
 companion (female); associate
towarzyszyć [to-va-zhi-shićh] v.
 accompany; escort; keep company; attend; go together
tożsamość [tozh-sa-mośhćh]

f. identity; sameness

tracić [tra-ćheećh] v. lose;
waste; shed (leaves); execute

tradycja [tra-di-tsya] f.
tradition; handing down orally
customs, beliefs, etc.

tradycyjny [tra-di-tsiy-ni] adj. m.
traditional

traf [traf] m. happenstance;
chance; luck; coincidence

trafem [tra-fem] adv. by chance

trafiać [tra-fyaćh] v. hit
(target); guess right; home

trafność [traf-nośhćh] f.
accuracy (of aim); rightness;
soundness; relevancy; fitness

trafny [traf-ni] adj. m. exact;
correct; right; fit; apt

tragarz [tra-gash] m. porter

tragedia [tra-ge-dya] f. tragedy;
very sad or tragic event

tragiczny [tra-geech-ni] adj. m.
tragic; disastrous; very sad

tragikomedia [tra-gee-ko-me-dya]
f. tragicomedy

trajkotać [tray-ko-taćh]
v. chatter; jabber; rattle;
gabble

trak [trak] m. square saw;
frame sawing machine

trakcja [tra-ktsya] f. traction

trakt [trakt] m. highway; course

traktat [tra-ktat] m. treaty

traktor [trak-tor] m. tractor

traktować [trak-to-vaćh] v.
deal; treat; negotiate; discuss

trampolina [tram-po-lee-na] f.
spring board; diving board

tramwaj [tram-vay] m. tramway

tramwajarz [tram-va-yash] m.
tramway worker

tran [tran] m. (cod or whale) oil;
cod liver oil; whale oil

trans [trans] m. trance; ecstasy

transakcja [trans-akts-ya] f.
transaction; deal

transatlantycki [trans-at-lan-tits-
-kee] adj. m. transatlantic

transformator [trans-for-ma-tor]
m. transformer; converter

transfuzja [trans-fooz-ya] f.
transfusion (of blood etc.)

transmisja [trans-mees-ya] f.
transmission; broadcast

transmitować [trans-mee-to-
-vaćh] v. transmit; broadcast

transparent [trans-pa-rent] m.
(marching) slogans; banner

transport [trans-port] m. transport; haulage; consignment

tranzyt [tran-zit] m. transit

tranzytowy [tran-zi-to-vi] adj. m.
transit-; through (traffic etc.)

trapez [tra-pez] m. trapeze

trapić [tra-peećh] v. molest;
pester; worry; annoy; bother

trasa [tra-sa] f. route; (bus) line

trasa podróży [tra-sa po-droo-
-zhi] f. itinerary

tratować [tra-to-vaćh] v.
trample; tread down

tratwa [trat-va] f. raft; float

trawa [tra-va] f. grass

trawić [tra-veećh] v. digest

trawienie [tra-vye-ńe] n.
digestion; consumption

trawnik [trav-ńeek] m. lawn

trąba [trown-ba] f. trumpet;
trunk (elephant); tornado;
twister; horn; whirlwind; ninny

trąba wodna [trown-ba vod-na]
f. waterspout; wind spout

trąbić [trown-beećh] v. bugle;
toot; hoot; roar; proclaim

trąbka [trownb-ka] f. horn; bugle

trącać [trown-caćh] v. jostle;
elbow; tip; knock; nudge;
strike; touch; nudge

trącić [trown-ćheećh] v.
jostle; smell; be fusty; be out
of date; border on (stupidity)

trąd [trownd] m. leprosy

trel [trel] m. trill

trelować [tre-lo-vaćh] v. trill

trema [tre-ma] f. stage fright

trener [tre-ner] m. coach; trainer

trening [tre-ńeeng] m. training

trenować [tre-no-vaćh] v. train;
coach; practice (shooting)

trepanacja [tre-pa-nats-ya] f.
trepanation

trepki [trep-kee] pl. sandals

tresować [tre-so-vaćh] v. train;
tame; drill; break in (horses)

tresura [tre-soo-ra] f. taming;
training (of animals)

treściwy [treśh-ćhee-vi]
adj. m. concise; substantial;
meaty; pithy; terse; brief; rich
treść [treśhćh] f. contents;
jist; substance; essence; pith;
marrow; tenor; purview; plot
trębacz [tran-bach] m. trumpeter
trędowaty [tran-do-va-ti] adj. m.
leprous; leper
triumfować [tree-oom-fo-vaćh]
v. triumph; achieve triumphs;
prevail; exult; jubilate; crow
trochę [tro-khan] adv. a little bit;
a few; some; awhile; a spell
trociny [tro-ćhee-ni] pl.
sawdust (of wood); scraps (of
writings, poetry, etc.)
trofea [tro-fe-a] pl. trophies
trojaki [tro-ya-kee] adj. m.
threefold; triple; treble; triplex
troje [tro-ye] num. three
troki [tro-kee] pl. straps
trolejbus [tro-ley-boos] m.
trolley-bus
tron [tron] m. throne; the throne
trop [trop] m. track; trace
tropić [tro-peećh] v. track
tropikalny [tro-pee-kal-ni] adj. m.
tropical; of the tropics
troska [tros-ka] f. care; anxiety;
worry; concern; solicitude
troskać się [tros-kaćh śhan] v.
care and worry about; be
concerned; take care
troskliwość [tros-klee-vośhćh]
f. thoughtfulness; care; heed
troskliwy [tros-klee-vi] adj. m.
careful; attentive; thoughtful
troszczyć się [trosh-chićh
śhan] v. care; be anxious
about; take care; look after
trotuar [tro-too-ar] m. sidewalk;
pavement (for pedestrians)
trójbarwny [trooy-barv-ni] adj. m.
tricolor; three-colored
trójca [trooy-tsa] f. trinity
trójka [trooy-ka] f. three
trójkąt [trooy-kownt] m. triangle;
set square
trójnasób [trooy-na-soop] three
times as much
trójnik [trooy-ńeek] m. three-
-way (pipe) connection; "T"

(tee) joint; "Y" joint; twye; tee
truchtem [trookh-tem] adv. by
jogging; by trot; at a trot
trucizna [troo-ćheez-na] f.
poison; venom
truć [trooćh] v. poison; bother
(slang); molest; worry
trud [troot] m. pains; toil
trudnić się [trood-ńeećh
śhan] v. occupy oneself; be
engaged; do (for a living)
trudno [trood-no] adv. with
difficulty; too bad; hard
trudność [trood-nośhćh] f.
difficulty; hardship handicap
trudny [trood-ni] adj. m. difficult;
hard; tough; laborious
trudzić [troo-dźheećh] v.
trouble; disturb; cause trouble
trujący [troo-yown-tsi] adj. m.
poisonous; toxic; poison-
trumna [troom-na] f. coffin
trunek [troo-nek] m. drink
trup [troop] m. corpse; cadaver
trupiarnia [troo-pyar-ńa] f.
mortuary; morgue
truskawka [troos-kav-ka] f.
strawberry
truteń [troo-teń] m. drone
trwać [trvaćh] v. last; persist;
stay; remain; linger on
trwały [trva-wi] adj. m. durable
trwanie [trva-ńe] n. duration
trwoga [trvo-ga] f. awe; fright
trwonić [trvo-ńeećh] v. waste;
squander; trifle away; fritter
away (money, time, energy,
opportunity, etc.)
trwożliwy [trvozh-lee-vi] adj. m.
timid; fearful; shy
trwożny [trvozh-ni] adj. m.
anxious; fearful; timid; shy
trwożyć [trvo-zhićh] v. startle;
frighten; scare; be frightened
tryb [trib] m. manner; mode;
mood; gear; procedure; course
trybuna [tri-boo-na] f. tribune;
stand; speaker's platform
trybunał [tri-boo-naw] m. tribunal
trychina [tri-khee-na] f. trichina;
trichinosis
trygonometria [tri-go-no-metr-ya]
f. trigonometry

tryk [trik] m. ram; trick
trykot [tri-kot] m. tricot
trykotaże [tri-ko-ta-zhe] pl.
  hosiery; knittings
trykotowy [tri-ko-to-vi] 1. adj. m.
  tricot; made of tricot
trykotowy [tri-ko-to-vi] 2. adj. m.
  knitted (goods, fabric, wear
trylion [tri-lyon] m. trillion
tryskać [tris-kać] v. spurt;
  spout; gush; jet; squirt; flow;
  eject; stream; burst forth
trywialny [tri-vyal-ni] adj. m.
  trivial; vulgar; coarse; trite
trzask [tshask] m. crack; bang
trzaska [tshas-ka] f. chip (wood)
trzaskać [tshas-kać] v. crack;
  bang; smash; shatter; knock;
  hit; strike; whack; crush
trząść [tshownśhćh] v. shake
trzcina [tshćhee-na] f. cane;
  reed (of bamboo etc.)
trzcina cukrowa [tshćhee-na
  tsook-ro-va] f. sugar cane
trzcinowy [tshćhee-no-vi]
  adj. m. cane (chair); made out
  of cane; reedy (area)
trzeba [tshe-ba] v. imp. ought to;
  one should; it is necessary
trzebić [tshe-beećh] v. clear;
  gut; geld; cut down; destroy
trzeci [tshe-ćhee] num. third
trzeć [tshećh] v. rub; grate
trzepaczka [tshe-pach-ka] f.
  whisk; beater; carpet beater
trzepać [tshe-paćh] v. hit dust
  out; beat (carpet); slap
trzepnąć [tshep-nownćh] v. hit;
  strike; spank; slap; wag; flip;
  flit off; smack
trzepotać [tshe-po-taćh] v. flap;
  flutter; flicker; toss
trzeszczeć [tshesh-chećh] v.
  crack; crackle; creak; crunch;
  rustle; decrepitate; jabber
trzewia [tshe-vya] pl. bowels;
  guts; intestines; entrails
trzewik [tshe-veek] m. shoe;
  slipper; skid; trig
trzeźwieć [tsheźh-vyećh] v.
  sober up; bring back to
  consciousness
trzeźwość [tsheźh-vośhćh]

f. sobriety; level-headedness
trzeźwy [tsheźh-vi] adj. m.
  sober; clear headed; level
  headed; wide awake
trzęsawisko [tshan-sa-vees-ko]
  n. bog; swamp; quagmire;
  slough
trzęsienie ziemi [tshan-śhe-ńe
  źhe-mee] n. earthquake
trzmiel [tshmyel] m. bumblebee
trznadel [tshna-del] m. yellow
  bunting; yellow hammer;
  bunting
trzoda [tsho-da] f. f. herd; flock;
  heard (of swine, pigs, etc.)
trzon [tshon] m. handle; hilt;
  core; main part; trunk; stem
trzonek [tsho-nek] m. shaft;
  shank; handle (of a hammer,
  axe, etc.); helve
trzonowy ząb [tsho-no-vi zownb]
  m. molar; grinder
trzpień [tshpyeń] m. pin
trzpiot [tshpyot] m. giddy; gay
trzustka [tshoost-ka] f. pancreas;
  sweetbread
trzy [tshi] num. three
trzydziestokrotny [tshi-dźhes-to-
  -krot-ni] adj. m. thirty-fold
trzydziestoletni [tshi-dźhes-to-
  -let-ńee] adj. m. thirty year
  old (man, oak, etc.)
trzydziesty [tshi-dźhes-ti] num.
  thirtieth
trzydzieści [tshi-dźheśh-ćhee]
  num. thirty; 30
trzykrotny [tshi-krot-ni] adj. m.
  threefold
trzylampowy [tshi-lam-po-vi] adj.
  m. three-lamp
trzyletni [tshi-let-ńee] adj. m.
  three year old (boy, car, etc.)
trzymać [tshi-maćh] v. hold;
  keep; cling; clutch; hold on to
trzynasty [tshi-nas-ti] num.
  thirteenth; 13th
trzynaście [tshi-naśh-ćhe]
  num. thirteen; 13
trzypiętrowy [tshi-pyant-ro-vi]
  adj. m. three-story high
  (house)
trzysta [tshis-ta] num. three
  hundred; 300

tu [too] adv. here; in here
tuba [too-ba] f. tube; horn
tubka [toob-ka] f. small tube
tuberkuliczny [too-ber-koo-leech-
  -ni] adj. m. tuberculous
tubylczy [too-bil-chi] adj. m.
  native; indigenous; local
tubylec [too-bi-lets] m. native;
  aboriginal; local inhabitant
tucznik [tooch-ńeek] m. porker
tuczyć [too-chićh] v. fatten
tulejka [too-ley-ka] f. socket
tulić [too-leećh] v. hug; fondle
tulipan [too-lee-pan] m. tulip
tułacz [too-wach] m. wanderer;
  vagrant; exile; homeless
  wanderer
tułaczka [too-wach-ka] f.
  homeless wandering;
  wandering life
tułać się [too-waćh śhan] v.
  wander; be homeless; be in
  exile
tułów [too-woov] m. torso
tum [toom] m. cathedral; minster
tuman [too-man] m. 1. dust
  -cloud; mint; 2. dummy;
  nitwit; duffer; addle-head
tunel [too-nel] m. tunnel
tupać [too-paćh] v. stamp
  one's foot; tramp
tupet [too-pet] m. nerve;
  chutzpa; self-assurance;
  impudence; nerve; cheek
tur [toor] m. bison; aurochs
turbina [toor-bee-na] f. turbine
turecki [too-rets-kee] adj. m.
  Turkish (saddle; fashion etc.)
turkawka [toor-kav-ka] f.
  turtledove; wild dove
turkot [toor-kot] m. rumble;
  rattle
turkotać [toor-ko-taćh] v.
  rumble; bump along; rattle
turkus [toor-koos] m. turquoise
turniej [toor-ńey] m. tournament
turysta [too-ris-ta] m. tourist
turystyczny [too-ris-tich-ni] adj.
  m. tourist; touring-
tusz [toosh] m. 1. shower; hit;
  2. India ink; mascara
tusza [too-sha] f. corpulence
tuszować [too-sho-vaćh] v. 1.

draw with ink; 2. cover up;
  hush up; stifle (a scandal etc.)
tutaj [too-tay] adv. here
tutejszy [too-tey-shi] adj. m.
  local (custom, man); of this
  place; of our (place, country)
tuzin [too-źheen] m. dozen
tuż [toosh] adv. near by; close
  by; just before; just after
tuż obok [toosh o-bok] adv. next
  too; near by; close by
twardnieć [tvard-ńećh] v.
  harden; stiffen; fix; bind
twardość [tvar-dośhćh] f.
  hardness; stiffness; severity
twardy [tvar-di] adj. m. hard
twarożek [tva-ro-zhek] m.
  cottage cheese; small cottage
  cheese; curds
twaróg [tva-rook] m. cottage
  cheese curds; cottage cheese
twarz [tvash] f. face;
  physiognomy; aspect
twarzowy [tva-zho-vi] adj. m.
  becoming; facial (bone etc.)
twierdza [tvyer-dza] f. fortress;
  stronghold; citadel
twierdzący [tvyer-dzown-tsi] adj.
  m. affirmative (answer etc.)
twierdzenie [tvyer-dze-ńe] n.
  affirmation; theorem; assertion
twierdzić [tvyer-dźheećh] v.
  assert; maintain; affirm; say
twornik [tvor-ńeek] m. armature
tworzyć [tvo-zhićh] v. create;
  form; compose; produce;
  make; bring to life
tworzywo sztuczne [tvo-zhi-vo
  shtooch-ne] n. plastic
twój [tvooy] pron. yours; your
twór [tvoor] m. creation; piece
  of work; origination; outgrowth; composition
twórca [tvoor-tsa] m. creator;
  author; maker; originator
twórczość [tvoor-chośhćh] f.
  creation; output; production
twórczy [tvoor-chi] adj. m.
  creative; originative; formative
ty [ti] pron. you (familiar form)
tyczka [tich-ka] v. pole; perch
tyczyć się [ti-chićh śhan] v.
  concern; regard; refer to

tyć [tićh] v. grow fat
tydzień [ti-dźheń] m. week
tyfus [ti-foos] m. typhus
tygiel [ti-gel] m. crucible
tygodnik [ti-god-ńeek] m.
  weekly (magazine etc.)
tygodniowy [ti-god-ńo-vi]
  adj. m. weekly (pay etc.)
tygrys [ti-gris] m. tiger; type of
  German tank in World War II
tygrysica [ti-gri-śhee-tsa] f.
  tigress
tyka [ti-ka] f. perch; pole
tyka miernicza [ti-ka myer-ńee-
  -cha] f. surveyor's rod
tykać [ti-kaćh] v. touch; affect;
  tick; strike; call by first name
tykwa [tik-va] f. pumpkin
tyle [ti-le] adv. so much; so
  many; that much (was done)
tylekroć [ti-le-kroćh] adv. so
  many times; that many times
tylko [til-ko] adv. only; but; just
tylko co [til-ko tso] adv. just
  now; a moment ago; this instant; just a minute ago
tylna straż [til-na strash] f. rear
  guard
tylny [til-ni] adj. m. back; hind
  (leg etc.); rear (light etc.)
tył [tiw] m. back; rear; stern
tym lepiej [tim le-pyey] adv. so
  much better
tymczasem [tim-cha-sem] adv.
  meantime; during; at the time
tymczasowo [tim-cha-so-vo] adv.
  provisionally; temporarily
tymczasowy [tim-cha-so-vi] adj.
  m. temporary; provisional
tynk [tink] m. plaster (work)
tynkować [tin-ko-vaćh] v.
  plaster; rough cast (a wall)
tynktura [tin-ktoo-ra] f. tincture;
  tinge; light color
typ [tip] m. type; model; guy
typowy [ti-po-vi] adj. m. typical;
  standard (article etc.)
tyrada [ti-ra-da] f. tirade
tyran [ti-ran] m. tyrant; bully
tyrania [ti-ra-ńya] f. tyranny
tyrański [ti-rań-skee] adj. m.
  tyrannical; tyrannous; bullying
tysiąc [ti-śhownts] num.

  thousand; 1,000
tysiąclecie [ti-śhownts-le-ćhe]
  n. millennium
tysiącletni [ti-śhownts-let-ńee]
  adj. m. millinery
tysięczny [ti-śhanch-ni] num.
  thousandth; 1,000th
tytan [ti-tan] m. titan; titanium;
  demon (of work etc.)
tytaniczny [ti-ta-ńeech-ni]
  adj. m. titanic; huge
tytoniowy [ti-to-ńo-vi] adj. m.
  tobacco; of tobacco leaves
tytoń [ti-toń] m. tobacco
tytularny [ti-too-lar-ni] adj. m.
  titular; nominal
tytuł [ti-toow] m. title
tytułowa strona [ti-too-wo-va
  stro-na] f. title page
tytułować [ti-too-wo-vaćh] v.
  entitle; address; style as a...

U

u [oo] adj. mbeside; at; with; by;
  on; from; in; (idiomatic)
u boku [oo bo-koo] exp.: at
  one's side (to have a helper, a
  sabre...)
ubarwić [oo-bar-veećh] v. color
ubawić się [oo-ba-veećh śhan]
  v. have fun; have a good
  laugh
ubezpieczać [oo-bez-pye-chaćh]
  v. insure; secure; protect
ubezpieczalnia [oo-bez-pye-chal-
  -ńa] f. health insurance
  center; insurance company
ubezpieczenie [oo-bez-pye-che-
  -ńe] n. insurance; protection
ubezpieczenie życia [oo-bez-pye-
  -che-ńe zhi-ćha] n. life
  insurance; life assurance
ubezpieczenie społeczne
  [oo-bez-pye-che-ńe
  spo-wech-ne] n. social
  security insurance
ubiec [oo-byets] v. run; pass
ubiegać się [oo-bye-gaćh

śhan] v. solicit; compete for
ubiegły [oo-**byeg**-wi] adj. m.
past; last (year,week etc.)
ubierać [oo-bye-rać] v. dress
ubijaczka [oo-bee-**yach**-ka] f.
stamper; compactor; kitchen
whisk; stamping machine
ubijać [oo-bee-yać] v. stamp;
churn; chip; kill; pack; ram
ubijać interes [oo-bee-yać
een-te-res] v. strike a bargain;
strike a deal
ubikacja [oo-bee-**kats**-ya] f.
toilet; rest room; powder
room; men's room; W.C.
ubiór [oob-yoor] m. attire; grab
ubliżać [oo-blee-zhać] v.
insult; offend; affront
ubliżający [oo-blee-zha-**yown**-tsi]
adj. m. offensive; insulting;
disparaging
uboczny produkt [oo-**boch**-ni pro-
-dookt] m. byproduct
ubogi [oo-bo-gee] adj. m. poor
ubolewać [oo-bo-le-vać] v.
deplore; feel sympathy for
ubolewanie [oo-bo-le-**va**-ńe] n.
regret; lamentation; sympathy
ubożeć [oo-bo-zheć] v.
become poor; become
impoverished
ubój [oo-booy] m. slaughter
ubóstwiać [oo-**boost**-vyać] v.
idolize; love; be crazy about
ubóstwo [oo-**boost**-vo] n.
poverty; destitution;
meagerness
ubóść [oo-boośhćh] v. gore
ubrać [oob-rać] v. dress
ubranie [oob-ra-ńe] n. clothes;
decoration; putting in a fix
ubytek [oo-bi-tek] m. decrease
ubytek krwi [oo-bi-tek **krvee**]
blood loss
ubywać [oo-bi-vać] v. retire;
go; lessen; reduce; decrease
ucałować [oo-tsa-**wo**-vać] v.
kiss (somebody good night,
good-bye, etc.)
ucho [oo-kho] n. ear; handle;
(needle) eye; ring (of anchors)
uchodzić [oo-kho-dźhećh] v.
go away; flee; pass (for)

uchodźca [oo-khodźh-tsa] m.
refugee; displaced person
uchować [oo-kho-vać] v.
save; preserve; save; retain;
keep; rear
uchronić [oo-khro-ńeećh] v.
guard; preserve; protect; keep
uchwalać [oo-khva-lać] v.
pass a law; resolve; decide
uchwała [oo-khva-wa] f.
resolution; vote; law
uchwycić [oo-khvi-ćheećh] v.
grasp; catch; seize; see; get
uchwyt [ookh-vit] m. handle
uchwytny [oo-khvit-ni] adj. m.
graspable; palpable; audible
uchybiać [oo-khib-yać] v. fail;
offend; transgress
uchybienie [oo-khib-bye-ńe] n.
offense; transgression; insult
uchylać [oo-khi-lać] v. put
aside; half-open; set ajar
uciążliwy [oo-ćhown-zhlee-vi]
adj. m. burdensome; heavy
ucichać [oo-ćhee-khać] v.
calm down; be hushed; abate
uciecha [oo-ćhe-kha] f. joy
ucieczka [oo-ćhech-ka] f.
escape; flight; desertion;
recourse
ucieleśnić [oo-ćhe-leśh-
-ńeećh] v. embody; personify
uciekać [oo-ćhe-kać] v. flee
uciemiężać [oo-ćhe-myan-
-zhać] v. oppress; burden;
tread down
ucierać [oo-ćhe-rać] v. wipe
off; grind; grate; level; pound
ucierpieć [oo-ćher-pyećh] v.
suffer from; be hard hit by;
sustain a loss of
ucieszny [oo-ćhesh-ni] adj. m.
funny; comical; droll; amusing
ucieszyć [oo-ćhe-shićh] v.
gladden; please; gratify;
delight; give joy; amuse
ucinać [oo-ćhee-nać] v. cut
off; clip; curtail; break off
ucisk [oo-ćheesk] m. oppression
uciskać [oo-ćhees-kać] v.
press down; pinch; oppress;
hurt; compress; screw down
uciszyć [oo-ćhe-shićh] v.

silence; quiet; still; soothe; lull
uciułać [oo-ćhoo-waćh] v.
scrape together; save; put
aside; store up (money, etc.)
uczcić [ooch-ćheećh] v. honor;
dignify; celebrate; do the
honor of; commemorate
uczciwy [ooch-ćhee-vi] adj. m.
honest; upright; straight
uczelnia [oo-chel-ńa] f. school;
college; academy; university
uczenie [oo-che-ńe] n. learning;
teaching; adv. learnedly
uczennica [oo-chen-ńee-tsa] f.
schoolgirl; (girl) pupil
uczeń [oo-cheń] m. schoolboy
uczepić [oo-che-peećh] v. hang
on; hitch; hook; attach; fasten
uczesać [oo-che-saćh] v. comb
(hair); brush hair; dress hair
uczesanie [oo-che-sa-ńe] n.
hairdo; hairstyle; coiffure
uczestniczyć [oo-chest-ńee-
-chićh] v. take part in; share
in; participate in
uczestnik [oo-chest-ńeek] m.
participant; (sport) competitor
uczęszczać [oo-chansh-chaćh]
v. frequent; attend (concerts);
go to (school...)
uczony [oo-cho-ni] m. scientist;
learned; erudite; scholarly man
uczta [ooch-ta] f. feast; banquet
uczucie [oo-choo-ćhe] n. feeling
uczuciowy [oo-choo-ćho-vi] adj.
m. sensitive; emotional;
sentimental
uczuć [oo-chooćh] v. feel;
realize; become aware of
uczyć [oo-chićh] v. teach; train
uczyć się [oo-chićh śhan] v.
learn; study; take lessons
uczynek [oo-chi-nek] m. deed
uczynić [oo-chi-ńeećh] v. do;
make (sb. rich; happy)
uczynność [oo-chin-noshćh]
f. kindness; helpfulness
uczynny [oo-chin-ni] adj. m.
obliging; helpful; cooperative
udany [oo-da-ni] adj. m.
successful; put-on; sham
udar słoneczny [oo-dar swo-
-nech-ni] m. sunstroke

udaremnić [oo-da-rem-ńeećh]
v. frustrate; foil; upset; defeat
udawać [oo-da-vaćh] v.
pretend; imitate
udawać się [oo-da-vaćh śhan]
v. go; succeed; manage; pan
out; make for
udeptać [oo-dep-taćh] v. tread
down; beat a path; tread on
uderzać [oo-de-zhaćh] v. hit
uderzenie [oo-de-zhe-ńe] n.
blow; stroke; hit; bump;
impact; slap; percussion
udo [oo-do] n. thigh
udobruchać [oo-do-broo-khaćh]
v. appease; win over; coax
udogodnić [oo-do-god-ńeećh]
v. facilitate; improve
udoskonalenie [oo-dos-ko-na-le-
-ńe] n. perfection;
improvement
udoskonalić [oo-dos-ko-na-
-leećh] v. perfect; improve
udostępnić [oo-dos-tanp-
-ńeećh] v. give access; put
within reach; facilitate
udowodnić [oo-do-vod-ńeećh]
v. prove; demonstrate;
substantiate; evidence
udowodnienie [oo-do-vod-ńe-
-ńe] n. evidence; proof;
demonstration
udręka [ood-ran-ka] f. anguish;
torment; distress; worry
udusić [oo-doo-śheećh] v.
strangle; smother; stifle;
throttle; suffocate; stew
udział [oo-dźhaw] m. share;
part; quota; participation
udziałowiec [oo-dźha-wo-vyets]
m. shareholder; partner
udzielać [oo-dźhe-laćh] v. give;
grant; furnish; apply
udzielenie [oo-dźhe-le-ńe] n.
giving; granting; dispensing
ufać [oo-faćh] v. trust; confide;
ufność [oof-noshćh] f.
confidence; trust; reliance
ufny [oof-ni] adj. m. confident;
trustful; hopeful; reliant;
sanguine
ufundować [oo-foon-do-vaćh]
v. found; set up; endow;

establish; make a gift
uganiać się [oo-ga-ńaćh
śhan] v. chase after; seek
(graces, job, etc.)
ugaszczać [oo-**gash**-chaćh] v.
entertain; treat; feast; treat to
uginać [oo-gee-naćh] v. bend
down; deflect; bow before
ugłaskać [oog-**was**-kaćh] v.
tame; humor; conciliate; coax
ugniatać [oog-**ńa**-taćh] v.
press down; exert pressure;
pinch; crush; oppress
ugoda [oo-go-da] f. agreement
ugodowiec [oo-go-do-vyets] m.
compromiser; advocate of
conciliation
ugodowy [oo-go-do-vi] adj. m.
conciliatory; amicable
ugodzić [oo-go-dźheećh] v.
hit; hire; come to terms
ugór [oo-goor] m. fallow
ugryźć [oog-riśhćh] v. bite
off; bite; sting
ugrzęznąć [oo-**gzhanz**-nownćh]
v. stick; be stuck; get bogged
uiszczenie [oo-eesh-che-ńe] n.
payment (of a bill, rent etc.)
uiścić [oo-**eeśh**-ćheećh] v.
pay up (a debt); pay; remit (a
sum); discharge (a debt)
ujadać [oo-ya-daćh] v. yelp;
bark; quarrel; wrangle
ujarzmić [oo-yazh-meećh] v.
subdue; enslave; enthrall;
subjugate; oppress
ujawniać [oo-yav-ńaćh] v.
reveal; disclose; expose;
unmask; show; lay open
ująć [oo-**yownćh**] v. conceive;
deduct; seize; grasp; lessen;
catch hold of; clasp; detain
ujednolicić [oo-yed-no-**lee**-
-ćheećh] v. standardize;
unify; make uniform
ujemny [oo-yem-ni] adj. m.
negative (value etc.);
unfavorable; detrimental
ujeżdżać [oo-yezh-dzhaćh] v.
break in (a horse); smooth (a
road by the wheels of cars)
ujeźdżalnia [oo-yezh-dzhal-ńa]
f. riding school; manege

ujęcie [oo-**yan**-ćhe] n. grasp
ujma [ooy-ma] f. detraction
ujmować [ooy-mo-vaćh] v.
seize restrain; embrace;
apprehend; express
ujmujący [ooy-moo-**yown**-tsi]
adj. m. winsome; engaging;
prepossessing
ujrzeć [ooy-zhećh] v. see;
glimpse; get a sight of
ujście [ooyśh-ćhe] n.
escape;(river) mouth;
withdrawal; retreat; outlet;
issue; vent (to indignation)
ukamienować [oo-ka-mye-**no**-
-vaćh] v. stone sb; stone to
death; lapidate
ukazać [oo-ka-zaćh] v. show
(appear); exhibit; reveal
ukąsić [oo-**kown**-śheećh] v.
bite; sting; bite off
ukąszenie [oo-k**own**-**she**-ńe] n.
bite; sting
uklęknąć [oo-klank-**nownćh**] v.
genuflect; kneel down
układ [ook-wat] m. scheme;
agreement; disposition;
system; arrangement
układać się [ook-**wa**-daćh
śhan] v. lay down; negotiate;
settle down; pan out
układanka [oo-kwa-dan-ka] f.
jigsaw puzzle; building blocks
układny [ook-**wad**-ni] adj. m.
polite; urbane; affable;
mannerly; courteous
ukłon [ook-won] m. bow
(greeting); salute
ukłonić się [oo-kwo-ńeećh
śhan] v. bow (to sb); tip
one's hat; greet
ukłucie [oo-kwoo-ćhe] n. prick;
sting; sharp pain; prod; twinge
ukochać [oo-ko-khaćh] v. take
a fancy; grow fond of; hug
ukochana [oo-ko-kha-na] adj. f.
beloved; darling; pet (female)
ukochany [oo-ko-kha-ni] adj. m.
beloved; darling; pet (male)
ukoić [oo-ko-eećh] v. soothe
ukojenie [oo-ko-ye-ńe] n. relief;
consolation; alleviation
ukończyć [oo-koń-chićh] v.

complete; finish; end (school
etc.); bring to an end
ukos [oo-kos] m. slant; incline
ukośny [oo-**kosh**-ni] adj. m.
oblique; sloping; skew;
diagonal; sidelong (glance)
ukracać [oo-kra-tsaćh] v. curb;
subdue; reform; check; put an
end; suppress; daunt sb
ukradkiem [oo-krad-kem] adv.
stealthily; by stealth; furtively
ukraiński [ook-ra-eeń-skee] adj.
m. Ukrainian; of Ukraine
ukrajać [oo-kra-yaćh] v. cut off
ukręcić [ook-ran-ćheećh] v.
twist off; roll up; wrench off
ukrop [ook-rop] m. boiling water;
feverish bustle
ukrócić [ook-**roo**-ćheećh] v.
repress; curb; reform; put an
end to
ukrycie [ook-ri-ćhe] n. hiding
place; hideaway; hideout;
cover
ukrywać [oo-**kri**-vaćh] v. hide;
cover up; conceal; hold back
ukryty [ook-ri-ti] adj. m. hidden;
concealed; put out of sight
ukrywać [ook-ri-vaćh] v. hide
ukształtować [ook-shtaw-to-
-vaćh] v. shape; fashion; cast
ukształtowanie [oo-kshtaw-to-va-
-ńe] n. configuration;
formulation; form; shape
ukuć [oo-koočh] m. hammer out
ul [ool] m. beehive; hive
ulać [oo-laćh] v. pour off; cast
(metal); pour off water
ulatać [oo-la-taćh] v. fly off
ulatniać się [oo-lat-ńaćh
śhan] v. evaporate; volatile;
vanish; melt away; leak;
escape; cease; disappear
ulatywać [oo-la-ti-vaćh] v. fly
away; leak (vapors, odors,
smells); rise in the air
uleczalny [oo-le-chal-ni] adj. m.
curable; remediable; medicable
uleczenie [oo-le-che-ńe] n. cure;
successful recovery
uleczyć [oo-le-chićh] v. heal
ulegać [oo-le-gaćh] v. yield
uległy [oo-leg-wi] adj. m.

submissive; docile; compliant
ulepszać [oo-lep-shaćh] v.
improve; better; ameliorate
ulepszenie [oo-lep-she-ńe] n.
improvement; amelioration
ulewa [oo-le-va] f. rainstorm
ulewać [oo-le-vaćh] v. pour off;
cast (metals); pour (water)
ulga [ool-ga] f. relief; solace
uleżeć się [oo-le-zhećh śhan]
v. mellow; settle; lie quiet
ulica [oo-lee-tsa] f. street
uliczka [oo-leech-ka] f. lane
ulicznica [oo-leech-ńee-tsa] f.
prostitute; streetwalker
ulicznik [oo-leech-ńeek] m.
gamin; guttersnipe; nipper
ulitować się [oo-lee-to-vaćh
śhan] v. have pity; take pity
ulotka [oo-lot-ka] f. handbill;
leaflet; throwaway
ultimatum [ool-tee-ma-toom] n.
ultimatum; final offer
(demand)
ultrafioletowy [ool-tra-fyo-le-to-
-vi] adj. m. ultraviolet
ulubieniec [oo-loo-bye-ńets]
favorite; darling; pet
ulubiony [oo-loo-byo-ni] adj. m.
beloved; favorite; pet
ulżyć [ool-zhićh] v. relive
ułamać [oo-wa-maćh] v. break
off; be broken off; come off
ułamek [oo-wa-mek] m. fraction;
fragment; mathematical
fraction
ułamkowy [oo-wam-ko-vi]
adj. m. fractional
(number, report etc.)
ułan [oo-wan] m. uhlan (Polish
light cavalryman (lancer)
ułaskawić [oo-was-ka-veećh] v.
pardon (a condemned person)
ułaskawienie [oo-was-ka-**vye**-ńe]
n. pardon; reprieve
ułatwić [oo-**wat**-veećh] v.
facilitate; simplify; make easier
ułatwienie [oo-wat-**vye**-ńe] n.
facilitation; simplification
ułomność [oo-**wom**-nośhćh]
f. deformity; defect; frailty
ułomny [oo-**wom**-ni] adj. m.
disabled; defective; lame;

faulty
ułożony [oo-wo-zho-ni] adj. m.
  arranged; well-mannered; set
umacniać [oo-mats-ńaćh] v.
  strengthen; fortify; secure
umaczać [oo-ma-chaćh] v. dip;
  wet; soak; sop; have hand in
umarły [oo-mar-wi] adj. m.
  deceased; dead
umartwiać [oo-mart-vyaćh] v.
  mortify (a person)
umarzać [oo-ma-zhaćh] v.
  amortize; discontinue; remit
umawiać się [oo-mav-yaćh
  śhan] v. make a date (or
  plan); appoint; fix (a price)
umeblować [oo-meb-lo-vaćh] v.
  furnish; fit out; fit up
umeblowanie [oo-meb-lo-va-ńe]
  n. furniture; furnishings
umiar [oom-yar] m. moderation
umiarkowany [oo-myar-ko-va-ni]
  adj. m. moderate; temperate
umieć [oo-myećh] v. know-
  -how; be able to
umiejętność [oo-mye-yant-
  -nośhćh] f. science; skill;
  know-how; art of; knack of
umiejscowić [oo-myey-stso-
  -veećh] v. locate; assign a
  place; fix a place
umierać [oo-mye-raćh] v. die
umieszczać [oo-myesh-chaćh]
  v. place; put; set; insert; seat
umilać [oo-mee-laćh] v. make
  pleasant; add charm; give
  charm; beguile (the time)
umilknąć [oo-meelk-nownćh] v.
  fall silent; cease talking
umiłowany [oo-mee-wo-va-ni]
  adj. m. beloved; favorite; dear
umizgać się [oo-meez-gaćh
  śhan] v. flirt; woo; court;
  ogle sb; make love (to sb)
umizgi [oo-meez-gee] pl. flirting;
  courtship; love making
umniejszać [oo-mńey-shaćh] v.
  diminish; lessen; belittle; abate
umocnić [oo-mots-ńeećh] v.
  strengthen; fortify; beef up
umocnienie [oo-mots-ńe-ńe] n.
  consolidation; fortification
umocować [oo-mo-tso-vaćh] v.

fasten; hitch; fix; secure
umorzyć [oo-mo-zhićh] v.
  absolve; amortize; extinguish
umowa [oo-mo-va] f. contract
umowny [oo-mov-ni] adj. m.
  contractual; conventional
umożliwić [oo-mozh-lee-veećh]
  v. make possible; enable
umówić = **umawiać**
umundurowanie [oo-moon-doo-
  -ro-va-ńe] n. uniforms;
  uniform
umyć [oo-mićh] v. wash up
umykać [oo-mi-kaćh] v. run
  away; escape; take flight
umysł [oo-misw] m. mind;
  intellect; brain; spirit
umysłowy [oo-mis-wo-vi] adj. m.
  mental; intellectual; brain
umyślnie [oo-miśhl-ńe] adv. on
  purpose; specially; purposely
umyślny [oo-miśhl-ni] adj. m.
  intentional; deliberate; special
umywać się [oo-mi-vaćh śhan]
  v. wash up; have a wash; be
  fit for comparison
umywalnia [oo-mi-val-ńa] f.
  washroom; washstand
unaocznić [oo-na-och-ńeećh]
  v. make evident; visualize
unarodowić [oo-na-ro-do-veećh]
  v. nationalize; put to state
  control; make national
unarodowienie [oo-na-ro-do-vye-
  -ńe] nationalization
uncja [oon-tsya] f. ounce
unia [ooń-ya] f. union
unicestwić [oo-ńee-tses-
  -tveećh] v. annihilate;
  frustrate; destroy entirely
unicestwienie [oo-ńee-tses-tvye-
  -ńe] n. annihilation; frust-
  ration; complete destruction
uniemożliwić [oo-ńe-mozh-lee-
  -veećh] v. make impossible
unieruchomić [oo-ńe-roo-kho-
  -meećh] v. immobilize; tie up
unieszkodliwić [oo-ńe-shkod-
  -lee-veećh] v. render harmless
unieść [oo-ńeśhćh] v. lift up
unieważnić [oo-ńe-vazh-
  -ńeećh] v. annul; void;
  cancel; repeal; abrogate

unieważnienie [oo-ńe-vazh-ńe-
-ńe] n. annulment; invali-
dation; nullification

uniewinnić [oo-ńe-veen-
-ńećh] v. acquit; exculpate;
excuse; clear of charge

uniewinnienie [oo-ńe-veen-ńe-
-ńe] n. acquittal

uniezależnić [oo-ńe-za-lezh
-ńećh] v. make independent

uniform [oo-ńee-form] m.
uniform

unikać [oo-ńee-kaćh] v. avoid;
shun; steer clear; abstain from

unikat [oo-ńee-kat] m. unique
item; rare specimen; curiosity

uniwersalny [oo-ńee-ver-sal-ni]
adj. m. universal; versatile

uniwersytet [oo-ńee-ver-si-tet]
m. university

uniżać się [oo-ńee-zhaćh
śhan] v. humble oneself; be
servile

uniżony [oo-ńee-zho-ni] adj. m.
humble; servile; cringing

unormować [oo-nor-mo-vaćh]
v. normalize; regulate;
regularize

unosić [oo-no-śheećh] v. carry
up; lift off; bear (a weight)

unowocześnić [oo-no-vo-
-cheśh-ńeećh] v. modernize

uodpornić [oo-od-por-ńeećh] v.
immunize; harden; inure

uogólnić [oo-o-gool-ńeećh] v.
generalize (rules, observations)

uogólnienie [oo-o-gool-ńe-ńe] n.
generalization

uosabiać [oo-o-sa-byaćh] v.
personify; embody; typify

uosobienie [oo-o-so-bye-ńe] n.
personification; embodiment

upadać [oo-pa-daćh] v. fall
down; collapse; topple over

upadek [oo-pa-dek] m. fall; drop

upadłość [oo-pad-wośhćh] f.
bankruptcy; insolvency

upadły [oo-pad-wi] adj. m. fallen;
bankrupt; insolvent

upajać [oo-pa-yaćh] v. elate;
intoxicate; fuddle; make drunk

upalny dzień [oo-pal-ni dźheń]
m. hot day; very hot day

upał [oo-paw] m. (intense) heat

upaństwowić [oo-pań-stvo-
-veećh] v. nationalize;
socialize

upaństwowienie [oo-pań-stvo-
-vye-ńe] n. nationalization

uparty [oo-par-ti] adj. m.
stubborn; obstinate; pigheaded

upatrywać [oo-pa-tri-vaćh] v.
look for; suspect; perceive

upełnomocnić [oo-pew-no-mots-
-ńeećh] v. give powers (of
attorney); empower;
commission

upewnić [oo-pev-ńeećh] v.
assure; reassure; make sure

upić się [oo-peećh śhan] v.
get drunk; be intoxicated

upierać się [oo-pye-raćh śhan]
v. persist; insist; stick to

upinać [oo-pee-naćh] v. fasten
on; pin up; tie (one's hair)

upiór [oop-yoor] m. ghost

upiorny [oo-pyor-ni] adj. m.
ghostly; weird; nightmarish;
ghastly; horrible; dreadful

upłynnienie [oo-pwin-ńe-ńe] n.
make fluid; flux; liquefaction

upływ [oop-wiv] m. run off;
(blood) loss; lapse; expiration

upływać [oo-pwi-vaćh] v. flow
away; pass; lapse; go by; flow

upłynąć [oo-pwi-nownćh] v.
elapse; pass; expire; sail away

upodobać [oo-po-do-baćh] v.
take a liking; take to; fancy

upodobanie [oo-po-do-ba-ńe] n.
liking; fancy; predilection for

upodobnić się [oo-po-dob-
-ńeećh śhan] v. assimilate;
conform to; become like

upoić [oo-po-eećh] v.
intoxicate; make drunk; elate

upojenie [oo-po-ye-ńe] n.
inebriation; rapture;
intoxication; ecstasy

upokorzenie [oo-po-ko-zhe-ńe] n.
humiliation; abasement

upokorzyć [oo-po-ko-zhićh] v.
humiliate; make eat crow;
abase; mortify; hurt the pride

upominać [oo-po-mee-naćh] v.
admonish; warn; scold; rebuke

upominek [oo-po-**mee**-nek] m.
gift; souvenir; present; token
uporać się [oo-**po**-rać śhan]
v. get over; cope with; settle;
negotiate; handle; manage
uporczywy [oo-por-chi-vi] adj. m.
stubborn; obstinate; severe
uporządkować [oo-po-zhownd-
-ko-vać] v. put in order; tidy
up; put straight; regulate
uposażenie [oo-po-sa-zhe-ńe] n.
pay; allowance; salary; wages
uposażyć [oo-po-**sa**-zhić] v.
endow; give allowance
upośledzenie [oo-po-śhle-dze-
-ńe] n. handicap (mental,
physical, etc.); wrong
upośledzony [oo-po-śhle-**dzo**-ni]
adj. m. feebleminded; deprived
upoważnić [oo-po-**vazh**-ńeeć]
v. authorize; commission;
entitle; empower; qualify for
upoważnienie [oo-po-vazh-ńe-
-ńe] n. authorization; full
powers; warrant; authority
upowszechniać [oo-pov-shekh-
-ńać] v. put into general
use; spread; disseminate
upór [oo-poor] m. obstinacy
upragniony [oo-prag-ńo-ni] adj.
m. desired; longed for
upraszać [oo-pra-shać] v.
request; beg; beseech
uprawa [oo-pra-va] f. culture;
cultivation; agriculture; tillage
uprawiać [oo-prav-yać] v.
cultivate; till (the soil)
uprawnić [oo-prav-ńeeć] v.
entitle; qualify; legalize
uprawniony [oo-prav-ńo-ni] adj.
m. entitled; qualified
uprosić [oo-pro-śheeć] v. get
by begging; persuade; ask to
do; request; entreat
uprościć [oo-prośh-ćheeć]
v. simplify; reduce; cancel
uprowadzić [oo-pro-**va**-
-dźheeć] v. abduct; kidnap;
lead away; take prisoner
uprzątać [oo-**pzhown**-tać] v.
clean up; tidy up; put away;
clear; remove; kill
uprząż [oop-zh**own**sh] f. harness

(horse); gear of draught
animals
uprzedni [oo-pzhed-ńee] adj. m.
previous; prior; foregoing
uprzedzać [oo-pzhe-dzać] v.
anticipate; warn; have bias
uprzedzenie [oo-pzhe-**dze**-ńe] n.
anticipation; prejudice; notice
uprzedzony [oo-pzhe-**dzo**-ni] adj.
m. prejudiced; forewarned
uprzejmość [oo-pzhey-
-mośhć] f. polite kindness;
courtesy; affability; favor
uprzejmy [oo-**pzhey**-mi] adj. m.
kind; polite; nice; suave;
affable; complaisant; bland
uprzemysłowić [oo-pzhe-mi-
-**swo**-veećh] v. industrialize
uprzemysłowienie [oo-pzhe-mi-
-swo-**vye**-ńe] n. industria-
lization; development of
industry
uprzykszać się [oo-pzhik-zhićh
śhan] v. get fed up with
uprzystępnić [oo-pzhis-**tanp**-
-ńeeć] v. facilitate; make
available; make accessible
uprzytomnić [oo-pzhi-tom-
-ńeeć] v. make realize;
impress upon (sb); perceive
uprzywilejowany [oo-pzhi-vee-le-
-yo-**va**-ni] adj. m. privileged
upuścić [oo-**poośh**-ćheeć]
v. let fall; let drop; bleed
upychać [oo-pi-khać] v. staff;
pack tight; cram; ram; fill
urabiać [oo-rab-yać] v. fashion
uraczyć [oo-ra-chić] v. treat
uradować [oo-ra-do-vać] v.
gladden; delight; rejoice
uradzić [oo-ra-**dźheeć**] v.
agree; decide upon a method;
resolve to do; contrive
uran [oo-ran] m. uranium
urastać [oo-ras-tać] v. grow
uratować [oo-ra-to-vać] v.
save; salvage; rescue
uraz [oo-ras] m. injury; complex;
resentment; grudge
uraza [oo-ra-za] f. grudge;
rancor; soreness; ill feeling
urazić [oo-ra-źheeć] v. hurt;
offend; wound sb's feelings

urągać [oo-**rown**-gaćh] v. insult
uregulować [oo-re-goo-**lo**-vaćh]
   v. settle; put in order; pay
urlop [oor-lop] m. leave;
   furlough; vacation; holiday
urna [oor-na] f. urn; ballot; box
uroczy [oo-ro-chi] adj. m.
   charming; enchanting; delightful; captivating; ravishing
uroczystość [oo-ro-**chis**-
   -tośhćh] f. celebration;
   festivity; feast; ceremony
uroczysty [oo-ro-**chis**-ti] adj. m.
   solemn; ceremonial; festive
uroda [oo-**ro**-da] f. beauty;
   loveliness; attraction; charm
urodzaj [oo-**ro**-dzay] m. good
   harvest; abundance; harvest;
   crop; good yield; yield
urodzajny [oo-ro-**dzay**-ni] adj. m.
   fertile; fecund
urodzenie [oo-ro-**dze**-ńe] n. birth
urodzić [oo-ro-d źheećh] v.
   give birth; breed; bear; yield a
   rich crop; be delivered
urodziny [oo-ro-**dźhee**-ni] n.
   birthday; birth; birthday party
uroić [oo-ro-eećh] v. imagine
urojenie [oo-ro-**ye**-ńe] n. fiction;
   fancy; illusion; delusion; dream
urojony [oo-ro-**yo**-ni] adj. m.
   imaginary; abstract; fictitious
urok [oo-rok] m. charm; spell
uronić [oo-ro-ńeećh] v. shed;
   drop; let fall; lose; shed; miss
urozmaicenie [oo-roz-ma-ee-**tse**-
   -ńe] n. variety; diversity;
   change; variation
urozmaicić [oo-roz-ma-ee-
   -ćheećh] v. diversity; vary;
   while away; beguile the time
uruchomić [oo-roo-kho-meećh]
   v. start; put in motion; set
   going; impel; launch; initiate
urwać [oor-vaćh] v. tear off;
   pull off; wrench away; deduct
urwis [oor-vees] m. urchin
urwisko [oor-**vees**-ko] n.
   precipice; crag; cliff; steep
   rock
urwisty [oor-**vees**-ti] adj. m.
   steep; precipitous; abrupt
urywek [oo-ri-vek] m. fragment

urząd [oo-zh**ownt**] m. office
urządzać [oo-zh**own**-dzaćh] v.
   arrange; settle; set up
urządzenie [oo-zh**own**-**dze**-ńe] n.
   furniture; installation; gear
urzec [oo-zhets] v. enchant;
   bewitch; fascinate; cast a
   spell; charm; captivate
urzeczywistnić [oo-zhe-chi-
   -veest-ńeećh] v. make real;
   fulfill; carry into effect
urzeczywistnienie [oo-zhe-chi-
   -veest-**ńe**-ńe] n. realization
urzędnik [oo-zh**and**-ńeek] m.
   official; white-collar worker
urzędowanie [oo-zh**an**-do-**va**-ńe]
   n. office hours; clerical duties
urzędowy [oo-zh**an**-**do**-vi] adj. m.
   official (document,capacity..)
urzynać [oo-zhi-naćh] v. cut off
usadowić się [oo-sa-**do**-veećh
   śhan] v. sit or settle down
uschły [oos-khwi] adj. m. dried
   up; withered; wasted away
usiąść [oo-**śhown**śhćh] v. sit
   down; take one's seat; perch;
   take a seat; alight
usidlać [oo-**śheed**-waćh] v.
   entrap; ensnare; enmesh;
   inveigle; entangle
usilny [oo-**śheel**-ni] adj. m.
   strenuous; intense; pressing
usiłować [oo-śhee-**wo**-vaćh] v.
   strive; try hard; attempt
usiłowanie [oo-śhee-wo-**va**-ńe]
   n. attempt; effort; endeavor
uskarżać się [oos-**kar**-zhaćh
   śhan] v. complain (against sb
   or sth); grumble (about..)
uskutecznić [oo-skoo-**tech**-
   -ńeećh] v. bring about;
   effect; perform
usłuchać [oo-**swoo**-khaćh] v.
   follow order (advice); obey
usługa [oo-**swoo**-ga] f. service;
   favor; good turn; help
usługiwać [oo-swoo-**gee**-vaćh]
   v. wait on; serve; attend
usłużyć [oo-**swoo**-zhićh] v. do
   a service; do a good turn
usnąć [oo-sn**own**ćh] v. fall
   asleep; go to sleep
uspokoić [oo-spo-**ko**-eećh] v.

calm down; soothe; set at
ease; pacify; tranquilize

uspołecznić [oos-po-**wech**-
-ńeećh] v. induce to socialize; civilize; collectivize

usposobić [oos-po-**so**-beećh] v.
dispose; predispose; incline

usposobienie [oos-po-so-**bye**-ńe]
n. disposition; temper; mood

usprawiedliwić [oos-pra-vyed-
-lee-veećh] v. justify; explain

usprawiedliwienie [oos-pra-vyed-
-lee-vye-ńe] n. excuse;
apology; plea; reason;
justification; vindication

usprawnić [oos-prav-ńeećh] v.
rationalize; make efficient

usta [oos-ta] n. mouth; lips

ustalenie [oo-sta-le-ńe] n.
determination; settlement

ustalić [oo-sta-leećh] v.
determine; settle; fix; set

ustały [oo-sta-wi] adj. m. settled
(fluid); tired (man, horse)

ustanawiać [oo-sta-na-vyaćh]
v. constitute; enact; set up

ustanowienie [oo-sta-no-vye-ńe]
n. instituting; establishing

ustatkować się [oo-stat-ko-
-vaćh **śhan**] v. settle down

ustawa [oo-sta-va] f. law; rule

ustawać [oo-sta-vaćh] v.
cease; be weary; hardly stand

ustawiać [oo-stav-yaćh] v.
arrange; place; put; set up

ustawiczny [oo-sta-veech-ni] adj.
m. constant; continual

ustawienie [oo-sta-vye-ńe] n.
disposition; installation

ustawodawca [oo-sta-vo-**dav**-tsa]
m. legislator

ustawodawstwo [oo-sta-vo-**dav**-
-stvo] n. legislation

usterka [oo-ster-ka] f. defect

ustęp [oos-tanp] m. rest-room;
paragraph; passage

ustępliwy [oos-tan-plee-vi] adj.
m. yielding; compliant

ustępować [oos-tan-po-vaćh]
v. yield; withdraw; recede;
cease; retreat; surrender

ustępstwo [oos-tanp-stvo] n.
concession; meeting half way

ustnik [oost-ńeek] m.
mouthpiece

ustny [oost-ni] adj. m. oral;
verbal; spoken

ustosunkowany [oo-sto-soon-ko-
-va-ni] adj. m. influential

ustrój [oos-trooy] m. structure;
government system; organism

ustrzec [oos-tzhets] v. guard;
avoid; safeguard; protect from

usunięcie [oo-soo-**ńan**-ćhe] n.
removal; withdrawal

usuwać [oo-**soo**-vaćh] v. clear
away; remove; dismiss; retire

usychać [oo-si-khaćh] v. wither

usypać [oo-si-paćh] v. pile up;
pour out; pour off (sand etc.)

usypiać [oo-sip-yaćh] v. put to
sleep; lull to sleep; send to
sleep; anaesthetize

uszanować [oo-sha-**no**-vaćh] v.
respect; spare (life etc.)

uszanowanie [oo-sha-no-**va**-ńe]
n. respect; respects

uszczelka [oosh-chel-ka] f.
gasket; seal; packing

uszczelniać [oosh-**chel**-ńaćh]
v. pack; caulk; stop (a leak
etc.); make water-tight; seal

uszczęśliwić [oosh-chan-**śhlee**-
-veećh] v. make happy;
delight; overwhelm with joy

uszczerbek [oosh-**cher**-bek] m.
harm; damage; loss; detriment

uszczuplić [oosh-**choop**-leećh]
v. curtail; reduce; lessen

uszczypliwy [oosh-chip-**lee**-vi]
adj. m. sarcastic; biting

uszko [oosh-ko] m. (small) ear;
(needle) eye; ravioli

uszkodzenie [oosh-ko-dze-ńe] n.
damage; injury; impairment

uszkodzić [oosh-**ko**-dźheećh]
v. damage; injure; impair; spoil

uszny [oosh-ni] adj. m. ear

uścisk dłoni [oośh-ćheesk
dwo-ńee] m. handshake

uścisnąć [oośh-**ćhees**-
-nownćh] v. embrace; grasp;
hug; squeeze (hand)

uśmiać się [oośh-myaćh
śhan] v. laugh heartily; have
a good laugh; sneer

uśmiech [oośh-myekh] m.
smile; (silly) smirk; simper
uśmiechać się [oośh-mye-
-khaćh śhan] v. smile; give a
smile; simper; grin; sneer
uśmiercić [oośh-myer-
-ćhećh] v. kill; put to death
uśmierzyć [oośh-mye-zhićh]
v. calm down; mitigate; pacify; alleviate; soothe; still
uśpić [oośh-peećh] v. put to
sleep; anesthetize; etherize
uświadomić [oośh-vya-do-
-meećh] v. instruct; initiate;
realize; inform; indoctrinate
uświadomienie [oośh-vya-do-
-mye-ńe] n. consciousness;
information; indoctrination
uświetnić [oośh-**vyet**-ńeećh]
v. give prestige; add splendor
utaić [oo-ta-eećh] v. conceal
utajony [oo-ta-yo-ni] adj. m.
secret; latent; potential
utalentowany [oo-ta-len-to-**va**-ni]
adj. m. talented; gifted
utarczka [oo-tarch-ka] f.
skirmish; encounter; squabble
utarg [oo-tark] m. receipts; take;
takings; sales (daily, etc.)
utargować [oo-tar-go-vaćh] v.
make a bargain; realize
utarty [oo-tar-ti] adj. m. usual;
well-worn; wide spread
utęsknienie [oo-tans-kńe-ńe] n.
longing; earnest desire
utknąć [oot-knownćh] v. get
stuck; stall; stick fast; get to
a stop; come to a dead stop
utlenić [oo-tle-ńeećh] v.
oxidize (metals) peroxide
(hair); become oxidized
utłuc [oot-woots] v. pound;
bruise; crush; pestle; mash
(potatoes etc.); grind
utonąć [oo-to-nownćh] v. be
drowned; sink; be lost
utopia [oo-top-ya] f. Utopia
utopić [oo-to-peećh] v. sink;
drown (an animal etc.)
utorować [oo-to-ro-vaćh] v.
clear a path; show the way
utożsamić [oo-tozh-**sa**-meećh]
v. identify with

utracić [oo-tra-ćheećh] v.
loose (health, job, etc.);
waste; forfeit a right etc.
utracjusz [oo-trats-yoosh] m.
spendthrift; squanderer
utrapienie [oo-trap-ye-ńe] n.
worry; torment; nuisance
utrata [oo-tra-ta] f. loss
utrącać [oo-trown-tsaćh] v.
chip; knock of; blackball
utrudniać [oo-trood-ńaćh] v.
make difficult; hinder
utrudnienie [oo-trood-ńe-ńe] n.
difficulty; hindrance
utrwalić [oo-trva-leećh] v.
make permanent; fix; record
utrzymanie [oo-tzhi-ma-ńe] n.
living; upkeep; board; support
utuczyć [oo-too-chićh] v.
fatten; grow fat; fatten up
utulić [oo-too-leećh] v.
comfort; console; nestle
(one's head in sb's lap etc.)
utwierdzić [oo-**tvyer**-dźheećh]
v. confirm; fix; set; consolidate; strengthen
utworzenie [oo-tvo-zhe-ńe] n.
formation; initiation; creation
utworzyć [oo-tvo-zhićh] v.
create; form; compose; initiate
utwór [oot-voor] m. work;
composition; production;
work; creation; formation
utyć [oo-tićh] v. become fat
utykać [oo-ti-kaćh] v. limp
utylitarny [oo-ti-lee-tar-ni] adj. m.
utilitarian; useful
utyskiwać [oo-tis-kee-vaćh] v.
complain; grumble (at, about)
uwaga [oo-va-ga] f. attention;
remark; notice; heed; note;
exp.: caution!; look out!
uwalniać [oo-val-ńaćh] v. set
free; rid; let off; dismiss
uważać [oo-va-zhaćh] v. pay
attention; be careful; mind;
take care; look after; watch
out; consider; reckon
uważny [oo-vazh-ni] adj. m.
careful; attentive; watchful
uwiąd [oov-yownt] m. atrophy
uwiązać [oo-**vyown**-zaćh] v.
attach; bind; tie; fasten

uwidocznić [oo-vee-doch-
-ńeećh] v. make evident;
show; expose
uwiecznić [oo-vyech-ńeećh] v.
perpetuate; immortalize
uwielbiać [oo-vyel-byaćh] v.
adore; worship; admire
uwielbienie [oo-vyel-bye-ńe] n.
adoration; admiration; worship
uwierać [oo-vye-raćh] v. (shoe)
pinch; rub; hurt
uwierzytelnić [oo-vye-zhi-tel-
-ńeećh] v. legalize; certify;
attest
uwierzytelnienie [oo-vye-zhi-tel-
-ńe-ńe] n. certification; ac-
creditation; authentication
uwięzić [oo-vyan-źheećh] v.
imprison; throw into prison
uwijać się [oo-vee-yaćh śhan]
v. be busy; bustle about;
hurry up; spin; whirl; dance
uwikłać [oo-veek-waćh] v.
entangle; involve; get
entangled; get trapped
uwłaczać [oov-wa-chaćh] v.
belittle; insult; outrage; affront
uwłosiony [oo-vwo-śho-ni] adj.
m. hairy; hirsute; pilose
uwodziciel [oo-vo-dźhee-ćhel]
m. seducer (of women);
inveigler
uwodzić [oo-vo-dźheećh] v.
seduce (men or women)
uwolnić [oo-vol-ńeećh] v. free
uwolnienie [oo-vol-ńe-ńe] n.
liberation; rescue; acquittal
uwydatnić [oo-vi-dat-ńeećh] v.
accentuate; set off; bring out
uwypuklić [oo-vi-pook-leećh] v.
accentuate; set off; protrude
uwzględnić [oovz-gland-ńeećh]
v. consider; comply; acquiesce
uwzględnienie [oovz-gland-ńe-
-ńe] n. allowance for;
compliance with; regard to
uzależnić [oo-za-lezh-ńeećh] v.
make dependent; subordinate
uzasadnić [oo-za-sad-ńeećh] v.
substantiate; justify; motivate
uzasadnienie [oo-za-sad-ńe-ńe]
n. justification; motive
uzbrajać się [ooz-bra-yaćh

śhan] v. arm oneself; equip
oneself (with tools, weapons)
uzbrojenie [ooz-bro-ye-ńe] n.
arming; armament; weapons
uzda [ooz-da] f. bridle
uzdolnić [ooz-dol-ńeećh] v.
enable; qualify; capacitate
uzdolnienie [ooz-dol-ńe-ńe] n.
talent; gift; aptitude
uzdolniony [ooz-dol-ńo-ni]
adj. m. gifted; talented;
capable; apt
uzdrawiać [ooz-dra-vyaćh] v.
heal; cure; bring back to
health; reorganize; sanify
uzdrowisko [ooz-dro-vees-ko] n.
health resort
uzębienie [oo-zan-bye-ńe] n.
dentition; toothing (of gears..)
uzgadniać [ooz-gad-ńaćh] v.
reconcile; coordinate; adjust
uziemienie [oo-źhe-mye-ńe] n.
grounding; earth
uzmysłowić [ooz-mi-swo-
-veećh] v. visualize; convey
(meaning); demonstrate
uznawać [ooz-na-vaćh] v.
acknowledge; do justice;
confess; recognize; admit
uznanie [ooz-na-ńe] n.
recognition; admission;
approval; esteem; regard
uzupełniać [oo-zoo-pew-ńaćh]
v. complete; fill up; make up
uzurpator [oo-zoor-pa-tor] m.
usurper (who takes and holds
power, position etc. by force)
uzyskać [oo-zis-kaćh] v. obtain;
gain; get; acquire; secure
użerać się [oo-zhe-raćh śhan]
v. fight over; quarrel; wrangle
użyczać [oo-zhi-chaćh] v.
grant; give; lend; spare; impart
użyć [oo-zhićh] v. use; exert;
take (medicine); profit; employ
użyteczny [oo-zhi-tech-ni]
adj. m. useful; serviceable;
helpful; effective
użytek [oo-zhi-tek] m. use
użytkownik [oo-zhit-kov-ńeek]
m. user (of apartment etc.)
używać [oo-zhi-vaćh] v. use;
enjoy; exercise a right; make

use; exert (strength etc.)
używalność [oo-zhi-val-
-nośhćh] f. use; enjoyment;
utilization; usufruct
używalny [oo-zhi-val-ni] adj. m.
usable; in working order
używany [oo-zhi-va-ni] adj. m.
used; second-hand; worn
używniać [oo-zhiźh-ńaćh] v.
fertilize; enrich (the soil)

W

w [v] prep. in; into; at
we [ve] prep. in; into; at
wabić [va-beećh] v. lure
wabik [va-beek] m. decoy; lure
wachlarz [vakh-lash] m. fan;
range or diversity (of
questions, subjects etc.)
wada [va-da] f. fault; defect;
flaw
wadliwy [wad-lee-vi] adj. m.
faulty; defective; imperfect
wafel [va-fel] m. wafer; cornet
waga [va-ga] f. weight; balance;
pair of scales; importance
wagary [va-ga-ri] pl. skipping
school; playing truant; the
wag
wagon [va-gon] m. car; wagon
wagon restauracyjny [va-gon res-
-taw-ra-tsiy-ni] dining car
wahać się [va-khaćh śhan] v.
hesitate; sway; rock; swing
wahadło [va-kha-dwo] n.
pendulum (swinging
backwards and forwards)
wahadłowy [va-khad-wo-vi] adj.
m. rocking; swinging;
oscillatory; pendular
wakacje [va-kats-ye] pl.
vacation; holidays; taking a
holiday; taking a vacation
walać [va-laćh] v. soil; stain;
dirty; roll; draggle; wallow
walc [valts] m. waltz
walcować [val-tso-vaćh] v. roll;

flatten; mill; laminate
walczyć [val-chićh] v. fight;
vie; straggle; be in conflict;
contend; wage war; combat
walec [va-lets] m. cylinder; roller
waleczność [va-lech-nośhćh]
f. bravery; valor; gallantry;
courage; prowess
waleczny [va-lech-ni] adj. m.
valiant; brave; gallant;
courageous
walić [va-leećh] v. demolish;
hit; pile; bring down; beat
walijski [va-leey-skee] adj. m.
Welsh; of Wales
walizka [va-leez-ka] f. suitcase;
valise; portmanteau
walka [val-ka] f. struggle; fight;
war; battle; wrestling
walny [val-ni] adj. m. general;
complete; decisive; signal;
outstanding; eminent
walor [va-lor] m. value; quality
waluta [va-loo-ta] f. currency
wał [vaw] m. 1. rampart; dike;
bank; 2.shaft; arbor; billow
wałach [va-wakh] m. gelding
wałek [va-wek] m. roller; shaft;
cylinder; rolling pin; wad; roll
wałęsać się [va-wan-saćh
śhan] v. rove; loaf; idle about
wałkoń [vaw-koń] m. loafer; do
nothing; idler
wałkować [vaw-ko-vaćh] v.
roll out; roll up; mangle;
debate; thresh out
wampir [vam-peer] m. vampire
wandal [van-dal] m. vandal
wanienka [va-ńen-ka] f. little
tub; bathtub; laboratory dish
wanna [van-na] f. bath tub
wapienny [va-pyen-ni] adj. m.
limy; limestone; calcareous
wapień [va-pyeń] m. limestone
wapno [vap-no] n. lime
wapń [vapń] m. calcium
warcaby [var-tsa-bi] pl. checkers;
draughts (game)
warchlak [varkh-lak] m. boar-
-cub; young wild boar; piglet
warchoł [var-khow] m. brawler;
discord sower; squabbler
warczeć [var-chećh] v. growl

warga [var-ga] f. lip; labium
wariant [var-yant] m. variant
wariactwo [var-yats-tvo] n.
madness; piece of folly; folly
wariat [var-yat] m. lunatic;
insane; madman; fool; crazy
man; crank
wariować [var-yo-vaćh] v. go
insane; rave; go mad; be mad
warkocz [var-koch] m. braid
warkot [var-kot] m. growl; whirr;
throb; rattle; drone
warowny [va-rov-ni] adj. m.
fortified; made into a fortress
warować [va-ro-vaćh] v. fortify
warstwa [vars-tva] f. layer;
stratum; coat; coating; class
warstwowy [var-stvo-vi] adj. m.
laminar; stratified; foliated
warsztat [varsh-tat] m.
workshop; workbench;
(weaver's) loom
warsztatowy [var-shta-to-vi] adj.
m. workshop- (equipment etc.)
warta [var-ta] f. watch; guard
wartki [vart-kee] adj. m. rapid;
fast (current); animated
wartko [vart-ko] adv. fast;
rapidly; impetuously
warto [var-to] adv. it's worth
(while); it's proper; it's worth
one's while; it pays
wartościowy [var-tośh-ćho-vi]
adj. m. valuable; precious
wartość [var-tośhćh] f. value;
worth; quality; power;
magnitude
wartownik [var-tov-ńeek] m.
guard; sentry; sentinel
warunek [va-roo-nek] m.
condition; requirement; term;
stipulation; circumstance
warunkowy [va-roon-ko-vi] adj.
m. conditional; contingent;
provisory
warząchew [va-zhown-khev] v.
ladle
warzyć [va-zhićh] v. cook;
brew; boil; nip; turn sour
warzywa [va-zhi-va] pl.
vegetables; pot herbs; true
garden produce
warzywny [va-zhiv-ni] adj. m.

vegetable; vegetable (garden)
wasz [vash] pron. your; yours
waśnić [vaśh-ńeećh] v. saw
discord (among men or
women) quarrel
waśń [vaśhń] f. quarrel
wata [va-ta] f. cotton wool
watować [va-to-vaćh] v. pad;
quilt; wad (a jacket etc.)
wawrzyn [vav-zhin] m. laurel
waza [va-za] f. vase; soup
tureen; tureenful
wazelina [va-ze-lee-na] f.
vaseline; petrolatum
wazon [va-zon] m. flower pot
ważki [vazh-kee] adj. m. grave;
weighty; ponderable
ważny [vazh-ni] adj. m.
important; valid; significant
ważyć [va-zhićh] v. weigh
ważyć się [va-zhićh śhan] v.
dare; weigh oneself; poise;
venture; rock oneself
wąchać [vown-khaćh] v. smell
wągr [vowngr] m. blackhead;
scolex; comedo; tapeworm
larva; pig measles
wąs [vowns] m. moustache;
whisker; barb; tentacle
wąski [vown-skee] adj. m.
narrow; tight (fitting); narrow-
(gage); bottle-neck
wąskotorowa kolej [vowns-ko-
-to-ro-va ko-ley] f. narrow
gauge railroad
wątek [vown-tek] m. weft; plot
wątły [vownt-wi] adj. m. frail
wątpić [vownt-peećh] v. doubt
wątpliwy [vownt-plee-vi] adj. m.
doubtful; open to doubt; toss-
up; questionable; precarious
wątroba [vown-tro-ba] f. liver
wątróbka [vown-troob-ka] f. liver
(dish); (calf's) liver
wąwóz [vown-voos] m. ravine;
gorge; gully; canyon; defile
wąż [vownsh] m. snake; hose
wbiec [vbyets] v. run in; run up
wbijać [vbee-yaćh] v. hammer
in; drive into; thrust into
wbrew [vbref] prep. in spite of;
in defiance; against
wbudować [vboo-do-vaćh] v.

build in; incorporate

w bród [v broot] adv. 1.in
abundance; 2. fording (river)

wcale [vtsa-le] adv. quite

wcale nie [vtsa-le ńe] not at all
(exp); not in the least

wchłaniać [vkhwa-ńаćh] v.
absorb; soak up; take in; soak
in; incept; imbibe

wchodzić [vkho-dźheećh] v.
enter; get in; set in; climb

w ciągu [v ćhown-goo] adv.
during; while; in time of

wciągać [vćhown-gaćh] v. pull
in; drag in; inhale; implicate

wciąż [vćhownsh] adv.
continually; constantly;
persistently; as ever

wcielać [vćhe-laćh] v.
incorporate; embody; merge;
incarnate; personify

wcielenie [vćhe-le-ńe] n.
incarnation; embodiment;
merger; incorporation

wcierać [vćhe-raćh] v. rub in

wcięcie [vćhan-ćhe] n. incision
notch; narrow waist; low cut
neck; dent; indentation

wciskać [vćhees-kaćh] v.
press in; squeeze in; wedge;
cram; push in; thrust in

w czas [v chas] on time

wczasy [vcha-si] pl. vacations

wczesny [vches-ni] adj. m. early;
in the small hours

wcześnie [vcheśh-ńe] adv.
early; at an early date

wczoraj [vcho-ray] adv.
yesterday; during yesterday

wczoraj wieczorem [vcho-ray
vye-cho-rem] adv. last night

wczuwać się [vchoo-vaćh
śhan] v. sympathize; get in
spirit; understand

wdarcie [vdar-ćhe] n. invasion

wdawać się [vda-vaćh śhan]
v. 1.intervene; 2.associate

wdech [vdekh] m. aspiration

wdowa [vdo-va] f. widow

wdowiec [vdo-vyets] m.
widower

w dół [v doow] adv. down;
downwards; downstairs; (go)

lower; (move) lower

wdrapać się [vdra-paćh śhan]
v. climb up; shin up (a tree)

wdrażać [vdra-zhaćh] v. train;
implant; accustom to; enter
upon; initiate; break in

wdychać [vdi-khaćh] v.
breathe; inhale; breathe in;
imbibe

wdzierać się [vdźhe-raćh
śhan] v. break in; struggle up
a hill; force one's way

wdziewać [vdźhe-vaćh] v. put
on (clothes); slip on; take (the
veil, the habit)

wdzięczność [vdźhanch-
-nośhćh] f. gratitude; thank-
fulness; indebtedness

wdzięczny [vdźhanch-ni] adj. m.
grateful; thankful; graceful;
cute; neat; charming

wdzięk [vdźhank] m. grace;
charm; attraction

według [ved-wook] prep.
according to; after; along;
near; next to; in accordance

wegetacja [ve-ge-tats-ya] f.
vegetation; bare existence

wegetarianin [ve-ge-tar-ya-ńeen]
m. vegetarian (man on a
meatless diet)

wegetować [ve-ge-to-vaćh] v.
exist barely; vegetate

wejrzeć [vey-zhećh] v. glance
in; look in; get an insight;
inspect; take a look inside

wejrzenie [vey-zhe-ńe] n. glance
in; (eye) expression; insight

wejście [veyśh-ćhe] n.
entrance; way in; admission
ticket; entry

wejściowy [veyśh-ćho-vi]
adj. m. entrance- (door, gate,
opening, etc.)

wejść [veyśhćh] v. enter; get
in; step in; walk in; go in

weksel [vek-sel] m. loan note

welon [ve-lon] m. veil

wełna [vew-na] f. wool

wełniany [vew-ńa-ni] adj. m.
woolen; worsted; wool-
(blanket, fabric, etc.)

weneryczna choroba [ve-ne-rich-

-na kho-ro-ba] f. venereal
disease
wenezuelski [ve-ne-zoo-el-skee]
adj. m. Venezuelan; of
Venezuela
wentyl [ven-til] m. vent; valve
wentylacja [ven-ti-lats-ya] f.
ventilation; ventilation system
wentylator [ven-ti-la-tor] m.
ventilator; ventilating-fan
weranda [ve-ran-da] f. porch
werbel [ver-bel] m. ruffle; drum
-call; drumbeat; drum
werbować [ver-bo-vaćh] v.
enlist; recruit; canvas
werbunek [ver-boo-nek] m. draft;
recruitment; enlisting;
recruiting
wersja [ver-sya] f. version
werwa [ver-va] f. verve; zip; pep
weryfikować [ve-ri-fee-ko-vaćh]
v. verify; confirm
wesele [ve-se-le] n. wedding
wesołość [ve-so-wośhćh] f.
joy; gaiety; glee; hilarity
wesoły [ve-so-vi] adj. merry;
gay; jolly; gleeful; funny
wespół [ves-poow] adv.
together; jointly; all together
westchnienie [vest-khńe-ńe] n.
sigh (of relief etc.)
wesz [vesh] louse
wet za wet [vet za vet] exp. tit
for tat; retaliate
weteran [ve-te-ran] m. veteran
weterynarz [ve-te-ri-nash] m.
vet; veterinary; farrier
wetknąć [vet-known̂ćh] v.
stick in; slip in; tuck away;
stuff; insert; shove
wewnątrz [vev-nowntsh] prep.
adv. inside; within; intra-
wewnętrzny [vev-nantzh-ni] adj.
m. inner; internal; inward
wezbrać [vez-braćh] v. swell
wezbrany [vez-bra-ni] adj. m.
flush; overflowing; swollen
wezwać [vez-vaćh] v. call in
wezwanie [vez-va-ńe] n. call
węch [vankh] m. smell; nose
wędka [vand-ka] f. fishing rod
wędkarz [vand-kash] m. angler
wędlina [vand-lee-na] f. meat

products; pork products
wędliniarnia [vand-lee-ńar-ńa] f.
pork-butcher's shop
wędrować [van-dro-vaćh] v.
wander; roam; rove; hike
wędrowiec [van-dro-vyets] m.
wanderer; tramp;rover
wędrówka [van-droov-ka] f.
migration; roam; tramp;
wandering; wayfaring
wędzić [van-dzheećh] v.
smoke; cure; meat; bloat fish
wędzidło [van-dźheed-wo] n.
(horse) bit; bridle; curb
wędzonka [van-dzon-ka] f. bacon
węgiel [van-gel] m. coal;
carbon; crayon
węgielny kamień [van-gel-ni ka-
-myeń] m. corner stone;
corner stone
węgieł [van-gew] m. corner;
quoin; coin
węgierski [van-ger-skee] adj. m.
Hungarian; of Hungary
węglan [van-glan] m. carbonate
węglowodan [van-glo-vo-dan] m.
carbohydrate (chemical
compound)
węglowodór [van-glo-vo-door] m.
hydrocarbon; rock oil etc.
węglowy [van-glo-vi] adj. m.
carbonic; coal (bed, seam,
field); carboniferous; carbon-
węgorz [van-gosh] m. eel
węzeł [van-zew] m. knot;
junction; noose; loop; snarl;
hitch; bend; tie; bond
węższy [vanzh-shi] adj. m.
narrower (than)
wgląd [vglownt] m. insight; view
wglądać [vglown-daćh] v. look
into; get an insight; inquire
wgłębiać się [vgwan-byaćh
śhan] v. sink; study; go into
(a matter); dig into
wgryźć się [vgrźhćh śhan]
v. penetrate; get teeth into...
wiać [vyaćh] v. blow; beat it
wiadomo [vya-do-mo] v. (imp.) it
is known; everybody knows
wiadomość [vya-do-mośhćh]
f. news; information; message
wiadomy [vya-do-mi] adj. m.

known; a certain; well known
wiadro [vya-dro] n. bucket; pail
wiadukt [vya-dookt] m. viaduct
wianek [vya-nek] m. flower
crown; wreath; maidenhead
wiara [vya-ra] f. faith; belief
wiarogodny [vya-ro-god-ni] adj.
m. reliable; credible; veracious
wiarołomny [vya-ro-wom-ni] adj.
m. unfaithful; treacherous
wiarus [vya-roos] m. veteran (old
guard); old campaigner
wiatr [vyatr] m. wind; gale;
breeze; (dog's or horse's) nose
wiatrak [vyat-rak] m. windmill
wiatrówka [vya-troov-ka] f. air
gun; wind breaker (jacket)
wiąz [vyowns] m. elm (Ulmus)
wiązać [vyown-zaćh] v.
tie; bind; make into bundles
wiązanie [vyown-za-ńe] n. tie;
truss; bond; link; fixation;
weave; bonding; setting
wiązanka [vyown-zan-ka] f.
garland; bunch; banquet;
cluster; volley of abuse
wiązka [vyownz-ka] f. bundle;
bunch; cluster; beam (of rays)
wibracja [vee-bra-tsya] f.
vibration; jarring; jar
wichrować się [vee-khro-vaćh
śhan] v. warp; curl
wicher [vee-kher] m. windstorm;
gale; strong wind
wichrzyciel [veekh-zhi-ćhel] m.
warmonger; firebrand; instigator; sedition-monger
wichrzyć [veekh-zhićh] v. make
trouble; create discord; tousle
wichura [vee-khoo-ra] f.
windstorm; gale; strong wind
wichura śnieżna [vi-khoo-ra
śhńezh-na] snowstorm with
a heavy snowfall; blizzard
wić [veećh] v. wind; meander;
build nest; curl; m. twig; osier
widelec [vee-de-lets] m. fork
widełki [vee-dew-kee] pl. fork
(small); forked branch
widełkowaty [vee-dew-ko-va-ti]
adj. m. forked; fork shaped
widły [veed-wi] pl. pitchfork
widmo [veed-mo] n. ghost;

phantom; spectrum; specter
widno [veed-no] adv. 1.
evidently; 2. in daylight; in
light (in a room, out of doors)
widnokrąg [veed-no-krownk] m.
horizon; sea-line; true horizon
widocznie [vee-doch-ńe] adv.
evidently; apparently; clearly
widoczność [vee-doch-
-nośhćh] f. visibility; field of
vision (visible space)
widoczny [vee-doch-ni] adj. m.
visible; evident; noticeable
widok [vee-dok] m. view; sight
widokówka [vee-do-koov-ka] f.
picture postcard
widowisko [vee-do-vees-ko] n.
show; spectacle; pageant
widownia [vee-dov-ńa] f.
audience; theater house;
scene; arena
widz [veets] m. spectator
widzenie [vee-dze-ńe] n. sight;
vision; visit; hallucination
widzialny [vee-dźhal-ni] adj. m.
visible (to the naked eye...)
widzieć [vee-dźhećh] v. see
wiec [vyets] m. meeting; rally
wieczerza [vye-che-zha] f.
supper; Lord's Supper
wieczność [vyech-nośhćh] f.
eternity; ages; eternal life
wieczny [vyech-ni] adj. m.
eternal; perpetual; endless
wieczorek [vye-cho-rek] m.
evening (party); nice evening
wieczorem [vye-cho-rem] exp. in
the evening; during the
evening
wieczorny [vye-chor-ni] adj. m.
evening- (dress, newspaper)
wieczorowy [vye-cho-ro-vi] adj.
m. nightly; evening
(performance)
wieczór [vye-choor] m. evening
wieczysty [vye-chis-ti] adj. m.
eternal; perpetual;
imperishable
wiedza [vye-dza] f. knowledge;
learning; erudition; science
wiedzieć [vye-dźhećh] v.
know; be aware; be conscious
wiedźma [vyedźh-ma] f. witch

wiejska droga [vyey-ska dro-ga]
f. village road; country road
wiejski [vyey-skee] adj. m.
village; rural; rustic; country
wiek [vyek] m. age; century
wiekowy [vye-ko-vi] adj. m.
secular; ancient; aged;
advanced in years; venerable
wiekuistość [vye-koo-ees-
-tośhćh] f. eternity; all time
wiekuisty [vye-koo-ees-ti] adj. m.
eternal; everlasting
wielbiciel [vyel-bee-ćhel] m.
devotee; admirer; idolator
(ladies' man)
wielbicielka [vyel-bee-ćhel-ka] f.
devotee; idolatress (woman)
wielbłąd [vyel-bwownd] m.
camel; dromedary (or bactrian)
wielce [vyel-tse] adv. very;
greatly; extremely; very much
wiele [vye-le] adj. m. many; a
lot; much; far out; a great
deal; how much?
wielebny [vye-leb-ni] adj. m.
reverend (Father etc.)
Wielkanoc [vyel-ka-nots] f.
Easter
wielkanocny [vyel-ka-nots-ni] adj.
m. Easter; of Easter
wielki [vyel-kee] adj. m. big;
large; great; vast; keen;
mighty; intense; important
wielkoduszny [vyel-ko-doosh-ni]
adj. m. magnanimous; noble-
minded; generous
wielkolud [vyel-ko-lood] m. giant
wielkomiejski [vyel-ko-myey-
-skee] adj. m. metropolitan;
urban; of a large city
wielkość [vyel-kośhćh] f.
greatness; size; dimension;
value; quantity; vastness
wielobarwny [vye-lo-barv-ni] adj.
m. multi-color (ed); colorful
wieloboczny [vye-lo-boch-ni] adj.
m. multilateral; polygonal
wielokrążek [vye-lo-krown-zhek]
m. set of pulleys; pulley-block
wielokrotny [vye-lo-krot-ni] adj.
m. repeated; multiple
wieloletni [vye-lo-let-ńee]
adj. m. long; years long; many

years (service...)
wielopiątrowy [vye-lo-pyan-tro-
-vi] adj. m. multi-story
wieloraki [vye-lo-ra-kee] adj. m.
manifold; varied; multiple
wieloryb [vye-lo-rib] m. whale
wielorybnik [vye-lo-rib-ńeek] m.
whaler; whale man; whaling
ship; whaling boat
wielostronny [vye-lo-stron-ni] adj.
m. multilateral; many-sided;
versatile; various
wielozgłoskowy [vye-lo-zgwos-
-ko-vi] adj. m. polysyllabic
wieloznaczny [vye-lo-znach-ni]
adj. m. equivocal; ambiguous
wielożeństwo [vye-lo-zheń-
-stvo] n. polygamy
wieniec [vye-ńets] m. wreath;
garland; crown; chaplet
wieńczyć [vyeń-chićh] v.
crown; garland; wreathe
wieprz [vyepsh] m. hog; pig
wieprzowina [vyep-zho-vee-na] f.
pork (meat)
wieprzowy [vyep-zho-vi] adj. m.
pork; pork's; pig's; hog's;
porcine
wiercenie [vyer-tse-ńe] n.
drilling; perforation; boring
wiercić [vyer-ćheećh] v. bore;
drill; pester; bother
wierność [vyer-nośhćh] f.
fidelity; loyalty; faith; truth
wierny [vyer-ni] adj. m. faithful;
true; loyal; exact
wiersz [vyersh] m. verse; poem
wiertarka [vyer-tar-ka] f. drill
wiertnictwo [vyert-ńeets-tvo] n.
drilling (activity)
wierutny [vye-root-ni] adj. m.
stark (liar); notorious; through-
and-through; rank; arrant; born
wierzący [vye-zhown-tsi] adj. m.
believer; believing Christian
wierzba [vyezh-ba] f. willow
wierzch [vyezhkh] m. top; brim
head; surface; cover; lid
wierzchni [vyezh-khńee] adj. m.
upper; top; outer; outside
wierzchołek [vyezh-kho-wek] m.
top; peak; summit; apex;
vertex; cusp

wierzyciel [vye-zhi-ćhel] m.
creditor; mortgagee; obligee
wierzycielka [vye-zhi-ćhel-ka] f.
creditor (woman)
wierzyć [vye-zhićh] v. believe;
trust; rely; believe in God
wierzytelność [vye-shi-tel-
-nośhćh] f. debt; claim
wieszać [vye-shaćh] v. hang
wieszadło [vye-shad-wo] v.
hanger; peg; coat-stand
wieszak [vye-shak] m. rack
wieszcz [vyeshch] m. bard; seer;
poet (leading, national)
wieszczy [vyesh-chi] adj. m.
prophetic; visionary
wieś [vyeśh] f. village;
countryside; hamlet; the
villagers
wieść [vyeśhćh] 1. f. news
2. v. lead; conduct; draw;
succeed; stand at the head
wieśniaczka [vyeśh-ńach-ka] f.
countrywoman; peasant
woman
wieśniak [vyeśh-ńak] m.
countryman; villager; yokel;
rustic; peasant
wietrzeć [vyet-zhećh] v. decay
wietrzyć [vyet-zhićh] v.
ventilate; smell; nose; aerate
wietrzenie [vyet-zhe-ńe] n.
ventilation; decay (of rocks)
wiewiórka [vye-vyoor-ka] f.
squirrel; squirrel fur
wieźć [vyeźhćh] v. carry (on
wheels, horse, sledge);
transport; convey; drive
wieża [vye-zha] f. tower; rook
wieżowiec [vye-zho-vyets] m.
skyscraper; high-rise (building)
wieżyczka [vye-zhich-ka] f.
turret; pinnacle; small tower
więc [vyants] conj. now; well;
therefore; so; consequently
więcej [vyan-tsey] adv. more
więdnąć [vyand-nownćh] v.
wither; fade; wilt
więcierz [vyan-ćhezh] m. fishing
net (set taut on hoops)
większość [vyank-shośhćh] f.
majority; the bulk; most
większy [vyank-shi] adj. m.

bigger; larger; greater
więzić [vyan-źheećh] v.
imprison; confine; detain;
restrain; keep locked up
więzienie [vyan-źhe-ńe] n.
prison; confinement; jail; gaol;
restraint
więzień [vyan-źheń] m.
prisoner; convict
więzy [vyan-zi] pl. fetters;
restrains; chains; bonds
wigilia [vee-geel-ya] f. Christmas
Eve; Christmas Eve supper
wiklina [vee-klee-na] f. osier
wikłać [veek-waćh] v. entangle
wikt [veekt] m. board; keep
wilczur [veel-choor] m. wolf dog
wilgoć [veel-goćh] f. humidity
wilgotny [veel-got-ni] adj. m.
moist; humid; damp; wet
wilia [veel-ya] f. see wigilia
wilk [veelk] m. wolf; wolf-skin
wilżyć [veel-zhićh] v. moisten
wina [vee-na] f. guilt; fault
winda [veen-da] f. elevator
winiarnia [vee-ńar-ńa] f.
wine-shop; vine vault; winery
winić [vee-ńeećh] v. accuse;
blame for; fix the blame on
winien [vee-ńen] adj. m.
indebted; owing; guilty; at
fault; in debit
winnica [venn-ńee-tsa] f.
vineyard; vine growing
plantation
winny [veen-ni] adj. m. guilty
winny [veen-ni] adj. m. of wine;
vinous; vine-; winy
wino [vee-no] n. wine; grapevine
winogrono [vee-no-gro-no] n.
grape
winorośl [vee-no-rośhl] f. vine
winowajca [vee-no-vay-tsa] m.
culprit; evildoer; the guilty one
winszować [venn-sho-vaćh] v.
congratulate (on having
success); wish well
wiosenny [vyo-sen-ni] adj. m.
spring- (flowers, month etc.)
wioska [vyos-ka] f. hamlet
wiosło [vyos-wo] n. oar; paddle
wiosłować [vyos-wo-vaćh] v.
row; paddle; pull an oar

wiosna [vyos-na] f. Spring (time)
wioślarz [vyosh-lash] m. oarsman; rower
wiotki [vyot-kee] adj. m. limp
wiór [vyoor] m. shaving; chip
wir [veer] m. whirl; eddy; vortex
wiraż [vee-rash] m. curve; bend
wirować [vee-ro-vaćh] v. whirl
wirówka [vee-roov-ka] f. centrifuge; hydro-extractor
wirtuoz [veer-too-os] m. virtuoso; maestro; great musician etc.
wirus [vee-roos] m. virus
wisieć [vee-shećh] v. hang; sag
wisiorek [vee-sho-rek] m. pendant
wiśnia [veesh-ńa] f. cherry (tree)
wiśniak [veesh-ńak] m. cherry -brandy; cherry liqueur
witać [vee-taćh] v. greet; welcome; meet to welcome; bid welcome
witamina [vee-ta-mee-na] f. vitamin (A, B, C, D, E etc)
witryna [vee-tri-na] f. shop window; glass case
wiza [vee-za] f. visa
wizerunek [vee-ze-roo-nek] m. likeness; image; picture; effigy
wizja [veez-ya] f. vision; view
wizyta [vee-zi-ta] f. call; visit; be on a visit
wizytówka [vee-zi-toov-ka] f. calling card; visiting card
wjazd [vyazt] m. (car) entrance
wjeżdżać [vyezh-dzaćh] v. drive in; ride to the top
wkleić [vkle-eećh] v. stick in
wklęsłodruk [vklan-swo-drook] m. copper plate print
wklęsły [vklans-wi] adj. m. concave; hollow; sunken
wkład [vkwat] m. input; deposit; investment; outlay; inset
wkładać [vkwa-daćh] v. put in
w koło [v ko-wo] adv. round; in circles; over and over again
wkoło [vko-wo] prep. round; about in circles
wkraczać [vkra-chaćh] v.

appear; step in; invade; intervene; enter; stalk
wkradać się [vkra-daćh shan] v. steal in; slip in; creep in
wkrapiać [vkrap-yaćh] v. put drops in; beat up
wkręcać [vkran-tsaćh] v. screw in; drive in; push into a job
wkroczyć [vkro-chićh] v. enter (formally); appear; invade
wkrótce [vkroot-tse] adv. soon
wkupić się [vkoo-peećh shan] v. buy way in; pay one's footing
wlać [vlaćh] v. pour in
wlatywać [vla-ti-vaćh] v. fly in; rush in; dart in; run in
wlec [vlets] v. drag; tow
wlepić [vle-peećh] v. 1. paste in; 2. glare at; stare at
wlewać [vle-vaćh] v. pour in
wleźć [vleżhćh] v. crawl in; climb up; barge in; step in
wliczenie [vlee-che-ńe] n. inclusion; counting in
wliczyć [vlee-chićh] v. count in; reckon in; include
w lot [v lot] adv. in a flash; quickly; in a harry
wlot [vlot] m. inlet; intake
wlot kuli [vlot koo-lee] m. bullet entry
władać [vwa-daćh] v. rule; wield (pen etc.); manage
władca [vwad-tsa] m. ruler
władny [vwad-ni] adj. m. sovereign; having the authority (or power)
władza [vwa-dza] f. authority
włamać się [vwa-maćh shan] v. break in; burglarize
włamanie [vwa-ma-ńe] n. burglary; house breaking
włamywacz [vwa-mi-vach] m. burglar; housebreaker; pick-lock
własnoręcznie [vwa-sno-ranch-ńe] adv. personally; with one's hand; with one's own hand; of one's own hand
własność [vwas-noshćh] f. property; characteristic feature
własnowolny [vwas-no-vol-ni]

adj. m. spontaneous; voluntary
własny [vvas-ni] adj. m. own;
very own; of one's own
właściciel [vvaśh-ćhee-ćhel]
m. proprietor; holder; owner
właściwy [vvaśh-ćhee-vi]
adj. m. proper; right; suitable;
due; adequate; becoming; fit
właściwość [vvaśh-ćhee-
-vośhćh] f. propriety;
characteristic; feature
właśnie [vvaśh-ńe] adv.
exactly; just so; precisely;
very; just as; just now; just
then; only just; quite so
właz [vvas] m. manhole; hatch
włazić [vva-źheećh] v. crawl
in; barge in; step in; go deep
włączać [vvown-chaćh] v.
include; switch on; plug in
włącznie [vvownch-ńe] adv.
inclusively; inclusive; including
włączenie [vvown-che-ńe] n.
inclusion; merger; incorporation; turning on (lights, motor)
włochaty [vvo-kha-ti] adj. m.
hairy; shaggy; hirsute; woolly
włos [vvos] m. hair; fur
włosień [vvo-śheń] m. trichina
włoski [vvos-kee] adj. m. Italian;
of Italy
włoskowaty [vvos-ko-va-ti] adj.
m. capillary; hairlike (tubes)
włoszczyzna [vvozh-chiz-na] pl.
vegetables; Italian studies
włościanin [vvośh-ćha-ńeen]
m. farmer; peasant; country
man; pl. country-folk
włożyć [vvo-zhićh] v. put in;
put on; clothe; invest
włóczęga [vvoo-chan-ga] m.
tramp; rover; vagrant; roam
włóczka [vvooch-ka] f. yarn
włócznia [vvooch-ńa] f. spear
włóczyć [vvoo-chićh] v. drag
włókienniczy [vvo-kyen-ńee-chi]
adj. m. textile (trade, fiber)
włókniarz [vvook-ńash] m.
weaver; textile worker
włóknisty [vvook-ńees-ti]
adj.m. fibrous; stringy; thready
włókno [vvook-no] n. fiber
wmawiać [vmav-yaćh] v. talk

into; persuade; make believe
wmieszać się [vmye-shaćh
śhan] v. interfere; join; mix;
mingle with; intervene in
wmuszać [vmoo-shaćh] v.
force (upon); press upon
wnet [vnet] adv. soon; directly;
shortly; before long presently
wnęka [vnan-ka] f. niche; recess
wnętrze [vnan-tzhe] n. interior
wnętrzności [vnantzh-nośh-
-ćhee] pl. bowels; intestines;
entrails
Wniebowzięcie [vńe-bo-vźhan-
-ćhe] n. Assumption
wnieść [vńeśhćh] v. carry
in; put in; infer; gather; bring
in; conclude
wnikać [vnee-kaćh] v.
penetrate; investigate
wnikliwy [vńee-klee-vi] adj. m.
penetrating; discerning; keen;
discriminating; piercing
wniosek [vńo-sek] m.
conclusion; proposition;
suggestion; motion
wnioskodawca [vńos-ko-dav-
-tsa] m. mover; giver or
proposer of a motion
wnioskować [vńos-ko-vaćh] v.
conclude; deduct; infer; gather
wnioskowanie [vńos-ko-va-ńe]
n. conclusion; inference
wnosić [vno-śheećh] v. carry
in; conclude; infer; gather
wnuczka [vnooch-ka] f.
granddaughter
wnuk [vnook] m. grandson
wnyk [vnik] m. snare
woalka [vo-al-ka] f. veil (hat)
wobec [vo-bets] prep. in the
face of; before; towards
woda [vo-da] f. water; froth; bull
wodnisty [vod-ńees-ti] adj. m.
watery; thin; wishy-washy;
weak; aqueous; hydrous
wodno-płatowiec [vod-no-pwa-
-to-vyets] m. hydroplane;
water plane
wodny [vod-ni] adj. m. water-
wodociąg [vo-do-ćhownk] m.
waterworks; water tap
wodolecznictwo [vo-do-lech-

-ńeets-tvo] n. hydrotherapy;
water cure

wodopój [vo-do-pooy] m.
watering spot; cow-pond;
horse-pond; water hole

wodorost [vo-do-rost] m.
seaweed; alga

wodorowa bomba [vo-do-ro-va
bom-ba] f. H-bomb

wodospad [vo-do-spat] m.
waterfall; cascade

wodotrysk [vo-do-trisk] m.
fountain; waterspout

wodować [vo-do-vaćh] v.
launch on water; splash down;
alight (on water)

wodowstręt [vo-do-vstrₐnt] m.
hydrophobia; rabies

wodór [vo-door] m. hydrogen

wodza [vo-dza] f. rein; hold;
sway; command

wodzić [vo-dźheećh] v. lead;
run; be the ringleader

wodzirej [vo-dźhee-rey] m.
dance leader; ringleader; bell-
wether; gang leader

w ogóle [vo-goo-le] adv.
generally; on the whole; in the
main; all in all; altogether

wojak [vo-yak] m. warrior;
soldier

wojenny [vo-yen-ni] adj. m.
military; war; wartime; of war

województwo [vo-ye-voodz-tvo]
n. province; voivodeship

wojłok [voy-wok] m. felt (thick)

wojna [voy-na] f. war; warfare

wojna domowa [voy-na do-mo-
-va] f. civil war

wojować [vo-yo-vaćh] v. wage
war; combat; contend

wojowniczy [vo-yov-ńee-chi]
adj. m. warlike; aggressive

wojownik [vo-yov-ńeek] m.
(tribal) warrior

wojsko [voy-sko] n. army; troops

wojskowość [voy-sko-
-vośhćh] f. military science;
the army; military service

wojskowy [voy-sko-vi] adj. m.
military; army (post etc.)

wokalny [vo-kal-ni] adj. m. vocal

wokoło [vo-ko-wo] adv. all

around; round; about

wola [vo-la] f. will; volition

woleć [vo-lećh] v. prefer

wolno [vol-no] adv. slowly

wolnomyśliciel [vol-no-mi-
-śhlee-ćhel] m. freethinker

wolność [vol-nośhćh] f.
liberty; freedom; independence

wolnościowy [vol-nośh-ćho-vi]
adj. m. for liberation

wolny [vol-ni] adj. m. free

wolt [volt] m. volt

woltomierz [vol-to-myesh] m.
voltmeter

wołać [vo-waćh] v. call; cry

wołanie [vo-wa-ńe] n. call; cry

wołowina [vo-wo-vee-na] f. beef

wonny [von-ni] adj. m. fragrant;
aromatic; sweet-smelling

wonieć [vo-ńećh] v. scent;
smell; be fragrant

woń [voń] f. fragrance

woreczek [vo-re-chek] m. small
bag; pouch; sack; cyst

worek [vo-rek] m. bag; sack

wosk [vosk] m. wax

woskować [vos-ko-vaćh] v.
wax

wozić [vo-źheećh] v. carry (on
wheels); transport; drive; cart

wozownia [vo-zov-ńa] f. coach
house; coach storage depot

woźnica [voźh-ńee-tsa] m.
coachman; driver; waggoner

wożenie [vo-zhe-ńe] n.
transport; transportation;
carriage

wódka [vood-ka] fr. vodka

wódz [voots] m. commander;
chief; leader; headman

wójt [vooyt] m. village mayor

wół [voow] m. ox; steer; bullock

wór [voor] m. (big) sack (full)

wówczas [voov-chas] adv. then;
that time; at the time

wóz [voos] m. car; cart; wagon

wózek [voo-zek] m. (small) car

wpadać [vpa-daćh] v. fall in;
rush in; drop in; run into

wpajać [vpa-yaćh] v. put in
(head); implant; instill

wpatrywać się [vpa-tri-vaćh
śhₐn] v. stare; look intently

wpełzać [vpew-zaćh] v. crawl in; creep in (into a cave etc.)

wpędzać [vpan-dzaćh] v. drive sb in; bring on sb...(death etc)

wpić się [vpeećh śhan] v. sink into; penetrate; bury (teeth)

wpierw [vpyerv] adv. first

wpis [vpees] m. enrollment

wpisać [vpee-saćh] v. write in

wpisowe [vpee-so-ve] n. registration fee; inscription fee

wplatać [vpla-taćh] v. twine in; weave; braid; intersperse

wplątać [vplown-taćh] v. entangle; implicate; involve

wpłacać [vpwa-tsaćh] v. pay in

wpłata [vpwa-ta] f. payment

wpław [vpwaf] adv. (swim) across

wpływ [vpwif] m. influence; income; effect; impact of

wpływać [vpwi-vaćh] v. flow in; influence; have effect

wpływowy [vpwi-vo-vi] adj. m. influential

w pobliżu [v po-blee-zhoo] adv. near; in the vicinity; close by

w poprzek [v po-pzhek] prep. adv. across; crosswise

wpół [vpoow] adv. in half; halfway; half past; half-; semi-

w pośród [v pośh-root] adv. among; in the midst of

wprawa [vpra-va] f. skill; practice; proficiency

wprawdzie [vprav-dźhe] adv. in truth; to be sure; indeed

wprawić [vpra-veećh] v. set in; train in; insert; put in

wprawny [vprav-ni] adj. m. skillful; trained; experienced

wprost [vprost] adv. directly; straight ahead; outright; simply; in a straight line

wprowadzenie [vpro-va-dze-ńe] n. introduction; initiation

wprowadzać [vpro-va-dzaćh] v. usher; introduce; lead in; put in; walk into; march into

wprzęgać [vpzhan-gaćh] v. harness (horse, river, etc)

wprzód [vpshoot] adv. ahead; before; first; in the first place

wpuszczać [vpoosh-chaćh] v. let in; admit; insert; allow to enter; give free passage

wpychać [vpi-khaćh] v. push in

wracać [vra-tsaćh] v. return

wrastać [vras-taćh] v. grow in

wraz [vras] prep. together

wrażenie [vra-zhe-ńe] n. 1. impression; sensation; feeling; thrill; 2. implant; engraft

wrażliwość [vrazh-lee--vośhćh] f. sensitivity; susceptibility; delicacy

wrażliwy [vrazh-lee-vi] adj. m. sensitive; thin-skinned; tender

wreszcie [vresh-će] adv. at last; finally; after all; eventually; last of all

wręcz [vranch] adv. down right

wręczać [vran-chaćh] v. hand in; hand over; deliver

wrodzony [vro-dzo-ni] adj. m. innate; inborn; inbred; congenital

wrogi [vro-gee] adj. m. hostile

wrogość [vro-gośhćh] f. hostility; ill-will; enmity; malevolence

wrona [vro-na] f. crow

wrota [vro-ta] n. gate

wrotki [vrot-kee] pl. roller skates

wróbel [vroo-bel] m. sparrow

wrócić [vroo-ćheećh] v. return

wróg [vrook] m. foe; enemy

wróżba [vroozh-ba] f. omen

wróżbiarz [vroozh-byash] m. fortune-teller; soothsayer

wróżka [vroozh-ka] f. fortune -teller; palmist; fairy

wróżyć [vroo-zhićh] v. tell fortunes; foretell; predict

wryć się [vrićh śhan] v. dig in; sink in; imbed into

wrzask [vzhask] m. scream; yell

wrzaskliwy [vzhas-klee-vi] adj. m. shrill; piercing; clamorous

wrzawa [vzha-va] f. noise

wrzący [vzhown-tsi] adj. m. boiling; scalding (hot)

wrzątek [vzhown-tek] m. boiling water

wrzeciono [vzhe-ćho-no] n. spindle; verge

wrzeć [vzhećh] v. boil; rage
wrzesień [vzhe-śheń] m.
September
wrzeszczeć [vzhesh-chećh] v.
shriek; yell;scream; cry
wrzos [vzhos] m. heather
wrzosowisko [vzho-so-vees-ko]
n. heat; moor
wrzód [vzhoot] m. abscess
wrzucać [vzhoo-tsaćh] v.
throw in; drop in; put in; cast
wsadzać [vsa-dzaćh] v. put in;
plant; stick; lock sb up
wschodni [vskhod-ńee] adj. m.
east; easterly; eastern
wschodzić [vskho-dźhećh] v.
shoot up; rise; sprout
**wschód słońca [vskhoot swoń-
-tsa]** m. sunrise
wsiadać [vśha-daćh] v. get in;
mount; get on board; take
one's seat; mount (a horse)
wsiąkać [vśhown-kaćh] v.
sink in; infiltrate
wskazany [vska-za-ni] adj. m.
advisable; indicated; desirable
wskazówka [vska-zoov-ka] f.
hint; direction; (clock) hand
**wskazujący palec [vska-zoo-
-yown-tsi pa-lets]** m. forefinger
wskazywać [vska-zi-vaćh] v.
point out; show; indicate
wskaźnik [vskaźh-ńeek] m.
index; pointer; indicator; signal
w skos [v skos] adv. slant
wskroś [vskrośh] prep. through
wskutek [vskoo-tek] prep. as a
result; due to; thanks to
wskrzesić [vskzhe-śhećh] v.
resuscitate; revive; wake;
bring back to life; recall
**wspaniałomyślny [vspa-ńa-wo-
-miśhl-ni]** adj. m. magnanimous; generous
**wspaniałość [vspa-ńa-
-wośhćh]** f. splendor; stateliness; grandeur; lordliness
wspaniały [vspa-ńa-wi] adj. m.
superb; glorious; grand; great;
smashing; magnificent; lordly;
gorgeous; luxurious; splendid
wsparcie [vspar-ćhe] n. support
wspierać [vspye-raćh] v.

support; prop up; assist; help
**wspinać się [vspee-naćh
śhan]** v. climb up; toil up hill;
climb mountains; rear
wspomagać [vspo-ma-gaćh] v.
help; aid; assist; succor
wspominać [vspo-mee-naćh] v.
remember; recall; mention
wspornik [vspor-ńeek] m.
cantilever (beam); bracket;
structural support
wspólnik [vspool-ńeek] m.
partner; accomplice; associate
wspólny [vspool-ni] adj. m.
common; joint; combined;
collective; united
**współczesność [vspoow-ches-
-nośhćh]** f. the present time
(day, age); simultaneousness
współczesny [vspoow-ches-ni]
adj. m. contemporary; modern;
present-day (music, writers)
współczucie [vspoow-choo-ćhe]
n. sympathy; compassion; pity
współcznnik [vspoow-chin-ńeek]
m. coefficient; factor
**współdziałać [vspoow-dźha-
-waćh]** v. cooperate; act
jointly; associate; concur
**współistnieć [vspoow-eest-
-ńećh]** v. coexist
**współistnienie [vspoow-eest-ńe-
-ńe]** n. coexistence
współpraca [vspoow-pra-tsa] f.
cooperation; team-work
współrzędna [vspoow-zhand-na]
f. coordinate axis
współudział [vspoow-oo-dźhaw]
m. participation; share
**współwłaściciel [vspoow-
-vwaśh-ćhee-ćhel]** m. joint
owner; joint proprietor
**współzawodnictwo [vspoow-
-za-vod-ńeets-tvo]** m.
competition; rivalry
**współzawodnik [vspoow-za-
-vod-ńeek]** m. competitor;
rival; contestant
współżyć [vspoow-zhićh] v.
get along; live together;
coexist; be in symbiosis
wstawać [vsta-vaćh] v. get up
wstawiać [vsta-vyaćh] v. set in

wstawiać się [vsta-vyaćh
śhan] v. get tipsy; plead for
someone; stand up for

wstąpić [vstown-peećh] v.
step in; drop in; step up; enter

wstążka [vstownzh-ka] f. ribbon

wstecz [vstech] adv. backwards

wsteczny [vstech-ni] adj. m.
reactionary; reverse; backward

wstęga [vstan-ga] f. (large)
ribbon (of a road, of a river);
band; sash; wreath; wisp

wstęp [vstanp] m. entrance;
admission; preface; opening

wstępny [vstanp-ni] adj. m.
introductory; initial; preliminary

wstręt [vstrant] m. aversion

wstrętny [vstrant-ni] adj. m.
hideous; foul; vile; nasty

wstrząs [vstzhowns] m. shock

wstrząsający [vstzhown-sa-
-yown-tsi] adj. m. shocking;
thrilling; startling

wstrzemięźliwość [vstzhe-
-myan-źhlee-vośhćh] f.
moderation; abstinence

wstrzemięźliwy [vstzhe-myan-
-źhlee-vi] adj. m. moderate

wstrzykiwać [vstzhi-kee-vaćh]
v. inject; give a shot

wstrzmać [vstzhi-maćh] v.
stop; abstain; put off; hold
back; delay; suspend; cease

wstyd [vstit] m. shame;
disgrace; dishonor; indecency

wstydliwy [vstid-lee-vi] adj. m.
shy; bashful; timid;
embarrassing; modest

wstydzić się [vsti-dźeećh
śhan] v. be ashamed; blush
for someone; feel shame for

wsunąć [vsoo-nownćh] v. slip
in; put in; insert into; tuck in

wsypa [vsi-pa] f. a bad break;
gaffe; give-away of a plot

wsypać [vsi-paćh] v. pour in;
tell on somebody; pour (grain)

wszakże [vshak-zhe] conj. adv.
yet; however; nevertheless

wszcząć [vshownćh] v. start;
begin; institute; enter (talks)

wszechmocny [vshekh-mots-ni]
adj. m. omnipotent; almighty

wszechnica [vshekh-ńee-tsa] f.
university

wszechstronny [vshekh-stron-ni]
adj. m. universal; versatile

wszechświat [vshekh-śhvyat]
m. universe; cosmos;
macrocosm

wszelki [vshel-ki] adj. m. every;
all; any (possible); whatever

wszerz [vshesh] adv. broadside

wszędzie [vshan-dźhe] adv.
everywhere; on all sides; all
over; far and near

wszystek [vshis-tek] adj. m.
whole; all; ever; the whole

wszywać [vshi-vaćh] v. sew in

wścibski [vśhćheeb-skee] m.
busybody; meddler; snooper

wściekać się [vśhćhe-kaćh
śhan] v. rage; rave; be
furious; become rabid

wścieklizna [vśhćhe-kleez-na]
f. rabies; madness; rabidness;
hydrophobia

wściekłość [vśhćhek-
-vośhćh] f. fury; rage;
tantrums; madness

w ślad [vśhlad] adv. following
in tracks; following closely

wśliznąć się [vśhleez-nownćh
śhan] v. sneak in; slip in

wśród [vśhroot] prep. among

wtaczać [vta-chaćh] v. roll in

wtajemniczyć [vta-yem-ńee-
-chićh] v. initiate; acquaint;
instruct (in the art of...)

wtargnąć [vtarg-nownćh] v.
invade; break into; interrupt

wtedy [vte-di] adv. then

wtem [vtem] adv. suddenly

wtenczas [vten-chas] adv. then;
at that time; at this junction

wtoczyć [vto-chićh] v. roll in

wtorek [vto-rek] m. Tuesday

wtórny [vtoor-ni] adj. m.
secondary; incidental;
repeated; derivative

wtrącać się [vtrown-tsaćh
śhan] v. meddle; cut into;
butt in; add (a remark)

wtyczka [vtich-ka] f. plug

wtykać [vti-kaćh] v. insert

w tył [v tiw] adv. back

wuj [vooy] m. uncle
wujenka [voo-yen-ka] f. aunt
wulgarny [vool-gar-ni] adj. m.
vulgar; coarse; low
wulkan [vool-kan] m. volcano
wulkanizować [vool-ka-ńee-zo-
-vaćh] v. vulcanize; cure
(rubber)
wwozić [v-vo-źheećh] v.
import; bring into an area
wwóz [v-voos] m. import;
importation
wy [vi] pron. you; you people
wybaczać [vi-ba-chaćh] v. 1.
forgive; pardon; 2. buckle out
of line; get out of line
wybawca [vi-bav-tsa] m. savior;
rescuer; liberator; redeemer
wybawić [vi-ba-veećh] v. save;
deliver; free; rescue; rid
wybebeszyć [vi-be-be-shićh] v.
gut (chicken etc.)
wybić [vi-beećh] v. knock out
(something); strike; cover; kill
wybiec [vi-byets] v. run out
wybieg [vi-byek] m. evasion;
runway; playground; fowl run
wybielić [vi-bye-leećh] v.
whitewash; bleach; coat with
tin; whiten; grow white
wybierać [vi-bye-raćh] v.
choose elect; select; pick out;
mine; extract; scoop; excavate
wybierak [vi-bye-rak] m. selector
(a technical term)
wybieralny [vi-bye-ral-ni] adj. m.
elective; eligible
wybitny [vi-beet-ni] adj. m.
prominent; eminent; marked
wybladły [vi-blad-wi] adj. m.
pale; dim; faded; colorless
wybłagać [vi-bwa-gaćh] v. get
by entreaty; impetrate
wyblakły [vi-blak-wi] adj. m.
faded; dim; dilute; weathered
wyboisty [vi-bo-ees-ti] adj. m.
rough; full of holes; bumpy
wyborca [vi-bor-tsa] m. voter
wyborczy [vi-bor-chi] adj. m.
electoral; election- (precinct...)
wyborny [vi-bor-ni] adj. m.
excellent; prime; choice;
splendid; delicious; exquisite

wyborowy [vi-bo-ro-vi] adj. m.
choice; select; first rate
wybory [vi-bo-ri] pl. election
wybór [vi-boor] m. choice;
option; selection; adoption
wybrany [vi-bra-ni] adj. m.
elected; chosen; selected
wybredny [vi-bred-ni] adj. m.
fastidious; particular; exacting
wybrnąć [vibr-nownćh] v. get
out; pull through; wade out
of; clear out of; extricate
wybrukować [vi-broo-ko-vaćh]
v. pave (a road, a street etc.)
wybryk [vi-brik] m. prank; freak;
antic; whim; frolic; caprice;
extravagance; escapade
wybrzeże [vi-bzhe-zhe] n. coast;
beach; seashore; seacoast
wybrzuszenie [vi-bzhoo-she-ńe]
n. bulge; swelling; knob; belly
wybuch [vi-bookh] m. explosion;
eruption; outbreak; outburst
wybudować [vi-boo-do-vaćh]
v. build; erect; raise; construct
wycelować [vi-tse-lo-vaćh] v.
take aim; level a gun at
wychodek [vi-kho-dek] m. privy
wychodzić [vi-kho-dźheećh] v.
get out; walk out; climb out
wychodźca [vi-khodźh-tsa] m.
emigrant; emigre
wychować [vi-kho-vaćh] v.
bring up; breed; rear; rise;
train; educate
wychowanek [vi-kho-va-nek] m.
pupil; alumnus; ward; foster
child
wychowanie [vi-kho-va-ńe] n.
upbringing; manners;
education; breeding
wychowawca [vi-kho-vav-tsa] m.
tutor; educator; foster father
wychudły [vi-khood-wi] adj. m.
gaunt; skinny; haggard;
emaciated; hollow-cheeked
wychwalać [vi-khva-laćh] v.
praise; exalt; extol; speak
highly of; crack up
wychylać [vi-khi-laćh] v. stick
out; empty (a glass) ; bend;
incline; lean out; hang out
wychylać się [vi-khi-laćh

śhan] v. lean out; stick one's neck out; hang out; appear; be visible

wyciąg [vi-ćhownk] m. extract; elevator; hoist; winch; excerpt

wyciągać [vi-ćhown-gaćh] v. pull out; stretch out; derive

wycie [vi-ćhe] n. howl; scream

wycieczka [vi-ćhech-ka] f. trip; excursion; outing; ramble; hike

wyciekać [vi-ćhe-kaćh] v. leak out; flow out; ooze out; scamper away; exude

wycieńczać [vi-ćheń-chaćh] exhaust; waste; emaciate

wycieńczenie [vi-ćheń-che-ńe] n. exhaustion; weakness; debility; emaciation

wycieraczka [vi-ćhe-rach-ka] f. wiper; doormat

wycierać [vi-ćhe-raćh] v. wipe; erase; efface; dust; wear out; blow (nose); rub

wycięcie [vi-ćhan-ćhe] n. opening; cut; decollete; notch; jag; neck-line; indentation

wycinać [vi-ćhee-naćh] v. cut out; carve out; fell; cut down

wycisk [vi-ćheesk] m. press; squeeze; beating (slang)

wyciskać [vi-ćhees-kaćh] v. squeeze out; impress; wring

wycofać [vi-tso-faćh] v. withdraw; remove; retract; call off; call back; recall; retire

wycofanie [vi-tso-fa-ńe] n. withdrawal; recall; retirement

wyczerpać [vi-cher-paćh] v. exhaust; drain; deplete; scoop

wyczerpanie [vi-cher-pa-ńe] n. exhaustion; depletion; fag; prostration; tiring out

wyczesywać [vi-che-si-vaćh] v. comb out; dress hair (beard etc.); comb hair

wyczuwać [vi-choo-vaćh] v. sense; feel; scent; ascertain; perceive by touch

wyczyn [vi-chin] m. feat; stunt

wyczyszczać [vi-chish-chaćh] v. clean; brush (clothes); clean out; polish; furbish

wyć [vićh] v. howl; roar; shriek

wyćwiczony [vićh-vee-cho-ni] adj. m. trained; skilled

wydać [vi-daćh] v. give away spend; pay; issue; betray

wydajność [vi-day-nośhćh] f. yield; productivity; output

wydajny [vi-day-ni] adj. m. productive; effective

wydalać [vi-da-laćh] v. dismiss; sack; expel; eliminate; excrete

wydalenie [vi-da-le-ńe] n. expulsion; dismissal

wydanie [vi-da-ńe] n. edition

wydarty [vi-dar-ti] adj. m. torn out; plucked out; snatched out

wydarzać się [vi-da-zhaćh śhan] v. happen; turn out well; occur; take place

wydarzenie [vi-da-zhe-ńe] n. event; happening; occurrence

wydatek [vi-da-tek] m. expense

wydatkować [vi-dat-ko-vaćh] v. spend; lay out funds; expend

wydatny [vi-dat-ni] adj. m. prominent; salient; distinct

wydawać [vi-da-vaćh] v. spend; give the change; give away; publish

wydawca [vi-dav-tsa] m. publisher; editor; publishing house or firm

wydawnictwo [vi-dav-ńeets-tvo] n. publication; publishing house; publishing firm

wydąć [vi-downćh] v. expand; puff up; inflate; blow up

wydech [vi-dekh] m. exhalation

wydeptać ścieżkę [vi-dep-taćh śhćhezh-kan] beat a path; thread a path (exp.)

wydłubywać [vi-dwoo-bi-vaćh] v. scrape out; poke; hollow out; extract; pick out

wydłużać [vi-dwoo-zhaćh] v. prolong; lengthen; elongate

wydma [vid-ma] f. dune; sand dune; snowdrift

wydobrzeć [vi-dob-zhećh] v. recover; get better; improve

wydobycie [vi-do-bi-ćhe] n. output; yield; production

wydobywać [vi-do-bi-vaćh] v. extract; mine; wring; get;

obtain; draw out; excavate

wydostać [vi-dos-taćh] v. bring out; extricate; obtain; pull out

wydra [vi-dra] f. otter; vulg.:bitch; hussy; minx; vixen

wydrapać [vi-dra-paćh] v. scratch out; erase a stain

wydrapać się [vi-dra-paćh śhan] v. climb up; scramble up (out); clamber up

wydrążać [vi-drown-zhaćh] v. hollow out; drill; excavate

wydrwić [vi-drveećh] v. jeer; mock; cheat; gibe; deride

wydrwigrosz [vi-drvee-grosh] m. swindler; fraud; take-in

wydusić [vi-doo-śheećh] v. squeeze out; extort; strangle

wydychać [vi-di-khaćh] v. breathe out; exhale; emit

wydymać [vi-di-maćh] v. puff out; inflate; belly out; blow up (a balloon); bulge

wydział [vi-dźhaw] m. department; section; division

wydziedziczyć [vi-dźhe-dźhee-chaćh] v. disinherit

wydzielać [vi-dźhe-laćh] v. emit; detach; distribute; secrete; give off; exhale

wydzielenie [vi-dźhe-le-ńe] n. secretion; assignment; elimination; emanation; issue

wydzieliny [vi-dźhe-lee-ni] pl. secreta; excretions; discharge

wydzielony [vi-dźhe-lo-ni] adj. m. emitted; segregated; allotted; rationed; secreted

wydzierać [vi-dźhe-raćh] v. tear out; roar out; blare out; scramble; vociferate; bellow

wydzierżawić [vi-dźher-zha-veećh] v. lease; farm out; rent; let out; take a lease

wydzirżawienie [vi-dźher-zha-vye-ńe] n. leasing; renting; farming out

wyegzekwować [vi-eg-zek-vo-vaćh] v. exact; enforce; carry out (a sentence etc.)

wyekwipowanie [vi-ek-vee-po-va-ńe] n. outfit; equipment

wyelegancieć [vi-e-le-gan--ćhećh] v. acquire; elegance; become elegant

wyeliminowanie [vi-e-lee-mee-no-va-ńe] n. elimination; exclusion

wyga [vi-ga] m. old experienced hand; sly fox; old stager

wygadać [vi-ga-daćh] v. blab out

wygadany [vi-ga-da-ni] adj. m. glib; eloquent; wordy; talkative

wyganiać [vi-ga-ńaćh] v. expel; chase out; turn out (cattle)

wygarniać [vi-gar-ńaćh] v. rake out; tell off; say openly; shoot

wygasać [vi-ga-saćh] v. extinguish; expire; go out; die out

wyginać [vi-gee-naćh] v. bend

wygląd [vig-lownd] m. appearance; aspect; air; looks; semblance

wyglądać [vig-lown-daćh] v. look out; appear; appear; look

wygładzać [vi-gwa-dzaćh] v. smooth; level; even; sleek

wygłodzić [vi-gwo-dźheećh] v. starve out; underfeed; famish

wygłosić [vi-gwo-śheećh] v. pronounce; utter; deliver (speech)

wygnać [vig-naćh] v. expel; banish

wygnanie [vig-na-ńe] n. exile

wygniatać [vi-gńa-taćh] v. press out; squeeze out; extort; kill

wygoda [vi-go-da] f. comfort

wygodny [vi-god-ni] adj. m. comfortable; cozy; handy

wygolony [vi-go-lo-ni] adj. m. clean-shaven; well shaven

wygotować [vi-go-to-vaćh] v. boil away; distill; prepare

wygórowany [vi-goo-ro-va-ni] adj. m. excessive; stiff (price)

wygrać [vi-graćh] v. win; score

wygramolić się [vi-gra-mo-leećh śhan] v. scramble up (out)

wygrana [vi-gra-na] f. winning; victory; prize; a win

wygryzać [vi-gri-zaćh] v. 1.bite out; corrode; 2.drive out by harassment; oust; bore a hole

wygrzebywać [vi-gzhe-bi-vaćh] v. dig out; unearth; rake out

wygrzewać się [vi-gzhe-vaćh śhan] v. bask; warm oneself

wygwizdać [vi-gveez-daćh] v. hiss off (stage); whistle away

wyjałowić [vi-ya-wo-veećh] v. sterilize; exhaust (brain, soil...)

wyjaśnić [vi-yaśh-ńeećh] v. explain; clear up; elucidate

wyjaśnienie [vi-yaśh-ńe-ńe] n. explanation; interpretation

wyjawić [vi-ya-veećh] v. disclose; reveal; bring to light

wyjazd [vi-yazt] m. departure

wyjąkać [vi-yown-kaćh] v. stammer out; stutter out; falter out

wyjątek [vi-yown-tek] m. exception; excerpt; extract

wyjątkowy [vi-yownt-ko-vi] adj. m. exceptional; unusual; unique

wyjechać [vi-ye-khaćh] v. drive away;leave; come out with

wyjeżdżać [vi-yezh-dzhaćh] v. leave; drive away; set out

wyjmować [viy-mo-vaćh] v. take out; remove; extract; excerpt

wyjście [viyśh-ćhe] n. exit; way out; departure; egress

wyka [vi-ka] f. vetch; tare

wykadzić [vi-ka-dźheećh] v. smoke out; fumigate; perfume

wykałaczka [vi-ka-wach-ka] f. toothpick

wykarczować [vi-kar-cho-vaćh] v. grub out; clear; dig up (trees)

wykaz [vi-kas] m. list; register; roll; schedule; docket

wykąpać [vi-kown-paćh] v. bathe

wykipieć [vi-keep-yećh] v. boil over (milk, water, soup etc.)

wyklęty [vi-klan-ti] adj. m. cursed; excommunicated

wykluczyć [vi-kloo-chićh] v. exclude; expel; shut out; except

wykład [vik-wat] m. lecture

wykładać [vi-kwa-daćh] v. lecture; lay out; display; cover

wykładnik [vi-kwad-ńeek] m. exponent; expression; ratio

wykładowca [vi-kwa-dov-tsa] m. lecturer; instructor

wykłuwać [vi-kwoo-vaćh] v. stab out; put out; tattoo; prick out

wykoleić [vi-ko-le-eećh] v. derail; lead astray; ditch (a train)

wykombinować [vi-kom-bee-no-vaćh] v. contrive; think out

wykonać [vi-ko-naćh] v. execute; do; fulfill; carry out; perform

wykonalny [vi-ko-nal-ni] adj. m. feasible; workable; realizable

wykonanie [vi-ko-na-ńe] n. execution; realization; fulfillment

wykonawczy [vi-ko-nav-chi] adj. m. executive; executory (details)

wykończenie [vi-koń-che-ńe] n. finish; trimming; last touch

wykończyć [vi-koń-chićh] v. finish off; dress; do sb in

wykop [vi-kop] m. excavation; potato lifting; flying kick

wykopać [vi-ko-paćh] v. dig out

wykopalisko [vi-ko-pa-lees-ko] n. find (archeological)

wykorzenić [vi-ko-zhe-ńeećh] v. root out; uproot; eradicate

wykorzystać [vi-ko-zhis-taćh] v. take advantage; exploit; use up

wykpić [vik-peećh] v. deride

wykraczać [vi-kra-chaćh] v. step over; break law; transgress

wykradać [vi-kra-daćh] v. steal; kidnap; purloin; pilfer; abduct

wykrajać [vi-kra-yaćh] v. cut out; carve out; make a low cut

wykres [vi-kres] m. graph; chart
wykreślić [vi-kreśh-leećh] v. trace; cross out; draw; erase
wykręcać [vi-kran-tsaćh] v. screw out; distort; elude; twist
wykręt [vi-krant] m. shift; excuse; dodge; quibble
wykrętny [vi-krant-ni] adj. m. shifty; evasive; sophistical
wykroczenie [vi-kro-che-ńe] n. offense; misdemeanor; delinquency
wykroić [vi-kro-eećh] v. cut out
wykruszyć [vi-kroo-shićh] v. crumble out; shell (corn etc.)
wykryć [vi-krićh] v. discover; detect; reveal (the truth etc.)
wykrztusić [vi-kzhtoo-śheećh] v. cough up; choke out; hawk up
wykrzknąć [vi-kzhik-nownćh] v. call out; shout; cry out
wykształcić [vi-kzhtaw-ćheećh] v. educate; train; shape; form
wykup [vi-koop] m. ransom
wykupić [vi-koo-peećh] v. buy up
wykurzać [vi-koo-zhaćh] v. smoke out (foxes, bees, etc.)
wykwintny [vi-kveent-ni] adj. m. elegant; exquisite; urbane
wyleczalny [vi-le-chal-ni] adj. m. curable; possible to cure
wyleczyć [vi-le-chićh] v. cure
wylew krwi [vi-lev krvee] hemorrhage; blood effusion
wylewać [vi-le-vaćh] v. pour out; overflow; spill; bail out water
wylęgać [vi-lan-gaćh] v. hatch
wylękły [vi-lank-wi] adj. m. frightened; scared; terrified
wyliczać [vi-lee-chaćh] v. count up; count out; recite
wylosować [vi-lo-so-vaćh] adj. m. draw by lots; toss for
wylot [vi-lot] m. flight departure; nozzle; exhaust; exit
wyludniać [vi-lood-ńaćh] v. depopulate; desolate; devastate

wyładować [vi-wa-do-vaćh] v. unload; discharge; cram; pack
wyładowanie [vi-wa-do-va-ńe] n. unloading; discharge
wyłamać [vi-wa-maćh] v. break out; break loose; break away
wyławiać [vi-wav-yaćh] v. fish out; spot out; catch (a sound)
wyłaniać [vi-wa-ńaćh] v. evolve; emerge; show; appoint; form
wyłączać [vi-wown-chaćh] v. exclude; switch off; disconnect
wyłącznik [vi-wownch-ńeek] m. switch; circuit-breaker; cut off
wyłączny [vi-wownch-ni] adj. m. exclusive; sole; only; entire
wyłudzić [vi-woo-dźheećh] v. coax; beguile; trick; fool
wyłom [vi-wom] m. breach; gap
wyłuskać [vi-voos-kaćh] v. husk; scale; fleece; shell; hull; pod
wymaczać [vi-ma-chaćh] v. soak
wymagać [vi-ma-gaćh] v. require; expect; demand; need; exact
wymaganie [vi-ma-ga-ńe] n. requirement; demand; requisite; need; want
wymawiać [vi-mav-yaćh] v. pronounce; reproach; cancel; express
wymazać [vi-ma-zaćh] v. erase; efface; blot out; smear; use up
wymiana [vi-mya-na] f. exchange
wymiar [vi-myar] m. dimension
wymiatać [vi-mya-taćh] v. sweep out; clean out; sweep
wymieniać [vi-mye-ńaćh] v. exchange; convert; replace
wymierać [vi-mye-raćh] v. die out; become extinct (gradually)
wymierzać [vi-mye-zhaćh] v. aim; measure; assess; survey; mete out
wymię [vi-myan] n. udder
wymijać [vi-mee-yaćh] v. pass by; evade

wymiotować [vi-myo-to-vaćh]
v. vomit; be sick; spew up
(one's food)

wymogi [vi-mo-gee] pl.
requirements; exigencies;
demands; needs; wants

wymowa [vi-mo-va] f.
pronunciation; significance (of
facts); eloquence

wymowny [vi-mov-ni] adj. m.
eloquent; telltale; telling

wymóc [vi-moots] v. extort;
compel; wring; force; prevail

wymówienie [vi-moov-ye-ńe] n.
notice (to quit or dismiss)

wymówka [vi-moov-ka] f.
reproach; pretext; excuse; put-
off; evasion; rebuke

wymusić [vi-moo-śhićh] v.
extort; wring; force; compel

wymuszenie [vi-moo-she-ńe] n.
extortion; blackmail; shake-
down; coercion; constraint

wymykać się [vi-mi-kaćh
śhan] v. escape; slip away;
sneak out; dodge; steal out

wymysł [vi-misw] m. fiction;
invention; fiction; abuse

wymyślać [vi-miśh-laćh] v.
think up; call names; invent;
abuse; devise; contrive

wymyślny [vi-miśhl-ni] adj. m.
clever; ingenious; fanciful;
cunning; sophisticated

wymywać [vi-mi-vaćh] v. wash
out; rinse; hollow out

wynagradzać [vi-na-gra-dzaćh]
v. reward; pay; indemnify;
recompense; make up; gratify

wynagrodzenie [vi-na-gro-dze-
-ńe] n. reward; pay; fee;
wages; reward; reparation

wynajdywać [vi-nay-di-vaćh] v.
find (out); invent; devise

wynajmować [vi-nay-mo-vaćh]
v. hire; rent; lease out

wynajem [vi-na-yem] m. lease;
rent; hire; letting out

wynalazca [vi-na-laz-tsa] m.
inventor; contriver

wynalazek [vi-na-la-zek] m.
invention; device; contrivance

wynaleźć [vi-na-leźhćh] v.
invent; discover; find

wynaradawiać [vi-na-ra-dav-
-yaćh] v. denationalize; divest

wynik [vi-ńeek] m. result; score

wyniosłość [vi-ńos-wośhćh]
f. eminence; haughtiness;
prance; rise; swell; knoll

wyniosły [vi-ńos-wi] adj. m.
lofty; high-handed; insolent

wyniszczać [vi-ńeesh-chaćh]
v. ruin; exhaust; weaken;
devastate; ravage; destroy

wynosić [vi-no-śheećh] v.
carry out; elevate; amount;
wear out; praise; nurse

wynudzać [vi-noo-dzaćh] v. get
by bothering; bore stiff

wynurzenie [vi-noo-zhe-ńe] n.
emergence; (personal)
outpouring; effusion

wyobraźnia [vi-o-braźh-ńa] f.
imagination; fancy; empty
fancy

wyobrażać [vi-o-bra-zhaćh] v.
imagine; picture; fancy; conceive; suppose; represent

wyobrażenie [vi-o-bra-zhe-ńe] n.
notion; idea; image; representation; picture; conception

wyodrębniać [vi-od-ranb-ńaćh]
v. single out; separate; isolate

wyodrębnienie [vi-od-ranb-ńe-
-ńe] n. separation; isolation

wyolbrzymiać [vi-ol-bzhi-
-myaćh] v. magnify;
exaggerate (very much)

wypaczyć [vi-pa-chićh] v. warp

wypad [vi-pat] m. sally; attack

wypadać [vi-pa-daćh] v. fall
out; rash out; become; turn
out; happen; occur; work out

wypadek [vi-pa-dek] m. accident;
case; event; chance; instance

wypadkowa [vi-pad-ko-va] f.
resultant (force, affect, etc)

wypakować [vi-pa-ko-vaćh] v.
unpack; cram;pack tight

wypalać [vi-pa-laćh] v. burn;
burn out; burn down; fire

wypaplać [vi-pap-laćh] v.
babble out; blurt out (the
truth, secret); spill the beans

wyparcie się [vi-par-ćhe śhan]

n. disclaimer; repudiation
wyparować [vi-pa-ro-vaćh] v.
evaporate; vanish into thin air
wypatrywać [vi-pa-tri-vaćh] v.
watch (for); look out; espy;
descry; strain one's eyes
wypełniać [vi-pew-ńaćh] v.
fulfill; fill up; while away; fill
in; perform; execute (a duty)
wypełnienie [vi-pew-ńe-ńe] n.
fulfillment; execution (of an
order, etc.); filler
wypędzać [vi-pan-dzaćh] v.
drive out; expel; discharge;
dislodge (an enemy, etc.)
wypiekać [vi-pye-kaćh] v. bake
wypierać [vi-pye-raćh] v. oust;
push out; force our; supplant
wypierać się [vi-pye-raćh
śhan] v. deny; repudiate;
disown; abjure; renounce
wypijać [vi-pee-yaćh] v. drink
(empty); drink to; drink off
wypinać [vi-pee-naćh] v.
extend; stretch out; show
one's back side
wypis [vi-pees] m. extract;
selected passage; selection
wypisywać [vi-pee-si-vaćh] v.
(write) extract; make out (a
check); fill in (a form)
wyplątać [vi-plown-taćh] v.
extricate; disentangle;
disengage; free from tangles
wyplątany [vi-plown-ta-ni] adj.
m. dis-embroiled; extricated
wyplenić [vi-ple-ńeećh] v.
weed out; root out; eradicate
wypluć [vi-plooćh] v. spit out
wypłacać [vi-pwa-tsaćh] v. pay
out; pay up; pay off; repay
wypłacalny [vi-pwa-tsal-ni] adj.
m. solvent; sound (financially)
wypłata [vi-pwa-ta] f. pay (day)
wypłoszyć [vi-pwo-shićh] v.
scare away; drive away (birds
etc.); rouse (game)
wypłowieć [vi-pwo-vyećh] v.
fade; discolor
wypłukać [vi-pwoo-kaćh] v.
rinse; wash out; swill out;
give a rinse
wypływ [vi-pwiv] m. outflow;

discharge; afflux; leakage
wypływać [vi-pwi-vaćh] v. flow
out; sail out; swim out; rise
wypocić [vi-po-ćheećh] v.
sweat out; perspire; be soaked
in sweat; exude
wypoczynek [vi-po-chi-nek] m.
rest; repose
wypoczywać [vi-po-chi-vaćh] v.
rest; have a rest; take a rest
wypogadzać się [vi-po-ga-
dzaćh śhan] v. clear up;
cheer up; brighten; uncloud
wypomnieć [vi-pom-ńećh] v.
reproach; remind; keep
reminding; upbraid; rebuke
wyporność [vi-por-nośhćh] f.
displacement; draught;
buoyancy
wyposażać [vi-po-sa-zhaćh] v.
equip; endow; fit out; stock
wyposażenie [vi-po-sa-zhe-ńe]
n. equipment; outfit; wages;
salary; dowry; furnishings
wyposażyć [vi-po-sa-zhićh] v.
endow; equip; fit out; stock
wypowiadać [vi-po-vya-daćh]
v. pronounce; declare; express
wypowiedzenie [vi-po-vye-dze-
-ńe] n. (discharge) notice;
(war) declaration; renun-
ciation; utterance; statement
wypożyczać [vi-po-zhi-chaćh]
v. lend out; borrow from; hire
to; hire from; lend to
wypożyczalnia [vi-po-zhi-chal-
-ńa] f. rental business; rental
agency
wypracowanie [vi-pra-tso-va-ńe]
n. (school) composition;
elaboration; essay; exercise
wyprać [vi-praćh] v. wash out
wypraszać [vi-pra-shaćh] v.
1.plead; pester; 2.show (the
door); give somebody the
gate; turn out; forbid
wyprawa [vi-pra-va] f.
expedition; excursion; outfit;
tanning; dowry; plaster
wyprawiać [vi-pra-vyaćh] v.
send; dispatch; tan; plaster;
give (a party); arrange
wyprężać [vi-pran-zhaćh] v.

stretch out, tense (a muscle
etc.); tauten (a rope, etc.)
wyprostować [vi-pros-to-vaćh]
v. straighten; set straight
wyprowadzać [vi-pro-va-dzaćh]
v. lead out; move out; trace
wypróbować [vi-proo-bo-vaćh]
v. test; try out; put to test
wypróżniać [vi-proozh-ńaćh]
v. empty; clear out; evacuate
wyprzedawać [vi-pzhe-da-vaćh]
v. sell out; clear out (stock)
wyprzedaż [vi-pzhe-dash] v.
(clearance) sale
wyprzedzać [vi-pzhe-dzaćh] v.
pull ahead; outrace; overtake
wyprzęgać [vi-pzhan-gaćh] v.
unharness; unhitch (a horse)
wypukły [vi-pook-wi] adj. m.
convex; bulging; cambered
wypuścić [vi-poośh-ćheećh]
v. let out; set free; let go;
omit; release; launch; lease
out; drop; set free; launch
wypychać [vi-pi-khaćh] v.
oust; push out; stuff; pack; fill;
cram; shove out; crowd; force
wypytywać [vi-pi-ti-vaćh] v.
question; ask questions;
inquire
wyrabiać [vi-ra-byaćh] v.
1. make; form; 2. play pranks
wyrachowany [vi-ra-kho-va-ni]
adj. m. scheming; thrifty
wyratować [vi-ra-to-vaćh] v.
rescue; save (a life etc.)
wyraz [vi-ras] m. word;
expression; look; term (of
praise, indignation, etc.)
wyraźny [vi-raźh-ni] adj. m.
explicit; clear; distinct
wyrażać [vi-ra-zhaćh] v.
express; say; signify
wyrażenie [vi-ra-zhe-ńe] n.
expression; utterance; phrase;
statement; formulation
wyrąb [vi-rownp] m. clearing;
felling; cutting; slash; fell
wyrąbać [vi-rown-baćh] v. cut
out (with axe); clear; hack out
wyręczać [vi-ran-chaćh] v. help
out; replace; relieve of tasks
wyrobnik [vi-rob-ńeek] m.

day-laborer; workman
wyrocznia [vi-roch-ńa] f. oracle
wyrodny [vi-rod-ni] adj. m.
degenerate; unnatural (son);
base; infamous; villainous
wyrodzić się [vi-ro-dźeećh
śhan] v. degenerate; deteriorate; spring from
wyrok [vi-rok] m. sentence;
verdict; judgment; pronouncement (by doctors, etc.)
wyrostek [vi-ros-tek] m.
outgrowth; stripling; teenager
wyrośnięty [vi-rośh-ńan-ti] adj.
m. grown up; overgrown
wyrozumiały [vi-ro-zoo-**mya**-wi]
adj. m. indulgent; lenient
wyrozumienie [vi-ro-zoo-**mye**-ńe]
n. sympathetic understanding
wyrób [vi-roob] m. manufacture
wyrównać [vi-roov-naćh] v.
equalize; pay up; smooth
wyrównanie [vi-roov-na-ńe] m.
leveling; balancing (accounts)
offset; payment; handicap
wyróżniać [vi-roozh-ńaćh] v.
distinguish; favor; single out
wyruszyć [vi-roo-shićh] v. start
out; set out; march out; sail
away; start on a journey
wyrwać [vir-vaćh] v. extract;
tear out; pull out; run away
wyrywki [vi-riv-kee] pl. random
wyryć [vi-rićh] v. engrave; root
up; dig out; gully; furrow;
incise; carve out; imprint
wyrzec się [vi-zhets śhan] v.
renounce; give up; forgo;
repudiate; surrender
wyrzucać [vi-zhoo-tsaćh] v.
expel; throw out; dump;
reproach; remove; eject
wyrzut [vi-zhoot] m. reproach
wyrzutnia [vi-zhoot-ńa] f. launch
(ing) pad; chute; launcher
wyrzutek [vi-zhoo-tek] m.
outcast; ruffian; wretch
wyrzynać [vi-zhi-naćh] v. cut
out; carve out; kill; massacre;
slaughter; bang; slap; whack
wysadzić [vi-sa-dźheećh] v.
set out; land; blow up; eject;
plant; disembark; help out

wyschnąć [vis-khnownćh] v.
dry up; go dry; shrivel up

wysepka [vi-sep-ka] f. islet

wysiadać [vi-śha-daćh] v. get
out (from car etc.); go bust;
get off; disembark

wysiadywać [vi-śha-di-vaćh]
v. sit out; hatch out; sit late

wysiedlać [vi-śhed-laćh] v.
expel (from home); resettle;
eject; displace; evacuate

wysilać [vi-śhee-laćh] v. exert

wysiłek [vi-śhee-wek] m. effort

wyskoczyć [vi-sko-chićh] v.
jump out; pop up; run out;
bale out; eject; protrude

wyskok [vis-kok] m. 1. fling;
freak; 2. cam; ledge; run out

wyskokowy [vis-ko-ko-vi] adj. m.
alcoholic; intoxicating

wyskrobać [vi-skro-baćh] v.
scratch out; erase; scratch

wyskubać [vi-skoo-baćh] v.
pluck out; pull out (hair etc.)

wysłać [vi-swaćh] v. send off;
dispatch; emit; let fly

wysłaniec [vi-swa-ńets] m.
messenger; envoy; deputy

wysłowić [vi-swo-veećh] v.
express; say; utter; speak

wysłuchać [vi-swoo-khaćh] v.
hear out; give a hearing

wysługiwać się [vi-swoo-gee-
-vaćh śhan] v. lackey; earn
seniority; get worn out

wysmarować [vi-sma-ro-vaćh]
v. smear; lubricate; soil; stain

wysmażony [vi-sma-zho-ni] adj.
m. well done (meat);cooked

wysmukły [vi-smook-wi] adj. m.
slender; slim and tall

wysoce [vi-so-tse] adv. highly

wysoki [vi-so-kee] m. tall; high;
soaring; lofty; towering

wysokość [vi-so-kośhćh] f.
height; altitude; level; extent

wysokościomierz [vi-so-kośh-
-ćho-myesh] m. altimeter

wyspa [vis-pa] f. island; isle

wyspać się [vis-paćh śhan] v.
sleep enough; sleep off

wyspowiadać się [vis-po-vya-
-daćh śhan] v. confess

wysrać się [vi-sraćh śhan] v.
(vulgar) shit

wyssać [vis-saćh] v. suck out;
suck dry; suck up; trump up

wystarać się [vi-sta-raćh
śhan] v. procure; obtain

wystarczyć [vi-star-chićh] v.
suffice; do enough; be enough

wystawa [vi-sta-va] f. exhibition;
display (window dressing)

wystawać [vi-sta-vaćh] v.
stand long time; stick out

wystawca [vi-stav-tsa] m.
exhibitor; signer (of check)

wystawiać [vi-stav-yaćh] v. put
out; stick out; sign (check);
expose; put up; draw up; rise

wystawienie [vi-sta-vye-ńe] n.
exposition; exposure; display

wystąpić [vi-stown-peećh] v.
step forward; perform; resign

wystąpienie [vi-stown-pye-ńe]
n. withdrawal; appearance

występ [vi-stanp] m. protrusion;
(stage) appearance; utterance

występek [vi-stan-pek] m.
felony; crime; vice; offense

występny [vi-stanp-ni] adj. m.
criminal; immoral; illicit

wystraszyć [vi-stra-shićh] v.
frighten away; terrify; scare

wystroić [vi-stro-eećh] v. dress
up; trig out; deck out; adorn

wystrzał [vi-stzhaw] m. shot

wystrzegać się [vi-stzhe-gaćh
śhan] v. avoid; beware; shun

wystrzelić [vi-stzhe-leećh] v.
fire a gun; shoot out; go off

wystrząpić [vi-stzhan-peećh] v.
ravel out; fray; unravel

wystygać [vi-sti-gaćh] v. cool
off; grow cold; get cold

wysuszyć [vi-soo-shićh] v. dry
up; wither; parch; shrivel

wysuwać [vi-soo-vaćh] v.
shove forward; protrude; put
out; put up; advance; propose

wyswobodzić [vi-svo-bo-
-dźheećh] v. liberate; deliver;
free from something

wysychać [vi-si-khaćh] v. dry
out; get perched; shrivel up

wysypać [vi-si-paćh] v. pour

out (sand); spill; scatter

wysypka [vi-sip-ka] f. (skin) rash; eruption; exanthema

wysysać [vi-si-saćh] v. suck

wyszczególnić [vi-shche-gool-ńeećh] v. specify; detail out

wyszeptać [vi-shep-taćh] v. whisper (not vibrating vocal chords); talk furtively

wyszkolić [vi-shko-leećh] v. train; school; educate; instruct

wyszpiegować [vi-shpye-go-vaćh] v. spy out that...; watch closely and secretly

wyszukać [vi-shoo-kaćh] v. find out; hunt up; search out

wyszukany [vi-shoo-ka-ni] adj. m. choice; unusual; elaborate

wyszydzać [vi-shi-dzaćh] v. scoff at; jeer; deride

wyszynk [vi-shink] m. liquor store; liquor retail on licence

wyszywać [vi-shi-vaćh] v. embroider; make design on fabric with needlework

wyścielać [vi-śhće-laćh] v. pad; line; strew; cushion

wyścig [viśh-ćheek] m. race; contest; rivalry; (horse) race

wyśledzić [vi-śhle-dźheećh] v. spy out; track out; detect

wyśliznąć się [vi-śhleez-nowńćh śhan] v. slip out; slide out; wriggle out

wyśmiać [viśh-myaćh] v. laugh at; deride; mock; ridicule

wyśmienity [viśh-mye-ńee-ti] adj. m. choice; excellent

wyśpiewać [vi-śhpye-vaćh] v. sing; say; sound praises; squeal during an investigation

wyświadczyć [viśh-vyad-chićh] v. do (favor); do (good); do (wrong)

wyświechtany [vi-śhvyekh-ta-ni] adj. m. well worn; beat up

wyświetlać [viśh-vyet-laćh] v. clear up; project (film)

wytaczać [vi-ta-chaćh] v. roll out; set forth; draw; turn

wytargować [vi-tar-go-vaćh] v. buy by haggling; haggle a lot

wytarty [vi-tar-ti] adj. m. worn

out; thread bare; shabby

wytchnąć [vi-tkhnownćh] v. rest up; relax; take a rest; have a rest; breathe

wytchnienie [vi-tkhńe-ńe] n. rest; break; relax; truce

wytępić [vi-tan-peećh] v. exterminate; eradicate; wipe out; extripate; root out

wytężać [vi-tan-zhaćh] v. strain; exert; put forth

wytknąć [vit-knownćh] v. put out; point out; reproach; trace

wytłuc [vi-twoots] v. kill off; break up; ruin; beat up

wytłumaczenie [vi-twoo-ma-che-ńe] n. explanation; excuse; justification; account

wytłumaczyć [vi-twoo-ma-chićh] v. explain; excuse; justify; account for

wytrawny [vi-trav-ni] adj. m. experienced; dry (wine); seasoned; mature; consummate

wytrącać [vi-trown-tsaćh] v. knock of; deduct; snatch

wytrwały [vi-trva-wi] adj. m. enduring; persevering; dogged

wytrwanie [vi-trva-ńe] n. endurance; persistence; lasting

wytrwać [vi-trvaćh] v. last; bear; persevere; endure; stand

wytrych [vi-trikh] m. pick-a-lock; pass-key; skeleton-key

wytrząść [vi-tzhownśhćh] v. shake out; empty; jolt

wytrzebić [vi-tzhe-beećh] v. devastate; exterminate; clear

wytrzeźwieć [vi-tzheźh-vyećh] v. sober up; get sober; sober down

wytrzymać [vi-tzhi-maćh] v. endure; stand; hold out; keep

wytrzymałość [vi-tzhi-ma-wośhćh] f. endurance; stamina; durability; strength

wytrzymały [vi-tzhi-ma-wi] adj. m. enduring; tough; durable

wytworny [vi-tvor-ni] adj. m. exquisite; elegant; stylish

wytwórca [vi-tvoor-tsa] m. producer; manufacturer; maker

wytwórczość [vi-tvoor-

-chośhćh] v. productivity;
output; product; producers

wytwórnia [vi-tvoor-ńa] f.
manufacture; factory; plant;
works; (textile) mill

wytyczna [vi-tich-na] f. directive;
guideline; guiding rule

wyuzdanie [vi-ooz-da-ńe] n.
unbridled license; without
restraint; adv. dissolutely

wywiad [vi-vyat] m. interview;
reconnaissance; espionage

wywiązać się [vi-wyown-zaćh
śhan] v. develop; arise;
discharge (duty); result; set in;
perform; implement; evolve

wywierać [vi-vye-raćh] v. exert

wywiercać [vi-vyer-tsaćh] v.
bore out; sink a well; drill a
hole; talk one's head off

wywlekać [vi-vle-kaćh] v. drag
out; tug; bring out; pull out

wywietrzać [vi-vyet-zhaćh] v.
ventilate; air; nose out

wywłaszczać [vi-vwash-chaćh]
v. expropriate; dispossess

wywłaszczenie [vi-vwash-che-
-ńe] n. expropriation; dis-
possession; disseizin

wywnioskować [vi-vńos-ko-
-vaćh] v. infer; draw a
conclusion; imply

wywodzić [vi-vo-dźheećh] v.
lead out; derive; lead nowhere

wywojować [vi-vo-yo-vaćh] v.
fight out; gain by force

wywołać [vi-vo-waćh] v. call;
cause; develop (film); recall

wywozić [vi-vo-źheećh] v.
take away; remove; export

wywód [vi-voot] m. deduction

wywóz [vi-voos] m. export;
removal; disposal; transport

wywracać [vi-vra-tsaćh] v.
overturn; overthrow; reverse;
upset; bring down; knock over

wywyższać [vi-vizh-shaćh] v.
exalt; elevate; extol; rise

wyzbyć się [viz-bićh śhan] v.
get rid of; sell out; get over

wyzdrowieć [vi-zdro-vyećh] v.
recover; get well; recuperate

wyziąbić [vi-źhan-beećh] v.
chill; let be cold; cool

wyzionąć [vi-źho-nownćh] v.
expire; give up (the ghost)

wyznaczać [vi-zna-chaćh] v.
mark out; appoint; point out

wyznanie [vi-zna-ńe] n. admission; confession; denomination; declaration; creed

wyznawać [vi-zna-vaćh] v.
profess (certain principles);
declare; hold a belief; confess

wyznawca [vi-znav-tsa] m.
believer; follower; advocate

wyzuć [vi-zooćh] v. deprive;
take off (shoe); strip; divest;
bereave; dispossess; despoil

wyzywać [vi-zi-vaćh] v.
challenge; tempt; call names;
abuse; revile; curse; abuse

wyzwalać [vi-zva-laćh] v.
liberate; free; let loose;
exempt; deliver; emancipate

wyzwolenie [vi-zvo-le-ńe] n.
liberation; release; exemption

wyzwolić [vi-zvo-leećh] v.
liberate; free; release; set free

wyzysk [vi-zisk] m. exploitation;
sweating (of labor)

wyzyskiwacz [vi-zis-kee-vach] m.
exploiter; slave driver

wyż [vizh] m. height; upland;
highland; high pressure area;
peak; atmospheric high

wyżarty [vi-zhar-ti] adj. m. over
-fed; corroded; bloated

wyżej [vi-zhey] adv. higher;
above; (mentioned) above;
(cited) above; higher up

wyżeł [vi-zhew] m. pointer

wyżerać [vi-zhe-raćh] v. eat
away; corrode; erode; eat up

wyżłobić [vi-zhwo-beećh] v.
hollow out; gully; erode;
groove; gutter; channel

wyżłobienie [vi-zhwo-bye-ńe] n.
groove; gully; erosion; channel

wyższość [vizh-shośhćh] f.
superiority; excellence;
predominance

wyższy [vizh-shi] adj. m. higher
(up); taller; superior; top
(floor); preponderant

wyżyć [vi-zhićh] v. use up;

hardly live; make ends meet;
pull through; survive; pull
through; find an outlet for...
wyżyć się [vi-zhićh śhan] v.
live up to; fulfill oneself
wyżymaczka [vi-zhi-mach-ka] f.
wringer (also machine)
wyżymać [vi-zhi-mać] v.
wring
wyżyna [vi-zhi-na] f. high
ground; upland; summit (of
glory); highland
wyżywić [vi-zhi-veećh] v. feed
wyżywienie [vi-zhi-vye-ńe] m.
food; board; subsistence; diet
wzajemny [vza-yem-ni] adj. m.
mutual; reciprocal; inter-
w zamian [v za-myan] adv. in
exchange; instead; in return
wzbić się [vzbeećh śhan] v.
soar (up); shoot up; rise
wzbogacić [vzbo-ga-ćheećh] v.
enrich; add to; dress; make
rich; make wealthy; treat
wzbraniać [vzbra-ńaćh] v.
forbid; prohibit
wzbroniony [vzbro-ńo-ni] adj. m.
forbidden; prohibited
wzbudzać [vzboo-dzaćh] v.
excite; inspire; arouse; stir
wzburzenie [vzboo-zhe-ńe] n.
agitation; unrest; tumult
wzburzyć [vzboo-zhićh] v. stir
up; agitate; dishevel; convulse
wzdąć [vzdownćh] v. puff out;
inflate; swell; bulge; fan
wzdłuż [vzdwoosh] prep. along
wzdrygać się [vzdri-gaćh
śhan] v. flinch; object;
shudder; boggle; give a start
wzdychać [vzdi-khaćh] v. sigh
wzgarda [vzgar-da] f. contempt
wzgardliwy [vzgard-lee-vi] adj.
m. disdainful; scornful
względność [vzgland-nośhćh]
f. relativity (of understanding)
względny [vzgland-ni] adj. m.
relative; indulgent; kind of
względy [vzglan-di] pl. favors
wzgórze [vzgoo-zhe] n. hill
wziąć [vźhownćh] v. take;
hold; help oneself to; possess
wziernik [vźher-ńeek] m.

peephole; scope; view finder;
spy hole; sight glass
wzięty [vźhan-ti] adj. m.
popular; in demand; in vogue
wzlot [vzlot] m. ascend; rise
wzmacniać [vzmats-ńaćh] v.
reinforce; brace up; fortify
wzmagać [vzma-gaćh] v. intensify; increase; enhance
wzmianka [vzmyan-ka] v.
mention; reference; notice
wzniesienie [wzńe-śhe-ńe] n.
elevation; height; erection
wznieść [vzńeśhćh] v. raise;
elevate; erect; lift; rear
wzniosły [vzńos-wi] adj. m.
lofty; noble; elevated; sublime
wznowić [vzno-veećh] v. renew; resume; reprint; re-edit
wznowienie [vzno-vye-ńe] n.
resumption; come back; renewal; reissue; revival
wzorowy [vzo-ro-vi] adj. m.
exemplary; model; perfect
wzór [vzoor] m. pattern; model;
formula; fashion; standard
wzrok [vzrok] m. sight; vision
wzrost [vzrost] m. growth
-size; height; increase; rise;
stature; increment; gain
wzruszać [vzroo-shaćh] v.
move; touch; affect; thrill; stir
wzruszający [vzroo-sha-yown-tsi]
adj. m. touching; moving;
pathetic; poignant; stirring
wzuć [vzoośh] v. put on (shoe)
wzuwacz [vzoo-vach] m. shoe
horn (for pulling boots)
wzwyż [vzvizh] adv. up;
upwards; more than; above
skok wzwyż [skok vzvizh] m.
high jump
wzywać [vzi-vaćh] v. call; call
in; summon; cite; ask in

Z

z [z] prep. with; off; together

ze [ze] prep. with; off; together; from (the ceiling etc.)

za [za] prep. behind; for; at; by; beyond; over (a wall)

zabarwić [za-bar-veećh] v. stain; dye; tint; color; tinge; tincture; add pigmentation

zabarwienie [za-bar-vye-ńe] n. color(ing); pigmentation; tinge

zabawa [za-ba-va] f. play; fun; party; game; recreation; ball; amusement; pastime; dance

zabawiać [za-bav-yaćh] v. entertain; amuse; divert; dwell; stay; last; take time

zabawka [za-bav-ka] f. toy; trifle

zabawny [za-bav-ni] adj. m. funny; comical; ridiculous

zabezpieczenie [za-bez-pye-che-ńe] n. protection; safety

zabezpieczyć [za-bez-pye-chićh] v. safeguard; secure; protect

zabić [za-beećh] v. kill; slay; slaughter; plug up; nail down; drive into; beat (a card)

zabieg [za-byek] m. measure; procedure; exertions; fuss

zabiegać [za-bye-gaćh] v. strive; try hard; court; woo; fuss over; exert oneself for

zabierać [za-bye-raćh] v. take away; take along; take on (up)

zabierać się [za-bye-raćh śhan] v. clear out; get ready for; start to do; begin;

zabijać [za-bee-yaćh] v. kill; deaden; wear out; exhaust

zabijaka [za-bee-ya-ka] m. bully; blusterer; swaggerer; hector

zabity [za-bee-ti] adj. m. killed; dead; out-and-out; thorough

zabliźniać [za-bleeźh-ńaćh] v. form cicatrize; scar up

zabłądzić [za-bwown-dźheećh] v. go astray; get lost; stray

zabłąkany [za-bwown-ka-ni] adj. m. lost; stray (bullet, man, steer, etc)

zabłocić [za-bwo-ćheećh] v. get muddy; muddy (shoes etc)

zabobon [za-bo-bon] m. superstition; belief in omens, stars, the supernatural, etc.

zaboleć [za-bo-lećh] v. ache

zaborca [za-bor-tsa] m. invader

zabójca [za-booy-tsa] m. killer

zabójczy [za-booy-chi] adj. m. murderous; seductive; lethal

zabójstwo [za-booy-stvo] n. killing; murder; homicide

zabór [za-boor] m. annexed territory; annexation; rape (of Belgium, Austria etc.)

zabraniać [za-bra-ńaćh] v. forbid; prohibit; interdict

zabrudzać [za-broo-dzaćh] v. dirty; soil; make a mess (of something); make grimy

zabudować [za-boo-do-vaćh] v. build over; build upon; close

zabudowania [za-boo-do-va-ńa] pl. (farm) buildings; (town, factory, etc.) buildings

zaburzenie [za-boo-zhe-ńe] n. disorder; rout; agitation

zabytek [za-bi-tek] m. relic; monument (of art, nature etc.)

zachcianka [zakh-ćhan-ka] f. fad; fancy; caprice; passing whim; megrim; crotchet

zachęta [za-khan-ta] f. encouragement; stimulus; incentive; spur; urge

zachłanność [za-khwan-nośhćh] f. greed; rapacity; cupidity; excessive desire

zachłysnąć się [za-khwis-nownćh shan] v. choke; swallow a bad way

zachmurzyć [za-khmoo-zhićh] v. cloud; become gloomy; overcloud; overcast

zachmurzenie [za-khmoo-zhe-ńe] n. cloudiness; clouds; gloom; gloominess; nebulosity

zachodzić [za-kho-dźheećh] v. call on; occur; arise; become; set; creep from behind; drop in; reach (a place); go far

zachodni [za-khod-ńee] adj. m. western; westerly

zachorować [za-kho-ro-vaćh] v. get sick; fall ill; be taken ill

zachowanie [za-kho-va-ńe] n. behavior; maintenance; retention; manners; behavior

zachowawczy [za-kho-**vav**-chi] adj. m. conservative

zachowywać [za-kho-vi-**vaćh**] v. preserve; maintain; keep; stick to; reserve for

zachowywać się [za-kho-vi-**vać śhan**] v. behave; last; survive; go on; remain

zachód [**za**-khoot] m. west; the West; sunset; pains; trouble; endeavor

zachód słońca [za-khoot swoń-tsa] m. sunset

zachrypnięty [za-khrip-**ńan**-ti] adj. m. hoarse; of a hoarse voice of a person

zachwalać [za-khva-laćh] v. praise; crack up; boost; cry up

zachwiać [zakh-vyaćh] v. rock; shake; unsettle (balance etc.)

zachwycać [za-khvi-tsaćh] v. fascinate; charm; delight; enchant; rouse admiration

zachwyt [zakh-vit] m. fascination; rapture; enchantment; ecstasy

zaciąg [za-ćhownk] m. recruitment; levy; draft; conscription; call-up

zaciągać [za-ćhown-gaćh] v. recruit; drag to; run in debt

zaciekać [za-ćhe-kaćh] v. leak; stain; run down; fill (up)

zaciekawić [za-ćhe-ka-veećh] v. interest; puzzle; intrigue

zaciekawienie [za-ćhe-ka-vye-ńe] n. interest; curiosity

zaciekły [za-ćhek-wi] adj. m. stubborn; bitter; rabid; stiff

zaciemnić [za-ćhem-ńeećh] v. obscure; dim; darken; black out (windows, etc.); cloud

zacieniać [za-ćhe-ńaćh] v. shade; darken; throw shade

zacierać [za-ćhe-raćh] v. efface; erase; hush up; cover up; obliterate; rub off

zacieśniać [za-ćheśh-ńaćh] v. tighten up; narrow; limit

zacięty [za-ćhan-ti] adj. m. obstinate; stubborn; dogged

zacinać [za-ćhee-naćh] v. notch; cut; lash; hack; taper;

set (teeth, lips); whip

zaciskać [za-ćhees-kaćh] v. tighten; clench; squeeze; clasp

zacisze [za-ćhee-she] n. retreat

zacny [zats-ni] adj. m. worthy; good; upright; respectable

zacofany [za-tso-fa-ni] adj. m. backward; old fashioned

zaczaić się [za-cha-eećh śhan] v. lie in ambush; lurk; hide

zaczarować [za-cha-ro-vaćh] v. enchant; bewitch; cast a spell

zacząć [za-chownćh] v. start; begin; fire away; go ahead

zaczepiać [za-chep-yaćh] v. hook on; accost; touch upon

zaczepny [za-chep-ni] adj. m. aggressive; offensive; provocative; truculent

zaczerpać [za-cher-paćh] v. scoop up; dip up; draw; lade

zaczerwienić [za-cher-vye-ńeećh] v. redden; blush; flush; color, paint, dye red

zaczynać [za-chi-naćh] v. start; begin; cut (into a new loaf)

zaćmienie [zaćh-mye-ńe] n. eclipse; obfuscation

zad [zad] m. posterior; rump

zadać [za-daćh] v. give; put; deal; associate; treat with

zadanie [za-da-ńe] n. task; charge; assignment; problem; job; work; stint; duty

zadatek [za-da-tek] m. earnest money; down payment; instalment; advance payment

zadławić [za-dwa-veećh] v. choke; strangle; throttle

zadłużyć się [za-dwoo-zhićh śhan] v. run into debt; incur debts; run up bills

zadłużenie [za-dwoo-zhe-ńe] n. debts; indebtedness; liabilities

zadowalający [za-do-va-la-yown-tsi] adj. m. satisfactory; fair

zadowolić [za-do-vo-leećh] v. satisfy; gratify; please; suffice

zadowolony [za-do-vo-lo-ni] adj. m. satisfied; content; pleased

zadra [za-dra] f. silver; splinter (in one's finger, etc.)

zadrapać [za-dra-paćh] v.

scratch open; make a scratch
zadrasnąć [za-dras-n<u>o</u>wnćh] v.
scratch; graze (arm, leg, etc.)
wound (sb's pride etc.);
zadrażnić [za-drazh-ńeećh] v.
irritate; embitter; inflame
zadrgać [zadr-gaćh] v. twitch;
vibrate; tremble; flicker
zadrwić [za-drveećh] v. sneer
zaduch [za-dookh] m. bad air;
stuffy air; stink; fustiness; fug
zaduma [za-doo-ma] f. meditation; reverie; musing; wist-
fulness; pensiveness
zadusić [za-doo-śheećh] v.
throttle; smother; choke;
strangle; suffocate
Zaduszki [za-doosh-kee] n. All
Souls' Day (Catholic holiday)
zadymka [za-dim-ka] f.
snowstorm; blizzard
zadyszany [za-di-sha-ni] adj. m.
breathless; panting
zadzierać [za-dźhe-raćh] v.
tear open; turn up; quarrel
zadzierżysty [za-dźher-zhis-ti]
adj. m. defiant; perky
zadziwiać [za-dźheev-yaćh] v.
astonish; amaze; astound
zadzwonić [za-dzvo-ńeećh] v.
ring; ring up; ring for
zagadka [za-gad-ka] f. puzzle;
riddle; crux; problem; quiz
zagadnienie [za-gad-ńe-ńe] n.
problem; question; issue
zagajnik [za-gay-ńeek] m. grove;
shrubbery; scrub; coppice;
copse; growth of young trees
zagiąć [za-gy<u>own</u>ćh] v. bend
zaginiony [za-gee-ńo-ni] adj. m.
lost; missing (person)
zaglądać [za-gl<u>own</u>-daćh] v.
peep; look up; look into
zagłada [za-gwa-da] f. extinction;
extermination; annihilation
zagłąbić [za-gw<u>an</u>-beećh] v.
plunge; sink; dip; immerse
zagłodzić [za-gwo-dźheećh] v.
starve to death; starve out
zagłuszać [za-gwoo-shaćh] v.
silence; jam; drown out; stifle
zagmatwać [za-gmat-vaćh] v.
entangle; confuse; embroil

zagniewany [za-gńe-va-ni]
adj. m. angry; cross; sore; in a
huff; in (high) dudgeon
zagospodarowywać [za-gos-po-
-da-ro-vi-vaćh] v. make
property productive; bring into
cultivation; manage (an estate)
zagotować [za-go-to-vaćh] v.
boil; start boiling; flare up
zagrabić [za-gra-beećh] v. rake
over; grab; seize; carve out
zagradzać [za-gra-dzaćh] v.
bar; fence; obstruct; intercept
zagranica [za-gra-ńee-tsa] f.
foreign countries;outside world
zagraniczny [za-gra-ńeech-ni]
adj. m. foreign; foreign (trade,
sojourn abroad, etc.)
zagrażać [za-gra-zhaćh] v.
threaten; impend; be imminent
zagroda [za-gro-da] f. farm house
with yard; enclosure
zagrodzić [za-gro-dźeećh] v.
fence in; bar; enclose; fence
around; obstruct; intercept
zagrożony [za-gro-zho-ni] adj. m.
threatened; endangered
zagrzebać [za-gzhe-baćh] v.
bury (in the grave,in the
past...); place alone
zagrzewać [za-gzhe-vaćh] v.
heat; warm up; animate;
inspirit; rouse; cheer
zahaczać [za-kha-chaćh] v.
hook (up, on, with); question;
accost; find fault; clasp
zahamować [za-kha-mo-vaćh]
v. restrain; put brakes on;
stop; check a motion
zaimek [za-ee-mek] m. pronoun
zainteresowanie [za-een-te-re-so-
-va-ńe] n. interest; concern
zaiste [za-ees-te] adv. truly;
indeed; very true; verily; yea
zajadać [za-ya-daćh] v. enjoy
eating; gorge; eat heartily
zajadły [za-yad-wi] adj. m. fierce;
rabid; bitter; unrelenting
zajazd [za-yazt] m. motel; inn;
zając [za-y<u>own</u>ts] m. hare
zająć [za-y<u>own</u>ćh] v. occupy
zajechać [za-ye-khaćh] v. drive
up; block; stump; pull in; stink

zajęcie [za-yan-će] v. interest; occupation; work; trade

zajmować [zay-mo-vać] v. occupy; replace; displace

zajmujący [zay-moo-yown-tsi] adj. m. interesting; absorbing

zajście [zayść-će] n. incident

zakalec [za-ka-lets] m. slack-baked bread (or cake)

zakatarzony [za-ka-ta-zho-ni] adj. m. suffering from a cold

zakatować [za-ka-to-vać] v. flog to death; torture to death

zakaz [za-kas] m. prohibition

zakazić [za-ka-źheeć] v. infect; contaminate; poison; pollute; spread a disease

zakazywać [za-ka-zi-vać] v. forbid; ban; suppress; prohibit; forbid to do something

zakaźny [za-kaźh-ni] adj. m. infectious; contagious

zakąska [za-kowns-ka] f. snack

zaklęcie [za-klan-će] n. spell; curse; incantation; charm; entreaty; entreaties

zakład pogrzebowy [za-kwat po-gzhe-bo-vi] m. funeral parlor

zakład [za-kwat] m. plant; shop; institute; bet; wager; fold

zakładać [za-kwa-dać] v. found; initiate; put on; lay

zakładka [za-kwad-ka] f. fold; bookmark; tuck; pleat; splice

zakładnik [za-kwad-ńeek] m. hostage (for ransom etc.)

zakłamanie [za-kwa-ma-ńe] n. hypocrisy; mendacity; pretense of virtue; dissimulation

zakłopotanie [za-kwo-po-ta-ńe] n. embarrassment; confusion

zakłócać [za-kwoo-tsać] v. disturb; unsettle; ruffle

zakłuwać [za-kwoo-vać] v. stab to death; prick; stick (a pig); cause a stabbing pain

zakochać się [za-ko-khać śhan] v. fall in love; become infatuated; become a lover of

zakochany [za-ko-kha-ni] adj. m. a person in love; infatuated; an enumerated man

zakomunikować [za-ko-moo-ńee-ko-vać] v. communicate; let know; convey a message; notify

zakon [za-kon] m. monastic order; convent; sisterhood

zakonnica [za-kon-ńee-tsa] f. nun; religious (woman)

zakonnik [za-kon-ńeek] m. monk

zakończenie [za-koń-che-ńe] n. end; ending; termination; tip

zakopać [za-ko-pać] v. bury

zakorkować [za-kor-ko-vać] v. plug up; cork up; jam (the traffic, a movement, etc.)

zakorzenić się [za-ko-zhe-ńeeć śhan] v. get roots in; take roots; strike roots; become deep-rooted

zakorzeniony [za-ko-zhe-ńo-ni] adj. m. rooted; deep rooted

zakradać się [za-kra-dać śhan] v. creep; steal; sneak

zakrapiać [za-krap-yać] v. put drops in; sprinkle; have a drink; instil (in one's eyes)

zakres [za-kres] m. range; field; scope; domain; sphere; realm

zakreślić [za-kreśh-leeć] v. outline; mark off; encircle

zakręcić [za-kran-ćheeć] v. turn; twist; turn off; curl

zakręt [za-krant] m. curve; bend turn; twist; (street) corner

zakrętka [za-krant-ka] f. turnbuckle; cap; nut; latch

zakrwawić [za-krva-veeć] v. stain with blood; draw blood

zakryć [za-krić] v. cover; hide

zakrzątnąć się [za-kzhownt-nownć śhan] v. get busy; bustle; try one's best; bestir oneself; start bustling

zakrztusić [za-kzhtoo-śheeć] v. choke (on food, fish bone)

zakrzywić [za-kzhi-veeć] v. bend; bend down; bend back

zaksięgować [za-kśhan-go-vać] v. post; enter in the books; to book (an item)

zakup [za-koop] m. purchase

zakurzony [za-koo-zho-ni] adj. m. dusty; covered with dust

zakuty [za-koo-ti] adj. m.

shackled; chained; thick-head-
ed; crass; grossly stupid
zakwitnąć [za-kveet-nownćh]
v. blossom out; go moldy
zalążek [za-lown-zhek] m. germ;
ovule; seed; origin; embryo
zalecać [za-le-tsaćh] v.
recommend; advise; enjoin;
counsel; prescribe; court; woo
zaledwie [za-led-vye] adv. barely;
scarcely; merely; but; only just
zalegać [za-le-gaćh] v. be
behind (in paying); lie useless;
fill (a space); surge
zaległy [za-leg-wi] adj. m.
unpaid; overdue; unfulfilled;
unaccomplished (duty, task)
zalepić [za-le-peećh] v. glue
up; paste up; gum up; paste
over; seal up; putty up
zalesienie [za-le-śhe-ńe] n.
forestation; afforestation
zaleta [za-le-ta] f. virtue;
advantage; quality; good point
zalew [za-lev] m. flood; bay;
invasion; deluge; lagoon
zalewać [za-le-vaćh] v. pour
over; flood; submerge; swarm;
spill; inundate; invade
zależeć [za-le-zhećh] v. depend on; be relative to
zależny [za-lezh-ni] adj. m.
dependent; contingent; subordinate; conditioned (by)
zaliczać [za-lee-chaćh] v.
include; count in; credit; rate;
accept; number; rate; reckon
zaliczka [za-leech-ka] f. earnest
money; down payment; pay-
ment on account; installment
zalotnica [za-lot-ńee-tsa] f. flirt;
coquette; kitten (slang)
zalotnik [za-lot-ńeek] m. suitor;
wooer; wheedler
zaloty [za-lo-ti] pl. courtship;
wooing; love making
zaludniać [za-lood-ńaćh] v.
populate; bring in population
zaludnienie [za-lood-ńe-ńe] n.
population; population density
załadować [za-wa-do-vaćh] v.
load up; embark; ship (goods)
załagodzić [za-wa-go-dźheećh]

v. mitigate; alleviate; soothe
załamać [za-wa-maćh] v. break
down; collapse; crash; slump
załamanie [za-wa-ma-ńe] n.
break down; (light) refraction
załatwiać [za-wat-vyaćh] v.
settle; transact; deal; dispose
załączać [za-wown-chaćh] v.
enclose; connect; annex; plug
in; include; subjoin
załącznik [za-wownch-ńeek] m.
enclosure; attachment; annex
załoga [za-wo-ga] f. crew;
garrison; staff; personnel
założenie [za-wo-zhe-ńe] n.
layout; foundation; assumption
założyciel [za-wo-zhi-ćhel] m.
founder; initiator; promoter
zamach [za-makh] m. attempt;
swing; sweep; coup d'etat;
spar; sparring motion
zamaczać [za-ma-chaćh] v.
steep; dip; wet; soak; drench
zamarzły [za-mar-zwi] adj. m.
frozen; frozen over; frozen to
death; frozen stiff; congealed
zamarznąć [za-mar-znownćh]
v. freeze up; freeze over;
freeze to death; congeal
zamaskować [za-mas-ko-vaćh]
v. mask; conceal; hide;
disguise; camouflage
zamaszysty [za-ma-shis-ti] adj.
m. brisk; vigorous; dashing;
swinging; sprawling; heavy
zamawiać [za-ma-vyaćh] v.
reserve; order (goods); book (a
seat); engage (workers)
zamazać [za-ma-zaćh] v. smear
over; soil up; daub; blur (a
picture); blur (outlines)
zamącić [za-mown-ćheećh] v.
ruffle (a water surface));
disturb; make turbid; stir
zamążpójście [za-mownzh-
-pooy-śhćhe] n. marriage
zamek [za-mek] m. lock; castle
zamek błyskawiczny [za-mek
bwis-ka-veech-ni] m. zipper
zamęt [za-mant] m. confusion;
disarray; muddle; welter
zamężna [za-manzh-na] adj. f.
married (woman in married

state); f. married woman
zamiana [za-mya-na] f. exchange
zamianować [za-mya-no-vaćh]
v. nominate; appoint; design
zamiar [za-myar] m. purpose
zamiast [za-myast] prep. instead
of; in place; in lieu
zamiatać [za-mya-taćh] v.
sweep; brush with a broom
zamieć [za-myećh] f.
violent snowstorm; blizzard;
snow in a windstorm
zamiejscowy [za-myeys-tso-vi]
adj. m. out of town; coming
from an other place
zamienić [za-mye-ńeećh] v.
change; convert; replace;
swap; turn into; exchange
zamienny [za-myen-ni] adj. m.
exchangeable; interchangeable
zamierać [za-mye-raćh] v. die
out; fade out; wither; die
away; decay; waste away
zamierzać [za-mye-zhaćh] v.
intend; mean; propose; think
zamierzenie [za-mye-zhe-ńe] n.
aim; purpose; plan; project
zamieszać [za-mye-shaćh] v.
stir up; blend; mix up; involve
zamieszanie [za-mye-sha-ńe] n.
confusion; disarray; turmoil;
stir; commotion; welter; to-do
zamieszkać [za-myesh-kaćh] v.
take up residence; put up; live
zamieszkiwać [za-myesh-kee-
-vaćh] v. inhabit; reside;
occupy; live; settle; put up
zamilknąć [za-meel-kno<u>wn</u>ćh]
v. became silent; be hushed
zamiłowanie [za-mee-wo-va-ńe]
n. predilection; fondness;
liking; relish; passion
zamknąć [zam-kno<u>wn</u>ćh] v.
close; shut; lock; wind up;
fence in; surround; clasp
zamoczyć [za-mo-chićh] v.
wet; soak; steep; drench; dip;
submerge; moisten
zamorski [za-mor-skee] adj. m.
overseas; from overseas
zamożny [za-mozh-ni] adj. m.
rich; wealthy; affluent; well-to-
-do; well-off; (man) of means

zamówić [za-moo-veećh] v.
order; reserve; commission;
book; engage; charm away
zamówienie [za-moo-**vye**-ńe] n.
order; commission (a work of
art); custom order
zamrażać [za-mra-zhaćh] v.
freeze; chill; refrigerate
zamroczyć [za-mro-chićh] v.
dim; gloom; confuse; darken;
cloud; bewilder; muddle
zamsz [zamsh] m. chamois;
suede; shammy-leather
zamulić [za-moo-leećh] v. fill
with slime; silt up (a harbor)
zamurować [za-moo-ro-vaćh] v.
brick over; brick up; wall up
zamydlić [za-mid-leećh] v. soap
over; pull the wool over eyes
zamykać [za-mi-kaćh] v. shut;
conclude; close (the view etc.)
zamysł [za-misw] m. design
zamyślać się [za-miśh-laćh
śhan] v. contemplate; muse;
ponder; plan; intend
zamyślenie [za-mi-śhle-ńe] n.
reverie; pondering; meditation
zanadto [za-nad-to] adv. too
much; excess; more than
enough; beyond measure
zaniechać [za-ńe-khaćh] v.
give up; wave; desist from
zanieczyścić [za-ńe-chiśh-
-ćheećh] v. soil; dirty; litter;
grime; pollute; contaminate
zaniedbanie [za-ńed-ba-ńe] n.
neglect; negligence; sloppiness
zaniemóc [za-ńe-moots] v.
become ill; fall ill; get sick
zaniemówić [za-ńe-moo-veećh]
v. become speechless (dumb)
zaniepokoić [za-ńe-po-ko-eećh]
v. alarm; upset; disturb
zaniepokojenie [za-ńe-po-ko-**ye**-
-ńe] n. anxiety; alarm; uneasiness; concern; disquiet
zanieść [za-ńeśhćh] v. carry
zanik [za-ńeek] m. wane
atrophy; disappearance
zanikać [za-ńee-kaćh] v.
disappear; vanish; decay;
wither; fade away; die out
zanim [za-ńeem] conj. before

zanocować [za-no-tso-vaćh] v.
stay over night; put up at
zanotować [za-no-to-vaćh] v.
note; write down;take down
zanurzyć [za-noo-zhićh] v. dip
zaocznie [za-och-ńe] adv. in
absence; (judgement or sentence) by default
zaognić [za-og-ńeećh] v.
inflame; irritate; excite; kindle
zaokrąglić [za-o-krowng-leećh]
v. round off; make even
zaopatrzenie [za-o-pa-tzhe-ńe] n.
supplies; equipment; provision
zaopatrzyć [za-o-pa-tzhićh] v.
provide; equip; supply; fit out;
furnish; stock; affix (a seal)
zaorać [za-o-raćh] v. plough
over(a field etc.); plough up
zaostrzyć [za-os-tzhićh] v.
sharpen; whet; tighten
(restrictions); stimulate (the
appetite); intensify
zaoszczędzić [za-osh-chan-
-dźheećh] v. save; spare
(trouble); put (money) by
zapach [za-pakh] m. smell;
aroma; flavor; odor; stench
zapadać [za-pa-daćh] v. fall in;
sink; set in; drop; settle
zapakować [za-pa-ko-vaćh] v.
pack up; stow away; pack off
zapalczywy [za-pal-chi-vi] adj. m.
hotheaded; impetuous
zapalenie [za-pa-le-ńe] n.
ignition; inflammation (of the
skin); setting fire
zapaleniec [za-pa-le-ńets] m.
fanatic; enthusiastic; hot head
zapalić [za-pa-leećh] v. switch
on light; set fire; animate
zapalniczka [za-pal-ńeech-ka] f.
(cigarette) lighter
zapalnik [za-pal-ńeek] m. fuse
zapalny [za-pal-ni] adj. m.
inflammable; combustible;
ardent; impetuous
zapał [za-paw] m. enthusiasm
zapałka [za-paw-ka] f. match
zapamiętać [za-pa-myan-taćh]
v. remember; memorize; keep
(something) in mind
zaparcie [za-par-ćhe] n.

constipation; denial
zaparzyć [za-pa-zhaćh] v. draw
(tea); brew; gall; make (tea);
heat (hay, etc.); infuse
zapas [za-pas] m. stock; store;
reserve; supply; fund; refill
zapasowy [za-pa-so-vi] adj. m.
spare; emergency (door, part,
etc.); reserve (fund, etc.)
zapaść [za-paśhćh] v. drop
sink; subside; collapse
zapaśnik [za-paśh-ńeek] m.
wrestler; contender
zapatrywać się [za-pa-tri-vaćh
śhan] v. have an opinion;
consider; stare;take example
zapatrywanie [za-pa-tri-va-ńe] n.
opinion; view; slant
zapełniać [za-pew-ńeećh] v. fill
up; stop a gap; fill (a space
etc.); crowd a street
zaperzyć się [za-pe-zhićh
śhan] v. flare up; be testy;
get mad; get on a high horse
zapewne [za-pev-ne] adv.
certainly; surely; doubtless; to
be sure; I should think
zapewnić [za-pev-ńeećh] v.
assure; secure; assert
zapewnienie [za-pev-ńe-ńe] n.
assurance; protestation;
assertion; affirmation
zapieczątować [za-pye-chan-to-
-vaćh] v. seal up (a letter);
seal; seal with wax
zapierać się [za-pye-raćh
śhan] v. deny; disavow;
resist; repudiate
zapinać [za-pee-naćh] v. button
up; fasten; buckle up
zapis [za-pees] m. registration;
bequest; record; notation
zapisać [za-pee-saćh] v. note
down ; prescribe; enroll;
bequeath; record; write down
zapisek [za-pee-sek] m. note
zaplątać [za-plown-taćh] v.
entangle; snarl; involve
zaplecze [za-ple-che] n.
hinterland; base (of supplies
etc.); subsidiaries
zapłacić [za-pwa-ćheećh] v.
pay; repay; requite; pay off

zapłakany [za-pwa-ka-ni] adj. m.
in tears; tearful; tear stained

zapłata [za-pwa-ta] f. payment

zapłodnić [za-pwod-ńeéch] v.
fertilize; inseminate; fecundate

zapłon [za-pwon] m. ignition

zapobiegać [za-po-bye-gaćh] v.
prevent; avert; ward off; stave
off; take precautions against

zapobiegliwy [za-po-bye-glee-vi]
adj. m. anticipating; thrifty
industrious; thrifty; provident

zapodziać [za-po-dźhaćh] v.
misplace; mislay; get lost

zapominać [za-po-mee-naćh] v.
forget; neglect; unlearn

zapomnienie [za-pom-ńe-ńe] n.
oblivion; forgetfulness

za pomocą [za po-mo-tsown]
adv. by means (of something);
with help (of a tool...)

zapomoga [za-po-mo-ga] f. hand
out; relief; benefit; grant

zapora [za-po-ra] f. dam;
(river) dam; obstacle; barrier;
check; (artillery) barrage

zapotrzebowanie [za-po-tzhe-bo-
-va-ńe] n. demand; order;
requisition; request

zapowiadać [za-po-vya-daćh] v.
announce; forecast; pretend

zapoznać [za-poz-naćh] v.
acquaint; introduce; instruct

zapożyczać [za-po-zhi-chaćh]
v. borrow (an idea, money);
adopt from; take from

zapracować [za-pra-tso-vaćh]
v. earn; get by hard work

zapracowany [za-pra-tso-va-ni]
adj. m. earned; overworked

zapraszać [za-pra-shaćh] v.
invite (to dinner etc.); offer

zaprawa [za-pra-va] f. mortar; v.
seasoning; training; work out

zaprawdę [za-praw-dan] adv.
indeed; to tell you the truth...

zaprawić [za-pra-veećh] v.
season; train; learn; dress;
spice; flavor; dress; train

zaproszenie [za-pro-she-ńe] n.
invitation (to dinner etc.)

zaprowadzić [za-pro-va-
-dźheećh] v. lead in; show

in; establish; initiate

zaprząg [za-pshownk] m. team

zaprzeczać [za-pshe-chaćh] v.
deny; contest; dispute

zaprzeczenie [za-pshe-che-ńe] n.
denial; negation; contradiction

zaprzepaścić [za-pshe-paśh-
ćheećh] v. loose; waste;
miss; bring to ruin; wreck

zaprzestać [za-pshes-taćh] v.
discontinue; stop; cease; quit

zaprząg [za-pshank] m. team;
cart; harness; yoke (of oxen);
carriage; turn-out; vehicle

zaprzyjaźnić się [za-pshi-yaźh-
ńeećh śhan] v. make friends

zaprzysiąc [za-pshi-śhownts] v.
swear by oath; vow; pledge

zaprzysiężony [za-pshi-śhan-
-zho-ni] adj. m. sworn in;
pledged; fanatic; ardent

zapusty [za-poos-ti] pl. carnival;
Shrovetide (Catholic holiday)

zapuszczać [za-poosh-chaćh] v.
let in (dye); grow (hair);
neglect; let down; sink into

zapychać [za-pi-khaćh] v. stuff;
cram; fill; block; crowd

zapytanie [za-pi-ta-ńe] n.
question; inquiry; query;asking

zapytywać [za-pi-ti-vaćh] v.
ask; question; interrogate

zarabiać [za-rab-yaćh] v. earn

zaradczy [za-rad-chi] adj. m.
preventive; remedial (measure)

zaradny [za-rad-ni] adj. m.
resourceful (man,boy etc.)

zaranie [za-ra-ńe] n. dawning

zarastać [za-ras-taćh] v.
overgrow; cicatrize (a wound)

zaraz [za-ras] adv. at once;
directly; right away; soon

zaraza [za-ra-za] f. infection;
plague; epidemic; pestilence

zarazek [za-ra-zek] m. virus;
germ; microbe; (disease)
bacteria; (microorganism)

zarazem [za-ra-zem] adv. at the
same time; as well; also

zarazić [za-ra-źheećh] v. infect

zarażenie [za-ra-zhe-ńe] n.
infection (with a disease etc.)

zardzewieć [zar-dze-vyećh] v.

rust; get rusty; corrode
zaręczyny [za-r<u>an</u>-chi-ni] n.
 betrothal; engagement
zarobek [za-ro-bek] m. gain;
 bread; earnings; wages;
 livelihood; living
zarobkować [za-rob-ko-vaćh] v.
 earn working; earn a living
zarodek [za-ro-dek] m. embryo
zarosły [za-ros-wi] adj. m.
 overgrown (with vegetation
 etc.); unshaven; shaggy
zarost [za-rost] m. beard; hair
zarośla [za-rośh-la] n. thicket
zarozumiały [za-ro-zoo-mya-wi]
 adj. m. conceited; uppish
zarówno [za-roov-no] adv.
 equally; as well; alike; both
zarumienić się [za-roo-mye-
 -ńeećh śh<u>an</u>] v. blush;
 flush; brown; get browned
zaryglować [za-rig-lo-vaćh] v.
 bolt a door; bar an entrance
zarys [za-ris] m. sketch; outline;
 broad lines; design; draft
zarząd [za-zh<u>own</u>d] m.
 management; administration;
 board (of directors, trustees)
zarządca [za-zh<u>own</u>d-tsa] m.
 administrator; manager
zarządzenie [za-zh<u>own</u>-dze-ńe]
 n. administrative order
zarzucać [za-zhoo-tsaćh] v. fill;
 give up; reproach; fling; cast
zarzut [za-zhoot] m. reproach;
 objection; accusation; blame
zasada [za-sa-da] f. principle;
 alkali; base; law; rule; tenet
zasadniczy [za-sad-ńe-chi] adj.
 m. fundamental; essential; basic; primary; primordial; vital
zasadzka [za-sadz-ka] f. ambush
zasądzić [za-s<u>own</u>-dźheećh] v.
 sentence (to imprisonment);
 adjudge to (somebody)
zasępiony [za-s<u>an</u>-pyo-ni] adj. m.
 gloomy; despondent; dejected
zasiadać [za-śha-daćh] v. take
 a seat; sit down; settle down
zasięg [za-śh<u>an</u>k] m. reach;
 scope; extent; range; radius
zasięgać rady [za-śh<u>an</u>-gaćh
 ra-di] v. consult; seek advice

zasiłek [za-śhee-wek] m.
 handout; grant; relief;
 subvention; allowance
zaskarżyć [za-skar-zhićh] v.
 sue; take legal proceedings
zasklepić się [za-skle-peećh
 śh<u>an</u>] v. scab; shut oneself
 up (in);seal up; vault; wall up
zaskoczyć [za-sko-chićh] v.
 surprise (an enemy); attack
 unawares; click; lock
zaskórny [za-skoor-ni] adj. m.
 subcutaneous; underground
 (water); subsoil (water)
zasłabnąć [za-swab-n<u>own</u>ćh] v.
 faint; get sick; grow faint;
 swoon; weaken; fall ill
zasłać [za-swaćh] v. cover
 (bed); strew; litter
zasłona [za-swo-na] f. blind; veil;
 screen; curtain; shield
zasłonić [za-swo-ńeećh] v.
 curtain shade; shield; cover up
zasługa [za-swoo-ga] f. merit
zasługiwać [za-swoo-gee-vaćh]
 v. deserve; be worthy; merit
zasłużony [za-swoo-zho-ni] adj.
 m. man of merit; just; fair
zasmucić [za-smoo-ćheećh] v.
 sadden; pain; distress; grieve
zasmucony [za-smoo-tso-ni] adj.
 m. sad; grieved; distressed
zasnąć [za-sn<u>own</u>ćh] v. fall
 asleep; sleep; drop off to
 sleep; fall to sleep
zasobnik [za-sob-ńeek] m.
 container; tank; storage tank
zasób [za-soop] m. store;
 resource; stock; supply
zaspa [zas-pa] f. snowdrift;
 dune; drifted sand; drifted
 snow; ridge of drifted snow
zaspać [zas-paćh] v. oversleep
zaspokoić [za-spo-ko-eećh] v.
 satisfy (a desire, a demand);
 quench; appease; provide
zastanowić się [za-sta-no-
 -veećh śh<u>an</u>] v. reflect;
 puzzle; ponder; wonder
zastaw [za-stav] m. pawn;
 deposit; security; forfeit; lien
zastawić [za-sta-veećh] v.
 1.bar; 2.pledge; 3.set a table;

cram a room; lay (snares)
zastąpić [za-**stown**-peećh] v.
 replace; bar passage; do duty
 for; supersede; stand for
zastępca [za-**stanp**-tsa] m.
 proxy; substitute; deputy
zastępczo [za-**stanp**-cho] adv.
 replacing; temporary; in lieu
zastępstwo [za-**stanp**-stvo] n.
 replacement; proxy; agency
zastosować [za-sto-**so**-vaćh] v.
 adopt (measures, etc.); apply;
 employ; make use; bring into
zastosować się [za-sto-**so**-vaćh
 śhan] v. comply; toe the line
zastosowanie [za-sto-so-va-**ńe**]
 n. application; use compliance
zastój [za-**stooy**] m. stagnation
zastraszyć [za-**stra**-shićh] v.
 intimidate; cow; bully; browbeat; use undue influence
zastrzał [za-**stshaw**] m. (knee)
 brace; strut; boom; cramp
zastrzec [za-**stshets**] v. reserve
 (for); stipulate; condition
zastrzeżenie [za-stshe-**zhe**-ńe] n.
 reservation; qualification
zastrzyk [za-**stshik**] m. injection;
 shot (in the arm); grouting
zastygnąć [za-stig-**nown**ćh] v.
 congeal; set; harden; petrify
zasuszyć [za-**soo**-shićh] v. dry
 up; wither; shrivel (the skin)
zasuwa [za-**soo**-va] f. bar;(door)
 bolt; valve; shutter; damper
zasuwka [za-**soov**-ka] f. small
 (door) bolt; damper; valve
zasypać [za-si-**paćh**] v. bury;
 cover; add (to soup); fill up
zasypiać [za-sip-**yaćh**] v. cat
 nap; doze off; fall asleep
zaszczepiać [za-**shche**-pyaćh]
 v. inoculate; graft; instill
zaszczycać [za-**shchi**-tsaćh] v.
 honor; dignify; favor; grace
zaszczyt [zash-**chit**] m. honor;
 distinction; privilege; dignity
zaszkodzić [za-shko-**dźhe**ećh]
 v. harm; hurt; damage; injure
zasznurować [za-shnoo-ro-
 -vaćh] v. tie up; lace (shoes);
 tighten one's stays
zaszyć [za-**shićh**] v. sew up

zaszyć się [za-shićh **śhan**] v.
 hide; burrow; conceal oneself
zaś [zaśh] conj. but; whereas;
 and; while; specially
zaślepić [za-śhle-**peećh**] v.
 blind; infatuate; blind to facts
zaślepiony [za-śhle-pyo-ni] adj.
 m. infatuated; fanatic; blind
zaślubić [za-śhloo-beećh] v.
 marry; get married
zaślubiny [za-śhloo-bee-ni] pl.
 wedding; marriage;nuptials
zaśmiecić [za-śhmye-ćheećh]
 v. litter (the street, etc.);
 clutter up (a room, etc.)
zaśniedziały [za-śhńe-dźha-
 -wi] adj. m. rusty; stagnant
zaśrubować [za-śhroo-bo-
 -vaćh] v. screw tight; screw
 on (a lid); screw up (a case)
zaświadczenie [za-śhvyad-che-
 -ńe] n. certificate; affidavit
zaświadczyć [za-śhvyad-
 -chićh] v. certify; attest;
 witness; record; give evidence
zaświecić [za-śhvye-ćheećh]
 v. put light on; light up; turn
 on light; shed light; shine
zataczać [za-ta-chaćh] v. roll
 in; describe (a circle); stagger;
 wheel; turn on a lathe
zataić [za-ta-eećh] v. conceal
 from; suppress; keep secret;
 hold back (one's breath); hide
zatamować [za-ta-mo-vaćh] v.
 dam up; stop; block; impede
zatańczyć [za-tań-chićh] v.
 dance; perform a dance
zatapiać [za-tap-yaćh] v. flood;
 sink; penetrate; inundate; submerge; immerse; scuttle
zatarasować [za-ta-ra-so-vaćh]
 v. obstruct; block up; bolt
zatarg [za-targ] m. conflict;
 clash; dispute; quarrel
zatem [za-tem] adv. then; consequently; therefore; and so
zatemperować [za-tem-pe-ro-
 -vaćh] v. sharpen (a pencil)
zatkać [za-tkaćh] v. stop up
 clog; clutter; block; chock up
zatlić się [za-tleećh **śhan**] v.
 catch fire; start smoldering

zatłoczony [za-two-cho-ni] adj.
m. crowded; crammed; congested; cluttered

zatoka [za-to-ka] f. bay; gulf

zatonąć [za-to-nownch] v. sink

zator [za-tor] m. (traffic) jam

zatracić [za-tra-cheech] v.
lose;waste; lose all sense of

zatroskać [za-tros-kach] v.
grieve; alarm; make anxious

zatrucie [za-troo-che] n.
poisoning; intoxication; toxaemia (blood poisoning)

zatruć [za-trooch] v. poison

zatrudniać [za-trood-ńach] v.
employ; engage; give work;
take on (workers); occupy

zatrzask [za-tshask] m. (door)
latch; (snap) fastener lock

zatrzymać [za-tshi-mach] v.
stop; retain; detain; arrest;
hold; bring to a stand still

zatwardzenie [za-tvar-dze-ńe] n.
constipation; costiveness

zatwierdzać [za-tvyer-dzach] v.
approve; ratify; affirm

zatwierdzenie [za-tvyer-dze-ńe]
n. ratification; approval;
assent; confirmation

zatwierdzić [za-tvyer-dźheech]
v. ratify; approve; confirm (a
nomination, etc.); validate

zatyczka [za-tich-ka] f. plug

zatykać [za-ti-kach] v. stop up;
plug up; insert a plug

zaufać [za-oo-fach] v. confide

zaufanie [za-oo-fa-ńe] n.
confidence; trust; faith;
reliance (in somebody)

zaufany [za-oo-fa-ni] adj. m.
reliable; confidential; trusted

zaułek [za-oo-wek] m.
alley; back street; lane;
recess; corner; nook

zauważyć [za-oo-va-zhich] v.
notice; catch sight; remark

zawada [za-va-da] f. obstruction;
nuisance; hindrance; obstacle

zawadiaka [za-vad-ya-ka] m.
bully; blusterer; swashbuckler

zawadzać [za-va-dzach] v.
hinder; scrape; touch; be a
drag; scrape against; impede

zawalać [za-va-lach] v. soil

zawalić [za-va-leech] v.
collapse; obstruct; bury; cover up; crush; bungle; clutter

zawartość [za-var-toshch] f.
contents; subject (of a book)

zawczasu [za-vcha-soo] adv. in
time; in advance; beforehand

zawczoraj [za-vcho-ray] adv. the
day before yesterday

zawdzięczać [za-vdźhan-chach] v. owe (gratitude); be
indebted (for something)

zawezwać [za-vez-vach] v. call;
summon; call in (a doctor etc.)

zawiadomić [za-vya-do-meech]
v. inform; give notice; let
know; notify; intimate

zawiadomienie [za-vya-do-mye-ńe] n. notification; information; notice; intimation

zawiadowca stacji [za-vya-dov-tsa stats-yee] m. stationmaster; superintendent

zawiasa [za-vya-sa] f. hinge

zawiązać [za-vyown-zach] v.
tie up; bind; set up (a club)

zawieja [za-vye-ya] f. blizzard;
snow-storm; cloud (of dust)

za wiele [za vye-le] adv. too
much; too many (expenses)

za widna [za veed-na] adv. in
day light; before dark

zawierać [za-vye-rach] v.
contain; include; contract;
conclude; shut; strike up

zawierucha [za-vye-roo-kha] f.
wind storm;gale;(war) clouds

zawieszenie broni [za-vye-she-ńe bro-ńee] n. armistice; truce;
cessation of hostilities

zawietrzna [za-vyetsh-na] f. lee
side (sheltered from the wind)

zawijać [za-vee-yach] v. wrap
up; tuck in; put in a port

zawikłać [za-veek-wach] v.
complicate; entangle; embroil;
tangle; confuse

zawiły [za-vee-wi] adj. m.
intricate; baffling; knotty; involved; complicated (problem)

zawinąć [za-vee-nownch] v.
wrap; take care of; pack

zawinić [za-**vee**-ńeeć] v. be
guilty; commit an offense
zawisły [za-**vees**-wi] adj. m.
dependent (on somebody etc.)
zawistnie [za-**veest**-ńe] adv.
with envy; jealously
zawistny [za-**veest**-ni] adj. m.
envious; jealous
zawiść [za-**veeśhć**] f. envy
zawitać [za-**vee**-tać] v. call
on; come and see (somebody)
zawlec [za-vlets] v. drag; tug;
cloud; (wrap with a mist)
zawodnik [za-**vod**-ńeek] m.
competitor (in sport); contestant; participant
zawodowiec [za-vo-**do**-vyets] m.
professional; specialist
zawody [za-**vo**-di] pl. (sport)
competition; match; race;
game; (sport) event
zawodzić [za-**vo**-dźheeć] v.
1. lead; 2. disillusion; lament
zawołać [za-vo-waćh] v. call
out for; call; exclaim; shout;
cry; cry out for; summon
zawołany [za-vo-**wa**-ni] adj. m.
excellent; perfect; born (poet)
zawozić [za-vo-źheeć] v.
convey; take to; cart; deliver;
give rides; carry; drive
zawód [za-voot] m. 1. profession; trade; vocation; craft
2. disappointment; deception
zawór [za-voor] m. valve; vent
zawrót głowy [za-vroot **gwo**-vi]
m. dizziness; vertigo; giddiness
zawstydzić [za-**vsti**-dźheeć]
v. shame; embarrass; overwhelm; put to shame
zawsze [zav-she] adv. always;
evermore; (for) ever; at all
times; for all times; still
zawszyć [zav-shićh] v. louse
up; infect with lice
zawziąć się [zav-źhownćh
śhan] v. be obstinate; persist;
set on; grow obstinate
zawziętość [zav-źhan-
-tośhćh] f. persistence; obstinacy; keenness; doggedness
zazdrosny [zaz-**dros**-ni] adj. m.
jealous; envious; resentful

zazdrość [zaz-**drośhćh**] f.
envy; jealousy
zaziębić się [za-**źhan**-beećh
śhan] v. catch a cold
zaznaczyć [za-zna-chićh] v.
mark; make a note; state
zaznać [zaz-nać] v. experience; taste; enjoy; undergo; taste (ill fortune, etc.)
zaznajomić [za-zna-yo-meećh]
v. acquaint; introduce to
zazwyczaj [za-zvi-**chay**] adv.
usually; generally; ordinarily
zażalenie [za-zha-le-ńe] n.
complaint; grievance
zażarty [za-zhar-ti] adj. m.
fierce; bitter; vehement
zażądać [za-**zhown**-daćh] v.
demand; require; order
zażenować [za-zhe-**no**-vaćh] v.
shame; embarrass; confuse;
abash; disconcert
zażyły [za-zhi-wi] adj. m.
familiar; intimate; close;
chummy; hob-nob (with)
zażywać pigułki [za-**zhi**-vaćh
pee-**goow**-kee] v. take pills
ząb [zownp] m. tooth; fang;
prong; cog; indentation
ząb mleczny [zownp mlech-ni]
m. milk tooth (of a child etc.)
ząb trzonowy [zownp tsho-**no**-vi]
adj. m. molar
ząbkować [zownb-ko-vaćh] v.
teethe; jag; cut one's teeth
zbaczać [zba-chaćh] v. deviate
zbankrutowany [zban-kroo-to-**va**-
-ni] adj. m. bankrupt; insolvent
zbawca [zbav-tsa] m. savior
zbawiciel [zba-**vee**-ćhel] m.
savior; redeemer; Saviour
zbawicielka [zba-vee-**ćhel**-ka] f.
savior; redeemer
zbawić [zba-veećh] v. save;
redeem; rescue; take (time)
zbawienie [zba-**vye**-ńe] n.
salvation; deliverance; rescue;
(spiritual) redemption; a saving
zbesztać [zbesh-taćh] v. scold
zbeszcześcić [zbez-**cheśh**-
-ćheećh] v. desecrate; defile;
profane; reprove sharply
zbędny [zb**an**d-ni] m.

superfluous; redundant;
needless; useless

zbieg [zbyek] m. fugitive; con-
fluence; deserter; escapee

zbieg okoliczności [zbyek o-ko-
-leech-**nosh**-ćhee] m. coincidence; an accidental occurrence at the same time

zbiegać [zbye-gaćh] v. run
down (stairs); escape; desert

zbiegowisko [zbye-go-**vees**-ko] n.
concourse; throng; crowd

zbieracz [zbye-rach] m. collector;
gatherer; (mushroom) picker

zbierać [zbye-raćh] v. gather;
pick; summon; clear; take in

zbieżny [zbyezh-ni] adj. m. con-
vergent; tapering; concurrent

zbijać [zbee-yaćh] v. knock
together; refute; beat down;
knock off; press together

zbiornik [zbyor-ńeek] m. tank;
reservoir; container; receptacle

zbiór [zbyoor] m. harvest;
collection; set; crop; class;
series; aggregation

zbiórka [zbyoor-ka] f. rally;
assembly; meeting; gathering

zbir [zbeer] m. thug; ruffian

zbity [zbee-ti] adj. m. close;
1.beaten up; 2. compact;
dense; firm; close

zblednąć [zbled-nownćh] v.
pale; grow pale; fade; turn
pale; become pale

z bliska [z blees-ka] adv. from
near; close up; from near by

zbliżać [zblee-zhaćh] v. nearby

zbliżyć się [zblee-zhićh **śhan**]
v. become close; approach; be
near; come up; draw near

zbliżenie [zblee-zhe-ńe] n.
rapprochement; close-up

zbliżony [zblee-zho-ni] adj. m.
approximate; nearing;
congenial; resembling

zbłądzić [zbwown-dźheećh] v.
go astray; make a mistake;
lose trail; wander off; loose
one's way; commit a blunder

zbocze [zbo-che] n. (hill) slope

zboczenie [zbo-che-ńe] n.
deviation; aberration; drift; sag

zbolały [zbo-la-wi] adj. m.
aching; sore; woeful; cheerless; wretched

zboże [zbo-zhe] n. corn; grain

zbój [zbooy] m. bandit; robber

zbór ewangielicki [zboor e-van-
-ge-leets-kee] m. Protestant
Church; Evangelical Church

zbratać się [zbra-taćh **śhan**] v.
fraternize; chum up (with)

zbroczony krwią [zbro-cho-ni
krvyown] adj. m. blood-stained

zbrodnia [zbrod-ńa] f. crime

zbrodniarz [zbrod-ńash] m.
criminal; felon; malefactor

zbroić [zbro-eećh] v. arm

zbroja [zbro-ya] f. armor

zbrojony beton [zbro-yo-ni be-
-ton] m. reinforced concrete

zbrojownia [zbro-yov-ńa] f.
arsenal; armory; gun room

zbryzgać [zbriz-gaćh] v.
spatter; bespatter; splash

zbrzydnąć [zbzhid-nownćh] v.
grow ugly; lose good looks

zbudować [zboo-do-vaćh] v.
build; rise; erect; lay out

zbudzić się [zboo-dźheećh
śhan] v. wake up; awake; be
stirred; be roused

zbujać [zboo-yaćh] v. fool;
hoax; pull one's leg

zburzyć [zboo-zhićh] v.
demolish; ruin; devastate

zbutwieć [zboo-tvyećh] v.
molder; rot; decompose;
decay; spoil; mildew

zbydlęcić [zbi-dlan-ćheećh] v.
bestialize; turn into a brute

zbyt [zbit] adv. too (much)

zbyt wiele [zbit vye-le] adv. too
much; excessively; over

zbyt [zbit] m. sale; market

zbyteczny [zbi-tech-ni] adj. m.
superfluous; needless; odd;
redundant; left over

zbytek [zbi-tek] m. frills; luxury;
pranks; follies; extravagance

zbytni [zbit-ńee] adj. m.
excessive; undue; more than
needed; superfluous

zbytnik [zbit-ńeek] m. rogue

zbywać [zbi-vaćh] v. dispose;

dismiss; put off (with an excuse); sell; lack; want

z czasem [z cha-sem] adv. with time; eventually; later

z dala [z da-la] adv. from far

z daleka [z da-le-ka] adv. from far; from afar; away from

zdalnie [zdal-ńe] adv. remote; from afar; by remote control

zdanie [zda-ńe] n. 1. opinion; judgment; sentence; clause; proposition; 2. giving back

zdanie sprawy [zda-ńe spra-vi] n. report; account; giving account; giving information

zdarzać się [zda-zhaćh śhan] v. happen; take place; occur

zdarzenie [zda-zhe-ńe] n. happening; event; incident

zdatność [zdat-nośhćh] f. fitness; capability; suitability

zdatny [zdat-ni] adj. m. able; fit; apt; suitable (for the purpose)

zdawać [zda-vaćh] v. entrust; submit; turn over; give up; pass (test); hand over

zdawać się [zda-vaćh śhan] 1. seem; 2. surrender; 3. rely

z dawien dawna [z da-vyen dav-na] adv. from way back

z dawna [z dav-na] adv. since a long time; from way back

zdążyć [zdown-zhićh] v. come on time; keep pace; tend

zdechlak [zdekh-lak] m. weakling

zdechły [zdekh-wi] adj. m. peaked; dead (animal); weakly; sickly (person)

zdecydować się [zde-tsi-do-vaćh śhan] v. decide; determine; make up one's mind

zdejmować [zdey-mo-vaćh] v. take off; strip (clothes); remove; snap (a photo)

zdenerwowany [zde-ner-vo-va-ni] adj. m. nervous; excited

zderzak [zde-zhak] m. bumper

zderzenie [zde-zhe-ńe] n. collision; clash; crash; smash-up; conflict (of interest, etc.)

zderzyć się [zde-zhićh śhan] v. collide; clash; run into

zdjęcie [zdyan-ćhe] n. snapshot

zdjęcie rentgenowskie [zdyan-ćhe rent-ge-nov-skye] n. X-ray picture; X-ray photograph

zdmuchiwać [zdmoo-khee-vaćh] v. blow off; blow out; blow away; puff away

zdobić [zdo-beećh] v. decorate

zdobycz [zdo-bich] f. booty; spoils; prey; prize; trophy

zdobyć [zdo-bićh] v. conquer

zdolność [zdol-nośhćh] f. ability; capacity; talent; aptitude; capability

zdolny [zdol-ni] adj. m. clever; able; capable; fit; competent

zdołać [zdo-waćh] v. be able

zdrada [zdra-da] f. treason

zdradliwy [zdrad-lee-vi] adj. m. treacherous; tricky; unsafe

zdradzać [zdra-dzaćh] v. betray

zdrajca [zdray-tsa] adj. m. traitor informer; turncoat; renegade;

zdrapać [zdra-paćh] v. scratch off; scrape off; loosen up

zdrętwieć [zdrant-vyećh] v. grow numb; stiffen; grow torpid; anchylose

zdrętwienie [zdrant-vye-ńe] n. numbness; stiffness; torpidity

zdrobniały [zdrob-ńa-wi] adj. m. diminutive; grown smaller

zdrojowisko [zdro-yo-vees-ko] n. spa; health resort; baths

zdrowie [zdrov-ye] n. health; good constitution; being well

zdrowotne jedzenie [zdro-vot-ne ye-dze-ńe] n. health food

zdrowy [zdro-vi] adj. m. healthy; sound; mighty; in good health

zdrożny [zdrozh-ni] adj. m. vicious; wicked; wrong; blameworthy; fatigued

zdrój [zdrooy] m. spring; spa

zdrów i cały [zdroov ee tsa-wi] m. safe and sound

zdrzemnąć się [zdzhem-nownćh śhan].v. doze off; sleep light; catnap; take a nap

zdumienie [zdoo-mye-ńe] n. astonishment; amazement

zdumiony [zdoo-myo-ni] adj. m. astonished; flabbergasted

zdun [zdoon] m. stove fitter

zdwajać [zdva-yać] v. double
zdychać [zdi-khać] v. die
zdyszany [zdi-sha-ni] adj. m.
breathless; panting for breath;
out of breath
zdziałać [zdźha-wać] v.
accomplish; achieve; manage
to do; do successfully
zdziczeć [zdźhee-cheć] v.
grow wild; become savage;
turn wild; fall into savagery
zdziecinnieć [zdźhe-ćheen-
-ńeć] v. grow childish (in
old age); grow senile
zdzierać [zdźhe-rać] v. strip
off; fleece; tear down; peel
zdzierstwo [zdźher-stvo] n.
exorbitance; extortion
zdziwaczeć [zdźhee-va-cheć]
v. become odd; grow whim-
sical; become freaky
zdziwić [zdźhee-veeć] v.
surprise; astonish; make
wonder; amaze; cause doubt
zdziwienie [zdźhee-vye-ńe] n.
surprise; wonderment; astonishment; sudden surprise
zebra [ze-bra] f. zebra
zebrać [ze-brać] v. gather;
clear; collect; unite; pick
zebranie [ze-bra-ńe] n. meeting
zecer [ze-tser] m. type setter
zechcieć [zekh-ćheć] v. be
willing; feel inclined; choose
zegar [ze-gar] m. clock; meter
zegar słoneczny [ze-gar swo-
-nech-ni] sundial
zegarek [ze-ga-rek] m. watch
zegarmistrz [ze-gar-meestsh] m.
watch-maker; clock-maker;
watch-maker's shop
zejście [zeyśh-ćhe] n. descent
zejść [zeyśhćh] v. descent
zejść się [zeyśhćh śhan] v.
meet (as prearranged); meet;
rendezvous; have a date
zelówka [ze-loov-ka] f. (shoe)
sole; bottom surface of a shoe
zelżeć [zel-zhećh] v. lighten
up; ease; let up; diminish;
abate; give; remit
zemdleć [zem-dlećh] v. faint;
pan out; swoon; feel weak

zemsta [zem-sta] f. revenge
zepchnąć [zep-khnownćh] v.
push down; drive out; shove
down; thrust down
zepsuć [zep-sooćh] v. damage;
spoil; worsen; pervert; harm;
injure; disarrange; pollute
zepsuty [zep-soo-ti] adj. m.
damaged; spoiled; corrupt;
bad; perverse; out of order
zerkać [zer-kaćh] v. squint at;
peep (into...); take a peep
zero [ze-ro] n. zero; nought; nil
zerwać [zer-vaćh] v. pick off;
snap loose; break off; sprain;
rip off; burst out; blow off
zerwanie [zer-va-ńe] n. rupture
zeskakiwać [ze-ska-kee-vaćh]
v. jump off; dismount; get off
zeskrobywać [ze-skro-bi-vaćh]
v. scrape off; erase; scrape
clean; scrape away; scratch
zesłać [ze-swaćh] v. deport;
send down; send into exile
zesłanie [ze-swa-ńe] n.
deportation; exile; penal
colony; transportation
zespolić [ze-spo-leećh] v. unite
zespół [ze-spoow] m. team;
group; gang; crew; troupe;
set; complex; co-operative
zestarzeć się [ze-sta-zhećh
śhan] v. grow old; get old;
age; stale (news, story)
zestawienie [ze-sta-vye-ńe] n.
comparison; balance sheet; list
zestrzelenie [ze-stshe-le-ńe] n.
shooting down; downing (of
an airplane, of a bird, etc.)
zeszłoroczny [ze-shwo-roch-ni]
adj. m. last year's (crop etc.)
zeszpecić [ze-shpe-ćheećh] v.
disfigure; make look ugly;
deface; mar the beauty of
zeszyt [ze-shit] m. notebook
ześlizgiwać się [ze-śhleez-gee-
vaćh śhan] v. glide down;
slip; slide down; skid down
zetknąć się [zet-knownćh
śhan] v. meet face-to-face;
get in touch; come into contact; meet; put in touch
zew [zef] n. call; appeal; slogan

zewnątrz [zev-nowntsh] adv. & prep. out; outside; outwards; outdoors; on the surface

zewnętrzny [zev-nantsh-ni] adj. m. exterior; external; outward

zewsząt [ze-vshownt] adv. from everywhere; from all points

zez [zes] m. squint; cross-eye

zeznawać [zez-na-vaćh] v. declare; testify; give evidence

zezować [ze-zo-vaćh] v. squint

zezwalać [zez-va-laćh] v. allow; give permission; permit

zezwolenie [zez-vo-le-ńe] n. permission; leave; license

zębaty [zan-ba-ti] adj. m. toothed; cogged; indented

zębate koło [zan-ba-te ko-wo] n. cog wheel; gear (wheel)

zęby [zan-bi] pl. teeth; cogs

zgadywać [zga-di-vaćh] v. anticipate; guess; make a guess

zgadzać się [zga-dzaćh śhan] v. agree; fit in; see eye-to-eye

zgaga [zga-ga] f. heartburn

zganić [zga-ńeećh] v. blame

zgarnąć [zgar-nownćh] v. rake; together; brush aside

zgasić [zga-śheećh] v. put out; extinguish; switch off; dim; stub out (a cigarette)

zgęszczenie [zgan-shche-ńe] n. condensation; compression

zgiełk [zgewk] m. uproar; clamor; turmoil; tumult

zgięcie [zgyan-ćhe] n. bend; fold; inflection; inflexion

zginać [zgee-naćh] v. bend (over); fold; stoop; bow

zgliszcza [zgleesh-cha] pl. cinders; ashes; site of fire

zgłaszać [zgwa-shaćh] v. notify;call for;tender;submit

zgłębiać [zgwan-beećh] v. probe; sound out; deepen; go deeply; get to the bottom

zgłodniały [zgwod-ńa-wi] adj. m. hungry; starving; hungering

zgłosić [zgwo-śheećh] v. notify; tender; lay a claim

zgłoska [zgwos-ka] f. syllable

zgłupieć [zgwoo-pyećh] v. grow silly; grow stupid; be

astounded; be astonished

zgnąbić [zgnan-beećh] v. depress; dispirit; oppress; dishearten; bring to ruin

zgnić [zgńeećh] v. rot; decay; putrefy; molder; ret

zgnieść [zgńeśhćh] v. crush; stub out; squash; suppress; quell; squeeze; crumble

zgnilizna [zgńee-leez-na] f. rot; corruption; foul smell

zgniły [zgńee-wi] adj. rotten; foul, corrupt; perverted

zgoda [zgo-da] f. concord; assent; consent; unity; harmony; approval; reconciliation

zgodnie [zgod-ńe] adv. according; in concert; peaceably; in unison; in compliance

zgodność [zgod-nośhćh] f. accord; agreement; unanimity; consistence; concordance

zgodny [zgod-ni] m. compatible; good-natured; unanimous

zgoić się [zgo-eećh śhan] v. heal up; heal over; heal a wound; become well again

zgon [zgon] m. death; decease

zgorszyć [zgor-shićh] v. horrify; scandalize; shock; arouse

zgorzkniały [zgosh-kńa-wi] adj. m. sour; embittered; acrimonious; soured (by misfortune)

zgotować [zgo-to-vaćh] v. prepare; cook; give (an ovation, a hearty welcome)

z góry [z goo-ri] adv. in advance

zgrabny [zgrab-ni] adj. m. skillful; clever; deft; smart; neat; shapely; slick; deft; well-built

zgraja [zgra-ya] f. gang; mob

zgromadzenie [zgro-ma-dze-ńe] n. assembly; congress; meeting; collection; congregation

zgromadzać się [zgro-ma-dzaćh śhan] v. assemble; gather

zgroza [zgro-za] f. horror

z grubsza [zgroob-sha] adv. roughly; approximately

zgryzota [zgri-zo-ta] f. grief

zgryźliwy [zgriźh-lee-vi] adj. m. sarcastic; peevish; harsh

zgrzać się [zgzhaćh śhan] v.

get hot; sweat; become hot
zgrzebło [zgzheb-wo] n.
horse-comb; harrow; curry-
comb; comb; stirrer
zgrzyt [zgzhit] m. screech; jar
zguba [zgoo-ba] f. loss;
doom; undoing; ruin; destruction; lost (property, object)
zgubić [zgoo-beech] v. lose;
undo; drop; bring to ruin;
destroy; unmake; fall out of
zgubić się [zgoo-beech shan]
v. get lost; get mixed up; be
mislaid; lose one another
zgubny [zagoob-ni] adj. m.
disastrous; fatal; ruinous;
calamitous; pernicious
zgwałcić [zgvaw-cheech] v.
rape; violate; force to do
ziarnisty [zhar-nees-ti] adj. m.
granular; grainy; whole grain
ziarno [zhar-no] n. grain; corn
ziele [zhe-le] n. weed; herb
zieleń [zhe-leń] f. greenery
zielonawy [zhe-lo-na-vi] adj. m.
greenish; of greenish color
zielony [zhe-lo-ni] adj. m. green;
young and inexperienced
(man); raw; sappy; unripe
ziemia [zhem-ya] f. earth; land
ground; native soil; native
land; district; the world
ziemianin [zhe-mya-ńeen] m.
squire; landowner; mortal
ziemianka [zhe-myan-ka] f.
1.dugout; 2. landowner's wife
ziemniak [zhem-ńak] m. potato
ziemski [zhem-skee] adj. m.
earthly; worldly; landed; land
ziewać [zhe-vach] v. yawn;
gape; give a yawn
zięba [zhan-ba] f. finch;
chaffinch
ziębić [zhan-beech] v. cool;
chill; expose to the cold
zięć [zhanch] m. son-in-law
zima [zhee-ma] f. winter
zimno [zheem-no] n. cold; chill
zimno [zheem-no] adv. coldly
zimny [zheem-ni] adj. m. cold
zimować [zhee-mo-vach] v.
hibernate; winter; pass the
winter; survive the winter

zioło [zho-wo] n. herb (mint,
sage, camomile, etc.)
ziszczać [zeesh-chach] v.
realize; fulfill; carry out (a
plan); materialize
zjadać [zya-dach] v. eat; eat
up; have food; ruin; drain
zjadliwy [zya-dlee-vi] adj. m.
biting; caustic; spiteful;
vicious; mordant; malignant
zjawa [zya-va] f. apparition;
ghost; vision; specter;
phantom; a becoming visible
zjawisko [zya-vees-ko] n. fact;
event; phenomenon; vision;
very unusual occurrence
zjazd [zyazt] m. meeting;
coming; descent; downhill
drive or slide; congress
zjednoczenie [zyed-no-che-ńe] n.
union; unification; association
zjeść [zyeshch] v. eat up;
devour; eat away (profits, etc)
zjeżdżać [zyezh-dzhach] v. ride
down; slide down; make way;
turn off the road; arrive; slip
zlecać [zle-tsach] v. order
commission to do; entrust to
do; instruct; charge with
zlecenie [zle-tse-ńe] n.
commission; order; errand;
message; instruction
z ledwością [z led-vosh-
-chown] adv. hardly; with
difficulty; with great pains
z lekka [z lek-ka] adv. lightly;
softly; slightly; gently
zlepek [zle-pek] m. agglomerate
zlew [zlef] m. sink; kitchen sink
zlewać [zle-vach] v. pour off;
decant; pour together; mix;
flunk; whip; blend (liquids)
zliczyć [zlee-chich] v. count up;
total; add up; reckon; tot up
zlikwidować [zlee-kvee-do-
-vach] v. liquidate; wind up;
destroy; suppress; abolish
zlodowacenie [zlo-do-va-tse-ńe]
n. freezing; glaciation
zlot [zlot] m. rally; flocking in
złagodzenie [zwa-go-dze-ńe] n.
mitigation; softening
złagodzić [zwa-go-dźheech] v.

mitigate; soothe; lessen;
soften; diminish the severity

złamać [zwa-maćh] v. break;
smash; overcome (resistance)

złamanie [zwa-ma-ńe] n. break;
fracture; prostration; collapse

złazić [zwa-źheećh] v. climb
down; get off; peel off

złączenie [zwown-che-ńe] n.
connection; junction; weld

złączyć [zwown-chićh] v. join;
link; fuse; weld; unite; bind

złe [zwe] n. evil; wrong; ill

zło [zwo] n. evil; devil; harm

złocenie [zwo-tse-ńe] n. gilding

złocić [zwo-ćheećh] v. gild

złoczyńca [zwo-chiń-tsa] m.
evildoer; criminal; malefactor

złodziej [zwo-dźhey] m. thief

złodziejka [zwo-dźhey-ka] f.
1. thief; 2. electrical adapter

złom [zwom] m. scrap; waste

złość [zwośćh] f. anger;
malice; spite; soreness; resentment; animosity against

złośliwy [zwośh-lee-vi] adj. m.
malignant; spiteful; malicious

złotnik [zwot-ńeek] m.
goldsmith; silversmith

złoto [zwo-to] n. gold; gold work

złoty [zwo-ti] adj. m. golden

złoty [zwo-ti] m. Polish money
unit (originally gold ducat)

złowić [zwo-veećh] v. catch
(an animal, a thief); net; hook
(a fish, a husband, etc.)

złowrogi [zwo-vro-gee] adj. m.
ominous; sinister; portentous

złoże [zwo-zhe] n. stratum; bed

złożony [zwo-zho-ni] adj. m.
complex; multiple; intricate

złuda [zwoo-da] f. illusion

złudny [zwood-ni] adj. m.
illusory; deceptive; illusive

zły [zwi] adj. m. bad; evil; ill;
vicious; cross; poor; rotten

zmagać się [zma-gaćh śhan]
v. struggle with; grapple with

zmaganie [zma-ga-ńe] n.
struggle; strife against

zmarły [zmar-wi] adj. m.
deceased; dead; defunct; the
late (husband, father, etc,)

zmarszczka [zmarshch-ka] f.
wrinkle; crease; fold; pucker

zmartwienie [zmar-tvye-ńe] n.
worry; sorrow; grief; trouble

**zmartwychwstać [zmar-tvikh-
-vstaćh]** v. rise from the dead

**zmartwychwstanie [zmar-tvikh-
-vsta-ńe]** n. resurrection

zmarznąć [zmar-znownćh] v.
freeze; freeze over; be cold

zmawiać się [zma-vyaćh śhan]
v. conspire; plot; arrange;
collude; enter into collusion

zmaza [zma-za] f. stain; blemish;
blot; wet dream; slur

zmazywać [zma-zi-vaćh] v.
wipe out; efface; erase; expiate; wipe off (a stain)

zmęczenie [zman-che-ńe] n.
fatigue; weariness; lassitude

zmiana [zmya-na] f. change;
variation; shift; relay; exchange; alteration; transition

zmiatać [zmya-taćh] v. sweep
up; carry away; dispatch

zmiażdżyć [zmyazh-dzhićh] v.
crush; everwhelm (the enemy)

zmienić [zmye-ńeećh] v. alter; change; modify; vary; exchange; replace; transform

zmierzać [zmye-zhaćh] v. aim;
tend towards; make one's
way; drive at; intend to do

zmierzch [zmyeshkh] m. dusk;
twilight; decline; fall; at dark;

zmierzyć [zmye-zhićh] v.
measure; gauge; take aim;
make for; estimate (a distance); eye up and down

zmieszanie [zmye-sha-ńe] n. mix
up; confusion; embarrassment

zmiłowanie [zmee-wo-va-ńe] n.
mercy; pity; disposition to
forgive or to be kind

zmniejszenie [zmńey-she-ńe] n.
reduction; decrease; relief

zmniejszyć [zmńey-shićh] v.
diminish; lessen; abate; reduce

zmoczyć [zmo-chićh] v. wet;
soak; moisten; drench

zmora [zmo-ra] f. nightmare;
ghost; curse (of war); bane

zmorzyć [zmo-zhićh] v.

overpower; overcome

zmordować [zmor-**do**-vaćh] v.
tire; wear; do in; tire out;
exhaust; tire to death; toil

zmowa [**zmo**-va] f. conspiracy;
collusion; plot; secret deal

zmrok [zmrok] m. dusk; twilight

zmurszały [zmoor-**sha**-wi] adj. m.
mouldy; decaying; crumbling;
rotten; mildew; musty

zmuszać [zmoo-**sha**ćh] v.
coerce; compel; force; oblige;
constrain; make do; get to do

zmykać [zmi-**ka**ćh] v. cut and
run; bolt; scoot off; scurry
away; scamper away

zmylić [zmi-**lee**ćh] v. fool;
mislead; lead into error;
deceive; lose way; outwit

zmysł [zmisw] m. sense;
instinct; knack; aptitude;
consciousness; pl. reason

zmysłowy [zmis-**wo**-vi] adj. m.
sensual; sensory; sense; lewd

zmyślać [zmiśh-**la**ćh] v. invent; trump up; fake up; cook
up; bluff; fabricate; brag

zmyślony [zmiśh-**lo**-ni] adj. m.
fictitious; invented; unreal

znaczący [zna-**chown**-tsi] adj. m.
significant; emphatic; telling

znaczek [zna-**chek**] m. mark;
stamp; badge; tick

znaczny [**znach**-ni] adj. m.
notable; goodly; prominent

znać [znaćh] v. know; know
how; adv. apparently

znajdować [znay-**do**-vaćh] v.
find; see; meet; experience

znajomość [zna-yo-**mo**śhćh]
f. acquaintance; knowledge

znajomy [zna-**yo**-mi] adj. m. well
acquainted; well-known; well-
known man; familiar

znak [znak] m. mark; sign;
stamp; signal; token; trace

znakomity [zna-ko-**mee**-ti] adj. m.
excellent; illustrious

znalazca [zna-**laz**-tsa] m. finder

znaleźne [zna-**leźh**-ne] n.
finder's reward; finder's share

znamienny [zna-**myen**-ni] adj. m.
significant; characteristic

znamię [zna-**my**a̲n̲] n. stigma;
mole; trait; birthmark

znany [zna-ni] adj. m. noted;
known; famed; familiar; well-
known; notorious; famous

znawca [**znav**-tsa] m. expert

znęcać się [zna̲n̲-tsa̲ćh śh**a̲n̲**]
v. torment; harass; ill-treat

znękany [zna̲n̲-**ka**-ni] adj. m.
dejected; harassed; wasted

znicz [**zn**eech] m. (holy) fire;
fireside; pilot-light

zniechęcać [źne-**kha̲n̲**-tsaćh] v.
discourage; sicken; indispose

zniecierpliwić się [źne-ćher-
-plee-veećh **śh**a̲n̲] v. grow
impatient; get vexed; lose
patience; become annoyed

znieczulić [źne-choo-**lee**ćh] v.
anesthetize; deaden; harden

zniedołężniały [źne-do-**wa̲n̲**-
-zhńa-wi] adj. m. impotent;
decrepit; infirm; disable; feeble
(old man); without force

zniekształcać [źne-**kshtaw**-
-tsaćh] v. deform; disfigure;
distort; put out of shape

zniemczać [**źn**em-chaćh] v.
Germanize; make into a German; force to accept German
identity or citizenship

znienacka [źne-**nats**-ka] adv. all
of a sudden; unawares

znienawidzieć [źne-na-**vee**-
-dźheećh] v. grow to hate;
loathe; come to detest

znieprawić [źne-pra-**vee**ćh] v.
deprave; demoralize; debauch

zniesienie [źne-**śh**e-ńe] n.
abrogation; abolition; repeal

zniesławienie [źne-swa-**vye**-ńe]
n. defamation; slander

zniewaga [źne-**va**-ga] f. insult

zniewalać [źne-**va**-laćh] v.
coerce; rape; captivate; win

znikać [**źn**ee-kaćh] v. vanish

zniewieściały [źne-vyeśh-**ćh**a-
-wi] adj. m. effeminate; sissy

znikąd [**źn**ee-**kownt**] adv. from
nowhere; out of nowhere

znikomy [źnee-**ko**-mi] adj. m.
perishable; negligible; minute

zniszczeć [**źn**eesh-chećh] v.

decay; go to ruin; be worn out
zniszczenie [zńeesh-che-ńe] n.
destruction; ravage; ruin;
havoc; annihilation
zniszczyć [zńeesh-chićh] v.
destroy; ruin; wear out;
ravage; annihilate; waste
zniweczyć [zńee-ve-chićh] v.
annihilate; wreck; lay waste
zniżać [znee-zhaćh] v. lower
zniżka [zneezh-ka] f. reduction;
decline; slump; drop; fall
znosić [zno-śheećh] v. annul;
endure; carry down; ware out
znośny [znośh-ni] adj. m.
tolerable; bearable; so-so; fair
znowu [zno-voo] adv. again;
anew; once again; afresh
znój [znooy] m. toil; sweat
znów [znoof] adv. again; anew
znudzenie [znoo-dze-ńe] n.
boredom; weariness; tedium;
till one is sick and tired
znużenie [znoo-zhe-ńe] n.
weariness; fatigue (people,
metals etc.); oppression
zobaczyć [zo-ba-chićh] v. see
zobojętnić [zo-bo-yant-ńeećh]
v. neutralize; make indifferent
zobojętnieć [zo-bo-yant-ńeećh]
v. grow indifferent; grow
listless; become apathetic
zobowiązać [zo-bo-vyown-
-zaćh] v. oblige; obligate;
bind to do; pin down to do
zobowiązanie [zo-bo-vyown-za-
-ńe] n. obligation; com-
mitment; engagement
zobrazować [zob-ra-zo-vaćh] v.
illustrate; describe; depict
zogniskować [zog-ńees-ko-
-vaćh] v. focus; concentrate
zohydzać [zo-khi-dzaćh] v.
defame; make loathsome; sicken of; render repugnant
zoolog [zo-o-log] m. zoologist
zorza północna [zo-zha poow-
-nots-na] f. aurora borealis
zostać [zos-taćh] v. remain;
stay; become; get to be; be
left; turn (green etc.)
zostawiać [zos-tav-yaćh] v.
leave; abandon; put aside

z powodu [z po-vo-doo] prep.
because of; owing to; due to
z powrotem [z pov-ro-tem] adv.
back; backwards; on the way
back (home, to work, etc.)
zrabować [zra-bo-vaćh] v. rob
z rana [z ra-na] adv. in the
morning; during the morning
zranić [zra-ńeećh] v. wound;
injure; hurt (feelings); mangle
zrastać [zras-taćh] v. grow into
one; fuse; heal up; blend
zrazu [zra-zoo] adv. at first
zrażać [zra-zhaćh] v. set
against; alienate; estrange;
antagonize; discourage
zrąb [zrownp] m. frame (work);
clearing; trunk; shell
zrąbać [zrown-baćh] v, hew;
cut down; hack; chop; pick to
pieces; prang (a target)
zrealizować [zre-a-lee-zo-vaćh]
v. realize; actualize; execute
zredagować [zre-da-go-vaćh] v.
draw up; compose; edit; draft
zresztą [zresh-town] adv.
1. moreover; besides; 2. after
all; though; anyway; in the
end; ah, well, no matter
zręczność [zranch-nośhćh] f.
cleverness; dexterity; skill
zrobić [zro-beećh] v. make; do;
turn; execute; perform
zrodzić [zro-dźheećh] v. give
birth; beget; originate
zrosnąć się [zros-nownćh
śhan] v. grow into one; fuse;
blend; set; heal up; knit
zrozpaczony [zros-pa-cho-ni] adj.
m. desperate; brokenhearted
zrozumiały [zro-zoo-mya-wi] adj.
m. intelligible; understandable
zrozumieć [zro-zoo-myećh] v.
understand; grasp (mentally);
see; make out; comprehend
zrozumienie [zro-zoo-mye-ńe] n.
understanding; sympathy; (legal) sense; mental grasp; comprehension; spirit; sense
zrównać [zroov-naćh] v. level;
make even; align; equalize
zrównoważyć [zroov-no-va-
-zhićh] v. balance; equalize;

equilibrate; compensate for

zróżniczkować [zroozh-ńeech--ko-vaćh] v. differentiate

zryć [zrićh] v. dig up; furrow

zrywać [zri-vaćh] v. rip; tear off; tear down; pick; quarrel

z rzadka [z zhad-ka] adv. rarely

zrządzenie losu [zzhown-dze-ńe lo-soo] n. fate; decree of fate

zrzeczenie się [zzhe-che-ńe śhan] n. resignation; renunciation; renouncement; abdication; relinquishment

zrzeszenie [zzhe-she-ńe] n. association; union

zrzęda [zzhan-da] m. grumbler

zrzucać [zzhoo-tsaćh] v. throw (down); buck off; drop; shed

zrzut lotniczy [zzhoot lot-ńee--chi] m. drop (from plane)

zsiadać [zśha-daćh] v. dismount; descend from; get off

zstąpić [zstown-peećh] v. descend; step down (one time); come down

zstępować [zstan-po-vaćh] v. descent; step down

zsyłać [zsi-waćh] v. deport; exile; send (down); inflict

zsyłka [zsiw-ka] f. deportation

zsypywać [zsi-pi-vaćh] v. heap up; pour off; shoot into

zszyć [zshićh] v. sew together

zubożeć [zoo-bo-zhećh] v. impoverish; grow poor; pauperize; reduce to poverty

zuch [zookh] m. brave fellow

zuchwalstwo [zookh-val-stvo] n. insolence; audacity; cheek; impudence; perkiness

zuchwały [zookh-va-wi] adj. m. insolent; impudent; bold

zupa [zoo-pa] f. soup

zupełny [zoo-pew-ni] adj. m. entire; whole; total; out and out; utter; outright; strict

zużycie [zoo-zhi-ćhe] n. consumption; wear and tear; waste; expenditure (of time)

zużytkować [zoo-zhit-ko-vaćh] v. utilize; use up; exploit

zużyty [zoo-zhi-ti] adj. m. worn out; used up; wasted; trite

zwać [zvaćh] v. call; name

zwalczyć [zval-chićh] v. overpower; overcome; cope; strive; stand against; subdue

zwalić [zva-leećh] v. demolish; fell; collapse; pile up; knock down; tumble down; dump

zwalniać [zval-ńaćh] v. release; loosen; let go; disengage; slow dawn; vacate

zwał [zvaw] m. heap; bank; pile

zwapnienie [zvap-ńe-ńe] n. calcification

zwarcie [zvar-ćhe] n. short (circuit); contraction; infighting adv. densely; closely

zwariować [zvar-yo-vaćh] v. go mad; go crazy; become insane; alter (a composition)

zwarzyć [zva-zhićh] v. boil; nip; frost damage; turn sour; blight

zważać [zva-zhaćh] v. pay attention; weigh (words); consider; give heed; have regard

zważyć [zva-zhićh] v. weigh; consider; give heed; regard

zwąchać [zvown-khaćh] v. smell out; get wind; sniff; scent; nose out; get wind of

zwątpić [zvownt-peećh] v. despair of; lose hope; give up

zwędzić [zvan-dźheećh] v. swipe; sneak; pinch; pilfer

zwęglić [zvang-leećh] v. carbonize; char; get charred

zwęzić [zvan-źheećh] v. narrow down; contract; restrict; confine; reduce width

zwiady [zvya-di] pl. reconnaissance; scouting; reconnoitring; surveying patrol

zwiastować [zvyas-to-vaćh] v. announce; herald; foreshadow

zwiastowanie [zvyas-to-va-ńe] n. Annunciation

zwiastun [zvyas-toon] m. harbinger; herald; omen; forerunner; precursor

związać [zvyown-zaćh] v. bind; fasten; join; tie up; strap; frame; lash together; link

związek [zvyown-zek] m. alliance; connection; bond;

compound; tie; trade union

zwichnąć [zveekh-nownćh] v.
strain; dislocate; disjoin;
luxate; warp; ruin (a career)

zwichnięcie [zveekh-ńan-će]
n. dislocation; luxation; sprain

zwiedzać [zvye-dzaćh] v. visit;
see the sights; tour (a
country); see; inspect

zwiedzanie [zvye-dza-ńe] n.
sightseeing; touring

zwierciadło [zvyer-ćhad-wo] n.
mirror; reflection; looking glass

zwierz [zvyesh] n. beast of prey

zwierzać się [zvye-zhaćh
śhan] v. disclose a secret;
confide in. ..

zwierzchnik [zvyezh-khńeek] m.
boss; superior; chief; lord;
master; suzerain; feudal lord

zwierzchnictwo [zvyezh-
-khńeets-tvo] n. sovereignty;
superior of rank; authority;
supreme power; control

zwierzę [zvye-zhan] n. animal

zwierzyna [zvye-zhi-na] f. game
(animals); game

zwierzyniec [zvye-zhi-ńets] m.
zoo; zoological garden; zodiac

zwieszać [zvye-shaćh] v. hang
low; let hang down; droop;
dangle; hang down

zwietrzeć [zvye-tshećh] v.
decompose; go stale; spoil

zwiewać [zvye-vaćh] v. cut
and run; blow away; run away

zwiędły [zvyand-wi] adj. m.
withered; wilted; faded

zwiędnąć [zvyand-nownćh] v.
wither (away); wilt; fade

zwiększyć [zvyank-shićh] v.
increase; magnify; heighten

zwięzły [zvyanz-wi] adj. m.
concise; brief; terse; compact

zwijać [zvee-yaćh] v. roll up;
wind up; coil; twist up; furl

zwilżać [zveel-zhaćh] v.
moisten; wet; dampen (often)

zwilżyć [zveel-zhićh] v.
moisten; wet; dampen (once)

zwinąć [zvee-nownćh] v. roll
up; wind up; coil up; twist up;
furl; take in (sails); fold

zwinny [zveen-ni] adj. m. agile;
nimble; deft; dexterous; lis-
some; light-fingered; light

zwisać [zvee-saćh] v. hang
down; droop; dangle; sag;
flag; overhang; beetle

zwlekać [zvle-kaćh] v. delay

zwłaszcza [zvwash-cha] adv.
particularly; chiefly; especially;
most of all; specially

zwłoka [zvwo-ka] f. delay;
respite; lag; postponement

zwłoki [zvwo-kee] n. corpse

zwodzić [zvo-dźheećh] v.
delude; deceive; mislead; let
down; lower

zwolenniczka [zvo-len-ńeech-ka]
f. adherent; follower; advocate

zwolennik [zvo-len-ńeek] m.
adherent; follower; advocate

zwolna [zvol-na] adv. slowly

zwolnieć [zvol-ńećh] v. slow
down; slack off; relax; slacken

zwolnienie [zvol-ńe-ńe] n.
1. dismissal; release; acquittal;
sack; exemption; 2. slowing

zwoływać [zvo-wi-vaćh] v. call
together; assemble; convene

zwój [zvooy] m. roll; reel; coil

zwracać [zvra-tsaćh] v. return;
give back; pay (attention)

zwrot [zvrot] m. 1. turn;
2. restitution; restoration; refund 3. revulsion; 4. phrase

zwrotka [zvrot-ka] f. stanza

zwrotnica [zvrot-ńee-tsa] f.
switch (large) steering

zwrotnik [zvrot-ńeek] m. tropic

zwrotny [zvrot-ni] adj. m.
flexible; returnable; repayable

zwrócić się [zvroo-ćheećh
śhan] v. turn (to); give back

zwycięski [zvi-ćhans-kee]
adj. m. victorious; triumphant;
triumphal; winning (team, etc.)

zwycięstwo [zvi-ćhans-tvo] n.
victory; triumph; win

zwyciężać [zvi-ćhan-zhaćh] v.
conquer; win; prevail; overcome; get the upper hand

zwyczaj [zvi-chay] m. custom;
habit; fashion; usage; practice

zwyczajny [zvi-chay-ni] adj. m.

usual; ordinary; common; normal; regular; plain; simple

zwyczajowy [zvi-cha-yo-vi] adj. m. customary; regular; usual

zwykły [zvik-wi] adj. m. common

zwyrodniały [zvi-rod-ńa-wi] adj. m. degenerate; degenerated

zwyrodnienie [zvi-rod-ńe-ńe] n. degeneration; degradation

zwyżka [zvizh-ka] f. rise (of prices); advance (of stocks)

zwyżka cen [zvizh-ka tsen] f. price rise; price increase

zygzak [zig-zak] m. zigzag

zysk [zisk] m. gain; profit

zyskać [zis-káćh] v. gain; earn

zyskowność [zis-kov-nośhćh] f. profitability; remunerativeness; lucrativeness

zyskowny [zis-kov-ni] adj. m. profitable; lucrative

zza [zza] prep. from behind

zziajać się [zźha-yaćh śhan] v. get out of breath; tire oneself out; become dog-tired

zzielenieć [zźhe-le-ńećh] v. turn green; become green

zziąbnąć [zźhanb-nownćh] v. feel cold; be chilled to the bone; become cold

zziębnięty [zźhanb-ńan-ti] adj. m. chilled (to the bone)

zżyć się [zzhićh śhan] v. become familiar (with); grow accustomed (to)

zżymać [zzhi-máćh] v. wring

zżynać [zzhi-naćh] v. cut down; reap (corn with a scythe); mow (the grass etc.)

zżywać się [zzhi-vaćh śhan] v. grow familiar; reconcile

Ź

źdźbło [źhdźhbwo] n. stalk; blade; trifle; a bit; a little

źle [źhle] adj. n. & adv. ill; wrong; badly; falsely; mistakenly; improperly; poorly

źrebak [źhre-bak] m. colt

źrebię [źhre-byan] n. foal; colt

źrenica [źhre-ńee-tsa] f. pupil

źródlany [źhrood-la-ni] adj. m. spring (water); of spring

źródło [źhrood-wo] n. spring; source; well; fountain head

źródłosłów [źhhrood-wo--swoof] m. root of a ward; etymology; radical of a word

źródłowy [źhrood-wo-vi] adj. m. original; spring (water)

Ż

żaba [zha-ba] f. frog

żaden [zha-den] pron. none; neither; not any; no one; no-

żagiel [zha-gyel] m. sail

żakiet [zha-kyet] m. jacket

żal [zhal] m. regret; grief; sorrow; remorse; grudge; rancor; compunction; soreness

żalić się [zha-leećh śhan] v. complain; lament; find fault

żaluzja [zha-looz-ya] f. blind

żałoba [zha-wo-ba] f. mourning

żałobny marsz [zha-wob-ni marsh] m. funeral march

żałosny [zha-wos-ni] adj. m. lamentable; wretched; plaintive; piteous; deplorable

żałość [zha-wośhćh] f. grief; desolation; sorrow; deep sorrow; emotional suffering

żałować [zha-wo-vaćh] v. regret; be sorry; mourn

żar [zhar] m. heat; glow; ardor

żarcie [zhar-ćhe] n. swill; dub

żargon [zhar-gon] m. jargon

żarliwość [zhar-lee-vośhćh] f. ardor; zeal; earnestness

żarliwy [zhar-lee-vi] adj. m. ardent; zealous; fervent

żarłoczny [zhar-woch-ni] adj. m. greedy; voracious; gluttonous

żarłok [zhar-wok] m. glutton

żarówka [zha-roof-ka] f. light bulb; electric bulb; bulb

żart [zhart] m. joke; jest; quip

żartować [zhar-to-vaćh] v. joke; make fun; poke fun; trifle; jest; make sport

żarzyć [zha-zhićh] v. glow; anneal; incandesce

żąć [zhownćh] v. mow; cut; reap (corn with a sickle)

żądać [zhown-daćh] v. demand; require; exact; stipulate; postulate; claim

żądanie [zhown-da-ńe] n. demand; claim (for damages); requirement; stipulation

żądło [zhownd-wo] n. sting; (snake) fang; dart

żądny [zhownd-ni] adj. m. eager (for); anxious; greedy; avid (of fame, honors, etc.)

żądny przygód [zhownd-ni pzhi-goot] adventurous (man)

że [zhe] conj. that; then; as

żebrać [zhe-braćh] v. beg

żebraczka [zhe-brach-ka] f. beggar; pauper (girl, woman)

żebrak [zhe-brak] m. beggar (men); pauper; mendicant

żebranina [zhe-bra-ńe-na] f. beggary; begging; alms

żebro [zhe-bro] n. rib; fin

żeby [zhe-bi] conj. so as; in order that; if; may; if only

żeglarski [zhe-glar-skee] adj. m. nautical; seaman's (life etc.)

żeglarstwo [zhe-glar-stvo] n. sailing; navigation; seamanship

żeglarz [zhe-glash] m. seaman; sailor; mariner; seafarer

żeglować [zhe-glo-vaćh] v. sail; navigate (the seas, the ocean)

żeglowny [zhe-glov-ni] adj. m. navigable (river, canal, etc.)

żegluga [zhe-gloo-ga] f. navigation; shipping; sailing

żegnać [zheg-naćh] v. bid farewell; bless; bid good-bye; see off; bid farewell

żelatyna [zhe-la-ti-na] f. jelly

żelazko [zhe-laz-ko] n. press-iron; cutting iron; edger

żelazny [zhe-laz-ni] adj. m. iron

żelazo [zhe-la-zo] n. iron; armor

żelazobeton [zhe-la-zo-be-ton] m. reinforced concrete

żelaztwo [zhe-las-tvo] n. scrap iron; hardware; iron junk

żelbet [zhel-bet] m. reinforced concrete; ferro-concrete

żeliwo [zhe-lee-vo] n. cast iron

żenić [zhe-ńeećh] v. marry

żenować [zhe-no-vaćh] v. embarrass; disconcert; nonplus

żeński [zheń-skee] adj. m. female; feminine; women's

żer [zher] m. food; prey; feeding

żerdka [zherd-ka] f. (small) perch

żerdź [zherdźh] f. perch; rod

żłobek [zhwo-bek] m. crib

żłobić [zhwo-beećh] v. channel; erode; furrow; groove

żłób [zhwoop] m. trough; crib

żmija [zhmee-ya] f. viper; adder; poisonous snake

żmudny [zhmood-ni] adj. m. uphill; toilsome; strenuous

żniwiarka [zhńe-vyar-ka] f. harvester; reaper

żniwo [zhńee-vo] n. harvest

żołądek [zho-wown-dek] m. stomach; belly; the abdomen

żołądź [zho-wowndźh] f. acorn

żołd [zhowd] m. (soldier's) pay

żołdactwo [zhow-dats-tvo] n. soldiery; the soldiery

żołnierz [zhow-ńesh] m. soldier

żona [zho-na] f. wife

żonaty [zho-na-ti] adj. m. married; family man

żółć [zhoowćh] f. bile

żółciowy [zhoow-ćho-vi] adj. m. gall; peevish; harsh; biting

żółknąć [zhoow-knownćh] v. turn yellow; become yellow

żółtaczka [zhoow-tach-ka] f. jaundice; the yellows

żółtawy [zhoow-ta-vi] adj. m. yellowish; nankeen; sallow

żółtko [zhoowt-ko] n. yolk

żółty [zhoow-ti] adj. m. yellow

żółto-blady [zhoow-to-bla-di] adj. m. yellow-pale; sallow

żółw [zhoowf] m. turtle; tortoise

żółwi krok [zhoow-vee krok] m. snail's pace; turtle's gait

żrący [zhr**own**-tsi] adj. m.
corrosive; caustic; biting

żubr [zhoobr] m. (European-
-Polish) bison; aurochs

żuchwa [zhookh-va] f. jawbone

żuć [zhooćh] v. chew up;
chew; masticate; manducate

żucie [zhoo-ćhe] n. chewing;
mastication; (the) chew;
chewing up

żuk [zhook] m. beetle; dung
beetle

żulik [zhoo-leek] m. swindler;
rogue; cheat; street urchin

żuławy [zhoo-**wa**-vi] pl.
marshlands; lowlands; fertile
lowlands (river delta)

żupa [zhoo-pa] f. salt-works

żupan [zhoo-pan] m. old Polish
costume; (hist.) district chief

żur [zhoor] m. soup of
fermented meal; sour soup

żuraw [zhoo-rav] m. crane;
gantry; water-crane

żurawina [zhoo-ra-vee-na] f.
cranberry; cranberry shrub

żurnal [zhoor-nal] m. fashion
magazine (for women or men)

żużel [zhoo-zhel] m. slag; cinder;
scoria; clinker; cinder track

żużlobeton [zhoo-zhlo-be-ton] m.
slag concrete

żwawo [zhva-vo] adj. m. briskly;
alertly; apace; jauntily

żwawy [zhva-vi] adj. m. brisk;
quick; lively; spry; sprightly

żwir [zhveer] m. gravel

życie [zhi-ćhe] n. life; pep;
upkeep; lifetime; animation

życiodajny [zhi-ćho-day-ni] adj.
m. life-giving; vivifying

życiorys [zhi-ćho-ris] m.
biography; life history

życzenie [zhi-che-ńe] n. wish;
desire;request; greeting

życzliwy [zhich-lee-vi] adj. m.
favorable; friendly; kindly

żyć [zhićh] v. be alive; live;
exist; subsist; get along

Żyd [zhid] m. Jew; Hebrew

żydowski [zhi-dov-skee] adj. m.
Jewish; Judaic; Yiddish

żydostwo [zhi-dos-tvo] n. Jewry

Żydówka [zhi-**doov**-ka] f. Jewess

żyjący [zhi-**yown**-tsi] adj. m.
living; pl. the living

żyjątko [zhi-**yownt**-ko] n.
animalcule; tiny animal

żylak [zhi-lak] m. varix

żylakowy [zhi-la-ko-vi] adj. m.
varicose; of varicose vein

żylasty [zhi-**las**-ti] adj. m.
venous; stringy; sinewy

żyletka [zhi-let-ka] f. (razor)
blade; safety razor blade

żyła [zhi-wa] f. vein; seam; core;
strand; streak; lode; string

żyłka [zhiw-ka] f. vein; streak

żyrafa [zhi-ra-fa] f. giraffe

żyrant [zhi-rant] m. endorser

żyrować [zhi-ro-vaćh] v.
endorse; sign as payee

żytni [zhit-ńee] adj. m. rye

żytniówka [zhit-**ńoov**-ka] f. corn
vodka; gin; rye vodka

żyto [zhi-to] n. rye

żywcem [zhiv-tsem] adv. alive

żywe srebro [zhi-ve **sreb**-ro] n.
mercury; restless person

żywica [zhi-**vee**-tsa] f. resin

żywiec [zhi-vyets] m. cattle for
slaughter; live bait

żywić [zhi-veećh] v. feed;
nourish; cherish; feel; foster

żywioł [zhi-vyow] m. element

żywiołowy [zhi-vyo-wo-vi] adj.
m. elemental; spontaneous;
impulsive; impetuous

żywność [zhiv-no**śhćh**] f.
food; provisions; eatables;
victuals; (animal) fodder

żywo [zhi-vo] adv. quickly;
briskly; exp. make it snappy!

żywopłot [zhi-vo-pwot] m. hedge

żywość [zhi-vo**śhćh**] f. animation; liveliness; vivacity; vitality; intensity; vigor; esprit

żywot [zhi-vot] m. life; womb;
belly; life (of a saint)

żywotnie [zhi-vot-ńe] adv.
vitally; exuberantly; luxuriantly

żywotność [zhi-vot-no**śhćh**]
f. vitality; liveliness; vivacity

żywotny [zhi-vot-ni] m. vital

żywy [zhi-vi] adj. m. alive; lively;
vivid; intense; gay; brisk; live;

acute; keen; bright
żyzność [zhiz-nośhćh] f.
   fertility; fruitfulness; richness
żyzny [zhiz-ni] adj. m. fertile;
   generous (soil); fruitful; fat;
   fecund; rich

Pogonowski
Phonetic Notation

PRONUNCIATION
AS IN COMMON,
EVERYDAY SPEECH

Complete Phonetics
for
English and Polish
Speakers

POGONOWSKI PHONETIC NOTATION
POLISH PRONUNCIATION
FOR ENGLISH SPEAKERS

Pronunciation related to familiar English sounds
Pronunciation explained with speech organ diagrams

GUIDE TO PRONUNCIATION
AS IN COMMON, EVERYDAY SPEECH

The phonetic transcription follows all
entries. It is subdivided into syllables.

In multi-syllable words the stressed syllables
are printed in bold letters.

Polish vowels are pure and consist of one
sound only.

Polish vowels are never drawled as happens
often in English.

Schematic Ellipse of the
Tip of the Tongue Positions
Of Six Basic Polish Vowels

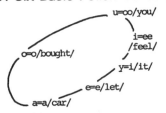

Polish nasalized vowels "ą" and "ę" are discussed on the next page.

Polish vowels:

A, a   as in: father, car;

                        in the phonetic guide: a

E, e,   as in: let, met, get;   -"-   : e

I, i,   as in: feel, keel;   -"-   : ee

O, o,   as in: bought, not;   -"-   : o

U, u,   as in: hook, too;   -"-   : oo

Y, y,   as in: it, big, bib;   -"-   : i

The two *Polish nasalized vowels* can not be exactly described by English sounds.

The two Polish nasalized vowels:

Ą, ą, shown in the phonetic guide as: <u>own</u> =
              French sound of "on."
it is a single nasalized sound composed of:
a clear "o" as in "bought" followed by "w"
and the ending with a trace of "n"

Ę, ę, shown in the phonetic guide as: <u>an</u> =
              French sound of "un."
it is a single nasalized sound composed of:
a clear "e" as in "pen" and the ending with
a trace of "n"

POLISH CONSONANTS

Most Polish consonants are to be read as in English. However, voiced consonants become unvoiced at the end of any Polish word and immediately in front or behind of any unvoiced cosonat.

There are *no silent* Polish letters, except "c" in "ch" pronounced as [kh].

UNVOICED
CONSONANTS:
(without sounding
the vocal cords)

p = p
t = t
k = k
k in kie = k̲
f = f
s = s
ś = śh
sz = sh
(sz = sh
c = ts
ć = ćh
cz = ch
h & ch = kh
I = I

VOICED
CONSONANTS:
(with sounding the
vocal cords)

b = b
d = d
g = g
g in gie = g̲
w = v
z = z
ź = źh
ż = zh
rz = zh)
dz = dz
dź = dźh
dż = dzh

GLIDES:
r = r
j = y
ł = w

NASALS:
m = m
n = n
n & ni = ń

PRONUNCIATION OF POLISH CONSONANTS SPELLED OR VOICED DIFFERENTLY THAN IN ENGLISH

cz = ch in the phonetic guide - it is pronounced exactly like "ch" in English.

sz = sh in the phonetic guide - it is pronounced exactly like "sh" in English.

szcz = shch pronounced exactly like in "fresh cheese" in English.

h & ch = kh pronounced like in Scottish "loch."

ń & ni = n with an apostrophe - a nasal consonant as in "onion," or Spanish "n" as in "manana". It also occurs in Polish when "n" is followed by the vowel "i."

ni = ń when the "i" is followed by a vowel

ni = ń + "ee" when the "i" is followed by a consonant.

j = y - a gliding consonant - pronounced exactly like "y" in the English word "yes."

ł = w - a gliding consonant - pronounced like "w" in English.

r = r - a gliding consonant - it is trilled with the tip of the tongue.

g = g - in Polish it is always pronounced as in the English word "good."

gie = g underlined indicates a trace of an "e" sound after "g" and before the sound of "e" as in "let."

kie = k underlined indicates a trace of an "ee" sound after "k" and before the "e" sound, as in "pet."

PRONUNCIATION OF POLISH PALATAL CONSONANTS

Polish palatal consonants are pronounced by touching the upper palate with the tongue. They are:

ć = ch with an apostrophe over the "c"

ci = ć when the "i" is followed by a vowel

ci = ć + "ee" when the "i" is followed by a consonant

ć is pronounced like "t" in nature.

dź = dźh with an apostrophe over the "z" - pronounced like "dz" while touching the tooth ridge.

dż = dzh - pronounced like "dzh" while touching the upper palate.

ś = śh with an apostrophe over the "s" - pronounced like "sh" while touching the tooth ridge.

si = ś when the "i" is followed by a vowel

si = ś + "ee" when the "i" is followed by a consonant

ź = źh with an apostrophe over the "z" - pronounced like "zh" while touching the upper palate.

zi = ź when the "i" is followed by a vowel

zi = ź + "ee" when the "i" is followed by a consonant

(ż = rz) = zh (note: a dot over the "z"). It is pronounced like the "s" in measure.

ść = śhćh with apostrophes over "s" and "c" - two consonants produced by touching the ridge of the teeth ridge with the tongue while pronouncing each consonant separately.

SPEECH ORGAN DIAGRAM
for Polish palatal consonants
not used in the English language.

Explosives: air compressed behind lips and teeth, then
suddenly released: dź, dzi, [dźh]
and ć, ci, [ćh]
Fricatives: air flow with a continuous friction:
ź, zi, [źh], and ś, si, [śh].
The tip of the tongue is at the tooth ridge.

POLISH SOUND "R"
is fluttered and may be pronounced
like the Scottish "r"

Mouth is slightly open; tip of the tongue is raised;
it vibrates on the exhaling impulse and strikes the
tooth-ridge; sides of the tongue touch back teeth.
The tongue does not glide as far back as is needed
in the English "r."

ZAPIS FONETYCZNY POGONOWSKIEGO
WYMOWA ANGIELSKA DLA POLAKÓW
ENGLISH PRONUNCIATION FOR POLES

**Pronunciation related to familiar Polish sounds
Pronunciation explained with speech organ diagrams.**

**Uproszczona wymowa wyrażona zapisem polskim
i wytłumaczona przekrojami narządów mowy.**

Nie ulega wątpliwości, że zapoznanie się z językiem angielskim w dużej mierze polega na zapoznaniu się z angielskimi dzwiękami, których wiele różni się od wymowy polskiej.

Akcent, rytm i intonacja mają zasadnicze znaczenie w porozumiewaniu się.

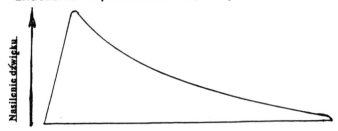

Często angielskie wyrazy można graficznie przedstawić powyższym wykresem dzwięku, intonacji, oraz akcentu (nacisku). Często początek słowa jest wymawiany w silniejszy sposób a następnie dźwięk *zamiera* ku końcowi słowa. Jednocześnie wymowa słów musi być jak najbardziej *swobodna*.

Należy unikać wszelkiego zmuszania się do mówienia w sposób sztuczny i nienaturalny.

Szkice narzadów mowy są pomocne w nauce wymowy słów angielskich. Ilustrują one różnice w używaniu narządów mowy przez mówiących po polsku i po angielsku. Ważne jest żeby pamiętać że przecinek u góry oznacza akcent na następującą po nim zgłoskę. Przecinek u dołu oznacza akcent słabszy, drugorzędny. Litery polskiego alfabetu są zastosowane jako podstawa znaków fonetycznych. Dwukropek zwiększa długość samogłoski.

Przy szkicach narządów mowy pokazane są angielskie samogłoski na obwodzie schematycznej elipsy ilustrującej pozycje języka. Oprocz dwunastu angielskich samogłosek, trzy postawowe dwugłoski angielskie zaznaczone są wewnątrz elipsy między początkową i końcową samogłoską dwugłoski. Początkowa część dwugłoski jest silniejsza niż końcowa. Cechą samogłosek angielskich, w przeciwieństwie do polskich, jest ich skłonność do przybierania dźwięków przejściowych i stawania się dwugłoskami. Trzeba pamiętać że w języku angielskim oznakowanie fonetyczne samogłosek może być tylko przybliżone. Zwłaszcza "e" fonetyczne jest mniej wyraźne niż po polsku. Samogłoska w końcówce, jak np. "nal" lub "bel" jest w fonetycznej wersji pominięta tak, że wymowa tych końcówek wymaga użycia dźwięku naturalnego zbliżonego do polskiego "y".

SPÓŁGŁOSKI ANGIELSKIE

Lista spółgłosek angielskich jest uzupełniona szkicami narządów mowy w układach odpowiadających dźwiękom, których się nie używa w języku polskim. Spółgłoski "seplenione" oznaczone literami "th" są jednymi z trudniejszych dźwięków angielskich. Jest ich pięć. Są one oznaczone podkreśleniem: s̲, t̲, d̲, dz̲, z̲. Wymowa ich jest wytłumaczona przy pomocy szkiców narządów mowy.

Angielskie "r" przypomina słabe rzężenie i jest inaczej a zarazem dużo słabiej wymawiane niż polskie "r". Angielskie "r" nie może być wymówione samodzielnie, jedynie przed lub po samogłosce.

Zmiękczone angielskie "n" [n̲] jak w "sing" [syn̲] różni się od polskiego "ń", które jest bliższe dźwiękowi w angielskim słowie "new" [ńju]. Zapis fonetyczny [n̲] zawiera w sobie ślad następującego dźwięku "g" lub "k."

Angielskie "h" jest prawie nieme w porównaniu do polskiego "h". Język i usta są w pozycji do następnego dźwięku i tylko lekkie tchnienie zaznacza dźwięk angielski "h."

Angielska przejściowa spółgłoska "w" [ł] jest niemożliwa do wypowiedzenia samodzielnie. Usta zaokrąglone w pozycji jak do "u," przejściowy dzwięk bliski jest polskiemu "ł." Usta i język szybko przechodzą do układu dla następującej samogłoski. W zapisie fonetycznym "ou" wymawia się jak

"oł" a dźwięk "au" jak "ał."
Poza omówionymi powyżej, spółgłoski angielskie i polskie nie różnią się.
Większość angielskich współgłosek czyta się tak samo jak w języku polskim.
Dźwięczne spółgłoski na końcu słów angielskich pozostają dźwięczne w przeciwieństwie do polskich.

SPÓŁGŁOSKI BEZDŹWIĘCZNE:

(bez dźwięku strun głosowych)

p = p
t = t
k & q = k
x = ks
f = f
th = t̲ & s̲
s = s
sh = sz
c = ts
ch = cz
hw = hł (why = hłaj)
h = prawie nieme

SPÓŁGŁOSKI DŹWIĘCZNE:

(z dźwiękiem strun głosowych)

b = b
d = d
g = g

w = v
th = d̲, dz̲ & z̲
z = z
zh = ż
dz = dz
dzh = dż
l = l

GŁOSKI PRZEJŚCIOWE:

r = r
y = j
w = ł

GŁOSKI NOSOWE:

m = m
n = n
ng & nk = n̲

PRZEKRÓJ NARZĄDÓW MOWY
ANGIELSKI DŹWIĘK "TH"

Angielska "sepleniona" spółgłoska "th": koniec i przód języka szeroko spłaszczony, widzialny między zębami; ciągły przelot powietrza między zębami i wargami.

Głoska bezdźwięczna: [s̲] bath [ba:s̲]
       [t̲] thank [t̲aenk]

Głoska dźwięczna: [d̲] those [d̲ouz]
  [dz̲] they [dz̲ej]
  [z̲] bathing [bej̲z̲yn̲g]

ANGIELSKI DŹWIĘK "R"

Andielska spółgłoska "r": usta nieco otwarte; koniec języka uniesiony wklęsłym podgięciem ku tyłowi, nie dotyka podniebienia; boki języka dotykają zębów; wymowa możliwa tylko w przejściu od lub do samogłski -- przypomina lekkie rzężenie.

SCHEMATYCZNA ELIPSA POZYCJI KOŃCA JĘZYKA DLA DWUNASTU SAMOGŁOSEK ANGIELSKICH (WYMOWA AMERYKAŃSKA)

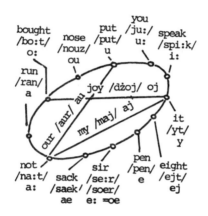

Trzy podstawowe dwugłoski angielskie -- diphtongs ['dyftons] -- są zaznaczone wewnątrz schematycznej elipsy pozycji końca języka przy wymawianiu dwunastu samogłosek angielskich.

STRUNY GŁOSOWE CZYLI FAŁDY GŁOSOWE VOCAL CHORDS OR RATHER VOCAL FOLDS

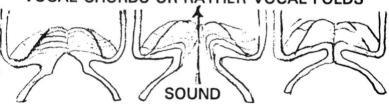

SOUND

PRODUCTION OF HUMAN VOICE

PRACTICAL

ENGLISH-POLISH

DICTIONARY

by

Iwo Cyprian Pogonowski

A

a [ej] art. jeden; pewien; pierwsza litera angielskiego alfabetu; pierwszej kategorii
A-O'k [ej okej] zupełnie gotów
aback [e'baek] adv. wstecz; w tył; do tyłu; nazad
abandon [e'baendon] v. opuszczać; porzucić; zarzucić; zaniechać; oddać się
abandonment [e'baendonment] s. opuszczenie; brak pohamowania; zrezygnowanie z
abashed [e'baeszt] adj. speszony; zmieszany (czymś)
abate ['ebejt] v. osłabiać; zmniejszać; mitygować; uciszyć; osłabić; anulować
abbey ['aebi] s. opactwo
abbreviate [e'bry:wjejt] v. skrócić; skracać
abbreviation [e'bry:wjejszyn] s. skrót; skrócenie; skracanie
ABC ['ej'bi:'si] alfabet
abdicate ['aebdykejt] v. zrzekać się (stanowiska); abdykować
abdomen ['aebdomen] s. brzuch
abduct [aeb'dakt] v. uprowadzić; uprowadzać; porwać; porywać (kogoś, coś)
abhor [eb'ho:r] v. mieć odrazę
abide, abode, abode [e'bajd, e'boud, e'boud]
abide [e'bajd] v. znosić; obstawać; dotrzymywać; czekać (na coś); trwać
ability [e'bylyty] s. zdolność
abject ['aebdżekt] adj. podły; nędzny, nikczemny, skrajny
abjure [eb'dżuer] v. poprzysiąc
able ['ejbl] adj. zdolny; zdatny; utalentowany; poczytalny
abnormal [aeb'no:rmel] adj. anormalny; nieprawidłowy
aboard [e'bo:rd] adv. na pokładzie; na statku; w

pociągu; w tramwaju, etc.
abode [e'boud] v. był posłuszny
abode [e'boud] s. mieszkanie; v. proszę zobaczyć: abide
abolish [e'bolysz] v. obalić; znieść; znosić; obalać
abolition [aebe'lyszyn] n. obalenie (ustawy, etc.); zniesienie (zwyczaju, etc.)
A-bomb ['ejbom] s. bomba atomowa; bomba jądrowa
abominable [e'bomynebl] adj. ohydny; wstrętny; obrzydliwy
abortion [e'bo:rszyn] s. przerwanie ciąży; poronienie
abound [e'baund] v. obfitować
about [e'baut] adv. naokoło; około; dookoła; po (czymś); o; wobec (kogś); przy
about [e'baut] prep. o; przy; odnośnie; naokoło; wokoło
about to [e'baut tu] gotów do
above [e'baw] adv. powyżej; w górze; wyżej; na górze
above [e'baw] prep. nad; ponad
above [e'baw] adj. powyższy
abrasive [e'brejsyw] adj. ścierny; s. ścierniwo
abreast [e'brest] adv. obok; rzędem; ramię przy ramieniu
abridge [e'brydż] v. skrócić
abroad [e'bro:d] adv. zewnątrz; za granicą; za granicę; w dal
abrogate ['aebrogejt] v. obalić; unicestwić; odwoływać; znosić (ustawę, zarządzenie etc.)
abrupt [e'brapt] adj. nagły; lapodarny; szorstki; urwany; ostry; os-chły; obcesowy
abscess ['aebses] s. wrzód; ropień (na skórze, etc.)
absence ['aebsens] s. brak; (czyjaś) nieobecność; niestawiennictwo (roztargnienie)
absent ['aebsent] adj. nieobecny; v. być nieobecnym
absent-minded ['aebsent-'majndyd] adj. roztargniony
absolute ['aebselu:t] adj. absolutny; zupełny; czysty (alkohol) nieodwołalny; prawdziwy
absolutely ['aebselu:tly] adv. absolutnie; oczywiście

absolve [eb'zolv] v. rozgrzeszyć;
darować; uwolnić; oczyś-
cić; zwolnić; zwalniać
absorb [eb'zorb] v. chłonąć;
wchłonąć; tłumić; absorbo-
wać; złagodzić (uderzenie)
abstain [eb'stejn] v. powstrzymywać się (od czegoś);
być abstynentem; pościć
abstention [eb'stenszyn] s.
wstrzymanie się (od jedze-nia);
powstrzymywanie sie
abstinence ['aebstynens] s.
wstrzemięźliwość; pow-
strzymywanie abstynencja
abstract ['aebstraekt] adj.
oderwany; abstrakcyjny; s.
abstrakcja; streszczenie; v.
streszczać; abstrahować; odrywać; ukraść; sprzątnąć;
wyabstrahować; wydobyć
absurd [eb'se:rd] adj. absurdalny;
bezsensowny; niedorzeczny
abundance [e'bandens] s.
obfitość; znaczna ilość; dostatek; zasobność
abundant [e'bandent] adj. obfity;
liczny; bogaty; zasobny (w
coś); płodny (urodzajny)
abuse [e'bju:s] s. nadużycie;
obelga; [e'bju:z] v. obrażać;
nadużywać; lżyć; obrzucać
obelgami (przekleństwami)
abyss [e'bys] n. otchłań;
przepaść; głębia; pierwotny
chaos (we wszechświecie)
acacia [e'kejsze] s. akacja
academic [,aeke'demyk] adj.
akademicki; jałowy; s. uczony
academy [e'kaedemy] s. akademia; uniwersytet
accelerate [aek'selerejt] v.
przyspieszać; przyśpieszyć
accelerator [aek'selerejter] s.
przyspieszacz; gaźnik; akce-
lerator; katalizator
accent ['aeksent] s. wymowa;
akcent; [aek'sent] v. ak-
centować; uwydatniać; da-
wać nacisk; znakować
accept [ek'sept] v. akceptować;
zgadzać się na; zechcieć
wziąć (przyjąć); uznać

acceptable [ek'septebl] adj. do
przyjęcia (możliwy); znośny;
zadawalający; mile widziany
access ['aekses] s. dostęp
accessible [aek'sesybl] adj.
dostępny; przystępny
accession [aek'seszyn] s.
wstąpienie; dostęp; dojście;
przystąpienie; objęcie (urzędu)
accessory [aek'sesery] s. dodatek; adj. dodatkowy; uboczn-
ny; pomocniczy (w zbrodni)
access road ['aekses roud] droga
dojazdowa (do miasta, etc.)
accident ['aeksydent] s. traf;
wypadek; katastrofa; awaria
accidental [,aeksy'dentl] adj.
przypadkowy; nieważny; mało
znaczący; uboczny
acclimatize [e'klajmetajz] v.
(za)aklimatyzować
accommodate [e'komedejt] v.
przystosować; pogodzić; za-
kwaterować; wygodzić; wy-
świadczyć (przysługą); załagodzić (spór, etc.)
accommodation [e,kome'dejszyn]
s. wygoda; dostosowanie;
kwatera; pogodzenie się;
ugoda; kompromis; usługa
accompaniment
[e'kampenyment] s.
towarzyszenie; akom-
paniament; dodatki
accompany [e'kampeny] v.
towarzyszyć; odprowadzać;
akompaniować
accomplice [e'komplys] s.
współsprawca; współwinny
accomplish [e'kamplysz] v.
dokonać; spełnić; zre-
alzować; udoslonalić
accomplished [e'kamplyszt] adj.
utalentowany; znakomity;
wykończony; z ogłądą;
skończony (artysta itp.)
accomplishment
[e'kamplyszment] s.
osiągnięcie; realizacja;
dokonanie; wykonanie; ogłada
accord [e'ko:rd] s. zgoda; v.
uzgadniać; dać; licować
according [e'ko:rdyng] prep.

według; zależnie od

accordingly [ə'ko:rdyngly] adv. odpowiednio; więc; zatem

accost [ə'kost]v. zaczepić (kogoś); zagadnąć (kogoś); przystąpić do kogoś

account [ə,kaunt] s. rachunek; sprawozdanie; v. wyliczać; wytłumaczyć; uważać; oceniać; być odpowiedzialnym

account for [ə'kaunt fo:r] v. dać powód; wytłumaczyć

accountant [ə'kauntent] s. księgowy, księgowa

accounting [ə'kauntyng] s. księgowość

accumulate [ə'kju:mju,lejt] v. gromadzić; zbierać; piętrzyć

accuracy ['aekjuresy] s. ścisłość; dokładność; celność (strzału)

accusative [ə'kju:zetyw] s. biernik (gramatyka)

accusation [aekju:zejszyn] s. oskarżenie; winienie (kogoś); posądzenie (o coś)

accuse [ə'kju:z] v. oskarżać

accused [ə'kju:zd] adj. oskarżony; oskarżona

accustom [ə'kastem] v. przyzwyczajać; przyzwyczaić

accustomed [ə'kastemd] adj. przyzwyczajony (do); zwykły; przywykły; zwyczajny

ace [ejs] s. as; oczko (in cards)

ache [ejk] s. ból; v. boleć

achieve [ə'czi:w] v. dokonać; osiągnąć (cel); zdobywać (sławę); dochodzic (do)

achievement [ə'czi:wment] s. osiągnięcie; wyczyn; zdobycz

aching ['ejkyng] adj. bolący

acid ['aesyd] adj. kwaśny; s. kwas; kwaśna substancja

acid trip ['aesyd tryp] halucynacje po narkotyku

acknowledge [ek'nołlydż] v. uznać; potwierdzić; przyznać (się); nagrodzić

acknowledgement [ek'nołlydżment] s. przyznanie; potwierdzenie; uznanie; dowód uznania

acoustics [ə'ku:styks] pl. akustyka

acquaint [ə'kłejnt] v. zaznajomić; zapoznać; zapoznawać (kogoś)

acquaintance [ə'kłejntens] s. znajomość; znajomy

acquiesce [,aekły'es] v. zgadzać się; przyzwalać (bez oporu); przychylić się (do prośby)

acquire [ə'kłajer] v. nabywać

acquisition [,aekły'zyszyn] s. nabytek; nabycie; zdobycz

acquit [ə'kłyt] v. zwolnić; wywiązać się; spławić; uniewinnić (kogoś); uiścić

acquittal [ə'kłytl] s. zwolnienie; uiszczenie; wywiązanie się

acre [ejker] s. akr; morga amery-kańska; 4047 m. kwadr.

acrid ['aekryd] adj. żrący; ostry; cierpki; kwaskowaty

acrimonious [,aekry'mounjes] adj. szorstki; zjadliwy; cierpki; zgorzkniały; tetryczny

acrobat ['aekrebaet] s. akrobata

across [ə'kros] adv. w poprzek; na krzyż; prep. przez; na przełaj; po drugiej stronie (rzeki, ulicy, itp.)

act [aekt] v. czynić; działać; postępować; s. czyn; akt; uczynek; akt sztuki; uchwała (parlamentu); ustawa

action ['aekszyn] s. działanie; czyn; akcja; ruch; proces

active ['aektyw] adj. czynny; obrotny; rzutki; ożywiony; żywy; ożywiony; bujny

activity [aek'tywyty] s. działalność; czynność; ożywienie; ruch

actor ['aekter] s. aktor

actress ['aektrys] s. aktorka

actual ['aekczuel] adj. istotny; faktyczny; bieżący; obecny

actually ['aekczuely] adv. rzeczywiście; obecnie; istotnie; faktycznie; nawet

acute [ə'kju:t] adj. ostry; przynikliwy; bystry

ad [aed] s. ogłoszenie (reklama) (pot. od advertisement)

adapt [e'daept] v. dostosować; przerobić; przystosować; dostrajać; nadawać się (do)
adaptation ['aedaep'tejszyn] s. przystosowanie; dostrojenie
add [aed] v. dodać; doliczyć
addict [aedykt] s. nałogowiec; v. oddawać; poświęcać się
addicted [e'dyktyd] adj. nałogowy; nałogowo poświęcający się (czemuś)
addition [e'dyszyn] s. dodawanie; dodatek; (in addition = ponadto)
additional [e'dyszynl] adj. dodatkowy; dalszy
address [e'dres] s. adres; mowa; odezwa; v. zwracać się; adresować (do); skierować (prośbą); przemawiać
addressee [,aedre'si:] s. adresat; adresatka (listu itp.)
adequate ['aedykłyt] s. stosowny; dostateczny; kompetentny; właściwy; trafny
adhere [ed'hjer] v. lgnąć; należeć; trzymać; przylegać
adhesion [ed'hi:żyn] s. lepkość; zrost; przyleganie; przywieranie do czegoś
adhesive [ed'hi:syw] adj. lepki; przylegający; s. plaster
adjacent [e'dżejsent] adj. przyległy; sąsiedni
adjective ['aeddżyktyw] s. przymiotnik; adj. dodatkowy
adjoin [e'ddżoyn] v. stykać się; sąsiadować; dołączać
adjourn [e'ddże:rn] v. odraczać; przesuwać; przerywać; zakończyć (obrady itp.)
adjust [e'ddżast] v. dostosowywać; uregulować; nastawić; pogodzić
administer [ed'mynyster] v. dawać; sprawować; administrować; zarządzać
administration [ed,myny'strejszyn] s. zarząd; rząd; administracja; ministerstwo; wymiar (kary itp.)
administrative [ed'mynystrejtyw] adj. administracyjny

administrator [ed'mynystrejtor] s. zarządca; administrator
admirable ['aedmerebl] adj. godny podziwu; zachwycający
admiral ['aedmyrel] s. admirał
admiration [aedmy'rejszyn] s. podziw; zachwyt; przedmiot podziwu (zachwytu)
admire [ed'majer] v. podziwiać
admirer [ed'majrer] s. wielbiciel; wielbicielka (kogoś,czegoś)
admissible [ed'mysybl] adj. dopuszczalny; do przyjęcia
admission [ed'myszyn] s. wstęp; dostęp; przyznanie; uznanie; (dopływ); bilet wstępu
admission ticket [ed'myszyn'tykyt] bilet wstąpu
admit [ed'myt] v. wpuszczać; uznać; przyjmować; dopuścić (do); przyznać (rację)
admittance [ed'mytens] s. dostęp; przyjęcie; przyznanie się; wstęp; dopuszczenie
admonish [ed'monysz] v. upominać; ostrzegać; pouczać; strofować; namówić
ado [e'du] s. wrzawa; kłopot; trudności; grymasy; cere giele; narzekania; fochy
adolescence [,aede'lesns] s. młodość (pokwitanie - dojrzałość); wiek młdzieńczy
adolescent [,aede'lesnt] adj. młodociany; dorastający
adopt [e'dopt] adoptować; przyjmować; akceptować; usynawiać; przybierać
adoption [e'dopszyn] s. adopcja; adaptacja; przyjęcie; przysposobienie; akceptacja; wybór; zastosowanie (pomysłu itp.)
adorable [e'do:rebl] adj. godny uwielbienia; bardzo miły
adoration [,aede:rejszyn] s. uwielbienie; wielka miłość
adore [e'do:r] v. czcić; uwielbiać; bardzo lubieć; kochać; oddawać cześć
adorn [e'do:rn] v. zdobić; upiększać; być ozdobą
adrift [e'dryft] adv. na fali; na wodzie bez steru; zdany na

laską losu
adult ['aedalt] adj. dorosły;
dojrzały; s. osoba dorosła
adulterate [ə'dalterejt] v.
fałszować (żywność itp.);
podrabiać; zatruwać
adultery [ə'daltery] s.
cudzołóstwo
advance [ed'waens] v. iść
(posuwać się) naprzód; po-
śpieszać; awansować;
przedkładać; popierać; pożyczać; adj. wysunięty;
wcześniejszy; w przodzie
advanced [ed'waenst] adj.
postępowy; światły; wysu-
nięty naprzód; stary; przedwczesny; czołowy; późny
advanced reservation [ed'waenst
rezerwejszyn] rezerwacja z
góry zamówiona (załatwiona)
advantage [ed'waentydż] s.
korzyść; pożytek; przewaga
advantageous [,aedwaen'tej-
dżes] adj.korzystny; zyskowny
adverb ['aedwe:rb] s. przysłówek
(oznaczający czas, sposób ...)
adversary ['aedwersery] s.
przeciwnik; wróg; oponent
adverse ['aedwe:rs] adj. wrogi;
przeciwny; szkodliwy; niechętny; niekorzystny
advertise ['aedwertajz] v.
ogłaszać; reklamować
advertisement ['edwertysment]
s. ogłoszenie; reklama
advertising ['aedwertajzyng] s.
reklama; ogłoszenie handlowe
advice [ed'wajs] s. rada;
informacje; porada; pouczenie
advisable [ed'wajzebl] adj.
wskazany; rozsądny; ostrożny
advise [ed'wajz] v. radzić;
powiadamiać; pouczać
adviser [ed'wajzer] s. doradca;
radca (prawny etc.)
advocate ['aedwekejt] v.
zalecać; bronić; s. rzecznik;
orędownik; adwokat (ka)
aerial ['eerjel] adj. powietrzny; s.
antena (radiowa etc.)
aeronautics [eere'no:tyks] pl.
aeronautyka; lotnictwo

aeroplane ['eereplejn] s. samolot
aesthetic [i:stetyk] adj.
estetyczny; wrażliwy na
piękno (sztukę itp.)
afar [e'fa:r] adv. daleko; z daleka
affair [e'feer] s. sprawa; interes;
romans; przedsięwzięcie
affect [e'fekt] v.
1. wpływać; oddziaływać;
wzruszać; 2, dotyczyć; udawać (ar-tystę, uczycia itp.)
affected [e'fektyd] adj.
dotknięty; przejęty; sztuczny
affection [e'fekszyn] s. uczucie;
przywiązanie; choroba; mi-
łość; afekt (do)
affectionate [e'fekszynyt] adj.
czuły; kochający; tkliwy (dla);
przywiązany (do)
affidavit [aef'ydejwyt] s.
poręczenie pod przysięgą
affinity [e'fynyty] s.
pokrewieństwo (z kimś);
przyciąganie; powinowactwo
affirm [e'fe:rm] v. potwierdzać;
zapewniać; zaręczać (że)
affirmation [,aefe:r'mejszyn] s.
twierdzenie; oświadczenie;
zapewnienie; zatwierdzenie
(wyroku w sądzie)
affirmative [e'fe:rmetyw] adj.
pozytywny; twierdzący
afflict [e'flykt] v. gnębić
affliction [e'flykszyn] s.
przygnębienie; choroba; ból;
cierpienie; schorzenie
affluence ['aefluens] s. dostatek;
bogactwo; obfitość; natłok
affluent ['aefluent] 1. adj. zamożny; 2. s. dopływ (rzeki)
afford [e'fo:rd] v. zdobyć się;
dostarczyć; stać na coś
affront [e'frant] v. znieważać
aficionado [e'fisienado] s.
entuzjasta (walki byków etc.)
aflame [e'flejm] adv. w ogniu; w
podnieceniu; w zapale
afraid [e'frejd] adj.
przestraszony; wyrażający
rezerwę; w strachu (przed)
African ['aefryken] adj.
afrykański
Afro ['aefro] s. (niby) styl

afrykański (uczesania, ubioru)
after ['a:fte:r] prep. po; za;
odnośnie; według; poniekąd
after all ['a:fte: o:l] prep. jednak;
przecież; mimo wszystko
after that ['a:fte: daet]
następnie; potem; po; za
afternoon ['a:fte:rnu:n] s.
popołudnie; adj. popołudniowy
afterwards ['aftełerdz] adv.
później; potem; następnie
again [e'gen] adv. ponownie;
znowu; na nowo; więcej;
ponadto; nadto; jeszcze
again and again [e'gen end
e,gen] wciąż; ciągle
against [e'genst] prep. przeciw;
wbrew; na; pod; na wypadek
age [ejdż] s. wiek; stulecie;
czasy; epoka; v. starzeć się
aged ['ejdżyd] adj. stary;
sędziwy; wiekowy; w po-
deszłym wieku; zniszczony
age ten [ejdż ten] w wieku lat
dziesięciu; dziesięć lat
agency ['ejdżensy] s. ajencja;
działanie; pośrednictwo
agenda [e'dżenda] s. agenda;
lista; porządek dzienny
agent ['ejdżent] s. pośrednik;
ajent; czynnik; przedstawiciel
aggravate ['aegrewejt] v.
pogarszać; rozjątrzać; denerwować; działać na nerwy
aggression [e'greszyn] s.
napaść; agresja; agresyw-
ność; napastliwość
aggressive [e'gresyw] adj.
napastliwy; zaczepny; agre-
sywny; napastniczy
aggressor [e'grese:r] s.
napastnik; agresor
aghast [e'gaest] adj. przerażony;
ogłupiały; skonsternowany
agile ['aedżyl] adj. zwinny;
obrotny; zręczny; ruchliwy
agitate ['aedżytejt] v. poruszać;
miotać; agitować; wzruszać
agitation [,aedżytejszyn] s.
poruszenie; agitacja; ruch;
podniecenie; wzruszenie
agitator ['aedżytejter] s. agitator;
mieszadło; trzęsarka

agnostic ['aegnostyk] s.
agnostyk; adj. agnostyczny
ago [e'gou] adv. przed; ... temu
agonize ['aegenajz] v. męczyć
się; (za) dręczyć się
agony ['aegeny] s. śmiertelna
męka; katusze; spazm; agonia
agree [e'gri:] v. godzić się;
zgadzać się; uzgadniać
agree about [e'gri: e'baut] v.
zgadzać się co do ...
agree to [e'gri: tu] zgadzać się
(na); wyrażać zgodę (na)
agreeable [e'gri:ebl] adj. zgodny;
miły; chętny; sympatyczny
agreement [e'gri:ment] s. zgoda;
umowa; porozumienie; układ
agricultural [,aegry'kalczeral] adj.
rolniczy; rolny
agriculture [,aegry'kalczer] s.
rolnictwo; uprawa ziemi
agriculturist [,aegry'kalczeryst] s.
rolnik
ague ['ejgju:] s. febra; dreszcze;
malaria; zimnica
ahead [e'hed] adv. naprzód;
dalej; na przedzie; z przodu
aid [ejd] s. pomoc; pomocnik; v.
pomagać; subwencjonować
aide [ejd] s. asystent; pomocnik
AIDS [ejdz] s. nabyta strata
odporności prowadząca do
zapadnięcia na raka, zapalenie
płóc, itd. (Acquired Immune
Defficieny Syndrome)
ailing ['ejlyng] s. choroba
aim [ejm] s. zamiar; cel; v.
celować (w coś); mierzyć;
wymierzyć; zamierzać; skierować; dążyć (do czegoś)
aimless ['ejmlys] adj. bezcelowy
air [eer] s. 1. powietrze; 2. mina;
postawa; wgląd; nastrój
air [eer] v. 1. wietrzyć;
2. obnosić się; nadawać
air base ['eerbejs] s. baza
lotnicza (wojskowa)
air brake ['eer,brejk] s. hamulec
na sprężone powietrze
air-conditioning [,eer-
-ken'dyszynyn] s. klimatyzacja
air compressor [,eer-kem'presor]
s. sprężarka (powietrza)

aircraft ['eer-kra:ft] s. samolot;
lotnictwo (wiedza, flota etc.)
aircraft carrier ['eer-kra:ft
'kaerje:r] s. lotniskowiec
airfield ['eer-fi:ld] s. lotnisko (do
startowania i lądowania)
air force ['eer fo:rs] s. lotnictwo
(wojskowe); siły lotnicze
airline ['eerlajn] s. linia lotnicza
(system transportu lotniczego)
airmail ['eermejl] s. poczta
lotnicza; przesyłka lotnicza
airplane ['eerplejn] s. samolot
airport ['eerpo:rt] s. lotnisko
air raid ['eerejd] atak lotniczy
air show ['eerszou] pokaz
lotniczy (samolotów, lotów)
airsickness ['eersyknys] s.
choroba powietrzna
airtight ['eertajt] adj.
hermetyczny
air traffic ['eer-traefyk] ruch
lotniczy (samolotów, poczty,
pasażerów; ładunków itp.)
airway ['eertej] linia lotnicza
airy ['eery] adj. przewiewny
aisle [ajl] s. przejście; nawa
boczna (kościoła)
ajar [e'dża:r] adv. uchylony; pół
otwarty; nieco otwarty
akin [e'kyn] adj. pokrewny
alacrity [e'laekryty] s. ochota;
gotowość (do); żwawość;
skwapliwość (do czegoś)
alarm [e'la:rm] s. popłoch;
strach; sygnał alarmowy;
trwoga; v. alarmować;
trwożyć; płoszyć
alarm clock [e'la:rm,klok] s.
budzik (zegar alarmowy)
alas ! [e'laes] excl. niestety
alcohol ['aelkehol] s. alkohol;
spirytus (ziemniaczany itp.)
alcoholic [,aelke'holyk] s.
alkoholik; adj. alkoholowy
alcove ['aelkouw] s. altanka;
alkowa; nisza; wnęka
alder ['o:lder] s. olcha; olsza
ale [ejl] s. piwo (gorzkie,
angielskie lub amerykańskie)
alert [e'le:t] adj. czujny; raźny;
żwawy; s. alarm; pogotowie
algae ['aeldżi:] pl. glony; algi

alias ['ejliaes] adv. inaczej; alias;
vel; s. pseudonim (autora itp.)
alibi ['aelybaj] s. alibi; wymówka;
v. usprawiedliwiać się
alien ['ejljen] adj. obcy
alienate ['ejljenejt] v.
odstręczać; odrywać (się);
zrażać; wyobcować (się)
alike [e'lajk] adj. jednakowy;
podobny; adv. tak samo;
jednako; podobnie; zarówno;
także; jednakowo
alimony ['aelimeny] s. alimenty
alive [e'lajw] adj. żywy; żyjący;
ożywiony; pełen życia
all [o:l] adj. & pron. cały;
wszystek; każdy (człowiek);
adv. całkowicie; w pełni;
zupełnie; s. wszystko
all of us [o:l ow as] my
wszyscy; my wszyscy razem
all at once [o:l at łans] wszyscy
na raz; wszyscy jednocześnie
all the better [o:l dy bete:r] tym
lepiej; tym bardziej
all told [o:l told] wszystkiego
razem; razem wziąwszy
alleged [e'ledżd] adj. rzekomy
alleviate [e'li:wjejt] v. łagodzić;
zmniejszać; złagodzić
alley ['aely] s. aleja; przejście;
zaułek; boczna ulica; tor
alliance [e'lajens] s. związek;
sojusz; powinowactwo; sko-
ligacenie; przymierze
allot [e'lot] v. przydzielać;
losować; wyznaczać; wya-
sygnować (na coś, kogoś)
allotment [e'lotment] s. przydział;
działka; asygnata; asygnacja
allow [e'lau] v. pozwalać;
użyczać; uznawać; uwzględniać; przyzwalać (na coś)
allow for [e'lau fo:r] v.
uwzględniać; dawać (czas)
allowance [e'lauens] s. przydział;
pozwolenie; kieszonkowe
alloy ['aeloj] s. stop; próba;
domieszka; stop kilku metali
all-round [o:l-raund] adj.
wszechstronny; uniwersalny
allude [e'lu:d] v. robić aluzje
allure [e'lju:] v. wabić; kusić;

oczarować; nęcić; znęcić;
zwabić; zwabiać (kogoś)
allusion [e'lu:żyn] s. aluzja
(do czegoś); przymówka (do);
przytyk; napomknienie (o)
ally [e'laj] v. sprzymierzać się;
łączyć; połączyć; skoligacić
ally ['aelaj] s. sprzymierzeniec;
sojusznik (wojskowy itp.)
almighty [o:l'majty] adj.
wszechmogący; ogromny;
straszliwy; wszechmocny
almond [am'end] s. migdał
almost ['o:lmoust] adv. prawie;
niemal; jak gdyby; o mało;
ledwo; zaledwie; ledwie
almost never ['o:lmoust 'newer]
prawie nigdy; rzadko kiedy
alms [a:mz] s. jałmużna
aloft [e'loft] adv. wysoko; hen;
w górze; w górę; do góry
alone [e'loun] adj. sam;
samotny; w pojedynkę; sam
jeden; jedyny; osamotniony
along [e'lo:ng] adv. naprzód;
wzdłóż; razem z sobą
alongside [e'lo:ngsajd] adv.
obok; wzdłóż; przy (molu,
burcie, chodniku, itp.)
aloof [e'lu:f] adv. z dala; na
uboczu; z daleka; na dystans
aloud [e'laud] adv. głośno
alphabet ['aelfebyt] s. alfabet
already [o:l'redy] adv. już;
(dużo) wcześniej; poprzednio;
uprzednio; wcześniej niż
also [o:lsou] adv. także; również
altar ['o:lter] s. ołtarz
alter ['o:lter] v. zmieniać
(styl, użytek, itp.); poprawiać; odmienić; przemienić
alteration [o:lte'rejszyn] s.
zmiana; poprawka; przemiana
alternate ['o:lternejt] v. zmieniać
się (kolejno); brać kolejno
alternate ['o:lternyt] adj. co
drugi; na zmianę; kolejny
alternating current [o:lter-
-nejtyn'karent] prąd zmienny
alternative [ol-ter'netywl] 1.
s. alternatywa (wybór) 2. adj.
alternatywny (dający wybór)
although [o:l'zou] conj. chociaż

altitude ['aeltytju:d] s.
wysokość (nad poziomem
morza); wysokie miejsce
altogether [o:lte'gedze:r] adv.
zupełnie; całkowicie
aluminum [e'lumynem] s.
aluminium (metal)
alumna [e'lamne] s. była
studentka; była wychowanka
alumnus [e'lamnes] s. były
student uczelni (uniwersytetu);
były wychowanek (szkoły)
always ['o:lłejz] adv. stale;
zawsze; ciągle; wciąż
am [aem] v. (ja) jestem
amass [e'maes] v. gromadzić
amateur ['aemecze:r] s.
miłośnik; amator; dyletant
amaze [e'mejz] v. zdumiewać;
zadziwiać; wprawić (wpra-
wiać kogoś) w zdumienie
amazement [e'mejzment] s.
zdumienie; osłupienie
amazing [e'mejzyng] adj.
zdumiewający; zadziwiający
ambassador [aem'baesede:r] s.
ambasador; przedstawiciel
amber ['aembe:r] s. bursztyn
ambient ['aembient] adj.
otaczający (coś, kogoś)
ambiguous [aem'bygjues] adj.
dwuznaczny; mętny; nie wyraźny; nie jasny; zagadkowy
ambition [aem'byszyn] s.
ambicja; chęć wybicia się
ambitious [aem'byszes] adj.
(bardzo) ambitny; żądny
ambulance ['aembjulens] s.
ambulans; wóz pogotowia
ambush ['aembusz] s. zasadzka
amen [ej'men] amen; tak jest!
amend [e'mend] v. poprawiać
amendment [e'mendment] s.
poprawa; ulepszenie (czegoś);
uzupełnienie; zmiana
amends [e'mendz] s.
odszkodowanie (za); zadośćuczynienie (za krzywdę)
American [e'meryken] s.
Amerykanin; adj. amerykański
amiable ['ejmjebel] adj. miły;
uprzejmy; sympatyczny
amicable ['aemykebl] adj.

polubowny; przyjacielski
amid [e'myd] prep. wśród;
pośród; między; pomiędzy
amidst [e'mydst] prep. wśród;
pośród; między; pomiędzy
amiss [e'mys] adv. na opak;
błędnie; źle; niefortunnie
ammo ['aemou] s. amunicja
ammunition [,aemju'nyszyn] s.
amunicja (proch, kule itp.)
amnesty [aemnysty] s.
ułaskawienie; amnestia
among [e'mang] prep. wśród;
pomiędzy; między; pośród
amongst [e'mangst] prep.
wśród; pomiędzy; między;
pośród; w otoczeniu
amount [e'maunt] v. wynosić;
s. suma; kwota; wynik
amount to [e'maunt tu] v.
wynosić (w sumie)
ample ['aempl] adj. rozległy;
dostatni; hojny; suty; obfity
amplifier ['aemplyfajer] s.
wzmacniacz; amplifikator
amplify ['aemplyfy] v.
rozszerzać (bardziej); wzmacniać; przesadzać; rozwinąć
amplitude ['aemplytju:d] s.
amplituda; wielkość; zasiąg;
zakres; obfitość
amply ['aemply] adv. obszernie;
szeroko; zupełnie (całkiem,
więcej niż) wystarczająco
amulet ['aemjulyt] s. amulet
amuse [e'mju:z] v. bawić;
ubawić; śmieszyć (kogoś);
zabawić; rozśmieszać
amusement [e'mju:zment] s.
rozrywka; zabawa
amusing [e'mju:zyng] adj. zabawny; śmieszny; pocieszny
an [aen; en] art. jeden; jakiś
anemia [e'ni:mja] s. anemia
anesthetic [e'nystetyk] s.
środek znieczulający
analogous [e'naeloges] adj.
analogiczny; zbieżny
analogy [e'naeledży] s.
podobieństwo; analogia
analysis [e'naelysys] s. analiza
analyze [e'naelajz] v.
analizować; rozpatrywać;

zanalizować (szczegółowo)
anathema [e'naetyma] s. klątwa
anatomize [e'naetemajz] v.
rozbierać; anatomizować
anatomy [e'naetemy] s. ana-
tomia (budowa organizmów)
ancestor ['aensester] s. przodek
ancestry ['aensestry] s.
przodkowie; starożytność
rodu; antenaci rodu
anchor ['aenker] s. kotwica
anchovy ['aenczewy] s. sardela
ancient ['ejnszent] adj.
starodawny; stary; sędziwy;
wiekowy; s. osoba stara
and [aend; end] conj. i; coraz
anecdote ['aenyk,dout] s.
dykteryjka; anegdota
anew [e'nju] adv. na nowo
angel ['ejndżl] s. anioł
anger ['eanger] s. gniew; złość;
v. gniewać; irytować
angina [aendżajna] s. angina
angle ['aengl] s. kąt; narożnik;
kątówka; v. kluczyć
Anglican ['aenglyken] adj.
anglikański (kościół)
Anglo-Saxon [aenglou-saeksen]
adj. anglo-saski (język itp.)
angry [aengry] adj. zagniewany
anguish [aenglysz] s. udręka;
męka; udręczenie; boleść;
ból (fizyczny, psychiczny)
angular ['aengjuler] adj. kanciasty; narożny; kątowy; gra-
niasty; szczupły; bez wdzięku
animal ['aenyml] s. zwierzę;
stworzenie; adj. zwierzęcy
animate ['aenymejt] v. ożywiać;
adj. ożywiony; żywy
animated cartoon ['aenymejtyd
'ka:rtu:n] film rysunkowy;
kreskówka (filmowa)
animation [,aeny'mejszyn] s.
ożywianie; ożywienie; ży-
wość; natchnienie
animosity [,aeny'mosyty] s.
uraza; niechęć; animozja
ankle ['aenkl] s. kostka u stopy;
staw między stopą i łydką
annex ['aeneks] v. przyłączać;
wcielać; s. przybudówka; załącznik (do czegoś)

annihilate [e'najelejt] v.
unicestwić; niszczyć; niweczyć; zniszczyć zupełnie
anniversary [,aeny've:rsery] s.
rocznica; adj doroczny (obchód tego samego zdarzenia)
annotation ['aene'tejszyn] s.
wąga; komentarz; przypis
announce [e'nauns] v.
zapowiadać; ogłaszać (pu-
blicznie); oznajmiać (coś)
announcement [e'naunsment] s.
zapowiedź; zawiadomienie
announcer [e'naunser] s.
1. zapowiadacz; 2. (radio)
speaker; konferansjer
annoy [e'noj] v. dokuczać;
drażnić; nękać (stale); trapić; martwić (ciągle)
annoyance [e'nojens] s. udręka;
przykrość; irytacja; kłopot
annoyed [e'nojd] adj.
rozgniewany; rozdrażniony;
strapiony; skłopotany
annual ['aenjuel] adj. coroczny;
s. rocznik; jednorocznik
annuity [e'njuyty] s. renta
roczna; renta dożywotnia
annul [e'nal] v. unieważniać;
anulować; skasować; pozbawić (czegoś); kasować
anodyne ['aenedajn] s. anodyna;
środek od bólu, łagodzący
anomalous [e'nomeles] adj.
nienormalny; nietypowy
anonym ['aenenym] s. anonim
anonymous [e'nonymes] adj.
bezimienny; anonimowy
another [e'na<u>dz</u>er] adj. & pron.
drugi; inny; jeszcze jeden
another time [e'na<u>dz</u>er,tajm]
kiedy indziej; innym razem
answer ['aenser] s. odpowiedź
answer for ['aenser fo:r] v.
odpowiadać za (przed kimś)
ant [aent] s. mrówka
antagonist [aen'taegenyst] s.
przeciwnik; przeciwniczka
antagonize [aen'taego'najz] v.
zrażać; narażać; zwalczać
antelope ['aentyloup] s. antylopa
anterior [aen'tierjer] adj.
poprzedni; uprzedni; w przo-

dzie; wcześniejszy; przed-
anthem ['aen<u>t</u>em] s. hymn
narodowy (religijny)
anti ['aenty] pre. przeciw-
anti-aircraft ['aentaj'e:rkra:ft] adj.
przeciwlotniczy (obronny)
antibiotic ['aentybajotyk] s.
antybiotyk (przeciw bakteriom)
antic ['aentyk] adj. dziwaczny;
groteskowy; s. figiel; dziwac-
twa; błazeństwo; głupi kawał
anticipate [aen'tysypejt] v.
przewidywać; uprzedzać
anticipation [aen'tysypejszyn]
s.uprzedzenie; przewidywanie;
przyśpieszenie; oczekiwanie
anticlimax ['aenty'klajmaeks] s.
rozczarowanie; zawód; spadek
anticyclone [,aenty'sajkloun] s.
antycyklon; wyż (atmosf.)
antidote ['aentydout] s. odtrutka;
antydotum (zapobiegające złu)
antifreeze ['aentyfri:z] s.
mieszanka niemarznąca
antiknock ['aentynok] s.
mieszanka przeciwstukowa
antipathy [aen'type<u>t</u>y] s. odraza;
niechęć (do kogoś)
antiquated ['aentyklejtyd] adj.
przestarzały; staroświecki
antique [aen'ti:k] adj. stary;
starożytny; staromodny
antiquity [aen'tykłyty] s.
starożytność; zabytki
antiseptic [aenty'septyk] adj.
antyseptyk; przeciwgnilny
antlers ['aentlerz] pl. rogi (np.
jelenia); rozgałęzione rogi
anvil ['aenwyl] s. kowadło
anxiety [aeng'zajety] s.niepokój;
troska; obawa; pragnienie
anxious ['aenkszes] adj.
zaniepokojony; zabiegający;
pragnący (usilnie czegoś)
anxious about ['aenkszes e'baut]
troskliwy o ...; niepokojący
się o ...; zabiegający o ...
anxious for ['aenkszes fo:r]
pragnący bardzo czegoś
anxious to ['aenkszes tu]
pragnący żeby; mający
ochotę na; chcący (czegoś)
any ['eny] pron. jakikolwiek;

któryś; jakiś; żaden; lada;
byle; jakaś; któraś; żadna
any farther ['eny fa:r<u>dz</u>er] trochę
dalej; nieco (jeszcze) dalej
any more ['eny mo:r] trochę
więcej; teraz; obecnie
anybody ['eny'body] pron. ktoś;
ktokolwiek; każdy; nikt
anyhow ['enyhau] adv. w każdym razie; jakkolwiek
anyone ['enyłan] pron.
ktokolwiek; każdy; ktoś; nikt
anything ['eny<u>tyng</u>] pron. coś;
cokolwiek; wszystko (oprócz);
nic; cokolwiek bądź
anything else ['eny<u>tyng</u> els]
jeszcze coś; coś więcej
anyway ['enyłej] adv. w każdym
razie; jakkolwiek; byle jak
anywhere ['enyhłeer] adv.
gdziekolwiek; byle gdzie;
nigdzie; (colloq.) at all
apart [e'pa:rt] adv. osobno;
niezależnie; na boku; od siebie
apart from [e'pa:rt,from]
niezależnie od ...; poza;
oprócz; prócz; inny niż
apartment [e'pa:rtment] s.
mieszkanie; izba; pokój
apartment house [e'pa:rtment
,haus] blok mieszkalny;
kamienica (czynszowa)
apathetic [aepe'<u>t</u>etyk] adj.
apatyczny; obojętny; bez
uczuć; nieczuły; bierny
ape [ejp] s. małpa (bezogonowa);
v. małpować; naśladować
(ruchy etc.); błaznować
apex ['ejpeks] s. szczyt; czubek;
wierzchołek; kulminacja
apiary ['ejpjery] s. pasieka
apiece [e'pi:s] adv. na osobę; od
sztuki; za sztukę; każdy
aplomb [e'plom] s. pewność
siebie; opanowanie; zimna
krew (wobec trudności)
apologize [e'poledżajz] v.
usprawiedliwiać; przepraszać
apology [e'poledży] s.
usprawiedliwienie; obrona
(ideologii etc.); przeprosiny
apoplexy ['aepepleksy] s.
apopleksja; udar

apostle [e'posl] s. apostoł
apostolic [,aepe'stolyk] adj.
apostolski; papieski
apostrophe [e'postrefy] s.
apostrof; apostrofa
appall [e'po:l] v. przerażać
apparatus [aepe'rejtes] s. aparat;
urządzenie; przyrząd; organ
apparent [e'paerent] adj. jawny;
pozorny; oczywisty; widoczny
appeal [e'pi:l] v. apelować;
odwoływać się (do wyższej
instancji); uciekać się do
appeal to [e'pi:l tu] v. zwracać
się do ...; zwracać się z
apelem; apelować do ...
appear [e'pier] v. ukazywać się;
zjawiać się; pokazywać się
appearance [e'pierens] s.
(zewnętrzny) wygląd; pozór;
wystąpienie; zjawienie się
appease [e'pi:z] v. łagodzić;
uśmierzać; zaspakajać; ulegać (prośbom); ugłaskać
append [e'pend] v. dołączać;
doczepiać; dodawać; zawieszać; przyczepić
appendicitis [ependy'sajtys] s.
zapalenie wyrostka robaczko-
wego (ślepej kiszki)
appendix [e'pendyks] s. dodatek;
uzupełnienie; ślepa kiszka
appetite ['aepitajt] s. apetyt
appetizing ['aepitajzing] adj.
apetyczny; smakowity
applaud [e'plo:d] v. oklaskiwać;
klaskać; bić brawo; przy-
klasnąć; (po)chwalić
applause [e'plo:z] s. aplauz;
oklaski; poklask; pochwała;
aprobata; klaskanie
apple ['aepl] s. jabłko
apple-pie ['aeplpaj] s. placek
jabłkowy; szarlotka
applesauce ['aepl so:s] s. puree
z jabłek; (slang) nonsens
apple tree ['aepltri:] s jabłoń
appliance [e'plajens] s. przyrząd;
urządzenie; akcesoria
applicant ['aeplykent] s. petent;
zgłaszający się; kandydat
application [,aeply'kejszyn] s.
podanie; użycie; zasto-

-sowanie; przykładanie;
pilność; sposób używania
apply [e'plaj] v. używać;
stosować; odnosić się; naciskać; być pilnym; prosić o
apply for [e'plaj fo:r] v. starać
się o ...; wnosić podanie o
apply to [e'plaj tu] v. zwracać
się do ...; zgłaszać się do (o
coś); stosować się
appoint [e'point] v. mianować;
wyznaczać; ustanawiać;
ustalić (datę, miejsce etc.)
appointment [e'pointment] s.
nominacja; oznaczenie czasu i
miejsca; umówione spotkanie
apportion [e'po:rszyn]
v. wyznaczyć; wydzielać;
przydzielać; wydać udziały
appraise [e'prejz] v. oceniać;
szacować; ustalić cenę
appreciate [e'pri:szjejt] v. cenić
wysoko; zyskiwać na war-
tości; ocenić; oszacować;
docenić; dobrze myśleć o
appreciation [e'pri:szjejszyn] s.
ocena; uznanie; wzrost
wartości; zrozumienie
czegoś; uznanie (jakości)
apprehend [,aepry'hend] v.
ująć; pojmać; rozumieć
apprehension [,aepry'henszyn] s.
obawa; pojęcie; aresztowanie;
lęk; zrozumienie; wrażenie
apprehensive [,aepry'hensyw]
adj. obawiający się; pojętny
apprentice [e'prentys] s.
czeladnik; uczeń; terminator
apprenticeship [e'prentsszyp] s.
termin; nauka rzemiosła
approach [e'proucz] v. zbliżać
się; podchodzić; s. dostęp
approach road [e'proucz,roud]
droga (rampa) dojazdowa
appropriate [e'prouprjejt] adj.
właściwy; odpowiedni; stosowny; przywłaszczyć sobie
appropriation [e'prouprejszyn] s.
asygnowanie; przywłasz-
czenie; przeznaczenie; kredyty;
przejęcie na własność
approval [e'pru:wel] s. aprobata;
uznanie; zatwierdzenie

approximate [e'proksymyt] adj.
zbliżony; przybliżony; mniej
więcej; v. zbliżać (się); być
około; przybliżać (coś)
apricot ['ejprykot] s. morela
April ['ejprel] s. kwiecień
apron ['ejpren] s. fartuch; płyta
przednia; przedpole
apropos [aepre'pou] adv. do tego
celu; w związku z tym
apt [aept] v. mieć skłonność
apt to [aept tu] v. być
skłonnym do ...; często coś
robić; być zdolnym
aquarium [e'kłerjem] s. akwarium
aquatic [e'kłaetyk] adj. wodny
aquatic sports [e'kłaetyk sports]
sporty wodne (żeglarstwo)
aqueduct ['aekłydakt] s.
wodociąg; akwedukt (rzym-ski
wraz z budowlą)
aquiline ['aekłylajn] adj. orli
Arabic [ae'rebyk] adj. arabski
arable ['aerebl] adj. orny
arbitrary ['a:rbytrary] adj.
dowolny; samowolny
arbor ['a:rber] s. altanka; wał
napędowy; oś maszyny; drzewo (krzaki) cieniste
arc [a:rk] s. łuk
arc lamp [a:rk lemp] lampa
łukowa (jarzeniowa)
arcade [a:r'kejd] s. arkada;
podcienie; przejście kryte
arch [a:rcz] s. łuk; sklepienie;
podbicie; v. tworzyć łuk
arch [a:rcz] adj. chytry;
wierutny; arcy...; figlarny
archaeologist [a:rky'oledżyst] s.
archeolog; badacz wykopalisk
archeology [a:rky'oledży] s.
archeologia
archaic [a:rkejyk] adj. archaiczny;
przestarzały; staroświecki
archangel ['a:rkejndżel] s.
archanioł; anioł wysokiej rangi
archbishop ['a:rczbyszep] s.
arcybiskup
archer ['a:rczer] s. łucznik
archery ['a:rczery] s. łucznictwo
(jako sztuka); łuki i strzały
architect ['a:rkytekt] s. architekt;
twórca; budowniczy

architecture ['a:rkytekczer] s.
architektura; styl budowy
archives ['a:rkajwz] pl. archiwa;
archiwum (miejsce i zbiory)
archway ['a:rcztej] s. sklepione
przejście; brama; łuk
arctic ['a:rktyk] adj. arktyczny;
polarny; bardzo zimny
ardent ['a:rdent] adj. rozpalony;
prążący; płonący; gorliwy
ardor ['a:rder] s. żar;
żarliwość; gorliwość; zapał
arduous ['a:rdżues] adj.
mozolny; wytrwały; stromy;
żmudny; wymagający wysiłku
are [a:r] v. są; jesteś; jesteście
area ['e:rje] s. obszar; zakres;
powierzchnia; teren; okolica;
strefa; część (domu, lasu)
Argentine ['a:rdżentajn] adj.
argentyński; z Argentyny
argot ['a:rgou] s. żargon
(złodziei, włóczęgów etc.)
argue ['a:rgju:] v. wykazywać;
rozumować; spierać się;
rozpatrywać; dowodzić;
udowadniać; kłócić się
argument ['a:rgjument] s.
argument; dowód; sprzeczka;
spór; debata; podsumowanie
argumentation [,a:rgjumen
'tejszyn] s. roztrząsanie;
argumentacja; rozumowanie;
debata; proces argumentacji
arid ['aeryd] adj. suchy; jałowy;
oschły; wypalony; spieczony
arise, arose, arisen [e'rajz;
e'rouz; e'ryzn]
arise [e'rajz] v. powstawać;
wstawać; wynikać; nada-
rzyć się; stać się
aristocrat ['aeryste,kraet] s.
arystokrata; arystokratka
arithmetic ['aeryt'metyk] s.
rachunki; arytmetyka; adj.
arytmetyczny; rachunkowy
ark [a:rk] s. arka; skrzynia
arm [a:rm] s. ramię; odnoga;
konar; rękaw; poręcz
arm [a:rm] s. broń (rodzaj);
uzbrojenie; v. uzbroić; opan-
cerzyć; nastawiać (zapłon);
przygotowywać się do walki

armament ['a:rmement] s.
uzbrojenie; zbrojenia; siły
zbrojne; wyposażenie wojska
armament race ['a:rmement,rejs]
wyścig zbrojeń
armchair [,a:rm'cze:r] s. fotel
armistice ['a:rmystys] s.
zawieszenie broni; rozejm
armor ['a:rmer] s. zbroja;
opancerzenie; v. zbroić w
płyty pancerne; opancerzać
armored car ['a:rmerd,ka:r]
samochód pancerny
arm-twisting ['a:rm'tłystyn]
napór na (kogoś); (wykrę-
canie ręki); nagabywanie
kogoś; narzucanie się
arms ['a:rmz] pl. broń;
uzbrojenie; herby; herb
arms race ['a:rmz,rejs] s.
wyścig zbrojeń
army ['a:rmy] s. wojsko; armia
aroma [e'roume] s. aromat
arose [e'rouz] v. powstał; wstał;
wynikł; zob. arise
around [e'raund] prep. dookoła;
naokoło; wokoło; adv. wokół;
tu i tam; około; wszędzie
arousal [e'rauzel] s. pobudzenie
do czynu (działania)
arouse [e'rauz] v. pobudzić;
budzić; wzniecać (uczucia)
arraign [e'rejn] v. pozwać;
oskarżyć; atakować pogląd
arrange [e'rejndż] v. układać;
szykować; porządkować;
ustalać; komponować
arrangement [e'rejndżment] s.
układ; ułożenie się; urządzenie; zaaranżowanie; porządek; szyk; plan; układ
array [e'rej] v. szykować;
przybrać; rozmieszczać; s.
szyk (bojowy); szereg; uszeregowanie; wystawa; strój
arrears [e'rierz] pl. zaległości;
długi; zaległe płace (płatności)
arrest [e'rest] s. areszt;
aresztowanie; zatrzymanie; v.
aresztować; zatrzymywać (i
sprawdzić); wstrzymywać;
przyciągać (uwagę etc.)
arrival [e'rajwel] s. przyjazd;

przybysz; rzecz nadeszła
arrive [e'rajw] v. przybyć;
  dojść; osiągnąć; wspólnie
  ustalać; zdobyć sławę etc.
arrive at [e'rajw,aet] v. dojść
  do ...; wspólnie ustalać
arrogance ['aeregens] s.
  zarozumiałość; buta;
  arogancja; wyniosłość
arrogant ['aeregent] adj. butny;
  arogancki; wyniosły
arrow ['aerou] s. strzała
arrow head ['aerou hed] s. grot
arse [a:rs] s. vulg. rzyć; zadek;
  dupa; dupsko
arsenal ['a:rsynl] s. arsenał
arsenic ['a:rsnyk] s. arszenik;
  arsen (pierwiastek chemiczny);
  ['a:rsenyk] adj. arsenowy
arson ['a:rsen] s. podpalenie
  (zbrodnia); podpalenie
art [a:rt] s. sztuka; chytrość;
  zręczność; rzemiosło; fortel
arterial [a:r'tyrjal] adj. tętniczy;
  magistralny; artaryjny
arterial road [a:r'tyrjal,roud]
  magistrala; główna szosa
artery [a:rtery] s. arteria; tętnica;
  arteria ruchu; magistrala
artful ['a:rtfull] adj. chytry;
  zręczny; pomysłowy; dowcipny; sprytny; cwany
artichoke ['a:rty,czouk] s.
  karczoch (jarzyna)
article ['a:rtykl] s. rodzajnik;
  artykuł; warunek; paragraf
  (dokumentu); temat
articulate [a:rtykjulejt] v.
  wyrażać jasno; artykułować;
  adj. artykułowany; wyraźny;
  łączony stawami; wygadany
artifact [,a:rty'faekt] s. wytwór
  ludzkiej ręki (jakikolwiek)
artificial [,a:rty'fyszel] adj.
  sztuczny; udany; symulowany
artillery [a:r'tylery] s. artyleria
artisan ['a:rtyzaen] s.
  wysokiej klasy rzemieślnik
artist ['a:rtist] s. artysta; artystka
artiste [a:r'ty:st] s. artysta;
  odtwórca; artysta estradowy
artless ['artlys] adj. niewinny;
  niedołężny; szczery; otwarty

as [aez; ez] adv. pron. conj. jak;
  tak; co; jako; jaki; skoro;
  żeby; choć; z (dniem, rokiem)
as ... as [ez ... ez] tak jak
as far as [ez fa:r ez] co do
as many [ez meny] tak wiele
as well [ez łel] również
as well as [ez łel ez] jak także;
  tak jak; jak również
as for [ez fo:r] co się tyczy
asbestos [aez'bestes] s. azbest
ascend [e'send] v. piąć się;
  iść w górę; wznosić się;
  wracać w przeszłość; wstępować (na tron); wsiąść na
ascension [e'senszyn] s.
  wznoszenie się; święcenie
  Wniebowstąpienia
ascent [e'sent] s. wzlot; wzrost;
  stok; postęp; wchodzenie
ascertain [aeser'tejn] v.
  stwierdzać; ustalać; konstatować; upewniać się
ascetic [e'setyk] s. asceta; adj.
  ascetyczny; surowo odmawia-
  jący sobie; ograniczający się
ascribe [e'skrajb] v. przypisywać; przypisać (coś
  komuś); przydzielić do
aseptic ['eseptyk] adj. jałowy;
  wyjałowiony; aseptyczny
ash [aesz] s. popiół; jesień
ashamed [e'szejmd] adj.
  zawstydzony; zażenowany
ashamed of [e'szejmd ow] adj.
  wstydzący się czegoś
ash can [aesz kaen] wiadro na
  śmieci; wiadro na popiół
ashen ['aeszen] adj. popielaty
ashes ['aeszyz] pl. popioły
ashore [e'szo:r] adv. na brzeg;
  na brzegu; na ląd; na lądzie
ash tray ['aesztrej] s. popielniczka (dla palaczy)
Ash Wednesday [,aesz'łenzdy]
  Środa Popielcowa
Asian [,ejż,jen] adj. Azjata;
  Azjatka; azjatycki; azjatycka
Asiatic [,ejży'atyk] adj. azjatycki
aside [e'sajd] adv. na stronę; na
  stronie; na boku; na uboczu
aside from [e'sajd,from] adv.
  oprócz; z wyjątkiem; poza;

prócz; w rezerwie; w zapasie
asinine ['aesynajn] adj. ośli;
głupi (jak osioł); idiotyczny
ask [ae:sk] v. pytać; zapytywać; prosić; zapraszać
ask a question ['ae:sk ej'kłesz-
czyn] v. stawiać pytanie; pytać; dowiadywać się o ...
ask to dinner ['ae:sk tu'dyner]
zapraszać na obiad
ask for ['ae:sk fo:r] prosić o ...
askance [as'kaens] adv. z ukosa;
zezem; niepewnie; podejrzliwie
askew [es'kju:] adv. krzywo;
skośnie; z ukosa; adj. krzywy
aslant [es'sla:nt] adv. ukośnie;
skośnie; na ukos; w poprzek
asleep [e'sli:p] adv. we śnie;
adj. śpiący; zdrętwiały;
ścierpły; nudny; martwy
asparagus [es'paereges] s.
szparag (jarzyna)
aspect ['aespekt] s. aspekt;
wygląd; wyraz; faza; postać;
strona; mina; przejaw; strona
(fasada) domu; zapatrywanie
aspen ['aespen] s. osika; osina
asphalt ['aesfalt] s. asfalt
aspire [es'pajer] v. dążyć;
marzyć; wzdychać do; mieć
aspiracje; być ambitnym
aspire after [es'pajer'a:fter]
aspirować; dążyć do (cze-
goś); mieć aspiracje żeby ...
ass [aes] s. osioł; wulg. dupa
assail [e'sejl] v. napadać (brutalnie); przystępować; atakować (argumentami); uderzać
assailant [e'sejlent] s. napastnik
assassin [e'saesyn] s. morderca
(najęty); zamachowiec
assassinate [e'saesynejt] v.
zamordować (podstępnie);
dokonać zamachu (na ...)
assassination [e,saesy'nejszyn]
s. morderstwo; zabójstwo;
zamach; skrytobójstwo
assault [e'sa:lt] s. napad; atak;
zgwałcenie; v. atakować; bić
assemblage [e'semblydż] s.
zebranie; zbiór; zmontowanie
assemble [e'sembl] v. zbierać;
montować; nagromadzać;

złożyć; wpasować (w coś)
assembly [e'sembly] s. zebranie;
zbiórka; montaż; legislatura
assembly line [e'sembly,lajn]
taśma montażowa; linia montażowa (w fabryce etc.)
assent [e'sent] s. zgoda; pogodzenie się; v. zgadzać się;
uznawać; wyrażać zgodę
assent to [e'sent tu] v. zgadzać
się na coś; zatwierdzać coś
assert [e'se:rt] v. twierdzić;
upominać się; dowieść; stawiać się; potwierdzić
assess [e'ses] v. szacować;
oceniać; wymierzać; opodatkować; nałożyć podatek na;
określić wysokość podatku
assets ['aesets] pl. własności;
aktywa (ściągalne); wartoś-
ciowi pracownicy
assign [e'sajn] v. przydzielać;
ustalać; odnosić; przekazywać; przypisywać (do pracy)
assignment [e'sajnment] s.
przydzielenie; przypisanie;
przekazanie; przydział; podział
assimilate [e'symylejt] v.
upodabniać; wcielać; wchłaniać; asymilować; przyswajać sobie; strawić
assist [e'syst] v. pomagać;
brać udział; być przy
assistance [e'systens] s. pomoc
(pieniężna); asysta; wsparcie
assistant [e'systent] s. asystent;
pomocnik; adj. pomocniczy
assizes [e'sajzyz] pl. okresowe
sesje sądu (wyjazdowe) w
Anglii (ich czas i miejsce)
associate [e'souszjejt] s. towarzysz; wspólnik; partner;
sprzymierzeniec; rzecz zwią-
zana z czymś; część (cze-
goś); v. łączyć; obcować;
kojarzyć; brać do spółki; adj.
towarzyszący (podrzędny)
association [e,souszy'ejszyn] s.
łączenie; współpraca; kojarzenie; przyłączenie się;
związek; organizacja
assort [e'so:rt] v. sortować;
dobierać; obcować; klasy-

-fikować; porządkować
assorted [e'so:rtyd] adj. dobrany;
posortowany; mieszany
assortment [e'so:rtment] s.
asortyment; wybór; sorto-
wanie; klasyfikacja
assume [e'sju:m] v. zakładać;
obejmować; przybierać; przypuszczać; wdziewać; uda-
wać; przedsiębrać; brać
assumption [e'sampszyn] s.
założenie; przypuszczenie;
przybranie; objęcie (władzy);
udawanie; symulowanie
assurance [e'szu:rens] s.
zapewnienie; pewność; za-
ufanie; ubezpieczenie
assure [e'szu:r] v. zapewniać;
ubezpieczać; zabezpieczać
assured [e'szu:rd] adj. pewny
(siebie); s. ubezpieczony
asthma [aesma] s. dusznica;
astma; dychawica (chroniczna)
astigmatic [,aestyg'maetyk] adj.
astygmatyczny
astir [e'ste:r] adv. poruszony; w
ruchu; na nogach; ożywiony
astonish [es'tonysz] v. zadziwiać; zdumiewać; zdziwić;
wprawić w zdumienie
astonished [es'tonyszt] adj.
zdumiony; bardzo zdziwiony
astonishment [es'tonyszment] s.
zdumienie; zdziwienie
astray [es'trej] adv. na błędną
drogę; na bezdrożu; na
manowce; w błąd
astride [es'trajd] adv. okrakiem;
rozstawionymi nogami
astringent [es'tryndżent] adj.
ściągający; surowy; wstrzymujący; s. środek wstrzymujący
astrodome ['aestre,doum] s.
astrokopuła (nad stadionem
sportowym)
astrologer [es'troledżer] s.
astrolog
astronomer [es'tronemer] s.
astronom
astronaut ['aestreno:t] s.
astronauta; kosmonauta
astute [es'tu:t] adj. bystry;
przebiegły; wnikliwy

asunder [e'sander] adv.
oddzielnie; na boki; na strony
asylum [e'sajlem] s. azyl (polityczny etc.); schronisko; przytułek; schronienie
at [aet; et] prep. w; na; u; przy;
pod; z; za; do; o; po
ate [ejt] v. jadłem; jadłeś; jadł
etc.; zob. eat
athlete ['eatli:t] s. atleta; siłacz;
sportowiec; wyczynowiec
athletic ['aet̲'letyk] adj.
atletyczny; sportowy
athletics [aet̲'letyks] pl. atletyka;
sport; wychowanie fizyczne
Atlantic [et'laentyk] adj.
atlantycki; s. Atlantyk
atlas ['aetles] s. atlas
atmosphere ['aetmesfier] s.
atmosfera; otoczenie; nastrój
atoll ['aetol] s. atol
atom ['aetem] s. atom
atom bomb ['aetem bom] s.
bomba atomowa
atomic [e'tomyk] adj. atomowy
atomic age [e'tomyk ejdż] epoka
atomowa; era atomowa
atomic pile [e'tomyk pajl] stos
atomowy; stos jądrowy
atomic weight [e'tomyk łejt]
ciężar atomowy
atomize ['aetemajz] v. rozbijać
na atomy; rozpylać
atomizer ['aetemajzer] s.
rozpylacz (cieczy, płynu)
atone [e'toun] v. odpokutować;
okupić; załagodzić
atrocious [e'trouszes] adj.
potworny; okropny; skandaliczny; bardzo okrutny; zły
atrocity [e'trosyty] s.
okrucieństwo; okrutny czyn;
ohyda; (colloq.) obrzydliwość
attach [e'taecz] v.
przywiązywać; przyczepiać;
przydzielać; łączyć;
przymocowywać; nalepiać
attachment [e'taeczment] s.
załącznik; przymocowanie;
więź; przywiązanie
attack [e'taek] v. napadać;
atakować; s. atak; uderzenie
attempt [e'tempt] v. usiłować;

czynić zamach; próbować; s.
próba; usiłowanie; zamach
attend [e'tend] v. uczęszczać;
leczyć; obsługiwać; towarzyszyć; iść razem
attendance [e'tendens] s.
obsługa; opieka; uczęszczanie
attendant [e'tendent] s. obecny;
służący; adj. towarzyszący
attention [e'tenszyn] s. uwaga;
uprzejmość; troska; opieka
attentive [e'tentyw] adj.
uważny; gorliwy; uprzejmy;
pilny; przywiązany
attest [e'test] v. poświadczyć;
stwierdzać; zalegalizować
attic ['aetyk] s. poddasze;
attyka; strych
attitude ['aetitu:d] s. postawa;
ustosunkowanie się; poza
attorney [e'te:rny] s. pełnomocnik; adwokat; prawnik
attract [e'traekt] v. przyciągać;
zwabić; być pociągającym;
zdobywać uznanie; urzekać
attraction [e'traekszyn] s.
przyciąganie; powab; urok;
atrakcja; siła przyciągania
attractive [e'traektyw] adj.
pociągający; przyciągający;
miły; urzekający
attribute ['aetrybju:t] s. przymiot;
cecha; właściwość
attribute [e'trybju:t] v.
przypisywać komuś (cze-
muś); odnosić do czegoś
attrition [e'tryszyn] s.
wyniszczenie; ścieranie;
skrucha; zużycie; starcie
auburn ['o:bern] adj. (barwa)
kasztanowa; złotobrązowa
auction ['o:kszyn] s. licytacja;
(publiczna) aukcja
auction off ['o:kszyn of] v.
licytować; sprzedawać na
licytacji; wystawiać na
(publiczną) licytację
audacious [o:'dejszes] adj.
odważny; śmiały; zuchwały
audacity [o:'daesyty] s.
śmiałość; odwaga; zuchwa-
łość; bezczelność
audible ['o:dybel] adj. słyszalny;

odbierany słuchem
audience ['o:djens] s. słuchacze
publiczność; audiencja
audit ['o:dyt] s. sprawdzenie
rachunków; rozliczenie; v.
kontrolować rachunki
aught [a:t] s. coś; nic; zero
August ['o:gest] s. sierpień
august ['o:gast] adj. wyniosły;
dostojny; majestatyczny
aunt [aent] s. ciotka; wujenka;
stryjenka
aurora [o:'ro:re] s. brzask;
jutrznia; jutrzenka; zorza
polarna; (rzymska bogini)
austere [o:s'tier] adj. surowy;
poważny; prosty; czysto użytkowy; bez ozdób; ponury
austerity [o:s'teryty] s.
surowość; powaga; prosto-
ta; srogość; charakter czysto
użytkowy; zaciskanie pasa
Australian [o:s'trejljen] adj.
australijski; s. Australijczyk
Austrian ['o:strjen] adj.
austriacki; s. Austriak
authentic [o:'tentyk] adj.
autentyczny; prawdziwy
author ['o:ter] s. autor; pisarz;
sprawca; twórca (dzieł etc.)
authoritative [o:'torytejtyw] adj.
stanowczy; miarodajny
authority [o:'toryty] s. władza;
autorytet; znaczenie; powaga;
moc rozkazywania; urząd
authorize ['o:terajz] v. upoważniać; zatwierdzać; dać
prawo (urząd); aprobować
authorship ['o:terszyp] s.
autorstwo; zawód pisarza
autobiography ['o:tebaj'ogrefy] s.
autobiografia
autograph ['o:tegraef] s. podpis;
autograf; podpis własny
automat ['o:temaet] n. automat;
automatem na monety do
sprzedaży (porcji) jedzenia
automatic [,o:te'maetyk] adj.
automatyczny; machinalny
automation [,o:te'mejszyn] s.
automatyzacja; robotyzacja
automobile ['o:temeby:l] s.
samochód; auto; sl. wóz

autumn ['o:tem] s. jesień
auxiliary [o:g'zyljery] adj.
pomocniczy; pomocny
avail [e'wejl] v. pomagać;
znaczyć; być przydatny
available [e'wejlebl] adj.
dostępny; osiągalny
avalanche ['aewelaencz] s.
lawina; v. spadać lawiną
avarice ['aewerys] s. chciwość;
skąpstwo; sknerstwo
avaricious [,aewe'ryszes] adj.
chciwy na pieniądze; skąpy
avenue ['aewynju:] s. bulwar;
aleja; ulica; dojazd; dojście
average ['aewerydż] adj. przeciętny; średni; s. średnia;
wartość średnia; przeciętna; v. osiągać średnio; obliczać średnią; wypośrodko-
wywać; pracować przeciąt-
nie, w średnim tempie
averse [e'we:rs] adj. niechętny;
czujący odrazę; przeciwny
aversion [e'werżyn] s. odraza;
niechęć; powód odrazy
avert [e'we:rt] v. odwracać (np.
myśli, oczy); oddalić (cios)
aviation [,ejwy'ejszyn] s. lotnictwo; aeronautyka
aviator ['ejwyejter] s. lotnik
avid ['ewyd] adj. chciwy;
zachłanny; bardzo chętny
avoid [e'woyd] v. unikać;
uchylać się; stronić
avow [e'wau] v. wyznawać
avowal [e'wauel] s. wyznanie;
przyznanie się; zeznanie
await [e'łejt] v. czekać;
oczekiwać; być w ocze-
kiwaniu; być zagrożonym
awake; awoke; awoke [e'łejk;
e'łouk; e'łouk]
awake [e'łejk] v. budzić się;
otwierać oczy na ...; adj.
czujny; przebudzony; na jawie
awaken [e'łejkn] v. budzić;
uświadamiać komuś (ko-
goś); adj. czynny; obudzony
award [e'ło:rd] v. przysądzać;
wyznaczać; s. nagroda;
zapłata; grzywna sądowa
aware [e'łeer] adj. świadomy

away [e'łej] adv. precz; z dala
awe [o:] s. lęk; nabożna cześć
awful ['o:ful] adj. straszny;
budzący lęk i szacunek
awhile ['ehłajl] adv. na krótko;
przez chwilę; na chwilę; na
króciutko; na krótki czas
awkward ['o:kłerd] adj. niezgrabny; niezdarny; kłopotliwy; nieporęczny; zakłopotany; trudny
(do prowadzenia); niewygodny
awning ['o:nyng] s. dach z
płótna; markiza; zasłona; stora
awoke [e'łouk] v. zbudzony;
proszę zobaczyć: awake
awry [e'raj] adv. skośnie;
krzywo; na opak; adj. krzywy;
błędny; opaczny; wypaczony
ax [aeks] s. siekiera; topór; v.
obcinać siekierą; redukować
axe [aeks] = ax
axes [aeksyz] pl. osie; siekiery
axis ['aeksys] s. oś; ośka
axle ['aeksel] s. oś (koła); ośka
(łącząca tylnie koła wozu)
azimuth ['aezymet] s. azymut
azure ['aeżer] s. błękit; lazur;
adj. błękitny; lazurowy

B

b [bi] b; druga litera alfabetu
angielskiego
babble ['baebl] v. paplać;
gadać; s. paplanina; gadanina
babe [bejb] s. niemowlę
baboon [be'bu:n] s. pawian
baby ['bejby] s. niemowlę
baby carriage ['bejby kaerydż] s.
wózek dziecinny
babyhood ['bejbyhud] s. wiek
niemowlęcy; niemowlęctwo
bachelor ['baeczeler] s. niezamężna; nieżonaty; stopień
uniwersytecki (najniższy); osoba posiadająca ten stopień
back [baek] s. tył; grzbiet; v.
cofać się; wycofać się

backbone ['baekboun] s. kręgosłup; stos pacierzowy
back-door ['baek'do:r] s. tylne
drzwi; adj. zakulisowy; potajemny; adv. od tyłu; tajemnie
backfire ['baek'fajer] s. wybuch
odwrotny; zawiść; v. spalić
na panewce; wypalać zapo-
biegawczo (małe połacie lasu)
background ['baekgraund] s. tło;
dalszy plan; przeszłość
back number ['baeknamber] s.
zaległy numer; stare wydanie
pisma (gazety, dziennika etc.)
back-seat ['baek'si:t] s. tylne
siedzenie (miejsce); wycofanie
się z akcji, działalności
backstairs ['baeksteerz] s. tylne
schody; adj. zakulisowy
backstroke ['baek'strouk] s.
pływanie na plecach; rzut
odbity od lewa w tenisie
back-tire ['baek'tajer] s. tylna
opona samochodowa (slang)
backward ['baekłerd] adj. tylny;
zacofany; zapóźniony
backwards ['baekłerds] adv. w
tyle; odwrotnie; do tyłu
back wheel ['baekhłil] s. tylne
koło (samochodu; ciężarówki)
bacon ['bejkn] s. słonina; wędzony i solony boczek; bekon
bacon and eggs ['bejkn end egz]
jajka z boczkiem
bacterium [baek'tierjem] s. bak-
teria; mikroorganizm
bacteria [baek'tjerie] pl. bakterie
bad [baed] adj. zły; niedobry;
przykry; sfałszowany; słaby;
zdrożny; niewłaściwy
bade [baed] v. proponował;
oferował cenę; kazał; zob. bid
badge [baedż] s. odznaka; oznaka (członkostwa, rangi etc.)
badger ['baedżer] s. borsuk; v.
zadręczać (narzekaniem)
badly ['baedly] adv. źle; bardzo;
w zły sposób; sl. świetnie
badly wounded ['baedly'łu:ndyd]
ciężko ranny; ciężko zraniony
badminton ['baedmynten] s. rodzaj tenisa (piłka z piórkiem)
bad mouth ['baedmous] v. ob-

mawiać; oczerniać; stawiać
(kogoś) w złym świetle
baffle ['baefl] v. udaremniać;
łudzić; niweczyć; skonfun-
dować; s. przegroda
bag [baeg] s. torba; worek;
sl. babsztyl; upodobanie;
v. pakować; zwędzić
baggage ['baegydż] s. bagaż
baggage check ['baegydż,czek]
kwit bagażowy
baggy ['baegy] adj. workowaty
bag-pipe ['baegpajp] s. kobza
bail [bejl] s. kaucja; poręka
bail out [bejl'ałt] v. zwolnić za
kaucją; wywinąć się z opresji
bailiff ['bejlyf] s. woźny
sądowy (powiatowy); ko-
mornik; rządca majątku
bait [bejt] s. przynęta; pokusa
bake [bejk] v. piec; wypalać
baker ['bejker] s. piekarz
bakery [bejkery] s. piekarnia
baking powder ['bejkyn,pałder]
proszek do pieczenia
balance ['baelens] s. waga
(przyrząd); bilans; równowaga;
v. równoważyć; bilansować;
wahać się; przeciwdziałać
balcony ['baelkeny] s. balkon
bald [bo:ld] adj. łysy; jawny
bale [bejl] s. zwój płótna; bela;
snop (siana); v. zob. bail
balk [bo:k] v. opierać się;
przeszkadzać; zniechęcać; s.
belka; miedza; zawada
ball [bo:l] s. 1. piłka; pocisk;
kłębek; kula (ziemska); 2. bal;
zabawa taneczna; gra
ballad ['baeled] s. ballada;
pieśń (sentymentalna, opi-
sowa, zwykle anonimowa)
ballast ['baelest] s. balast; v.
obciążać balastem
ball-bearing ['bo:lbearyn] łożysko
kulkowe (też jedna z kulek)
ballet ['baelej] s. balet; zespół
baletowy (tancerzy)
ball game [bo:lgejm] s. rozgrywka w piłkę; sl. położenie
ballistic [be'lystyk] adj. balis-
tyczny (swobodnie spadający)
balloon [be'lu:n] s. balon

ballot ['baelet] s. (tajne)
głosowanie; kartka do głosowania; v. tajnie głosować
ballot box ['baeletboks] s. urna
wyborcza
ball-point pen ['bo:l-point-pen] s.
kulkowy pisak; długopis
balm [ba:m] s. balsam
balmy ['ba:my] adj. błogi; bal-
samiczny; łagodzący
balustrade [,baeles'trejd] s.
poręcz; balustrada
bamboo [baem'bu:] s. bambus
ban [baen] s. zakaz; klątwa; v.
zabraniać; wyjąć spod prawa
banana [be'na:ne] s. banan
band [baend] s. szajka; kapela;
zespół muzyczny; taśma; v.
wiązać się; przepasywać
opaską; zrzeszać (w celu)
bandage ['baendydż] s. bandaż;
v. bandażować; obandażo-
wać; nakładać bandaże
bandit ['baendyt] s. bandyta
bandmaster ['baend,ma:ster] s.
kapelmistrz
bandstand [baendstaend] s.
estrada (zwykle na dworze)
bang [baeng] s. huk; zryw;
uciecha; bęc; v. trzaskać;
walnąć (z wielkim hukiem)
banish ['baenysz] v. wygnać;
usunąć; wykluczać; wypę-
dzać; pozbywać się (kogoś)
banishment ['baenyszment] s.
wygnanie; banicja
banisters ['baenystez] pl.
banistry (schodów); poręcze
banjo ['baendżou] s. rodzaj
gitary okrągłej, pokrytej skórą
bank [baenk] s. brzeg; ławica;
nasyp; skarpa; bank; stół roboczy; rząd; nachylenie toru;
zasób; zbiór; wał przeciw-
powodziowy; v. prowadzić
bank; składać w banku; piętrzyć; pochylać; sl. polegać;
obwałować; pochylić jezdnię
bank bill [baenk,byl] s. banknot
banker ['baenker] s. bankier
banking ['baenkyng] s. banko-
wość; transakcje banku
banknote ['baenknout] s.

banknot; papierowy pieniądz
bank-rate ['baenkrejt] s. stopa
dyskontowa; stopa procentowa (obciążająca pożyczki)
bankrupt ['baenkrept] s. bankrut
banner ['baener] s. chorągiew;
transparent; tytuł (czołowy)
banns [baenz] pl. zapowiedzi
banquet ['baenkłyt] s. bankiet
baptism ['baeptyzem] s. chrzest
baptize ['baeptajz] s. chrzcić
bar [ba:r] s. belka; drąg; rogatka;
krata; bariera; v. zagradzać;
hamować; prep. oprócz
bar [ba:r] s. izba adwokacka,
sądowa; adwokatura; bar; bufet z wyszynkiem; szynkwas
barb [ba:rb] s. haczyk; docinek;
kolec; skaza (na odlewie);
szew; cierń; grot
barbarian [ba:r'baerjen] s. barbarzyńca; adj. barbarzyński
barbed wire ['ba:rbd,łajer] drut
kolczasty (do zasieków etc.)
barber ['ba:rber] s. fryzjer
(męski); golibroda
barbershop ['ba:rber,szop] s.
zakład fryzjerski (męski)
barbiturate [ba:r'buczeret] lek
uspakajający; nasenny lek
bare [beer] adj. nagi; goły; łysy;
v. obnażać; odkrywać
barefoot ['beerfut] adj. & adv.
boso; bosy; bosa
bareheaded ['beerhedyd] adj. z
gołą głową; bez czapki
barely ['beerly] adv. ledwie;
otwarcie; ubogo; zaledwie
bargain ['ba:rgyn] s. ubicie targu;
dobre (okazyjne) kupno; v. targować się (o cenę); spodziewać się; dobijać targu
barge [ba:rdż] s. barka; v.
pakować się; trynić się
bark [ba:rk] s. kora drzewna;
szczeknięcie; barka rzeczna; v.
zdzierać korę; garbować
korę; szczekać; pyskować;
kaszleć; warkliwie mówić;
wyszczekać; zakaszleć
barley ['ba:rly] s. jęczmień
barmaid ['ba:rmejd] s. bufetowa;
kelnerka; szynkarka

barn [ba:rn] s. stodoła; stajnia; obora; wozownia; remiza
barometer [be:romyter] s. barometr; ciśnieniomierz
barracks ['baereks] pl. koszary; baraki; budynki koszarowe
barrel ['baerel] s. beczka; lufa; rura; cylinder; walec; bęben
barren ['baeren] adj. jałowy; wyczerpany; nieurodzajny; pustynny; niewydajny; nudny; nudzący; pozbawiony (czegoś)
barricade [,baery'kejd] s. barykada; v. barykadować się
barrier ['baerjer] s. zapora; zastawa; rogatka; ogrodzenie
barrister ['baeryster] s. adwokat; adwokatka; obrońca; obrończyni (głównie w Anglii)
barrow ['baerou] s. taczki
bartender ['ba:rtender] s. barman; bufetowy; bufetowa; barmanka; sprzedający wódkę
barter ['ba:rter] v. wymieniać; handlować; s. handel wymienny (bez pieniędzy)
base [bejs] s. podstawa; nasada; adj. podły; nędzny; niski
baseball ['bejsbo:l] s. (sport) palant amerykański (grany piłką i maczugą)
baseless ['bejslys] adj. bezpodstawny; nieuzasadniony
basement ['bejsment] s. suterena; piwnica; podziemie
bashful ['baeszful] adj. wstydliwy; nieśmiały; trwożliwy; lękliwy
basic ['bejsyk] adj. podstawowy; zasadniczy; zasadowy
basin ['bejsn] s. miednica; zbiornik; dorzecze; zagłębie
basis ['bejsys] pl. fundamenty; podstawy; podłoże; grunt; zasada; główna część
bask [baesk] v. wygrzewać się na słońcu (plażować); wylegiwać się; pławić się
basket ['ba:skyt] s. kosz; koszyk; v. wrzucać do kosza
basketball ['ba:skytbo:l] s. koszykówka (gra); piłka do koszykówki

bass [bejs] s. bas (głos, śpiewak, instrument)
bass [baes] s. okoń; łyko lipowe (sandałowe); okoń morski lub rzeczny
bastard ['baesterd] s. bękart; nieślubne dziecko; adj. nieślubny; nędzny; kiepski
baste [bejst] v. fastrygować; polewać tłuszczem pieczeń
bat [baet] s. nietoperz; maczuga; kij; v. mrugać; hulać (slang)
bath [ba:s] s. kąpiel; łazienka
bathe [bejz̲] v. kąpać; moczyć; rosić; przemywać; wykąpać
bathing [bejz̲yng] s. kąpanie
bathing cap ['bejz̲yngkaep] czepek kąpielowy
bathing suit ['bejz̲yng sju:t] strój kąpielowy; kostium kąpielowy
bathing trunks ['bejz̲yng tran̲ks] spodenki kąpielowe
bathrobe ['ba:z̲roub] s. płaszcz kąpielowy (z frotte)
bathroom ['ba:z̲ru:m] s. łazienka; ubikacja; ustęp; klozet
bath towel ['ba:z̲ tałel] ręcznik kąpielowy (z frotte)
bathtub ['ba:z̲tab] s. wanna
baton ['baeton] s. buława; pałka; batuta; pałeczka dyrygenta
battalion [be'taeljen] s. batalion; taktyczny pododdział pułku
batter ['baeter] v. tłuc; walić
battered ['baeterd] adj. pobity
battery ['baetery] s. bateria (elektryczna lub armat); komplet; pobicie; zestaw armat
battle ['baetl] s. bitwa; walka
battleship ['baetlszyp] s. okręt wojenny (opancerzony)
baulk [bo:k] s. przeszkoda; rozczarowanie; v. przeszkadzać; zob. balk
bawl [bo:l] v. wrzeszczeć; drzeć się; krzyczeć; zwymyślać; głośno szlochać
bay [bej] adj. czerwono-brązowy; gniady (koń); s. wawrzyn; laur (drzewo); pl. laury
bay [bej] s. zatoka; wnęka; przęsło; v. ujadać; wyć
bay window ['bej'łyndoł] okno

we wnęce (alkowie)
bazaar [be'za:r] s. bazar
be; was; been [bi:; łoz; bi:n]
be [bi:] v. być; żyć; trwać;
dziać się; istnieć; stawać
się; zdarzać się; pozostawać
be reading [bi:'ry:dyn̲] czytać
właśnie; być w trakcie
czytania (gazety etc.)
beach [bi:cz] s. brzeg; plaża
beachhead ['bi:czhed] s.
przyczółek (nad wodą)
beach-wear ['bi:człe:r] s. odzież
plażowa; kostiumy; płaszcze
beacon ['bi:ken] s. sygnał
(ogniowy); latarnia morska
bead [bi:d] s. paciorek; koralik;
v. nawlekać korale; perlić
się; ozdabiać paciorkami
beak [bi:k] s. dziób; belfer
beam [bi:m] s. belka; dźwigar;
promień; radosny uśmiech;
v. promieniować; nadawać
sygnał; rozpromieniać się
bean [bi:n] s. fasola; bób;
ziarnko; łeb; animusz
bear; bore; borne [beer; bo:r;
bo:rn]
bear [beer] s. niedźwiedź; v.
dźwigać; ponosić; znosić;
podtrzymywać; trzymać się;
rodzić; mieć (potomstwo);
nosić się; zachowywać się
beard [bierd] s. broda (zarost)
bearer ['beerer] s. nosiciel;
okaziciel (legitymacji);
zwiastun; karawaniarz
bearing ['beeryn̲g] s. zachowanie; wzgląd; wspornik;
rodzenie; łożysko
beast [bi:st] s. bestia; bydlę
beastly ['bistly] adj. bydlęcy;
potworny; sl. przykry; niemiły; adv. straszliwie; okrutnie
beast of prey ['bi:st ow prej] s.
drapieżnik (mięsożerny)
beat; beat; beaten[bi:t; bi:t;
bi:tn]
beat [bi:t] v. bić; bić się;
ubijać; tłuc; trzepotać; zbić;
kuć; karać biciem (batem)
beat it ! ['bi:t,yt] excl. precz!;
wynoś się!; wynoście się!

beaten ['bi:tn] adj. ubity;
wydeptany (przemarszem, ko-
pytami); wyczerpany; znany
beatnik [bi:tnyk] s. nonkonformista; (-tka)
beautiful ['bju:teful] adj. piękny;
cudny; wspaniały; świetny
beautify ['bju:tyfaj] v.
upiększać; upiększyć
beauty ['bju:ty] s. piękność;
piękno; uroda; piękna kobieta
beauty parlor ['bju:ty'pa:rler]
salon kosmetyczny
beaver ['bi:wer] s. bóbr;
przedsiębiorczy człowiek
because [bi'ko:z] conj. dlatego;
że; gdyż; adv. z powodu
beckon ['beken] v. skinąć;
nęcić; s. skinienie
become; became; become
[bi'kam; bi'kejm; bi'kam]
become [bi'kam] v. stawać się;
nadawać się; zostawać
kimś (czymś); pasować do
becoming ['bikamyn̲g] adj.
stosowny; odpowiedni;
twarzowy; właściwy
bed [bed] s. łoże; łożysko;
klomb; grządka; ławica;
podkład; nocleg
bedclothes ['bedklouz̲] s. pościel; prześcieradła; kołdry
bedding ['bedyn̲g] s. pościel
bed linen ['bed,lynyn] s. pościel;
bielizna pościelowa
bedridden ['bed,rydn] adj.
obłożnie chory; złożony
chorobą; nie mogący wstać z
łóżka; przykuty do łóżka
bedroom ['bedrum] s. sypialnia
bedside ['bedsajd] przy łożu
bedsore ['bedso:r] s. odleżyna
bed spread ['bed'spred] s.
narzuta wierzchnia na łóżko
bedtime ['bedtajm] s. pora do
spania; pora snu
bee [bi:] s. pszczoła
beech [bi:cz] s. buk; adj.
bukowy; z drzewa bukowego
beef [bi:f] s. wołowina; siła;
narzekanie; wyrzekanie (slang)
beefsteak ['be:f'stejk] s. befsztyk
(do smażenia lub pieczenia)

beefy ['bi:fy] adj. krzepki;
flegmatyczny; muskularny
beehive ['bi:hajw] s. ul
beekeeper ['bi:kiper] s.
pszczelarz; hodowca pszczół
beeline ['bi:lajn] s. najkrótsza
droga; linia powietrzna
been [bi:n] v. były; zob. be
beer [bier] s. piwo
beet [bi:t] s. burak
beetle ['bi:tl] s. tłuczek; ubijak;
v. ubijać; wystawać; zwisać
beetroot ['bi:tru:t] s. burak
befall [by'fo:l] v. zdarzać się
(komuś); przydarzać się (komuś); przytrafiać się
before [by'fo:r] adv. przedtem;
dawniej; z przodu; na przedzie
beforehand [by'fo:rhend] adv.
uprzednio; przedtem; z góry
befriend [by'frend] v. zaprzy-
jaźniać się; wspomagać
beg [beg] v. prosić; żebrać
began [by'gaen] v. zaczęty;
proszę zobaczyć: begin
beget; begot; begotten [by'get;
by'got; by'gotn]
beget [by'get] v. płodzić;
rodzić; powodować; wywo-
ływać; stawać się ojcem
beggar ['beger] s. żebrak
begin; began; begun [by'gyn;
by'gaen; by'gan]
begin [by'gyn] v. zaczynać
zapoczątkować; rozpocząć
beginner [by'gyner] s.
początkujący; nowy (człowiek)
beginning [by'gynyng] s.
początek; rozpoczęcie
begun [by'gan] v. p.p.
proszę zobaczyć: begin
behalf [by'hae:f] s. w imieniu
kogoś; poparcie dla kogoś;
w czyimś interesie; dla
behave [by'hejw] v. zachowywać się; prowadzić się
behavior [by'hejwjer] s.
postępowanie; zachowanie się
behind [by'hajnd] adv. w tyle; z
tyłu; do tyłu; prep. za; poza;
s. tyłek; pupa
being ['by:yng] s. byt; istnienie;
istota (ludzka)

belated [by'lejtyd] adj.
spóźniony; zapóźniony;
późny; opóźniony
belch [belcz] v. zionąć; odbijać
się; s. bekanie; buchanie; huk;
odbijanie się
belfry ['belfry] s. dzwonnica
Belgian ['beldżen] adj. belgijski
belief [by'li:f] s. wiara; wierzenie;
zaufanie; przekonanie
believe [by'li:w] v. wierzyć;
sądzić; mieć przekonanie;
zakładać; uważać
believer [by'li:wer] s. wyznawca;
wierzący; zwolennik
bell [bel] s. dzwon; dzwonek
belligerent [by'lydżerent] adj.
wojujący; wojowniczy; wojenny; s. strona walcząca
bellow ['belou] v. ryczeć; s. ryk;
ryczenie; porykiwanie
bellows ['belouz] s. miech;
płuca; przedmiot podobny do
miecha; dmuchawa
belly ['bely] s. brzuch; żołądek
belong [bylong] v. należeć
belongings [bylongynz] pl.
rzeczy; bagaż; przynależności
beloved [by'lawd] adj. ukochany;
drogi; s. kochana osoba
below [by'lou] adv. niżej; w
dole; na dół; pod spodem;
prep. poniżej; pod; w piekle
belt [belt] s. pas; pasek; strefa;
v. bić pasem; opasywać
bench [bencz] s. ława; ławka;
stół; terasa; miejsce sędziego
bend; bent; bent [bend; bent;
bent]
bend [bend] s. zgięcie; krzywa;
v. giąć; wyginać; przeginać;
zginać; naginać
beneath [by'ni:s] prep. pod; pod
spodem; na dół; poniżej
benediction [,beny'dykszyn] s.
błogosławieństwo
benefactor [,beny'faekter] s.
dobroczyńca; dobrodziej
beneficent [bi'nefysent] adj.
dobroczynny
beneficial [,beny'fyszel] adj.
pożywny; korzystny; zbawienny; dobroczynny

benefit ['benyfyt] s. korzyść; dobrodziejstwo; pożytek; zasiłek; dobro

benevolent [by'newelent] adj. dobroczynny; życzliwy; łaskawy

bent [bent] s. sitowie; skłonność; zgięcie; adj. skłonny; zgięty; zdecydowany; uparty; wygięty; wykrzywiony

benzene ['benzi:n] s. benzen

benzine ['benzi:n] s. (lekka) benzyna (do czyszczenia)

bequeath [by'kłyg] v. zostawiać w spadku; przekazać potomości; zapisać w testamencie

bequest [by'kłest] s. zapis; spadek; spuścizna; legat

bereave; bereft; bereaved [by'ri:w; by'reft; by'ri:wd]

bereave [by'ri:w] v. pozbawiać; odzierać; wyzuwać; osieroić; porwać

bereft [by'reft] adj. osierocony; pozbawiony; wyzuty

beret ['berej] s. beret

berry ['bery] s. jagoda; ikra

berth [be:rg] s. koja; łóżko; stoisko; miejsce postoju statku

beseech; besought; besought [by'si:cz; by'so:t; by'so:t]

beseech [by'si:cz] v. błagać; upraszać; zaklinać

beside [by'sajd] adv. poza tym; ponadto; inaczej; prep. obok; przy; w pobliżu; w porównaniu; na równi z ...

besides [by'sajdz] adv. prócz tego; poza tym; prep. oprócz; poza; ponadto; w dodatku

besiege [by'si:dż] v. oblegać

best [best] adj. & adv. najlepszy; najlepiej; v. okpiwać

best wishes [best'łyszys] najlepsze życzenia

best of all [best,ow'o:l] najlepszy; najlepiej; a najlepiej

bestow [by'stou] v. podarować; składać; nadawać; użyczać; darzyć; obdarzyć

bet [bet] s. zakład; v. zakładać się; iść o zakład

betray [by'trej] v. zdradzić;

myślić; zawodzić; dawać dowód; świadczyć

betrayal [by'trejel] s. zdrada

betrayer [by'trejer] s. zdrajca

better ['beter] adv. lepiej; lepszy; v. poprawić; przewyższyć; prześcignąć; prześcigać

better than ['beter dzaen] exp. więcej (slang); ponad; lepiej

between [by'tli:n] prep. miądzy; adv. w pośrodku; tymczasem

beverage ['bewerydż] s. napój

beware [by'łe:r] v. strzec się

beware of the dog [by'łe:r ow dy dog] strzec się psa; zły pies

bewilder [by'łylder] v. zmieszać (kogoś); oszałamiać

bewilderment [by'łylderment] s. zaczarowanie; oszołomienie; chaos; dezorientacja

bewitch [by'łycz] v. zaczarować; oczarować; ująć (kogoś czymś)

beyond [by'jond] adv. & prep. za; poza; dalej niż; nad; ponad; dalej (położony etc.)

bias ['bajes] s. uprzedzenie; fałsz; kierunek; ukos; odchylenie; v. skłonić; nachylić; uprzedzić; usposabiać

biased ['bajest] adj. stronniczy; uprzedzony; nastawiony

bib [byb] s. śliniak; v. popijać

Bible ['bajbl] s. Biblia

bicycle ['bajsykl] s. rower

bid [byd] v. oferować cenę; licytować; kazać; s. oferta na licytacji; stawka; zaproszenie; odzywka; zapowiedź

bid farewell [,byd'fa:rłel] v. żegnać się (z kimś); pożegnać kogoś

bier [bjer] s. mary (pod trumną)

big [byg] adj. & adv. duży; wielki; ważny; głośny; godny

big business [byg'byznys] wielkie interesy; wielkie korporacje

big wig [byg łyg] s. wielka szyszka; ważniak; gruba ryba

bigamy ['bygemy] s. bigamia; dwużeństwo

bigness ['bygnys] s. wielkość; duży rozmiar; grubość

bigot ['byget] s. bigot; bigotka; świętoszek; zapaleniec
bigoted ['bygetyd] adj. zajadły; sfanatyzowany
bike [bajk] s. rower
bilateral [baj'laeterel] adj. dwustronny; obustronny
bile [bajl] s. żółć; zgorzkniałość; tetryczność
bilious ['byljes] adj. żółciowy; zrzędny; popędliwy; tetryczny
bill [byl] s. dziób; pika; cypel
bill [byl] s. rachunek; kwit; afisz; plakat; v. ogłaszać; afiszować; oblepiać afiszami
billboard ['byl,bo:rd] s. tablica ogłoszeniowa
billfold ['byl,fould] s. portfel (na dokumenty i pieniądze)
billiards ['byljerdz] s. bilard
billion ['byljen] s. tysiąc milionów (USA); miliard
bill of exchange ['byl,ow 'eksczendż] weksel
billow ['bylou] s. bałwan; kłąb; v. piętrzyć; falować; bałwanić się
bin [byn] s. skrzynia; paka; v. pakować; chować do skrzyni
bind [bajnd] v. wiązać; zobowiązywać; opatrywać; oprawiać; obszywać; uwiązać
binding ['bajndyng] adj. wiążący; s. połączenie; oprawa (książki); oprawianie; wiązanie; obszycie; zaciskanie
binoculars [bajnokjulez] pl. lornetka (polowa, teatralna)
biography [baj'ografy] s. biografia; opis życia i działalności
biology [baj'oledży] s. biologia
birch [be:rcz] s. brzoza
bird [be:rd] s. ptak; dziwak
bird of passage ['be:rd ow paesydż] przelotny ptak
bird of prey ['be:rd ow prej] drapieżny ptak
bird's eye view ['be:rds aj,wju] widok z lotu ptaka
birth [be:rt] s. urodzenie
birth control ['be:rt kon,troul] kontrola urodzin

birthday ['be:rtdej] s. urodziny; początek czegoś
birthday party ['be:rtdej pa:rty] przyjęcie urodzinowe
birthplace ['be:rt-plejs] miejsce urodzenia
biscuit ['byskyt] s. bułka; sucharek lekkostrawny
bishop ['byszep] s. biskup
bison ['bajsn] s. bizon
bit [byt] s. wędzidło; ostrze; wiertło; ząb; szczypta; odrobina; kawałek; 12 1/2 centów; moment; krótki czas; najprostsza informacja w komputerze jak: "tak" lub "nie"
bitch [bycz] s. suka; wulg. kurwa
bite; bit; bitten [bajt; byt; bitn]
bite [bajt] v. gryźć; kąsać; docinać; dokuczać; s. pokarm; przynęta; ukąszenie; ciętość; lekki posiłek; odrobina czegoś do jedzenia
bitter ['byter] adj. gorzki; ostry; zły; zgorzkniały; przykry
blab [blaeb] v. paplać; gadać; s. plotkarz; plotkarka; gaduła
black [blaek] adj. czarny; ponury; s. murzyn; v. czernić
blackberry ['blaekbery] s. jeżyna
blackbird ['blaekbe:rd] s. kos
blackboard ['blaekbo:rd] s. tablica (szkolna)
blacken ['bleakn] v. czernić
black eye ['blaekaj] s. podbite oko
blackhead ['blaekhed] s. wągier
blackmail ['blaekmejl] s. szantaż; wymuszenie; v. szantażować
black-market ['blaek ma:rkyt] s. czarny rynek
blackout ['blaekaut] s. zaciemnienie (miasta, okien)
black pudding ['blaek'pudyng] s. kaszanka; kiszka
blacksmith ['blaeksmys] s. kowal (wiejski)
bladder ['blaeder] s. pęcherz
blade [blejd] s. źdźbło; liść; ostrze; płetwa; klinga; wesołek
blame [blejm] s. wina; nagana; v. łajać; ganić; winić

blame for ['blejm for] v. winić
za (coś)
blameless ['blejmlys] adj. bez
winy; niewinny
blank [blaenk] adj. biały; pusty;
czysty; nie wypełniony; s.
puste miejsce; nie wypełniony
formularz; ślepak
blanket ['blaenkyt] s. koc
wełniany; ciepły koc
blasphemy ['blaesfymy] s. bluź-
nierstwo; pogarda dla Boga
blast [bla:st] s. wybuch; podmuch; odgłos eksplozji; prąd
powietrza; v. wysadzić w
powietrze; detonować; niszczyć; przeklinać; uderzać
blast furnace ['bla:st,fe:rnys] s.
wielki piec hutniczy
blatant ['blejtent] adj. krzykliwy;
ryczący; przesadny
blaze [blejz] s. błysk; płomień;
wybuch; v. płonąć
bleach [bli:cz] v. wybielać
bleak [bli:k] adj. ponury; smutny;
wystawiony do wiatru
blear [blier] adj. mętny;
zamglony; niewyraźny
bleat [bli:t] v. beczeć
bleed; bled; bled [bli:d; bled;
bled]
bleed [bli:d] v. krwawić
blemish ['blemysz] s. plama;
wada; skaza; v. zniekształcić; splamić; poplamić; pobrudzić; zepsuć; być skazą
blend; blent; blent [blend; blent;
blent]
blend [blend] v. mieszać się;
łączyć się; s. mieszanina
bless [bles] v. błogosławić;
udzielić błogosławieństwa
bless my soul ['bles,maj'so:l]
excl. o Boże!
blessed ['blesyd] adj. błogo-
sławiony; święty; kojący
blessing ['blesyng] s. błogosławieństwo; aprobata; dobra
rzecz; dar boski; szczęście
blew [blu:] v. zob. blow
blight [blajt] s. zniszczenie;
zaraza; v. niszczyć
blind [blajnd] adj. ślepy; v.

oślepić; s. zasłona
blind alley ['blajnd,alej] ślepa
ulica
blindfold ['blajnd,fould] adj. &
adv. na ślepo; z zawiązanymi
oczami; na oślep; v. zawiązywać oczy; s. zasłona oczu
blink [blynk] v. mrugać; s. błysk
oka; mignięcie; migotanie
bliss [blys] s. radość; błogość
blithe ['blajz] adj. wesoły
blizzard ['blyzerd] s. śnieżyca;
zawieja; zadymka; zamieć
bloat [blout] v. nadymać;
nabrzmiewać; uwędzić;
wędzić
bloater ['blouter] s. śledź
wędzony; pikling
block [blok] s. blok; kloc; zeszyt;
przeszkoda; v. tamować;
wstrzymywać; tarasować;
zatykać; zablokować;
blokować; tamować
block up ['blokap] v.
zablokować; zablokowywać;
zamurować; zatkać
blockade [blo'kejd] s. blokada; v.
blokować; robić zator
blonde [blond] s. blondynka
blood [blad] s. krew; ród;
pokrewieństwo
bloodshed ['bladszed] s. rozlew
krwi
bloodshot ['bladszot] adj.
nabrzmiały krwią; zaszły krwią
blood vessel ['blad,wesl] s.
naczynie krwionośne
bloody ['blady] adj. krwawy
bloom [blu:m] s. kwiecie; v.
kwitnąć; rozkwitać
blooming [blu:myng] adj.
kwitnący; przeklęty (slang)
blossom ['blosem] v. kwitnąć;
s. kwiecie; kwiat
blot [blot] s. plama; v. plamić
blot out ['blot aut] v. wymazać;
usunąć; wykreślać; zamazy-
wać; ukrywać
blotter ['bloter] s. bibularz; rejestr
aresztowań; suszka
blotting paper ['blotyng,pejper]
bibuła; suszka
blouse [blauz] s. bluza

blow; blew; blown [blou; blu; bloin]

blow [blou] s. silny cios; nagły atak; nagłe nieszczęście; szok; dmuchnięcie; podmuch; rzut; rozkwit; v. dmuchać; zakwitać; rozkwitać; popychać podmuchem; wybuchać; stapiać; trąbić; chwalić się; rozrzutnie wydawać pieniądze; popełniać błąd; odchodzić; rozbić; rozwalić

blow drier ['blou,drajer] s. suszarka do włosów

blow gun ['blou,gan] s. rura do strzelania pneumatycznego; pistolet pneumatyczny

blowout ['blou'aut] s. rozerwanie opony; libacja; bankiet

blowup ['blou'ap] s. eksplozja; wybuch gniewu; sprzeczka; powiększona fotografia

blue [blu:] adj. niebieski; błękitny; siny; ponury; v. farbować na niebiesko; pomalować na niebiesko; s. błękit; lazur

bluebell ['blu:bel] s. dzwonek (kwiat)

blues [blu:s] pl. smutek; przygnębienie; smutne piosenki

bluff [blaf] s. oszustwo; nabieranie; blaga; bluff; adj. szorstki; stromy; v. wprowadzać w błąd; bluffować

bluish ['blu:ysz] adj. niebieskawy

blunder ['blander] s. ciężki błąd; v. popełniać błąd (gafę)

blunt [blant] adj. tępy; nieczuły; v. stąpić; przytępić

blur [ble:r] s. plama; v. zatrzeć; splamić; zamazać

boar [bo:r] s. dzik; odyniec

board [bo:rd] s. deska; władza naczelna; tablica; rada; pokład

boarder ['bo:rder] s. pensjonariusz; pasażer; stołownik

boardinghouse ['bo:rdyng,haus] s. pensjonat

boarding school ['bo:rdyng,sku:l] s. szkoła z internatem

boardwalk ['bo:rd łok] s. chodnik z desek

boast [boust] v. chwalić się; s. samochwalstwo; przechwałki

boat [bout] s. łódź; statek

boat race ['bout,rejs] s. regaty; wyścigi łodzi

bob [bob] v. kiwać sie; krótko strzyc; szturchnąć; s. wisiorek; kłąb włosów; wahadło; pion; szturchnięcie

bobby ['boby] s. angielski policjant

bobsled ['bob sled] s. bobslej; sanki z kierownicą etc.

bodice ['bodys] s. stanik

bodily ['bodyly] adj. & adv. osobiście; fizycznie; całkowicie; gremialnie; cieleśnie

body ['body] s. ciało (ludzkie, fizyczne, astralne); karoseria; korpus; grupa; gromada; ogół

bodyguard ['bodyga:rd] s. straż przyboczna; ochrona osobista

bog [bog] s. bagno; moczary

boil [bojl] v. wrzeć; kipieć; gotować; s. wrzenie; czyrak

boil over ['bojl,ouwer] v. wygotować; wygotować się

boiled eggs ['bojld egs] gotowane jajka

boiler ['bojler] s. kocioł

boisterous ['bojsteres] adj. hałaśliwy; niesforny; burzliwy; gwałtowny; porywisty

bold [bould] adj. śmiały; zuchwały; zauważalny; wyraźny; wyrazisty

bolster ['boulster] s. miękka podkładka; poduszka; v. miękko podeprzeć

bolt [boult] s. zasuwa; bolec; piorun; wypad; rygiel; ucieczka; v. zasuwać; rzucić się; wypaść; czmychać

bomb [bom] s. bomba; v. bombardować; atakować bombami; adj. bombowy

bombard [bom'ba:rd] v. bombardować (artylerią lub bombami)

bond [bond] s. więź; obligacja

bone [boun] s. kość; ość

bonfire ['bonfajer] s. płonący stos; ognisko (obozowe etc.)

bonnet ['bonyt] s. czapka (damska); czepek

bonny ['bony] adj. piękny; ładny

bonus ['bounes] s. premia

bony ['bouny] adj. kościsty

book [buk] s. książka; rejestr; v. księgować; rezerwować; aresztować; rejestrować

booked up ['bukt ap] adj. wyprzedany; pełny

bookcase ['bukkejs] s. półka na książki; biblioteczka

booking clerk ['bukyn,klerk] s. kasjer kolejowy

booking office ['bukyn,ofys] biuro biletowo-rezerwacyjne

bookkeeper ['buk,ki:per] s. księgowy; księgowa

bookkeeping ['buk,ki:pyng] s. księgowość

booklet ['buklyt] s. książeczka

bookseller ['buk,seler] s. księgarz

book shop ['bukszop] s. księgarnia

bookstore ['buksto:r] s. księgarnia

bookworm ['buk,łerm] s. mól książkowy

boom [bu:m] s. huk; nagła zwyżka; bom; bariera; v. zwyżkować; podbijać ceny

boomerang ['bu:meraeng] s. bumerang; v. działać jak bumerang

boor [bu:r] s. prostak; gbur; chłop; prostaczka

boost [bu:st] v. forsować; podnosić znaczenie; zachwalać; wzmacniać; rozreklamować; podsadzić (kogoś)

boot [bu:t] s. but; cholewa

booth [bu:s] s. budka; stragan

booty ['bu:ty] s. łup; zdobycz

booze ['bu:z] s. alkohol pitny

border ['bo:rder] s. granica; brzeg; rąbek; lamówka; skraj; kresy; v. obrębiać; graniczyć; oblamować; obszar

bore [bo:r] v. wiercić; drążyć; nudzić; zanudzać; s. otwór; nudy; nudziarz; natręt; rzecz nieznośna; nudziarstwo

bore [bo:r] v. zob. bear

born [bo:rn] adj. urodzony

borough ['be:rou] s. miasteczko

borrow ['borou] v. (za)pożyczać

bosom ['busem] s. (łono) pierś

boss [bo:s] s. szef; v. rządzić

botany ['boteny] s. botanika

botch [bocz] s. fuszerka; łatanina; partactwo; v. partaczyć; fuszerować

both [bous] pron. & adj. obaj; obydwaj; obie; obydwie; oboje

bother [bodzer] s. kłopot; v. niepokoić; dokuczać; dręczyć; zawracać głowę

bother about [,bodzer e'baut] v. kłopotać się czymś

bottle ['botl] s. butelka

bottom ['botem] s. dno; spód; dolina; głąb; dolna część; adj. dolny; spodni; podstawowy; v. sięgać dna; wstawiać dno; osiągać dno

bough [bau] s. konar; gałąź

bought [bo:t] v. zakupiony; zob. buy (zakupiony, przekupiony)

boulder ['boulder] s. głaz

bounce [bauns] v. odbijać się; podskakiwać; odskoczyć; blagować; s. gwałtowne odbicie; odskok; samochwalstwo; chełpliwość

bound [baund] s. granica; adj. będący w drodze; v. graniczyć; być zobowiązanym

boundary [baundry] s. linia graniczna; adj. graniczny

boundless [baundlys] adj. bezgraniczny; niezmierzony

bountiful ['bauntyful] adj. obfity; hojny; szczodry

bouquet [bu:'kej] s. bukiet kwiatów; zapach (wina)

bout [baut] s. okres; runda; próba sił; atak (choroby)

bow [bau] s. łuk; kabłąk; smyczek; ukłon; v. zginać się; kłaniać się; wygiąć w kabłąk; schylić się

bowels ['bauelz] pl. trzewia; wnętrzności; kiszki

bower ['bauer] s. altana; chatka; kotwica przednia

bowl [boul] s. miska; czerpak;

box   329   break down

stadion; szala; v. grać kulami
(w kręgla); toczyć koło
box [boks] s. skrzynka; pudełko;
loża; boks; v. pakować;
oddzielać; uderzać pięścią
boxer ['bokser] s. pięściarz;
bokser
boxing ['boksyng] s. boks;
pięściarstwo
box office ['boks,ofys] s. kasa w
teatrze; kasa biletów wstępu
boy [boj] s. chłopak; służący
boycott ['bojkot] s. bojkot; v.
bojkotować
boyfriend ['boj-frend] s.
przyjaciel (dziewczyny);
kochanek
boyhood ['bojhud] s. wiek chłopięcy; dzieciństwo chłopca
boyish ['bojysz] adj. chłopięcy
boy-scout ['boj-skaut] s. harcerz
bra [bra:] s. biustnik; stanik;
biustonosz
brace [brejs] s. klamra; korba;
podpora; wiązanie; kleszcze;
v. wzmacniać; krzepić; podpierać; spiąć klamrą; związać; ścisnąć; napiąć
brace up [brejs ap] v. wytężyć
się; zebrać siły; orzeźwić
bracelet ['brejslyt] s. bransoletka;
kajdanek
bracket ['braekyt] s. wspornik;
ramię; nawias; grupa; klamra;
podpórka; konsola; v. brać w
nawiasy; grupować
brag [braeg] v. chełpić się
braggart ['braegert] s. samoch-
wała; pyszałek; bufon;
fanfaron
braid [brejd] s. warkocz; wstążka; plecionka; v. pleść;
opasywać; obszywać
brain [brejn] s. mózg; rozum
brain wave ['brejn,łejw] s.
świetny pomysł; świetna
myśl; natchnienie
brake [brejk] s. hamulec
bramble ['braembel] s. krzak
jagody; krzak jeżyny; jeżyna
branch [bra:ncz] s. gałąź;
odnoga; filia; v. odgałęziać
się; zbaczać; rozwidlać się

brand [braend] s. głownia;
żagiew; wypalony znak na
skórze; piętno; żelazne
narzędzie do wypalania znaku;
znak własności; znak fir-
mowy; marka towaru; pochodzenie towaru; gatunek towaru; v. naznaczać; piętno-
wać; wryć (w pamięć)
brand new [,braen'nju] adj.
nowiutki; nowiusieńki; jak
spod igły
brandy ['braendy] s. wódka ze
spirytusu winnego
brass [braes] s. mosiądz; spiż;
ranga; starszyzna; instrumenty
dęte; forsa; pieniądze; czelność; śmiałość; przedmio-
ty z mosiądzu
brass band [,braes'baend] s.
kapela dęta; orkiestra dęta
brassiere [bre'zier] s. biustnik;
stanik; biustonosz
brat [braet] s. brzdąc; bachor
brave [brejw] adj. dzielny; odważny; śmiały; v. stawiać
czoło; odważyć się
brazen ['brejzn] adj. mosiężny;
brązowy; bezczelny; bez-
wstydny; cyniczny
Brazilian [bre'zyljen] adj.
brazylijski; s. Brazylijczyk
breach [bry:cz] s. naruszenie;
wyłom; zerwanie; niedotrzy-
manie; v. przełamać (się);
zrobić wyłom; przerwać się
bread [bred] s. chleb; forsa
(slang); środki utrzymania
bread and butter [bred-en-bater]
chleb z masłem; środki
utrzymania
breadth [breds] s. szerokość;
rozmach; szerokość poglą-
dów; rozpiętość (skrzydeł)
break; broke; broken [brejk;
brouk; brouken]
break [brejk] v. łamać; rujnować; przegrywać; potłuc; urwać; przerwać; s. załamanie;
wyłom; nagła zmiana; wada
break away ['brejk ełej] v.
oderwać (się); uciekać
break down ['brejk dałn] v.

załamać (się); s. zaparcie się; upadek; rozbiór; awaria

break in ['brejkyn] v. włamać (się); wtargnąć; wtrącić się

break off ['brejkof] v. urwać; odłamać; zerwać stosunki

break out ['brejkaut] v. wyrwać (się); pokryć się pryszczami

break up ['brejkap] v. połamać (się); rozpadać się; rozejść się; rozebrać; rozdrobnić

breakable ['brejkebel] adj. kruchy; łamliwy; łatwy do zbicia, stłuczenia

breakfast ['brekfest] s. śniadanie; v. jeść śniadanie

breast [brest] s. pierś

breaststroke ['brest,strouk] pływanie żabką

breath [breṣ] s. oddech; tchnienie; dech; oddychanie; powiew; podmuch

breathe [bri:z] v. oddychać; tchnąć; żyć; dać wytchnąć; powiewać; natchnąć; wionąć; szepnąć

breathing ['bri:zyng] s. oddech; wytchnienie; adj. żywy

breathless [breslys] adj. bez tchu; zasapany; zadyszany; zziajany

bred [bred] zob. breed; wychowany

breeches ['bry:czyz] pl. spodnie do jazdy konnej; bryczesy

breed; bred; bred [bri:d; bred; bred]

breed [bri:d] v. rodzić; rozmnażać; hodować; płodzić; s. chów; rasa; ród; plemię; ród ludzki

breeder ['bri:der] s. hodowca; rozsadnik (choroby); rozpłodnik; reproduktor

breeding [bri:dyng] s. hodowla; obejście; dobre wychowanie

breeze [bri:z] s. wietrzyk; zwada; podmuch wiatru; v. wiać; śmigać; odejść; oszukać

brevity ['brewyty] s. zwięzłość; krótkość; krótkotrwałość

brew [bru:] v. warzyć (piwo); knuć; s. napój uwarzony;

preparat; warzenie; parzenie; odwar; napar

brewery [bru:ery] s. browar

bribe [brajb] v. dawać łapówkę; przekupywać; s. łapówka

bribery ['brajbery] s. przekupstwo; łapownictwo; korupcja

brick [bryk] s. cegła; kostka; adj. ceglany; v. obmurować; zamurować (okno; drzwi etc.)

bricklayer ['bryk,lejer] s. murarz

brickwork ['bryklork] s. murowanie; wykonana robota murarska

brickyard ['brykja:rd] s. cegielnia

bridal ['brajdel] adj. ślubny; weselny; s. ślub; wesele

bride [brajd] s. panna młoda

bridegroom ['brajdgru:m] s. pan młody; nowożeniec

bridesmaid ['brajdzmejd] s. druhna; drużka

bridge [brydż] s. most; mostek; brydż; grzbiet; v. łączyć mostem; zapełnić lukę

bridgehead ['brydżhed] s. przyczółek mostowy; przyczółek

bridle ['braidl] s. uździenica; uzda; cuma; cugiel; wodza; v. kiełznać; powściągać; opanowywać; okiełznać

bridle path ['brajdl,paṣ] s. ścieżka do jazdy konnej

brief [bri:f] s. streszczenie; zestawienie; odprawa; krótkie majtki; v. zwięźle streścić; pouczyć; informować; zrobić odprawę; mówić krótko; adj. krótkotrwały; treściwy; zwięzły; krótki

briefcase ['bri:f,kejs] s. teczka

brigade [bry'gejd] s. brygada

bright [brajt] adj. jasny; świetny; bystry; adv. jasno

brighten ['brajtn] v. rozjaśnić; błyszczeć; promieniować

brightness [brajtnys] s. jasność; światło; blask; żywość

brilliance ['bryljens] s. blask; wielkie zdolności; świetność; jasność; blichtr

brilliancy ['bryljensy] s. świetność; blichtr; połysk; jasne
światło; blask; jasność
brilliant ['bryljent] adj.
lśniący; błyszczący; świetny; wybitny; znakomity
brim [brym] s. brzeg (naczynia);
rondo (kapelusza); v.
napełniać po brzegi
brimful ['brym'ful] adj. pełen po
brzegi; przepełniony
bring; brought; brought [bryng;
bro:t; bro:t]
bring [bryng] v. przynosić;
przyprowadzać; powodować;
zmusić (się); ściągnąć
bring an action ['bryng an
'aekszyn] v. wszczynać
działanie, akcję
bring about ['bryng e'baut] v.
uskutecznić; wywoływać;
dokonać; spowodować
bring forth ['bryng,fo:rs] v.
ujawniać; wywoływać; uro-
dzić; wydawać na świat
bring in ['bryng yn] v.
wprowadzać; przynosić;
wydawać (wyrok etc.)
bring up [bring ap] v. poruszyć;
przynieść na górę; przy-
sunąć; wychowywać
brink [brynk] s. skraj; brzeg
brisk [brysk] adj. żywy; raźny;
rześki; trzaskający; wesoły
bristle ['brysl] s. szczecina
British ['brytysz] adj. brytyjski; s.
Anglik; Brytyjczyk
brittle ['brytl] adj. kruchy
broach [broucz] v. żłobić;
zaczynać; poruszać; s.
szydło; rożen; iglica
broad [bro:d] adj. szeroki; z
rozmachem; wyraźny; obszerny; rozległy; s. szeroka
płaszczyzna; wulg. kobieta;
adv. szeroko; z akcentem
broadcast ['bro:dka:st] s.
transmitować; rozsiewać;
szerzyć; s. transmisja
broad-minded ['bro:d'majndyt]
adj. pobłażliwy; z otwartą
głową; tolerancyjny
brochure ['broszjuer] s. broszura

broke [brouk] adj. złamany; bez
grosza; zob. break
broken [brouken] adj. połamany;
zepsuty; zob. break
broker [brouker] s. pośrednik;
ajent; makler; taksator;
handlarz narkotyków
bronchia ['bronkje] pl. oskrzela
bronchitis ['bron'kajtys] s.
bronchit
bronze [bronz] s. brąz; spiż; adj.
brązowy; spiżowy; v. brązo-
wać; brązowieć
brooch [broucz] s. brosza; spinka
brood [bru:d] s. wyląg; potomstwo; v. wysiadywać; tkwić;
rozmyślać ponuro; być
pogrążonym w myślach
brook [bruk] s. potok; strumyk;
v. ścierpieć
broom [bru:m] s. miotła; v.
zamiatać; wymiatać; ob-
miatać
broth [bros] s. rosół; bulion
brothel ['brodzel] s. burdel
brother ['bradzer] s. brat
brotherhood ['bradzer,hud] s.
braterstwo; związek
zawodowy
brothers and sisters ['bradzers
,en'systers] rodzeństwo
brotherly ['bradzerly] adj.
braterski
brought [bro:t] adj. przyniesiony;
zob. bring
brow [brau] s. brew; czoło;
nawis; szczyt; brzeg (prze-
paści); pomost; kładka
brown [braun] adj. brunatny;
brązowy; palony; kasztano-
waty; pakunkowy (papier); v.
brązowieć; opalać się;
przyrumieniać (mięso)
brown paper ['braun,pejpe:r] s.
papier pakunkowy
brown sugar [braun 'szuger] s.
melasa
bruise [bru:z] s. siniak; stłuczenie; v. tłuc; otłuc; posinia-
czyć; połamać kości; ranić;
zgnieść; wyklepać
brunette [bru:'net] s. brunetka
brush [brasz] s. szczotka;

pędzel; draśnięcie; v.
szczotkować; otrzepać;
pędzlować
brush up ['brasz ap] v.
wygładzić; odświeżyć;
zgarnąć szczotką
Brussels sprouts ['brazls,spraut]
s. brukselka (jarzyna)
brutal ['bru:tl] adj. brutalny;
zmysłowy; zwierzęcy
brutality [bru:'taelyty] s.
brutalstwo; brutalność
brute [bru:t] s. bydlę; zwierzę
ludzkie; adj. tępy; brutalny;
bezduszny; bydlęcy; nieokrzesany; zwierzęcy
bubble ['babl] s. bąbel; bańka;
kipienie; wrzenie; v. kipieć;
burzyć się; wydzielać bańki;
musować; bulgotać
buck [bak] s. kozioł; fircyk;
dolar; adj. rogowy; męski;
zwykły (szeregowy); v. skakać narowiście; opierać się
bucket ['bakyt] s. wiadro;
czerpak (koparki); tłok; miska
buckle ['bakl] v. spinać; łączyć;
wichrować; s. spinka; kla-
merka; sprzączka
buckle on ['bakl on] v. poza-
pinać się; zapiąć pas;
przypiąć
buckskin ['bakskyn] s. wypra-
wiona skóra koźla (sarnia)
bud [bad] s. pączek; zawią-
zek; zarodek; v. pączkować;
wyrastać; być w zarodku;
rozwijać się; dobrze
zapowiadać się
Buddhist ['budyst] s. buddysta
buddy ['bady] s. bliski kolega
budget ['badżyt] s. budżet; v.
budżetować; asygnować
buffalo ['bafelou] s. bawół
buffer ['bafer] s. bufor; zderzak;
odbój
buffet ['bafyt] s. bufet; cios;
kułak; szturchaniec; raz;
uderzenie
buffet ['befej] s. niski kredens;
dania barowe
bug [bag] s. owad; pluskwa;
defekt; amator; insekt; robak

bugle ['bju:gl] s. róg (do
trąbienia); v. trąbić; zatrąbić
build; built; built [byld; bylt; bylt]
build [byld] v. budować;
rozbudowywać; stworzyć;
wznosić
builder ['bylder] s. budowniczy
building ['byldyng] s. budowla
built [bylt] adj. zbudowany; zob.
build
bulb [balb] s. cebula; żarówka
bulge [baldż] v. wzdymać;
wybrzuszać; wydymać; wy-
trzeszczać; s. wypukłość;
wzdęcie; wzdymanie się;
wybrzuszenie; przewaga
bulk [balk] s. masa; kolos;
większość; cielsko; wielka
ilość (towaru); v. groma-
dzić; komasować
bulky ['balky] adj. wielki; otyły;
ciężki; masywny; nieporęczny
bull [bul] s. byk; duży samiec;
głupstwo; nonsens = bull-shit
[bul-szyt] (wulg.)
bullet ['bulyt] s. kula (nabój)
bulletin ['buletyn] s. komunikat;
biuletyn
bulletin board ['buletyn,bo:rd] s.
tablica na ogłoszenia
bullion ['buljen] s. złoto i srebro
w sztabach
bully ['buly] v. dręczyć;
tyranizować; s. awanturnik;
kłótnik; najęty drab; adj.
byczy; żywy; wesoły; świetny; kapitalny
bum [bam] s. włóczęga; nierób;
popijawa; zadek; v. włóczyć
się; cyganić; pić; adj. marny
bumblebee ['bambl-bi:] s. trzmiel
bump [bamp] v. zderzyć się;
łupnąć; odbić z łomotem;
nabić guza; s. zderzenie;
grzmotnięcie; guz; wybój;
wstrząs; uderzenie; wy-
pukłość; zdolności
bumper ['bamper] s. zderzak;
pełny kielich; rekord
bun [ban] s. ciastko drożdżowe;
kok (włosów)
bunch [bancz] s. pęk; banda;
zgraja; guz; v. składać w

pęki; skupiać się; kulić się

bunch of grapes ['bancz,ow grejps] kiść (gałązka) winogron; pęk winogron

bundle ['bandl] s. tłumok; wiązka; v. pakować (w tobół)

bundle up ['bandl,ap] v. zawinąć się; zebrać; zbierać

bungalow ['baŋgelou] s. domek letni parterowy

bungle ['baŋgl] s. partactwo; v. partaczyć; bałaganić

bunion ['banjen] s. zapalenie stawu w stopie (bolesny guz)

bunk ['baŋk] s. koja; banialuki

bunk bed ['baŋk,bed] s. łóżko piętrowe; łóżko do podnoszenia

bunny ['bani] s. królik; truś

buoy ['boj] s. boja; znak pływający; pława; v. znaczyć bojami

buoyant ['bojent] adj. utrzymujący się na powierzchni wody; pławny; sprężysty; pogodny

burden ['be:rdn] s. brzemię; ciężar; obowiązek; v. obciążać; przygniatać; obładowywać

bureau ['bjurou] s. komoda; biuro; sekretarzyk; urząd

bureaucracy [bju'rokresy] s. biurokracja

burglar [be:rgler] s. włamywacz

burglary ['be:rglery] s. włamanie (zwłaszcza w nocy)

burial ['berjel] s. pogrzeb

burly ['be:rly] adj. krzepki; tęgi; duży i silny

burn; burnt; burnt [be:rn; be:rnt; be:rnt]

burn [be:rn] v. palić; płonąć; zapalić; poparzyć; wypalać; s. oparzelizna; dziura wypalona; oparzenie

burner ['be:rner] s. palnik

burning ['be:rnyŋg] s. palenie

burnt [be:rnt] v. spalony; zob. burn (przypalony, opalony ...)

burst; burst; burst [be:rst; be:rst; be:rst]

burst [be:rst] v. rozsadzać;

rozrywać; s. wybuch; pęknięcie; salwa; zryw; szał; grzmot; hulanka

burst of laughter ['be:rst ,ow'lafter] wybuch śmiechu

burst into flames ['be:rst ,yntu'flejms] buchać ogniem

burst into tears ['be:rst ,yntu'tiers] wybuchnąć płaczem; zalać się łzami

bury ['bery] v. pochować; zagrzebać; pogrzebać; chować; zakopywać

bus [bas] s. autobus

bush [busz] s. krzak; gąszcz

bushel ['buszel] s. korzec (8 galonów); v. przerabiać

bushy ['buszy] adj. nastroszony; krzaczasty; gęsty

business ['byznys] s. interes; zajęcie; sprawa; przedsiębiorstwo; transakcja; handel; adj. handlowy; urzędowy

business hours ['byznys,aurs] godziny urzędowe

business letter ['byznys,leter] oficjalny list

businesslike ['byznys,lajk] adj. rzeczowy; solidny; poważny; praktyczny; dokładny

businessman ['byznysman] s. przedsiębiorca; człowiek interesów; handlowiec

business trip ['byznys,tryp] podróż służbowa

businesswoman ['byznys'łumen] s. kobieta interesu; właścicielka przedsiębiorstwa

bus stop ['bas-stop] s. przystanek autobusowy

bust [bast] s. popiersie; biust; v. :ujnować; psuć; rozwalić; niszczyć; bankrutować; wybuchnąć

bustle ['basl] v. krzątać się; zapędzać do pracy; s. rozgardiasz; krzątanina; bieganina

busy ['byzy] adj. zajęty; skrzętny; wścibski; ruchliwy

busybody ['byzy,body] adj. wścibski; złośliwy; plotkarz; intrygant

but [bat] adv. conj. prep. lecz; ale; jednak; natomiast; tylko; inaczej niż; z wyjątkiem

but for [ˈbat foːr] exp. oprócz; bez; gdyby nie

but now [ˈbat nau] exp. dopiero teraz; dopiero w tej chwili

but once [ˈbat łans] exp. tylko raz; chociaż tylko raz

butcher [ˈbuczer] s. rzeźnik; kat; v. zarzynać; mordować; masakrować; brutalnie zabijać; partaczyć

butt [bat] 1. s. drzewce; kolba; nasada; niedopałek papierosa; pośladki; cel; przedmiot kpin; ofiara; tarcza; v. bóść; trącać; przytykać; 2. s. styk; zetknięcie; uderzenie głową (bykiem)

butt in [ˈbat yn] v. wtrącać się; przerywać rozmowę

butter [ˈbater] s. masło; v. smarować masłem; przychlebiać

buttercup [ˈbaterkap] s. jaskier

butterfly [ˈbaterflaj] s. motyl; adj. motyli

buttocks [ˈbateks] pl. pośladki

button [ˈbatn] s. guzik; przycisk dzwonka; v. zapinać

button up [ˈbatn ap] v. zapinać się; zapinać na guziki

buttonhole [ˈbatnhoul] s. dziurka od guzika; v. zmuszać do słuchania

buttress [ˈbatrus] s. podpora

buxom [ˈbaksem] adj. dorodny; okazały; pełny (biust); ładna (babka)

buy; bought; bought [baj; boːt; boːt]

buy [baj] v. kupować; przekupić; okupić

buyer [bajer] s. nabywca

buzz [baz] s. brzęczenie; v. brzęczeć; przelatywać nisko

buzzard [ˈbazed] s. myszołów

by [baj] prep. przy; koło; co(dzień); przez; z; po; w (nocy); o; według

by myself [ˈbaj majself] ja sam

by and large [ˈbaj end ˈlaːrdż] adv. ogólnie mówiąc; ogólnie biorąc

by twos [ˈbaj,tuz] dwójkami

by the dozen [ˈbaj dy ˈdazn] tuzinami

by the end [ˈbaj dy ,end] przy końcu; ku końcowi; z końcem; pod koniec

by land [ˈbaj,laend] lądem

by bus [ˈbaj,bas] autobusem

by day [ˈbaj,dej] za dnia

by-and-by [ˈbaj-end-baj] s. przyszłość; adv. wnet; po chwili

bye-bye ! [ˈbajˈbaj] excl. pa !

by-election [,baj-eˈlekszyn] s. wybory uzupełniające

bygone [ˈbajgon] adj. miniony; przestarzały; s. zdarzenia minione

bygones [ˈbajgonz] pl. przeszłość; dawne urazy; dawne zatargi

bylaw [ˈbajloː] s. przepis; zarządzenie (miejscowe etc.)

by-name [ˈbajnejm] s. przydomek

bypass [ˈbaj-pas] s. droga dojazdowa; objazd; v. objeżdżać; ominąć

by-product [,baj-ˈprodact] s. produkt uboczny

byroad [,baj-ˈroud] s. boczna droga; droga drugorzędna

bystander [,baj-ˈstander] s. przygodny widz

bystreet [,baj-ˈstriːt] s. boczna ulica (drugorzędna)

byte [bajt] s. osiem bitów (zob. "bit"); 256 układów jednostek informacji; informacja wyrażająca literę w tekscie; zakodowanie jednej litery; odczytanie kodu jednej litery; jakakolwiek liczba jest zazwyczaj oznaczona w komputerze grupą "baytów;" jeden "byte" może zapisać w pamięci komputera cyfrę od zera do 255

byway [ˈbaj-łej] s. boczna droga; boczne przejście

byword [ˈbaj-,łeːrd] s. przysłowie; przydomek

(pogardliwy)
by work ['baj-,łe:rk] s. praca
uboczna poza zajęciem
głównym

C

c [si:] litera "c"; trzecia litera
alfabetu angielskiego
cab [kaeb] s. taksówka;
dorożka-szoferka; budka
maszynisty
cabaret [,kaebe'rej] s. lokal
taneczny; kabaret; serwis na
tacy
cabbage ['kaebydż] s. kapusta
cabin ['kaebyn] s. kabina;
chatka; prymitywnie zbudowany domek
cabinet ['kaebynyt] s. szafka;
rada ministrów; adj. tajny
cabinetmaker ['kaebynyt,mejke:r]
s. stolarz meblowy
cable ['kejbl] s. przewód; lina;
depesza; v. depeszować;
umocowywać liną; przesyłać
kablem
cable-car ['kejbl,ka:r] s. wóz
linowy; kolejka linowa
cabman ['kaebmen] s.
taksówkarz
cabstand ['kaeb staend] s. postój
taksówek
cackle ['kaekl] v. gdakać;
gęgać; chichotać; s. gda-
kanie; gęganie; chichot
cacti ['kaektaj] pl. kaktusy
cactus ['kaektes] s. kaktus
cad [kaed] s. ordynus; cham
cafe ['kaefej] s. kawiarnia; kawa;
restauracja; bar
cafeteria [,kaefy'tierja] s.
restauracja samoobsługowa
cage [kejdż] s. klatka; kosz; v.
zamykać w klatce
cake [kejk] s. ciastko; kostka
(mydła); smażony placek (z
ryby)

cake tin ['kejk,tyn] s. forma na
ciastko
calamity [ke'laemyty] s.
nieszczęście; klęska; niedola
calculate ['kaelkjulejt] v.
rachować; sądzić; oceniać
calculation [,kaelkju'lejszyn] s.
liczenie; ostrożność
calendar ['kaelynder] s.
kalendarz; terminarz
calf [kaef] s. cielak; łydka
caliber ['kaelyber] s. średnica
wewnętrzna; kaliber; wzorzec;
sprawdzian
call [ko:l] v. wołać; wzywać;
telefonować; odwiedzać; zawijać do portu; wyzywać; s.
krzyk; wezwanie; apel; powołanie; wizyta; nazwanie;
żądanie; sygnał
call for help ['ko:l,fo:r help]
wołanie o pomoc; wzywanie
pomocy
call names ['ko:l,nejmz] przezywać; wyzywać; ubliżać
call back ['ko:l,baek]
odtelefonować; odwołać z
powrotem
call at ['ko:l,aet] odwiedzać
call for ['ko:l,fo:r] żądać;
chodzić po coś (żeby
otrzymać)
call on ['ko:l,on] odwiedzać
(kogoś); prosić o
wypowiedź
call up ['ko:l,ap] telefonować
wywoływać (duchy etc.)
caller ['ko:ler] s. gość;
odwiedzający; adj. rześki;
świeży
calling ['ko:lyng] s. zawód;
powołanie; zatrudnienie; fach
callous ['kaeles] adj. stwardniały;
nieczuły; zrogowaciały
calm [ka:m] adj. spokojny; cichy;
opanowany; s. spokój; cisza;
opanowanie; v. uspokajać;
uciszać; uciszyć się
calm down ['ka:m,dałn] v.
uciszyć się; uspokoić się
calorie ['kaelery] s. kaloria
calves [ka:wz] pl. cielaki; łydki
camber ['kaember] v. wyginać;

s. wygięcie; wypukłość (jezdni)
came [kejm] v. przyszedł; zob. come
camel ['kaemel] s. wielbłąd
camera ['kaemere] s. aparat fotograficzny; prywatna izba
camomile ['kaemoumajl] s. rumianek
camouflage ['kaemufla:ż] s. maskowanie; v. maskować (wojsk.)
camp [kaemp] s. obóz; v. obozować; rozlokowywać w namiotach
camp out [kaemp aut] v. obozować w namiocie
campaign [kaem'pejn] s. kampania; akcja; v. odbywać kampanię; agitować
camp bed ['kaemp,bed] s. łóżko polowe; łóżko składane
camper ['kaemper] adj. obozujący; s. wóz lub przyczepa do obozowania; mieszkalny wóz (turystyczny)
camping ['kaempyng] s. obozowanie; życie obozowe
camping ground ['kaempyng ,graund] s. obozowisko; miejsce do obozowania
campus ['kaempes] s. teren uniwersytecki lub szkolny
can [kaen] s. puszka blaszana; ustęp; v. móc; konserwować; wyrzucać; umieć; zdołać; potrafić
Canadian [ke'nejdjen] adj. kanadyjski; s. Kanadyjczyk
canal [ke'nael] s. kanał; kanalik
canard [kae'na:rd] s. kaczka dziennikarska; plotka
canary [ke'nery] s. kanarek
cancel ['kaensel] v. znosić; kasować; odwoływać; skreślać; anulować
cancer ['kaenser] s. rak (choroba); nowotwór
candid ['kaendyd] adj. szczery; bezstronny; otwarty
candidate ['kaendydyt] s. kandydat; kandydatka
candied ['kaendyd] adj.

pocukrzony; lukrowany
candle ['kaendl] s. świeca
candlestick ['kaendlstyk] s. świecznik; lichtarz
candy ['kaendy] s. cukierki; lukier; cukier lodowaty
cane [kejn] s. trzcina; laska; pałka; v. chłostać; wyplatać trzciną; ukarać trzciną
canned [kaend] adj. zakonserwowany w puszce
cannery [kaenery] s. fabryka konserw
cannibal ['kaenybel] s. ludożerca; adj. ludożerczy
cannon ['kaenen] s. działo
cannot ['kaenot] v. nie móc (od can not); nie potrafić
canoe [ke'nu:] s. czółno; kajak; łódka; v. pływać kajakiem; wiosłować
canopy ['kaenepy] s. baldachim; okap; firmament; sklepienie
cant ['kaent] s. żargon; frazes
can't [ka:nt] v. nie móc (od can); nie potrafić
canteen [kaen'ti:n] s. manierka; menażka; kantyna
canvas ['kaenwes] s. płótno impregnowane
canvass ['kaenwes] s. badanie; zapobieganie; v. zabiegać; badać; starać się o głosy
cap [kaep] s. czapka; pokrywa; wieko; kapiszon; beret
cap [kaep] v. wkładać czapkę lub nakrywkę; wieńczyć; zakładać spłonkę; zakasować; nakrywać
capability [,kaepe'bylyty] s. zdolność; zdatność; możliwość
capable ['kejpebl] adj. zdolny
capacity [ke'paesyty] s. zdolność; kompetencja; pojemność; właściwość; nośność; objętość
cape [kejp] s. 1. peleryna; 2. przylądek
caper [kejper] v. wywijać kozły; s. hołubiec; sus; skok
capital ['kaepytl] s. stolica; kapitał; adj. główny;

zasadniczy; stołeczny; fatalny
capital crime ['kaepytl,krajm] s.
morderstwo
capitalism ['kaepytlyzem] s.
kapitalizm
capital letter ['kaepytl,leter] s.
duża litera
capital punishment ['kaepytl
'panyszment] kara śmierci
capricious [ke'pryszes] adj.
kapryśny
capsize [kaep'sajz] v. wywracać
(statek) dnem do góry
capsule ['kaepsju:l] s. kapsułka;
torebka; pochewka; kabinka
captain ['kaeptyn] s. kapitan;
naczelnik; v. dowodzić
caption ['kaepszyn] s. nagłówek;
napis; poświadczenie; aresztowanie; pojmanie
captivate ['kaeptywejt] v. ująć;
czarować; urzekać; zniewa-
lać; oczarować
captive ['kaeptyw] s. jeniec
captivity ['kaeptywyty] s.
niewola
capture ['kaepczer] s.
owładnięcie; łup; zdobycz; v.
pojmać; owładnąć
car [ka:r] s. samochód; wóz
caravan ['kaerewaen] s.
karawana; wóz kryty;
przyczepka mieszkalna
carbohydrate ['ka:rbe'hajdrejt] s.
węglowodan
carbon ['ka:rben] s. węgiel;
kopia (kalka)
carbon dioxide ['ka:rben daj
'oksajd] s. CO2; dwutlenek
węgla
carbon paper ['ka:rben,pejper] s.
kalka
carburetor ['ka:rbjurejter] s.
gaźnik
car carrier [ka:r-'kaerjer] s. wóz
do przewozu aut
carcass ['ka:r-kes] s. ścierwo;
padlina; szkielet
card ['ka:rd] s. karta; bilet;
pocztówka; legitymacja; atut
cardboard ['ka:rdbo:rd] s.
tektura; adj. tekturowy
card box ['ka:rdboks] s. karton

cardigan ['ka:rdygen] s. wełniana
kurta (kamizelka)
cardinal ['ka:rdynl] adj. główny;
s. kardynał
card index ['ka:rd yndeks] s.
kartoteka
car papers [ka:r pejpers] s.
dokumenty samochodowe
care [keer] s. opieka; troska;
ostrożność; zgryzota; dozór;
uwaga; niepokój
care of [keer ow] c/o; adres (u
kogoś)
care for [keer fo:r] v. dbać o
kogoś; lubić; kochać; mieć
ochotę; przepadać za
career [ke'rier] s. kariera; zawód;
tok; pęd; bieg; v. cwałować
carefree [keerfri:] adj. beztroski
careful [keerful] adj. ostrożny;
troskliwy; dbały; pieczołowity
careless [keerles] adj. niedbały;
nieuważny; nieostrożny
caress [ke'res] s. pieszczota; v.
pieścić; popieścić
caretaker ['keertejker] s.
dozorca; stróż
careworn ['keerlo:rn] s.
zgnębiony kłopotami
carfare ['ka:rfeer] s. opłata za
jazdę
cargo ['ka:rgou] s. ładunek
caricature [,kaeryke'czjuer] s.
karykatura; v. karykaturować
car mechanic [ka:r-my'kaenyk] s.
mechanik samochodowy
carnation ['ka:r'nejszyn] 1. s. &
adj. ciemno-czerwony; cielisty;
2. goździk ogrodowy
carnival ['ka:rnywel] s. karnawał;
zapusty
carnivorous [ka:r'nyweres] adj.
mięsożerny
carol ['kaerel] s. kolęda; v.
kolędować
carp [ka:rp] s. karp; v. czepiać
się; ganić; przycinać
car parking ['ka:r-pa:rkyng] s.
parking samochodowy
carpenter ['ka:rpynter] s. cieśla;
stolarz
carpet ['ka:rpyt] s. dywan; v.
wyściełać dywanem

carriage [´kaerydż] s. wagon;
powóz; postawa; kareta; chód
carrier [´kaerjer] s. firma
przewozowa; nośnik; tragarz;
rozsadnik (zakażenia);
lotniskowiec; okaziciel
carrion [´kaerjen] s. padlina
carrot [´kaeret] s. marchewka
carry [´kaery] v. nosić; wozić;
zanieść; unosić
carry off [´kaery,of] v.
uprowadzić; zabrać;
zdobywać (nagrodę)
carry on [´kaery,on] v.
kontynuować; wytrwać;
awanturować się
carry out [´kaery,aut] v.
wykonać; przeprowadzić;
spełnić
cart [´ka:rt] s. wóz
cartel [´ka:rtel] s. kartel
carter [´ka:rter] s. woźnica
cart horse [´ka:rt,hors] s. koń
pociągowy
carton [´ka:rten] s. karton
cartoon [ka:r´tun] s. karykatura;
v. rysować karykatury
cartoonist [ka:r´tunyst] s.
karykaturzysta
cartridge [´ka:rtrydż] s. nabój
cartwheel [´ka:rt-hłi:l] s. kołodziej
carve [´ka:rw] v. rzeźbić;
krajać; cyzelować; pociąć
na części
carver [´ka:rwer] s. snycerz
carving [´ka:rwyng] s. rzeźba
cascade [kaes´kejd] s.
wodospad; v. spadać jak
wodospad
case [kejs] s. 1. wypadek;
sprawa; dowód; 2. skrzynia;
pochwa; torba; 3. sprawa
sądowa; v. zamykać w
pochwie; otaczać czymś;
oszalować; oprawić
casement [´kejsment] s. rama
okienna; okno z kwaterami
cash [kaesz] s. gotówka;
pieniądze; v. spieniężać;
inkasować; płacić (gotówką)
cash on delivery [kaesz on
dy´lywery] zapłata przy
odbiorze; C.O.D.

cashier [kae´szjer] s. kasjer
cash register [kaesz ´redżyster]
s. kasa (zmechanizowana)
casing [´kejsyng] s. 1. powłoka;
pochwa; 2. obudowa; oprawa;
3. łuska; 4. opancerzenie
cask [kaesk] s. beczułka
casket [kaeskyt] s. trumna; urna;
szkatuła
cassock [´kaesek] s. sutanna
cast; cast; cast [ka:st; ka:st;
ka:st]
cast [ka:st] s. rzut; odlew; gips;
odcień; v. rzucać; łowić;
odlewać; powalić; dzielić
role teatralne
castaway [´ka:st,e´łej] s.
wyrzutek; rozbitek
cast down [ka:st dałn] adj.
przygnębiony; v. de-
prymować
caste [ka:st] s. kasta
cast iron [ka:stajren] s. żeliwo
castle [´ka:sl] s. zamek
castor oil [´ka:ster,ojl] s. olej
rycynowy
cast steel [´ka:st,sti:l] s. lana stal
casual [´kaeżuel] adj. przypadkowy; niedbały; dorywczy;
nie planowany; niechlujny
casualty [´kaeżuelty] s.
wypadek; ofiara wypadku;
lista strat; nieszczęście
cat [kaet] s. kot; jędza
catalog [´kaetelog] s. katalog
catamaran [,kaeteme´raen] s.
dwu-czółnowa łódź
cataract [´kaeteraekt] s.
katarakta; ulewa; wodospad
catarrh [ke´ta:r] s. katar
catastrophe [ka´taestrefy] s.
katastrofa
catch; caught; caught [kaecz;
ko:t; ko:t]
catch [kaecz] v. łapać; łowić;
ujmować; słyszeć; wybuch-
nąć; nabawić się; usidlić;
uchwycić; s. łup; połów
catch cold [kaecz kold] v.
zaziębiać się
catch fire [kaecz fajer] v.
zapalać się
catch up [kaecz ap] v. dogonić

catching [kaeczyŋg] adj.
zaraźliwy; s. tryby; uchwyt;
zazębienie
category ['kaetygery] s.
kategoria
cater ['kejter] v. dostarczać
żywności; obsługiwać
caterpillar ['kaetepyler] s. gąsienica (traktora, czołgu)
cathedral [ke'ti:drel] s. katedra
Catholic ['kaetelyk] adj. katolicki;
s. katolik
cattle [kaetl] s. bydło rogate
caucus ['ko:kes] s. tajne narady
partyjne; klika
caught [ko:t] złapany; zob. catch
cauldron ['ko:ldren] s. kocioł
cauliflower ['kaulyflauer] s.
kalafior
cause [ko:z] s. przyczyna;
sprawa; racja; motywacja;
proces; powód; v. spowodować; być przyczyną
causeless [ko:zles] adj.
przypadkowy; bezpodstawny
caustic ['ko:styk] adj. żrący;
gryzący; złośliwy; do-
kuczliwy; uszczypliwy
caution ['ko:szyn] s. ostrożność; przezorność; roztropność; uwaga; v. ostrzegać
cautious ['ko:szes] adj. ostrożny;
rozważny; roztropny; uważny
cavalry ['kaewelry] s. kawaleria
cave [kejw] s. pieczara; jaskinia;
v. zapadać się; drążyć
cavern ['kaewen] s. jama;
jaskinia; grota; pieczara
cavity ['kaewyty] s. wklęsłość;
dziura (w zębie); dół; jama;
wydrążenie
cease [sy:s] v. ustawać;
przestawać; położyć kres
ceaseless [sy:slys] adj.
bezustanny; ciągły; nie-
przerwany
cedar ['si:der] s. cedr
cede [si:d] v. ustąpić; cedować
ceiling ['sy:lyŋg] s. sufit; pułap;
górna granica
celebrate ['selybrejt] v.
święcić; uczcić; sławić;
obchodzić

celebrated ['selybrejtyd] adj.
sławny; słynny; głośny
celebration ['selybrejszyn] s.
obchód; odprawianie; święcenie; celebrowanie
celebrity ['sylebryty] s. sławna
osoba; sława; znakomita
osobowość
celery ['selery] s. seler (jarzyna)
celibacy ['selybesy] s.
bezżeństwo; celibat
cell [sel] s. cela; komórka
cellar ['seler] s. piwnica
Celtic [keltyk] adj. celtycki
cement [sy'ment] s. cement; v.
cementować; kleić; utwierdzać; spoić; złączyć
cemetery ['semytry] s. cmentarz
censor ['sensor] s. cenzor
censorship ['senserszyp] s.
cenzura
censure ['senszer] s. nagana;
krytyka; v. krytykować
cent [sent] s. cent
centenary [sentynery] adj.
stuletni; s. stulecie; setna
rocznica
centennial ['sen'tenjel] s.
stulecie; adj. stuletni
center ['senter] s. ośrodek;
centrum; v. ześrodkowywać;
centrować; skupiać się
centigrade ['sentygrejd] adj.
stustopniowy (termometr)
centimeter ['sentymi:ter] s.
centymetr
central ['sentral] adj. środkowy;
czołowy; s. centrala
Central Europe ['sentral juerop]
Europa Środkowa
central heating ['sentrel hi:tyŋg]
centralne ogrzewanie
centralize ['sentrelajz] v.
centralizować; ześrod-
kowywać
century ['senczury] s. stulecie
cereals ['syerjelz] pl. zboża
cerebral ['syrybrel] adj. mózgowy
ceremonial [,sery'mounjel] adj.
ceremonialny; s. rytuał; ceremoniał; ceremonialność
ceremonious [,sery'mounjes] adj.
drobiazgowy; ceremonialny

ceremony ['serymeny] s.
ceremonia; v. sztywno się
zachowywać

certain ['se:rtyn] adj. niejaki;
pewien; pewny; ustalony;
jakiś

certainly ['se:rtnly] adv. na
pewno; oczywiście; bez-
względnie

certainty ['se:rtynty] s.
pewność; pewnik; rzecz
pewna

certificate [se'rtyfykyt] s.
świadectwo; poświadczenie;
dyplom; metryka; v. za-
świadczać; dyplomować

certify ['se:rtyfaj] v.
zaświadczać; zapewniać;
uznawać za

certitude ['se:rtytju:d] s.
pewność; przeświadczenie

chafe [czejf] v. trzeć; otrzeć;
irytować; s. tarcie; otarcie;
irytacja; rozdrażnienie; złość

chaff [cza:f] s. 1. sieczka;
2. żart; naciąganie; v.
wyśmiewać żartobliwie;
naciągać

chagrin ['szaegryn] s. smutek;
rozczarowanie; v. upokarzać;
rozczarowywać boleśnie

chain [czejn] s. łańcuch;
syndykat; trust; v. wiązać na
łańcuchu; mierzyć; uwiązać;
zakuć

chair [czeer] s. krzesło; stołek;
fotel; katedra; v. prze-
wodniczyć; sadzać na
krześle

chair lift ['czeerlyft] s. wyciąg
linowy

chairman ['czeermen] s.
przewodniczący; prezes

chalk [czo:k] s. kreda; v. pisać
kredą

challenge ['czaelyndż] s.
wyzwanie; zadanie; v. wy-
zywać; zarzucać; wzywać;
korcić; prowokować; rzucać
wyzwanie

chamber ['czejmber] s. izba;
komora; sala; pokój; v.
wydrążyć

chambermaid ['czejmbermejd] s.
pokojowa

chameleon [ke'my:ljen] s.
kameleon

chamois ['szaemła:] s. giemza;
ircha; zamsz

champagne ['szaem'pejn] s.
szampan

champion ['czaempjen] s. mistrz;
obrońca; v. bronić; walczyć
o ...; popierać; adj.
przewyższający wszystkich

championship ['czaempjenszyp]
s. mistrzostwo

chance [cza:ns] s. okazja;
przypadek; szczęście; szansa;
ryzyko; adj. przypadkowy;
przygodny; v. zdarzać się;
ryzykować; próbować; przytrafić się; natknąć się

chancellor [cza:seler] s. kanclerz;
pierwszy sekretarz
(ambasady); najwyższy sędzia

chandelier [szaendy'ljer] s.
żyrandol; świecznik

change [czejndż] s. zmiana;
wymiana; drobne; v. zmienić;
przebierać (się); wymieniać;
rozmieniać (na drobne)

change one's mind ['czejndż
,łans'majnd] zmienić czyjeś
zdanie (przekonania etc.)

change trains ['czejndż,trejns] v.
przesiąść się (na kolei)

changeable ['czejndżebl] adj.
zmienny; ulegający zmianom

channel ['czaenl] s. kanał;
koryto; łożysko; v. żłobić;
przesyłać drogą (urzędową)

chaos ['kejos] s. chaos

chap [czaep] s. chłop; chłopiec;
człek; v. pękać; powodować
pęknięcia (warg); zary-
sowywać

chapel ['czaepel] s. kaplica

chaplain ['czaeplyn] s. kapelan

chaps [cza:ps] pl. skórzane
nogawice (kowboja); ochra-
niacze (chaparillos)

chapter ['czaepter] s. rozdział;
oddział; v. dzielić na rozdziały

character ['kaerykter] s.
charakter; typ; cecha;

reputacja; moralność; facet;
znak; usposobienie
characteristic ['kaerykterystyk]
adj. charakterystyczny;
typowy; s. cecha; własność;
właściwość
characterize ['kaerykterajz] v.
charakteryzować (opisywać)
charge [cza:rdż] s. ciężar;
ładunek (naboju, baterii); obowiązek; piecza; podopieczny;
zarzut; opłata; należność;
koszt; szarża; godło; v. ładować; nasycać; obciążać;
żądać; liczyć sobie; oskarżać; atakować; szarżować
charge account [cza:rdż e'kaunt]
s. otwarty kredyt (w banku)
charge card [cza:rdż 'kard] s.
karta kredytowa do zakupów
chariot ['czaerjet] s. wóz;
rydwan
charitable ['czaerytebl] adj.
litościwy; dobroczynny
charity ['czaeryty] s. miłosierdzie; dobroczynność
charm [cza:rm] s. czar; urok;
amulet; urok; wdzięk; v.
czarować; oczarować
charming [cza:rmyng] adj.
czarujący
chart [cza:rt] s. wykres; mapa
morska; v. robić wykres;
wytyczać; pokazywać (jak)
charmless [cza:rmlys] adj. bez
wdzięku
charter [cza:rter] s. statut;
przywilej; dyplom; akt nadania
prawa do ...; v. nadawać; zakładać na statutach; wynajmować statek lub samolot
charter plane [cza:rter plejn] s.
wynajęty grupowo samolot
charwoman ['cza:rłumen] s.
sprzątaczka; dochodząca;
sprzątaczka; posługaczka
chase 1. [czejs] s. pościg;
pogoń; polowanie; łowy;
teren polowania; v. gonić;
ścigać; polować; wyganiać
chase 2. [czejs] s. łożysko;
wgłębienie; wykop; v. żłobić
chasm ['kaezem] s. otchłań

chaste [czejst] adj. czysty;
niewinny; nieskażony;
cnotliwy
chastity ['czaestyty] s.
niewinność; prostota;
dziewictwo
chat [czaet] s. pogawędka;
awędzenie; v. gawędzić; gadać; rozmawiać
chatter [czaeter] v. szczebiotać;
klapać; s. szczebiot; klapanie;
klekot; paplanie; terkot
chatterbox [czaeterboks]
s.trajkotka; gaduła; pleciuga
chauffeur ['szoufer] s. zawodowy kierowca; przenośny
piecyk
cheap [czi:p] adj. tani; marny
cheapen [czi:pen] v. tanieć;
obniżać wartość; spadać
na cenie
cheat [czi:t] s. oszust; oszustka;
v. oszukiwać; zdradzać (w
małżeństwie); okpiwać
check [czek] s. wstrzymanie;
przerwa; sprawdzenie; czek;
kwit; szach; adj. szachow-
nicowy; kontrolny; pod-
kreślony; v. hamować;
sprawdzać; zakreślać;
nadawać; zgadzać się;
szachować; ganić; kryty-
kować; opanowywać
check in [czek yn] v.
wmeldowywać się (w pracy,
w wojsku, w hotelu, etc.)
check out [czek aut] v.
wymeldowywać się; zapłacić
za hotel
checked [czekt] adj. w kratkę
checkroom [czekrum] s.
przechowalnia (bagażu);
szatnia
cheek [czi:k] s. policzek;
bezczelne gadanie; śmia-
łość; v. mówić bezczelnie
do kogoś; stawiać się
cheeky ['czi:ky] adj. bezczelny;
zuchwały; pełen tupetu; z
tupetem; impertynencki
cheer [czier] s. brawo; hurra;
radość; jadło; v. krzyczeć;
rozweselać; dodawać otuchy

cheer on ['czier on] v.
zachęcać; zagrzewać;
dodawać otuchy
cheer up ['czier ap] v.
pocieszać; nabrać otuchy;
rozpogodzić
cheerful ['czierful] adj. pogodny;
wesoły; ochoczy;
rozweselający
cheerless ['czierlys] adj. ponury;
smutny; przybity
cheery ['cziery] adj. wesoły;
radosny; pogodny
cheese ['czi:z] s. ser
chef [czef] s. kuchmistrz
chemical ['kemykel] adj.
chemiczny; s. substancja
chemiczna
chemicals ['kemykels] pl.
chemikalia; leki; lekarstwa
chemise [sze'mi:z] s. damska
koszula luźna i długa
chemist ['kemyst] s. chemik;
aptekarz
chemistry ['kemystry] s. chemia
cheque [czek] s. czek (poza
USA)
chequered ['czekerd] adj.
kratkowany; urozmaicony;
burzliwy
cherish ['czerysz] v. lubić;
tulić; żywić (uczucie);
miłować
cherry ['czery] s. czereśnia;
wiśniowy kolor; vulg.
prawiczka; adj. wiśniowy;
vulg. prawiczy; czerwony
chess [czes] s. szachy
chess-board [czes-bo:rd] s.
szachownica
chess man ['czesmen] s. figurka
szachowa
chest [czest] s. skrzynia;
komoda; pierś; płuca; kufer;
skrzynka
chestnut ['czesnat] s. kasztan
chest of drawers ['czest
,ow'dro:ers] s. komoda
chew [czu:] v. żuć;
przeżuwać; besztać;
gderać; s. żucie; tytoń do
żucia; prymka
chewing gum ['czu:yng,gam] s.

guma do żucia
chewy [czu:y] adj. nadający się
do żucia
chicken ['czykyn] s. kurczę; adj.
tchórzliwy; bojący się
chicken out ['czykyn aut] v.
stchórzyć; ustąpić ze
strachu
chide; chid; chidden [czajd; czyd;
czydn]
chide [czajd] v. łajać; droczyć
się; skarżyć; besztać
chicken pox ['czykyn poks] s.
ospa wietrzna
chief [czy:f] s. wódz; szef; adj.
główny; naczelny
chilblain ['czylblejn] s.
odmrożenie (zob. frost bite)
child [czajld] s. dziecko
childish ['czajldysz] adj.
dziecinny
childless ['czajldlys] adj.
bezdzietny
childlike ['czajldlajk] adj.
dziecięcy; jak dziecko
children ['czyldren] pl. dzieci
chill [czyl] s. chłód; dreszcz; v.
studzić; mrozić; oziębiać
chilly [czyly] adj. chłodny; adv.
chłodno; zimno
chime ['czajm] s. dzwony
grające; rytm; kurant; v. bić
w dzwony; wydzwaniać;
rymować; zabrzmieć
chimney ['czymny] s. komin;
wylot; szkło lampy naftowej
chimney sweeper ['czymny
,słi:per] s. kominiarz;
kominiarski
chin [czyn] s. broda; podbródek;
v. podciągać brodę do
drążka
china ['czajna] s. porcelana
chinese ['czaj'ni:z] adj. chiński;
Chinese s. Chińczyk
chink ['czynk] 1. s. brzęk; v.
pobrzękiwać; brzęczeć; 2. s.
szpara; szczelina; v. zapychać
szpary
chip [czyp] s. drzazga; odłamek;
skrawek; v. otłuc; obijać;
dokuczać; nabierać; ciosać;
ćwierkać; piszczeć; nogą

podstawiać; złuszczać się;
odłupać

chirp [czy:rp] s. świergot; v.
ćwierkać; szczebiotać

chisel ['czyzl] s. dłuto; przecinak;
v. ciąć; rzeźbić; oszukać

chivalrous ['czywelres] adj.
rycerski

chivalry ['czywelry] s. rycerstwo;
rycerskość

chive [czajw] s. szczypiorek

chlorine ['klo:ry:n] s. chlor

chloroform ['klo:refo:rm] s.
chloroform; v. maczać w
chloroformie; usypiać
chloroformem

chock [czok] s. klin; v. osadzać
na klinach; adv. szczelnie;
ciasno; mocno; w pełni

chocolate ['czoklyt] s. czekolada;
adj. czekoladowy (kolor etc.)

choice [czojs] s. wybór;
wybranka; adj. wyborowy;
doborowy

choir ['kłajer] s. chór

choke [czouk] v. dusić;
zadusić; tłumić; dławić; s.
duszenie; dławik; gardziel;
przewężenie; odgłosy
duszenia; zawór

choke down [czouk dałn] v.
dławić; zmniejszać gardziel

choke up [czouk ap] v. zatykać
(rurę); zadławić (motor etc.)

choose; chose; chosen [czu:z;
czouz; czouzn]

choose [czu:z] v. wybierać;
woleć; postanowić; obrać;
zadecydować

chop [czop] v. rąbać; obcinać;
s. rąbnięcie; kotlet; krótka fala

chop down [czop dałn] v.
powalić (drzewo etc.);
ściąć; zrąbać

chord [ko:rd] s. struna; cięciwa;
struna głosowa

chorus ['ko:res] s. chór; v.
mówić chórem; śpiewać
chórem

chose [czouz] v. wybrał; zob.
choose

chow [czau] s. jadło (slang)

Christ [krajst] Chrystus

christen ['krisn] v. ochrzcić

Christian ['krystjen] adj.
chrześcijański; s. chrześcijanin (slang: cywilizowany)

Christianity [krys'czaenyty] v.
chrześcijaństwo

Christian name ['krystjen,nejm]
s. imię (inne niż nazwisko)

Christmas ['krysmas] s. Boże
Narodzenie

Christmas Day ['krysmas dej]
Dzień Bożego Narodzenia

Christmas Eve ['krysmas i:w]
wilia; wigilia Bożego
Narodzenia

chromium ['kroumjem] s. chrom

chronic ['kronyk] adj. chroniczny;
straszliwy (ból)

chronicle ['kronykl] s. kronika

chronological [krone'lodżykel]
adj. chronologiczny

chubby ['czaby] adj. pucołowaty;
pyzaty; mały i gruby

chuck [czak] v. rzucać;
gdakać; klinować; cmokać;
zwężać strumień wody w
rurze s. zawór wodny; klin

chuckle [czakl] v. chichotać; s.
chichot; zduszony śmiech

chum [czam] v. przyjaźnić się
blisko; s. serdeczny kolega;
współlokator

church [cze:rcz] s. kościół

churchyard ['cze:rcz,ja:rd] s.
cmentarz; dziedziniec kościelny; adj. cmentarny

churn [cze:rn] v. robić masło;
kłócić się; burzyć się;
kotłować się; pienić się; s.
maślnica; maślniczka; bańka
na mleko

chute [szu:t] s. koryto zrzutowe;
spadek; wodospad; zsyp; ryn-
na; spadochron; tor zjeżdżalni
dla dzieci

chutzpah [hucpa] s. nachal-
ność; śmiałość; tupet (po
nowohebrajsku)

cider ['sajder] s. wino z jabłek

cigar [sy'ga:r] s. cygaro

cigarette [sige'ret] s. papieros

cigarette lighter [sy'gae'ret'lajter]
s. zapalniczka

cinder ['synder] s. popiół; żużel;
v. spalać na żużel
Cinderella [,synde'rele] s.
kopciuszek; Kopciuszek
cinder track ['synder-traek] s.
bieżnia żużlowa; tor żużlowy
cinécamera ['syni-'kaemere] s.
aparat filmowy
cinema ['syneme] s. kino
cinema projector ['syneme
,prodżekter] s. rzutnik filmowy
cipher ['sajfer] s. cyfra; szyfr;
zero; monogran; v. szyfrować; rachować
circle ['se:rkl] s. koło; krąg;
obwód; v. otaczać; kręcić
się w koło; opasywać; krążyć; okrążać
circuit ['se:rkyt] s. obwód;
okrężna; okólna (podróż)
circular ['se:rkjuler] s. okólnik;
adj. okrągły; kolisty
circulate ['se:rkjulejt] v. krążyć;
cyrkulować; puszczać w
obieg; być w obiegu
circulation ['se:rkjulejszyn] s.
krążenie; obrót; nakład
circumference [se'rkamfyrens] s.
obwód (koła etc.)
circumcision [se:rkem'syżyn] s.
obrzezanie; obcięcie napletka
circumscribe [,se:rkem'skrajb] v.
opisywać; zakreślać
circumstance ['se:rkemstaens] s.
okoliczności; szczegóły
circus ['se:rkes] s. cyrk; okrągły
plac; rondo; desant (sl.)
cistern ['systern] s. zbiornik na
wodę; cysterna
citation [saj'tejszyn] s. cytat;
przytoczenie; wzmianka
pochwalna; pochwała
cite [sajt] v. cytować;
przytaczać; pozywać;
wymieniać w komunikacie;
pozywać do sądu
citizen ['sytyzn] s. obywatel
citizenship ['sytyzenszyp] s.
obywatelstwo; cnoty oby-
watelskie
city ['syty] s. (wielkie) miasto;
centrum finansowe; ośrodek
city center ['syty,senter] s.

centrum miasta
city guide ['syty'gajd] s. plan
miasta; przewodnik po
mieście
city hall ['syty,ho:l] s. zarząd
miasta; magistrat
civics ['sywyks] s. nauka praw i
obowiązków obywatela
civil ['sywl] adj. społeczny;
uprzejmy; obywatelski; cywilny (kodeks)
civilian [sy'wyljen] adj. cywilny;
s. cywil; obywatel
civility [sy'wylyty] s.
uprzejmość; grzeczność
civilization [,sywylaj'sejszyn] s.
cywilizacja; całość kultury
civilize ['sywylajz] v.
cywilizować; ucywilizować
civil marriage ['sywl'maerydż] s.
ślub cywilny
civil rights ['sywl,rajts] s. prawa
obywatelskie
civil service ['sywl'se:rwys] s.
służba państwowa
civil war ['sywl,ło:r] s. wojna
domowa
clack [klaek] v. klekotać;
gdakać; s. klekot; wieko
clad [klaed] adj. odziany; zob.
clothe
claim [klejm] v. żądać;
twierdzić; s. żądanie; twierdzenie; działka; skarga; zażalenie; dług
claimant [klejment] s. rościciel;
pretendent; adj. pilny; rażący
clammy ['klaemy] adj. mokro-
-lepki; wilgotny i zimny
clamor ['klaemer] s. zgiełk;
krzyk; v. krzyczeć; robić
wrzawę; wymuszać krzykiem
clamorous ['klaemeres] adj.
zgiełkliwy; krzykliwy
clamp [klaemp] s. klamra; zacisk;
v. zaciskać (jak) klamrą
clan [klaen] s. klan; szczep
szkocki; v. tworzyć klikę
clandestine [klaen'destyn] adj.
potajemny; skryty; tajny
clang [klaeng] s. dźwięk;
szczęk; klekot; v.
dźwięczeć; szczękać; kle-

clank 345 clemency

kotać; rozbrzmiewać; brzękać; dzwonić
clank [klaenk] s. chrzęst; brzęk;
v. brzękać; chrzęścić
clap [klaep] s. huk; klaskanie; v.
łopotać; oklaskiwać; klepać
claret ['klaeret] s. czerwone
wino; bordo; slang: krew
clarify ['klaeryfaj] v. wyjaśniać;
rozjaśniać; oczyszczać
clarity ['klaeryty] s. czystość;
jasność; przejrzystość;
klarowność
clash [klaesz] s. brzęk; starcie;
v. brzęczeć; ścierać się;
kolidować; uderzać w coś
clasp [klaesp] s. klamra; uchwyt;
okucie; v. spinać; ściskać
clasp knife ['klaesp-najf] s.
scyzoryk; kozik; nóż składany
class [klaes] s. klasa; lekcja;
rocznik; grupa; kurs; kategoria; v. klasyfikować;
segregować; sortować
classmate ['kla:s,mejt] s. kolega
szkolny
classroom ['kla:s,ru:m] s. klasa
(w szkole); sala szkolna
class struggle [,kla:s'stragl] s.
walka klas w społeczeństwie
classic ['klaesyk] s. klasyk;
studia klasyczne; adj. klasyczny; uznany autorytet;
klasyk
classical ['klaesykel] adj.
klasyczny; typowy; huma-
nistyczny
classification [klaesyfy'kejszyn]
s. klasyfikacja; klasyfikowanie
classify ['klaesyfaj] s.
klasyfikować; sortować;
zaklasyfikować
clatter ['klaeter] v. brzęczeć;
klapać; s. brzęk; łoskot; gwar
clause [klo:z] s. klauzula; zdanie;
punkt umowy
claw [klo:] s. pazur; szpon; łapa;
kleszcze; v. drapać; wy-
drapać; łapać w szpony
clay [klej] s. glina; sl. trup
clean [kli:n] adj. czysty;
wyraźny; zgrabny; adv.
całkiem; zupełnie; po prostu;

v. oczyścić; opróżniać; ogo-
łocić; wygrać; uprzątnąć;
dużo zyskać (sl.)
clean out ['kli:n aut] v.
oczyścić; opróżniać;
wyczyścić
clean up ['kli:n ap] v.
posprzątać; wygrać; zrobić
na czysto; robić porządek
cleaner ['kli:ner] s. czyściciel;
oczyszczalnik; właściciel
pralni; pralnia chemiczna
cleaning ['kli:nyng] s.
czyszczenie; sprzątanie;
porządki
cleanliness ['klenlynys] s.
czystość; zamiłowanie do
czystości
cleanly ['klenly] adj. czysty; adv.
czysto; schludnie
cleanness ['kli:nnys] s.
czystość; zamiłowanie do
czystości
cleanse [klenz] v. czyścić;
zmywać (grzechy);
oczyszczać
clear [klier] adj. jasny; czysty;
bystry; adv. jasno; wyraźnie;
z dala; zupełnie; dokładnie; s.
wolna przestrzeń
clear away ['klier,elej] v. usunąć
(przeszkodę etc.)
clear up ['klier,ap] v. wyjaśnić
clear-cut ['klier,kat] adj.
wyraźny; czysty; poprawny
clearing ['klieryng] s.
karczowisko; rozrachunek;
obrachunek
clearly ['klierly] adv. wyraźnie;
jasno; oczywiście
cleave; cleft; cleft [kli:w; kleft;
kleft]
cleave [kli:w] v. 1. łupać;
pękać; rozdwajać; 2.
trzymać się wiernie; nie
odstępować
clef [klef] s. klucz (muzyczny)
cleft [kleft] s. szczelina;
pęknięcie; zob. cleave
clemency ['klemensy] s.
miłosierdzie; łagodność
(klimatu etc.)

clench [klencz] v. ściskać;
zaciskać; zewrzeć się; ubić
(targu); s. uścisk;
zaciśnięcie; zagięcie
clergy ['kle:rdży] s.
duchowieństwo; kler
clergyman ['kle:rdżymen] s.
duchowny; ksiądz; pastor
clerical ['klerykel] adj.
urzędniczy; duchowny;
biurowy
clerk [kla:rk] s. subiekt;
urzędnik; pisarz; ekspedient
clever ['klewer] adj. zdolny;
sprytny; zręczny; pomysłowy;
uprzejmy
click [klyk] v. szczękać;
cmokać; trzaskać; dopiąć
swego; wygrać; s. trzask;
zatrzask; klamka; mlaśnięcie;
klekot; brzęk
client ['klajent] s. klient
cliff [klyf] s. urwisko; stroma
ściana; ściana skalna
climate ['klajmyt] s. klimat
climax ['klajmaeks] s. szczyt;
zakończenie; v. stopniować;
szczytować; kulminować
climb [klajm] s. wspinaczka;
miejsce wspinania; v. piąć
się; wspinać; wzbijać się;
wdrapać się
climb up [klajm ap] v. wspinać
się w górę; wdrapywać się
climber [klajmer] s. taternik;
karierowicz; pnącze (roślina)
clinch [klyncz] v. zaciskać;
zaginać; zanitować;
zakończyć
cling; clung; clung [klyng; klang;
klang]
cling [klyng] v. trzymać się;
chwytać się; czepiać się;
trwać
clinic ['klynyk] s. klinika;
poradnia; adj. kliniczny
clink [klynk] s. dzwonienie;
ciupa; v. dzwonić (kluczami
etc.)
clip [klyp] 1. s. sprzączka; v.
spinać; 2. s. strzyżenie;
nożyce; v. strzyc; orżnąć
clippings ['klypyns] pl. wycinki (z

gazet); okrawki; obrzynki
cloak [klouk] s. płaszcz; maska;
v. okryć płaszczem;
wdziewać
clock [klok] s. zegar ścienny
clockwise ['klokłajz] adj. (obrót)
w prawo wg. zegarka
clod [klod] s. gruda; ziemia;
gamoń; v. obrzucać
grudkami ziemi
clog [klog] s. kłoda; chodak; v.
zatykać; zapychać;
zawadzać
cloister ['klojster] s. krużganek;
klasztor
close [klouz] v. zamykać;
zatykać; zakończyć;
zwierać; zgodzić się; s.
zakończenie; koniec; miejsce
ogrodzone; adv. szczelnie;
blisko; prawie; adj. zamknięty;
skąpy; gęsty; bliski; ścisły;
ekskluzywny
close to ['klous tu] przy; tuż
obok
close by ['klous baj] obok
close down ['klouz dałn] v.
zamykać; kończyć
(działalność etc.)
close in [klouz yn] v.
nadchodzić; ogarniać;
okrążyć; otoczyć
closet ['klozyt] s. pokoik; klozet;
kredens
close-up ['klousap] s. zdjęcie
zbliżone; zbliżenie
closing time ['klouzyng,tajm] s.
koniec pracy; zamknięcie
(sklepu); koniec urzędowania
clot [klot] s. skrzep; v. ścinać
się; skrzepnąć; zsiadać się
cloth [klos] s. materiał; szmata;
szafa; obrus; sukno; żagiel
cloth-bound [klos baund] s.
oprawny w płótno
clothe [klouz] s. materiał; sukno;
v. przywdziewać;
zamaskować
clothes [klouz] pl. ubranie;
pościel; pranie; odzież; ubiór
clothes brush ['klouz,brasz] s.
szczotka do ubrań
clothes hanger ['klouz,hanger] s.

wieszak do ubrań
clothesline ['klous,lajn] s. sznur
na bieliznę do suszenia
clothespin ['klouz,pyn] s. spinacz
do bielizny
clothing [klouzyng] s. odzież;
osłona; bielizna; odzienie
cloud [klaud] s. chmura; obłok;
zasępienie; tuman; kłąb dymu;
v. chmurzyć; sępić; rzucać
cień; ufarbować
cloudy ['klaudy] adj. chmurny;
posępny; zamglony; mętny
clove [klouw] s. goździk; ząbek
czosnku; zob. cleave
clover [klouwer] s. koniczyna
clown [klaun] s. błazen; prostak;
v. błaznować; wygłupiać się
club [klab] s. klub; pałka; kij; v.
bić pałką; zbijać; łączyć;
zrzeszać; stowarzyszać się
clue [klu:] s. klucz; ślad; wątek;
v. informować (o wątku)
clumsy ['klamzy] adj. niezgrabny;
nietaktowny; niekształtny
clung [klang] v. przywarty; zob.
cling
cluster ['klaster] s. grono; kiść;
pęk; kupka; v. tworzyć pęki;
skupiać się; zbierać się
clutch [klacz] s. chwyt; szpon;
sprzęgło; v. trzymać się
kurczowo
clutch pedal ['klacz,pedl] s.
pedał sprzęgła
coach [koucz] s. wóz pasażerski;
trener; v. jechać wozem;
trenować; uświadamiać;
pouczać
coagulate [kou'aegjulejt] v.
stężać; skrzepnąć; koagu-
lować
coal [koul] s. węgiel
coal-field ['koul'fi:ld] s. zagłębie
węglowe
coalition [,koue'lyszyn] s.
związek; koalicja; przymierze
coal mine [koul-majn] s. kopalnia
węgla
coal pit ['koul-pyt] s. kopalnia
węgla; szyb kopalniany
coarse [ko:rs] adj. pospolity;
gruboziarnisty; szorstki

coast [koust] s. brzeg; v. jechać
bez napędu; płynąć brzegiem
coast-guard ['koustga:rd] s.
straż przybrzeżna
coat [kout] s. marynarka; surdut;
powłoka; v. okrywać; pokry-
wać warstwą; powlekać
(farbą)
coat hanger ['kouthaenger] s.
wieszak (do ubrania)
coating [koutyng] s. powłoka;
warstwa; pokrycie
coat of arms ['kout ow,a:rms] s.
herb; godło
coax [kouks] v. namówić
pochlebstwem; udobruchać;
przymilać się; wycyganiać;
wyczarowywać (z butelki)
cob [kob] s. głąb; kucyk; łabędź
samiec; kaczan; kutwa;
bochenek
cobra ['koubre] s. kobra
cobweb ['kobłeb] s. pajęczyna
cock [kok] s. kogut; kurek; kran;
kutas (wulg.); v. postanowić;
nastroszyć; napiąć; odwo-
dzić; podnieść; zadzierać;
wznieść
cock-and-bull ['koken'bul] exp. o
żelaznym wilku
cockchafer ['kok,czejfer] s.
chrząszcz
cockle ['kokl] s. kąkol;
piecyk
cockpit ['kokpyt] s. kokpit; kabina; arena do walki kogutów
cockroach ['kokroucz] s.
karaluch
cocksure ['kokszuer] adj. pewny
siebie; zarozumiały
cocktail ['koktejl] s. cocktail
coco ['koukou] s. palma
kokosowa; kokos
cocoa ['koukou] s. kakao
coconut ['koukenat] s. orzech
kokosowy
cocoon [ke'ku:n] s. kokon;
oprzęd
cod [kod] s. dorsz; sztokfisz;
wątłusz; v. wystrychnąć na
dudka
coddle ['kodl] v. podgotować;

pieścić; tuczyć; zepsuć
code [koud] s. kodeks; szyfr; v.
szyfrować; pisać szyfrem
cod-liver oil ['kod,lywer ojl] s.
tran (lekarski)
coerce [kou'e:rs] przymusić;
zniewalać
coexist ['kouyg'zyst] v.
współistnieć; koegzystować
coexistence ['kouyg'zystens] s.
współistnienie; współżycie
coffee ['kofy] s. kawa
coffee bean ['kofy-bi:n] s. ziarno
kawy
coffee mill ['kofy-myl] s. młynek
do kawy
coffeepot ['kofy-pot] s.
maszynka do kawy
coffin ['kofyn] s. trumna
cogwheel ['kog-hił] s. koło
zębate; tryb
coherence [kou'hierens] s. sens;
spoistość; związek logiczny
coherency [kou'hierensy] s.
sens; zwartość; spójność
coherent [kou'hierent] adj.
logiczny; zwarty; spoisty
cohesive [kou'hi:syw] adj.
spoisty; zwarty; kleisty
coiffure [kła:'fjuer] s. fryzura;
styl uczesania
coil [kojl] s. zwój; cewka; lok; v.
zwijać; skręcać; wić się
coin [koyn] s. moneta; v. bić
monety; spieniężać; ukuć
(nowe pojęcie); tłoczyć
coinage [koynydż] s. bicie
monety; monety; system
monetarny; wymysł; nowe
słowo
coincide [kouyn'sajd] v. zbiegać
się; pokrywać się;
przystawać do siebie;
pasować
coincidence [kou'ynsydens] s.
zbieg okoliczności;
zgodność; przystawanie;
zgodność faktów
coke [kouk] s. koks; kokaina;
Coca-Cola; v. koksować
cold [kould] s. zimno;
przeziębienie; adj. zimny;
chłodny; mroźny

cold storage room [kould-
-storedż,ru:m] chłodnia
colic ['kolyk] s. kolka (w
brzuchu); ostry ból w brzuchu
collaborate [ke'laeberejt] v.
współpracować;
kolaborować
collaboration [ke'laeberejszyn] s.
współpraca; kolaboracja
collapse [ke'laeps] s. załamanie
się; upadek; runięcie;
zawalenie się; v. załamać się;
upaść; opaść; zawalić się;
załamywać
collapsible [ke'laepsebl] adj. składany (mebel, stół, łóżko etc.)
collar ['koler] s. kołnierz; szyjka;
pierścień; obroża; chomąto;
piana (na piwie); v. wkładać
obrożę; pojmać; ująć
collarbone ['koler-boun] s.
obojczyk
colleague ['koli:g] s. kolega (po
fachu); współpracownik
collect ['ke'lekt] v. zbierać;
odbierać; inkasować
collected ['ke'lektyd] adj.
skupiony; opanowany;
spokojny
collection ['ke'lekszyn] s. zbiór;
kolekcja; inkaso;
zainkasowane pieniądze
collective ['ke'lektyw] adj.
zbiorowy; wspólny; s.
kolektyw
collector ['ke'lektor] s. inkasent;
poborca; zbieracz
college ['kolydż] s. uczelnia;
kolegium; zrzeszenie;
akademia
collegiate [ke'ly:dżiet] adj.
uniwersytecki; studencki;
kolegialny; kolegiacki
collide [ke'lajd] v. zderzyć się;
kolidować; wejść w kolizję
colliery ['koljery] s. kopalnia
węgla
collision [ke'lyżen] s. zderzenie;
kolizja
colloquial [ke'loukłjel] adj.
potoczny (język); familiarny
colon ['koulen] s. grube jelito;
dwukropek

colonel ['kə:nl] s. pułkownik
colonial [kə'lounjəl] adj.
kolonialny; s. mieszkaniec
kolonii
colonialism [kə'lounjəlyzem] s.
kolonializm
colonist ['kolenyst] s. osadnik;
mieszkaniec kolonii
colonize ['kolenajz] v. osiedlać;
kolonizować
colony ['koleny] s. kolonia
color ['kaler] s. barwa; farba;
koloryt; v. barwić; farbować;
koloryzować; rumienić się
color bar ['kaler ba:r] s.
oddzielenie ras
colored ['kaleret] adj. barwny;
kolorowy
colorful ['kalerful] adj. pstry;
barwny; żywy; kolorowy
coloring ['kaleryng] s. koloryt;
kolorowanie; rumieńce
colorless ['kalerlys] adj.
bezbarwny; nudny; monotonny
color-line ['kalerlajn] s. przedział
rasowy
color print ['kaler,prynt] s.
chromodruk
colt [koult] s. źrebak
column ['kolem] s. kolumna;
stos; trzon; szpalta; formacja
coma ['koume] s. omdlenie;
koma; śpiączka; ogon
(komety)
comb [koum] s. grzebień;
grzbiet (fali); v. czesać;
kłębić się
combat ['kombet] s. walka; v.
zwalczać; walczyć
combatant ['kombetent] adj.
walczący; s. kombatant;
bojownik
combination [komby'nejszyn] s.
kombinacja; zespół; związek
combine [kembajn] v. połączyć;
powiązać; skombinować;
łączyć w sobie
combine-harvester [kembajn-
-'ha:rwyster] s. kombajn
combustible [kem'bastebl] adj.
palny; s. paliwo; materiały
pędne; opał; adj. popędliwy
combustion [kem'bastszyn] s.

spalanie; zapłon
come; came; come [kam; kejm;
kam]
come [kam] v. przybyć;
pochodzić; wynosić; dziać
się; być
come about ['kam,e'baut] v.
zdarzyć się; stać się;
odwracać się
come across ['kam,e'kros] v.
natknąć się; dać się
przekonać
come along ['kam,e'long] v.
pośpieszyć się; nadejść
come around ['kam,e'raund] v.
zmienić zdanie; odwiedzić
come at ['kam,et] v. podejść;
dotrzeć; przyjść o
(czwartej...)
come by ['kam,baj] v. dojść do
czegoś; minąć; nabyć
come for ['kam,for] v. przyjść
po coś
come loose ['kam,luz] v.
obluźniać się
come off ['kam,of] v. odpaść;
odlecieć; puszczać; mieć
miejsce
come on ['kam,on] v. chodźże;
przestań; daj spokój
come round ['kam,raund] v.
zmienić zdanie; przechytrzyć;
obejść
come to see ['kam tu si:] v.
odwiedzić; przyjść z wizytą
come up to ['kam ap tu] v.
podejść do ...; wejść na
sam (szczyt)
come-and-go ['kam-en-'go] s.
bieganina; ruch tam i z
powrotem
comeback ['kam-'baek] s.
powrót; bystra odpowiedź;
poprawa
comedian [ke'mi:djen] s. komik
comedy ['komydy] s. komedia
comer ['kamer] s. przybysz
comet ['komyt] s. kometa
comfort ['kamfert] s. wygoda;
pociecha; v. pocieszać;
czynić wygodnym; dodawać
otuchy
comfortable ['kamfertebl] adj.

wygodny; zadowolony; spokojny

comforter ['kamferter] s. pocieszyciel; kołdra; smoczek

comical ['komykel] adj. zabawny; śmieszny; komiczny

comic strips ['komyk,stryps] s. seryjne obrazkówki; kreskówki

comma ['kome] s. przecinek

command [ke'maend] v. rozkazywać; kazać; rozporządzać; panować nad; dowodzić; s. rozkaz; nakaz; komenda; dowództwo

commander [ke'maender] s. dowódca; komendant; kapitan (fregaty)

commander-in-chief [ke'maender yn'czi:f] głównodowodzący

commandment [ke'maendment] s. przykazanie (boskie)

commend [ke'mend] v. chwalić; zalecać; polecać opiece

commendable [ke'mendebl] adj. chwalebny; godny polecenia

comment ['koment] s. objaśnienie; v. robić uwagi krytyczne lub złośliwe; wypowiadać zdanie

comment on ['koment on] v. komentować; oceniać (utwór)

commentary ['komentery] s. komentarz; uwaga; notatka

commentator ['komentejter] s. komentator; sprawozdawca

commerce ['kome:rs] s. handel

commercial [ke'me:rszel] adj. handlowy; s. ogłoszenie (w radio ...)

commissar ['komy'sa:r] s. komisarz w b. ZSRR

commission [ke'myszyn] s. zlecenie; misja; urząd; v. delegować; powierzać; objąć; zlecać; zamianować; upoważniać

commissioner [ke'myszener] s. delegat; pełnomocnik; komisarz rządowy; członek komisji rządowej

commit [ke'myt] v. powierzać; przekazywać; odsyłać;

popełniać; wciągać; zobowiązywać się; oddawać w opiekę; zamykać w (domu wariatów); obiecywać

commitment [ke'mytment] s. zobowiązanie; dopuszczenie się; przekazanie; zaangażowanie się

committee [ke'myti:] s. komitet; komisja; opiekun (umysłowo chorego)

commodity [ke'modyty] s. towar; rzecz przydatna; artykuł handlu

common ['komen] adj. wspólny; publiczny; ogólny; pospolity; zwyczajny; prosty

Common Wealth of Independent States ['komen łels ow ,yndy'pendet stejc] s. Wspólnota Niezależnych Państw

commoner ['komener] s. człowiek z gminu; nie szlachcic

common law marriage ['komen, ,lo:'maerydż] pożycie na wiarę

common market ['komen' ma:rkyt] wspólny rynek (Zach. Europa)

commonplace ['komen-plejs] s. banał; adj. banalny; oklepany

common sense ['komen,sens] zdrowy rozsądek

commonwealth ['komen,łels] s. wspólnota; rzeczpospolita

commotion [ke'mouszyn] s. zamieszki; tumult; poruszenie

commune ['komju:n] s. gmina; komuna; v. obcować; rozmawiać

communicate [ke'mju:ny,kejt] v. dzielić się; komunikować się; łączyć się; przenosić (ciepło, zimno etc.)

communication [ke,mju:ny 'kejszyn] s. łączność; komunikacja; porozumiewanie się; zakomunikowanie

communicative [ke'mju:nykejtyw] adj. otwarty; rozmowny; towarzyski; przystępny

communion [kə'mju:njen] s.
obcowanie; uczestnictwo;
wspólnota; komunia; wyznanie
wiary

communism ['komju,nyzem] s.
komunizm; ruch
komunistyczny

communist ['komjunyst] s.
komunista; adj. komunistyczny

community [kə'mju:nyty] s.
środowisko; społeczność;
gmina; kolektyw; wspólnota;
koło; zakon

commute [kə'mju:t] v.
zamieniać; zastępować;
łagodzić; dojeżdżać do
pracy; brać bilet okresowy

comose ['koumous] adj.
włochaty; puszysty; włóknisty

compact [kəm'paekt] adj. gęsty;
zbity; zwarty; v. ubijać;
zbijać; zagęszczać; s.
puderniczka

compact ['kempaekt] s. ugoda;
porozumienie; puderniczka;
samochód średniej wielkości
(USA)

companion [kəm'paenjen] s.
towarzysz; (coś) do pary

companionship [kəm'
paenjenszyp] s. koleżeństwo;
towarzystwo

company ['kampeny] s.
towarzystwo; załoga; goście;
partnerzy; spółka; kompania;
trupa teatralna

comparable ['komperebl] adj.
porównywalny; wytrzymujący
porównanie

comparative [kəm'paeretyw] adj.
porównawczy; względny;
stosunkowy; s. stopień
wyższy (przymiotnika)

compare [kəm'peer] v.
porównywać; dawać się
porównać; stopniować
(gram.)

comparison [kəm'paeryson] s.
porównanie; zestawienie

compartment [kəm'pa:rtment] s.
przedział; przegroda; komora
wodoszczelna

compass ['kampes] s. kompas;

busola; obwód; obręb; cyrkiel;
zasięg; v. obchodzić;
otaczać; ogarniać; osiągać;
dopiąć

compassion [kəm'paeszyn] s.
litość; współczucie

compassionate [kəm'paeszynyt]
adj. litościwy; v. litować się

compatible [kəm'paetebl] adj.
zgodny; licujący; do
pogodzenia

compatriot [kəm'paetryet] s.
rodak; ziomek; rodaczka

compel [kəm'pel] v. zmuszać;
wymuszać (coś); wzbudzać

compensate ['kompen,sejt] v.
wyrównywać; nagradzać;
wypłacić odszkodowanie;
kompensować

compensation [,kompen'sejszyn]
s. rekompensata;
wynagrodzenie;
odszkodowanie; wyrównanie

compete [kəm'pi:t] v.
konkurować; rywalizować;
ubiegać się

compete for [kəm'pi:t,fo:r] v.
(o coś) współzawodniczyć;
współubiegać się;
prześcigać się

competence ['kompytens] s.
fachowość; kwalifikacja;
uzdolnienie; zasobność;
dobrobyt

competent ['kompytent] adj.
właściwy; kwalifikowany;
odpowiedni; kompetentny

competition [,kompy'tyszyn] s.
konkurencja; konkurs; zawody;
współzawodnictwo; turniej

competitor [kəm'petyter] s.
rywal; konkurent;
współzawodnik;
współzawodniczka; rywalka

compile [kəm'pajl] v. zbierać;
zestawiać; kompilować

complacent [kəm'plejsnt] adj.
zadowolony (z siebie, ze
świata); błogi

complain [kəm'plejn] v. żalić
się; narzekać; skarżyć;
wnosić zażalenie; wnosić
skargę

complaint [kəm'plejnt] s. skarga; zażalenie; dolegliwość

complete [kəm'pli:t] adj. całkowity; zupełny; kompletny; v. uzupełniać; udoskonalić; ukończyć; wypełnić (formularz)

completion [kəm'pli:szyn] s. ukończenie; uzupełnienie; udoskonalenie; spełnienie (woli, testamentu)

complex [kəm'pleks] adj. złożony z dwu lub więcej części; zawiły; skomplikowany; s. połączona grupa (np. budynków; impulsów, itd.); obsesja

complexion [kəm'plekszyn] s. cera; płeć; postać; aspekt (charakter); wygląd

complicate ['komply,kejt] v. wikłać; splatać; komplikować

complicated ['kemlpy,kejtyd] adj. skomplikowany; powikłany

compliment ['komplyment] s. komplement; gratulacje; ukłony; uszanowanie; v. mówić komplementy; gratulować

complimentary ['komply'mentery] adj. pochlebny; okazowy; grzecznościowy

comply [kəm'plaj] v. zastosować się; spełnić; podporządkować się; uczynić zadość; przestrzegać

comply with [kəm'plaj,łys] s. spełniać; przestrzegać czegoś

component [kəm'pounent] s. składnik; część składowa; siła składowa; adj. składowy

compose [kəm'pouz] v. składać; układać; tworzyć; komponować; skupiać (myśli); uspokoić; załagodzić; uspakajać się

composed [kəm'pouzd] adj. opanowany; spokojny; stateczny

composer [kəm'pouzer] s.

kompozytor; kompozytorka

composition [,kempe'zyszyn] s. skład; układ; ugoda; wypracowanie; budowa; usposobienie

composure [kəm'pouźer] s. spokój; opanowanie; zimna krew; przytomność umysłu

compote ['kompout] s. kompot (z puszki); kompotiera

compound [kom'paund] adj. złożony; sprężony; s. związek (chem.); mieszanka; złożenie; v. mieszać; składać; powiększać; łączyć; zawrzeć; załatwić

comprehend [,kompry'hend] v. pojmować; rozumieć; zawierać

comprehensible [,kompry 'hensebl] adj. zrozumiały; pojętny

comprehensive [,kompry 'hensyw] adj. obszerny; szeroki; rozumowy; wyczerpujący; ogólny; wszechstronny

compress [kəm'pres] v. ściskać; streszczać; s. kompres; okład

comprise [kəm'prajz] v. włączać; obejmować; składać się

compromise ['kompre,majz] s. kompromis; ugoda; kompromitacja; narażenie; v. załatwić ugodowo; kompromitować

compulsion [kəm'palszyn] s. przymus; siła przymusu

compulsory [kəm'palsery] adj. przymusowy; przymuszający

compunction [kəm'pankszyn] s. skrucha; żal za grzechy

computation [,kompju'tejszyn] s. obliczenie; kalkulacja

computer [kəm'pju:ter] s. kalkulator; komputer; przelicznik

comrade ['komraed] s. kolega; druh; współpracownik

comradeship ['komraedszyp] s. koleżeństwo; braterstwo

con [kon] adv. (głosować)
przeciw; v. wkuwać (lekcje);
oszukiwać; w błąd
wprowadzać; s. aresztant;
skazaniec

concave ['kon'kejw] adj.
wklęsły; wklęśnięty

conceal [ken'si:l] v. taić;
ukrywać; przemilczać;
zataić

concede [ken'si:d] v.
przyznawać; ustępować;
poddawać się

conceit [ken'si:t] s. próżność;
zarozumiałość; mniemanie;
koncept

conceited [ken'si:tyd] adj.
próżny; zarozumiały

conceivable [ken'si:webl] adj.
wyobrażalny; zrozumiały

conceive [ken'si:w] v.
wymyślić; wyobrażać;
rozumieć; ujmować; zajść
w ciążę; pojąć; redagować

concentrate ['konsentrejt] v.
skupiać się; stężać; s.
roztwór

concentration ['kensentrejszyn]
s. skupienie (się); stężenie;
koncentracja; skoncentrowanie

conception [ken'sepszyn] s.
pomysł; poczęcie (dziecka);
początek

concern [ken'se:rn] s. interes;
troska; związek; v. tyczyć
się; dotyczyć; obchodzić;
niepokoić się o ...; wchodzić
w grę

concerned [ken'se:rnd] adj.
zainteresowany; zaaferowany;
strapiony; niespokojny

concert ['konsert] s. koncert;
porozumienie; v. ułożyć;
ukartować; porozumieć się

concession [ken'seszyn] s.
koncesja; ustępstwo;
przyzwolenie

conciliate [ken'syly,ejt] v.
zjednywać; jednać; godzić;
łagodzić; pogodzić;
udobruchać

conciliatory [ken'syljeto:ry] adj.
pojednawczy

concise [ken'sajs] adj. zwięzły;
treściwy; krótki i węzłowaty

conclude [ken'klu:d] v.
zakończyć; zawierać;
wnioskować; postanawiać;
kończyć się

conclusion [ken'klu:żyn] s.
zakończenie; wynik;
postanowienie; wniosek;
konkluzja; zawarcie układu;
wynik ostateczny

conclusive [ken'klu:syw] adj.
rozstrzygający; dowodny

concord ['konko:rd] s. zgoda;
jedność; harmonia; v.
zgadzać się

concrete ['konkri:t] s. beton;
konkret; adj. rzeczywisty;
realny; zwarty; stały;
konkretny; specyficzny;
betonowy

concur [ken'ke:r] v. zgadzać
się; schodzić się;
współdziałać

concurrence [ken'ke:rens] s.
zgodność; zbieżność;
zgoda

concussion [ken'kaszyn] s.
wstrząs (mózgu); uderzenie

condemn [ken'dem] v. potępiać;
skazywać; krytykować;
wybrakować

condemnation [,kendem'nejszyn]
s. potępienie; skazanie

condense [ken'dens] v.
kondensować; zgęszczać;
streszczać

condenser [ken'denser] s.
kondensator; skraplacz

condescend [,kondy'send] v.
zniżać się; raczyć;
zezwalać; zachowywać się z
wyższością

condition [ken'dyszyn] s. stan;
warunek; zastrzeżenie;
poprawka; v.
uwarunkowywać;
zastrzegać; naprawiać;
przygotowywać;
przyzwyczajać;
klimatyzować

conditional [ken'dyszynl] adj.
warunkowy; uzależniony;

zależny
condole [ken'doul] v. składać
  kondolencje; współczuć;
  ubolewać
condolence [ken'doulens] s.
  wyrazy współczucia;
  kondolencje
condom [kan'dem] s.
  prezerwatywa; kondon
conduct [kon'dakt] s.
  prowadzenie; sprawowanie;
  prowadzenie się; sprawowanie
  się; kierownictwo; v.
  prowadzić; wieść;
  przewodzić; dyrygować;
  dowodzić
conduction [kon'dakszyn] s.
  przewodzenie (fiz.)
conductor [kon'dakter] s.
  kierownik; przewodnik;
  dyrygent; przewód;
  odgromnik; piorunochron
cone [koun] s. stożek; szyszka;
  v. nadawać kształt stożka
confection [ken'fekszyn] s.
  sporządzanie; konfitura;
  słodycze; konfekcja (damska)
confectioner [ken'fekszyner] s.
  cukiernik; właściciel cukierni
confectionery [ken'feksznery] s.
  cukiernia; wyroby cukiernicze
confederacy [ken'federesy] s.
  konfederacja; sojusz; związek;
  spisek; sprzysiężenie
confederate [ken'federyt] adj.
  sprzysiężony; v. jednoczyć;
  spiskować; knuć;
  sprzymierzać
confederation [ken,fede'rejszyn]
  s. sprzymierzenie;
  skonfederowanie; konfederacja
confer [ken'fe:r] v. naradzać
  się; nadawać; przyznawać
conferee [,konfe'ri:] s. uczestnik
  konferencji; nagrodzony
conference ['konferens] s.
  narada; liga; zebranie; zjazd
confess [ken'fes] v. wyznać;
  przyznać się; spowiadać się
confession [ken'feszen] s.
  wyznanie; spowiedź;
  przyznanie się; religia
confessor [ken'feser] s.

spowiednik; ksiądz spowiednik
confide [ken'fajd] v. ufać
  (komuś); zwierzać się;
  powierzać
confidence ['konfydens] s.
  zaufanie; bezczelność;
  pewność; ufność;
  zwierzenie; śmiałość
confident ['konfydent] adj.
  dufny; bezczelny; przekonany
confidential [,konfy'denczel] adj.
  tajny; poufny; zaufany;
  poufały; intymny
confine ['konfajn] v. ograniczać;
  odosabniać; s. kres; granica
confinement [kon'fajnment] s.
  uwięzienie; ograniczenie;
  odosobnienie; połóg; poród
confirm [ken'fe:rm] v.
  potwierdzać; zatwierdzać;
  umacniać; bierzmować;
  utwierdzać; pokrzepić
confirmation [,konfer'mejszyn] s.
  potwierdzenie; zatwierdzenie;
  bierzmowanie; pokrzepienie
confiscate ['konfyskejt] v.
  konfiskować; skonfiskować
conflagration [,konfle'grejszyn] s.
  pożar; pożoga
conflict ['konflykt] s. zatarg;
  starcie; konflikt; kolizja
conform [kon'fo:rm] v.
  dostosować; upodabniać;
  dostrajać
conformity [kon'fo:rmyty] s.
  zgodność; dostosowanie się
confound [kon'faund] v.
  mieszać; zawieść;
  pokrzyżować; poplątać
confound it! [kon'faund,yt] exp.
  do licha!; niech to diabli
  wezmą!
confront [ken'frant] v. stawiać
  czoło; konfrontować;
  unaocznić
confuse [ken'fju:z] v. zmieszać
  (kogoś, siebie); wikłać;
  gmatwać
confusion [ken'fju:żyn] s. nieład;
  zamieszanie; bałagan; chaos
congeal [ken'dżi:l] v. mrozić;
  ścinać; marznąć;
  zakrzepnąć

congestion [ken'dżestczyn] s.
przeludnienie; przeciążenie
(ruchu); przekrwienie
conglomerate [ken'glomerejt] v.
skupiać; zlewać w jedną
masę
congratulate [ken'graetju,lejt] v.
gratulować; składać
(komuś) gratulacje;
pogratulować
congratulation [ken,
graetju'lejszyn] s. gratulacje;
gratulowanie; gratulacja
congregate ['kongry,gejt] adj.
zbiorowy; v. skupiać; zbierać
(się); gromadzić (się)
congregation [,kongry'gejszyn] s.
zbieranie; zgromadzenie
congress ['kongres] s. zjazd;
zebranie; parlament USA
conjecture [ken'dżekczer] s.
domysł; przypuszczenie; v.
przypuszczać; mniemać
conjugal ['kondżugel] adj.
małżeński
conjugate ['kondżu,gejt] v.
odmieniać się; kopulować;
parzyć się; adj. połączony
conjugation [,kondżu'gejszyn] s.
koniugacja; zespalanie się;
kopulacja; odmiana
czasownika
conjunction [ken'dżankszyn] s.
zbieg; związek; skojarzenie;
spójnik; połączenie
conjunctive mood [ken'
dżanktyw,mu:d] s. tryb
łączący
conjure [kan'dżuer] v. zaklinać;
błagać; robić sztuczki
conjure ['kandżer] v. czarować
conjurer ['kandżerer] s.
czarownik; magik; kuglarz
connect [ke'nekt] v. łączyć;
wiązać; mieć połączenie
connected [ke'nektyd] adj.
zwarty (logiczny);
ustosunkowany
connection(xion) [ke'nekszyn] s.
połączenie; pokrewieństwo
connive [ke'najw] v. pobłażać;
tolerować nadużycie; być w
zmowie

connoisseur ['kony':ser] s.
znawca; fachowiec
conquer ['konker] v. zdobyć;
zwyciężyć; pokonać
conqueror ['konkerer] s.
zdobywca; zwycięzca
conquest ['konkłest] s. podbój;
zdobycie; zawojowanie
conscience ['konszyns] s.
sumienie; świadomość zła i
dobra
conscientious [,konszy'enszes]
adj. sumienny; skrupulatny
conscious ['konszes] adj.
przytomny; świadomy;
naumyślny
consciousness ['konszysnys] s.
świadomość; całość
myśli i uczuć
conscript ['konskrypt] s. & adj.
poborowy; s. rekrut; v.
rekwirować; brać do wojska
consecrate ['konsy,krejt] v.
poświęcać; adj.
poświęcony
consecutive [ken'sekjutyw] adj.
kolejny; nieprzerwany;
skutkowy
consensus [ken'senses] s.
zgoda; jednomyślność
consent [ken'sent] s. zgoda; v.
zgadzać się; przyzwalać
consequence ['konsykłens] s.
wynik; znaczenie;
konsekwencja
consequently ['konsykłently] adv.
a zatem; przeto; tym samym;
w skutek tego; więc
conservative [ken'se:rwatyw]
adj. ostrożny; zachowawczy;
konserwatywny; s.
konserwatysta; środek
konserwujący
conserve [ken'se:rw] v.
konserwować; zachowywać;
zabezpieczać; s. konserwa
owocowa
consider [ken'syder] v.
rozważać; rozpatrywać;
uważać; szanować; mieć
wzgląd; sądzić
considerable [ken'syderebl] adj.
znaczny; adv. znacznie

considerate [ken'syderyt] adj.
myślący; uważający;
troskliwy

consideration [ken,syde'rejszyn]
s. wzgląd; rozważanie;
warunek; uprzejmość;
rekompensata

consign [ken'sajn] v. przekazać;
powierzać; złożyć do
(banku, grobu ...)

consignment [ken'sajnment] s.
przesyłka; powierzenie

consist [ken'syst] v. składać
się; polegać; zgadzać się

consistency [ken'systensy] s.
konsystencja; solidność;
stałość; zgodność;
logiczność

consistent [ken'systent] adj.
zgodny; stały; konsekwentny

consolation [,konse'lejszyn] s.
pocieszenie; pociecha;
ukojenie

console [ken'soul] v. pocieszać;
s. konsola; wspornik; podpora

consolidate [ken'solydejt] v.
utwierdzać; scalać;
jednoczyć

consonant ['konsenent] s.
spółgłoska; adj. spółgłoskowy;
zgodny; harmonijny

conspicuous [ken'spykjues] adj.
widoczny; zwracający uwagę

conspiracy [ken'spyresy] s. spise
k; konspiracja; zmowa; umowa

conspirator [ken'spyreter] s.
spiskowiec; konspirator

conspire [ken'spajer] v.
konspirować; spiskować;
uknuć

constable ['kanstebl] s. policjant;
posterunkowy

constant ['konstent] adj. stały;
trwały; s. liczba stała

consternation [,konste:r'nejszyn]
s. przerażenie; osłupienie

constipation [,konsty'pejszyn] s.
zatwardzenie; zaparcie

constituency [ken'stytjuensy] s.
okręg wyborczy; wyborcy

constituent [ken'stytjuent] adj.
składowy; s. wyborca;
część; składowa; element

constitute ['konsty,tju:t] v.
stanowić; ustanawiać;
wyznaczać

constitution [,konsty'tju:szyn] s.
statut; konstytucja; struktura;
założenie; układ psychiczny

constitutional [,konsty'tu:szenl]
adj. zasadniczy; istotny;
zdrowotny; s. przechadzka dla
zdrowia

constrain [ken'strejn] v.
wymuszać; zmuszać;
ograniczać; więzić;
zniewalać; przymuszać

constraint [ken'strejnt] s.
przymus; skrępowanie;
ograniczenie swobody
(ruchów)

construct [ken'strakt] v.
budować; tworzyć; rysować
(figury geom.)

construction [ken'strakszyn] s.
budowa; konstrukcja; układ;
konstruowanie; ujęcie;
interpretacja

constructive [ken'straktywy] adj.
twórczy; konstruktywny

consul ['konsel] s. konsul

consular ['konsjuler] adj.
konsularny

consulate ['konsjulyt] s.
konsulat; uprawnienia konsula

consulate general ['konsjulut
'dżeneral] s. konsulat
generalny

consult [ken'salt] v. radzić się;
informować się

consultation [,konsel'tejszyn] s.
porada; konsultacja

consultative [ken'saltetyw] adj.
doradczy; konsultatywny

consume [ken'sju:m] v.
spożywać; zużywać;
trawić; niszczyć; marnieć;
uschnąć

consumer [ken'sju:mer] s.
konsumer; spożywca;
odbiorca

consummate [ken'samyt] adj.
doskonały; wielkiej miary;
skończony

consummate ['konsemejt] v.
spełniać małżeństwo

consumption [ken'sampszyn] s.
zużycie; suchoty; pylica
contact ['kontaekt] s.
styczność; stosunki;
znajomości; v. kontaktować;
porozumiewać się; stykać
się; zetknąć się
contact lenses ['kontaekt,lenzys]
pl. szkła kontaktowe
contagious [ken'tejdżes] adj.
zaraźliwy; zakaźny;
udzielający się
contain [ken'tejn] v. zawierać;
opanowywać się; wiązać;
hamować
container [ken'tejner] s.
zasobnik; zbiornik; naczynie
contaminate [ken'taemynejt] v.
zakazić; skalać;
deprawować
contamination [ken'
taemynejszyn] s. konta-
minacja; zakażenie; skażenie;
ujemny wpływ
contemplate ['kontemplejt] v.
oglądać; rozważać; liczyć
się z (czymś); medytować;
planować
contemplation ['kontemplejszyn]
s. oglądanie; kontemplacja;
rozważanie; planowanie;
medytacja
contemplative ['kontemplejtyw]
adj. kontemplacyjny;
zamyślony
contemporary [ken'temperery]
adj. & s. współczesny
(rówieśnik)
contempt [ken'temt] s. pogarda;
lekceważenie; obraza (sądu
etc.)
contemptible [ken'temtebl] adj.
godny pogardy, lekceważenia
contemptuous [ken'temtjues]
adj. pogardliwy; nadęty;
lekceważący
contend [ken'tend] v. spierać
się; walczyć; rywalizować;
upierać się
content 1. [ken'tent] adj.
zadowolony; s. zadowolenie;
v. zadowalać
content 2. ['kontent] s.

zawartość; treść; obję-
tość; pojemność; po-
wierzchnia; kubatura; istota
contented [ken'tentyd] adj.
zadowolony; zaspokojony
contents ['kontents] s.
zawartość (pojemnika, książki); treści
contest ['kontest] s. rywalizacja;
spór; v. walczyć; spierać
się; ubiegać; kwestionować
context ['kontekst] s. kontekst
continent ['kontynent] s.
kontynent; część świata
continental ['kontynentl] adj.
kontynentalny; s. mieszkaniec
kontynentu
continual [ken'tynjuel] adj.
ciągły; powtarzający się; stały
continuance [ken'tynjuens] s.
ciągłość; trwanie; przebieg;
ciąg dalszy; odroczenie; pobyt
continuation [ken'tynju'ejszyn] s.
kontynuacja; ciąg dalszy
continue [ken'tynju:] v.
kontynuować; ciągnąć dalej;
trwać; ciągnąć się;
odroczyć; upierać się
continuous [ken'tynjues] adj.
nieprzerwany; stały; ciągły
contort [ken'to:rt] v. skręcać;
wykrzywiać; zwichnąć;
przekrzywić
contour ['kontuer] s. zarys;
kontur; warstwica; v.
konturować
contraceptive [,kontre'septyw] s.
środek zapobiegający zapłod-
nieniu; środek antykoncepcyjny; adj. antykoncepcyjny
contract ['kontraekt] s. umowa;
układ; kontrakt; obietnica
contract [ken'traekt] v.
ściągać; kurczyć; zobo-
wiązywać
contractor [ken'traekter] s.
przedsiębiorca (budowlany
etc.); kontrahent
contradict [,kontre'dykt] v.
zaprzeczać; posprzeczać się
contradiction [,kontre'dykszyn] s.
sprzeczność; zaprzeczenie
contradictory [,kontre'dyktery]

adj. sprzeczny; przekorny;
kłótliwy; zaprzeczający
contrary ['kontrery] adj.
przeciwny; s. przeci-
wieństwo; adv. w przeci-
wieństwie
contrariwise ['kontrery,łajz] adv.
odwrotnie; natomiast
contrast [ken'traest] v.
przeciwstawiać; kontras-
tować; s. kontrast;
przeciwieństwo
contribute [ken'trybjut] v.
przyczynić się; dostarczyć;
współdziałać; zasłużyć się
contribution [,kontry'bju:szyn] s.
przyczynek; wkład; ofiara;
kontrybucja; datek; wsparcie
contributor [ken'trybjuter] s.
ofiarodawca; współpracownik
(pisarz); współpracowniczka
contrite [ken'trajt] adj.
skruszony; pełen skruchy
contrivance [ken'trajwens] s.
pomysł; sztuczka; fortel;
wynalazek; wynalazczość;
pomysłowość
contrive [ken'trajw] v.
wymyślić; wynaleźć;
doprowadzić do czegoś;
zaplanować; wykombinować
control [ken'troul] v. sprawdzać;
rządzić; kontrolować; opanować; s. kontrola; sterowanie; regulowanie; ster;
władza
controller [ken'trouler] s.
kontroler; regulator; zarządca
controversial [,kentre'we:rżel]
adj. sporny; sprzeczający się
controversy ['kontre,we:rsy] s.
spór; kłótnia; polemika;
dysputa
contuse [ken'tju:z] v. stłuc;
kontuzjować
convalesce [,konwe'les] v.
wyzdrowieć i odzyskać siły
convalescence [,konwe'lesens] s.
wyzdrowienie
convalescent [,konwe'lesnt] s.
rekonwalescent; ozdrowieniec
convenience [ken'wi:njens] s.
wygoda; korzyść;

dogodność
convenient [ken'wi:njent] adj.
wygodny; łatwy do
osiągnięcia
convent ['konwent] s. zakon
convention [ken'wenszyn] s.
zjazd; zgromadzenie; układ;
umowa; konwent; zebranie
conventional [ken'wenszynl] adj.
zwyczajowy; konwencjonalny;
umowny; powszechnie stosowany; klasyczny
conversation [,konwer'sejszyn] s.
rozmowa; konwersacja
converse [ken'we:rs] v.
rozmawiać; obcować; pro-
wadzić rozmowę
converse ['konwe:rs] s.
rozmowa; adj. odwrotny; s.
rzecz odwrotna
conversion [ken'we:rżyn] s.
odwrócenie; przemiana;
nawrócenie; przeistoczenie
convert [ken'we:rt] v. zmieniać;
nawracać; przekształcać;
odwracać; przemieniać; przystosować
convert ['konwert] s. neofita
convertible [ken'we:rtybl] adj.
wymienialny; s. otwarty samochód z podnoszonym dachem;
kabriolet
convey [ken'wej] v. przewozić;
przenosić; przesyłać; przekazywać; komunikować;
zapisywać
conveyance [ken'wejens] s.
przewóz; przenoszenie;
uzmysławianie; pojazd;
przekazanie
conveyor belt [ken'wejer,belt] s.
przenośnik taśmowy
convict ['konwykt] s. skazaniec;
więzień; v. udowadniać;
przekonywać; uznać winnym
conviction [ken'wykszyn] s.
przeświadczenie; przekonanie;
zasądzenie; skazanie
convince [ken'wyns] v.
przekonać; przekonywać
convoy ['konwoj] s. konwój;
eskorta; straż
convoy [kon'woj] v.

konwojować
convulsion [ken'walszyn] s.
drgawki; wstrząs; konwulsje
convulsive [ken'walsyw] adj.
konwulsyjny; niepohamowany
cook [kuk] s. kucharz;
kucharka;v. gotować;
preparować
cookbook [kuk'buk] s. książka
kucharska
cooking [kukyng] s. gotowanie
cool [ku:l] adj. chłodny; oziębły;
spokojny; v. chłodzić; stu-
dzić; ochłonąć; s. chłód
cooler ['ku:ler] s. chłodnica;
element chłodzący; więzienie
coolness ['ku:lnys] s. chłód;
zimna krew; opanowanie;
spokój
co-op [kou'op] s. spółdzielnia
cooperate [kou'operejt] v.
współpracować; współ-
działać
cooperation [kou,ope'rejszyn] s.
współpraca; współdziałanie;
kooperacja; spółdzielczość
cooperative [kou,ope'rejtyw] adj.
spółdzielczy; uspołeczniowy;
uczynny; współpracujący
cooperator [kou'ope,rejter] s.
współpracownik; spółdzielca
coordinate [kou'o:rdynejt] adj.
współrzędny; współrzędna
cop [kop] s. policjant (slang); v.
złapać; wygrać; buchnąć;
nakryć; porwać; ukraść
(slang)
copartner [kou'pa:rtner] s.
uczestnik; wspólnik;
udziałowiec (we wspólnym
interesie)
cope ['koup] v. uporać; dawać
sobie radę; pokrywać;
borykać się; zwieńczać; s.
kapa; peleryna
copilot ['kou'pajlot] s. kopilot;
zastępca pilota
copious ['koupjes] adj. obfity;
suty; bogaty; płodny;
obfitujący
copper ['koper] s. miedź; v.
miedziować; s. (slang) glina;
policjant; miedziak; kocioł z

miedzi
copy ['kopy] v. kopiować;
przepisywać; naśladować;
s. kopia; odpis; odbitka;
egzemplarz; wzór; model;
rękopis do druku
copybook ['kopy,buk] s. zeszyt
copyright ['kopy,rajt] s. prawo
autorskie; v. chronić prawem
autorskim
coral ['korel] s. koral
cord [ko:rd] s. sznur; lina; v.
wiązać; ustawiać w sągi
cordial ['ko:rdżel] adj. serdeczny;
nasercowy; s. lek nasercowy
cordiality [,ko:rdy'aelyty] s.
serdeczność; kordialność
corduroys ['ko:rde,rojz] pl.
sztruksowe spodnie
core [ko:r] s. rdzeń; v. usuwać
rdzeń; wycinać rdzeń
cork [ko:rk] s. korek; v.
korkować
corkscrew ['ko:rk,skru:] s.
korkociąg; adj. w kształcie
korkociągu
corn [ko:rn] s. 1. ziarno; zboże;
kukurydza; 2. nagniotek
corner ['ko:rner] s. róg;
narożnik; kąt; zakręt; v.
zapędzać do kąta; zmuszać;
monopolizować
cornered ['ko:rnerd] adj. rogaty;
schwytany; zapędzony w
ślepą ulicę
cornet ['ko:rnyt] s. kornet;
trąbka (mosiężna)
corn-flakes ['ko:rn,flejks] pl.
płatki z kukurydzy
coronary disease ['korenery
dy'zi:z] s. choroba wieńcowa
coronation [,kore'nejszyn] s.
koronacja
coroner ['korener] s. sędzia
śledczy; lekarz sądowy
(oględziny zwłok)
corporal ['ko:rperel] adj. cielesny;
osobisty; s. kapral
corporation [,ko:rpe'rejszyn] s.
korporacja; zrzeszenie; osoba
prawna zbiorowa
corpse [ko:rps] s. trup; zwłoki
corpulent ['ko:rpjulent] adj. tęgi;

otyły; gruby; tłusty

corral [ke'rael] s. ogrodzenie dla bydła; tabór; v. zamykać w ogrodzeniu; łapać; ustawiać tabor; wpędzać do ogrodzenia

correct [ke'rekt] adj. poprawny; v. korygować; karcić; prostować; leczyć; naprawiać

correction [ke'rekszyn] s. poprawka; korekta; kara

correspond [,korys'pond] v. odpowiadać; korespondować

correspondence [,korys'pondens] s. zgodność; korespondencja

correspondent [,korys'pondent] s. korespondent; adj. odpowiedni; zgodny z; odpowiadający

corridor ['korydo:r] s. korytarz

corrigible ['korydżybl] adj. dający się poprawiać; uległy

corroborate [ke'robe,rejt] v. potwierdzić; potwierdzać

corrode [ke'roud] v. zżerać; rdzewieć; niszczeć; niszczyć

corrosion [ke'roużyn] s. korozja; zżeranie; niszczenie

corrugate ['korugejt] v. marszczyć; fałdować; karbować

corrugated iron ['korugejtyd 'ajron] s. pofałdowana blacha

corrupt [ke'rapt] adj. zepsuty; sprzedajny; v. korumpować; psuć się

corruption [ke'rapszyn] s. zepsucie; korupcja; rozkład; fałszowanie

corset ['ko:rsyt] s. gorset; sznurówka; v. wkładać gorset

cosmetic [koz'metyk] s. kosmetyk; adj. kosmetyczny

cosmetician [koz'metyszyn] s. kosmetyczka

cosmonaut ['kozme,no:t] s. kosmonauta; astronauta (w USA)

cost; cost; cost [kost; kost; kost]

cost [kost] v. kosztować; s. koszt; strata; cena

costly ['kostly] adj. kosztowny; wspaniały; drogi; cenny

costume ['kostju:m] s. kostium; strój; przystroić w kostium

cosy ['kouzy] adj. przytulny; v. przytulić się

cot [kot] s. łóżko składane; szałas; schronienie

cottage ['kotydż] s. chata; dworek; domek letniskowy

cottage cheese ['kotydż,czi:z] s. biały ser krowi z kwaśnego mleka

cotton ['kotn] s. bawełna; v. polubić; kapować; adj. bawełniany

cotton wool ['kotn,łul] s. wata

couch [kaucz] s. tapczan; posłanie; łóżko; v. rozsiadać się; mówić

cougar ['ku:ger] s. puma; kuguar

cough [kof] s. kaszel; v. kaszleć; wykaszleć; zakaszleć

could [kud] v. mógłby; zob. can

council ['kaunsyl] s. rada; konsylium; sobór; zarząd (miejski etc.)

councilor ['kaunsyler] s. radny; radca; członek zarządu

counsel ['kaunsel] s. rada; zamysł; radca prawny; v. radzić; doradzać; przyjmować radę

count [kaunt] v. liczyć; sądzić; liczyć się; znaczyć; s. rachuba; liczenie; suma; zarzut; hrabia

countdown [kaunt-dałn] s. liczenie do startu (rakiety)

count in [kaunt yn] v. brać w rachubę; wliczać; włączyć

count out [kaunt aut] v. wyliczyć; nie brać w rachubę

countenance ['kauntynens] s. mina; wyraz twarzy; śmiałość; pewność siebie; animusz; fantazja; v. zachęcać; popierać; zatwierdzać; usankcjonować

counter ['kaunter] s. 1. kantor; lada; licznik; żeton;

2. przeciwieństwo; cios
odbijający; napiętek; adj.
przeciwny; przeciwległy;
podwójny; v. sprzeciwiać się;
reagować; uderzać; adv.
przeciwnie; na przekór; wbrew
(instrukcjom, poleceniom etc.)
counteract [,kaunter'aekt] v.
przeciwdziałać;
neutralizować
counterbalance ['kaunter
,baelens] s. przeciwwaga
counterespionage ['kaunter
'espje,na:ż] s. kontrwywiad
counterfeit ['kaunterfyt] adj.
fałszywy; podrobiony; v.
udawać; fałszować
counterintelligence ['kaunter
yn'tylydżens] s. kontrwywiad
counterpart ['kaunter,pa:rt] s.
odpowiednik; duplikat
countess ['kauntys] s. hrabina;
hrabianka
countless ['kauntlys] adj.
niezliczony; nie do zliczenia
country ['kantry] s. kraj;
ojczyzna; wieś; prowincja
country house ['kantry-'haus] s.
dom wiejski; dom na wsi
countryman ['kantrymen] s.
rodak; wieśniak; człowiek ze
wsi; mieszkańcy wsi
countryside ['kantry,sajd] s.
okolica; krajobraz; ludzie ze
wsi
country town ['kantry,tałn] s.
miasteczko; duża wieś
county ['kaunty] s. powiat;
hrabstwo; adj. powiatowy
couple ['kapl] s. para; v. łączyć;
parzyć się; żenić
coupling ['kaplyng] s. złącze;
skojarzenie; sprzęgło
coupon ['ku:pon] s. odcinek;
kupon wymienny (w sklepie,
banku ...)
courage ['karydż] s. odwaga
courageous [ke'rejdżes] adj.
odważny; śmiały; dzielny;
waleczny
courier ['kurjer] s. posłaniec;
goniec; kurier; agent
turystyczny

course [ko:rs] s. bieg; kierunek;
ruch naprzód; droga; danie;
kolejność; bieżnia; warstwa;
kurs; ciąg; v. gnać; pędzić;
ścigać; uganiać się
court [ko:rt] s. podwórze; hala;
dwór; hotel; sąd; v. zalecać
się; wabić; zabiegać
courteous ['ke:rcjes] adj.
grzeczny; uprzejmy i miły
courtesy ['ke:rtysy] s.
grzeczność; uprzejmość;
kurtuazja; (darmowa) usługa;
gest przez grzeczność; adj.
grzecznościowy
courtly ['ko:rtly] adj. układny;
wytworny; dworski; dostojny
court-martial ['ko:rt'ma:rszel] s.
sąd wojenny; v. sądzić
sądem wojskowym
court of justice
['ko:rt,ow'dżastys] s. sąd
courtroom ['ko:rt,ru:m] s. sala
sądowa (rozpraw)
courtship ['ko:rtszyp] s. zaloty;
umizgi do kobiety
courtyard ['ko:rt,ja:rd] s.
podwórze; dziedziniec
cousin ['kazyn] s. kuzyn;
kuzynka; krewny; cioteczny
brat (siostra)
cover ['kawer] s. koc; wieko;
oprawa; osłona; koperta;
nakrycie (stołu); pokrycie; v.
kryć; pokryć (klacz);
ubezpieczać; dać opis;
nakrywać; rozlać; chować;
przejechać
coverage ['kawerydż] s. pokrycie
ubezpieczeniem; zasięg
radiowy; omówienie w prasie
covering ['kaweryng] s. osłona;
pokrycie (dachu); przykrycie
covert ['kawert] s. schronienie;
adj. ukryty; potajemny;
przebrany
covet ['kawyt] v. pożądać
(cudzego); patrzeć z
zawiścią
covetous [kawytes] adj. chciwy;
pożądliwy; łapczywy;
zawistny
cow [kał] s. krowa; v.

zastraszyć się; przestraszyć
coward ['kauerd] s. tchórz; adj.
tchórzliwy; bojaźliwy
cowardice ['kauerdys] s.
tchórzostwo; tchórzliwość
cowardly ['kauerdly] adj.
tchórzliwy; adv. tchórzliwie
cowboy ['kałboj] s. konny
pastuch; pastuch bydła;
krowiarz
cower ['kauer] v. skulić się;
kucnąć; przykucać na ziemi
cowherd ['kał,he:rd] s. pasterz
bydła; pastuszka
cowhide ['kał,hajd] s. krowia
skóra; skóra wołowa
cowshed ['kał,szed] s. krowia
szopa; obora
cowslip ['kał,slyp] s. pierwiosnek
(kwiat bagienny)
coxcomb ['koks,koum] s. błazen;
fircyk; pajac; głupi
zarozumialec
coxswain ['kok,słejn] s. sternik
na regatach
coy [koj] adj. skromny;
nieśmiały; ostrożny; cichy;
udający
cozy [kouzy] adj. wygodny;
przytulny; s. okrycie czajnika
crab [kraeb] s. krab; rak; (wulg.)
menda; v. łowić kraby;
krytykować; rujnować;
narzekać
crab louse ['kraeb,laus] s. wesz
łonowa
crack [kraek] s. trzask; rysa;
szpara; próba; dowcip; v.
trzaskać; żartować; łupać;
uderzyć; rujnować; spowo-
dować pęknięcie; adj.
wysokiej jakości; doskonały
crack a joke ['kraek e 'dżok] v.
palnąć żart; palnąć kawał
crack a smile ['kraek,e'smajl] v.
(slang) uśmiechnąć się
cracker ['kraeker] s. sucharek;
petarda; łupacz; kłamstwo
crackpot ['kraekpot] s. wariat;
bez piątej klepki (slang)
crackle ['kraekl] v. trzeszczeć;
s. trzeszczenie; pajęczyna;
porcelana zdobiona

cradle ['krejdl] s. kołyska;
kolebka; wywrotka; v. kraść
w kołysce; kołysać; kosić
(kosa z ramą); płukać złoto
craft [kraeft] s. rzemiosło;
branża; sztuka; cech;
podstęp; chytrość;
biegłość; pojazd
craftsman ['kraftsmen] s.
rzemieślnik; mistrz w swoim
zawodzie
crafty ['kra-fty] adj. sprytny;
zręczny; podstępny;
przebiegły
crag [kraeg] s. skała (stroma);
turnia; nawis skalny
cram [kraem] v. tłoczyć;
napychać; opychać;
wytłaczać; wkuwać (się); s.
tłok; ciżba; wkuwanie do
egzaminu; ścisk; kłamstwo;
uczenie się do egzaminu
intensywnie i w pośpiechu
cramp [kraemp] s. skurcz;
klamra; zwornik; v. ściskać;
krępować; ograniczać; adj.
ściśnięty; stłoczony;
nieczytelny; sztuczny;
uchwycomy w imadło
cranberry ['kraenbery] s.
żurawina; brusznica błotna
crane [krejn] s. żuraw; dźwig;
v. podnosić; wyciągać szyję
crank [kraenk] s. korba; dziwak;
bzik; v. puszczać w ruch
(korba); kręcić; wydąbić
crank up ['kraenk,ap] v.
zapuszczać (motor);
uruchomić (motor)
crap [kraep] s. gra w kości;
brednie; bzdury; nonsens
crape [krejp] s. krepa
crash [kraesz] s. huk; łomot;
upadek; katastrofa; ruina;
krach; samodział; v. trzaskać;
huczeć; roztrzaskiwać;
wpaść na ...; adv. z hukiem;
z trzaskiem; z łomotem; z
hałasem
crash helmet ['kraesz,helmyt] s.
kask ochronny (motocyklisty)
crash landing ['kraesz,laendyng]
s. rozbicie się przy lądowaniu

crate [krejt] s. stare pudło;
skrzynia; paka; v. pakować w
skrzynie; wkładać do pak
crater ['krejter] s. krater
crave [krejw] v. pożądać;
pragnąć; prosić usilnie; błagać
crawfish ['kro:fysz] s. rak; v.
wycofywać się (rakiem)
crawl [kro:l] v. pełzać; czołgać
się; wlec; roić się; s.
czołganie; pływanie kraulem;
ciarki; basen do hodowli
raków
crayfish ['krejfysz] s. rak
(rzeczny); rak morski bez
kleszczy
crayon ['krejen] s. kredka;
rysunek kredką; v. rysować
kredką; szkicować;
narysować węglem
crazy ['krejzy] adj. zwariowany;
pomylony; walący się (np.
dom)
crazy about ['krejzy,e'baut]
zwariowany na punkcie
czegoś
creak [kri:k] v. skrzypieć;
trzeszczeć; s. skrzypienie;
pisk; zgrzyt; trzask;
trzeszczenie; pisknięcie;
zgrzytnięcie
cream [kri:m] s. śmietana;
śmietanka; krem; v. ustać
się; zbierać śmietankę;
zabielać
cream cheese ['kri:m,czi:z] s. ser
śmietankowy (biały i miękki)
creamy ['kri:my] adj.
śmietankowy; jak śmietana
crease ['kri:s] s. fałda; kant
(spodni); v. fałdować;
plisować; prasować; zmiąć;
pomiąć
create [kry:'ejt] v. tworzyć;
wywoływać;
zapoczątkowywać;
powodować
creation [kry'ejszyn] s.
stworzenie; kreacja; świat;
wszechświat
creative [kry'ejtyw] adj. twórczy;
wynalazczy; tworzący
creator [kry'ejter] s. twórca

creature ['kry:czer] s. stwór;
istota; kreatura (dominowana)
credentials [kry'denszelz] pl.
dokumenty; listy
uwierzytelniające
(tożsamość posła etc.)
credibility gap [,kredy'bylyty
gaep] s. niedowierzanie; luka
w zaufaniu; brak zaufania
credible ['kredybl] adj.
wiarogodny; wiarygodny
credit ['kredyt] s. kredyt; wiara;
autorytet; powaga; uznanie;
chluba; v. dawać wiarę;
zapisywać na rachunek;
zaliczać; przypisywać (coś
komuś)
creditable ['kreditebl] adj.
zaszczytny; godny pochwały;
chlubny
credit card ['kredyt ka:rd] karta
kredytowa do zakupów
creditor ['kredyter] s. wierzyciel
(handlowy, prywatny etc.)
credulous ['kredjules] adj.
łatwowierny; zbyt łatwowierny
creed [kri:d] s. wiara; wierzenia;
głębokie przekonania
creek [kri:k] s. potok; zatoka
creep; crept; crept [kri:p; krept;
krept]
creep [kri:p] v. pełzać; wkradać
się; mieć ciarki; s. pełzanie;
ciarki; obsuwanie; poślizg;
nędzny typ; pełzanie się
creeper ['kri:per] s. pnącz
cremate [krymejt] v. spalać
zwłoki na popiół
crept [krept] v. podpełzał; zob.
creep
crescent ['kresnt] s. półksiężyc;
rogalik; adj. półksiężycowy;
rosnący; przybywający
cress [kres] s. rzeżucha
crest [krest] s. czub; grzebień;
grzywa; pióropusz; kita; hełm;
klejnot; grzbiet; v. formować
grzbiet; osiągnąć szczyt
crestfallen [krest-folen] adj. z
opadniętym czubem;
speszony; zawstydzony;
przygnębiony
crevasse [kry'waes] s. szczelina;

pęknięcie (w lodowcu etc.)
crevice ['krewys] s. szczelina;
rysa; pęknięcie; szpara
crew [kru:] s. załoga; drużyna;
zgraja; zob. crow
crib [kryb] s. żłób z pętami;
stajnia; obora; ciupka; pokoik;
domek; kojec; plagiat; v.
stłaczać; wyposażać w
żłoby; ocembrować;
zwądzić; używać
ściągaczki
cricket ['krykyt] s. świerszcz;
krykiet; v. grać w krykieta
crime [krajm] s. zbrodnia
criminal ['krymynl] s. zbrodniarz;
kryminalista; adj. zbrodniczy;
kryminalny
crimson ['krymzn] s. & adj.
karmazyn(owy); v. zabarwiać
na karmazynowo;
zaczerwieniać się
cringe [kryndż] s. uniżoność;
v. kulić; kurczyć się; kłaniać
się; płaszczyć się (usłużnie)
cripple ['krypl] s. kulawy; kaleka;
v. okulawić; osłabiać; kuleć;
utykać; okaleczyć;
przeszkadzać
crisis ['krajsys] s. przesilenie;
kryzys; krytyczna sytuacja
crises ['krajsi:z] pl. przesilenia;
kryzysy; opały
crisp [krysp] adj. rześki;
chrupki; energiczny; v. robić
kruchym; marszczyć;
kędzierzawić; fryzować;
ufryzować
critic ['krytyk] s. krytyk
recenzent; recenzentka
critical ['krytykel] adj.
krytykujący; krytyczny; trudny
do nabycia; ważny (moment)
criticism ['krytysyzem] s.
krytyka; krytycyzm;
znajdowanie błędów
criticize ['krytysajz] v.
krytykować; ganić;
znajdować błędy
croak [krouk] v. rechotać;
krakać; s. rechot; rechotanie;
krakanie
crochet ['krouszej] v. robić na

szydełku; szydełkować
crockery ['krokery] s. naczynia
gliniane (słoje, dzbany etc.)
crocodile ['krokedajl] s. krokodyl;
adj. krokodylowy
crocus ['kroukes] s. krokus;
szafran (z rodziny irysów)
crook [kruk] s. hak; zagięcie;
krzywizna; kanciarz; v.
krzywić; wyginać; kraść;
kantować
crooked ['krukyd] adj.
zakrzywiony; krzywy;
wypaczony; zgarbiony;
cygański; szachrajski;
oszukańczy; zgięty; wygięty
crop [krop] s. plon; biczysko;
bacik; całość; przycinanie;
krótko strzyżone włosy;
ucinek; v. strzyc; skubać;
zbierać; zasiewać; obrodzić;
wyłaniać się; uprawiać
ziemię; obradzać
crop up ['krop ap] v. nagle
zjawiać się; wyskoczyć
nagle
cross [kros] s. krzyż;
skrzyżowanie; mieszaniec;
kant; cygaństwo; v. żegnać
się; krzyżować; przecinać
coś; iść w poprzek;
przekreślać; udaremnić; adj.
poprzeczny; skośny;
krzyżujący; przeciwny;
gniewny; opryskliwy
cross out ['kros,aut] v.
wykreślać; skreślać;
przekreślać
cross-examination ['kros-
-ig'zaemynejszyn] s.
przesłuchanie; badanie (w
śledztwie)
crossing ['krosyng] s.
skrzyżowanie; przejście lub
przejazd na drugą stronę
(rzeki itp.)
crossroads ['krosroudz] pl.
rozstaje; skrzyżowanie dróg
crossword puzzle ['krosłord-'pazl]
s. krzyżówka
crouch [kraucz] v. kulić się;
kurczyć; przysiąść;
gotować się do skoku

crow [krou] s. kruk; wrona;
pianie; wesoły pisk; v. piać;
piszczeć wesoło; krzyczeć z
radości

crowbar ['krouba:r] s. drąg;
lewar; łom (do podważania
etc.)

crowd [kraud] s. tłum; tłok;
banda; mnóstwo; v. tłoczyć;
natłoczyć; napierać;
wpychać; śpieszyć;
przepełniać

crowded ['kraudyd] adj.
zatłoczony; zapchany;
przeludniony

crown [kraun] s. korona;
wieniec; v. wieńczyć;
koronować

crucial ['kru:szel] adj.
decydujący; przełomowy;
krytyczny

crucifixion [,kru:sy'fykszyn] s.
ukrzyżowanie; krucyfiks

crucify [kru:syfaj] v.
ukrzyżować; torturować;
znęcać się

crude [kru:d]adj. surowy;
szorstki; niepożyty; obskurny

cruel [kruel] adj. okrutny

cruelty ['kruelty] s.
okrucieństwo; znęcanie się
(nad kimś)

cruet ['kru:yt] s. flaszeczka;
ampułka; buteleczka (na ocet
etc.)

cruise [kru:z] v. krążyć; lecieć;
podróżować; s. wycieczka
morska; przejażdżka; rejs

crumb [kram] s. okruch; (slang)
drań; v. kruszyć; drobić;
dodawać okruszyn; obtoczyć
(w bułce)

crumble ['kramb] v. kruszyć
(się)

crumple ['krampl] v. zmiąć;
zmarszczyć; załamywać się

crumple up ['krampl,ap] v.
pomiąć; zawalić się;
załamać się

crunch [krancz] v. miażdżyć;
chrupać; s. chrupanie;
chrzęst; kłopotliwa sytuacja

crunchy [kranchy] adj.

chrupiący; chrzęszczący;
kłopotliwy

crusade [kru:'sejd] s. wyprawa
krzyżowa; iść z krucjatą

crusader [kru:'sejder] s.
krzyżowiec; aktywny działacz

crush [krasz] v. kruszyć;
miażdżyć; miąć; s.
miażdżenie; tłok; ciżba;
zadurzenie się

crusher [kraszer] s. łamacz;
miażdżarka; druzgocący cios

crust [krast] s. skorupa; skóra;
v. zaskorupiać (się)

crutch [kracz] s. kula; podpórka;
laska; v. podpierać się

cry [kraj] s. krzyk; płacz; wrzask;
okrzyk; hasło; v. krzyczeć;
płakać; urągać; ujadać

cry-baby ['kraj,bejby] s. mazgaj;
beksa; płaksa (dziecinna)

crying ['krajyng] s. wołanie;
płacz; adj. płaczący;
skandaliczny

cry of rage ['kraj,ow'rejdż] s.
krzyk szału (wściekłości)

crypt [krypt] s. krypta

crystal ['krystl] s. kryształ;
szkiełko od zegarka; adj.
kryształowy

crystalline ['krystelajn] adj.
krystaliczny; kryształowy

crystallize ['krystelajz] v.
krystalizować się

cub [kab] s. szczenię (dzikiego
zwierza); zuch; młodzik

cube [kju:b] s. sześcian; kostka;
(slang) facet; v. podnosić do
sześcianu; obliczać
kubaturę; formować w
sześciany

cube root ['kju:b,ru:t] s.
pierwiastek sześcienny

cubicle ['kju:bykl] s. pokoik;
mała sypialnia; małe
mieszkanie

cuckoo ['kuku] s. kukułka;
głuptas; kukanie; dureń

cucumber ['kju:kamber] s.
ogórek

cuddle ['kadl] v. tulić; pieścić;
kulić się; gnieździć się

cudgel ['kadżel] s. pałka; bić

pałką, kijem

cue [kju:] s. wskazówka; nastrój; ogonek (do sklepu); kij bilardowy; warkocz; v. dać wskazówkę

cuff [kaf] s. mankiet; kajdanki; v. bić pięścią; uderzać; kułakować; potarmosić; szturchać

cuff links ['kaf,lynks] pl. spinki do mankietów

culminate ['kalmynejt] v. szczytować; kulminować

culmination [,kalmy'nejszyn] s. kulminacja; punkt szczytowy

culprit ['kalpryt] s. oskarżony; winowajca; winowajczyni

cultivate ['kaltywejt] v. uprawiać; rozwijać; kultywować; pielęgnować; spulchniać

cultivation [,kalty'wejszyn] s. uprawa; kultura; kultywowanie; kultura duchowa

cultivator ['kaltywejter] s. plantator; kultywator; rolnik

cultural ['kalczerel] adj. kulturalny; kulturowy

culture ['kalczer] s. kultura; uprawa; v. uprawiać; hodować; kształcić; hodować bakterie

cultured ['kalczerd] adj. kulturalny; oczytany; wykształcony

cumulative ['kju:mjulejtyw] adj. łączny; kumulacyjny; skumulowany; kumulujący się

cunning ['kanyng] s. chytrość; przebiegłość; adj. chytry; przebiegły; miły; ładny

cup [kap] s. kubek; kielich; czasza; filiżanka; v. wgłębiać; stawiać bańki

cup board ['kaberd] s. kredens; szafka; półka na kubki

cupola ['kju:pele] s. kopuła; piec kopułowy; żeliwiak

cur [ke:r] s. kundel; szelma

curable ['kjuerebl] adj. uleczalny; wyleczalny

curate ['kjueryt] s. wikary

curb [ke:rb] s. krawężnik; łańcuszek; wędzidło; oszczep; twarda spuchlizna; v. okiełznać; hamować; ograniczać

curd [ke:rd] s. twaróg; tłuszcz

curdle [ke:rdl] v. ścinać; zsiadać się; formować w grudki

cure [kjuer] s. kuracja; lek; lekarstwo; v. uleczyć; wyleczyć; zaradzić; wykurować

cure-all ['kjuero:l] s. panaceum; lek na wszystkie dolegliwości

curfew ['ke:rfju:] s. godzina policyjna; capstrzyk

curio ['kjuerjou] s. okaz; osobliwość; unikat; rzadkość

curiosity [,kjur'josyty] s. ciekawość; osobliwość

curl [ke:rl] s. kędzior; lok; pukiel; skręt; spirala; wir; v. kręcić; skręcać; zwijać; marszczyć; złościć; skulić się

curling iron ['ke:rlyng,ajren] s. rurki do fruzowania

curl up ['ke:rl ap] v. zwinąć (się)

curly ['ke:rly] adj. kędzierzawy; kręty; falujący; kręcony

currant ['karent] s. porzeczka; rodzynek bez pestki

currency ['karensy] s. waluta; obieg; potoczność; popularność

current ['karent] adj. bieżący; obiegowy; obiegający; powszechnie znany; panujący (pogląd); s. prąd; bieg; nurt; tok; strumień; natężenie prądu

curriculum [ke'rykjulem] s. plan studiów; program nauki

curriculum vitae [ke 'rykjulem,wajti:] s. życiorys

curse [ke:rs] s. przekleństwo; klątwa; v. przeklinać; wyklinać; kląć; bluźnić; złorzeczyć

cursed [ke:rsyd] adj. przeklęty; cholerny; adv. paskudnie;

cholernie; po diable
curt [ke:rt] adj. krótki; zwięzły;
lakoniczny; szorstki; suchy
curtail [ke:r'tejl] v. obcinać;
skracać; zmniejszać;
uszczuplać
curtain ['ke:rtn] s. zasłona;
firanka; kurtyna; v. zasłaniać
curtsy ['ke:rtsy] s. dyg; v.
dygać; złożyć głęboki ukłon
curve [ke:rw] s. krzywa;
krzywizna; krzywka; wyginać
(się); wykrzywiać (się);
zakręcać
cushion ['kuszyn] s. poduszka
custody ['kastedy] s. opieka;
nadzór; areszt; przetrzymanie
custom ['kastem] s. zwyczaj;
klientela; zrobiony na
zamówienie; nawyk; stałe
zaopatrywanie się
customary ['kastemery] adj.
zwyczajny; zwyczajowy; s.
zbiór praw
customer ['kastemer] s. klient
customhouse ['kastem-haus] s.
komora celna; urząd celny
custom-made ['kastem-mejd] adj.
zrobiony na zamówienie
customs ['kastemz] pl. cło
customs clearance ['kastemz
klierenz] s. odprawa celna
customs declaration ['kastemz
,dekle'rejszyn] s. deklaracja
celna (przy przekraczaniu
granicy etc.)
customs examination ['kastemz
ig,zamy'nejszyn] s. rewizja
celna (bagażu, towarów etc.)
cut; cut; cut [kat; kat; kat]
cut [kat] s. cięcie; przecięcie;
wycięcie; ścięcie; odrzynek;
krój; styl (krawiecki); wykop;
drzeworyt; v. ciąć; zaciąć;
skaleczyć; ranić; krajać;
kroić; przycinać; kosić;
rżnąć; rzeźbić; szlifować;
wycinać; obcinać; uciąć;
ścinać
cut down ['kat,dałn] v. obniżać;
redukować; wyciąć w pień
(wroga)
cut in ['kat,yn] v. wtrącać się

cut off ['kat,of] v. odcinać;
przerywać (dopływ);
wydziedziczać
cut out ['kat,aut] v. wykroić;
przestać; zaprzestać (palić);
wyciąć; wyrżnąć
cut up ['kat,ap] v. posiekać;
skrytykować; wypatroszyć;
siec; rozciąć
cute [kju:t] adj. miły; ładny;
chytry; sprytny; ciekawy;
bystry
cuticle ['kju:tykl] s. naskórek
cuticle scissors ['kju:tykl-'syzez]
s. nożyczki od naskórka
cutlery ['katlery] s. wyroby
nożownicze; sztućce
cutlet ['katlyt] s. kotlet (bity);
kotlet mielony (mięsny, rybi)
cut-off ['katof] s. odcięcie;
skrót; wyłącznik; wycinek;
zawór (wodny; parowy;
gazowy etc.)
cutout ['kat aut] = cut-off
cutpurse ['kat pe:rs] s.
rzezimieszek; kieszonkowiec;
opryszek
cutter ['kater] s. kuter;
przecinek; przykrawacz;
odcinacz; kamieniarz; mistrz
kamieniarski
cutting ['katyng] adj. bolesny;
przenikliwy; cięty; s. sadzonka
cutthroat ['kat,trout] s. zbój;
bandyta; adj. zbójecki;
bandycki; morderczy;
bezlitosny
cycle [sajkl] s. cykl; okres;
obieg; rower; v. jechać na
rowerze; obiegać cyklicznie
(tam i nazad, w koło itp.)
cyclist ['sajklyst] s. rowerzysta;
rowerzystka; cyklista;
cyklistka
cyclone ['sajkloun] s. cyklon
cylinder ['sylynder] s. walec;
(maszyny do pisania); cylinder;
bęben (rewolweru etc.)
cynic ['synyk] s. cynik
cynical ['synykel] adj. cyniczny
(pomysł, program, człowiek)
cynicism ['syny,syzem] s.
cynizm

cypress ['sajprys] s. cyprys
cyst [syst] s. cysta; torbiel
czar [za:r] s. car; (od nafty,
 sportu, walki z narktukami,
 komisarz generalny USA)
Czech [czek] adj. czeski
Czechoslovak ['czekou,slouwaek]
 adj. czechosłowacki

D

d [di] czwarta litera alfabetu
 angielskiego; oznaczenie centa
dab [daeb] v. musnąć; klepać;
 dotknąć; dziobnąć; s.
 muśnięcie; klaps;
 stuknięcie; dziobnięcie; plama;
 bryzg; odrobina
dabble ['daebl] v. moczyć;
 babrać; pluskać (się);
 interesować (się)
dabbler ['daebler] s. amator;
 amatorka; dyletant; dyletantka
dachshund ['daekshund] s.
 jamnik; a. jamniczy; jamnika
dad [daed] s. tato; tatuś
daddy ['daedy] s. tatuś
daffodil ['daefedyl] s. żółty
 narcyz; żonkil; adj. bladożółty
daffy ['daefy] adj. zwariowany
daft ['daeft] adj. pomylony;
 głupkowaty; zwariowany
dagger ['daeger] s. sztylet;
 odsyłacz; v. sztyletować
daily ['dejly] adj. codzienny; adv.
 codziennie; s. dziennik
dainty ['dejnty] adj. wyszukany;
 wyborowy; delikatny;
 gustowny; miły; wybredny
daiquiri ['daikery] s. rum z
 sokiem cytrynowym, cukrem i
 lodem (po amerykańsku)
dairy ['deery] s. mleczarnia
dairyman ['deerymen] s.
 mleczarz; właściciel mleczarni
daisy ['dejzy] s. stokrotka; ładny
 okaz (człowieka)
dale [dejl] s. dolina

dally ['daely] v. marudzić;
 igrać; flirtować; tracić czas
dam [daem] s. tama; zapora
damage ['daemydż] s. szkoda;
 uszkodzenie; odszkodowanie;
 (slang) koszt; v. uszkodzić;
 ponieść szkody; uwłaczać
dame [dejm] s. dziewczyna;
 kobieta; pani (starsza)
damn [daem] v. potępiać;
 przeklinać; adj. przeklęty
damnation [daem'nejszyn] s.
 potępienie (kogoś, czegoś;
 excl. psiakrew; cholera; a
 niech to piorun trzaśnie!
damp [daemp] v. zwilżyć;
 skropić; stłumić; ostudzić;
 amortyzować; butwieć; s.
 wilgoć; czad; przygnębienie;
 zwątpienie; depresja
dampen ['daempen] v.
 wilgotnieć; zwilgotnieć;
 zwilżyć; ostudzić
dance [da:ns] s. taniec; zabawa
 taneczna; v. tańczyć;
 skakać; kazać tańczyć;
 huśtać; kręcić się
dancer ['da:nser] s. tancerz;
 tancerka; baletnica
dancing ['da:nsyng] s. taniec;
 adj. tańczący; do tańca
dandelion ['daendylajon] s.
 mniszek lekarski; mlecz
dandruff ['daendref] s. łupież
danger ['dejndżer] s.
 niebezpieczeństwo; groźba
dangerous ['dejndżeres] adj.
 niebezpieczny; groźny; niepewny (grunt, interes etc.)
dangle ['daengl] v. dyndać;
 bujać; kręcić się; nadskakiwać (komuś, koło kogoś)
Danish [dejnysz] adj. duński
dapper ['daeper] adj. wytworny;
 elegancki; dobrze ubrany;
 zwinny; fertyczny
dare [deer] v. śmieć; ważyć
 się; wyzywać; s. wyzwanie
daring ['deeryng] adj. śmiały;
 śmiałość; odwaga
dark [da:rk] adj. ciemny; ponury;
 s. ciemność; mrok; cień;
 murzyn; tajemniczość; brak

ninformacji; niewiedza
dark-brown ['da:rk braɪn] adj.
ciemno-brązowy
darken [da:rkn] v. zaciemniać
darkness ['da:rknys] s.
ciemność; ciemnota; mrok;
śniadość (cery); ciemności
darling ['da:rlyng] s. kochanie;
ulubieniec; adj. kochany;
ulubiony; ukochany
darn [da:rn] v. cerować; s. cera;
adj. (slang) przeklęty
dart [da:rt] s. żądło; szybki ruch;
oszczep; zryw; v. pędzić;
rzucać; wybuchać; strzelać
dash [daesz] v. roztrzaskać;
rzucać się; rzucić (czymś)
pędzić; popisywać się;
zakropić; opryskać;
niweczyć (coś); mieszać;
onieśmielać (kogoś); odbić;
naszkicować; s. uderzenie;
zderzenie; plusk; barwna
plama; szczypta; przymieszka;
myślnik; kreska; pęd; skok;
rozmach; popęd; popis
dash-board ['daeszbo:rd] tablica
rozdzielcza; zestaw zegarów
(lotniczych, samochodowych
etc.); błotnik (samochodowy)
dashing [daeszyng] adj. dziarski;
z werwą; z rozmachem
data ['dejtə] pl. dane; podstawa
odniesienia; dane liczbowe
data processing ['dejtə
'prousesyng] s. przetwarzanie
danych (na komputerze)
date [dejt] v. datować (list)
nosić datę; chodzić z kimś;
s. data; spotkanie; randka;
umówienie się; termin; palma
daktylowa; daktyl
date from ['dejt,from] data z ...
(dnia, miejsce, miasto etc.)
dative case ['dejtyw,kejs] s.
trzeci przypadek; celownik
datum ['dejtem] s. dana (fakt;
szczegół); punkt wyjściowy
daub [do:b] v. babrać; mazać;
oblepiać; s. tynk; polepa;
plama; kicz sknocony; gips
daughter ['do:ter] s. córka
daughter-in-law ['do:ter,yn lo:] s.

synowa, (żona syna)
dawdle ['do:dl] v. próżniaczyć;
mitrężyć; wałkonić się
dawdle away ['do:dl,a'łej] v.
marnować czas; tracić czas
dawn [do:n] v. świtać;
zaświtać; dnieć; jaśnieć;
s. świt; brzask; zaranie;
zdanie sobie sprawy
day [dej] s. dzień; doba
daybreak ['dejbrejk] s. świt;
brzask; świtanie
day by day ['dej,baj dej] exp.
dzień w dzień; dzień po dniu
daydream ['dejdri:m] s. marzenie;
sen na jawie; v. marzyć; budować zamki na lodzie
day in day out ['dej,yn'dej aut]
exp. codziennie; dzień w
dzień (robić to samo, etc.)
daylight ['dejlajt] s. światło
dzienne; biały dzień
day nursery ['dej,ne:rsery] s.
żłobek (dzienny)
day off ['dej of] s. dzień wolny
days to come ['dejs,tu kam] exp.
przyszłość (niedaleka)
day's work ['dejz,łe:rk] s.
dniówka; dzienna praca
daytime ['dejtajm] s. dzień od
świtu do zmroku
daze [dejz] v. oszałamiać;
otumaniać; oślepiać; s.
oszołomienie; otumanienie
dazzle [daezl] v. oślepiać;
olśniewać; zamaskować; s.
oślepiający blask
dead [ded] adj. & s. zmarły;
martwy; wymarły; matowy
dead body [ded'body] s. zwłoki
dead center ['ded'senter] s.
punkt martwy, zwrotny
deaden ['deden] v. zabijać siły,
uczucia etc.; tłumić; osłabiać; stępiać; zmartwieć;
złagodzić (cios); obumrzeć;
pozbawiać blasku, połysku,
zapachu; znieczulać
dead end ['dedend] s. ślepa
(ulica, ostateczny koniec)
deadline ['dedlajn] s.
nieprzekraczalny termin; ostateczna granica (czegoś)

deadlock ['dedlok] s. impas;
martwy punkt; v. powo-
dować impas (zastój)
deadly [dedly] adj. śmiertelny;
adv. śmiertelnie; nieludzko
deadweight ['dedłejt] s. ciężar
własny (urządzenia); kula u
nogi; kamień u szyi
deaf [def] adj. głuchy
deafen [defn] v. ogłuszać
deafening [defnyng] adj.
ogłuszający (hałas)
deal; dealt; dealt [di:l; delt; delt]
deal [di:l] v. zajmować się;
traktować o; załatwiać
(coś); przestawać z (kimś);
postępować; handlować;
rozdzielać (karty); s. ilość;
sprawa; sporo; wiele
deal with ['di:l łyt] v.
postępować z ...; mieć do
czynienia (z kimś, czymś)
dealer ['di:ler] s. kupiec;
handlarz; rozdający karty
dealing ['di:lyng] s.
postępowanie z; stosunki;
transakcje; konszachty
dealt [delt] zob. deal
dean [di:n] s. dziekan
dear [dier] adj. kochany; drogi
dear Sir ['dier,se:r] exp.
Szanowny Panie; Drogi Panie
dear me! [dier mi] exp. ojej! mój
Boże! czyżby! ależ nie!
death [des] s. śmierć; zgon
deathly [desly] adj. śmiertelny;
trupi; adv. śmiertelnie;
grobowo; trupio
debar ['dyba:r] v. wykluczać;
zabraniać (komuś); za-
kazywać (komuś czegoś)
debase [dy'bejs] v. obniżać;
poniżać; fałszować; upadlać
debate [dy'bejt] v. roztrząsać;
rozważać; debatować; s.
debata; spór; rozprawa
debauchery ['dy'bo:czery] s.
rozpusta; wyuzdanie; roz-
wiązłość; rozwiązłe życie
debit ['debyt] s. debet;
obciążenie rachunku
debrief [dy'bri:f] s. przesłuchania
po (akcji); v. przesłuchiwać

po (akcji wojskowej etc.)
debris ['dejbri:] pl. gruzy
debt [det] s. dług
debtor ['deter] s. dłużnik;
dłużniczka (czyjaś)
decade ['dekejd] s.
dziesięcioletni okres
decadence ['dekejdens] s.
dekadencja; chylenie się ku
upadkowi; schyłek; upadek
decapitate [dy'kaepytejt] v.
ścinać głowę; pozbawić
wodza (przywództwa)
decay [dy'kej] v. gnić;
rozpadać się; psuć się; s.
upadek; ruina; zanik; rozkład;
gnicie; uwiąd; niszczenie
decease [dy'si:s] v. umierać; s.
zgon; śmierć; zejście
deceased [dy'si:st] adj. zmarły;
s. nieboszczyk; nieboszczka
deceit [dy'si:t] s. oszukaństwo;
podstęp; złuda; fałsz
deceitful [dy'si:tfel] adj.
kłamliwy; zwodniczy; oszukańczy; podstępny; fałszywy
deceive [dy'si:w] v. okłamywać;
zwodzić; łudzić; zawodzić
deceiver [dy'si:wer] s.
oszukaniec; zwodziciel; kłamca
decelerate [dy:'selerejt] v.
zwalniać szybkość (cze-
goś); zmniejszać szybkość
December [dy'sember] s.
grudzień (mieśiąc)
decency ['di:snsy] s.
przyzwoitość; obyczajność;
dobre obyczaje
decent ['di:sent] adj. przyzwoity;
porządny; skromny; znośny
deception [dy'sepszyn] s.
łudzenie; okłamywanie; podstęp; zawód; szachrajstwo;
oszukanie; oszukaństwo
decide [dy'sajd] v. rozstrzygać;
postanawiać; decydować się
(na coś); zadecydować;
skłaniać się (ku czemuś)
decided [dy'sajdyd] adj.
zdecydowany; stanowczy; definitywny; kategoryczny
decimal ['desymel] adj.
dziesiętny (system, ułamek);

s. ułamek dziesiętny
decipher [dy'sajfer] v.
odcyfrować (depeszę, etc.);
rozszyfrować; rozwiązać
decision [dy'syżyn] s.
rozstrzygnięcie (czegoś);
postanowienie (o czymś); decyzja; zdecydowanie; stanowczość; wygrana na punkty;
ustalenie; rezolutność
decisive [dy'sajsyw] adj.
decydujący; rozstrzygający;
zdecydowany; stanowczy
deck [dek] s. pokład; pomost;
podłoga; talia; v. pokrywać
pokładem; przystrajać
deck chair ['dek czeer] s. leżak
(do opalania się na statku)
declaration [dekle'rejszyn] s.
deklaracja; zapowiedź;
oświadczenie (oficjalne)
declare [dy'kle:r] v. deklarować;
oświadczać; zeznawać; wy-
powiadać (wojnę); ogłaszać
(coś); uznawać (za niewin-
nego); stwierdzać; wykazać;
dawać (coś) do oclenia
declension [dy'klenszyn] s.
deklinacja (gram.); przypad-
kowanie; odchylenie; upadek
decline [dy'klajn] v. uchylać
(się); pochylać (się); skłaniać
(się); iść ku schyłkowi; opadać; obniżać; podupadać;
marnieć; słabnąć; zanikać;
zamierać; przypadkować; odrzucać (propozycję etc.); s.
schyłek; utrata; spadek
declivity [dy'klywyty] s.
pochyłość; spadzistość;
stok (góry etc.); skłon
decode [dy'koud] v. rozszyfrować; rozszyfrowywać
decorate ['dekerejt] v. ozdabiać;
odznaczać; udekorować; odnowić; upiększać (coś)
decompose [,dy:kem'pouz] v.
rozkładać (się); rozłożyć (na
części etc.); gnić
decoration [,deke'rejszyn] s.
ozdoba; odznaczenie; medal
decorative [,deke'rejtyw] adj.
ozdobny; dekoracyjny

decorator ['dekerejter] s.
dekorator; architekt wnętrz
decoy ['dy:koj] s. wabik;
przynęta; v. wabić (w pułapkę, w sidła); usidlać; zwabiać; wciągać w pułapkę; zaciągać sidła (na lisy etc.)
decrease ['dy:kri:s] v.
zmniejszać; słabnąć; ob-
niżać; s. zmniejszenie;
spadek (cen, wartości etc.)
decree [dy'kri:] s. dekret;
rozporządzenie; wyrok rozwodowy; postanowienie o se-
paracji; zrządzenie (losu); v.
zarządzać; rozporządzać; nakazywać (coś) dekretem
decrepit [dy'krepyt] adj.
zgrzybiały; wyniszczony
decry [dy'kraj] v. potępić;
okrzyczeć; zohydzić; obgadać; oczernić (kogoś)
dedicate ['dedykejt] v.
dedykować; poświęcać; in-
augurować; przeznaczyć na
dedication ['dedykejszyn] s.
dedykacja; poświęcenie; otwarcie; przeznaczenie
deduce [dy'du:s] v.
wnioskować; dedukować;
wywodzić (rodowód etc.)
deduct [dy'dakt] v. potrącać;
odciągać (kwotę etc.); odejmować; odtrącać (kogoś)
deduction [dy'dakszyn] s.
potrącenie; odciągnięcie;
wnioskowanie; wniosek; **wy-
dedukowanie; wywód**
deed [di:d] s. czyn; wyczyn; akt;
v. przekazywać aktem (własność); przekazywać (ko-
muś) pieniądze etc.
deep [di:p] adj. głęboki; s.
głębia; adv. głęboko
deepen ['di:pn] v. pogłębiać
deep-freeze ['di:p,fri:z] s.
(głębokie) zamrożenie
deeply ['di:ply] adv. głęboko
deep-rooted ['di:p'ru:tyd] adj.
głęboko zakorzeniony
deer [dier] s. jeleń; sarna; łoś;
łania; daniel; renifer
deface [dy'fejs] v. szpecić;

zniekształcać; zacierać
defame [dy'fejm] v. zniesławić
defeat [dy'fi:t] v. pokonać;
pobić (przeciwnika); uni-
cestwić; udaremnić; unie-
możliwić; unieważnić prawnie; s. klęska; udaremnienie
defect [dy'fekt] s. brak; wada;
błąd; defekt; skaza; man-
kament; przywara; v. od-
paść; skłonić do odstęp-
stwa; odstąpić (od czegoś)
defective [dy'fektyw]
adj. wadliwy; wybrakowany
defence [dy'fens] = defense
defend [dy'fend] v. bronić
defendant [dy'fendent] s.
pozwany; oskarżony; obrońca
defender [dy'fender] s. obrońca
(w prawie i sporcie)
defensive [dy'fensyw] adj.
obronny; defensywny (układ);
s. defensywa; (być) w defen-
sywie; stanowisko obronne
defense [dy'fens] s. obrona
defenseless [dy'fenslys] adj.
bezbronny (człowiek etc.)
defer [dy'fe:r] v. odraczać;
ustępować; ulegać; mieć
wzgląd; skłaniać się (przed)
defiant [dy'fajent] adj.
zbuntowany; nieufny; bun-
towniczy; prowokujący
deficiency [dy'fyszynsy] s. brak;
niedobór; należność nie-
zapłacona; niedostatek; słabość (natury człowieka etc.)
deficit ['defysyt] s. deficyt;
niedobór; nadwyżka rozchodu
defile ['dy:fail] v. kalać;
plugawić; brukać; bez-
cześcić; iść szeregami; defilować; s. wąwóz; przełęcz
define [dy'fajn] v. określać;
definiować; zakreślać (granice); precyzować (coś)
definite ['defynyt] adj.
określony; wyraźny; pewny;
jasny; prostolinijny; okreś-
lający; sprecyzowany
definition [,defy'nyszyn] s.
określenie; definicja; ostrość (konturów, obrazu etc.);

czystość; oznaczenie
definitive [dy'fynytyw] adj.
ostateczny; definitywny; stanowczy; rozstrzygający; kon-
kluzywny; definiujący
deflate [dy'flejt] v. wypuszczać
powietrze (z dętki); zmniejszać (obieg, znaczenie etc.)
deform [dy'fo:rm] v. szpecić;
zniekształcać; oszpecać
deformed [dy'fo:rmd] adj.
ułomny; szpetny; zniekształ-
cony; zdeformowany
defrost ['dy:frost] v. odmrozić
defunct ['dy'fankt] adj. zmarły;
zlikwidowany; już nie istniejący; wymarły; rozwiązany
defy [dy'faj] v. stawiać czoło;
rzucać wyzwania (by zrobić,
wykazać); przeciwstawiać
degenerate [dy'dżeneryt] adj.
zwyrodniały; s. degenerat
degrade [dy'grejd] v. poniżać;
obniżać; wyrodnieć; spod-
leć; upadlać; znieważać
degree [dy'gri:] s. stopień (np.
naukowy, ciepła etc.)
dejected [dy'dżektyd] adj.
przygnębiony; zgaszony
(człowiek); zdeprymowany;
strapiony (złą wieścią)
dejectedly [dy'dżektydly] adv. z
przygnębieniem; z niechęcią
delay [dy'lej] v. odraczać;
opóźniać; zwlekać; s. od-
roczenie; zwłoka; opóźnienie
delegate ['delegejt] s. zastępca;
wysłannik; v. delegować;
udzielać delegacji; zlecać
(władzę); udzielać (władzy,
pełnomocnictwa komuś)
delegation [,dely'gejszyn] s.
delegacja; grupa delegatów
deliberate [dy'lyberejt] adj.
rozmyślny; spokojny; powolny; umyślny; [dy,ly'berejt] v.
rozmyślać; rozważać (coś);
obradować; naradzać się
delicacy [dy'delykesy] s.
delikatność; smakołyk; takt
delicate ['delykyt] adj. delikatny;
wyśmienity; taktowny
delicatessen [,delyka'tesn] s.

sklep z delikatesami
delicious [dy'lyszes] adj.
rozkoszny; bardzo smaczny
delight [dy'lajt] s. rozkosz; v.
zachwycać się; rozkoszować
się (czymś); lubować się
delightful [dy'lajtful] adj.
zachwycający; czarujący; cza-
rowny; niezapomniany
delinquency [dy'lynkłensy] s.
zaniedbanie; wina; przestępstwo; niepłacenie należności;
przestępczość; wykroczenie
delinquent [dy'lynkłent] a. winny;
zaniedbany; zalegający z za-
płatą (podatkiem); s. winowajca; przestępca (nieletni);
osoba zalegająca etc.
deliver [dy'lywer] v. doręczać;
zdawać; wydawać; wygła-
szać; zadawać; uwalniać;
ratować; wybawić; wyzwo-
lić; podawać; oddawać
deliverance [dy'lywerens] s.
uwolnienie; wygłoszenie
deliverer [dy'lywerer] s. zbawca;
oswobodziciel; wybawca
delivery [dy'lywery] s. dostawa;
wydawanie; wygłaszanie;
podanie; poród; przekazanie
deluge ['delju:dż] s. potop
delusion [dy'lu:żyn] s. urojenie;
zwodzenie; ułuda; iluzja
delusive [dy'lu:syw] adj. złudny;
oszukańczy; bałamutny;
zwodniczy; iluzoryczny
demand [dy'ma:nd] s. zadanie;
popyt; v. zadać; dopytywać
się; wymagać; domagać się
demeanor [dy'mi:ner] s.
zachowanie się; postępo-
wanie; postawa (wobec)
demented [dy'mentyd] adj.
obłąkany; oszalały; umysłowo
chory; opętany
demi- ['demy] pref. pół-
demilitarized ['dy:myłyterajzd]
adj. zdemilitaryzowany
demise [dy'majz] s. zgon;
przekazanie spadku; v.
przekazywać (coś) testa-
mentem lub zgonem
demobilize [dy:,moubyłajz] v.

demobilizować (wojsko etc.);
zdemobilizować (żołnierzy)
democracy [dy'mokresy] s.
demokracja (równość praw)
democrat ['dymokreat] s.
demokrata; demokratka
democratic [,deme'kraetyk] adj.
demokratyczny
demolish [dy'molysz] v. burzyć;
niszczyć; obalać (teorię);
demolować; zburzyć (coś)
demon ['di:men] s. diabeł;
demon; doskonały zawodnik
sportowy, gracz, tenisista
demonstrate ['demenstrejt] v.
wykazywać; udowadniać;
demonstrować; urządzać
manifestację etc.
demonstration [,demen'strejszyn]
s. wykazywanie; okazywanie;
demonstracja; zademonstro-
wanie; manifestacja
demonstrative [dy'menstrejtyw]
adj. wylewny; dowodowy;
wskazujący (coś); dowodzący (czegoś); ekspansywny
demurrage [dy'me:rydż] s.
przestój; opłata za postojowe
den [den] s. nora; jaskinia;
ustronie; cicha pracownia
denial [dy'najel] s. zaprzeczenie;
odmowa; wyparcie się
denomination [dynomy'nejszyn]
s. nazwa; miano; określenie;
wyznanie (rel.); kategoria
denounce [dy'nauns] v.
oskarżać; donosić; wypo-
wiadać; denuncjować
dense [dens] adj. gęsty; zwarty;
tępy (człowiek); niepojętny
density ['densyty] s. gęstość;
zwartość; głupota; tępota;
spoistość; szczelność
dent [dent] s. wgłębienie; wrąb;
wklęśnięcie; sl. znaczenie; v.
szczerbić; wyginać
dental ['dentl] adj. zębowy;
dentystyczny; stomatologiczny
dentist ['dentyst] s. dentysta;
dentystka; stomatolog
denture [denczer] s. (sztuczne)
uzębienie; szczęka
deny [dy'naj] v. zaprzeczyć;

odrzucić; odmawiać; **wypie-**
rać się; dementować; przeczyć (czemuś); odmówić
depart [dy'pa:rt] v. odjeżdżać;
odbiegać; robić dygresję;
zejść (zs swiata); odejść
department [dy'pa:rtment] s.
wydział; ministerstwo; dział
department store [dy'pa:rtment
,sto:r] s. dom towarowy
departure [dy'pa:rczer] s. odjazd;
rozstanie; odchylenie
depend on [dy'pend on] v.
polegać na ...; zależeć od
depend upon [dy'pend,apon] v.
być zależnym od ...; być na
utrzymaniu (kogoś)
depends [dy'pends] v. zależy
deplorable [dy'plo:rebl] adj.
godny pożałowania; opłakany
deplore [dy'plo:r] v. ubolewać;
boleć nad ...; wyrażać ubolewanie, żal, współczucie
depolarize [dy'poulerajz] v.
depolaryzować; rozwiać
(czyjeś) złudzenia
depopulate [dy'popjulejt] v.
wyludniać; pustoszyć; wy-
ludniać się; opustoszyć
deport [dy'po:rt] v. zsyłać;
deportować (złoczyńcą);
zsyłać; zachowywać się
depose [dy'pouz] v. składać;
zeznawać; usunąć (z tronu)
deposit [dy'pozyt] s. osad;
warstwa; kaucja; depozyt; v.
składać do depopzytu; osadzać; deponować; nawar-
stwiać; złożyć (jaja ...)
depositor [dy'pozyter] s.
depozytor; deponent
depot [depou] s. stacja kolejowa;
skład; remiza; kadra
depraved [dy'prejwd] adj.
zdeprawowany; zepsuty
moralnie; deprawowany
depreciate [dy'pry:szy,ejt] v.
obniżać wartość; de-
waluować; ujmować znacze-
nie; ujemnie mówić (o kimś)
depress [dy'pres] v.
przygnębiać; deprymować;
spychać w dół (ceny); zni-

żać (cenę etc.); martwić
depressed [dy'prest] adj.
przygnębiony; przygnieciony;
zmartwiony; zatroskany; prrzy-
płaszczony; zahamowany
depression [dy'preszyn] s.
przygnębienie; depresja
deprive [dy'prajw] v. odzierać;
wykluczać; umartwiać się;
pozbawiać; odwołać (z urzędu etc.); odbierać
depth [deps] s. głębokość;
głębia; głębina; dno (nędzy)
deputy ['depjuty] s. zastępca;
deputowany; poseł; wice-
derail [dy'rejl] v. wykoleić (się)
(czyjś plan, zamiar etc.)
derange [dy'rejndż] v.
pomieszać; rozstrajać; psuć;
zakłócać; powodować obłęd;
wprowdzić (nieład, chaos)
deride [dy'rajd] v. wyśmiewać
derision [dy'ryżyn] s.
szyderstwo; pośmiewisko;
drwina; wyszydzanie kogoś
derisive [dy'rajsyw] adj. kpiący;
ironiczny; wart śmiechu
derive [dy'rajw] v. uzyskiwać;
czerpać; wywodzić; wypro-
wadzić (ród); pochodzić (z)
derogatory [dy'rogeto:ry] adj.
pomniejszający; uszczupla-
jący; uwłaczający; szkodliwy
descend [dy'send] v. zejść;
spaść; zstąpować z; zni-
żać się; pochodzić (od); opadać; zwalić się (na kogoś)
descendant [dy'sendent] s.
potomek (przodka, rodziny,
grupy, narodu, etc.)
descent [dy'sent] s. zejście;
spadek; pochodzenie; nagły
atak; lądowanie; obniżka
describe [dys'krajb] v.
opisywać; określać; prze-
rysowywać; dawać rysopis
description [dy'skrypszyn] s.
opis; sposób opisywania
desegregate [dy'segrygejt] v.
(Am) znieść podział rasowy
desert ['desert] adj. pustynny;
pusty; s. pustynia; pustkowie
desert [dy'ze:rt] v. porzucać;

opuszczać; dezerterować; s.
zasłużenie; zasługa; nagroda;
zasłużona kara (opinia)
deserted [dy'ze:rted] adj.
opuszczony; bezludny
deserter [dy'ze:rter] s. dezerter;
dezerterka; zbieg; zbiegła
desertion [dy'ze:rszyn] s.
opuszczenie; dezercja;
porzucenie (kogoś, czegoś)
deserve [dy'ze:rw] v.
zasługiwać na ...; mieć
zasługi wobec (kogoś)
design [dy'zajn] s. zamiar; plan;
szkic; v. pomyśleć; za-
mierzać; przeznaczać; projektować; zamyślać; uplano-
wać; kreślić; szkicować
designate ['dezygnejt] v.
wyznaczać; określać; za-
mianować; desygnować
designer [dy'zajner] s. projektant;
konstruktor; rysownik;
intrygant; projektodawca;
autor; autorka; kreślarz
desirable [dy'zajerebl] adj.
pożądany; pociągający; atrak-
cyjny; celowy; mile (dobrze)
widziany; wskazany
desire [dy'zajer] v. pożądać;
pragnąć; życzyć sobie
desirous [dy'zajeres] adj. żądny;
pragnący czegoś; spragniony
desk [desk] s. biuro; referat;
pulpit; ambona; ławka szkolna
desk set ['desk set] s. zestaw
przyborów do pisania
desolate ['deselyt] adj.
opuszczony; posępny; wyludniony; zdewastowany
desolate ['deselejt] v.
pustoszyć; wyludniać;
opuszczać; (z)dewastować
desolation [,dese'lejszyn] s.
wyludnienie; spustoszenie;
pustka; żałość; strapienie
despair [dys'peer] s. rozpacz
despairingly [dys'peeryngly] adv.
rozpaczliwie; beznadziejnie
desperate ['desperyt] adj.
rozpaczliwy; beznadziejny;
beznadziejnej; zaciekły
desperation [,despe'rejszyn] s.

rozpacz; desperacja
despise [dys'pajz] v. pogardzać;
gardzić; (z)lekceważyć
despite [dys'pajt] s. przekora;
złość; prep. pomimo; wbrew;
na przekór (komuś; czemuś)
despond [dys'pond] v.
przygnębiać się; stracić
otuchę; s. przygnębienie
despondent [dys'pondent] adj.
przygnębiony; zniechęcony
despot ['despot] s. despota;
despotka; władca absolutny
dessert [dy'ze:rt] s. deser;
legumina; ciastka
destination [desty'nejszyn] s.
miejsce przeznaczenia
destine ['destyn] v. przeznaczać
(z góry); przeznaczyć
destiny ['destyny] s.
przeznaczenie (wypadków, ludzi); (nieunikniony) los
destitute ['destytju:t] adj. bez
środków; całkowicie pozbawiony środków; w nędzy
destroy [dy'stroj] v. burzyć;
niweczyć; zabijać; zgładzać
destroyer [dy'strojer] s.
kontrtorpedowiec; niszczyciel
destruction [dys'trakszyn] s.
zniszczenie; ruina; zguba;
zagłada (powód, środki etc.)
destructive [dy'straktyw] adj.
niszczycielski; s. niszczyciel
detach [dy'taecz] v. odczepić;
odłączyć; odpiąć; odwią-
zać; odkomenderować; od-
lepiać (coś); urwać (z)
detached [dy'taeczt] adj.
odosobniony; obojętny; niezależny (od); na dystans
detail ['di:tejl] s. szczegół;
wyszczególnienie; v. wyłuszczać; przydzielać do zadań
detain [dy'tejn] v. wstrzymywać; więzić (kogoś);
przeszkadzać (komuś)
detect [dy'tekt] v. wykrywać;
wyśledzić; przychwycić na
detection [dy'tekszyn] s.
wykrywanie; wyśledzenie
detective [dy'tektyw] s.

detektyw; adj. detek-
tywistyczny; śledczy
detention [dy'tenszyn] s.
areszt; więzienie; zatrzymanie;
przetrzymanie; opóźnienie
deter [dy'te:r] v. odstraszać od;
pohamować; onieśmielać
detergent [dy'te:rdżent] s. & adj.
czyszczący (środek)
deteriorate [dy'tierjerejt] v.
psuć; marnieć; tracić na
wartości; pogarszać się
determination [dyte:rmy'nejszyn]
s. określenie; postanowienie;
ustalenie; orzeczenie; wygaśnięcie (umowy); dawkowanie
determine [dy'te:rmyn] v.
rozstrzygać; określać; postanawiać; ustalać; zdefi-
niować; zadecydować (o)
determined [dy'te:rmynd] adj.
zdecydowany; stanowczy;
zdeterminowany (człowiek)
deterrent [dy'terent] adj.
odstraszający; s. (czynnik)
odstraszający; środek
zaradczy (zapobiegawczy)
detest [dy'test] v. nienawidzić;
czuć wstręt; nie cierpieć
detestable [dy'testebl] adj.
wstrętny; nienawistny;
obmierzły; znienawidzony
detonate [’detounejt] v.
wybuchać; powodować
gwałtowny wybuch (czegoś)
detour [’dy:tuer] s. objazd
devaluation [,dy:waelju'ejszyn] s.
dewaluacja; zdewaluowanie
detriment [’detryment] s. ujma;
szkoda; uszczerbek; krzywda
devaluate [’dy:waelju:ejt] v.
dewaluować; obniżać war-
tość; zdewaluować (coś)
devastate [’dewestejt] v.
pustoszyć; niweczyć (coś);
dewastować; zniweczyć
develop [dy'welop] v. rozwijać
(się); wywoływać (zdjęcia)
development [dy'welepment] s.
rozwój; rozbudowa; osiedle;
wywołanie (filmu); ewolucja
deviate [’di:wyejt] v. zbaczać;
odchylać; schodzić z drogi

device [dy'wajs] s. plan; pomysł;
urządzenie; dewiza; hasło;
środek (wiodący do celu)
devil [’dewl] s. czart; diabeł
devilish [’dewlysz] adj.
szatański; diabelski; demo-
niczny; adv. diabelsko
devise [dy'wajz] v. zapisać
(komuś); wymyślać; wyna-
leźć; obmyślać; knuć
devoid [dy'woyd] adj.
pozbawiony (czgoś); próżny;
czczy; wolny (od czegoś)
devote [dy'wout] v. poświęcać; ofiarować; odda-
wać się; przeznaczyć (na)
devoted [dy'wouted] adj. oddany (komuś, czemuś); przywiązany (do kogoś, czgoś)
dew [dju:] s. rosa; świeżość;
powiew; v. rosić; zraszać
dew point [’dju:point]
temperatura powstawania rosy
dexter [’dekster] a. prawy
dexterity [deks'teryty] s.
zręczność; bystrość;
sprawność (ciała, umysłu)
dexterous [’deksteres] s.
zręczny; zwinny; sprawny
diabetes [,daje'by:ty:z] s.
cukrzyca; choroba cukrowa
diagnose [’dajeg,nouz] v.
rozpoznać (chorobę)
diagonal [daj'aegnl] adj.
przekątny; skośny; s.
przekątnia; przekątna
diagram [’dajegraem] s. wykres;
schemat; diagram; plan
dial [’dajel] s. tarcza numerowa
(zwł. zegarowa); v. mierzyć;
nakręcać (numer telefonu)
dial tone [’dajel,toun] s. sygnał
połączenia (telefonicznego)
dialect [’dajelekt] s. gwara;
narzecze; dialekt
dialogue [’dajelog] s. rozmowa;
dialog (na scenie etc.)
diameter [dai'aemyter] s.
średnica; długość średnicy
diamond [’dajemond] s. diament;
romb; a. diamentowy; romboidalny; s. boisko do gry w
palanta amerykańskiego

diaper ['dajeper] s. pieluszka;
wzór romboidalny; v. przewijać; ozdabiać (coś) w romby
diaphragm ['dajefraem] s.
przepona; membrana; przesło-
na; damska przerwatywa
diarrhea [daje'rye] s. biegunka
diary ['daiery] s. dziennik
dice [dajs] v. grać w kości;
kratkować; pl. od die = kostka do gry (towarzyskiej)
dictate [dyk'tejt] s. nakaz; v.
dyktować; narzucać (wolę)
dictation [dyk'tejszyn] s. dyktat;
dyktowanie; wyraźny nakaz
dictator [dyk'tejter] s. dyktator;
dyktujący dyktando; dyktujący
na głos (tekst, list etc.)
dictatorship [dyk'tejterszyp] s.
dyktatura; władza nieograni-
czona (dyktatora, partii)
dictionary ['dykszeneeri] s.
słownik; mała encyklopedia
did [dyd] v. zrobić; zob. do
die [dajj] v. umierać; zdechnąć;
zginąć; s. matryca; sztanca;
proszę zobaczyć; pl. dice
die-hard ['daj-ha:rd] adj. twardy;
nieustępliwy; s. zagorzały
bojownik (szermierz etc.)
diet ['dajet] v. dieta; zjazd; sejm;
v. trzymać na diecie
differ ['dyfer] v. różnić się;
niezgadzać się (z opinią etc.);
mieć inną opinię (o czymś)
difference ['dyferens] s. różnica;
sprzeczka; nieporozumienie
different ['dyferent] adj.
różny; odmienny; niezwykły
difficult ['dyfykelt] adj. trudny;
ciężki; niełatwy (do)
difficulty ['dyfykelty] s.
trudność; przeszkoda
diffident ['dyfydent] adj.
(bardzo) nieśmiały; bez wiary
we własne siły; bez zaufania
do siebie samego
diffuse [dy'fju:z] adj. rozwlekły;
rozproszony; v. rozlewać;
szerzyć; rozpraszać
dig; dug; dug [dyg; dag; dag]
dig [dyg] v. kopać; ryć; ro-
umieć; ocenić; bawić się;

kuć się; grzebać się; s.
szarpnięcie; przytyk; kujon;
szturchnięcie; docinek
digest [dy'dżest] v. trawić;
przetrawiać; s. streszczenie;
skrót; przegląd; zbiór praw
digestible [dy'dżestebl] adj.
strawny; łatwy do strawienia
(przyswojenia czegoś))
digestion [dy'dżestszyn] s.
trawienie; wygotowanie
diggings ['dygynz] s. kopalnia
(złota); mieszkanie
dignified ['dygnyfajd] adj. dostojny; godny; (człowiek) pełen godności (dostojeństwa)
dignity ['dygnyty] s. godność;
dostojeństwo; powaga; tytuł;
zaszczyt; stanowisko; ranga
digress ['daj'gres] v. zbaczać;
odbiegać od rzeczy (tematu)
digs [dygz] s. mieszkanie; pokój;
buda; melina (złodziejska)
dihedral [daj'hi:drel] adj. m. (o
kącie) dwuścienny
dike [dajk] s. tama; grobla; rów;
v. osuszać rowem; otamo-
wać; ochronić tamą
dilapidated [dy'laepydejtyd] adj.
zniszczony; walący się
dilate [daj'lejt] v. rozszerzać;
rozwodzić się; rozciągać
diligence ['dylydżens] n.
pilność; przykładanie się do
pracy; pracowitość
diligent ['dylydżent] adj. pilny;
przykładający się do pracy
dill [dyl] s. koper ogrodowy
dill-pickle ['dyl,pykl] s. kiszony
ogórek; ogórek z koperkiem
dilute [daj'lju:t] v. rozpuszczać;
rozcieńczać; rozrzedzać; adj.
rozpuszczony; rozcieńczony;
rozrzedzony; rozwodniony;
wypłukany; wybladły; spłowiały; wyblakły; wyjałowiony
dim [dym] v. przyćmić;
zaciemnić; zamglić; adj.
przyćmiony; blady; zamazany;
niewyraźny; nikły; ciemny
dime [dajm] s. dziesięciocentowa
moneta (Stany Zjednoczone)
dimension [dy'menszyn] s.

wymiar; rozmiar; wielkość
diminish [dy'mynysz] v.
zmniejszać; zwężać (coś);
uszczuplać; niknąć; maleć
diminutive [dy'mynjutyw] adj. &
s. drobniutki; zdrobniały;
zdrobnienie; malutka kobieta
dimple ['dympl] s. dołek (w
twarzy); v. robić dołki; mieć
dołki (w twarzy etc.)
dine [dajn] v. jeść obiad;
jeść; mieć na obiedzie
diner [dajner] s. stołówka;
wagon restauracyjny; osoba
jedząca; restauracja
dining car ['dajnyng,ka:r] s.
wagon restauracyjny
dining room ['dajnyng,ru:m] s.
jadalnia; pokój jadalny
dinner ['dyner] s. obiad
dinner-jacket ['dyner,dżaekyt] s.
smoking (tuxedo)
dinner-party ['dyner,pa:rty] s.
przyjęcie; obiad proszony
dip [dyp] v. zanurzać; czerpać;
farbować; pogrążać; płu-
kać; nachylać się; opadać;
zamoczyć; wykąpać (coś
w czymś s. zanurzenie; zamoczenie; rozczyn; nachylenie;
obniżenie; łojówka; sos do
maczania; skok do wody
diphtheria [dyfteria] s. dyfteryt;
błonica (choroba)
diploma [dy'plouma] s. dyplom
diplomacy [dy'ploumesy] s.
dyplomacja; takt
diplomat ['dyplemaet] s. dy-
plomata; człowiek taktowny
diplomatic [,dyple'maetyk] adj.
dyplomatyczny; taktowny
direct [dy'rekt] v. kierować;
kazać; zarządzić; dowodzić;
zaadresować; nakierować;
wymierzać; polecić; dyrygować; adj. prosty; bezpośredni; otwarty; szczery; wyraźny; adv. wprost; prosto; bezpośrednio; otwarcie
direct current [dy'rekt'karent] s.
prąd stały (elektryczny)
direction [dy'rekszyn] s.
kierunek; kierowanie; kierow-

nictwo; zarząd; wskazówka;
administracja; adres
directions [dy'rekszyns] pl.
instrukcje; przepisy; przepis
directly [dy'rektly] adv.
bezpośrednio; wprost; od
razu; zaraz; skoro tykło;
natychmiast; dokładnie
director [dy'rektor] s. dyrektor;
reżyser; celownik; kierownik;
zarządzający; nadzorca
directory [dy'rektery] s. książka
adresowa, telefoniczna (lub
przepisów); skorowidz
dirigible ['dyrydżebl] adj. & s.
sterowy; sterowiec
dirt [de:rt] s. brud; błoto;
świństwo; ziemia; język
plugawy; mówienie osz-
czerstw; plotki; śmieci
dirt-cheap [de:rt'czi:p] adv. za
bezcen; adj. bardzo tani; tani
jak barszcz; śmiesznie tani
dirty [de:rty] adj. brudny;
sprośny; podły; wstrętny
disability [,dyse'bylyty] s.
inwalidztwo; niemoc; niemożność; niezdolność (do)
disabled [dys'ejbld] s. kaleka;
inwalida wojenny
disadvantage [dysed'wa:ntydż]
s. niekorzyść; wada; strata;
szkoda; niekorzystne położenie; v. szkodzić; zaszkodzić (komuś w czymś)
disadvantageous [dysaedwa:n
tejdżes] adj. niekorzystny;
szkodliwy; ujemny
disagree [dyse'gri:] v. nie
zgadzać się; różnić się; nie
służyć (jedzenie, klimat)
disagreeable [,dyse'gri:ebl] adj.
nieprzyjemny; niemiły
disagreement [,dyse'gri:ment] s.
niezgoda; różnica
disallow [,dyse'lau] v. nie
pozwalać; nie dopuszczać
disappear [,dyse'pier] v. znikać;
zapodziewać się; przepaść
disappearance [,dyse'pierens] s.
zniknięcie; zanik; zginięcie
disappoint [dyse'point] v.
zawieść; rozczarować; nie

spełnić (oczekiwań, nadzieii)
disappointment [dyse'pointment]
s. zawód; rozczarowanie
disapproval [dyse'pru:wel] s.
potępienie; niechęć; dez-
aprobata; niepochwalenie
disapprove [dyse'pru:w] v.
potępiać (kogoś, coś); ganić; źle widzieć (kogoś);
disarm [dys'a:rm] v. rozbroić;
unieszkodliwić (kogoś);
odebrać broń (komuś)
disarmament [dys'a:rmement] s.
rozbrojenie; a. rozbrojeniowy
disarrange [dyse'rejndż] v.
rozstrajać; dezorganizować
disarray [,dyse'rej] v.
wprowadzać nieład; roz-
strajać; s. nieład; zamieszanie; bałagan; niekompletny
strój; wywracać; rozebrać
disaster [dy'za:ster] s.
nieszczęście; klęska (żywio-
łowa etc.); katastrofa
disastrous [dy'za:stres] adj.
katastrofalny; zgubny; fatalny
disband [dis'baend] v.
rozpuścić (wojsko); pójść
w rozsypkę; rozbiegać się
disbelief ['dysby'li:f] s. niewiara;
niedowierzanie; nieufność
disbelieve ['dysby'li:w] v. nie
wierzyć; niedowierzać
disc [dysk] s. krążek; tarcza;
płyta; dysk; płyta gramofonowa; krążek (metalowy etc,)
discard [dys'ka:rd] v. wyrzucać;
(coś niepotrzebnego); odrzucać; zarzucać; zaniechać
discard ['dyska:rd] s. odrzucenie;
odrzucona (rzecz lub osoba);
odpadek; rzecz wybrakowana
discern [dy'se:rn] v. rozróżniać;
odróżniać; rozpoznawać
discharge [dys'cza:rdż] v.
rozładować; odciążać; zwalniać; wypuścić; wystrzelić;
s. rozładowanie; wystrzał;
zwolnienie; wydzielina; odpływ (czegś); odchody; ropa
(z wrzodu, z rany etc.)
disciple [dy'sajpl] s. uczeń;
wyznawca; jeden z apostołów

discipline ['dyscyplyn] s. dyscyplina; karność; v. karać;
ćwiczyć; musztrować
disc-jockey [dysk'dżoki] s.
nadający przez radio muzykę z
płyt; (disc jockey)
disclaim [dys'klejm] v. wypierać
się (czegoś); rezygnować (z
czegoś); zrzekać się
disclose [dys'k-ouz] v.
odsłaniać; ujawniać; wyjawiać; odkryć; odsłonić (coś)
discolor [dys'kaler] v. odbarwiać
discomfort [dys'kamfert] s.
niewygoda; niepokój; v.
sprawiać niewygody lub złe
samopoczucie; krępować; żenować; deranżować kogoś
discompose [,dyskem'pouz] v.
zaniepokoić; niepokoić; mieszać; zmieszać (kogoś)
disconcert [,dysken'ser:t] v.
żenować; krzyżować plany
disconnect ['dyske'nekt] v.
odłączyć; oderwać; odcze-
pić; odhaczyć (od czegoś)
disconnected ['dyske'nektyd]
adj. bez związku; bezładny;
rozłączony; chaotyczny
disconsolate [dys'konselyt] adj.
niepocieszony; posępny
discontent ['dysken'tent] s.
niezadowolenie; adj. niezadowolony; v. wywoływać niezadowolenie; wywoływać rozgoryczenie (czyjeś)
discontented ['dysken'tentyd]
adj. niezadowolony; rozgo-
ryczony; zniecierpliwiony
discontinue ['dysken'tynju:] v.
zaprzestawać; przerywać;
ustawać; zakończyć (coś);
zaniechać (czegoś)
discord ['dysko:rd] s. niezgoda;
różnica; dysonans; niesnaski
discordance ['dysko:rdens] s.
niezgodność; dysonans
discotheque ['dyskoutek] s.
dyskoteka; nocny lokal z
muzyką z płyt do tańca
discount ['dyskaunt] s.
dyskonto; rabat; odjęcie; v.
potrącać; odliczać; nie da-

wać wiary (komuś, czemuś)
discourage [dys'karydż] v.
zniechęcać (do czegoś); odstraszać; być przeciwnym
discover [dys'kawer] v.
wynaleźć; odkryć; odsła-
niać; (nagle) zobaczyć
discoverer [dys'kawerer] s.
odkrywca; wynalazca
discredit [dys'kredyt] v.
dyskredytować; przynosić
ujmę; pozbawiać zaufania; s.
utrata zaufania i dobrego
imienia; niewiara (w coś); zła
opinia (o kimś, o czymś)
discreet [dys'kri:t] a. rozsądny;
dyskretny; z rezerwą
discrepancy [dys'krepensy] s.
sprzeczność; rozbieżność
discretion [dys'kreszyn] s.
swoboda decyzji; rozwaga;
powściągliwość; dyskrecja
discriminate [dys'krymynejt] v.
odróżniać; dyskryminować;
robić różnicę; wyróżniać
discriminate against [dys'
krymynejt e'gejnst]
wprowadzać dyskryminację
w stosunku do (kogoś)
discrimination [dys,krymy
'nejszyn] s. odróżnienie;
niejednakowe traktowanie
discuss [dys'kas] v.
dyskutować (o); roztrząsać
(coś); debatować (o czymś)
discussion [dys'kaszyn] s.
dyskusja; debata; debaty
disdain [dy'dejn] s. pogarda;
wzgarda; v. gardzić (kimś,
czymś); lekceważyć
disease [dy'zi:z] s. choroba
diseased [dy'zi:zd] adj. chory;
schorzały; cierpiący na ...
disembark [‚dysym'ba:rk] v.
wyładować; wysiadać; lądować (samolotem, statkiem)
disengage [‚dysen'gejdż] v.
odczepiać; wyłączać; odwik-
łać; rozłączyć; odhaczyć
disengaged [‚dysen'gejdżd] adj.
wolny; nie zajęty; zwolniony
disentangle [‚dysyntaengl] v.
wyplątać; rozplątać; wywik-

łać (się); rozwikłać (coś)
disfavor ['dys'fejwer] s. niełaska;
dezaprobata; v. odnosić się
nieprzychylnie; z niechęcią
traktować; dezaprobować
disfigure [dys'fyger] v.
zniekształcić; zeszpecić
disgrace [dys'grejs] s. hańba;
niełaska; v. hańbić; zniesławić; pozbawiać łaski; narobić (komuś, sobie) wstydu
disgraceful [dys'grejsfel] adj.
haniebny; hańbiący; sromotny; niecny; shameless
disguise [dys'gajz] v. przebierać;
ukrywać; maskować; zata-
ić; s. charakteryzacja; udawanie; pozory; zamaskowanie;
maska; nadanie pozorów
disgust [dys'gast] s. odraza;
wstręt; obrzydzenie; v.
budzić odrazę, wstręt, obrzydzenie, rozgoryczenie, oburzenie (na kogoś, na coś)
disgusting [dys'gastyng] adj.
wstrętny; obrzydliwy; oburzający; odrażający (czymś)
dish [dysz] s. półmisek; naczynie; potrawa; danie; v. nakładać; podawać; drążyć; ok-
piwać; nakładać na półmisek
dishes ['dyszyz] pl. statki;
naczynia; smaczne potrawy
dish-cloth ['dysz,klos] s. ścierka
do wycierania talerzy
disheveled [dy'szeweld] adj.
rozczochrany; zaniedbany
dishonest [dys'onyst] adj.
nieuczciwy; (człowiek) nie
godny zaufania (czyjegoś)
dishonesty [dys'onysty] s.
nieuczciwość; nieuczciwy
postępek; oszustwo
dishonor [dys'oner] s. hańba;
dyshonor; niehonorowanie;
hańbiący czyn; v. hańbić
dishonorable [dys'onerebl] adj.
haniebny; podły; (człowiek)
bez czci i wiary
dishwasher [dysz,łoszer] s.
pomywacz; pomywaczka
dish-water [dysz,ło:ter] s. pomyje
disillusion [‚dysy'lu:żyn] s.

rozczarowanie; otrzeźwienie
disincline [,dysyn'klajn] v.
zniechęcać; mieć niechęć
disinclined [,dysyn'klajnd] adj.
zniechęcony; źle usposobiony
disinfect [,dysyn'fekt] v.
odkażać; zdezynfekować
disinfectant [,dysyn'fektent] s.
środek odkażający
disinherit ['dysyn'heryt] v.
wydziedziczyć; wydziedziczać (kogoś z czegoś)
disintegrate [dys'yntegrejt] v.
rozpadać (się); rozkładać (się); rozdrobnić (coś)
disinterested [dys'yntrystyd] adj.
bezinteresowny; nie zainteresowany; obiektywny
disjoint [dys'dżoint] v.
rozłączać; rozdzielać; zwichnąć; rozerwać
disk [dysk] s. krążek; tarcza; płyta gramofonowa; dysk
dislike [dys'lajk] v. nie lubić; mieć odrazę; s. odraza; niechęć; awersja; wstręt
dislocate ['dyslekejt] v.
zwichnąć; przesunąć; zatrącić (porządek etc.)
disloyal [,dys'lojel] adj.
niewierny; nielojalny; zdradziecki (wobec kogoś etc.)
dismal ['dyzmel] adj.
nieszczęsny; ponury; posępny
dismantle [dys'maentl] v.
rozmontowywać; ogołacać; odzierać; rozbroić; pozbawiać; demontować (coś)
dismay [dys'mej] s. trwoga; przestrach; v. przerażać; konsternować; skonsternować
dismember [dys'member] v.
rozczłonkować; rozebrać na części; dokonać rozbioru
dismiss [dys'mys] v. odprawiać; zwalniać; odsuwać od siebie; przenieść w stan spoczynku
dismissal [dys'mysel] s.
zwolnienie; dymisja; rozejście się; pożegnanie; pozbycie się
dismount ['dys'maunt] v.
zsiadać z konia; wyjmować z oprawy; wysadzać z siodła

disobedience [dyse'bi:djens] s.
nieposłuszeństwo; opór
disobedient [dyse'bi:djent] adj.
nieposłuszny; oporny
disobey [,dyse'bej] v. nie słuchać; być nieposłusznym
disoblige [,dyse'blajdż] v.
lekceważyć; bagatelizować
disorder [dys'o:rder] s.
nieporządek; zamieszki; zaburzenie; nieład; zamęt
disorderly [dys'o:rderly] adj.
nieporządny; niesforny; gorszący; burzliwy; bezładny
disown [dys'oun] v. wypierać się; zaprzeczać; nie uznawać
disparage [dys'paerydż] v.
poniżać; ubliżać; dyskredytować; uwłaczać; lekceważyć; mówić ubliżająco (o)
dispassion [dys'paeszyn] s.
beznamiętność; obiektywizm
dispassionate [dys'paeszynyt] adj. beznamiętny; obiektywny
dispatch [dys'paecz] s. wysyłka; wysyłanie; sprawność; szybkość; szybkie załatwianie; v. wysyłać; załatwiać; dobijać (ranne zwierzę, człowieka)
dispel [dys'pel] v. rozwiewać (obawy); rozpędzać (chmury)
dispensable [dys'pensebl] adj.
zbędny; niekonieczny; możliwy do uchylenia (ślub)
dispense [dys'pens] v.
wydzielać; wymierzać; wydawać; udzielać; sporządzać (lekarstwo w aptece)
dispense with [dys'pens tys] v.
pomijać; obyć się (bez)
disperse [dys'pe:rs] v.
rozpraszać; rozpędzać; rozjeżdżać się; rozsiewać; płoszyć; rozszczepić (światło)
displace [dys'plejs] v. przemieszczać; wypierać; usuwać; przełożyć; przekładać
display [dys'plej] v. wystawiać; popisywać się; s. wystawa; popis; pokaz (czegoś); parada
displease [dys'pli:z] v. urażać; drażnić; gniewać; dotykać; oburzać (kogoś); irytować

displeased [dys'pli:zd] adj. urażony; zirytowany; niezadowolony; obrażony; poirytowany
displeasure [dys'pleżer] s. niezadowolenie; gniew; irytacja (na kogoś, na coś)
disposal [dys'pouzel] s. rozkład; zbyt; sprzedaż; przekazanie; rozporządzenie; niszczenie
dispose [dys'pouz] v. rozmieszczać; rozporządzić; pozbyć się (czegoś); sprzedać (coś); usunąć; niszczyć; nakłanić; usposabiać (do)
disposed [dys'pouzd] adj. skłonny; usposobiony (dobrze, pogodnie, wesoło, źle etc.)
disposition [dys'pouzyszyn] s. skłonność; pociąg; zarządzenie; dyspozycje; rozporządzanie; popęd; żyłka (do czegś)
disproportionate [,dyspre'po:rsznyt] adj. nieproporcjonalny; niewspółmierny
dispute [dys'pju:t] s. spór; kłótnia; v. sprzeczać się; kłócić się; kwestionować
disqualify [dys'kłolyfaj] v. dyskwalifikować
disquiet [dys'kłajet] v. niepokoić; s. niepokój; adj. niespokojny; zaniepokojony
disregard [,dysry'ga:rd] v. pomijać; lekceważyć; s. lekceważenie (kogoś, czegoś)
disrepute [,dysry'pju:t] s. niesława; hańba; zła reputacja
disrespectful [,dysry'spektfel] adj. niegrzeczny; niedelikatny
disrupt [dys'rapt] v. rozrywać; rozdzierać; przerwać; obalić
dissatisfaction ['dyssaetys'faekszyn] s. niezadowolenie
dissatisfied [dys,satys'fajd] adj. niezadowolony (z czegoś)
dissension [dy'senszyn] s. waśń; niezgoda; swary
dissent [dy'sent] s. różnica; rozbieżność zdań; odstępstwo; v. różnić się (w zapatrywaniach, opiniach etc.)
dissimilar ['dy'symyler] adj. niepodobny; różny

dissipate [dy'sypejt] v. rozpraszać; marnować; trwonić; marnotrawić; rozgonić; hulać; zabawić się
dissociate [dy'souszjejt] v. rozłączać (się)(od); zrywać (z kimś, z czymś)
dissolute ['dyselu:t] adj. rozwiązły; rozpustny
dissolution [,dys'elu:szyn] s. rozkład; zanik; rozpuszczenie; rozwiązanie (spółki etc.); śmierć; zgon; rozpad
dissolve [dy'zolw] v. rozpuszczać; rozkładać; niszczyć; rozwiązywać; zanikać; skasować (bilet)
dissuade [dy'słejd] v. odradzać; odwodzić (kogoś); wyperswadować (komuś, coś)
distance ['dystens] s. odległość; odstęp; oddalenie; v. zdystansować (się) (od)
distant ['dystent] adj. daleki; odległy (od); powściągliwy; z rezerwa (wobec); nie widzący
distaste [,dys'tejst] s. niesmak; niechęć; odraza; awersja
distasteful [,dys'tejstful] adj. odstręczający; wstrętny; przykry; odrażający (od siebie)
distend [dys'tend] v. rozdymać; rozszerzać; nabrzmiewać; rozdąć; nadąć; nadymać
distill [dy'styl] v. przekraplać; (prze)destylować; przesączać (coś); kapać (czymś)
distinct [dys'tynkt] adj. odmienny (od kogoś, czegoś); odrębny; wyraźny; dobitny
distinction [dys'tynkszyn] s. rozróżnienie; wyróżnienie się; wytworność; podział (na); individual style, character
distinctive [dys'tynktyw] adj. odróżniający się; charakterystyczny; wyróżniający się
distinguish [dys'tyngłysz] v. dostrzec; rozróżniać; klasyfikować; zauważyć; odznaczyć
distinguished [dystyngłyszt] adj. wybitny; znakomity; dystyngowany; odznaczający się

distort [dys'to:rt] v. wykrzywiać; wykręcać; przekręcać; fałszywie przedstawiać; zniekształcać (fakty etc.)

distract [dys'traekt] v. odrywać; rozproszyć; oszołomić

distracted [dys'traektyd] adj. oszalały; w rozterce; skłopotany; roztargniony; rozproszony (przez kogoś, coś)

distraction [dys'traekszyn] s. dystrakcja; roztargnienie; rozrywka; rozterka; szaleństwo; zamieszanie; odwrócenie uwagi (czyjejś od czegoś)

distress [dys'tres] s. męka; strapienie; niedostatek; potrzeba; niebezpieczeństwo

distressed [dys'trest] adj. umęczony; udręczony; w niedoli; dotknięty nędzą

distribute [dys'trybju:t] v. udzielać; rozmieszczać; rozdać; rozprowadzać (ludzi)

distribution [dys'trybju:szyn] s. rozdział; podział; dystrybucja; roznoszenie; a. rozdzielczy

district ['dystrykt] s. okręg; powiat; dystrykt; dzielnica; rejon (kaju, państwa)

distrust [dys'trast] s. nieufność; niedowierzanie; v. nie ufać; niedowierzać; podejrzewać (kogoś o coś)

disturb [dys'te:rb] v. przeszkadzać; niepokoić; zakłócać; mącić; zaburzyć; denerwować (kogoś)

disturbance [dys'te:rbens] s. zakłócenie; zaburzenie; poruszenie; burda; awantura; rozruchy; wstrząs; niepokoje

disuse [dys'ju:z] s. zarzucenie; nieużywanie (kogoś, czegoś)

ditch [dycz] s. rów; v. kopać; drenować; utknąć w rowie; rzucać (do morza samolot)

dive [dajw] v. nurkować; zanurzać się; skakać z trampoliny do wody; s. nurkowanie; zanurzenie; melina; lot nurkowy samolotu; pikowanie samolotem; (licha) knajpa

diver ['dajwer] s. nurek; skoczek z trampoliny; ptak nurkujący

diverge [daj'we:rdż] v. rozchodzić się; odchylać się; zbaczać (z drogi, na bok etc.); odbiegać (od); rozbiegać się

diverse [daj'we:rs] adj. odmienny; rozmaity; inny; zmienny; urozmaicony

diversion [daj'we:rżyn] s. odchylenie (od) objazd; rozrywka; dywersja (wojskowa)

diversion [dy'we:rżyn] s. zboczenie; dywersja; rozrywka; odwrócenie uwagi; oderwanie uwagi (od kogoś, od czegoś)

diversity [daj'we:rsyty] s. rozmaitość (poglądów etc.); różnorodność; urozmaicenie

diversity [dy'we:rsyty] s. odmienność (charakterów); różnorodność; rozmaitość

divert [daj'we:rt] v. odwracać (uwagą); odrywać; rozerwać (się); rozbawić; bawić

divide [dy'wajd] v. dzielić; rozdzielać; oddzielać; różnić

divide by [dy'wajd,baj] v. dzielić przez (liczbę, mianownik)

divine [dy'wajn] adj. boski; boży; v. wróżyć; przepowiadać

diving ['dajwyng] s. skakanie z trampoliny; pikowanie w locie

divinity [dy'wynyty] s. bóstwo; boskość; teologia

divisible [dy'wyzebl] adj. podzielny (przez, na etc.)

division [dy'wyżyn] s. podział; rozdział; dzielenie; dział; wydział; oddział; dywizja

divorce [dy'wo:rs] s. rozwód; rozdzielenie; v. rozwodzić się; oddzielać; a. rozwodowy

dizzy ['dyzy] adj. wirujący; oszołomiony; zawrotny; oszołomiający v. oszołomiać

do [du:] v. czynić; robić; wykonać; zwiedzać; przyrządzać; spełniać obowiązek

do away ['du,ełej] v. znieść; pozbyć się; zabić (kogoś); skasować (mecz, lot etc.)

do not ['du not] = don't [dont]
nie (rób); nie (idź); nie (stój)

do in ['du,yn] v. uwięzić; zlikwidować; zabić; wykończyć

do up ['du,ap] v. przerobić; odnowić; upiększyć się zmęczyć; upudrować etc.

do well [,du'łel] v. mieć się dobrze; powodzić się; być w (bardzo) dobrej sytuacji

do without [,du'łysout] v. obywać się bez; obyć się bez

do you know? [du: ju nou] expr. czy pan wie? czy pani zna? czy pan słyszał? czy wiesz?

docile ['dousajl] adj. uległy; posłuszny; pojętny; skory do nauki; potulny; giętki; łagodny; podatny (do czegoś)

dock [dok] s. dok; basen; molo; miejsce oskarżonego; v. umieścić w doku; cumować przy molu (w porcie)

dockyard [dokja:rd] s. stocznia

doctor ['dakter] s. lekarz; doktor (medycyny, filozofii etc.)

doctorate ['dokteryt] s. doktorat

doctrine ['daktryn] s. doktryna

document ['dokjument] s. dokument; v. poprzeć dokumentami; udokumentować

documentary [,dokju'mentery] s. adj. dokumentalny (film etc.)

dodge [dodż] v. uchylić; uniknąć; zwodzić; s. unik; kruczek; sztuczka; odskok; kiwanie (w grze w piłkę etc.)

doe [dou] s. łania; pl. does [douz] łanie

does [daz] v. on czyni; robi; proszę zobaczyć: do

dog [dog] s. pies; samiec; klamra; uchwyt; sl. facet

dog-catcher [dog'kaeczer] s. rakarz; oprawca; hycel

dogged ['dogyd] adj. uparty; zawzięty; wytrwały

doggie ['dogi] s. psina

dogma ['dogme] s. dogmat

dog-tired ['dog'tajerd] adj. skonany; ledwo żywy ze zmęczenia; bardzo zmęczony

doings ['du:yngs] pl. sprawki;

uczynki; wyprawiania; psoty

dole [doul] s. zasiłek; zapomoga; smutek; v. mało dawać

doll [dol] s. lalka; (slang) dziewczyna; v. wystroić się

dollar ['doler] s. dolar

dollish ['dolysz] adj. lalkowaty; lalkowata; lalusiowaty

dolorous ['douleres] adj. smętny; żałosny; zbolały; boleściwy

dolphin ['dolfyn] s. delfin

domain [de'mejn] s. dziedzina; majątek ziemski; posiadłość; zakres (władzy, wpływów)

dome [doum] s. kopuła; sklepienie; v. nakrywać sklepieniem (kopułą)

domestic [de'mestyk] adj. domowy; krajowy; domatorski; s. służący; służąca

domesticate [de'mestykejt] v. oswajać; zadomowić

domicile ['domysajl] s. miejsce zamieszkania; v. osiedlać; zamieszkać na stałe

dominate ['domynejt] v. dominować; górować; przewyższać; panować; mieć zwierzchnictwo (nad)

domination ['domynejszyn] s. władza; panowanie; przewaga

domineer [,domy'nier] v. dominować; rządzić się; rozkazywać; tyranizować; panoszyć się (nad otoczniem etc.)

domineering [,domy'nieryng] adj. tyranizujący; apodyktyczny; despotyczny; władczy

donate [dou'nejt] v. podarować

donation [dou'nejszyn] s. darowizna; donacja; dar

done [dan] adj. zrobiony; uczyniony; proszę zobaczyć: do

donkey ['donky] s. osioł

donor ['douner] s. donator; dawca (krwi etc.); darujący

doom [du:m] s. zguba; zły los; śmierć; potępienie; przeznaczenie; v. potępiać; skazać na zgubę; przesądzać

Doomsday ['du:mzdej] s. dzień sądu ostatecznego

door [do:r] s. drzwi; brama

door handle ['do:r,haendl] s.
klamka do drzwi (do bramy)
doorkeeper ['do:r,ki:per] s.
dozorca; portier; odźwierny
doorknob ['do:r,nob] s. klamka
doormat ['do:r,maet] s.
wycieraczka (przy drzwiach)
doorway ['do:r,łej] s. wejście
dope [doup] s. maź; lakier;
narkotyk; informacja (poufna);
głupiec (slang); naiwniak; v.
narkotyzować; zaprawiać;
fałszować; sfałszować
dormitory ['do:rmytry] s. dom
studencki; sypialnia
dose [dous] s. dawka; dodatek;
dawkowanie; v. dawkować
(lekarstwo); mieszać; fałszować (wino alkoholem);
leczyć; dozować; wydzielać
dot [dot] s. kropka; punkt; v.
kropkować; rozsiewać
dote [dout] v. wariować;
kochać przesadnie; mówić
od rzeczy; dziecinnieć
double ['dabl] adj. podwójny;
dwukrotny; dwojaki; fałszywy;
v. podwajać; adv. podwójnie;
w dwójnasób; dwojako
double up ['dabl,ap] v. składać
się we dwoje; zsuwać się
(razem); przybiegać; dzielić
pokój (na dwie osoby)
double bed ['dabl,bed] podwójne
łóżko (podwójnej szerokości)
double-breasted ['dabl,brestyd]
adj. dwurzędowy (płaszcz);
dwurzędowa (marynarka)
double-decker ['dabl-'deker] s.
dwupokładowiec; dwupoklado-
wy (statek, okręt, dom etc.)
double-park ['dabl-'pa:rk] v.
parkować podwójnie na jezdni przy chodniku)
double-room ['dabl,ru:m] s. pokój
dwuosobowy (w hotelu etc.)
doubt [daut] s. wątpliwość;
niedowierzanie; v. wątpić;
powątpiewać; niedowierzać
doubtful ['dautful] adj. wątpliwy;
niepewny; niezdecydowany
doubtless ['dautlys] adv.
niewątpliwie; bez wątpienia

douche [du'sz] s. natrysk
dough [dou] s. ciasto; (slang)
forsa; pieniądze
doughnut ['dounat] s. pączek (z
dziurą w środku
dove [daw] s. gołąb(ica)
down [dałn] s. wydma; puch;
meszek; puszek; piórka
down [dałn] adv. na dół; niżej;
nisko; v. obniżać; poniżać;
przewrócić; strącić; połknąć
downcast ['dałnka:st] adj.
przybity; przygnębiony; ze
spuszczonymi oczyma
downfall ['dałnfo:l] s. upadek;
klęska; ruina; zguba
downhill ['dałn'hyl] adj.
opadający; s. spadek; adv. na
dół; z góry na dół
downpour ['dałnpo:r] s. ulewa
downright ['dałnrajt] adv.
zupełnie; całkowicie; gruntownie; wprost; wręcz; stanowczo; adj. zupełny; szczery;
otwarty; uczciwy; jawny
downstairs ['dałn'steerz] adv. na
dół; w dole; na dole; pod nami
downtown ['dałntałn] s. centrum
miasta; adv. w śródmieściu;
w centrum; adj. śródmiejski
downwards ['dałnłodz] adv. w
dół; ku dołowi; na dół; z góry
downy ['dałny] adj. puszysty;
(slang) chytry; falisty; puchaty
dowry ['dałry] s. posag; wiano;
dar wrodzony; talent (do)
doze [douz] s. drzemka; v.
drzemać; zdrzemnąć się
dozen ['dazn] s. tuzin
drab [draeb] s. & adj. brudno-
-brunatny; nudny; szary; monotonny; brudas; prostytutka;
flądra v. puszczać się
draft [dra:ft] s. szkic; brulion;
zarys; przekaz; pobór; rysunek; ciąg w kominie; v.
szkicować; projektować; rysować; odkomenderować
draftsman ['dra:ftsmen] s.
kreślarz (techniczny);
rysownik; projektodawca
drag [draeg] v. wlec; ciągnąć;
s. pogłębiarka; pojazd; wle-

czenie (po); opór czołowy
dragon ['draegen] s. smok
dragonfly ['draegenflaj] s. ważka
drain [drejn] v. odwadniać; wysączać; ociekać; osuszać;
wuczerpać; s. dren; spust;
ściek; rów odwadniający
drainage ['drejnydż] s.
odwadnianie; wody ście-
kowe; obszar odpływowy
(rzeki, strumienia etc.)
drainpipe ['drejnpajp] s. dren
drake [drejk] s. kaczor
drama ['dra:ma] s. dramat
dramatic [dre'maetyk] adj.
dramatyczny; jak w sztuce;
żywy; uderzjący; frapujący
drank [draenk] s. pijak; pijany;
proszę zobaczyć: drink
drape [drejp] v. upinać; spadać
fałdami; drapować; s. kotara
drastic ['draestyk] adj. dra-
astyczny; gwałtowny; surowy
draught [draeft] s. przeciąg;
ciąg (w kominie); haust; łyk;
dawka; zanurzenie statku;
wyporność; adj. pociągowy
draw; drew; drawn [dro:; dru:;
dro:n]
draw [dro:] v. ciągnąć; pociągać (skutki etc); wyciągać;
przyciągać (uwagę); odcią-
gnąć; czerpać (pociechę);
wdychać; ściągać (wodze);
spuszczać (wodę); napinać
(łuk); mieć wyporność;
wlec; rysować; kreślić
draw near [dro:nier] v. zbliżać
się; przybliżać się (do)
drawback [dro:baek] s. strona
ujemna; przeszkoda; wada
etc.; v. cofać się (draw back)
draw up [dro:,ap] v. podciągać
(się); redagować; zbliżać
się; zrównać się; ustawiać
drawer ['dro:er] s. szuflada;
kreślarz; rysownik; bufetowy
drawers ['dro:ers] pl. kalesony;
majtki (damskie, dziecięce ...)
drawing ['dro:yng] s. rysunek
drawing pen ['dro:yng,pen] s.
grafion; piórko kreślarskie
drawing room ['dro:yng,ru:m] s.

salon; wagon salonowy
drawn [dro:n] adj. nierozstrzygnięty; ciągniony; wychudzony; wyciągnięta (szabla
etc.); proszę zobaczyć: draw
drawn-out [dro:n aut] adj.
przewlekły; przeciągający się;
wyciągnięty (z pochwy etc.)
dread [dred] s. strach; postrach;
lęk; v. bać się bardzo; lękać
się; adj. straszny; straszliwy
dreadful [dredful] adj. przera-
żliwy; okropny; straszny; sl.
bardzo zły, irytujący etc.
dream; dreamt; dreamt [dri:m;
dremt; dremt]
dream [dri:m] v. śnić; marzyć;
s. sen; marzenie; mrzonka;
urojenie; miła nadzieja
dreamt [dremt] v. mieć sen,
marzenie (o); zob. dream
dreamy ['dri:my] adj. kojący;
marzycielski; mglisty; niewyraźny (obraz); sl. wspaniały
dreary ['dryery] adj. posępny;
ponury; smętny; melancholijny
dregs [dregz] pl. osady; męty
drench [drencz] v. zmoczyć;
przemoczyć; s. ulewa
dress [dres] s. ubiór; strój; szata;
suknia; v. ubierać; stroić;
opatrywać; czyścić; cze-
sać; przyprawiać; wykań-
czać; wyprawiać; wygarbo-
wać; przygotować (do)
dress down ['dres dałn] v.
besztać; czyścić (konia)
dress up ['dres,ap] v. stroić
dressing ['dresyng] s. przyprawa;
opatrunek; nawóz; ubiór
dressing-case ['dresyng,kejs] s.
neseser (z kosmetykami etc.)
dressing-gown ['dresyn-gołn] s.
podomka; szlafrok
dressing-room ['dresyng,ru:m] s.
garderoba; ubieralnia; umywalnia; (schowek z ubraniami)
dressing-table ['dresyng,tejbl] s.
toaleta (mebel z lustrem etc.)
dressmaker ['dresmejker] s.
krawiec damski; krawcowa
drew [dru:] zob. draw
dribble ['drybl] v. kapać; ślinić

się; wolno toczyć; odbijać (piłkę); dryblować; s. kapanie; cieknąca ślina (dziecka)

drift [dryft] s. dryf; znoszenie; bierność; prąd; dążność; treść; zamieć; zaspa; nanos; v. dryfować; znosić; plątać się; nanosić; płynąć z prądem; być biernym

drill 1. [dryl] s. świder; wiertarka; dryl; musztra; v. wiercić; świdrować; ćwiczyć; musztrować; drążyć; sortować (wagony etc.)

drill 2. [dryl] s. rowek do siania; siewnik rzędowy; rząd; v. siać; obsadzać w rowkach

drink; drank; drunk [drynk; draenk; drank]

drink [drynk] v. pić; przepijać; s. napój; woda (morze)

drinking water ['drynkyng,ło:ter] s. woda pitna (do picia)

drip [dryp] v. kapać; ociekać; ciec; s. kapanie; okap; piła (sl.); nudziara; kapka; kropla (płynu, cieczy, wody etc.)

drip-dry ['dryp,draj] s. bielizna nie wymagająca prasowania (schnąca na wieszaku etc.)

dripping ['drypyng] s. tłuszcz spod pieczeni; adj. kapiący; ociekający; przemoczony

drive; drove; driven [drajw; drouw; drywn]

drive [drajw] v. pędzić; gnać; wieźć; powozić; prowadzić; napędzać; jechać; wbijać; drążyć; s. przejażdka; obława; napęd; droga; dojazd; energia; pościg (za)

drive at [drajw et] v. kierować (dyskusją, rozmowę ku ...)

drive out ['drajw, aut] v. wyjeżdżać (z garażu); wypędzać; wuganiać (kogoś)

drive-in ['drajw,yn] s. obsługa w samochodzie, w banku, jadłodajni etc.; kino; sklep; poczta

drive-in movies [drajw,yn mu:wiz] kino do oglądania siedząc w (swoim) samochodzie

driven [drywn] v. napędzany;

proszę zobaczyć: drive

driver [drajwer] s. kierowca

driving license ['drajwyng ,lajsens] s. prawo jazdy

drizzle ['dryzl] s. mżący deszcz; mżawka; kapuśniaczek; v. mżyć; adj. mżący (deszcz)

drone [droun] s. truteń; buczenie; brzęczenie; dudniący mówca; v. zbijać bąki; buczeć; dudnić (monotonnie)

droop [dru:p] v. opadać; zwisać; zwieszać (głowę); omdlewać; s. zwis; spadek (tonu); utrata (otuchy)

drop [drop] v. kapać; ciec; upuszczać; spadać; opadać; s. kropla; cukierek; spadek (temperatury, terenu etc.); łuk; kieliszek; zniżka; kotara; upadek; uskok; obniżenie

drop in ['drop,yn] v. wpaść do kogoś; wejść na chwilę

dropout [dropaut] s. osoba przerywająca (studia, gimnazjum lub szkołę wstępną)

drove [drouw] zob. drive

drown [draun] v. tonąć; topić; tłumić; głuszyć; zagłuszać

drowsy ['drauzy] adj. senny; śpiący; ospały; na pół śpiący; usypiający (kogoś)

drudge [dradż] s. niewolnik; popychadło; v. harować

drug [drag] s. lek; lekarstwo; v. narkotyzować; przesycać

drug-addict ['drag,aedykt] s. narkoman; narkomanka

drugstore ['drag,stor] s. apteka; drogeria (z kosmetykami etc.)

drum [dram] s. bęben; v. bębnić; zwoływać bębnieniem; zjednywać (poparcie)

drummer ['dramer] s. dobosz

drunk [drank] adj. pijany; proszę zobaczyć: drink

drunkard ['drankerd] s. pijak; pijaczka (nałogowa)

drunken driving ['dranken 'drajwyng] s. kierowanie po pijanemu (samochodem etc.)

dry [draj] adj. suchy; wytrawny (wino); v. osuszać; suszyć;

zeschnąć; wyjaławiać; wycierać; konserwować (mięso)
dry up [draj,ap] v. wycierać; wysychać; zapomnieć (co mówić); zaniemówić
dry-clean ['draj kli:n] v. oczyścić chemicznie (sucho)
dry goods ['drajgudz] pl. materiały do szycia; konfekcja
dual ['dju:el] adj. podwójny; dwoisty; dwudzielny; wspólny
duchess ['daczys] s. księżna
duck [dak] s. kaczka; unik; v. zanurzyć; zrobić unik (przed kimś, czymś); nurkować
duct [dakt] s. przewód; kanał
dud [dad] s. (slang) poroniony pomysł; safanduła; nieuk; niewypał; strach na wróble; adj. niezdolny; przegrany
dude [d(j)u:d] s. elegancik; laluś; turysta; goguś; wycieczkowicz (na wsi)
dude ranch ['du:d,ra:ncz] ranczo wakacyjne (dla mieszczuchów)
due [dju:] adj. należny; płatny; należyty; adv. w kierunku na (wschód); s. to co się należy; należności; opłata; składka
due to ['dju:,tu] exp. z powodu
duel ['dju(:)el] s. pojedynek
dug [dag] 1. s. cycek; wymię; proszę zobaczyć: dig
dug 2. [dag] s. dójka
dugout ['dagaut] s. ziemianka; łódź drążona; okop; schron
duke [dju:k] s. książę
dull [dal] adj. tępy; głuchy; ospały; ociężały; niemrawy; nudny; ponury; ciemny; nieostry; v. tępić; tłumić
duly ['dju:ly] adv. właściwie; należycie; punktualnie; we właściwy sposób; słusznie
dumb [dam] adj. niemy; milczący; głupi; v. odbierać mowę
dumbfounded [dam'faundyd] adj. osłupiony; osłupiały; oniemiały
dummy ['damy] s. imitacja; makieta; atrapa; sl. bałwan; manekin; dureń; głupiec; niemowa; adj. udany; pozorny; sztuczny; podstawiony; symu-

lujący; imitowany; na niby
dump [damp] s. śmietnisko; hałda; magazyn; v. zwalać; rzucać; zarzucać (towarem)
dun [dan] s. wierzyciel; inkasent długów; bezwzględne żądanie zapłaty; v. (wielokrotnie) napastować o spłatę długu; adj. ciemnobrązowy; szarobrązowy
dune [dju:n] s. wydma; diuna
dung [dang] s. nawóz; gnój; bagno moralne; v. nawozić; użyźniać ziemię; gnoić
dungeon ['dandżen] s. loch; baszta; v. więzić w lochu lub baszcie zamkowej etc.
dupe [du:p] s. ofiara; łatwo wystrychnięty na dudka; v. oszukać; okpić; nabrać
duplicate ['dju:plykyt] adj. podwójny; s. duplikat; w dwu egzemplarzach; v. podwajać; duplikować (niepotrzebnie)
duplicity [dju:'plysyty] s. dwulicowość; fałszywość; podstęp; fałsz; obłuda
durable ['djuerebl] adj. trwały
duration [dju'rejszyn] s. trwanie; czas trwania (czegoś)
duress [dju'res] s. przymus
during ['djueryng] prep. podczas; w czasie; w ciągu; przez; za
dusk [dask] s. zmierzch; mrok; cień; adj. ciemny; mroczny; v. zaćmić; zamroczyć
dust [dast] s. pył; kurz; prochy; pyłek; v. odkurzać; trzepać; kurzyć się; posypywać
dust bowl [dast,boul] s. kraj suszy i zamieci piaskowych
dust-cover ['dast,kawer] s. obwoluta; pokrowiec od kurzu
duster ['daster] s. odkurzacz; wiatr z kurzem; zmiotka
dust-pan ['dast,paen] s. śmietniczka; łopatka na śmieci, odpadki etc.
dust-storm ['dast,sto:rm] s. wicher z tumanami kurzu
dusty ['dasty] adj. zakurzony; pokryty kurzem; suchy; nudny; nieciekawy; niewyraźny
Dutch [dacz] adj. holenderski; w

niełasce; skąpy; niemiecki
duty ['dju:ty] s. powinność;
obowiązek; szacunek; służba;
uległość; cło; podatek od
sprzedaży; funkcja; obowiązki
dwarf [dło:rf] s. karzeł;
krasnoludek; adj. karłowaty; v.
pomniejszać; karleć; skar-
leć; skarłowacieć; zmniejszać wzrost (wymiar)
dwell; dwelt; dwelt [dłel; dłelt;
dłelt]
dwell [dłel] v. mieszkać; zatrzymywać się; rozwodzić się (o
czymś); przeciągać (rozmowę); zwlekać; przystanąć
dwelling [dłelyng] s. mieszkanie;
pomieszczenie mieszkalne
dwelt [dłelt] v. mieszkał ...;
proszę zobaczyć: dwell
dwindle [dłyndl] v. maleć;
topnieć; marnieć; kurczyć
się; tracić znaczenie; poniej-
szać (coś); zwyrodnieć
dye [daj] v. barwić; farbować;
s. barwa; barwnik; farba
dying ['dajyng] v. umierający;
zanikający; zob. die
dyke [dajk] s. grobla; rów; tama;
v. ogroblić; ochronić tamą
dynamic [daj'naemyk] adj.
dynamiczny; energiczny; z
wigorem; z energią (siłą)
dynamics [daj'naemyks] s.
dynamika (sił fizycznych
działających razem w ruchu)
dynamite ['dajne,majt] s.
dynamit; v. wysadzać (w
powietrze) dynamitem
dynamo ['dajne,mou] s. dynamo
dynasty ['dajnesty] s. dynastia
dysentery ['dysnetry] s.
czerwonka; dyzenteria (krwawa i ostre bóle brzucha)

E

● [i:] piąta litera angielskiego

alfabetu
each [i:cz] pron. każdy (z dwu
lub więcej); za (sztukę)
each other ['i:cz,o̲dzer] siebie;
nawzajem (dwie osoby); sobie
eager ['i:ger] adj. gorliwy; ostry;
żądny; ożywiony pragnieniem;
żywy; niecierpliwy; pragnący
eagerness ['i:gernys] s.
gorliwość; skwapliwość;
pochopność; pragnienie
eagle ['i:gl] s. orzeł; a. orli
ear [ier] s. ucho; słuch; kłos
(zboża); adj. uszny; dotyczący
uszu (leczenia uszu etc.)
eardrum ['ierdram] s. bębenek
ucha; błona bębenkowa (ucha)
early ['e:rly] adj. wczesny; adv.
wcześnie; przedwcześnie
earn [e:rn] v. zarabiać (pracą, etc.); zasługiwać; zapracować; zdobywać (sławę)
earnest ['e:rnyst] adj. poważny;
gorliwy; nie żartujący; s. zadatek (dowód kupna domu)
earnings ['e:rnyn̲z] pl. zarobki
earphone ['ierfoun] s. słuchawka;
loki ułożone na uszach
earring ['ieryng] s. kolczyk
earshot ['ier,szot] w zasięgu
głosu; w zasięgu słuchu
earth [e:rs̲] s. ziemia; świat;
gleba; planeta ziemska
earthen ['e:rs̲en] adj. ziemisty;
gliniany; wypiekany z gliny
earthenware ['e:rs̲en,łe:r] s.
wyroby garncarskie (z gliny)
earthly ['e:rs̲ly] adj. ziemski
earthquake ['e:rs̲,kłejk] s.
trzęsienie ziemi
earthworm ['e:rs̲,łe:rm] s.
(glista); dżdżownica
ease [i:z] v. łagodzić; uspokoić
(się) odciążyć; ostrożnie ruszać; s. spokój; wygoda; beztroska; ulga (od); łatwość
easel ['i:zl] s. sztaluga
easily ['i:zyly] adv. łatwo; lekko;
swobodnie; bez trudności
east [i:st] s. wschód; adj.
wschodni; adv. na wschód
Easter ['i:ster] s. Wielkanoc

eastern ['i:stern] adj. wschodni; ku wschodowi; ze wschodu
eastward ['i:stłerd] adv. ku wschodowi; na wschód; adj. wschodni (wiatr, kierunek)
easy [i:zy] adj. łatwy; beztroski; wygodny; adv. łatwo; swobodnie; lekko; s. odpoczynek
easy chair ['i:zy,czeer] s. fotel (klubowy, wygodny) miękki
eat; ate; eaten [i:t; ejt; i:tn]
eat [i:t] v. jeść (posiłek)
eat up ['i:t,ap] v. wyjeść
eaten [i:tn] adj. zjedzony; proszę zobaczyć: eat
eau-de-Cologne ['oudeke'loun] s. woda kolońska (pachnąca)
eaves [i:wz] pl. okap (dachu)
eavesdropping ['i:wzdropyng] s. podsłuchiwanie (rozmowy)
ebb-tide ['ebtajd] s. odpływ w morze; v. odpływać (jak morze, ocean etc.)
ebony ['ebeny] s. heban
eccentric [ik:sentryk] adj. dziwaczny; s. ekscentryk; dziwak; mimośród; dziwaczka
ecclesiastic [ik,ly:zi'aestyk] adj. kościelny; s. duchowny
echo ['ekou] s. echo; v. odbijać się echem; powtarzać za kimś (czyjeś słowa); odbijać głos (od powierzchni)
eclipse [i'klyps] s. zaćmienie; v. zaciemniać; zaćmiewać
ecology [i'koledży] s. ekologia; związek między środowiskiem a organizmem (część biologii i inżynierii)
economic [,i:ke'nomyk] adj. ekonomiczny; gospodarczy
economical [,i:ke'nomykel] adj. oszczędny; ekonomiczny
economics [,i:ke'nomyks] pl. nauka o ekonomii (gospodarce)
economist [i'konemyst] s. ekonomista; specjalista od działania gospodarki
economize [i:kone,majz] v. oszczędzać; zmniejszać wydatki i marnotrawstwo; gospodarowac oszczędnie; używac (coś) wydajnie

economy [i'konemy] s. ekonomia; gospodarka; gospodarowanie; zapobiegliwość
economy class [i'konemy,kla:s] s. druga klasa (w pociągu, samolocie); klasa turystyczna
ecstasy ['ekstesy] s. zachwyt; ekstaza; uniesienie; siódme niebo; wielka radość
eddy ['edy] s. wir; v. wirować
edelweiss ['ejdl,wajs] s. szarotka (kwiat górski, tatrzański)
edge [edż] s. ostrze; krawędź; kraj; v. ostrzyć; obszywać; wyślizgać się; przysuwać po trochu; posuwać bokiem
edging ['edżyng] s. brzeg; obszywka; lamówka; skraj
edgy ['edży] adj. nerwowy; podniecony; o ostrych kantach
edible ['edybl] adj. jadalny
edict ['i:dykt] s. edykt; dekret
edifice ['edyfys] s. budowla; gmach (duży i imponujący)
edifying ['edyfajyng] adj. pouczający, poprawiający (zwłaszcza moralnie)
edit ['edyt] v. redagować; wydawać; zarządzać gazetą
edition [i'dyszyn] s. wydanie; nakład (książki, gazety etc.)
editor [e'dyter] s. redaktor; wydawca; pisarz "od redakcji"
editorial [,edy'to:rjel] s. artykuł od redakcji (wydawcy); adj. redakcyjny; redaktorski
educate ['edju:kejt] v. kształcić; wychowywać (w szkole); płacić za szkołę
education [,edju'kejszyn] s. wykształcenie; nauka; oświata; nauczanie (formalne); wychowanie; tresura; wiedza
educational [,edju'kejszenl] adj. kształcący; wychowawczy
educator ['edju,kejter] s. wychowawca; wychowawczyni
eel [i:l] s. węgorz (ryba)
effect [i'fekt] s. skutek; wynik; wrażenie; wpływ; zanczenie; powodowanie; v. wykonywać; spełnić; powodować
effects [i'fekts] pl. ruchomości;

dobytek (osobiste); manatki
effective [i'fektyw] adj. skuteczny; wydajny; rzeczywisty; imponujący; wchodzący w życie; będący w mocy (w sile)
effeminate [i'femynyt] adj. zniewieściały; nie męski; słaby; delikatny; wrażliwy
effervescent [,efer'wesnt] adj. musujący; kipiący (pęcherzmi powietrza); tryskający życiem
efficacy ['efykesy] s. skuteczność; dawanie porządnych wyników (skutków etc.)
efficiency [i'fyszency] s. wydajność; skuteczność; sprawność (przy minimum nakładów, wysiłków i strat)
efficient [i'fyszent] adj. skuteczny; wydajny; sprawny
effigy ['efydży] s. wizerunek; podobizna; czyjaś kukła
effort [efert] s. wysiłek; usiłowanie; wyczyn; próba; popis; wynik pracy i wysiłków
effusive [i'fju:syw] adj. wylewny; wylany; ekspansywny; niepowstrzymany; wulkaniczny
egg [eg] s. jajko; v. zachęcać; namawiać; podbechtać; podniecać (kogoś czymś)
egg-cup ['eg,kap] s. kieliszek na jajko; kieliszek do jaj
egghead ['eg,hed] s. intelektualista (nieżyciowy)
egoism ['egou,yzem] s. egoizm
egress ['i:gres] s. wyjście; wyjazd; uchodzenie; wypływ
Egyptian [i'dżypszen] adj. egipski
eiderdown ['ajder,dałn] s. kaczy puch; kołdra; pierzyna
eight [ejt] num. osiem; s. ósemka; ośmioro; ośmiu (wioślarzy, sportowców)
eighteen ['ejt'i:n] num. osiemnaście; osiemnaścioro; osiemnastka (w drużynie etc.)
eightfold ['ejt,fould] num. ośmiokrotny; adv. ośmiokrotnie; osiem razy (robić)
eighty ['ejty] num. osiemdziesiąt; s. osiemdziesiątka
either ['ajdzer] pron. każdy (z

dwu); obaj; obie; oboje; jeden lub drugi; adv. także; też
either ... or ['ajdzer ... o:r] albo ...albo (jeden albo drugi)
ejaculate [i'dżaekju,lejt] v. zawołać; krzyknąć nag- le; wytrysnąć (nasienie)
eject [i'dżekt] v. wyrzucać (się); eksmitować; usuwać
elaborate [i'laebe,rejt] v. opracować; adj. wypracowany; staranny; skomplikowany
elapse [i'laeps] v. minąć; przeminąć; przemijać
elastic [i'laestyk] adj. sprężysty; rozciągliwy; elastyczny; s. guma; gumka (do majtek ...)
elated [i'lejtyd] adj. podniecony; uniesiony; entuzjastyczny; (bardzo) dumny, szczęśliwy
elbow ['elboł] s. łokieć; zakręt; kolanko; v. szturchać; przepychać się; zakręcać
elbow grease ['elboł,gri:s] s. ciężka praca; wysiłek
elder ['elder] s. człowiek starszy; adj. starszy (z dwóch); należący do starszyzny
elderly ['elderly] adj. podstarzały; starszy; starszawy
eldest ['eldyst] adj. najstarszy (syn w rodzeństwie etc.)
elect [i'lekt] v. wybrać; postanawiać; decydować; adj. wybrany (ale jeszcze nie na stanowisku); wyborowy
election [i'lekszyn] s. wybór; wybory (głosowaniem)
elector [i'lekter] s. wyborca (uprwniony) elektor; członek kolegium wyborczego
electric [i'lektryk] adj. elektryczny; przyciągający jak bursztyn; elektryzujący
electrical engineer [e'lektry kel,endży'nier] s. inżynier elektryk (dyplomowany)
electric chair [i'lektryk,cze:r] s. krzesło elektryczne (do egzekucji w Ameryce w USA)
electrician [ilek'tryszen] s. elektryk (monter) (instalator)
electricity [ilek'trysyty] s.

elektryczność; prąd elektryczny; energia elektryczna
electrify [i'lektryfaj] v.
elektryfikować; elektryzować
electrocute [i'lektrekju:t] v.
uśmiercić prądem elektrycz-
nym (wykonac egzekucją)
electron [i'lektron] s. elektron
elegance ['elygens] s. elegancja
elegant ['elygent] adj. elegancki;
dostojny; doskonały
element ['elyment] s. żywioł;
pierwiastek; część składowa; ogniwo; część podsta-
wowa; składnik; element
elemental [,ely'mentl] adj.
żywiołowy; zasadniczy; elementarny; podstawowy; ko-
nieczny; pierwotny
elementary [,ely'mentery] adj.
elementarny; zasadniczy;
niepodzielny; pierwiastkowy
elementary school [,ely'mentery
sku:l] s. szkoła powszechna
elephant ['elyfent] s. słoń
elevate ['ely,wejt] v. podnosic;
unosić; wynosić (wzwyż)
elevation [ely'wejszyn] s.
wysokość; godność; fasa-
da (domu); podwyższenie
elevator ['ely,wejter] s. winda;
dźwig; wyciąg; spichlerz
eleven [i'lewn] num. jedenaście;
s. jedenastka; jedenaścioro
eleventh [i'lewnt] num.
jedenasty; jedenastka
eligible ['elydżebl] adj. nadający
się; odpowiedni na wybór
eliminate [i'lymy,nejt] v. usuwać; wydzielać; pozbywać
się; nie brać pod uwagę;
opuszczać; wyeliminować
elimination [i,lymy'nejszyn] s.
eliminacja; pozbycie się
elk [elk] s. łoś (rogacz)
ell [el] s. łokieć (miara)
ellipse [i'lyps] s. elipsa
elm [elm] s. wiąz (drzewo)
elongate [i'longejt] v. wydłużać
się; adj. wydłużony
elope [i'loup] v. uciekać z
ukochanym (potajemnie)
eloquence ['eloukłens] s.

elokwencja; krasomówstwo
eloquent ['eloktłent] adj.
elokwentny; wymowny (też w
piśmie); kroasowówczy
else [els] adv. inaczej; bo
inaczej; w przeciwnym razie;
poza tym; jeszcze; jeśli nie;
(będziesz) adj. różny; inny
elsewhere [els'hłer] adv. gdzie
indziej; w innym miejscu
elude [i'lu:d] v. ujść; wymknąć się; obejść prawo;
uchylić się; ukrywać się
elusive [ilu:syw] adj.
nieuchwytny; wymykający się
emanate ['eme,nejt] v. wydobywać; pochodzić; wy-
dzielać się; emanować
emancipate [i'maens,ypejt] v.
wyzwolić; wyemancypować
embalm [im'ba:lm] v. zabalsa-
amować; napełnić aromatem
embankment [im'baenkment] s.
nasyp; grobla; nabrzeże
embargo [em'ba:rgou] s. zakaz
handlowania, wjazdu, wyjazdu
embark [im'ba:rk] v. ładować
(się); wsiadać (na statek);
załadować (wojsko, towar;
rozpoczynać; przedsięwziąć
embark upon [im'ba:rk e'pon] v.
rozpoczynać; przedsięwziąć
embarrass [im'baeres] v. za-
kłopotać; wikłać; przeszkadzać; powodować zadłuże-
nie; zażenować; skrępować
embarrassing [im'baeresyng] adj.
żenujący; kłopotliwy;
krępujący; zawstydzający
embarrassment [im'baeresment]
s. zakłopotanie; powikłanie;
skrępowanie; zaaferowanie
embassy ['embesy] s. ambasada
embed [im'bed] v. osadzić; sadzić; wmurować; wryć; za-
lać; wkopać; wbijać w coś
embedded [im'bedyd] adj.
osadzony; wsadzony; wryty;
wmurowany; wbity; wkopany
embellish [im'belysz] v.
upiększać; ozdabiać; podko-
lorowywać; dekorować; po-
prawić (opowiadanie etc.)

embers ['emberz] pl. niewygasłe
węgle; żar; palące się polana
embezzle [ym'bezl] v. sprzeniewierzać (własność cudzą);
zdefraudować (pieniądze)
embitter [im'byter] v.
rozgoryczać; zatruwać; pogarszać; rozjątrzać (kłótnię)
emblem ['emblem] s. godło;
wzór; symbol; emblemat
embody [im'body] v. wcielać;
uosabiać; zawierać; włą-
czać; ucieleśniać (coś)
embolden [im'boulden] v.
ośmielać; rozzuchwalać;
dodać (komuś) śmiałości
embolism [embelyzem] s. zator
embrace [im'brejs] v. uścisnąć
się; obejmować; przystępować; imać się; korzystać z;
s. uścisk; objęcie; włączenie
(do jakiejś kategorii)
embroider [im'brojder] v. haf-
haftować; wyszywać; upiększać (ubarwiać) opowiadanie
embroidery [im'brojdery] s. haft;
hafciarstwo; upiększanie
(ubarwianie) opowiadania
embryo ['embry'ou] s. płód;
zarodek; embrion; adj.
zarodkowy; nierozwinięty
emerald ['emereld] s. szmaragd
emerge [y'me:rdż] v. wynurzać
się; wyłaniać; wyniknąć; nasunąć się (komuś coś); wy-
łonić się z wody (z morza);
wyjść na jaw; wynikać z;
nabawiać (kłopotów komuś)
emergency [y'me:rdżensy] s.
nagła potrzeba; stan wyjątkowy; stan pogotowia
emergency brake [y'me:rdżensy
,brejk] s. ręczny hamulec w
samochodzie (zapasowy)
emergency call [y'me:rdżensy
,kol] s. wzywanie pogotowia
emergency exit [y'me:rdżensy
,eksyt] s. wyjście zapasowe
emergency landing [y'me:r
dżensy,laendyng] s. przy-
musowe lądowanie (samolotu)
emigrant ['emygrent] s. wychodźca; emigrant; adj. wy-

chodźczy; emigracyjny
emigrate ['emygrejt] v. emi-
grować; wywędrować; prze-
prowadzać się (dokądś)
emigration [,emy'grejszyn] s.
emigracja; wychodźctwo
emigre ['emygrej] s. emigrant
(polityczny); adj. emigracyjny
eminent ['emynent] adj. dostojny; wybitny; wyniosły; wysoki; znakomity; sławny
eminently ['emynently] adv.
szczególnie; wybitnie; wysoce
emit [y'myt] v. wydawać; wysyłać (światło, fale radiowe,
ciepło, opinie); wypuszczać
(banknoty); nadawać przez
radio (audycję); emitować
emotion [y'mouszyn] s. wzruszenie; emocja; uczucie (miłości, strachu, gniewu, obu-
rzenia, współczucia etc.)
emotional [y'mouszynel] adj.
emocjonalny; poruszający
uczucia (czyjeś); uczuciowy
emperor ['emperer] s. cesarz
emphasis ['emfesys] s. nacisk;
emfaza; uwypuklenie; uwydat-
nienie; siła wyrażenia;
wzmocnienie akcentu (na)
emphasize ['emfesajz] v.
podkreślać; kłaść nacisk;
uwypuklać; uwydatniać coś
emphatic [ym'faetyk] adj. dobitny; wyraźny; stanowczy;
emfatyczny; mówiący z naciskiem; zdecydowany; niedwuznaczny; wymowny; znaczący
empire ['empajer] s. cesarstwo;
imperium; adj. empirowy
emplacement [ym'plejsment] s.
umiejscowienie; stanowisko
employ [ym'ploj] v. zatrudniać;
używać; zajmować się;
poświęcać (czas); posłu-
giwać się; zastosować coś
employee [,emploj'i:] s.
pracownik; siła (robocza)
employer [em'plojer] s. szef;
pracodawca; pracodawczyni
employment [ym'plojment] s.
zatrudnienie; używanie;

zajęcie; praca (najemna)
employment agency [ym'ploj ment'ejdżensy] agencja pośrednictwa pracy; biuro zatrudnienia bezrobotnych
empower [ym'pałer] v. upełnomocnić; upoważniać; umożliwiać (coś, komuś)
empress ['emprys] s. cesarzowa
emptiness ['emptynys] s. pustka
empty ['empty] adj. pusty; próżny; gołosłowny; bezsensowny; czczy; v. wypróżniać; wysypywać; wylewać brudy
emulate ['emjulejt] v. rywalizować; współzawodniczyć
enable [y'nejbl] v. umożliwiać; upoważniać; dawać możność; upoważniać (kogoś)
enact [y'naekt] v. postanawiać; uchwalać; grać (rolę); odgrywać (sztukę); uprawomocnić; wydawać zarządzenia; zagrać role (na scenie)
enamel [y'naemel] s. emalia; szkliwo (na zębach etc.)
encase [yn'kejs] v. wsadzać do pochwy; oprawiać; obramować; wpakowywać; pokryć
enchant [yn'czaent] v. zaczarować; oczarować (kogoś czymś); zachwycać (czymś)
encircle [yn'se:rkl] v. otaczać; okalać; okrążać; okrążyć; otoczyć (armie wroga etc.)
enclose [yn'klouz] v. ogradzać; zamykać; dołączać; załączać; zawierać (w sobie); okrążyć (wroga); opasać
enclosure [yn'kloużer] s. ogrodzenie; załącznik; płot
encore! [en'ko:r] s. bis! (zagrać, zaśpiewać na bis); bisowanie
encounter [yn'kaunter] s. spotkanie; potyczka; pojedynek; v. natknąć się (na trudności); spotkać się; potykać się (niespodziewanie); mieć utarczkę; utarczka
encourage [yn'ka:rydż] v. zachęcać; ośmielać; popierać; dodawać odwagi; pomagać; udzielać poparcia

encouragement [yn'ka:rydżment] s. zachęta; ośmielenie; popieranie; dodanie odwagi komuś
encroach [yn'kroucz] v. wdzierać się; naruszać; wkraczać na cudze; targnąć się na cudze (mienie, własność etc.)
encumber [yn'kamber] v. krępować; tarasować; obarczać; zawadzać; utrudniać; obciążać (kogoś długami etc.)
end [end] s. koniec; cel; skrzydłowy w piłce nożnej; v. kończyć (się); skończyć; dokończyć; położyć kres
endanger [yn'dejndżer] v. narażać, wystawiać kogoś na niebezpieczeństwo
endear [yn'dier] v. czynić drogim, lubianym; przymilać się; zdobywć serce (czyjeś)
endeavor [yn'dewer] v. starać się; usiłować; dążyć; zabiegać o; s. usiłowanie; wysiłek; dążenie do; zabiegi o; próba
ending ['endyng] s. zakończenie; końcówka (wyrazu)
endless ['endlys] adj. nie kończący się; nieskończony; bezustanny; ustawiczny; bezkresny; wieczny; ciągły
endorse [yn'do:rs] v. potwierdzać; popierać; żyrować; podżyrować; notować na odwrocie; indosować coś
endow [yn'dał] v. uposażyć; wyposażyć; ufundować; zapisywać; obdarzyć kogoś
endurance [yn'djuerens] s. wytrzymałość; cierpliwość
endure [yn'djuer] v. znosić (ból; bez skargi); cierpieć; wytrzymać; przetrwać; ostać się; trwać; ścierpieć
enema ['enyme] s. lewatywa
enemy ['enymy] s. wróg; przeciwnik; adj. wrogi; nieprzyjacielski; przeciwny
energetic [,ene:r'dżetyk] adj. energiczny; z wigorem
energy ['enerdży] s. energia
enervate ['ene:rwejt] v. osłabiać (nerwowo, na zdrowiu); wy-

czerpywać; pozbawiać (sił)
enervate [y'ne:rwyt] adj. słaby;
bez energii; wyczerpany
enfold [yn'fould] v. zawijać;
obejmować; zapakowywać
enfranchise [yn'fraenczajz] v.
wyzwalać; nadawać prawo
wyborcze; uwalniać; uwłaszczać (niewolników etc.)
engage [yn'gejdż] v. zajmować;
angażować; skłaniać; ścierać się; zaręczyć; zobowiązywać się; nawiązać (walkę)
engaged [yn'gejdżd] adj. zajęty;
zaręczony; włączony
engagement [yn'gejdżment] s.
zobowiązanie; zaręczyny
engine ['endżyn] s. silnik;
parowóz; maszyna; motor
engine-driver ['endżyn,drajwer]
s. maszynista (kolejowy)
engineer [,endży'nier] s. inżynier; v. planować; zręcznie
prowadzić: budowę, operacje
engineering [,endży'nieryng] s.
technika; mechanika; inżynieria; zarząd dróg, maszyn
engine trouble ['endżyn'trabl] s.
zepsucie silnika (samochodowego); kłopot z silnikiem
English ['ynglysz] adj. angielski
(język, mowa); angielszczyzna
english ['ynglysz] v. uderzyć
piłkę fałszem; zanglizować;
zangielszczyć; s. fałsz; podkręcona piłka (w tenisie)
engorge [yn'go:rdż] v. pożerać
engrave [yn'grejw] v. rytować;
ryć; grawerować; wyryć;
wyrytować (napis, litery,
wzór, plaskorzeźbę etc.)
engraving [yn'grejwyng] s.
sztych; rytownictwo; grawiura
engross [yn'grous] v. zaabsorbować sobą; pochłaniać; monopolizować (rozmowę, całkowitą uwagę itd.)
engulf [yn'galf] v. pochłonąć w
przepaść; porwać w odmęt
enigma [y'nygme] s. zagadka
enjoin [yn'dżoyn] v. nakazywać;
zarządzać; zakazywać; rozkazywać; zalecać; zabraniać

enjoy [yn'dżoj] v. cieszyć się;
rozkoszować; mieć (przyjemność, użytek); posiadać
enjoyment [yn'dżojment] s.
uciecha; rozkosz; przyjemność; posiadanie, korzystanie z uprawnień etc.
enlarge [yn'la:rdż] v. powiększać; poszerzać; rozdąć;
rozwijać; zwalniać z ciupy
enlargement [yn'la:rdżment] s.
powiększenie; poszerzenie
enlighten [yn'lajtn] v. oświecać; oświetlać; objaśniać
enlist [yn'lyst] v. zaciągać (się);
werbować (do wojska); mobilizować kogoś dla sprawy
enliven [yn'lajwn] v. ożywiać
enmesh [yn'mesz] v. wplatać
(w sieć); usidlać; usidlić
enmity ['enmyty] s. wrogość;
nieprzyjaźń; nienawiść
enormous [y'no:rmes] adj.
olbrzymi; ogromny; kolosalny
enough [y'naf] adj., s. & adv.
dosyć; dość; na tyle; nie
więcej; wystarczająco
enounce [y'nauns] v. ogłaszać;
wymawiać; wypowiadać;
wymówić; wygłaszać mowę
enquire [yn'kłajer] v. pytać o;
dowiadywać się o; rozpytywać się (o coś, o kogoś)
enquiry [yn'kłajry] s. pytanie;
śledztwo; zapytanie; badania
enrage [yn'rejdż] v. rozwścieczać; doprowadzać (czymś,
kogoś) do wściekłości
enraged [yn'rejdżd] adj. rozwścieczony; rozwścieczona
enrapt [yn'raept] adj. zachwycony; pogrążony w zachwycie
enrapture [yn'raepczer] v. zachwycać; oczarowywać (kogoś); porywać publiczność
enrich [yn'rycz] v. wzbogacać;
użyźniać; ozdobić; poprawić jakość; ozdabiać
enroll(l) [yn'roul] v. zaciągać
(się); zapisywać (się)
ensue [yn'su:] v. wynikać;

nastepować po kimś, po czymś; wypływać (z)

ensure [yn'szuer] v. zabezpieczać; zapewniać; zagwarantować; asekurować

entangle [yn'taengel] v. gmattwać; wplątać; zmieszać; komplikować; powikłać

enter ['enter] v. wchodzić; wpisywać; penetrować; wkładać; wstępować;

enter into ['enter,yntu] v. wdawać się; brać udział w; zawierać (układ z kimś)

enter upon ['enter,apon] v. wchodzić w posiadanie; przystąpować do tematu; zaczynać (pertraktacje etc.)

enterprise ['enterprajz] s. przedsięwzięcie; przedsiębiorstwo; przedsiębiorczość; zadanie; inicjatywa

enterprising ['enterprajzyng] adj. przedsiębiorczy; ryzykujący

entertain [,enter'tejn] v. zabawiać; przyjmować; rozerwać (towarzystwo); żywić (podejrzenia); nosić się; brać pod uwagę; ugościć

entertainer [,enter'tejner] s. artysta (kabaretowy)

entertainment [,enter'tejnment] s. rozrywka; zabawa; uciecha

enthusiasm [yn'tju:zjaezem] s. zapał; entuzjazm do

enthusiast [yn'tju:zaest] s. entuzjasta; zapaleniec

enthusiastic [yn'tu:zy'aestyk] adj. entuzjastyczny; zapalony

entice [yn'tajs] v. znęcić; zwabić; kusić (nagrodą)

entire [yn'tajer] adj. cały; całkowity; nietknięty

entirely [yn'tajerly] adv. całkowicie; jedynie; wyłącznie; kompletnie; niepodzielnie

entitle [yn'tajtl] v. uprawniać; tytułować; nazwać; nadawać coś; upoważniać do

entity ['entyty] s. byt; istnienie; jednostka; istota

entrails ['entrejlz] pl. jelita; wnętrzności; wnętrze ziemi

entrance ['entrens] s. wejście; wstęp (za opłatą); dostęp; wjazd; pozwolenie wstępu

entrance [,en'traens] v. przejmować; wprawiać w trans; zachwycać (kogoś)

entrance fee ['entrens,fi:] opłata za wstęp; bilet wstępu

entreat [yn'tri:t] v. błagać

entreaty [yn'tri:ty] s. błaganie; usilna prośba; modlitwa

entrust [yn'trast] v. powierzać

entry ['entry] s. wejście; wpis; hasło (słownika); uczestnik wyścigu; wkroczenie; wstęp

entry permit ['entry,per'myt] pozwolenie wejścia, wjazdu

enumerate [y'nju:merejt] v. wliczać; sporządzać wykaz

envelop [yn'welep] v. owijać; otaczać; ogarniać; okryć (całkiem); ukryć; objąć

envelope ['enweloup] s. koperta; otoczka; teczka (papierowa)

envenom [yn'wenem] v. zatruwać; zaognić; podsycić

enviable ['enwjebl] adj. godzien zazdrości; godny pożądania

envious [enwjes] adj. zazdrosny; zawistny; pełen zazdrości

environment [ynwajerenment] s. otoczenie; środowisko

environmental pollution [yn'wajerenmentel pel'u:szyn] zanieczyszczenie środowiska

environs [yn'wajerenz] s. okolice podmiejskie; przedmieścia

envoy ['enwoj] s. wysłannik

envy ['enwy] s. zawiść; zazdrość; przedmiot zazdrości; niezadowolenie z powodzenia drugiego człowieka

epic ['epyk] adj. epicki; s. epos

epidemic [,epy'demyk] s. epidemia; adj. epidemiczny

epidermis [,epy'de:rmys] s. naskórek; skóra (powierzchnia)

epilepsy ['epylepsy] s. epilepsja; padaczka (choroba)

epilogue ['epylog] s. epilog

episode ['epysoud] s. epizod

epitaph ['epytaef] s. napis na grobie (ku pamięci zmarłego)

epoch 397 essential

epoch [i:'pok] s. epoka (czyjaś)
equal ['i:kłeł] adj. równy; jednaki;
jednakowy; jednostajny; zrównoważony; równy (stanem); v.
równać się; dorównywać komuś; wyrównywać (coś)
equality [i'kłolyty] s. równość
equalize [i'kłełajz] v. wyów-
nywać; równać; zrównywać
(się); (s)kompensować (coś)
equanimity [,i:kłe'nymyty] s.
opanowanie; spokój ducha;
równowaga psychiczna
equate [i'kłejt] v. równać;
przyrównywać do; stawiać
na równi (z kimś, z czymś)
equation [i'kłejżyn] s. równanie;
równoważenie; bilansowanie
equator [i'kłejter] s. równik
equilibrium [,i:kły'lybrjem] s.
równowaga; stan równowagi
equip [i'kłyp] v. wyposażać;
zaopatrywać; uzbrajać; ekwipować (kogoś w coś)
equipment [i'kłypment] s. wyposażenie; ekwipunek; sprzęt
equitable ['ekłytebl] adj. słuszny;
sprawiedliwy; godziwy
equivalent [i'kływelent] adj.
równowartościowy; równo-
znaczny; równej wielkości; s.
równoważnik; równowart-
tość; równoważność
era ['yere] s. era (historyczna)
erase [y'rejz] v. wycierać; wy-
mazywać; zatrzeć; zacierać;
wytrzeć; wyskrobać (coś)
erect [y'rekt] adj. prosty; wy-
prężony; sztywny; najeżony;
nastroszony; zadarty; pionowy; v. budować; stawiać
erection [y'rekszyn] s. podniesienie; wyprostowanie; najeże-
nie; erekcja; budowla; montaż
erosion [y'roużyn] s. wyżeranie;
żłobienie; erozja; nadżerka
ermine ['e:rmyn] s. gronostaj
erotic [y'rotyk] adj. erotyczny;
miłosny; s. erotyk; erotoman;
wiersz erotyczny
err [e:r] v. błądzić; być w
błędzie; grzeszyć; zgrzeszyć
errand ['erand] s. posyłka;

zlecenie; cel; sprawunek
erratic [y'raetyk] adj. błędny;
nieobliczalny; dziwny; s.
dziwak; ekscentryk
erroneous [y'rounjes] adj.
błędny; mylny; fałszywy
error ['erer] s. błąd; pomyłka
erudite ['erudajt] adj. uczony; s.
erudyta (b. oczytany etc.)
erupt [y'rapt] v. wybuchać;
wyrzucać; przerzynać (się);
wysypywać się; wybuchać
lawą; mieć wysypkę skórną
eruption [y'rapszyn] s. wybuch;
przerzynanie się; wysypka
escalation [,eske'lejszyn] s.
wzmożenie; rozszerzenie się
escalator ['eskelejter] s. ruchome
schody; ruchoma skala płac
(wg kosztów utrzymania etc.)
escape [ys'kejp] s. ucieczka; wyciekanie; wychodzenie; ocalenie; v. wymknąć się; zbiec;
wyjść cało; uchodzić; ratować się ucieczką
escort ['esko:rt] s. eskorta;
konwój; mężczyzna towarzyszący kobiecie; kawaler; v.
eskortować; kowojować
escort [i'sko:rt] v. eskortować
especial [ys'peszel] adj. szczególny; wyjątkowy; specjalny;
główny; osobliwy (przypadek)
especially [ys'peszely] adv.
szczególnie; zwłaszcza
espionage [,espje'na:dż] s.
wywiad; szpiegostwo; szpiegowanie; śledzenie kogoś
esprit [es'pri:] s. żywość;
życie; dowcip; duch; poczucie
humoru; duma (zespołowa)
espy [ys'paj] v. spostrzegać;
wyśledzić; wykombinować
essay ['esej] s. esej; szkic
literacki; próba; v. próbować;
wypróbować; poddać próbie
essence ['esens] s. esencja;
istota czegoś; wyciąg;
treść; istotna treść; sedno
sprawy; olej; ekstrakt
essential [y'senszel] adj. niezbędny; istotny; zasadniczy;
zupełny; podstawowy; konie

czny; eteryczny; s. cecha
istotna, nieodzowna, zasad-
nicza; rzecz podstawowa
establish [ys'taeblysz] v. zakładać; osądzać; ustalać;
wprowadzać; udowodnić;
ufundować; ustanawiać
establishment [ys'taeblyszment]
s. założenie; osadzenie;
ustalenie; ustanowienie;
zakład; gospodarstwo; koła
rządzące; organizacja
państwowa lub wojskowa;
firma; przedsiębiorstwo
estate [ys'tejt] s. majątek; stan
majątkowy; położenie w życiu
estate tax [ys'tejt,taeks] s.
podatek spadkowy, od nie-
ruchomości (majątkowy)
esteem [ys'ti:m] v. cenić;
szanować; poważać; s. po-
ważanie; szacunek; dobra
opinia; wielkie uznanie
estimate ['estymejt] v. oceniać;
szacować; s. szacunek;
kosztorys; ocena; opinia;
oszacowanie; obliczenie
estimation [,esty'mejszyn] s.
szacowanie; poważanie;
szacunek; zdanie; mniemanie;
sąd
estrange [ys'trejndż] v.
odstręczać; zrażać;
zniechęcać
estray [ys'trej] s. stworzenie
bezpańskie, zgubione
estuary ['estjuery] s. ujście
(rzeki) do morza (oceanu)
eternal [y'ternl] adj. wieczny;
odwieczny; bez początku i
końca
eternity [y'ternyty] s.
wieczność; trwanie bez
końca i odpoczynku
ether ['i:ter] s. eter
ethics ['etyks] pl. etyka
ethnic ['etnyk] adj. etniczny;
pogański; odrębny
zwyczajami i językiem
etymology [,ety'moledży] s.
etymologia; pochodzenie i
rozwój słów
eulogy ['ju:ledży] s. mowa;

pochwała (pogrzebowa)
eunuch ['ju:nek] n. eunuch;
rzezaniec; człowiek
wykastrowany
European [,ju:re'pi:en] adj.
europejski; s. Europejczyk
evacuate [y'waekjuejt] v.
ewakuować; opróżniać;
wypróżniać; wydalać;
usuwać; wycofywać się
evacuation [y,waekju'ejszyn] s.
ewakuacja; wypróżnienie (się)
evade [y'wejd] v. ujść;
uniknąć; obchodzić;
wymykać się; wykręcać się;
pomijać
evaluate [y'waeljuejt] v.
obliczać; oceniać;
analizować
evaporate [y'waeperejt] v.
parować; ulatniać się;
poddawać parowaniu;
wyparować; umrzeć
evasion [y'wejżyn] s. uniknięcie;
wymknięcie się; obejście;
wykręt; oszustwo
(podatkowe)
evasive [y'wejsyw] adj.
wykrętny; wymijający;
nieuchwytny
eve [i:w] s. wilia; wigilia
even ['i:wen] adj. równy;
jednolity; parzysty; adv.
nawet; v. równać;
wyrównać; zemścić się;
wygładzać; ujednostajnić
even-handed ['i:wen,haendyd]
adj. sprawiedliwy; bezstronny
evening ['i:wnyng] s. wieczór
evening dress ['i:wnyn,dres] s.
strój wieczorowy
evening paper ['i:wnyn'pejper]
gazeta wieczorna
evensong ['i:wensong] s.
nieszpory; pieśń wieczorna
event [y'went] s. wydarzenie;
możliwość; wynik; rezultat;
zawody (sportowe);
konkurencja
eventful [y'wentful] adj.
burzliwy; pamiętny; pełen
wydarzeń
eventual [y'wenczuel] adj. w

końcu pewny
eventually [y'wenczuely] adv. w
końcu na pewno
ever ['ewer] adv. w ogóle;
niegdyś; kiedyś; jak tylko; ile
tylko; kiedykolwiek; jeszcze
wciąż
ever after [,ewer'after] do tego
czasu; już od tego czasu
ever since [,ewer'syns] od tego
czasu; od kiedy (był etc.)
everlasting [,ewerlastyng] adj.
wieczny; ciągły; nieustanny
evermore ['ewer'mo:r] adv.
zawsze; na zawsze; na wieki
every ['ewry] adj. każdy;
wszelki; co (dzień, noc, rano)
every other day ['ewry,odzer,dej]
co drugi dzień
everybody ['ewrybody] pron.
każdy; wszyscy (ludzie)
everyday ['ewrydej] adj.
codzienny; powszedni; zwykły
everyone ['ewryłan] pron. każdy;
wszyscy; każda rzecz
everything ['ewrytyng] pron.
wszystko (co jest etc.)
everywhere ['ewryhłer] adv.
wszędzie; gdziekolwiek
evidence ['ewydens] s. znak;
dowód; świadectwo;
oczywistość; jasność; v.
świadczyć; dowodzić
(czegoś); manifestować
evident ['ewydent] adj.
oczywisty; widoczny; jawny;
jasny
evil ['i:wl] adj. zły; fatalny
evildoer ['i:wl-duer] s. złoczyńca
evince [y'wyns] v. wykazywać;
okazywać (życzenie);
przejawiać
evoke [y'wouk] v. wywoływać;
wydobywać; zdobywać
(odpowiedź)
evolution [,ewe'lu:szyn] s.
rozwój; ewolucja; rozwinięcie
(się); pierwiastkowanie
evolve [y'wolw] v. rozwijać;
wypracowywać; wytwarzać
(ciepło etc.); rozwijać się
stopniowo
ewe [ju:] s. owca

ex- [eks] pref. były; była; prep.
bez; ze; s. (litera) "x"
exacerbate [eks'aeserbejt] v.
drażnić; pogorszyć;
irytować
exact [yg'zaekt] adj. dokładny;
ścisły; v. wymagać;
ściągać; egzekwować;
wymuszać
exactitude [yg'zaektytju:d] s.
ścisłość; dokładność;
punktualność
exactly [yg'zaektly] adv.
dokładnie; ściśle; właśnie;
zgadza się; punktualnie; ostro
exactness [yg'zaektnys] s.
dokładność; precyzja
exaggerate [yg'zaedżerejt] v.
przesadzać; wyolbrzymiać
exaggeration [yg'zaedże'rejszyn]
s. przesada; wyolbrzymienie
exalt [yg'zo:lt] v. wywyższać;
podnosić; wychwalać;
chwalić
exam [yg'zaem] s. egzamin
(slang); klasówka; egzamin w
szkole lub na uniwersytecie
examination [yg,zaemy'nejszyn]
s. egzamin; badanie; rewizja
examine [yg'zaemyn] v. badać;
sprawdzać; egzaminować;
rozpatrywać; rewidować;
przesłuchiwać;
przeprowadzać śledztwo
example [yg'za:mpl] s. przykład;
wzór; precedens
exasperate [yg'za:sperejt] v.
rozjątrzać; rozgoryczać;
pogarszać; powodować
rozpacz
excavate ['ekskewejt] v. kopać;
odkopać; wykopać; drążyć;
pogłębiać; wybierać (ziemię)
exceed [yk'si:d] v.
przewyższać; celować;
przekraczać
exceedingly [ek'si:dyngly] adv.
niezmiernie; nadzwyczajnie
excel [yk'sel] v. przewyższać;
wybijać się; celować (w
czymś)
excellence [yk'selens] s.
wyższość; doskonałość;

zaleta

excellent [yk'selent] adj.
doskonały; wyborny; świetny;
celujący

except [yk'sept] conj. chyba że;
żeby; oprócz; poza; wyjąwszy

except [yk'sept] v. wykluczać;
wyłączać; prep. z wyjątkiem;
pominąwszy; wyjąwszy;
chyba że

exception [yk'sepszyn] s.
wyjątek; wyłączenie; zarzut;
obiekcja

exceptional [yk'sepszenl] adj.
nadzwyczajny; wyjątkowy

excess [yk'ses] s. nadmiar;
nadwyżka; a. nadmierny; nad-

excess fare [yk'ses,fe:r] s.
dopłata do biletu

excessive [yk'sesyw] adj.
nadmierny; zbytni;
nieumiarkowany

excess luggage [yk'ses,lagydż]
nadwyżka bagażu

exchange [yks'czendż] s.
wymiana; zamiana; giełda;
centrala telefoniczna; v.
wymienić; zamienić (się); a.
wymienny; walutowy

excitable [yk'sajtebl] adj.
pobudliwy; pobudzający;
podniecający

excite [yk'sajt] v. pobudzać;
podniecać; prowokować

excited [yk'sajtyd] adj.
podniecony; zdenerwowany

excitement [yk'sajtment] s.
podniecenie; zdenerwowanie

exciting [yk'sajtyng] adj.
emocjonujący; pasjonujący

exclaim [yks'klejm] v. zawołać;
wykrzyknąć; zaprotestować

exclamation [,ekskla'mejszyn] s.
okrzyk; krzyk; wykrzyknik

exclamation mark [,ekskla
'mejszyn,ma:rk] wykrzyknik

exclude [yks'klu:d] v.
wykluczać; wydalać;
usuwać

exclusion [yks'klu:żyn] n.
wykluczenie; wydalenie;
usunięcie; wyłączenie

exclusive [yks'klu:syw] adj.
modny; wykluczający;
wyłączny; jedyny;
ekskluzywny

excursion [yks'ker:żyn] s.
wycieczka; dygresja; a.
wycieczkowy

excuse [yks'kju:z] v.
usprawiedliwiać;
przepraszać; darować;
zwalniać; s.
usprawiedliwienie; wymówka;
pretekst

excuse me [yks'kju:z,mi]
przepraszam; przepraszam
pana

excusable [iks'kju:zebl] adj.
usprawiedliwiony; wybaczalny

execute ['eksykju:t] v. wykonać
(wyrok, plan); stracić
(skazańca); nadawać
ważność

execution [,eksy'kju:szyn] s.
wykonanie; egzekucja;
stracenie

executive [yg'zekjutyw] adj.
wykonawczy; s. władza
wykonawcza; stanowisko
kierownicze

exemplary [yg'zemplery] adj.
wzorowy; przykładny;
przykładowy; wymierzony dla
odstraszenia

exempt [yg'zempt] v. zwalniać;
adj. wolny; zwolniony; s.
osoba zwolniona; człowiek
zwolniony

exercise ['eksersajz] s.
ćwiczenie; wykonywanie
(zawodu); korzystanie; v.
ćwiczyć; używać;
wykonywać; spełniać;
pełnić

exercise book ['eksersajz,buk] s.
zeszyt (szkolny)

exert [yg'ze:rt] v. wytężać
(się); wysilać (się);
wywierać (nacisk, wpływ
etc.) zabiegać

exertion [yg'ze:rszyn] s.
wytężenie; wysiłek;
wywieranie

exhale [eks'hejl] v. wyziewać;
wydychać; zionąć; parować

exhaust [yg'zo:st] v. wydychać;
wyczerpywać; wyciągać;
wypróżniać; odgazować; s.
wydech; wydmuch; rura
wydechowa; opróżnianie (z
powietrza); aspirator; rura
wydechowa (auta)

exhaust fumes [yg'zo:st,fjums]
gazy wydechowe (z motoru)

exhaustion [yg'zo:stszyn] s.
wyczerpanie; opróżnienie;
zużycie; pochłonięcie;
zmęczenie

exhaust-pipe [yg'zo:st,pajp] s.
rura wydechowa (w aucie)

exhibit [yg'zybyt] s. wystawa;
pokaz; eksponaty; v.
wystawiać; okazywać;
pokazywać; wykazywać;
popisywać się czymś;
przedkładać; mieć wystawę

exhibition [,eksy'byszyn] s.
wystawa; wystawianie;
pokazywanie; pokaz;
widowisko; popis

exhibitor [yg'zybyter] s.
wystawca; wystawczyni

exile ['eksajl] s. wygnanie;
tułaczka; emigracja;
wygnaniec; v. wygnać na
banicję

exist [yg'zyst] v. istnieć; być;
żyć; egzystować; zdarzać
się

existence [yg'zystens] s.
istnienie; byt; egzystencja

existent [yg'zystent] a.
istniejący; będący; znajdujący
się

exit ['eksyt] s. wyjście;
odejście; ujście; wylot;
swobodne wyjście; v.
wychodzić; kończyć (slang);
schodzić ze sceny

exit visa ['eksyt,wyza] s. wiza
wyjazdowa

exorbitant [yg'zo:rbytent] adj.
wygórowany; nadmierny;
przesadny

exotic [eg'zotyk] adj.
egzotyczny; s. egzotyk;
egzotyczna roślina;
egzotyczny wyraz

expand [yks'paend] v.
rozszerzać; powiększać;
wzrastać; rozprężać;
rozwijać; rozruszać;
rozpościerać; powiększać

expanse [yks'paens] s. bezmiar;
rozległa przestrzeń; ekspansja

expansion [yks'paenszyn] s.
rozszerzanie; rozprężanie się;
ekspansja; rozpościeranie;
rozwijanie (się); ilość
ekspansji

expansive [yks'paensyw] adj.
rozszerzalny; rozległy;
rozprężalny; obszerny;
wylewny

expect [yks'pekt] v. spodziewać
się; przypuszczać; zgadywać

expectation [,ekspek'tejszyn] s.
oczekiwanie; nadzieja; widoki;
prospekt; przewidywanie

expedient [yks'pi:djent] adj.
celowy; wygodny;
oportunistyczny; korzystny; s.
środek; zabieg; sposób;
wybieg; fortel

expedition [,ekspy'dyszyn] s.
wyprawa; ekspedycja;
sprawność; szybkość;
pośpiech; marsz do akcji

expel [yks'pel] v. wypędzać;
wydalać; usuwać; wyrzucać

expend [yks'pend] v. wydawać;
zużywać; poświęcać czas

expense [yks'pens] s. koszt;
wydatek; rachunek; strata;
ofiara

expensive [yks'pensyw] adj.
drogi; kosztowny; wysoko
wyceniony

experience [yks'pierjens] s.
doświadczenie; przeżycie; v.
doświadczać; doznawać;
poznać (coś); przeżywać;
przechodzić

experienced [yks'pierjenst] adj.
doświadczony; doznany

experiment [yks'peryment] s.
próba; eksperyment;
doświadczenie; v.
eksperymentować; robić
doświadczenia

expert ['ekspe:rt] s. biegły;

ekspert; znawca; adj. biegły; światły; mistrzowski; wykonany przez eksperta

expiration [,ekspi'rejszyn] s. wygaśnięcie; upłynięcie; wydech; wyzionięcie ducha; śmierć

expire [yks'pajer] v. wygasać; upływać; wydychać; wyzionąć ducha; umierać; kończyć się

explain [yks'plejn] v. wyjaśnić; objaśnić; wytłumaczyć

explanation [,eks'plaenejszyn] s. wyjaśnienie; wytłumaczenie

explicable ['eksplykebl] adj. dający się wyjaśnić

explicit [yks'plysyt] adj. jasny; wyraźny; szczery; otwarty; definitywny; wygadany

explode [yks'ploud] v. wybuchać; eksplodować; demaskować (fałsz); obalić (teorię etc.)

exploit [yks'ploit] v. użytkować; eksploatować; wyzyskiwać

exploit ['eksploit] s. wyczyn

exploration [,eksplo:'rejszyn] s. oszukiwanie; badanie

explore [yks'plo:r] v. badać; sondować; wybadać; przebadać

explorer [yks'plo:rer] s. badacz; sonda; odkrywca; odkrywczyni

explosion [yks'ploużyn] s. eksplozja; wybuch (kłótni etc.)

explosive [yks'plousyw] s. materiał wybuchowy; adj. wybuchowy; mogący wybuchnąć

exponent [yks'pounent] adj. interpretujący; s. eksponent; wyraziciel; interpretator; wykładnik (potęgi); przedstawiciel

export [yks'po:rt] v. wywozić; eksportować; s. wywóz; eksport; towar wywozowy; wywożenie

expose [yks'pouz] v. wystawiać (na wpływ); poddawać (czemuś); odsłaniać; demaskować; eksponować;

naświetlać; narażać (dziecko); zrobić zdjęcie

expose [,ekspou'zej] s. zdemaskowanie; odsłonięcie skandalu

exposition [,ekspe'zyszyn] s. wystawa; wykład; przedstawienie; wyjaśnienie; opis; naświetlenie; ekspozycja; porzucenie (dziecka)

exposure [yks'poużer] s. wystawienie (na zimę etc.); ujawnienie; zdemaskowanie; naświetlenie; jedno zdjęcie na filmie

exposure-meter [yks'poużer 'mi:ter] s. światłomierz

expound [yks'paund] v. wykładać; wyjaśnić szczegółowo; przedstawić

express [yks'pres] s. ekspres; przesyłka pośpieszna; adj. wyraźny; umyślny; dokładny; adv. pośpiesznie; ekspresem

expression [yks'preszyn] s. wyrażenie; wyraz; ekspresja; ton; wydawanie; wytłoczenie; zwrot; wyciśnięcie; wyżymanie

expressive [yks'presyw] adj. wyrażający; wyrazisty; ekspresyjny; pełen wyrazu

expressly [yks'presly] adv. wyraźnie; kategorycznie; naumyślnie; specjalnie; formalnie

express way [yks'pres,łej] s. droga przelotowa (bez skrzyżowań jednopoziomowych)

expulsion [yks'palszyn] s. wydalenie; wyrzucenie; wypędzenie; wygnanie; wyparcie

exquisite ['ekskłyzyt] adj. wyborowy; wyborny; wyśmienity; nadzwyczajny; ostry; przeszywający; s. laluś; goguś; piękniś

extent ['ekstent] adj. pozostały; jeszcze istniejący

extemporaneous [eks,tempe
'rejnjes] adj. zaimprowizowany
extend [yks'tend] v. wyciągać
(się); rozciągać (się);
przeciągać (się); rozszerzać
(się); dawać i udzielać;
przedłużać; powiększać;
rozpościerać się
extendible [yks'tendybl] adj.
rozszerzalny; rozciągalny
extension [yks'tenszyn] s.
rozciąganie; wyciąganie;
rozwinięcie; przedłużenie;
zasiąg; rozmiar; zakres;
skrzydło (domu)
extensive [yks'tensyw] adj.
obszerny; rozległy;
ekstensywny
extent [yks'tent] s. obszar;
rozmiar; zasiąg; miara;
stopień; wysokość;
oszacowanie
extenuate [yks'tenjuejt] v.
zmniejszać; łagodzić
exterior [eks'tierjer] s.
powierzchowność; wygląd
zewnętrzny; strona
zewnętrzna; fasada
exterminate [yks'te:rmynejt] v.
tępić (np. pogląd);
wyniszczyć
external [eks'te:rnal] adj.
zewnętrzny; zagraniczny
extinct [yks'tynkt] adj. wygasły;
zgasły; zanikły; wymarły
extinguish [yks'tyngłysz] v.
zgasić; zagasić; niszczyć;
unicestwić; umierać; tępić
extirpate ['ekster,pejt] v.
wykorzeniać; plewić; tępić
extol [yks'tol] v. wysławiać;
wynosić pod niebiosa
extort [yks'tort] v. wymuszać;
zdzierać (pieniądze);
wydrzeć
extra ['ekstre] adj. specjalny;
dodatkowy; luksusowy;
nadzwyczajny; ponad normę;
adv. nadzwyczajnie;
dodatkowo; s. dodatek;
dopłata; rzecz szczególnie
dobra; statysta
extra charge ['ekstre,cza:rdż] s.

dopłata; nadpłata
extract ['ekstraekt] s. wyciąg;
ekstrakt; wyjątek; wypis
extract [yks'traekt] v.
wyciągać; wydobywać;
wypisywać
extraction [eks'traekszyn] s.
wyciągnięcie; wydobycie;
wyrwanie (zęba);
pochodzenie; ród
extradite ['ekstredajt] v.
wydawać (przestępcę przez
granicę) do miejsca zbrodni
extraordinary [yks'tro:rdnery] adj.
niezwykły; nadzwyczajny
extravagance [yks'traewygens]
s. przesada; rozrzutność;
nieumiarkowanie; głupstwo;
niedorzeczność;
ekstrawagancja
extravagant [yks'traewegent]
adj. rozrzutny; przesadny;
zwariowany; wygórowany;
szalony
extravaganza [yks,traewe
'gaenze] s. ekstrawagancja;
fantazja
extreme [yks'tri:m] adj. skrajny;
krańcowy; najdalszy; ostatni;
s. kraniec; ostateczna granica;
ostateczność; skrajność
extremity [yks'tremyty] s.
koniec; kraniec; skrajność;
krańcowość; kończyna;
krytyczne położenie; potrzeba;
ostateczność
extrude [yks'tru:d] v. wypierać;
wyrzucać; przeciągać lub
ciągnąć odlew; wytłoczyć
exuberant [yg'zju:berent] adj.
wybujały; pełen życia;
kwitnący; wylewny; płodny;
obfity
exult [yg'zalt] v. triumfować;
unosić się radością
eye [aj] s. oko; wzrok; v.
patrzeć
eyeball ['ajbo:l] s. gałka oczna w
oczodołach za powiekami
eye to eye ['aj,tu'aj] exp. oko w
oko
eyebrow ['ajbrau] s. brew
eyeglasses ['ajgla:sys] pl.

okulary; lupy; monokle
eyelash ['ajlaesz] s. rzęsa
eyelid ['ajlyd] s. powieka
eyesight ['aj-sajt] s. wzrok
eyewash ['ajłosz] s. woda do
oczu; mydlenie oczu (slang)
eyewitness ['aj'łytnes] s.
świadek naoczny

F

f [ef] szósta litera angielskiego
alfabetu; stopień "f" failure =
niedostatecznie
fable [fejbl] s. bajka
fabric ['faebryk] s. tkanina;
materiał; osnowa; szkielet;
budowa; wytwór; a. sukienny
fabricate ['faebrykejt] v.
tworzyć; wymyślać;
zmyślać; montować;
wyssać z palca; sfałszować
fabulous ['faebjules] adj.
bajeczny; legendarny;
fantastyczny
facade [fe'sa:d] s. fasada
face [fejs] s. twarz; oblicze;
mina; grymas; czelność;
śmiałość; powierzchnia lica;
prawa strona; obuch; v.
stawiać czoła; stanąć
wobec; napotykać; stać
frontem do ...; wykładać
powierzchnię; oblicować
face-lifting ['fejs-lyftyng] v.
operacyjnie usuwać
zmarszczki
facet ['faesyt] s. ścianka
(brylantu)
facetious [fe'si:szes] adj.
żartobliwy; krotochwilny
facilitate [fe'sylytejt] v.
ułatwiać; udogadniać;
uprzystępniać
facility [fe'sylyty] s. łatwość;
zręczność; udogodnienia;
układność; swada;
zgodność

facsimile [faek'simily] s.
dokładna reprodukcja; kopia
fact [faekt] s. fakt; stan
rzeczywisty; podstawa
twierdzenia
factor ['faekter] s. czynnik;
współczynnik; część;
okoliczność
faculty ['faekelty] s. zdolność;
władza; wydział; fakultet;
grono profesorskie; dar; zmysł
fad [faed] s. moda; kaprys;
konik; bzik; chwilowa moda;
dziwactwo
fade [fejd] v. więdnąć;
blednąć; zanikać; płowieć;
pełznąć
fail [feil] v. chybić; zawodzić;
nie udać się; brakować;
bankrutować; omieszkać;
słabnąć; załamać się;
zamierać; zepsuć się
failure ['fejljer] s. niepowodzenie;
brak; upadek; zawał (serca);
niezdara; stopień
niedostateczny; pechowiec
faint [fejnt] adj. słaby; omdlały;
bojaźliwy; s. omdlenie; v.
mdleć; słabnąć; zasłabnąć
fair [feer] adj. piękny; jasny;
uczciwy; honorowy; czysty;
pomyślny; niezły; adv. prosto;
honorowo; pomyślnie;
pięknie; v. wypogadzać się;
wygładzać; przepisywać na
czysto; s. targ; targi; jarmark;
targowisko
fairly ['feerly] adv. słusznie;
uczciwie; całkowicie; zupełnie;
dość; rzetelnie; wręcz; po
prostu
fair play ['feer'plej] szlachetne
postępowanie; czysta gra
fairness ['feernys] s. piękność;
jasność; sprawiedliwość;
bezstronność; uczciwość;
uroda
fairy ['feery] s. czarodziejka; adj.
zaczarowany; czarodziejski
fairy-tale ['feerytejl] s. bajka
faith [fejs] s. wiara; zaufanie;
wierność; wyznanie;
słowność

faithful ['fejgful] adj. wierny;
uczciwy; sumienny;
skrupulatny
faithless ['fejslys] adj. niewierny;
wiarołomny; zdradziecki
fake [fejk] v. fałszować;
oszukiwać; podrabiać; s.
fałszerstwo; oszustwo; kant;
lipa; szwindel
falcon ['fo:lken] s. sokół
fall; fell; fallen [fo:l; fel:; fo:len]
fall [fo:l] v. padać; opadać;
wpadać; marnieć; zdarzać
się; przypadać; s. upadek;
spadek; jesień; opad; schyłek;
obniżka
fall back ['fo:l,baek] v.cofać się
fall ill ['fo:l,yl] v. zachorować;
rozchorować się
fall in love ['fo:l,yn'law] v.
zakochać się
fallout ['fo:laĥt] s. skutek
uboczny; pył radioaktywny;
wrażenie na publiczności i
prasie (z wypowiedzi, planów)
fall out ['fo:l,aĥt] v. poróżnić
się; rozejść sięl (komenda)
fall short ['fo:l,szo:rt]
nieosiągnąć;
niewywiązywać się
fallen ['fo:len] upadły; zob. fall
false [fo:ls] adj. fałszywy;
kłamliwy; adv. zdradliwie;
fałszywie
falsehood ['fo:lshud] s. fałsz;
kłamstwo; nieprawda;
kłamliwość
falsify ['fo:lsyfaj] v. fałszować
przekręcać; kłamać;
zawodzić; podrabiać;
oszukać
falter ['fo:lter] v. chwiać się;
wahać się; potykać się;
jąkać się; s. chwiejność;
jąkanie
fame [fejm] s. sława; wieść;
fama
famed [fejmd] adj. sławny;
znany; głośny; słynący z
familiar [fe'myljer] adj. zażyły;
poufały; znany; obeznany
familiarity [fe,myly'aeryty] s.
zażyłość; poufałość;

obeznanie; znajomość
familiarize [fe'myljerajz] v.
obeznać; obznajomić;
oswoić; spoufalić;
spopularyzować
family ['faemyly] s. rodzina; adj.
rodzinny
family name ['faemyly,nejm] s.
nazwisko
family tree ['faemyly,tri:] s.
drzewo genealogiczne
famine ['faemyn] s. głód; klęska
głodu; ogólne braki
wszystkiego
famish ['faemysz] v. głodzić;
wygłodnieć; głodować;
morzyć głodem
famous ['fejmes] adj. znany;
sławny; znakomity; świetny;
nie byle jaki
fan [faen] v. wachlować;
rozdmuchiwać; wiać;
rozpościerać; wywiewać; s.
wachlarz; wentylator; wialnia;
żagiel i śmigło (wiatraka);
entuzjasta; miłośnik; kibic; a.
wachlarzowaty
fanatic [fe'naetyk] adj. zagorzały;
fanatyczny; s. fanatyk
fanciful ['faensyful] adj.
dziwaczny; kapryśny;
fantastyczny; zmyślony;
wyszukany; fantazyjny
fancy ['faensy] s. urojenie;
złudzenie; fantazja; kaprys;
humor; pomysł; chętka; a.
pstry
fancy dress ball ['faensy'dres
,bo:l] s. bal kostiumowy
fancy-free ['faensy,fri:] adj.
wolny od trosk; nie zakochany
fancy work ['faensy,łe:rk] s.
robótki ręczne
fang [faeng] s. ząb jadowity;
kieł; sztyft; korzeń; v. dławić
pompę
fantastic [faen'taestyk] adj.
fantastyczny; s. fantasta
fantasy ['faentsy] s. fantazja;
wyobraźnia; kaprys
far [fa:r] adv. daleko
far away ['fa:r,ełej] adv. hen;
daleko; adj. daleki; odległy

far from ['fa:r,from] adv.
bynajmniej; daleko od
fare [feer] s. pasażer; bilet
pasażerski; pożywienie;
potrawa; v. być w położeniu;
mieć się; wieść się; czuć
się; odżywiać się; jadać;
podróżować
farewell [,feer'łel] s. pożegnanie;
adj. pożegnalny; v. żegnaj; do
widzenia
farfetched [,fa:r'feczt] adj.
przesadny; naciągany;
wyszukany; nierozsądny
far-flung [,fa:r'flang] adj. szeroko
rozrzucony; rozgałęziony;
zakrojony na szeroką skalę
farm [fa:rm] s. ferma;
gospodarstwo rolne; kolonia
hodowlana; v. uprawiać;
dzierżawić; wydzierżawiać;
wynajmować;
poddzierżawiać; prowadzić
gospodarstwo
farmer ['fa:rmer] s. rolnik;
farmer; dzierżawca; hodowca
farmhand ['fa:rm,haend] s.
parobek; robotnik rolny
farmhouse ['fa:rm,haus] s.
dworek; gospodarski dom
mieszkalny
farming ['fa:rmyng] s. rolnictwo;
gospodarka rolna; dzierżawa
farm worker [,fa:rm'łe:rker] s.
robotnik rolny; parobek
farmyard ['fa:rm,ja:rd] s.
podwórze fermy; podwórze
gospodarskie na fermie
farsighted ['fa:r'sajtyd] adj.
przewidujący; dalekowidz;
dalekowzroczny
farther ['fa:rdzer] adj. dalszy;
adv. dalej; ponadto; poza tym;
prócz tego
farthest ['fa:rdzest] adj.
najdalszy; adv. najdalej;
najpóźniej
fascinate ['faesynejt] v.
urzekać; czarować;
fascynować; hipnotyzować
zachwycić
fascination [,faesy'nejszyn] s.
urok; czar; oczarowanie;

olśnienie
fascist ['faeszyst] s. faszysta;
adj. faszystowski;
faszystowska
fashion ['faeszyn] s. moda;
fason; kształt; wzór; sposób;
v. kształtować; fasonować;
modelować; urabiać
fashionable ['faesznebl] adj.
modny; s. człowiek wytworny
fast [faest] adj. szybki;
przytwierdzony; mocny;
twardy; zwodniczy; adv.
mocno; pewnie; trwale; v.
pościć; s. post
fasten ['faesn] v. umocować;
zamykać; przymocować
fastener ['faesner] s.
przymocowanie (np.
gwóźdź); spinacz; zatrzask;
zasuwka
fastidious [fes'tydjes] adj.
wybredny; grymaśny;
wymagający
fat [faet] s. tłuszcz; tusza; adj.
tłusty; tuczny; głupi; tępy;
urodzajny; zyskowny
fatal ['fejtl] adj. fatalny;
śmiertelny; nieuchronny
fate ['fejt] s. los; przeznaczenie;
zguba; fatum; v. los rządzi ...
father ['fa:dzer] s. ojciec
fatherhood ['fa:dzerhud] s.
ojcostwo; starszeństwo (w
służbie)
father-in-law ['fa:dzerynlo:] s.
teść; ojciec męża lub żony
fatherland ['fa:dzerlaend] s.
ojczyzna; ojczysty kraj
fatherly ['fa:dzerly] adj.
ojcowski; jak ojciec; dobrotliw
fathom ['faedzem] s. sążeń
fathomless ['faedzemlys] s.
bezdenny; niezgłębiony
fatigue [fe'ti:g] s. zmęczenie
(człowieka lub materiału);
służba porządkowa; v.
trudzić; męczyć
fatten ['faetn] v. tuczyć; tyć;
użyźniać ziemię; utyć;
utuczyć
fattening ['faetnyng] adj.
tuczący

fatty ['faety] adj. tłuszczowy; s.
tłuścioch; grubas
faucet ['fo:syt] s. kurek (od
wody); czop; tuleja
fault ['fo:lt] s. błąd; wada; wina;
uskok; usterka; brak; defekt
faultless ['fo:ltlys] adj.
bezbłędny; nienaganny;
doskonały
faulty ['fo:lty] adj. wadliwy;
nieprawidłowy; nieścisły;
błędny
favor ['fejwer] s. łaska;
uprzejmość; upominek; v.
sprzyjać; zaszczycać;
faworyzować
favorable ['fejwerebl] adj.
życzliwy; łaskawy;
sprzyjający; korzystny (dla
kogoś, czegoś)
favorite ['fejweryt] s. ulubieniec;
faworyt; adj. ulubiony
fawn [fo:n] v. ocielić; łasić się;
przymilać (się); płaszczyć się
(przed kimś); s. jelonek;
sarenka; adj. brunatny; płowy
FAX ['faeks] s. elektroniczna
transmisja kopii dokumentów;
system przesyłania kopii
dokumentów przez telefon
(zob. facsimile)
fear [fier] s. strach; obawa; v.
bać się; obawiać się
fearful ['fierful] adj. okropny;
straszny; wystraszony;
bojaźliwy; bojący się; pełen
strachu
fearless ['fierlys] adj.
nieustraszony; bardzo
odważny
feasible ['fi:zebl] adj. wykonalny;
możliwy do przeprowadzenia
feast [fi:st] s. święto; odpust;
biesiada; v. ucztować; sycić
się; ugaszać pragnienie
feat [fi:t] s. wyczyn; czyn
(bohaterski); (dokazana) sztuka
feather ['fedzer] s. pióro; v.
zdobić piórami
featherbed ['fedzerbed] s.
piernat; pierzyna; lekka praca
feathered ['fedzerd] adj.
upierzony; pokryty piórami

feathery ['fedzery] adj. puchaty;
miękki jak puch; leciutki
feature ['fi:czer] s. cecha; rys;
atrakcja; film
długometrażowy; v.
cechować; odgrywać
February ['februery] s. luty
fed [fed] adj. karmiony; zob.
feed
federal ['federel] adj. związkowy;
federalny
federation [,fede'rejszyn] s.
federacja; konfederacja
fee [fi:] s. opłata; wpisowe;
należność; honorarium; v.
płacić honorarium; płacić
wpisowe
feeble ['fi:bl] adj. słaby
feed [fi:d] fed [fi:d; fed; fed]
feed [fi:d] v. karmić; paść;
zasilać; s. pasza; obrok;
zasilacz; posuw
feeder [fi:der] s. boczna (droga);
dopływ; przewód zasilający
feel; felt [fi:l; felt; felt]
feel [fi:l] v. czuć (się);
odczuwać; macać; dotykać
feel well ['fi:l,tel] v. czuć się
dobrze; być zdrowym
feel bad ['fi:l,baed] v. czuć się
źle
feeler ['fi:ler] s. macka; sonda;
próbny balon; szperacz
feeling ['fi:lyng] s. dotyk;
uczucie; odczucie; poczucie;
takt; wrażliwość; adj.
wrażliwy; czuły;
współczujący; szczery;
wzruszony
feet [fi:t] pl. stopy; nogi
feign [fejn] v. udawać;
symulować; znaleźć
wymówkę
fell [fel] v. ścinać (drzewo);
zob. fall
felloe ['felou] s. dzwono (koła)
fellow ['felou] s. towarzysz;
człowiek; chłop; gość; facet;
odpowiednik; wykładowca;
adiunkt
fellow being ['felou bi:yng] s.
bliźni
fellow citizen ['felou'sytyzen] s.

współobywatel
fellowship ['felouszyp] s. udział;
wspólnota; związek;
towarzystwo; przyjaźń; cech
felon ['felen] s. przestępca; adj.
okrutny; zły; zbrodniczy
felony ['feleny] s. przestępstwo;
zbrodnia
felt [felt] czuły; zob. feel
felt [felt] s. wojłok; filc
female ['fi:mejl] s. kobieta;
niewiasta; samica; adj.
żeński; kobiecy; wewnętrzny
(gwint)
feminine ['femynyn] adj. żeński;
kobiecy; zniewieściały; s.
rodzaj żeński; a. rodzaju
żeńskiego
fen [fen] s. bagno; trzęsawisko;
nizina bagienna
fence [fens] s. płot; ogrodzenie;
szermierka; v. ogrodzić;
fechtować się; odpowiadać
wykrętnie
fencing ['fensyng] s. szermierka;
płot; ogrodzenie; paserstwo
fend for ['fend,fo:r] v.
zaspokajać potrzeby;
utrzymywać
fend off ['fend,of] v. odbijać;
odparowywać; chronić;
ochraniać
fender ['fender] s. błotnik;
zderzak; zasłona
fennel ['fenel] s. koper
ferment ['fe:rment] s. ferment;
ermentacja; v. wywoływać
fermentację; podniecać;
fermentować
fermentation [,fe:rmen'tejszyn] s.
fermentacja; ferment
fern [fe:rn] s. paproć
ferocity [fe'rosyty] s. dzikość;
okrucieństwo; srogość
ferry ['fery] v. przeprawiać
promem; kursować; s. prom
ferryboat ['ferybout] s. prom
fertile ['fe:rtajl] adj. żyzny;
płodny; zapłodniony;
obfitujący
fertility [fer'tylyty] s. żyzność;
płodność; urodzajność
fertilize ['fe:rtylajz] v. użyźniać

nawozić; zapładniać;
zapylać
fertilizer ['fe:rtylajzer] s. nawóz
sztuczny
fervent ['fe:rwent] adj. żarliwy;
gorący; płomienny; gorliwy
fester ['fester] v. jątrzyć (się);
ropieć; gnić; s. ropiejąca
rana; mały wrzód; ropniak;
zajad
festival ['festewel] adj.
świąteczny; odświętny; s.
święto
festive ['festyw] adj. uroczysty;
wesoły; radosny; biesiadny
festivity [fes'tywyty] s.
wesołość; zabawa;
uroczystość
fetch [fecz] v. iść po coś;
przynieść; przywieźć; s.
odległość
fetish [fet'ysz] s. fetysz
fetter ['feter] v. skuć; spętać
feud [fju:d] s. lenno; waśń
rodowa; wojna między
klanami
feudal ['fju:dl] adj. feudalny
fever ['fy:wer] s. gorączka
feverish ['fy:werysz] adj.
gorączkowy;
rozgorączkowany
few [fju:] adj. & pron. mało;
kilka; niewielu; nieliczni; kilku;
kilkoro
fiance [fi'a:nsej] s. narzeczony(a)
fib [fyb] s. kłamstwo; v.
cyganić; okładać; s. cios;
uderzenie
fiber ['fajber] s. włókno; siła
ducha; charakter; łyko;
budowa
fibrous ['fajbres] adj. włóknisty;
łykowaty
fickle ['fykl] adj. zmienny;
niestały; płochy; wietrzny
fiction ['fykszyn] s. fikcja;
urojenie; beletrystyka; wymysł
fictitious [fyk'tyszes] a. fikcyjny;
urojony; fałszywy
fiddle ['fydl] v. grać na
skrzypcach; baraszkować; s.
skrzypce
fiddler ['fydler] s. skrzypek;

skrzypaczka

fidelity [fy'delyty] s. wierność;
dokładność; ścisłość

fidget ['fydżyt] v. wiercić się;
niepokoić się; s. niepokój;
człowiek niespokojny

fidgety ['fydżyty] adj. wiercący
się; niespokojny; niecierpliwy

field [fi:ld] s. pole; boisko;
drużyna; dziedzina; v.
ustawiać na boisku;
zatrzymać (piłkę);
poprowadzić do akcji

field-events ['fi:ld,ywents] pl.
lekkoatletyka

field-glasses ['fi:ld,glasys] pl.
lornetka polowa

field-gun ['fi:ld,gan] s. działo
polowe

fiend [fy:nd] s. zły duch; szatan;
demon; nałogowiec;
zagorzalec

fierce [fiers] adj. dziki; srogi;
zażarty; wściekły; zawzięty;
nieopanowany; gwałtowny

fiery ['fajery] adj. ognisty;
płomienny; palący; zapalny;
burzliwy; popędliwy;
choleryczny

fife [fajf] s. piszczałka; v. grać
na piszczałce (na fujarce)

fifteen ['fyf'ti:n] num.
piętnaście; piętnaścioro;
piętnastka

fifteenth ['fyf'ti:nt] num.
piętnasty; jedna piętnasta
część

fiftieth ['fyftjet] num.
pięćdziesiąty; jedna
pięćdziesiąta

fifty ['fyfty] num. pięćdziesiąt

fig [fyg] s. figa; strój

fight; fought; fought [fajt; fo:t;
fo:t]

fight [fajt] s. walka; bitwa;
zapasy; bój; duch do walki;
mecz bokserski; v. walczyć
(przeciw lub o coś); bić się

fighter ['fajter] s. bojownik;
zapaśnik; samolot myśliwski

figurative ['fygjurejtyw] adj.
obrazowy; przenośny;
symboliczny

figure ['fyger] s. kształt; postać;
wizerunek; cyfra; wzór; v.
figurować; liczyć;
rachować; oznaczać cenami;
wyobrażać; przedstawiać

figure out ['fyger,aut] v.
obliczać; wynosić; składać
się na

figure skating ['fyger,skejtyng] s.
jazda figurowa na łyżwach

filament ['fylement] s. włókno;
nitka; drucik jarzeniowy; żyła
mineralna

file [fajl] s. rejestr; archiwum;
seria; pilnik; v. archiwować;
defilować; piłować pilnikiem;
wnosić (podanie, skargę);
iść rzędem (rzędami);
maszerować

fill [fyl] v. napełniać;
plombować ząb; osadzać; s.
wypełnienie; napicie i
najedzenie do syta; nasyp;
ładunek; porcja

fill in ['fyl,yn] v. zapełniać;
wypełniać (formularze,
blankiety)

fill up ['fyl,ap] v. wypełniać;
zapełniać; nabierać benzyny

fillet ['fylyt] s. wstążki; zraz
zawijany; dzwonko; v.
przepasywać; wycinać filety

fillet ['fylej] v. dzielić na
dzwonka; wycinać dzwonka

filling ['fylyng] s. nadziewka;
plomba; wątek; zapas
benzyny

filing station ['fylyng,st'ejszyn] s.
stacja benzynowa

filly ['fyly] s. źrebica; koza;
młoda dziewczyna; dzierlatka

film [fylm] s. powłoka; błona;
warstwa; film; mgiełka;
bielmo; v. pokrywać błoną;
filmować

filter ['fylter] s. filtr; sączek; v.
filtrować; przeciekać

filth [fyls] s. brud; plugastwo

filthy ['fylsy] adj. brudny;
plugawy; niegodziwy;
sprośny

fin [fyn] s. płetwa; v. obcinać
płetwy; ruszać płetwami

finagle ['fy'nejgl] v. oszukiwać;
wyłudzać; nabierać
final ['fajnl] adj. końcowy;
ostateczny; s. finał (sport,
egzamin etc.); coś
ostatecznego
finally ['fajnly] adv. w końcu;
wreszcie; na końcu;
ostatecznie
finance [faj'naens] s. finanse;
skarbowość; v. finansować;
udzielać pożyczki
financial [faj'naenszel] adj.
pieniężny; finansowy
financier [,fynaen'sjer] s.
finansista; v. spekulować;
sprzeniewierzać pieniądze
finch [fyncz] s. łuszczak; ptak z
krótkim dziobem
find; found; found [fajnd; faund;
faund]
find [fajnd] v. znajdować;
konstatować; dowiedzieć się
find out ['fajnd,aut] v. wykryć;
wynaleźć; dowiedzieć się
finder ['fajnder] s. znalazca;
odkrywca; wizjer; dalekomierz
finding ['fajndyng] s. odkrycie;
stwierdzenie; dane; wniosek
fine [fajn] adj. piękny; misterny;
czysty; przedni; wyszukany;
dokładny; adv. świetnie;
wspaniale; s. grzywna; kara;
v. ukarać grzywną
finery ['fajnry] s. szyk; elegancja;
strojny ubiór
finger ['fynger] s. palec; kciuk;
v. przebierać w palcach;
wskazywać palcem; brać
palcami
finger nail ['fynger,nejl] s.
paznokieć
finger print ['fynger,prynt] odcisk
palca
finish ['fynysz] s. koniec;
wykończenie; v. kończyć;
skończyć; wykończyć;
dokończyć
finite ['fajnajt] adj. skończony;
ograniczony; końcowy
Finnish ['fynysz] adj. fiński
fir [fe:r] s. jodła; jedlina
fire ['fajer] s. ogień; pożar

fire alarm ['fajer,e'la:rm] s.
sygnał pożarowy; alarm
pożarowy
firearm ['fajera:rm] s. broń palna
(armaty, strzelby etc.)
firebug ['fajer,bag] s. świetlik;
robaczek świętojański
fire brigade ['fajerbry,gejd] s.
straż pożarna
fire department ['fajer
,dy'pa:rtment] s. miejska straż
pożarna; straż ogniowa
fire engine ['fajer'endżyn] s. wóz
straży ogniowej (pompa)
fire escape ['fajerys,kejp] s.
wyjście zapasowe; schody
zapasowe
fire extinguisher ['fajer
yks,tyngłyszer] s. gaśnica
fireman ['fajermen] s. strażak
fireplace ['fajer-plejs] s. kominek;
palenisko
fireproof ['fajerpru:f] adj.
ogniotrwały; ognioodporny
fireside ['fajersajd] s. przy
kominku; kominek; ognisko
domowe
firewood ['fajerłud] s. drzewo
opałowe; drewno opałowe
fireworks ['fajerłe:rks] pl. ognie
sztuczne; hałaśliwe sceny
firm [fe:rm] s. firma; adv.
mocno; adj. pewny;
stanowczy; trwały; v. ubijać;
osadzać (mocno); umacniać
się
firmness ['fe:rmnys] s. stałość;
trwałość; stanowczość;
jędrność; moc; energia
first ['fe:rst] adj. pierwszy; adv.
najpierw; po raz pierwszy;
początkowo; na początku
first of all ['fe:rst,ow'o:l] przede
wszystkim; najpierw
first aid ['fe:rst,ejd] pierwsza
pomoc; doraźna pomoc;
opatrunek
first aid kit ['fe:rst,ejd kyt]
podręczna apteczka; zestaw
pierwszej pomocy
(opatrunków etc.)
firstborn ['fe:rstbo:rn] adj.
pierworodny (syn, dziecko)

first class ['fe:rst'klas] s.
pierwsza klasa; a. najlepszej
jakości
first-class ['fe:rst'klas] adj.
pierwszorzędny; wspaniały
first floor ['fe:rst flo:r] s. parter;
w Anglii pierwsze piętro
first hand ['fe:rst,haend] adj.
bezpośredni; z pierwszej ręki
firstly ['fe:rstly] adv. po
pierwsze; najpierw
first name ['fe:rst,nejm] s. imię
(chrzestne)
first-rate ['fe:rst,rejt] adj.
pierwszorzędny; adv.
pierwszorzędnie; bardzo
dobrze
firth [fe:rs] n. odnoga morska;
zatoka (zwłaszcza w Szkocji)
fish [fysz] s. ryba; v. łowić ryby
fish-bone ['fyszboun] s. ość
fisherman ['fyszemen] s. rybak
fishery ['fyszery] s.
rybołówstwo; teren połowu
lub hodowli
fishing ['fyszyng] s.
wędkarstwo; rybołówstwo;
połów
fishing line ['fyszyng,lajn] s.
linka; żyłka od wędki
fishing rod ['fyszyng,rod] s.
wędka
fishing tackle ['fyszyng,taekl] s.
sprzęt rybacki
fishmonger ['fyszmanger] s.
handlarz ryb; sklep z rybami
fission ['fyszyn] s. dzielenie;
rozbicie (atomu);
rozszczepienie; rozerwanie
fissure ['fyszer] s. szczelina;
pęknięcie; v. rozszczepiać;
pękać; łupać (się)
fist [fyst] s. pięść; v. uderzać
fit [fyt] s. atak (choroby, gniewu
etc.); krój; dopasowanie; adj.
dostosowany; odpowiedni;
nadający się; gotów; zdatny;
dobrze leżący; v. sprostać;
dobrze leżeć; przygotować
się
fit on [fyt on] v. przymierzać
fit out [fyt aut] v. zaopatrywać;
s. wyposażenie; umeblowanie

fitness ['fytnys] s.
stosowność; kondycja;
trafność (uwagi);
przyzwoitość
fitter ['fyter] s. monter; krawiec
dokonujący przymiarek;
ślusarz
fitting ['fytyng] s. okucie;
oprawa; przymiarka; adj.
odpowiedni; właściwy;
trafny; stosowny
five [fajw] num. pięć; pięcioro;
piąta (godzina); piątka (numer
obuwia)
fix [fyks] v. umocować;
przyczepiać; ustalać;
utkwić; zgęszczać; tężeć;
krzepnąć; urządzić kogoś
(źle); usytuować;
zaaranżować wynik
(zapasów); s. kłopot; dylemat;
położenie nawigacyjne (statku,
samolotu etc.)
fix up [fyks,ap] v. naprawić;
uporządkować; ulokować
(kogoś)
fixed [fykst] adj. trwały; stały;
nieruchomy; niezmienny
fixedly ['fyksydly] adv. stale;
trwale; uporczywie
fixture ['fyksczer] s. urządzenie
przymocowane
fizz [fyz] s. syk; napój musujący;
v. syczeć; musować
flabbergast ['flaebergaest] v.
zdumieć; odebrać mowę (ze
zdumienia); oszołamiać
flabby ['flaeby] adj. zwiotczały;
obwisły; miękki; słaby;
niedbały; bez charakteru
flag [flaeg] s. flaga; chorągiew;
lotka; v. wywieszać flagę;
sygnalizować
flagstone ['flaeg,stoun] s. płyta
brukowa; płyta chodnikowa
flak [flaek] s. artyleria
przeciwlotnicza (niemiecka)
flake [flejk] s. płatek; łuska;
iskra; v. prószyć;
odpryskiwać łuszczyć;
padać płatkami
flake off ['flejk,of] v. złuszczyć
(się); odpadać płatkami

flame 412 fling

flame [flejm] s. płomień;
miłość; v. zionąć;
błyszczeć; płonąć; opalać;
migotać; być podnieconym
flank [flaenk] s. bok; flanka; v.
flankować; strzec flanki
flannel ['flaenl] s. flanela; v.
wycierać flanelą; ubierać we
flanelą (lekka wełna)
flap [flaep] s. trzepot; klapnięcie;
klapa; poła; płat; pokrywa; v.
trzepotać; zwisać; klapnąć;
uderzyć czymś płaskim
flare [fleer] v. błyszczeć;
sygnalizować; popisywać
się; rozszerzać się; s. jasny
płomień
flare up [fleer ap] s. wybuch;
błysk; v. wybuchnąć
(gniewem, płomieniem);
reagować gwałtownie
flash [flaesz] s. błysk; blask; adj.
błyskotliwy; fałszywy;
gwarowy; v. zabłysnąć;
sygnalizować; pędzić;
mknąć; wysyłać
(natychmiastowo
wiadomości)
flashbulb ['flaeszbalb] s.
żarówka (do zdjęć); flesz
flashlight ['flaeszlajt] s. latarka
(elektryczna)
flashy ['flaeszy] adj. błyskotliwy
(chwilowo); jaskrawy;
krzykliwy
flask [flaesk] s. flaszka; flakon;
kolba; opleciona flaszka wina
flat [flaet] adj. płaski; płytki;
nudny; równy; stanowczy;
oczywisty; matowy;
bezbarwny; adv. płasko;
stanowczo; dokładnie; s.
płaszczyzna; równina;
mieszkanie; przedziurawiona
dętka; v. rozpłaszczyć;
matować
flatten ['flaetn] v. spłaszczyć
(się); matowieć; wietrzeć;
równać
flatter ['flaeter] v. pochlebiać
flattery ['flaetery] s.
pochlebstwo; schlebianie
komuś

flavor ['flejwer] s. smak; zapach;
v. dawać smak; mieć
posmak
flaw [flo:] s. skaza; rysa;
pęknięcie; v. psuć; pękać
flawless ['flo:les] adj. bez skazy;
(przedstawienie) bez usterek
flax [flaeks] s. len
flaxen [flak'sn] adj. płowy; lniany
flea [fli:] s. pchła
fled [fled] zob. flee
fledgling ['fledżlyng] s. świeżo
opierzony ptak; żółtodziób
flee; fled; fled [fli:; fled; fled]
flee [fli:] v. uciekać; pierzchać
fleece [fli:s] s. runo; wełna;
czupryna; puch; v. strzyc;
skubać; pokrywać puchem
fleet [fli:t] s. flota; park
pojazdów; v. mknąć;
przemknąć; mijać; adj.
płytki; adv. płytko
flesh [flesz] s. ciało; miąższ
fleshy ['fleszy] adj. mięsisty;
tłusty; cielesny; zmysłowy
flew [flu:] zob. fly
flexible [fl'eksybl] adj. giątki;
gibki; układny; obrotny;
elastyczny; łatwo
przystosowujący się;
ustępliwy; poddający się
flick [flyk] s. przytyk;
śmignięcie; smuga; v.
śmignąć; trzepnąć; rzucać
się; trzepotać się; zapalać
zapalniczkę
flicker ['flyker] s. mig; miganie;
drganie; trzepot; v. migać;
drgać; trzepotać; machać;
lekko się poruszać
flier ['flajer] s. lotnik; ulotka;
pośpieszny pociąg etc.
flight [flajt] s. lot; przelot;
ucieczka; kondygnacja
schodów
flight engineer ['flajt,endży'nier]
s. mechanik pokładowy
flimsy ['flymzy] adj. cienki;
wątły; słaby (papier,
wymówka ...)
flinch [flyncz] v. uchylać się;
cofać się; drgać; s. unik
fling; flung; flung [flyng; flang;

flang]
fling [flyŋg] v. rzucać (się);
powalić; wypaść; wierzgać
fling open ['flyŋ,oupen] v.
rozewrzeć (gwałtownie)
flint [flynt] s. krzemień;
krzesiwo; kamyk do
zapalniczki
flip [flyp] v. prztykać; rzucać;
wyprztykiwać; s. prztyk
flippant ['flypent] adj.
niepoważny; impertynencki
flipper ['flyper] s. płetwa nożna;
graba; łapa; błona pławna
flirt [fle:rt] v. flirtować;
machać; s. flirciarz; flirciarka;
machnięcie (raptowne)
flirtation [,fle:r'tejszyn] s. flirt;
powierzchowny romans
flit [flyt] v. biegać; fruwać;
wyjechać; poruszać się
zwinnie
float [flout] v. unosić się;
pływać na powierzchni;
spławiać; puszczać w obieg;
lansować; s. pływak; tratwa;
platforma na kołach; gładzik
do tynku; niezdecydowany
ruch
flock [flok] s. trzoda; stado;
tłum; v. tłoczyć się; iść
tłumem; gromadzić się
floe [flou] s. kra (lodowa)
flog [flog] v. chłostać; smagać;
bić; biczować się
flood [flad] s. powódź; wylew;
potok; v. zalewać nawadniać
floodlights ['flad,lajts] pl.
reflektory (szeroko-stożkowe)
flood tide ['fladtajd] s. przypływ
(morza); fala powodziowa
floor [flo:r] s. podłoga; dno
floor cloth ['flo:rklo:s] s. szmata
do podłogi; linoleum
floor lamp ['flo:r,laemp] s. lampa
stojąca na podłodze
floor show ['flo:r,szou] s.
przedstawienie kabaretowe
flop [flop] s. klapanie; klapa;
fiasko; v. klapnąć; załamać
się; zrobić klapę; a.
dziadowski
florist ['floryst] s. kwiaciarz;

kwiaciarka; hodowca kwiatów
flounder ['flaunder] s. flądra;
brnięcie; v. brnąć; brodzić;
błądzić; wystąkać (mową)
flour [flauer] s. mąka; v. mleć
na mąkę; dodawać mąki
(posypywać)
flourish ['flarysz] s. fanfara;
wymachiwanie; v. kwitnąć;
zdobić kwiatami;
wymachiwać
flow [flou] s. strumień; prąd;
przepływ; dopływ; v. płynąć;
lać się; zalewać; ruszać się
płynnie
flower [flauer] s. kwiat; v.
kwitnąć; być w rozkwicie
flown [floun] zob. fly
fluctuate ['flaktjuejt] v. falować;
wahać się; być
niezdecydowanym
flu [flu:] s. grypa; influenca
fluent ['fluent] adj. płynny; biegły
i wymowny (mówca, pisarz)
fluff [flaf] s. puch; v. trzepać;
knocić
fluffy ['flafy] adj. puszysty; lekki
fluid ['flu:yd] s. płyn; adj.
płynny; płynnie poruszający
się
flung [flaŋg] zob. fling
flunk [flaŋk] v. oblać (egzamin);
spalić (ucznia); nie zdać;
zawalić
flurry ['fle:ry] s. wichura; ulewa;
śnieżyca; podniecenie;
rozgardiasz; v. oszałamiać;
denerwować; wprowadzać
zamieszanie
flush [flasz] v. rumienić się;
napełniać; spłukiwać; s.
rumieniec; rozkwit; blask; adj.
wylewający się; krzepki;
rumiany; równy; etc.; adv.
równo; prosto; gładko; pełno;
poziomo; sowicie (wyposażać
w pieniądze)
fluster ['flaster] s. podniecenie;
niepokój; v. podniecać;
oszałamiać; kręcić się
flute [flu:t] s. flet; rowkowanie
flutter ['flater] s. trzepotanie;
dygotanie; niepokój; v.

trzepotać; drzeć; dygotać;
płoszyć; powodować
trzepotanie
flux [flaks] s. prąd; przepływ;
potok; płynność; krwotok;
przypływ; pasta do lutowania
fly [flaj] s. mucha; klapka
fly; flew; flown [flaj; flu; floun]
v. latać; lecieć; powiewać;
uciekać; przewozić
samolotem; puszczać
(latawca)
fly across [,flaj e'kros] v.
przelatywać (przez)
flyblown ['flaj-bloun] adj.
popstrzony przez muchy
fly into a rage ['flaj,yntu ej'rejdż]
v. wpaść w pasję
flyer ['flajer] s. lotnik
flying ['flajyng] adj. latający;
lotny; lotniczy; krótkotrwały;
samolotowy; pośpieszny
flying boat ['flajynbout] s.
hydroplan (do wodowania)
flying buttress ['flajyn,batrys] s.
łuk przyporowy
flying machine ['flajyng,meszi:n]
s. samolot
flying time ['flajyng,tajm] s. czas
przelotu; czas lotu
fly weight ['flaj,łejt] s. waga
musza (112 funtów lub mniej)
flywheel ['flajhłi:l] s. koło
zamachowe (do regulowania
szybkości)
foal [foul] s. źrebię
foam [foum] s. piana; v. pienić
się; a. pianowy; piankowy
foamy ['foumy] adj. pieniący się;
pienisty; spieniony
focus ['foukes] s. ognisko;
ogniskowa; v. skupiać;
ogniskować; koncentrować;
ześrodkowywać
fodder ['foder] s. pasza
foe [fou] s. wróg; przeciwnik
fog [fog] s. mgła; v. otumaniać
foggy ['fogy] adj. mglisty
foible ['fojbl] s. słabostka; lekka
słabość charakteru;
słabość; wątłość
foil [fojl] s. folia; tło; floret; trop;
ślad; v. udaremnić; zacierać

(ślad); niweczyć
fold [fould] s. fałda; zagięcie;
zagroda (owiec); v. składać;
zaginać (się); splatać;
zamykać owce (w owczarni);
fałdować
folder ['foulder] s. składana
teczka; broszura; falcownik
folding ['fouldyng] adj. składany;
rozsuwany; s. fałd; fałda
folding boat ['fouldyng bout]
składana łódź (turystyczna)
folding chair ['fouldyng,czeer]
składane krzesło (kampingowe)
foliage ['fouljydż] s. listowie;
liście (rosnące); ulistnienie
folk [fouk] s. ludzie; krewni; lud;
rasa; adj. ludowy;
folklorystyczny
folklore ['fouklo:r] s. folklor
folksy ['fouksy] adj. towarzyski;
prosty; ludzki
folk song ['fouksong] s. pieśń
ludowa (regionalna etc.)
follow ['folou] v. iść za;
następować za; śledzić;
rozumieć (kogoś); wnikać;
gonić; wynikać
follower ['folouer] s. stronnik;
zwolennik; uczeń; pomocnik
following ['folouyng] s.
zwolennicy; adj. następujący;
następny; s. orszak; świta;
posłuch; autorytet
folly ['foly] s. szaleństwo
foment [fou'ment] v. podżegać;
podsycać; nagrzewać;
pobudzać
fond [fond] adj. kochający;
czuły; łatwowierny; głupio
czuły
fondle ['fondl] v. pieścić
fondness ['fondnys] s. czułość;
miłość; zamiłowanie; pociąg
food [fu:d] s. żywność;
strawa; pokarm; jedzenie; a.
żywnościowy; odżywczy
fool [fu:l] s. głupiec; głuptas;
błazen; v. błaznować;
wyśmiewać; oszukiwać;
okpiwać; partaczyć
foolhardy ['fu:l,ha:rdy] adj.
szaleńczy; wariacki;

lekkomyślny; nieroztropny; gwałtowny

foolish ['fu:lysz] adj. głupi

foolishness ['fu:lysznys] s. głupota; głupstwo; bzdura; nonsens

foolproof ['fu:l,pru:f] adj. niezawodny; nie do zepsucia

foot [fut] s. stopa; dół; spód; miara (30.5 cm); piechota; v. płacić

foot the bill ['fut,ty'byl] v. zapłacić rachunek

football ['fut,bo:l] s. piłka nożna; futbol; piłka do nożnej

foot brake ['fut,brejk] s. hamulec nożny w (samochodzie)

foothills ['fut,hylz] pl. podgórze (przy łańcuchu górskim)

foothold ['fut,hould] s. oparcie (dla nóg); miejsce gdzie można stanąć; pewna pozycja

footing ['futyng] s. fundament; ostoja; podstawa; położenie

footpath ['futpas] s. ścieżka dla pieszych; chodnik

footprint ['futprynt] s. ślad stopy

footstep ['fut,step] s. odgłos kroku; ślad; długość kroku

for [fo:r] prep. dla; zamiast; z; do; na; żeby; że; za; po; co do; co się tyczy; jak na; mimo; wbrew; po coś; z powodu; conj. ponieważ; bowiem; gdyż; albowiem; dlatego że

for two years ['fo:-tu-je:rs] przez dwa lata

forbade [fe:r'bejd] zob. forbid

forbear; forbore; forborne [fo:'beer; fe'bo:r; fe'bo:rn]

forbear ['fo:r'beer] v. znosić cierpliwie; powstrzymywać (się); s. wyrozumiałość; przodek

forbid; forbade; forbidden [fer'byd; fe:r'bejd; fer'bydn]

forbid [fer'byd] v. zakazywać; zabraniać; nie dopuszczać; uniemożliwiać; nie pozwalać

forbidding [fe'rbydyng] adj.

odpychający; posępny; ponury

forbore [fer'bo:r] zob. forbear

forborne [fer'bo:rn] zob. forbear

force [fo:rs] s. siła; moc; potęga; sens; v. zmuszać; pędzić; wpychać; forsować

forced landing ['fo:rst,laendyng] przymusowe lądowanie

forceps ['fo:rsyps] pl. kleszcze; szczypce; szczypczyki

forcible ['fo:rsybl] adj. gwałtowny; przymusowy; przekonywujący; mocny; dosadny; bezprawny

ford [fo:rd] v. przeprawiać się brodem; s. bród (płytkie miejsce)

fore [fo:r] adj. przedni; adv. na przedzie; s. przednia część

foreboding [fo:r'boudyng] s. przeczucie (złego); złe przeczucie

forecast ['fo:r-ka:st] v. przewidywać; s. przewidywanie

forefather ['fo:r,fa:dzer] s. przodek; antenat

forefinger ['fo:rfynger] s. palec wskazujący

forefoot ['fo:r-fut] s. przednia noga (zwierzęcia)

foregone [fo:r'gon] adj. przesądzony; miniony

foreground ['fo:rgraund] s. pierwszy plan (obrazu)

forehead ['fo:ryd] s. czoło

foreign ['foryn] adj. obcy; obcokrajowy; cudzoziemski

foreign currency [,foryn'karensy] s. obca waluta

foreigner ['foryner] s. cudzoziemiec; cudzoziemka; obcokrajowiec

foreign policy ['foryn,polysy] polityka zagraniczna

foreign trade ['foryn,trejd] handel zagraniczny

foreleg ['fo:rleg] s. przednia noga (zwierzęcia)

foreman ['fo:rmen] s. majster; sztygar; starszy przysięgły

foremost ['fo:r,maust] adj. główny; przedni; adv. przede

wszystkim; w pierwszym
rzędzie

forenoon ['fo:rnu:n] s.
przedpołudnie; a.
przedpołudniowy

foresee ['fo:rsi:] v.
przewidywać; przewidzieć;
wiedzieć z góry

foresight ['fo:rsajt] s.
przezorność; przewidywanie;
muszka celownika (przy
strzelbie etc.)

forest ['foryst] s. las; v.
zalesiać; a. leśny; w lesie

forester ['foryster] s. leśniczy;
leśnik; ptak leśny; ćma
leśna

forestry ['forystry] s. leśnictwo;
lasy; wiedza o lesie

foretaste ['fo:rtejst] s.
przedsmak; zapowiedź tego
co ma nastąpić

foretell; foretold; foretold [fo:rtel;
fo:'tould; fo:'tould]

foretell [fo:rtel] v.
przepowiadać; zapowiadać;
wróżyć

forever [fe'rewer] adv. wiecznie;
na zawsze; ustawicznie

foreword ['fo:rłe-rd] v.
przedmowa; przedsłowie;
słowo wstępne

forfeit ['fo:rfyt] s. grzywna; fant;
zastaw; utrata; v. stracić (w
skutek konfiskaty); utracić

forge ['fo:rdż] s. kuźnia; huta;
v. kuć; fałszować; posuwać
się z trudem; wykuwać sobie
przyszłość

forgery ['fo:rdżery] s.
fałszerstwo; podrobiony
dokument

forget; forgot; forgotten [fer'get;
fer'got; fer'gotn]

forget [fer'get] v. zapominać;
pomijać; przeoczyć;
zaniedbać

forgetful [fer'getful] adj.
zapominający; zapominalski;
niepomny

forget-me-not [fer'getmyna:t] s.
niezapominajka

forgive; forgave; forgiven

[fer'gyw; fer'gejw; fer'gywn]

forgive [fer'gyw] v. przebaczać;
darować; odpuszczać

forgiveness [fer'gywnys] s.
przebaczenie; darowanie;
wybaczenie

forgiving [fer'gywyng] adj.
wyrozumiały; pobłażliwy

forgo [fo:r'gou] v.
powstrzymywać się;
obchodzić się bez czegoś;
zrzekać się czegoś

forgot [fer'got] zob. forget

fork [fo:rk] s. widły; widelec;
widełki; v. rozwidlać (się);
brać na widły; spulchniać
(ziemią)

forlorn [fer'lo:rn] adj.
zapuszczony; opuszczony;
beznadziejny; rozpaczliwy;
niepocieszony

form [fo:rm] v. formować (się);
kształtować (się); utworzyć
(się); organizować (się);
wytworzyć; s. forma; kształt;
postać; formuła; formułka;
formularz; blankiet; styl; układ

formal ['fo:rmel] adj. formalny;
urzędowy; oficjalny; s. strój
wieczorowy

formation ['fo:rmejszyn] s.
formacja; szyk; układ;
tworzenie (się); kształtowanie;
formowanie (się);
powstawanie; budowa

formative ['fo:rmetyw] adj.
formujący; kształtujący;
tworzący (się); słowotwórczy

former ['fo:rmer] adj. & pron.
oprzedni; były; miniony;
dawny; s. formierz; giser;
wzornik

formerly ['fo:rmerly] adv.
dawniej; przedtem; poprzednio

formidable ['fo:rmydebl] adj.
straszny; potężny; ogromny

formulate ['fo:rmjulejt] v.
formułować; wyrażać;
redagować

fornicate ['fo:rnykejt] v.
cudzołożyć; spółkować bez
ślubu

forsake; forsook; forsaken

[fer'sejk; fer'suk; fer'sejken]
forsake [fer'sejk] v. opuszczać;
porzucać; poniechać;
zaprzeć się

fort [fo:rt] s. fort

forth [fo:rs̱] adv. naprzód; dalej;
wobec; na zewnątrz etc.

forthcoming [fo:rs̱'kamyng] adj.
zbliżający się; nadchodzący

forthwith ['fo:rs̱'tys̱] adv.
bezzwłocznie; natychmiast

fortieth ['fo:rtyjes̱] num.
czterdziesty; czterdziesta
(część)

fortify ['fo:rtyfaj] s. wzmacniać;
fortyfikować; umacniać

fortnight ['fo:rtnajt] s. dwa
tygodnie (czternaście nocy)

fortran ['fo:rtraen] = formula
translation, język dla
programów na komputery

fortress ['fo:rtrys] s. twierdza;
forteca; warownia

fortunate ['fo:rcznyt] adj.
szczęśliwy; pomyślny;
udany

fortunately ['fo:rcznytly] adv. na
szczęście; szczęśliwie

fortune ['fo:rczen] s. szczęście;
los; majątek; traf; ślepy los

forty ['fo:rty] num. czterdzieści;
czterdziestka; czterdzieścioro

forward ['fo:rłerd] adj. przedni;
naprzód; postępowy;
wczesny; chętny; gotowy; v.
przyśpieszać; ekspediować;
s. napastnik (w sporcie); gracz
w ataku

forwards ['fo:rłerds] adv.
naprzód; dalej; adj. frontowy;
śmiały

foster-child ['foster,czajld] s.
wychowanek; wychowanka

fought [fo:t] zob. fight

foul [faul] adj. zgniły; plugawy;
wstrętny; adv. nieuczciwie;
wbrew regułom; s.
nieuczciwość; v. zawalać
(się); zabrudzić (się);
plugawić się; kalać

found [faund] v. 1. uzasadniać;
zakładać; odlewać; 2. zob.
find

foundation [faun'dejszyn] s.
podstawa; założenie;
fundament; fundacja;
podwalina

founder ['faunder] s. odlewnik;
założyciel; v. zatonąć;
przepaść; okulawić;
zatopić

foundling ['faundlyng] s.
podrzutek; znajda

fountain ['fauntyn] s. fontanna;
źródło; wodotrysk; pijalnia

fountain-pen ['fauntyn,pen] s.
wieczne pióro

four [fo:r] num. cztery; czwórka;
czworo

fourscore ['fo:rskor] nom.
osiemdziesiąt

four-stroke engine ['fo:r,strok
'endżyn] motor cztero-
taktowy

fourteen ['fo:rti:n] num.
czternaście; czternaścioro;
czternastka

fourth ['fo:rs̱] num. czwarty

fourthly [fo:rs̱ly] adv. po
czwarte; na czwartym miejscu

fowl [faul] s. drób; ptaki

fox [foks] s. lis; v. przechytrzyć

fraction ['fraekszyn] s. ułamek;
część; odłam; frakcja

fracture ['fraekczer] s. złamanie;
v. złamać; łamać się

fragile ['fraedżajl] adj. kruchy;
łamliwy; słabowity; wątły

fragment ['fraegment] s.
fragment; urywek; odłamek;
okruch

fragrance ['frejgrens] s. zapach;
woń; aromat

fragrant ['frejgrent] adj.
pachnący; aromatyczny;
wonny

frail [frejl] adj. kruchy; wątły;
lekkomyślny; s. kosz;
plecionka

frailty ['frejlty] s. słabość;
wątłość; chwila słabości

frame ['frejm] s. oprawa; rama;
struktura; szkielet; v.
oprawiać; kształtować;
wrabiać

frame of mind ['frejm,ow'majnd]

s. nastrój; nastawienie psychiczne; usposobienie do czegoś

frame-house ['frejm,haus] s. drewniany dom (typowy w USA)

framework ['frejm,łe:rk] s. struktura; zrąb; szkielet; wiązanie

franchise ['fraenczajz] s. przywilej; prawo do prowadzenia filii lub firmy, do głosowania

frank [fraenk] adj. szczery; otwarty; v. wysyłać bez opłaty

frankness ['fraenknys] s. szczerość; otwartość

frantic ['fraetyk] adj. wariacki; szalony; zapamiętały

fraternal [fre'te:rnl] adj. braterski; bratni; bracki

fraternity [fre'te:rnyty] s. braterstwo; korporacja studencka

fraud [fro:d] s. oszustwo; oszust

fray [frej] v. strzępić; wycierać; s. bójka; burda

freak [fri:k] s. kaprys; wybryk; potwór; a. fantazyjny

freckle ['frekl] s. pieg; v. pokrywać piegami; powodować piegi

free [fri:] adj. wolny; bezpłatny; nie zajęty; v. uwolnić; wyzwolić; oswobodzić; adv. wolno; swobodnie; bezpłatnie

free and easy ['fri:,end'i:zy] adj. beztroski; bez ceremonii

freedom ['fri:dem] s. wolność; swoboda; nieskrępowanie; prawo do

freemason ['fri:,mejsn] s. mason; wolnomularz

free port ['fri:,port] s. wolnocłowy port

freethinker ['fri:tynker] s. wolnomyśliciel; wolnomyślicielka

freeway ['fri:łej] s. szosa przelotowa wielopasmowa

freewheel ['fri:hłi:l] s. wolne koło (np. od roweru)

freeze; froze; frozen [fri:z; frouz; frouzn]

freeze [fri:z] v. marznąć; zamarznąć; krzepnąć; przymarznąć; mrozić; wyrugować (konkurenta)

freezing point ['fri:zyn,point] s. punkt zamarzania

freight [frejt] s. przewóz; fracht; v. przewozić; frachtować statek; adj. towarowy (pociąg)

freighter ['frejter] s. frachtowiec; statek towarowy

French [frencz] adj. francuski

frenzy ['frenzy] s. szał; szaleństwo; v. doprowadzać do szału

frequency ['fri:kłensy] s. częstość; częstotliwość

frequent ['fri:kłent] adj. częsty; rozpowszechniony; v. uczęszczać; odwiedzać; bywać

fresh [fresz] adj. świeży; nowy; zuchwały; niedoświadczony; adv. świeżo; niedawno; dopiero co

freshman ['freszmen] s. student pierwszego roku

freshness ['fresznys] s. świeżość; zuchwałość; zuchwalstwo

freshwater ['fresz,ło:ter] adj. słodkowodny; s. słodka woda

fret [fret] v. gryźć się; niepokoić się; s. rozdrażnienie; niepokój; zdenerwowanie; irytacja

fretful ['fretful] adj. rozdrażniony; drażliwy; nerwowy; wzburzony

friar ['frajer] s. mnich; zakonnik; biała plamka

friction ['frykszyn] s. tarcie; ścieranie się; ucieranie

Friday ['frajdy] s. piątek

fridge [frydż] s. lodówka (slang)

fried [frajd] adj. smażony

friend [frend] s. znajomy; znajoma; przyjaciel; kolega; klient

friendly ['frendly] adj. przyjazny; przychylny; życzliwy

friendship ['frendszyp] s.
przyjaźń osobista; dobra
znajomość; znajomość
powierzchowna; stosunki
koleżeńskie lub handlowe

fright [frajt] s. strach;
przerażenie; strach na wróble

frighten ['frajtn] v. straszyć

frightened ['frajtnd] adj.
przestraszony; zastraszony;
wylękniony

frightful ['frajtful] adj. straszny;
przerażający; straszliwy;
alarmujący; nieprzyjemny;
wstrętny

frigid ['frydżyd] adj. zimny;
lodowaty; oziębły; zimna
(kobieta)

frill [fryl] v. plisować; s.
falbanka; pl. fochy; fanaberie;
niepotrzebne ozdóbki

fringe [fryndż] v. frędzla;
obrąbek; v. obrębiać;
obramowywać; ograniczać;
wystrzępić

frisk [frysk] v. brykać s. sus;
podskok; skok; v. rewidować

frisky ['frysky] adj. rozbrykany;
ożywiony; samowolny

fro [frou] exp. to and fro; tu i
tam; tam i z powrotem

frock [frok] s. sukienka; habit;
mundur; surdut; anglez

frog [frog] s. żaba; strzałka
(w kopycie konia); vulg.
Francuz

frolic ['frolyk] s. wybryk; figiel;
swawola; v. dokazywać;
swawolić; figlować; adj.
rozbawiony; swawolny;
figlarny

frolicsome ['frolyksem] adj.
figlarny; swawolny;
rozbawiony

from [from] prep. od; z; przed
(zimnem); że; (ponieważ;
żeby)

from under [from ander] prep.
spod (czegoś)

from ... to [from ... tu] exp. stąd
... dotąd; od ... do

front [frant] s. przód; front;
czoło; adj. przedni; frontowy;

czołowy; v. stawiać czoło;
stać frontem; konfrontować

front-door ['frant,do:r] s. główne
drzwi wejściowe

frontier ['frantjer] s. granica; a.
pograniczny

front-page ['frant,pejdż] s.
strona tytułowa; a. sensacyjny

front tire ['frant,tajer] s. przednia
opona (samochodu)

front-wheel ['frant,hłi:l] s.
przednie koło (wozu)

front wheel drive ['frant,hłi:l
'drajw] s. napęd na przednie
koła (auta etc.)

frost [frost] s. mróz; przymrozek;
oziębłość; v. zmrozić;
oszronić

frostbite ['frost,bajt] s.
odmrożenie (nosa, ręki, stopy)

frosted ['frostyd] adj. matowy;
oszroniony; matowy odcień

frosty ['frosty] adj. mroźny;
oszroniony; lodowaty

froth [froś] s. piana; szumowiny;
v. pienić się; ubijać białko

frothy ['froŝy] adj. spieniony

frown [fraun] v. marszczyć
brwi; s. zachmurzone czoło;
wyraz dezaprobaty;
niezadowolona mina

froze [frouz] zob. freeze

frozen food ['frouzn,fu:d] s.
mrożonki; mrożona
żywność

frugal ['fru:gel] adj. oszczędny;
tani; skromny (posiłek etc.)

fruit [fru:t] s. owoc; v.
owocować; a. owocowy

fruitcake ['fru:t,kejk] s.
świąteczne ciasto z
kandyzowanymi owocami i
orzechami

fruitful ['fru:tful] adj. owocny;
owocujący; zyskowny;
wydajny

fruitless ['fru:tlys] adj.
bezowocny; bezpłodny;
nieudany

frustrate [fra'strejt] v.
udaremnić; zniechęcić;
zawieść

fry [fraj] v. smażyć; s. narybek

frying pan [frajyn,paen] s.
patelnia

fuel [fjuel] s. paliwo; opał

fugitive ['fju:dżytyw] s. zbieg;
adj. zbiegły; przelotny

fulfill [ful'fyl] v. spełnić;
wykonać; dokonać;
skończyć

fulfillment [ful'fylment] s.
spełnienie; wykonanie;
dokonanie; wypełnienie;
wysłuchanie

full [ful] adj. pełny; pełen;
zapełniony; całkowity;
kompletny; cały; adv. w pełni;
całkowicie

full board ['ful'bo:rd] s. pełne
utrzymanie; wikt i opierunek

full moon ['ful'mu:n] s. pełnia
księżyca

fullness [ful'nys] s. pełność;
dokładność;
drobiazgowość

full-time ['ful'tajm] adj.
pełnoetatowy; całkowicie
zajęty

fumble ['fambl] v. szperać;
partaczyć; s. gmeranie;
partactwo; niezdarność;
niezdarne zagranie

fume [fju:m] v. dymić; kopcić;
s. dym (ostry); wyziew
(przykry); gazy spalinowe;
zapach; woń; napad gniewu;
wybuch gniewu

fun [fan] s. uciecha; zabawa;
wesołość; śmiech; powód
do wesołości

in fun ['yn,fan] adv. żartem

make fun [mejk fan] v.
dokuczać; kpić;
wyśmiewać się

function ['fankszyn] v. działać;
funkcjonować; s. działanie;
funkcja; praca; obowiązek;
impreza; uroczystość;
czynność

functionary ['fanksznery] s.
urzędnik; funkcjonariusz

fund [fand] s. fundusz

fundamental [,fande'mentel] adj.
podstawowy; s. zasada;
podstawa; nakaz

funeral ['fju:nerel] s. pogrzeb;
adj. pogrzebowy; żałosny

funereal [fju'njerjel] adj. żałobny;
pogrzebowy

funicular railway [fju'nykjuler
,rejłłej] kolejka linowa

funk ['fank] s. strach; trema;
tchórz (człowiek); v. mieć
pietra; zląknąć się;
stchórzyć

funky ['fanky] adj. tchórzliwy

funnel ['fanl] s. lej; lejek; komin
(maszyny parowej etc.)

funny ['fany] adj. zabawny;
śmieszny; dziwny;
humorystyczny

fur [fe:r] s. futro; v. okładać

furious ['fjuerjes] adj. wściekły;
rozjuszony; gwałtowny;
zaciekły

furl [fe:r] v. składać (się);
złożyć (się); s. zwitek;
zawinięcie

furnace ['fe:rnys] s. piec
(centralny); palenisko; piekło

furnish ['fe:rnysz] v. zaopatrzyć;
dostarczyć; umeblować;
wyposażyć; uzbrajać;
meblować

furniture ['fe:rnyczer] s.
umeblowanie; urządzenie

furrier ['farjer] s. kuśnierz

furrow ['farou] s. bruzda;
zmarszczka; koleina; v. orać;
przeorać; ryć; zryć; pruć;
żłobić

further ['fe:rdzer] adv. dalej;
dodatkowo; adj. dalszy;
dodatkowy; v. pomagać;
ułatwiać; posuwać naprzód;
sprzyjać; popierać

further more ['fe:rdzermo:r] adv.
ponadto; oprócz tego; w
dodatku

furtive ['fe:rtyw] adj. skryty;
potajemny; ukradkowy;
skradający się

furuncle ['fjuerankl] s. czyrak

fury ['fjuery] s. szał; furia; pasja;
gwałtowna siła; jędza;
megiera; siła burzy; siła wiatru

fuse [fju:z] v. stopić; s.
zapalnik; bezpiecznik; korek

fuselage ['fju:zyla:ż] s. kadłub (samolotu) bez skrzydeł i ogona

fusion ['fju:żen] s. stopienie; spawanie; zlewanie się

fuss [fas] v. niepokoić; denerwować; krzątać się; s. wrzawa; zamieszanie; krzątanina

fussy ['fasy] adj. grymaśny; hałaśliwy; nieznośny; zrzędny

futile ['fju:tajl] adj. daremny; bezskuteczny; próżny

future ['fju:tczer] s. przyszłość; adj. przyszły (czas ...)

fuzzy ['fazy] adj. kędzierzawy; kręty; puszysty; niewyraźny; zamazany (obraz, pojęcie etc.)

G

g [dżi:] siódma litera angielskiego alfabetu

gab [gaeb] s. gadanie (slang)

gable ['gejbl] s. szczyt (dachu); trójkąt płaszczyzn dachu

gad-fly ['gaedflaj] s. giez; bąk; osoba zaczepna jak giez

gag [gaeg] s. knebel; v. kneblować; nałożyć kaganiec; zamknąć debatę; oszukiwać

gage [gejdż] s. wskaźnik; miara; rękojmia; v. mierzyć; oceniać; zestawiać; sądzić

gaiety ['gejety] s. wesołość

gaily ['gejly] adv. wesoło

gain [gejn] s. zysk; zarobek; korzyść; v. zyskiwać; zdobywać; pozyskiwać; wygrywać; osiągać; mieć korzyść; wyprzedzać

gait [gejt] s. chód; bieg (konia)

gaiter ['gejter] s. kamasz; getr

galaxy ['gaeleksy] s. galaktyka; plejada; rój

gale [gejl] s. poryw wiatru; sztorm; wybuch śmiechu; zefir

gall [go:l] s. żółć; złość; gorycz; tupet; otarcie; v. urazić

gallant ['gaelent] s. bawidamek; galant; adj. piękny; dzielny; waleczny; szarmancki

gallery ['gaelery] s. arkady; galeria; krużganek; balkon; chór

galley ['gaely] s. galera; kuchnia na statku; szufelka

galley proof ['gaely,pru:f] s. odbitka na korektę (szczotkowa)

gallon ['gaelen] s. miara płynu (ok. 4,5 litra)(am. gal.=3,78 l)

gallop ['gaelep] v. galopować; s. galop; cwał; galopada

gallows ['gaelouz] s. szubienica; kobylica; szelki; a. szubieniczny

galore [ga'lo:r] s. mnóstwo; adv. w bród; bardzo wiele

gamble ['gaembl] s. hazard; ryzyko; v. uprawiać hazard; ryzykować; igrać; spekulować

gambler ['gaembler] s. gracz--hazardzista; ryzykant

gambol ['gaembel] v. podskakiwać; s. podskok; skok

game [gejm] s. gra; zabawa; zawody; sztuczki; machinacje; adj. dzielny; odważny; kulawy; v. uprawiać hazard

gamekeeper ['gejm,ki:per] s. gajowy; leśnik

gander ['gaender] s. gąsior

gang [gaeng] s. banda; szajka; grupa; v. łączyć się w bandę

gangster ['gaengster] s. gangster; bandyta

gangway ['gangłej] s. przejście; kładka; chodnik w kopalni

gaol = jail [dżejl] s. więzienie; ciupa; v. uwięzić; wsadzać do więzienia

gaoler = jailer ['dżejler] s. dozorca więzienny; strażnik więzienny

gap [gaep] s. szpara; luka;
otwór; przerwa; odstęp;
wyrwa; przełęcz; wyłom
gape [gejp] v. gapić się;
ziewać; s. ziewanie; gapienie
się
garage [gaera:dż] s. garaż; v.
garażować; zagarażować
garbage ['ga:rbydż] s. odpadki;
śmieci; bezwartościowe
publikacje
garden ['ga:rdn] s. ogród; v.
uprawiać ogród
gardener ['ga:rdner] s. ogrodnik
gardening ['ga:rdenyng] s.
ogrodnictwo (warzywne,
kwiatowe etc.)
gargle ['ga:rgl] v. płukać gardło;
s. płyn do płukania gardła
garland ['ga:rlend] s. girlanda
garlic ['ga:rlik] s. czosnek
garment ['ga:rment] s. część
ubrania; szaty; v. odziewać
garnish ['ga:rnysz] v. ozdabiać;
s. ozdoba; przybranie
(potraw); upiększenia literackie
garret ['gaeret] s. poddasze;
strych; mansarda; sl. łeb
garrison ['gaerysn] s. załoga;
garnizon; v. garnizonować
garter ['ga:rter] s. podwiązka
gas [gaes] s. gaz; benzyna
gaseous ['gejzjes] adj. gazowy
gash [gaesz] v. skaleczyć się; s.
szrama; skaleczenie; blizna
gasket ['gaeskyt] s. uszczelka
gas-meter ['gaes,mi:ter] s.
gazomierz; zegar gazowy
gasoline ['gaesely:n] s. gazolina;
benzyna
gasp [ga:sp] v. ciężko dyszeć;
sapać; s. ciężki oddech
gas station ['gaes,stejszyn] s.
stacja benzynowa
gas-stove ['gaes'stouw] s.
kuchenka gazowa; kuchnia
gazowa
gate [gejt] s. brama; furtka;
wrota; szlaban; ilość
publiczności; wpływy kasowe
ze wstępu
gateway ['gejtłej] s. przejście;
wjazd; brama wjazdowa

gather ['gaedzer] v. zbierać;
wnioskować; wzbierać;
narastać
gather speed ['gaedzer spi:d]
nabierać szybkości;
rozpędzać się
gathering ['gaedzeryng] s.
zebranie; nagromadzenie;
ropień
gaudy [go:dy] adj. jaskrawy;
krzykliwy; s. obchód
(uroczysty)
gauge [gejdż] s. wskaźnik;
miara; skala; v. kalibrować;
oceniać; szacować;
oszacować
gaunt [go:nt] adj. chudy;
nędzny; wycieńczony;
ponury; posępny
gauze ['go:z] s. gaza; siateczka;
mgiełka; gaza metalowa
gave [gejw] zob. give
gay [gej] adj. wesoły; jaskrawy;
pstry; rozpustny; s. pederasta;
pedzio; pedał
gaze [gejz] s. spojrzenie; v.
przyglądać się;
przypatrywać się
gaze at [gejz aet] v. wpatrywać
(się) w kogoś, w coś
gear [gier] v. włączyć (napęd);
s. przybory; bieg; układ
gear change ['gier,czeindż]
zmiana biegów
gearbox ['gier,boks] s. skrzynka
biegów; skrzynia biegów
gearing ['gieryng] s. przekładnia;
mechanizm napędowy
gear wheel ['gier-hłi:l] s. tryb;
koło zębate
geese [gi:s] pl. gęsi
gem [dżem] s. klejnot; perła
gender ['dżender] s. rodzaj;
płeć; wytwór; potomstwo
general ['dżenerel] adj. ogólny;
powszechny; generalny;
naczelny; główny; nieścisły;
ogólnikowy; s. generał; wódz
generalize ['dżenerelajz] v.
uogólniać; mówić ogólnikami
generally ['dżenerely] adv.
ogólnie; zazwyczaj;
powszechnie; najczęściej; w

ogóle
generate ['dżenerejt] v. rodzić;
wytwarzać; płodzić;
wywoływać
generation [,dżenerejszyn] s.
powstawanie; pokolenie
generator ['dżenerejter] s.
prądnica; sprawca; generator
generosity [,dżene'rosyty] s.
szczodrość;
wspaniałomyślność
generous ['dżeneres] adj. hojny;
wielkoduszny; suty; obfity;
bogaty; żyzny; mocny;
krzepiący
genial ['dżi:njel] adj. wesoły;
łagodny; miły; jowialny;
ożywczy
genitive [dżenytyw] s. (gram.)
dopełniacz; adj. wesoły;
łagodny
genius [dżi:njes] s. geniusz;
duch; talent; duch epoki etc.
genocide ['dżenousajd] s.
ludobójstwo (systematyczne
mordowanie)
gentle ['dżentl] adj. łagodny;
delikatny; subtelny; stopniowy
gentleman ['dżentlmen] s. pan;
człowiek honorowy;
dżentelmen
gentlemanly ['dżentlmenly] adj.
dżentelmeński; honorowy
gentleness ['dżentlnys] s.
łagodność; delikatność
gentlewoman ['dżentl,łumen] s.
szlachcianka; dama; dama
dworu
gentry ['dżentry] s.
ziemiaństwo; szlachta;
światek
genuine ['dżenjuyn] adj.
prawdziwy; autentyczny;
szczery
geography [dży'ogrefy] s.
geografia; fizyczne cechy
rejonu
geologist [dży'oledżyst] s.
geolog
geology [dży'oledży] s. geologia
geometry [dży'omytry] s.
geometria
germ [dże:rm] s. zarodek;

zarazek; nasienie; pączek
German ['dże:rmen] adj.
niemiecki (język, człowiek); s.
Niemiec
germinate ['dże:rmynejt] v.
kiełkować; rozwijać się
gerund [dżerend] s. rzeczownik
odsłowny (z końcówką "ing")
gestation ['dżes'tejszyn] s. ciąża
gesticulate ['dżes'tykjulejt] v.
gestykulować; mówić na
migi
gesture ['dżeszczer] s. gest
get; got; got [get; got; got]
get [get] v. dostać; otrzymać;
nabyć; zawołać; łupać;
przynieść; zmusić; musić;
mieć; dostać się; wpływać;
wsiadać
get about [,get e'baut] v.
poruszać się; rozchodzić się
get along [,get e'long] v. dawać
sobie radę; współpracować
get away [,get e'łej] v. uciec;
odejść; wyjeżdżać;
oderwać się
get in [,get'yn] v. wejść;
wsiąść
get off [,get'of] v. wysiąść
get on [,get'on] v. wdziewać;
posuwać się; robić dalej
get out [,get'aut] v. wysiąść;
wyjmować; wyciągać;
wynosić się
get to [,get'tu] v. dotrzeć;
przyjść; musieć; być
zmuszonym
get together [,get te'gedzer] v.
zebrać się; s. zebranie
get up [,get'ap] v. wstać;
zbudzić się
get-up ['getap] s. wygląd; ubiór
get ready [,get'redy] v.
przygotować (się);
przygotowywać się
get to know ['get,tu'nou] v.
zapoznać się (bliżej)
geyser ['gajzer] s. gejzer
ghastly ['ga:stly] adj. ohydny;
upiorny; blady; adv. okropnie
gherkin ['ge:rkyn] s. korniszon
ghost [goust] s. duch; cień;
widmo

ghostly ['goustly] adj. upiorny
giant ['dżajent] s. olbrzym
gibbet ['dżybyt] s. szubienica
gibe ['dżajb] s. kpina; drwina; v.
    kpić; szydzić; wyśmiewać
giblets ['dżyblyts] pl. podróbki
    (np. kurze); podroby
giddy ['gydy] adj. zawrotny;
    mający zawrót głowy;
    roztrzepany; v. przyprawiać o
    zawrót głowy
gift [gyft] s. dar; upominek;
    talent; uzdolnienie; a.
    darowany
gifted ['gyftyd] adj.
    utalentowany; mający
    naturalne zdolności
gigantic [dżaj'gantyk] adj.
    olbrzymi; gigantyczny;
    kolosalny
giggle ['gygl] s. chichot; v.
    chichotać; głupio śmiać się
gild [gyld] v. złocić; pozłocić;
    nadać lepszego wyglądu
gill [gyl] s. skrzela; wąwóz;
    potok; jedna czwarta galona
gilt [gylt] adj. pozłacany; s.
    złocenie; pozłocenie
gin [dżyn] s. jałowcówka
ginger ['dżyndżer] s. imbir
ginger bread ['dżyndżer,bred] s.
    piernik; przesadne dekoracje
gingerly ['dżyndżerly] adj.
    ostrożny; delikatny; adv.
    ostrożnie; delikatnie;
    nieśmiało
gipsy ['dżypsy] s. cygan
giraffe [dży'ra:f] s. żyrafa
gird; girt; girt [ge:rd; ge:rt; ge:rt]
gird [ge:rd] v. opasać; kpić; s.
    kpina
girder ['ge:rder] s. dźwigar;
    belka; wzdłużnik
girdle ['ge:rdl] s. pas; v. opasać;
    okrążyć; opasywać lekkim
    gorsetem
girl [ge:rl] s. dziewczyna;
    ukochana
girlfriend [ge:rl'frend] s.
    przyjaciółka; dobra znajoma;
    kochanka
girlhood ['ge:rlhud] s. wiek
    dziewczęcy; dziewczęta (kraju

etc.)
girl scout ['ge:rl skaut] s.
    harcerka
girl's name ['ge:rls,nejm] s.
    panieńskie nazwisko
girt [ge:rt] zob. gird
girth [ge:rt] s. popręg; obwód
gist [dżyst] s. treść; istota;
    sedno; esencja; osnowa; sens;
    główna treść
give; gave; given [gyw; gejw;
    gywn]
give [gyw] v. dać; dawać; być
    elastycznym; zawalić się;
    ustąpić; s. elastyczność;
    ustępstwo pod naciskiem
give away [,gyw e'łej] v.
    wydawać; zdradzać;
    wydawać córkę
give in [,gyw'yn] v. ustępować;
    podawać (nazwisko);
    uznawać w końcu
give up [,gyw'ap] v. poddać
    się; ustąpić; zaniechać; dać
    za wygraną
give way [,gyw'łej] v. zrobić
    miejsce; ustąpić; obsunąć
    się
glacier ['glaesjer] s. lodowiec
glad [glaed] adj. rad; wesoły;
    radosny; dający radość;
    ochoczy
gladly ['glaedly] adv. z
    przyjemnością; chętnie;
    właściwie
gladness ['glaednys] s.
    wesołość; pogoda ducha;
    przyjemność
glamorous ['glaemeres] adj.
    czarujący; wspaniały;
    fascynujący
glance [gla:ns] v. spojrzeć;
    ześliznąć się; błyszczeć;
    połyskiwać; s. rzut oka;
    błysk; połysk; rykoszet;
    odbicie się
glance at ['glan:s et] v. spojrzeć
    na (coś); rzucić spojrzenie
gland [glaend] s. gruczoł
glare [gleer] v. błyskać; razić;
    wlepiać wzrok; s. błysk; blask
glass [gla:s] s. szkło; szklanka;
    lampka; kieliszek; szyba etc.

glasses ['gla:sys] pl. okulary;
szkła
glassy ['gla:sy] adj. szklisty;
szklany; przezroczysty; bez
wyrazu
glaze [glejz] v. szklić; oszklić
glazier ['glejzjer] s. szklarz
gleam [gli:m] s. połysk; v.
połyskiwać; zjawić się nagle
glee [gli:] s. wesele; radość
glen [glen] s. dolina (zaciszna)
glib [glyb] adj. gładki; żwawy;
płynny; wygadany (zanadto)
glide ['glajd] s. poślizg;
szybowanie; v. ślizgać się;
szybować; powodować
poślizg
glider ['glajder] s. szybowiec
glimmer ['glymer] v. migotać;
słabo świecić; s. słabe
światło; migotanie; słabe
postrzeganie
glimpse [glymps] s. mignięcie;
przelotne spojrzenie; v. ujrzeć
w przelocie; zerknąć
glint [glynt] s. błysk; odblask; v.
błysnąć; zamigotać
glisten ['glysn] s. połysk; v.
połyskiwać; lśnić; iskrzyć
się
glitter ['glyter] v. świecić się;
błyszczeć; s. połysk; blask;
pretensjonalność
gloat ['glout] v. napawać się;
źle patrzeć; pożerać oczami
gloat over ['glout,ower] v.
napawać się (cudzym
nieszczęściem); unosić się
globe [gloub] s. globus; kula
ziemska; jabłko królewskie;
gałka
gloom [glu:m] s. smutek; mrok;
przygnębienie; v. zasmucać
(się); zaciemniać (się);
posępnieć
gloomy ['glu:my] adj. ponury;
mroczny; posępny;
przygnębiony
glorify ['glo:ryfaj] v. chwalić;
wychwalać; gloryfikować
glorious ['glo:rjes] adj. sławny;
wspaniały; przepiękny;
chlubny

glory ['glo:ry] s. chwała; sława;
v. szczycić się; chlubić się;
chwalić się; chełpić się
gloss [glos] s. połysk; v.
polerować; interpretować
(błędnie)
glossary ['glosery] s. słownik
(przy tekście); glosariusz
glossy [glosy] adj. lśniący
glove [glaw] s. rękawiczka
glow [glou] v. żarzyć się;
pałać; s. jarzenie; zapał;
żarliwość; łuna; rumieniec;
jasność
glowworm ['glou,łe:rm] s.
robaczek świętojański
glue [glu:] s. klej; v. kleić;
zalepiać; wlepiać (oczy);
zlepić
glutton ['glatn] s. żarłok
gluttonous ['glatnes] adj.
żarłoczny; jedzący zbyt dużo
gluttony ['glatny] s.
żarłoczność; zwyczaj
jedzenia za dużo
glycerine [,glyse'ry:n] s.
gliceryna
gnarled ['na:rld] adj. sękaty;
wykrzywiony; węzłowaty
gnash [naesz] v. zgrzytać
zębami jak w złości
gnat [naet] s. komar; owad
gnaw [no:] v. gryźć; wgryzać;
ogryzać; nękać (stałym
bólem)
gnome [noum] s. gnom;
chochlik; zdanie wyrażające
myśl ogólną; przysłowie;
sentencja
go; went; gone [gou; łent; gon]
go [gou] v. iść; chodzić;
jechać; stać się; być na
chodzie
go about [,gou e'baut] v. zająć
się (czymś); afiszować się
go along [,gou e'long] v.
towarzyszyć; zgadzać się;
iść sobie
go away [,gou e'łej] v. iść
precz; odchodzić; wyjeżdżać
go back [,gou'bek] v. wracać;
cofać się; sięgać wstecz
go by [,gou'baj] v. mijać

go on [,gou'on] v. iść naprzód; ciągnąć dalej; kontynuować

go out [,gou'aut] v. wychodzić (z kimś); gasnąć; bywać (u ludzi)

go through [,gou'tru] v. przechodzić; brnąć przez; przebrnąć

go under [,gou'ander] v. tonąć; ulegać; zniknąć; umrzeć

goad [goud] s. kolec; bodziec; v. popędzać; drażnić; prowokować; doprowadzać do zrobienia

goal [goul] s. cel; meta; bramka

goalie [gouli] s. bramkarz

go-between [,gouby'tły:n] s. pośrednik; stręczyciel

goblet ['goblyt] s. kieliszek; czara; puchar; kielich na nóżce

goblin ['goblyn] s. chochlik

god [god] s. Bóg; bożek; bóstwo

godchild ['godczajld] s. chrześniak; chrześniaczka

goddess ['godys] s. bogini

godfather ['god,fadzer] s. ojciec chrzestny; v. trzymać do chrztu

godless ['godlys] adj. bezbożny; grzeszny; niegodziwy; nikczemny

godmother ['god,madzer] s. matka chrzestna

goggles ['goglz] pl. okulary ochronne; gogle; okrągłe okulary

going ['gouyng] s. chodzenie; jazda; tempo; adj. ruchliwy; istniejący

going rate ['gouyn,rejt] bieżący kurs (dolara, oprocentowania)

gold [gould] s. złoto; adj. złoty

gold digger ['gould,dyger] poszukiwacz złota; naciągaczka

golden ['gouldn] adj. złoty

gold-plated ['gould,plejtyd] s. plater złoty; adj. platerowany

goldsmith ['gould,smys] s. złotnik

golf [golf] s. golf; v. grać w golfa

golf course ['golf,ko:rs] s. pole golfowe

gondola ['gondele] s. gondola (np. balonu); otwarty, niski wagon towarowy

gone [gon] v. zob. go

good [gud] adj. dobry; s. dobro; pożytek; zaleta; wartość; better ['beter] lepszy; best [best] najlepszy

good at it ['gud,et'yt] dobry w tym; dobrze to robi

good-bye [,gud'baj] s. do widzenia; pożegnanie

good-for-nothing ['gudfe:r ,nasyng] s. nicpoń; hultaj; łobuziak

good-looking ['gud'lukyng] adj. przystojny; ładny

good-natured ['gud'nejczerd] adj. dobroduszny; poczciwy

goodness ['gudnys] s. dobroć

good will ['gud'łyl] s. dobra wola; wartość reputacji firmy

goose [gu:s] s. gęś; pl. geese [gi:s] gęsi; gęsie mięso; dureń

gooseberry ['gusbery] s. agrest

gooseflesh ['gu:sflesz] s. gęsia skórka (z zimna, strachu etc.)

gopher ['goufer] s. suseł; v. grzebać; ryć; plądrować gospodarkę

gore [go:r] v. bóść; klinować; s. klin w krawiectwie; posoka

gorge ['go:rdż] s. wąwóz; żarłoczność; treść żołądka; przejedzenie; gardziel; v. obżerać się; pożerać; połykać; opychać się

gorgeous ['go:rdżes] adj. wspaniały; okazały; suty; ozdobny; wystawny; cudowny

gospel ['gospel] s. ewangelia

gossip ['gosyp] s. plotka; plotkarz; plotkarka; v. plotkować; pisać popularne artykuły

got [got] zob. get

Gothic ['gotyk] adj. gotycki

gotten ['gotn] = got; zob. get

gourd 427 grapefruit

gourd [go:rd] s. bania; tykwa
gourmet ['guermej] n. smakosz
gout [gaut] s. gościec; podagra
govern ['gawern] v. rządzić;
kierować; dowodzić;
trzymać w ryzach
governess ['gawernys] s.
guwernantka; nauczycielka;
instruktorka
government ['gawernment] s.
rząd; ustrój; okręg; a.
rządowy
governor ['gawerner] s.
gubernator; zarządca;
naczelnik; szef
gown [gaun] s. suknia; toga; v.
układać togę; ubierać suknię
grab [graeb] v. łapać;
zagarniać; grabić; s. łapanie;
chwyt; zagarnięcie; porwanie
grace [grejs] s. łaska; wdzięk;
przyzwoitość; v. czcić;
ozdabiać; dodawać wdzięku;
zaszczycić
graceful ['grejsful] adj. pełen
wdzięku; wdzięczny; łaskawy
gracious ['grejszes] adj. łaskawy;
miłosierny; exp. goodness
gracious! ['gudnys'grejszes]
Boże miłosierny
grade [grejd] s. stopień; klasa;
nachylenie; v. stopniować;
dzielić na stopnie;
cieniować; równać teren;
niwelować; profilować
grade crossing ['grejd'krosyng] s.
skrzyżowanie dróg; przejazd
przez tory (jednopoziomowy)
grade school ['grejd'sku:l] s.
szkoła podstawowa
gradient ['grejdjent] s.
nachylenie; stopień
nachylenia
gradual ['graedżuel] adj.
stopniowy; po trochu
graduate ['graedżuejt] s.
absolwent; v. stopniować;
ukończyć studia; adj.
podyplomowy (kurs)
graduation [,graedżu'ejszyn] s.
ukończenie wyższych
studiów; stopniowanie;
cechowanie; podziałka

graft [gra:ft] v. szczepić;
dawać łapówkę;
przeszczepiać; s. szczepienie;
łapówka; przeszczep; szufla
(pełna ziemi)
grain [grejn] s. ziarno; zboże;
odrobina; grań; włókno; słój;
v. granulować; ziarnować
gram [graem] s. gram; 1/28 uncji
grammar ['graemer] s. gramatyka
grammar school ['graemer-,sku:l]
s. szkoła podstawowa
grammatical [gre'maetykel] adj.
gramatyczny (poprawny)
gramme [graem] s. gram (ang.)
gramophone ['graemefoun] s.
patefon; gramofon
grand [graend] adj. wielki;
główny; wspaniały; świetny;
okazały; (slang): 1000
dolarów; całkowity
grandchild ['graen,czajld] s.
wnuk
granddaughter ['graen,do:ter] s.
wnuczka
grandeur ['graendżer] s.
wielkość; dostojność;
okazałość; wspaniałość;
majestat; blask; pompa
grandfather ['graend,fa:dzer] s.
dziadek
grandma ['graenma:] s. babcia
grandmother ['graen,madzer] s.
babka
grandpa ['graenpa:] s. dziadzio
grandparents ['graen,paerents]
pl. dziadkowie
grandson ['graensan] s. wnuk
grandstand ['graen'staend] s.
główna trybuna; v.
popisywać się
granny ['graeny] s. babunia
grant [gra:nt] v. nadawać;
udzielać; uznawać; zgadzać
się na; przekazywać; s.
pomoc; przekazanie tytułu
własności; darowizna
granulated ['graenjulejtyd] adj.
ziarnisty; rozdrobniony;
granulowany
grape [grejp] s. winogrona
grapefruit ['grejp-fru:t] s.
grejpfrut (owoc lub drzewo)

grape-sugar ['grejp,szuger] s.
cukier gronowy

grapevine ['grejp-wajn] s.
winorośl; poczta pantoflowa;
szeptanka; źródło kaczek
prasowych

graph [graef] s. wykres; krzywa

graphic ['graefyk] adj. graficzny;
plastyczny; obrazowy
(dosadny)

grasp [gra:sp] v. łapać;
chwytać; pojmać;
pojmować; dzierżyć; s.
chwyt; uchwyt; pojęcie;
panowanie; zrozumienie;
kontrola

grass [gra:s] s. trawa; (slang):
marijuana; "pot"; haszysz

grasshopper ['gra:s,hoper] s.
konik polny (z czterema
skrzydłami)

grass widower ['gra:s,łydouer] s.
słomiany wdowiec

grate [grejt] s. krata; ruszt; v.
trzeć; ucierać; zgrzytać;
skrzypieć; irytować; być
irytującym

grateful ['grejtful] adj.
wdzięczny; dobrze widziany

grater ['grejter] s. tarko; tarło;
raszpla; tarnik do drzewa

gratification [,graetyfy'kejszyn] s.
zaspokojenie; wynagrodzenie;
gratyfikacja; łapówka

gratify ['graetyfaj] v. dogadzać;
uprzyjemniać; zadawalać;
przekupywać; wynagradzać

grating ['grejtyng] s. krata; adj.
zgrzytliwy; ochrypły

gratis ['grejtys] adv. gratis;
bezpłatnie; adj. bezpłatny;
gratisowy; darmowy

gratitude ['graetytju:d] s.
wdzięczność (za pomoc etc.)

gratuitous [gre'tjuites] adj.
bezpłatny; niepotrzebny

gratuity [gre'tjuity] s. napiwek;
zasiłek przy zwolnieniu

grave ['grejw] s. grób; adj.
poważny; v. wyryć; wryć;
wykopać

gravel ['grawel] s. żwir; piasek;
v. posypywać żwirem;

kłopotać

graveyard ['grejwja:rd] s.
cmentarz; nocna zmiana w
pracy

gravitation [,graewy'tejszyn] s.
ciążenie (ciał); grawitacja

gravity ['graewyty] s. siła
ciężkości; ciężkość;
powaga (np. sytuacji); ciężar
(gatunkowy)

gravy ['grejwy] s. sos miąsny;
sok; dodatkowy zysk; osobista
korzyść

gray [grej] adj. szary; zob. grey;
v. szarzeć; s. szary kolor

graze [grejz] v. paść; drasnąć;
s. draśnięcie; muśnięcie;
odarcie

grazing land ['grejzyng,laend] s.
pastwisko; pastwiska

grease [gri:s] s. tłuszcz; smar; v.
brudzić; smarować;
nasmarować smarem
(samochód etc.)

grease gun ['gri:s,gan] s.
smarownica wtryskowa;
towotnica

greasy ['gri:sy] adj. tłusty; śliski

great [grejt] adj. wielki; duży;
świetny; znakomity;
wspaniały; zamiłowany;
doniosły

greatcoat ['grejt'kout] s. palto;
płaszcz; opończa

great grandchild ['grejt'graend
,czajld] s. prawnuk

great grandfather ['grejt'graend
fa:dzer] s. pradziadek

great grandmother ['grejt'graend
madzer] s. prababka

greatness ['grejtnys] s.
wielkość; ogrom;
wielkoduszność; powaga

greed [gri:d] s. chciwość;
zachłanność; żądza (władzy)

greedy [gri:dy] adj. chciwy;
zachłanny; łakomy; łapczywy;
żądny; żarłoczny; spragniony

Greek [gri:k] adj. grecki;
(niezrozumiały); s. język
grecki; Grek

green [gri:n] adj. zielony;
naiwny; młody;

niedoświadczony; świeży; s.
zieleń; zielenina; trawnik; v.
zielenić; naciągać
greenback ['gri:nbaek] s. (slang)
dolar (banknot)
greenhorn ['gri:nhorn] s.
nowicjusz; żółtodziób
greenhouse ['gri:nhaus] s.
cieplarnia
greenish ['gri:nysz] adj.
zielonkawy
greet ['gri:t] v. kłaniać się;
pozdrawiać; ukazać się;
dojść do (uszu);
zaprezentować się
greeting ['gri:tyng] s.
pozdrowienie; powitanie;
pozdrowienia
grew [gru:] zob. grow
grey [grej] adj. szary; siwy; s.
szarość; v. szarzeć; siwieć
(ortografia brytyjska)
greyhound ['grejhaund] s. chart
(wysoki, chudy, szybki pies)
grid [gryd] s. krata; sieć; siatka;
sieć wysokiego napięcia
grief [gri:f] s. zmartwienie;
zgryzota; smutek; żal
grievance ['gri:wens] s. uraza;
krzywda; skarga; zażalenie
grieve [gri:w] v. martwić;
krzywdzić; smucić;
zasmucić
grievous ['gri:wes] adj.
dręczący; przykry; ciężki;
smutny
grill [gryl] s. rożen; krata;
potrawa z rusztu; v. smażyć
na rożnie; przesłuchiwać
grim [grym] adj. srogi; ponury;
okrutny; groźny; odrażający
grimace [gri'mejs] s. grymas; v.
grymasić
grime [grajm] s. brud; v. brudzić
(sadzą, smarem etc.)
grimy ['grajmy] adj. brudny;
wysmarowany; zatłuszczony
grin [gryn] v. szczerzyć zęby;
uśmiechać się; s. uśmiech
grind; ground; ground [grajnd;
graund; graund]
grind [grajnd] v. ostrzyć;
toczyć; mleć; zgrzytać;

trzeć; harować; s. mlenie;
harówka; kujon; ciężka
rutyna; kucie się
grindstone ['grajnd,stoun] s.
kamień szlifierski; harówka
grip [gryp] s. uchwyt; trzonek;
rękojeść; rączka; łapka;
uścisk dłoni; władza; moc;
wywieranie wrażenia;
opanowanie (tematu); v.
chwycić; złapać; mocno
trzymać w rękach;
opanować sytuację; ująć
rozumem
gripes [grajps] pl. kolka
gristle ['grysl] s. chrząstka
grit [gryt] s. żwir; piasek;
odwaga; wytrzymałość;
charakter; v. zgrzytać;
skrzypieć; posypywać
groan [groun] s. jęk; v. jęczeć
grocer ['grouser] s. właściciel
sklepu spożywczego
groceries ['grouserys] pl. towary
spożywcze
grocery ['grousery] s. sklep
spożywczy; artykuł
spożywczy
groin [grain] s. pachwina
groom [grum] s. parobek; pan
młody; v. obrządzać;
przygotowywać do objęcia
stanowiska
groove [gru:w] s. bruzda; rowek;
rutyna; v. żłobić; rowkować;
nacinać zwojnik; gwintować
grope [group] v. szukać po
omacku; iść po omacku;
iść na ślepo
gross [grous] adj. gruby;
ordynarny; prostacki;
całkowity; hurtowy; tłusty;
niesmaczny; spasły; wybujały;
s. 12 tuzinów; v. uzyskać
brutto ...
ground [graund] s. grunt; ziemia;
podstawa; podłoże; teren; dno
(morza); osad; powód;
przyczyna; dno; v. 1. osiąść
na mieliźnie; uziemiać;
gruntować; zagruntować; 2.
zob. grind
ground control ['graund,ken

'troul] kontrolna stacja (lotów)
ground crew ['graund,kru:] s.
załoga, ekipa na ziemi
ground floor ['graund,flo:r] s.
parter (bliski poziomu gruntu)
ground glass ['graund,glas] s.
tłuczone szkło
groundhog ['graundhog] s.
świstak (amerykański)
groundless ['graundlys] adj.
bezpodstawny; gołosłowny
groundnut ['graundnat] s.
orzeszek ziemny
ground staff ['graund,staf] s.
personel naziemny (lotnictwa)
groundwork ['graundłerk] s.
podstawa; podłoże; zasada;
fundament; tło; osnowa;
kanwa (utworu)
group [gru:p] s. grupa; v.
grupować; rozsegregowywać
na grupy
grove [grouw] s. gaj
grow; grew; grown [grou; gru:;
groun]
grow [grou] v. rosnąć; stawać
się; dojrzewać; hodować;
sadzić
growl [graul] s. ryk; pomruk;
warczenie; v. mruknąć;
warknąć; burczeć; warczeć;
odburknąć; gderać;
mrukliwie odpowiadać
grown [groun] v. zob. grow
grown-up ['groun,ap] adj.
dorosły; s. człowiek dorosły
growth [grous] s. rozwój;
wzrost; uprawa; narośl;
porost; przyrost
grub [grab] v. karczować;
dłubać; harować; wcinać
(jedzenie)
grubby ['graby] adj. brudny;
niechlujny; robaczywy
grudge [gradż] v. żałować;
skąpić; zazdrościć; mieć
niechęć; s. żal; uraza;
niechęć
gruel [gruel] s. kaszka; kleik; v.
wymęczyć; zadawać bobu
(komuś)
gruesome ['gru:sem] adj.
okropny

gruff [graf] adj. burkliwy;
gburowaty; ochrypły; gruby
(głos)
grumble ['grambl] v. narzekać;
utyskiwać; gderać; skarżyć
się; s. narzekanie; pomruk;
szemranie
grumbler ['grambler] s. zrzęda
grunt [grant] s. kwik; v.
kwiczeć; chrząkać;
wymruczeć
guarantee [,gaeren'ti:] v.
gwarantować; poręczać; s.
poręczyciel; poręka; rękojmia
guarantor [,gaeren'to:r] s.
poręczyciel; poręczycielka
guard [ga:rd] v. pilnować;
chronić; s. strażnik; opiekun;
obrońca; bezpiecznik
guard against ['ga:rd,e'genst] v.
zabezpieczać się przed ...
guardhouse ['ga:rdhaus] s.
wartownia; tymczasowy
areszt
guardian ['ga:rdjen] s. opiekun;
kustosz; adj. opiekuńczy
guardianship ['ga:rdjenszyp] s.
opieka; opiekuństwo; kuratela
guess [ges] v. zgadywać;
przypuszczać; myśleć; s.
zgadywanie; przypuszczenie;
zgadnięcie
guest [gest] s. gość
guest house ['gesthaus] s.
pensjonat; osobny domek dla
gości
guest room ['gestru:m] s. pokój
gościnny; gościnna sypialnia
guidance ['gajdens] s.
kierownictwo; poradnictwo;
kierowanie
guide [gajd] s. przewodnik;
doradca; v. wskazywać
drogę; prowadzić
guidebook ['gajdbuk] s.
przewodnik (książka) dla
turystów
guild [gyld] s. cech; związek
guildhall ['gyld'ho:l] s. dom
cechowy; ratusz; dom
związkowy
guile [gajl] s. oszustwo
guileless ['gajllys] adj. szczery;

otwarty (w postępowaniu)
guilt [gylt] s. wina; przestępstwo
guiltless ['gyltlys] adj. niewinny;
wolny od zarzutu
guilty ['gylty] adj. winny
guinea pig ['gynypyg] s. świnka
morska; przedmiot
eksperymentów
guitar [gy'ta:r] s. gitara
gulf [galf] s. zatoka; przepaść;
wir; v. pochłaniać
gull [gal] s. mewa; v. oszukiwać
gullet [galyt] s. przełyk; gardło;
gardziel
gully ['galy] s. wąwóz; ściek;
kanał; v. żłobić; wyżłobić;
poryć
gulp [galp] s. łyk; duży kęs
gulp down ['galpdałn] v. łukać;
dławić się; hamować łzy
gum [gam] s. dziąsło; guma; v.
kleić; wydzielać żywicę
gun [gan] s. strzelba; armata;
pistolet; działo; wystrzał
armatni
gunpowder ['gan,pałder] s. proch
strzelniczy; proch armatni
gurgle ['ge:rgl] v. bulgotać;
bełkotać; s. bulgotanie;
szemranie
gush [gasz] s. ulewa; wylew; v.
tryskać; lać się; wytrysnąć
gust [gast] s. podmuch; wybuch
gut [gat] s. kiszka; v. patroszyć;
wypalić wnętrze (domu)
guts [gats] pl. wnętrzności
gutter ['gater] v. wyżłobić;
okapywać; s. rynna;
rynsztok; rów; wyżłobienie;
adj. rynsztokowy; brukowy
(dziennik)
guy [gaj] s. facet; człek; cuma;
v. cumować; uwiązać
gym [dżym] s. sala
gimnastyczna; gimnastyka
(przedmiot w szkole)
gymnasium [dżym'nejzjem] s.
sala gimnastyczna; hala
sportowa
gymnastics [dżym'naestyks] s.
gimnastyka; ćwiczenia
fizyczne
gynecologist [,gajny'koledżyst]

s. ginekolog
gypsy ['dżypsy] s. cygan;
cyganka; cyganeria; język
cygański
gyrate [,dżaje'rejt] v. wirować;
kręcić się (wzdłuż koła lub
spirali)

H

h [ejcz] ósma litera angielskiego
alfabetu (prawie niema)
haberdasher ['haeberdaeszer] s.
kupiec galanteryjny; szmuklerz
habit ['haebyt] s. zwyczaj; nałóg;
usposobienie;
przyzwyczajenie; habit; v.
odziewać się
habitation [,haeby'tejszyn] s.
miejsce zamieszkania;
zamieszkiwanie
habitual [he'bytjual] adj. zwykły;
nałogowy; zwyczajny
hack [haek] v. siekać; rąbać;
kopać; kaszleć; s. szrama;
motyka; szkapa; najemnik;
taksówka; adj. wynajęty;
spowszedniały; banalny;
oklepany; szablonowy
hacksaw ['haekso:] s. piła do
metalu (z drobnymi ząbkami)
had [haed] zob. have
haddock ['haedek] s. łupacz
h(a)emorrhage ['hemerydż] s.
krwotok; mieć krwotok
hag [haeg] s. wiedźma;
czarownica; brzydka, zła
kobieta
haggard ['haegerd] adj.
wynędzniały; strapiony;
wychudły
hail [hejl] s. grad; powitanie; v.
grad pada; witać;
pozdrawiać; zawołać; walić
jak gradem
hair [heer] s. włos; włosy
hairbrush ['heerbrash] s.
szczotka do włosów

haircut ['heerkat] s. ostrzyżenie; styl ostrzyżenia włosów
hairdo ['heerdu:] s. uczesanie; fryzura; styl uczesania
hairdresser ['heer,dreser] s. fryzjer damski
hair dryer ['heer,drajer] s. suszarka do włosów (elektryczna)
hairless ['heerlys] adj. bezwłosy; łysy; wyłysiały
hairpin ['heerpyn] s. szpilka do włosów
hairy [heery] adj. włochaty
half [ha:f] s. połowa; adj. pół; adv. na pół; po połowie
half an hour ['ha:f,en'aur] s. pół godziny
half brother ['ha:f,bra<u>dz</u>er] s. przyrodni brat
half-breed ['ha:f,bri:d] s. mieszaniec
half time ['ha:f'tajm] s. przerwa; pół etatu; a. półetatowy
halfway ['ha:f'łej] adv. w pół drogi; w połowie drogi
hall [ho:l] s. sień; sala; hala; dwór; gmach publiczny; westybul
halloo! [he'lu:] excl. okrzyk w celu zwrócenia uwagi; v. krzyczeć; wołać
halo ['hejlou] s. nimb; aureola
halt [ho:lt] v. zatrzymać; utykać; kuleć; wahać się; s. postój; przystanek; utykanie
halter ['ho:lter] s. kantar pastewny; stryczek; v. nakładać kantar
halve [ha:w] v. przepołowić; podzielić się po połowie
ham [haem] s. szynka
hamburger ['haembe:rger] s. siekany kotlet wołowy; bułka z siekanym kotletem wołowym
hamlet ['haemlyt] s. wioska; sioło; malutka wieś
hammer ['haemer] s. młotek; v. bić młotkiem; walić
hammock ['haemok] s. hamak
hamper ['haemper] v. zawadzać; krępować; s. kosz z wiekiem

hamster ['haemster] s. chomik
hand [haend] s. ręka; dłoń; pismo; v. podać; zwijać; pomagać; a. podręczny; przenośny
hand back ['haend,baek] v. oddać; podać do tyłu
hand down ['haend,dałn] v. przekazać; dać w spadku; podać w dół
hand in ['haend,yn] v. wręczyć
hand over ['haend,ouwer] v. wręczyć; podać; dostarczyć
handbag ['haendbaeg] s. damska torebka
handbill ['haendbyl] s. ulotka
handbook ['haend-buk] s. podręcznik; poradnik
hand brake ['haend,brejk] s. hamulec ręczny
handcuff ['haendka:f] s. kajdany; v. zakuwać w kajdany
handful ['haendful] s. garść; garstka; kłopotliwa osoba
handicap ['haendykaep] s. przeszkoda; upośledzenie; trudność
handicraft ['haendykra:ft] s. rzemiosło; rękodzieło (tkactwo, etc.)
handkerchief ['hendkerczy:f] s. apaszka; chustka do nosa
handle ['haendl] s. trzonek; rękojeść; uchwyt; sposób; v. dotykać; manipulować; traktować; załatwiać; dać radę; handlować; zarządzać; kontrolować
handlebar ['haendlba:r] s. kierownica od (roweru)
hand luggage ['haend,lagydż] s. bagaż ręczny
handmade ['haend'mejd] adj. ręcznie zrobiony
handrail ['haend,rejl] s. poręcz; bariera; balustrada
handshake ['haend,szejk] s. uścisk dłoni (w pozdrowieniu, targu)
handsome ['haensem] adj. przystojny; szczodry; znaczny (datek)
handwork ['haend,łe:rk] s. robota

ręczna; praca fizyczna
handwriting ['haend,rajtyŋg] s.
pismo; charakter pisma
handy ['haendy] adj. zręczny;
wygodny; bliski; pod ręką
hang; hung; hung [haeŋg; haŋg;
haŋg]
hang [haeŋg] v. wieszać;
powiesić; rozwiesić;
wywiesić; zwisać; s.
nachylenie; pochyłość;
powiązanie; orientacja
hang around ['haeŋg e'raund] v.
wałąsać się; obijać się
hang out ['haeŋg'aut] v.
wywieszać; wychylać się
hang up ['haeŋg,ap] v. zaczepić
sie; powiesić słuchawkę;
opóźniać (pracę);
wstrzymywać
hangar ['haenger] s. hangar
hang-glider ['haeŋg'glajder] s.
lotnia; skrzydło Rogali
hangings ['haeŋynz] s. kotary;
portiery; draperie; obicia;
firanki
hang loose ['haen,lu:z] v. być
rozluźniony w akcji
(sportowej); zwisać
swobodnie
hangover ['haeŋg,ouwer] s.
(slang) kac; przeżytek
hanky-panky ['haeŋky-'paenky]
s. hokus-pokus; też:
rozwiązłość
haphazard ['haep'haezerd] s. los
szczęścia; przypadek; adj.
przypadkowy; dorywczy; adv.
przypadkowo; na chybił trafił
happen ['haepen] v. zdarzać
się; trafić się; przypadkowo
być (gdzieś); mieć
(nie)szczęście
happen on ['haepen,on] v.
przypadkiem spotkać;
natknąć się na
happening ['haepenyŋg] s.
wydarzenie; wypadek;
zdarzenie
happily ['haepyly] adv.
szczęśliwie; na szczęście;
trafnie
happiness ['haepynys] s.

szczęście; zadowolenie;
radość
happy ['haepy] adj. szczęśliwy;
zadowolony; właściwy
(wybór); mądra (rada);
radosny
happy-go-lucky ['haepy,gou'laky]
adj. beztroski
harass ['haeres] v. niepokoić;
trapić; dręczyć; nękać
harbor ['ha:rber] s. przystań;
port; v. gościć; dawać
schronienie; zawijać do portu
harelip ['heer'lyp] s. zajęcza
warga
hard [ha:rd] adj. twardy; surowy;
trudny; ciężki; ostry; adv.
usilnie; wytrwale; ciężko; z
trudem; siarczyście
hard by ['ha:rd,baj] adv. blisko;
tuż obok; w pobliżu
hard up ['ha:rd,ap] v. być w
kłopotach pieniężnych
hard of hearing [ha:rd,ow
'hieryŋg] adj. głuchawy
harden ['ha:rdn] v. twardnieć;
uodparniać; stabilizować
hardheaded ['ha:rd'hedyd] adj.
trzeźwy; praktyczny; twardy
człowiek
hardhearted ['ha:rd'ha:rtyd] adj.
nieczuły; niemiłosierny
hardly ['ha:rdly] adv. ledwie;
zaledwie; prawie; z trudem;
surowo; chyba nie; rzadko
hardness ['ha:rdnys] s.
twardość; wytrzymałość;
odporność
hardship ['ha:rdszyp] s.
trudność; trudy; męka; znój
hardware ['ha:rdłeer] s. wyroby
żelazne; towary żelazne
hare [heer] s. zając; królik
harebell ['heer-bel] s. dzwonek
okrągłolistny
hark [ha:rk] v. słuchaj; uważaj;
odejdź; słuchaj uważnie
harm [ha:rm] s. szkoda;
krzywda; v. szkodzić;
krzywdzić
harmful ['ha:rmful] adj.
szkodliwy; szkodzący;
zadający ból

harmless ['ha:rmlys] adj.
nieszkodliwy; niewinny
harmonious [ha:rmounjes] adj.
harmonijny; melodyjny; zgodny
harmonize ['ha:rmenajz] v.
uzgadniać; harmonizować
harmony ['ha:rmeny] s. harmonia
(dźwięków, ludzi); zgoda
harness ['ha:rnys] s. uprząż; v.
zaprzęgać; zużytkować
(wiatr ...)
harp [ha:rp] s. harfa; v. gadać
w kółko; grać na harfie
harpoon [ha:'rpu:n] s. harpun; v.
ugodzić harpunem
harrow ['haerou] s. brona; v.
bronować; dręczyć;
szarpać; ranić; pustoszyć;
niszczyć
harsh [ha:rsz] adj. szorstki;
żrący; ostry; cierpki; przykry;
surowy; nieprzyjemny
hart [ha:rt] s. rogacz (dorosły)
(powyżej pięcioletni)
harvest ['ha:rwyst] s. żniwa;
zbiory; zbiór; urodzaj; plony; v.
zbierać (zboże); zbierać
(plony); sprzątać z pól
harvester ['ha:rwyster] s.
żniwiarz; żniwiarka
(mechaniczna)
has [haez] (on, ona, ono) ma;
zob. have
hash [haesz] s. siekane mięso;
v. siekać; knocić;
przemieszać
haste [hejst] s. pośpiech
hasten [hejstn] v. przyśpieszać;
spieszyć; być szybkim
hasty ['hejsty] adj. pośpieszny;
prędki; porywczy; niecierpliwy
hat [haet] s. kapelusz
hatch [haecz] v. wysiadywać;
wylęgać; wykluwać; knuć;
zakreskować; s. wyląg; łuk;
drzwiczki; śluza; kreska
hatchet ['haeczyt] s. toporek
hatchet man ['haeczyt,men] s.
człowiek przeprowadzający
czystkę (odrabiający brudną
robotą)
hate [hejt] s. nienawiść; v.
nienawidzieć; nie znosić

hateful ['hejtful] adj.
nienawistny; zasługujący na
nienawiść
hatred ['hejtryd] s. nienawiść
haughtiness ['ho:tynys] s.
pyszność; hardość;
zarozumialstwo
haughty ['ho:ty] adj. hardy;
pyszny; zarozumiały;
wzgardliwy
haul [ho:l] s. wleczenie;
holowanie; ładunek; połów;
zysk; v. wlec; ciągnąć;
holować; wozić;
transportować; taszczyć
haunch [ho:ncz] s. biodro z
udem
haunt [ho:nt] v. nawiedzać; s.
miejsce często odwiedzane;
melina; spelunka; legowisko
have; had; had [haew; haed;
haed]
have [haew] v. mieć;
otrzymać; zawierać; nabyć;
musieć
have-not ['haew,nat] adj. nie
posiadający; biedny
have on ['haew on] v. mieć na
sobie; być ubranym w
have to do ['haew,tu'du] v.
musieć (coś) robić
haven ['hejwn] s. przystań;
port; v. dawać schronienie;
wprowadzać do portu
havoc ['haewek] s. spustoszenie
hawk [ho:k] s. jastrząb; packa;
chrząknięcie; v. polować z
jastrzębiem; sprzedawać na
ulicy; chrząkać głośno
hawthorn ['ho:torn] s. głóg
hay [hej] s. siano
haycock ['hejkok] s. stóg siana
hay-fever ['hej'fi:wer] s.
uczulenie; katar sienny
hayloft ['hej-loft] s. strych na
siano (w stodole etc.)
hayrick ['hejryk] s. stóg siana
haystack ['hejsta:k] s. stóg siana
(w polu, na łące etc.)
hazard ['haezerd] s. przypadek;
traf; ryzyko; v. ryzykować
hazardous ['haezerdes] adj.
ryzykowny; hazardowny;

haze   435   heavy

niebezpieczny
haze [hejz] s. lekka mgła
hazel ['hejzl] s. leszczyna; kolor
orzechowy
hazel-nut ['hejzl-nat] s. orzech
laskowy
hazy ['hejzy] adj. mglisty;
zamglony; nieco podchmielony
H-bomb ['ejcz bom] s. bomba
wodorowa
he [hi:] pron. on
head [hed] s. głowa; łeb; szef;
naczelnik; nagłówek; szczyt;
v. prowadzić; kierować (się)
head over heels ['hed,ouwer
hi:ls] do góry nogami; na łeb
na szyję; panicznie; w panice
headache ['hedejk] s. ból głowy
headgear ['hedgi:r] s. nakrycie
głowy; ubiór głowy
heading ['hedyng] s. nagłówek
headland ['hedlend] s. przylądek
(daleko wysunięty w morze)
headlights ['hedlajts] pl. główne
światła samochodu
headline ['hedlajn] s. nagłówek
(w gazecie); wiadomość w
skrócie
headlong ['hedlong] adv. na łeb
na szyję; na złamanie karku;
na oślep; głową w przód
headmaster ['hedma:ster] s.
dyrektor (szkoły)
heads or tails ['heds,o:r'tejlz]
orzeł czy reszka
headphones ['hedfouns] pl.
słuchawki (radiowe,
gramofonowe)
headquarters ['hed'kło:terz] pl.
kwatera główna; główne biuro
headstrong ['hedstrong] adj.
zawzięty; uparty;
bezwzględny
headway ['hedłej] s. postęp
heal [hi:l] v. leczyć; łagodzić;
uspakajać; wyleczyć się
heal up ['hi:l,ap] v. zagoić
health [hels] s. zdrowie
health resort [hels ry'zo:rt] s.
uzdrowisko
healthy ['helsy] adj. zdrowy;
potężny; spowodowany
zdrowiem

heap [hi:p] s. kupa; gromada; v.
gromadzić; ładować na stos;
obsypywać dużą ilością
hear; heard; heard [hier; he:rd;
he:rd]
hear [hier] v. słyszeć; usłyszeć;
słuchać; dowiedzieć się
heard [he:rd] zob. hear
hearing ['hieryng] s. słuch;
posłuch; przesłuchanie;
rozprawa; zasięg głosu;
słyszenie
hearsay ['hiersej] s. pogłoska
hearse [he:rs] s. karawan
heart [ha:rt] s. serce; odwaga;
otucha; sedno; symbol serca
heartbreaking ['ha:rtbrejkyng]
adj. rozdzierający serce
heartburn ['ha:rtbe:rn] s. zgaga;
pieczenie w żołądku
hearth [ha:rs] s. palenisko
heartless ['ha:rtlys] adj. nieczuły;
bez serca
heart transplant ['ha:rt,traens
'pla:nt] przeszczepienie serca
hearty ['ha:rty] adj. serdeczny;
szczery; otwarty; pożywny;
obfity; solidny; dobry; krzepki;
rześki
heat [hi:t] s. gorąco; upał; żar;
ciepło; uniesienie; pasja;
popęd płciowy (zwierząt)
heater ['hi:ter] s. grzejnik; piec
heath [hi:s] s. wrzos; wrzosiec;
wrzosowisko
heathen [hi:zen] adj. pogański;
s. poganin; ciemniak
heather ['hedzer] s. wrzos
heating ['hi:tyng] s. ogrzewanie
heave; hove; hove [hi:w; houw;
houw]
heave [hi:w] v. unosić;
dźwigać; podważać;
nabrzmiewać; wyciągać;
sapać; s. dźwignięcie;
przesunięcie
heaven ['hewn] s. niebo; raj;
niebiosa
heavenly ['hewnly] adj. niebieski;
niebiański; boski
heaviness ['hewynys] s.
ciężkość; ociężałość
heavy ['hewy] adj. ciężki; duży;

ponury; zrozpaczony
heavy-handed ['hewy'haendyd]
adj. niezgrabny; nietaktowny;
bezwzględny
heavy traffic ['hewy'traefyk]
ciężki ruch (np. kołowy)
heavyweight ['hewyłejt] s. waga
ciężka
hectic ['hektyk] adj. gorący;
dziki; niszczący;
rozgorączkowany
hedge [hedż] s. płot; żywopłot;
ogrodzenie; zapora;
ubezpieczenie; v. ogradzać;
wykręcać się; ubezpieczać
się w spekulacji
hedgehog ['hedżhog] s. jeż;
świnka morska
heed [hi:d] s. troska; dbałość;
uwaga; wzgląd; ostrożność;
v. uważać; baczyć
heedful ['hi:dful] adj. uważny;
ostrożny
heedless ['hi:dlys] adj. niedbały;
nieostrożny; nieuważny
heel [hi:l] s. pięta; obcas;
przechył; łajdak; v. dotykać
piętą; podbijać obcas;
zaopatrywać; przechylać się;
tupać obcasem
he goat ['hi:gout] s. kozioł
heifer ['hefer] s. jałówka
height [hajt] s. wysokość;
wzniesienie; wyniosłość;
szczyt; najwyższa granica
heighten [hajtn] v. podnosić;
podwyższać; powiększać
heinous ['hejnes] adj. potworny;
ohydny; nienawistny; haniebny
heir [eer] s. spadkobierca;
dziedzic; następca
heiress ['eerys] s.
spadkobierczyni; następczyni;
dziedziczka (majątku, tytułu)
held [held] zob. hold
helicopter ['helykopter] s.
śmigłowiec; helikopter
hell [hel] s. piekło; psiakrew!
miejsce nędzy i okrucieństwa
hello ['he'lou] excl. halo!
cześć! czołem! dzień dobry!
helm [helm] s. ster; v. sterować
helmet ['helmyt] s. hełm; kask

help [help] v. pomagać;
usługiwać; nakładać
(jedzenie); s. pomoc;
pomocnik; robotnik
helper ['helper] s. pomocnik
helpful ['helpful] adj. pomocny;
przydatny; użyteczny
helping ['helpyng] s. porcja
(jedzenia); udzielanie pomocy
helpless ['helplys] adj. bezradny;
bez pomocy; słaby
helplessness ['helplysnys] s.
bezradność; słabość
helter-skelter ['helter'skelter]
adv. łapu-capu; na łeb na
szyję; s. popłoch; bezładny
pośpiech (w bałaganie)
hem [hem] s. brzeg; obrąbek;
chrząkanie; v. obrąbiać;
otoczyć; pochrząkiwać;
wahać się
hem in ['hem,yn] v. okrążyć;
zamknąć; obrąbić
hemisphere ['hemysfier] s.
półkula (zachodnia,
wschodnia, etc.)
hemline ['hemlajn] s. obrąbek
spódnicy
hemlock ['hemlek] s. szalej;
cykuta jadowita; drzewo tsuga
hemp [hemp] s. konopie; adj.
konopny (sznur etc.)
hemstitch ['hemstycz] s.
mereżka; v. mereżkować
(ozdobnie)
hen [hen] s. kura; kwoka; baba
hence [hens] adv. stąd; odtąd; a
więc; przeto; dlatego
henceforth [hens'fo:rs] adv.
odtąd; na przyszłość; od
teraz
hen coop ['henku:p] s. kurnik
hen house ['henhaus] s. kurnik
henpecked ['henpekt] s.
pantoflarz; adj. będący pod
pantoflem
her [he:r] pron. ją; jej; adj. jej;
(należący) do niej
herald ['hereld] s. zwiastun; v.
zwiastować; wprowadzać
heraldry ['hereldry] s. heraldyka;
pompa; ceremonia
herb [he:rb] s. zioło

(jednoroczne)

herd [he:rd] s. trzoda; stado; pastuch; v. iść stadem; zganiać w stado; paść; popędzać stadem

herdsman ['he:rdzmen] s. pasterz; pastuch

here [hier] adv. tu; tutaj; oto

here you are [‚hier'ju:‚a:r] exp. tu pan mal proszą bardzol

hereafter ['hier'a:fter] adv. odtąd; poniżej; potem; w życiu pozagrobowym; s. przyszłość; przyszłe życie

hereby ['hier'baj] adv. przez to; w ten sposób; skutkiem tego; w pobliżu

hereditary [hy'redytery] adj. dziedziczny; odziedziczony; tradycyjny; przekazany dziedzicznie

herein ['hier'yn] adv. tutaj; tam że; wobec tego; w tych warunkach; w tym (rozdziale)

hereof ['hier'of] adv. tego; o tym; w odniesieniu do tego

heresy ['herysy] s. herezja

heretic ['heretyk] s. heretyk; heretyczka

hereupon ['hiere'pon] adv. potem; skutkiem tego; o tym

herewith ['hier'tyş] adv. niniejszym; w ten sposób

heritage ['herytydż] s. spuścizna; spadek; dziedzictwo

hermit ['he:rmyt] s. pustelnik; odludek; eremita; pustelnica

hero ['hierou] s. bohater

heroic ['hierouyk] adj. bohaterski; heroiczny; epicki; bardzo wymowny; podniosły

heroine ['hierouyn] s. bohaterka

heroism ['hierouyzem] s. bohaterstwo (w czynach i cechach)

heron ['heren] s. czapla

herring ['heryng] s. śledź

hers [he:rz] pron. jej

herself [he:r'self] pron. ona sama; ona sobie; ja sama

hesitate ['hezytejt] v. wahać się; być niepewnym;

zatrzymać się

hesitation [‚hezytejszyn] s. wahanie; być niezdecydowanym

hew; hewed; hewn [hju:; hju:d; hju:n]

hew [hju:] v. rąbać; ciosać; kuć; wyrąbywać (ścieżką)

hewn [hju:n] zob. hew

hey [hej] excl. hej! ejże!

heyday ['hejdej] s. pełnia; rozkwit; świetny nastrój

hi [haj] excl. hej! (pozdrowienie); cześć! czołem!

hiccup; hiccough ['hykap] s. czkawka; v. mieć czkawkę

hid [hyd] zob.hide

hidden [hydn] zob. hide

hide; hid; hidden [hajd; hyd; hydn]

hide [hajd] v. chować; ukrywać; s. kryjówka; skóra (zwierzęca)

hide-and-seek ['hajd‚en si:k] exp. zabawa w chowanego

hideous ['hydjes] adj. ohydny; wstrętny; paskudny; odrażający

hiding ['hajdyng] s. kryjówka; skórobicie; lanie; manto

hiding place ['hajdyng'plejs] s. kryjówka; melina

hi-fi ['haj'faj] = high fidelity ['haj fy'delyty] wiernie odtwarzający dźwięk (aparat)

high [haj] adj. wysoki; wyniosły; silny; cienki (głos)

highbrow ['hajbrau] s. intelektualista; a. intelektualny

high diving ['hajdajwyng] s. skakanie z wieży do wody

high jump ['hajdżamp] s. skok wzwyż (w sporcie)

highlands ['hajlend] s. podgórze; góry; górzysty kraj

highlights ['hajlajts] pl. główne punkty (np. programu)

highly ['hajly] adv. wysoko; wysoce; wielce; zaszczytnie

highness ['hajnys] s. wysokość (tytuł); wyniosłość

high-pitched ['haj'pyczt] adj. wysoki; ostry; cienki (głos);

spadzisty; stromy (dach)
high-powered ['haj'pałerd] adj.
potężny
high-pressure ['haj'preszer] adj.
wysokiego ciśnienia;
nachalny
highroad ['haj'roud] s. szosa;
główna droga
high-school ['haj'sku:l] s.
gimnazjum; szkoła średnia
high-strung ['haj'strang] adj.
nerwowy; napięty; wrażliwy
high-tide ['haj'tajd] s. przypływ
highway ['haj'łej] s. szosa
highwayman ['haj,łejmen] s.
rozbójnik
hijack ['hajdżaek] v. rabować;
grabić
hike [hajk] v. włóczyć się;
wędrować; wyciągać do
góry; s. wycieczka; podwyżka
hilarious [hy'leerjes] adj. wesoły;
hałaśliwie wesoły
hill [hyl] s. górka; pagórek;
kopiec; v. sypać kopiec
hillbilly ['hylbyly] s. prowincjusz
hillside ['hyl'sajd] s. stok
hilly ['hyly] adj. pagórkowaty;
górzysty
hilt [hylt] s. rękojeść; garda
him [hym] pron. jego; go; jemu;
mu
himself [hym'self] pron. się;
siebie; sobie; sam; osobiście;
we własnej osobie
hind [hajnd] s. parobek; łania;
adj. tylni; zadni
hinder ['hynder] v.
przeszkadzać;
powstrzymywać
hind leg ['hajnd,leg] s. tylnia
noga
hindrance ['hyndrens] s.
przeszkoda; zawada;
zawadzanie
hindsight ['hajnd,sajt] s.
zrozumienie co trzeba było
zrobić
hinge [hyndż] s. zawiasa; v.
obracać; zależeć; zawiesić
na zawiasach; wisieć na
zawiasach
hinny [hyny] s. muł (z oślicy i

ogiera); v. rżeć
hint [hynt] s. aluzja; przytyk;
wskazówka; v. napomknąć;
dać do zrozumienia; zrobić
aluzję
hinterland ['hynter,laend] s.
zaplecze; daleki teren
hip [hyp] s. biodro; naroże;
dachu; chandra; adj.
biodrowy; współczesny;
stylowy
hip to [hyp,tu] adj.
poinformowany o (slang)
hippie [hypi:] s. nonkonformista;
adj. zbuntowany przeciw
tradycji (wyobcowany)
hippopotamus [hype'potemes] s.
hipopotam
hire [hajer] s. najem; opłata za
najem; v. najmować;
wynajmować; dzierżawić;
odnajmować
hire out ['hajer aut] v.
wynajmować (się do pracy,
na służbę ...)
hire purchase ['hajer'pe:rczys]
wynajem - zakup na raty
his [hyz] pron. jego
hiss [hys] v. syczeć; gwizdać;
s. syk; gwizd; głoska sycząca
historian [hys'to:rjen] s. historyk;
historyczka
historic [hys'toryk] adj.
historyczny; sławny w historii
history ['hystory] s. historia;
dzieje; przeszłość (znana)
hit [hyt] s. uderzenie; przytyk;
sukces; sensacja; v. uderzyć;
utrafić; natrafić; zabić
hit and run ['hyt,en'ran] adj.
uciekający od wypadku
(drogowego); walczący
podjazdowo; dorywczy i
niepewny
hit man ['hytmen] s. najemny
zabójca; najemny morderca
hit or miss [hyt o:r mys] adv. na
chybił trafił; przypadkiem
hit upon ['hyte'pon] v. natrafić
(na coś, na kogoś)
hitch [hycz] s. zaciśnięcie;
węzeł; przeszkoda;
szarpnięcie; uchwyt; służba

(wojskowa); v. doczepić;
uczepić; pociągnąć;
szarpnąć; przywiązać;
zaczepić się; ciągnąć
szarpiąc
hitchhike ['hycz,hajk] v. jechać
autostopem
hitchhiker ['hycz,hajker] s.
jadący autostopem
hither ['hydzer] adv. dotąd; tutaj;
adj. bliżej
hitherto ['hydzer'tu] adv.
dotychczas; do tej pory
hive [hajw] s. ul; rojowisko; v.
umieszczać w ulu; wchodzić
do ula; zbierać do ula
hoard [ho:rd] v. gromadzić;
zbierać; s. zapas; zbiór; skarb
hoarfrost ['ho:r'frost] s. szron
(na trawie, włosach etc.)
hoarse [ho:rs] adj. zachrypnięty;
v. zachrypnąć; mieć
chrapliwy głos
hoax [houks] v. bujać;
nabierać; s. bujda; kaczka;
kawał
hobble ['hobl] s. pęta; utykanie;
v. utykać; kuleć; pętać
hobby ['hoby] s. hobby; pasja
(np. filatelistyka)
hobbyhorse ['hobyho:rs] s. konik
na kiju do zabawy (na
biegunach)
hobgoblin ['hob,goblyn] s.
skrzat; chochlik
hobnob ['hobnob] v. być za pan
brat; blisko się zadawać
hobo ['haubou] s. włóczęga
hock [hok] s. pęcina; v.
zastawić (się) w lombardzie
hockey ['hoky] s. hokej
hoe [hou] s. motyka; graca; v.
gracować; okopywać
motyką
hog [hog] s. wieprz; człowiek
zachłanny; v. łapać dla siebie;
jechać środkiem; wyginać
łukowato w środku;
zagarniać sobie
hoist [hojst] s. dźwig; wyciąg;
v. wyciągać ładunek w górę;
wywieszać (flagą);
podciągać do góry

hold; held; held [hould; held;
held]
hold [hould] v. trzymać;
posiadać; zawierać;
powstrzymywać; uważać;
obchodzić; wytrzymywać;
trwać; s. chwyt; pauza;
pomieszczenie; więzienie;
twierdza; silny wpływ; uchwyt
hold back ['hould,baek] v.
powstrzymać; zataić;
wahać się
hold on ['hould,on] v. trzymać
się; wytrzymywać
powstrzymać
holdup ['hould'ap] s.
zatrzymanie; zator; napad
rabunkowy
holder ['houlder] s. właściciel;
posiadacz; uchwyt
holding ['houldyng] s.
posiadłość; portfel akcji;
dzierżawa; uchwyt; ujęcie;
trzymanie
hole [houl] s. dziura; nora; dołek;
v. dziurawić; przedziurawiać;
przekopywać (tunel)
holiday ['holedy] s. święto;
wakacje; urlop; adj. wesoły;
radosny
holiday maker ['holedy,mejker] s.
wczasowicz; letnik; turysta;
wycieczkowicz; letniczka
holler ['holer] v. wrzeszczeć;
krzyczeć (po prostacku)
hollow ['holou] s. dziupla; dziura;
kotlina; dolina; adj. wklęsły;
dziurawy; fałszywy; głuchy;
pusty; czczy; głodny;
nieszczery; adv. pusto
hollow out ['holou,aut] v.
drążyć; wydrążyć; żłobić
holly ['holy] s. ostrokrzew
holy ['holy] adj. święty
homage ['homydż] s. hołd
home [houm] s. dom; ojczyzna;
kraj; schronisko; bramka; adj.
domowy; rodzinny; krajowy;
wewnętrzny; ojczysty
homeless ['houmlys] adj.
bezdomny; bez dachu nad
głową
homely ['houmly] adj. swojski;

pospolity; nieładny; prosty;
skromny; niewybredny;
niewyszukany

homemade ['houm'mejd] adj.
domowego wyrobu; krajowy

homesick ['houm-syk] adj.
stęskniony za domem
rodzinnym; stęskniony za
(czymś swoim)

homesickness ['houm,syknys] s.
nostalgia; tęsknota za domem

home team ['houm-ti:m] s.
drużyna miejscowa (sportowa)

home trade ['houm-trejd] s.
handel wewnętrzny

homewards ['houmłedz] adv. ku
domowi (ojczyźnie); do domu

homework ['houmłerk] s. zadanie
domowe; odrabianie lekcji

homicide ['homy,sajd] s. zabójca;
zabójstwo

honest ['onyst] adj. uczciwy;
prawy; przyzwoity; szczery;
adv. naprawdę

honesty ['onesty] s. zacność;
prawość; rzetelność;
uczciwość

honey ['hany] s. miód; słodycz

honeycomb ['hany,koum] s.
(woskowy) plaster pszczeli; v.
dziurawić; przenikać

honeymoon ['hany,mu:n] s.
miodowy miesiąc; v. spędzić
miodowy miesiąc

honk [honk] s. krzyk gęsi; głos
trąbki, klaksonu; v. trąbić;
(slang: wymyślać)

honorary ['onerery] adj.
honorowy (np. urząd);
bezpłatny

honor ['oner] s. cześć;
uczciwość; cnota; tytuł
sędziego; v. czcić;
zaszczycać; honorować

honorable ['onerebl] adj.
czcigodny; uczciwy;
szanowny; honorowy;
zaszczytny

hood [hud] s. kaptur; kapturek;
maska; buda; v. zaopatrywać
w kaptur; przykrywać

hoodlum ['hu:dlem] s. opryszek;
chuligan; łobuz

hoodwink ['hudłynk] v. oczy
mydlić; zmylić; zawiązywać
oczy

hoof ['hu:f] s. kopyto; v. kopać;
iść; tańczyć; iść pieszo

hook [huk] s. hak; v. zahaczyć;
zakrzywić (się); złapać
(męża)

hoop [hu:p] s. obręcz; v.
otaczać obręczą;wykrzyknąć

hooping-cough ['hu:pyng-kof] s.
koklusz; krztusiec; zob.
whooping cough

hoot [hu:t] s. hukanie; odgłosy
niezadowolenia; v. hukać
gwizdać; wyć; trąbić;
wygwizdać

hooves [hu:wz] pl. kopyta

hop [hop] s. chmiel; skok;
potańcówka; v.
podskakiwać; poderwać
(się); przeskakiwać

hope [houp] s. nadzieja; v. mieć
nadzieję; spodziewać się;
ufać; żywić nadzieję

hopeful ['houpful] adj. pełen
nadziei; ufny; obiecujący;
rokujący nadzieją

hopeless ['houplys] adj.
beznadziejny; rozpaczliwy;
zrozpaczony; zdesperowany

horde [ho:rd] s. horda; gromada

horizon [he'rajzen] s. horyzont;
widnokrąg; warstwa
oznaczona

horizontal [,hory'zontel] adj.
poziomy; horyzontalny;
widnokręgowy; s. płaszczyzna
pozioma; poziom równy i
płaski

horn [ho:rn] s. róg; trąbka;
syrena; kula (siodła); v.
bóść; przebóść; wmieszać
się

hornet ['ho:rnyt] s. szerszeń

horny ['ho:rny] adj. rogowy;
zrogowaciały; rogaty; jak róg

horoscope ['hore,skoup] s.
horoskop

horrible ['horebl] adj. straszny;
okropny; szokujący; paskudny

horrid ['horyd] adj. straszny;
ohydny; odrażający; paskudny

horrify ['horyfaj] v. przerażać; oburzać; ciężko szokować

horror ['horer] s. groza; wstręt; odraza; przerażenie; dreszcz

horse ['ho:rs] s. koń; konnica; jazda; kozioł z drzewa

horseback ['ho:rs,baek] s. grzbiet koński; adv. konno

horsefly ['ho:rs,flaj] s. giez

horsehair ['ho:rs,heer] s. włosie końskie; sztywna tkanina

horseman ['ho:rsmen] s. jeździec

horse opera ['ho:rs'opere] s. film kowbojski (nie-realistyczny)

horseplay ['ho:rs,plej] s. ordynarna zabawa (brutalna)

horsepower ['ho:rs,pałer] s. koń mechaniczny = 746 watów

horse race ['ho:rs,rejs] s. wyścigi konne

horseradish ['ho:rs,raedysz] s. chrzan; adj. chrzanowy

horseshoe ['ho:rs,szu] s. podkowa; a. w kształcie podkowy

horticulture ['ho:rty,kaltczer] s. ogrodnictwo

hose [houz] s. pończochy; wąż do podlewania (wiedza i praktyka)

hosiery ['haouzery] s. trykotaże; pończochy

hospitable ['hospytebl] adj. gościnny; szczodry dla gości

hospital ['hospytl] s. szpital; lecznica; a. szpitalny

hospitality [,hospy'taelyty] s. gościnność

host [houst] s. gospodarz; żywiciel; chmara; czereda; tłum

hostage ['hostydż] s. zakładnik; zastaw; zakładniczka

hostel ['hostel] s. dom studencki; bursa; zajazd

hostess ['houstys] s. gospodyni; stewardesa; fordanserka

hostile ['hostajl] adj. wrogi; nieprzyjemny; antagonistyczny

hostility [hos'tylyty] s. wrogość; stan wojny; ostra opozycja

hot [hot] adj. gorący; palący; pieprzny; ostry; nielegalny; świeży; pobudliwy; adv. gorąco

hotbed ['hot,bed] s. inspekty; wylęgarnia; siedlisko; rozsadnik

hot dog ['hot,dog] s. kiełbaska w bułce; kiełbaska smażona

hotel [hou'tel] s. hotel

hothead ['hot,hed] s. człowiek zapalczywy; raptus; a. porywczy

hothouse ['hot,haus] s. cieplarnia; oranżeria

hot-pants [,hot'paents] exp. obcisłe damskie szorty; vulg. panna puszczalska

hot water bottle [hot'ło:ter'botl] s. gorąca butelka

hound [haund] s. ogar; łajdak; v. tropić; szczuć; podjudzać

hour ['auer] s. godzina; pora

hourly ['auerly] adj. cogodzinny; adv. co godzinę; ustawicznie; z godziny na godzinę

house [haus] s. dom; zajazd; teatr; widzowie; v. gościć; dawać pomieszczenie; mieszkać

housekeeper ['haus,ki:per] s. najęta gosposia; pomoc domowa

housekeeping ['haus,ki:pyng] s. gospodarka domowa

housemaid ['haus,mejd] s. pokojówka; pomoc domowa

housewife ['haus,łajf] s. gospodyni (nie pracująca poza domem)

housework ['haus,łe:rk] s. prace domowe; sprzątanie i gotowanie

housing ['hauzyng] s. pomieszczenie; kolonia; osłona; pokrywa; czaprak; obudowa

hove [houw] zob. heave

hover ['hower] v. unosić się; kręcić się; być w niepewności; s. stan niepewności; unoszenie się; wahanie się; przywieranie

how [hau] adv. jak; jak? sposób
how do you do ['hau,du'ju:du]
exp.: dzień dobry! dobry
wieczór! (jak się pan(i) ma ?)
how are you ['hau,a:r'ju] exp.:
jak się pan(i) ma?
how about ['hau,e'baut] exp.:
może? pozwolisz? etc.
how much ['hau,macz] exp.: ile?
how many ['hau,meny] exp.: ile?
ilu? jak wielu?
how much is it? ['hau,macz'yz
,yt] ile to kosztuje?
however [hau'ewer] adv.
jakkolwiek; jednak; niemniej
howl [haul] s. wycie; ryk; v.
wyć; wyganiać (gonić)
wrzaskiem
howler ['hauler] s. gruby błąd
hub [hab] s. piasta; ośrodek;
slang: mąż; środek
(rozgrywki)
hubbub ['habbab] s. zgiełk;
gwar; awantura; wrzawa;
tumult
hubby ['haby] s. mężulek (slang)
huckleberry ['hakelbery] s.
borówka amerykańska (krzak
i jagoda)
huddle together ['hadl,tu'gedzer]
v. przytulać się; tulić się
huddle up ['hadl,ap] v. skulić
się; zwinąć się w kłębek
hue [hju:] s. barwa; odcień
hug [hag] s. uścisk; chwyt
zapaśniczy; v. ściskać;
przyciskać; tulić (się);
uściskać
huge [hju:dż] adj. ogromny
hull [hal] s. łuska; kadłub; v.
łuszczyć; godzić w kadłub
hullabaloo ['halebelu:] s.
harmider; zgiełk; wrzawa;
gwar
hullo [he'lou] excl. hola! halo!
hum [ham] v. nucić; buczeć;
mruczeć; chrząkać; s.
pomruk; chrząkanie; wahanie
się; blaga
human ['hju:men] adj. ludzki; s.
istota ludzka
humane ['hju:mejn] adj. ludzki;
humanitarny; litościwy

humanitarian [hju,maeny'teerjen]
adj. humanitarny; s. filantrop
humanity [hju'maenyty] s.
ludzkość; rasa ludzka; cechy
ludzkie; dobre uczynki
humble ['hambl] adj. pokorny;
uniżony; skromny; v.
upokarzać; poniżać;
poniżyć
humbleness ['hamblnys] s.
pokora; bezpretensjonalność
humbug ['hambag] s. oszustwo;
blaga; bujda; oszust; blagier;
v. blagować; oszukiwać;
nabierać; wyłudzać
opowiadaniem bredni
humdrum ['hamdram] adj. nudny;
banalny; monotonny; s.
szarzyzna; banalność;
nudziarz
humidity [hju'mydyty] s. wilgoć;
wilgotność (powietrza etc.)
humiliate [hju'myly,ejt] v.
upokarzać; poniżać;
martwić
humiliation [hju,:myly,ejszyn] s.
upokorzenie; poniżenie
humility [hju'mylyty] s.
skromność; pokora ducha
humming-bird ['hamyng,byrd] s.
koliber
humor ['hju:mer] s. humor;
nastrój; kaprys; wesołość; v.
dogadzać; zaspakajać;
zadowalać; ustępować;
dostosować się do
zachcianek etc.
humorous ['hju:meres] adj.
śmieszny; pocieszny; pełen
humoru; zabawny; komiczny
hump [hamp] s. garb; v. garbić
się; wyginać w łuk
humpback ['hampbaek] s. garbus
hunchback ['hancz,baek] s.
garbus; garb na plecach
hundred ['handred] num. sto; s.
setka; niezliczona ilość
hundredth ['handredt] num.
setny; jedna setna
hundredweight ['handred,łejt] s.
cetnar angielski
hung [hang] zob. hang
Hungarian [han'geerjen] adj.

węgierski; s. Węgier
hunger ['hanger] s. głód; v.
głodować; łaknąć; głodzić
hunger strike ['hanger-strajk] s.
strajk głodowy
hungry ['hangry] adj. głodny;
zgłodniały; pożądliwy; ubogi;
jałowy; nieurodzajny; łaknący
hunt [hant] s. polowanie; teren
łowiecki; v. polować; gonić;
przeszukiwać; szukać
hunter ['hanter] s. myśliwy
hunting ['hantyng] s. polowanie;
adj. myśliwski
hunting ground ['hantyng
,graund] s. teren myśliwski
huntsman ['hantsmen] s.
myśliwy; łowca
hurdle ['he:rdl] s. opłotki; v.
porać się; skakać przez
płotki; grodzić; przebijać się
hurdler ['he:rdler] s. zawodnik
wyścigów (z płotkami)
hurdle race ['he:rdl,rejs] s.
wyścigi (z płotkami; przez
płotki)
hurl [he:rl] s. rzut; v. rzucać
hurrah [he'ra:] excl.: hura!
hurray [he'rej] excl.: hura! v.
krzyczeć hura (z radości)
hurricane ['haryken] n. huragan;
orkan tropikalny
hurried ['haryd] adj. pośpieszny
hurry ['hary] s. pośpiech
hurry up! ['hary,ap] v. śpiesz
się! ruszaj się!
hurt; hurt; hurt [he:rt; he:rt;
he:rt]
hurt [he:rt] v. ranić; kaleczyć;
urazić; uszkodzić; boleć;
dokuczać; s. skaleczenie;
rana; szkoda; krzywda; uraz;
uszkodzenie; ból; ujma; ranka
husband ['hazbend] s. mąż; v.
gospodarować oszczędnie;
wydawać za mąż
husbandry ['hazbendry] s.
rolnictwo; uprawa; hodowla
hush [hasz] s. cisza; spokój;
milczenie; v. cicho! szal
uciszyć się; milczeć;
tuszować (coś); ululać;
załagodzić

hush up ['hasz,ap] v. siedzieć
cicho; zatuszować (coś)
husk [hask] s. łuska; v.
łuszczyć; wyłuszczać;
złuszczać
husky ['hasky] adj. krzepki;
suchy; zachrypnięty;
łuszczasty; s. pies eskimoski;
język eskimoski
hustle ['hasl] s. pośpiech;
krzątanina; bieganina;
popychanie; v. śpieszyć się;
krzątać się; popychać;
pchać się; szturchać;
popędzać; wypchnąć
hut [hat] s. chata; barak;
chałupa; v. mieszkać w
chałupie
hutch [hacz] s. skrzynia; klatka;
domek; kurnik; chlewik; v.
wkładać coś do skrzyni
hybrid ['hajbryd] s. mieszaniec;
adj. mieszany; mieszanego
pochodzenia
hydrant ['hajdrent] s. hydrant
hydraulic ['haj'dro:lyk] adj.
hydrauliczny
hydro ['hajdrou] adj. wodo-;
wodoro-; wodny
hydrocarbon ['hajdrou'ka:rben] s.
węglowodór
hydrochloric acid [,hajdrou'klo:
ryk,asyd] s. kwas solny
hydrogen ['hajdrydżen] s. wodór
hydrogen bomb ['hajdrydżen
,bom] s. bomba wodorowa
hydroplane ['hajdrou,plejn] s.
wodnopłatowiec; ślizgacz
hyena [haj'y:ne] s. hiena
hygiene ['hajdżi:n] s. higiena
hymn [hym] s. hymn; v.
śpiewać hymn; chwalić
hymnem
hyphen ['hajfen] s. łącznik; v.
używać łącznika
hypnotize ['hypne,tajz] v.
hipnotyzować
hypocrisy [hy'pokresy] s.
hipokryzja; udawanie cnoty
hypocrite ['hypekryt] s.
hipokryta; obłudnik; obłudnica
hypocritical [,hypou'krytkel] adj.
obłudny; hipokrytyczny;

dwulicowy; udający cnotę

hypodermic [,hajpe'de:rmyk] adj.
podskórny (zastrzyk)

hypothesis [haj'potysys] s.
hipoteza; niesprawdzona teoria

hysterectomy [,histe'rektemy] s.
wycięcie macicy

hysteria [hys'tyerje] s. histeria;
wybuch podniecenia

hysterical [hys'terykel] adj.
histeryczny; podlegający
histerii

hysterics [hys'teryks] pl. atak
histerii

hysterotomy [,histe'rotemy] s.
operacja macicy

I

I [aj] pron. ja; dziewiąta litera
angielskiego alfabetu

I-beam ['aj,bi:m] s. belka
dwuteówka (stalowa)

ice [ajs] s. lód; lody; v.
zamrażać; mrozić; lukrować

Ice Age ['ajsejdż] s. epoka
lodowa; epoka lodowcowa

iceberg ['ajsbe:rg] s. góra
lodowa (na morzu)

ice-cream ['ajskri:m] s. lody

icicle ['ajsykl] s. sopel

ice floe ['ajs-flou] s. kra

icing ['ajsyn] s. lukier

icon ['ajkon] s. ikona

icy ['ajsy] adj. lodowaty

idea [aj'die] s. idea; pojęcie;
pomysł; wyobrażenie; myśl;
plan

ideal [aj'diel] adj. idealny; s.
ideał; model doskonały

idealize [aj'dielajz] v.
idealizować; wyidealizować

identical [aj'dentykel] adj. taki
sam; identyczny;
tożsamościowy; zupełnie
podobny

identification [ajdentyfy'kejszyn]
s. utożsamienie; identyfikacja;

stwierdzenie tożsamości

identification papers [aj,dentyfy
'kejszyn'pejpers] s. dowód
tożsamości; dowód osobisty

identify [aj'dentyfaj] v.
utożsamić; identyfikować

identity [aj'dentyty] s.
tożsamość; identyczność

identity card [aj'dentyty ka:rd] s.
dowód osobisty

ideological [,ajdje'lodżykel] adj.
ideologiczny

idiom ['ydjem] s. wyrażenie
zwyczajowe; wyrażenie
idiomatyczne; dialekt; typowy
styl

idiot ['ydjet] s. idiota; dureń

idiotic [,ydy'otyk] adj. idiotyczny;
bardzo głupi

idle ['ajdl] adj. niezajęty;
bezczynny; jałowy; zbyteczny;
leniwy; pusty; czczy; v.
próżnować; być na wolnym
biegu; być bez pracy; obijać
się

idle away ['ajdl,e'łej] v.
marnować (czas); roztrwonić
czas

idleness ['ajdlnys] s.
bezczynność; lenistwo;
próżniactwo; daremność;
bezpodstawność

idol ['ajdl] s. bożyszcze; bałwan;
posąg bożka

idolize ['ajdelajz] v. ubóstwiać;
uwielbiać; bałwochwalić

idyll ['ydyl] s. sielanka; idylla;
opis raju na wsi (w poezji)

if [yf] conj. jeżeli; jeśli; gdyby;
o ile; czy; żeby (tylko)

iffy [yffy] adj. wątpliwy (slang)

igloo ['iglu:] s. eskimoska chata
kopulasta ze śniegu

ignite [yg'najt] v. zapalić

ignition [yg'nyszyn] s. zapłon;
zapalenie; elektryczny zapłon

ignition key [yg'nyszyn,ki:] s.
klucz do zapłonu (w aucie)

ignoble [yg'noubl] adj. nędzny;
podły; haniebny; niecny;
marny; niegodziwy; niskiego
pochodzenia

ignorance ['ygnerens] s.

nieświadomość; ignorancja;
nieuctwo; ciemnota;
obskurantyzm
ignorant ['ygnerent] adj.
nieświadomy; ciemny; bez
wykształcenia; zdradzający
ignorancję
ignore [yg'no:r] v. pomijać;
lekceważyć; odrzucać; nie
zważać
ill [yl] adj. zły; chory; słaby;
lichy; s. zło; adv. źle; nie
bardzo; kiepsko; niepomyślnie
ill-advised ['yled'wajzd] adj.
nierozsądny; nierozważny
ill-affected ['yle'fektyd] adj. źle
usposobiony; nieżyczliwy
ill-bred ['yl'bred] adj. źle
wychowany; grubiański
illegal [y'li:gel] adj. bezprawny;
nielegalny; samowolny;
przeciw prawu i ustawom
illegible [y'ledżybl] adj.
nieczytelny; źle napisany
(wydrukowany)
illegitimate [,yly'dżytymejt] adj.
bezprawny; nieprawny;
nieprawowity; nieślubny
ill-fated ['yl-fejtyd] adj. fatalny;
nieszczęśliwy; nieszczęsny
ill-humored ['yl'hju:merd] adj. w
złym humorze
illicit [y'lysyt] adj. bezprawny;
niedozwolony; niewłaściwy
illiterate [y'lyteryt] s. analfabeta;
adj. niepiśmienny
ill-judged ['yl'dżadżd] adj.
nierozważny; nierozsądny
ill-mannered ['yl'maenerd] adj.
źle wychowany; grubiański
ill-natured ['yl'nejczerd] adj. zły;
złośliwy; opryskliwy
illness ['ylnys] s. choroba
illogical [y'lodżykel] adj.
nielogiczny; nierozsądny
ill-tempered ['yl'temperd] adj. w
złym humorze; zły; kłótliwy
ill-timed ['yl'tajmd] adj. nie na
czasie; niefortunny
ill-treat ['yl'tri:t] v. maltretować;
znęcać się (nad kimś)
illuminate [y'lju:mynejt] v.
oświetlać; oświecać;

uświetniać
illumination [y'lju:my'nejszyn] s.
oświecenie; oświecanie;
uświetnianie; rozjaśnienie
illusion [y'lu:żyn] s. złudzenie;
iluzja; złuda
illusive [y'lu:syw] s. złudny;
iluzyjny; iluzoryczny;
zwodniczy
illusory [y'lu:sery] adj. złudny;
iluzoryczny; zwodniczy
illustrate ['yles,trejt] v.
wyjaśniać; ilustrować
illustration [,yles'trejszyn] s.
lustracja; ilustrowanie
illustrative ['yles,trejtyw] adj.
objaśniający; ilustrujący
(przykład, zdarzenie etc.)
illustrious [y'lastrjes] adj.
znakomity; wybitny; sławny
ill will ['yl'łyl] s. niechęć
image ['ymydż] s. wizerunek;
obraz; wcielenie; v.
wyobrażać; odzwierciedlać;
ucieleśniać; dawać obraz
(wyobrażenie)
imagery ['ymydżery] s.
wizerunki; podobizny; gra
wyobraźni; porównanie przez
przykłady
imaginable [y'maedżynebl] adj.
wyobrażalny; możliwy; do
pomyślenia
imaginary [y'maedżynery] adj.
urojony; zmyślony;
nierzeczywisty
imagination [y,maedży'nejszyn]
s. wyobraźnia; fantazja;
urojenie; tworzenie nowych
pomysłów
imagine [y'maedżyn] v.
wyobrażać sobie;
przypuszczać; myśleć
imbecile ['ymby,syl] adj.
upośledzony; głupi;
niedorozwinięty; cherlawy; s.
człowiek upośledzony;
imbecyl (niedorozwinięty)
imitate ['ymytejt] v.
naśladować; małpować;
imitować; wzorować się
imitation [,ymy'tejszyn] s.
naśladowanie;

naśladownictwo; imitacja;
falsyfikat; podróbka
immaterial [,yme'tierjel] adj.
nieistotny; bezcielesny; błahy
immature [,yme'tjuer] adj.
niedojrzały; niewyrobiony;
niedorosły
immeasurable [y,meżerebl] adj.
niezmierzony; ogromny;
bezmierny
immediate [y'mi:djet] adj.
bezpośredni;
natychmiastowy; pilny; nagły
immediately [y'mi:djetly] adv.
natychmiast; bezpośrednio
immense [y'mens] adj. olbrzymi;
ogromny; świetny; kapitalny
immerse [y'me:rs] v. zanurzać;
pogrążać; ochrzcić przez
zanurzenie
immigrant ['ymygrent] s.
imigrant; adj. imigrujący;
osadniczy
immigrate ['ymygrejt] v.
imigrować; przywędrować;
sprowadzać osadników
immigration [,ymy'grejszyn] s.
imigracja; urząd imigracyjny
imminent ['ymynent] adj.
nadchodzący; groźny;
nadciągający; bliski
immobile [y'moubajl] adj.
nieruchomy; przytwierdzony
na stałe
immoderate [y'moderyt] adj.
nieumiarkowany;
niepohamowany; nadmierny
immodest [y'modyst] adj.
nieskromny; bezczelny;
zuchwały
immoral [y'morel] adj.
niemoralny; nieetyczny;
rozpustny
immorality [ym'e-ral'ety] s.
rozpusta; niemoralność
immorality [,yme'raelyty] s.
niemoralność; rozpusta
immortal [y'mo:rtl] adj.
nieśmiertelny; wiekopomny
immortality [,ymo:r'taelyty] s.
nieśmiertelność
immovable [y'mu:webl] adj.
nieruchomy; niezmienny;

nieczuły; nieugięty;
niewzruszony
immune [y'mju:n] adj. odporny;
uodporniony; wolny (od
przepisów)
imp [ymp] s. skrzat; diablik
impact ['ympaekt] v. wgniatać;
s. zderzenie; uderzenie;
wpływ; wstrząs; kolizja;
działanie
impair [ym'peer] v. uszkadzać;
osłabiać; nadwyrężać;
umniejszać
impart [ym'pa:rt] v. dawać;
udzielać; zakomunikować
impartial [ym'pa:rszel] adj.
bezstronny; sprawiedliwy
impartiality ['ym,pa:rszy'aelyty]
s. bezstronność;
sprawiedliwość
impassable [ym'pa:sebl] adj.
nieprzebyty; nie do przebycia
impassive [ym'paesyw] adj.
niewzruszony; obojętny;
nieczuły
impatience [ym'pejszens] s.
zniecierpliwienie;
niecierpliwość; irytacja (z
powodu czegoś)
impatient [ym'pejszent] adj.
niecierpliwy; zniecierpliwiony;
palący się do; podrażniony
impeach [ym'pi:cz] v.
zakwestionować; podawać
w wątpliwość; oskarżyć;
postawić w stan oskarżenia
impediment [ym'pedyment] s.
przeszkoda; utrudnienie
impend [ym'pend] v. grozić;
zbliżać się; zagrażać (z
bliska)
impenetrable [ym'penytrebl] adj.
nieprzeniknony; niedostępny;
niezgłębiony; nie do przebycia
imperative [ym'peretyw] adj.
stanowczy; rozkazujący;
konieczny; naglący; niezbędny
imperceptible [,ym-pe'rseptebl]
adj. niedostrzegalny;
nieuchwytny
imperfect [ym'pe:rfykt] adj.
niedoskonały; niedokończony;
wadliwy; niezupełny;

niedokonany
imperial [ym'pierjel] adj. cesarski;
imperialny; dostojny;
rozkazujący; majestatyczny
imperialism [ym'pierjelyzem] s.
imperializm (budowanie
imperium)
imperil [ym'peryl] v. zagrażać;
narazić na
niebezpieczeństwo
imperiuos [ym'pierjes] adj.
władczy; naglący; nakazujący
imperishable [ym'peryszebl] adj.
niezniszczalny;
nieprzemijający; trwały;
wieczysty
impermeable [ym'pe:rmiebl] adj.
nieprzemakalny;
nieprzenikniony;
nieprzepuszczający
impersonal [ym'pe:rsenl] adj.
nieosobowy; nieosobisty
impersonate [ym'pe:rsenejt] v.
wcielać; uosabiać;
odgrywać kogoś;
personifikować
impertinence [ym'pe:rtynens] s.
niestosowność;
impertynencja;
niewłaściwość; natręctwo;
nietakt
impertinent [ym'pe:rtynent] adj.
niestosowny; impertynencki;
bezczelny; natrętny; bez
związku
imperturbable [,ympe:r'te:rbebl]
adj. niewzruszony; spokojny
impervious [ym'pe:rwjes] adj.
nieprzepuszczalny;
niedostępny
impetuous [ym'petjues] adj.
popędliwy; porywczy;
gwałtowny
implacable [ym'plekebl] adj.
nieubłagany; nieprzejednany
implant [ym'pla:nt] v.wszczepić;
wpoić; zaszczepić
implement ['ymplyment] s.
narzędzie; środek; sprzęt; v.
uzupełniać; urzeczywistniać;
wykonać; uprawomocniać;
spełniać
implicate ['ymplykejt] v.

uwikłać; owijać; włączać;
wplątać; wmieszać
implication [,ymply'kejszyn] s.
uwikłanie; włączenie; sugestia
implicit [ym'plysyt] adj.
rozumiejący się sam przez się;
niezaprzeczalny; domniemany;
ślepy
implore [ym'plo:r] v. błagać
impromptu ym'promptju:] adj.
improwizowany; nie
przygotowany; powiedziany z
głowy; adv. bez
przygotowania; z głowy
imply [ym'plaj] v. zawierać w
sobie; mieścić; sugerować;
zakładać; nasuwać wniosek
impolite [,ympo'lajt] adj.
nieuprzejmy; niegrzeczny
import [ym'po:rt] s. import;
treść; v. oznaczać;
importować; przywozić z
zagranicy; a. importowy
import ['ympo:rt] s. treść;
znaczenie; ważność;
doniosłość
importance [ym'po:rtens] s.
znaczenie; ważność;
doniosłość
important [ym'po:rtent] adj.
ważny; znaczący; doniosły
importation [,ympo:r'tejszyn] s.
przywóz; importowanie
importune [ym'po:rtju:n] v.
dokuczać; żądać
natarczywie; narzucać się;
naprzykrzać się
impose [ym'pouz] v. nadawać;
narzucać; oszukiwać;
imponować; nakładać
obowiązek
impose upon [,ym'pouz e'pon] v.
narzucać się komuś;
okpiwać
imposing [ym'pouzyng] adj.
imponujący; wspaniały;
okazały
impossibility [ym,posy'bylyty] s
niemożliwość
impossible [ym'posybl] adj.
niemożliwy (do zrobienia,
zniesienia)
impostor [ym'poster] s. oszust

(podszywający się); szarlatan
impotence ['ympotens] s.
niemoc; zniedołężnienie
(płciowe); nieudolność;
niesprawność
impotent ['ympotent] s. bezsilny;
impotent; nieudolny
impracticable [ym'praektykebl]
adj. niewykonalny; krnąbrny
impregnate ['ympregnejt] v.
zapładniać; impregnować;
nasycać; wpoić; zaszczepić;
nasiąkać
impress [ym'pres] v. odcisnąć;
wycisnąć; robić wrażenie; s.
odcisk; odbicie; piętno
impression [ym'preszyn] s.
wrażenie; druk; odbicie;
nakład
impressive [ym'presyw] adj.
robiący wrażenie; uderzający;
podniosły; wstrząsający;
frapujący
imprint [ym'prynt] v. odbijać;
wpajać; wydrukować;
wbijać w pamięć; wyryć w
pamięci
imprint ['ymprynt] s. odbicie;
nadruk; odcisk; piętno; znak
firmowy
imprison [ym'pryzn] v. uwięzić
imprisonment [ym'pryznment] s.
uwięzienie (kara więzienia)
improbable [ym'probebl] adj.
nieprawdopodobny
improper [ym'proper] adj.
niewłaściwy; nieprzyzwoity;
zdrożny
improve [ym'pru:w] v.
poprawić; udoskonalić;
ulepszać (jakość)
improvement [ym'pru:wment] s.
poprawa; udoskonalenie;
wykorzystanie (sposobności)
improvise ['ymprowajz] v.
improwizować; sklecić na
poczekaniu
imprudent [ym'pru:dent] adj.
nierozsądny; nieopatrzny;
nierozważny; nieoględny;
niebaczny
impudence ['ympjudens] s.
bezwstyd; bezczelność;

tupet
impudent ['ympjudent] adj.
bezwstydny; bezczelny;
zuchwały; z tupetem
impulse ['ympals] s. impuls;
poryw; popęd; pęd; siła
napędowa; bodziec
impulsive ['ympalsyw] adj.
impulsywny; porywczy;
pobudliwy
impunity [ym'pju:nyty] s.
bezkarność; swoboda od
skutków (kary)
impure [ym'pjur] adj. nieczysty;
zanieczyszczony
impute [ym'pju:t] v. oskarżać;
przypisywać (zbrodnię, błąd)
in [yn] prep. w; we; na; za; po;
do; u; nie-
in and out ['yn,end'aut] exp.: na
wylot; wchodzić i wychodzić
in a week ['yn,ej'ti:k] exp.: za
tydzień; w ciągu tygodnia
in my opinion ['yn,maj e'pynjen]
exp.: według mnie; moim
zdaniem
in order that ['yn,o:rder'daet]
exp.: ażeby; w celu; po to
żeby
in pairs ['yn,peers] exp.: parami
in Shakespeare ['yn,Szekspir] u
Szekspira; w sztukach
Szekspira
inability [,yne'byłyty] s.
niezdolność; niemożność
inaccessible [ynaek'sesybl] adj.
niedostępny; nieprzystępny
inaccurate [yn'aekjuryt] adj.
nieścisły; niedokładny
inactive [yn'aektyw] adj.
bezczynny; bierny; obojętny;
inertny
inadequate [yn'aedykłyt] adj.
nieodpowiedni;
niewystarczalny
inadmissible [,yned'mysebl] adj.
niedopuszczalny; nie do
przyjęcia
inadvertent [,yned'we:rtent] adj.
nieuważny; niedbały;
nierozmyślny; mimowolny;
nieumyślny
inalterable [yn'o:lterebl] adj.

inanimate

449

inclusive

niezmienny
inanimate [yn'aenymyt] adj.
martwy; nieożywiony;
bezduszny; nieorganiczny
inappropriate [,yne'prouprjyt] adj.
niewłaściwy; niestosowny
inapt [yn'aept] adj. niezdatny
inarticulate [,yna:r'tykjulyt] adj.
nieartykułowany; niewyraźny;
niemy; słabo mówiący
inasmuch [,ynez'macz] adv. o
tyle; ponieważ; wobec tego;
że; skoro; zważywszy; jako
inasmuch as [,ynez'macz,aez]
adv. gdyż; o tyle że; o tyle o
ile; zważywszy
inattentive [,yne'tentyw] adj.
nieuważny; nie uważający
inaudible [yn'o:debl] adj.
niesłyszalny; nieuchwytny dla
ucha
inaugural [y'no:gjurel] adj.
inauguracyjny
inaugurate [y'no:gjurejt] v.
otwierać uroczyście;
inaugurować; uroczyście
zapoczątkowywać
inborn ['yn'bo:rn] adj. wrodzony;
przyrodzony; z natury
incalculable [yn'kaelkjulebl] adj.
nieobliczalny; nieprzewidzialny
incapable [yn'kejpebl] adj.
niezdolny; nie będący w
stanie
incapacitate ['ynke'paesytejt] v.
czynić niezdatnym;
dyskwalifikować; uznać za
niezdatnego
incapacity [,ynke'paesyty] s.
niezdolność; nieudolność
incarnate [yn,ka:rnejt] adj.
wcielony; v. wcielać;
ucieleśniać (się); być
wcieleniem
incautious [yn'ko:szes] adj.
nierozważny; niebaczny
incendiary [yn'sendjery] adj.
zapalający; podżegający; s.
podpalacz; podżegacz
incense ['ynsens] s. kadzidło
incense [yn'sens] v.
rozwścieczać; doprowadzać
do szału

incertitude [yn'se:rtytju:d] s.
niepewność; niepokój
incessant [yn'sesnt] adj.
ustawiczny; bezustanny; stały
incest ['ynsest] s. kazirodztwo;
adj. kazirodczy
inch [yncz] s. cal (2.54 cm); v.
posuwać cal po calu
incident ['ynsydent] s. zajście;
wydarzenie; incydent; adj.
padający; związany;
prawdopodobny
incidental [,ynsy'dentl] adj.
przypadkowy; uboczny;
drugorzędny
incidentally [,ynsy'dently] adv.
przypadkowo; ubocznie;
nawiasem mówiąc;
mimochodem; przy
sposobności
incinerate [yn'synerejt] v. palić;
spopielić; palić na popiół
incise [yn'sajz] v. naciąć;
wyryć; wyrzeźbić;
wygrawerować
incision [yn'syżyn] s. nacięcie;
cięcie; ciętość; bystrość;
ostrość
incisive [yn'sajsyw] adj.
przenikliwy; ostry; tnący;
bystry; sieczny; zjadliwy;
wcinający się
incisor [yn'sajzer] s. siekacz
(ząb); każdy z przednich
zębów między kłami
incite [yn'sajt] v. zachęcać;
podburzać; podżegać;
namawiać
inclement [yn'klement] adj.
surowy; ostry (klimat etc.)
inclination [ynkly'nejszyn] s.
skłonność; nachylenie;
pociąg
incline [yn'klajn] v. mieć
skłonność; pochylać się
inclose [yn'klous] v. ogrodzić;
załączyć; włączyć;
zamknąć
include [yn'klu:d] v. zawierać;
włączać; wliczać (w cenę);
obejmować
inclusive [yn'klu:syw] adj.
włączony; obejmujący; adv.

włącznie
incoherent [,ynkou'hierent] adj.
bez związku;
nieskoordynowany
income ['ynkam] s. dochód
income tax ['ynkam,taeks] s.
podatek dochodowy
incoming ['yn,kamyŋg] adj.
nadchodzący; następujący;
przyrastający; s. przybycie;
dochód
incomparable [yn'komperebl] adj.
niezrównany; nie do
porównania; nieporównywalny
incompatible [,ynkem'paetebl]
adj. niezgodny; sprzeczny
incompetent [yn'kompytent] adj.
niekompetentny; nieudolny
incomplete [,ynkem'pli:t] adj.
niezupełny; nieukończony
incomprehensible [yn,kompry
'hensebl] adj. niepojęty;
niezrozumiały
inconceivable [,ynken'si:webl]
adj. niepojęty;
niprawdopodobny
inconclusive [,ynken'klu:syw]
adj. nieprzekonywujący;
nierozstrzygający; nie
decydujący
inconsequent [yn'konsykłent]
adj. bez związku;
niekonsekwentny; nielogiczny
inconsiderable [,ynken'syderebl]
adj. nieznaczny; niepokaźny
inconsiderate [,ynken'syderyt]
adj. bezwzględny;
nierozważny
inconsistent [,ynken'systent] adj.
niejednolity; niekonsekwentny;
niezgodny; bez związku
inconsolable [,ynken'soulebl] adj.
niepocieszony; nieutulony
inconstant [yn'konstent] adj.
zmienny; niestały; nieregularny
inconvenience [,ynken'wi:njens]
s. niewygoda; kłopot; v.
niepokoić; przeszkadzać;
sprawiać kłopot;
deranżować
inconvenient [,ynken'wi:njent]
adj. niewygodny; niedogodny;
kłopotliwy; uciążliwy

incorporate [yn'korperejt] v.
jednoczyć; wcielać;
zrzeszać; [yn'ko:rperyt] adj.
zrzeszony
incorporated [yn'ko:rperejtyd]
adj. zarejestrowany;
zalegalizowany; wcielony;
złączony
incorrect [,ynke'rekt] adj.
niepoprawny; nieścisły;
błędny
incorrigible [yn'korydżybl] adj.
niepoprawny; nie do
poprawienia
increase [yn'kri:s] v. wzrastać;
zwiększać się; pomnażać
się; wzmagać się;
rozmnażać się; ['ynkri:s] s.
wzrost; przyrost; podwyżka;
mnożenie się
increasingly [yn'kri:syŋgly] adv.
coraz więcej; coraz bardziej;
coraz to; wciąż
incredible [yn'kredebl] adj. nie do
wiary; niewiarygodny;
nieprawdopodobny; nie do
pomyślenia
incredulous [yn'kredjules] adj. nie
incriminate [yn'krymynejt] v.
obwiniać; oskarżać;
pomawiać; objąć (kogoś)
oskarżeniem
incubator ['ynkjubejter] s.
wylęgarka; inkubator
incur [yn'ke:r] v. narażać się;
ponieść; zaciągać; natknąć
się na
incurable [yn'kjuerebl] adj.
nieuleczalny; s. człowiek
nieuleczalnie chory
indebted [yn'detyd] adj. dłużny;
zobowiązany; wdzięczny;
zawdzięczający
indecency [yn'di:sensy] s.
nieskromność;
nieprzyzwoitość
indecent [yn'di:sent] adj.
nieprzyzwoity; obrażający
moralność
indecision [,yndy'syżyn] s.
chwiejność;
niezdecydowanie
indecisive [,yndy'sajsyw] adj.

nierozstrzygnięty;
niezdecydowany; chwiejny;
nie rozstrzygający
indecisiveness [,yndy'sajsywnys]
s. chwiejność;
niezdecydowanie
indeed [yn'di:d] adv. naprawdę;
istotnie; rzeczywiście;
faktycznie; wprawdzie; co
prawda; właściwie
indefatigable [,yndy'faetygebl]
adj. niestrudzony;
niezmordowany
indefinite [yn'defynyt] adj.
nieokreślony; niewyraźny;
nie sprecyzowany
indelible [yn'delybl] adj.
niezatarty; trwały; nie do
zmazania
indelicate [yn'delykyt] adj.
niedelikatny; nietaktowny;
niestosowny
indemnify [yn'demnyfaj] v.
dawać odszkodowanie;
zabezpieczać przed (np.
szkodą); powetować
indemnity [yn'demnyty] s.
odszkodowanie;
zabezpieczenie przed ...;
wynagrodzenie
indent [yn'dent] v. naciąć;
wyciąć; wyrżnąć; zamówić;
zawierać umowę; tłoczyć; s.
wgłębienie; nacięcie;
karbowanie
indent ['yndent] s. wcięcie;
nacięcie; karbowanie;
zamówienie
independence [,yndy'pendens] s.
niezależność;
niepodległość;
niezależność materialna
independent [,yndy'pendent] adj.
niepodległy; niezależny
(materialnie); osobny;
oddzielny
indescribable [,yndys'krajbebl]
adj. nieopisany; nie do
opisania (poza możliwościami
opisania)
indeterminate [,yndy'te:rmynyt]
adj. nieokreślony;
niewyraźny

index ['yndeks] s. wskaźnik;
indeks; v. umieszczać w
spisie (indeksie); robić indeks
Indian ['yndjen] adj. indiański;
hinduski
Indian Summer ['yndjen'samer]
exp.: słoneczne dni w jesieni;
babie lato
India-rubber ['yndje'raber] s.
guma (naturalna, elastyczna)
indicate ['yndykejt] v.
wskazywać; stwierdzać;
wymagać
indication [,yndy'kejszyn] s.
wskazówka; wskazanie; znak
indicative [yn'dyketyw] adj.
oznajmiający; dowodzący
indicator ['yndykejter] s.
wskaźnik; indykator; licznik
indict [yn'dajt] v. oskarżyć
indictment [yn'dajtment] s.
oskarżenie; akt oskarżenia
indifference [yn'dyferens] s.
obojętność; nieistotność;
błahość
indifferent [yn'dyfrent] adj.
obojętny; mierny; błahy;
neutralny
indigent ['yndydżent] adj. ubogi;
biedny; s. biedak; biedaczka
indigestible [,yndy'dżestebl] adj.
niestrawny; źle strawny
indigestion [,yndy'dżestczyn] s.
niestrawność
indignant [yn'dygnent] adj.
oburzony (na
niesprawiedliwość ...)
indignation [,yndyg'nejszyn] s.
oburzenie
indirect [,yndy'rekt] adj.
pośredni; okrężny;
nieuczciwy
indiscreet [,yndys'kri:t] adj.
nierozważny; niedyskretny
indiscretion [,yndys'kreszyn] s.
nierozwaga; niedyskrecja;
uchybienie (słowem, czynem)
indiscriminate [,yndys'krymynyt]
adj. bezkrytyczny; pomieszany
indispensable [,yndys'pensebl]
adj. nieodzowny; niezbędny;
konieczny; niezastąpiony
indisposed [,yndys'pouzd] adj.

niezdrów; niedysponowany;
niechętny; bez zapału;
niedomagający
indisposition [ˌyndyspe'zyszyn] s.
niedyspozycja; niechęć;
odraza; dolegliwość;
niedomaganie
indisputable [ˌyndys'pju:tebl] adj.
bezsporny; niezaprzeczalny
indistinct [ˌyndys'tynkt] adj.
niewyraźny; niejasny; mętny
individual [ˌyndy'wydjuel] adj.
pojedynczy; odrębny; s.
jednostka; osobnik; okaz;
człowiek
individualist [ˌyndy'wydjuelyst] s.
indywidualista; indywidualistka
indivisible [ˌyndy'wyżebl] adj.
niepodzielny; nieskończenie
mały
indolence ['yndelens] s. lenistwo;
opieszałość; próżniactwo
indolent ['yndelent] adj. leniwy;
opieszały; obojętny;
niebolesny
indomitable [yn'domytebl] adj.
nieposkromiony; nieugięty
indoor ['yndo:r] adj. domowy;
wewnętrzny; pokojowy;
zakładowy
indoors ['yndo:rz] adv. w domu;
pod dachem; do domu; do
mieszkania
indorse [yn'do:rs] v. potwierdzić
(podpisem)
induce [yn'dju:s] v. skłonić;
namówić; powodować;
wnioskować; pobudzić;
nakłonić
induct [yn'dakt] v. wprowadzać;
tworzyć; brać do wojska
indulge [yn'daldż] v. pobłażać;
znosić; ulegać; dogadzać;
używać sobie; dawać upust;
zaspokajać
indulgence [yn'daldżens] s.
dogadzanie; nałóg; oddawanie
się; pobłażanie; odpust;
uleganie
indulgent [yn'daldżent] adj.
pobłażliwy; ulegający;
folgujący
industrial [yn'dastrjel] adj.

przemysłowy (towar, robotnik)
industrial area [yn'dastrjel'eerje]
s. teren przemysłowy
industrial city [yn'dastrjel'syty] s.
miasto przemysłowe
industrialist [yn'dastrjelyst] s.
przemysłowiec
industrialize [yn'dastrjelajz] v.
uprzemysławiać
industrious [yn'dastrjes] adj.
skrzętny; pilny; pracowity
industry ['yndastry] s. przemysł;
pilność; pracowitość;
skrzętność; gałąź
przemysłu; właściciele i
zarządcy przemysłu
ineffective [ˌyny'fektyw] adj.
bezskuteczny; niesprawny
inefficient [ˌyny'fyszent] adj.
niewydajny; niesprawny
inequality [ˌyny'kłolyty] s.
nierówność;
niewystarczalność;
zmienność (krajobrazu);
niestałość
inert [y'ne:rt] adj. bezwładny;
ociężały; obojętny; opieszały
inertia [y'ne:rszja] s. inercja;
bezwład; ociężałość
inestimable [yn'estymebl] adj.
nieoceniony; bezcenny
inevitable [yn'ewytebl] adj.
nieunikniony; nieuchronny
inexact [ˌynyg'zaekt] adj.
nieścisły; niedokładny
inexcusable [ˌynyks'kju:zebl] adj.
niewybaczalny;
nieusprawiedliwiony; nie do
darowania
inexhaustible [ˌynyg'zo:stebl] adj.
niewyczerpany; nieprzebrany;
niestrudzony; bez dna
inexpensive [ˌynyks'pensyw] adj.
niedrogi; niekosztowny; tani
inexperience [ˌynyks'pierjens] s.
niedoświadczenie; brak
wprawy
inexplicable [yn'eksplykebl] adj.
niewytłumaczalny;
niewyjaśniony; zagadkowy
inexpressible [ˌyneks'presebl]
adj. niewysłowiony;
niewyrażalny; niewymowny

inexpressive [,ynyks'presyw] adj.
bez wyrazu
infallible [yn'faelebl] adj.
nieomylny; niezawodny;
niechybny; bezbłędny; zawsze
słuszny
infamous ['ynfemes] adj.
haniebny; niesławny;
hańbiący; podły
infamy ['ynfemy] s. hańba;
niesława; podłość; utrata
praw obywatelskich
infancy ['ynfensy] s.
niemowlęctwo; dzieciństwo
infant ['ynfent] s. niemowlę;
dziecko; noworodek; a.
dziecinny
infantile ['ynfentajl] adj.
dziecięcy; infantylny;
niemowlęcy
infantry ['ynfentry] s. piechota
(wojsko)
infatuated with [yn'faetjuejtyd
łys] adj. szalejący za ...;
rozkochany w ...; nierozsądnie
zakochany
infect [yn'fekt] v. zakazić;
zarazić; zatruwać
infection [yn'fekszyn] s.
zakażenie; zarażenie; zaraza
infectious [yn'fekszes] adj.
zakaźny; zaraźliwy;
infekcyjny
infer [yn'fe:r] v. wnioskować;
zawierać w sobie pojęcie
inference ['ynferens] s. wniosek;
konkluzja; domniemanie
inferior [yn'fierjer] adj. niższy;
podrzędny; pośledni
inferior to [yn'fierjer,tu] adj.
ustępujący; gorszy
inferiority [yn,fiery'oryty] s.
niższość; poczucie
niższości
infernal [yn'fe:rnel] adj. piekielny;
diabelski; szatański
infest [yn'fest] v. nawiedzać;
trapić; być utrapieniem
infidelity [,ynfy'delyty] s.
niewiara; niewierność
infiltrate ['ynfyltrejt] v. wsiąkać;
przesiąkać; przenikać
infinite ['ynfynyt] adj.

nieskończony; bezgraniczny;
niezliczony; ogromny;
bezkresny
infinitive [yn'fynytyw] s.
bezokolicznik; adj.
nieokreślony
infinity [yn'fynyty] s.
nieskończoność
infirm [yn'fe:rm] adj. słaby;
niedołężny; dotknięty
niemocą
infirmary [yn'fe:rmery] s. szpital;
lecznica; izba chorych
infirmity [yn'fe:rmyty] s. niemoc;
słabość; zniedołężnienie
inflame [yn'flejm] v. zapalić;
rozognić; pobudzać;
zagrzewać
inflammable [yn'flaemebl] adj.
zapalny; pobudliwy; palny
inflammation [,ynfle'mejszyn] s.
zapalenie; zaognienie
inflammatory [yn'flaemeto:ry]
adj. podżegający; zapalny
inflate [yn'flejt] v. nadąć;
rozdąć; powodować inflację
inflation [yn'flejszyn] s. inflacja;
nadymanie; nadmuchanie;
zwyżka cen
inflect [yn'flekt] v. zginać;
skrzywić; odmienić; naginać
inflection [yn'flekszyn] s. fleksja;
modulacja; końcówka;
wygięcie; nadgięcie;
odchylenie
inflexible [yn'fleksebl] adj.
sztywny; nieugięty;
nieelastyczny
inflict [yn'flykt] v. żądać;
narzucać; zsyłać (na kogoś)
infliction [yn'flykszyn] s. zadanie
(ciosu); narzucanie;
przykrość; nieszczęście;
strapienie
influence ['ynfluens] s. wpływ;
v. wywierać wpływ;
oddziaływać
influential [,ynflu'enszel] adj.
wpływowy (polityk etc.)
influenza [,ynflu'enza] s. grypa;
influenca
inform [yn'fo:rm] v.
powiadomić; nadawać;

donosić; ożywić
inform against [yn'fo:rm e'genst]
v. donosić na (kogoś)
information [,ynfer'mejszyn] s.
wiadomość; wiedza;
objaśnienie; informacja;
doniesienie
information desk [,ynfer'mejszyn
,desk] punkt informacyjny (w
banku, hotelu, na wystawie)
information officer [,ynfer
'mejszyn 'ofyser] oficer
informacyjny (w banku etc.)
informative [yn'fo:rmetyw] adj.
objaśniający; pouczający
informer [yn'fo:rmer] s.
donosiciel; konfident;
konfidentka
infuriate [,yn'fjuerjejt] v.
rozwścieczać; rozjuszać
infuse [yn'fju:z] v. lewać;
zalewać; zaparzać; dodać
(odwagi)
ingenious [yn'dżi:njes] adj.
pomysłowy; dowcipny
(pomysł)
ingenuity [,yndży'njuyty] s.
pomysłowość;
oryginalność; dowcip
ingot ['yngot] s. sztaba
ingratiate [yn'grejszjejt] v.
wkradać się w łaski czyjeś
ingratitude [yn'graetytju:d] s.
niewdzięczność
ingredient [yn'gri:djent] s.
składnik (mieszanki etc.)
ingress ['yngres] s. wejście
inhabit [yn'haebyt] v.
zamieszkiwać; mieszkać
inhabitable [yn'haebytebl] adj.
mieszkalny (godny
zamieszkania)
inhabitant [yn'haebytent] s.
mieszkaniec; mieszkanka
inhale [yn'hejl] v. wdychać;
zaciągać się (dymem);
wziewać
inherent [yn'hierent] adj.
nieodłączny; właściwy;
wrodzony
inherit [yn'heryt] v. dziedziczyć;
być spadkobiercą
inheritance [yn'herytens] s.

spadek; spuścizna;
dziedzictwo
inhibit [yn'hybyt] v.
wstrzymywać; wzbraniać;
zakazywać
inhibition [,ynhy'byszyn] s.
zakaz; zahamowanie;
wstrzymanie
inhospitable [yn'hospytebl] adj.
niegościnny
inhuman [yn'hju:men] adj.
nieludzki; okrutny; brutalny
initial [y'nyszel] adj.
początkowy; v. znaczyć
własnymi inicjałami
initiate [y'nyszjejt] v.
zapoczątkować;
wprowadzać; zainicjować;
wtajemniczać; s. nowicjusz
initiation [y,nyszy'ejszyn] s.
wprowadzenie;
zapoczątkowanie
initiative [y'nyszjejtyw] s.
inicjatywa; adj. początkowy
inject [yn'dżekt] v. wstrzyknąć
injection [yn'dżekszyn] s.
zastrzyk; wstrzyknięcie; a.
wtryskowy
injudicious [,yndżu'dyszes] adj.
nierozważy; nieroztropny
injure ['yndżer] v. zranić;
uszkodzić; krzywdzić;
zepsuć
injurious [yn'dżuerjes] adj.
szkodliwy; krzywdzący;
obelżywy; przynoszący ujmę;
obraźliwy
injury ['yndżery] s. szkoda;
krzywda; rana; uszkodzenie
injustice [yn'dżastys] s.
niesprawiedliwość; krzywda
ink [ynk] s. atrament; tusz
inkling ['ynklyng] s. wzmianka;
podejrzenie; przypuszczenie
ink-pot ['ynk,pot] s. kałamarz
inland ['ynlend] s. wnętrze kraju;
adj. w głębi kraju;
wewnętrzny; adv. w głębi; w
głąb kraju; w głębi kraju
inlet ['ynlet] s. wstawka; zatoka;
wlot; wejście; a. wlotowy
inmate ['ynmejt] s. mieszkaniec;
lokator; współ-(więzień etc.)

inmost ['ynmoust] adj. głęboko
utajony; skryty; najtajniejszy
inn [yn] s. gospoda; oberża
innate ['y'nejt] adj. wrodzony
inner ['yner] adj. wewnętrzny
innermost ['ynermoust] adj.
głęboko ukryty; najskrytszy
inner tube ['yner,tju:b] s. dętka
(samochodowa, rowerowa)
innkeeper ['yn,ki:per] s.
oberżysta; właściciel zajazdu
innocence ['ynesns] s.
niewinność; naiwność;
prostoduszność
innocent ['ynesynt] adj.
niewinny; naiwny;
nieszkodliwy; niemądry; s.
prostaczek; niewiniątko;
głuptas
innovation [,ynou'wejszyn] s.
innowacja; wprowadzenie
zmian
innuendo [,ynju'endou] s.
insynuacja
innumerable [y'nju:merebl] adj.
niezliczony; bez liku
inoculate [y'nokjulejt] v.
szczepić; wpajać; oczkować
rośliny
inoffensive [,yne'fensyw] adj.
nieszkodliwy; spokojny;
obojętny
inopportune [yn'oper,tju:n] adj.
niewczesny; nie w porę; nie
na czas; nieodpowiedni
inpatient ['ynpejszent] s. pacjent
leżący w szpitalu
inquest ['ynkłest] s. śledztwo
inquire [yn'kłajer] v. pytać się;
dowiadywać się; dociekać
inquiry [yn'kłajry] s. badanie;
zasięganie informacji;
śledztwo; poszukiwanie;
ankieta; wywiad
inquisitive [yn'kłyzytyw] adj.
badawczy; ciekawski;
wścibski
insane [yn'sejn] adj. chory
umysłowo; zwariowany; bez
sensu
insanity [yn'saenyty] s. obłęd
insatiable [yn'sejsjzebl] adj.
nienasycony; niezaspokojony;

chciwy
insatiate [yn'sej'szjyt] adj.
nienasycony; niezaspokojony
inscribe [yn'skrajb] v. wpisać;
napisać; umieszczać na
liście
inscription [yn'skrypszyn] s.
napis; dedykacja
insect ['ynsekt] s. owad
insecure [,ynsy'kjuer] adj.
niepewny; niezabezpieczony
insemination [yn,semy'nejszyn]
s. zapłodnienie; zasianie
insensible [yn'sensybl] adj.
nieświadomy; bez zmysłów;
w stanie omdlenia;
niedostrzegalny
insensitive [yn'sensytyw] adj.
nieczuły; niewrażliwy
inseparable [yn'seperebl] adj.
nierozłączny; nieodstępny
insert [yn'se:rt] v. wstawiać;
wkładać; s. wkładka;
wstawka
insertion [yn'se:rszyn] s.
wkładka; wstawka; włożenie;
wstawienie; przyczep;
przyczepienie
inshore [yn'szo:r] adv. blisko
brzegu; przy brzegu; adj.
przybrzeżny; bliski brzegu
inside ['ynsajd] s. wnętrze; adj.
wewnętrzny; adv. wewnątrz
inside [yn'sajd] adv. wewnątrz
inside out ['ynsajd'aut] exp.: na
lewą stronę (np. marynarki)
insidious [yn'sydjes] adj.
podstępny; zdradziecki;
zdradliwy
insight ['ynsajt] s. wgląd;
intuicja; wnikliwość
insignificant [,ynsyg'nyfykent]
adj. mało znaczący; błahy
insincere [,ynsyn'sier] adj.
nieszczery; zwodniczy;
dwulicowy
insinuate [yn'synjuejt] v.
insynuować; podsuwać;
sugerować
insipid [yn'sypyd] adj. mdły;
tępy; bez sensu; głupi; ckliwy
insist [yn'syst] v. nalegać;
nastawać; utrzymywać;

obstawać
insist on [yn'syst,on] v.
domagać się; upierać się;
nastawać
insolent ['ynselent] adj.
bezczelny; zuchwały; butny;
wyniosły
insoluble [yn'soljubl] adj.
nierozpuszczalny; nie do
rozwiązania
insolvent [yn'solwent] adj.
niewypłacalny; s. bankrut;
bankrutka
insomnia [yn'somnja] s.
bezsenność (nie normalna)
insomuch [,ynsou'macz] adv. o
tyle; do tego stopnia; tak
dalece
inspect [yn'spekt] v. oglądać;
doglądać; mieć nadzór;
badać
inspection [yn'spekszyn] s.
przegląd; oglądanie; inspekcja;
doglądanie; sprawdzanie;
kontrola
inspector [yn'spekter] s.
inspektor; nadzorca; kontroler
inspiration [,ynspe'rejszyn] s.
natchnienie; wdech;
wdychanie
inspire [yn'spajer] v. natchnąć;
podsunąć; zainspirować;
wdychać
instability [ynste'bylyty] s.
niestałość; chwiejność;
nietrwałość
install [yn'sto:l] v. instalować;
wprowadzać na stanowisko
installation [,ynsto:'lejszyn] s.
instalacja; wprowadzenie na
stanowisko; zamontowanie
instal(l)ment [yn'sto:lment] s.
część całości; rata
instance ['ynstens] s. wypadek;
przykład; v. przytaczać
przykład
instant ['ynstent] adj. nagły;
natychmiastowy; bieżący; s.
moment; chwila (szczególna)
instantaneous [,ynsten'tejnjes]
adj. natychmiastowy;
momentalny; zdarzający się w
momencie

instantly [yn'stently] adv.
natychmiast; momentalnie
instead [yn'sted] adv. zamiast
tego; natomiast; w miejsce
instead of [yn'sted,ow] adv.
zamiast (kogoś, czegoś)
instigate ['ynstygejt] v.
podżegać; podjudzać;
prowokować
instigator ['ynstygejter] s.
podżegacz; prowokator;
poduszczyciel
instil(l) [yn'styl] v. wsączać;
wpajać (uczucia etc.);
wkraplać
instinct ['ynstynkt] s. instynkt;
adj. tchnący (czymś); pełen
instinctive [yn'stynktyw] adj.
instynktowny; odruchowy
institute ['ynstytju:t] s. instytut;
v. zakładać; ustanawiać;
zarządzać (śledztwo etc.)
institution [,ynsty'tju:szyn] s.
instytucja; ustanowienie
instruct [yn'strakt] v. uczyć
instruction [yn'strakszyn] s.
pouczenie; nauka; instrukcja
instructive [yn'straktyw] adj.
pouczający; kształcący
instructor [yn'strakter] s.
nauczyciel; wykładowca;
instruktor
instructress [yn'straktrys] s.
nauczycielka; instruktorka
instrument ['ynstrument] s.
instrument; przyrząd;
dokument
insubordinate [,ynseb'o:rdnyt]
adj. niesforny; nieposłuszny
insufferable [yn'saferebl] adj.
nieznośny; nie do zniesienia
insufficient [,ynse'fyszent] adj.
niedostateczny; nieodpowiedni
insulate ['ynsjulejt] v. izolować;
oddzielać; odosabniać
insult ['ynsalt] s. zniewaga
insult [yn'salt] v. lżyć;
znieważać; uchybiać;
zelżyć
insupportable [,ynse'po:rtebl]
adj. nie do zniesienia;
nieznośny; nieuzasadniony
insurance [yn'szuerens] s.

ubezpieczenie; a.
ubezpieczeniowy
insurance policy [yn'szuerens
'polysy] s. polisa
ubezpieczeniowa; polisa
asekuracyjna
insure [yn'szuer] v. ubezpieczać
(się); asekurować;
zabezpieczać
insurmountable [,ynse:r
'mauntebl] adj. niepokonany
insurrection [,ynse'rekszyn] s.
powstanie; insurekcja
intact [yn'taekt] adj. nietknięty;
nieuszkodzony
integrate ['yntygrejt] v. scalić;
uzupełniać; całkować
integrity [yn'tegryty] s.
uczciwość; rzetelność;
czystość; prawość;
niepodzielność
intellect ['yntylekt] s. rozum;
umysł; rozsądek; wybitne
umysły
intellectual [,ynty'lekczuel] adj.
intelektualny; umysłowy; s.
intelektualista; inteligent
intelligence [yn'telydżens] s.
inteligencja; informacja;
wywiad; wiadomości; nowiny
intelligent [yn'telydżent] adj.
inteligentny; łatwo uczący się
intelligentsia [yn'tely'dżencja] s.
inteligencja (warstwa
ludności kraju)
intelligible [yn'telydżybl] adj.
zrozumiały; jasny; wyraźny
intemperate [yn'temperyt] adj.
nieumiarkowany; bez umiaru
intend [yn'tend] v. zamierzać;
przeznaczać; mieć na myśli
intense [yn'tens] adj. napięty;
usilny; gorliwy; wytężony;
uczuciowy
intensify [yn'tensyfaj] v. wzmóc;
wzmocnić; napiąć;
wzmagać
intensity [yn'tensyty] s.
intensywność; wzmożenie;
natężenie
intensive [yn'tensyw] adj.
intensywny; wzmożony; silny;
wzmacniający

intent [yn'tent] s. plan; zamiar;
adj. uważny; zamierzający;
zajęty; pochłonięty;
zdecydowany
intent on [yn'tent on] adj.
pochłonięty; zajęty czymś
intention [yn'tenszyn] s. zamiar;
cel; zamierzenie (czynu)
intentional [yn'tenszenel] adj.
umyślny; celowy; zamierzony
inter [yn'te:r] v. grzebać
intercede [,ynte:r'si:d] v.
wstawiać się; orędować
intercept ['ynte:rsept] v.
przechwycić; przejąć;
przerwać; udaremnić;
podsłuchać
intercession [,ynter'seszyn] s.
wstawiennictwo;
orędownictwo
interchange [,ynte:r'czejndż] s.
wzajemna wymiana; v.
wymieniać się; zmieniać się
intercourse ['ynterko:rs] s.
stosunek; obcowanie;
spółkowanie
interdict [,ynter'dykt] s. zakaz; v.
zakazywać; zabraniać
interest ['yntryst] s.
zainteresowanie; ciekawość;
odsetki; interes; procent; v.
zainteresować
interested ['yntrystyd] adj.
zaciekawiony; zainteresowany
interesting ['yntrystyng] adj.
ciekawy; interesujący
interfere [,ynter'fier] v. wtrącać
się; wdawać się; kolidować;
zakłócać; dokuczać
interfere with [,ynter'fier,tys] v.
mieszać się do kogoś
interference [,ynter'fierens] s.
wtrącanie się; zakłócenie
interior [yn'tierjer] adj.
wewnętrzny; środkowy; s.
wnętrze; głąb kraju; głąb
duszy (serca)
interior decorator [yn'tierjer
'dekerejter] s. architekt
wnętrz; sprzedawca mebli
interjection [,ynter'dżekszyn] s.
okrzyk; wykrzyknik
interlude [ynter'lu:d] s. przerwa;

antrakt

intermarriage ['ynter'maerydż] s.
małżeństwo w obrębie
własnego rodu, szczepu,
plemienia

intermediary [,ynter'mi:diery] adj.
pośredni; pośredniczący; s.
pośrednik; pośredniczka;
średnie stadium; pośrednia
forma; pośredni produkt;
agent

intermediate [,ynter'mi:djet] adj.
pośredni; środkowy; średni;
s. pośrednik; v.
pośredniczyć

intermingle [,ynter'myngl] v.
mieszać (się); pomieszać
(się)

intermission [,ynter'myszyn] s.
przerwa; pauza; antrakt

intermittent [,ynter'mytent] adj.
przerywany; niemiarowy

intern [yn'te:rn] v. internować;
odbywać praktykę lekarską

intern ['ynte:rn] s. praktykant
lekarski w szpitalu

internal ['ynte:rnl] adj.
wewnętrzny; krajowy;
domowy

international [,ynter'naeszenl]
adj. międzynarodowy; s.
międzynarodówka; zawody
międzynarodowe; zawodnik
międzynarodowy

interpose [,ynter'pouz] v.
wstawać; wtrącać (się);
przerywać

interpret [yn'ter:pryt] v.
tłumaczyć i objaśniać;
interpretować; rozumieć
(opacznie etc.)

interpretation [yn,te:rpry'tejszyn]
s. interpretacja; tłumaczenie;
sposób zrozumienia

interpreter [yn'te:rpryter] s.
tłumacz (ustny)

interrogate [yn'teregejt] v.
wypytywać; przesłuchiwać

interrogation [yn,tere'gejszyn] s.
przesłuchanie; pytanie

interrogative [,ynte'rogetyw] adj.
pytający (np. ton)

interrupt [,ynte'rapt] v.
przerywać; zasłaniać (widok)

interruption [,ynte'rapszyn] s.
przerwa (w czynności etc.)

intersect [,ynte:r'sekt] v.
przecinać (się); pokrzyżować
(się)

intersection [,ynter'sekszyn] s.
przecinanie się; skrzyżowanie

interval ['ynterwel] s. odstęp;
przerwa; antrakt; okres
(pogody)

intervene [,ynter'wi:n] v.
wdawać się; interweniować;
zdarzyć się; zajść; być
między (dwoma etc.)

intervention [,ynter'wenszyn] s.
interwencja; wdanie się

interview ['ynterwju:] s. wywiad;
rozmowa; v. mieć wywiad;
widzieć się z kimś (dla
wywiadu)

interviewer ['ynterwju:er] s.
przeprowadzający wywiad

intestines [yn'testynz] pl.
wnętrzności; jelita

intimacy ['yntymesy] s.
zażyłość; intymność;
poufałe stosunki (płciowe);
poufałość

intimate ['yntymyt] adj. zażyły;
wewnętrzny; intymny; v.
zawiadamiać; dawać do
zrozumienia; s. serdeczny
przyjaciel

intimation [,ynty'mejszyn] s.
zawiadomienie; danie do
zrozumienia; napomknięcie;
znak (czegoś)

intimidate [yn'tymydejt] v.
zastraszyć; onieśmielić

into ['yntu:] prep. do; w; na

intolerable [yn'tolerebl] adj.
nieznośny; nie do zniesienia

intolerant [yn'tolerent] adj.
nietolerancyjny; nie znoszący
czegoś (cudzych przekonań)

intoxicate [yn'toksykejt] v. upić;
upajać; odurzać się

intransitive [yn'traensytyw] adj.
& s. nieprzechodni

intrepid [yn'trepyd] adj.
nieustraszony; śmiały;
odważny

intricate ['yntrykyt] adj. zawiły;
trudny do zrozumienia
intrigue [yn'tri:g] s. intryga;
potajemna miłość; v.
intrygować; potajemnie
utrzymywać stosunek
miłosny; zaciekawiać
introduce [,yntre'dju:s] v.
wprowadzać (coś lub
kogoś); przedstawiać;
rozpoczynać; wsuwać;
wysuwać; wkładać;
zapoznawać
introduction [,yntre'dakszyn] s.
wstęp; wprowadzenie;
włożenie; wsunięcie;
przedstawienie (kogoś);
przedmowa; innowacja etc.
introductory [,yntre'daktery] adj.
wstępny; wprowadzający
intrude [,yn'tru:d] v. wpychać
(się); wciskać (się); wedrzeć
(się); narzucać (się) (komuś)
intruder [yn'tru:der] s. natręt;
intruz; nieproszony gość
intrusion [yn'tru:żyn] s.
wciśnięcie (się); wepchnięcie
(się); narzucanie (się); wdarcie
(się) w cudze prawa
intuition [,yntju'yszyn] s. intuicja;
przeczucie; wyczucie
inundate ['ynan,dejt] v.
zalewać; zatopić;
zasypywać (prośbami)
inutile [yn'ju:tyl] adj.
niepotrzebny; bezcelowy;
bezużyteczny
invade [yn'wejd] v. najeżdżać;
wdzierać się; zalewać;
owładać; ogarnąć;
wtargnąć
invader [yn'wejder] s.
najeźdźca; okupant
invalid [yn'weli:d] s. chory;
inwalida; kaleka; człowiek
słaby
invalid [yn'waelyd] adj.
nieważny; nieprawomocny
invalidate [yn'waelydejt] v.
unieważniać (prawnie etc.)
invaluable [yn'waeljuebl] adj.
bezcenny; nieoceniony
invariable [yn'weeryebl] adj.

niezmienny; stały;
równomierny
invariably [yn'w-eryebly] adv.
niezmiennie; stale;
równomiernie
invasion [yn'wejżyn] s. inwazja;
najazd; wdarcie się
invective [yn'wektyw] s.
inwektywa; obelga; napaść
(słowna); obelżywe słowa
invent [yn'went] v. wynaleźć;
wymyślić; zmyślić (coś na
kogoś)
invention [yn'wenszyn] s.
wynalazek; wymysł;
zmyślenie
inventive [yn'wentyw] adj.
pomysłowy; wynalazczy
inventor [yn'wentor] s.
wynalazca (w nauce,
mechanice etc.)
inverse [yn'we:rs] adj. odwrotny;
s. odwrotność (czegoś)
inversion [yn'we:rżyn] s.
odwrócenie; inwersja;
homoseksualizm; wynicowanie
invert [yn'we:rt] v. odwrócić;
przestawić; s.
homoseksualista
inverted commas [yn'we:rtyd
'komes] cudzysłów
invest [yn'west] v. inwestować;
wyposażać; oblegać;
obdarzać
investigate [yn'westygejt] v.
badać; prowadzić
dochodzenie
investigation [yn,westy'gejszyn]
s. badanie; dochodzenie;
śledztwo; rozpatrzenie;
dociekanie
investigator [yn'westygejtor] s.
badacz; agent (prokuratury)
investment [yn'westment] s.
inwestycja; lokata; oblężenie;
osaczenie; obleczenie
invincible [yn'wynsebl] adj.
niepokonany; niezwyciężony
inviolable [yn'wajelebl] adj.
nienaruszalny; nietykalny;
niepogwałcony; niezniszczalny
invisible [yn'wyzybl] adj.
niewidoczny; niewidzialny

invitation [,ynwy'tejszyn] s.
zaproszenie (pisemne, słowne)
invite [yn'wajt] v. zapraszać;
wywoływać; ściągać;
nęcić; zachęcać; prosić o
(radę)
invoice ['ynwois] s. faktura; v.
fakturować
invoke [yn'wouk] v. wzywać;
odwoływać się; wywoływać
involuntary [yn'wolentery] adj.
mimowolny; nieumyślny;
bezwiedny (czyn, ruch etc.)
involve [yn'wolw] v. gmatwać;
wikłać; mieszać;
komplikować; obejmować;
wymagać
invulnerable [yn'walnerebl] adj.
nie do zranienia;
nienaruszalny; nie do zdobycia
inward ['ynłerd] adj.
wewnętrzny; adv. wewnątrz;
w sercu etc.
inwards ['ynłerds] adv.
wewnątrz; w duchu; w myśli
iodine ['ajoudi:n] s. jod
I.O.U. = I owe you ['ajou'ju:] s.
kwit; skrypt dłużny
irascible [y'raesybl] adj. gniewny;
popędliwy; wybuchowy; skory
do gniewu
irate [aj'rejt] adj. rozgniewany;
zirytowany; zły; wściekły
iridescent [,yry'desnt] adj.
mieniący się; tęczowy
iris ['ajerys] s. tęczówka
Irish ['ajerysz] adj. irlandzki; s.
Irlandczyk
irk [e:rk] v. drażnić; być
przykrym; męczyć
irksome [e:rksem] adj.
nieprzyjemny; przykry
iron ['ajern] s. żelazo; żelazko;
(pistolet; rewolwer); adj.
żelazny; v. zakuwać;
prasować
ironic(al) [aj'ronyk(el)] adj.
ironiczny; drwiący;
uszczypliwy
ironing ['ajernyng] s. prasowanie
(bielizna etc.)
ironmonger ['ajern,manger] s.
handlarz wyrobów żelaznych;

właściciel sklepu żelaznego
iron mold ['ajern,mould] s. plama
od rdzy
ironworks ['ajernłe:rks] s. huta
żelaza; przetwórnia żelaza
irony ['ajereny] s. ironia
irradiate [y'rjedjejt] v.
oświetlać; naświetlać;
oświecać; rozjaśniać;
rozpromieniać
irrational [y'raesznel] adj.
nieracjonalny; nierozumny;
niewymierny; s. liczba
niewymierna
irreconcilable [y'rekesajlebl] adj.
nieprzejednany; nie dający się
pogodzić (z wiarą etc.)
irrecoverable [,yry'kawerebl] adj.
niepowetowany; nie do
odzyskania; stracony
bezpowrotnie
irredeemable [,yry'di:mebl] adj.
niewymienny; beznadziejny;
nieodwracalny; nieodkupny
irrefutable [y'refjutebl] adj.
niezbity; nieodparty
irregular [y'regjuler] adj.
nieregularny; nierówny;
nieporządny; nielegalny;
nieprawidłowy
irrelevant [y'relywent] adj.
nieistotny; niestosowny;
oderwany; od rzeczy; nie do
rzeczy
irremovable [,yry'mu:webl] adj.
nieusuwalny; nie do pokonania
irreparable [y'reperebl] adj.
niepowetowany; nie do
naprawienia
irreplaceable [,yry'plejsebl] adj.
niezastąpiony; nie do
zastąpienia
irrepressible [,yry'presybl] adj.
niepohamowany; nieodparty
irreproachable [,yry'proczebl] adj.
nienaganny; bez zarzutu
irresistible [,yry'zystybl] adj.
nieodparty; porywający;
gwałtowny
irresolute [y'rezelu:t] adj.
niezdecydowany; chwiejny
irrespective [,yrys'pektyw] adj.
niezależny; adv. niezależnie;

bez względu na ...; bez szacunku

irresponsible [,yrys'ponsybl] adj. nieobliczalny; nieodpowiedzialny

irretrievable [,yry'tri:webl] adj. bezpowrotnie stracony

irreverent [y'rewerent] adj. lekceważący; uchybiający

irrevocable [y'rewokebl] adj. nieodwołalny; nie do odwołania

irrigate ['yrygejt] v. nawadniać; przepłukiwać; odświeżać

irritable ['yrytebl] adj. drażliwy; wrażliwy; nerwowy; przewrażliwiony; skory do gniewu

irritate ['yrytejt] v. denerwować; irytować; drażnić; rozdrażniać; unieważniać prawnie

irritation [,yry'tejszyn] s. irytacja; rozdrażnienie

is [yz] v. jest; zob. be

island ['ajlend] s. wyspa; wysepka (na bruku)

isle [ajl] s. wyspa; v. żyć na wyspie; zrobić (jak) wyspę

isn't ['yznt] = is not; exp.: nie jest (w domu etc.)

isn't it? ['yznt yt] nieprawda? czy nie prawda?

isolate ['ajselejt] v. odosabniać; izolować; osamotniać

isolated ['ajselejtyd] adj. odosobniony; osamotniony

isolation [,ajse'lejszyn] s. odosobnienie; izolacja; wyodrębnienie; osamotnienie

issue ['yszu:] s. wydanie; przydział; zeszyt; spór; problem; argument; wynik; koniec; ujście; wyjście; wypływ; potomstwo; upuszczenie; dochód; v. wysyłać; wypuszczać; wydawać; dawać w wyniku; wychodzić; pochodzić; emitować

isthmus ['ysmes] s. przesmyk; międzymorze; cieśń; węzina

it [yt] pron. to; ono

Italian [y'taeljen] adj. włoski

italics [y'taelyks] pl. kursywa; pismo pochyłe

itch ['ycz] s. swędzenie; świerzb; chętka; v. czuć swędzenie; swędzić; mieć ochotę

item ['ajtem] s. pozycja; punkt programu; artykuł; wiadomość; adv. podobnie; także; też dotyczy

itemize ['ajte,majz] v. wyszczególniać (rachunek, spis)

itinerary [aj'tynerery] s. marszruta; szlak; przewodnik; adj. podróżny; drogowy

its [yts] pron. jego; jej; swój

itself [yt'self] pron. sią; siebie; sobie; sam; sama; samo

ivory ['ajwery] s. kość słoniowa; klawisz fortepianu; biel kremowa; adj. z kości słoniowej; biały

ivy ['ajwy] s. bluszcz

J

j [dżej] dziewiąta litera angielskiego alfabetu

jab [dżaeb] s. szturchaniec; dźgnięcie; v. szturchać; dźgać

jack [dżaek] s. lewarek; dźwignia; przyrząd; walet; flaga; gniazdo elektr.; złącze

jack up ['dżaek,ap] v. podnieść lewarkiem; wyśrubowanie (cen)

jackal [dżaeko:l] s. szakal; sługus; harować na kogoś

jackass ['dżaekaes] s. osioł; dureń; bałwan; menda; niedojda

jackdaw ['dżaekdo:] s. kawka

jacket [dżaekyt] s. marynarka; żakiet; kurtka; okładzina; obwoluta; osłona;

v.okrywać; nakładać okładzinę; wkładać do teki

jack-in-the-box ['dżaek-yn-dy -boks] s. figura wyskakująca z pudełka; typ ognia sztucznego

jack-nife ['dżaeknajf] s. scyzoryk; nóż składany

jack-of-all-trades ['dżaek,ow'o:l ,trejds] majster do wszystkiego; majster klepka

jackpot ['dżaek,pot] s. główna wygrana; pula

jackscrew [dżaekskru:] s. lewar śrubowy (podnośnik)

jag [dżaeg] s. ostry występ; zadarcie; nacięcie; podniecenie; popijawa; zabawa; v. poszarpać; postrzępić; ząbkować

jagged [dżaegyd] adj. postrzępiony; wyszczerbiony; szczerbaty

jaguar [dżaegjuer] s. jaguar

jail [dżejl] s. ciupa; więzienie; v. więzić; uwięzić (kogoś)

jam [dżaem] s. tłok; zator; korek; zła sytuacja; v. stłoczyć; zablokować; zaciąć; zagłuszyć

janitor ['dżaenitor] s. portier; dozorca; sprzątacz biurowy

January ['dżaenjuery] s. styczeń; a. styczniowy (dzień etc.)

Japanese [,dżaepe'ni:z] adj. japoński; s. Japończyk

jar [dża:r] s. słój; słoik; zgrzyt; kłótnia; drganie; v. zgrzytać; drażnić; wstrząsać; kłócić się; trząść; razić

jaundice ['dżo:ndys] s. żółtaczka; v. powodować zazdrość (żółtaczkę)

javelin ['dżaewlyn] s. oszczep

jaw [dżo:] s. szczęka; v. ględzić; gadać; wstawiać mowę

jaw-bone ['dżo:boun] s. kość szczękowa; v. nakłaniać słowami (pod presją)

jay [dżej] s. sójka; dudek; pleciuga; gaduła (arogancki)

jay-walker ['dżej,ło:ker] s.

nieprawidłowo przechodzący jezdnię; roztrzepaniec

jazz [dżaz] s. muzyka jazzowa; (slang) mowa lub czyny oceniane lekceważąco; v. grać w stylu jazzu; adj. zgrzytliwy; krzykliwy

jazz it up ['dżaz,yt'ap] exp. ożyw to; popraw to; przystrój to

jazz up ['dżaz,ap] v. (slang) ożywiać; upiększać; ulepszać (coś)

jazzy [dżazy] adj. w stylu jazz'u; podobny do jazz'u; (slang) żywy, ostentacyjny

jealous ['dżeles] adj. zazdrosny; baczny (nadzór); zawistny

jealousy ['dżelesy] s. zazdrość; zawiść; wybuch zazdrości

jeep [dżi:p] s. łazik; samochód terenowy (silnie zbudowany)

jeer [dżier] s. kpina; szyderstwo; drwina; v. drwić; kpić; wykpiwać (ordynarnie i złośliwie)

jelly ['dżely] s. galareta; kisiel; v. zgalarecieć; robić galaretę

jellyfish ['dżelyfysz] s. meduza; człowiek słabej woli

jeopardize ['dżepe,dajz] v. narazić na niebezpieczeństwo

jerk [dże:rk] s. szarpnięcie; skręt; skurcz; pchnięcie; bzik; frajer; v. szargać; targać; pchnąć; rzucać się; wzdrygać się

jerky ['dże:rky] adj. urwany; trzęsący; bzikowaty; spazmatyczny

jersey ['dże:rzy] s. sweter

jest [dżest] s. żart; dowcip; zabawa; pośmiewisko; v. żartować; dowcipkować; przekomarzać się

jester ['dżester] s. błazen; trefniś; błazen nadworny

jet [dżet] s. strumień; wytrysk; płomień; dysza; rozpylacz; odrzutowiec; v. tryskać; a. czarny jak smoła

jet engine [,dżet'endżyn] s.

motor odrzutowy
jet-lag ['dżet,laeg] s. ujemny efekt zmiany czasu na pasażera samolotu odrzutowego
jet plane ['dżet,plejn] s. samolot odrzutowy; odrzutowiec
jet-propelled ['dżet-pre,peld] adj. odrzutowy
jet set ['dżet,set] s. złota młodzież; prominenci
jetty [dżety] s. grobla; molo; adj. czarny jak smoła
Jew [dżu:] s. Żyd
jewel ['dżu:el] s. klejnot; drogi kamień; ozdabiać klejnotami; osadzać na kamieniach (zamontować)
jeweler ['dżu:eler] s. jubiler; właściciel sklepu jubilerskiego
jewelry ['dżu:elry] s. klejnoty; biżuteria; kosztowności
Jewess ['dżuys] s. Żydówka (członkini narodu żydowskiego); żydówka (wyznawczyni religii mojżeszowej)
Jewish ['dżu:ysz] adj. żydowski; hebrajski; judaistyczny; w stylu żydowskim; s. Yidysz, język żydowski
Jewry ['dżuery] s. Żydzi; Żydostwo; getto
Jewishness ['dżu:ysznys] s. żydowskość; żydowskie cechy
jibe [dżajb] v. zgadzać się; pasować (do czegoś); harmonizować
jiffy ['dżyfy] s. mig; chwileczka; momencik; sekundka
jiggle ['dżygl] v. kołysać; lekko huśtać; wstrząsać zrywnie
jig [dżyg] s. skoczny taniec; osadzarka; prowadnica
jig is up [dżyg yz ap] exp. beznadziejna sytuacja; koniec
jigsaw ['dżyg,so:] s. laubzega; włośnica
jigsaw puzzle ['dżyg,so:'pazl] s. składanka
jilt [dżylt] v. porzucić uwiedzionewgo lub

uwiedzioną s. kokietka; uwodzicielka
jimmy ['dżymy] s. krótki łom do podważania; v. otwierać podważając
jingle ['dżyngl] v. brzękać; szczękać; dzwonić; s. brzęk; szczęk; wierszyk (rymy); dzwonek
jingo ['dżyngou] s. szowinista; szowinistka
jingoism ['dżyngou'yzem] s. dżyngoism; szowinizm
jink [dżynk] v. unikać; wymknąć się; oszukiwać; s. unik; kiwnięcie (kogoś)
jitters ['dżyterz] s. pl. zdenerwowanie; trema
job [dżob] s. robota; zajęcie; zadanie; posada; v. pracować; robić; handlować; wynajmować
job [dżob] v. ukłuć; dźgnąć; dziobnąć; s. dźgnięcie; praca; dziobnięcie; zadanie; robota; fach
jobless ['dżoblys] adj. bezrobotny; bez pracy
job-work ['dżobłerk] s. praca na akord (zob. piece-work)
jockey ['dżoky] s. dżokej; v. oszukać; nabrać; pchać się na pozycję
jocular ['dżokjuler] adj. wesoły; żartobliwy; krotochwilny
jocularity [,dżokju'laeryty] s. wesołość; żartobliwość; żarty; krotochwilność; figlarność
jocund ['dżoukend] adj. wesoły
jog [dżog] s. potrącenie; poruszenie; trucht; róg; występ; v. potrącać; poruszać; przebiedować; biec truchtem; telepać się
jog-trot ['dżog'trot] s. trucht; a. monotonny; jednostajny
join [dżoyn] v. łączyć; przyłączać się; przytykać się do; spotykać się; brać udział
joiner ['dżojner] s. stolarz
joint [dżoynt] v. spajać; łączyć; ćwiartować;

kantować; s. spojenie; fuga;
złącze; zestawienie; zawiasa
francuska; część; lokal;
melina; a. wspólny;
połączony; dzielący się z
kimś

joint stock ['dżoynt‚stok] adj.
akcyjny (bank); udziałowy

joke [dżouk] s. żart; dowcip;
figiel; v. żartować z kogoś;
dowcipkować; wyśmiać;
zadrwić

joker ['dżouker] s. żartowniś;
dowcipniś; gość; facet;
dżoker; pułapka; trudność

jolly ['dżoly] adj. wesoły; miły;
podochocony; adv. szalenie;
bardzo; v. przychlebiać;
nabierać; zachęcać;
mitygować; ugłaskać

jolt [dżoult] v. wstrząsać;
podrzucać; s. wstrząs;
podrzucenie; szarpnięcie;
podskok

jostle ['dżosl] v. rozpychać
(się); roztrącać; szarpać się;
walczyć (z kimś); s.
pchnięcie; starcie;
szturchnięcie; tłok; ścisk

jot down ['dżot‚dałn] v. zapisać
naprędce; zanotować
pośpiesznie

journal ['dże:rnl] s. dziennik;
czasopismo; czop; oś w
łożysku

journalism ['dże:rnlyzem] s.
dziennikarstwo

journey ['dże:rny] v.
podróżować; s. podróż;
jazda; wycieczka

journeyman ['dże:rnymen] s.
czeladnik (nauczony rzemiosła)

jovial ['dżouwjel] adj. wesoły;
jowialny; pełen dobrego
humoru

joy [dżoj] s. radość; uciecha

joyful ['dżojful] adj. radosny;
wesoły; zadowolony (bardzo)

joyous ['dżojes] adj. = joyful

jubilant ['dżu:bylent] adj.
triumfujący; rozradowany

jubilee ['dżu:byli:] s. jubileusz;
wielka radość; a.

jubileuszowy

judge [dżadż] v. sądzić;
osądzać; rozsądzać; s.
sędzia; znawca; znawczyni;
człowiek biegły w ocenach

judgment ['dżadżment] s. sąd;
sądzenie; wyrok; rozsądek;
opinia; ocena; decyzja

judicial [dżu'dyszel] adj. sądowy;
sędziowski; bezstronny;
krytyczny; sądownie
zrzeszony

judicious [dżu'dyszes] a.
rozsądny; rozumny;
wykazujący rozum

jug [dżag] s. dzbanek; koza;
ciupa; v. gotować; wsadzać
do kozy, ciupy; dusić
(potrawkę)

juggle ['dżagl] v. żonglować;
cyganić; robić sztuczki; s.
kuglarstwo; żonglerka

juggler ['dżagler] s. kuglarz;
żongler; oszust; kanciarz

jugglery ['dżaglery] s.
kuglarstwo; podstęp;
oszukaństwo; żonglerka

juice [dżu:s] s. sok; treść;
benzyna; elektryczność; v.
wyciskać sok; doić

juicy ['dżu:sy] adj. soczysty;
jędrny; barwny; deszczowy

juke-box ['dżuk‚boks] s.
automat-gramofon (na
monety)

July [dżu:laj] s. lipiec

jumble ['dżambl] s. pomieszać;
kotłować; s. mieszanina;
galimatias; bigos; trzęsąca
jazda

jumble-sale ['dżambl‚sejl] s.
wyprzedaż wysortowanych
towarów (często dobroczynna)

jump [dżamp] s. skok; sus;
podskok; wyskok; v. skakać;
podskoczyć; wskoczyć;
wyskoczyć; wyprzedzać;
podnosić cenę; wykoleić;
poderwać się; rzucać się

jumper ['dżamper] s. skoczek;
typ sukni (bez rękawów)

jumpy ['dżampy] adj. nerwowy;
zmienny; nierówny; kapryśny

junction ['dżankszyn] s.
połączenie; złącze; stacja
węzłowa; węzeł;
skrzyżowanie (dróg)
juncture ['dżankczer] s.
połączenie; stan rzeczy;
krytyczna chwila; chwila;
przesilenie
June [dżu:n] s. czerwiec
jungle ['dżangl] s. dżungla;
gąszcz zarośli, lian etc.
junior ['dżu:njer] s. junior;
młodszy; student trzeciego
roku (USA); a. młodszy; z
młodszych
junk [dżank] s. złom; szmelc;
narkotyki; v. wyrzucać
junkie ['dżanki] s. narkoman
jurisdiction [,dżurys'dykszyn] s.
wymiar sprawiedliwości;
sądownictwo; zasięg władzy
jurisprudence [,dżurys'pru:dens]
s. prawoznawstwo
juror ['dżuerer] s. sędzia
przysięgły; ławnik;
zaprzysiężony; juror
jury ['dżuery] s. sąd
przysięgłych; sąd konkursowy
just [dżast] adj. sprawiedliwy;
słuszny; dokładny; adv.
właśnie; po prostu; zaledwie;
przecież; dokładnie; moment
wcześniej; ściśle; równie;
tak samo
just now ['dżast,nał] exp.:
właśnie teraz; przed chwilą
justice ['dżastys] s.
sprawiedliwość; słuszność;
sędzia (pokoju, sądu
najwyższego)
justification [,dżastyfy'kejszyn]
s. uzasadnienie;
usprawiedliwienie; wykazanie
justify ['dżastyfaj] v.
usprawiedliwić;
wytłumaczyć; umotywować;
uzasadnić; dać dowody
justly ['dżastly] adv. słusznie;
poprawnie; właściwie;
sprawiedliwie
jut [dżat] s. występ; v.
wystawać
jut out ['dżat,aut] v. wystawać;

sterczeć (na zewnątrz);
występować
juvenile ['dżu:wynajl] adj.
małoletni; nieletni; s.
wyrostek; młodzik; podrostek
juvenile court ['dżu:wynajl,ko:rt]
s. sąd dla nieletnich
juvenile delinquent ['dżu:wynajl
,dy'lynkłent] s. młodociany
przestępca
juxtaposition [,dżakstepe'zyszyn]
s. zestawienie; bezpośrednie
sąsiedztwo (tuż obok)

K

k [kej] jedenasta litera
angielskiego alfabetu
kangaroo [,kaenge'ru:] s. kangur;
a. samosądny; nielegalny
kayak ['kajaek] s. kajak; a.
kajakowy
keel [ki:l] s. stępka; kil; v.
wywracać do góry stępką
keen [ki:n] adj. ostry; dotkliwy;
żywy; cięty; serdeczny;
gorliwy; zapalony; bystry;
przenikliwy; wrażliwy; czuły
keen on ['ki:n,on] adj. palący się
do ...; czujący miętę
keep; kept; kept [ki:p; kept;
kept]
keep [ki:p] v. dotrzymywać;
przestrzegać; dochować;
obchodzić; strzec; pilnować;
utrzymywać; prowadzić;
trzymać (się);
powstrzymywać się;
mieszkać; kontynuować; s.
utrzymanie; jedzenie; wikt;
umocnienie
keep away ['ki:p,e'łej] v.
trzymać się z daleka;
odstraszać
keep back ['ki:p,baek] v.
powstrzymać; nie zbliżać się
keep down ['ki:p,dałn] v.
trzymać w ryzach; tłumić;

kulić się; utrzymywać na niskim poziomie

keep in ['ki:p,yn] v. zatrzymywać; nie wychodzić; pozostawać; nie pokazywać się

keep off ['ki:p,of] v. nie dopuszczać; trzymać się z dala

keep on ['ki:p,on] v. kontynuować; iść dalej; nudzić; męczyć

keep on doing ['ki:p,on'du:yng] v. robić dalej; nie przestawać; nie dawać spokoju; nudzić

keep out ['ki:p,ałt] v. nie wchodzić; trzymać się na uboczu; nie pozwolić wejść; odpędzać

keep talking ['ki:p'to:kyng] v. mówić dalej; kontynuować rozmowę

keep time ['ki:p'tajm] v. być punktualnym; zapisywać czas pracy

keep to oneself ['ki:p,tu'łanself] v. trzymać się na uboczu; żyć w odosobnieniu

keep up ['ki:p,ap] v. dotrzymywać; utrzymywać w porządku; nie dawać iść spać; trzymać się w dobrym stanie; czuwać

keep up with ['ki:p,ap'łys] v. śledzić; dotrzymywać (kroku)

keeper ['ki:per] s. opiekun; dozorca; strażnik; konserwator; klamra; kotwica magnesu; skobel

keeping ['ki:pyng] s. opieka; zgoda; harmonia; a. do przechowywania

keepsake ['ki:psejk] s. upominek; pamiątka od kogoś

keg [keg] s. beczułka; 100 funtów

kennel ['kenl] s. psiarnia; psia buda; ściek; v. trzymać w budzie; mieszkać w norze

kept [kept] v. zob. keep

kerb stone ['ke:rb,stoun] s.

krawężnik (ang.) zob. curb

kerchief ['ke:rczyf] s. chustka (na głowę); chustka do nosa

kernel ['ke:rnl] s. jądro; ziarno; sedno sprawy; istotna rzecz

ketchup ['keczap] s. sos pomidorowy (gotowy) do mięsa

kettle ['ketl] s. kocioł; czajnik; imbryk na herbatę

kettledrum ['ketl,dram] s. bęben kocioł (półkolisty) miedziany

key [ki:] s. klucz; klawisz; klin; ton; rafa; wysepka; v. stroić; zamykać kluczem lub zwornikiem; adj. ważny; kontrolujący

keyboard ['ki:bo:rd] s. klawiatura (maszyny do pisania etc.)

keyhole ['ki:houl] s. dziurka od klucza (w drzwiach etc.)

keynote ['ki:nout] s. nuta kluczowa; myśl przewodnia

keystone ['ki:stoun] s. zwornik; zasada; główna część

kick [kyk] s. kopniak; kopnięcie; wierzgnięcie; wykop; strzał; odrzut; skarga; narzekanie; przyjemność; uciecha; krzepa; miłe podniecenie; opór; v. kopać; wierzgać; skrzywić się; protestować; opierać się

kickback ['kykbaek] s. łapówka za kontrakt; dawanie łapówki

kick downstairs ['kykdałn'steerz] v. degradować; zrzucać ze schodów (kopniakiem)

kick-off ['kykof] s. rozpoczęcie meczu; pierwszy strzał

kick out ['kyk ałt] v. wyrzucić; wykopać; pozbyć się

kick the bucket ['kyk,dy'bakyt] v. umrzeć; odwalić kitę; wyciągnąć nogi; wykitować

kid [kyd] s. koźlę; dzieciak; smyk; młodzik; blaga; bujda; v. urodzić koźlę; bujać; nabierać; żartować; dowcipkować

kid glove ['kydglaw] s. rękawiczka; a. balowy; delikatny

kidnap ['kydnaep] v. porywać; uprowadzać; ukraść dziecko

kidnapper ['kydnaeper] s. porywacz (dziecka, zakładnika)

kidney ['kydny] s. nerka; rodzaj; a. w kształcie nerki

kidney bean ['kydny,bi:n] s. fasola szparagowa; piesza

kill [kyl] v. zabijać; uśmiercać; wybić; zatrzymać (piłkę, motor); ścinać (piłkę); s. upolowane zwierzę; zabicie; mord

killjoy ['kyldżoj] s. człowiek psujący innym zabawę lub humor

kill time [,kyl'tajm] v. zabijać czas; marnować czas

killer ['kyler] s. zabójca; morderca; narzędzie śmierci

kiln [kyln] s. piec do wypalania lub wysuszania cegieł etc.

kilogram(me) ['kylougraem] s. kilogram; a. kilogramowy

kilometer ['kyle,mi:ter] s. kilometr; a. kilometrowy

kilt [kylt] s. spódniczka męska (szkocka); v. podkasać; plisować pionowo

kin [kyn] s. rodzina; krewni; ród; adj. spokrewniony; pokrewny

kind [kajnd] s. rodzaj; jakość; gatunek; charakter; natura; adj. grzeczny; uprzejmy; życzliwy; łagodny; wyrozumiały

kindergarten ['kynder,ga:rtn] s. przedszkole (do sześciu lat wieku)

kindhearted ['kajnd'ha:rtyd] adj. dobrotliwy; współczujący

kindle ['kyndle] v. rozpalić; rozżarzyć; rozniecać; podniecać; zapalać się

kindly ['kajndly] adv. uprzejmie; życzliwie; adj. dobry; dobrotliwy; życzliwy

kindness ['kajndnys] s. dobroć; uprzejmość; łaskawość; życzliwość; życzliwy postępek

kindred ['kyndryd] s. krewni; pokrewieństwo; adj.

pokrewny

king [kyng] s. król

kingdom ['kyngdom] s. królestwo; monarchia; świat (roślin etc.)

king-size ['kyngsajz] adj. wielki; duży; królewskich wymiarów

kingly ['kyngly] adj. królewski

kinsman ['kynzmen] s. krewny; powinowaty (mężczyzna)

kipper ['kyper] s. śledź wędzony; ryba suszona; v. suszyć; wędzić i solić; zasuszać (ryby)

kiss [kys] s. całus; v. całować; pocałować; lekko dotknąć

kit [kyt] s. przybory; narzędzia; wyposażenie; zestaw; komplet; torba; bagaż; cebrzyk; kubeł; komplet (narzędzi)

kitchen ['kyczn] s. kuchnia

kitchenette ['kyczynet] s. kuchenka (mała w kawalerce)

kite [kajt] s. latawiec; v. szybować

kitten ['kytn] s. kotek

knack [naek] s. spryt; sztuczka; chwyt; dryg; talent

knapsack ['naepsaek] s. plecak

knave [nejw] s. łajdak; łotr; szelma; walet; naciągacz; kanalia

knavery ['nejwery] s. łajdactwo; szelmostwo; niegodziwość

knead ['ni:d] v. miesić; gnieść; masować; kształtować (charakter)

knee ['ni:] s. kolano; v. klękać

kneecap ['ni:kaep] s. rzepka (kolana)

knee-deep ['ni:di:p] adj. po kolana

knee-jerk ['ni:dże:rk] s. odruch kolanowy; automatyczna reakcja

kneel; knelt; knelt [ni:l; nelt; nelt]

kneel [ni:l] v. klękać

knelt [nelt] zob. kneel

knew [nju:] zob. know

knickerbockers ['nikerbokers] s. pumpy; krótkie spodnie spięte pod kolanami

knickknack ['niknaek] s. cacko;
fatałaszek; przysmaczek
knife [najf] s. nóż; v. krajać;
kłuć nożem; zakłuć;
zadźgać nożem
knight [najt] s. rycerz; v.
nadawać szlachectwo;
nobilitować
knit; knit; knit [nyt; nyt; nyt]
knit [nyt] v. robić na drutach;
dziać; marszczyć (brwi);
łączyć; ściągać;
powodować zrośnięcie
(kości); spajać (cementem)
knitting [nytyng] s. dzianie;
trykotarstwo; dziewiarstwo
knives [najwz] pl. noże; pl. od
knife
knob [nob] s. guzik; guz; gałka;
sęk; uchwyt; pokrętło; rączka
knock [nok] s. stuk; uderzenie;
pukanie; v. stukać; pukać;
zapukać; uderzyć; zderzyć;
szturchać; zderzyć się
knock down ['nok,dałn] v.
powalić; obniżać cenę;
rozkręcać
knock out ['nok,aut] v.
nokautować; wybijać;
wymęczyć
knock over ['nok,ower] v.
przewracać; przewrócić
knocker ['noker] s. kołatka na
drzwiach; malkontent;
opukiwacz
knot [not] s. węzeł; kokarda;
sęk; zgrubienie; dystans
morski 1853 m; v. wiązać;
zawiązywać; komplikować;
motać
knotty ['noty] adj. węzłowaty;
sękaty; zawiły; zagadkowy
know; knew; known [nou; nju:
noun]
know [nou] v. wiedzieć; umieć;
znać; móc odróżniać;
poznać
know-how ['nouhau] s.
umiejętność; znajomość
rzeczy
knowingly ['nouyngly] adj.
świadomie; naumyślnie;
chytrze

knowledge ['noulydż] s. wiedza;
nauka; znajomość; zasięg
wiedzy
knowledgeable ['nolydżebl] adj.
dobrze poinformowany; mądry
knuckle ['nakl] s. staw palca;
kastet; uderzać kośćmi
palców
kosher ['kouszer] adj. koszerny;
v. koszerować (mięso)
kotow ['kou,tał] = kowtow
kowtow ['koł,tał] v. bić czołem;
płaszczyć się; s. ukłon
starochiński czołem do ziemi
Kraut [kraut] adj. szkopski
(niemiecki); kapuściany
kudos ['kju:dos] s. nagroda lub
uznanie za znaczne
osiągnięcie; sława (slang)
Ku Klux Klan ['kju:,kluks'klaen]
s. rasistowska tajna
organizacja w USA przeciw
Murzynom, Żydom i katolikom
kulak [ku:'la:k] s. zamożny
chłop; kułak

L

l [el] dwunasta litera alfabetu
angielskiego; klauzura; kolanko
(rury); kątownik
lab [laeb] s. (slang) laboratorium;
a. laboratoryjny
label ['lejbl] s. nalepka; etykieta;
naklejka; przezwisko; v.
przylepiać etykiety (na coś,
komuś); przezywać
labor ['lejber] s. praca; robota;
trud; mozół; wysiłek; klasa
robotnicza; poród; v. ciężko
pracować; mozolić się;
borykać się; łudzić się;
brnąć; opracować;
rozwodzić się; rodzić;
szczegółowo opracować
laboratory [lae'boretery] s.
laboratorium; pracownia
laborious [le'bo:rjes] adj.

pracowity; mozolny;
wypracowany; ciężko
pracujący
labor union ['lejber'ju:njen] s.
związek zawodowy
laborer ['lejberer] s. robotnik
płatny na godzinę (fizyczny)
laborite ['lejberajt] s. członek
partii pracy (w Anglii)
lace [lejs] s. sznurówka;
sznurowadło; koronka; v.
sznurować; przetykać;
koronkować; urozmaicać;
chłostać; zakrapiać (wódką);
młócić; bić; walić
lack [laek] s. brak; niedostatek;
v. brakować; nie mieć
czegoś; być bez czegoś
laconic [le'konyk] adj.
lakoniczny; zwięzły; treściwy
lacquer ['laeker] s. lakier; v.
lakierować; emaliować
lad [laed] s. chłopak; chłopiec
ladder ['laeder] s. drabina; v.
pruć; rozpruć; puszczać
oczka
ladder proof ['laeder,pru:f] adj.
nie prujące się (np.
pończochy); nie puszczający
oczek
laden ['lejdn] adj. obciążony;
obarczony; pogrążony (w
smutku)
lading ['lejdyng] s. fracht;
załadowanie; ładunek (statku)
ladle ['lejdl] s. warząchew;
czerpak; chochla; v. czerpać;
nalewać warząchwią
(czerpakiem)
lady ['lejdy] s. pani; dama
lady killer ['lejdy,kyler] s.
pożeracz serc niewieścich
ladylike ['lejdylajk] adj.
wytworny; zniewieściały
lag [laeg] s. zaleganie;
opóźnienie; zwłoka; v.
zalegać; wlec się z tyłu; nie
nadążać
lag behind ['laeg,by'hajnd] v.
pozostawać w tyle; zalegać
lager ['la:ger] s. wystałe piwo
lagoon [le'gu:n] s. laguna
laid [lejd] zob. lay

lain [lejn] zob. lie
lair [leer] s. barłóg; legowisko;
szałas; v. iść na legowisko
lake [lejk] s. jezioro; a. jeziorny
lamb [laem] s. jagnię; baranina
lame [lejm] adj. kulawy; ułomny;
v. okulawić; okaleczyć
lament [le'ment] s. lament;
biadanie; v. lamentować;
biadać; opłakiwać;
narzekać; ubolewać;
zawodzić; być w żałobie
lamentable ['laementebl] adj.
opłakany; godny ubolewania;
żałosny; wyrażający
ubolewanie
lamentation [,laemen'tejszyn] s.
lament; biadanie; lamentacja
lamp [laemp] s. lampa; latarka;
kaganek; v. świecić;
oświetlać; gapić się;
zobaczyć; widzieć
lamppost ['laemp,poust] s. słup
latarniany; latarnia uliczna
lamp shade ['laempszejd] s.
abażur
lance [la:ns] s. lanca; lansjer;
lancet; v. kłuć; przebijać
lancą lub lancetem; rozcinać
land [laend] s. ląd; ziemia; grunt;
kraj; v. wyciągać na ląd;
wyładować; zdobyć (np.
nagrodę)
landholder ['laend,houlder] s.
właściciel ziemski;
dzierżawca
landing ['laendyng] s. lądowanie;
pomost; przystań; półpiętrze
landing field ['laendyng,fi:ld] s.
lotnisko polowe; lądowisko
landing gear ['laendyng,gier] s.
podwozie (z kołami -
samolotu)
landing stage ['laendyng, stejdż]
s. pomost pływający;
wyładunek
landlady ['laend,lejdy] s.
właścicielka domu, hotelu
etc.; gospodyni (pensjonatu)
landlord ['laend,lo:rd] s.
właściciel domu

czynszowego; gospodarz
odnajmujący pokój
landmark ['laendma:rk] s. punkt
orientacyjny; słup graniczny
landowner ['laend,ołner] s.
właściciel ziemski
landscape ['laendskejp] s.
krajobraz; v. kształtować
teren i ogród (upiększać)
landslide ['laendslajd] s.
osuwisko; lawina głazów
landslip ['laendslyp] s. osuwisko;
obsunięcie się ziemi
lane [lejn] s. tor; uliczka; szlak;
przejście; linia ruchu
kołowego; trasa (samolotu)
language ['laengłydż] s. mowa;
język mówiony i pisany
languid ['laengłyd] s. ospały;
omdlały; słaby; ociężały;
powolny; rozmarzony; tęskny
languish ['laengłysz] v.
omdlewać; marnieć; ginąć z
tęsknoty; mieć wyraz zadumy
languor ['laenger] s. omdlenie;
osłabienie; ociężałość;
ospałość; tęsknota;
rozmarzenie; powolność;
brak wigoru; słabość
lank [laenk] adj. mizerny;
wysoki; chudy; wychudzony;
prosty; gładki; długi i płaski
lanky ['laenky] adj. wychudzony;
wysoki i chudy
lanolin ['laenolyn] s. lanolina
lantern ['laentern] s. latarnia
lap [laep] s. łono; podołek; poła;
okrążenie; zanadrze; dolinka;
chlupotanie; lura; v. spowijać;
otulać; zakładać (jak
dachówki); wystawać;
chłeptać; chlupotać;
chlupać
lapel [le'pel] s. klapa (płaszcza)
dochodząca kołnierza
lapse [laeps] s. lapsus; upływ;
okres; omyłka; v. potknąć
się; odstąpić; omylić się;
upłynąć; stracić ważność;
minąć; przechodzić;
pogrążyć się w stan ...
larceny ['la:rseny] s. kradzież
larch [la:rcz] s. modrzew

lard [la:rd] s. smalec; v.
szpikować; naszpikowywać;
ozdabiać cytatami
larder ['la:rder] s. spiżarnia
large [la:rdż] adj. wielki; rozległy;
obfity; hojny
largely ['la:rdżly] adv. znacznie;
hojnie; suto; w dużym
stopniu; w dużej ilości;
głównie
lark [la:rk] s. skowronek;
zabawa; uciecha; v. figlować;
żartować; przeskakiwać
larva ['la:rwa] s. larwa
larynx ['laerynks] s. krtań
lascivious [le'sywjes] adj.
lubieżny; wzbudzający
lubieżność
lash [laesz] s. bicz; uderzenie;
nagana; rzęsa; v. chłostać;
machać; walić; pędzić;
uwiązać
lass [laes] s. dziewczyna;
dziewczę; młoda kobieta
lasso [lae'su:] s. lasso; v.
chwytać na lasso
last [laest] adj. ostatni; ubiegły;
ostateczny; adv. po raz
ostatni; ostatnio; wreszcie; w
końcu; v. trwać;
wytrzymać; wystarczyć;
długo służyć; s. koniec; kres;
wytrzymałość; kopyto
szewskie; ostatnie dziecko
last but one ['laest,bat'łan] exp.:
przedostatni
lasting ['la:styng] adj. stały;
trwały; długotrwały
lastly [la:stly] adv. w końcu; na
końcu; w konkluzji;
ostatecznie
last night ['laest,najt] exp.:
wczoraj wieczór
last name ['laest,nejm] s.
nazwisko
latch [laecz] s. zasuwka; rygiel;
zatrzask; v. zamykać na
zasuwkę, rygiel lub zatrzask
latch onto ['laecz,ontu] v.
uczepić się kogoś
late [lejt] adj. & s. późny;
spóźniony; były; zmarły; adv.
późno; poniewczasie;

niegdyś
lately ['lejtly] adv. ostatnio
later on ['lejter,on] adv. później;
potem; dalej
lath [laes] s. łata; deseczka; v.
pokrywać łatami (do
tynkowania)
lathe [lejz] s. tokarnia; koło
garncarskie; v. toczyć (na
tokarni); obrabiać (na
obrabiarce)
lather ['laedzer] s. piana;
mydliny; v. mydlić (brodę);
zapienić (się); prać; łoić
Latin ['laetyn] adj. łaciński; s.
łacina; łacinnik
latitude ['laetytju:d] s.
szerokość (geograficzna);
szerokość poglądów; zakres;
rozmiary; wolność; swoboda
(np. działania); tolerancja
latter ['laeter] adj. drugi;
końcowy; schyłkowy; ostatni
latterly ['laeterly] adv. ostatnio;
niedawno; później
lattice ['laetys] s. kratownica; v.
kratować; ułożyć w kratę
laudable ['lo:debl] adj.
chwalebny; godny pochwały
laugh [laef] v. śmiać się;
zaśmiać się; roześmiać się
laugh at ['laef,et] v.
wyśmiewać; uśmiać się (z
czegoś)
laugh away ['laef,e'łej] v. zbyć
śmiechem
laugh off ['laef,of] v. obrócić w
żart; pokryć zmieszanie
śmiechem
laughter ['laefter] s. śmiech
launch [lo:ncz] v. puszczać w
ruch; spuszczać na wodę;
miotać; rzucać; zadawać;
wydawać; s. szalupa;
spuszczenie na wodę (statku,
okrętu etc.)
launching pad ['lo:nczyng,paed]
s. wyrzutnia (rakiet)
launderette [lo:n'dret] s. pralnia
samoobsługowa
laundry ['lo:ndry] s. pralnia;
bielizna do prania
laurel ['lorel] s. wawrzyn; laur; v.

wieńczyć wawrzynem
lava ['la:we] s. lawa
lavatory ['laewetery] s.
umywalnia; ustęp; umywalka
lavender ['laewynder] s.
lawenda; v. wkładać lawendę
w bieliznę; a. lawendowy
lavish ['laewysz] adj. hojny;
suty; rozrzutny; v. nie
szczędzić (pieniędzy,
miłości)
law [lo:] s. prawo; ustawa;
reguła; sądy; posłuszeństwo
prawu
lawful ['lo:ful] adj. legalny;
słuszny; prawowity; z
prawego łoża; prawnie uznany
lawless ['lo:lys] adj. bezprawny;
łamiący prawo; rozpustny
lawn [lo:n] s. trawnik; murawa
lawn mower ['lo:n,mołer] s.
kosiarka do strzyżenia trawy
lawsuit ['lo:sju:t] s. proces
(sądowy); sprawa sądowa
lawyer ['lo:jer] s. prawnik;
adwokat; radca prawny
lax [laeks] adj. luźny;
nieszczelny; niedbały;
nieścisły; mający
rozwolnienie; wolny
laxative ['laeksetyw] adj. & s.
przeczyszczający (środek)
laxity ['laeksyty] s. luźność;
nieścisłość;
niedokładność; niedbalstwo;
rozwiązłość
lay; laid; laid [lej; lejd; lejd]
lay [lej] v. kłaść; uspokajać;
układać; skręcać (się);
zaczaić się; spać z kimś; s.
położenie; układ; spanie (z
kimś); adj. świecki; laicki;
niefachowy; lay- zob. lie
layout ['lejout] s. rozkład; plan;
założenie; układ
lay out ['lej,aut] v. układać;
projektować; powalić;
(slang) zabić; wydatkować;
wyłożyć
lay up ['lejap] v. zbierać;
gromadzić; przechowywać
layer ['lejer] s. warstwa; odkład;
kura niosąca; zakładający się;

pokład

layman ['lejmen] s. człowiek
świecki; laik

lazy ['lejzy] adj. leniwy;
próżniaczy; ociężały

lead [led] s. ołów; v. pokrywać
ołowiem; obciążać ołowiem

lead; led; led [li:d; led; led]

lead [li:d] v. prowadzić;
kierować; dowodzić;
naprowadzać; nasunąć;
namówić; dyrygować;
przewodzić; s. kierownictwo;
przewodnictwo; przewaga;
prym; wskazówka; przykład;
powodzenie

leaden ['ledn] adj. ołowiany;
ciężki; ociężały; ponury; szary

leader ['li:der] s. przywódca;
lider; przewodnik; prowadzący

leadership ['li:der,szyp] s.
przywództwo; kierownictwo;
przewodnictwo; umiejętność
przewodzenia

leading ['li:dyng] adj.
kierowniczy; naczelny;
główny; s. kierownictwo;
prowadzenie; przewodnictwo;
przywództwo

leaf [li:f] s. liść; kartka; pl.
leaves [li:wz]

leaflet [li:flyt] s. listek; ulotka
(często złożona)

league [li:g] s. liga; związek;
mila; v. łączyć (się) w ligę

leak [li:k] s. dziura; otwór;
przeciekanie; v. cieknąć;
przeciekać; wyciekać
(sekrety); wysączać;
zaciekać

leakage [li:kydż] s. przeciekanie
(sekretów); wyciekanie
(pieniędzy); rozproszenie

leaky ['li:ky] adj. dziurawy;
nieszczelny; cieknący;
niedyskretny; nie
dochowujący sekretu

lean; leant; leant [li:n; lent; lent]

lean [li:n] v. nachylać (się);
pochylać (się); opierać (się)
(o coś); adj. chudy; s. chude
mięso; nachylenie;
skłonność

leant [lent] v. zob. lean

leap; leapt; leapt [li:p; lept; lept]

leap [li:p] v. skakać;
przeskoczyć; s. skok;
podskok

leapt [lept] v. zob. leap

leap-year ['li:pje:r] s. rok
przestępny

learn; learnt; learnt [le:rn; le:rnt;
le:rnt]

learn [le:rn] v. uczyć się;
dowiadywać się; zapamiętać

learned ['le:rnyd] adj. uczony

learner ['le:rner] s. uczący się;
uczeń; uczennica

learning ['le:rnyng] s. nauka;
wiedza; erudycja;
umiejętności

learnt [le:rnt] v. zob. learn

lease [li:s] s. dzierżawa; v.
dzierżawić; wydzierżawiać

leash [li:sz] s. smycz

least [li:st] adj. najmniejszy; adv.
najmniej; w najmniejszym
stopniu; s. najmniejsza rzecz;
drobnostka najmniej ważna

leather ['ledzer] s. skóra; adj.
skórzany; v. pokrywać skórą;
oprawiać w skórę; sprać
(rzemieniem)

leave; left; left [li:w; left; left]

leave [li:w] v. zostawiać;
opuszczać; odchodzić;
odjeżdżać; pozostawiać; s.
pożegnanie; urlop; pozwolenie

leaven [lewn] s. drożdże

leaves [li:wz] pl. liście; zob. leaf

lecture ['lekczer] s. wykład;
nagana; v. wykładać;
udzielać nagany; przemawiać
do sumienia

lecturer ['lekczerer] s.
wykładowca (na uczelni, w
klasie etc.)

led [led] v. zob. lead

ledge [ledż] s. występ; stopień;
półka; gzyms; listwa; rafa

lee [li:] s. strona zawietrzna;
osłona; adj. zawietrzny;
osłonięty

leech [li:cz] s. pijawka

leek [li:k] s. por

leer [lier] s. spojrzenie z ukosa;

v. łypać okiem znacząco
(chytrze, złośliwie,
pożądliwie)
left [left] adj. lewy; adv. na
lewo; s. lewa strona; zob.
leave
left-hand ['left,haend] s. lewa
ręka; adj. lewoskrętny;
lewostronny
left-handed ['left'haendyd] s.
mańkut; adj. leworęki;
niezgrabny; wątpliwy;
nieszczery
left side ['left,sajd] s. lewa
strona (drogi, samochodu etc.)
leg [leg] s. noga; nóżka;
podpórka; odcinek; kończyna;
udziec
legacy [legesy] s. spadek;
spuścizna; dziedzictwo; zapis
legal ['li:gel] adj. prawny;
prawniczy; ustawowy; legalny
legation [li'gejszyn] s. poselstwo
(włącznie z posłem)
legend ['ledżend] s. legenda
legendary ['ledżendery] adj.
legendarny; tradycyjny
legible ['ledżebl] adj. czytelny;
łatwo czytelny
legion ['li:dżen] s. legion; legia;
wojsko; wielka ilość;
mnóstwo; tłumy; mnogość
legislation [,ledżys'lejszyn] s.
prawodawstwo;
ustawodawstwo
legislative ['ledżysletyw] adj.
prawodawczy; ustawodawczy
legislator ['ledżyslator] s.
prawodawca; poseł do
parlament (sejmu, senatu etc.)
legitimate [ly'dżytymyt] adj.
ślubny; prawowity; słuszny;
uzasadniony; logiczny;
rozsądny
leg-pull ['legpu:l] s. kawał; żart;
sztuczka; naciąganie
leisure ['li:żer] s. wolny czas;
swoboda od zajęć; wolne
chwile
leisurely ['li:żerly] adv.
swobodnie; bez pośpiechu;
adj. mający czas; spokojny;
robiony w wolnym czasie

lemon ['lemen] s. cytryna;
tandeta; adj. cytrynowy; z
cytryn
lemonade ['lemenejd] s.
lemoniada (z soku
cytrynowego etc.)
lend; lent; lent [lend; lent; lent]
lend [lend] v. pożyczać;
użyczać; udzielać
length [lenks] s. długość
lengthen ['lenksen] v.
przedłużać; wydłużać (się);
podłużać
lengthwise ['lensłajz] adv. adj.
wzdłuż; na długość
lenient ['li:njent] adj.
wyrozumiały; łagodny
lens [lenz] s. soczewka;
obiektyw; lupa
lent [lent] s. post; zob. lend
leopard ['leperd] s. lampart
leper ['leper] s. trędowaty;
trędowata
leprosy ['lepresy] s. trąd
less [les] adj. mniejszy; adv.
mniej; s. coś mniejszego;
prep. bez; nie tak dużo (wiele)
lessen [lesn] v. zmniejszać (się);
maleć; pomniejszać
lesser ['leser] adj. mniejszy
lesson [lesn] s. lekcja; nauczka;
urywek z Biblii; wykład
lest [lest] conj. ażeby nie; że
let; let; let [let; let; let]
let [let] v. zostawić;
wynajmować; dawać;
puszczać; pozwalać
let alone ['let,e'loun] v.
zostawić w spokoju; dać
spokój
let down ['let,dałn] v. robić
zawód; spuszczać;
opuszczać; upokorzyć;
odmawiać pomocy
let go ['let,gou] v. wypuszczać;
zwalniać; pozwolić odejść
let know ['let,nou] v.
zawiadomić; donieść;
powiadomić
let up ['let,ap] v. zelżeć;
złagodnieć; s. zelżenie
lethal ['li:sel] adj. śmiertelny;
zgubny; śmiercionośny

letter ['leter] s. litera; list;
czcionka; v. drukować;
oznaczać literami;
kaligrafować
letter-box ['leter,boks] s.
skrzynka pocztowa
letter-carrier ['leter'kaerjer] s.
listonosz
lettuce ['letys] s. sałata
(główiasta); liście sałaty
leukemia [lju'ki:mie] s. białaczka;
leukemia
level ['lewl] s. poziom;
płaszczyzna; równina;
poziomnica; adj. poziomy; adv.
poziomo; równo; v.
zrównywać; celować
level crossing ['lewl'krosyng] s.
skrzyżowanie dróg (kolizyjne)
w jednej płaszczyźnie
lever ['li:wer] s. dźwignia;
lewar; v. podważać;
podnosić dźwigiem
(lewarem)
levity ['lewyty] s.
lekkomyślność
levy ['lewy] v. pobierać;
nakładać (podatek); s. pobór
lewd [lu:d] adj. zmysłowy;
lubieżny; pożądliwy; sprośny
liability [,laje'bylyty] s.
odpowiedzialność;
obowiązek; obciążenie;
zadłużenie; ryzyko
liable ['lajebl] adj.
odpowiedzialny; podlegający;
podatny; skłonny; narażony;
mający widoki
liable to ['lajebl,tu] adj. skłonny
do ...; adv. łatwo (zgnije)
liaison [ly'ejzo:n] s. łączność;
związek; romans (nielegalny)
liar ['lajer] s. kłamca; łgarz
libation [laj-bej'szyn] s. libacja
libel ['lajbel] s. paszkwil;
oszczerstwo; zniesławienie
(publiczne w piśmie, filmie
etc.); v. zniesławiać
liberal ['lyberel] s. liberał; a.
liberalny; hojny; tolerancyjny
liberate ['lyberejt] v. uwalniać;
zwalniać; wyzwalać
liberation [lyberejszyn] s.

uwalnianie; oswobodzenie
liberator ['lyberejter] s.
oswobodziciel; wyzwoliciel
liberty ['lyberty] s. wolność;
swoboda; nadużywanie
wolności
librarian [laj'breerjen] s.
bibliotekarz
library ['lajbrery] s. biblioteka;
księgozbiór
lice [lajs] pl. wszy; zob. louse
license(ce) ['lajsens] s. licencja;
pozwolenie; upoważnienie;
swoboda; rozpusta; v.
upoważniać; udzielać
pozwolenia; nadużywać
wolności
licensee [,lajsen'si:] s. posiadacz
zezwolenia; koncesjonariusz;
właściciel licencji
lichen ['lajken] s. liszaj
lick [lyk] s. liźnięcie; odrobina;
cios; raz; wybuch; energia; v.
lizać; polizać; wylizać; bić;
smarować
licking ['lykyng] s. (slang) bicie;
pobicie; młocka
lid [lyd] s. wieko; powieka;
pokrywa; nakrywka;
przykrywka
lie; 1. lay; lain [laj; lej; lejn]
lie [laj] v. leżeć; s. układ;
położenie; konfiguracja;
legowisko
lie; 2. lied; lied [laj; lajd; lajd]
lie [laj] v. kłamać; s. kłamstwo;
łgarstwo; fałsz
lie down ['laj,dałn] v. kłaść się;
położyć się; nie reagować
lie in ['laj,yn] v. być w połogu;
leżeć w (łóżku)
lie over ['laj,ouwer] v. być
odroczonym; zostać przez
noc
lieutenant [lef'tenant; lu:tenant]
s. porucznik
life [lajf] s. życie; życiorys; zob.
pl. lives
life assurance ['lajfe'szuerens] s.
ubezpieczenie na życie
life belt ['lajfbelt] s. pas
ratunkowy
lifeboat ['lajfbout] s. łódź

ratunkowa
lifeguard ['lajfga:rd] s. ratownik
life insurance ['lajn,yn'szuerens]
s. ubezpieczenie na życie
life jacket ['lajfdżaekyt] s. kurta
ratownicza; kamizelka
ratunkowa
lifeless ['lajflys] adj. bez życia;
martwy; zamarły; wymarły
lifelike ['lajflajk] adj. jak żywy
(człowiek, osoba, stworzenie)
life sentence ['lajf,sentens] s.
kara dożywocia (wyrok)
life-style ['lajfstajl] s. styl życia;
modła życia; sposób życia
lifetime ['lajf,tajm] s. życie; całe
życie
lift [lyft] s. dźwig; winda;
przewóz; podniesienie;
wzniesienie; v. podnieść;
dźwignąć; podnosić się;
kraść; spłacić (np. dom);
kopnąć; buchnąć;
awansować
lift-off ['lyft,of] s. start lotu (np.
rakiety)
ligament ['lygement] s. ścięgno
ligature ['lygeczuer] s.
przywiązanie; ligatura;
podwiązanie; bandaż; nić
chirurgiczna
light; lit; lit [lajt; lyt; lyt]
light [lajt] s. światło;
oświetlenie; ogień; adj.
świetny; jasny; łatwy; lekki;
błahy; słaby; beztroski;
niefrasobliwy; lekkomyślny;
v. świecić; oświecać;
zapalać; ujawniać;
poświęcić; rozjaśnić;
przyświecić; wsiadać;
zsiadać; wpaść; wyjechać;
adv. lekko
lightheaded ['lajt'hedyd] adj.
lokkomyślny; majaczący;
roztargniony
light up ['lajtap] v. zaświecić;
rozjaśnić; oświecić
lighten ['lajtn] v. ulżyć; zelżyć;
oświecać; rozjaśnić się;
błysnąć; błyskać się
lighter ['lajter] s. zapalniczka;
latarnik; lampiarz

lighthouse ['lajthaus] s. latarnia
morska
lighting ['lajtyng] s. oświetlenie;
oświetlanie
light-minded ['lajt'majndyd] adj.
lekkomyślny; roztargniony
lightness ['lajtnys] s. jasność;
lekkość; łagodność;
łatwość; lekkomyślność
lightning ['lajtnyng] s.
błyskawica; piorun; a.
błyskawiczny
lightning rod ['lajtnyng,rod] s.
piorunochron; odgromnik
lightweight ['lajt-łejt] s. waga
lekka; adj. lekkiej wagi; błahy;
(127 do 135 funtowy bokser)
light-year ['lajt,je:r] s. rok
świetlny (ok. 6x10^12 mil =
10x10^12 km)
lignite ['lygnajt] s. węgiel
brunatny; lignit
like [lajk] v. lubieć; upodobać
sobie; (chcieć); mieć
zamiłowanie, ochotę; adj.
podobny; analogiczny;
typowy; adv. podobnie; w ten
sam sposób; s. drugi taki sam;
rzecz podobna; conj. jak; tak
jak; po; w ten sposób; niby
to; niczym
like that ['lajk'dzaet] adv. tak; w
ten sposób; właśnie tak
likelihood ['lajklyhud] s.
prawdopodobieństwo
likely ['lajkly] adj. możliwy;
prawdopodobny; odpowiedni;
nadający się; obiecujący; adv.
pewnie; prawdopodobnie
likeness ['lajknys] s.
podobieństwo; podobizna;
pozory
likewise ['lajkłajz] adv. także;
również; podobno; podobnie;
w ten sam sposób; też
liking ['lajkyng] s. sympatia;
upodobanie; zamiłowanie
lilac ['lajlek] s. bez; adj. lila;
liliowy; blado siny
lily ['lyly] s. lilia; a. jak lilia
lily of the valley ['lyly,ow'dy
,waely] s. konwalia
limb [lym] s. kończyna; konar;

brzeg; krawędź; ramię; noga;
skrzydło
lime 1. [lajm] s. wapno; v.
wapnić; adj. wapienny
lime 2. [lajm] s. lipa; cytrus
(dzika cytryna); a. cytrusowy
limelight ['lajmlajt] s. światło
wapienne; światło
reflektorów; widok publiczny
limestone ['lajmstoun] s.
wapień; a. z wapienia
limey ['lajmy] s. (slang)
Brytyjczyk (wulg.) zwłaszcza
marynarz
limit ['lymyt] s. granica; kres; v.
ograniczać; ustalać granice
limitation [,lymy'tejszyn] s.
ograniczenie; zastrzeżenie;
prekluzja; przedawnienie
limited liability ['lymytyd
,laje'bylyty] s. ograniczona
odpowiedzialność
limp [lymp] adj. wiotki; bez sił;
osłabiony; v. kuleć; chromać
line [lajn] s. linia; kreska; bruzda;
lina; sznur; przewód; granica;
zajęcie; zainteresowania;
szereg; rząd; linka; v.
liniować; wyścielać; podbić
podszewką; służyć za
podszewkę
lineup ['lajnap] s. uszeregowanie;
rząd; ustawianie w rząd
line up ['lajnap] v. ustawić w
rząd; uszeregować
lineaments ['lynjements] pl. rysy
twarzy; cechy szczególne
linear ['lynjer] adj. liniowy;
linijny; wąski i długi
linen ['lynyn] s. płótno; bielizna;
adj. lniany; płócienny
linen closet ['lynen'klozyt] s.
schowek na bieliznę
liner ['lajner] s. samolot
pasażerski; statek pasażerski
linger ['lynger] v. ociągać się;
zwlekać; pozostawać w tyle;
marudzić; tkwić; wlec życie
lingerie ['le:nżeri] s. damska
bielizna; damskie artykuły
bieliźniane
lining ['lajnyng] s. podszewka;
podkład; okładzina;

zawartość
link [lynk] s. ogniwo; więź;
spinka; 20,1 cm; połączyć;
zczepiać; związać; sprzęgać
links [lynks] pl. wydmy; boisko
golfowe; wydmy piaszczyste
lion [lajon] s. lew; a. lwi; lwie
lioness [lajonys] s. lwica
lip [lyp] s. warga; brzeg; ostrze;
bezczelne gadanie; v. dotykać
wargami; mruczeć
lipstick ['lypstyk] s. kredka do
warg; pomadka do ust
liquid ['lykłyd] s. płyn; adj.
płynny; niestały; nieustalony
liquor ['lyker] s. napój
alkoholowy; sok; odwar;
bulion
liquorice ['lykorys] s. lukrecja
lisp [lysp] v. seplenić; seplenić
jak niemowlę; s. seplenienie
list [lyst] s. lista; spis; listwa;
krawędź; v. wciągać na
listę; obramowywać;
przechylać (się); pochylać
(się); s. pochylenie; przechył
listen ['lysen] v. słuchać;
usłuchać; przysłuchiwać się
listen in ['lysen,yn] v.
podsłuchiwać; posłuchać
(radia etc.)
listen to ['lysen,tu] v. usłuchać
kogoś (czyjejś rady)
listener ['lysener] s. słuchacz
listless ['lystlys] adj. apatyczny;
obojętny; zobojętniały; bierny
(z powodu choroby)
lit [lyt] zob. light
liter ['li:ter] s. litr
literal ['lyterel] adj. literalny;
dosłowny; prozaiczny;
literowy; rzeczowy (umysł)
literary ['lyterery] adj. literacki;
obeznany w literaturze
literature ['lytereczer] s.
literatura; piśmiennictwo
lithe [lajs] adj. giętki; gibki;
łatwo gnący się
litter ['liter] s. śmieci;
podściółka; barłóg; v.
śmiecić; podścielać;
urodzić szczeniaki;
porozrzucać niechlujnie

litter bin ['lyter,byn] s. śmietnik; kosz na śmieci

little ['lytl] adj. mały; niski; nieduży; adv. mało; niewiele

little bit ['lytl,byt] adv. trochę; bardzo mało; troszeczkę

little one ['lytl,łan] s. dziecko; dziecina; dzieciątko

little by little ['lytl,baj'lytl] exp. po trochu; stopniowo; pomału; pomalutku

live [lyw] v. żyć; mieszkać; przeżywać; przetrwać; ocalić

live [lajw] adj. żywy; żyjący; ruchliwy; energiczny

live on ['lyw,on] v. żyć z czegoś; żyć czymś

live wire ['lajw'łajer] s. przewód pod napięciem

livelihood ['lajwly,hud] s. utrzymanie; środki do życia

lively ['lajwly] adj. żywy; wesoły; ożywiony; żwawy; gorący; rześki; pełen życia; jaskrawy

liver ['lywer] s. wątroba; wątróbka; a. wątroby

livery ['lywery] adj. wątrobiany; chory na wątrobę; opryskliwy; s. liberia; utrzymanie konia; wynajem (wozów)

lives [lajws] pl. żywoty; zob. life

livestock ['lajwstok] s. żywy inwentarz; zwierzęta domowe

livid ['lywyd] adj. siny; wściekły; posiniaczony

living ['lywyng] s. życie; utrzymanie; tryb życia

living room ['lywyn,ru:m] s. salon; bawialnia; pokój

lizard ['lyzerd] s. jaszczurka

load [loud] s. ładunek; waga; ciężar; obciążenie; v. ładować; załadować; naładować; obciążać; nasycać; fałszować

load up ['loud,ap] v. brać ładunek; opychać się

loader ['louder] s. ładowniczy; maszyna do ładowania

loading ['loudyng] s. ładunek; ładowanie; a. ładunkowy

(pomost)

loaded words ['loudyd,łe:rds] s. słowa tendencyjne (niesprawiedliwe) (uwłaczające)

loaf [louf] s. bochenek; głowa (cukru); pl. loaves [louwz]; v. wałęsać się; marnować czas

loafer ['loufer] s. włóczęga; łazik; próżniak; nierób; wałkoń; wygodny bucik sportowy

loam [loum] s. gleba ilasta; ił; zaprawa gliniana (murarska)

loan [loun] s. pożyczka; v. pożyczać

loath [lous] adj. niechętny

loathe [lous] v. nienawidzieć; czuć wstręt

loathsome ['loussem] adj. wstrętny; obrzydliwy; ohydny

loaves [louwz] zob. loaf

lobby ['loby] s. przedpokój; kuluar; v. urabiać senatora lub posła na czyjąś korzyść (przekupywać)

lobbyist ['lobyst] s. interwencjonalista kuluarowy (często oficjalnie rejestrowany w USA); lobbyista

lobe [loub] s. płat (np. płucny)

lobster ['lobster] s. homar

local ['loukel] adj. lokalny; miejscowy; s. oddział związku zawodowego

locality [lou'kaelyty] s. okolica; miejscowość; strefa; rejon

localize ['lokelajz] v. umiejscowić; lokalizować

locate ['loukejt] v. umieścić; znaleźć; osiedlić się

located ['lokejtyd] adj. zamieszkały; umieszczony; znaleziony

location ['loukejszyn] s. położenie; ulokowanie; miejsce zamieszkania; miejsce zaznaczone

loch [lok] s. jezioro; wąska zatoka (zwłaszcza w Szkocji)

lock [lok] s. zamek; zamknięcie; śluza; lok; v. zamykać (na klucz); przechodzić śluzę

lock in ['lokyn] v. zamykać (wewnątrz); otaczać (górami)

locker ['loker] s. szafka; kabina; skrzynia; schowek

lock out ['lokaut] v. wykluczać; s. lokaut (lockout)

locksmith ['loksmys] s. ślusarz

locomotive ['louke,moutyw] s. lokomotywa; adj. ruchomy

locust ['loukest] s. szarańcza; akacja

lodge [lodż] s. chata; loża; kryjówka; domek myśliwski; nora; v. przenocować; zdeponować; umieszczać; wnosić (skargę etc.)

lodger ['lodżer] s. lokator

lodging ['lodżyng] s. mieszkanie (tymczasowe,wynajęte etc.)

loft [loft] s. strych; poddasze; chór; v. podbić piłkę golfową

lofty ['lofty] adj. wzniosły; wyniosły; wysoki; dumny; hardy

log [log] s. kłoda; kloc; log; dziennik operacyjny (statku, szybu); v. wycinać drzewa; ciąć na kłody; wciągać do dziennika okrętowego etc.

logbook ['logbuk] s. dziennik pokładowy; książka raportowa

log cabin ['log,kaebyn] s. chata (z belek) (z okrąglaków)

logic ['lodżyk] s. logika

logical ['lodżykel] adj. logiczny; rozumujący poprawnie

loin [loin] s. lędźwie; polędwica; comber; krzyże; biodra

loiter [lojter] v. marudzić; wałęsać się; guzdrać; mitrężyć; kręcić się podejrzanie

loll [lol] v. rozwalać się; opierać się niedbale; wywieszać (język psa); zwisać

loneliness ['lounlynys] s. samotność; osamotnienie; odludność

lonely ['lounly] adj. samotny

lonesome ['lounsom] adj. osamotniony; odludny

long [long] adj. długi; długotrwały; v. tęsknić; pragnąć (czegoś); adv. długo; dawno

long ago [,long'egou] adv. dawno temu; adj. dawno miniony

long before ['long,befor] adv. dużo wcześniej; znacznie wcześniej

long since ['long,syns] adv. dawno temu; od dawna

long distance call ['long'dystans ,kol] s. telefon międzymiastowy; rozmowa międzymiastowa

longing ['longyng] s. pragnienie; tęsknota; ochota; adj. tęskny

long jump ['long,dżamp] s. skok w dal

longshoreman ['long,szo:rmen] s. doker; robotnik portowy

long-sighted ['lon'sajtyd] adj. dalekowzroczny; przewidujący

long spun ['lon'span] a. rozwlekły

long-term ['lon'term] adj. długoterminowy; długofalowy

long-winded ['lon'tyndyd] adj. gadatliwy; długo mówiący; (koń) ze zdrowymi płucami

look [luk] s. spojrzenie; wygląd; v. patrzeć; wyglądać

look after ['luk,a:fter] v. doglądać; opiekować się (kimś)

look around ['luk,e'raund] v. rozglądać się; poszukiwać wzrokiem

look at ['luk,et] v. patrzeć na (kogoś, coś)

look for ['luk,fo:r] v. szukać

look forwards ['luk fo:rterds] v. oczekiwać; cieszyć się

look into ['luk,yntu] v. badać; wglądać

look on ['luk,on] v. przypatrywać się; przyglądać się; kibicować

look out ['luk,aut] v. być w pogotowiu; mieć się na baczności; uważać; wyjrzeć; wyszukać

look over ['luk,ouwer] v.

przeglądać; przejrzeć

look up ['luk,ap] v. szukać; odwiedzać; patrzeć w górę

looker-on ['luker'on] s. widz; przyglądający się; kibic

looking-glass ['lukynglas] s. lustro; zwierciadło

lookout ['luk,aut] s. widok; uwaga; czaty; czujność

loom [lu:m] s. krosna; warsztat tkacki; v. wynurzać się; zagrażać; grozić; zamajaczyć

loop [lu:p] s. pętla; węzeł; supeł; v. robić pętlę, kokardę; podwiązywać; splatać (się)

loophole ['lu:p,houl] s. strzelnica; droga ucieczki (od podatków); wykręt; luka; furtka

loose [lu:s] adj. luźny; rozluźniony; obluźniony; wolny; na wolności; rzadki; sypki; rozwiązły; s. upust; v. luzować; obluźniać; zwalniać

loosen ['lu:sn] v. rozluźniać (się); obluźniać (się); rozwalniać; leczyć zatwardzenie

loot [lu:t] s. łupy; (nadużycia urzędnika); v. plądrować; szabrować

lop [lop] v. obcinać; ciąć; zwisać; plątać się; wałęsać się; s. ścięcie; obcięte (gałęzie)

lop off ['lop,of] v. obciąć

lope [loup] v. biec susami; pędzić krótkim galopem; s. krótki galop; sus

lord [lo:rd] s. pan; władca; magnat; Bóg; v. grać pana; nadawać tytuł lorda

lorry ['lory] s. ciężarówka; platforma; lora; przyczepa

lose; lost; lost [lu:z; lost; lost]

lose [lu:z] v. stracić; schudnąć; zgubić; zabłądzić; niedosłyszeć; spóźnić się; przegrać; być pokonanym, pozbawionym

loss [los] s. strata; utrata; zguba; ubytek; szkoda; kłopot

lost [lost] adj. stracony; zgubiony; zob. lose

lot [lot] s. doba; las; losowanie; udział; działka; parcela; grupa; zespół; partia; sporo; wiele; v. parcelować; dzielić; losować; adv. bardzo dużo

loth [lous] adj. niechętny; wstrętny; z ciężkim sercem

lotion ['louszyn] s. płyn (leczniczy)

lottery ['lotery] s. loteria

lotto ['lotou] s. loteryjka

loud [laud] adj. głośny; smrodliwy; krzykliwy; adv. na cały głos; głośno; w głośny sposób

loudspeaker ['laud'spi:ker] s. głośnik; megafon

lounge [laundż] v. próżnować; wylegiwać; łazić; s. lokal; salonik; hall; włóczęga; wolny krok; wygodna kanapa

louse [laus] s. wesz; pl. lice

lousy ['lauzy] adj. zawszony; wstrętny; dobrze zaopatrzony (slang)

lout ['laut] s. gbur; prostak

love [law] s. kochanie; miłość; lubienie; ukochana; ukochanie; gra na zero; v. kochać; lubić; być przywiązanym; pieścić; umizgać się

love-affair ['lawefeer] s. romans; przygoda miłosna; osobiste troski w sprawach miłosnych

loveless ['lawlys] adj. niekochany; nie kochający; bez miłości; nie kochany przez nikogo

lovely ['lawly] adj. śliczny; uroczy; rozkoszny; przyjemny (bardzo)

lovemaking ['law,mejkyng] s. zaloty; umizgi; spółkowanie

lover ['lawer] s. kochanek; miłośnik; amator czegoś

loving ['lawyng] adj. kochający; s. kochanie; miłość

low [lou] s. ryk (bydła); v. ryczeć; adj. niski; niewysoki; słaby; przygnębiony; cichy; podły; mały; adv. nisko;

niewysoko; słabo; skromnie;
cicho; szeptem; marnie; podle

lower ['louer] adj. niższy; dolny;
młodszy; adv. niżej; v.
obniżać; zniżać; spuszczać;
poniżyć; ściszyć;
zmniejszyć; osłabić; opadać;
spadać; ryczeć (jak bydło)

low-grade ['lougrejd] adj.
niskoprocentowy; niskiej
jakości; kiepski; tandetny

lowland ['loulend] pl. nizina; adj.
nizinny

lowly ['louly] adj. skromny; adv.
skromnie; bez pretensji

low-necked ['lou,nekyd] adj.
dekoltowany (głęboko)

low-pressure ['lou'preszer] s.
niskie ciśnienie; adj.
niskoprężny; pod niskim
ciśnieniem

low tide ['lou'tajd] s. odpływ
(morza)

loyal [lojel] adj. lojalny; wierny
(krajowi, ideałem etc.)

loyalty ['lojelty] s. lojalność;
wierność

lozenge ['lozyndż] s. romb;
tabletka; pastylka

lubber ['laber] s. niezdara;
niedołęga; niezdarny marynarz

lubricant ['lu:brykent] s. smar;
adj. smarujący; smarowniczy

lubricate ['lu:brykejt] v.
smarować; oliwić; robić
śliskim

lubrication ['lu:brykejszyn] s.
smarowanie; oliwienie

lubricity [lu:'brysyty] s.
smarowność; lubieżność

lucid ['lu:syd] adj. świecący;
jasny; błyszczący; klarowny;
przezroczysty; czysty;
oczywisty

luck [lak] s. los; traf; szczęście;
szczęśliwy traf; powodzenie

luckily ['lakyly] adv. na
szczęście; szczęśliwie

luckless ['laklys] adj.
niefortunny; nieszczęśliwy

lucky ['laky] adj. szczęśliwy

lucky fellow ['laky'felou] s.
szczęściarz

ludicrous ['lu:dykres] adj.
śmieszny; nonsensowny;
absurdalny; komicznie głupi

lug [lag] v. wlec; pociągać;
przytłaczać; s. wleczenie;
szarpanie; ucho; uchwyt

luggage ['lagydż] s. bagaż;
walizki

luggage carrier ['lagydż'kaerjer]
s. bagażowy

luggage rack ['lagydż'raek] s.
półka na walizki

luggage slip ['lagydż'slyp] s.
kwit bagażowy

luggage van ['lagydż'waen] s.
wóz bagażowy

lukewarm ['lu:kło:rm] adj.
ciepławy; letni; obojętny;
oziębły; niezainteresowany

lull [lal] v. ukołysać; uciszyć;
uśmierzyć; s. cisza; zastój

lullaby ['lalebaj] s. kołysanka

lumbago [lam'bejgou] s.
lumbago; ischias

lumbar ['lamber] adj. lędźwiowy

lumber ['lamber] s. budulec
(drewniany); rupiecie; graty; v.
zwalać; wycinać; ciężko
stąpać; poruszać się
ociężale

lumberjack ['lamber'dżaek] s.
drwal (przygotowujący do
tartaku)

lumber mill ['lambermyl] s. tartak

luminous ['lu:mynes] adj.
świetlny; jasny; świecący;
wyjaśniający; zrozumiały

lump [lamp] s. bryła; gruda;
masa; hurt; guz; niezdara;
niedołęga; v. zwalać;
gromadzić; dojść do ładu;
zcierpieć; znosić

lump of ['lamp,ow] s. kawałek

lump sugar ['lamp,szu:ger] s.
gruda cukru

lump sum ['lamp,sam] s. suma
całościowa

lunar ['lu:nar] adj. księżycowy;
mierzony ruchem księżyca

lunar module ['lu:nar,modjul] s.
kapsuła do lądowania na
Księżycu

lunatic ['lu:netyk] s. wariat

(chory umysłowo); lunatyk;
adj. obłąkany; zwariowany
lunch [lancz] s. obiad
(popołudniowy); v. jeść
obiad; gościć obiadem
lunch-hour ['lancz'auer] s.
przerwa obiadowa (w
południe)
lung [laŋg] s. płuco
lunge [landż] s. wypad;
pchnięcie; v. pchnąć; zrobić
wypad; spowodować wypad
lurch [le:rcz] v. opuszczać w
potrzebie; słaniać się na
nogach; przechylać się; s.
nagłe przechylenie się (na
bok); trudna sytuacja
lure [ljuer] s. przynęta; wabik;
urok; powab; v. kusić;
nęcić; wabić; przywabiać
lurk [le:rk] v. czaić się; s. czaty;
ukrycie
luscious ['laszes] adj. słodziutki;
ckliwy; soczysty
lush [lasz] adj. bujny; soczysty;
miękki i pełen soku
lust [last] s. żądza; lubieżność;
namiętność; pożądliwość;
v. pożądać (namiętnie)
luster ['laster] s. blask; połysk;
świecznik; świetność; v.
glansować; wyświecać
lusty ['lasty] adj. krzepki; pełen
wigoru (młodzieńczego)
lute [lu:t] s. lutnia; glina; v.
lepić gliną; kitować
luxate ['laksejt] v. zwichnąć
(np. nogę, staw)
luxuriant [lag'zjuerjent] adj.
wybujały; płodny; kwiecisty
(styl); bogato zdobiony
luxurious [lag'żjuerjes] adj.
zbytkowny; luksusowy;
zmysłowy
luxury ['lakszery] s. zbytek;
luksus; rozkosz; a. od zbytku
lying ['lajyŋg] adj. kłamliwy; zob.
lie; s. kłamstwo; adj. leżący;
zob. lie; s. leżenie; posłanie;
pozycja leżąca
lying-in [,lajyŋg'yn] adj.
położniczy; połogowy; s.
połóg

lymph [lymf] s. limfa;
szczepinka; wysięk; serum;
(czysta woda)
lynch [lyncz] v. zlinczować; s.
linczowanie; zabijanie bez
wyroku
lynx [lyŋks] s. ryś
lyre ['lajer] s. lira
lyric ['lirik] adj. liryczny; s. słowa
pieśni; poemat liryczny; tekst
piosenki
lysol ['lajsol] s. lizol

M

m [em] trzynasta litera alfabetu
angielskiego; cyfra rzymska:
1000
ma'am [maem] s. pani (madam)
mac [maek] s. nieprzemakalny
materiał (płaszcz) mackintosh
macaroni ['maeka;rouny] s.
makaron rurkowaty
machine [me'szi:n] s. maszyna;
machina (polityczna); v.
obrabiać maszynowo; adj.
maszynowy
machine-made [me'szi:nmejd]
adj. maszynowy; maszynowo
robiony
machine-gun [me'szi:ngan] s.
karabin maszynowy
machinery [me'szi:nery] s.
maszyneria; aparat
machinist [me'szi:nyst] s.
maszynista (np. tokarz,
szwaczka)
macho [ma:czou] s. bardzo
męski mężczyzna (slang)
mack [maek] s. zob. mac
mackintosh ['maekyntosz] s.
zob. mac
mad [maed] adj. obłąkany;
szalony; zły; wściekły; v.
doprowadzać do obłędu; być
obłąkanym
madam ['maedem] s. pani;
(panienka); (w zwrocie: proszę

pani)
madcap ['maedkaep] s.
narwaniec
madden ['maedn] v.
rozwścieczać; szaleć;
wściekać się; wariować
made [mejd] v. zrobiony; zob.
make; (wykombinowany,
fabryczny)
madman ['maedmen] s. wariat;
szaleniec; furiat; obłąkaniec
madness ['maednys] s. obłęd;
obłąkanie; furia;
wściekłość; wścieklizna;
szał; szaleństwo
magazine [maege'zi:n] s.
czasopismo; magazynek (na
kule); skład broni dla wojska
maggot ['maeget] s. dziwactwo;
chimera; larwa
magic ['maedżyk] s. magia; adj.
magiczny; działający jak magia
magician [me'dżyszyn] s.
czarodziej; magik
magistrate ['maedżystrejt] s.
sądownik; stróż prawa
magnanimous [maeg'neanymes]
adj. wielkoduszny
magnet ['maegnyt] s. magnes
magnetic [maeg'netyk] adj.
magnetyczny; przyciągający
magnificence [maeg'nyfysns] s.
wspaniałość; świetność;
okazałość
magnificent [maeg'nyfysnt] adj.
okazały; wspaniały
magnify ['maegnyfaj] v.
powiększać; potęgować;
wyolbrzymiać
magpie ['maegpaj] s. sroka;
gaduła
mahogany [me'hogeny] s.
mahoń; z mahoniu
maid [mejd] s. dziewczyna;
dziewka; panna; służąca
maiden ['mejden] s. dziewczyna;
panna; adj. panieński;
dziewiczy; świeży; nowy
maidenly ['mejdenly] adj.
dziewczęcy; panieński
maiden name ['mejden,nejm] s.
nazwisko panieńskie
mail [mejl] s. poczta; kolczuga;

v. wysyłać pocztą
mailbag ['mejl,baeg] s. worek
pocztowy
mailbox ['mejl,boks] s. skrzynka
pocztowa
mailman [mejlmen] s. listonosz
mail-order house ['mejl,order
,haus] s. firma sprzedająca
przez pocztę (z katalogu)
maim [mejm] v. okaleczyć
main [mejn] s. główny
(przewód); adj. główny;
najważniejszy
mainland ['mejnlaend] s.
kontynent (w odróżnieniu od
bliskich wysp)
mainly ['mejnly] adv. głównie;
przeważnie; po większej
części
main road ['mejnroud] s. główna
droga; główna szosa
main street ['mejn,stri:t] s.
główna ulica
maintain [men'tejn] v.
utrzymywać (w dobrym
stanie); trzymać (pozycją);
podtrzymywać;
zachowywać; twierdzić;
mieć na utrzymaniu; bronić;
pomagać
maintenance ['mejntenens] s.
utrzymanie; utrzymywanie;
poparcie; wyżywienie
maize [mejz] s. kukurydza
majestic [medżestyk] adj.
majestatyczny
majesty ['maedżysty] s.
majestat; godność;
wielkość
major ['mejdżer] s. major;
pełnoletni; przedmiot
kierunkowy specjalizacji; adj.
większy; główny; ważniejszy;
pełnoletni; starszy; v.
specjalizować się w studiach
majorette ['mejdżeret] s.
tancerka na defiladach i w
przerwach meczów w USA
majority [me'dżoryty] s.
większość; a.
większościowy
major road ['mejdżer,roud] s.
główna droga; ważniejsza

droga
make; made; made [mejk; mejd; mejd]
make [mejk] v. robić; tworzyć; sporządzać; powodować; wynosić; doprowadzać; ustanawiać; starać się; postanowić etc.
make a bed [mejk e bed] exp. pościelić łóżko
make-believe ['mejk,by'li:w] s. udawanie; pozory
make off ['mejkof] v. uciec; uciekać; gwizdnąć coś komuś
make up ['mejkap] v. uzupełnić; wynagrodzić; sporządzić; zmontować; ucharakteryzować
makeup ['mejkap] s. makijaż; charakteryzacja; układ (graficzny); stan (kogoś, czegoś)
make up your mind ['mejk,ap'jo:r ,majnd] exp.: zdecyduj się (czego chcesz, co wolisz, na co nasz ochotę, gdzie jedziesz, etc.)
maker ['mejker] s. wytwórca; sprawca; producent; fabrykant; konstruktor; (Maker = Bóg)
makeshift ['mejkszyft] s. namiastka; urządzenie prowizoryczne; adj. prowizoryczny
malady ['maeledy] s. choroba
male [mejl] s. mężczyzna; samiec; adj. męski; samczy; wewnętrzny; obejmowany
malediction [,maely'dikszyn] s. przekleństwo; złorzeczenie
malefactor ['maelyfaekter] s. złoczyńca; zbrodniarz
malevolent [me'lewelent] adj. niechętny; wrogi
malice ['maelys] s. złośliwość; zła wola; zły zamiar
malicious [me'lyszys] adj. złośliwy; zły; powodowany złością
malignant [me'lygnent] adj. złośliwy; zjadliwy

malnutrition ['maelnju'tryszyn] s. niedożywienie
malt [mo:lt] s. słód; v. słodować; adj. słodowy; scukrzony
maltreat [mael'tri:t] v. poniewierać; maltretować
mamma [me'ma:] s. mama; gruczoł mlekowy
mammal [me'ma:l] s. ssak; a. ssakowy
man [maen] s. człowiek; mężczyzna; mąż; v. obsadzać (np. załogą); pl. men [men]
manacle ['maenekl] s. kajdany; v. zakuwać w kajdany
manage ['maenydż] v. kierować; zarządzać; posługiwać się; obchodzić się; opanowywać; poskramiać; radzić sobie
manageable ['maenydżebl] adj. do pokierowania (możliwy, łatwy)
management ['maenydżment] s. zarząd; kierownictwo; dyrekcja; posługiwanie się; obchodzenie się; sprawne zarządzanie
manager ['maenydżer] s. kierownik; zarządzający; gospodarz
manageress ['maenydżeres] s. kierowniczka
mandate ['maendejt] s. mandat; pełnomocnictwo do sprawowania funkcji pochodzącej z wyboru; pismo władzy wyższej; grzywna; rozkaz; komenda; wola wyborców przekazana wybranemu reprezentantowi
mandatory ['maendetery] adj. zawierający mandat; nakazany przez władze; obowiązujący; obowiązkowy
mane [mejn] s. grzywa
maneuver [me'nu:wer] s. manewr; v. manewrować; manipulować
manger ['mejndżer] s. żłób; koryto

mangle ['maengl] s. magiel; v. maglować; poszarpać; pokaleczyć; poprzekręcać

manhood ['maenhud] s. męskość; ludność męska; wiek męski

mania ['mejnjə] s. bzik; obłęd; mania; zbytni entuzjazm; szał

maniac ['mejnjaek] s. maniak; szaleniec; adj. umysłowo chory

manifest ['maenyfest] adj. jawny; oczywisty; v. manifestować; ujawniać; s. manifest okrętowy (szczegółowa lista ładunku)

manifold ['maenyfould] adj. różnorodny; wieloraki; wielokrotny; v. powielać (tekst)

manipulate [me'nypjulejt] v. manipulować; umiejętnie, zręcznie pokierować (niesprawiedliwie)

mankind [,maen'kajnd] s. ludzkość; rodzaj ludzki

mankind ['maenkajnd] pl. mężczyźni; cały rodzaj męski

manly ['maenly] adj. dzielny; mężny; męski; adv. po męsku

manner ['maener] s. sposób; zwyczaj; zachowanie (się); wychowanie; maniera; procedura; rodzaj

manoeuvre [me'nu:wer] s. manewr; v. manewrować (pisownia brytyjska)

man-of-war ['maenew'ło:r] s. okręt wojenny; uzbrojony statek

manor ['maener] s. dwór; rezydencja (w Anglii: duży majątek)

man power ['maen,pałer] s. siła robocza; rezerwy ludzkie

mansion ['maenszyn] s. rezydencja; pałac; duży dwór

manslaughter ['maen,slo:ter] s. zabójstwo (bez premedytacji)

mantelpiece ['maentlpi:s] s. gzyms kominka (obramowanie)

manual ['maenjuel] s. podręcznik; manuał; adj.

ręczny; ręcznie zrobiony

manufacture [,maenju'faekczer] v. wyrabiać; s. sposób; produkcja; produkt (zwłaszcza masowy)

manufacturer [,maenju'faek ,czerer] s. wytwórca; producent; fabrykant; przedsiębiorstwo wytwórcze

manure [me'njuer] s. nawóz; v. nawozić (gnój)

manuscript ['maenjuskrypt] s. rękopis; adj. ręcznie pisany

many ['meny] adj. dużo; wiele

many-sided ['meny'sajdyd] adj. wielostronny; wieloboczny; wszechstronny

map [maep] s. mapa; plan; v. planować; robić mapą

maple ['mejpl] s. klon

marble ['ma:rbl] s. marmur; kulka do zabawy; adj. marmurowy; v. marmurkować (np. papier)

March [ma:rcz] s. marzec

march [ma:rcz] s. marsz; v. maszerować

mare [meer] s. klacz; kobyła

margarine ['ma:rdże,ri:n] s. margaryna

margin ['ma:rdżyn] s. margines; brzeg; krawędź; nadwyżka; rezerwa

marine [me'ri:n] adj. morski; s. marynarka; żołnierz piechoty desantowej (USA)

mariner ['maeryner] s. marynarz; żeglarz

maritime ['maerytajm] adj. morski

mark [ma:rk] s. marka (pieniądz); ślad; znak; oznaczenie; nota; cenzura; cel; uwaga; v. oznaczać; określać; notować; zwracać uwagę

marked [ma:rkt] adj. wybitny; wyraźny; znaczny

mark out ['ma:rk,aut] v. wyznaczać; wytyczać (np. granicę)

market ['ma:rkyt] s. rynek; zbyt; targ; v. robić zakupy; sprzedawać na targu

marketing ['ma:rkytyng] s.

organizowanie rynku; handlowanie

market-place ['ma:rkytplejs] s. rynek; plac targowy

marksman ['ma:rksmen] s. strzelec (doborowy)

marmalade ['ma:rmelejd] s. marmolada (pomarańczowa)

marmot ['ma:rmet] s. świstak

marriage ['maerydż] s. małżeństwo (skojarzenie); a. ślubny

marriageable ['maerydżebl] adj. na wydaniu; odpowiedni do małżeństwa

marriage certificate [,maerydż ,ser'tyfykyt] s. świadectwo ślubu

married ['maeryd] adj. żonaty; zamężna; małżeński; ślubny

married couple ['maerys,kapl] s. & adj. para małżeńska

marrow ['maerou] s. szpik (kostny); dynia

marry ['maery] v. poślubić; udzielać ślubu; ożenić (się); brać ślub; pobierać się; wychodzić za mąż

marsh [ma:rsz] s. moczary; bagno; błota; a. bagienny

marshal ['ma:rszel] s. marszałek; mistrz ceremonii; komisarz policji; v. uszykować; (uroczyście); przetaczać wagony; uporządkować; uszykować

marshy ['ma:rszy] adj. bagnisty; bagienny; błotnisty

marten ['ma:rtyn] s. kuna

martial ['ma:rszel] adj. wojenny; wojowniczy; wojskowy

martyr ['ma:rter] s. męczennik; v. zamęczać; zadręczać

marvel ['ma:rwel] s. cudo; cud; v. podziwiać; dziwić się

marvelous ['ma:rwyles] adj. cudowny; zdumiewający

mascot ['maesket] s. maskotka

masculine ['maeskjulyn] adj. męski; płci męskiej

mash [maesz] s. zacier; papka; mieszanka; v. warzyć; tłuc na papkę; umizgać się

mashed potatoes ['maeszt,pe 'tejtous] s. gniecione ziemniaki

mask [ma:sk] s. maska; v. zamaskować; maskować

mason ['mejsn] s. murarz; kamieniarz; v. wymurować; murować

masonry ['mejsnry] s. murarstwo; obmurowanie; kamieniarstwo

masque [ma:sk] s. maskarada; pantomima (amatorska)

mass [maes] s. msza; masa; rzesza; v. gromadzić; zrzeszać

massacre ['maeseker] s. masakra; v. masakrować; urządzić rzeź

massage ['maesa:ż] s. masaż; v. masować; zrobić masaż

massif ['maesyw] s. masyw (górski); zwarta roślinność

massive ['maesyw] adj. masywny; ciężki; zwarty; bryłowaty

mast [ma:st] s. maszt

master ['ma:ster] s. mistrz; nauczyciel; pan; gospodarz; szef; kapitan statku; panicz; v. panować; kierować; nabywać (np. wprawy); owładnąć

master key ['ma:sterki:] s. wytrych

masterly ['ma:sterly] adj. mistrzowski

master of ceremony ['ma:ster ,ow sere'mouny] s. mistrz ceremonii

masterpiece ['ma:sterpi:s] s. arcydzieło

master-ship ['ma:sterszyp] s. mistrzostwo; władza; panowanie; zwierzchnictwo

mastery ['ma:stery] s. władza; panowanie; mistrzostwo

mat [maet] s. mata; v. plątać; adj. matowy (bez połysku)

match [maecz] s. zapałka; lont; mecz; dobór; małżeństwo; v. swatać; współzawodniczyć; dobierać; dorównywać

matchless ['maeczlys] adj.

niezrównany; nie mający
równego
matchmaker ['maecz,mejker] s.
swat; swatka; aranżujący
mecze
mate [mejt] s. kolega; małżonek;
samiec; pomocnik; v. łączyć
ślubem; parzyć (się);
pobierać się; zadawać mata
(w szachach)
material [me'tierjal] s. materiał;
tworzywo; tkanka; adj.
materialny; cielesny
maternal [me'te:rnl] adj.
macierzyński; matczyny
maternity [me'te:rnyty] s.
macierzyństwo; adj.
położniczy
maternity hospital [me'te:rnyty
'hospytl] s. szpital położniczy
mathematician [,maetyme
'tyszyn] s. matematyk
mathematics [,maety'maetyks] s.
matematyka
math [maes] s. matematyka
(slang)
matriculate [me'trykjulejt] v.
immatrykulować; zdawać
wstępny egzamin (uniw.);
zapisać się na ...
matrimony ['maetrymeny] s.
małżeństwo; akt ślubu
matron ['mejtren] s. matrona;
kobieta zamężna; (gospodyni)
matter ['maeter] s. rzecz;
treść; materiał; substancja;
sprawa; kwestia; v. znaczyć;
mieć znaczenie; odgrywać
rolę
matter-of-fact ['maeter,ow'faekt]
adj. rzeczowy; praktyczny
mattress ['maetrys] s. materac
mature [me'tjuer] adj. dojrzały;
płatny; v. dojrzewać; stawać
się płatnym (np. pożyczka)
maturity [me'tjueryty] s.
dojrzałość; termin płatności
mauve [mouw] s. kolor różowo-
liliowy; adj. różowo-liliowy
maw [mo:] s. żołądek; wole
maxim ['maeksym] s. maksyma
maximum ['maeksymem] s.
maksimum

May [mej] s. maj
may [mej] v. być może; **might**
[majt] mógłby
maybe ['mejbi:] adv. być może;
może być; możliwe że
may I? ['mej aj] czy mogę?
may-bug ['mejbag] s. chrabąszcz
mayor [meer] s. burmistrz
maypole ['mejpoul] s. słup do
tańca "gaik", 1-go maja
maze [mejz] s. labirynt;
gmatwanina; v. w błąd
wprowadzić; oszołomić;
dezorientować; mieszać
mazurka [me'ze:rke] s. mazur;
mazurek
me [mi:] pron. mi; mnie; mną;
(slang) ja
meadow ['medou] s. łąka
meager ['mi:ger] adj. chudy;
cienki; skromny; nie
obradzający
meal [mi:l] s. posiłek; grubo
mielona mąka; czas posiłku
mealtime ['mi:l-tajm] s. pora
posiłku (ustalona zwyczajem)
mealy ['mi:ly] adj. mączysty;
nieszczery; słodziutki; obleśny
mean; meant; meant [mi:n;
ment; ment]
mean [mi:n] v. myśleć;
przypuszczać; znaczyć; s.
przeciętna; średnia; środek;
adj. ubogi; nędzny; podły;
marny; skąpy; tandetny
meaning ['mi:nyng] s. znaczenie;
sens; treść; adj. znaczący;
mający zamiar
meaningless ['mi:nynglys] adj.
bez sensu; bez znaczenia
meant [ment] przeznaczony; zob.
mean
meantime ['mi:n'tajm] adv.
tymczasem; w tym samym
czasie
meanwhile ['mi:n,hłajl] adv.
tymczasem
measles ['mi:zlz] s. odra
measure ['meżer] s. miara;
miarka; środek; zabieg;
sposób; v. mierzyć; mieć
rozmiar; oszacować; być ...
wzrostu

measureless ['meżerlys] adj.
bezmierny; nieskończony
measurement ['meżerment] s.
wymiar; miara; mierzenie
meat [mi:t] s. mięso; danie
mięsne; treść (książki etc.)
mechanic [my'kaenyk] s.
mechanik; rzemieślnik;
technik
mechanical [my'kaenykel] adj.
mechaniczny
mechanics [my'kaenyks] s.
mechanika
mechanism ['mekenyzem] s.
mechanizm; maszyneria
mechanize ['mekenajz] v.
zmechanizować
medal ['medl] s. medal
meddle [medl] v. wmieszać się;
wtrącać się w cudze sprawy
mediate ['my:djejt] adj.
pośredni; v. pośredniczyć;
zapośredniczyć; doprowa-
dzić pośrednictwem do ...
mediator ['my:djejtor] s.
rozjemca; mediator
medical ['medykel] adj. lekarski;
medyczny
medical certificate ['medykel
,sertyfykyt] s. świadectwo
lekarskie
medicated ['medykejtyd] adj.
leczony; zaprawiony
substancją leczniczą
medicinal [me'dysynl] adj.
leczniczy; lekarski; medyczny
medicine ['medysyn] s.
medycyna; lek; lekarstwo; v.
leczyć lekarstwami
medieval [,medy'i:wel] adj.
średniowieczny
mediocre ['my:djouker] adj.
mierny; średni; przeciętny
meditate ['medytejt] v.
obmyślać; rozmyślać;
medytować
meditation [,medy'tejszyn] s.
rozmyślanie; planowanie
meditative ['medytejtyw] adj.
zadumany; zamyślony;
medytacyjny; kontemplacyjny
Mediterranean [,medyter'rejnjen]
adj. śródziemnomorski

medium ['mi:djem] s. środek;
średnia; przewodnik; środek
obiegowy; środowisko;
rozpuszczalnik; sposób;
środkowa droga; adj. średni;
adv. średnio
medley ['medly] s. mieszanina;
pstrokacizna; rozmaitości
meek [mi:k] adj. potulny;
łagodny; skromny; bez wigoru
meet; met; met [mi:t; met; met]
meet [mi:t] v. spotykać;
zbierać się; gromadzić; iść
na kompromis; zgadzać się;
zaspokajać; s. spotkanie;
zbiórka; miejsce spotkania;
spotkanie sportowe; zawody
(na bieżni etc.)
meet with ['mi:t,łys] v. spotkać
się z (kimś); doświadczyć
meeting ['mi:tyng] s. spotkanie;
połączenie się; posiedzenie;
zgromadzenie; wiec; zawody;
konferencja; pojedynek
melancholy ['melenkely] s.
melancholia; adj. smutny;
melancholijny; zasmucający;
ponury
mellow ['melou] adj. słodki;
miękki; soczysty; uleżały;
złagodzony (wiekiem);
łagodny; wesoły; pogodny;
podchmielony; dojrzały; miły;
świetny; przyjemny; v.
dojrzewać; zmiękczać;
uleżeć się; łagodnieć;
łagodzić
melodious [my'loudjes] adj.
melodyjny; harmonijny
melody ['meledy] s. melodia;
piosenka
melon ['melen] s. melon
melt [melt] s. stop; stopienie;
topnienie; wytop; v. topić;
topnieć; roztapiać (się);
rozpuszczać; przetapiać;
odlewać; wzruszać;
roztkliwiać
melting point ['meltyng'point] s.
temperatura topnienia
member ['member] s. członek;
człon (odróżniający się)
membership ['memberszyp] s.

członkostwo; przynależność;
skład członkowski
membrane ['membrejn] s. błona;
przepona; membrana
memoir ['memła:r] s. pamiętnik;
życiorys; autobiografia
memorable ['memerebl] adj.
pamiętny; znaczny
memorial [my'mo:riel] s. pomnik;
memoriał; petycja; posąg (na
pamiątką)
memorize ['memerajz] v.
zapamiętywać; uczyć się na
pamięć
memory ['memery] s. pamięć;
wspomnienie
men [men] pl. mężczyźni;
robotnicy; zob. man
menace ['menes] s. groźba;
zagrożenie; v. grozić;
zagrażać
mend [mend] s. naprawa;
naprawka; v. reperować;
zaszyć
menial ['mi:njel] s. sługa;
służalec; adj. czarno-roboczy;
służalczy; służebny
menopause ['mene.po:z] s.
przekwitanie; klimakterium
menstruation [,menstru'ejszyn] s.
menstruacja; miesiączka;
period
mental ['mentl] adj. umysłowy;
pamięciowy; psychiatryczny;
s. (slang) umysłowo chory
mental hospital ['mentl'hospytl]
s. szpital psychiatryczny
mentality [men'taelyty] s.
umysłowość; mentalność
mention ['menszyn] v.
wspominać wymieniać;
nadmieniać; wzmiankować;
s. wzmianka
menu ['menju:] s. jadłospis
meow [mi:'au] v. miauczeć jak
kot
mercantile ['me:rkentajl] adj.
handlowy; kupiecki
mercenary ['me:rsynery] adj.
najemny; wyrachowany; s.
najemnik; żołnierz najemny
merchandise ['me:rczendajz] s.
towar(y); v. handlować

merchant ['me:rczent] s. kupiec;
handlowiec; adj. handlowy;
kupiecki
merciful ['me:rsyful] adj.
miłosierny; litościwy
merciless ['me:rsylys] adj.
bezlitosny; niemiłosierny
mercurial [me:r'kjuerjel] adj.
rtęciowy; żywy; bystry;
rozgarnięty; zmienny
mercy ['me:rsy] s. miłosierdzie;
litość; łaska; rzecz
pomyślna
mercy killing ['me:rsy'kylyng] s.
eutanazja; zabójstwo z litości
mere [mjer] adj. zwykły;
zwyczajny; nie więcej niż
merely ['mjerly] adv. tylko;
jedynie; zaledwie; po prostu
merge [me:rdż] v. roztapiać
(się); zlewać; łączyć (się)
merger ['me:rdżer] s. połączenie;
zlanie się; fuzja
meridian [me'rydjen] s. południk;
zenit; szczyt; adj. południowy;
szczytowy
merit ['meryt] s. zasługa; zaleta;
odznaczenie; v. zasługiwać
meritorious [,mery'to:rjes] adj.
chwalebny; zasłużony
mermaid ['me:rmejd] s. rusałka;
syrena
merriment ['meryment] s.
uciecha; radość; wesołość
merry ['mery] adj. wesoły;
radosny; podochocony;
odświętny; podchmielony
merry-go-round ['merygou,raund]
s. karuzela
merry-making ['mery,mejkyn] s.
zabawa; uciecha; weselenie
się
mesh [mesz] s. siatka; sieć;
układ siatkowy; v. łapać w
sieć; zazębiać; wplątać
mess [mes] s. nieporządek;
bałagan; bród; świństwo;
paskudztwo; paćka; papka;
zupa; bigos; posiłek wspólny;
stołówka; wspólny stół; v.
zababrać; zapaskudzić;
zabrudzić; zabałaganić;
pokpić; sfuszerować; obijać

się; bawić; dawać jeść
(posiłek); stołować się
(wspólnie)
mess up [‚mes'ap] v. zepsuć;
zaprzepaścić; sknocić;
zagmatwać; pobrudzić;
zabałaganić
message ['mesydż] v.
wiadomość; orędzie; morał;
wypowiedź; v.
komunikować; podawać;
posłać
messenger ['mesyndżer] s.
posłaniec; zwiastun
messy ['mesy] adj. kłopotliwy;
zapaskudzony; sfuszerowany;
brudny; upaćkany; niechlujny
met [met] v. zob. meet
metal [metl] s. metal; v.
pokrywać metalem; a.
metalowy
metallic [my'taelyk] adj.
metaliczny; metalowy;
metalurgiczny
meteor ['mi:tjer] s. meteor
meteorology [‚mi:tjero'ledży] s.
meteorologia
meter ['mi:ter] s. metr; licznik; v.
mierzyć; a. metrowy
method ['meted] s. metoda;
metodyka; metodyczność;
sposób
methodical [me'todykel] adj.
metodyczny; systematyczny
meticulous [my'tykjules] adj.
drobiazgowy; szczegółowy;
drobnostkowy; pedantyczny
metric system ['metryk'system]
s. system metryczny
metropolitan [‚metre'polyten] adj.
wielkomiejski; metropolitalny;
s. mieszkaniec metropolii;
metropolita (duchowny)
mew [mju:] v. miauczeć;
pierzyć się
Mexican ['meksyken] adj.
meksykański; s. Meksykanin;
Meksykanka
miaow [mi:'au] v. miauczeć
mica ['maike] s. mika; łuszczyk
mice [majs] pl. myszy; zob.
mouse
micron ['majkron] s. mikron

microphone ['majkrefoun] s.
mikrofon
microscope ['majkreskoup] s.
mikroskop
mid [myd] adj. środkowy; prep.
w; podczas; pośród; między-
midday ['myddej] adj.
południowy; s. południe
mid summer [‚myd'samer] exp.:
w środku lata
middle ['mydl] s. środek; kibić;
stan; adj. środkowy; v.
składać w środku; kopać na
środek
middle aged ['mydl'ejdżd] adj. w
średnim wieku
Middle Ages ['mydl'ejdżys] s.
średniowiecze
middle class ['mydl‚kla:s] s.
klasa średnia; klasa
średniozamożna; a. ze
średniozamożnej klasy
middle name ['mydl‚nejm] s.
drugie imię
middle sized ['mydl‚sajzd] adj.
średniej wielkości; średni
middleweight ['mydl‚łejt] s. waga
średnia; adj. średniej wagi
(148 do 160 funtów)
middling ['mydlyng] adj. średni;
przeciętny; adv. średnio
midge [mydż] s. muszka
midget ['mydżyt] s. karzełek;
maleństwo; adj. miniaturowy
midland ['mydlend] s. środek
kraju; adj. leżący w środku
kraju; w głębi kraju
midmost ['mydmoust] adj.
leżący w samym środku;
prep. pośród
midnight ['mydnajt] s. północ;
adj. północny; o północy
midway ['myd'łej] s. połowa
drogi; adv. w połowie drogi
midwife ['mydłajf] s. położna;
akuszerka
might [majt] s. moc; potęga; v.
mógłby; zob. may
mighty ['majty] adj. potężny;
adv. bardzo; wielce
migrate ['maj‚grejt] v.
wędrować; przesiedlać się
migratory ['maj‚gretery] adj.

wędrowny (ptak etc.)

mild [majld] adj. łagodny;
powolny; potulny; słaby;
delikatny

mildew ['myldju:] s. pleśń; v.
pleśnieć; rdzewieć (o
zbożu)

mildly ['majldly] adv. łagodnie;
umiarkowanie; oględnie

mildness ['majldnys] s.
łagodność; nieostrość

mile [majl] s. mila; 1,609 km

mil(e)age ['majlydż] s. milaż;
odległość w milach

milestone ['majlstoun] s. kamień
milowy

military ['mylytery] adj.
wojskowy; pl. wojskowy;
wojsko

milk [mylk] s. mleko; v. doić
(krowy); wykorzystać;
eksploatować; podsłuchiwać
(telefon)

milkmaid ['mylk,mejd] s. dojarka;
mleczarka

milkman ['mylkmen] s. mleczarz

milk-shake ['mylkszejk] s.
mieszany napój mleczny

milksop ['mylksop] s.
maminsynek; fajtłapa; oferma;
niedołęga

milky ['mylky] adj. mleczny;
zniewieściały; koloru mleka

mill [myl] s. młyn; huta; fabryka;
(1/1000); walcownia;
krawędź ząbkowana; v.
mleć; frezować; pilśnić;
kręcić się

miller ['myler] s. młynarz

millet ['mylyt] s. proso

milliner ['mylyner] s. modniarka;
modystka

million ['myljen] num. milion

millionaire ['myljeneer] s. milioner

millionth ['myljent] num.
milionowy; jedna milionowa
(część)

milt [mylt] s. mlecz rybi; v.
zapładniać ikrę

mimic ['mymyk] s. naśladowca;
imitator; v. naśladować;
małpować; adj.
naśladowniczy; udany;

mimiczny; zmyślony; fikcyjny

mince [myns] v. siekać; mówić
bez ogródek; cedzić (słowa);
drobić nogami; s. siekane
mięso; nadzienie mięsne

mincing ['mynsyng] adj.
mizdrzący się; afektowany;
sztucznie zachowujący się
(wykwintny)

mind [majnd] s. umysł; pamięć;
zdanie; opinia; postanowienie;
zamierzenie; v. pamiętać;
zważać; przejmować się;
baczyć; mieć coś
przeciwko; być posłusznym

mind your own business ['majnd
,jo:'ołn'byznys] pilnuj swego
nosa; nie wtrącaj się

minded ['majndyd] adj.
nastawiony na; skłonny do;
gotów; gotowy

mindful ['majndful] adj. pomny;
dbały; uważający; troskliwy

mindless ['majndlys] adj.
nierozumny; niedbały; nie
uważający

mine [majn] pron. mój; moje;
moja; s. kopalnia; podkop;
mina; bomba; v. kopać;
podkopywać; eksploatować;
minować

miner ['majner] s. górnik

mineral ['mynerel] s. mineralny;
adj. zawierający minerały

mingle ['myngl] v. mieszać się;
przyłączać się (do innych)

miniature ['mynjeczer] s.
miniatura; adj. miniaturowy

minimum ['mynymem] s.
minimum; adj. minimalny;
najmniejszy

mining ['majnyng] s. górnictwo;
adj. górniczy; kopalniany

miniskirt ['myny,ske:rt] s.
spódnica (mini) (b. krótka)

minister ['mynyster] s.
duchowny; minister; v.
stosować; przyczyniać się;
udzielać; pomagać

ministry ['mynystry] s.
duszpasterstwo; kler;
duchowieństwo;
ministerstwo; gabinet

ministrów; służba; pomoc;
posługa
mink ['my<u>nk</u>] s. norka; adj. z
norek; z futer norek
minor ['majner] adj. mniejszy;
mało ważny; młodszy;
nieletni; s. człowiek
niepełnoletni
minority [maj'noryty] s.
mniejszość;
niepełnoletniość
minster ['mynster] s. katedra;
kościół klasztorny
minstrel ['mynstrel] s. bard;
śpiewak przebrany za
murzyna
mint [mynt] s. mięta; mennica;
majątek; źródło; v. bić
pieniądze; wymyślać;
tworzyć; kuć
minute ['mynyt] s. minuta;
chwilka; notatka; v.
szkicować; protokołować;
[maj'nju:t] adj. szczegółowy;
bardzo mały; znikomy
miracle ['myrekl] s. cud; a.
cudowny
miraculous [my'raekjules] adj.
cudowny; nadprzyrodzony
mirage ['myra:dż] s. miraż;
fatamorgana; złudzenie
wzrokowe
mire ['majer] s. muł; błoto;
bagno; v. grzęznąć (w
trudnościach); zabłocić się
mirror ['myrer] s. zwierciadło; v.
odzwierciedlać
mirth [me:r<u>s</u>] s. wesołość;
radość; uciecha (pełna
śmiechu)
miry ['majry] adj. błotnisty;
mulisty; bagnisty
mis- [mys] przedrostek: nie; źle;
(błędnie) nie-; źle-
misadventure ['mysed'wenczer]
s. niepowodzenie; zła
przygoda
misanthrope ['myze<u>n</u>troup] s.
mizantrop; wróg ludzkości
misapply ['myse'plaj] v.
nadużyć; źle zastosować
misapprehend ['mys,aepry'hend]
v. nie pojąć; źle zrozumieć

misbehave ['mysby'hejw] v.
nieodpowiednio zachowywać
się
miscalculate ['mys'kaelkjukejt] v.
przeliczyć się; przerachować
się
miscarriage [mys'kaerydż] s.
poronienie; omyłka;
niepowodzenie
mischief ['myscnyf] s. szkoda;
krzywda; psota; utrapienie;
złośliwość; figiel;
figlarność; licho; szkodnik;
bieda; niezgoda
mischievous ['mysczywes] adj.
szkodliwy; niegodziwy;
niesforny; niegrzeczny; psotny
misdeed ['mys'di:d] s.
przestępstwo; zły czyn
(karygodny)
misdemeano(u)r ['mysdy'mi:ner]
s. wykroczenie; złe
sprawowanie
miser ['majzer] s. sknera;
chciwiec; skąpiec; kutwa
miserable ['myzerebl] adj.
nędzny; chory; marny;
żałosny
miserably ['myzerebly] adv.
nędznie; marnie; żałośnie
misfortune [mys'fo:rczen] s.
nieszczęście; pech; zły los
misgiving [mysgywy<u>ng</u>] s. złe
przeczucie; obawa;
powątpiewanie
misguide [,mys'gajd] v.
wprowadzać w błąd;
sprowadzać na manowce
mishap ['myshaep] s. (mały,
nieważny) wypadek
(niepowodzenie)
misinform ['mysyn'form] v. źle
informować; zwieść z drogi
misjudge ['mys'dżadż] v. źle
osądzić; źle ocenić; mieć
fałszywe mniemanie; nie
doceniać
mislay [mys'lej] v. zatracić; zob.
lay; zagubić; zapodziać
mislead [mys'li:d] v.
wprowadzić w błąd; zob.
lead; zbałamucić
mismanage [,mys'maenydż] v.

źle prowadzić; źle
pokierować
misplace [,mys'plejs] v.
zatracić; położyć nie na
miejscu
misprint [,mys'prynt] v. błędnie
wydrukować; s. omyłka
drukarska; błąd drukarski
mispronounce ['myspre'nauns] v.
błędnie wymawiać; źle
wymawiać
misrepresent ['mysrepry'zent] v.
przekręcić; błędnie
przedstawić; fałszywie
przedstawić
Miss [mys] s. panna; panienka
miss [mys] v. chybić; nie
trafić; nie znaleźć; nie
dostać; brakować; tęsknić;
zacinać się; s. pudło;
niepowodzenie; opuszczenie;
chybienie
miss out ['mys,aut] v.
wypuścić (słowo); chybić;
nie dostać
missile ['mysajl] s. pocisk;
rakieta; adj. nadający się do
rzucania (oszczep, rakieta etc.)
missing ['mysyng] adj.
nieobecny; brakujący;
zaginiony
mission ['myszyn] s. misja;
delegacja; v. wysłać z misją;
zakładać misje; a. misyjny
missionary ['myszynery] s.
misjonarz; adj. misjonarski
misspelling ['mys'spelyng] s.
błąd ortograficzny
mist [myst] s. lekka mgiełka; v.
zachodzić parą (mgiełką)
mistake [mys'tejk] s. omyłka;
nieporozumienie; v. pomylić
(się) (co do faktu lub
człowieka); źle zrozumieć;
mylić się
mistaken [mys'tejken] adj.
mylny; błędny; pomylony; nie
mający zrozumienia sytuacji
mistakenly [mys'tejknly] adv.
błędnie; pomyłkowo;
nierozsądnie
Mister ['myster] s. pan
(używane z nazwiskiem);

skrót Mr. (bez nazwiska
niegrzecznie!)
mistletoe ['mysltou] s. jemiołka;
jemioła; liście jemioły
mistress ['mystrys] s. kochanka;
nauczycielka; [myzys] s. pani;
(skrót Mrs.); zob. Mister
mistrust [mys'trast] v.
podejrzewać; nie ufać; s.
niedowierzanie; nieufność
misty ['mysty] adj. mglisty;
zamglony; niejasny;
nieokreślony
misunderstanding ['mysande:r
'staendyng] s. nieporozumienie
misuse ['mys'ju:z] v.
nadużywać; źle używać;
['mys'ju:s] s. nadużycie; złe
użycie
mite [majt] s. molik; kruszyna;
drobiazg; grosz (wdowi);
berbeć; mała sumka
pieniędzy
mitigate ['mytygejt] v. koić;
uśmierzać; łagodzić;
łagodnieć; ukoić; złagodzić
mitten ['mytn] s. rękawiczka bez
palców; (slang) rękawica
bokserska (zimowa etc.)
mix [myks] v. mieszać;
obcować; współżyć; s.
mieszanka; mieszanina;
zamieszanie
mix-up ['myks'ap] s.
gmatwanina; plątanina;
zamieszanie; bójka
mixed up with ['mykst'ap,łys]
adj. zamieszany (w coś)
mixture ['myksczer] s.
mieszanka; mieszanina;
mikstura
moan [moun] s. jęk; v. jęczeć;
lamentować; mówić jęcząc
moat [mout] s. fosa; rów; v.
opasywać fosą
mob [mob] s. tłum; motłoch;
banda; v. napastować;
atakować tłumnie; stłoczyć
się
mobile ['moubajl] adj. ruchomy;
ruchliwy; zmienny; s. rzeźba -
kompozycja wisząca
(abstrakcyjna)

mock [mok] v. wykpić;
przedrzeźniać; zmylić;
stawiać czoło; żartować z
kogoś; s. kpiny;
przedrzeźnianie;
naśladownictwo; adj.
fałszywy; udany; pozorny
mockery ['mokery] s. kpiny;
śmiech; pośmiewisko;
pokrzywianie się
mode [moud] s. sposób; tryb;
moda; rzecz modna (lub
zwyczajowa)
model ['modl] s. model; wzór;
modelka; manekin; v.
modelować
moderate ['moderyt] adj.
umiarkowany; średni; s.
człowiek umiarkowany (w
poglądach etc.)
moderate ['moderejt] v.
powściągać; uspokoić (się);
prowadzić (zebranie)
moderation [,mode'rejszyn] s.
umiarkowanie; umiar; spokój
modern ['modern] adj.
współczesny; nowoczesny;
nowożytny
modernize ['modernajz] v.
unowocześnić (się);
modernizować
modest ['modyst] adj. skromny
modesty ['modysty] s.
skromność
modification [,modyfy'kejszyn] s.
modyfikacja; łagodzenie z
lekka
modify ['modyfaj] v.
modyfikować; zmieniać
częściowo; łagodzić
modulate ['modjulejt] v.
modulować; regulować;
dostosowywać
module ['modju:l] s. moduł;
kabina (astronauty)
moist [mojst] adj. wilgotny
moisten [mojsen] v. wilgnąć;
zwilżać (sobie usta etc.);
wilgotnieć
moisture ['mojszczer] s. wilgoć;
wilgotność; lekkie
zamoczenie
molar [mouler] s. trzonowy

(ząb); adj. trzonowy
molasses [me'laesyz] s. pl.
melasa; ciemny, gęsty syrop z
trzciny cukrowej
mole [moul] s. kret; grobla;
molo; znamią; brodawka etc.
molecule ['molykju:l] s. molekuła;
cząsteczka
molest [mou'lest] v.
napastować; dokuczać;
molestować; naprzykrzać się
mollify ['molyfaj] v. łagodzić;
miękczyć; miąknąć;
uśmierzać
moment ['moument] s. chwila;
moment; waga; znaczenie;
motyw; powód; doniosłość;
ważność
momentary ['moumentery] adj.
chwilowy; mijający; lada
chwila
monarch ['monerk] s. monarcha;
król; duży motyl tropikalny
monarchy ['monerky] s.
monarchia
monastery ['monestery] s.
klasztor (głównie męski);
miejsce zamieszkania mnichów
(zakonnic)
Monday ['mandy] s.
poniedziałek; a.
poniedziałkowy
monetary ['manytry] adj.
monetarny; pieniężny;
walutowy
money ['many] s. pieniądze
money-order ['many,o:rder] s.
przekaz pieniężny
monger ['manger] s. handlarz;
przekupień; kupiec
monk [mank] s. mnich
monkey ['manky] s. małpa
(ogoniasta); v. dokazywać;
małpować; wygłupiać się
monkey business ['manky
'byznys] s. małpie figle
(dokuczliwe)
monkey wrench ['manky'rencz]
s. francuski klucz
(dostosowywalny)
monolog(ue) ['monelog] s.
monolog; a. monologowy
monopolize [me'nopelajz] v.

monopolizować; skupiać na
sobie uwagę wszystkich etc.
monopoly [me'nopely] s.
monopol
monotonous [me'notnes] adj.
monotonny; jednolity
monotony [me'notny] s.
monotonia
monster ['monster] s. potwór;
adj. olbrzymi; potworny;
okrutny
monstrous ['monstres] adj.
potworny; ogromny; okrutnie
zły
month [mant] s. miesiąc
monthly ['mantly] adj.
miesięczny; adv. miesięcznie;
co miesiąc; na miesiąc; s.
miesięcznik
monument ['monjument] s.
pomnik
moo [mu:] v. ryczeć; s. ryk
(krowy)
mood [mu:d] s. humor; nastrój;
(gram.) tryb; usposobienie
moody [mu:dy] adj. ponury;
mający humory; markotny
moon [mu:n] s. księżyc; a.
księżycowy
moonlight ['mu:nlajt] s. światło
księżyca; v. mieć kilka posad
równocześnie
moonlit ['mu:nlyt] adj.
oświetlony księżycem
moonshine ['mu:nszajn] s.
światło księżyca; alkohol
pędzony nielegalnie lub
przemycony
Moor [muer] adj. mauretański;
s. Maur
moor [muer] s. otwarty teren
łowiecki; wrzosowisko; bagno;
trzęsawisko; v. cumować;
umocować; przybijać do
brzegu
moorings ['mueryns] pl. kotwica
martwa; miejsce
przycumowania
moose [mu:s] s. łoś
amerykański
mop [mop] s. szmata do podłóg;
grymas; v. wycierać;
zgarniać; robić miny;

spuścić manto
moral ['morel] s. morał; pl.
moralność; adj. moralny;
obyczajny
morale [me'rael] s. nastrój; duch
(w wojsku, narodzie)
morality [me'raelyty] s.
moralność; moralizowanie;
etyka
moralize ['morelajz] v.
umoralniać; moralizować
morass [me'raes] s. moczary;
bagno; mokradła; grzęzawiska
morbid ['mo:rbyd] adj.
chorobliwy; chorobowy;
niezdrowy; schorzały
more [mo:r] adv. bardziej;
więcej; adj. liczniejszy; dalszy
morel [mo'rel] s. (grzyb) smardz;
psianka; a. psiankowaty
more or less ['mo:r,or'les] adv.
mniej więcej; w przybliżeniu
moreover [mo:'rouwer] adv. co
więcej; prócz tego; nadto;
poza tym
morgue [mo:rg] s. morga (na
zwłoki); kostnica; a. kostnicy
morning ['mo:rnyng] s. rano;
poranek; przedpołudnie
morose [mo'rous] adj. ponury;
zasępiony; przygnębiony;
markotny
morphine ['mo:rfi:n] s. morfina;
a. morfinowy
morsel ['mo:rsel] s. kęs; kąsek;
kawałek; smakołyk; v. dzielić
na kawałki; rozdrabniać;
rozparcelowywać
mortal ['mo:rtl] s. śmiertelnik;
adj. śmiertelny; straszny
mortality [mo:'rtaelyty] s.
śmiertelność; liczba ofiar
mortar ['mo:ter] s. moździerz;
zaprawa murarska; v.
tynkować; kłaść zaprawę;
strzelać z moździerza;
związać zaprawą
mortgage ['mo:rgydż] s.
hipoteka; v. hipotekować
mortician [mo:r'tyszen] s.
przedsiębiorca pogrzebowy
mortification [mo:rtyfy'kejszyn]
s. upokorzenie; umartwianie

się; wstyd; gangrena
mortify ['mo:rtyfaj] v.
zamierzać; ranić (uczucia);
upokarzać; umartwiać (się);
powściągać; zgangrenować
mortuary ['mo:rtjuery] s.
trupiarnia; kostnica; a.
pogrzebowy
mosaic [mou'zejyk] s. mozaika;
adj. mozaikowy; mojżeszowy
mosque [mosk] n. meczet
mosquito [mes'ki:tou] s. komar;
moskit; a. moskitowy
moss [mos] s. mech; v.
pokrywać mchem
(torfowiskiem)
most [moust] adj. największy;
najliczniejszy; adv. najbardziej;
najwięcej; s. największa
ilość; maksimum
mostly ['moustly] adv.
przeważnie; głównie; po
największej części
moth [mos] s. ćma; mól
moth-eaten ['mos,i:tn] adj.
zjedzony przez mole;
przestarzały
mother ['madzer] s. matka; v.
matkować
mother country ['madzer'kantry]
s. ojczyzna; kraj rodzinny
motherhood ['madzer,hud] s.
macierzyństwo
mother-in-law ['madzer,yn'lo:] s.
teściowa
motherly ['madzerly] adj.
macierzyński
mother tongue ['madzer,tang] s.
język ojczysty
motif [mou'ti:f] s. motyw
(artystyczny); główny temat
motion ['mouszyn] s. ruch;
wniosek; stolec; v. kierować
skinieniem, znakiem; skinąć
na kogoś znaczącym gestem
motionless ['mouszenlys] adj.
bez ruchu; unieruchomiony
motion picture ['mouszyn
'pykczer] s. film ruchomy
motivate ['moutywejt] v.
uzasadniać; pobudzać
kogoś; zachęcać
motive ['moutyw] s. motyw;

podnieta; adj. napędowy;
poruszający
motor ['mouter] s. motor; adj.
ruchowy; mechaniczny;
samochodowy; v. jeździć;
przewozić samochodem;
prowadzić wóz
motorbike ['mouter,bajk] s.
motocykl; rower z motorkiem
motorboat ['mouter,bout] s.
motorówka; łódź motorowa
motorcycle ['mouter,sajkl] s.
motocykl
motorcyclist ['mouter,sajklyst] s.
motocyklista
motoring ['mouteryng] s. jazda
samochodem; automobilizm
motorist ['mouteryst] s.
automobilista; kierowca
motorize ['mouterajz] v.
motoryzować; zmotoryzować
mottle ['motl] s. cętka; plama; v.
cętkować; nakrapiać;
upstrzyć
motto [motou] s. motto; dewiza
mould [mould] s. pleśń;
ziemia; modła; forma; v.
pleśnieć; odlewać;
kształtować; urabiać
moulder ['moulder] v. gnić;
próchnieć; niszczyć się;
kruszyć się; zgłupieć; s.
odlewacz
mouldy ['mouldy] adj.
spleśniały; zgniły; stęchły;
przeżyty; nudny
moult [moult] v. linieć; s.
linienie
mound [maund] s. hałda; kopiec
mount [maunt] s. oprawa;
podstawa; wierzchowiec; v.
stanąć (na); wsiąść (na
konia); podnieść; wchodzić;
oprawić; osadzić;
wyposażyć; zmontować;
wyreżyserować
mountain ['mauntyn] s. góra;
sterta; adj. górski; górzysty
mountaineer [,maunty'nier] s.
góral; alpinista
mountainous ['mauntynes] adj.
górzysty; olbrzymi; zawrotny
mourn [mo:rn] v. być w żałobie;

opłakiwać; pogrążać się w smutku

mournful ['mo:rnful] adj. żałobny; ponury; przygnębiony

mourning ['mo:rnyŋg] s. żałoba

mouse [maus] s. mysz; pl. **mice** [majs]; podbite oko; v. myszkować

moustache [mos'ta:sz] s. wąsy

mouth [mauš] s. usta; ujście; wylot; v. mówić przesadnie (z patosem)

mouth [mouš] v. deklamować; brać w usta; robić złą minę

mouthful ['mauȿful] s. pełne usta; kąs; dźwięk trudny do wymówienia; ważne słowa; dużo czegoś; v. powiedzieć do rzeczy

mouthpiece ['mauȿpi:s] s. ustnik; rzecznik; kiełzno

mouthwash ['mauȿłosz] s. woda do ust; płukanka do ust

move [mu:w] s. ruch; pociągnięcie; krok; zmiana mieszkania; przeprowadzka; v. ruszać się; posuwać; przesuwać; postępować; przeprowadzać się; wzruszać; nakłonić; zwracać się; wnosić; zrobić ruch; działać

move in ['mu:wyn] v. wprowadzać się; wtargnąć; wejść

move on ['mu:w,on] v. jechać dalej; iść dalej; ruszyć (w drogę)

move out ['mu:w,aut] v. wyprowadzać się; wynieść się

movement [mu:wment] s. ruch; poruszenie; przemieszczenie; mechanizm; wypróżnienie

movies ['mu:wyz] s. (slang) kino; film niemy; film

moving ['mu:wyŋg] adj. ruchomy; wzruszający; s. przeprowadzka

moving violation ['mu:wyn, waje'lejszyn] przestępstwo drogowe w czasie jazdy (autem)

mow; mowed; mown [moł; mołd; mołn]

mow [moł] v. kosić (trawą)

mower ['mołer] s. kosiarz

mown [mołn] v. zob. **mow**

Mr. [myster] s. pan (używane z nazwiskiem)

Mrs. [mysyz] s. zamężna pani (używane z nazwiskiem)

much [macz] adj. & adv. wiele; bardzo; dużo; sporo; niemało

much too much [,macz'tu,macz] exp.: dużo za dużo; zbyt dużo

mucus ['mju:kes] s. śluz

mud [mad] s. błoto; brud

muddle ['madl] v. nurzać się; mącić; bełtać; mieszać; brnąć; wikłać się; s. powikłanie; trudne położenie; nieład; zamęt

muddle through ['madl,tru:] v. przebrnąć; wybrnąć z kłopotów

muddy ['mady] adj. zabłocony; błotnisty; mętny; v. błocić; mącić

muff [maf] s. zarękawek; fuszerka; fuszer; v. fuszerować

muffle [mafl] v. tłumić; owinąć; otulić; s. pysk (przeżuwaczy, gryzoni)

muffler ['mafler] s. tłumik; szal; rękawica bokserska; szalik

mug [mag] s. dzban; kubek; gęba

mulberry ['malbery] s. morwa

mule [mju:l] s. muł (zwierzę)

mull [mal] v. rozmyślać; pokpić; sfuszerować; zagrzać i zaprawić (np. piwo); s. bałagan; muślin; przylądek; tabakiera

mullion ['malion] s. pręt; drążek okienny; słupek okienny

multiple ['maltypl] s. wielokrotna; adj. wielokrotny; złożony

multiplication [,maltyply'kejszyn] s. mnożenie; rozmnażanie się

multiplication table [,maltyply 'kejszyn tejbl] s. tabliczka

mnożenia
multiply ['maltyplaj] s. mnożyć
(się); rozmnażać się;
pomnożyć
multitude ['maltytju:d] s.
mnóstwo; tłum; pospólstwo;
mnogość
mumble ['mambl] s. mruknięcie;
bąknięcie; v. mruknąć;
bąknąć; żuć bezzębnymi
dziąsłami; mamrotać
mummy ['mamy] s. mumia;
miazga; brunatny barwik;
mamusia
mumps ['mamps] s. (choroba)
świnka; zapalenie ślinianki
munch [mancz] v. chrupać;
schrupać
municipal [mju:'nysypel] adj.
miejski; samorządowy;
komunalny
municipality [mju:,nysy'paelyty]
s. zarząd miasta; miasteczko
mural ['mjuerel] s. malowidło
ścienne; fresk; adj. ścienny
murder ['me:rder] s. mord;
morderstwo; v. mordować;
paskudzić (rolę)
murderer ['me:rderer] s.
morderca
murderess ['me:rderys] s.
morderczyni
murderous ['me:rderes] adj.
morderczy; śmiercionośny
murmur ['me:rmer] s. mruczenie;
pomruk; pomrukiwanie; szmer;
szmeranie; sarkanie; v.
mruczeć; szmerać
muscle ['masl] s. mięsień;
muskuł; v. pchać się na siłę
muscle bound ['masl,baund] adj.
z zerwanymi mięśniami
muscular ['maskjuler] adj.
mięśniowy; krzepki;
muskularny; wykonany
muskułami etc.
muse [mju:z] v. dumać; s.
zaduma
museum [mju:'zjem] s. muzeum
mush [masz] s. papka; kulesza (z
kukurydzy); v. iść po śniegu
mushroom ['maszrum] s. grzyb;
pieczarka polna; dorobkiewicz;

v. zbierać grzyby; rozszerzać
się (jak grzyby po deszczu)
music ['mju:zyk] s. muzyka;
nuty; konsekwencje postąpku
(slang)
musical ['mju:zykel] adj.
muzyczny; muzykalny; s.
komedia lub film muzyczny
music hall ['mju:zykho:l] s. teatr
rewiowy
musician ['mju:zyszen] s. muzyk
(zawodowy)
music stand ['mju:zyk,staend] s.
pulpit (na nuty)
musk [mask] s. piżmo
musket ['maskyt] s. muszkiet
muskrat ['mask,raet] s.
piżmoszczur; futro
piżmoszczura
Muslim ['muslym] adj.
muzułmański; s. muzułmanin
muslin ['mazlyn] s. muślin
musquash ['maskłosz] s. (muskrat) piżmowiec; piżmoszczur
mussel ['masl] s. małż
must [mast] s. moszcz winny;
stęchlizna; szał; v. musieć;
adj. konieczny; nieodzowny
mustache ['mastasz] s. wąsy
mustard ['masterd] s. musztarda
muster ['master] v.
musztrować; zbierać (się); s.
przegląd; zebranie; zbiór; apel;
zebrani
muster in ['master,yn] v.
zaciągać się do wojska
(powołać)
muster out ['master,aut] v.
zwalniać z wojska
musty ['masty] adj. stęchły;
zapleśniały; zbutwiały;
przestarzały
mute [mju:t] adj. niemy; v.
tłumić
mutilate ['mju:tylejt] v.
okaleczyć; psuć; okroić
(tekst książki)
mutineer [,mju:ty'nier] s.
buntownik; winny buntu
mutinous ['mju:tynes] adj.
buntowniczy; zbuntowany
mutiny ['mju:tyny] s. bunt; v.
buntować

mutter ['mater] v. mamrotać;
mruczeć; szemrać (przeciw);
szeptać; pomrukiwać; s.
mamrot; pomruk; szemranie;
narzekanie
mutton ['matn] s. baranina; a.
barani
mutton chop ['matn,czop] s.
kotlet barani
mutual ['mju:tjuel] adj.
wzajemny; wspólny;
obustronny
muzzle ['mazl] s. wylot lufy;
pysk; kaganiec; v. nakładać
kaganiec (psu, dziennikarzowi)
my [maj] pron. mój; moje; moja;
moi
myelitis [,maje'lytys] s. zapalenie
rdzenia pacierzowego
myriad ['myryed] s. krocie; roje;
10000; miriada; adj.
niezliczony; wielostronny
myrrh [me:r] s. mirra
myrtle ['me:rtl] s. mirt
myself [maj'self] pron. ja sam;
sam osobiście; siebie; sobie
mysterious [mys'tierjes] adj.
tajemniczy; niezgłębiony
mystery ['mystery] s. tajemnica;
tajemniczość; misterium
mystify ['mystyfaj] v.
wprowadzać w błąd;
okrywać tajemnicą
myth [mys] s. mit; postać
mityczna; bajka; mistyfikacja
mystic ['mystyk] s. mistyk; adj.
mistyczny; tajemniczy

N

n [en] czternasta litera
angielskiego alfabetu
nab [naeb] v. capnąć; złapać;
przydybać; aresztować;
przyłapać
nag [naeg] v. gderać;
dokuczać; dręczyć; s.
szkapa; kucyk; konik

nail [nejl] s. gwóźdź;
paznokieć; pazur; v.
przybijać; utkwić (wzrok);
ujawnić (kłamstwo);
przygwoździć; chwytać
naive [na:'i:w] adj. naiwny
naked ['nejkyd] adj. nagi; goły;
goła (prawda etc.); obnażony
name [nejm] s. imię; nazwa;
nazwisko; v. nazywać;
mianować; wymieniać;
naznaczyć (datę)
nameless ['nejmlys] adj.
bezimienny; nieznany;
niesłychany; nieopisany;
anonimowy
namely ['nejmly] adv.
mianowicie; właśnie; żeby
(wyjaśnić)
nanny ['naeny] s. niańka; koza
nanny-goat ['naeny,gout] s. koza
(żywicielka, mlekodajna)
nap [naep] v. drzemać;
zdrzemnąć się; s. drzemka;
meszek; puch; włos;
stroszenie meszku
nape [nejp] s. kark
nappy ['naepy] adj. mocny;
podchmielony; puszysty; v.
napój; piwo; półmisek;
serwetka
narcosis [na:r'kousys] s.
narkoza; uśpienie
narkotykami
narcotic [na:r'kotyk] adj.
narkotyczny; s. narkotyk;
narkoman
narrate [nae'rejt] v. opowiadać
(coś); opowiedzieć
narration [nae'rejszyn] s.
opowiadanie; opowieść
narrative ['naeretyw] adj.
narracyjny; s. opowiadanie
narrator [nae'rejter] n. narrator;
opowiadający; opowiadacz
narrow ['naerou] adj. wąski;
ciasny; ograniczony;
przesmyk; cieśninia; v.
zwężać; ścieśniać;
kurczyć się; zmniejszać się;
redukować do ...
narrow-minded ['naerou
'majndyd] s. ciasny;

ograniczony

nasty ['na:sty] adj. obrzydliwy; wstrętny; nieznośny; groźny; brudny; nieprzyzwoity

nation ['nejszyn] s. naród; kraj; państwo

national ['naeszenl] adj. narodowy; państwowy; s. członek narodu; obywatel; ziomek

nationality [,naesze'naelyty] s. narodowość; obywatelstwo

nationalize ['naesznelajz] v. upaństwowić; nadawać obywatelstwo (imigrantom)

native ['nejtyw] adj. rodzinny; krajowy; miejscowy; wrodzony; naturalny; prosty; s. tubylec; autochton; człowiek miejscowy

native language ['nejtyw 'laengłydż] s. ojczysty język

nativity [ne'tywyty] s. narodzenie

natural ['naeczrel] adj. naturalny; przyrodniczy; przyrodzony; doczesny; fizyczny; przyrodni; pierwotny; nieślubny; dziki; s. biały klawisz (pianina); kasownik (muzyczny)

naturalize ['naeczerelajz] v. naturalizować (się); aklimatyzować (się); robić naturalnym; przyswajać sobie; pozbawiać cech nadprzyrodzonych

naturally ['naeczrely] adv. naturalnie; z przyrodzenia; oczywiście

natural-science ['naeczerel 'sajens] s. przyroda; nauka przyrody; przyrodoznawstwo

nature ['nejczer] s. natura; przyroda; usposobienie; rodzaj

naught [no:t] s. nic; zero

naughty ['no:ty] adj. niegrzeczny; nieposłuszny; nieprzyzwoity

nausea ['no:sje] s. nudność; mdłość; choroba morska; obrzydzenie; wstręt; chęć wymiotowania

nauseating ['no:sjejtyng] adj. obrzydliwy; przyprawiający o mdłości, wymioty etc.

nautical ['no:tykel] adj. marynarski; morski

nautical mile ['no:tykel,majl] s. mila morska; 1853 m

naval ['nejwel] adj. morski

naval base ['nejwel,bejz] s. baza morska (wojskowa)

nave [nejw] s. 1. nawa; 2. piasta (u koła)

navel ['nejwel] s. pępek (ośrodek)

navigable ['naewygebl] adj. spławny; żeglowny; sterowny; przydatny do żeglugi

navigate ['naewygejt] s. żeglować; kierować (np. balonem)

navigation [,naewy'gejszyn] s. żegluga; podróż morska; nawigacja

navigator ['naewygejter] s. żeglarz; nawigator

navy [nejwy] s. marynarka wojenna; granatowy kolor

nay [nej] adv. nie; nawet; co więcej; s. sprzeciw

near [nier] adj. bliski; dokładny; v. zbliżać się; adv. blisko; prawie; oszczędnie

nearby ['nier'baj] adj. pobliski; sąsiedni; adv. w pobliżu

nearly ['nierly] adv. prawie; blisko; oszczędnie; nie całkiem

nearness ['niernys] s. bliskość

nearsighted ['nier-sajtyd] s. krótkowzroczny

neat [ni:t] adj. schludny; zgrabny; proporcjonalny

neatness ['ni:tnys] s. schludność; prostota; porządek; gustowność; dobre proporcje

necessary ['nesysery] adj. konieczny; potrzebny; wynikający

necessitate [ny'sesytejt] v. wymagać; czynić koniecznym

necessity [ny'sesyty] s. potrzeba; konieczność;

artykuł pierwszej potrzeby; niedostatek; los; zrządzenie losu

neck [nek] s. szyja; kark; szyjka; przesmyk; v. pieścić się

necklace ['neklys] s. naszyjnik

neck-tie ['nektaj] s. krawat

née [nej] z domu (nazwisko panieńskie)

need [ni:d] s. potrzeba; trudność; bieda; v. potrzebować; musieć; cierpieć biedę

needful [ni:dful] adj. potrzebujący; potrzebny; konieczny

needle ['ni:dl] s. igła; v. kłuć

needless ['ni:dlys] adj. niepotrzebny; zbyteczny; zbędny

needy ['ni:dy] adj. będący w potrzebie, w biedzie etc.

negate [ny'gejt] v. zaprzeczać; negować; anulować

negation [ny'gejszyn] s. zaprzeczenie; odmowa; niebyt

negative ['negetyw] adj. przeczący; negatywny; odmowny; ujemny; s. zaprzeczenie; odmowa; forma przecząca; wartość ujemna; negatyw; v. sprzeciwić się; odrzucać (np. plan)

neglect [ny'glekt] v. zaniedbywać; nie zrobić; s. zaniedbanie; pominięcie; lekceważenie

negligent ['neglydżent] adj. niedbały; opieszały; nieuważny

negotiate [ny'gouszjejt] v. pertraktować; omawiać; załatwiać; przezwyciężać; przebić się przez; uporać się; przekazać lub sprzedać

negotiation [ny,gouszy'ejszyn] s. pertraktacje; omawianie w celu osiągnięcia porozumienia

neigh [nej] s. rżenie; v. rżeć

neighbor ['nejber] s. sąsiad

neighborhood ['nejberhud] s. sąsiedztwo; sąsiedzi; okolica

neighboring ['nejberyng] adj.

sąsiedni; sąsiadujący

neither ['ni:dzer] pron. & adj. żaden (z dwóch); ani jeden ani drugi; ani ten ani tamten; conj. też nie; jeszcze nie

neither ... nor ['ni:dzer ... no:r] exp. ani ... ani

neon ['ni:en] s. neon; a. neonowy

neon sign ['ni:en,sajn] s. reklama neonowa

nephew ['nefju:] s. siostrzeniec; bratanek

nerve [ne:rw] s. nerw; siła; energia; odwaga; opanowanie; zuchwalstwo; tupet; czelność; v. dodawać sił, odwagi

nervous ['ne:rwes] adj. nerwowy

nervousness ['ne:rwesnys] s. nerwowość; zdenerwowanie

nest [nest] s. gniazdo; wyląg; v. budować; gnieździć się

nestle ['nesl] v. skulić; stulić się; przytulić się; urządzić się

nestle down ['nesl,dałn] v. usadawiać się (wygodnie)

nestle close up to ['nesl'klouz ,ap'tu] v. przytulić się (do kogoś lu czegoś)

net [net] adj. czysty; netto; s. siatka; sieć; v. łowić siecią; trafić w siatkę; zarobić na czysto (na sprzedaży etc.)

nettle ['netl] s. pokrzywa; v. parzyć pokrzywą; drażnić; irytować; docinać (komuś); dopiekać

network ['net,łe:rk] s. sieć (np. elektryczna)

neurosis [njue:rousys] s. nerwica; zaburzenia psychiczne

neuter ['nju:ter] adj. nijaki; neutralny; bezstronny; bezpłciowy; s. człowiek bezstronny; rodzaj nijaki

neutral ['nju:trel] adj. bezstronny; neutralny; obojętny; pośredni; nieokreślony; bezpłciowy; s. państwo neutralne

neutrality [nu'traelyty] s.

neutralność; obojętność
neutralize [ˈnyːtrelajz] v.
neutralizować;
unieszkodliwiać; zobojętniać
neutron [ˈnuːtron] s. neutron
never [ˈnewer] adv. nigdy; chyba
nie; wcale; ani nawet
nevermore [ˈnewerˈmoːr] adv.
nigdy więcej; przenigdy
nevertheless [ˌneverð̲yˈles] adv.
niemniej; jednak; pomimo tego
new [njuː] adj. nowy; świeży;
nowoczesny; adv. znowu; na
nowo
newborn [ˈnjuːˌboːrn] adj. nowo
urodzony; s. noworodek
newcomer [njuːˈkemer] adj.
nowoprzybyły; s. przybysz
news [njuːz] s. nowiny;
wiadomości; aktualności;
zdarzenia
newscast [ˈnjuːzˌkaːst] s.
nadawanie wiadomości
newspaper [ˈnjuːsˌpejper] s.
dziennik (gazeta); tygodnik
newsreel [ˈnjuːsriːl] s. kronika
filmowa
newsstand [ˈnjuːstaend] s. kiosk
z gazetami
new year [ˈnjuːjeːr] s. nowy rok;
pierwszy stycznia
New Year's Eve [ˈnjuːˌjeːrsˈiːw]
s. Sylwester (31 grudnia)
next [nekst] adj. następny;
najbliższy; sąsiedni; adv.
następnie; potem; z kolei; tuż
obok; prep. obok; najbliżej
next but one [ˈnekstˌbatˈłan] adj.
przedostatni
next day [ˈnekstˌdej] exp.:
następnego dnia
next door [ˈnekstˌdoːr] adj. (dom)
obok; sąsiedni (budynek)
next to [ˈnekstˌtu] prep. obok
nibble at [ˈnydlˌet] v. obgryzać;
nadgryzać; brać (przynętę);
s. ogryzanie; dziobanie
nice [najs] adj. miły;
sympatyczny; przyjemny;
uprzejmy; ładny; wybredny;
dokładny
nicely [ˈnajsly] adv. przyjemnie;
miło; grzecznie; ściśle;

dokładnie; skrupulatnie
nicety [ˈnajsyty] s. delikatność;
subtelność; zawiłość;
drobiazgowość;
dokładność; drobny
szczegół; małe rozróżnienie;
precyzja; akuratność
niche [nycz] s. nisza; v. chować
(się) w niszy
nick [nyk] s. karb; otłuczenie;
moment; v. karbować;
podcinać; przecinać; trafić;
natrafić; odgadnąć;
oszukać; złapać; otłuc
nickel [ˈnykl] s. nikiel; 5 centów
USA; v. niklować
nick-nack [ˈnykˌnaek] (= knickknack) ozdóbka; świecidełko
nickname [ˈnyknejm] s.
zdrobniałe imię; przezwisko; v.
nazywać zdrobniale;
przezywać
niece [niːs] s. siostrzenica;
bratanica
niggard [ˈnyged] s. sknera; adj.
żałujący (czegoś); skąpiący
night [najt] s. noc; wieczór
night cap [ˈnajtkaep] s. kieliszek
przed snem; czepek do spania;
szklanka wina przed snem
nightclub [ˈnajtklab] s. nocny
lokal (rozrywkowy)
nightgown [ˈnajtgałn] s. damska
koszula nocna; nocny ubiór
nightingale [ˈnajtyŋgejl] s.
słowik; a. słowiczy; słowika
nightly [ˈnajtly] adv. co noc; w
nocy; adj. nocny; jak noc
nightmare [ˈnajtmeer] s.
koszmar; przerażające
doświadczenie
night school [ˈnajtskuːl] s. szkoła
wieczorowa
nightshirt [ˈnajtszeːrt] s. koszula
nocna
nighty [ˈnajty] s. koszulka nocna
(dziecinna, kobieca)
nil [nyl] s. nic; zero
nimble [ˈnymbl] adj. zwinny;
zgrabny; bystry; żywy;
żwawy
nine [najn] num. dziewięć; s.
dziewiątka; dziewięcioro

ninepins ['najnpynz] pl. kręgle

nineteen ['najn'ti:n] num.
dziewiętnaście;
dziewiętnastka

nineteenth ['najn'ti:n<u>s</u>] num.
dziewiętnasty; dziewiętnasta
część

ninetieth ['najnty<u>s</u>] num.
dziewięćdziesiąty

ninety ['najnty] num.
dziewięćdziesiąt;
dziewięćdziesiątka

ninth ['najn<u>s</u>] num. dziewiąty

ninthly ['najn<u>s</u>ly] adv. po
dziewiąty (raz)

nip [nyp] v. uszczypnąć;
przychwycić; odszczepić;
stłumić; zmrozić; buchnąć;
ukraść; popędzić; polecieć;
ucinać; niszczyć; s.
ukąszenie; uszczypnięcie

nip off ['nypof] v. zmykać;
odszczepić się

nipple ['nypl] s. brodawka
sutkowa; smoczek; złącze
gwintowane rury; wzniesienie;
pagórek; bańka; złącze;
nasuwka

niter ['najter] s. saletra

nitrogen ['najtrydżen] s. azot

no [nou] adj. nie; żaden; adv.
nie; bynajmniej; nic; wcale nie;
s. odmowa; sprzeciw

no one ['nou,łan] adj. żaden; ani
jeden; nikt (w ogóle)

nobility [nou'byłyty] s.
szlachetność; szlachta

noble [noubl] adj. szlachetny;
szlachecki; wspaniały;
wielkoduszny; s. szlachcic

nobleman [noublmen] s.
szlachcic

nobody ['noubedy] s. nikt;
człowiek bez znaczenia

nod [nod] v. skinąć głową;
ukłonić się; drzemać
przyzwalać skinieniem; być
nachylonym

noise ['nojz] s. hałas; zgiełk;
wrzawa; szum; odgłos; szmer;
v. rozgłaszać coś; rozgłosić

noiseless ['nojzlys] adj. cichy;
bezszelestny; niehałaśliwy

noisy ['nojzy] adj. hałaśliwy;
krzykliwy; wrzaskliwy

nomadic ['noumaedyk] adj.
wędrowny; koczowniczy;
wędrujący

nominal ['nomynl] adj.
nominalny; imienny;
symboliczny; tylko z nazwy

nominate ['nomynejt] v.
mianować; wyznaczać;
obierać

nomination [,nomy'nejszyn] s.
nominacja

nominative ['nomynetyw] s.
mianownik (gram.); ta sprawa
(sądowa)

non- [non] prefix nie-; bez-

nonalcoholic ['non,aelke'holyk]
adj. bezalkoholowy

noncommissioned ['nonke
'myszend] adj. bez rangi
oficerskiej (podoficer)

noncommittal ['nonke'mytl] adj.
wymijający; nie
zobowiązujący (się)

nonconducting ['nonken'daktyng]
adj. nieprzewodzący

nonconformist ['nonken'fo:rmyst]
s. dyskontent; nonkonformista

nondescript ['nondyskrypt] adj.
nieokreślony; s. człowiek
nieokreślony (trudny do
opisania)

none [non] pron. nikt; żaden;
nic; adv. wcale nie; bynajmniej
nie

nonexistence [,nony'ksystens] s.
niebyt; nieistnienie

nonfiction [,non-'fykszyn] s.
reportaże; opowieść
prawdziwa; opisy faktów (w
dziennikach etc.)

nonsense ['nonsens] s.
niedorzeczność; nonsens;
głupstwo

nonskid ['nonskyd] adj.
przeciwślizgowy; nie
ślizgający się (samochód,
opona etc.)

nonsmoker ['non'smouker] s.
osoba niepaląca; przedział dla
niepalących (w pociągu etc.)

nonstop ['non'stop] adj.

bezpośredni; bez lądowania;
bez postoju; nieprzerwany (lot)

nonunion ['non'ju:njen] adj. nie
należący do związku
zawodowego; nie uznający
związku zawodowego

nonviolence ['non'wajelens] s.
(polityka) bez gwałtów

noodle ['nu:dl] s. makaron;
kluska; cymbał;pała; głupek;
łeb

nook [nuk] s. kącik; zakątek

noon [nu:n] s. południe

noose [nu:s] s. pętla; stryczek;
sidła; lasso; v. usidlić; zrobić
pętlę

nor [no:r] conj. też nie

norm [no:rm] s. norma; wzorzec;
standard

normal ['no:rmel] adj. normalny;
prostopadły; prawidłowy; s.
stan normalny; prostopadła

normalize ['no:rmelajz] v.
normalizować; unormować

Norman ['no:rmen] adj.
normański; s. Normandczyk;
Normandka

north [no:rs] adv. na północ; s.
północ; adj. północny

northeast [no:rs'i:st] adj.
północno-wschodni

northerly ['no:rdzerly] adj.
północny; adv. na północ

northerner ['no:rdzerner] s.
człowiek z północnych stanów

northward ['no:rslerd] adj.
północny; adv. na północ

northwest ['no:rs'lest] adj.
północny-zachodni; adv. na
północny-zachód; s. północny-
zachód

Norwegian [no:rli:dżen] adj.
norweski; s. Norweg

nose [nouz] s. nos; węch; wylot;
dziób; v. węszyć; pocierać
nosem; wtykać nos

nosegay ['nouzgej] s. wiązanka;
bukiet

nostril ['noustryl] s. nozdrze;
chrapy; dziura w nosie

nosy ['nouzy] adj. wścibski;
śmierdzący; aromatyczny;
stęchły; cuchnący; s. nosacz

wielki

not [not] adv. nie; ani (jeden)

not a [not ej] adv. żaden

notable ['noutebl] adj.
znakomity; sławny; wybitny;
s. dostojnik; wybitny człowiek

notary public ['noutery'pablyk] s.
notariusz

notation [nou'tejszyn] s.
znakowanie; notacja; symbol

notch [nocz] s. nacięcie; karb;
przełęcz; v. nacinać;
karbować; rowkować; s.
krok (dalej)

note [nout] s. nuta; znak;
znamię; uwaga; notatka;
banknot; v. zapisywać;
zauważać

note down ['nout'dałn] v.
zanotować; zapisywać

notebook ['noutbuk] s. zeszyt;
notatnik; notes; notesik

noted ['noutyd] adj. znany;
znakomity; wybitny

notepaper ['nout,pejper] s. papier
listowy; blok

noteworthy ['nout,le:rsy] adj.
godny uwagi; wybitny;
osobliwy

nothing ['nasyng] s. nic;
drobiazg; adv. nic; nie; w
żaden sposób; bynajmniej nie;
wcale nie

nothing but ['nasyng'bat] s. nic
tylko ... (coś najlepszego)

notice ['noutys] v. zauważyć;
spostrzec; traktować
grzecznie; powiadamiać; s.
zawiadomienie; uwaga;
recenzja; spostrzeżenie

noticeable ['noutysebl] adj.
godny uwagi; widoczny

notification [,noutyfy'kejszyn] s.
zawiadomienie; zgłoszenie

notify [noutyfaj] v. zawiadomić

notion ['nouszyn] s. pojęcie;
wyobrażenie; zamiar;
wrażenie

notorious ['nou'to:rjes] adj.
notoryczny; osławiony; jawny

notwithstanding [,noutlys
'staendyng] adv. jednakże;
niemniej; mimo; prep. pomimo

(tego); mimo

nought [no:t] s. nic; zero

noun [naun] s. rzeczownik

nourish ['narysz] v. żywić; karmić; utrzymywać

nourishing ['naryszyng] adj. pożywny; pokrzepiający

nourishment ['naryszment] s. pokarm; pożywienie; żywienie; karmienie; żywność; jedzenie

novel ['nowel] s. powieść; opowieść; nowela; adj. nowy; nowatorski; osobliwy; oryginalny

novelist ['nowelyst] s. powieściopisarz

novelty ['nowelty] s. nowość; innowacja; oryginalność

November [nou'wember] s. listopad; adj. listopadowy

novice ['nowys] s. nowicjusz; neofita; początkujący

now [nał] adv. teraz; obecnie; dopiero co; otóż; a więc; s. teraźniejszość; chwila obecna; chwila dzisiejsza

now and again ['nał,ende'gejn] exp.: od czasu do czasu

now and then ['nał,end'dzen] exp.: nieraz; od czasu do czasu; czasem; co jakiś czas

nowadays ['nałe,dejz] adv. obecnie; dzisiaj; s. obecne czasy; dzisiejsze czasy

nowhere ['nouhłer] adv. nigdzie; s. niepowodzenie etc.

no way [noułej] adv. bynajmniej; wcale nie

noxious ['nokszes] adj. szkodliwy; niezdrowy (moralnie etc.)

nozzle ['nozl] s. dysza; rozpylacz; dziób; wylot (rury)

nuclear ['nu:kli:er] adj. jądrowy; o napędzie nuklearnym

nuclear fission ['nu:kli:er'fyszyn] s. rozszczepienie jądra

nuclear power plant ['nu:kli:er 'pałer'pla:nt] s. elektrownia atomowa

nuclear reactor ['nu:kli:er ,ri:'aekter] s. reaktor nuklearny

nucleus ['nu:kljes] s. jądro

nude [nju:d] adj. nagi; goły; nie ważny (prawnie); s. człowiek nagi; nagość; akt

nudge [nadż] v. trącać lekko; s. trącenie łokciem

nugget ['nagyt] s. bryłka; złoty samorodek

nuisance ['nju:sns] s. zawada; naruszenie porządku publicznego; osoba sprawiająca zawadę

null and void ['nal,end'woid] exp.: nieważny; bez znaczenia; unieważniony; nic nie znaczący

numb [nam] adj. ścierpły; zdrętwiały; odrętwiały; v. drętwieć; odurzać; paraliżować; zdrętwieć

number ['namber] s. liczba; numer; ilość; v. liczyć; numerować; wyliczać; zaliczać

numberless ['namberlys] adj. niezliczony; bez numeru

number plate ['namber'plejt] s. płyta z numerem rejestracji samochodu, motoru etc.

numeral ['nju:merel] adj. liczbowy; cyfrowy; s. liczebnik; cyfra (pisana, mówiona etc.)

numerous ['nju:meres] adj. liczny; obfity; liczebny; rytmiczny

nun [nan] s. zakonnica; mniszka

nunnery ['nanery] s. zakon żeński

nuptials ['napszels] pl. zaślubiny; gody; wesele; ślub

nurse [ne:rs] s. pielęgniarka; pielęgniarz; mamka; osłona; v. pielęgnować; leczyć; opiekować się; żywić; podsycać; szanować; obejmować; karmić; pić powoli; (piersią) niańczyć

nursery ['ne:rsery] s. pokój dziecinny; żłobek; przedszkole; ochronka; wylęgarnia; szkółka (roślin, drzewek)

nursery school ['ne:rsery'sku:l] s.
przedszkole

nursing bottle ['ne:rsyng'botl] s.
flaszka do karmienia

nursing home ['ne:rsyn'houm] s.
przytułek - lecznica dla starych
i kalekich; dom zdrowia

nut [nat] s. orzech; bzik; dziwak;
nakrętka; zakrętka; v. szukać
i zbierać orzechy

nutcracker ['natkraeker] s.
dziadek do orzechów

nutmeg ['natmeg] s. gałka
muszkatołowa

nutria ['nju:trje] s. nutria (futro);
nutrie

nutrient ['nju:trjent] adj.
pożywny; odżywczy; s.
odżywka

nutriment ['nju:tryment] s.
środek odżywczy; jedzenie;
pokarm

nutrition [nju'tryszyn] s.
odżywianie; pokarm; nauka o
diecie

nutritious [nju'tryszes] adj.
pożywny; odżywczy

nuts ['nats] adj. (slang)
zwariowany; głupi;
zwariowany na punkcie
czegoś; bardzo zakochany;
excl.: (wyrażające) wstręt,
szyderstwo, lekceważenie

nutshell ['natszel] s. łupka od
orzecha; istota rzeczy; sama
treść (w paru słowach)

nutty ['naty] adj. orzechowy;
pomylony; zbzikowany;
dziwaczny; zwariowany;
pikantny; zakochany

nuzzle ['nazl] v. wsadzać nos
(w coś); ryć; węszyć;
wtulać się (twarzą w czyjeś
ramię); pocierać nosem lub
ryjem

nylon ['najlon] s. nylon;
pończochy nylonowe

nymph [nymf] s. nimfa

nymphomania [,nymfe'mejnia] s.
nimfomania (kobieca
nieposkromiona żądza
miłości; chorobliwy stan
podniecenia erotycznego
kobiety;) snębica

nymphomaniac [,nymfe'menjek]
s. nimfomanka; adj. typowy
dla nimfomanki

O

o [ou] piętnasta litera
angielskiego alfabetu; zero

oak [ouk] s. dąb; a. dębowy

oar [o:r] s. wiosło; v. wiosłować

oarsman ['o:rzmen] s. wioślarz

oasis [ou'ejsys] s. oaza; zielone i
żyzne miejsce wśród
pustynnej okolicy

oat [out] s. owies

oatmeal ['outmi:l] s. owsianka

oath [ous] s. przysięga;
przekleństwo;
świętokradztwo etc.

obedience [e'bi:djens] s.
posłuszeństwo

obedient [e'bi:djent] adj.
posłuszny

obey [e'bej] v. słuchać; być
posłusznym (rozsądkowi etc.)

obituary [e'bytjuery] s. nekrolog;
adj. pośmiertny; żałobny

object ['obdżykt] s. przedmiot;
rzecz; cel; śmieszny człowiek;
dopełnienie; v. zarzucać coś;
być przeciwnym; sprzeciwiać
się

objection [eb'dżekszyn] s.
zarzut; sprzeciw; przeszkoda;
trudność; wada; niechęć

objective [eb'dżektyw] s. cel;
obiektyw; adj. przedmiotowy;
obiektywny; rzeczywisty

obligation [obly'gejszyn] s.
zobowiązanie; obowiązek;
obligacja; dług (wdzięczności)

oblige [e'blajdż] v.
zobowiązywać; spełniać
prośbę

obliging [e'blajdżyng] adj.
uprzejmy; uczynny; usłużny

oblique [e'bli:k] adj. pośredni;

ukośny; skośny; kręty;
nieszczery; potajemny; v. iść
na ukos

obliterate [e'blyterejt] s.
zacierać; zamazywać;
wykreślić; zniszczyć;
skasować (znaczek etc.)

oblivion [e'blywjen] s.
zapomnienie; niepamięć

oblivious [o'blywjes] adj.
zapominający; niepomny;
nieświadomy; dający
zapomnienie

oblong ['oblong] adj. podłużny;
s. podłużny przedmiot

oboe ['oubou] s. obój (instr.
muzyczny)

obscene [ob'si:n] adj. sprośny;
nieprzyzwoity; niemoralny

obscure [eb'skjuer] adj. ciemny;
skromny; niejasny; ukryty;
nieznany; v. zaciemniać;
przyciemniać; zaćmiewać

obsequies ['obsykłyz] pl. pogrzeb

observance [eb'ze:rwens] s.
obrzęd; zwyczaj;
przestrzeganie; szacunek;
poszanowanie; rytuał

observant [eb'ze:rwent] adj.
uważny; postrzegający;
spostrzegawczy; bystry;
czujny

observation [,obzer'wejszyn] s.
obserwacja; spostrzeżenie;
uwaga; spostrzegawczość

observatory [eb'ze:rweto:ry] s.
obserwatorium; punkt
obserwacyjny

observe [eb'ze:rw] v.
obserwować; przestrzegać;
obchodzić; zauważać;
wypowiedzieć uwagą;
zbadać

observer [eb'ze:rwer] s.
obserwator; człowiek
przestrzegający praw

obsess [eb'ses] v. opętać;
prześladować; nie dawać
spokoju; nawiedzać

obsession [eb'seszyn] s. obsesja;
opętanie; natręctwo
(myślowe)

obsolete ['obseli:t] adj.

przestarzały; szczątkowy;
zarzucony

obstacle ['obstekl] s. przeszkoda;
zawada

obstetrics [ob'stetryks] s.
położnictwo

obstinacy ['obstynesy] s. upiór

obstinate ['obstynyt] adj. uparty;
uporczywy; zawzięty;
wytrwały

obstruct [eb'strakt] v. tamować;
zagradzać; zasłaniać;
wstrzymywać; wywoływać
zator; zawadzać

obtain [eb'tejn] v. uzyskać;
trwać; panować;
obowiązywać

obtainable [eb'tejnebl] adj.
osiągalny (do nabycia etc.);
możliwy do nabycia

obtrusive [eb'tru:syw] adj.
natarczywy; natrętny

obvious ['obwjes] adj.
oczywisty; rzucający się w
oczy

occasion [e'kejżyn] s.
sposobność; okazja; powód

occasional [e'kejżenl] adj.
przypadkowy; okazyjny;
okolicznościowy; rzadki

Occident ['oksydent] s. Zachód
(jako kultura, ekonomia etc.) -
całość geograficzna

occult [o'kalt] adj. tajemny

occupant ['okjupent] s.
mieszkaniec; posiadacz
(faktyczny)

occupation [,okju'pejszyn] s.
okupacja; zawód; zajęcie;
zajmowanie; zamieszkiwanie

occupy ['okjupaj] v. okupować;
zajmować (się czymś);
zatrudniać

occur [e'ke:r] v. zdarzać się;
przychodzić na myśl;
pojawiać się; dziać się;
trafić się

occurrence [e'karens] s.
wydarzenie; przypadek;
występowanie

ocean ['ouszen] s. ocean; a.
oceaniczny

o'clock [e'klok] adv. na zegarze;

według zegara
October [ok'touber] s.
październik; a.
październikowy

ocular ['okjuler] adj. oczny;
naoczny; na oko; okiem; s.
okular

oculist ['okjulyst] s. okulista

odd [od] adj. nieparzysty;
dziwny; dziwaczny;
zbywający; pozostały;
dodatkowy; od pary

odds [ods] pl. szanse; fory;
nadwyżka; różnica; drobne
szczegóły; spór; nierówność
(w grze); sprzeczność

odds-and-ends ['ods,end'ends]
exp.: resztki; rupiecie

oddity ['odyty] s. osobliwość;
dziwak; dziwactwo; dziwna
rzecz

odor ['ouder] s. odór; woń;
ślad; reputacja; sława;
posmak

of [ow] prep. od; z; o; w

of Cracow [ow'Krakau] exp.: z
Krakowa (pochodzeniem etc.)

of charity [ow'czaeryty] exp.: z
miłosierdzia

off [of] adv. od; z; na boku;
precz; z dala; przy; prep. z
dala

offshore [of'szo:r] adv. przy
wybrzeżu; adj. od lądu (na
morze)

offense [e'fens] s. obraza;
zaczepka; przekroczenie;
ofensywa

offend [e'fend] v. obrażać;
razić; występować przeciw
(np. prawu); zawinić;
wykroczyć

offender [e'fender] s. winowajca;
przestępca; strona winna

offensive [e'fensyw] adj.
obraźliwy; drażniący;
przykry; cuchnący; zaczepny;
s. ofensywa; postawa
zaczepna

offer ['ofer] s. oferta; propozycja
(np. ślubu); v. ofiarować
(się); oświadczyć (się);
oferować; nastręczyć się;

nadarzyć się; występować z
propozycją

offering ['oferyng] s. ofiara

office ['ofys] s. biuro; urząd;
obowiązek; służba
urzędowania; posada; funkcja;
stanowisko; gabinet

officer ['ofyser] s. urzędnik;
oficer; policjant; v. obsadzać
kadrą; dowodzić; kierować

official [e'fyszel] s. urzędnik; adj.
urzędowy; oficjalny

officious [e'fyszes] adj.
narzucający się; natrętny;
gorliwy; nieurzędowy;
nieoficjalny

offish ['ofysz] adj. chłodny;
sztywny; z rezerwą;
nieprzystępny

offset [o':fset] s. offsetowy
druk; gałąź; odgałęzienie;
odrośl; potomek;
wyrównanie; kompensata; v.
wynagradzać; rozrastać się

offspring ['o:fspryng] s.
potomek; wynik; potomstwo

often ['o:fn] adv. często

oh! [ou] excl. och! ach!

oil [ojl] s. oliwa; olej; ropa; nafta;
farba olejna; v. oliwić
smarować; przetapiać;
pochlebiać

oilcloth ['ojlklog] s. cerata

oily ['ojly] adj. oleisty; olejny;
tłusty; obleśny; służalczy

ointment ['oyntment] s. maść

O.K., okay ['ou'kej] adv. w
porządku; tak; adj. b. dobry;
s. zgoda; v. zaaprobować
(coś)

old [ould] adj. stary;
staroświecki; doświadczony;
były; s. dawne czasy; dawno
temu

old age ['ould,ejdż] s. starość

old-age ['ould ejdż] adj. dawny;
stary; starczy

old-fashioned ['ould'faeszend]
adj. staromodny; staroświecki

old-time ['ould,tajm] adj. dawny

old town ['ould,taln] s.
starówka; stare miasto

olive ['olyw] s. oliwka; drzewo

oliwne; (kolor) oliwkowy;
oliwa stołowa
olive-branch ['olywbra:ncz] s.
gałązka oliwna
Olympic Games [ou'lympyk,
gejms] pl. igrzyska olimpijskie
ombudsman [om'bu:dz‚men] s.
rzecznik ludu - załatwia skargi
na biurokratów
omelet(te) ['omlyt] s. omlet
omen ['oumen] s. omen;
wróżba; znak; v. być
wróżbą; być znakiem
ominous ['omynes] adj.
złowieszczy; źle wróżący
omission [e'myszyn] s.
opuszczenie; zaniedbanie
omit [ou'myt] v. opuszczać;
pomijać; zaniedbywać
omnipotent [om'nypetent] adj.
wszechmocny; wszechmogący
omniscient [om'nysjent] adj.
wszechwiedzący
on [on] prep. na; ku; przy; nad;
u; po; adv. dalej; przed siebie;
naprzód; przy sobie
on and on ['on‚end'on] exp.:
coraz dalej; bez końca; wciąż
on demand [‚on dy'ma:nd] exp.:
na żądanie
on the street ['on‚dy'stri:t] exp.:
na ulicy
on to ['ontu] exp.: na; do
once [łans] adv. raz; nagle;
naraz; zaraz; kiedyś;
niegdyś; dawniej; s. raz; conj.
raz; gdy; skoro; od razu;
zarazem etc.
one [łan] num; jeden; adj.
pierwszy; pojedynczy; jedyny;
pewien; s. dowcip; kieliszek;
jedynka; pron. ten; który;
ktoś; niejaki
one Adams ['łan‚aedems] exp.:
pewien Adams; niejaki Adams
one day ['łan‚dej] exp.: pewnego
dnia; kiedyś; niegdyś
one by one ['łan‚baj'łan] adv.
pojedynczo; jeden za drugim
one another [‚łan e'nadzer] adv.
jeden drugiego; wzajemnie
oneself [łan'self] pron. się;
siebie; sobie; sam; osobiście;

samodzielnie; samotnie
one-sided ['łan'sajdyd] adv.
jednostronny
one-up-manship ['łan-‚ap-
'menszyp] s. "wyścig"
nerwów (w zatargu etc.)
one-way ['łan‚łej] adj.
jednokierunkowy (ruch)
onion ['anjen] s. cebula
onlooker ['onluker] s. widz
only ['ounly] adj. jedyny;
jedynak; adv. tylko; jedynie;
ledwo; dopiero; conj. tylko że;
cóż z tego, kiedy ...
onward ['onłerd] adj. naprzód; ku
przodowi; adv. naprzód; dalej;
dalej naprzód
ooze [u:z] v. sączyć się;
wydzielać się; ciec; s. szlam;
muł; wyciek; rzadkie błoto
opaque [ou'pejk] adj.
nieprzezroczysty; matowy;
mętny; niejasny; s. rzecz
matowa, nieprzezroczysta
open ['oupen] adj. otwarty;
rozwarty; dostępny;
wystawiony; jawny;
odsłonięty; wakujący; wolny;
v. otworzyć; zwierzyć się;
umożliwić; rozpoczynać;
rozchylić; udostępnić
open air ['oupen‚eer] s. świeże
powietrze; wolna przestrzeń
opener ['oupener] s. otwieracz
(np. puszek); przyrząd do
otwierania
open-handed ['oupn'haendyd]
adj. szczodry; hojny
open-hearted ['oupn‚ha:rtyd] adj.
szczery; serdeczny
opening ['oupnyng] s. otwór;
wylot; otwarcie; początek;
zbyt; adj. początkowy;
wstępny
openly ['oupnly] adv. otwarcie;
szczerze; publicznie; bez
ogródek; po prostu; wprost
(powiedzieć)
open-minded ['oupn'majndyd]
adj. z otwartą głową; bez
przesądów; bezstronny
opera ['opere] s. opera
opera glasses ['operegla:sys] s.

lornetka (teatralna)

operate ['operejt] v. działać;
zadziałać; oddziałać;
pracować; operować (kimś,
kogoś); wywoływać;
prowadzić; kierować;
obsługiwać; spekulować

operation [,ope'rejszyn] s.
działanie; czynności;
operacja; obsługiwanie; akcja

operative ['operejtyw] adj.
skuteczny; działający;
praktyczny; operacyjny; s.
pracownik; agent; mechanik;
robotnik; detektyw; agent
wywiadu

operator ['operejter] s. operator;
pracownik; obsługujący
maszynę; telefonista;
kierownik; przemysłowiec;
finansista; spekulant

opinion [e'pynjen] s. pogląd;
opinia; zdanie; zapatrywanie;
sąd

opponent [e'pounent] s.
przeciwnik; oponent; adj.
przeciwny; przeciwległy

opportunity [,oper'tju:nyty] s.
sposobność; okazja

oppose [e'pouz] v.
przeciwstawiać; sprzeciwiać
się

opposed [e'pouzd] adj.
przeciwny; przeciwdziałający

opposite ['epezyt] adj.
przeciwny; przeciwległy;
odmienny; adv. naprzeciwko;
naprzeciw; s. przeciwieństwo;
odwrotność

opposition [,ope'zyszyn] s.
sprzeciw; opór; opozycja;
przeciwstawienie (się);
przeciwieństwo; a.
opozycyjny

oppress [e'pres] v. przygniatać;
uciskać; ciemiężyć; gnębić;
nużyć; męczyć

oppression [e'preszyn] s. ucisk

oppressive [e'presyw] adj.
uciążliwy; dręczący;
gnębicielski; ciężki; duszny;
deprymujący

opt [opt] v. wybierać z dwu

alternatyw; optować na rzecz
czegoś

optical ['optykel] adj. optyczny;
wzrokowy; pomocny w
widzeniu

optician [op'tyszen] s. optyk

optimism ['optymysem] s.
optymizm; pogodny pogląd na
życie

optimize ['optymajz] v. używać
najwydajniej, najsprawniej

option ['opszyn] s. możność
wyboru; opcja; wybór; v.
wybrać alternatywę

or [o:r] conj. lub; albo; czy; ani;
inaczej; czyli; s. złoto; adj.
złoty

or else ['o:rels] exp.: bo jak nie
...; w przeciwnym razie

oral ['o:rel] adj. ustny; doustny;
s. egzamin ustny

orange ['oryndż] s. pomarańcza;
adj. pomarańczowy

orangeade ['oryn'dżejd] s.
oranżada (z pomarańcz,
cukru)

orator ['oreter] s. mówca

orbit ['o:rbyt] s. orbita; oczodół;
v. latać na orbicie (ziemi,
słońca etc.)

orchard ['o:rczerd] s. sad

orchestra ['o:rkystra] s. orkiestra

ordain [o:r'dejn] v. wyświęcać;
mianować; nakazywać;
przeznaczać; zarządzać;
nakazać

ordeal [o:r'di:l] s. ciężka próba;
ciężkie doświadczenie

order ['o:rder] s. rozkaz;
zlecenie; zarządzenie; przekaz;
porządek; szyk; układ; stan;
zakon; order; obrzęd;
zamówienie; zadanie; v.
rozkazywać; zamawiać;
komenderować; zarządzać;
wyświęcać; porządkować

orderly ['o:rderly] s. posługacz;
ordynans; adj. adv. porządny;
czysty; dokładny; skromny;
spokojny; dyżurny

ordinal ['o:rdynl] s. liczebnik
porządkowy; adj. porządkowy

ordinary ['o:rdnry] adj.

zwyczajny; zwykły;
przeciętny; pospolity; typowy;
s. rzecz zwykła, codzienna,
przeciętna
ore [o:r] s. ruda; kruszec; a.
kruszcowy; rudowy
organ ['o:rgen] s. narząd; organ;
organy; czasopismo
organic ['o:rgaenyk] adj.
organiczny;
usystematyzowany
organization [,o:rgenaj'zejszyn] s.
organizacja; organizowanie;
struktura; zrzeszenie
organize ['o:genajz] v.
organizować; zrzeszyć;
nadawać ustrój
organizer ['o:genajzer] s.
organizator
orgasm ['o:rgaesem] s. orgazm;
punkt kulminacyjny aktu
seksualnego; paroksyzm
orgy ['o:rdży] s. orgia
Orient ['o:rjent] adj. orientalny;
wschodni; s. Wschód (bliski)
orient ['o:rjent] v. orientować;
ukierunkowywać; ustawiać
origin ['orydżyn] s. pochodzenie;
początek; źródło; geneza
original [e'rydżynel] adj.
oryginalny; początkowy; s.
oryginał; dziwak
originality [e,rydży'naelyty] s.
oryginalność
originate [e'rydżynejt] v.
zapoczątkować; powstawać
ornament ['o:rnament] s.
ozdoba; v. ozdabiać;
upiększać
ornamental [,o:rne'mentl] adj.
ozdobny; dekoracyjny;
zdobniczy; upiększający
orphan ['o:rfen] s. sierota; adj.
sierocy; osierocony
orphanage ['o:rfenydż] s.
sierociniec; sieroctwo
orthodox ['o:tedoks] adj.
prawowierny; prawosławny
oscillate ['osylejt] v. drgać;
wahać się; oscylować
osmose ['osmous] s. osmoza;
prznikanie równoważące obie
strony (membrany, przedziału)

ostentatious [,osten'tejszes] adj.
ostentacyjny; wystawny;
okazały
ostracize ['ostre'sajz] v.
wykluczać z towarzystwa;
skazywać na wygnanie
ostrich ['ostrycz] s. struś
other ['adzer] pron. inny; drugi;
adv. inaczej; odmiennie
otherwise ['adzerłajz] adv.
inaczej; poza tym; skądinąd
ought [o:t] v. powinien; trzeba
żeby; należy; zobowiązany
ounce [auns] s. uncja; odrobina;
lampart; 1/16 funta
our ['aur] adj. nasz
ours ['auerz] pron. nasz
ourselves [auer'selwz] pl. pron.
my; my sami; (dla) nas etc.
oust [aust] v. usuwać;
wypierać; wyrzucać;
wywłaszczać
out [aut] adv. na zewnątrz;
precz; poza; na dworze; poza
domem; nieobecnym (być)
out-and-out [auten'aut] adj.
całkowity; adv. całkowicie
out of ['autow] adv. z; bez;
poza; nie (modne, rozsądne)
outbalance [aut'baelens] v.
przeważyć; przewyższać
outbid [aut'byd] v.
przelicytować; dać więcej
(niż inny)
outbreak ['autbrejk] s. wybuch
(np. wojny, epidemii)
outburst ['autbe:rst] s. wybuch
(np. gniewu, wulkanu)
outcast ['autka:st] s. wyrzutek;
wygnaniec; adj. wygnany
outcome ['autkam] s. wynik;
rezultat; konsekwencje
outcry ['autkraj] s. okrzyk;
wrzawa; silny protest
outdoors ['aut'do:rz] adj. na
wolnym powietrzu; s. wolna
przestrzeń; adv. zewnątrz
(domu)
outer ['auter] adj. zewnętrzny
outermost ['auter'moust] adj.
najbardziej zewnętrzny
outfit ['autfyt] s. wyposażenie;
drużyna; zespół; towarzystwo;

zestaw narzędzi; v.
wyposażyć; zaopatrywać;
wyekwipować

outgoing ['aut,gouyng] adj.
odchodzący; odjeżdżający;
przyjazny; komunikatywny;
towarzyski

outgrow [aut'grou] v.
przerastać; wyrastać z ...;
wyróść (z roli)

outing ['autyng] s. wycieczka
(na otwarte morze, do lasu
etc.); wypad

outlast [aut'la:st] v. przetrwać
(coś, kogoś); wytrwać
dłużej

outlaw ['aut-lo:] v. zakazywać;
wyjmować spod prawa; s.
przestępca; banita; notoryczny
kryminalista

outlet ['autlet] s. wylot; rynek
zbytu; wyjście; ujście

outline ['autlajn] s. zarys; szkic;
v. konturować; szkicować;
przedstawiać (plany etc.)

outlive [aut'lyw] v. przeżyć;
przetrwać; wytrwać dłużej

outlook ['autluk] s. widok;
pogląd; obserwacja; widoki
(na przyszłość); czaty

outnumber [aut'namber] v.
przewyższać liczebnie; być
liczniejszym

out-of-date [autew'dejt] adj.
przestarzały; niemodny

outpatient ['aut,pejszent] s.
pacjent dochodzący (z domu)

output ['autput] s. wydajność;
wydobycie; moc; produkcja

outrage ['autrejdż] s. gwałt;
zniewaga; v. gwałcić;
znieważać; urągać
(zdrowemu rozsądkowi)

outrageous [aut'rejdżes] adj.
wołający o pomstę; bezecny;
gwałtowny; skandaliczny;
obrażający

outright [aut'rajt] adj. całkowity;
zupełny; stanowczy;
bezpośredni; adv. od razu;
całkowicie; zupełnie; otwarcie

outrun [aut'ran] v. przegonić;
prześcignąć

outside ['aut'sajd] s. okładka;
fasada; strona zewnętrzna; na
dworze; adj. zewnętrzny; inny
niż; adv. zewnątrz; oprócz; z
wyjątkiem; poza (czymś)

outside on the right ['aut'sajd
'on,dy'rajt] exp.: na zewnątrz
po prawej

outsider ['aut'sajder] s. człowiek
obcy; niewtajemniczony; laik;
obcy zawodnik

outsize ['autsajz] s. wielkość
nietypowa, za duża

outskirts ['aut,ske:rts] s. krańce;
kraj; peryferie

outspoken [aut'spouken] adj.
szczery; otwarcie
wypowiedziany, bez ogródek,
prosto w oczy

outspread [aut'spred] adj.
rozpostarty; rozpowszechniony

outstanding ['autstaendyng] adj.
wybitny; wyróżniający się;
otwarty; niezałatwiony;
zaległy; wystający; sterczący

outstretched [aut'streczt] adj.
rozpostarty; wyciągnięty

outward ['autłerd] adj.
zewnętrzny; powierzchowny;
pozorny; cielesny; s. strona
zewnętrzna; wygląd
zewnętrzny; adv. na zewnątrz

outweigh [aut'łej] v. przeważyć

outwit [aut'łyt] v. przechytrzyć

oval ['ouwel] s. owal; adj.
owalny; owalnego kształtu

oven ['own] s. piekarnik; piec

over ['ouwer] prep. na; po; w;
przez; ponad; nad; powyżej;
adv. na drugą stronę; po
powierzchni; całkowicie; od
początku; zbytnio; znowu; raz
jeszcze (odrabiać zadanie
etc.)

over again ['ouwer,e'gejn] adv.
na nowo; jeszcze raz

over-and-over ['ouwer,end
'ouwer] adv. w kółko

overall ['ouwero:l] adj. ogólny;
wszystko obejmujący; s.
kombinezon roboczy

overboard ['ouwerbo:rd] adv.
(zaniechać) za burtę

(wyrzucić)

overburden [,ouwe'rbe:rden] v.
przeładowywać; s. ciężar
pokładów (np. nad kopalnią);
nadmiar ciężaru; ciężar
warstw

overcast ['ouwerka:st] adj.
zachmurzony; mroczny;
ponury; obrębiony; v.
mroczyć; chmurzyć (się);
obrębiać

overcharge [,ouwer'cza:rdż] v.
przeciążać; zdzierać
(pieniądze); stawiać za
wysokie ceny

overcoat ['ouwerkout] s. płaszcz

overcome [,ouwer'kam] v.
pokonać

overcrowd [,ouwer'kraud] v.
zatłoczyć; przepełniać

overdo [,ouwerdu:] v.
przeciążać; przesadzać;
przegotowywać; niszczyć
przesadą; robić za dużo

overdraw [,ouwer'dro:] v.
wyczerpać (konto);
przesadzać; pisać czeki bez
pokrycia

overdue [,ouwer'dju:] adj.
zaległy; zapóźniony (pociąg)

overestimate [,ouwer'esty,mejt]
v. przeceniać; s. za wysoka
ocena; zbyt duże oczekiwania

overflow [,ouwer'flou] v.
przepełniać; przelewać; s.
wylew; przelew; kanał
przelewowy etc.

overgrow [,ouwer'grou] v.
obrastać; przerastać; rosnąć
nadmiernie; róść zbyt szybko

overhang ['ouwer'haeng] v.
zwisać; sterczeć; zagrażać;
s. występ; zwis; nawis
(dachu); występ (skały); zwis
(skalny etc.)

overhaul [,ouwer'ho:l] v.
gruntownie naprawić;
gruntownie zbadać; s.
gruntowny remont

overhead ['ouwer'hed] s.
wydatki administracyjne; adv.
powyżej; na górze; adj. górny

overhear [,ouwer'hier] v.

usłyszeć przypadkiem;
podsłuchać

overheat ['ouwerhi:t] v.
przegrzać; s. nadmierne
gorąco; przegrzanie

overjoyed [,ouwer'dżojd] adj.
nieposiadający się z radości

overlap [,ouwer'laep] v.
zachodzić na siebie; s.
zachodzenie (na siebie)

overload [,ouwer'loud] v.
przeładować; s. nadmierny
ciężar; przeciążenie (dachu)

overlook [,ouwer'luk] v.
przeoczyć; puszczać płazem;
mieć widok z góry;
nadzorować; wybaczyć; s.
widok z góry; nadzór

overlord ['ouwerlo:rd] s. suzeren;
samodzierżca

over-night ['ouwer'najt] adv.
przez noc; poprzedniego
wieczora; adj. nocny; na noc

overpass [,ouwer'pa:s] s.
skrzyżowanie wiaduktem;
przejazd wiaduktem; v.
przecinać; przekraczać;
przewyższać;
przezwyciężać; pomijać (w
kolejce etc.)

overrate ['ouwer'rejt] v.
przeceniać; spodziewać się
zbyt dużo

overrule [,ouwer'ru:l] v.
opanować; uchylać;
odrzucać; unieważniać;
zmieniać czyjeś
postanowienie

overrun [,ouwer'ran] v.
najechać; zalewać;
przelewać; s. przekraczanie
ceny umówionej

overseas ['ouwer'si:z] adv. za
morzem; do krajów
zamorskich; adj. zamorski

oversee ['ouwer'si:] v.
dozorować; doglądać

overseer ['ouwer'si:er] s.
nadzorca

overshadow ['ouwer'szaedou] v.
przyćmiewać; zaćmiewać

oversight ['ouwersajt] s.
przeoczenie

oversleep ['ouwer'sli:p] v.
zaspać; przespać

over-strain ['ouwer'strejn] v.
przemęczać s. przeciążenie;
przemęczenie

overtake ['ouwer'tejk] v.
doganiać przeganiać;
zaskoczyć

overthrow ['ouwer'srou] v.
przywrócić; obalić; pobić; s.
obalenie

overtime ['ouwertajm] s. godziny
nadliczbowe; adv.
nadprogramowo; adj.
nadprogramowy; v.
prześwietlić;
przeeksponować

overtone ['ouwertoun] s.
niedomówienie; sugestia;
akcent; główna nuta

overture ['ouwer,tjuer] s.
rozpoczęcie rokowań;
propozycja; uwertura; v.
proponować

overturn [,ouwer'te:rn] v.
wywracać; obalać; s.
przewracanie; przewrót;
podbój

overweight [,ouwer'łejt] s.
nadwaga; dodatkowa waga;
otyłość; adj. ponad normalną
wagę

overwhelm [,ouwer'hłelm] v.
przygniatać przywalać;
zalewać; rujnować; ogarniać

overwork ['ouwer'łe:rk] v.
przepracowywać się;
przeciążać pracą; zmuszać
do za ciężkiej pracy;
przemęczać się; s. nadmierna
praca

ovulate ['ouwjulejt] v.
jajeczkować; wytwarzać jaja

owe [oł] v. być winnym;
zawdzięczać

owing ['ołyng] adj. dłużny;
należny; prep. z powodu;
skutkiem

owing to ['ołyng,tu] prep.
ponieważ

owl [aul] s. sowa

own [ołn] v. mieć; posiadać;
przyznawać (się); adj.

własny; rodzony

owner ['ołner] s. właściciel

ownership ['ołnerszyp] s.
własność; posiadanie

ox [oks] s. wół; pl. oxen

oxen ['oksen] pl.woły; zob. ox

oxide ['oksajd] s. tlenek

oxidation [oksy'dejszyn] s.
utlenianie; oksydacja

oxidize [oksydajz] v. utleniać

oxygen [oksydżen] s. tlen

oyster ['ojster] s. ostryga

ozone ['ouzoun] s. ozon

P

p [pi:] szesnasta litera
angielskiego alfabetu

pa [pa:] s. tato

pace [pejs] s. krok; chód; v.
kroczyć; mierzyć krokami;
ustalać rytm kroku; ćwiczyć
krok (np. konia); przebywać
(drogą); chodzić (tam i z
powrotem)

pacer ['pejser] s. regulator rytmu
(serca, kroku etc.)

pacific [pe'syfyk] adj. spokojny;
pokojowy

pacify ['paesyfaj] v. uspakajać;
zaspokajać

pack [paek] s. pakunek; tłumok;
tobół; stek; sfora; okład; kupa;
v. pakować; opakować;
owijać; stłoczyć; napychać;
objuczyć; zbierać w stado

pack up ['paek,ap] v. spakować

package ['paekydż] s. pakunek;
paczka

package deal ['paekydż'di:l] s.
przyjęcie złożonej propozycji
bez zmian

packer ['paeker] s. pakier;
przedsiębiorca od pakowania
artykułów spożywczych;
maszyna do pakowania

packet ['paekyt] s. pakiet; v.
zawijać

packing ['paekyŋg] s.
pakowanie; opakowanie;
uszczelka; okładzina; tampon
packthread ['paektred] s. szpagat
pact [paekt] s. pakt; układ
pad [paed] s. wyściółka; notes;
blok (papieru); bibularz; łapa;
podkładka; v. wyściełać;
wywoływać; rozdymać
padding ['paedyŋg] s. obicie;
wyściółka; podbicie;
podszycie; rozwadnianie
tekstu
paddle ['paedl] s. wiosełko
kajakowe; v. wiosłować
paddock ['paedek] s. wybieg
(koński)
padlock ['paedlok] s. kłódka; v.
zamykać na kłódkę
pagan ['pejgen] s. poganin; adj.
pogański
page [pejdż] s. stronica; karta;
paź; goniec
pageant ['paedżent] s. widowisko (np. historyczne)
paid [pejd] adj. zapłacony;
płatny; zob. pay
pail [pejl] s. wiadro
pain [pejn] s. ból; cierpienie;
trud; starania; v. zadawać
ból; boleć; dolegać
painful ['pejnful] adj. bolesny;
przykry
painless [pejnlys] adj. bezbolesny
paint [pejnt] s. farba; szminka; v.
malować
paintbrush ['pejntbrasz] s. pędzel
painter ['pejnter] s. malarz
painting ['pejntyŋg] s.
malarstwo; obraz
pair [peer] s. para; parka; stadło;
v. dobierać do pary;
stanowić parę
pajamas [pe'dża:mez] pl. piżama
pal [pael] s. kumpel; druh;
przyjaciel
palace ['paelys] s. pałac
palate ['paelyt] s. podniebienie
pale [pejl] s. pal; granica; adj.
blady; v. otaczać palami;
blednąć; spowodować
blednięcie
pallor ['paeler] s. bladość

palm [pa:m] s. palma; dłoń;
piędź; v. ukrywać w dłoni;
dotykać dłonią
palpitation [,paelpy'tejszyn] s.
palpitacja; mocne bicie serca;
kołatanie serca; drżenie;
dygotanie
pamper ['paemper] v.
rozpieszczać; przekarmiać;
zbyt pobłażać
pamphlet ['paemflyt] s. broszura
natury polemicznej na tematy
bieżące, kontrowersyjne etc.
pan [paen] s. patelnia; rondel;
rynka; szalka; panewka; gęba;
kra; v. gotować na patelni;
udawać się; krytykować
pancake ['paen,kejk] s.
naleśnik; adj. płaski
pane [paen] s. szyba; krata;
ścianka; płaszczyzna
panel ['paenl] s. tafla; otoczyna;
płyta; wstawka; tablica
(rozdzielcza); komitet; lista
(przysięgłych, lekarzy etc.);
czaprak
pang [paeŋg] s. ostry ból; męka;
wyrzuty (sumienia etc.)
panhandler [,paen'haendler] s.
kwestarz; ksiądz z tacą
panic ['paenyk] s. panika;
popłoch; v. wpaść w panikę;
wywoływać panikę; poddać
się panice
pan-Slavism ['paen'sla:wyzem] s.
panslawizm
pansy ['paensy] s. bratek
pant [paent] s. zadyszka; v.
sapać; dyszeć
panther ['paenter] s. pantera
panties ['paentyz] pl. majtki
(damskie)
pantry ['paentry] s. spiżarnia
pants [paents] pl. spodnie;
kalesony
panty hose ['paenty'houz] s.
rajstopy; pończochy z
majtkami
pap [paep] s. papka; bzdury;
sutka; brodawka piersiowa
papa ['pa:pe] s. papa; tata
paper ['pejper] s. papier; gazeta;
tapeta; rozprawa naukowa;

papierowe pieniądze; adj.
papierowy; rzekomy; v.
zawinąć w papier;
tapetować

paper-back ['pejper,baekt] adj. w
papierowej okładce; s.
kieszonkowe wydanie książki

paper bag ['pejper,baeg] s. torba
papierowa

paper-hanger ['pejper,haenger] s.
tapeciarz

paper-hangings ['pejper
,haengyngs] pl. tapety

paper money ['pejper'many] s.
papierowe pieniądze

paperweight ['pejper,łejt] s.
przycisk

par [pa:r] s. stan równości;
norma

parable ['paerebl] s.
przypowieść

parachute ['paere,szu:t] s.
spadochron

parachutist ['paere,szu:tyst] s.
spadochroniarz

parade [pe'rejd] s. parada;
pochód; rewia; defilada; v.
popisywać się; obnosić się
(z czymś)

paradise ['paere,dajs] s. raj; adj.
rajski

paragraph ['paere,gra:f] s. ustęp;
odnośnik; notatka; v. dzielić
na ustępy; pisać notatkę

parallel ['paere,lel] adj.
równoległy; odpowiedni
(czemuś); s. równoległa;
równoleżnik; porównanie; v.
być równoległym; kłaść
równolegle; zestawiać;
znaleźć odpowiednik

paralyze ['paere,lajz] v.
paraliżować; porażać

paralysis [pe'raelysys] s. paraliż

paramount ['paere,maunt] adj.
główny; najważniejszy;
kapitalny; najwyższy

parasite ['paere,sajt] s. pasożyt

parcel ['pa:rsl] s. paczka; działka;
v. dzielić; pakować w paczki

parch ['pa:rcz] v. wysuszać
(się); prażyć; cierpieć z
pragnienia

parchment ['pa:rczment] s.
pergamin

pardon ['pa:rdn] s. ułaskawienie;
przebaczenie; v. przebaczać;
darować; ułaskawiać

pardon me ['pa:rdn,mi:] exp.:
przepraszam

pardonable ['pa:rdnebl] adj.
wybaczalny

pare [peer] v. obcinać; obierać;
obskrobać

parent ['peerent] s. ojciec;
matka; rodziciel; rodzicielka

parental [pe'rentl] adj.
rodzicielski

parenthesis [pe'rentysys] s.
nawias

parentheses [pe'renty,si:s] pl.
nawiasy

parings ['peerynz] pl. łupiny;
obrzynki

parish ['paerysz] s. parafia

parishioner [pe'ryszener] s.
parafianin

park [pa:rk] s. park; postój
samochodów; v. parkować

parking ['pa:rkyng] s. postój
samochodów; parkowanie

parking garage ['pa:rkyng
'gaera:ż] s. garaż parkingowy

parking lot ['pa:rkyn,lot] s. plac
parkingowy

parking meter ['pa:rkyn'mi:ter] s.
licznik do płacenia za parking
(na ograniczony czas)

parking ticket ['pa:rkyn'tykyt] s.
mandat karny za złe
parkowanie lub za
niezapłacenie

parkway ['pa:rkłej] s.
czteroliniowa szosa
przedzielona roślinnością

parliament ['pa:rlyment] s.
parlament

parliamentary [,pa:rly'mentery]
adj. parlamentarny

parlor ['pa:rler] s. salon; sala;
pokój (przyjęć)

parquet ['pa:rkej] s. parkiet; v.
wyłożyć parkietem

parrot ['paeret] s. papuga; v.
powtarzać jak papuga

parsley ['pa:rsly] s. pietruszka; a.

pietruszkowy
parry ['paery] v. parować;
odpierać; s. odparcie
parson ['pa:rsn] s. proboszcz
parsonage ['pa:rsnydż] s.
plebania
part [pa:rt] s. część; ustęp;
udział; rola; strona; przedział
(włosów); v. rozchodzić (się);
rozdzielać; dzielić; pękać;
robić (przedział); wyjeżdżać;
adj. mniejszy niż całość
partake [pa:r'tejk] v. brać udział;
dzielić coś z kimś; zob. take
partaken [pa:r'tejkn] v. zob.
partake
partial ['pa:rszel] adj. stronniczy;
częściowy; mający słabość
do ...; niepełny
partiality [,pa:rszy'aelyty] s.
stronniczość; upodobanie
participant [pa:r'tysypent] s.
uczestnik; adj. uczestniczący
participate [pa:r'tysypejt] v.
brać udział
particle ['pa:rtykl] s. cząstka;
odrobina; partykuła
particular [per'tykjuler] adj.
szczególny; szczegółowy;
specjalny; prywatny;
grymaśny; dokładny;
uważny; dziwny;
niezwyczajny; ostrożny; s.
szczegół; fakt
particularity [per,tykju'laeryty] s.
osobliwość;
szczegółowość;
drobiazgowość;
wybredność
particularly [per,tykju'laerly] adv.
osobliwie; szczególnie
particulars [per'tykjulers] s. dane
osobiste
parting ['pa:rtyng] s. przedziałek
(włosów); rozstanie; rozdział;
pożegnanie; rozdroże; zgon
partition [pa:r'tyszyn] s. podział;
rozbiór; rozdział; v. dzielić;
przegradzać
partition off [pa:rtyszyn,of] v.
oddzielać
partly ['pa:rtly] adv. częściowo;
po części; poniekąd

partner ['pa:rtner] s. wspólnik
partnership ['pa:rtnerszyp] s.
spółka
partook [pa:r'tuk] v. zob. partake
partridge ['pa:trydż] s.
kuropatwa
part-time ['pa:rt,tajm] adv. na
niepełnym etacie; na
niepełnym czasie; adj.
niepełnoetatowy
party ['pa:rty] s. partia; przyjęcie
towarzyskie; towarzystwo;
grupa; strona; uczestnik;
osobnik
pass [pa:s] s. przełęcz; odnoga
rzeki; przepustka; wypad;
bilet; umizg; sztuczka; v.
przechodzić; mijać; pomijać;
zdać; przekazać; wymijać;
wyprzedzać; przeprowadzić;
przewyższać; spędzać;
puszczać w obieg; podawać;
odchodzić; umierać; dziać
się; krążyć
pass away ['pa:se,łej] v.
odchodzić; umierać
pass by ['pa:s,baj] v. mijać;
pomijać
pass for ['pa:s,fo:r] v. udawać
(kogoś)
pass out ['pa:s,aut] v. zemdleć;
umrzeć; wyjść
pass round ['pa:s,raund] v.
podawać w koło (np.
gościom)
pass through ['pa:s,tru] v.
przechodzić (przez, na
wskroś)
passable ['paesebl] adj. nadający
się do przebycia; (stopień)
dostateczny; znośny
passage ['paesydż] s. przejście;
przejazd; przeprawa; przelot;
upływ; korytarz; urywek
tekstu
passenger ['paesyndżer] s.
pasażer; pasażerka
passer-by ['pa:ser'baj] s.
przechodzień
passion ['paeszyn] s.
namiętność; pasja; Męka
Pańska; stan bierny
passionate ['paeszenyt] adj.

namiętny; porywczy;
zapalczywy; żarliwy; ognisty
passive ['paesyw] adj. bierny; s.
strona bierna
passport ['pa:s,po:rt] s. paszport
password ['pa:s,ło:rd] s. hasło
past [pa:st] adj. przeszły;
miniony; ubiegły; prep. za;
obok; po; przed; adv. obok; s.
przeszłość; czas przeszły
paste [pejst] s. pasta; ciasto; klej
mączny; klajster; masa;
makaron; uderzenie (slang); v.
przylecieć; oblepiać; obić
(kogoś)
pasteboard ['pejst,bo:rd] s.
karton; tektura; adj.
tekturowy; kartonowy; lichy
pastime ['pa:s,tajm] s. rozrywka
(po pracy etc.)
pastry ['pejstry] s. wyroby
cukiernicze; ciastka
pastry shop ['pejstry szop] s.
sklep wyrobów cukierniczych
past tense ['pa:st tens] s. czas
przeszły (gram.)
pasture ['pa:sczer] s. pastwisko
pat [paet] s. głaskanie; klepanie;
krążek (np. masła); v.
pogłaskać; poklepać;
pochwalić (kogoś); adv.
trafnie; w sam raz; adj. trafny;
biegły; na czasie; zupełnie
właściwy
patch [paecz] s. łata; plama;
skrawek; półko; zagon;
grządka; klapka (na oko);
przepaska; v. łatać; załatać;
szyć z łat; sztukować;
naprawić; skleić; załagodzić
patch pocket ['paecz,pokyt] s.
naszywana kieszeń
patchwork ['paecz,łe:rk] s.
łatanina; szachownica
pate [pejt] s. slang: głowa; łeb;
pała; szczyt głowy
patent ['paetnt] s. patent; v.
opatentować; a.
patentowany; opatentowany;
oczywisty
patent ['pejtnt] adj. jasny;
otwarty; oczywisty; chroniony
patentem

patent-leather ['paetnt'ledzer] s.
skóra lakierowana
paternal [pe'te:rnl] adj. ojcowski;
po ojcu
paternity [pe'te:rnyty] s.
ojcostwo; pochodzenie po
ojcu; autorstwo (książki,
planu etc.)
path [pa:s] s. ścieżka; tor;
droga ruchu; zob. paths
pathetic [pe'tetyk] adj. żałosny;
smutny; uczuciowy;
wzruszający; rozrzewniający
paths [pa:sz] pl. ścieżki; tory;
drogi ruchu
patience ['pejszens] s.
cierpliwość; pasjans
patient ['pejszent] adj. cierpliwy;
wytrwały; s. pacjent;
pacjentka; chory; chora
patio ['pa:ti:o] s. ogródek
wewnętrzny; taras
patriarch ['pejtry,a:rk] s.
patriarcha
patriot ['pejtryet] s. patriota
patriotic [,paetry'otyk] adj.
patriotyczny
patriotism ['paetrye,tyzem] s.
patriotyzm
patrol [pe'troul] v. patrolować;
s. patrolowanie; patrol
patrolman [pe'troulmen] s.
policjant (drogowy USA)
patron ['pejtren] s. klient;
opiekun; patron
patronage ['paetrenydż] s.
opieka; poparcie; klientela;
rozdawanie posad;
protekcjonalność; przywileje;
posady
patronize ['paetre,najz] v.
popierać; protegować;
traktować protekcjonalnie
patsy ['paecy] s. oferma przez
wszystkich zawsze
nadużywana
patter ['paeta] s. stukot; trajkot;
trajkotanie; gwara; klepanie;
szybka recytacja; żargon; v.
stukać; bębnić; trajkotać;
klepać (np. pacierze);
odklepywać; kłapać; gadać
pattern ['paetern] s. próbka;

wzór; układ; materiał na
suknię lub ubranie (USA);
zespół; cechy
charakterystyczne; ślady kul
(na tarczy); v. wzorować;
modelować; ozdabiać
wzorami

paunch ['pa:ncz] s. (duży)
brzuch; żołądek krowy

paunchy ['pa:nczy] adj.
brzuchaty; z wydatnym
brzuchem

pause [po:z] s. przerwa; pauza;
v. robić przerwę; wahać się

pave [pejw] v. brukować;
torować drogę

pavement ['pejwment] s. bruk;
posadzka; materiał do
brukowania

pavement-cafe ['pejwment
'kaefej] s. kawiarnia za
stolikami na chodniku

paw [po:] s. łapa; (slang) tatuś;
v. uderzać łapą lub kopytem;
miętosić w łapach; macać
(poufale)

pawn [po:n] s. zastaw; fant;
pionek; v. zastawiać; dawać
w zastaw

pawnbroker ['po:n,brouker] s.
lichwiarz pożyczający pod
zastaw; właściciel lombardu

pawnshop ['po:n-szop] s.
lombard; sklep zastawniczy

pay; paid; paid [pej; peid; peid]

pay [pej] v. płacić; zapłacić;
wynagradzać; udzielać
(uwagi); dawać (dochód);
opłacać (się); s. płaca;
zapłata; pobory;
wynagrodzenie; adj. płatny
(np. automat telefoniczny);
opłacalny

pay back ['pej baek] v. zwrócić
dług; odpłacać

payday ['pej dej] s. dzień
wypłaty

pay down ['pej dałn] v. dawać
zadatek; płacić pierwszą ratę
gotówką

pay for ['pej,fo:r] v. płacić (za
coś)

pay in ['pej,yn] v. wpłacać

pay off ['pej,of] v. spłacać

pay out ['pej,aut] v.
wydatkować; wypuszczać
linę (na statku); wypłacać;
płacić

pay up ['pej,ap] v. wyrównywać
(dług); zapłacić

payable ['pejebl] adj. płatny;
dochodowy; opłacający się

payee ['pej'i:] s. odbiorca
płatności

payer ['pejer] s. płatnik

payment ['pejment] s.
płatność; wypłata; zapłata

pea [pi:] s. groch; ziarnko grochu

peace [pi:s] s. pokój; pojednanie;
spokój

peaceful ['pi:sful] adj. spokojny;
pokojowy

peach [pi:cz] s. brzoskwinia;
wspaniała rzecz, dziewczyna,
człowiek; v. (slang) sypać;
donosić (na kogoś)

peacock ['pi:,kok] s. paw; v.
pysznić się jak paw; chodzić
jak paw; paradować

peak [pi:k] s. (ostry) szczyt;
wierzchołek; daszek (u
czapki); szpic; garb (krzywej)

peak hour ['pi:k'auer] s. godzina
szczytu ruchu

peal [pi:l] s. huk; łoskot; bicie w
dzwony; huczny śmiech;
zespół dzwonów; v. huczeć;
bić w dzwony; grać (coś)
hucznie

peanut ['pi:nat] s. orzeszek
ziemny; drobnostka; a.
drobny; prowincjonalny

pear [peer] s. gruszka

pearl [pe:rl] s. perła

peasant ['pezent] s. chłop;
wieśniak; adj. chłopski

peat [pi:t] s. torf

peat bog ['pi:t'bog] s. torfowisko

pebble ['pebl] s. kamyk; otoczak;
v. granulować; obrzucać
kamykami

peck [pek] v. dziobać; wcinać
(jedzenie); dziobnąć;
cmoknąć (męża); stukać;
wydziobać; dłubać;
odziobać; s. dziobnięcie;

cmok; ślad dziobania
peculiar [py'kju:ljer] adj.
szczególny; dziwny; osobliwy;
charakterystyczny; dziwaczny
peculiarity [py'kju:li'aeryty] s.
właściwość; cecha;
osobliwość; dziwaczność
pedal ['pedl] s. pedał; nuta
pedałowa; v. pedałować;
naciskać pedał; ['pi:dl] adj.
pedałowy; nożny
peddle ['pedl] v. sprzedawać po
domach; być domokrążcą;
wydzielać po trochu
peddler ['pedler] s. domokrążcą
pedestal ['pedystl] s. piedestał;
podstawa; v. stawiać na
piedestał
pedestrian [py'destrjen] adj.
pieszy; przyziemny;
prozaiczny; s. piechur; pieszy
człowiek
pedestrian crossing [py'destrjen
'krosyng] s. przejście dla
pieszych; zebra; pasy
pedigree ['pedygri:] s. rodowód;
drzewo genealogiczne
peddlar ['pedler] s. przekupień;
handlarz
peek ['pi:k] v. podglądać
peel [pi:l] s. skóra; skórka; łupa;
v. obierać; zdzierać;
łuszczyć się; (slang)
rozbierać (się)
peep [pi:p] v. zerkać;
podglądać; wynurzać (się);
wychodzić niepostrzeżenie
peeping Tom ['pi:pyng,tom] s.
podglądający natręt
peer [pier] s. równy (komuś)
stanem, pochodzeniem etc.
peerless ['pierlys] adj.
niezrównany
peevish ['pi:wysz] adj. drażliwy;
zły; gniewny; zirytowany
peg [peg] s. czop; kołek;
zatyczka; szpunt; v.
zakołkować; przymocować
kołkami
pelican ['pelyken] s. pelikan
pelt [pelt] s. futro; kanonada;
grzmocenie; pośpiech; v.
ostrzeliwać; obrzucać;

obsypywać gradem; rzucać
zniewagi; obsypywać
zniewagami; walić
pelvis ['pelwys] s. miednica; a.
miedniczny
pen [pen] s. pióro; kojec;
ogrodzenie; schron; (slang)
więzienie; v. pisać; układać
list; zamykać w ogrodzeniu
penal ['pi:nl] adj. karny; karalny
penalty ['penlty] s. kara
penalty kick ['penlty,kik] s. karny
strzał (do bramki)
penance ['penens] s. pokuta
pence [pens] pl. grosze; zob.
penny
pencil ['pensl] s. ołówek; v.
rysować; pisać
pencil sharpener ['pensl'sza:rp-
ner] s. strugaczka do ołówka
pendant ['pendent] s. wisiorek;
proporzec; adj. wiszący;
zwisający; nierozstrzygnięty;
toczący się; do
rozstrzygnięcia
pending ['pendyng] adj.
niezałatwiony; będący w toku;
wiszący; prep. aż do; podczas
penetrate ['peny,trejt] v.
przenikać; przepajać;
przedostawać się przez;
wtargnąć; zanurzyć
penetration [,peny'trejszyn] s.
penetracja; przenikanie;
przenikliwość
pen friend ['penfrend] s. znajomy
z listów
penguin ['pengłyn] s. pingwin
penholder ['pen,houlder] s.
piórnik; obsadka; stojak na
pióro
penicillin [,peny'sylyn] s.
penicylina
peninsula [py'nynsjule] s.
półwysep
penitent ['penytent] s. żałujący
grzesznik; pokutnik; adj.
żałujący; skruszony
penitentiary [,peny'tenszery] s.
więzienie; adj. karany
więzieniem; poprawczy
penknife ['pen,najf] s. scyzoryk
pennant ['penent] s. proporzec

penniless ['penylys] adj. w
nędzy; bez grosza
penny ['peny] s. cent; grosz; pl.
pennies ['penyz]; Br. pl. pence
[pens]
penny-worth ['penyłe:rs̲] s.
wartość centa; exp.: za
centa
pen pal [pen pael] s. znajomy (a)
z listów
pension ['penszyn] s. renta;
emerytura; pensjonat; v.
wyznaczać pensję;
pensjonować
pension off ['penszyn,of] v.
przenosić na emeryturę
pensioner ['penszener] s. emeryt;
emerytka; rencista; rencistka
pensive ['pensyw] adj.
zamyślony
penthouse ['pent,haus] s.
mieszkanie z ogrodem na
szczycie budynku;
przybudówka na dachu
people ['pi:pl] s. ludzie;
ludność; lud; v. zaludniać
pep [pep] s. animusz; werwa;
wigor; adj. ożywiony; wesoły;
dowcipny; dodający animuszu
pep pills ['pep,pyls] pl. pigułki
podniecające
pep up ['pep,ap] v. ożywić;
dodać animuszu
pepper ['peper] s. pieprz;
papryka; v. pieprzyć; kropić;
zasypywać kulami; dać lanie
per [pe:r] prep. przez; za; na;
według; co do; za
pośrednictwem
perceive [per'si:w] v.
uświadamiać sobie; odczuć;
dostrzegać; spostrzegać
percent [per'sent] s. odsetek; od
sta
percentage [per'sentydż] s.
odsetek; procent; od sta
perceptible [per'septebl] adj.
dostrzegalny
perception [per'sepszyn] s.
spostrzeganie; percepcja
perch [pe:rcz] s. okoń; grzęda;
żerdź; prąt; v. siedzieć na
grzędzie; sadzać na grzędzie

percussion [per'kaszyn] s.
uderzenie; zderzenie; bicie
(bębna)
peremptory [per'emptery] adj.
stanowczy; apodyktyczny;
ostateczny; nieodwołalny
perfect ['pe:rfykt] adj.
doskonały; zupełny; v.
udoskonalić; wykończyć
perfect tense ['perfykt'tens] s.
gram. czas przeszły dokonany
perfection [per'fekszyn] s.
doskonałość; szczyt;
wykończenie; udoskonalenie
perforate ['pe:rferejt] v.
przedziurawiać; dziurkować;
przenikać; przebijać się
perform [per'fo:rm] v.
wykonywać; odgrywać;
spełniać; występować
performance [per'fo:rmens] s.
przedstawienie; wyczyn;
wykonanie; spełnienie
performer [per'former] s.
wykonawca
perfume ['pe:rfju:m] s. perfuma;
zapach; [pe'rfju:m] v.
perfumować
perhaps [per'haeps, praeps] adv.
może; przypadkiem
peril ['peryl] s.
niebezpieczeństwo; ryzyko; v.
narazić na
niebezpieczeństwo
perilous ['peryles] adj.
niebezpieczny; ryzykowny
period ['pieried] s. okres; period;
menstruacja; kropka; kres;
pauza; miesiączka; a. stylowy
periodic [,piery'odyk] adj.
okresowy; periodyczny
periodical [,piery'odykel] s.
czasopismo; periodyk; adj.
okresowy; periodyczny
perish ['perysz] v. zgiąć;
niszczyć; nękać; trapić;
gnębić; ginąć (przedwczesną
śmiercią)
perishable ['peryszebl] adj.
zniszczalny; s. łatwo psujący
się towar
perjury ['pe:rdżery] s.
krzywoprzysięstwo; złamanie

obietnicy

perm [pe:rm] s. trwała ondulacja

permanent ['pe:rmenent] adj.
trwały; permanentny

permanent wave ['pe:rmenent
,łejw] s. trwała ondulacja

permeable ['pe:rmjebl] adj.
przepuszczalny; przenikalny

permission [per'myszyn] s.
pozwolenie; zezwolenie

permit [per'myt] s. pisemne
zezwolenie; pozwolenie; v.
pozwalać; zezwalać;
dopuszczać

pernicious [pe:rnyszes] adj.
szkodliwy; zgubny

perpendicular [,pe:rpen'dykjuler]
adj. prostopadły; s.
prostopadła; pion

perpetual [per'petjuel] adj.
wieczny; wieczysty; trwały;
dożywotni

persecute ['pe:rsy,kju:t] v.
prześladować

persecution [,pe:rsy'kju:szyn] s.
prześladowanie

persecutor ['pe:rsy,kju:ter] s.
prześladowca

persevere [,pe:rsy'wier] v.
wytrwać

persist [pe'rsyst] v. obstawać;
wytrwać; upierać się

persistence [per'systens];
persistency [per'systency] s.
wytrwałość; uporczywość;
trwałość

persistent [per'systent] adj.
wytrwały; uporczywy; trwały

person ['pe:rson] s. osoba;
człowiek

personage ['pe:rsonydż] s.
osobistość; ważny człowiek

personal ['pe:rsenel] adj.
osobisty; robiący osobiste
uwagi; s. wiadomość
osobista

personality [,pe:rse'naelyty] s.
osobowość;
powierzchowność; postawa;
indywidualność; pl.
wycieczki (uwagi) osobiste

personify [pe:r'sony,faj] v.
uosabiać; personifikować

personnel [,pe:rse'nel] s.
personel

personnel manager [,pe:rse'nel
'maenydżer] s. kierownik
oddziału personalnego;
personalny

perspiration [,pe:rspy'rejszyn] s.
pocenie się; pot

perspire [,pe:r'spajer] v. pocić
się; wypacać się

persuade [pe:r'słejd] v.
przekonywać; namawiać

persuasion [pe:r'słejżyn] s.
perswazja; przekonywanie;
namawianie; przekonanie;
wyznanie; wierzenie

persuasive [pe:r'słejsyw] adj.
przekonywujący; s. motyw;
pobudka (do czegoś)

pert [pe:rt] adj. śmiały;
arogancki; (slang) żwawy

pertain [per'tejn] v. należeć do
czegoś; być właściwym
czemuś; odnosić się;
wchodzić w zakres

pertinent ['pe:rtynent] adj.
stosowny; trafny; słuszny;
odnoszący się do czegoś lub
kogoś

perusal [pe'ru:zal] s.
przestudiowanie; dokładne
przeczytanie

peruse [pe'ru:z] v. czytać
uważnie; studiować (np.
twarz)

pervade [per'wejd] v. przenikać;
owładnąć; ogarniać; szerzyć
się

perverse [per'we:rs] adj.
przewrotny; przekorny;
wyuzdany

pesky ['pesky] adj. (slang)
dokuczliwy; natrętny; cholerny

pessimism ['pesy,myzem] s.
pesymizm; spodziewanie się
najgorszego

pest [pest] s. plaga; zaraza

pet [pet] s. faworyt; ulubieniec
(np. pies); adj. ulubiony; v.
(slang) pieścić; być w złym
nastroju; gniewać się;
migdalić; wypieścić

petal ['petl] s. płatek

petition [py'tyszyn] s. petycja;
    prośba; podanie; v. prosić;
    wnosić podanie
petrify ['petry,faj] v. zamieniać
    (się) w kamień; powodować
    kostnienie
petroleum [py'trouljem] s. ropa
    naftowa; olej skalny
pet shop ['petszop] s. sklep
    zwierzątek pokojowych
petticoat ['petykout] s. halka;
    spódniczka; kobieta; adj.
    kobiecy
petty ['pety] adj. drobny
petty cash [,pety'kaesz] s.
    gotówka podręczna
pew [pju:] s. ławka (kościelna)
pewter ['pju:ter] s. stop cyny z
    ołowiem; naczynie cynowe
pharmacy ['fa:rmesy] s. apteka;
    farmacja
phase [fejz] s. faza (np.
    rozwojowa); aspekt
pheasant ['feznt] s. bażant
philanthropist [fy'laentrepyst] s.
    filantrop; filantropka
philatelist [fy'laetelyst] s.
    filatelist; filatelistka
philologist [fy'loledżyst] s.
    filolog; lingwista;
    językoznawca
philology [fy'loledży] s. filologia;
    językoznawstwo; lingwistyka
philosopher [fy'losefer] s. filozof
philosophize [fy'lose,fajz] v.
    filozofować
philosophy [fy'losefy] s. filozofia
phlegm [flem] s. flegma; śluz;
    plwocina; spokój
phone [foun] s. telefon (slang)
phonetic [fou'netyk] adj.
    fonetyczny
phony [founy] adj. fałszywy;
    udawany; s. rzecz fałszywa,
    podrabiana; ktoś udający
photo ['foutou] s. fotka;
    fotografia; v. fotografować
photograph ['foute,gra:f] s.
    fotografia; zdjęcie; v.
    fotografować
photographer [fe'togrefer] s.
    fotograf; fotografik
photography [fe'tegrefy] s.

fotografia; fotografika
phrase [frejz] s. wyrażenie;
    zwrot; v. wyrażać;
    wypowiadać wyrażeniami lub
    słowami
physical ['fyzykel] adj. fizyczny;
    cielesny
physician ['fyzyszyn] s. lekarz
physicist ['fyzysyst] s. fizyk
physics ['fyzyks] s. fizyka
physique [fy'zi:k] s. budowa
    ciała; rozwój; wygląd fizyczny;
    kondycja; siła muskularna
piano [py'aenou] s. fortepian;
    pianino
pick [pyk] v. wybierać;
    dorabiać; kopać;
    krytykować; dłubać;
    obierać; zbierać; usuwać;
    oskubać; wydziobać;
    kraść; okraść; s. kilof;
    dłuto; wybór; czółenko; nitka
pick-off ['pyk,of] v. zedrzeć;
    wystrzelać pojedynczo
    (wrogów)
pick out ['pyk,aut] v. wybrać;
    dobrać; doszukiwać się
pick over ['pyk,ouwer] v.
    przebierać; wybrać co lepsze
pick up ['pyk,ap] v. podnosić;
    brać; nauczyć się; zarabiać;
    odnaleźć; odzyskać;
    przyjść do siebie; poznać
    się; s. adapter; lekka
    ciężarówka
picket ['pykyt] s. palik; kół;
    pikieta; posterunek; v.
    rozstawiać pikiety strajkowe;
    służyć jako pikieta;
    zabezpieczać pikietami
pickle ['pykel] s. kiszony ogórek;
    marynata; kłopot; łobuz; v.
    marynować; kisić;
    wytrawiać
pickpocket ['pyk,pokyt] s.
    złodziej kieszonkowy;
    kieszonkowiec
picnic ['pyknyk] s. piknik;
    majówka; v. brać udział w
    pikniku, majówce, posiłku na
    dworze
pictorial [pyk'to:rjel] adj.
    obrazowy; ilustrowany;

malowniczy; malarski; s.
(czaso)pismo ilustrowane;
ilustracja (trzywymiarowa)
techniczna
picture ['pykczer] s. obraz; film;
rysunek; rycina; portret;
widok; v. odmalowywać;
przedstawiać; opisywać;
wyobrażać sobie; dawać
obraz czegoś
picturesque [,pykcze'resk] adj.
malowniczy; żywy i przyjemny
pie [paj] s. placek; szarlotka;
pasztet; paszstecik; (ptak)
sroka
piece [pi:s] s. kawałek; część;
sztuka; moneta; utwór; v.
łączyć; zeszyć; łatać;
naprawiać
piecework ['pi:s,łe:rk] s. robota
na akord
pier [pier] s. pomost ładunkowy;
molo; falochron; filar (np.
mostu)
pierce [piers] v. przewiercać;
wnikać; przedziurawiać;
przebijać; przedostawać się
piercing [piersyng] adj.
przeszywający; ostry;
rozdzierający; przenikający
piety ['pajety] s. pobożność
pig [pyg] s. wieprz;
świnia;prosię; v. prosić się
pigeon ['pydżyn] s. gołąb; v.
oszukiwać
pigeon-hole ['pydżyn,houl] s.
przegródka; v. umieszczać w
przegródkach
pigheaded ['pyg'hedyd] adj.
uparty; głupi
pigskin ['pyg,skyn] s. świńska
skóra; (slang) piłka; siodło
pigtail ['pyg,tejl] s. warkocz
pike [pajk] s. rogatka; dzida;
pika; szpic; ostrze; szczupak
pile [pail] s. stos; sterta; kupa;
pal; słup; puszek; meszek;
włos; v. układać w stos;
gromadzić na kupę; stawiać
w kozły
pile up ['pail,ap] v. walić na
kupę; s. zwalenie na kupę
piles [pailz] pl. hemoroidy

pilfer ['pylfer] v. ukraść;
zwędzić; buchnąć
pilgrim ['pylgrym] s. pielgrzym
pilgrimage ['pylgrymydż] s.
pielgrzymka
pill [pyl] s. pigułka; tabletka
pillar ['pyler] s. filar; słup;
podpora
pillbox ['pylboks] s. bunkier;
pudełeczko na pigułki;
kapelusz
pillion ['pyljen] s. tylne siodełko
(np. na motocyklu)
pillory ['pylery] s. pręgierz; v.
stawiać pod pręgierzem
pillow ['pylou] s. zagłówek;
jasiek; poduszka; podkładka;
v. spoczywać; opierać (np.
głowę)
pillowcase ['pylou,kejs] s.
poszewka
pillow slip ['pylou,slyp] s.
poszewka
pilot ['pajlet] s. pilot; sternik; v.
pilotować; sterować;
przeprowadzić
pimp [pymp] s. stręczycielka;
alfons; v. stręczyć
pimple ['pympl] s. pryszcz;
wągier
pin [pyn] s. szpilka; sztyft;
sworzeń; kołek; kręgiel; v.
przyszpilić; przymocować
pincers ['pynserz] pl. kleszcze;
obcęgi
pinch [pyncz] v. szczypać;
gnieść; cisnąć; przycisnąć;
przyskrzynić; krępować;
dokuczać; doskwierać;
podważać łomem; s.
uszczypnięcie; szczypta; łom;
(slang) aresztowanie; obława;
kradzież
pinch bar ['pyncz ba:r] s. łom (ze
stopką)
pine [pajn] s. sosna; ananas; v.
usychać
pineapple ['pajnaepl] s. ananas
pinion ['pynjen] s. kółko zębate;
wrzeciono zębate; wał
przekładni; koniec pióra; lotka;
v. podcinać (skrzydła);
pętać; przywiązywać

pink [pynk] s. różowy kolor;
radykał (komunizujący);
goździk; v. urazić do
żywego; przekłuwać

pinnacle ['pynekl] s. szczyt;
wieżyczka; v. zwieńczać;
postawić na szczycie;
stanowić szczyt

pint [pajnt] s. półkwarcie; 0.47
litra; 1/8 galona

pioneer [,paje'nier] s. pionier;
saper; v. torować drogę

pious [pajes] adj. pobożny

pip [pyp] s. pestka; oczko;
gwiazdka; ziarnko; punkcik;
pypeć; dźwięk gwizdka; v.
piszczeć; wykluwać się;
pobić; trafić; postrzelić

pipe [pajp] s. rura; rurka;
przewód; piszczałka; (slang)
łatwizna; drobiazg; v.
doprowadzać rurami;
włączyć; połączyć;
prowadzić dźwiękiem fujarki;
grać na fujarce; grać na
kobzie; gwizdać; piszczeć

pipeline ['pajp,lajn] s. rurociąg;
(slang) informator; v.
przesyłać rurociągiem

piper [pajper] s. kobziarz

pipes [pajps] s. kobza

pirate [pajeryt] s. korsarz; pirat;
statek piracki; maruder; v.
grabić; uprawiać korsarstwo;
wydawać bezprawnie
(książki)

piss [pys] v. szczać (wulg.) s.
szczyny (wulg.)

piss off [pys'of] v. wkurzyć;
irytować (wulg.)

pistol ['pystl] s. pistolet

piston ['pysten] s. tłok

pit [pyt] s. dół; jama; kopalnia;
pestka; v. puszczać do walki;
robić dołki; wkładać do dołu;
wyjmować pestki

piston-stroke ['pysten,strouk] s.
suw tłoka

pitch [pycz] v. rozbijać (obóz);
umieszczać; rzucać;
ustawiać; chwiać się;
upaść ciężko; kołysać (na
fali); przechylać; wybierać;

ostro pracować; rzucać się
na ...; smołować; s. stopień;
najwyższy punkt; wzniesienie;
wzdłużne kołysanie statku;
spadek dachu; odstęp między
(falami, zębami kół etc.); skok
(uzwojenia, śruby); smoła

pitcher ['pyczer] s. dzban;
rzucający piłką

piteous ['pytjes] adj. żałosny;
nędzny

pitfall ['pytfo:l] s. pułapka;
wilczy dół

pith [pys] s. miękisz; rdzeń;
tężyzna; moc; v. wyjmować
rdzeń; przecinać rdzeń w
celu zabijania bydła (w rzeźni)

pitiable ['pytjebl] s. żałosny;
godny pożałowania

pitiful ['pytyful] adj. litościwy;
żałosny; nędzny

pitiless ['pytylys] adj. bezlitosny

pity ['pyty] s. litość;
współczucie; szkoda; v.
litować się; współczuć;
żałować kogoś

pivot ['pywet] s. czop; oś;
ośrodek; v. obracać się jak
na osi

pivotal ['pywetel] s. adj.
centralny; kardynalny;
kluczowy; decydujący

placard ['plaeka:rd] s. afisz;
plakat; [ple'ka:rd] v. rozlepiać
plakaty

place [plejs] s. miejsce;
miejscowość; plac; ulica;
dom; mieszkanie; zakład;
krzesło; posada; v.
umieszczać; położyć;
ulokować; dać stanowisko;
pokładać; powierzyć;
określać

placid ['plaesyd] adj. łagodny;
spokojny

plagiarism ['plejdżje,ryzem] s.
plagiat; popełnienie plagiatu

plague [plejg] s. plaga; dżuma;
zaraza; v. dręczyć

plaice [plejs] s. płastuga
pospolita

plaid [plaed] s. sukno; pled w
kratę; rysunek w kratę

plain [plejn] adj. wyraźny; prosty; gładki; szczery; płaski; równy; adv. jasno; szczerze; s. równina

plainclothes man ['plejn,kloʒmen] s. tajny policjant

plaintiff ['plejntyf] s. powód (zaskarżający); powódka

plaintive ['plejntyw] adj. żałosny; płaczliwy

plait [plejt] s. plecionka; warkocz; fałda; zakładka; v. pleść; splatać; fałdować

plan [plaen] s. plan; v. planować; zamierzać

plane [plejn] s. płaszczyzna; równina; poziom; samolot; płat (skrzydła); strug; wiórnik; gładzik; platan (owoc); v. ślizgać; ześlizgiwać się; heblować

planet ['plaenyt] s. planeta

plank ['plaenk] s. deska; tarcica; punkt programu (politycznego w USA); v. pokrywać deskami

plank down ['plaenk,dałn] v. wybulić gotówkę

plant ['pla:nt] s. roślina; fabryka; zakład; wtyczka; (slang) oszustwo; włamanie; kant; v. zasadzać; zakładać; umieszczać; pozorować; ukrywać; wtykać; sadzić (rośliny)

plantation [plaen'tejszyn] s. plantacja

planter ['pla:nter] s. plantator; maszyna do sadzenia; skrzynka na kwiaty

plaque [plaek] s. tablica (pamiątkowa); odznaka

plaster ['pla:ster] s. tynk; wyprawa wapienna; przylepiec; v. tynkować; wyprawiać; powlekać; zalepiać; oblepiać

plaster cast ['pla:ster,ka:st] s. odlew gipsowy; opatrunek gipsowy

plaster of Paris ['pla:ster of 'paerys] s. gips

plastic ['plaestyk] s. plastyk; sztuczne tworzywo; adj. plastyczny; giętki

plastics ['plaestyks] s. tworzywa sztuczne

plate [plejt] s. talerz; danie; płyta; taca; tafla; v. platerować; opancerzać

platform ['plaet,fo:rm] s. platforma; podium; trybuna; rampa; program polityczny

platinum ['plaetynem] s. platyna

platter ['plaeter] s. półmisek

plausible ['plo:zebl] adj. pozornie słuszny, prawdziwy, uczciwy; obłudnie przymilny

play [plej] s. gra; zabawa; sztuka; v. grać; bawić się; zagrać; udawać

play back ['plej,baek] v. reprodukować; przegrywać

playboy ['plej,boj] s. lekkoduch

player ['plejer] s. gracz; muzyk; aktor; zawodnik

playful ['plejful] adj. wesoły; żartobliwy; figlarny; filuterny; swawolny; rozbawiony; zabawny; rozbrykany; ożywiony

playground ['plej,graund] s. boisko; park

playhouse ['plej,haus] s. teatr

playmate ['plej,mejt] s. towarzysz zabaw (dziecinnych, intymnych)

play-off ['plejof] s. rozgrywka poremisowa

play off ['plej,of] v. rozgrywać partię poremisową

plaything ['plejtyng] s. zabawka

playwright ['plej,rajt] s. dramaturg

plea [pli:] s. usprawiedliwienie; wywód; apel; prośba

plead [pli:d] v. bronić; błagać; powoływać się

plead guilty ['pli:d'gyłty] v. przyznawać się do winy

pleasant ['plesnt] s. przyjemny; miły; wesoły

please [pli:z] v. podobać się; zadowalać

please! [pli:z] v. proszę

pleased [plizd] adj. zadowolony

pleasing ['pli:zyng] adj.
przyjemny; miły
pleasure ['pleżer] s.
przyjemność; adj.
rozrywkowy
pleat [pli:t] s. fałda; v. plisować
pledge [pledż] v. zobowiązywać
(się); zastawiać; s. zastaw;
gwarancja; przyrzeczenie
plenipotentiary [,plenype
'tenszery] s. pełnomocnik; adj.
pełnomocny
plentiful ['plentyful] adj. obfity;
liczny
plenty ['plenty] s. obfitość;
mnóstwo; adv. zupełnie; aż
nadto; adj. obfity; liczny;
obszerny
pliable ['plajebl] adj. giętki
pliers ['plajerz] pl. szczypce
plight [plajt] s. trudności; stan;
położenie; przyrzeczenie; v.
ręczyć; dawać słowo
plod [plod] v. mozolić się;
ślęczeć; s. harowanie; kucie
plod along ['plod,e'long] v. wlec
się; mozolić się; trudzić się
plot [plot] s. osnowa; fabuła;
spisek; działka; wykres; mapa;
v. knuć; spiskować; nanosić
na mapę; planować; dzielić
plough [plau] s. pług; v. orać
plow [plau] s. pług; v. orać
plowshare ['plau-szeer] s.
lemiesz
pluck [plak] v. wyrwać;
zerwać; szarpnąć
pluck up courage ['plak,ap
'karydż] exp.: zdobyć się na
odwagę
plucky ['plaky] adj. śmiały;
odważny
plug [plag] s. czop; zatyczka;
kurek; reklama; świeca
(silnika); v. zatykać
plug up ['plag,ap] v. zatykać
plum [plam] s. śliwka; rodzynka;
gratka; adv. pionowo
plumage ['plu:mydż] s.
upierzenie
plumb [plam] adj. pionowy;
zupełny; adv. pionowo;
prosto; dokładnie; zupełnie; s.

pion murarski; sonda; v.
pionować; sondować
plumber ['plamer] s. hydraulik
plumbing ['plambyng] s.
instalacja wodociągowo-
ściekowa budynku
plume [plu:m] s. pióro;
pióropusz; v. ozdabiać
piórami; czyścić pióra
plummet ['plamyt] s. pion
murarski; v. spadać pionowo
plump [plamp] adj. pulchny; tęgi;
stanowczy; otwarty; v.
tuczyć; tyć; wypełniać (się);
ciężko upaść; upuścić;
rzucić; popierać w wyborach
masowym głosowaniem; adv.
prosto; nagle; ciężko; s.
upadek
plum pudding ['plam'pudyng] s.
budyń świąteczny
plunder ['plander] s. grabież;
rabunek; łup; v. plądrować;
łupić grabić
plunge [plandż] v. pogrążać
(się); zanurzać (się);
wpadać; spadać; s. skok do
wody; pływalnia
plunk [plank] v. brząkać;
wybulić; ciskać; rzucać;
upaść ciężko; szarpać
(struny); strzelić do kogoś;
s. brząk; adv. z brząkiem;
prościutko; s. sl. dolar
pluperfect ['plu:pe:rfykt] adj.
zaprzeszły; s. czas zaprzeszły;
plusquamperfectum
plural ['pluerel] s. liczba mnoga;
adj. pluralny; mnogi
plus [plas] prep. plus; więcej;
adj. dodatni; dodatkowy; s.
znak plus; dodatek
plush [plasz] s. plusz; adj.
pluszowy; okazały
ply [plaj] v. uprawiać gorliwie;
używać czegoś; zasypywać
(np. pytaniami); kursować po
...; s. warstwa; grubość;
skłonność; pasmo
plywood ['plaj,łud] s. sklejka;
dykta
pneumatic [nju'maetyk] adj.
pneumatyczny

pneumonia [nju'mounje] s.
zapalenie płuc
poach [poucz] v. uprawiać
kłusownictwo; grzęznąć;
rozrabiać; udeptywać;
rozmiękać; gotować jajko na
miękko bez skorupki
poached egg ['pauczt,eg] s. jajko
gotowane na miękko bez
skorupki
poacher ['pouczer] s. kłusownik
pocket ['pokyt] s. kieszeń;
dziura (powietrzna); v.
wkładać do kieszeni
pocketbook ['pokyt,buk] s.
portfel
pocketknife ['pokyt,najf] s.
scyzoryk
pocket money ['pokyt,many] s.
kieszonkowe
pod [pod] s. strączek; kokon;
stadko; obsada; v. rodzić
strączki; łuszczyć; spędzać
razem
poem [pouim] s. wiersz; poemat
poet [pouyt] s. poeta
poetess ['pouytys] s. poetka
poetic [pou'etyk] adj. poetyczny;
poetycki; poetycznie piękny
poetry ['pouytry] s. poezja
pogrom ['pougrem, pe'grom] s.
pogrom
poignant ['pojnent] adj.
przejmujący; uszczypliwy;
cięty; ostry; dotkliwy;
wzruszający
point [point] s. punkt; ostry
koniec; szpiczaste narzędzie;
przylądek; kropka; pointa;
cecha; sedno; sens; v.
zaostrzać; celować;
wskazywać; punktować;
kropkować; dowodzić;
dążyć; pokazywać
point at ['point,aet] v.
wycelować; wskazać
point of view ['point,ow'wju:] s.
punkt widzenia
point out ['point,aut] v.
wskazywać; uwydatnić
point to ['point,tu] v. wskazać
kierunek (kogoś, coś)
pointed ['pointyd] adj. spiczasty;

ostry; cięty; zjadliwy
point-blank ['point'blaenk] adj.
(strzelać) na wprost;
bezpośredni;
bezceremonialny; bez ogródek;
adv. bezpośrednio; z bliska;
wprost; bez ogródek; w
prostej linii; bez zastanowienia
się
pointer ['pointer] s. wskaźnik;
wskazówka
pointless ['poyntlys] adj. tępy;
bez sensu; bez znaczenia
poise [pojz] s. równowaga;
postawa; swoboda; stan
zawieszenia; stan
niepewności; v.
równoważyć; ważyć w
rękach; zawisnąć w
powietrzu; być
przygotowanym do ataku
poison ['pojzn] s. trucizna; v.
truć; zatruć; zakazić
poisonous ['pojznes] adj. trujący;
jadowity; szkodliwy
poke [pouk] v. wtykać;
wpychać; szturchać;
dłubać; sterczeć; wtrącać
się; plątać
poker ['pouker] s. pogrzebacz;
poker
polar ['pouler] adj. polarny
polar bear ['pouler beer] s. biały
niedźwiedź
Pole [poul] s. Polka; Polak
pole [poul] s. biegun; słup;
żerdź; dyszel; maszt
pole jump ['poul dżamp] s. skok
o tyczce
police [pe'li:s] s. policja; v.
rządzić; pilnować;
utrzymywać porządek
policeman [pe'li:smen] s.
policjant
police officer [pe'li:s,ofyser] s.
policjant
police station [pe'li:s,stejszyn] s.
komisariat
policewoman [pe'li:s,łumen] s.
policjantka
policy ['polysy] s. polityka
rządzenia; polityka
postępowania; mądrość

polityczna; polisa
ubezpieczeniowa
polio ['pouljou] s. polimyelitis
[,poliou,maje'lajtis] paraliż
dziecięcy; choroba Haine-
Medina
Polish ['poulysz] adj. polski
(język, obywatel etc.)
polish ['polysz] v. polerować;
gładzić; pochlebiać;
nabierać połysku; s. pasta (do
butów); połysk; politura; polor
polite [pe'lajt] adj. grzeczny;
uprzejmy; kulturalny
politeness [pe'lajtnys] s.
grzeczność; ogłada; kultura;
uprzejmość
political [pe'lytykel] adj.
polityczny
politician [,poly'tyszyn] s.
polityk; politykier
politics ['polytyks] s. polityka
poll [poul] s. głosowanie;
rejestrowanie głosów; wyniki
głosowania; lista; wykaz; lokal
wyborczy; urny wyborcze;
ankieta; głowa; tył głowy;
obuch; v. oddawać głosy;
obliczać głosy; rejestrować;
dostawać głosy; strzyc
włosy; obcinać rogi
pollen ['polyn] s. pył kwiatowy
pollute [pe'lju:t] v.
zanieczyszczać; skazić
pollution [pe'lju:szyn] s.
skażenie; zanieczyszczenie
pomp [pomp] s. pompa
pompous ['pompes] adj.
napuszony; nadęty;
pompatyczny
pond [pond] s. staw
ponder ['ponder] v. rozważać;
rozmyślać; przemyśliwać;
dumać; zastanawiać się;
zadumać się
ponderous ['ponderes] adj.
ciężki; niezgrabny
pontoon [pon'tu:n] s. ponton
pony ['pouny] s. kuc; bryk; v.
odpisywać; ściągać;
zrzynać
poodle ['pu:dl] s. pudel (pies)
pool [pu:l] s. kałuża; sadzawka;

pływalnia; v. składać się
razem; zbierać się w grupę
poor [puer] adj. biedny; ubogi;
lichy; marny; słaby; kiepski;
nędzny; skromny
poorhouse ['puer,haus] s.
przytułek
poorly ['puerly] adv. licho;
kiepsko; skąpo; skromnie;
biednie; ubogo; adj. niezdrów
pop [pop] s. trzask; puknięcie;
strzał; napój musujący;
lombard; tatuś (slang); v.
strzelać; pukać; nagle
wyrzucać; nagle wsadzać;
skakać; wściekać się
popcorn ['pop,ke:rn] s. sucha
prażona kukurydza
pop in ['pop,yn] v. wskoczyć
pop out ['pop,aut] v.
wyskoczyć
pope [poup] s. papież
poplar ['popler] s. topola
poppy ['popy] s. mak
popular ['popjuler] adj. ludowy;
rozpowszechniony; popularny
(tani)
popularity [,popju'laeryty] s.
popularność
populate ['popjulejt] v. zaludniać
population ['popjulejszyn] s.
ludność
populous ['popjules] adj. ludny;
gęsto zaludniony
porch [po:rcz] s. weranda;
ganek; portyk
porcupine ['po:rkjupajn] s. jeż;
jeżozwierz; kolczatka
pore [po:r] v. rozmyślać;
ślęczeć; wpatrywać się; s.
por (skóry)
pore over ['po:r,ouwer] v.
rozmyślać nad czymś;
ślęczeć (nad książką);
zagłębiać się
pork [po:rk] s. wieprzowina
porous ['po:res] adj. porowaty
porpoise ['po:rpes] s. morświn;
ssak morski
porridge ['porydż] s. owsianka
port [po:rt] s. port; przystań;
otwór; otwór ładunkowy;
postawa; trzymanie się;

prezentowanie (broni); wino
porto; lewa burta; sterowanie
w lewo
portable ['po:rtebl] adj.
przenośny; polowy
porter ['po:rter] s. tragarz;
kolejarz od sypialnego wagonu
portion ['po:rszyn] s. część;
porcja; udział; posag; los; v.
dzielić; przydzielać
portion out ['po:rszyn,aut] v.
wydzielać; wyposażać
portly ['po:rtly] adj. dostojny;
godny; tęgi; postawny;
okazały
portrait ['po:rtryt] s. portret
pose [pouz] v. pozować;
upozować; stawiać (np.
problem); kłopotać
(zapytaniem); s. poza
posh [posz] adj. elegancki;
szykowny; v. wyelegantować
się
position [pe'zyszyn] s. położenie;
stanowisko; postawa;
twierdzenie; umieszczenie; v.
umieszczać; ulokować
positive ['pozetyw] adj.
pozytywny; stanowczy;
ustanowiony; zupełny;
dodatni; pozytywistyczny; s.
znak dodatni; wartość
dodatnia; pozytyw
possess [pe'zes] v. posiadać;
opanować; opętać;
przejać
possessed [pe'zest] adj. opętany
possession [pe'zeszyn] s.
posiadanie; posiadłość;
własność; dobytek;
opanowanie
possessor [pe'zeser] s.
posiadacz; właściciel
possibility [pose'byłyty] s.
możliwość; możność;
ewentualność
possible ['posebl] adj. możliwy;
ewentualny
possibly ['posebly] adv. może; w
ogóle możliwe; możliwie
post [poust] s. słup; posada;
posterunek; poczta; v.
ogłaszać; wywieszać;

zalepiać plakatami
postage ['poustydż] s. opłata
pocztowa
postage stamp ['poustydż
,staemp] s. znaczek pocztowy
postal ['poustel] adj. pocztowy
postal order ['poustel'o:rder] s.
przekaz pocztowy
postcard ['poust,ka:rd] s.
pocztówka
post code ['poust,koud] = zip-
-code [,zyp'koud] pocztowy
numer kierunkowy
poste restante ['poust'resta:nt]
s. list lub przesyłka do
odebrania na poczcie
poster ['pouster] s. plakat
posterity [po'teryty] s.
potomność
post-free ['poust'fri:] adj. wolny
od opłaty pocztowej
posthumous ['post,jumes] adj.
pośmiertny
postman ['poustmen] s. listonosz
postmark ['poust,ma:rk] s.
stempel pocztowy
postmaster ['poust,ma:ster] s.
naczelnik poczty
post office ['poust,ofys] s.
poczta
post office box ['poust,ofys
'boks] s. skrytka pocztowa
postpaid ['poust,pejd] s. opłata
pocztowa z góry uiszczona
postpone [poust'poun] v.
odłożyć; odroczyć;
odwlekać
postscript ['pous,skrypt] s.
dopisek; postscriptum
posture ['posczer] s. postawa;
stan; położenie; v. przybrać
postawą; pozować
postwar ['poust'ło:r] adj.
powojenny
posy ['pouzy] s. bukiet
pot [pot] s. garnek; imbryk;
czajnik; nocnik; doniczka;
wazonik; rondel; dzban; kocioł;
kufel; słój; puchar; więcierz;
łuza; szklanka; haszysz; v.
wsadzać do garnka;
polować; strzelać
potato [po'tejtou] s. ziemniak

potent ['potent] adj. potężny;
skuteczny; jurny
potion ['pouszyn] s. dawka;
napój
potter ['poter] s. garncarz; v.
grzebać się; włóczyć się;
łazić
potter about ['poter,e'baut] v.
włóczyć się
pottery ['potery] s. wyroby
gancarskie; gancarstwo
potty ['poty] adj. marny; lichy;
błahy; łatwy; stuknięty;
pomylony; zbzikowany
pouch [paucz] s. worek; torba;
brzuszysko; ładownica;
sakiewka; v. nadawać formę
worka; łykać
poulterer ['poulterer] s. handlarz
drobiu
poultice ['poultys] s. okład; v.
kłaść okład
poultry ['poultry] s. drób
pounce [pauns] s. szpon; nagły
atak z góry; v. rzucać się na
coś; trybować;
pumeksować; posypywać
(rysunek) proszkiem
(kolorowym)
pound [paund] s. funt (pieniądz,
waga); stuk; tupot; uderzenie;
tłuczenie; walnięcie;
ogrodzenie; magazyn; areszt;
v. tłuc; walić; tupać;
biegać; więzić; zamykać
pour [po:r] v. wysypać;
posypać; lać; polać; wylać;
rozlać; nalać
pour out ['po:r,aut] v. wysypać;
wylać
pout [paut] v. dąsać się;
wydymać; s. wydęcie warg;
kwaśna mina
poverty ['powerty] s. bieda;
ubóstwo
powder ['pałder] s. proch; pył;
puder; proszek; v.
posypywać; pudrować;
proszkować
powder room ['pałder,ru:m] s.
toaleta damska
power ['pałer] s. potęga; moc;
energia; siła; własność;

władza; mocarstwo; v.
napędzać; wspomagać;
dostarczać energii
power brake ['pałer,brejk] s.
serwohamulec; wspomagany
hamulec
powerful ['pałerful] adj. potężny;
mocny
powerless ['pałerlys] adj.
bezsilny
power plant ['pałer,plaent] s.
siłownia
power station ['pałer,stejszyn] s.
elektrownia
powwow ['pał,łał] v. naradzać
się co do taktyki; leczyć; s.
sejmik Indian; odprawa
oficerska; czarownik indiański
practicable ['praektykebl] adj.
wykonalny; możliwy do
przeprowadzenia
practical ['praektykel] adj.
praktyczny
practice ['praektys] s. praktyka;
ćwiczenie; v. praktykować;
uprawiać; ćwiczyć
practise ['praektys] v. = practice
practitioner [praek'tyszener] s.
zawodowiec; praktykujący
lekarz
prairie ['preery] s. preria
praise [prejz] s. pochwała; v.
chwalić; sławić
praiseworthy ['prejz,łe:r<u>s</u>y] adj.
chwalebny; godny pochwały
pram [praem] s. ręczny wózek
prance [praens] v. stawać dęba;
tańczyć; paradować;
hasać; kazać koniowi
stawać dęba
prank [prae<u>n</u>k] s. psota; figiel; v.
wystroić; popisywać się
prattle ['praetl] v. paplać; s.
paplanina
prawn ['pro:n] s. krewetka; v.
łowić krewetki
pray [prej] v. modlić się;
prosić; błagać
prayer ['prejer] s. modlitwa;
prośba
prayer book ['prejer,buk] s.
modlitewnik; książka do
nabożeństwa

pre- [pri:-] prefix. przed-; z góry

preach [pri:cz] v. głosić; kazać; wygłaszać

preacher [pri:czer] s. kaznodzieja; pastor

precarious [pry'keeries] adj. niepewny; nieubezpieczony; dowolny

precaution [pry'ko:szyn] s. przezorność; środek ostrożności

precede [pry:'si:d] v. poprzedzać; mieć pierwszeństwo

precedence [pry'si:dens] s. pierwszeństwo; nadrzędność

precedent [pry'si:dent] adj. uprzedni; poprzedzający

precedent ['presydent] s. precedens

precept ['pry:sept] s. nakaz; przykazanie; nauka moralna; reguła

precinct ['pry:synkt] s. okręg (wyborczy); obręb; granice

precious ['preszes] adj. drogi; cenny; afektowany; wyszukany; wspaniały; adv. bardzo; niezwykle

precipice ['presypys] s. przepaść

precipitate [pry'sypytejt] s. opad; osad; v. przyspieszać (zdarzenia); skraplać (się); rzucać; spadać

precipitation [pry,sypy'tejszyn] s. opady; przyspieszanie; pochopność; upadek; strącanie

precipitous [pry'sypytes] adj. przepaścisty; spadzisty

precis ['prejsi:] s. skrót; v. robić skrót

precise [pry'sajs] adj. dokładny; wyraźny; v. precyzować; wyszczególniać

precision [pry'syżyn] s. precyzja; dokładność

precocious [pry'kouszes] adj. przedwczesny; przedwcześnie rozwinięty; kwitnący

preconceived ['pry:ken'si:wd]

adj. uprzedzony do; powzięty z góry

predatory ['predetery] adj. łupieżczy; grabieżczy; drapieżny

predecessor ['pry:dyseser] s. poprzednik; przodek

predetermine ['pry:dy'te:rmyn] v. z góry ustanowić; z góry określić; z góry zadecydować

predicament [pry'dykement] s. kłopot; kłopotliwe położenie

predicate ['predy,kejt] v. opierać się na czymś; łączyć się z czymś; przypisywać czemuś; orzekać o czymś; mieścić pojęcie czegoś; ['predykt] s. cecha; orzecznik; adj. orzeczeniowy; dopełnienie orzeczenia

predict [pry'dykt] v. przepowiadać

prediction [pry'dykszyn] s. przepowiednia

predisposition ['pri:dyspe,zyszyn] s. skłonność; predyspozycja

predominant [pry'domynent] adj. przeważający; panujący; górujący

predominate [pry'domynejt] v. górować; przewyższać

preface ['prefys] s. przedmowa; wstęp

prefect ['pry:fekt] s. prefekt

prefer [pry'fe:r] v. woleć; przedkładać; dawać awans

preferable ['preferebl] adj. lepszy

preferably ['preferebly] adv. raczej

preference ['preferens] s. pierwszeństwo; uprzywilejowanie; możność wyboru; rzecz bardziej lubiana, upodobana

preferment [pry'fe:rment] s. wybór; awans

prefix ['pry:fyks] s. przedrostek; prefiks; tytuł przed nazwiskiem; v. umieszczać przedrostek; umieszczać na wstępie

pregnancy ['pregnensy] s. ciąża

pregnant ['pregnent] adj.
brzemienny; doniosły;
sugestywny; płodny; ciężarna
(kobieta)

prejudice ['predżudys] s.
uprzedzenie; szkoda; v.
uprzedzać się do kogoś;
szkodzić (komuś);
rozpowszechniać uprzedzenie

prejudiced ['predżudyst] adj.
uprzedzony; mający
uprzedzenie

preliminary [pry'lymynery] adj.
wstępny; przygotowawczy; s.
wstęp

prelude ['prelju:d] s. wstęp;
preludium; v. grać preludium;
dawać wstęp do czegoś

premature [,preme'tjuer] adj.
przedwczesny; przedwcześnie
dojrzały

premeditate [pry'medy,tejt] v.
obmyślać; rozważać

premier ['premjer] adj. pierwszy;
najważniejszy; premier; prezes
rady ministrów

premises ['premysys] pl. lokal;
obejście

premium ['pri:mjem] s. nagroda;
premia

preoccupied [pry:'okju,pajd] adj.
pochłonięty; zaabsorbowany

preparation [,prepe'rejszyn] s.
przygotowywanie;
przyrządzanie

prepare [pry'peer] v.
przygotowywać (się);
szykować (się); przyrządzać

prepay ['pry'pej] v. opłacać z
góry

preposition [,prepe'zyszyn] s.
przyimek

prepossess [,pry:po'zes] v.
wpoić; usposobić; natchnąć

prepossessing [prype'zesyng]
adj. miły; sympatyczny

preposterous [pry'posteres] adj.
niedorzeczny; absurdalny

prerequisite [pry'rekłyzyt] adj. &
s. (warunek) wstępny;
podstawowy

prescribe [prys'krajb] v.
przepisać; nakazać;

zaordynować

prescription [prys'krypszyn] s.
nakaz; przepis; recepta

presence ['presens] v.
obecność

presence of mind
['prezens,ow'majnd] v.
przytomność umysłu

present ['preznt] s. upominek;
prezent; teraźniejszość; adj.
obecny; niniejszy;
teraźniejszy; v. stawiać się;
nadarzyć się

present tense ['presnt,tens] s.
czas teraźniejszy

presentation [,prezen'tejszyn] s.
przedstawienie; ofiarowanie;
podarek; darowanie;
przedłożenie

presentiment [pry'zentyment] s.
przeczucie

presently ['prezently] adv.
wkrótce; niebawem; zaraz

preservation [,preze:r'wejszyn] s.
zachowanie; ochrona;
zabezpieczenie

preserve [pry'ze:rw] v.
zachowywać; chronić;
przechowywać;
konserwować; ochraniać; s.
konserwa; rezerwat

preside [pry'zajd] v.
przewodniczyć

president ['prezydent] s.
prezydent

press [pres] s. prasa; dzienniki;
tłocznia; druk; drukarnia;
nacisk; tłok; ścisk; pośpiech;
v. cisnąć; ściskać;
przyciskać; ciążyć;
pracować; naglić; narzucać;
wciskać; tłoczyć

press in ['pres-yn] v. wciskać

pressing ['presyng] adj. naglący;
natarczywy

pressure ['preszer] s. ciśnienie;
napór; parcie

prestige [pres'ty:dż] s. prestiż
(szacunek i uznanie)

presumable [pry'zju:mebl] adj.
przypuszczalny

presume [pry'zju:m] v.
przypuszczać;

wykorzystywać (kogoś);
ośmielać się
presumedly [pry'zju:mydly] adv.
przypuszczalnie
presuming [pry'zju:my**ng**] adj.
zarozumiały
presumption [pry'zampszen] s.
przypuszczenie; założenie;
zarozumiałość
presumptuous [pry'zamptjues]
adj. zarozumiały
presuppose [pry'se:pouz] v.
przypuszczać; zakładać z
góry; stawiać warunek
pretend [pry'tend] v. udawać;
pretendować
pretender [pry'tender] s.
pretendent
pretense [pry'tens] s. udawanie;
pozór; pretensja;
pretensjonalność
pretension [pry'tenszyn] s.
aspiracje; roszczenie;
pretensjonalność; pretensja
preterite ['preteryt] adj. przeszły;
s. czas przeszły
pretext ['pry:tekst] s. pretekst;
pozór
pretext [pry'tekst] v. wymawiać
się; powoływać się
pretty ['pryty] adj. ładny; adv.
dość; dosyć
prevail [pry'wejl] v. przeważać;
brać górą; przekonać;
panować (np. zwyczaj)
prevalent ['prewelent] adj.
panujący; przeważający
prevent [pry'went] v. zapobiec;
powstrzymywać
prevention [pry'wenszyn] s.
zapobieganie; środek
zapobiegający
preventive [pry'wentyw] adj.
zapobiegawczy; prewencyjny
previous ['pry:wjes] adj.
poprzedni; wcześniejszy od
...; przedwczesny; nagły;
pochopny
previous to ['pry:wjes,tu] adv.
przed czymś
previously ['pry:wjesly] adv.
wcześniej
prewar ['pri:'ło:r] adj.

przedwojenny
prey [prej] s. zdobycz; łup;
ofiara; v. grabić; trawić
price [prajs] s. cena; koszt; v.
wyceniać
priceless ['prajslys] adv.
bezcenny; nieoceniony
prick [pryk] s. ukłucie; (wulg.)
penis; v. kłuć; przekłuwać
prick up one's ears
[pryk,ap'łans,eerz] v.
nadstawiać uszu; postawić
uszy
prickle ['prykl] s. kolec; cierń; v.
ukłuć; jeżyć się
prickly ['prykly] adj. kolczasty
pride [prajd] s. duma; pycha;
ambicja; chluba; v. być
dumnym z czegoś; chełpić
się; pysznić się
priest [pri:st] s. kapłan;
duchowny
prim [prym] adj. sztywny;
pedantyczny; sztuczny;
wyszukany; przesadny
primarily ['prajmeryly] adv.
głównie; przede wszystkim
primary ['prajmery] adj. główny;
zasadniczy; pierwotny; s.
wybór kandydatów (USA)
primary school ['prajmery,sku:l]
s. szkoła podstawowa
prime ['prajm] adj. pierwszy;
najważniejszy; główny; v.
przygotować
prime minister ['prajm-'mynyster]
s. premier
primer ['prajmer] s. elementarz;
podręcznik (elementarny)
primitive ['prymytyw] adj.
prymitywny; pierwotny
primrose ['prymrous] s.
pierwiosnek
prince ['pryns] s. książę
princess [pryn'ses] s. księżna;
księżniczka
principal ['prynsepel] adj.
główny; s. kierownik;
zleceniodawca; kapitał;
sprawca
principality [prynsy'paelyty] s.
księstwo
principle ['prynsepl] s. zasada;

reguła; podstawa; źródło;
składnik
prink [prynk] v. stroić się;
muskać się
print [prynt] s. ślad; odcisk;
druk; pismo; fotka; v.
wycisnąć; wytłoczyć;
wydrukować; być w druku;
drukować się; odbić
printed matter ['prynted'maeter]
v. druki; materiały drukowane
printer ['prynter] s. drukarz
printing ['pryntyng] s. druk;
drukowanie; nakład; a.
drukarski
printing ink ['pryntyng,ynk] s.
farba drukarska
printing office ['pryntyn,ofys] s.
drukarnia
prior ['prajer] adj. wcześniejszy;
ważniejszy; s. przeor
prior to ['prajer,tu] adv. przed
czymś; wcześniej od
czegoś
priority ['praj'oryty] s.
pierwszeństwo;
starszeństwo; priorytet
prison ['pryzn] s. więzienie
prisoner ['pryzner] s. więzień
privacy ['prajwesy] s.
odosobnienie; samotność;
utrzymanie w dyskrecji
(tajemnicy); życie prywatne,
intymne, osobiste
private ['prajwyt] adj. prywatny;
tajny; ukryty; s. szeregowiec;
(private parts = genitalia)
private hotel ['prajwyt,hou'tel] s.
pensjonat
privation [praj'wejszyn] s.
prywacja; niedostatek
privilege ['prywylydż] s.
przywilej; prawdziwa
satysfakcja
privileged ['prywylydżd] adj.
uprzywilejowany; zaszczycony
prize [prajz] v. podważyć;
zajmować; cenić; s. nagroda;
premia; wygrana; łup; a.
kapitalny
prizefighter ['prajz,fajter] s.
zawodowy bokser
prizewinner ['prajz,łyner] s.

laureat; zdobywca nagrody
pro [prou] s. zawodowiec
(slang); adv. za; dla; prep. pro
(forma etc.)
probability [proba'bylyty] s.
prawdopodobieństwo; widoki;
szanse
probable ['probebl] adj.
prawdopodobny; wiarygodny;
mający szanse
probation [pro'bejszyn] s. okres
próbny; próba; zawieszenie
kary
probe [proub] s. sonda; v.
sondować; zagłębiać się;
badać w śledztwie
problem ['problem] s. problem;
zadanie; zagadnienie; a.
problemowy
procedure [pre'si:dżer] s.
postępowanie; procedura
(sądowa)
proceed [pre'si:d] v. iść dalej;
postępować; kontynuować;
zaskarżać
proceed from [pre'si:d,from] v.
wychodzić z ...; iść dalej z
...
proceedings [pre'si:dyngs] pl.
sprawozdanie (z sesji etc.)
proceeds ['prosi:dz] pl. zysk;
dochody; przychód (ze
sprzedaży)
process ['prouses] s. przebieg;
proces; postęp; v. obrabiać;
przerabiać; załatwiać;
procesować; poddawać
procesowi; mleć
procession [pre'seszyn] s.
pochód; procesja;
kontynuowanie; prowadzenie
dalej; dalszy rozwój
proclaim [pre'klejm] v.
proklamować; ogłaszać;
zakazywać; wskazywać;
wprowadzać ograniczenia
proclamation [,prokle'majszyn] s.
proklamacja; obwieszczenie
procrastinate [pre'kraesty,nejt] v.
zwlekać; odkładać na
później
procure [pre'kjuer] v. postarać
się; stręczyć do nierządu

prodigal ['prodygel] adj.
marnotrawny; s. marnotrawca;
utracjusz
prodigious [pre'dydżes] adj.
niezwykły; cudowny; olbrzymi
prod [prod] v. szturchać; kłuć;
drażnić; popędzać; s.
dźgnięcie; bodziec; szpikulec
prodigy ['prodydży] s. dziwo;
cud; genialne dziecko etc.
produce ['produ:s] s. produkty;
plony; wynik; produkcja;
wydajność; wydobycie;
produkty rolne
produce [pre'dju:s] v.
wytwarzać; produkować;
dostarczać; wydobywać;
wystawiać; okazywać
producer ['produ:ser] s.
wytwórca (filmowy);
producent
product ['predakt] s. produkt;
wynik; iloczyn; wytwór
(natury etc.)
production [pre'dakszyn] s.
wytwórczość; wydobycie;
produkcja; utwór; produkty; a.
produkcyjny
productive [pre'daktyw] adj.
wydajny; produktywny;
produkcyjny; urodzajny; żyzny
profess [pre'fes] v. twierdzić;
zapewniać; udawać;
wyznawać; uprawiać
(zawód); być profesorem
professed [pre'fest] adj. jawny;
rzekomy; zawodowy
profession [pre'feszyn] s. zawód;
wyznanie; zapewnienie;
oświadczenie; śluby zakonne
professional [pre'feszenl] s.
zawodowiec; adj. zawodowy;
fachowy; należący do
wolnego zawodu
professor [pre'feser] s. profesor;
wyznawca; nauczyciel (tańca)
proficiency [pre'fyszensy] s.
biegłość; sprawność
proficient [pre'fyszent] adj.
biegły; sprawny; s. mistrz;
biegły; znający (obcy język);
fachowiec
profile ['proufajl] s. profil; szkic

biograficzny; v. przedstawiać
z profilu; profilować
profit ['profyt] s. zysk; dochód;
korzyść; pożytek; v.
korzystać; być korzystnym;
przydawać się; mieć zyski
profitable ['profytebl] adj.
korzystny; intratny; zyskowny
profiteer [,profy'tier] v.
paskować; spekulować; s.
paskarz; spekulant (na
czarnym rynku etc.)
profound [pro'faund] adj.
głęboki; gruntowny; s.
otchłań
profusion [pro'fju:żyn] s.
obfitość; rozrzutność;
nadmiar
prognoses [prog'nousi:z] pl.
prognozy; rokowania
prognosis [prog'nousys] s.
prognoza; rokowanie
program ['prougraem] s.
program; plan; audycja;
przedstawienie; v. planować
progress ['prougres] s. postęp;
bieg; rozwój; kolejne etapy
etc.
progress [pre'gres] v. robić
postępy; iść naprzód; być
w toku
progressive [pre'gresyw] adj.
postępowy; stopniowy; s.
postępowiec
prohibit [pro'hybyt] v.
zakazywać; zabraniać
prohibition [,prouy'byszyn] s.
zakaz; prohibicja
project ['prodżekt] s. projekt;
plan; przedsięwzięcie;
schemat
project [pro'dżekt] v.
projektować; miotać;
rzutować; sterczeć;
wystawać; wyświetlać (na
ekranie)
projection [pro'dżekszyn] s. rzut;
planowanie; projektowanie;
rzutowanie; wystawanie;
projekcja; wyświetlanie
projector [pro'dżekter] s. rzutnik;
aparat projekcyjny
proletariat [,proule'teerjet] s.

proletariat; robotnicy
przemysłowi
prolific [pre'lyfyk] adj. płodny
prologue ['proulog] s. prolog
prolong [prou'long] v.
przedłużać; wydłużać;
prolongować (spłaty)
promenade [,promy'nejd] s.
przechadzka; przejażdżka;
deptak; promenada; v.
przechadzać się
prominent ['promynent] adj.
wydatny; wybitny; sterczący;
wystający; wyróżniający się;
sławny
promiscuous [pre'myskjues] adj.
mieszany; różnorodny;
niewybredny w stosunkach
płciowych
promise ['promys] s. obietnica;
przyrzeczenie; v. obiecywać;
przyrzekać; zaręczać;
zapewniać; robić obietnice;
zapowiadać się
promising ['promysyng] adj.
obiecujący; rokujący nadzieje
promontory ['promento:ry] s.
przylądek; wyrostek
promote [pre'mout] s. popierać;
promować; awansować;
(slang) oszukiwać;
kombinować
promoter [pre'mouter] s.
organizator; krzewiciel;
inspirator
promotion [pre'mouszyn] s.
popieranie; ułatwienie; awans;
promowanie; lansowanie
prompt [prompt] adj. szybki;
natychmiastowy; v.
nakłaniać; pobudzać;
podpowiadać; suflerować;
adv. punktualnie; co do
minuty
prompter ['prompter] s. sufler (w
teatrze); podżegacz
promptly ['promptly] adv.
natychmiast; z miejsca;
bezzwłocznie; punktualnie
prone [proun] adj. leżący twarzą
w dół; stromy; skłonny
prong [prong] s. ząb (wideł); róg;
v. kłuć; przebijać;

zaopatrywać w zęby
pronoun ['prounaun] s. zaimek
pronounce [pre'nauns] v.
oświadczać; wymawiać;
mieć wymowę; wypowiadać
się
pronto ['prontou] adv. (slang)
prądko; już; natychmiast;
zaraz
pronunciation [pra,nansy'ejszyn]
s. wymowa; zapis fonetyczny
proof [pru:f] s. dowód; próba
(np. złota); sprawdzian;
wypróbowanie; korekta;
próbna odbitka; adj. odporny;
wypróbowany; sprawdzony;
nieprzemakalny
prop(up) ['prop,ap] v. podpierać;
s. podpórka; ostoja; oparcie
propagate ['prope,gejt] v.
rozmnażać (się); rozszerzać;
propagować; przekazywać
propagation [,prope'gejszyn] s.
rozmnażanie się;
propagowanie
propel [pre'pel] v. napędzać;
poruszać; pędzić
propeller [pre'peler] s. śmigło;
śruba (okrętowa)
proper ['proper] adj. właściwy;
własny; przyzwoity
properly ['properly] adv.
właściwie; słusznie;
przyzwoicie
property ['property] s.
własność; właściwość;
cecha; nieruchomość
prophecy ['profysy] s. proroctwo
prophet ['profyt] s. prorok;
apostoł
proportion [pre'po:rszyn] s.
proporcja; stosunek; rozmiar;
część; v. dostosowywać;
rozdzielać; dawkować;
dozować
proportional [pre'po:rsznl] adj.
proporcjonalny (do czegoś)
proposal [pre'pouzel] s.
propozycja; projekt;
oświadczyny
propose [pre'pouz] v.
proponować; przedkładać;
zamierzać

proposition [,prope'zyszyn] s.
propozycja; sąd; zagadnienie;
twierdzenie; v. robić
nieprzyzwoite propozycje

proprietary [pre'prajetery] adj.
należący; będący własnością
prywatną; s. właściciel;
własność

proprietor [pre'prajeter] s.
właściciel; posiadacz;
gospodarz

propulsion [pre'palszyn] s.
napęd; bodziec; popędzanie

prose [prouz] s. proza; v. nudzić

prosecute ['prosy,kju:t] v.
ścigać prawnie; prowadzić
(np. studia); nie zaniedbywać;
pilnować

prosecution [,prosy'kju:szyn] s.
oskarżenie

prosecutor ['prosy,kju:ter] s.
prokurator; oskarżyciel

prospect ['prospekt] s. widok;
perspektywa; ewentualny
klient; potencjalne złoża; v.
przeszukiwać (okolice);
próbnie eksploatować
kopalnię; szukać złota etc.;
badać (teren etc.)

prospective [pres'pektyw] adj.
przyszły; ewentualny

prospectus [pres'pektes] s.
prospekt (nowego
przedsiębiorstwa)

prosper ['prosper] v.
prosperować; sprzyjać
powodzeniu

prosperity [pros'peryty] s.
dobrobyt; powodzenie;
koniunktura; pomyślność

prosperous ['prosperes] adj.
mający powodzenie;
kwitnący; pomyślny;
zamożny

prostate [pros'tejt] s. prostata;
gruczoł krokowy

prostitute ['prosty,tu:t] s.
prostytutka; v. prostytuować
(się); adj. wszeteczny;
rozpustny

prostrate ['prostrejt] v. powalić
(np. ze zmęczenia); adj.
leżący twarzą w dół;
powalony; wyczerpany;
bezsilny; kłaniający się;
leżący plackiem

protect [pre'tekt] v. chronić;
bronić; ochraniać;
zabezpieczać

protection [pre'tekszyn] s.
ochrona; opieka; protekcja; list
żelazny; wymuszanie
pieniędzy przez grożenie
gwałtem

protective [pre'tektyw] adj.
ochronny; zapobiegawczy

protector [pre'tekter] s. opiekun;
protektor; ochraniacz

protest [pro'test] v.
protestować; zapewniać;
oponować

protest ['proutest] s. protest

protestant ['protystent] s.
ewangelik; protestant

protestation [proutes'tejszyn] s.
uroczyste zapewnienie;
protest; zaprotestowanie

protocol ['proute,kol] s.
początkowa forma
dokumentu; protokół
dyplomatyczny; etykieta

prototype ['proute,tajp] s.
prototyp; model

protract [pre'traekt] v.
przeciągać; przedłużać;
wystawiać; przedstawiać w
skali

protrude [pre'tru:d] v.
wystawać; wysuwać;
sterczeć

proud [praud] adj. dumny;
napawający dumą; piękny;
szczęśliwy

prove [pru:w] v. udawadniać;
wykazać (się);
uprawomocnić; poddawać
próbie; okazywać się

proverb ['prowe:rb] s.
przysłowie; przypowieść

proverbial [pre'we:rbjel] adj.
przysłowiowy

provide [pre'wajd] v.
zaopatrywać;
przygotowywać; postarać
się; sprzyjać; postanowić;
zaplanować

provide for [pre'wajd,fo:r] v.
zaopatrywać (kogoś)
provided that [pre'wajdyd,daet]
exp.: pod warunkiem że ...; o
ile
providence ['prowydens] s.
opatrzność; oszczędność;
przezorność; skrzętność
province ['prowyns] s.
prowincja; zakres; dziedzina
provincial [pre'wynszel] adj.
zaściankowy; prowincjonalny;
s. człowiek z prowincji
provision [pro'wyżyn] s.
klauzula; dostawa;
przygotowanie się; (pl.)
prowianty; v. prowiantować;
zaopatrywać w żywność;
zaprowiantować
provisional [pro'wyżenl] adj.
prowizoryczny; tymczasowy
provocation [,prowe'kejszyn] s.
prowokacja; rozdrażnienie;
podniecenie; spowodowanie
provocative [pro'woketyw] adj.
prowokujący; zaciekawiający;
drażniący; wyzywający
provoke [pre'wouk] v.
prowokować podniecać;
pobudzać; wywoływać;
podżegać; jątrzyć
prowl [praul] v. grasować; s.
grasowanie (po łup)
proxy ['proksy] s. zastępstwo;
pełnomocnik
prude [pru:d] s. świętoszka
prudence ['pru:dens] s. rozwaga;
roztropność; ostrożność
prudent ['pru:dent] s. rozważny;
roztropny; ostrożny
prudish ['pru:dysz] adj.
pruderyjny; przesadnie
skromny
prune [pru:n] s. śliwka
(suszona); v. obcinać (np.
gałązki); oczyszczać (z
czegoś)
psalm [sa:m] s. psalm
pseudonym ['sju:de,nym] s.
pseudonim; fikcyjne nazwisko
psyche ['sajki:] s. dusza; duch;
umysł (zwierciadło odchylone)
psychiatrist [saj'kajetryst] s.

psychiatra
psychiatry [saj'kajetry] s.
psychiatria
psychological [,sajke'lodżykel]
adj. psychologiczny
psychologist [saj'koledżyst] s.
psycholog
psychology [saj'koledży] s.
psychologia
pub [pab] s. Br. knajpa
puberty ['pju:berty] s.
dojrzałość płciowa
public ['pablyk] s. publiczność;
adj. publiczny; obywatelski
publication [,pably'kejszyn] s.
opublikowanie; ogłoszenie;
publikacja; wydanie książki
public house ['pablyk,haus] s.
szynk; oberża
publicity [pab'lysyty] s. rozgłos;
reklama; a. reklamowy
publish ['pablysz] v.
publikować; wydawać;
ogłaszać; rozgłaszać;
wydawać drukiem
publisher ['pablyszer] s.
wydawca; nakładca
publishing house
['pablyszyng,haus] s. firma
wydawnicza
pudding ['pudyng] s. budyń
puddle ['padl] s. kałuża
puff [paf] v. pykać; sapać;
dmuchać; reklamować;
pudrować; s. puszek;
pyknięcie; dmuchnięcie; blaga
reklamowa; pierzyna; kłąb
dymu; zwój włosów
puff paste ['paf,pejst] s.
francuskie ciasto
puffy ['pafy] adj. dychawiczny;
nadęty; pękaty; napuszony;
otyły; porywisty
pull [pul] v. pociągnąć;
szarpnąć; wyrwać;
wyciągać; przeciągać;
wiosłować; ściągnąć
pull down ['pul,daln] v.
spuścić; rozbierać (np.
budynek); osłabiać; ściągać
(storę etc.)
pull for ['pul,fo:r] v. popierać
pull in ['pul,yn] v. wciągać

pull off ['pul,of] v. ściągać;
zdobywać; potrafić; zdołać;
stanąć
pull out ['pul,aut] v. wyrwać;
wycofać; s. wycofanie się
pulley ['puli] s. bloczek; blok
krążkowy; v. podnosić
bloczkiem
pullover ['pul,ouwer] s. pulower
pulp [palp] s. miazga; miąższ;
papka; v. rozcierać na miazgę
pulpit ['pulpyt] s. ambona;
kazalnica; kaznodzieja; kazanie
pulpy ['palpy] adj. papkowaty;
miąższowy
pulsate [pal'sejt] v. tętnić;
pulsować; drgać; trząść
się
pulse [pals] s. tętno; puls; v.
tętnić; pulsować
pulverize ['palwerajz] v.
proszkować (się); rozpylać;
ścierać w proch; zemleć na
proch
pump [pamp] v. pompa; lakierek;
v. pompować; pytać
uporczywie
pump gun ['pamp,gan] s.
strzelba (do repetowania)
pumpkin ['pampkyn] s. dynia
pun [pan] s. gra słów
(dwuznacznych); v. robić
kalambury
punch [pancz] s. uderzenie
(pięścią); poncz; przebijak;
krzepa; siła; sztanca; kułak;
rozmach; v. dziurkować;
tłoczyć; walić; szturchać
punctual ['panktjuel] adj.
punktualny; punktowy
punctuate ['panktju,ejt] v.
przestankować; przerywać
punctuation [,panktju'ejszyn] s.
interpunkcja
punctuation mark [,panktju
'ejszyn ma:rk] s. kropka; znak
przestankowy
puncture ['pankczer] s. przebicie;
punkcja; v. przekłuwać;
przedziurawiać; przebić
pungent ['pandżent] adj. kłujący;
ostry; cierpki; zjadliwy;
gryzący; sarkastyczny;

pikantny
punish ['panysz] v. karać; dać
bobu
punishment ['panyszment] s.
kara; sromotna klęska (na
boisku)
pupil ['pju:pl] s. źrenica; uczeń;
wychowanek; małoletni;
niepełnoletni
puppet ['papyt] s. kukiełka;
marionetka; a. kukiełkowy;
marionetkowy
puppet show ['papyt,szou] s.
występy marionetek
puppet state ['papyt,stejt] s.
państwo marionetkowe
puppy ['papy] s. szczenię;
szczeniak; piesek;
zarozumialec
purchase ['pe:rczes] s. zakup;
kupno; dźwignia; v. kupić;
okupić; nabywać; podnosić
(np. kotwicę); sprawiać sobie
purchaser [pe:rczeser] s.
nabywca; kupujący
pure [pjuer] adj. czysty; zupełny;
szczery; niewinny; nie
zepsuty; zwykły; czystej krwi
purgative ['pe:rgetyw] adj.
przeczyszczający; s. środek
na przeczyszczenie
purgatory ['pe:rgetery] s.
czyściec; adj. oczyszczający
purge [pe:rdż] v. przeczyszczać;
oczyścić; usuwać; dawać
na przeczyszczenie;
oczyszczenie; czystka; środek
przeczyszczający; rafinowanie;
klarowanie
purify ['pjuery,faj] v. oczyszczać
(się); klarować; rafinować
purity ['pjueryty] s. czystość
purloin [pe:rloyn] v. okraść;
ściągać; porwać
purple ['pe:rpl] s. purpura; adj.
purpurowy; v. robić
purpurowym; robić
szkarłatnym
purpose ['pe:rpes] s. cel; zamiar;
skutek; decyzja; wola; v.
zamierzać; mieć na celu;
planować
purposeful ['pe:rpesful] adj.

celowy; znaczący; rozmyślny;
zdecydowany; stanowczy
purposeless ['pe:rpeslys] adj.
bezcelowy; bezsensowny;
daremny; próżny (wysiłek
etc.)
purposely ['pe:rpesly] adv.
naumyślnie; celowo;
rozmyślnie
purr [pe:r] v. mruczeć;
pomrukiwać; s. mruczenie;
pomruk
purse [pe:rs] s. sakiewka;
torebka damska; kiesa;
nagroda; v. ściągać (się);
marszczyć (czoło)
pursue [per'sju:] v. ścigać;
tropić; iść dalej; uprawiać
(np. zawód); działać wg
planu; prześladować;
kontynuować; towarzyszyć;
spełniać (obowiązek)
pursuer [per'sju:er] s. ścigający;
prześladowca; dążący do
czegoś
pursuit [per'sju:t] s. pościg;
pogoń; zawód; zajęcie;
rozrywka
pursy [pe:rsy] adj. dychawiczny;
wydęty; otyły; ściągnięty
purvey [pe:r'wej] v. dostarczyć;
zaopatrywać; być dostawcą
purveyor [pe:rwejer] s. dostawca
pus [pas] s. ropa
push [pusz] s. pchnięcie; suw;
nacisk; wypad; wysiłek;
**energia; dryg; bieda; kryzys;
zdecydowanie; v. pchać;
posunąć; szturchnąć;
nakłonić; dopingować;
odpychać; spychać;
pomiatać; robić karierę;
ponaglać
push along ['pusz,e'long] v. iść
dalej; ciągnąć się dalej;
jechać dalej; spieszyć się
push around ['pusz,e'raund] v.
pomiatać kimś
pusher ['puszer] s. popychacz
(uliczny); sprzedawca
narkotyków
puss [pus] s. kociak;
dziewczyna; (slang) gęba; kot

(tygrys)
pussycat ['pusy,kaet] s. kociak;
pliszka; (wulg.) narząd płciowy
żeński
put; put; put [put; put; put]
put [put] v. kłaść; stawiać;
umieszczać; wsadzać;
pouczać; przedkładać;
ujmować; wystawiać;
dodawać; wlewać;
szacować; nakładać;
opierać; składać; narażać;
wypychać (np. kule); zanosić
(np. prośby); s. rzut; adj.
nieruchomy (pozostający na
miejscu)
put back ['put,baek] v.
przestawić do tyłu; odłożyć
z powrotem
put down ['put,dałn] v. położyć;
stłumić; spuścić w dół;
zapisywać
put forth ['put,fo:rs] v.
wydobyć; wytężyć (siły);
wydawać (pismo)
put off ['put,of] v. odłożyć;
odroczyć; zbywać;
odwieść; pozbyć się
put on ['put,on] v. wdziewać;
przybierać; tyć; udawać;
dodawać
put out ['put,aut] v. zwichnąć;
zgasić; wytężyć (się);
produkować; wydawać;
wysunąć (ręką etc.)
put together [,put'tugedzer] v.
łączyć; montować;
powiązać; zbierać (myśli);
kojarzyć; zliczyć
put up ['put,ap] v. ustawiać;
wywieszać; cierpieć;
wetknąć; schować;
dźwigać do góry; ustawić
putrefy ['pju:try,faj] v. gnić;
ropieć; ulegać zepsuciu
putrid ['pju:tryd] adj. zgniły;
zepsuty; cuchnący;
śmierdzący; wstrętny;
obrzydliwy
putty ['paty] s. kit; szpachlówka;
v. szpachlować; zakitować
putty knife ['paty,najf] s.
szpachla

puzzle ['pazl] s. zagadka;
łamigłówka; zakłopotanie; v.
intrygować; wprawiać w
zakłopotanie; odgadnąć;
wymyślić
puzzler ['pazler] s. łamigłówka
pajamas [pe'dże:mes] pl. piżama
pyramid ['pyremyd] s. piramida;
ostrosłup; v. zarabiać na
spekulacji; wznosić (się)
piramidalnie; budować jak
piramidę
python ['pajsen] s. pyton

Q

q [kju:] siedemnasta litera
alfabetu angielskiego (q. =
kwarta)
quack [kłaek] s. znachor;
szarlatan; kwakanie; v.
uprawiać znachorstwo;
gadać jak szarlatan; kwakać
quad [kłod] (skrót) s. kwadrat;
czworokąt
quadrangle [kło'draengl] s.
czworokąt
quadruped ['kładru,ped] adj.
czworonożny
quadruple [kło'drupl] adj.
czterokrotny; cztery razy
większy; czterokrotnie
większy
quadruplets [kło'dru:plets] s.
czworaczki
quail [kłejl] s. przepiórka; v.
drżeć przed czymś
quaint [kłejnt] adj. malowniczy;
trochę dziwaczny
quake [kłejk] s. trzęsienie (ziemi);
v. trząść się (np. z zimna, ze
strachu etc.)
quaky [kłejky] adj. trzęsący się;
grząski
qualification [,kłolyfy'kejszyn] s.
warunek; określenie;
kwalifikacja; uzdolnienie (do
pracy)

qualified ['kłolyfajd] adj.
wykwalifikowany;
uwarunkowany; kwalifikujący
się
quality ['kłolyty] s. jakość;
gatunek; właściwość; zaleta
qualm [kło:m] s. mdłości;
nudności; obawa; wyrzuty;
skrupuły
quandary ['kłondery] s.
zakłopotanie; kłopot; dylemat
quantity ['kłontyty] s. ilość;
wielkość; hurt; obfitość
quarantine ['kłorenti:n] s.
kwarantanna; v. izolować
quarrel ['kło:rel] s. kłótnia;
zerwanie; spór; sprzeczka; v.
kłócić się; sprzeczać się;
zerwać z sobą; robić
wyrzuty
quarrelsome ['kłorelsem] adj.
kłótliwy; swarliwy
quarry ['kłory] s. kamieniołom;
kopalnia odkrywkowa; łup;
zdobycz; płytka; szybka; v.
łamać; wygrzebywać;
wydobywać; eksploatować;
szperać (za wiadomościami)
quart [kło:rt] s. jedna czwarta
galonu (0.946 l.); kwarta piwa
quarter ['kło:ter] v.
ćwiartować; kwaterować;
rozpłatać; stacjonować; s.
ćwierć; ćwiartka; kwadrans;
kwartał; kwatera; 25 centów
(moneta); kwadra (księżyca);
dzielnica; mieszkanie; strona
świata; czynniki wpływowe;
(pl.) sfery (rządzące); kwartał
quarterly ['kło:terly] adj.
kwartalny; adv. kwartalnie; s.
kwartalnik; pismo kwartalne
quartet(te) [kło:r'tet] s. kwartet;
czwórka
quarto ['kło:rtou] s. format
ćwiartkowy
quartz [kłe:rts] s. kwarc
quash [kło:sz] v. unieważnić;
zdławić; stłumić; zgnieść
quasi ['kła:zy] conj. prawie;
niemal; jak gdyby; niby;
poniekąt
quaver ['kłejwer] s. drżenie

głosu; tryl; v. drżeć; drgać;
wibrować; trelować
quavery ['kłejwery] adj. drżący
quay [ki:] s. molo; nadbrzeże
queasy ['kłi:zy] adj. przeczulony;
mdlejący; grymaśny;
wrażliwy
queen [kłi:n] s. królowa;
królówka
queen bee ['kłi:n,bi:] s. królowa
pszczoła
queer [kłir] adj. dziwny;
dziwaczny; nieswój;
podejrzany; fałszywy; s.
pederasta; v. zepsuć;
wpakować w złą sytuację;
mdlić
quench ['kłencz] v. gasić;
tłumić; nagle oziębiać
(metal)
querulous ['kłerules] adj.
narzekający; zrzędny;
płaczliwy
query ['kłiery] s. zapytanie;
pytajnik; znak zapytania; v.
pytać; kwestionować
quest [kłest] s. poszukiwanie;
śledztwo; v. szukać
question ['kłesczyn] s. pytanie;
zagadnienie; kwestia;
wątpliwości; v. wypytywać;
przesłuchiwać; badać;
kwestionować; pytać się;
przeegzaminować
questionable ['kłesczenebl] adj.
wątpliwy (moralnie); sporny;
niepewny; niejasny
question mark ['kłesczyn,ma:rk]
s. znak zapytania
questionnaire [,kłejstje'neer] s.
kwestionariusz
queue [kju:] s. warkocz; ogonek;
kolejka; v. czekać w kolejce;
czekać w ogonku
queue up ['kju:,ap] v. ustawiać
się w kolejce
quibble ['kłybl] s. kruczek; v.
szukać wykrętów
quibbler ['kłybler] s. krętacz;
matacz
quick [kłyk] adj. prędki; szybki;
bystry; pomysłowy; żywy;
lotny; rudonośny; adv.

szybko; chyżo; v.
przyspieszać; ożywiać (się);
zwiększać szybkość
quicken ['kłyken] v.
przyspieszać;
pobudzać; ożywiać się;
wrócić do życia
quickie divorce ['kłyky dy'wo:rs]
s. rozwód błyskawiczny (w
stanie Newada; w Meksyku
etc.)
quickly ['kłykly] adv. szybko;
prędko; z pośpiechem
quickness ['kłyknys] s.
prędkość; ostrość
quicksand ['kłyk,saend] s.
grząski piasek
quicksilver ['kłyk,sylwer] s.
rtęć; żywe srebro
quick-tempered ['kłyk'temperd]
adj. porywczy
quick-witted ['kłyk'łytyd] adj.
bystry; rozgarnięty
quid [kłyd] s. funt szterling;
prymka; kawałek do żucia
quiet ['kłajet] adj. spokojny;
cichy; s. spokój; cisza; v.
uspokoić (się); uciszyć (się);
uspokajać; ściszyć;
ucichnąć
quiet down ['kłajet dałn] v.
uspokajać; przyciszyć;
ucichnąć
quietness ['kłajetnys] s. spokój;
cisza; łagodność;
skromność
quietude [kłajetju:d] s. spokój
(ducha)
quill [kłyl] s. lotka; dutka; kolec;
szpulka; pióro
quilt [kłylt] s. pikowana kołdra;
pikowana narzuta; v.
pikować; watować; robić
kołdry; zszywać; sprawić
lanie
quince [kłyns] s. pigwa
quinine ['kłajnajn] s. chinina
quintal ['kłyntl] s. cetnar; **kwintal**
quintuple ['kłyntjupl] adj.
pięciokrotny
quintuplets ['kłyntjuplyts] pl.
pięcioraczki
quit [kłyt] v. przestać; odejść;

odjechać; zabrać się;
wyprowadzać się;
opuszczać; porzucać;
rezygnować; adj. wolny;
uwolniony

quite [kłajt] adv. całkowicie;
zupełnie; raczej; wcale

quiver ['kływer] s. kołczan;
drżenie; drganie; v. drżeć;
drgać; trzepotać skrzydłami

quixotic ['kłyks,otyk] s. marzyciel
w stylu Don Kichota

quiz [kłyz] s. klasówka; egzamin;
badanie; przesłuchiwanie;
kawał; v. egzaminować;
badać; przesłuchiwać;
przeglądać; kpić

quota ['kłouta] s. udział;
kontyngent; norma

quotation [kłou'tejszyn] s.
cytata; cytowanie; notowanie;
przytaczanie (bieżącej ceny)

quotation marks
[kłou'tejszyn,ma:rks] pl.
cudzysłów

quote [kłout] v. cytować;
przytaczać; umieszczać w
cudzysłowie; notować;
podawać kurs; powoływać
się na kogoś

quotient ['kłouszent] s. iloraz

R

r [a:r] osiemnasta litera
angielskiego alfabetu

rabbi ['raebaj] s. rabin

rabbit ['raebyt] s. królik

rabble ['raebl] s. motłoch

rabid ['raebyd] adj. wściekły;
szalony; rozjuszony;
rozzłoszczony

rabies ['raebi:z] s. wścieklizna;
wodowstręt

raccoon [ra'ku:n] s. pracz
pospolity

race [rejs] s. rasa; plemię;
szczep; ród; rodzaj; bieg;

gonitwa; wyścigi; prąd;
kanał; v. ścigać (się); gonić
(się); pędzić; iść w zawody

racer ['rejser] s. wyścigowiec

racial ['rejszel] adj. rasowy

racing ['rejsyng] adj.
wyścigowy; s. wyścigi; biegi

racist ['rejsyst] s. rasista

rack [raek] s. ruina; zagłada;
zniszczenie; koło tortur;
wieszak; drabina stajenna;
półka; stojak; zębatka; szybki
kłus; v. niszczeć; łamać
kołem; torturować; cedzić;
szarpać; męczyć; dręczyć

racket ['raekyt] s. rakieta; rak;
zabawa; hulanka; awantura;
hałas; afera; granda;
nieuczciwe interesy; kant; v.
hałasować; hulać;
bumblować; zabawiać się;
awanturować się

racketeer [,raeky'tier] s.
szantażysta; opryszek; v.
szantażować; robić grandę

racoon [re'ku:n] s. szop

racy ['rejsy] adj. typowy; cięty;
żywy; dosadny; aromatyczy;
pikantny; nieprzyzwoity

radar ['rejder] s. radar

radiance ['rejdjens] s.
promieniowanie; blask;
promienność

radiant ['rejdjent] adj.
promieniujący; promienny;
rozpromieniony; rzucający
promienie

radiate ['rajdyejt] v.
promieniować (ciepłem,
światłem etc.)

radiation [,redy'ejszyn] s.
promieniowanie; źródło
promieniowania

radiator ['rejdy'ejter] s. grzejnik;
kaloryfer; chłodnica
(samochodowa); radiowa
antena nadawcza;
radioaktywna substancja
wydzielająca promienie

radical ['raedykel] s. pierwiastek;
radykał; adj. zasadniczy;
radykalny; podstawowy;
pierwiastkowy; korzeniowy

radio ['rejdjou] s. radio; adj.
radiowy; v. nadawać przez
radio; wysyłać drogą radiową
radioactive ['rejdjou'aektyw] adj.
radioaktywny;
promieniotwórczy
radio set ['rejdjou,set] s. aparat
radiowy; odbiornik radiowy
radiotherapy ['rejdjou-'terepy] s.
radioterapia
radish ['raedysz] s. rzodkiewka
radius ['rejdjes] s. promień
raffle ['raefl] s. loteria fantowa;
rupiecie; v. sprzedawać na
loterii; kupować los
raft [raeft] s. tratwa; (slang)
mnóstwo; v. spławiać na
tratwie; robić tratwę
rafter [raefter] s. krokiew
rag [raeg] s. szmata; łachman;
łupek; dachówka; v. (slang)
besztać; dokuczać
rage [rejdż] v. szaleć;
wściekać się; s. szał;
wściekłość; namiętność
ragged [raegyd] adj. szmatławy;
obdarty; podarty; poszarpany;
kosmaty; zapuszczony;
zaniedbany; wadliwy;
chropowaty
raid [rejd] s. obława; nalot;
najazd; v. urządzać obławę;
najeżdżać; dokonywać
napadu
rail [rejl] s. poręcz; szyna; kolej;
listwa; erekcja (slang); v.
ogradzać poręczami; kłaść
szyny; przewozić koleją;
drwić; gorzko narzekać;
pomstować
rail in ['rejl,yn] v. przywozić
koleją (materiały, towar)
rail off ['rejl,of] v. wywozić
koleją (ludzi, towary etc.)
railing ['rejlyng] s. sztachety;
ogrodzenie; poręcz; balustrada
railroad ['rejlroud] s. kolej; v.
przewozić koleją; przepychać
pospiesznie (np. ustawę);
(slang) wpakować niesłusznie
do więzienia
railway ['rejłłej] s. kolej; tor
kolejowy; tor na szynach

railway man ['rejłłej,men] s.
kolejarz
rain [rejn] s. deszcz; v. pada
deszcz; spadać deszczem
rainbow ['rejn,boł] s. tęcza
raincoat ['rejnkout] s. płaszcz
nieprzemakalny
rainfall ['rejn,fo:l] s. opad; ilość
opadów
rainproof ['rejn,pru:f] adj.
nieprzemakalny
rainy ['rajny] adj. deszczowy;
dżdżysty; mokry od deszczu
rainy day ['rejny,dej] exp.:
czarna godzina
raise [rejz] v. podnosić;
wskrzeszać; wznosić;
wynosić; hodować;
wychowywać; wysuwać;
wytaczać; wzniecać;
zrywać; wywoływać;
budzić; zbierać (np.
fundusze); wydobywać;
przerywać (np. oblężenie);
znosić (zakaz); s. podwyżka
(płac); podwyższenie
raisin ['rejzyn] s. rodzynek
rake [rejk] v. grabić;
przegrzebać; grzebać;
ostrzeliwać (wzdłuż);
obrzucać wzrokiem;
nachylać do tyłu; uganiać
się za zwierzyną; s. grabie;
grabki; rozpustnik
rake-off ['rejk,of] s. nielegalna
prowizja; łapówka
rake out ['rejk,aut] v.
wygrzebywać; wygarniać
(popiół etc.)
rakish ['rejkisz] adj. zgrabny;
rozpustny; hulaszczy;
(pozornie) szybki (okręt) (z
wyglądu)
rally ['raely] v. zbierać (się);
skupiać (się); przyjść do
siebie; ochłonąć; okrzepnąć;
ulegać poprawie (giełda);
żartować z kogoś; s.
zbiórka; wiec; okrzepnięcie;
ożywienie walki bokserskiej;
wymiana ciosów; poprawa
(koniunktury)
ram [raem] s. tryk; baran; taran;

tłok; dźwig hydrauliczny;
bijak; v. uderzyć; zderzyć
się; ubijać; wtłaczać; bić
taranem; upychać; ugniatać;
najechać; zanudzać

ramble ['raemb] v. włóczyć się;
przechadzać się; piąć się
(np. o bluszczu); mówić bez
związku; odbiegać od tematu;
s. wędrówka

ramify ['raemyfaj] v. rozgałęziać
(się); s. odgałęzienie (się)

ramp [raemp] s. rampa; v.
rzucać się; stawać na
tylnych łapach; opadać
pochyło; szaleć

rampart [raempa:rt] s. wał;
szaniec; v. umacniać
(szańcem)

ramshackle ['raem-szaekl] adj.
zrujnowany; walący się; w
ruinie

ran [raen] v. zob. run

ranch [raencz] s. rancho
(gospodarstwo hodowlane); v.
prowadzić rancho (farmę
etc.)

rancher ['raenczer] s. właściciel
rancha

rancid ['raensyd] adj. zjełczały
(tłuszcz, oliwa etc.)

rancor ['raenker] s. uraza;
zajadłość; zawziętość;
złość

rancorous [raenkeres] adj.
urażony; złośliwy

random ['raendem] adj. na chybił
trafił; przypadkowy; pierwszy
lepszy; nieplanowany

rang [raeng] v. zob. ring

range [rejndż] s. skala; zasięg;
rozpiętość; nośność;
strzelnica; pasmo; obszar;
wędrówka; pastwisko; piec
kuchenny; v. ustawiać;
układać; klasyfikować;
wędrować; nastawiać
teleskop; mieć zasięg;
wstrzeliwać się; ciągnąć
się; zaliczać się; rozciągać
się; sięgać; nieść

range finder ['rejndż,fajnder] s.
dalekomierz; odległościomierz

ranger [rejndżer] s. strażnik
leśny; policjant; komandos;
wędrowiec; desantowieć etc.

rank [raenk] s. ranga; stan;
stanowisko; v. ustawiać
rzędem; układać;
klasyfikować; zaszeregować;
przewyższać rangą; mieć
rangę; adj. wybujały; zjełczały;
śmierdzący; zupełny;
jaskrawy; obrzydliwy;
sprośny; wierutny

ransack ['raensaek] v.
przetrząsać; plądrować;
grzebać

ransom ['raensem] s. okup;
zwolnienie za okupem; v.
wykupić; zwalniać za
okupem

rant [raent] v. deklamować z
patosem; s. tyrada;
bombastyczna mowa

rap [raep] v. dać klapsa;
stukać; krytykować; s.
klaps; kołatanie; nagana;
zarzut; skazanie na więzienie;
odrobina

rapacious [re'pejszes] adj.
drapieżny; chciwy

rape [rejp] s. zgwałcenie
(kobiety); zniewolenie;
splądrowanie; uprowadzenie
v. gwałcić (kobietę);
uprowadzać; plądrować;
pogwałcić neutralność

rapid ['raepyd] adj. prędki;
szybki; bystry; stromy

rapidity ['raepydyty] s.
szybkość; bystrość; rwący
nurt (rzeki)

rapids ['raepyds] pl. progi (na
rzece); wodospad

rapt [raept] adj. zaabsorbowany;
zachwycony; urzeczony;
oczarowany

rapture ['raepczer] s. zachwyt;
uniesienie; wzięcie żywcem
do nieba

rare [reer] adj. rzadki;
niedopieczony (np. kotlet); na
pół surowy; niedosmażony;
adv. rzadko

rarity ['reeryty] s. rzadkość

rascal ['raeskal] s. hultaj; łobuz;
adj. hulatajski
rascally ['raeskely] adj. hultajski;
łobuzerski
rash [raesz] s. wysypka skórna;
ulewa; powódź; adj.
pochopny; popędliwy;
nieprzemyślany
rasher ['raeszer] s. płatek (np.
szynki)
rasp [raesp] s. raszpla; pilnik;
zgrzytanie; v. drapać;
skrobać; drażnić; chrapliwie
mówić
raspberry [ra:zbery] s. malina
rat [raet] s. szczur; łamistrajk;
donosiciel; v. polować na
szczury; zdradzać; donosić;
zaprzedawać
rats [raets] pl. szczury; bzdura
rate [rejt] s. stopa; stosunek;
proporcja; wysokość;
poziom; szybkość; cena;
stawka; opłata; podatek;
stopień; klasa; v. szacować;
oceniać; ustalać; zaliczać;
opodatkować; zasługiwać;
besztać; wymyślać
rate of exchange ['rejt of
yks'czejndż] s. kurs wymiany
rate of interest [,rejt of 'yntryst]
s. stopa procentowa
rather ['raedzer] adv. raczej;
chętniej; dość; nieco; do
pewnego stopnia; poniekąd;
zamiast
ratify ['raetyfaj] v. zatwierdzać;
ratyfikować
ration ['raeszyn] s. przydział;
porcja; racja; v. racjonować;
sprzedawać na kartki
rational ['raeszynl] adj. rozumny;
rozsądny; racjonalny;
wymierny; sensowny
rationalize ['raeszyne,lajz] v.
racjonalizować;
usprawiedliwiać
rattle ['raetl] v. grzechotać
szczękać; brzęczać; stukać;
trzaskać; terkotać; paplać
wiersze; s. grzechotanie;
terkot; stuk; paplanina; gaduła
rattler ['raetler] s. grzechotnik

rattlesnake ['raetl,snejk] s.
grzechotnik
ravage ['raewydż] s.
spustoszenie; zniszczenie; v.
pustoszyć; niszczyć;
plądrować
rave [rejw] v. bredzić;
majaczyć;
szaleć; wściekać się; wyć;
zachwycać się; s. wrzask;
wycie; zaślepienie; przesadna
pochwała (entuzjastyczna)
raven ['rejwn] s. kruk; adj.
kruczy; ['raewen] s. grabież;
łup; v. pożerać; szukać łupu;
mieć szalony apetyt
ravenous ['raewynes] adj.
wygłodniały; zgłodniały;
żarłoczny; drapieżny
ravine [re'wi:n] s. parów; jar;
wąwóz
raving ['rejwyng] adj. bredzący;
szalony; porywający (np.
pięknością); s. atak furii;
bredzenie; majaczenie
ravish ['raewysz] v. porywać
(kobietę); gwałcić (kobietę)
raw [ro:] adj. surowy; otwarty
(np. rana); wrażliwy;
nieokrzesany; brutalny;
nieprzyzwoity; s. gołe ciało;
surówka; v. ocierać (skórę)
ray [rej] s. promień; promyk;
(ryba) płaszczka; v.
promieniować; naświetlać;
prześwietlać; wysyłać
promienie (światła etc.)
rayon ['rejon] s. sztuczny jedwab
raze [rejz] v. zburzyć; zatrzeć;
otrzeć (skórę)
razor ['rejzer] s. brzytwa
razor blade ['rejzer'blejd] s.
żyletka; ostrze brzytwy
re [ri:] prep. w sprawie; tyczy;
dotyczy; przedrostek: znowu;
od nowa
reach [ri:cz] v. osiągać;
wyciągnąć (np. rękę);
dosięgnąć; dotrzeć;
docierać; sięgnąć; s.
sięgnięcie; zasięg; połać;
przestrzeń; pobliże; granice
reach out ['ri:cz,aut] v.

wyciągnąć (rękę etc.)
react [ri:'aekt] v. reagować;
oddziaływać; przeciwdziałać
reactor [ri:'aekter] s. reaktor (np.
jądrowy)
read; read; read [ri:d; red; red]
read [ri:d] v. czytać;
tłumaczyć; interpretować
read out ['ri:d,aut] v. wydalać
kogoś; wyczytywać
readout ['ri:daut] s. odczyt
wyników komputera
read to [ri:d tu] v. czytać
komuś
reader ['ri:der] s. czytelnik;
korektor; czytanka; wypisy;
recenzent (wydawnictwa)
readily ['redyly] adv. łatwo;
chętnie; ochoczo; bez trudu
readiness ['redynys] s.
gotowość; pogotowie;
obrotność; ciętość;
przytomność umysłu
reading ['ri:dyng] s. czytanie;
oczytanie; interpretacja;
lektura; czytelnictwo; adj.
czytający
readjust ['ri:e'dżast] v.
dopasować na nowo
ready ['redy] adj. gotów;
gotowy; przygotowany; adv.
w przygotowaniu; gotowy; v.
przygotowywać
ready-made ['redy'mejd] s.
konfekcja; adj. gotowy
ready-to-wear ['redy,tu'łeer] s.
odzież fabrycznej produkcji
reaffirm ['ry:eferm] v.
potwierdzić (ponownie)
real [ryel] adj. rzeczywisty;
realny; istotny; prawdziwy;
autentyczny; faktyczny
real estate ['ryel,es'tejt] s.
nieruchomość; realność
realism ['ryelyzem] s. realizm
realistic ['ryelystyk] s. adj.
realistyczny
reality [ry'aelyty] s.
rzeczywistość; realizm;
prawdziwość
realization [,ryelaj'zejszyn] s.
realizacja; spełnienie;
wykonanie; spieniężenie;

uświadomienie sobie
realize ['ry:e,lajz] v.
urzeczywistnić; realizować;
uprzytamniać; zdawać sobie
sprawę; uzyskiwać;
zdobywać (majątek)
really ['ryely] adv. rzeczywiście;
naprawdę; doprawdy;
faktycznie; istotnie
realm [relm] s. królestwo;
dziedzina; sfera; zakres
realpolitik [rej'a:lpouly'tyk] s.
polityka egoistyczna
realtor ['ryelter] s. pośrednik
sprzedaży nieruchomości
realty ['ryelty] s. nieruchomość
reap [ry:p] v. żąć; zbierać
plony, owoce pracy etc.
reaper ['ry:per] s. żniwiarz;
żniwiarka
reappear ['ry:e'pier] v. zjawić
się ponownie; znowu ukazać
się
rear [rier] s. tył; tyły; ustęp; v.
stawać dęba; hodować;
wychowywać; wznosić (się);
wybudować; wystawiać
rear guard ['rier,ga:rd] s. tylna
straż
rear-light ['rier,lajt] s. tylne
światło samochodu
rearm ['ry:'a:rm] v. ponownie
uzbrajać
rearmament ['ry:'a:rmement] s.
remilitaryzacja
rearmost [rie:r,moust] adj.
końcowy; ostatni
rear-view mirror ['rier,wju:'myrer]
s. (tylne) lusterko w
samochodzie (do sprawdzania
ruchu za samochodem)
rearrange ['ry:erejndż] v.
przestawić; zmieniać
(porządek); poprawić (fryzurę
etc.)
rearwards ['rierłedz] adv. wstecz;
ku tyłowi; na tył
reason ['ri:zn] s. rozum; powód;
uzasadnienie; motyw;
przesłanka; rozsądek; v.
rozumować; rozważać;
wnioskować; rozprawiać;
przekonywać; dowodzić

reason out ['ri:zn,aut] v.
przemyślać; wyrozumować;
dociekać

reason with ['ri:zn,łyg] v.
przekonywać kogoś

reasonable ['ri:znabl] adj.
rozumny; rozsądny;
umiarkowany; słuszny;
racjonalny

reassure [,ry:a'szuer] v.
zapewniać; upewniać;
ubezpieczać na nowo;
uspakajać; przywracać
zaufanie; upewniać na nowo

reassuring [,ry:a'szueryng] adj.
uspakajający

rebate [ry'bejt] s. rabat; zwrot
(części kwoty); v. udzielać
rabatu; potrącać (z
rachunku); zamortyzować
przytępiać

rebel ['rebel] s. buntownik; v.
buntować się; adj.
zbuntowany; buntowniczy

rebellion [ry'beljen] s. bunt;
powstanie

rebellious [ry'beljes] adj.
zbuntowany; buntowniczy;
niesforny; oporny

rebirth [ry'be:rg] s. odrodzenie;
odżywanie

re-book ['ry:buk] v. zamawiać
na nowo (program teatralny,
bilety lotnicze etc.)

rebound [ry'baund] s. odbicie;
odskok; rykoszet; v.
odskakiwać; odbijać (się)
(sobie na kimś)

rebuff [ry'baf] s. ofuknięcie;
odrzucenie; v. ofuknąć; dać
odprawę; odesłać z kwitkiem

rebuild ['ry:byld] v.
odbudowywać;
przebudowywać

rebuke [ry'bju:k] s. nagana; v.
upominać; łajać

recall [ry'ko:l] v. odwoływać;
przypominać (sobie);
wycofywać; cofać
(obietnicę); s. nakaz powrotu

recap ['ry:kaep] s. opona
ponownie gumowana; v.
ponownie wulkanizować

opony; powtarzać dla
podsumowania

recapture ['ri:'kaepczer] v.
odzyskać; s. odzyskanie

recede [ry'si:d] v. cofać się;
oddalać się; mdleć; słabnąć

receipt [ry'si:t] s. pokwitowanie;
odbiór; recepta

receive [ry'si:w] v. otrzymywać;
dostawać; odbierać;
przyjmować (np. gości)

receiver [ry'si:wer] s. odbiornik
(radiowy); słuchawka
(telefoniczna); odbiorca;
syndyk; zarządca upadłości

recent ['ri:snt] adj. niedawny;
świeży; nowy

recently ['ri:sntly] adv.
niedawno; świeżo; ostatnio;
współcześnie

reception [ry'sepszyn] s.
przyjęcie; odbiór; recepcja

reception desk [ry'sepszyn,desk]
s. biuro do przyjmowania
interesantów; portiernia; biuro
przyjęć

receptionist [ry'sepszynyst] s.
recepcjonistka; sekretarka
przyjmująca klientów; portier

recess [ry'ses] s. przerwa
(między lekcjami); ferie;
wgłębienie; nisza; wnęka; v.
odraczać; wkładać do wnęki;
robić wnęką; rozjeżdżać się
na ferie

recession [ry'seszyn] s.
cofnięcie; recesja
(gospodarcza); wgłębienie;
wnęka; kryzys; zastój

recipe ['rysypy] s. przepis;
recepta

recipient [ry'sypjent] adj.
odbiorczy; s. odbiorca;
zdobywca nagrody; osoba
obdarowana

reciprocal [ry'syprekel] adj.
wzajemny; odwrotny; s.
odwrotność (w matematyce)

recital [ry'sajtl] s.
przedstawienie; opowiadanie;
recytacja; koncert;
deklamowanie utworu

recite [ry'sajt] s. recytować

wiersz; wyliczać
reckless ['reklys] adj.
(niebezpiecznie) lekkomyślny;
nie uważający; na oślep;
wariacki; brawurowy;
szaleńczy; zuchowaty
reckon ['reken] v. liczyć;
sądzić; myśleć że; polegać
na
reckon up ['reken,ap] v. zliczać;
zsumować; podsumowywać
reckon with ['reken,łys] v.
liczyć się (z kimś)
reckoning ['rekenyng] s.
obliczanie (położenia);
rachuba; obrachunek;
kalkulacja; rozliczenie
reclaim [ry'klejm] v. odzyskiwać
(pod uprawę); użyźniać;
przerabiać odpadki;
wyprowadzać z (zaniedbania,
błędu etc.); zażądać zwrotu;
dochodzić
recline [ry'klajn] v. kłaść się;
wyciągać się; złożyć (np.
głowę); spoczywać na pół
leżąc
recognition [,rekeg'nyszyn] s.
rozpoznanie; uznanie;
pozdrowienie; dowód uznania
recognize ['rekeg,najz] v.
rozpoznawać; pozdrowić;
uznawać; przyznawać;
udzielać (głosu)
recoil [ry'kojl] v. wzdrygać się;
cofać się; kopać (np. kolbą);
odskoczyć; odbijać; s.
odskok; odrzut; odbicie;
wzdrygnięcie się
recollect [reke'lekt] v.
wspominać; przypominać
sobie; zbierać na nowo;
przypominać sobie z trudem
recollection [,reke'lekszyn] s.
wspomnienie; pamięć
recommend [reke'mend] v.
polecać; zalecać; dobrze
świadczyć
recommendation
[,rekemen'dejszyn] s.
polecenie; zlecenie
recompense ['rekem,pens] v.
odpłacać; dawać

odszkodowanie; s.
wynagrodzenie;
zadośćuczynienie;
odszkodowanie; rekompensata
reconcile ['rekensajl] v. godzić
(sprzeczności); zażegnać
(spór); pojednać; pogodzić
się
reconciliation [,reken,syły'ejszyn]
s. pojednanie; pogodzenie
reconsider [,ri:ken'syder] v.
ponownie rozważyć;
reasumować
reconstruct [,ri:ken'strakt] v.
odbudowywać; odtwarzać
reconstruction ['ri:ken'strakszyn]
s. rekonstrukcja; odbudowa
record ['ryko:rd] v. zapisywać;
notować; rejestrować;
zaznaczać; nagrywać; s.
zapiska; archiwum; rejestracja;
dokument; przeszłość
(czyjaś); pamięć o kimś;
nagranie; rekord
recorder [ry'ko:rder] s.
rejestrator; aparat zapisujący;
pisak; pisarz archiwista
record holder ['reko:rd,houlder]
s. rekordzista; mistrz
recording ['reko:rdyng] s.
nagranie (płyta)
record player ['reko:rd,plejer] s.
adapter
recourse [ry'ko:rs] s. uciekanie
się (ratunek)
recover [ry'kawer] v. odzyskać;
nadrabiać; powetować sobie;
uzyskać przywracać;
wyzdrowieć; ochłonąć;
przyjść do siebie
recovery [ry'kawery] s.
odzyskanie (pozycji);
wyzdrowienie; poprawa
(gospodarcza)
recreation [,rekry'ejszyn] s.
rozrywka; zabawa;
odtworzenie
recruit [ry'kru:t] s. rekrut;
poborowy; v. werbować;
uzupełniać (stan zatrudnienia)
rectangle ['rektaengl] s.
prostokąt; a. prostokątny
rectify ['rektyfy] v. prostować

(np. błąd); poprawiać (np. plan); usuwać (np. nadużycia)

rector ['rekter] s. proboszcz; rektor

rectory ['rektery] s. probostwo

recur [ry'ke:r] v. powtarzać się; przypominać się; nawiązywać do czegoś (wielokrotnie)

recurrent [ry'karent] adj. powracający; nawracający

recycle [,ry'sajkl] v. puścić w obieg drugi raz; używać wielokrotnie

red [red] adj. czerwony; s. czerwień; lewicowiec; komunista; radykał (skrajny); forsa (sl.)

red-bait ['redbejt] v. oskarżać o komunizm (USA)

red-blooded ['red,bladyd] adj. męski; krzepki; jurny

redden ['reden] v. zaczerwienić się; zarumienić się

reddish ['redysz] adj. czerwonawy

redeem [ry'di:m] v. wykupywać; okupywać; wybawiać; zbawiać; odkupić; zamienić; kompensować

redemption [ry'dempszyn] s. wykup; okupienie; odkupienie; wybawienie; umorzenie; zbawienie

red-handed ['red'haendyd] adj. splamiony krwią; exp.: na gorącym uczynku

red letter day ['red'leter,dej] s. dzień specjalny; dzień świąteczny

redouble [ry'dabl] v. podwoić (się); zwijać się

reduce [ry'dju:s] v. zmniejszać (się); chudnąć; redukować; ograniczać; obniżać; dostosowywać; sprowadzać; doprowadzać; rozcieńczać; osłabiać; odtleniać; wytapiać

reduction [ry'dakszyn] s. zmniejszenie; redukcja; obniżka; sprowadzenie;

dostosowanie; odtlenienie; wytapianie

redundant [ry'dandent] adj. niepotrzebny; zbędny; zbyteczny

reed [ri:d] s. trzcina; słoma; fujarka; strzała; płocha tkacka; stroik (muzyczny)

reeducation ['ry:edju'kejszyn] s. przeszkolenie ponowne

reef [ri:f] s. rafa; skała podwodna; ref; v. refować

reek [ri:k] s. odór; para; dym; v. śmierdzieć; parować; dymić; wędzić; ociekać (krwią)

reel [ri:l] s. szpula; cewka; rolka; chwianie się; kręcenie się; v. nawijać; odwijać; rozwijać; recytować; chwiać się; zataczać się; kręcić się; dostawać zawrotu głowy; dawać zawrót głowy; zachwiać się na nogach

reel off ['ri:l,of] v. odwijać

reel up ['ri:l,ap] v. nawijać

reelect ['ri:y'lekt] v. ponownie wybierać

reenter ['ri:'enter] v. ponownie wchodzić (w posiadanie etc.)

reentry ['ri:'entry] s. ponowne wejście; rewindykacja

re-establish [,ry:ys'taeblysz] v. ponownie: zakładać; ustanawiać; ustalać; wprowadzać

refer [ry'fe:r] v. odsyłać; powiązywać; skierować; odwoływać; cytować; odnosić się; dotyczyć; powoływać się

referee [refe'ri:] s. sędzia sportowy; rozjemca; v. sędziować

reference ['refrens] s. odsyłacz; odnośnik; odwoływanie się; aluzja; informacja; referencja; stosunek; związek; wgląd; przelotna wzmianka

reference book ['referens,bu:k] s. tekst podręczny; podręcznik

reference library ['referens laj'brery] s. biblioteka

podręczna naukowo-
informacyjna
referendum [,refe'rendem] s.
referendum
refill [ry:'fyl] s. ponowne
napełnienie; wypełnienie;
nowy zapas; v. ponownie
napełniać, wkładać,
zapełniać etc.
refine [ry'fajn] v. oczyszczać;
rafinować; wysubtelniać;
rozprawiać subtelnie
refinement [ry'fajnment] s.
rafinowanie; wyrafinowanie;
subtelność; wytworność
refinery [ry'fajnery] s. rafineria
reflect [ry'flekt] v. odbijać;
odzwierciedlać; rozmyślać;
zastanawiać się;
krytykować; przynosić
(zaszczyt, ujmę)
reflection [ry'flekszyn] s. odbicie;
odzwierciedlenie; odbicie
światła; zarzut; rozwaga;
namysł; wzmianka; pomysł;
wstyd
reflex ['ry:fleks] s. odruch;
refleks; odbicie;
odzwierciedlenie; adj.
refleksyjny; odbity; wygięty;
v. poddawać refleksom;
wyginać wstecz
reflexive [ry'fleksyw] adj.
odbijający; pełen zadumy;
refleksyjny
reform [ry'fo:rm] v.
reformować; poprawiać;
usuwać; ulegać reformie; s.
reforma; poprawa
reformation [,refer'mejszyn] s.
reformacja; poprawa
reformer [ry'fo:rmer] s.
reformator (moralności,
warunków etc.)
refract [ry'fraekt] v. załamywać
światło; wyginać promień
światła
refractory [ry'fraektery] adj.
oporny; uporczywy; krnąbrny;
odporny; ogniotrwały
refrain [ry'frejn] v.
powstrzymywać się; s. refren
refresh [ry'fresz] v. odświeżyć;

wzmacniać; pokrzepiać
refreshment [ry'freszment] s.
odpoczynek; wytchnienie;
odświeżenie; zakąska
refrigerator [ry'frydże,rejter] s.
lodówka; chłodnia
refuel ['ry:'fjuel] v. zaopatrzyć
w paliwo; dodać paliwa
refuge ['refju:dż] s. schronienie;
azyl; przytułek; v. schronić
się
refugee [,refju'dżi:] s. zbieg;
uchodźca; uciekinier
refund [ry'fand] s. zwrot; spłata;
v. zwracać pieniądze
refusal [ry'fju:zel] s. odmowa;
prawo opcji; wbijanie do oporu
refuse [ry'fju:z] v. odmawiać;
odrzucać; adj. odpadowy; s.
odpadki; rupiecie
refute [ry'fju:t] v. zbijać (np.
twierdzenie)
regain [ry'gejn] v. odzyskać;
wrócić (do zdrowia)
regal ['ry:gel] adj. królewski
regard [ry'ga:rd] v. spoglądać;
zważać; uważać; dotyczyć;
s. wzgląd; spojrzenie;
szacunek; uwaga;
pozdrowienia; ukłony
regarding [ry'ga:rdyng] prep.
odnośnie; co się tyczy; w
sprawie
regardless [ry'ga:rdlys] adv. w
każdym razie; adj. nie
zważający; bez względu (na
kłopoty etc.); nie licząc się (z
wydatkami)
regard of [ry'ga:rd,ow] exp.: co
się tyczy; w sprawie etc.
regent ['ri:dżent] s. regent;
opiekun; członek zarządu
regime [ry'żi:m] s. ustrój; reżym;
tryb życia; system; rządy
regiment ['redżyment] s. pułk;
zastęp; v. organizować;
koszarować; wcielać do
pułku
region ['ri:dżen] s. okolica; sfera;
rejon; obszar; dzielnica
register ['redżyster] v.
rejestrować; zapamiętywać;
wysyłać polecony list;

prowadzić rejestr;
wstrzeliwać się; wyrażać
minami
registered letter
['redżysterd,leter] s. list
polecony
registration [,redżys'trejszyn] s.
rejestracja; meldunek; ilość
zarejestrowana
regret [ry'gret] s. ubolewanie;
żal; v. żałować czegoś
regrettable [ry'gretebl] adj.
godny ubolewania
regular ['regjuler] adj. regularny;
stały; zawodowy; poprawny;
przepisowy; s. regularny
(żołnierz, ksiądz etc.); stały
gość; wierny partyjniak
regularity [,regju'laeryty] s.
regularność;
systematyczność
regulate ['regjulejt] v.
regulować; przystosowywać
do wymogów
regulation [,regju'lejszyn] s.
przepis; regulowanie; adj.
przepisowy; zwykły
rehearsal [ry'he:rsel] s. próba;
powtarzanie
rehearse [ry'he:rs] v. odbywać
próbę; powtarzać
reign [rejn] v. panować;
władać; s. władza;
panowanie
rein [rejn] v. kierować wodzami;
trzymać na wodzach
reins [rejns] pl. wodze
reindeer ['rejn,dier] s. renifer
reinforce [,ri:yn'fors] v.
wzmocnić; popierać; dodać
sił
reject [ry'dżekt] v. odrzucić;
odpalić; zwracać; ['rydżekt]
s. wybrakowany towar;
niezdatny do wojska; coś
odrzuconego
rejection [ry'dżekszyn] s.
odrzucenie; odmowa;
wybrakowany towar; oblanie
studenta; odkosz
rejoice [ry'dżojs] v. radować;
cieszyć się; weselić się
rejoicing [ry'dżojsyng] s.

radość; uradowanie; adj.
uradowany
rejoin ['ri:dżoyn] v. ponownie
łączyć (się); zestawiać
połamane części;
odpowiadać na zarzut
relapse [ry'laeps] s. nawrót;
pogorszenie; v. ponownie
popadać; zapadać z
powrotem
relate [ry'lejt] v. opowiadać;
referować; łączyć się
related [ry'lejtyd] adj. bliski;
spokrewniony;
spowinowacony; związany;
pokrewny; powinowaty
relation [ry'lejszyn] s.
sprawozdanie; opowiadanie;
stosunek; związek;
pokrewieństwo;
powinowactwo; krewny
relationship [ry'lejszynszyp] s.
stosunek; pokrewieństwo;
powinowactwo; zależność
relative ['reletyw] adj. względny;
stosunkowy; podrzędny;
zależny; dotyczący; adv.
odnośnie; w sprawie; s.
krewny; zaimek względny
relax [ry'laeks] v. odprężać
(się); osłabnąć; rozluźniać
się; łagodnieć; odpoczywać
relaxation [,ry:laek'sejszyn] n.
odprężenie; odpoczynek;
rozrywka; złagodzenie
relay [ry'lej] s. bieg rozstawny;
wzmacniacz; v. przekazywać;
zmieniać (tor); kłaść na
nowo
relay race [ry'lej,rejs] s. bieg
rozstawny; bieg sztafetowy
release [ry'li:z] v. wypuszczać;
uwalniać; zwalniać; s.
zwolnienie; uwolnienie;
puszczenie (do druku); spust;
wyzwalacz; wypuszczenie
(filmu)
relent [ry'lent] v. łagodnieć;
mięknąć; dać się wzruszyć
relentless [ry'lentlys] adj.
nieugięty; bezlitosny;
nieprzejednany; nieustępliwy;
srogi

relevant ['relewent] adj. istotny; trafny; na miejscu; należący do rzeczy

reliability [ry,laje'bylyty] s. rzetelność; solidność; pewność

reliable [ry'lajebl] adj. pewny; solidny; rzetelny

reliance [ry'lajens] s. zaufanie; otucha

reliant [ry'lajent] adj. ufny w siebie; liczący na kogoś; zależny od czegoś

relic ['relyk] n. zabytek; relikwie; pozostałość; resztka

relief [ry'li:f] n. odprężenie; ulga; urozmaicenie; zapomoga; pomoc; zmiana (np. warty); płaskorzeźba; uwypuklenie

relieve [ry'li:w] v. nieść pomoc, ulgę; ulżyć (sobie); oddać mocz; ożywić; zmieniać wartę; zluzować; uwypuklić (na tle czegoś); uwydatnić

religion [ry'lydżyn] s. religia; obrządek; wyznanie; zakon

religious [ry'lydżes] adj. pobożny; religijny; zakonny; s. zakonnik; zakonnica

relinquish [ry'lynkłysz] v. porzucać; wyrzekać się czegoś; zaniechać; zrzekać się; rezygnować; wypuścić coś z rąk

relish ['relysz] s. smak; posmak; przyprawa; przysmak; urok; zamiłowanie; v. smakować w czymś; czynić smaczniejszym; przyprawiać; mieć dobry smak; być przyjemnym; dodawać smaku

reluctance [ry'laktens] s. niechęć; opór (magnetyczny); wstręt

reluctant [ry'laktent] adj. niechętny; oporny

rely on [ry'laj,on] v. polegać na czymś lub kimś; liczyć na

remain [ry'mejn] v. pozostawać

remains [ry'mejns] pl. pozostałości; resztki; przeżytki; zwłoki; szczątki

remainder [ry'mejnder] s. reszta; pozostałość; remanent

remand [ry'maend] v. odsyłać (do niższej instancji lub więzienia); s. odesłanie do więzienia; człowiek odesłany z powrotem

remark [ry'ma:rk] v. zauważyć; zrobić uwagę; s. uwaga

remarkable [ry'ma:rkebl] adj. wybitny; godny uwagi

remedy ['remydy] s. lekarstwo; środek; rada; v. leczyć; zaradzać; naprawiać

remember [ry'member] v. pamiętać; przypominać; pozdrawiać; modlić się za kogoś; mieć w pamięci

remembrance [ry'membrens] s. wspomnienie; pamiątka; pamięć; pozdrowienie; ukłony

remind [ry'majnd] v. przypominać coś komuś; przypomnieć

reminder [ry'majnder] s. przypomnienie; upomnienie; ponaglenie; ktoś przypominający

reminiscent [,remy'nysnt] adj. przypominający; wspominający; pełen wspomnień

remiss [ry'mys] adj. niedbały; ospały; niechlujny

remit [ry'myt] s. przekazywać (pieniądze); darować (dług); odpuszczać (grzechy); odsyłać; przywracać; łagodzić; łagodnieć; słabnąć

remittance [ry'mytens] s. przesyłka pieniężna; wypłata

remnant ['remnent] s. resztka; pozostałość; ślad czegoś

remodel [ry'modl] v. przerabiać; odnowić; przemodelować

remonstrate ['remenstrejt] v. protestować

remorse [ri'mo:rs] s. wyrzuty sumienia; skrupuły

remorseless [ri'mo:rslys] adj. bezlitosny; nieskruszony

remote [ry'mout] adj. odległy; zdalny; mało prawdopodobny; obcy

removal [ry'mu:wl] s. usunięcie;
przeprowadzka
remove [ry'mu:w] v. usuwać;
przewozić; zdejmować;
przeprowadzać się;
opuszczać; s. przeprowadzka;
odległość; stopień;
oddalenie
remover [ry'mu:wer] s. usuwacz
(plam); środek do usuwania
renaissance [ry'nesens] s.
odrodzenie; renesans; a.
renesansowy
rend; rent; rent [rend; rent; rent]
rend [rend] v. drzeć; targać;
wydzierać; urągać;
rozdzierać
render ['render] v. uczynić;
zrobić; oddawać; okazywać;
składać; wydawać; płacić;
odpłacać; oczyszczać;
wytapiać; tynkować; s.
odpłata (np. w naturze);
pierwsza warstwa tynku
rendezvous ['ra:ndy,wu:] s.
randka; umówione spotkanie;
miejsce spotkań
renew [ry'nu:] v. odnawiać;
ponawiać; wznawiać;
odświeżać; prolongować
renewal [ry'nu:el] s. odnowienie
(np. kontraktu)
renounce [ry'nauns] v. zrzekać
się; zrezygnować; wyrzekać
się; wypowiadać;
odstąpować; nie uznawać
renovate [ry'nowejt] v.
odnowić; naprawić
renown [ry'naun] s. sława;
rozgłos; pogłoska
renowned [ry'naund] adj. sławny
rent 1. [rent] v. zob. rend
rent 2. [rent] s. komorne;
czynsz; renta; najem;
rozdarcie; szczelina; rozłam;
parów; v. wynajmować;
dzierżawić; pobierać czynsz;
być wynajmowanym
rental ['rentl] s. czynsz;
komorne; wypożyczanie; adj.
czynszowy
rental agency ['rentl'ejdżensy] s.
biuro wynajmu (narzędzi,

mieszkań etc.)
rent free ['rent'fri:] adj. wolny od
opłaty czynszowej
repair [ry'peer] v. pójść;
uczęszczać; naprawiać;
reperować; remontować;
powetowć; wynagrodzić; s.
naprawa; remont; stan
repair shop [ry'peer,szop] s.
warsztat naprawy
reparation [repa'rejszyn] s.
naprawa; remont;
odszkodowanie
repartee [repa:r'ti:] s. riposta;
cięta odpowiedź; odcinanie
się
repay [ry:'pej] v. spłacić;
zwrócić; wynagrodzić;
odwzajemnić się; oddać
repeat [ry:'pi:t] v. powtarzać
(się); repetować; odbijać się;
robić powtórkę; robić
ponownie; odtwarzać; s.
powtórka; powtórzenie;
powtórne zamówienie; a.
powtórny; wielokrotny
repel [ry'pel] v. odpierać;
odrzucać; odtrącać; budzić
odrazą, niechęć, wstręt etc.
repent [ry'pent] v. żałować
repentance [ry'pentens] s.
skrucha; żal
repentant [ry'pentent] adj.
żałujący; pełen skruchy
repetition [,repy'tyszyn] s.
powtórzenie; powtórka
replace [ry'plejs] v. zastępować;
zwracać oddawać;
umieszczać z powrotem;
przywrócić; wymienić
replacement [ry'plejsment] s.
zastępstwo; zastępca;
zastąpienie; wymiana (części)
replenish [ry'plenysz] v.
ponownie napełniać;
wypełniać; uzupełniać
replay [ry'plej] v. ponownie
rozgrywać; ['ry:plej] s.
ponowna rozgrywka
reply [ry'plaj] v. odpowiadać; s.
odpowiedź
report [ry'po:rt] v. opowiadać;
meldować; dawać

sprawozdanie; zdawać
sprawę; pisać sprawozdanie;
referować; s. raport;
sprawozdanie; komunikat;
opinia; huk; wybuch; pogłoska
reporter [ru'po:rter] s.
dziennikarz; sprawozdawca;
reporter
repose [ry'pouz] s. odpoczynek;
spokój; v. odpoczywać;
spoczywać; polegać;
opierać; pokładać
represent [,repry'zent] v.
przedstawiać;
reprezentować; wyobrażać;
grać (kogoś)
representation [,repryzen'tejszyn]
s. przedstawicielstwo;
reprezentacja; przedstawienie;
wyobrażenie
representative [,repry'zentetyw]
adj. przedstawiający;
reprezentujący; wyobrażający;
s. przedstawiciel; reprezentant
(poseł na sejm)
repress [ry'pres] v. tłumić;
hamować; powstrzymywać;
poskromić
reprieve [ry'pri:w] v. zawieszać;
odraczać; dawać odroczenie;
s. odroczenie; darowanie;
zmiana kary (śmierci)
reprimand ['reprymaend] v.
karcić; udzielać nagany; s.
nagana
reproach [ry'proucz] v. robić
wyrzuty; wymawiać; s.
wyrzut; zarzut; wymówka
reproachful [ry'prouczful] adj.
pełen wyrzutu
reproduce [,rypre'du:s] v.
odtwarzać; reprodukować;
rozmnażać; wznawiać
reproduction [,ri:pre'dakszyn] s.
reprodukcja; rozmnażanie się;
płodzenie
reproof [ry'pru:f] s. nagana
reprove [ry'pru:w] v. ganić
reptant ['reptent] adj. pełzający
reptile ['reptajl] s. gad; płaz;
gadzina; adj. pełzający;
gadzinowy
republic [ry'pablyk] s. republika;

rzeczpospolita
republican [ry'pablyken] adj.
republikański; s. republikanin
repugnance [ry'pagnens] s.
odraza; niechęć;
niezgodność; sprzeczność
repugnant [ry'pagnent] adj.
odrażający; oporny;
sprzeczny; niezgodny
repulse [ry'pals] v. odpierać;
odrzucać; odtrącać; s.
odparcie; odrzucenie; odmowa
repulsive [ry'palsyw] adj.
odrażający; wstrętny;
odpychający; budzący odrazę
reputable ['repjutebl] adj.
szanowany; zaszczytny
reputation [,repju'tejszyn] s.
reputacja; sława; dobre imię
repute [ry'pju:t] s. reputacja;
sława; v. uważać za coś
request [ry'kłest] s. prośba;
życzenie; żądanie;
zapotrzebowanie; v. prosić o
pozwolenie; upraszać;
poprosić o przysługę
require [ry'kłajer] v. żądać;
nakazywać; wymagać; być
wymaganym
required [ry'kłajerd] adj.
obowiązkowy; wymagany;
żądany
requirement [ry'kłajerment] s.
wymaganie; żądanie; potrzeba
requisite ['rekłyzyt] adj.
wymagany; s. rzecz
konieczna, potrzebna; rekwizyt
requisition [,rekły'zyszyn] s.
żądanie; nakaz;
zapotrzebowanie; v.
wydawać zapotrzebowanie;
zapotrzebowywać;
rekwirować; zażądać
dostaw
requite [ry'kłajt] v.
odwzajemniać się;
wynagradzać; zemścić się
rescue ['reskju:] v. ratować;
wybawiać; odbijać z
więzienia; s. ratunek; odbicie
z więzienia; odebranie
przemocą
research [ry'se:rcz] s.

poszukiwanie; badanie
researcher [ry'se:rczer] s. badacz
(naukowy etc.); badaczka
resemblance [ry'zemblens] s.
podobieństwo
resemble [ry'zembl] v. być
podobnym (z wyglądu)
resent [ry'zent] v. czuć urazę
resentful [ry'zentful] adj.
urażony; obrażony; zawzięty
resentment [ry'zentment] s.
uraza; złość; oburzenie;
obraza
reservation [‚rezer'wejszyn] s.
zastrzeżenie; zarezerwowanie;
miejsce zarezerwowane;
rezerwat (np. indiański);
rezerwa; zapas; ograniczenie
reserve [ry'ze:rw] v. odkładać;
zastrzegać; rezerwować; s.
rezerwa; zapas; rezerwat;
zastrzeżenie; warunek
reserved [ry'ze:rwd] adj.
zarezerwowany;
powściągliwy; pełen rezerwy;
z rezerwą; zastrzeżony
reservoir ['reserwła:r] s. zbiornik;
zbiór; pokład kopalniany; v.
składać w zbiorniku
reside [ry'zajd] v. mieszkać;
tkwić; spoczywać w;
osadzać się
residence ['rezydens] s. miejsce
zamieszkania; pobyt (stały)
residence permit
['rezydens,per'myt] s. prawo
pobytu
resident ['rezydent] s. stały
mieszkaniec; adj. zamieszkały;
umiejscowiony; zamieszkujący
residue ['rezydju:] s. reszta;
pozostałość; reszta
spadkowa
resign [ry'zajn] v. zrzekać się;
wyrzekać się; godzić się z
losem
resignation [‚rezyg'nejszyn] s.
dymisja; zrzeczenie się;
wyrzeczenie się; pogodzenie
się (z losem)
resigned [ry'zajnd] adj.
zrezygnowany; w stanie
spoczynku

resin ['rezyn] s. żywica; v.
zaprawiać żywicą
resist [ry'zyst] v. opierać się;
stawiać opór; być opornym;
powstrzymywać się
resistance [ry'zystens] s. opór;
sprzeciw; wytrzymałość;
odporność; opornica; a.
oporowy
resistant [ry'zystent] adj.
odporny; opierający się; s.
coś lub ktoś odporny,
opierający się
resolute ['rezelu:t] adj. rezolutny;
śmiały; zdecydowany
resolution [‚rese'lu:szyn] s.
uchwała; postanowienie;
rezolucja; śmiałość;
rozłożenie; rozwiązanie;
rozkład (sił)
resolve [ry'zolw] s.
postanowienie; decyzja;
stanowczość; v. rozkładać;
rozwiązywać; uchwalać;
decydować; postanawiać;
usuwać; przemieniać;
skłaniać
resolved [ry'solwd] adj.
zdecydowany; śmiały
resonance ['resnens] s.
oddźwięk; odgłos; rezonans
resonant [reznent] adj.
rezonujący; rozbrzmiewający
resort [ry'zo:rt] v. uciekać się;
uczęszczać; s. uzdrowisko;
uczęszczanie; ucieczka;
uciekanie się; ratunek;
wyjście
resort to [ry'zo:rt,tu] v. uciekać
się do ...
resound [ry'zaund] v.
rozbrzmiewać; odbijać;
opiewać; obiegać;
wypowiadać się; odbijać się
echem
resource [ry'so:rs] s. zasoby;
środki; bogactwa;
zaradność; pomysłowość;
zasoby naturalne
resourceful [ry'so:rsful] adj.
zaradny; pomysłowy
respect [rys'pekt] v. szanować;
dotyczyć; zważać; s.

wzgląd; szacunek; poważanie;
związek; łączność;
pozdrowienia
respectable [rys'pektebl] adj.
chwalebny; godny szacunku;
poważny; pokaźny
respectful [rys'pektful] adj. pełen
szacunku
respectfully [rys'pektfuly] adv. z
poważaniem; z uszanowaniem
respecting [rys'pektyng] prep.
odnośnie do ...
respective [rys'pektyw] adj.
odpowiedni; poszczególny
respectively [rys'pektywly] adv.
odpowiednio; każdemu z
osobna; kolejno
respiration [,respy'rejszyn] s.
oddech; oddychanie
respite ['respajt] s. wytchnienie
(krótkie); odroczenie; v.
odraczać (stracenie);
przynosić (krótką) ulgę
resplendent [rys'plendent] adj.
błyszczący silnie; jasny
respond [rys'pond] v.
odpowiadać; reagować; być
czułym
respondent [rys'pondent] adj.
odpowiadający; wrażliwy; s.
pozwany; obrońca
response [rys'pons] s.
odpowiedź; odzew; reakcja;
oddźwięk; odezwanie się
responsibility [rys,ponse'byłyty]
s. odpowiedzialność
responsible [rys'ponsebl] adj.
odpowiedzialny (wobec, przed)
rest [rest] s. odpoczynek;
spokój; przerwa; przystanek;
podpórka; pomieszczenie;
schronienie; reszta; v.
spoczywać; odpoczywać;
dawać odpoczynek;
uspokoić; być spokojnym;
podpierać się; polegać
restaurant ['resterent] s.
restauracja; jadłodajnia
restful ['restful] adj. spokojny;
uspokajający; wypoczęty
restless ['restlys] adj.
niespokojny; bezsenny;
niesforny

restlessness ['restlysnys] s.
niepokój; zniecierpliwienie
restoration [,reste'rejszyn] s.
odnowienie; rekonstrukcja;
restytucja; odtworzenie
restore [rys'to:r] v. przywracać;
uleczyć; odnawiać;
restaurować; restytuować;
zwracać; rekonstruować;
odtwarzać
restrain [rys'trejn] v.
powstrzymywać;
powściągać; krępować;
ograniczać; trzymać w
ryzach
restraint [rys'trejnt] s.
skrępowanie; uwięzienie;
zamknięcie w szpitalu
psychiatrycznym;
wstrzemięźliwość; umiar
restrict [rys'trykt] v. ograniczać
do; zamykać (w granicach)
restriction [rys'trykszyn] s.
ograniczenie
rest room ['rest,rum] s. ustęp;
toaleta
result [ry'zalt] s. rezultat; wynik;
v. wynikać; dawać w
wyniku; wypływać;
pochodzić
result in [ry'zalt,yn] v. kończyć
się na
resultant [ry'zaltent] adj.
wynikający; (np. siła)
wypadkowa
resume [ry'zju:m] v. wznawiać;
ponownie podejmować;
obejmować; zajmować;
odzyskiwać; ciągnąć dalej;
streszczać; odzyskać
resumption [ry'zampszyn] s.
wznowienie; odzyskanie;
podjęcie na nowo; powrót do
czegoś
resurrection [,reze'rekszyn] s.
odżycie; zmartwychwstanie;
wskrzeszenie; wznowienie
(zwyczaju)
retail ['ri:tejl] s. detal; adj.
detaliczny; v. sprzedawać
detalicznie; szczegółowo
opowiadać; adv. detalicznie
retailer [ri:'tejler] s. sklepikarz;

detalista; plotkarz
retain [ry'tejn] v. zatrzymywać;
zapamiętywać; zgodzić (do
pracy); zachowywać
(tradycję)
retaliate [ry'taeliejt] v.
odwzajemnić się; brać
odwet
retaliation [ry,taely'ejszyn] s.
odwet; zemsta; odpłata
retard [ry'ta:rd] v. opóźniać;
zwalniać; zahamować;
wstrzymywać
retell ['ri:'tel] v. ponownie
opowiedzieć; powtórzyć
retention [ry'tenszyn] s.
zatrzymanie (np. moczu);
zdolność zatrzymywania;
pamięć
retinue ['retynu:] s. orszak;
świta; czeladź; poczet
(dostojnika)
retire [ry'tajer] v. wycofywać
(się); iść na spoczynek;
pensjonować; s. sygnał
odwrotu
retired [ry'tajerd] adj.
emerytowany; ustronny;
odosobniony
retirement [ry'tajerment] s.
przejście w stan spoczynku;
ustronie; odosobnienie;
wycofanie (weksla); odwrót
retort [ry'to:rt] v. odpłacać się;
odcinać się; odparować;
ripostować; s. retorta;
riposta; odwet; odwrócenie
(oskarżenia); cięta odpowiedź
retrace [ry'trejs] v. odtworzyć;
przypomnieć sobie; badać
początek
retrace [ry:'trejs] v. ponownie
liniować; kopiować
retract [ry'traekt] v. cofnąć się;
odwołać; chować się;
wciągać (się) (pazury)
retreat [ry'tri:t] v. cofać się; s.
odwrót; wycofanie się w
zacisze; kryjówka;
odosobnienie; przytułek;
ustronie
retribution [,retry'bju:szyn] s.
odpłata; kara; nagroda

retrieve [ry'tri:w] v. odzyskać;
powetować; odszukać;
uratować; uprzytomnić
sobie; aportować; s.
odzyskanie; odszukanie;
powetowanie; uratowanie;
ruch wsteczny (powrotny)
retrospect ['retrespekt] s.
spojrzenie wstecz; rozważanie
przeszłości; v. rzucać okiem
wstecz; nawiązywać do
(przeszłości); patrzeć w
przeszłość
retrospective ['retrespektyw] adj.
retrospektywny; działający
wstecz; z mocą retroaktywną
return [ry'te:rn] v. wracać;
przynosić dochód; złożyć
(zeznanie); obracać w ...;
oddawać; odwzajemnić;
odpowiedzieć; wybrać; s.
powrót; nawrót; dochód; zysk;
zwrot; rewanż; sprawozdanie
(np. podatkowe)
return flight [ry'te:rn,flajt] s. lot
powrotny
return ticket [ry'te:rn,tykyt] s.
powrotny bilet
reunification ['ri:ju:nyfy'kejszyn]
s. ponowne zjednoczenie
reunion ['ri:'ju:njen] s. zjazd;
ponowne połączenie; zebranie
revaluation [ri:'wael'juejszyn] s.
ponowna ocena;
przewartościowanie (po
ponownej ocenie)
revaluate [ri:'waelju':ejt] v.
ponownie ocenić;
przewartościować (dom w
celach podatkowych)
revamp [ry:'waemp] v.
przerobić; reorganizować;
rewidować; okapować
(buty); odnowić
reveal [ry'wi:l] v. ujawniać;
objawiać; odsłaniać; s. rama
okna w karoserii
revel ['rewl] s. zabawa; hulanka;
v. hulać; używać sobie
revelation [,rewy'lejszyn] s.
ujawnienie; objawienie;
odsłonięcie; rewelacja;
odkrycie

revenge [ry'wendż] s. zemsta;
mściwość; v. pomścić;
zemścić się (za zniewagę,
krzywdę etc.)

revengeful [ry'wendżful] adj.
mściwy

revenue ['rewy,nu:] s. dochód (z
podatków)

revenue office ['rewy,nu:'ofys] s.
urząd podatkowy (finansowy)

revere [ry'wier] v. czcić;
odnosić się z czcią

reverence ['rewerens] s. cześć;
szacunek; wielebność

reverend ['rewerend] adj.
czcigodny; wielebny; s.
duchowny

reverse [ry'we:rs] s.
odwrotność; rewers; tył;
niepowodzenie; wsteczny
bieg; adj. odwrotny;
przeciwny; wsteczny; v.
odwracać; zmieniać
kierunek; obalać (np. przepis)

reverse gear [ry'we:rs,gier] s.
wsteczny bieg (w
samochodzie)

reverse side [ry'we:rs,sajd] s.
odwrotna strona

review [ry'wju:] v. przeglądać;
pisać recenzje; przeglądać w
myśli; dokonywać przeglądu;
s. recenzja; przegląd; rewia;
ponowny przegląd

reviewer [ry'wju:er] s. recenzent;
krytyk

revile [ry'wajl] v. wyzywać;
wymyślać; przezywać

revise [ry'wajz] v. przejrzeć;
zrewidować; przerabiać

revision [ry'wyżyn] s. rewizja;
przejrzane wydanie; przeróbka

revival [ry'wajwel] s. ożywienie;
odżywanie; powrót do życia;
powrót do stanu
użyteczności

revive [ry'wajw] v. wskrzeszać;
przywracać do życia;
wznawiać; ożywiać;
odżywać; wracać do
przytomności

revolt [ry'woult] s. bunt;
powstanie; v. buntować się;

wzdrygać się; mieć odrazą;
budzić odrazę

revolution [,rewe'lu:szyn] s.
obrót; rewolucja

revolutionary [,rewe'lu:sznry] adj.
rewolucyjny; s. rewolucjonista

revolutionist [,rewe'lu:szynyst] s.
rewolucjonista

revolutionize [,rewe'lu:szn,ajz] v.
zrewolucjonizować;
wywoływać rewolucją

revolve [ry'wolw] v. obracać;
krążyć; obracać się;
obmyślać

revolving [ry'wolwyng] adj.
obrotowy

reward [ry'ło:rd] s. nagroda;
wynagrodzenie; v.
wynagradzać

rheumatism ['ru:metyzem] s.
reumatyzm; gościec stawowy

rhubarb ['ru:ba:rb] s. rabarbar;
(slang) kłótnia

rhyme [rajm] s. rym; v.
rymować się

rhythm ['rytm] s. rytm

rhythmic ['rytmyk] adj.
rytmiczny; miarowy

rib [ryb] s. żebro; żeberko;
wręga; v. żeberkować;
nabierać; wyśmiewać;
droczyć się; płytko orać

ribbed [rybd] adj. żebrowany

ribbon ['ryben] s. taśma; pasek;
strzęp; wstążka; v. drzeć na
strzępy, paski; ozdabiać
wstążką; wić się wstęgą

rice [rajs] s. ryż

rich [rycz] adj. bogaty;
kosztowny; suty; obfity;
tuczący; pożywny; soczysty;
mocny (zapach); pełny; tłusty
(np. pokarm); pocieszny
(zdarzenie)

riches ['ryczyz] pl. bogactwo;
bogactwa

richness ['rycznys] s. bogactwo;
pełnia

rick [ryk] s. stóg; v. ustawiać w
stogi; stawiać stóg

rickets ['rykyts] s. choroba
angielska; krzywica; rachityzm

rickety ['rykyty] adj. chwiejny;

koślawy; rachityczny

rid; rid; ridded [ryd; ryd; 'rydyd]

rid [ryd] v. uwalniać się od ...; oczyszczać się; pozbywać się

ridden ['rydn] v. zob. ride

riddle ['rydl] s. zagadka; v. zadawać zagadki; mówić zagadkami; rozwiązywać zagadki

ride; rode; ridden [rajd; roud; 'rydn]

ride [rajd] v. pojechać; jechać (też statkiem); jeździć; tyranizować; wozić; nosić; dokuczać; s. przejażdżka; jazda; nabieranie (kogoś); droga

rider ['rajder] s. jeździec; dżokej; poprawka; dodatek; klauzula; ciężarek przesuwany; nasadka; poprawka na dokumencie

ridge [rydż] s. grzbiet (też góry); krawędź; kalenica; pasmo górskie; wał; skiba; grobla; v. pokrywać skibami; robić krawędzie; marszczyć

ridicule ['rydy,kju:l] v. wyśmiewać się; s. kpiny

ridiculous [ry'dykju:les] adj. śmieszny; bezsensowny

riding ['rajdyng] s. konna jazda; adj. jadący; do konnej jazdy

rife [rajf] adj. częsty; rozpowszechniony; pełen

riff-raff [ryf-raf] pl. motłoch; swołocz

rifle [rajfl] s. karabin; gwintówka; gwint; strzelec; v. gwintować (lufę); strzelać; ograbić; okraść; pokrzyżować

rift [ryft] s. szczelina; różnica zdań; v. rozszczepiać się; pęknąć; popękać

rig [ryg] v. zaopatrywać; klecić; montować; stroić; robić kanty; manipulować ceny; s. sprzęt (wiertniczy); wóz z koniem; kostium; machlojka

right [rajt] adj. prawa; prawy; poprawny; prawoskrętny; prosty (też kąt); właściwy; słuszny; dobry; odpowiedni; prawidłowy; w porządku; zdrowy; adv. w prawo; na prawo; prosto; bezpośrednio; bezzwłocznie; dokładnie; słusznie; dobrze; s. prawa strona; prawo; dobro; słuszność; sprawiedliwość; pierwszeństwo; v. naprostować; naprawić; sprostować; odpłacać; mścić; usprawiedliwiać

right ahead ['rajt,e'hed] exp.: wprost; na wprost; przed siebie

right away ['rajt,e'łej] exp.: zaraz; natychmiast; już teraz

righteous ['rajtszes] adj. sprawiedliwy; prawy; słuszny

rightful ['rajtful] adj. słuszny; sprawiedliwy; prawowity; należny z prawa; prawy

right-hand ['rajt,haend] adj. praworęki; położony na prawo

right-handed ['rajt-'haendyd] adj. praworęczny; dostosowany do prawej ręki; idący wg. ruchu zegara; obracający się w prawo (gwint etc.)

right of way ['rajt,ow'łej] exp.: prawo pierwszeństwa na drodze; prawo przejazdu; grunt pod drogą (kolej) (pod szosą etc.)

rightist ['rajtyst] s. prawicowiec; adj. prawicowy

rightly ['rajtly] adv. sprawiedliwie; słusznie; poprawnie; właściwie; na miejscu

rigid ['rydżyd] adj. sztywny; nieugięty; surowy; nieustępliwy

rigor ['ryger] s. rygor; surowość; zesztywnienie

rigorous ['rygeres] adj. surowy; rygorystyczny

rim [rym] s. brzeg; krawędź; obręcz; powierzchnia wody (przy żeglowaniu); v. robić krawędź; posuwać wzdłuż krawędzi; dawać oprawę (do okularów)

rind [rajnd] s. kora; łupina; skórka (owocu, sera, etc.); v. zdzierać (korę, jarzynę)

ring [ryng] s. pierścień; obrączka; kółko; koło; zmowa; szajka; słój; arena; ring (bokserski); v. otaczać; kołować; krajać w kółko

ring; rang; rung [ryng; raeng; rang]

ring [ryng] v. dzwonić; dźwięczeć; brzmieć; rozbrzmiewać; wydzwaniać; telefonować; wybijać czas na zegarze kontrolnym; sprawdzać monetę dźwiękiem; s. dzwonek; dzwony; dźwięk; brzęk; telefonowanie

ring off ['ryng,of] s. skończyć rozmowę telefoniczną

ring the bell ['ryng,dy'bel] v. dzwonić (do drzwi etc.)

ring up ['ryng,ap] v. wybijać kwotę (na kasie rejestracyjnej); zatelefonować (do kogoś)

ringleader ['ryng,li:der] s. prowodyr; herszt

rink [rynk] s. ślizgawka; tor jazdy na wrotkach; boisko do gry w kule

rinse [ryns] s. płukać s. wypłukanie

rinse out ['ryns,aut] v. wypłukać; przepłukiwać

riot ['rajot] s. zgiełk; zamęt; rozruchy; bunty; rozpusta; hulanka; rozprężenie; orgia; v. buntować się; robić rozruchy, zamieszki; hulać; używać sobie; uprawiać rozpustę

riotous ['rajetes] adj. buntowniczy; rozpustny; hulaszczy; hałaśliwy; bujny; oporny; niesforny

rip [ryp] v. odrywać; zrywać; łupać; rozpruwać; piłować wzdłuż; pękać; pędzić; s. rozprucie; rozpustnik; hulaka; szkapa; rzecz nie warta nic;

wir; wzburzona powierzchnia wody

ripe [rajp] adj. dojrzały

ripen ['rajpn] v. dojrzewać; przyspieszać dojrzewanie

ripeness ['rajpnys] s. dojrzałość

ripple ['rypl] s. zmarszczki (na wodzie); fale (na włosach); falowanie; grzebień do lnu; v. marszczyć; falować; rozczesywać; rozwodzić się

rise; rose; risen [rajz; rouz; 'ryzn]

rise [rajz] v. podnieść się; stanąć; wstawać; powstać; buntować się; wzbierać; wzbijać się; wzmagać się; sprostać; s. wschód; wznoszenie się; podwyżka; wzrost; powodzenie; początek; stopień

risen ['ryzn] v. zob. rise

riser [rajzer] s. osoba wstająca; pionowy przewód (też rura); podstawka stopnia (na schodach)

rising ['rajzyng] s. wzniesienie; powstanie; zmartwychwstanie; bąbel; pryszcz; zaczynanie ciasta; adj. podnoszący się; wzrastający; wschodzący

risk [rysk] s. ryzyko; niebezpieczeństwo; v. narażać się; ryzykować; ponosić ryzyko

risky ['rysky] adj. niebezpieczny; ryzykowny; pikantny; drastyczny

rite [rajt] s. obrządek; obrzęd (ślubny); rytuał

rival ['rajwel] s. rywal; współzawodnik; v. rywalizować

rivalry ['rajwelry] s. rywalizacja; współzawodnictwo

river ['rywer] s. rzeka

river boat ['rywer,bout] s. statek rzeczny; łódź rzeczna

riverside ['rywer,sajd] s. brzeg rzeki

rivet ['rywyt] s. nit; v. nitować; utkwić; przykuć

rivulet ['rywjulyt] s. rzeczułka; mały strumień; mały potok

road [roud] s. droga; kolej; reda; v. topić

road hog ['roud,hog] s. pirat drogowy (lekceważący przepisy)

road map ['roud,maep] s. mapa drogowa; mapa samochodowa

roadside ['roud,sajd] s. bok drogi; adj. przydrożny

road sign ['roud,sajn] s. znak drogowy

roam [roum] v. włóczyć się; s. włóczęga; wędrówka

roar [ro:r] v. ryczeć; huczeć; s. ryk; huk (armat); ryk (śmiechu)

roars of laughter ['ro:rs,ow'lafter] exp.: wybuchy śmiechu

roast [roust] v. piec; opiekać; przypiekać; wypalać; ośmieszać; krytykować ostro; s. pieczeń; pieczenie; kpiny; krytyka ostra; adj. pieczony

roast beef ['roust,bi:f] s. pieczeń wołowa

roast meat ['roust,mi:t] s. pieczone mięso

rob [rob] v. grabić; rabować; ograbić; pozbawiać (czegoś)

robber ['rober] s. rabuś

robbery ['robery] s. rabunek

robe [roub] s. podomka; suknia; szata; płaszcz kąpielowy; toga; v. przyodziewać; przyoblekać

robin ['robyn] s. drozd; rudzik

robot ['roubot] s. robot

robust ['roubast] adj. krzepki; trzeźwy; szorstki; hałaśliwy; ciężki; silny; mocny

rock [rok] s. kamień; skała; farba; kołysanie; taniec (rock and roll); pl. kostki lodu w napoju; v. kołysać się; bujać się; huśtać się; wstrząsać; wypłukiwać piasek; płukać (się); a. kamienny; skalisty

rocker ['roker] s. biegun; łyżwa holenderka

rocket ['rokyt] s. rakieta; v. wznosić się

rocket power ['rokyt'pałer] s. napęd rakietowy

rocketry ['rokytry] s. broń rakietowa; technika rakietowa

rocking chair ['rokyng,czeer] s. krzesło na biegunach

rocky ['roky] adj. skalisty; chwiejny; kamienisty; skalny

rod [rod] s. pręt; drąg; wędka; (pręt = 5.029m)

rode [roud] v. zob. ride

rodent ['roudent] s. gryzoń

roe [rou] s. sarna; łania; ikra we wnętrzu ryby; sperma ryby

rogue [roug] s. łobuz; łajdak; psotnik; słoń samotnik

roguish ['rougysz] adj. psotny; figlarny; łobuzerski

role [roul] s. rola

roll [roul] s. rolka; zwój; zwitek; rulon; bułka; rożek; spis; wykaz; rejestr; lista; wokanda; wałek; walec; wałek; kołysanie (się); werbel; huk; v. toczyć; wałkować; tarzać; grzmieć; dudnić; rozlegać się; zataczać beczkę; toczyć koło; wręcić; obracać; wymawiać "r"; rozwałkowywać; wałkować

roll up ['roul,ap] v. zawinąć (rękawy); kłębić się podjeżdżać; skumulować (się)

roller ['rouler] s. wałek; rolka; kółko; długa tocząca się fala; narzędzie do wałkowania

roller coaster ['rouler'kouster] s. kolejka wysokogórska; wesołe miasteczko

roller-skate ['rouler'skejt] s. wrotka

rolling mill ['roulyn,myl] s. walcownia

Roman ['roumen] adj. rzymski

romance [rou'maens] s. romans średniowieczny; powieść miłosna; sprawa miłosna; adj. romański; v. romansować; koloryzować; przesadzać; pisać romanse

romantic [rou'maentyk] adj. romantyczny; s. romantyk

romp [romp] s. urwis; zbytki;
swawole; figle; igraszki; v.
figlować; dokazywać;
uganiać; łatwo wygrać
(wyścigi)
rompers ['rompers] pl.
kombinezon do zabawy dla
dziecka
roof [ru:f] s. dach; v. pokrywać
dachem
roof over ['ru:f,ouwer] v.
pokrywać dachem
rook [ruk] s. gawron; szuler;
wieża (w szachach); v.
ograć; oszukać; zdzierać
skórę
room [rum] s. pokój; miejsce;
mieszkanie; izba; wolna
przestrzeń; sposobność;
powód; v. dzielić pokój lub
mieszkanie; mieszkać lub
odnajmować pokój
room-mate ['rum,mejt] s.
współmieszkaniec;
współlokator
roomy ['rumy] adj. przestronny;
obszerny
roost [ru:st] s. grzęda; v.
siedzieć na grzędzie
rooster [ru:ster] s. kogut
root [ru:t] s. korzeń; nasada;
podstawa; istota; źródło;
sedno; pierwiastek; v.
posadzić; zakorzenić; ryć;
szperać; wygrzebywać;
popierać; dopingować
root out ['ru:t,aut] v.
wykorzenić; wyrwać z
korzeniami
rope [roup] s. sznur; powróz;
lina; stryczek; v. związać;
przywiązać; łapać na lasso;
ogradzać sznurami; ciągnąć
na linie; przyciągać;
zdobywać; obśliznąć
rope off ['roup,of] v. ogradzać
linami
rose [rous] s. róża; kolor
różowy; rozetka; v.
zaróżowić; zob. rise
rosy ['rouzy] adj. różowy
rot [rot] s. zgnilizna; rozkład;
zepsucie; głupstwa; brednie;

motylica; v. gnić; butwieć;
rozkładać się
rotary ['routery] adj. rotacyjny;
obrotowy
rotate ['routejt] v. obracać (się);
kolejno zmieniać (się);
wirować; adj. kółkowy
rotation [rou'tejszyn] s. rotacja;
ruch obrotowy; obracanie
(się); płodozmian; ciągła
wymiana; kolejne następstwo
rotor ['router] s. wirnik
rotten ['rotn] adj. zgniły;
zepsuty; zdemoralizowany;
lichy; kiepski; marny; chory na
motylicę; do niczego; do
chrzanu
rotund [rou'tand] adj. okrągły;
zaokrąglony; szumny;
przysadkowy
rough [raf] adj. szorstki;
chropowaty; ostry; nierówny;
wyboisty; nieokrzesany;
brutalny; drastyczny; cierpki;
nieprzyjemny; nieociosany;
surowy; gruby; burzliwy;
gwałtowny; hałaśliwy; ciężki;
pobieżny; przybliżony;
prymitywny; wstępny;
szkicowy; adv. ostro;
szorstko; grubiańsko; z
grubsza; s. nierówny teren;
stan naturalny - nieobrobiony;
hacel; chuligan; v. być
szorstkim; szorstko
postępować; hartować (się);
jeżyć (się); burzyć (się);
szlifować z grubsza;
pasować z grubsza; obrabiać
z grubsza; szkicować;
przebiedować; ujeżdżać
(konia); robić coś z grubsza;
podkuwać hacelami
roughness ['rafnys] s.
szorstkość; grubiaństwo;
chamstwo
rough-neck ['rafnek] s. członek
obsługi szybu; łobuz; brutal;
chuligan
round [raund] adj. okrągły;
zaokrąglony; kolisty; okrężny;
tam i nazad; kulisty;
sferyczny; adv. wkoło; kołem;

dookoła; prep. dookoła; s.
koło; obwód; kula; obrót;
krąg; bieg; cykl; ciąg; zasięg;
seria; objazd; obchód; runda;
zaokrąglenie; pasmo (np.
trudności); przechadzka; v.
zaokrąglać; wygładzać;
okrążyć; obchodzić;
opływać
round off ['raund,of] v.
zaokrąglać
round out ['raund,aut] v.
zaokrąglać się; tyć
round up ['raund,ap] v. spędzać
(bydło)
round-up ['raund'ap] s.
spędzanie bydła
roundabout ['raundebaut] adj.
okrężny; s. rondo; karuzela
round trip ['raund,tryp] s. podróż
tam i nazad
rouse [rauz] v. pobudzić;
wzniecać; ruszyć; ożywiać;
podsycać; wyrywać;
wypłoszyć; obudzić się;
otrząsnąć się
roustabout ['rauste,baut] s.
robotnik portowy; robotnik
przemysłu naftowego
route [ru:t] s. droga; trasa;
marsz; szlak
routine [ru:'ti:n] s. rutyna; tok
zajęć
rove [rouw] v. wałęsać się;
błądzić wzrokiem; łowić;
skręcać włókno; s.
niedoprzęd
rover ['rouwer] s. wędrowiec;
włóczęga; korsarz; pirat
row [roł] s. szereg; rząd; jazda
łodzią; v. wiosłować
row [rał] s. zgiełk; hałas; kłótnia;
bójka; burda; nagana; bura; v.
besztać; pokłócić się
row-boat ['roł,bout] s. łódź
wiosłowa
rower ['rołer] s. wioślarz
rowing boat ['rołyngbout] s.
łódź wiosłowa
royal ['rojel] adj. królewski
royalty ['rojelty] s.
królewskość; honorarium
autorskie

rub [rab] v. trzeć; potrzeć;
wytrzeć; wycierać; głaskać;
nacierać; s. tarcie; nacieranie
rub down ['rab,dałn] v.
nacierać; wcierać
rub in ['rab,yn] v. wcierać;
wytykać
rub off ['rab,of] v. zetrzeć
rub out ['rab,aut] v. wymazać
rubber ['raber] s. guma;
masażysta; pl. kalosze; v.
pokrywać gumą; odwracać
(głowę)
rubberneck ['raber,nek] s.
ciekawski; turysta; gapa
rubber plant ['raber,plaent] s.
kauczukowa roślina
rubbish ['rabysz] s. śmieć;
gruz; tandeta; nonsens;
brednie; głupstwa; bzdury
rubble ['rabl] s. gruz; rumowisko
skalne; kamień łamany
ruby ['ru:by] s. rubin
rucksack ['ruksaek] s. plecak
rude [ru:d] adj. szorstki;
niegrzeczny; ostry; surowy;
prosty; pierwotny; nagły;
gwałtowny; krzepki
ruder ['rader] s. ster
ruddy ['rady] adj. rumiany;
czerstwy; czerwony; v.
rumienić się
ruff [raf] s. kołnierz; kreza;
batalion; bojownik; bicie
atutem; v. przebić atutem
ruffian ['rafjen] s. zbój; łotr
ruffle ['rafl] s. kreza; żabot;
mankiet koronkowy; kłopot;
zamieszanie; marszczenie; v.
marszczyć (powierzchnię);
rozwiewać; rozczochrać;
nastroszyć; wzburzyć (się)
rug [rag] s. pled; kilim; dywan
rugby ['ragby] s. (sport) rugby
ruin [,ruyn] s. ruina; v. rujnować
(się); zniszczyć (się)
rule [ru:l] s. przepis; prawo;
reguła; zasada; rządy;
panowanie; postanowienie;
miarka; linijka; v. rządzić;
panować; kierować;
orzekać; postanawiać;
liniować

rule out ['ru:l,aut] v. wykluczać
ruler ['ru:ler] s. władca; liniał; linijka
rum [ram] s. rum; adj. dziwny
rumble ['rambl] v. dudnić; grzmieć; turkotać; s. huk; grzmot; dudnienie; tylne miejsce w pojeździe na bagaż lub służącego
ruminant ['ru:mynent] adj. przeżuwający; s. przeżuwacz
rummage ['ramydż] s. szperanie; przetrząsanie; wyprzedaż resztek; v. wygrzebać; przetrząsać
rumor ['ru:mer] s. pogłoska; słuchy; v. puszczać pogłoski
rump [ramp] s. zad; kuper; comber; kadłub
rumple ['rampl] v. zmiąć; zmiętosić; mierzwić; czochrać
run; ran; ran [ran; raen; raen]
run [ran] v. biec; biegać; pędzić; spieszyć się; jechać; płynąć; kursować; obracać się; działać; funkcjonować; pracować; uciekać; zbiec; prowadzić; toczyć się; wynosić (sumę); rozpływać się; łzawić; głosić; spotykać; narzucać się; molestować; zderzyć się; sprzeciwiać się; wpaść etc.; s. bieg; przebieg; bieganie; rozbieg; rozpęd; przebieg; passa; sekwens; okres; seria; ciąg; dostęp; wybieg; pastwisko; zjazd; tor
run about [ran,e'baut] v. biegać tu i tam; s. wędrowiec; adj. wędrowny
run across [ran,e'kros] v. spotkać przypadkowo
run after [ran,aefter] v. gonić
run away [ran,e'łej] v. uciekać; ponieść
run down [ran,dałn] v. przejechać; wyczerpać; wytropić
run in [ran,yn] v. wpaść na ...; dotrzeć
run off [ran,of] v. uciekać; recytować; drukować
run out [ran,aut] v. skończyć się; wygasnąć; drukować
run over [ran,ouwer] v. przejechać; przepełniać
run up [ran,ap] v. dobiec; dojść do ...; dodać; wyśrubować; s. dochodzenie do celu
rung [rang] s. poprzeczka; szczebel; szprycha; v. zob. ring
runner ['raner] s. goniec; biegacz; posłaniec; woźny; akwizytor; łopatka; obsługujący maszynę; chodnik; przemytnik; płoza; łożysko ślizgowe; wałek
running ['ranyng] adj. bieżący; biegający; będący w biegu; cieknący; ropiejący; w ruchu; ruchomy; ciągły; nieustanny; pochyły; nieprzerwany; s. bieg; wyścig; kandydowanie; funkcjonowanie; ropienie; kierownictwo
running board ['ranyng,bo:rd] s. stopień; pomost
runway ['ran,łej] s. bieżnia (do lądowania); tor (jezdny)
rupture ['rapczer] s. złamanie; zerwanie; przepuklina; v. przerywać; zrywać; poderwać się (mieć przepuklinę)
rural ['ruerel] adj. wiejski
ruse [ru:z] s. podstęp
rush [rasz] v. pędzić; poganiać; ponaglać; rzucać się na coś; przeskakiwać; wysyłać pospiesznie; zdobywać szturmem; zdzierać (pieniądze); słać sitowiem; s. pęd; ruch; pośpiech; napływ; atak; intensywny popyt; sitowie
rush hour ['rasz,auer] s. godzina szczytu; chwila uderzenia
Russia [rasz'e] s. Rosja
Russian ['raszyn] adj. rosyjski; s. Rosjanin
rust [rast] s. rdza (zbożowa); v. rdzewieć; niszczyć się

rust-eaten ['rast,i:tn] adj.
zardzewiały
rustic ['rastik] adj. wiejski;
prostacki; s. wieśniak;
prostak
rustle ['rasl] v. szeleścić;
kraść bydło; krzątać się; s.
szelest
rusty ['rasty] adj. zardzewiały;
zaniedbany; wyszły z wprawy;
podniszczony
rut [rat] s. koleina; bruzda; utarty
szlak; rutyna; nawyk; rowek;
wyżłobienie; ruja; bokowisko;
rykowisko
ruthless ['ru:tlys] adj. bezlitosny;
bezwzględny; niemiłosierny
rutted ['ratyd] adj. rozjeżdżony;
wyjeżdżony
rutty ['raty] adj. wyjeżdżony
rye [raj] s. żyto; żytniówka
rye whisky ['raj,hłysky] szkocka
żytnia wódka

S

s [es] dziewiętnasta litera
alfabetu angielskiego
's skrót: is, has, us
saber ['sejber] s. szabla; pałasz;
v. ciąć; ranić; ścinać
sable ['sejbl] s. soból; czerń;
adj. czarny; sobolowy (z futer)
sabotage ['saebeta:ż] s.
sabotaż; v. sabotować
sabre ['sejber] s. szabla; zob.
saber
saccharin ['saekeryn] s.
sacharyna
sack [saek] s. worek; torebka;
sak; luźny płaszcz;
plądrowanie; v. pakować do
worków; zwalniać z pracy;
plądrować
sacrament ['saekrement] s.
sakrament
sacred ['sejkryd] adj.
poświęcony; nienaruszalny

sacrifice ['saekryfajs] s. ofiara;
wyrzeczenie (się); v.
ofiarowywać; poświęcać;
wyrzekać się w zamian za
coś innego
sacrilegious [,saekry'lydżes] adj.
świętokradzki
sad [saed] adj. smutny; bolesny;
posępny; ponury; okropny
sadden ['saedn] v. zasmucać
(się); posmutnieć
saddle ['saedl] s. siodło; v.
siodłać; obarczać; wkładać
ciężar (komuś) (na kogoś)
sadness ['saednys] s. smutek
safe [sejf] adj. pewny;
bezpieczny; s. schowek
bankowy; kasa pancerna;
spiżarnia wietrzona; (slang):
kondon
safeguard ['sejfga:rd] v.
ochraniać; zabezpieczać;
gwarantować; s.
zabezpieczenie; gwarancja
safety ['sejfty] s.
bezpieczeństwo;
zabezpieczenie; bezpiecznik;
adj. dający bezpieczeństwo
safety belt ['sejfty,belt] s. pas
bezpieczeństwa (np. w
samochodzie)
safety lock ['sejfty,lok] s. zamek
bezpieczeństwa
safety pin ['sejfty,pyn] s. agrafka
safety razor ['sejfty,rejzer] s.
maszynka do golenia się
żyletkami (które się wymienia
po użyciu)
safety-valve ['sejfty,waelw] s.
klapa bezpieczeństwa; zawór
bezpieczeństwa
sag [saeg] v. obwisać; zwisać;
wyginać (się); przechylać
się; spadać w cenie; s. zwis;
wygięcie; spadek (ceny)
sagacity [se'gaesyty] s.
rozwaga; mądrość;
roztropność; bystrość
said [sed] v. zob. say
sail [sejl] s. żagiel; podróż
morska; v. żeglować;
kroczyć okazale; sterować
okrętem; bawić się modelem

statku
sail-boat ['sejl,bout] s. żaglówka
sailing-ship ['sejlyng,szyp] s.
statek żaglowy
sailor ['sejlor] s. żeglarz;
marynarz
saint [sejnt] s. & adj. święty
sake [sejk] s. czyjeś dobro;
wzgląd
salad ['saeled] s. sałatka
salary ['saelery] s. pensja;
pobory; wynagrodzenie
sale [sejl] s. sprzedaż;
wyprzedaż
saleslady ['sejls'lejdy] s.
sprzedawczyni
salesman ['sejlsmen] s.
sprzedawca
sales manager [,sejls'maenydżer]
s. kierownik działu sprzedaży
saliva [se'lajwa] s. ślina
sallow ['saelou] adj. ziemisty;
blady; żółtawy; v. dawać
żółtawy odcień; s. iwa
(wierzba)
sally ['saely] s. wypad;
wycieczka z oblężenia;
docinek (cięty)
sally out ['saely,aut] v.
wyruszać w podróż
salmon ['saemen] s. łosoś; adj.
łososiowy; łososiowego koloru
saloon [se'lu:n] s. bar; szynk;
sala (zabaw); salon (na
okręcie)
salt [so:lt] s. sól; adj. słony; v.
solić
saltcellar ['so:lt,seler] s.
solniczka
salt-free ['so:lt,fri:] adj. bezsolny;
pozbawiony soli
salty ['so:lty] adj. słony
salutation [,saelju:'tejszyn] s.
pozdrowienie; przywitanie
salute [se'lu:t] s. pozdrowienie;
salutowanie; honory
wojskowe; salwa (powitalna);
v. pozdrowić; powitać;
salutować; odbierać
defiladę; przejść przed
kompanią honorową
salvation [sael'wejszyn] s.
zbawienie; ratunek;

wybawienie
salve [sa:w] v. natrzeć;
złagodzić; uspokoić; s.
maść; balsam
same [sejm] adj. ten sam; taki
sam; jednostajny; monotonny;
adv. tak samo; identycznie;
bez zmiany; pron. to samo
sample ['sa:mpl] s. próbka;
wzór; v. próbować; dawać
próbki
sanatorium [,saene'to:rjem] s.
sanatorium
sanctify ['saenkty,faj] v.
uświęcać; poświęcać
sanctimonious [,saenkty
'mounjes] adj.
świętoszkowaty
sanction ['saenkszyn] v.
usankcjonować; s. sankcja
sanctuary ['saenkczuery] s.
przybytek; azyl
sand [saend] s. piasek; v.
posypywać piaskiem;
obrabiać papierem ściernym
sandal ['saendl] s. sandał;
rzemyk; v. wkładać **sandały**;
przywiązywać rzemykiem
sandwich ['saendłycz] s.
kanapka; sandwicz; v.
wkładać (między)
sandy ['saendy] adj. piaskowy;
piaskowego koloru
sandy beach ['saendy,bi:cz] s.
plaża
sane [sejn] adj. zdrowy na
umyśle; rozsądny; normalny
sang [saeng] v. zob. sing
sanitarium [,saeny'teerjem] s.
sanatorium
sanitary ['saenytery] adj.
higieniczny; zdrowy
sanitary napkin ['saenytery
'naepkyn] s. podpaska
higieniczna
sanitation [,saeny'tejszyn] s.
higiena; kanalizacja;
urządzenia sanitarne
sank [saenk] v. zob. sink
Santa Claus [,saenta'klo:z] s.
Dziadek Mróz; Święty Mikołaj
sap [saep] s. żywica; sok;
głupiec; kujon; nudziarstwo;

sapa; podkopywanie; v.
wyciągać soki; usuwać biel
z drzewa; podkopywać;
podmywać; kopać sapę
sappy ['saepy] s. soczysty; pełen
wigoru; energiczny
sarcasm ['sa:rkaezem] s.
sarkazm
sardine [sa:r'di:n] s. sardynka
sash [saesz] s. szarfa; rama
okienna do pionowego
suwania okien; v. instalować
ramy okienne
sash window ['saesz'łyndou] s.
suwane okno
sat [saet] v. zob. sit
Satan ['sejtn] s. szatan
satchel ['saeczel] s. torba z
rzemieniami na plecy
satellite ['saete,lajt] s. satelita
satin ['saetyn] s. atłas; adj.
atłasowy; v. satynować
(papier)
satire ['saetajer] s. satyra
satirize ['saety,rajz] v.
wykpiwać; wyśmiewać;
satyryzować
satisfaction [,saetys'faekszyn] s.
zadowolenie; satysfakcja;
spłacenie długu; zaspokojenie
satisfactory [,saetys'faektery]
adj. zadowalający; odpowiedni
satisfy ['saetys,faj] v.
zaspokoić; uiścić; spełnić;
zadowalać; odpowiadać;
przekonywać
Saturday ['saeterdy] s. sobota
sauce [so:s] s. sos; kompot; v.
przyprawiać jedzenie;
nagadać komuś; stawiać
się
sauce-box ['so:s,boks] s.
impertynent; zuchwalec
saucepan ['so:spen] s. patelnia;
rondel
saucer ['so:ser] s. spodek
saunter ['so:nter] s. przechadzka;
v. przechadzać się; chodzić
powolnym krokiem
sausage ['sosydż] s. kiełbasa
save [sejw] v. ratować;
oszczędzać; zachowywać
pozory; zbawiać; uniknąć;

zyskiwać (czas); prep.
oprócz; wyjąwszy; poza;
pominąwszy; conj. że; poza
tym; chyba że; z wyjątkiem
save for a car ['sejw,fo:r'ej,ka:r]
exp.: oszczędzać na
samochód
saver ['sejwer] s. osoba
oszczędzająca; przedmiot
oszczędzający (np. czas)
saving ['sejwyng] adj.
zbawienny; oszczędny; prep.
wyjąwszy
savings-bank ['sejwynz'baenk] s.
kasa oszczędności
savior ['sejwjer] s. zbawca;
zbawiciel
savor ['sejwer] s. smak; aromat;
powab; v. mieć smak;
pachnieć; smakować;
nadawać smak
savory ['sejwery] adj. smaczny;
apetyczny; smakowity;
pikantny; aromatyczny
saw; sawed; sawn [so:; so:d;
so:n]
saw [so:] v. zob. see; piłować;
s. piła
sawdust ['so:,dast] s. trociny
sawmill ['so:,myl] s. tartak
Saxon ['saeksn] adj. saksoński;
saski; s. Sas
say; said; said [sej; sed; sed]
say [sej] v. mówić; powiedzieć;
odprawiać; twierdzić
say-so ['sejso] s. prawo decyzji;
zapewnienie; ostatnie słowo
saying ['sejyng] s. powiedzonko;
powiedzenie
scab [skaeb] s. strup; parch;
świerzb; łamistrajk
scaffold ['skaefeld] s.
rusztowanie; platforma;
estrada; szafot; v. stawiać
rusztowanie
scaffolding ['skaefeldyng] s.
rusztowanie
scald [sko:ld] v. oparzyć;
wyparzyć; pasteryzować; s.
oparzenie
scale [skejl] s. skala; podziałka;
układ; drabina; szalka; łuska;
kamień nazębny; v. wyłazić;

wdzierać się; mierzyć
(podziałką); ważyć;
łuszczyć; łuskać; złuszczać
się
scale down ['skejl,daln] v.
zmniejszać (proporcjonalnie)
scale up ['skejl,ap] v.
powiększać (proporcjonalnie)
scales ['skejls] pl. waga
scalp ['skaelp] s. skalp; skóra na
głowie; v. oskalpować;
złośliwie krytykować
scan [skaen] v. badawczo
przeglądać; skandować;
mieć rytm
scandal ['skaendl] s. skandal;
zgorszenie; oszczerstwo; plotki
scandalous ['skaendeles] adj.
skandaliczny; gorszący;
oszczerczy
Scandinavian [,skaendy'nejwjan]
adj. skandynawski
scant [skaent] adj. skąpy;
ograniczony; ledwo
wystarczający; niedostateczny
scapegoat ['skejp,gout] s. kozioł
ofiarny
scar [ska:r] s. blizna; szrama;
wyrwa; urwisko; v.
pokiereszować (się);
zabliźniać się
scar over ['ska:r,ouwer] v.
zabliźnić
scarce [skeers] adj. rzadki;
niewystarczający
scarcely ['skeersly] adv.
zaledwie; ledwo; z trudem; z
trudnością
scarcity ['skeersyty] s.
niedostatek; niedobór; brak
scare [skeer] s. popłoch; panika;
strach; v. nastraszyć;
przestraszyć; siać popłoch
scare away ['skeere,łej] v.
odstraszać
scarecrow ['skeer,krou] s.
straszydło; strach na wróble
scarf [ska:rf] s. szalik; chustka
na szyję; szarfa
scarfs [ska:rfs] pl. styk; złącza
scarlet ['ska:rlyt] s. szkarłat; adj.
szkarłatny
scarlet fever ['ska:rlyt,fi:wer] s.

szkarlatyna; płonica
scarp [ska:rp] s. skarpa; urwisko
scarred [ska:rd] adj. poznaczony
bliznami; poszarpany
scarves [ska:rwz] pl. zob. scarf;
chusty na szyję; szarfy etc.
scathing ['skejzyng] adj.
kostyczny; zjadliwy; niszczący
scatter ['skaeter] v. rozpraszać
(się); rozsypywać; rozrzucać;
rozwiewać; posypywać;
rozpierzchnąć (się)
scavenge ['skaewyndż] v.
czyścić; oczyszczać;
wyrzucać spaliny; być
zamiataczem ulic
scenario [sy'na:riou] s.
scenariusz; plan zdarzeń
rzeczywistych lub
zmyślonych
scene [si:n] s. scena; miejsce
zdarzeń; widowisko; widok;
obraz; awantura publiczna
scenery [si:nery] s. widok;
krajobraz; dekoracje sceniczne
scent [sent] v. węszyć;
wietrzyć; wydawać zapach;
s. zapach; nos (węch);
perfumy
sceptic ['skeptyk] s. sceptyk;
adj. sceptyczny;
powątpiewający
sceptical ['skeptykel] adj.
sceptyczny; powątpiewający
we wszystko
schedule ['skedżul] s. rozkład
jazdy; wykaz; zestawienie;
tabela; taryfa; harmonogram;
lista; plan; v. planować;
wciągać na listę; naznaczać
wg planu
scheme [ski:m] s. intryga;
podstęp; plan
scholar ['skoler] s. uczony;
stypendysta; uczeń; student
scholarship ['skolerszyp] s.
poziom naukowy; stypendium;
erudycja; systematyczna
wiedza
school [sku:l] s. szkoła; katedra;
nauka; ławica; adj. szkolny; v.
szkolić; kształcić; nauczać;
wyćwiczyć; tworzyć

ławicę; karcić; sprawdzać naukę
schoolboy ['sku:l,boj] s. uczeń
schoolgirl ['sku:l,ge:rl] s. uczennica
schooling ['sku:lyŋg] s. nauka; szkolenie; wykształcenie
schoolmaster ['sku:l,ma:ster] s. kierownik szkoły
schoolmate ['sku:l,mejt] s. kolega szkolny
school of driving ['sku:l,ow'drajwyŋg] s. nauka jazdy (samochodem)
schooner ['sku:ner] s. skuner; szklanka na piwo
science ['sajens] s. wiedza; nauka; umiejętność
scientific ['sajentyfyk] adj. naukowy; umiejętny
scientist ['sajentyst] s. uczony; przyrodnik; naukowiec
scissors ['syzez] s. nożyce; nożyczki
scoff [skof] v. szydzić; kpić; drwić; s. pośmiewisko; szyderstwo; kpiny; drwiny
scold [skould] v. besztać; skrzyczeć; obrugać; łajać; złorzeczyć; s. jędza; sekutnica; megiera
scone [skon] s. placek trójkątny z jęczmiennej mąki
scoop [sku:p] v. zaczerpnąć; wygarnąć; wybrać; s. czerpak; szufelka; chochla; kubeł; sensacyjna wiadomość
scooter ['sku:ter] s. skuter; hulajnoga
scope [skoup] s. zasięg; zakres; dziedzina; meta; sposobność; możliwość
scorch [sko:rcz] v. spalić; przypiekać; przypalać; dopiekać; wypłowieć; pędzić samochodem jak szalony; s. poparzenie
score [sko:r] v. zdobyć (punkt); podkreślić; zanotować; zapisać; wygrać; osiągnąć; strzelić bramkę; s. ilość (zdobytych punktów lub

bramek); zacięcie; rysa; znak; dwadzieścia
scorn [sko:rn] s. lekceważenie; wzgarda; v. lekceważyć; gardzić; odrzucać z pogardą
scornful ['sko:rnful] adj. pogardliwy (i zagniewany); odrzucający z gniewem i pogardą
Scot [skot] adj. szkocki
Scotch [skocz] adj. szkocki
scot-free ['skot'fri:] adj. cały; nietknięty; niezraniony; gratis; bezpłatny
scoundrel ['skaundrel] s. kanalia; łotr
scour ['skauer] v. podmyć; szorować; przepłukiwać; poszukiwać; grasować; przetrząsać; s. podmycie; przemywanie; przepłukiwanie
scout [skaut] s. harcerz; zwiadowca; v. iść na zwiady; robić rekonesans
scoutmaster ['skaut,ma:ster] s. harcmistrz
scowl [skaul] v. chmurzyć się; patrzeć spode łba; groźnie patrzeć; s. zła mina; groźne spojrzenie; krzywa mina
scramble ['skraembl] s. ubijanie się; gramolenie się; dobijanie się; robienie jajecznicy; v. ubijać się; gramolić się; dobijać się; robić jajecznicę
scrambled eggs ['skraembld,egs] s. jajecznica
scrap [skraep] s. szmelc; odpadki; skrawki; wycinki; bójka; v. wyrzucać na szmelc; odrzucać; wycofać; bić się
scrape [skrejp] s. skrobanie; tarapaty; szurnięcie; ciułanie; draśnięcie; v. skrobać; drasnąć; ciułać; szurnąć
scrape off ['skrejp,of] v. zeskrobać
scrape out ['skrejp,aut] v. wyskrobać
scrape together [skrejp, tu'gedzer] v. uciułać
scrap iron ['skraep,ajern] s. złom

żelazny
scrappy ['skraepy] adj.
niejednolity; bez związku;
fragmentaryczny
scratch [skraecz] s. draśnięcie;
zadrapanie; rozdarcie;
skrobanie; linia startu; adj. do
pisania (np. brulion);
brulionowy; v. drapać (się);
zadrasnąć; gryzmolić;
wydrapać; wykreślić
scream [skri:m] s. krzyk; pisk;
gwizd; kawał; v. krzyczeć
przenikliwie; śmiać się
hałaśliwie i histerycznie
screech [skri:cz] s. zgrzyt; pisk;
skrzypienie; v. zgrzytać;
piszczeć; skrzypieć
screen [skri:n] s. zasłona; osłona;
siatka na komary; ekran; sito;
siewnik; filtr (światła); v.
zasłaniać; osłaniać;
zabezpieczać; wyświetlać;
przesiewać; sortować;
badać; przesłuchiwać;
filmować; izolować
screw [skru:] s. śruba; propeler;
śmigło; zwitek; wyzyskiwacz;
dusigrosz; (slang): stosunek
płciowy; v. przyśrubować;
wyduszać; naciskać;
wykrzywiać; zabałaganić;
obracać się; (slang):
spółkować; wkopać
(kogoś); oszukać
screwdriver ['skru:,drajwer] s.
śrubokręt; wódka z sokiem
pomarańczowym
scribble ['skrybl] s. gryzmoły;
bazgranina; v. gryzmolić;
bazgrać; pisać naprędce
script [skrypt] s. rękopis;
scenariusz
scripture ['skrypczer] s. Pismo
Święte
scroll [skroul] s. zwitek; krzywa;
spirala
scrub [skrab] s. zarośla; zagajnik; karłowate drzewo; pętak;
niepozorny człowiek;
szorowanie; v. szorować;
oczyszczać; adj. lichy; marny;
maławy

scruple ['skrupl] s. skrupuł; v.
wahać się; mieć skrupuły
scrupulous ['skru,pjules] adj.
sumienny; dokładny;
skrupulatny; pedantyczny
scrutinize ['skru:tynajz] v. badać
szczegółowo
scrutiny ['skru:tyny] s. dokładne
badanie
scuff [skaf] s. włóczenie nogami;
wytarte miejsca; v.
powłóczyć nogami;
wycierać; rozrzucać;
porysować; musnąć;
zedrzeć; zdzierać; szurać
scuffle [skafl] s. włóczenie
nogami; szamotanie się;
utarczka; bójka; v. szamotać
się; bić się; powłóczyć
nogami; szurać; zaszurać
sculptor ['skalpter] s. rzeźbiarz
sculpture ['skalpczer] s. rzeźba;
v. rzeźbić
scum [skam] s. szumowiny; v.
zbierać szumowiny;
wytarzać
scurf [ske:rf] s. łupież; strup;
parchy
scurvy ['ske:rwy] s. szkorbut;
adj. podły; nędzny
scuttle ['skatl] s. wiaderko;
szybka ucieczka; właz; v.
pędzić; uciekać; robić
dziury w dnie; zatapiać
scuttlebutt ['skatelbat] s. kadź;
pogłoska
scythe [sajz] s. kosa; v. kosić
sea [si:] s. morze; fala
sea breeze ['si:'bri:z] s. wiatr od
morza
seafarer ['si:,feerer] s. żeglarz;
podróżnik morski
seafood ['si:fu:d] s. potrawy
morskie (ryby, skorupiaki)
sea gull ['si:gal] s. mewa
seal [si:l] s. foka; futro foki;
uszczelka; zagadka; plomba;
pieczątka; piętno; znak; v.
polować na foki;
uszczelniać; plombować;
pieczętować; zalakować
seal up ['si:l,ap] v.
zaplombować; uszczelnić;

zamknąć; zalakować;
zapieczętować

sea level ['si:,lewl] s. poziom
morza

sealskin ['si:lski:n] s. futro z fok

seam [si:m] s. szew; rąbek;
pokład; blizna; szpara;
szczelina; v. łączyć szwami;
pękać; pokiereszować

seaman ['si:men] s. marynarz;
żeglarz

seamstress ['semstrys] s.
szwaczka

seaplane ['si:,plejn] s. hydroplan

seaport ['si:,po:rt] s. port morski

sea-power ['si:,pałer] s. potęga
morska

search [se:rcz] s. poszukiwanie;
badanie; szperanie; rewizja; v.
badać; dociekać; szukać;
przetrząsać; rewidować

searching ['se:rczyng] adj.
badawczy; przenikliwy

seashore ['si:,szo:r] s. wybrzeże;
brzeg morski

seasick ['si:,syk] adj. chory na
morską chorobę

seaside ['si:'sajd] s. wybrzeże
morskie

season ['si:zn] s. pora roku;
pora; sezon; v. zaprawiać;
przyprawiać; okrasić

seasonable ['si:znebl] adj.
stosowny; odpowiedni;
właściwy na porę roku; w
porę

seasonal ['si:zenl] adj. sezonowy

seasoned ['si:znd] adj.
zaprawiony; wdrożony;
przyprawiony; pikantny;
wystały

seasoning ['si:znyng] s.
przyprawa

season ticket ['si:sn'tykyt] s.
abonament; karta wstępu;
bilet (np. na serię
przedstawień)

seat [si:t] s. siedzenie; ławka;
krzesło; miejsce siedzące;
siedlisko; siedziba; gniazdo; v.
posadzić; usadowić;
wybierać (do sejmu); siąść;
osadzić

seat belt ['si:t,belt] s. pas
ochronny w samolocie lub
samochodzie; pas
bezpieczeństwa

seaward ['si:łerd] adv. ku
(otwartemu) morzu; adj.
skierowany ku morzu

seaweed ['si:łi:d] s. wodorost

seaworthy ['si:,łe:rsy] adj. zdatny
do podróży morskiej (m.in.
wodoszczelny)

secession [sy'seszyn] s. secesja;
oddzielenie się

seclude [sy'klu:d] v. odosabniać
(się)

secluded [sy'klu:dyd] adj.
odosobniony

seclusion [sy'klu:żyn] s.
odosobnienie; ustronie; zacisze

second ['sekend] adj. drugi;
wtórny; powtórny; ponowny;
zastępczy; zapasowy;
drugorzędny; v. poprzeć;
sekundować; s. sekunda;
moment; chwila; drugi;
sekundant; delegat; zastępca

secondary ['sekendery] adj.
drugorzędny; wtórny;
pochodny

secondary school ['sekendery
,sku:l] s. szkoła średnia

second floor ['sekend,flo:r] s.
pierwsze piętro

secondhand ['sekend,haend] adj.
z drugiej ręki; używany

secondly ['sekendly] adv. po
drugie

second-rate ['sekend'rejt] adj.
drugorzędny; lichy; kiepski

secrecy ['si:krysy] s. tajemnica;
skrytość; dyskrecja

secret ['si:kryt] adj. tajny;
tajemny; sekretny; skryty;
ustronny; dyskretny; s.
tajemnica; sekret; pl.
wstydliwe części ciała

secretary ['sekretry] s. sekretarz;
sekretarka; sekretarzyk

secretary of state
['sekretry,ow'stejt] s. minister
spraw zagranicznych USA

secrete [sy'kri:t] v. wydzielać;
ukrywać

secretion [sy'kri:szyn] s.
wydzielina; wydzielanie;
ukrycie
section ['sekszyn] s. część;
wycinek; etap; oddział; grupa;
dział; ustęp; paragraf; sekcja;
przekrój; żelazo profilowe;
przedział; drużyna robocza; v.
dzielić na części; robić
przekrój
sector ['sekter] s. wycinek;
odcinek
secular ['sekjuler] adj. świecki;
wiekowy; stuletni; s. ksiądz
świecki
secularize ['sekjulerajz] s.
sekularyzować
secure [sy'kjuer] v.
zabezpieczać (się);
umacniać; uzyskiwać;
zapewniać sobie; adj.
spokojny; bezpieczny; pewny
security [sy'kjueryty] s.
bezpieczeństwo;
zabezpieczenie; pewność;
zastaw; papier wartościowy;
zbytnia ufność
sedan [sy'daen] s. samochód 4
-osobowy
sedate [sy'dejt] v. uspokajać
(lekarstwami); adj. spokojny;
opanowany; zrównoważony
sedative ['sedetyw] adj. & s.
(środek) uspokajający,
nasenny
sediment ['sydyment] s. osad;
nanos; skała osadowa
seduce [sy'du:s] v. uwodzić
seduction [sy'dakszyn] s.
uwodzenie; pokusa; ponęta;
powab
seductive [sy'daktyw] adj.
kuszący; nęcący
sedulous ['sedjules] adj. pilny;
skrzętny; staranny; skwapliwy
see; saw; seen [si:; so:; si:n]
see [si:] v. zobaczyć; widzieć;
ujrzeć; zauważyć;
spostrzegać; doprowadzić;
odprowadzić; zwiedzać;
zrozumieć; odwiedzać;
przeżywać; dożyć;
uważać; zastanawiać się;

dopilnować
see off ['si:,of] v. odprowadzać
see out ['si:,aut] v. odprowadzić
do drzwi
see through ['si:,tru:] v.
przeprowadzić do końca;
doczekać się końca
see to ['si:,tu:] v. troszczyć się
o...
seed [si:d] v. obsiewać;
obsypywać się; zasiewać;
wybierać; s. nasienie;
zarodek; plemię
seek; sought; sought [si:k; so:t;
so:t]
seek [si:k] v. szukać; starać
się; chcieć; żadać;
nastawać; usiłować;
próbować; przetrząsać;
dążyć
seek out ['si:k,aut] v.
odszukiwać; wykrywać
seem [si:m] v. zdawać się;
robić wrażenie; okazywać
się; mieć wrażenie
seeming [si:myng] adj. pozorny;
widoczny
seemingly ['si:myngly] adv. na
pozór; widocznie
seemly [si:mly] adj. właściwy;
przyzwoity
seen [si:n] v. zob. see
seep [si:p] v. sączyć się;
wyciekać
seer [sier] s. jasnowidz; prorok;
prorokini
seesaw ['si:so:] s. huśtawka (na
desce); adj. wahadłowy;
huśtawkowy; s. huśtać się;
wahać się; adv. (poruszać
czymś) do góry i na dół
segment ['segment] s. odcinek;
segment; v. podzielić na
części
segregate ['segry'gejt] v.
oddzielać; segregować
segregation ['segry'gejszyn] s.
oddzielenie; segregacja
seize [si:z] v. uchwycić;
złapać; zrozumieć;
owładnąć; skorzystać;
zaciąć się; zatrzeć się;
zablokować się

seizure ['si:zer] s. zagarnięcie;
zawładnięcie; zajęcie; napad;
atak apopleksji; zatarcie;
zablokowanie; atak drgawek

seldom ['seldem] adv. rzadko; z
rzadka

select [sy'lekt] v. wybierać;
wyselękcjonować; adj.
wybrany; doborowy;
ekskluzywny

selection [sy'lekszyn] s. wybór;
dobór; selekcja

self [self] prefix samo;
automatycznie; s. jaźń;
osobowość; własne dobro;
pl. selves [selwz]

self-acting ['self'aektyng] adj.
samoczynny

self-command ['self,ke'ma:nd] s.
spokój; panowanie nad sobą;
opanowanie

self-confidence ['self,konfydens]
s. pewność siebie; tupet

self-conscious ['self'konszes]
adj. nieśmiały; zażenowany

self-control ['self,ken'troul] s.
zimna krew; opanowanie

self-defense ['self,dy'fens] s.
samoobrona

self-employment ['self
,ym'plojment] s.
samozatrudnienie

self-government ['self
'gawenment] s. samorząd;
autonomia

self-interest ['self'yntryst] s.
interesowność; własne
dobro

selfish ['selfysz] adj. samolubny;
egoistyczny

self-made ['self'mejd] adj. przez
samego siebie osiągnięty

self-possessed ['self,pe'zest] adj.
opanowany; spokojny

self-reliant ['self,ry'lajent] adj. na
sobie polegający

self-respect ['self,rys'pekt] s.
poczucie własnej godności

self-righteous ['self'rajczes] adj.
nadmiernie pewny siebie

self-service ['self'se:rwys] s.
samo-obsługa

sell; sold; sold [sel; sould; sould]

sell [sel] v. sprzedawać;
zaprzedawać;
sprzeniewierzyć; wykiwać;
mieć zbyt; być na sprzedaż;
wyprzedawać

sell out ['selaut] v.
wyprzedawać

seller ['seler] s. sprzedawca

selves [selwz] pl. zob. self

semblance ['semblens] s. pozór;
podobieństwo

semen ['si:men] s. nasienie

semester [sy'mester] s. półrocze;
semestr

semicolon ['semy'koulen] s.
średnik

semifinal ['semy'fajnl] s. półfinał

senate ['senyt] s. senat

senator ['seneter] s. senator

send; sent; sent [send; sent;
sent]

send [send] v. posyłać;
wysyłać; nadawać;
transmitować; wystrzeliwać;
sprawiać; wywoływać

send away ['send,e'łej] v.
odprawiać; wypędzać

send for ['send,fo:r] v. zawołać;
zamawiać; kazać przynieść

send in ['send,yn] v. posłać;
nadesłać

send off ['send'o:f] v. wysyłać;
odprowadzać (np. na
lotnisko); pożegnać kogoś
(na stacji)

sender ['sender] s. nadawca;
nadajnik (np. radiowy)

send-off ['send'o:f] s.
pożegnanie

senior ['si:njer] adj. starszy (np.
rangą); s. starszy człowiek;
senior; student ostatniego
roku

sensation [sen'sejszyn] s.
wrażenie; doznanie; uczucie;
sensacja

sensational [sen'sejszenl] adj.
sensacyjny; wrażeniowy

sense [sens] s. zmysł; poczucie;
uczucie (np. zimna);
świadomość (czegoś);
rozsądek; znaczenie; sens; v.
wyczuwać; czuć; rozumieć

senseless ['senslys] adj. bez
   sensu; nierozumny;
   nieprzytomny
sensibility [,sensy'bylyty] s.
   wrażliwość
sensible ['sensybl] adj. rozsądny;
   świadomy; przytomny;
   wrażliwy; odczuwalny;
   poznawalny; sensowny
sensitive ['sensytyw] adj.
   wrażliwy; delikatny
sensual ['senszuel] adj.
   zmysłowy (też seksualnie)
sensuous ['senszues] adj.
   zmysłowy (nie seksualnie)
sent [sent] v. zob. send
sentence ['sentens] s. zdanie;
   powiedzenie; wyrok;
   sentencja; v. wydawać
   wyrok; skazywać
sentiment ['sentyment] s.
   sentyment; uczucie; opinia;
   zdanie; życzenie;
   sentymentalność
sentimental [,senty'mentl] adj.
   uczuciowy; sentymentalny
sentimentality
   [,senty'ment'aelyty] s.
   uczuciowość; czułostko-
   wość; sentymentalność
sentry ['sentry] s. posterunek;
   wartownik
separable ['seperebl] adj.
   rozłączny
separate ['seperejt] v.
   rozłączyć; rozdzielić;
   oddzielić; oderwać;
   odseparować (się);
   odgrodzić; rozszczepić
separate ['sepryt] adj. odrębny;
   oddzielny; osobny;
   indywidualny; poszczególny
separation [,sepe'rejszyn] s.
   separacja; rozdzielenie;
   oddzielenie; rozłączenie
September [sep'tember] s.
   wrzesień
septic ['septyk] adj. septyczny;
   zakaźny
sepulcher ['sepelker] s. grób; v.
   składać do grobu
sequel ['si:kłel] s. ciąg dalszy;
   wynik; następstwo

sequence ['si:kłens] s.
   następstwo; kolejność;
   porządek; progresja
serene [sy'ri:n] adj. pogodny;
   spokojny; s. spokojne morze;
   pogodne niebo etc.; v.
   rozpogodzić
sergeant ['sa:rdżent] s. sierżant
serial ['sierjel] adj. seryjny;
   periodyczny; kolejny;
   odcinkowy
series ['sieri:z] s. seria; szereg;
   rząd
serious ['sierjes] adj. poważny
sermon ['se:rmen] s. kazanie;
   nagana
serpent ['se:rpent] s. wąż
serum ['sierem] s. surowica
servant ['se:rwent] s. służący;
   sługa; służąca; urzędnik
   (państwowy)
serve [se:rw] v. służyć;
   odbywać służbę (też
   kadencją, praktykę etc.);
   nadawać się; obsłużyć;
   podawać; sprzedawać;
   dostarczyć; wręczyć;
   potraktować; postąpować;
   spełniać funkcje; sprawować
   urząd; odbywać karę
   (więzienia); zaserwować
service ['se:rwys] s. służba;
   obsługa; praca; urząd;
   zaopatrzenie; instalacja;
   uprzejmość; grzeczność;
   przysługa; pomoc;
   użyteczność; nabożeństwo;
   serw; serwis (stołowy);
   wręczenie; v. doglądać;
   naprawić; kryć (samice)
serviceable ['se:rwysebl] adj.
   pożyteczny; użyteczny;
   praktyczny; wygodny; mocny;
   trwały
service-station ['se:rwys
   -'stejszyn] s. stacja obsługi i
   sprzedaży benzyny
session ['seszyn] s. posiedzenie;
   siedzenie; półrocze
set; set; set [set; set; set]
set [set] v. stawiać; ustawiać;
   wstawić; urządzić;
   umieszczać; przykładać;

nastawiać; osadzać; wbijać;
wyznaczać; ustalać; sądzić;
nakrywać; składać;
wysadzać (czymś); ścinać
się; okrzepnąć; adj. zastygły;
nieruchomy; zdecydowany;
stały; ustalony; s. seria;
garnitur; skład; komplet;
zespół; grupa; szczepek;
zachód; ustawienie; układ;
twardnienie; gęstość;
rozstęp; oszalowanie
set at ease ['set,et'i:z] v.
uspokoić
set-back ['setbaek] s.
pogorszenie; nawrót;
zahamowanie
set free ['set,fri:] v. uwolnić
set off ['set,of] v. uwydatnić;
wyodrębnić; wystrzelić;
wysadzić; wywołać;
wyruszyć; wyjeżdżać
set out ['set,aut] v. wystawiać;
ozdabiać; wykładać;
wyruszać; zacząć się
set to ['set,tu] v. zabierać się
(do czegoś)
set up ['set,ap] v. ustawiać;
zakładać; zaczynać;
zaopatrywać; rościć;
wysuwać; przywracać;
podnosić; założyć; podawać
się (za kogoś)
settee [se'ti:] s. kanapa; sofa
setting ['setyng] s. otoczenie;
oprawa; ułożenie; układ;
inscenizacja
settle [setl] v. osiedlić (się);
umieścić (się); uregulować;
osadzić (się); ustalić;
rozstrzygnąć; zapłacić (dług);
zamieszkać; usadowić (się);
uspokoić (się); zawierać
(umowę); układać (się)
settle down ['setl,dałn] v.
ustatkować się; osiedlić się;
zabrać się do czegoś
settlement ['setlment] s. osiedle;
osada; kolonia; osiadanie;
sedymentacja; załatwienie;
rozstrzygnięcie; ustalenie
settler ['setler] s. osadnik;
kolonista

set-up ['set,ap] s. postawa;
układ; drużyna; dodatki do
alkoholu; (slang): ukartowane
zawody; łatwa sprawa
seven ['sewn] num. siedem; s.
siódemka
seventeen ['sewn'ti:n] num.
siedemnaście; s.
siedemnastka
seventh ['sewent] adj. siódmy
seventy ['sewnty] num.
siedemdziesiąt; s.
siedemdziesiątka
sever ['sewer] v. odrywać;
odłączyć; zrywać; urywać;
rozchodzić się
several ['sewrel] adj. kilku; kilka;
kilkoro
severe [sy'wier] adj. surowy;
srogi; ostry; dotkliwy; bolesny;
zacięty
severity [sy'weryty] s.
surowość; srogość;
ostrość; zaciętość; ciężki
stan
sew; sewed; sewn [sou; soud;
soun]
sew [sou] v. szyć; uszyć
sewage ['sju:ydż] s. ścieki
sewer ['suer] s. kanał ściekowy;
v. kanalizować
sewer ['souer] s. osoba szyjąca
sewerage ['su:erydż] s.
kanalizacja; system
kanalizacyjny
sewing ['souyng] s. szycie
sewing-machine ['souyng
me,szi:n] s. maszyna do
szycia
sewn [soun] v. zob. sew
sex [seks] s. płeć
sex appeal ['sekse'pi:l] s.
atrakcyjność płciowa;
seksapil
sexton ['seksten] s. grabarz
sexual ['seksziuel] adj.
seksualny; płciowy
Seym [sejm] s. Sejm, parliament
shabby ['szaeby] adj. brudny;
skąpy; odrapany; wytarty;
nędzny; podły
shack [szaek] s. buda; szałas;
dom

shack up ['szaek,ap] v. spędzać
noc z kimś (slang)
shackle ['szaekl] s. kajdany;
klamra; pęta; v. zakuwać;
sczepiać
shade [szejd] s. cień; odcień;
abażur; stora; pl. ustronie;
piwnica na wino; v.
zasłaniać; zamroczyć;
cieniować
shadow ['szaedou] s. cień
(czyjś); v. pokrywać cieniem;
śledzić kogoś
shady ['szejdy] adj. cienisty;
nieczysty; mętny
shaft [szaeft] s. drzewce; trzon;
strzała; promień; wał;
trzonek; dyszel; szyb
shaggy ['szaegy] adj. włochaty;
krzaczasty
shake; shook; shaken [szejk;
szuk; szejken]
shake [szejk] potrząsać;
uścisnąć dłoń; grozić
(palcem); wstrząsać; drżeć;
dygotać; s. dygotanie;
dreszcze; drżenie; potrząsanie
shake-up ['szejkap] s.
otrząśnięcie (się); czystka
(slang)
shaky ['szejky] adj. drżący;
rozklekotany; słaby;
zachwiany; chwiejący się
shale [szejl] s. łupek
shall [szael] v. będę; będziemy;
musisz; musi; muszą (zrobić)
shallow ['szaelou] s. mielizna;
adj. płytki; powierzchniowy; v.
spłycać; płycieć; obniżać
poziom (wody)
sham [szaem] adj. fałszywy;
oszukańczy; sztuczny;
udawany; symulowany;
upozorowany; s. poza;
symulowanie; symulant;
pozór; udawanie; v. udawać;
symulować
shambles ['szaemblz] pl. jatki;
rzeź
shame [szejm] s. wstyd; v.
wstydzić się
shame on you! ['szejm,on'ju:]
exp.: wstydź się!

shameful ['szejmful] adj.
sromotny; haniebny
shameless ['szejmlys] adj.
bezwstydny; bezczelny
shampoo [szaem'pu:] s.
szampon; mycie głowy
szamponem; v. myć
szamponem
shank [szaenk] s. goleń;
trzonek; uchwyt
shape [szejp] v. kształtować;
rzeźbić; modelować;
formułować; wyobrazić; s.
kształt; kondycja; postać;
zjawa; widmo; model
shaped ['szejpt] adj.
ukształtowany
shapeless ['szejplys] adj.
bezkształtny; nieforemny;
niezgrabny
shapely ['szejply] adj. kształtny;
foremny; zgrabny
share [szeer] s. udział; należna
część; lemiesz; v.
rozdzielić; dzielić (się);
podzielać; brać udział
share-holder ['szeer,houlder] s.
akcjonariusz
shark [sza:rk] s. rekin
sharp [sza:rp] adj. ostry; bystry;
pilny; wyraźny; chytry;
dominujący; inteligentny; adv.
punktualnie; szybko; biegiem
sharpen ['sza:rpen] v. ostrzyć;
temperować; obostrzyć;
zaostrzyć
sharpener ['sza:rpner] s.
temperówka; narzędzie do
ostrzenia
sharpness ['sza:rpnys] s.
ostrość; bystrość;
chytrość; pilność
sharp-witted ['sza:rp'łytyd] adj.
bystry; dowcipny; rozgarnięty
shatter ['szaeter] v. gruchotać;
roztrzaskać; niweczyć;
szarpać
shave; shaved; shaven [szejw;
szejwd; szejwn]
shave [szejw] v. golić (się);
oskrobać; strugać; s.
golenie; muśnięcie
shaven [szejwn] v. zob. shave

shaving ['szejwyng] v. golenie; skrobanie; wiórkowanie; s. wiór

shawl [szo:l] s. szal

she [szi:] pron. ona

sheaf [szi:f] s. snop; wiązka; wiązanka; plik; pl. sheaves [szi:wz]

shear; sheared; shorn [szier; szierd; szo:rn]

shear [szier] v. ścinać; ucinać; ostrzyć; s. ścinanie; pl. nożyce (shears)

sheath [szi:s] s. pochwa; futerał; powłoka; prezerwatywa

sheaves [szi:wz] pl. od sheath

shed [szed] s. szopa; buda; v. zrzucać; strącać; pozbywać (się); pogubić; ronić; przelewać (krew); wydzielać; promieniować

sheep [szi:p] pl. owce

sheep dog ['szi:p,dog] s. owczarek

sheepish ['szi:pysz] adj. bojaźliwy; nieśmiały; zakłopotany; zbaraniały; ogłupiały

sheer [szier] v. schodzić z kursu; skręcać nagle; adj. zwykły; jawny; czysty; zwyczajny; stromy; prostopadły; pionowy; przejrzysty; przewiewny; lekki; adv. zupełnie; pionowo; stromo

sheet [szi:t] s. arkusz; prześcieradło; gazeta; tafla; obszar; warstwa; v. pokrywać prześcieradłem; okrywać brezentem

sheet iron ['szi:t,ajren] s. blacha stalowa

shelf [szelf] s. półka; rafa; mielizna; pl. shelves [szelwz]

shell [szel] s. łupina; skorupa; powłoka; osłona; pancerz; muszla; szkielet; łuska; pocisk; granat; gilza; v. ostrzeliwać z armat; wyłuskiwać

shellfish ['szel,fysz] s. skorupiak; mięczak

shelter ['szelter] s. schronienie;

ochrona; osłona; v. chronić; osłaniać; udzielać schronienia; zabezpieczać

shelve [szelw] v. odkładać (na półkę); wkładać do szuflady; opadać (wzdłuż stoku)

shelves [szelwz] pl. zob. shelf

shepherd ['szeperd] s. pastuch; pasterz; v. paść; (pilotować) prowadzić

shield [szi:ld] s. tarcza; osłona; v. osłaniać; ochraniać

shift [szyft] v. zmieniać (np. biegi); przesuwać; przełączyć; zwalić; s. przesunięcie; zmiana; szychta; wykręt; wybieg

shiftless ['szyftlys] adj. niezaradny

shifty ['szyfty] adj. zmienny; fałszywy; chytry

shilling ['szylyng] s. szyling

shin [szyn] s. goleń; v. kopać w goleń

shine; shone; shone [szajn; szon; szon]

shine [szajn] v. zabłyszczeć; zajaśnieć; oczyścić na połysk; s. jasność; blask; (slang): granda; awantura; sympatia

shingle ['szyngl] s. gont; szyld; wywieszka; kamyk; v. pokryć gontami; krótko ostrzyc

shingles ['szynglz] pl. półpasiec

shiny ['szajny] adj. błyszczący; wypolerowany

ship [szyp] s. okręt; statek; samolot; v. załadować; zaokrętować; posyłać

shipment ['szypment] s. załadunek; przesyłka; fracht

shipowner ['szyp,ołner] s. armator

shipping ['szypyng] s. flota handlowa; żegluga; załadunek; usługi żeglugowe; przesyłka; adj. spedycyjny; okrętowy

shipping company ['szypyng 'kampeny] s. firma okrętowa; armator

shipwreck ['szyp,rek] s. rozbicie statku; v. ulec rozbiciu;

spowodować rozbicie statku; rozbić się

ship-wrecked ['szyp,rekt] s. rozbitek

shipyard ['szyp,ja:rd] s. stocznia

shire ['szajer] s. hrabstwo (powiat)

shirk [sze:rk] v. uchylać się; wymigiwać się; s. nieróbь; wymigiwacz

shirt [sze:rt] s. koszula

shirt sleeves ['sze:rt,sli:wz] pl. rękawy od koszuli; bez marynarki; adj. prosty; domowy

shit [szyt] v. wulg.: srać; s. gówno

shitty ['szyty] adj. wulg.: zasrany

shiv [sziw] s. majcher (slang)

shiver ['szywer] v. drżeć; trząść się; rozbijać się w kawałki; s. dreszcz; kawałek

shock [szok] s. wstrząs; cios; uderzenie; starcie; porażenie; czupryna; kopka; v. wstrząsać; gorszyć; oburzać; porazić

shock absorber ['szok-eb,so:rber] s. tłumik drgań; amortyzator

shocking ['szokyng] adj. okropny; wstrętny; skandaliczny; oburzający; niestosowny

shoddy ['szody] adj. tandetny

shoe; shod; shod [szu:; szod; szod]

shoe [szu:] s. but; półbucik; trzewik; okucie; podkowa; nakładka (hamulca); obręcz; nasada; v. obuwać; podkuwać

shoehorn ['szu:,ho:rn] s. łyżka do butów; wzuwacz

shoelace ['szu:,lejs] s. sznurowadło

shoemaker ['szu:,mejker] s. szewc

shoestring ['szu:,stryng] s. sznurowadło; bardzo mały kapitał

shoeshine ['szu:,szajn] s. czyszczenie butów (na połysk)

shone [szon] v. zob. shine

shook [szuk] v. zob. shake

shoot; shot; shot [szu:t; szot; szot]

shoot [szu:t] v. strzelić; wystrzelić; zastrzelić; rozstrzelać; zrobić zdjęcie; nakręcić film; mknąć; przemknąć; spłynąć; rwać; kiełkować; s. pęd; kiełek; polowanie; progi; plac zwozu śmieci

shooter ['szu:ter] s. strzelec; rewolwer

shooting ['szu:tyng] adj. mknący; pędzący; strzelający

shooting gallery ['szu:tyng,gaelery] s. strzelnica

shooting-star ['szu:tyng,sta:r] s. spadająca gwiazda

shooting-party ['szu:tyng,pa:rty] s. wyprawa łowiecka; polowanie

shop [szop] s. sklep; pracownia; warsztat; zakład; v. robić zakupy

shopkeeper ['szop,ki:per] s. kupiec; sklepikarz

shoplifter ['szop,lyfter] s. złodziej sklepowy

shopping center ['szopyng,senter] s. skupisko sklepów; ośrodek zakupów

shopping mall ['szopyng,mol] s. skupisko sklepów wzdłuż krytej hali; pasaż handlowy

shop window ['szop'lyndoł] s. wystawa

shore [szo:r] s. brzeg; wybrzeże; podpora; v. podpierać; podstemplować

shorn [szo:rn] v. zob. shear

short [szo:rt] adj. krótki; niski; zwięzły; oschły; niecały; niewystarczający; adv. krótko; nagle; za krótko; s. skrót; zwarcie; pl. szorty

shortage ['szo:rtydż] s. brak; niedobór; deficyt

short circuit ['szo:rt'se:rkyt] s. krótkie spięcie; zwarcie

shortcoming ['szo:rt'kamyng] s. wada; niedociągnięcie; brak; niedobór

shorten ['szo:rtn] v. skracać
shorthand ['szo:rthaend] s.
stenografia
shortly ['szo:rtly] adv. wkrótce;
niebawem
shortness ['szo:rtnys] s.
krótkość; niedobór
shorts ['szo:rts] pl. szorty;
kalesony (krótkie)
short story ['szo:rt,sto:ry] s.
nowela
short-sighted ['szo:rt'sajtyd] adj.
krótkowzroczny;
nieprzewidujący
short-term ['szo:rt'term] adj.
krótkoterminowy; krótkotrwały
short-winded ['szo:rt'łyndyd] adj.
zasapany; krótko mówiący
shot [szot] v. zob. shoot;
ładować broń; s. strzał;
pocisk; śrut; zastrzyk;
docinek; adj. mieniący się
shotgun ['szotgan] s.
dubeltówka; śrutówka;
strzelba
should [szud] v. tryb warunkowy
od shall
shoulder ['szoulder] s. ramię;
plecy; łopatka; pobocze; v.
brać na ramię; rozpychać się
shout [szałt] s. krzyk; okrzyk;
wrzask; v. krzyczeć;
wykrzykiwać
shove [szaw] v. popychać;
posuwać (coś); s. pchnięcie
shovel ['szawl] s. łopata; szufla;
v. przerzucać łopatą lub
szuflą
show; showed; shown [szou;
szoud; szoun]
show [szou] v. pokazywać;
wskazywać; s. wystawa;
przedstawienie; pokaz
show around ['szou,e'raund] v.
oprowadzać
show off ['szou,o:f] v.
popisywać się; paradować;
starać się imponować
show up ['szou,ap] v.
demaskować; zjawiać się;
ukazywać się
show business ['szou'byznyz] s.
przemysł widowiskowy

shower ['szałer] s. tusz;
prysznic; przelotny deszcz;
grad; stek; v. przelotnie
kropić; obsypywać;
oblewać
shower bath ['szałer,ba:t] s.
tusz; prysznic
shown [szołn] v. zob. show
showy ['szoły] adj. ostentacyjny;
okazały
shrank [szraenk] v. zob. shrink
shred [szred] s. strzęp; v. ciąć
na strzępy
shrew [szru:] s. złośnica;
sekutnica; sorek
shrewd [szru:d] adj. przenikliwy
(np. obserwator)
shriek [szri:k] v. wrzeszczeć;
piszczeć; rechotać; s.
wrzask; pisk; gwizd (ostry)
shrill [szryl] adj. ostry;
przenikliwy; przeraźliwy; v.
rozlegać się przenikliwie; adv.
przenikliwie
shrimp [szrymp] s. krewetka;
karzełek; v. łowić krewetki
shrine [szrajn] s. przybytek;
relikwiarz; v. umieszczać w
przybytku
shrink; shrank; shrunk [szrynk;
szraenk; szrank]
shrink [szrynk] v. kurczyć (się);
wzbraniać (się); wzdrygać
się; s. kurczenie się; (slang):
psychiatra
shrinkage ['szrynkydż] s.
kurczenie się; ubytek na
wadze
shrivel ['szrywl] v. kurczyć (się)
shroud [szraud] s. całun; kir;
zasłona; płaszcz
Shrovetide ['szrouwtajd] s.
(święto) ostatki; zapusty
Shrove Tuesday
['szrouw'tju:zdy] s. tłusty
wtorek
shrub [szrab] s. krzew; krzak
shrubbery ['szrabery] s. krzaki
shrubby ['szraby] adj. krzaczasty
shrug [szrag] s. wzruszenie
ramion; v. wzruszyć
ramionami
shrunken ['szrankn] v. zob.

shrink
shudder ['szader] s. dreszcz;
(slang): nudziarz; v. zadrżeć;
wzdrygać się
shuffle ['szafl] v. wlec się;
powłóczyć; kręcić;
tasować; mieszać; s. krok
suwany; krętactwo; tasowanie
(kart); wleczenie się; szuranie
shun [szan] v. unikać;
wystrzegać się; s.
baczność; uwaga
shut; shut; shut [szat; szat; szat]
shut [szat] v. zamykać (się);
przytrzasnąć; adj. zamknięty
shut down ['szat,dałn] s.
zamknięcie; wstrzymanie
pracy; v. zamykać; kłaść
koniec; zasłaniać; (o
zakładzie) stanąć
shut up ['szat,ap] v.
pozamykać; zamknąć gębę;
zamilknąć; bądź cicho;
wulg.: stul pysk!
shutter ['szater] s. okiennica;
zasłona; migawka; regulator
organów; v. zamykać
okiennice
shy [szaj] adj. płochliwy;
wstydliwy; nieśmiały;
nieufny; ostrożny; skąpy;
szczupły; v. płoszyć się;
stronić; rzucać; s. rzut (w
coś)
shyness ['szajnys] s.
skromność; nieśmiałość
shyster ['szajster] s. chytry
(polityk) bez zasad; adwokat-
krętacz
sick [syk] adj. chory; znudzony;
chorowity; skażony zarazkami;
chorobowy
sickbed ['sykbed] s. łóżko
chorego; łoże boleści
sick benefit ['syk'benefyt] s.
zasiłek chorobowy
sicken ['sykn] v. zaczynać
chorować; wywoływać
obrzydzenie; brzydzić (się)
sickle ['sykl] s. sierp
sick leave ['sykli:w] s. zwolnienie
lekarskie; urlop chorobowy
sickly ['sykly] adj. chorowity;

słabowity; niezdrowy;
chorobliwy; ckliwy
sickness ['syknys] s. choroba;
wymioty; nudności
sick room ['syk-ru:m] s. izba
chorych; pokój chorego
side [sajd] s. strona; adj.
uboczny; v. stać po czyjejś
stronie
side by side ['sajd,baj'sajd] exp.:
obok siebie; jeden przy drugim
side arms ['sajda:rmz] pl. broń
boczna (np. szable)
sideboard ['sajdbo:rd] s. kredens
sidecar ['sajd,ka:r] s. przyczepa
do motocykla
sided ['sajdyd] adj. stronny;
mający strony
side dish ['sajd,dysz] s.
przystawka
side-kick ['sajdkyk] s. (slang):
kompan; pomagier
side road ['sajd,roud] s. boczna
droga
side line ['sajd,lajn] v. odsuwać
na bok; zapobiegać
sidewalk ['sajd-ło:k] s. chodnik;
trotuar
sidewalk café ['sajdło:kaefej] s.
kawiarnia na chodniku
side-wards ['sajdłedz] adv.
bokiem; w bok
sideways ['sajdłejz] adv. bokiem;
na poprzek; adj. boczny
side with ['sajd,tys] v. brać
czyjąś stronę
siege [si:dż] s. oblężenie
sieve [syw] s. sito; rzeszoto;
przetak; v. przesiewać
sift [syft] v. przesiewać;
przebierać; oddzielać;
prószyć; posypywać
sigh [saj] s. westchnienie; v.
wzdychać
sight [sajt] s. wzrok; widok;
celownik; przeziernik
sighted ['sajtyd] adj.
spostrzeżony
sightly ['sajtly] adj. dający dobry
widok; miły; przyjemny
sightseeing ['sajtsi:yng] s.
zwiedzanie; adj. turystyczny
sightseeing tour ['sajtsi:yng,tu:r]

s. zwiedzanie z wycieczką;
wycieczka krajoznawcza
sightseer ['sajtsi:er] s. turysta;
zwiedzający
sign [sajn] s. znak; omen; godło;
napis; wywieszka; szyld;
skinienie; oznaka; objaw;
ślad; znak drogowy; hasło;
odzew; v. znaczyć;
naznaczyć; podpisać;
skinąć
sign up ['sajn,ap] v. zapisywać
się
sign out ['sajn,aut] v.
wypisywać się
signal ['sygnl] s. sygnał; znak; v.
sygnalizować; zapowiadać;
dawać znak
signature ['sygnyczer] s. podpis;
sygnatura; klucz
signature-tune ['sygnyczer,tju:n]
s. oznaczenie tonacji
signboard ['sajnbo:rd] s.
wywieszka; szyld; godło
signet ['sygnyt] s. sygnet;
pieczątka; v. pieczętować
significance [syg'nyfykens] s.
wyraz; ważność; znaczenie
significant [syg'nyfykent] adj.
istotny; znaczący; doniosły;
znamienny; ważny
signification [,sygnyfy'kejszyn] s.
znaczenie
signify ['sygnyfaj] v. znaczyć;
mieć znaczenie; oznaczać;
zaznaczać
signpost ['sajn,poust] s.
drogowskaz
silence ['sajlens] s. milczenie;
cisza; v. nakazywać
milczenie; cicho!
silencer ['sajlenser] s. tłumik
silent ['sajlent] adj. milczący;
cichy; małomówny
silk [sylk] s. jedwab; adj.
jedwabny
silken ['sylkn] adj. jedwabny;
jedwabniczy
silky ['sylky] adj. jedwabisty
sill [syl] s. próg; podkład;
parapet
silly ['syly] s. głupiec; adj. głupi;
ogłupiały

silver ['sylwer] s. srebro; v.
posrebrzać; adj. srebrny;
srebrzysty
silvery ['sylwry] adj. srebrzysty
similar ['symyler] adj. podobny
similarity [,symy'laeryty] s.
podobieństwo
simmer ['symer] v. wolno
gotować (się); burzyć się
wewnątrz; s. gotowanie na
wolnym ogniu
simple ['sympl] adj. prosty;
zwykły; naturalny; szczery;
naiwny; głupkowaty;
zwyczajny
simpleton ['symplten] s.
prostaczek; kiep; głuptas
simplicity [sym'plysyty] s.
prostota
simplification [,symplyfy'kejszyn]
s. uproszczenie
simplistic ['symplystyk] adj. zbyt
upraszczający
simplify ['symplyfaj] v.
uprościć; ułatwić
simply ['symply] adv. po prostu
simulate ['symjulejt] v. udawać;
naśladować
simultaneous [symel'tejnjes] adj.
równoczesny; jednoczesny
sin [syn] s. grzech; v. grzeszyć
since [syns] adv. odtąd; potem;
conj. skoro; ponieważ; od
czasu jak
sincere [syn'sier] adj. szczery
sincerely [syn'sierly] adv.
szczerze
sincerity [syn'seryty] s.
szczerość
sinew ['synu:] s. ścięgno
sinews ['synu:s] pl. muskulatura;
siła; moc
sinewy ['synuy] adj. muskularny;
mocny
sinful ['synful] adj. grzeszny
sing; sang; sung [syng; saeng;
sang]
sing [syng] v. śpiewać; wyć;
zawodzić; bzykać; świstać;
opiewać; s. śpiew; świst
singe [syndż] v. opalać;
osmalać
singer ['synger] s. śpiewak

single ['syngl] adj. pojedynczy;
jeden; samotny; szczery;
uczciwy; s. bilet w jedną
stronę; gra pojedyncza; v.
wybierać; wyróżniać
single out ['syngl,aut] v.
wybierać
single-handed ['syngl'haendyd]
adj. adv. w pojedynkę; na
własną rękę; samodzielny;
samodzielnie
single room ['syngl'ru:m] s.
pojedynczy pokój
single ticket ['syngl'tykyt] s.
bilet w jedną stronę
singles bar ['syngls,ba:r] s. bar
dla samotnych
singular ['syngjuler] adj.
osobliwy; niezwykły;
pojedynczy; s. liczba
pojedyncza
singularity [,syngju'laeryty] s.
osobliwość; niezwykłość;
niezwykły człowiek
sinister ['synyster] adj.
zbrodniczy; złowieszczy; lewy
sink; sank; sunk [synk; saenk;
sank]
sink [synk] v. zatonąć; zatopić;
zagłębić (się); opuścić;
obniżyć; pogrążyć; zanikać;
zmaleć; wykopywać;
ukrywać; wyryć;
zainwestować;
amortyzować; s. zlew; ściek;
bagno zepsucia
sinking ['synkyng] s. uczucie
mdłości (np. z przerażenia)
sinner ['syner] s. grzesznik
sip [syp] s. łyk; popijanie; v.
popijać
sir [se:r] s. pan; v. nazywać
panem; exp.: proszę pana!
sirloin ['se:rloin] s. polędwica
sister ['syster] s. siostra
sister-in-law ['syster yn,lo:] s.
szwagierka
sit; sat; sat [syt; saet; saet]
sit [syt] v. siedzieć;
przesiadywać; usiąść;
zasiadać; obradować; leżeć;
pozować
sit down ['syt,dałn] v. usiąść

sit up ['syt,ap] v. wyprostować
się siedząc; czuwać; usiąść
prosto
site [sajt] s. miejsce; plac (np.
budowy); położenie; v.
umieszczać
sitting ['sytyng] s. posiedzenie;
sesja
sitting-room ['sytyng,ru:m] s.
bawialnia; salon
situated ['sytjuejtyd] adj.
umieszczony; stojący;
usytuowany
situation [,sytu'ejszyn] s.
położenie; posada; sytuacja
six [syks] num. sześć; s.
szóstka
sixteen ['syks'ti:n] num.
szesnaście; s. szesnastka
sixth [sykst] num. adj. szósty; s.
jedna szósta
sixthly ['sykstly] adv. po szóste
size [sajz] s. wielkość; numer;
format; klajster; krochmal;
rzadki klej; v. sortować **wg**
wielkości; oceniać
wielkość; nadawać się;
krochmalić; usztywnić klejem
sized-up ['sajzd,ap] adj. oceniony
(co do wielkości, siły lub
ważności)
sizzle ['syzl] v. skwierczeć; s.
skwierczenie
skate [skejt] s. łyżwa; wrotka;
płaszczka; szkapa; pętak;
patałach; v. ślizgać się;
jeździć na wrotkach
skater ['skejter] s. łyżwiarz;
wrotkarz
skeleton ['skelytn] s. szkielet
skeptic ['skeptyk] adj.
sceptyczny; s. sceptyk
sketch ['skecz] s. szkic; skecz;
zarys; v. szkicować;
przedstawić w ogólnych
zarysach (w krótkich
słowach); robić wstępny
rysunek
sketch block ['skecz,blok] s.
szkicownik
sketchbook ['skecz,bu:k] s.
szkicownik
ski [ski:] s. narta; wyrzutnik

bomb; v. jeździć na nartach
skid [skyd] s. deska; płoza;
podpórka; klin hamowniczy;
poślizg; zarzucenie; v.
ślizgać się; zarzucać;
umieszczać na płozach;
hamować
skier ['ski:er] s. narciarz
skiing ['skiyng] s. narciarstwo;
jazda na nartach
ski lift ['ski lyft] s. wyciąg
narciarski
skill [skyl] s. zręczność;
wprawa
skilled ['skyld] adj.
wykwalifikowany; wykonany
fachowo
skillful ['skylful] adj. zręczny;
wprawny
skillet ['skylyt] s. patelnia;
(slang): draka
skim [skym] v. zbierać
(śmietankę); szumować;
przebiegać wzrokiem;
puszczać po powierzchni;
szybować; s. zbieranie; mleko
zbierane; adj. zbierany
skimmer ['skymer] s.
warzechew; cedzidło
skimp [skymp] v. skąpić
skimpy ['skympy] adj. skąpy; za
mały; niewystarczający
skin [skyn] s. skóra; skórka;
cera; szawłok; (slang): oszust;
v. zdzierać skórę; pokrywać
naskórkiem; ściągać z siebie
skin-deep ['skyn'di:p] adj.
powierzchowny
skin diver ['skyn'dajwer] s.
płetwonurek
skindiving ['skyn'dajwyng] s.
sportowe nurkowanie (z
płetwami)
skinny ['skyny] adj. chudy; skóra
i kości
skip [skyp] v. skakać;
przeskakiwać; odskakiwać;
pomijać; (slang): uciekać; s.
skok; przeskok; kapitan
sportowy
skipper ['skyper] s. szyper;
kapitan statku; skoczek;
kapitan drużyny

skirt ['ske:rt] s. spódnica; poła;
wulg.: kobietka; przepona;
brzeg; v. jechać brzegiem;
obchodzić; leżeć na skraju
skit ['skyt] s. skecz; satyra;
mnóstwo
skoal [skoul] excl.: na zdrowie!
skull [skal] s. czaszka
sky [skaj] s. niebo; klimat
skyjack ['skaj,dżaek] s. porwanie
samolotu w locie; v. porwać
samolot w locie (uprowadzać)
skyjacker ['skaj,dżaeker] s. pirat
powietrzny
skylark ['skajla:rk] s. skowronek;
v. dokazywać; swawolić
skylight ['skajlajt] s. okno dające
górne światło; okno w suficie
skyscraper ['skaj,skrejper] s.
drapacz chmur
skyward ['skajterd] adv. ku
niebu
slab [slaeb] s. płytka; v. krajać
na płytki (kromki)
slack [slaek] adj. luźny; wolny;
rozlazły; opieszały; ospały;
leniwy; niedbały; v. zluźniać;
zwalniać; popuszczać;
zaniedbywać; gasić (np.
ogień); s. luźna część;
lenistwo; zastój;
bezczelność; miał węglowy;
zwis; impertynencja
slacken ['slaeken] v. rozluźniać
(się); zwalniać; poluźniać
(się); popuszczać;
zaniedbywać
slacks [slaeks] pl. (luźne)
spodnie
slain [slejn] adj. zabity; v. zob.
slay
slake [slejk] v. gasić (np.
wapno); wywierać (np.
zemstą)
slam [slaem] v. zatrzasnąć (się);
(slang): krytykować ostro;
pobić; s. trzaśnięcie; ostra
krytyka; ciupa
slang [slaeng] s. gwara; żargon;
slang; adj. gwarowy;
żargonowy; v. nawymyślać
komuś
slangy [slaengy] adj. gwarowy

slant [sla:nt] s. pochyłość;
skos; tendencja; punkt
widzenia; spojrzenie; adj.
ukośny; v. iść skośnie;
pochylać (się); odchylać
(się); być nachylonym

slap [slaep] s. klaps; plaśnięcie;
v. plasnąć; dać klapsa;
uderzyć; narzucić; adv.
nagle; prościutko; regularnie

slapstick ['slaep,styk] s. laska
arlekina; błazeńska komedia

slash [slaesz] v. pokiereszować;
przeciąć; chłostać; smagać;
walić; ciąć; s. cięcie;
szrama; przecięcie; wyrąb;
odpadki drzewne; porosłe
(krzakami) moczary

slate [slejt] s. łupek; dachówka
łupkowa; tabliczka do pisania;
lista (kandydatów w USA); v.
pokrywać dachówkami;
umieszczać na liście
kandydatów; łajać;
wymyślać; krytykować

slate pencil ['slejt'pensl] s. rysik

slattern ['slaete:rn] s. brudas;
flejtuch; kocmołuch

slaughter ['slo:ter] v. rżnąć;
zabijać; wymordować; s.
ubój; rzeź; masakra

Slav [sla:w] adj. słowiański

slave [slejw] adj. niewolniczy; s.
niewolnik; v. harować

slavery ['slejwery] s.
niewolnictwo

slay; slew; slain [slej; slu:; slejn]

slay [slej] v. zabić; uśmiercać

sled [sled] s. sanie; v. wozić
saniami

sledge hammer ['sledż-haemer]
s. oburęczny młot

sleek [sli:k] adj. gładki; ulizany;
v. gładzić; wygładzać

sleep; slept; slept [sli:p; slept;
slept]

sleep [sli:p] v. spać;
spoczywać; dawać nocleg;
s. sen; spanie; drzemka

sleep off ['sli:p,of] v. odespać

sleeper ['sli:per] s. człowiek
śpiący; dźwigar; potencjalny
przedmiot rozgłosu; truteń;

leń; wtyczka (szpiegowska
etc.)

sleeping-bag ['sli:pyng,baeg] s.
śpiwór

sleeping car ['sli:pyng,ka:r] s.
wagon sypialny

sleeping partner ['sli:pyng
'pa:rtner] s. cichy wspólnik

sleeping pill ['sli:pyng,pyl] s.
pigułka nasenna

sleepless ['sli:plys] adj. bezsenny

sleepwalker ['sli:p,ło:ker] s.
lunatyk

sleepy ['sli:py] adj. śpiący

sleet [sli:t] s. słota; deszcz ze
śniegiem; gołoledź

sleeve [sli:w] s. rękaw; tuleja;
łuska; nasadka; tuba; zanadrze

sleeved ['sli:wd] adj. z rękawami

sleigh [slej] v. saneczkować
(się); jechać saniami

slender ['slender] adj. wysmukły;
szczupły; wiotki; nikły;
skromny; niewielki; słaby

slept [slept] v. zob. sleep

slew [slu:] v. zob. slay

slice [slajs] s. kromka; płatek;
plasterek; kawałek; łopatka
kuchenna; v. krajać na
kromki,
kawałki etc.; przecinać;
wiosłować; wyjmować
łopatką

slick [slyk] adj. gładki; tłusty;
oślizgły; miły; pociągający;
pierwszorzędny; adv. gładko;
prościutko; s. tłusta plama
(na morzu); szerokie dłuto

slicker ['slyker] s. gładki płaszcz
od deszczu; oszust

slid [slyd] v. zob. slide

slide; slid; slid [slajd; slyd; slyd]

slide [slajd] v. suwać (się);
sunąć (się); ślizgać (się); s.
ślizganie się; suwak;
prowadnica ślizgowa;
poślizg; przeźrocze; zrzutnia

slide rule ['slajd,ru:l] s. suwak
logarytmiczny

slight [slajt] adj. wątły; niewielki;
drobny; skromny; nieznaczny;
v. lekceważyć; s.
lekceważenie

slim [slym] adj. szczupły; wysmukły; słaby; (slang): chytry; v. wyszczuplać; odchudzać (się)

slime [slajm] s. szlam; muł; śluz; płynna smoła ziemna; v. zamulać; odmulać; zwilżać (np. śliną)

slimy ['slajmy] adj. mulisty; zamulony; obleśny; oślizgły

sling; slung; slung [slyng; slang; slang]

sling [slyng] s. proca; rzut; pętla (np. do ładowania dźwigiem); temblak; rzemień do strzelby itp.; v. rzucać; strzelać z procy; podnosić na pętli; zawieszać na (np. rzemieniu)

slinger ['slynger] s. procarz

slinky ['slynky] adj. ukradkowy; (slang): mający ruchy węża

slip; slipped; slipped [slyp; slypt; slypt]

slip [slyp] v. pośliznąć (się); wyśliznąć (się); ześliznąć (się); popełnić nietakt; zrobić błąd; przepuścić (np. okazję); wymknąć się; zerwać się; zapomnieć; spuszczać (np. ze smyczy); s. poślizg; potknięcie; pomyłka; błąd; przemówienie się; zsuw; halka; świstek (papieru); pochylnia

slip off ['slyp,of] v. zdejmować; rozbierać się; ześlizgiwać się; spadać

slip on ['slyp,on] v. wdziewać

slip out ['slyp,aut] v. wymknąć się

slip up ['slyp,ap] s. błąd; zachwianie się; przemówienie się; zsuw; ślizg; v. zrobić błąd; pomylić się; potknąć się

slipper ['slyper] s. pantofel

slippery ['slypery] adj. śliski; niebezpieczny; ryzykowny; nieuczciwy; nieczysty; drażliwy; delikatny; wykrętny; chytry

slit; slit; slit [slyt; slyt; slyt]

slit [slyt] v. rozszczepić;

rozedrzeć wzdłuż; s. szpara; szczelina; rozcięcie

slobber ['slober] s. ślina; rozczulenie; v. oślinić się; rozczulić się

slogan ['slougen] s. slogan; hasło; powiedzonko (np. reklamowe)

sloop [slu:p] s. slup (łódź)

slop [slop] v. rozlewać; przepełniać płynem; rozpryskiwać; s. kałuża; brudna woda; pomyje; lura

slop over ['slop,ouwer] v. przelewać się przez wierzch

slope [sloup] s. pochyłość; spadek; nachylenie; spadzistość; stok; skarpa; zbocze; pochylnia; v. być pochylonym; mieć nachylenie; nachylać; pochylać; wałąsać się; łazikować

sloping [sloupyng] adj. pochyły; skośny

sloppy ['slopy] adj. błotnisty; pochlapany; zaniedbany; rozlazły; ckliwy

slot [slot] s. szczelina; rozcięcie; trop; ślad; v. rozciąć; naciąć; wyżłobić

sloth [slous] s. lenistwo; leniwiec

slot-machine ['slotme,szi:n] s. (grający lub sprzedający) automat na monety

slouch [slaucz] s. przygarbienie; niedbała postawa; wałkoń; v. garbić się; iść ociężale; opuszczać rondo kapelusza

slough [slou] s. bagno; trzęsawisko

slough [slaw] v. lenieć; zrzucać skórę

sloven ['slawn] s. niechlujny; brudas; flejtuch; fuszer; partacz

slovenly ['slawnly] adj. niechlujny; partacki

slow [sloł] adj. powolny; niegorliwy; nieskory; opieszały; leniwy; tępy; nudny; adv. wolno; powoli

slow down ['sloł,dałn] v. zwalniać; przyhamować

slow-motion ['sloł'mouszyn] s.
zwolnione tempo; adv. w
zwolnionym tempie
slow-worm ['sloł,łe:rm]s. padalec
sluggish ['slagysz] adj. ospały;
leniwy; powolny
sluice [slu:s] s. śluza; ściek;
rynna; v. puszczać wodę (ze
stawu etc.); spłukiwać;
zalewać; chlusnąć; spływać
ze śluzy
slums [slamz] s. dzielnica nędzy
slumber ['slamber] v. spać
lekko; drzemać; s. sen;
drzemka; spokój;
bezczynność
slung [slang] v. zob. sling
slush [slasz] s. chlapa; odpadki
tłuszczowe; smar; fundusz z
odpadków; tajny fundusz na
przekupstwo; v. opryskać;
wysmarować; pokrywać
zaprawą
slut [slat] s. flejtuch; kocmołuch;
plucha; pinda; szmata; flądra;
suka
sly [slaj] adj. szczwany; chytry;
filuterny
slyboots ['slajbu:ts] s. urwis;
spryciarz; chytrus (udający
głupiego)
smack [smaek] s. posmak;
odrobina; trzask; mlaśnięcie;
cmoknięcie; klaps;
jednomasztowiec; v. cmokać;
strzelać z bata; dać w pysk;
oblizywać (wargi)
smacking ['smaekyng] adj.
zgrabny; raźny; mocny (wiatr)
small [smo:l] adj. mały; drobny;
niewielki; skromny; ciasny;
nieliczny; nieznaczny;
małostkowy; adv. drobno; na
małą skalę; cicho; s. drobna
rzecz; mała część
small change ['smo:l,czejndż] s.
drobne (pieniądze)
small hours ['smo:l,auers] pl.
bardzo wczesne godziny ranne
smallish ['smo:lysz] adj. maławy
small of the back
['smo:l,ow'dy,baek] s. krzyże
smallpox ['smo:l,poks] s. ospa

smart [sma:rt] adj. dotkliwy;
cięty; zręczny; żwawy;
dowcipny; szykowny; zgrabny;
elegancki; v. piec; palić (np.
w oczy); cierpieć; szczypać;
parzyć; odczuwać boleśnie;
pokutować
smart aleck ['sma:rt,alek] s.
Jędrek-mędrek
smash [smaesz] v. rozbić;
rozwalić; roztrzaskać;
zmiażdżyć; potłuc; palnąć;
rozgromić; upadać;
zbankrutować; ścinać piłkę
smashing ['smaeszyng] adj.
nadzwyczajny; niezwykły
smattering ['smaeteryn] s.
znajomości po łebkach;
wiedza powierzchowna
smear [smier] v. osmarować;
zasmarować; wlepić komuś
smary; s. plama; smar
smell; smelt; smelled [smel;
smelt; smeld]
smell [smel] s. węch; woń;
zapach; odór; smród; v.
pachnieć; trącić; mieć
zapach; śmierdzieć; mieć
powonienie; obwąchiwać;
czuć zapach; zwietrzyć;
zwąchać; poczuć
smelt [smelt] v. zob. smell;
stapiać; wytapiać (metal); s.
stynka (ryba)
smile [smajl] v. uśmiechać się;
s. uśmiech
smite; smote; smitten [smajt;
smout; 'smytn]
smite [smajt] v. uderzać;
porazić; powalić; zabić;
nękać; karać; oczarować
smith [smys] s. kowal
smithy [smysy] s. kuźnia
smitten ['smytn] v. zob. smite
smock [smok] s. chałat; kitel; v.
ubierać chałat; ozdabiać
rysunkiem szachownicy
smog [smog] s. mgła
zanieczyszczona dymem
(Londyn, Los Angeles)
smoke [smouk] s. dym; palenie;
papieros; v. dymić; kopcić;
wykurzać; wyjawiać;

wykadzać; okadzać;
okopcić; uwędzić;
przypalać; palić (tytoń)
smoke-dried ['smouk,drajd] adj.
wędzony
smoker ['smouker] s. palący;
palacz
smoking ['smoukyng] s. palenie
(tytoniu)
smoking car ['smoukyng,ka:r] s.
wagon dla palących
smoking compartment
['smoukyngkaem,pa:rtment] s.
przedział dla palących
smoky ['smouky] adj. dymiący;
przydymiony; zadymiony;
okopcony
smolder ['smoulder] v. tlić się;
s. tlenie się; dym
smooch [smu:cz] v. brudzić;
walać; całować się;
ściskać się; migdalić się
smooth [smu:s] adj. gładki;
spokojny; łagodny; v. gładzić;
łagodzić; adv. gładko; s.
wygładzenie
smooth down ['smu:s,dałn] v.
wygładzić; uspokajać (się)
smother ['smadzer] v. stłumić;
stłamsić; obcałowywać;
zatuszować; okrywać
smudge [smadż] v. poplamić;
zabrudzić; s. plama; kleks;
brud
smuggle ['smagl] v. przemycać
smuggler ['smagler] s.
przemytnik
smut [smat] v. poplamić; s.
brud z sadzy; sprośności;
tłuste kawały; śnieć
smutty ['smaty] adj. sprośny;
brudny od sadzy
snack [snaek] s. zakąska
snack bar ['snaek,ba:r] s. bufet;
bar
snafu [snae'fu:] v. zabałaganić;
s. bałagan (slang)
snail [snejl] s. ślimak
snake [snejk] s. wąż; v. wić
się; wlec (za sobą); pełzać
jak wąż; przybierać kształt
węża
snap [snaep] v. łapać zębami;

warczeć; błysnąć; urwać;
złamać; chwytać; zapalić
się do; przerwać szorstko;
poprawić się; mieć się na
baczności; zatrzasnąć (się);
strzelać z bicza; pstryknąć;
sfotografować; śpiesznie
załatwiać; machnąć ręką
lekceważąco; s. ugryzienie;
warknięcie; trzask; zatrzask;
dociskacz; zdjęcie; rzecz
łatwa; adj. prosty; łatwy;
doraźny; nagły
snap bolt ['snaep,boult] s.
zatrzask u drzwi
snap fastener ['snaep,fa:sner] s.
zatrzask
snappish ['snaepysz] adj.
zgryźliwy; kostyczny
snappy ['snaepy] adj. zgryźliwy;
kostyczny; żwawy; prędki
snapshot ['snaepszot] s. zdjęcie
migawkowe; strzał na chybił
trafił
snare [sneer] v. usidłać; łapać
w sidła; s. sidła; pułapka
snarl [sna:rl] s. warknięcie;
plątanina; v. warczeć; plątać
(się); zaplątać; robić zator
snatch [snaecz] v. złapać;
wyrwać; s. złapanie; urywek;
strzęp; mig
sneak [sni:k] v. chyłkiem
zakradać się; przemykać się;
zerkać; zwiać; s. podły
tchórz
sneakers ['sni:kers] pl. trzewiki;
trampki
sneer [snier] v. uśmiechać się
szyderczo; kpić; drwić; s.
szyderstwo; szydercze
spojrzenie
sneeze [sni:z] v. kichać; s.
kichnięcie
sniff [snyf] v. prychać;
pociągać nosem; krzywić się
na coś; powąchać;
obwąchać; zwąchać;
wyczuć; s. prychnięcie;
pociągnięcie nosem
sniffle ['snyfl] s. katar;
pociąganie nosem; v.
pociągać nosem

snipe [snajp] s. bekas; strzał z ukrycia; v. z ukrycia: strzelać, trafić, zabić

sniper ['snajper] s. strzelec wyborowy; strzelec z ukrycia

snivel ['snywel] s. śluz z nosa; biadolenie; udawanie; v. smarkać się; skamleć; biadolić; płakać; rozczulać się

snob [snob] s. człowiek wywyższający się

snoop [snu:p] v. myszkować; wścibiać nos; s. szpicel

snoop around ['snu:p,e'raund] v. przemyszkowywać; szpiegować

snooze [snu:z] s. drzemka; v. drzemać; zdrzemnąć się

snore [sno:r] v. chrapać; s. chrapanie

snort [sno:rt] v. parskać; s. parsknięcie

snout [snaut] s. ryj; pysk; morda; wylot

snow [snou] s. śnieg; (slang): kokaina; heroina; v. ośnieżyć; śnieg pada; zasypać śniegiem; pobić na głowę; omamiać

snowball ['snoubo:l] s. kula śnieżna; v. bić się śniegiem; rosnąć jak lawina

snow blindness ['snou'blajndnys] s. śnieżna ślepota

snowdrift ['snou'dryft] s. zaspa śnieżna

snowdrop ['snoudrop] s. śnieżyczka

snow job ['snou,dżob] s. naciąganie pochlebstwami

snow-white ['snou'hłajt] adj. śnieżnobiały

snowy ['snoły] adj. śnieżny; śniegowy

snub [snab] v. ofuknąć; dać po nosie; traktować lekceważąco; nagle zatrzymać; adj. perkaty, zadarty (nos); s. bura; ofuknięcie; ostra odprawa; afront; ucieranie nosa komuś; przywodzenie kogoś do porządku

snuff [snaf] s. tabaka; proszek do zażywania przez nos; zapach; opalony koniec knota; v. zażywać tabakę; pociągać nosem; czyścić koniec knota

snug [snag] adj. przytulny; wygodny; ukryty; v. tulić się; zrobić przytulnym

snuggle ['snagl] v. przytulić się

so [sou] adv. tak; a więc; w takim razie; a zatem; też; tak samo; bardzo to; także; excl.: to tak! no, no!

so far ['sou fa:r] adv. jak dotąd; jak do tej pory

soak [souk] v. moczyć (się); nasycać (się); przenikać; namoknąć; (slang): wyciągać (od kogoś) pieniądze; mocno uderzyć; s. moczenie (się); woda do moczenia; popijawa; zastaw

soap [soup] s. mydło; pochlebstwo; wazelinowanie się (komuś); v. mydlić (się); pochlebiać; adj. mydlany; mydlarski

soap box ['soup,boks] s. skrzynia od mydła; mównica (np. uliczna); v. przemawiać na ulicy, w parku etc.

soap opera ['soup'opere] s. (popołudniowe) przedstawienie radiowe lub telewizyjne pełne małżeńskich kryzysów, tragedii, cierpień, płaskiej czułostkowości i melodramatycznych zakończeń

soar [so:r] v. wznosić się; osiągać wyżyny; iść w górę (np. ceny)

sob [sob] v. łkać; szlochać; s. łkanie; szloch

sober ['souber] adj. trzeźwy; wstrzemięźliwy; stateczny; zrównoważony; rzeczowy; poważny; spokojny; v. trzeźwieć; wytrzeźwieć; wytrzeźwiać; otrzeźwieć; opanować się

sober up ['souber,ap] v.
wytrzeźwieć
sober-minded ['souber,majndyd]
adj. stateczny; zrównoważony
so-called ['sou-ko:ld] adj. tak
zwany
soccer ['soker] s. piłka nożna
sociable ['souszebl] adj.
towarzyski; przyjacielski;
gromadny; stadny
social ['souszel] adj. społeczny;
socjalny; s. zebranie
towarzyskie
social democrat ['souszel
'demekraet] s.
socjaldemokrata
socialism ['souszelyzem] s.
socjalizm
social security
['souszelsy'kjueryty] s.
ubezpieczenia społeczne
socialist ['souszelyst] s.
socjalista; adj. socjalistyczny
social worker ['souszel'łerker] s.
pracownik społeczny;
pracownik urzędu opieki
społecznej
socialize ['souszelajz] v.
upaństwowić; uspołecznić
social welfare ['souszel,łelfeer] s.
opieka społeczna
society [so'sajety] s.
towarzystwo; społeczeństwo;
społeczność; spółka (np.
akcyjna)
sock [sok] s. skarpetka; cios;
szturchaniec; v. cisnąć w
kogoś; uderzyć; walnąć;
adv. prosto (np. w nos)
socket ['sokyt] s. oprawka;
oczodół; zębodół; gniazdko;
wydrążenie
sod [sod] s. darń; darnina;
wulg.: skurwysyn; sodomita
sofa ['soufe] s. kanapa; sofa
soft [soft] adj. miękki; delikatny;
przyciszony; łagodny; słaby;
głupi; wygodny
soft drink ['soft,drynk] s. napój
bezalkoholowy
soft goods ['soft,gu:ds] pl.
tekstylia
soften ['so:fen] v. zmiękczyć;

osłabić; złagodzić;
złagodnieć; zmięknąć
soil [sojl] s. gleba; rola; ziemia;
brud; plama; v. zabrudzić;
powalać; poplamić;
wysmarować
sojourn ['sedże:rn] s. pobyt; v.
przebywać; zatrzymywać
(się)
sold [sould] adj. sprzedany; v.
zob. sell
soldier ['souldżer] s. żołnierz
najemnik; adj. żołnierski; v.
służyć w wojsku
sole [soul] s. podeszwa;
podwalina; zelówka; stopa;
spodek; sola; adj. jedyny;
wyłączny
solemn ['solem] adj. solenny;
uroczysty; poważny
solicit [se'lysyt] v. prosić;
zwracać się (o coś);
nagabywać; ubiegać się;
zwracać (np. uwagę)
solicitor [se'lysyter] s. radca
prawny; akwizytor; agent
firmowy
solicitous [se'lysytes] adj.
pragnący; troszczący się o ...;
niepokojący się
solicitude [se'lysytju:d] s. troska;
pieczołowitość; troskliwość
solid ['solyd] adj. stały;
masywny; lity; trwały; mocny;
rzetelny; solidny; s. ciało stałe;
bryła
solidarity [,soly'daeryty] s.
solidarność
solidity [so'lydyty] s.
masywność; trwałość;
rzetelność
soliloquy [se'lylekły] s. monolog;
mówienie do siebie
solitary ['solytery] adj. samotny;
odosobniony; odludny;
pojedynczy; wyjątkowy; s.
pustelnik; odludek; samotnik
solitude ['solytju:d] s.
samotność; osamotnienie;
odludne miejsce
solo ['soulou] adv. w pojedynkę;
adj. jednoosobowy; s. solo
soloist ['soulouyst] s. solista

soluble ['soljubl] adj.
rozpuszczalny; możliwy do
rozwiązania

solution [so'ljuszyn] s. rozczyn;
roztwór; rozwiązanie
(problemu)

solve [solw] v. rozwiązywać
(np. problemy)

solvent ['solwent] adj.
wypłacalny; rozpuszczający; s.
rozpuszczalnik

somber ['somber] adj. mroczny;
ciemny; posępny; ponury

some [sam] adj. jakiś; pewien;
niejaki; nieco; trochę; kilku;
kilka; kilkoro; niektórzy;
niektóre; sporo; niemało; nie
byle jaki; adv. niemało; mniej
więcej; jakieś; pron.
niektórzy; niektóre; kilku; kilka

some more ['sam,mor] exp.:
nieco więcej

somebody ['sambedy] pron.
ktoś; s. ktoś ważny

someday ['samdej] adv. kiedyś

somehow ['samhał] adv. jakoś;
w jakiś sposób

someone ['samłan] pron. ktoś;
s. ktoś

somersault ['samerso:lt] s. salto;
koziołek

something ['samsyng] s. coś;
coś niecoś; ważna osoba;
adv. trochę; nieco; (slang): co
się zowie

sometime ['samtajm] adj. były;
adv. kiedyś; swego czasu

sometimes ['samtajmz] adv.
niekiedy; czasem; czasami

someway ['sam,łej] adv. jakoś

somewhat ['samhłot] adv. nieco;
do pewnego stopnia; niejako

somewhere ['samhłe:r] adv.
gdzieś

son [san] s. syn

song [song] s. pieśń; śpiew

song-bird ['songbe:rd] s. ptak
śpiewający

song-book ['songbuk] s.
śpiewnik

sonic ['sonyk] adj. dźwiękowy

sonic boom ['sonyk,bu:m] s.
grzmot samolotu

przekraczającego szybkość
dźwięku

son-in-law ['san,ynlo:] s. zięć

sonnet ['sonyt] s. sonet

soon [su:n] adv. wnet;
niebawem; wkrótce; zaraz;
niedługo

sooner ['su:ner] adv. wcześniej;
chętnie

soot [sut] s. sadza; kopeć; v.
brudzić sadzą; użyźniać
sadzą

soothe [su:z] v. uspokajać;
uciszać

soothing ['su:zyng] adj. kojący;
uspokajający; uśmierzający

sooty ['suty] adj. okopcony;
zakopcony; czarny jak sadza

sophisticated [se'fystykejtyd]
adj. wyszukany;
wyrafinowany; wymyślny;
doświadczony

sophomore ['sofemo:r] s. student
drugiego roku

sorcerer ['so:rserer] s.
czarownik; czarodziej

sorceress ['so:rserys] s.
czarodziejka

sorcery ['so:rsery] s. czary

sordid ['so:rdyd] adj. brudny (np.
zysk); nikczemny; podły;
skąpy

sore [so:r] adj. bolesny;
drażliwy; wrażliwy; dotkliwy;
dotknięty; złoszczący się;
zmartwiony; adv. srodze;
bardzo; okrutnie

sore throat ['so:r,trout] s.
zapalenie gardła; angina

sorrow ['sorou] s. zmartwienie;
żal; smutek; narzekanie; v.
martwić się; boleć za ...

sorrowful ['sorouful] adj.
smutny; zmartwiony; przykry

sorry ['so:ry] adj. żałujący;
zmartwiony; przygnębiony;
nędzny; marny

sorority [se'ro:ryty] s. korporacja
studentek (w USA)

sort [so:rt] s. rodzaj; gatunek;
sorta; v. sortować

sortie ['so:rty] s. wypad
wojskowy; lot bojowy

so-so ['sou-sou] adj. taki sobie;
adv. tak sobie
sought [so:t] v. zob. seek
soul [soul] s. dusza
soulless ['soullys] adj. bezduszny
sound [saund] s. dźwięk; ton;
szmer; cieśnina wodna;
pęcherz pławny; sonda; v.
dźwięczeć; brzmieć; grać
(na trąbce); bić na alarm;
głosić; opukiwać;
wymawiać; zabierać głos;
chwalić się; sondować;
zanurzać się do dna
soundless ['saundlys] adj.
bezdźwięczny
soundproof ['saundpru:f] adj.
dźwiękoszczelny
sound wave ['saundłejw] s. fala
dźwiękowa
soup [su:p] s. zupa
sour ['sauer] adj. kwaśny;
skwaszony; cierpki; v.
kisnąć; kwasić się;
zniechęcać się
source [so:rs] s. źródło
south [saus] adj. południowy; s.
południe; adv. na południe
southeast ['saus'i:st] s.
południowy wschód; adj.
południowo-wschodni; adv. na
południowy wschód
southern ['sadzern] adj.
południowy; s. południowiec
southernmost [,sadzern'moust]
adj. najbardziej na południe
southward ['sausłerd] adv. ku
południowi; na południe
southwest ['saus'łest] s.
południowy zachód; adj.
południowo-zachodni; adv. na
południowy zachód
southwesterly ['saus'łesterly]
adj. południowo-zachodni
souvenir ['su:wenier] s. pamiątka
sovereign ['sawryn] s. suweren;
władca; adj. suwerenny;
wyniosły; najwyższy
sovereignty ['sawrenty] s.
suwerenność;
zwierzchnictwo; najwyższa
władza
Soviet ['souwjet] adj. sowiecki;

radziecki
sow; sowed; sown [sou; soud;
soun]
sow [sou] v. siać; zasiewać;
posiać
sow [sau] s. maciora; koryto
odlewnicze
sown [soun] v. zob. sow
spa [spa:] s. zdrojowisko; zdrój
mineralny; (USA) sport
zdrowotny za opłatą
space [spejs] s. przestrzeń;
miejsce; obszar; odstęp;
okres; przeciąg (czasu);
chwila; v. robić odstępy;
rozstawiać
spacecraft ['spejs,kra:ft] s.
pojazd międzyplanetarny
spaceship ['spejs,szyp] s. statek
międzyplanetarny (kosmiczny)
space suit ['spejs,sju:t] s.
kombinezon międzyplanetarny
spacious ['spejszes] adj.
przestronny; obszerny
spade [spejd] s. łopata; v.
kopać łopatą
spades [spejdz] pl. piki (w
kartach)
spadework ['spejd-łe:rk] s. praca
przygotowawcza
span; spanned; spanned [spaen;
spaend; spaend]
span [spaen] v. sięgać (np.
przez rzekę); rozciągać się
(np. nad rzeką); obejmować
(pamięcią); mierzyć piędzią;
posuwać się stopniowo;
łączyć brzegi; s. piędź;
rozpiętość; prześwit;
przęsło; przeciąg (czasu);
zasięg; rozciągłość; para;
zaprzęg
spangle ['spaengl] s.
świecidełko; błyskotka; v.
pokrywać świecidełkami;
błyszczeć świecidełkami
spangled ['spaengld] adj. pokryty
(świecidełkami)
Spanish ['spaenysz] adj.
hiszpański
spank [spaenk] s. klaps; v.
dawać klapsa; popędzać
klapsami; iść kłusem

spanking [spaenkyng] s.
skórobicie; lanie; adj. chyży;
zamaszysty; silny; solidny;
świetny; adv. bardzo (slang)

spanner ['spaener] s. ścięgno
(mostu); klucz do nakrętek;
gąsienica miernikowa

spare [speer] v. oszczędzać;
zaoszczędzić; odstępować;
obywać się; zachować;
przeznaczać; szanować
(uczucia); szczędzić; adj.
zapasowy; oszczędny;
skromny; drobny; szczupły;
wolny (np. czas); s. część
zapasowa; koło zapasowe

spare time ['speer,tajm] s. wolny
czas

spare tire ['speer,tajer] s. koło
zapasowe

sparing ['speeryng] adj.
oszczędny; wstrzemięźliwy

spark [spa:rk] s. iskra; zapłon;
wesołek; zalotnik; v. iskrzyć
się; sypać iskrami; zapalać
się; dawać początek;
zalecać się; grać galanta

spark plug ['spa:rk,plag] s.
świeca samochodowa
(zapłonowa)

sparrow ['spaerou] s. wróbel

sparse [spa:rs] adj. rzadki; z
rzadka; rozsiany; szczupły

spasm ['spaezem] s. skurcz;
spazm; napad (kaszlu)

spastic ['spaestyk] adj.
skurczowy; spazmatyczny;
chory na paraliż kurczowy

spat [spaet] v. zob. spit; kłócić
się; dawać klapsy; składać
jaja (przez ostrygi); s. jaja
mięczaków; kłótnia; klaps;
lekki cios

spatial ['spejszel] adj.
przestrzenny

spawn [spo:n] s. ikra; skrzek;
nasienie; v. składać (ikrę,
skrzek); wylągać się;
płodzić; zasiewać grzybnią

spayed [spejd] adj. (samica) z
usuniętymi jajnikami;
bezpłodna; wytrzebiona

speak; spoke; spoken [spi:k;
spou:k; 'spouken]

speak [spi:k] v. mówić;
przemawiać; szczekać na
rozkaz; grać; sygnalizować
do ataku

speak out ['spi:k,aut] v.
wypowiadać (się); mówić
otwarcie; mówić głośno

speak up ['spi:k,ap] v.
wypowiedzieć się bez
osłonek

speaker ['spi:ker] s. mówca;
głośnik; marszałek sejmu;
przewodniczący

spear [spier] s. dzida; włócznia;
oszczep; kopia; oścień;
źdźbło; v. przebijać dzidą;
kłuć; wystrzelić w górę

spearhead ['spierhed] s. ostrze
dzidy; czołówka; v.
prowadzić; być na czele

special ['speszel] adj. specjalny;
wyjątkowy; osobliwy;
dodatkowy; nadzwyczajny; s.
dodatkowy autobus;
nadzwyczajne wydanie;
reklamowa dzienna zniżka
ceny w sklepie

specialist ['speszelyst] s.
specjalista; specjalistka

specialize ['speszelajz] v.
wyspecjalizować (się); wyszczególniać; ograniczać;
precyzować; różniczkować
(się); ograniczać (się)

specially ['speszely] adv.
specjalnie; szczególnie

specialty [,speszy'aelyty] s. 1.
specjalność; specjalna cecha

specialty ['speszelty] s. 2.
fach; specjalizacja; umowa

species ['spi:szi:z] s. gatunek;
rodzaj; postać (czegoś)

specific [spy'syfyk] adj.
(ściśle) określony; wyraźny; gatunkowy; właściwy;
charakterystyczny; swoisty;
specyficzny; szczególny

specify ['spesyfaj] v.
wyszczególniać; precyzo-
wać; konkretyzować; spo-
rządzić specyfikacją

specimen ['spesymyn] s. okaz;

przykład; wzór; typ; próba;
numer okazowy

speck [spek] s. plamka; cętka;
punkcik; skaza; pyłek; ziarnko;
odrobina; zdziebło

spectacle ['spektekl] s.
widowisko

spectacles ['spektekls] pl.
okulary

spectacular [spek'taekjuler] adj.
widowiskowy; efektowny;
sensacyjny; okazały; s. film
widowiskowy "wielki"

spectator ['spektejter] s. widz

specter ['spekter] s. widmo;
upiór

speculate ['spekjulejt] v.
spekulować; rozmyślać
nad ...; rozważać

speculation [,spekju'lejszyn] s.
spekulacja; domysł;
rozmyślanie

sped [sped] v. zob. speed

speech [spi:cz] s. mowa;
przemówienie; język;
wymowa; przemowa

speechless ['spi:czlys] adj.
(chwilowo) niemy; oniemiały;
(slang): pijany (kompletnie)

speed; sped; sped [spi:d; sped;
sped]

speed [spi:d] v. pośpieszyć;
popędzić; pędzić; odprawić;
kierować śpiesznie;
popierać (np. sprawę); s.
szybkość; prędkość; bieg

speedboat ['spi:dbout] s.
ślizgacz

speed limit ['spi:d,lymyt] s.
ograniczenie szybkości

speedometer [spi'domyter] s.
szybkościomierz

speed up ['spi:d,ap] v.
przyśpieszyć; s.
przyśpieszenie

speedy ['spi:dy] adj. szybki

spell; spelled; spelt [spel; speld;
spelt]

spell [spel] v. przeliterować
(poprawnie); napisać
ortograficznie; znaczyć;
mozolnie odczytywać;
sylabizować; zaczarować;

urzec; dać (wytchnienie);
odpoczywać; zaczarować;
pracować na zmiany; s.
chwila pracy; chwila; okres;
pewien czas; zaklęcie; czar

spellbound ['spelbaund] adj.
zaczarowany; urzeczony;
oczarowany

spelling ['spelyng] s. pisownia

spelt [spelt] v. zob. spell

spend; spent; spent [spend;
spent; spent]

spend [spend] v. wydawać (np.
pieniądze); spędzać (czas);
zużywać (się);
wyczerpywać; tracić (np.
siły); składać ikrę

spent [spent] v. wyczerpany;
wydany; zob. spend

sperm [spe:rm] s. sperma;
nasienie męskie

spew [spju:] v. wypluwać;
wymiotować; wyrzucać z
siebie

sphere [sfier] s. kula; globus;
ciało niebieskie; sfera (np.
działalności)

spice [spajs] s. wonne korzenie;
pikanteria; v. przyprawiać
korzeniami; dodawać
pikanterii

spick-and-span [spyk'n,span] adj.
nowy; świerzy; porządny i
czysty

spicy ['spajsy] adj. korzenny;
zaprawiony korzeniami;
aromatyczny; pikantny; nieco
nieprzyzwoity; elegancki;
żywy; ostry

spider [spajder] s. pająk

spike [spajk] s. ćwiek; bretnal;
kolec; gwóźdź do szyn;
szpic; ostrze; fanatyk religijny;
kłos; v. przymocowywać
gwoździami; zaostrzać
końce; ranić kolcami;
zagważdżać armatę;
zaprzeczać pogłoskom;
odpierać; zakrapiać
alkoholem; wspinać się na
słup ostrymi okuciami (na
butach)

spiky ['spajky] adj. kolczasty;

wydłużony; ostro zakończony; fanatyczny religijnie

spill; spilled; spilt [spyl; spyld; spylt]

spill [spyl] v. rozlewać (się); rozsypywać (się); uchylać żagiel z wiatru; wyśpiewać; wygadać (się); powiedzieć wszystko; popsuć sprawę; s. rozlanie; rozsypanie; ilość rozlana; ilość rozsypana; odłamek; zatyczka; upadek; fidybus do zapalania świec

spilt [spylt] v. zob. spill

spin; spun; spun [spyn; span; span]

spin [spyn] v. snuć; prząść; kręcić (się); puszczać bąka; toczyć na tokarni; łowić ryby na błyszczkę; zawirować; s. kręcenie (się); zawirowanie; ruch wirowy; przejażdżka; korkociąg (w locie)

spinach ['spynycz] s. szpinak

spinal column ['spajnel'kolem] s. stos pacierzowy; kręgosłup

spinal cord ['spajnel'ko:rd] s. rdzeń kręgowy

spindle ['spyndl] s. wrzeciono; oś; wał; 14400 jardów lnu; 15120 jardów bawełny; v. mieć kształt wrzecionowaty

spine [spajn] s. kręgosłup; grzbiet; cierń

spinning mill ['spynyng,myl] s. przędzalnia

spinster ['spynster] s. stara panna

spiny ['spajny] adj. ciernisty; kolczasty; trudny

spiral ['spajerel] s. spirala; adj. spiralny; v. poruszać się spiralnie; szybko iść w górę (np. ceny); nadawać kształt spirali

spire ['spajer] s. iglica; hełm wieży; zwój; spirala; ostry szczyt; szpic; pęd; v. strzelać w górę; nakładać hełm na wieżę

spirit ['spyryt] s. duch; intelekt; umysł; zjawa; odwaga;

nastawienie; nastrój; v. zachęcać; ożywiać; rozweselać; zabierać (potajemnie)

spirits ['spyryts] s. spirytus; alkohol

spirited ['spyrytyd] adj. ożywiony; z werwą; napisany z zacięciem

spiritual ['spyryczuel] adj. duchowy; duchowny; natchniony; s. murzyńska pieśń religijna

spit; spat; spat [spyt; spaet; spaet]

spit [spyt] v. pluć; zionąć; splunąć; wypluć; lekceważyć; fuknąć; parsknąć; mżyć; kropić; pryskać; nadziewać na rożen; s. plucie; ślina; parskanie; mżenie; jaja owadów; rożen; językowaty półwysep; głębokość łopaty

spite [spajt] s. złość; uraz; złośliwość; v. zrobić na złość; in spite of = wbrew; pomimo

spiteful ['spajtful] adj. złośliwy; mściwy

spittle ['spytl] s. plwocina; ślina

splash [splaesz] v. chlapać; pryskać; plusnąć; rozpryskać; upstrzyć; s. rozprysk; plusk; zakropienie; plamka; sensacja

splash down ['splaesz,dałn] v. wodować; s. wodowanie

spleen [spli:n] s. śledziona; przygnębienie; splin; złość

splendid ['splendyd] adj. wspaniały; świetny; doskonały

splendor ['splender] s. wspaniałość; przepych; blask

splint [splynt] s. łupek; szyna; patyk; kość piszczelowa; v. wstawiać w szyny złamaną kość

splinter ['splynter] s. drzazga; odłamek

split; split; split [splyt; splyt; splyt]

split [splyt] v. łupać; pękać; rozszczepiać (się); dzielić; oddzielać (się); odchodzić; s. pęknięcie; rozszczepienie; rozdwojenie; odejście

splitting ['splytyng] adj. rozsadzający; ostry; gwałtowny

splutter ['splater] v. pryskać; opryskać; mówić bezładnie; s. pryskanie; szybka gadanina; zgiełk

spoil; spoilt; spoiled [spojl; spojlt; spojld]

spoil [spojl] v. psuć (się); zepsuć (się); (slang): kraść; sprzątnąć; przetrącić

spoils [spojls] pl. łupy (też w polityce)

spoilsport ['spojl'spo:rt] s. psujący zabawę

spoilt ['spojlt] v. zob. spoil

spoke [spouk] v. zob. speak; s. szczebel; szprycha

spoken ['spoukn] v. zob. speak

spokesman ['spouksmen] s. rzecznik

sponge [spandż] s. gąbka; wycior; tampon; pieczeniarz; pasożyt; v. myć gąbką; chłonąć; łowić gąbki; wyłudzać; wsysać; pasożytować

sponger ['spandżer] s. pasożyt; pieczeniarz (slang)

sponge cake ['spandż'kejk] biszkopt

spongy ['spandży] adj. gąbczasty

sponsor ['sponser] s. patron; organizator; gwarant; ojciec chrzestny; v. wprowadzać; być gwarantem; popierać; opłacać (np. program telewizyjny)

spontaneous [spon'tejnjes] adj. spontaniczny; samorzutny; naturalny; odruchowy

spook [spuk] s. zjawa; duch; upiór

spool [spu:l] s. cewka; rolka; szpulka; v. nawijać (na rolkę etc.)

spoon [spu:n] s. łyżka; v. czerpać (łyżką); durzyć się w kimś

spoon out ['spu:n,aut] v. drążyć; nabierać

spoon-fed ['spu:n,fed] adj. rozpieszczony; łyżką karmiony

spoonful ['spu:nful] s. łyżka czegoś

sporadic [spe'raedyk] adj. sporadyczny; rzadki; rzadko zdarzający się

spore [spo:r] s. zarodnik; v. wytwarzać zarodniki

sport [spo:rt] s. sport; zawody; zabawa; rozrywka; sportowiec; (slang): człowiek dobry, elegancki, lubiący zakładać się; v. bawić się; uprawiać sport; obnosić się z czymś; popisywać się; wyśmiewać się

sportive ['spo:rtyw] adj. żartobliwy

sportsman ['spo:rtsmen] s. sportowiec; myśliwy

sporty ['spo:rty] adj. (slang): sportowy; krzykliwy (ubiór); modny

spot [spot] s. plama; skaza; kropka; cętka; plamka; miejsce; lokal; odrobina; punkt; dolar; krótkie ogłoszenie; v. plamić (się); umiejscowić (np. zepsucie); poznawać; wyróżniać; rozmieszczać; adj. gotowy; gotówkowy; dorywczy

spotless ['spotlys] adj. bez skazy

spotlight ['spotlajt] s. reflektor szczelinowy; v. rzucać światło (na coś)

spouse [spauz] s. małżonek; małżonka

spout [spaut] s. wylot; rynna; wylew; dziobek; strumień; pochyłe koryto; v. wyrzucać z siebie płyn; tryskać; chlusnąć; recytować

sprain [sprejn] s. bolesne wykręcenie (nie zwichnięcie); v. wykręcić

sprang [spraeng] v. zob. spring

sprat [spraet] s. szprotka (śledź); v. łowić szproty

sprawl [spro:l] v. rozwalać się; gramolić się; rozłazić się; rozrzucać; być rozrzuconym; s. rozwalenie się; rozłażenie się; rozkrzewianie się

spray [sprej] s. rozpylony płyn; krople z rozpylacza; płyn do rozpryskiwania; spryskiwacz; grad (kul); gałązka; v. opryskiwać; rozpryskiwać (się)

spread; spread; spread [spred; spred; spred]

spread [spred] v. rozpościerać (się); rozszerzać (się); posiać; rozsmarowywać; rozkładać; pokrywać; nakrywać; rozklepywać; s. rozpostarcie; rozpiętość; zasięg; szerokość; pasta; narzuta; (slang): smarowidło na chleb

sprig [spryg] s. gałązka; latorośl; młokos; szyft; v. ozdabiać gałązkami

sprightly ['sprajtly] adj. żywy; dziarski; wesoły

spring; sprang; sprung [spryng; spraeng; sprang]

spring [spryng] v. skakać; sprężynować; wypłynąć; puścić pędy (pąki); zaskoczyć; spowodować wybuch; paczyć się; puszczać oczko; pękać; s. wiosna; skok; sprężyna; źródło; zdrój; prężność; adj. wiosenny; sprężynowy; źródlany

springboard ['spryng,bo:rd] s. trampolina; odskocznia

springtime ['spryngtajm] s. wiosna

sprinkle ['sprynkl] v. posypać; pokropić; s. deszczyk

sprint [sprynt] s. krótki bieg; krótki zrywny wysiłek; v. biec na krótki dystans

sprinter ['sprynter] s. sprinter; biegacz krótkodystansowy

sprout [spraut] s. pęd; odrośl;

v. puszczać pędy; wyrastać

spruce [spru:s] s. świerk; smrek; adj. elegancki; schludny; v. stroić się

sprung [sprang] v. zob. spring

spun [span] v. zob. spin

spur [spe:r] v. pogardliwie odtrącać; pośpieszyć; popędzać; s. odtrącenie z pogardą

sputter ['spater] v. pryskać (śliną); bełkotać; s. pryskanie; plwociny; bełkot

spy [spaj] s. szpieg; tajniak; szpiegowanie; v. szpiegować; wybadać; czatować; wypatrzyć

squabble ['skłobl] s. sprzeczka; v. sprzeczać się

squad [skłod] s. oddział; grupka; (lotny) patrol; wóz patrolowy; v. formować grupki

squall [skło:l] s. szkwał; kłopot; wrzask; v. wiać gwałtownie; wrzeszczeć

squander ['skłonder] s. marnotrawstwo; v. trwonić; marnotrawić

square [skłeer] s. kwadrat; czworobok (budynków); plac; kątownik; węgielnica; adj. kwadratowy; prostokątny; prostopadły; uporządkowany; zupełny; uczciwy; v. robić kwadratowym, prostym; podnosić do kwadratu; płacić (dług); adv. w sedno; rzetelnie; wprost

squash [skłosz] v. ubijać (się); gnieść (się); miażdżyć; s. miazga; tłok; rodzaj tenisa; napój owocowy; mała dynia

squat; squat; squat [skłot; skłot; skłot]

squat [skłot] v. kucać; przycupnąć; nielegalnie koczować na gruncie; adj. przysadzisty; niski; szeroki; s. osoba przysadzista; kucki

squeak [skłi:k] v. piszczeć; skrzypieć; mówić piskliwie; (slang): zdradzać (sekrety); sypać; przepychać się z

trudnością; s. pisk; trudne
osiągnięcie czegoś

squeal [skli:l] v. piszczeć;
kwiczeć; (slang):
awanturować się; sypać;
wydawać (kogoś); s. pisk;
kwik; sypanie (kogoś,
czegoś)

squeamish ['skli:mysz] adj.
wybredny; pruderyjny;
przesadny; wrażliwy

squeegee ['skli:dżi:] s. przyrząd
w kształcie litery T do
usuwania wody z mytych szyb

squeeze [skli:z] v. ściskać;
wyciskać; wygniatać;
wciskać; odciskać;
ścieśnić; s. ucisk; nacisk;
odcisk; tłok; ściśnięcie

squeezer ['skli:zer] s. wyciskacz
(soku)

squid [skłyd] s. przynęta z
mątwy; kałamarnica (ryba)

squint [skłynt] s. zez; ukośne
spojrzenie; zerknięcie;
skłonność; v. mrużyć oczy;
wysilać wzrok; zezować;
skłaniać się; adj. zezowaty;
zerkający

squirm [skłe:rm] v. wić się (z
bólu); płonąć (ze wstydu);
kręcić się niespokojnie; s.
skręcanie się

squirrel ['skłe:rel] s. wiewiórka

squirt [skłe:rt] v. strzykać;
tryskać; s. strzykawka;
struga; pętak

stab [staeb] v. dźgnąć;
pchnąć; ugodzić; ranić; s.
pchnięcie; dźgnięcie; rana
kłuta

stability [ste'bylyty] s. stałość;
stateczność; stabilność;
równowaga

stabilize ['stejbylajz] v. ustalać;
stabilizować

stable ['stejbl] s. stajnia;
stadnina; v. trzymać konie w
stajni; adj. stały; stanowczy;
trwały

stack [staek] s. stóg; stos;
sterta; komin; kupa; v.
układać w stogi; ustawiać w

kozły; układać podstępnie
przeciwko komuś

stadium ['stejdjem] s. stadion;
faza; stadium (czegoś)

staff [staef] s. laska; drzewce;
sztab; personel; adj.
sztabowy; v. obsadzać
personelem

stag [staeg] s. rogacz; jeleń;
samotny mężczyzna

stage [stejdż] s. scena; stadium;
etap; rusztowanie; pomost;
postój; v. wystawiać;
odegrać (sztukę); urządzać;
inscenizować; adj. teatralny;
sceniczny

stagecoach ['stejdż-koucz] s.
dyliżans

stage-manager ['stejdż
'maenydżer] s. reżyser

stagflation ['staegflejszyn] s.
stagnacja, rosnące bezrobocie
i inflacja jednocześnie

stagger ['staeger] v. zataczać
się; wahać się; chwiać się;
układać w zygzak lub w
odstępach; porażać; s. układ
skośny, zachodzący na siebie
w odstępach lub
zygzakowaty; zataczanie się;
pl. zawroty głowy

staggering ['staegeryng] adj.
przerażający; oszałamiający;
rozbrajający

stagnant ['staegnent] adj.
zastały; stojący; będący w
zastoju

stain [stejn] v. plamić (się);
brudzić; szargać; barwić;
kolorować; farbować;
drukować tapety; s. plama;
barwnik; bejca do drewna

stained ['stejnd] adj. zabarwiony
(np. szkło)

stainless ['stejnlys] adj.
nierdzewny (stal); nieskalany

stair [steer] s. stopień; pl.
schody

staircase ['steer,kejs] s. klatka
schodowa

stairway ['steerlej] s. schody

stake [stejk] s. słup; słupek;
kołek; palik; stawka;

kowadełko blacharskie; v.
przytwierdzać kołkami;
wytaczać; przywiązywać do
słupa; stawiać na coś
stake out ['stejk,aut] v. wziąć
pod obserwację; wyznaczać
granicę
stake-out ['stejkaut] s. zasadzka
(slang)
stale [stejl] adj. stęchły;
nieświeży; zwietrzały;
czerstwy; przestarzały; v.
czuć nieświeżym
stalk [sto:k] v. kroczyć;
podkradać się; podchodzić;
s. (majestatyczny) chód;
podkradanie się;
podchodzenie; wysoki komin;
łodyga; nóżka (kieliszka)
stall [sto:l] v. działać
opóźniająco; zwlekać;
przewlekać; kręcić;
zwodzić; przetrzymywać;
dławić motor; utykać;
grzęznąć; trzymać bydło w
oborze; zaopatrywać w
przegrody; s. stajnia; obora;
stragan; kiosk; przegroda;
komora (w kopalni); (slang):
trik; kruczek
stallion ['staeljen] s. ogier
stalwart ['sto:łłert] s. bojownik
partyjny; adj. dzielny; krzepki;
stanowczy
stammer ['staemer] v. jąkać
się; s. jąkanie się
stamp [staemp] v. stemplować;
wytłaczać; tupać; kruszyć;
wbijać (w pamięć);
przylepiać znaczki pocztowe;
s. stempel; pieczątka;
znaczek; piętno; cecha;
pokrój; tupnięcie; ubijak do
kruszenia (rudy)
stanch [staencz] v. tamować
krwotok; adj. wierny; stały;
krzepki; szczelny
stand; stood; stood [staend;
stud; stud]
stand [staend] v. stać; stanąć;
wytrzymać; znosić;
przetrzymać; zostać;
utrzymywać się; stawiać

opór; znajdować się; być;
postawić; (slang): płacić; s.
stanie; stanowisko; stojak;
trybuna; postój; łan; ława dla
świadków; unieruchomienie;
umywalka
stand back ['staend,baek] v.
stać w tyle; zachowywać
rezerwę
stand by ['staendbaj] v.
popierać; być w stanie
pogotowia
stand off ['staend,of] v. cofać
się
stand-off ['staend,of] s.
nierozegrana (równowaga sił)
stand out ['staend,aut] v.
wyróżniać się;
kontrastować; wytrwać
stand up ['staend,ap] v.
wstawać; powstawać;
stawać w obronie; nie
ustępować; stawiać czoło
standard ['staenderd] s.
sztandar; norma; miernik;
wzorzec; wskaźnik; stopa
(życiowa); próba; słup;
podpórka; adj.
znormalizowany; normalny;
typowy; przeciętny;
wzorcowy; klasyczny; literacki
(język)
standardize ['staenderdajz] v.
normalizować;
dostosowywać do normy;
mierzyć wzorcem;
porównywać z wzorcem
standing ['staendyng] adj.
stojący; na pniu; pionowy;
stały; s. stanie; stanowisko;
znaczenie; poważanie;
reputacja; czas trwania
standing room ['staendyng,ru:m]
s. miejsce stojące
standoffish ['staend'ofysz] adj.
nieprzystępny; trzymający się
z dala
standpoint ['staend,point] s.
punkt widzenia; punkt
obserwacyjny
standstill ['staendstyl] s. zastój;
przerwa; martwy punkt;
unieruchomienie

stank [staenk] v. zob. stink

star [sta:r] s. gwiazda; gwiazdor; gwiazdka; v. ozdabiać gwiazdkami; być gwiazdorem; adj. gwiezdny; występujący w głównej roli

starboard ['sta:rberd] s. prawa burta; v. sterować na prawo

starch [sta:rcz] s. skrobia; sztywność; krochmal; v. nakrochmalić; (slang): siła

starchy ['sta:rczy] adj. nakrochmalony; skrobiowaty; sztywny

stare [steer] v. patrzeć; gapić się; wpatrywać się; zwracać uwagę; s. nieruchomy wzrok; wytrzeszczone oczy; zagapione spojrzenie

stare at ['steer,aet] v. gapić się na ...

stark [sta:rk] adj. sztywny; zupełny; czysty; wierutny; ponury; posępny; adv. zupełnie; całkowicie

starling ['starlyng] s. szpak

starlit ['sta:rlyt] adj. gwiaździsty; oświetlony gwiazdami; wygwieżdżony

starry ['sta:ry] adj. gwiaździsty; usiany gwiazdami; promienny; marzycielski; rozmarzony

star-spangled ['sta:r-spaengld] adj. usiany gwiazdami (flaga USA)

start [sta:rt] v. zacząć; ruszyć; startować; zerwać się; podskoczyć; wyruszyć; zabierać się; uruchamiać; obsuwać; rozpoczynać; wszczynać; s. początek; start; wymarsz; poderwanie się; obsunięcie się; zdobywanie przewagi

starter ['sta:rter] s. starter; rozrusznik; startujący zawodnik; pierwsze danie; kierownik ruchu

startle ['sta:rtl] v. zaskoczyć; zaniepokoić; podrywać; wzdrygać się; przestraszać; s. zaniepokojenie; poderwanie się

startling ['sta:rtlyng] adj. sensacyjny; zdumiewający; niepokojący

starvation [sta:r'wejszyn] s. głód; głodowanie; głodzenie; przymieranie głodem

starve [sta:rw] v. głodować; zagłodzić; przymierać z głodu, zimna; łaknąć; zmuszać (głodem, brakiem)

stash [staesz] v. (slang): chować na potem; s. schowanie; schowek

state [stejt] s. państwo; stan; zajęcie; parada; pompa; ceremoniał; stan prac; adj. państwowy; stanowy; uroczysty; paradny; formalny; v. stwierdzać; wyrażać (też symbolami); określać

state department ['stejt,dy'pa:rtment] s. (w USA) ministerstwo spraw zagranicznych

stately ['stejtly] adj. uroczysty; okazały; adv. uroczyście; okazale

statement ['stejtment] s. wyrażenie; twierdzenie; sprawozdanie; wyciąg; oświadczenie; deklaracja; zeznanie

state room ['stejt,rum] s. prywatny pokój; kabina; przedział

stateside ['stejt,sajd] adj. amerykański; w stanach

statesman ['stejtsmen] s. mąż stanu

statesmanship ['stejtsmenszyp] s. rozum polityczny

static ['staetyk] adj. statyczny; nieruchomy

station ['stejszyn] s. stacja; stanowisko; stan; pozycja życiowa; godność; punkt; stacja telewizyjna, radiowa etc.

stationary ['stejsznery] adj. niezmienny; stały; nieruchomy; pozycyjny

stationery ['stejszn,ery] s. pl. materiały piśmienne; papier

listowy
station master ['stejszyn,ma:ster]
s. naczelnik stacji
station wagon ['stejszyn,łaegn]
s. samochód typu kombi
statistics [ste'tystyks] s.
statystyka
statue ['staeczu:] s. posąg
statute ['staetjut] s. ustawa;
prawo; statut; nakaz
staunch [sto:ncz] v. tamować
krwotok; tamponować; adj.
oddany; wierny; zagorzały
stay; stayed; staid [stej; stejd;
stejd]
stay [stej] s. pobyt; zwłoka;
odroczenie; opóźnienie;
zawieszenie; podpora; wanta;
zatrzymanie; przerwa;
wytrzymałość; v. zostać;
przebywać; wytrzymać;
odraczać; kłaść kres;
zaspokajać (głód)
stay away ['stej,ełej] v. trzymać
się z dala
stay up ['stej,ap] v. nie siadać
stay with ['stej,łyg] v. mieszkać
u kogoś
stead [sted] s. miejsce; na
miejsce; pożyteczność
steadfast ['sted,fa:st] adj. stały;
nieruchomy; niezachwiany;
niewzruszony; mocny; pewny
steady ['stedy] adj. mocny; silny;
pewny; stały; rzetelny; równy;
stateczny; excl.: powolil
prostol naprzódl stój!; v.
dawać równowagę;
odzyskiwać równowagę; s.
podpora; (slang): ukochany
steak [stejk] s. stek; befsztyk;
płat (np. mięsa)
steal; stole; stolen [sti:l; stoul;
stoulen]
steal [sti:l] v. kraść; wykraść;
wejść ukradkiem; zakradać
się; skradać się; s. kradzież;
rzecz ukradziona; rzecz
kupiona prawie, że za darmo;
darmocha (slang)
stealth [stelş] s. tajemniczość;
ukradkowość
stealthy ['stelşy] adj. ukradkowy;

tajemny
steam [sti:m] s. para; v.
parować; dymić; płynąć
pod parą; gotować w parze;
umieszczać pod parą
steam up ['sti:m,ap] v. zamglić
(się); zajść mgłą lub parą
steamer ['sti:mer] s. parowiec
steamship ['sti:m,szyp] s.
parowiec
steel [sti:l] s. stal; pręt stalowy;
adj. stalowy; ze stali; v.
pokrywać stalą; hartować
steel works ['sti:l,łe:rks] s.
stalownia
steep [sti:p] v. moczyć się;
rozmiękczać; impregnować;
pogrążyć się; rozpijać się;
adj. stromy;
nieprawdopodobny;
wygórowany; przesadny
steepen ['sti:pn] v. nagle
podnosić ceny; robić
stromym
steeple ['sti:pl] s. strzelista
wieża; ostra wieżyczka
steer [stier] v. sterować;
kierować; prowadzić; s.
wskazówka; młody wół na
mięso
steering wheel ['stieryng,hłi:l] s.
kierownica; koło sterowe
stem [stem] s. pień; łodyga;
szpulka; trzon; trzonek; nóżka;
v. pochodzić; tamować;
powstrzymywać; iść pod
prąd; zwalczać
stench [stencz] s. smród; odór;
fetor
stenographer [ste'negraefer] s.
stenograf; stenografistka
step [step] s. krok; stopień;
takt; szczebel; schodek; v.
stąpać; kroczyć; iść;
tańczyć; podnosić;
wzmagać; przyciskać nogą;
mierzyć (krokami)
stepchild ['step,czajld] s. pasierb
stepfather ['step,fa:dzer] s.
ojczym
stepmother ['step,madzer] s.
macocha
stereo ['steriou] s. stereoskop;

dwugłośnikowe radio-adapter;
adj. stereofoniczny

sterile ['sterajl] adj. wyjałowiony;
jałowy; sterylny; bezpłodny

sterilize ['stery,lajz] v.
wyjałowić; wysterylizować

sterling ['ste:rlyng] s. pieniądz
pełnowartościowy; adj.
solidny; niezawodny

stern [ste:rn] adj. surowy; srogi;
s. rufa; zad; zadek; tył;
pośladki

sternness ['ste:rnys] s.
surowość; srogość

stew [stu:] v. gotować; dusić
(się); martwić się; wkuwać
się; s. potrawa duszona;
kłopot; staw na ryby

steward ['stu:erd] s. zarządca;
ekonom; kelner; v. zarządzać;
być stewardem

stewardess ['stu:erdys] s.
stewardessa

stew pan ['stu:,paen] s. rondel;
garnek

stick; stuck; stuck [styk; stak;
stak]

stick [styk] v. wtykać;
przekłuwać; kłuć; wbijać;
zarzynać; przyklejać;
naklejać; utkwić; utknąć;
ugrzęznąć; przyczepiać (się);
trzymać się (tematu);
oszukiwać; s. pałka; patyk;
laska; kij; tyczka; żerdź

stick out ['styk,aut] v.
wystawiać; sterczeć; zadać

stick to ['styk,tu] v. trzymać się
(tematu); przylepiać

stick up ['styk,ap] v.
terroryzować (bronią); brać
w obronę; podnosić;
przeciwstawiać się

sticky ['styky] adj. lepki; kleisty;
grząski; parny; (slang): marny;
nieprzyjemny

stiff [styf] adj. sztywny; twardy;
kategoryczny; zdrętwiały;
"słony"; wygórowany; trudny;
ciężki; silny; s. (slang): trup;
umrzyk; niedojda; włóczęga;
facet; pedant

stiffen ['styfn] v. usztywniać;

podnieść (wymagania);
zgęszczać; zesztywnieć

stifle [stajfl] v. dusić (się);
tłumić; przygaszać;
tuszować

stile [stajl] s. przełaz; kołowrót;
pionowa rama drzwi

still [styl] adj. spokojny; cichy;
nieruchomy; martwy
(przedmiot); milczący; adv.
jeszcze; jednak; wciąż; dotąd;
niemniej; mimo to; v.
uspokoić (się); uciszyć;
destylować; s. destylarnia
(też wódki)

stillness ['stylnys] s. cisza;
spokój; bezruch

stilt [stylt] s. szczudło

stilted ['styltyd] adj. na
szczudłach; nienaturalny;
sztuczny; na wspornikach

stimulant ['stymjulent] s.
bodziec; podnieta; alkohol;
środek podniecający;
zachęta; adj. pobudzający

stimulate ['stymjulejt] v.
pobudzać; zachęcać

stimulating ['stymjulejtyng] adj.
podniecający; pobudzający

stimulation ['stymjulejszyn] s.
podnieta; zachęta; podniecenie

stimulus ['stymjules] s. bodziec;
zachęta; podnieta

sting; stung; stung [styng;
stang; stang]

sting [styng] v. kłuć; parzyć;
kąsać; szczypać; palić;
rwać; gryźć; s. żądło;
ukłucie; poparzenie; piekący
ból; uszczypliwość;
zjadliwość

stingy ['styndży] adj. skąpy

stink; stank; stunk [stynk;
staenk; stank]

stink [stynk] v. cuchnąć;
śmierdzieć; zasmradzać;
wyganiać smrodem; (slang):
poczuć smród; s. smród

stipulate ['stypjulejt] v.
zażądać; uwarunkować;
zastrzegać w umowie

stir [ste:r] v. ruszać; poruszać;
grzebać; mieszać; wzniecać;

podniecać; s. poruszenie;
podniecenie; ruch; (slang):
więzienie

stirrup ['styrep] s. strzemię;
pociągiel; okucie do wspinania
się

stitch [stycz] s. szew; ścieg;
oczko; kłucie; v. szyć;
zaszyć; zeszywać

stoat [stout] s. gronostaj;
zaszywać niewidocznym
ściegiem

stock [stok] s. zapas; zasób;
bydło; pień; trzon; kłoda;
łożysko; ród; rasa; surowiec;
kapitał udziałowy; akcje
giełdowe; obligacje; wywar; v.
zaopatrywać;
zagospodarować; zarybiać;
mieć na składzie; adj.
typowy; seryjny; w stałym
zapasie; repertuarowy

stockade [sto'kejd] s. palisada;
częstokół; obóz

stockbroker ['stok,brouker] s.
makler giełdowy

stock exchange
['stok,eks'czejndż] s. giełda

stockholder ['stok,houlder] s.
akcjonariusz; udziałowiec

stocking ['stokyng] s.
pończocha

stocky ['stoky] adj. krępy

stock market ['stok-'ma:rkyt] s.
giełda

stole [stoul] v. zob. steal; s.
stula; etola

stolen ['stouln] v. zob. steal

stolid ['stolyd] adj. obojętny;
flegmatyczny

stomach ['stamek] s. żołądek;
brzuch; apetyt; ochota; v.
jeść; przełykać (obelgę);
znosić

stone [stoun] s. kamień; głaz;
skała; pestka; adj. kamienny;
v. ukamienować; obkładać
(mur) kamieniem; wyjmować
pestki; upijać (się) na umór

stonewall ['stoun-ło:l] v.
odmówić zaciekle
jakiejkolwiek kooperacji

stoneware ['stoun-łeer] s.

naczynia kamionkowe

stony ['stouny] adj. kamienny;
kamienisty; skamieniały;
pestkowy

stood [stud] v. zob. stand

stool [stu:l] s. stołek; sedes;
taboret; stolec; klęcznik;
podnóżek; pniak puszczający
pędy; wabik; v. puszczać
pędy

stoop [stu:p] v. schylać się;
ugiąć się; poniżyć się;
raczyć; garbić się; s.
pochylenie; przygarbione
plecy; weranda; taras (przy
domu)

stooping ['stu:pyng] adj.
przygarbiony

stop [stop] v. zatrzymywać;
powstrzymywać;
wstrzymywać; zatykać;
zaplombować; zagrodzić;
zablokować; zamknąć;
zaprzestawać; nie dopuścić;
stanąć; przestać; exp.:
przestań! stój! dosyć tego!;
s. zatrzymanie (się); stop;
postój; przystanek; zatkanie;
zator; zatyczka; zderzak;
ogranicznik

stop by ['stop,baj] v. wstąpić
do kogoś na chwilę

stopover ['stop'ouwer] s.
zatrzymanie się w podróży

stoppage ['stopydż] s.
wstrzymanie; zatrzymanie
(się); zatwardzenie

stopper ['stoper] s. korek;
zatyczka; v. zatykać;
umocować liną

stopping ['stopyng] s. plomba (w
zębie); zatrzymanie; zatkanie

storage ['sto:rydż] s. skład;
przechowywanie;
magazynowanie

store ['sto:r] s. zapas; sklep;
skład; mnóstwo; składnica; v.
magazynować; mieścić w
sobie; zaopatrywać;
wyposażać

store up ['sto:r,ap] v.
zamagazynować; zachować

storehouse ['sto:rhaus] s. skład;

magazyn; skarbnica; kopalnia

storekeeper ['sto:r,ki:per] s. sklepikarz; kupiec

storey ['sto:ry] (=story) s. piętro

storeyed ['sto:rjed] adj. piętrowy (angielska pisownia)

storied ['sto:rjed] adj. piętrowy

stork [sto:rk] s. bocian

storm [sto:rm] s. burza; wichura; sztorm; zawierucha; szturm; v. szaleć (burza etc.); wpaść do pokoju; wypaść z pokoju (jak burza); rzucać gromy; szturmować; brać szturmem

stormy ['sto:rmy] adj. burzliwy; zwiastujący burzę

story ['sto:ry] s. opowiadanie; opowieść; powiastka; historia; bajka; anegdota; gawęda; zmyślanie; nowela; piętro

story teller ['sto:ry,teler] s. gawędziarz; kłamczuch

stout [staut] adj. dzielny; krzepki; gruby; s. mocne np. porto (wino); mocne piwo; tęga osoba

stove [stouw] s. piec (też kuchenny); cieplarnia; v. zob. stave; hodować w cieplarni

stow [stou] v. wypełniać; układać szczelnie; mieścić; wsuwać; chować; przesłać (slang)

stow away ['stou,e'łej] v. jechać na gapę

stowaway ['stouełej] s. pasażer na gapę

straggling ['straeglyng] adj. sporadyczny; rozpościerający się; rzadki

straight [strejt] adj. prosty; bezpośredni; celny; szczery; otwarty; rzetelny; zwykły; s. prosta linia; prosty odcinek (toru); adv. prosto; wprost; na przełaj; po prostu; pod rząd; należycie; nieprzerwanie; ciągiem

straightaway ['strejt,ełej] adv. natychmiast; bez zwłoki

straight ahead ['strejt,ehed] adv. na wprost

straighten ['strejtn] v. wyprostować (się); poprawić (się)

straightforward [strejt'fo:rłerd] adj. łatwy; jasny; prosty; prostolinijny; szczery; uczciwy

strain [strejn] v. prężyć; naprężać; naciągać; wytężać; odkształcać; nadużywać; nadwerężać; przeciążać; robić gwałtowne wysiłki; cedzić; przecedzać; s. naprężenie; napięcie; obciążenie; przemęczenie; zwichnięcie; nadwerężenie; wysiłek; odkształcenie; rasa; odmiana; rys

strainer ['strejner] s. sito; sączek; cedzidło; rozciągacz; napinacz

strait [strejt] v. ścieśniać; być w trudnościach

straited circumstances ['strejtyd, ser'kamstensys] s. kłopoty pieniężne

straiten ['strejtn] v. zbiednieć; zubożeć

strait jacket ['strejt'dżaekyt] s. kaftan bezpieczeństwa

straits [strejts] pl. cieśnina morska; kłopoty finansowe; braki czegoś

strand [straend] s. skręt; zwitek; pasmo; nitka; warkocz; sznur; rys; kosmyk; brzeg; plaża; v. splatać; osadzać na mieliźnie; osiąść na mieliźnie

strange [strejndż] adj. obcy; dziwny; niezwykły; nieznany; niewprawny

stranger ['strejndżer] s. obcy; nieznajomy; człowiek nieobeznany; exp. panie tego!

strangle ['straengl] v. dusić; trzymać za gardło; zadusić

strap [straep] s. rzemień; pasek; rzemyk; taśma; uchwyt; rączka; chłosta; bicie; v. na pasku umocowywać; ostrzyć; bić paskiem; zalepiać plastrem

strategic [stre'ti:dżyk] adj.

strategiczny
strategy ['straetydży] s.
strategia; taktyka
straw [stro:] s. słoma
strawberry ['stro:bery] s.
truskawka
stray [strej] v. zabłądzić;
zabłąkać się; schodzić na
manowce; s. zbłąkane
zwierzę; dziecko bez opieki;
adj. zabłąkany
strays [strejs] pl. zaburzenia
atmosferyczne (np. w radiu)
streak [stri:k] s. smuga; pasek;
pasmo; prążek; rys;
pierwiastek; passa; v.
rysować paski, prążki;
błyskawicznie poruszać się;
wpadać nagle dokądś
streaky ['stri:ky] adj.
prążkowany; w paski;
zmienny; nierówny (slang)
stream [stri:m] s. strumień;
potok; rzeka; struga; prąd; v.
płynąć (strumieniami);
ociekać; tryskać; powiewać
street [stri:t] s. ulica
streetcar ['stri:tka:r] s. tramwaj
strength [strenks] s. moc; siła;
stężenie; natężenie; ilość;
skład (ludzi)
strengthen ['strenksn] v.
wzmocnić (się); wzmagać;
dać przewagę
strenuous [strenjues] adj.
męczący; żmudny; mozolny;
wytężony; zawzięty;
pracowity; energiczny; silny
stress [stres] s. nacisk; akcent;
napór; wysiłek; v. kłaść
nacisk; podkreślać; naciskać
stretch [strecz] v. naciągać
(się); naprężać; napinać;
nadużywać; przeciągać;
rozciągać (się); ciągnąć się;
sięgać; powiesić (kogoś); s.
napięcie; rozciąganie;
przeciąganie się; nadużycie;
połać; okres służby; przeciąg
czasu; prosty odcinek toru;
(slang): pobyt w więzieniu
stretcher ['streczer] s. nosze
strew; strewed; strewn [stru:;

stru:d; stru:n]
strew [stru:] s. posypać;
rozrzucić; porozrzucać
strewn [stru:n] v. zob. strew
stricken ['stryken] v. zob. strike;
adj. dotknięty; nawiedzony;
rażony; udręczony
stride; strode; stridden [strajd;
stroud; strydn]
stride [strajd] v. kroczyć;
przekroczyć; stać okrakiem
(nad czymś); s. krok; rozkrok
strife [strajf] s. spór; walka;
współzawodnictwo
strike; struck; stricken [strajk;
strak; strykn]
strike [strajk] v. uderzać; bić
(monetę); walić; kuć;
wykrzesać; zapalić (zapałkę);
natrafić; zastrajkować;
porzucać robotę; chwytać
(przynętę); s. strajk;
strychulec; wybicie monety;
natrafienie (żyły, np.
złotodajnej); chwycenie
przynęty; nieudane uderzenie
palantem; zwalenie wszystkich
kręgli naraz
strike off ['strajk off] v.
odrapywać; ścinać;
wykreślać; drukować kilka
egzemplarzy
strike out ['strajk,aut] v.
uderzać na odlew; zacząć;
ukuć; wymyślić
striker ['strajker] s. strajkujący;
młotek (w dzwonku)
striking ['strajkyng] adj.
uderzający
string; strung; strung [stryng;
strang; strang]
string [stryng] v. zawiązać;
przywiązać; zaopatrzyć w
struny; stroić; napinać;
podniecać; powiesić kogoś;
ciągnąć się (klej);
obwieszać; s. sznurek;
szpagat; powróz;
sznurowadło; tasiemka;
cięciwa; struna; żyła; włókno;
rząd; stek (głupstw)
strip [stryp] v. obdzierać;
ogołacać; obnażać;

zdzierać; rozbierać (się);
wydobyć do końca; ścierać
(gwint); ciąć na paski; s.
pasek; skrawek; seria
komiksów

strip-tease ['strypti:z] s.
rozbieranie się na scenie

striped ['strajpt] adj. pasiasty; w
pasy

stripes [strajps] pl. paski; prążki;
naszywki; chłosta; cięgi

strive; strove; striven ['strajw;
strouw; strywn]

strive [strajw] v. starać się;
usiłować; dążyć; borykać
się; zwalczać

striven ['strywn] v. zob. strive

strode [strode] v. zob. stride

stroke [strouk] s. uderzenie;
cios; cięcie; raz; porażenie;
ciąg; pociągnięcie (pióra); rys;
kreska; ruch (wiosła); wysiłek;
suw; skok (tłoka); takt;
głaskanie; v. znaczyć;
przekreślać; nadawać
tempo; głaskać; ugłaskać

stroke of luck ['strouk,ow'lak]
exp.: los szczęścia

stroll [stroul] v. przechadzać
się; spacerować; wędrować;
s. przechadzka

stroller ['strouler] s. spacerowicz;
włóczęga; aktor wędrowny;
wózek (dziecięcy)

strong [strong] adj. mocny; silny;
będący w liczbie ...;
mocarstwowy; potężny;
trwały; solidny; wyskokowy;
przekonywający; ordynarny

strongbox ['strong,boks] s. sejf;
kasa ogniotrwała

strongroom ['strong,rum] s.
skarbiec

strove [strouw] v. zob. strive

struck [strak] v. zob. strike

structure ['strakczer] s. budowa;
struktura; budowla; wiązanie;
splot; v. nadawać kształt

struggle ['stragl] v. szarpać się;
szamotać się; walczyć;
usiłować; s. walka; borykanie

strum [stram] v. rzępolić;
brzdąkać; s. brzdęk;

brzdąkanie

strung [strang] v. zob. string;
adj. napięty

strut [strat] v. kroczyć
majestatycznie; rozpierać; s.
krok majestatyczny; zastrzał;
rozpora

stub [stab] s. pniak; korzeń;
resztka; niedopałek; grzbiet
(biletu); v. karczować; gasić
(papierosa)

stubble ['stabl] s. rżysko;
ściernisko; twardy zarost

stubborn ['stabern] adj. uparty

stuck [stak] v. zob. stick

stud [stad] s. sworzeń;
gwóźdź; guz; trzon; słup;
rozpórka; ogier; stadnina; v.
nabijać (np. gwoździami,
guzami); usiewać
czymś; być rozsianym;
podpierać (słupami)

student ['stu:dent] s. student;
badający coś; znawca
czegoś

studio ['stju:djou] s. studio;
pracownia

studio couch ['stju:djou,kaucz] s.
tapczan

studious ['stu:djes] adj. pilny;
staranny; dbały; wyszukany

study ['stady] s. pracownia;
gabinet; nauka; przedmiot
nauki, starań, troski, zadumy,
marzenia; v. badać;
studiować; dociekać; uczyć
się

stuff [staf] v. napychać;
opychać (się); tuczyć (się);
faszerować; wpychać;
wkuwać; s. materia; materiał;
glina; rzecz; rupiecie (brednie)

stuffing ['stafyng] s. nadzienie;
farsz; nadziewka; wyściółka

stuffy ['stafy] adj. zatęchły;
duszny; ciężki; nudny;
zatkany (nos); (slang): ważny;
tępy; skwaszony; zły;
purytański

stumble ['stambl] v. potykać
(się); utykać; natknąć się;
zawahać (kogoś); mieć
skrupuły; czuć się

dotkniętym; s. potknięcie się
stumble-bum ['stambl,bam] s.
(slang): zawalidroga; próżniak
stumbling block
['stamblyng,blok] s.
przeszkoda; zawada; szkopuł;
trudność
stump [stamp] s. pniak; głąb;
kikut; ogarek; resztka;
niedopałek; kulas; krzykactwo;
agitacja (polityczna); klocek;
przysadkowaty człowiek; v.
karczować; obcinać;
zdumieć (się); agitować;
wyzwać kogoś; chodzić na
protezie
stun [stan] v. ogłuszyć;
oszołomić; s. oszołomienie
(uderzenie hukiem)
stung [stang] v. zob. sting
stunk [stank] v. zob. stink
stunning ['stanyng] adj.
nadzwyczajny; szlagierowy;
kapitalny
stupefy ['stu:pyfaj] v. ogłupiać;
odurzać; wprawiać w
osłupienie
stupid ['stu:pyd] adj. głupi;
odurzony; nudny; s. głupiec
stupidity ['stu:pydyty] s. głupota;
głupstwo
stupor ['stu:per] s. osłupienie;
odurzenie; apatia
sturdy ['ste:rdy] adj. krzepki;
dzielny; solidny; s. motylica
stutter ['stater] v. jąkać (się); s.
jąkanie się
sty [staj] s. chlew; burdel;
jęczmień (w oku); v. żyć w
chlewie; trzymać w chlewie
style [stajl] s. styl; maniera;
sposób; fason; wzór; kształt;
rylec; szyjka; tytuł; nazwa;
format; wskazówka; v.
formować stylowo; określać
mianem
stylish ['stajlyзz] adj. szykowny;
stylowy; wytworny
suave [sła:w] adj. gładki;
łagodny; uprzejmy
subdivision [,sabdy'wyżyn] s.
dzielnica (miasta, osiedla);
podział

subdue [seb'du:] s. ujarzmiać;
poskramiać; przyciszać;
tłumić; łagodzić; podbijać
subject ['sabdżykt] s. podmiot;
przedmiot; temat; treść;
tworzywo; [sab'dżekt] motyw;
poddany; osobnik; v.
podporządkować; ujarzmić;
podbić; narazić; poddać
czemuś; adj. poddany; uległy;
podległy; narażony; podatny;
podlegający; ujarzmiony; adv.
pod warunkiem; z
zastrzeżeniem; z
uwzględnieniem czegoś
subjective [seb'dżektyw] adj.
subiektywny; podmiotowy
subjunctive mood
[seb'dżanktyw,mu:d] s. tryb
warunkowy
sublime [se'blajm] adj. wzniosły;
wyniosły; podniosły
submachine-gun
['sabme'szi:ngan] s.
(automatyczny) pistolet
maszynowy
submarine [sabme'ri:n] s. łódź
podwodna
submariners [sabme'ri:ners] pl.
załoga łodzi podwodnej
submerge [seb'me:rdż] v.
zalewać; zatapiać; zanurzać
(się); zakrywać
submission [seb'myszyn] s.
uległość; poddanie się;
przedłożenie (opinii)
submissive [seb'mysyw] adj.
uległy
submit [seb'myt] v. poddawać
(się); przedkładać
subnormal [sab'no:rmel] adj.
niżej normy; cofnięty w
rozwoju
subordinate [se'bo:rdnyt] adj.
zależny; podporządkowany; s.
podwładny; [se'bo:rdnejt] v.
podporządkowywać
subordinate clause
[se'bo:rdnyt,klo:z] s. zdanie
podrzędne
subscribe [seb'skrajb] b.
zaprenumerować;
podpisywać (np. obraz);

pisać się na coś; dawać na
cel

subscribe for [seb'skrajb,fo:r] v.
zapisywać się na (nową)
książkę

subscribe to [seb'skrajb,tu] v.
abonować gazetę

subscriber [seb'skrajber] s.
abonent; człowiek popierający

subscription [seb'skrypszyn] s.
prenumerata; przedpłata;
podpisanie; zgoda pisemna;
podpis dołączony

subsequent ['sabsykłent] adj.
następny

subsequently ['sabsykłently] adv.
następnie

subside [seb'sajd] v. klęsnąć;
opadać; osadzać się;
osiadać; uspokajać się

subsidiary [seb'sydjery] adj.
pomocniczy; subsydiowany
(zależny); s. pomocnik

subsidiary company
[seb'sydjery'kampeny] s. firma
zależna od innej firmy

subsidize ['sabsydajz] v.
zasiłkować; zasilać;
opłacać; przekupywać

subsidy ['sabsydy] s. zasiłek
(państwowy); subwencja;
danina

subsist [seb'syst] v. istnieć;
egzystować; utrzymywać się
przy życiu; żyć czymś

subsistence [seb'systens] s.
utrzymanie; istnienie

substance ['sabstens] s. istota;
treść; sens; sedno;
substancja; znaczenie;
rzeczywistość; majątek

substandard [sab'staenderd] adj.
poniżej poziomu; ordynarny
(język)

substantial [sab'staenszel] adj.
materialny; rzeczywisty;
solidny; zasadniczy; ważny;
bogaty; wpływowy;
konkretny; treściwy

substantive ['sabstentyw] adj.
rzeczywisty; niezależnie
istniejący; zasadniczy;
poważny; rzeczownikowy;

wyrażający istnienie; s.
rzeczownik

substitute ['sabstytut] s.
namiastka; zastępca

substitution [,sabsty'tuszyn] s.
zastępstwo; zastąpienie

subtitle ['sabtajtl] s. podtytuł;
napis na filmie

subtle ['satl] adj. subtelny;
delikatny; cienki; rzadki;
chytry; bystry

subtract [sab'traekt] v.
odejmować

suburb ['sabe:rb] s.
przedmieście

suburban [se'be:rben] adj.
podmiejski

subway ['sabłej] s. kolejka
podziemna

succeed [sek'si:d] v. mieć
powodzenie; udawać się;
następować po kimś

success [sek'ses] s. powodzenie;
sukces; rzecz udana; człowiek
mający sukces

successful [sek'sesful] adj.
udały; mający powodzenie

succession [sek'seszyn] s.
następstwo; kolej; kolejność;
sukcesja; spadkobiercy; szereg

successive [sek'sesyw] adj.
kolejny

successor [sek'seser] s.
następca; dziedzic;
spadkobierca

succumb [se'kam] v. ulegać
(pokusie); poddawać się;
umierać

such [sacz] adj. taki; tego
rodzaju; pron. taki; tym
podobny

suck [sak] v. ssać; korzystać;
wyzyskiwać; wchłaniać;
wciągać; (slang): nabierać;
dać się nabrać; podlizywać
się komuś; s. ssanie;
wciąganie; (slang): łyk

suckle ['sakel] v. karmić piersią;
dawać pierś; ssać pierś

suckling ['saklyng] s. osesek;
młode w okresie ssania

sudden ['sadn] adj. nagły

sudden death ['sadn,det] s.

nagła śmierć; rozstrzygnięcie w następnej rozgrywce
suddenly ['sadnly] adv. nagle; raptownie; nieoczekiwanie
suds [sadz] pl. mydliny; (slang): piwo
sue [su:] v. skarżyć; zaskarżać; pozywać; upraszać; ubiegać się
suede [słejd] s. zamsz
suet ['su:yt] s. łój; adj. łojowy
suffer ['safer] v. cierpieć; ucierpieć; ścierpieć; doznać (czegoś); zostać straconym
suffer from ['safer,from] v. być chorym (na coś)
sufferable ['saferebl] adj. znośny
sufferer ['saferer] s. cierpiący
suffice [se'fajs] v. wystarczyć
sufficiency [se'fyszensy] s. wystarczająca ilość; zapasy
sufficient [se'fyszent] adj. dostateczny; wystarczający
suffix ['safyks] s. przyrostek
suffocate ['safokejt] v. udusić; zadusić
sugar ['szuger] s. cukier; słodkie dziecko; (slang): forsa; v. słodzić
sugar-cane ['szugerkejn] s. trzcina cukrowa
suggest [se'dżest] v. sugerować; proponować; nasuwać; podsuwać; poddawać (myśl)
suggestion [se'dżesczyn] s. sugestia; wskazówka; myśl; poddawanie; podsuwanie; ślad (czegoś)
suggestive [se'dżestyw] adj. przypominający; nasuwający (myśl); dwuznaczny
suicide [,su:y'sajd] s. samobójstwo; samobójca; v. popełnić samobójstwo
suit [su:t] v. dostosować; odpowiadać; służyć; wybrać; być odpowiednim; zadowalać; pasować; s. garnitur; ubranie; komplet; skarga; proces; prośba; zaloty; staranie się; zestaw

suit yourself ['su:tjor,self] exp.: rób co chcesz
suitable ['su:tebl] adj. właściwy; stosowny; odpowiedni
suitcase ['su:tkejs] s. walizka
suite [sli:t] s. świta; orszak; szereg; zestaw (mebli); apartament; garnitur; komplet; suita
suitor ['su:ter] s. zalotnik; petent; pretendent; strona; konkurent
sulfate ['salfejt] s. siarczan; v. zakwaszać; zamieniać na siarczan
sulfur ['salfer] s. siarka; v. siarkować
sulk [salk] v. być w złym humorze; s. zły humor; człowiek w złym humorze
sulky ['salky] adj. w złym humorze; ponury; s. jednokonny dwukołowy wózek
sullen ['salen] adj. ponury; posępny; flegmatyczny; powolny
sulphur ['salfer] s. siarka; v. siarkować
sultry ['saltry] adj. parny; duszny; gwałtowny; gorący; namiętny
sum [sam] s. suma; w sumie; rachunek; v. dodawać; zbierać; podsumowywać
sum up ['sam,ap] v. dodawać; zbierać; podsumowywać
summarize ['samerajz] v. streszczać; zbierać; podsumowywać
summary ['samery] s. streszczenie; skrót; adj. pobieżny; doraźny; krótki
summer ['samer] s. lato; v. spędzać lato
summer resort ['samer ry'so:rt] s. letnisko
summer school ['samer,sku:l] s. szkoła w lecie, w czasie wakacji
summit ['samyt] s. szczyt
summon ['samen] v. wzywać (oficjalnie); zdobywać się (na odwagą)

summons ['samens] pl.
wezwanie urzędowe; v.
doręczać wezwanie
urzędowe

sumptuous ['samptjues] adj.
wspaniały; wystawny;
okazały; zrobiony z
przepychem

sun [san] s. słońce; v.
nasłoneczniać (się)

sun-bath ['sanba:s] s. kąpiel
słoneczna (brit.)

sunbathe ['sanbejz] v. opalać
się

sunbeam ['sanbi:m] s. promień
słońca

sunburn ['sanbe:rn] s. opalenizna

Sunday ['sandy] s. niedziela

sundial ['sandajel] s. zegar
słoneczny

sundries ['sandryz] pl. różności;
rozmaitości

sundry ['sandry] adj. różny;
rozmaity

sung [sang] v. zob. sing

sunglasses ['san,gla:sys] pl.
okulary od słońca

sunk [sank] v. zob. sink

sunken ['sanken] v. zob. sink;
adj. zapadnięty; zatopiony;
podwodny

sunny ['sany] adj. słoneczny

sunny side up ['sany,sajd ap]
exp.: jaja sadzone

sunrise ['san-rajz] s. wschód
słońca

sunshade ['sanszejd] s. parasol
od słońca

sunset ['sanset] s. zachód
słońca

sunshine ['sanszajn] s. blask
słońca; pogoda; wesołość

sunstroke ['sanstrouk] s.
porażenie słoneczne

sup [sap] s. łyk; v. częstować
kolacją; zjeść kolację; pić
małymi łykami

super ['su:per] adj.
pierwszorzędny; wspaniały;
kwadratowy; prefix: nad-;
prze-; s. statysta; nadzorca;
szlagier; przebój (filmowy);
najlepszy gatunek

superabundant
['su:per,e'bandent] adj.
nadmierny; przebogaty

superb [se'pe:rb] adj. wspaniały

super-duper [,su:per-'du:per] adj.
(slang): b. dobry; luksusowy;
bardzo elegancki

superficial [,su:per'fyszel] adj.
powierzchowny;
powierzchniowy

superfluous [su'pe:rflues] adj.
zbędny; zbyteczny

super-highway ['su:per'haj,łej] s.
(m. in. 4-pasmowa) autostrada

superhuman [,su:per'hju:man]
adj. nadludzki

superintend [,su:peryn'tend] v.
nadzorować; doglądać;
kierować

superintendent
[,su:peryn'tendent] s.
nadzorca; dozorca;
nadinspektor

superior [su:'pierjer] adj. wyższy;
nieprzeciętny; pierwszorzędny;
przewyższający; lepszy;
nadęty; wyniosły; s.
zwierzchnik; przełożony;
starszy rangą

superiority [su:,pie:ry'oryty] s.
wyższość

superlative [su:'pe:rlatyw] adj.
najwyższy; s. szczyt;
superlatyw; stopień
najwyższy

superman ['su:permen] s.
nadczłowiek

supermarket ['su:per'ma:rkyt] s.
supersam; duży sklep
samoobsługowy
(żywnościowy)

supernatural [,su:per'naeczerel]
adj. nadprzyrodzony

supernumerary
[,su:per'nju:meryry] adj.
nadliczbowy; nieetatowy; s.
statysta

superscription [,su:per'skrypszyn]
s. napis u góry; nadpis; adres;
napis

supersede [sju:per'si:d] v.
zastąpić; wypierać;
zajmować miejsce

supersonic [,su:per'sonyk] adj.
ultradźwiękowy;
ponaddźwiękowy

superstition [su:per'styszyn] s.
zabobon; przesądy

supervise ['su:perwajz] v.
nadzorować; doglądać

supervisor ['su:perwajzer] s.
inspektor; nadzorca

supper ['saper] s. wieczerza;
kolacja

supple ['sapl] adj. giętki; gibki;
v. stawać się gibkim

supplement ['saplyment] s.
dodatek; uzupełnienie; v.
uzupełniać

supplementary [,saply'mentery]
adj. dodatkowy; uzupełniający

supplication [,saply'kejszyn] s.
błaganie; prośba

supplier [se'plajer] s. dostawca

supply [se'plaj] s. zapas;
aprowizacja; zaopatrzenie;
dostarczenie; dostawy;
kredyty; podaż; dopływ;
zasilanie; v. dostarczać;
zaopatrywać; zaradzić;
zastępować

support [se'po:rt] s. utrzymanie;
podtrzymanie; podpora;
poparcie; pomoc; wspornik;
dźwigar; rama; łożysko;
podłoże; ostoja; v.
podtrzymywać; utrzymywać;
podpierać; popierać;
wytrzymywać; znosić;
tolerować

suppose [se'pouz] v.
przypuszczać; zakładać;
sądzić

supposed [se'pouzd] adj.
domniemany; przypuszczalny;
rzekomy

supposedly [se'pouzdly] adv.
rzekomo; przypuszczalnie

supposition [sape'zyszyn] s.
przypuszczenie; domniemanie

suppress [se'pres] v. tłumić;
zgniatać; znosić;
zatrzymywać (krwawienie);
usuwać; taić

suppression [se'preszyn] s.
stłumienie; zgniecenie;

zniesienie; usunięcie;
przemilczenie; zatajenie

suppurate ['sapjurejt] v. ropieć

supremacy [se'premesy] s.
zwierzchnictwo; przewaga;
najwyższa władza; supremacja

supreme [se'pri:m] adj.
najwyższy; doskonały;
ostateczny

surcharge [se:r'cza:rdż] s.
nadpłata; nadmierny ciężar;
dodatkowy ciężar; opłata
(karna); przeładowanie; v.
ściągać opłatę podatkową;
nakładać grzywnę;
przeładować; przedrukować
(znaczek)

sure [szuer] adj. pewny;
niezawodny; niemylny;
bezpieczny; exp.: na pewno!;
zgadza się!; adv. z
pewnością; pewnie; na
pewno; niezawodnie;
niechybnie

sure enough ['szuer,y'naf] adv.
faktycznie

surely ['szuerly] adv. pewnie; z
pewnością

surety ['szuerty] s. ręczyciel;
gwarancja; zabezpieczenie;
kaucja; pewność

surf [se:rf] s. (łamiące się) fale
przybrzeżne

surface ['se:rfys] s.
powierzchnia; v. wypływać
na powierzchnię; wykańczać
powierzchnię

surfboard ['se:rfbo:rd] s.
pojedyncza deska; narta
wodna; v. jeździć na desce
na falach ku brzegowi

surf-riding ['se:rf,rajdyng] s.
zjeżdżanie z fal ku brzegowi

surge [se:rdż] s. gwałtowny
impuls; fala uskokowa;
falowanie; fala; v. nagle
wzbierać; drgać; popuścić;
kołysać; huśtać;
ześlizgiwać się

surgeon ['se:rdżen] s. chirurg

surgery ['se:rdżery] s. chirurgia;
operacja; sala operacyjna

surgical ['se:rdżykel] adj.

chirurgiczny
surly ['se:rly] adj. grubiański;
zgryźliwy
surmise ['se:rmajz] s. domysł; v.
domyślać się czegoś
surmount [ser'maunt] v.
pokonywać; wychodzić na
(górą); przechodzić przez;
pokrywać; wznosić się
surmounted by [ser'mauntyd baj]
adj. pokonany przez
surname ['se:rnejm] s. nazwisko;
przydomek; [se:r'nejm] v.
przezywać; nadawać
przydomek
surpass [se:r'paes] v.
przewyższać; przechodzić
(oczekiwania)
surpassing [se:r'paesyng] adj.
nieprześcigniony;
niezrównany
surplus ['se:rplas] s. nadwyżka;
nadmiar; superata; nadwyżka
produkcyjna; wartość
dodatkowa; adj. stanowiący
nadwyżką; nadwyżkowy;
zbywający
surprise [ser'prajz] s.
niespodzianka; zaskoczenie;
zdziwienie; v. zaskoczyć;
zdziwić; zmuszać; złapać na
gorącym uczynku; adj.
nieoczekiwany;
niespodziewany
surprised [ser'prajzd] adj.
zaskoczony; złapany na
gorącym uczynku
surrender [se'render] s. poddanie
się; wyrzeczenie się; v.
poddawać się; oddawać się;
wyrzekać się czegoś
surround [se'raund] v. otaczać;
okrążać
surroundings [se'raundyngs] pl.
otoczenie
survey [se:r'wej] s. przegląd;
oględziny; inspekcja; pomiary;
plan (topograficzny); opis;
ankieta; statystyka; v.
przeglądać; robić pomiary;
wymierzać; oglądać
surveying [se:r'wejyng] s.
miernictwo

surveyor [se:r'wejer] s.
mierniczy; inspektor celny
survival [ser'wajwel] s.
przeżycie; przeżytek
survive [ser'wajw] v. przeżyć;
dalej żyć
survivor [ser'wajwer] s. człowiek
pozostały przy życiu
susceptible [se'septybl] adj.
wrażliwy; drażliwy; podatny;
dopuszczający
suspect [ses'pekt] v.
podejrzewać kogoś; s. adj.
['saspekt] podejrzany
suspected [ses'pektyd] adj.
podejrzany
suspend [ses'pend] v. zawiesić;
powstrzymać (się chwilowo)
suspended [ses'pendyd] adj.
zawieszony w czynnościach
suspenders [ses'penders] pl.
podwiązki; szelki
suspense [ses'pens] s.
niepewność; zawieszenie;
nierozstrzygnięcie
suspension [ses'penszyn] s.
zawieszenie; zawiesina;
wstrzymanie
suspension bridge [ses'penszyn,
brydż] s. wiszący most
suspicion [ses'pyszyn] s.
podejrzenie; v. podejrzewać
suspicious [ses'pyszes] adj.
podejrzany; nieufny
sustain [ses'tejn] v.
podtrzymywać; dźwigać;
cierpieć; doznawać;
ponosić; potwierdzać;
utrzymywać; uznawać
(słuszność)
sustenance ['sastynens] s.
pożywienie; utrzymanie
swab [słob] s. wycior; wacik
chłonący; ścierka na kiju;
(slang): gamoń; epolet; v.
wycierać; ścierać;
wyszorować
swab up ['słob,ap] v. wytrzeć
swagger ['słaeger] v.
paradować; dumnie chodzić;
chełpić się; pysznić się;
odstraszyć; nakłaniać
strachem

swallow ['sɫoɫou] v. połykać (np.
zniewagą); przełykać; dać
się nabrać; odwołać (słowa);
s. przełykanie; łyk; kęs;
przełyk; jaskółka

swam [sɫaem] v. zob. swim

swamp [sɫomp] s. bagno; v.
zalewać; pochłaniać;
przysłaniać; grzęznąć

swampy ['sɫompy] adj. bagnisty;
błotnisty

swan [sɫon] s. łabędź

swap [sɫop] v. zamieniać (się);
wymieniać (się); s. zamiana;
wymiana

swarm [sɫo:rm] s. mrowie;
mnóstwo; rój; v. roić (się);
wyroić; obfitować (w coś);
wspinać się; wdrapywać się

swarthy ['sɫo:rty] adj. śniady;
smagły

swathe [sɫejz] v. spowijać; s.
zawinięcie; bandaż

sway [sɫej] v. kołysać (się);
chwiać (się); zachwiać (się);
rządzić czymś; władać; s.
chwianie się; władza

swear [sɫeer; swore; sworn [sɫeer;
sɫo:r; sɫo:rn]

swear [sɫeer] v. przysięgać;
poprzysiąc

sweat [sɫet] s. poty; pot;
harówka; v. pocić się;
pracować ciężko; (slang):
harować; szwejsować;
fermentować;
wyświechtywać monety;
wydzielać (żywicą)

sweat out [sɫet,aut] v.
wypacać (się); (slang):
ciężko pracować; wyduszać
z kogoś coś; wyciągać
pieniądze szantażem;
wyciągać odpowiedzi
torturami; odsiadywać
więzienie

sweater ['sɫeter] s. sweter;
wyzyskiwacz robotników

sweatshop ['sɫet,szop] s. zakład
wyzyskujący robotników

sweatshirt ['sɫet,sze:rt] s.
koszula trykotowa

Swedish ['sɫi:dysz] adj. szwedzki

sweep; swept; swept [sɫi:p;
sɫept; sɫept]

sweep [sɫi:p] v. zamiatać;
wymiatać; zmiatać;
oczyszczać; wygrywać (np.
wszystkie medale); porywać
(słuchaczy); przewalić się
przez coś (burza, wichura,
powódź); ogarniać;
obejmować; rozciągać się;
sunąć uroczyście; ślizgać
się; śmigać; zwalać (kogoś
z nóg); ostrzeliwać; etc.; s.
zamiatanie; zdobycie;
zagarnięcie; ogołocenie;
śmieci; śmignięcie;
machnięcie; zasięg; robienie
zakrętu; etc.

sweeper ['sɫi:per] s. zamiatacz;
zamiataczka; zmiotka

sweeping ['sɫi:pyng] adj. szeroki;
wspaniały; rozległy; daleko
idący

sweepings ['sɫi:pyngs] pl. śmieci

sweepstake ['sɫi:pstejk] s.
wyścigi; loteria; nagroda
(zbiorowa) w wyścigach

sweet [sɫi:t] adj. słodki;
przyjemny; miły; rozkoszny;
dobrze osłodzony; deserowy;
melodyjny; świeży; łagodny;
zakochany

sweeten ['sɫi:tn] v. słodzić;
osładzać; stawać się
słodkim; (slang): zwiększać
stawkę; zwiększać zastaw

sweetheart ['sɫi:t-ha:rt] s.
ukochana; ukochany

sweetness ['sɫi:tnys] s. słodycz

sweet pea ['sɫi:tpi:] s. groszek
pachnący

swell; swelled; swollen [sɫel;
sɫeld; 'sɫoulen]

swell [sɫel] v. puchnąć;
wzdymać (się); nadymać
(się); wydymać (się);
rozdymać; wzbierać;
wzrastać; potęgować się; s.
wydęcie; zgrubienie;
nabrzmienie; wzbieranie;
wzburzona fala (morze);
(slang): wytworniak; gruba
ryba

swelling ['słelyŋg] s. spuchlizna; wzdęcie; obrzęk; wezbranie (rzeki)

swept [słept] v. zob. sweep

swerve [słe:rw] s. odchylenie; zboczenie; v. zbaczać; odchylać (się)

swift [słyft] adj. prędki; rączy; chyży; żywy; s. nawijak przędzy; traszka; jaszczurka; jerzyk

swiftness ['słyftnys] s. prędkość; chyżość

swim; swam; swum [słym; słaem; słam]

swim [słym] v. płynąć; przepłynąć; pływać (w wyścigach); pławić; ociekać czymś; unosić się na powierzchni; iść z prądem; kręcić się (w głowie); s. pływanie; nurt (życia); woda (do pływania); głębia; pęcherz pławny

swimmer ['słymer] s. pływak

swimming ['słymyŋg] s. pływanie

swimming pool ['słymyŋg,pu:l] s. pływalnia

swimming suit ['słymyŋg,sju:t] s. kostium kąpielowy

swindle ['słyndl] s. oszustwo; v. oszukiwać

swine [słajn] s. świnia

swing; swung; swung [słyŋg; słaŋg; słaŋg]

swing [słyŋg] v. huśtać (się); kołysać (się); wahać (się); bujać (się); machać; wywijać; przerzucać (się) na coś; porywać (za sobą); pociągać (za sobą); s. huśtanie (się); kołysanie (się); ruch wahadłowy; zmiana pracy; objazd (terenu); rytm; przerzucanie się; kołyszący chód; taniec (swing)

swing bridge ['słyŋg,brydż] s. most wahadłowy

swing door ['słyŋg,do:r] s. drzwi wahadłowe

swing wheel ['słyŋg,hłi:l] s. koło rozpędowe (zamachowe)

swipe [słajp] s. uderzenie; cios z

rozmachu; v. walić z rozmachem; slang: ukraść; zwędzić; porwać; walić

swirl [słe:rl] s. wir; wirowanie; skręt; lok; trąba powietrzna; kłębiący się dym; zwój (koronek); upięcie warkocza dookoła głowy; v. wirować; kręcić się; unosić się (wirując)

Swiss [słys] adj. szwajcarski

switch [słycz] s. pręt; zwrotnica; przekładnia; wyłącznik; przełącznik; kontakt; śmignięcie; v. bić prętem; machać; wyrywać; zmieniać; przełączać; włączać (np. światło); rozłączać (się); wyłączać (się)

switch off ['słycz,of] v. wyłączać

switch on ['słycz,on] v. włączać

switchboard ['słyczbo:rd] s. tablica rozdzielcza; łącznica (telefoniczna etc.)

swivel ['sływl] s. połączenie przegubowe (zawiasowe); oś; v. obracać (się) na połączeniu zawiasowym

swivel bridge ['sływl,brydż] s. most obrotowy

swivel chair ['sływl,cze:r] s. krzesło ruchome (na przygubie i na kółkach)

swollen ['słoulen] v. zob. swell; adj. opuchnięty; wzdęty; wezbrany

swoon [słu:n] v. zemdleć; omdleć; zamierać; s. omdlenie

swoop down on ['słu:p,dałn on] v. zaatakować z góry; runąć na coś

swoop up ['słu:p,ap] v. porywać; s. spadnięcie; porwanie

swop [słop] v. zamieniać; wymieniać; s. zamiana; wymiana

sword [so:rd] s. pałasz; szpada; miecz; szabla; bagnet (slang)

swordfish [so:rd'fysz'] s.

miecznik (ryba)
swordsman ['so:rdzmen] s.
szermierz
swore [sło:r] v. zob. swear
sworn [sło:rn] v. zob. swear; adj.
zaprzysiężony; przysięgły
swum [słam] v. zob. swim
swung [słang] v. zob. swing
sycamore ['sykemo:r] s. jawor;
klon; figowiec
syllable ['sylebl] s. sylaba;
zgłoska
syllabus ['sylebes] s. program
(nauki; kursu)
symbol ['symbel] s. symbol; v.
symbolizować
symbolic [,sym'bolyk] adj.
symboliczny
symbolism ['symbelyzem] s.
symbolizm
symmetric [sy'metryk] adj.
symetryczny
symmetry ['symytry] s. symetria
sympathetic [,sympe'tetyk] adj.
współczujący; życzliwy;
sympatyczny; współbrzmiący;
współczulny; łatwy do
zahipnotyzowania
sympathize ['sympetajz] v.
współczuć; mieć
zrozumienie; sympatyzować z
kimś
sympathy ['sympety] s.
współczucie; solidarność;
sympatia
symphony ['symfeny] s.
symfonia
symposium [sym'pouzjem] s.
sesja; konferencja; sympozjum
symptom ['symptem] s.
symptom; objaw
symptomatic [,sympte'maetyk]
adj. znamienny;
symptomatyczny
synagogue ['synegog] s.
bożnica; bóżnica; synagoga
synchronism ['synkre,nyzem] s.
synchronizm; równoczesność
synchronize ['synkrenajz] s.
działać równocześnie;
synchronizować; pokazywać
jednakowo (czas); uzgadniać
(zegary)

syndic ['syndyk] s. pełnomocnik;
przedstawiciel
synonym ['synenym] s. synonim
synod ['syned] s. synod
synonymous [sy'nonymes] adj.
równoznaczny z czymś
synopsis [sy'nopsys] s.
streszczenie
syntax ['syntaeks] s. składnia
synthesis ['syntysys] s. synteza
syntheses ['syntysi:z] pl. syntezy
synthetic [syn'tetyk] adj.
sztuczny; syntetyczny
synthesize ['synty,sajz] v.
wyciągać syntezę
synthetize ['synty,tajz] v.
wyciągać syntezę
syphilis ['syfylys] s. kiła; syfilis
syphon ['sajfn] s. syfon
syringe ['syryndż] s. strzykawka;
v. strzykać (wodą)
syrup ['syrep] s. syrop
system ['systym] s. system;
układ; metoda; sieć
(kolejowa); organizm
(człowieka); formacja; ustrój
systematic [,systy'maetyk] adj.
systematyczny
systematize ['systyme,tajz] v.
systematyzować
systemic [sys'temyk] adj.
układowy
systole ['systely] s. normalny
rytmiczny skurcz serca
systolic [sys'tolyk] adj.
skurczowy

T

t [ti:] dwudziesta litera alfabetu
angielskiego
tab [taeb] s. patka; wieszak
(przyszyty); język (buta);
naszywka; języczek; ucho;
przywieszka; rachunek;
kontrola; pilnowanie; v.
prowadzić ewidencję;
tabelować; zaopatrywać w

table 616 taint

(języczek lub ucho etc.)
table ['tejbl] s. stół; stolik;
tablica; tabela; tabliczka (np.
mnożenia); płyta; płaskowyż;
blat; v. kłaść na stole;
odraczać (na długo);
wciągać na agendę; adj.
stołowy
tablecloth ['tejbl,kloş] s. obrus
tableland ['tejbl-laend] s.
płaskowyż
tablespoon ['tejbl-spu:n] s. łyżka
stołowa (do zupy)
tablespoonful ['tejblspu:nful] s.
pełna łyżka (pół uncji)
tablet ['taeblyt] s. tabletka;
tabliczka (do pisania)
tabloid ['taeb'loid] s. gazeta,
zwykle małego wymiaru,
zawierająca krótkie
ilustrowane, często
sensacyjne, wiadomości
bieżące (przeważnie w
skrócie); gazeta brukowa,
sensacyjna, często płacąca
wysokie wynagrodzenia za
rewelacje skandaliczne; adj.
ściśnięty; prasowany
tabloid journalism ['taeb'loid
'dźe:rne,lysem] s.
wiadomości dziennikarskie
podawane w skrócie;
polowanie na rewelacje
skandaliczne dotyczące
zwykle znanych osobistości
taboo [te'bu:] s. tabu; v.
zakazywać; adj. zakazany
tacit ['taesyt] adj. milczący;
cichy; niemy
taciturn ['taesyte:rn] adj.
małomówny
tack [taek] s. gwóźdź
tapicerski;
papiak; pluskiewka; fastryga;
kurs (polityki); taktyka; stan
lepki; prowiant; żywność;
jedzenie; v. przyczepiać;
przybijać (lekko);
fastrygować; zmieniać kurs;
lawirować; hałasować
tackle ['taekl] s. zestaw
przyborów (do łowienia,
golenia); wielokrążek;

takielunek; złapanie i
trzymanie; v. zewrzeć się;
borykać (się); złapać i
trzymać; zmagać (się); brać
się do czegoś (ostro);
umocowywać; porać (się)
tacky ['taeky] adj. lepki;
niemodny; marny
tact [taekt] s. takt; wyczucie;
dotyk
tactful ['taektful] adj. taktowny
tactics ['taektyks] pl. taktyka
tactile ['taektajl] adj. dotykowy;
dotykalny
tactless ['taektlys] adj.
nietaktowny
tad [taed] s. berbeć
tadpole ['taedpoul] s. kijanka
tag [taeg] s. skuwka; etykieta;
kartka; strzęp; przywieszka;
znaczek tożsamości; marka;
mandat karny (pisany); ucho;
igliczka; wieszadło (przyszyte);
błyszczka; dodatek; morał;
frazes; banał; cytat; refren;
ogon; zabawa w gonionego; v.
przyczepiać: skuwkę, kartkę,
znaczek, markę, ucho,
wieszadło, igliczkę, ogon;
dawać: mandat karny, morał;
bawić się w gonionego;
tańczyć odbijanego;
wymierzać wyrok;
przeznaczać; włóczyć się za
kimś; dołączyć do czegoś
tail [tejl] s. ogon; tył; koniec;
tren; poła; pośladki;
buńczuk; warkocz; świta;
cień (chodzący za kimś); v.
dodawać ogon; obrywać
ogonki; śledzić (krok w
krok); zamykać pochód
tailcoat ['tejl,kout] s. frak
taillight ['tejl,lajt] s. tylne
światło (wozu)
tailor ['tejler] s. krawiec; v. szyć
odzież
tailor-made ['tejlermejd] adj.
uszyty na zamówienie
tail wind ['tejlłynd] s. wiatr w
plecy
taint [tejnt] s. skaza; zaraza;
plama; v. plamić; kazić;

zepsuć; plugawić
taintless ['tejntlys] adj. bez skazy
take; took; taken [tejk; tuk; 'tejkn]
take [tejk] s. brać; wziąć; łapać;chwytać; zdobywać (twierdzą); zajmować (miejsce); rezerwować; zażywać; pić; jeść; odczuwać; rozumieć; pojechać; notować; zrobić (zdjęcie); zadać sobie (trud); dostawać (napadu); przyjmować (radę, karę etc.); mierzyć swoją temperaturę; godzić się (na traktowanie); nabierać (połysku); iść (za przykładem); s. połów; zdjęcie; wpływy (do kasy)
take along [,tejke'long] v. zabrać ze sobą
take down ['tejk,dałn] v. zdejmować; rozmontowywać
take-in ['tejk'yn] s. oszukanie; naciąganie
take off ['tejk,of] v. rozbierać; kasować; małpować; wystartować; odjąć; usunąć
takeoff ['tejkof] s. start; skok; skocznia; karykatura; parodia; naśladowanie; odbicie; lista materiałów
take out ['tejk,aut] v. podejmować (poza domem); wyprowadzać; wynieść; wyrywać; wykupić; odjąć; oddzielić
takeover ['tejkouwer] s. opanowanie firmy przez manipulacje giełdowe lub finansowe
take over ['tejk,ouwer] v. przejmować (firmę); przyjmować (obowiązki); dominować
take up ['tejk,ap] v. ponosić; wchłonąć; wziąć (miejsce); zacząć (uczyć się); zadawać się; brać; ścieśniać; besztać
taken ['tejkn] v. zob. take; adj. zabrany; porwany; zdobyty;

nabrany; oszukany
talc [taelk] s. talk; v. posypywać talkiem
tale [tejl] s. opowiadanie; plotka; wymysł
talent ['taelent] s. talent (do czegoś); dar; uzdolnienie
talk [to:k] v. mówić; rozmawiać; plotkować; namawiać; s. rozmowa; dyskusja; pogadanka; plotka; gadanie; mowa
talkative ['to:ketyw] adj. rozmowny; gadatliwy
talk-to ['to:k,tu] s. bura
tall [to:l] adj. wysoki; (slang): nieprawdopodobny
tall talk ['to:l,to:k] s. przechwałki
tallow ['taelou] s. łój; v. tuczyć; smarować łojem
talon ['taelen] s. szpon; pazur; rygiel; łapa ludzka; palec
tame [tejm] v. oswajać; poskramiać; ujarzmić; okiełznać; łagodzić; przytłumić; upokorzyć
tamper ['taemper] s. ubijak; v. majstrować; manipulować; zmieniać coś nielegalnie
tan [taen] s. opalenizna; kolor (brązowy) brunatny; kora garbarska; v. garbować; opalać się (na słońcu); brązowieć; wyłoić komuś skórę
tangent ['taendżent] adj. styczny; s. styczna; szczegół oderwany; zmiana tematu (od rzeczy); zmiana kierunku rozmowy
tangerine [taendże'ri:n] s. mandarynka
tangle ['taengl] s. plątanina; v. plątać (się); wikłać (się); (slang): pobić się z kimś
tank [taenk] s. tank; zbiornik; cysterna; czołg; (slang): więzienie; v. nabierać do zbiornika; (slang): popić sobie
tankard ['taenkerd] s. kufel
tanner ['taener] s. garbarz
tantalize ['taentelajz] v. dręczyć (zwodną) nadzieją; łudzić

tantrum ['taentrem] s. napad
złości

tap [taep] v. stukać;
odszpuntować; napoczynać;
robić punkcje; naciąć;
ciągnąć sok;
wykorzystywać; gwintować;
podsłuchiwać (telefon); s.
czop; szpunt; kurek; zawór;
gwintownik; zaczep; odczep

tape [tejp] s. taśma; tasiemka;
tasiemiec; (slang): wódka; v.
wiązać taśmą (przylepcem);
mierzyć; (slang): oceniać
kogoś

tape measure ['tejp,meżer] s.
miara na taśmie (krawiecka)

taper ['tejper] s. stopniowe
zwężanie (się); stożek;
ubytek; osłabianie; stoczek;
świeczka

taper off ['tejper,of] v. zwężać
się stopniowo; cichnąć
stopniowo; kończyć się
spiczasto

tape recorder ['tejp-ry,ko:rder] s.
magnetofon

tape recording ['tejp-ry,ko:rdyng]
s. nagranie na taśmę

tapestry ['taepystry] s. gobelin;
arras; v. zdobić gobelinami

tapeworm ['tejpłe:rm] s. soliter;
tasiemiec

tar [ta:r] s. smoła; dziegieć; ter;
v. smołować; terować

target ['ta:rgyt] s. cel; obiekt;
tarcza strzelnicza; v.
kierować do celu; celować;
ustalać cel

tariff ['taeryf] s. cło; taryfa;
cennik; v. clić wg taryfy;
układać taryfę celną

tarnish ['ta:rnysz] v. matowieć;
przyćmiewać; brudzić (się);
brukać (się); tracić połysk; s.
matowienie; skaza

tart ['ta:rt] adj. cierpki;
zgryźliwy; s. ciastko
owocowe; (slang): kurewka

tartan ['ta:rten] s. materiał w
kratę szkocką

task ['taesk] s. zadanie
(specjalne); lekcja zadana;

przedsięwzięcie; v.
wyznaczać zadanie;
wystawiać na próbę; rugać

task force ['taesk,fo:rs] s. oddział do specjalnego zadania

taskmaster ['taesk,ma:ster] s.
nadzorca (kontrolujący
wykonanie zadania)

tassel ['taesel] s. kutas; kitka; v.
ozdabiać kutasami, kitkami

taste [tejst] s. smak; gust;
posmak; zamiłowanie; v.
smakować; kosztować;
czuć smak; mieć smak;
doznawać (czegoś)

tasteful ['tejstful] adj. gustowny;
w dobrym smaku

tasteless ['tejstlys] adj. bez
gustu; bez smaku

tasty ['tejsty] adj. smakowity;
smaczny

ta-ta [tae'-ta:] exp. do widzenia;
pa! pa!

tattoo [te'tu:] v. bębnić
palcami; tatuować; s.
capstrzyk; tatuaż

taught [to:t] v. zob. teach

taunt [to:nt] v. urągać;
wymyślać komuś;
zwymyślać kogoś; s.
urąganie; wymyślanie; adj.
wysoki (np. maszt)

taut [to:t] adj. napięty;
naprężony; w dobrej formie;
w dobrym stanie

tax [taeks] s. podatek; wysiłek;
ciężar; obciążenie; v.
opodatkować; obarczać;
obciążać; nadwerężać;
sprawdzać; wymagać
wysiłku; zarzucać coś

taxation [taek'sejszyn] s.
opodatkowanie

tax collector ['taekske,lekter] s.
poborca podatkowy

taxi ['taeksy] s. taksówka; v.
jechać taksówką; wieźć
taksówką

taxi driver ['taeksydrajwer] s.
taksówkarz

taximeter ['taeksy,mi:ter] s.
licznik (w taksówce);
taksometr

taxpayer ['taeks,pejer] s.
podatnik
tax return ['taeks,ry'te:rn] s.
podatek (zapłata ze
sprawozdaniem)
tea [ti:] s. herbata; herbatka;
podwieczorek; v. pić i
częstować herbatą
tea-bag ['ti:baeg] s. woreczek
papierowy z herbatą
teach; taught; taught [ti:cz; to:t;
to:t]
teach [ti:cz] v. uczyć; nauczać;
wykładać
teacher ['ti:czer] s. nauczyciel
teacup ['ti:kap] s. filiżanka na
herbatę
teakettle ['ti:,ketl] s. imbryk;
czajnik
team [ti:m] s. zespół; drużyna;
zaprząg; v. zaprzęgać;
jeździć zaprzęgiem
team up ['ti:map] v. łączyć się
razem (do pracy etc.)
teamwork ['ti:młe:rk] s. praca
zespołowa
teapot ['ti:pot] s. mały czajnik
tear; tore; torn [teer; to:r; to:rn]
tear [teer] v. drzeć; targać;
rwać; kaleczyć; wydrzeć
(ranę); pędzić; s. dziura;
rozdarcie; wybuch pasji;
kropla; łza; (slang): hulanka
tea-room ['ti:ru:m]s. herbaciarnia
tease [ti:z] v. drażnić; nudzić;
s. dokuczanie; nudziarstwo
teat [tyt] s. cycek (wulg.:
kobiecy)
technical ['teknykel] adj.
techniczny; formalny;
spekulacyjny
technician [tek'nyszyn] s.
technik
technique [tek'ni:k] s. technika
malowania, rzeźby etc.
tedious ['ti:dies] adj. nudny
teem [ti:m] v. roić się;
obfitować; opróżniać;
wylewać
teen [ti:n] s. szkoda; zgryzota
teenager ['ti:,nejdżer] s.
nastolatek; nastolatka
teens [ti:nz] pl. wiek 12 do 18

lat
teeny ['ti:ny] adj. maleńki
teeth [ti:s] pl. zęby; zob. tooth
teethe [ti:z] v. ząbkować
teetotaler [ti:'toutler] s.
abstynent
telegram ['telygraem] s. telegram
telegraph ['telygra:f] s. telegraf
telephone ['telyfoun] s. telefon;
v. telefonować
telephone booth ['telyfoun,bu:s]
s. kabina telefoniczna
telephone call ['telyfoun,ko:l] s.
rozmowa telefoniczna
telephone directory
['telyfoundy,rektory] s.
książka telefoniczna
telephone exchange ['telyfoun
-eks,czejndż] s. centrala
telefoniczna na zagranicę
telephone kiosk ['telyfoun-kiosk]
s. kiosk telefoniczny
teleprinter ['tely,prynter] s.
dalekopis
telescope ['telyskoup] s.
teleskop
teletypewriter [,tely'tajprajter] s.
dalekopis
televise ['telywajz] v. nadawać
przez telewizję
television ['telywyżyn] s.
telewizja
television set ['telywyżyn,set] s.
telewizor; odbiornik
telewizyjny
televisor ['telywajzer] s.
telewizor
tell; told; told [tel; tould; tould]
tell [tel] v. (o kimś; o czymś):
mówić; opowiadać;
powiedzieć; wskazywać;
pokazywać; kazać; poznać;
sprawdzić; policzyć;
poznawać; wiedzieć;
donieść; oskarżyć;
skarżyć; mieć znaczenie;
odbijać się na kimś;
odróżniać
teller ['teler] s. narrator; kasjer;
liczący głosy
telltale ['teltejl] s. plotkarz;
okoliczność ostrzegawcza;
wskaźnik odchylenia (steru);

aparat sprawdzający,
ostrzegawczy; adj.
ostrzegawczy; wymowny
temper ['temper] s.
usposobienie; humor; gniew;
złość; domieszka;
mieszanka; stan;
hartowność; v. łagodzić;
hartować
temperament ['temprement] s.
temperament; usposobienie;
skala temperowana;
temperatura skali
temperance ['temperens] s.
umiarkowanie;
powściągliwość;
abstynencja;
wstrzemięźliwość
temperate ['temperyt] adj.
umiarkowany; powściągliwy;
wstrzemięźliwy
temperature ['tempereczer] s.
temperatura; ciepłota
tempest ['tempyst] s. burza; v.
zaburzać
tempestuous [tem'pestjues] adj.
burzliwy
temple ['templ] s. świątynia;
skroń; ucho od okularów;
rozciągacz tkacki
temporal ['temperel] adj.
doczesny; czasowy;
skroniowy; s. kość
skroniowa
temporary ['temperery] adj.
chwilowy; tymczasowy
tempt [tempt] v. kusić; nęcić
temptation [temp'tejszyn] s.
pokusa; kuszenie
tempting ['temptyng] adj.
ponętny; nęcący; kuszący
ten [ten] num. dziesięć; s.
dziesiątka
tenacious [ty'nejszes] adj.
wytrwały; nieustępliwy;
trwały; wierny; czepny;
ciągliwy; mocny; spoisty
tenant ['tenent] s. lokator;
dzierżawca; v. zamieszkiwać;
dzierżawić
tend [tend] v. skłaniać się;
zmierzać; służyć; doglądać;
obsługiwać

tendency ['tendensy] s.
skłonność; tendencja
tender ['tender] adj. delikatny;
miękki; kruchy; wrażliwy;
czuły; niedojrzały; młody;
młodociany; uważający;
dbały; łamliwy; drażliwy;
wywrotny; v. oferować;
przedłożyć; założyć; s.
oferta; środek płatniczy;
dozorca; tender; statek
pomocniczy-zaopatrzeniowy
tenderloin ['tenderloin] s.
polędwica
tenderness ['tendernyss] s.
czułość; dbałość;
delikatność
tendon ['tenden] s. ścięgno
tendril ['tendryl] s. wąs; wić
tenement house
['tenyment,haus]
s. dom czynszowy
tennis ['tenys] s. tenis
tennis court ['tenys'ko:rt] s. kort
tenisowy
tense [tens] s. czas (np.
przyszły); adj. naprężony;
napięty
tension ['tenszyn] s. naprężenie;
napięcie; prężność
tent [tent] s. namiot
tentacle ['tentekl] s. macka;
czułek
tenth [teng] adj. dziesiąty
tenthly ['tengly] adv. po
dziesiąte
tepee ['ti:pi:] s. namiot indiański
(stożkowy)
tepid ['tepyd] adj. letni;
ciepławy; bez zapału
term [te:rm] s. okres; czas
trwania; przeciąg; semestr;
kadencja; termin; wyrażenie;
określenie; kres; v.
określać; nazywać
terms [te:rms] pl. warunki
(kontraktu, porozumienia);
stosunki wzajemne
terminal ['te:rmynel] adj.
końcowy; terminowy;
ostateczny; s. zakończenie;
końcówka; uchwyt;
końcowa stacja

terminate ['te:rmynejt] v.
skończyć; zakończyć;
kończyć (się); ograniczać;
upływać; rozwiązywać
(umowę); ustawać;
wygasać; wymawiać pracę

termination [,te:rmy'nejszyn] s.
koniec; wypowiedzenie
(pracy); wygaśnięcie;
zakończenie; końcówka

terminus ['te:rmynes] s.
końcowa
stacja; kres; koniec; granica

termite ['te:rmajt] s. termit

terrace ['teres] s. taras; terasa;
ulica wzdłuż zbocza; v. robić
terasy

terraced ['terest] adj.
uformowany w terasy

terrible ['terybl] adj. straszliwy;
straszny; okropny

terrific [te'ryfyk] adj.
przerażający; (slang):
fantastyczny; pierwszej klasy

terrify ['teryfaj] v. przerażać

territorial [,tery'torjel] adj.
terytorialny

territory ['teryto:ry] s. obszar;
rejon; terytorium bez praw
stanu (np. w USA)

terror ['terer] s. terror;
przerażenie; postrach

terrorize ['tereraiz] v. siać
strach; przerażać;
terroryzować

terse [te:rs] adj. zwięzły;
dosadny

test [test] s. próba; sprawdzian;
test; egzamin; odczynnik;
skorupa; v. sprawdzać;
poddawać próbie;
oczyszczać (metal)

testament ['testement] s.
testament

testify ['testyfaj] v. świadczyć;
dawać świadectwo;
zaświadczać; poświadczać

testimonial [,testy'mounjel] s.
świadectwo (moralności);
polecenie; nagroda w uznaniu
zasług

testimony ['testymouny] s.
świadectwo

testy ['testy] adj. drażliwy;
popędliwy; pobudliwy

tetanus ['tetenes] s. tężec

text [tekst] s. tekst

textbook ['tekstbuk] s.
podręcznik

textile ['tekstail] s. tkanina; adj.
tkacki; tekstylny

texture ['teksczer] s. budowa;
tkanina; struktura; tkanie

than [dzaen] conj. aniżeli; niż;
od

thank [taenk] v. dziękować; s.
podziękowanie; dzięki

thank you ['taenkju:] exp.:
dziękuję

thank you very much
['taenkju:'wery,macz] exp.:
bardzo dziękuję

thankful ['taenkful] adj.
wdzięczny; dziękczynny

thankless ['taenklys] adj.
niewdzięczny

thanks ['taenks] pl.
podziękowanie; dzięki

Thanksgiving Day
['taenksgywyng,dej] s. dzień
święta dziękczynienia (USA)

that [daet] adj. & pron. pl. those
[dzous]; tamten; tamta;
tamto; ten; ta; to; ów; owa;
owo; pl. tamci; tamte; ci; te;
owi; owe; adv. tylu; tyle; conj.
że; żeby; aby; skoro

thatch [taecz] s. strzecha; v.
pokrywać strzechą

thaw [to:] s. odwilż;
rozkrochmalenie się; v. tajać;
odtajać; taje; jest odwilż

the [przed samogłoską dy; przed
spółgłoską de:; z naciskiem
dy:] przyimek określony
rzadko kiedy tłumaczony; ten;
ta; to; pl. ci; te; ten właśnie
etc.; adv. tym; im ... tym

theater ['tieter] s. teatr; kino;
widownia; amfiteatr

theatrical [ti:'aetrykel] adj.
teatralny; sceniczny; aktorski

theatricals [ti:'aetrykels] pl.
przedstawienie (amatorskie)

theatrics [ti:'aetryks] s. sztuka
teatralna

thee [ḏi:] archaiczna forma ty,
używana przez kwakrów
theft [teft] s. kradzież
their [ḏzeer] zaimek: ich
theirs [ḏzeers] zaimek
dzierżawczy: ich
them [ḏzem] przypadek zależny
od they (np.: im, nimi, nich)
theme [ṯi:m] s. temat; zadanie;
wypracowanie
themselves [ḏzem'selwz] pl. oni
sami; one same
then [ḏzen] adv. wtedy;
wówczas; po czym; potem;
następnie; później; zatem;
zaraz; poza tym; ponadto;
conj. a więc; no to; wobec
tego; ale przecież; adj.
ówczesny; s. przedtem;
uprzednio; dotąd; odtąd
theologian [ṯie'loudżjen] s.
teolog
theology [ṯi:'oledży] s. teologia
theoretical [ṯie'retykel] adj.
teoretyczny
theory [ṯiery] s. teoria
therapy [ṯerepy] s. leczenie;
terapia
there [ḏzeer] adv. tam; w tym;
co
do tego; oto; właśnie; potem;
tędy; dlatego; z tego; na to; s.
ta miejscowość; to miasto;
to miejsce
thereabout ['ḏzeerebaut] adv. w
tych stronach; gdzieś tam
mniej więcej; coś około tego
thereafter ['ḏzeera:fter] adv.
później; odtąd
there are [ḏzeer'a:r] exp.: są
thereby ['ḏzeer'baj] adv. przez
to; w ten sposób; skutkiem
tego
therefore ['ḏzeer,fo:r] adv.
dlatego; zatem więc
therein [,ḏzeer'yn] adv. w tym;
w nim; w niej
there is [,ḏzeer'ys] exp.: jest
thereupon ['ḏzeer,e'pon] adv.
skutkiem tego
therewith [,ḏzeer'łys] adv. tym; z
tym; w następstwie tego
there you are [,ḏzeer'ju:,a:r]

exp.: proszę; tu jest to!; tu
pan to ma! etc.
thermometer [ter'momyter] s.
termometr
thermos ['termos] s. termos
these [ḏi:z] pl. od this
thesis ['ṯi:sys] s. teza; praca
dyplomowa; pl. theses ['ṯi:si:z]
they [ḏzej] pl. pron. oni; one (ci;
którzy)
they say [ḏzej sej] exp.: podobno
(mówią)
thick [tyk] adj. gruby; gęsty;
zbity; rzęsisty; stłumiony;
niewyraźny; mętny; ponury;
tępy; ochrypły; (slang): blatny;
spoufalony; s. gruba część;
dureń; głuptas; adv. gęsto;
grubo; ochryple; tępo
thicken ['tykn] v. pogrubiać
(się); zagęszczać (się)
thicket ['tykyt] s. gąszcz;
gęstwina
thickness ['tyknys] s. grubość;
warstwa; gęstość
thief [ṯi:f] s. złodziej; pl. thieves
[ṯi:ws]
thigh [taj] s. udo
thimble ['tymbl] s. naparstek;
końcówka (metalowa liny)
thimbleful ['tymblful] s. odrobina,
naparstek
thin [tyn] adj. cienki (sos, głos
etc.); rzadki; szczupły; słaby
(kolor etc.); (slang): paskudny;
v. rozcieńczać; szczupleć;
przerzedzać (się)
thine [tajn] zob. thy; stara forma:
twój; twoje
thing [tyng] s. rzecz; przedmiot;
uczynek; coś; krzyk mody;
warunek; urojenia;
przywidzenia; pl. zwierzęta;
rzeczy; odzież; ubrania;
ruchomości; sytuacja;
koniunktura; wszystko;
nieruchomości; głupstwa
think [tynk] thought; thought [tynk]
'to:t; 'to:t]
think [tynk] v. myśleć;
pomyśleć; zastanawiać się;
rozważać; rozmyślać (się);
wymyślić; wyobrażać

sobie; uważać za; mieć
zdanie; mieć za; zapomnieć
(rozmyślnie); mieć na myśli;
rozwiązywać; etc.
think over ['tynk'ouwer] v.
przemyśliwać; zastanawiać
się
think up ['tynk,ap] v.
wymyślać; wykombinować;
rozwiązać
third [te:rd] adj. trzeci
third degree [,te:rd dy'gri:] exp.:
trzeci stopień
(przesłuchiwania na policji -
głupi, przykry i męczący)
thirdly ['te:rdly] adv. po trzecie
third party [,te:rd'pa:rty] s.
strona trzecia; osoby trzecie
third-rate ['te:rd'rejt] adj.
trzeciorzędny
Third World ['te:rd'łe:rld] s.
trzeci świat (poza Europą,
Chinami, Indią oraz Ameryką)
thirst ['te:rst] s. pragnienie;
żądza; v. pragnąć
thirsty ['te:rsty] adj. spragniony;
żądny; suchy; wyschnięty;
(slang): ciężki
this [tys] adj. & pron. pl. these
[ti:z] ten; ta; to; tak; w ten
sposób; tyle; obecny; bieżący;
adv. tak; tak daleko; tyle; tak
dużo
thistle ['tysl] s. oset
thorn ['to:rn] s. kolec; cierń;
krzak cierniowy; v. kłuć;
drażnić
thorny ['to:rny] adj. kolczasty;
ciernisty; drażliwy
thorough ['terou] adj. dokładny;
zupełny; całkowity; sumienny;
adv. na wskroś; na wylot
thoroughbred ['te:rou,bred] adj.
rasowy; czystej krwi; s. koń
rasowy
thoroughfare ['te:rou,feer] s.
arteria komunikacyjna;
przejazd; ulica
thoroughly ['te:rouly] adv.
zupełnie; dokładnie;
całkowicie; na wskroś;
sumiennie; gruntownie
those [douz] pl. od that

thou [dau] biblijne: ty
though [tou] conj. chociaż;
choćby; gdyby; adv. jednak;
pomimo tego; przecież
thought [to:t] v. zob. think; s.
myśl; namysł; zastanowienie
się; pomysł; oczekiwanie;
rozwaga; zamiar; pl. zdanie;
pogląd; odrobina; troszkę
thoughtful ['to:tful] adj.
zamyślony; zadumany;
rozważny; uważający; dbały;
uprzejmy; (oryginalnie)
myślący
thoughtless ['to:tlys] adj.
bezmyślny; nieuważający;
nierozważny
thousand ['tauzend] num. tysiąc
thousandth ['tauzendt] adj.
tysięczny
thrash [traesz] s. młócić; walić;
bić; prać; dyskutować; s.
młócenie; walenie
thrashing [traeszyng] s. młocka;
lanie
thread [tred] s. nić; nitka;
przędza; sznurek; wątek;
żyłka; krok (śruby); zwojnik
(nici); gwint; v. nawlekać
(igłą); przetykać; nacinać
gwint (zwojnik); przepychać
się
threadbare [tredbeer] adj.
wytarty; wyświechtany;
wyszarzały
threat [tret] s. groźba; pogróżka
threaten ['tretn] v. grozić;
zagrażać; odgrażać się
threatening ['tretnyng] adj.
grożący; zagrażający; groźny
three [tri:] num. trzy; s. trójka
threefold ['tri:fold] adj. potrójny
threescore ['tri:sko:r] num.
sześćdziesiąt
three-stage ['tri:stejdż] adj.
trójfazowy; trzystopniowy
thresh [tresz] v. młócić;
roztrząsać; obgadać
szczegółowo; omówić
gruntownie; s. młocka
thresher ['treszer] s. młockarnia
threshing ['treszyng] s. młócenie
threshing machine

['treszyng,me'szi:n] s.
młockarnia
threshold ['treszould] s. próg
threw [tru:] v. zob. throw
thrice [trajs] adv. trzykrotnie
thriftless [tryftlys] adj. rozrzutny
thrifty ['tryfty] adj. oszczędny;
rozrastający się; kwitnący
thrill [tryl] v. przejmować (się);
drgać; s. dreszcz; dreszczyk;
drganie; powieść
sensacyjna; szmer (serca)
thriller ['tryler] s. dreszczowiec;
powieść sensacyjna
(kryminalna); sztuka
sensacyjna; opowieść
sensacyjna
thrilling ['trylyng] adj.
podniecający; przejmujący;
sensacyjny
thrive; throve; thriven [trajw;
trouw; trywn]
thrive [trajw] v. dobrze: rosnąć,
chować się, rozwijać się,
miewać się; kwitnąć;
prosperować
thro [tru:] = through
throat [trout] s. gardło; szyja;
wlot; gardziel; wąskie
przejście; v. żłobić;
żłobkować; mówić gardłowo
throb [trob] v. pulsować;
drgać; bić; tętnić; rwać; s.
pulsowanie; drganie; bicie
serca; dreszcz; warkot
maszyny
thrombosis [trom'bousys] s.
skrzep
throne [troun] s. tron; v.
tronować; wprowadzać na
tron
throng [tro:ng] s. tłum; tłok;
rzesza; masa; v. tłoczyć się;
zatłaczać; napierać na
throstle [trosl] s. drozd;
przędzarka
throttle ['trotl] s. gardziel;
dławik; przepustnica; zawór
dławiący; v. dusić;
regulować dławikiem
through [tru:] prep. przez;
poprzez; po; wskroś; na
wylot; ze; z; skutkiem; na

skutek; za; dzięki; z powodu;
adv. na wskroś; na wylot;
adj. przelotowy; bezpośredni;
skończony (np. życiowo)
throughout [tru:'aut] prep.
poprzez; przez cały; od
początku do końca;
wszędzie; całkowicie; adv. na
wskroś
throve [trouw] v. zob. thrive
throw; threw; thrown [trou; tru:;
troun]
throw [trou] v. rzucać; ciskać;
zarzucać; zrzucać; skręcać;
powalić; narzucać;
modelować na kole;
odrzucać; marnować; s. rzut;
ryzyko; szal; narzuta; uskok
throw up ['trou,ap] v.
wymiotować; rzucać w
górę; podrzucać
thrown ['troun] v. zob. throw
thru [tru:] = through
thrum [tram] v. rzępolić;
bębnić; robić z nitek;
odcinać luźne nitki; s.
brzdąkanie; odcięta nitka;
krajka
thrush [trasz] s. drozd; choroba
strzałki kopyta końskiego;
pleśniawka
thrust; thrust; thrust [trast; trast;
trast]
thrust [trast] v. wpychać;
wsadzać; wtykać; wrazić;
pchać (się); przepychać się;
wysuwać (się); szturchać;
przebijać; wepchnąć;
narzucać (się); wtrącać
(się); zadawać pchnięcie;
pchnąć; s. pchnięcie;
dźgnięcie; wypad;
wypchnięcie; nacisk; siła:
napędu, ciągu, pędu; zrzut;
parcie; uwaga; przytyk
thud [tad] s. łomot; łoskot
(głuchy); v. łomotać; upadać
z łoskotem
thug [tag] s. bandyta; zbir
thumb [tam] s. kciuk; duży
palec; władza (domowa);
talent ogrodniczy; zasada
(praktyczna); v. kartkować;

brudzić palcami; niszczyć;
walać; **grać niezgrabnie;**
prosić o podwiezienie;
wyprosić (gestem)
thumb a lift [tam a lyft] v.
prosić o podwiezienie
(autostopem)
thumbtack ['tam-taek] s.
pinezka; pluskiewka
thump [tamp] s. grzmotnięcie; v.
grzmocić; walić; iść ciężko
thunder ['tander] s. grzmot;
burza; grom; piorun; v.
grzmieć; rzucać gromy;
piorunować; miotać
(groźby)
thunderstorm ['tander-sto:rm] s.
burza z piorunami
thunderstruck ['tander-strak] adj.
rażony piorunem; oszołomiony
Thursday ['te:r-zdej] s. czwartek
thus [tas] adv. tak; w ten
sposób; tak więc; a zatem
thus far ['tas,fa:r] adv. jak dotąd
thus much ['tas,macz] adv. tyle
thwart [tlo:rt] v. udaremnić;
pokrzyżować; psuć szyki;
adj. poprzeczny; przeciwny;
niepomyślny; s. poprzeczna
ławka wioślarska
thy [taj] pron. twój; twoje; zob.
thine
tick [tyk] s. kleszcz; tykanie;
moment; wsyp; kredyt;
sprawne działanie; v. tykać;
kupować na kredyt;
sprzedawać na kredyt;
(slang): ustalać sprawne
działanie
tick away ['tyke'lej] v. znaczyć
tykaniem
tick off ['tykof] v. odliczać;
besztać; odfajkować
ticker ['tyker] s. telegraf;
zegarek; serce (slang)
ticket ['tykyt] s. bilet; kwit;
znaczek; wywieszka; lista
kandydatów (USA); v.
zaopatrywać w bilet,
etykietką; umieszczać na
liście kandydatów
ticket office ['tykyt'ofys] s. kasa
biletowa

tickle ['tykl] v. łaskotać;
łechtać; swędzić;
rozśmieszać; bawić;
cieszyć; s. łaskotanie;
łechtanie; swędzenie
tidal wave ['tajdełłejw] s.
olbrzymia fala przypływu
skutkiem trzęsienia ziemi
tide [tajd] s. przypływ i odpływ
morza; fala; okres; v.
przypływać falą; płynąć z
falą; wybrnąć
tidy ['tajdy] adj. schludny;
czysty; niemały; spory; s.
zbiornik na odpadki; pokrowiec
na mebel; v. oporządzić;
sporządzać; oporządzać
(się); porządkować
tie [taj] v. wiązać; zawiązać;
przywiązać; łączyć;
sznurować; remisować;
zawrzeć ślub; unieruchomić;
s. węzeł; krawat; podkład
kolejowy; próg; remis; sznur;
rozgrywka; półbucik
tie up ['taj,ap] v. zawiązywać;
unieruchamiać
tier [tier] s. piętro; rząd; węzeł;
zwój; kondygnacja; rzecz
wiążąca; fartuszek; v.
spiętrzać się (też warstwami)
tiger ['tajger] s. tygrys; jaguar;
kuguar; zawadiaka; pracujący
zapamiętale
tight [tajt] adj. zaciśnięty;
mocny; zwarty; szczelny;
spoisty; obcisły; wąski;
nabity; wstawiony; zalany;
skąpy; niewystarczający;
silny; mocny; uparty; adv.
zwarcie; ciasno; szczelnie;
obciśle; mocno; silnie
tighten ['tajtn] v. zaciskać (się);
uszczelniać; napinać (się)
tightfisted ['tajt-,fystyd] adj.
sknera; kutwa
tight fitting ['tajt-fytyng] adj.
obcisły; opięty
tightrope ['tajt-roup] s. lina
akrobatyczna
tights [tajts] pl. trykot baletnicy,
akrobaty etc.; w Anglii
rajstopy

tigress ['tajgrys] s. tygrysica
tile [tajl] s. dachówka; kafelek; dren; (slang): cylinder; v. pokrywać dachówkami; wykładać kaflami (płytami)
till [tyl] prep. aż do; dopiero; dotychczas; aż; dopóki nie; dotąd; v. uprawiać (ziemię); s. szufladka na pieniądze; kasa podręczna
tilt [tylt] s. przechylenie; przechył; nachylenie; natarcie kopią; plandeka; daszek; v. przechylać (się); nachylać (się); nacierać kopią; (pełnym) pędem lecieć; zaopatrywać w daszek
timber ['tymber] s. drzewo; budulec; drewno; belka; wręga; las; charakter; v. zaopatrywać w budulec; podpierać belką
timberland ['tymber'laend] s. obszar lasu budulcowego
timber-work ['tymberłe:rk] s. konstrukcja drewniana
timber yard ['tymber,ja:rd] s. skład (drzewa) budulca
time [tajm] s. czas; pora; raz; takt; v. obliczać czas zużyty; ustalać czas; wybierać czas; robić we właściwym czasie; nastawiać (przyrząd); regulować (zegar); synchronizować; harmonizować; trzymać takt; excl.: czas! (zamykać lokal etc.)
time and again ['tajm end,e'gen] exp.: ciągle; ustawicznie
time bomb ['tajm,bom] s. bomba zegarowa
timely ['tajmly] adv. na czasie; w porę; adj. aktualny; odpowiedni; właściwy; punktualny
timetable ['tajm,tejbl] s. rozkład jazdy, zajęć etc.
timeless ['tajmlys] adj. wieczny; ponadczasowy (niekończący się)
timid ['tymyd] adj. nieśmiały; bojaźliwy

timidity [ty'mydyty] s. bojaźliwość
timorous ['tymeres] adj. bojaźliwy
tin [tyn] s. cyna; blacha; puszka blaszana; blaszanka; folia cynowa; pieniądze; adj. cynowany; blaszany; dziadowski (kubek); v. cynować
tinfoil ['tynfojl] s. folia metalowa; cynfolia; staniol
tinge [tyndż] s. odcień; lekkie zabarwienie; v. zabarwiać lekko
tingle ['tyngl] s. mrowienie; świerzbienie; kłucie; v. czuć kłucie, mrowienie; kłuć
tinkle ['tynkl] v. dzwonić; brzęczeć; siusiać; s. dzwonienie
tinned [tynd] adj. cynowany
tint [tynt] s. odcień; zabarwienie; v. zabarwiać
tinware ['tynłeer] s. wyroby blaszane
tiny ['tajny] adj. drobny; malusieńki; malutki
tip [typ] s. koniec (np. palca); koniuszek; szczyt; zakończenie; skuwka; okucie; napiwek; poufna informacja; wiadomość; rada; wskazówka; trącenie; przechylenie; skład śmieci; v. wykańczać koniec; okuwać; przechylać (się); ważyć; przewracać (się); dać napiwek; informować (poufnie); trącać lekko; dotykać; uderzać ukosem (piłkę); przeważać
tip off ['typ,of] v. ostrzegać
tip-off ['typof] s. poufne ostrzeżenie; (informacja)
tipster ['typster] s. człowiek udzielający poufnych informacji (o wyścigach etc.)
tipsy ['typsy] adj. podchmielony; pijany; chwiejny; niepewny
tiptoe ['typtou] s. koniec palca u nogi; v. chodzić na palcach; adv. na palcach (u nóg)

tire ['tajer] v. męczyć (się);
nudzić (się); nakładać
obręcz, oponę; przystroić; s.
obręcz; opona; strój

tired ['tajerd] adj. zmęczony;
znużony; znudzony

tireless ['tajerlys] adj.
niestrudzony

tiresome ['tajersem] adj.
męczący; nudny

tissue ['tyszu:] s. tkanka;
tkanina; siatka; bibułka

tissue paper ['tyszu:,pejper] s.
bibułka; papier toaletowy;
papier płótnowany

tit [tyt] s. sikora

tit for tat ['tyt,fo:r'taet] exp.:
wet za wet

titbit ['tytbyt] s. smakołyk

titillate ['tytylejt] s. łechtać

title ['tajtl] s. tytuł; nagłówek;
napis; tytuł rodowy; tytuł
prawny; prawo; czystość
złota w karatach

titled ['tajtld] adj. utytułowany

titter ['tyter] v. chichotać; s.
chichot

tittle-tattle ['tytl-'taetl] v.
plotkować; s. plotkowanie

to [tu:; tu] prep. do; aż do; ku;
przy; w stosunku do; w
porównaniu z; w stosunku jak;
stosownie do; dla; wobec;
względem; za (zależnie od
ustaleń zwyczajowych)

toad [toud] s. ropucha

to and fro ['tu:end'frou] exp.:
tam i z powrotem

toast [toust] s. grzanka; toast; v.
robić grzanki; wznosić toast

tobacco [te'baekou] s. tytoń

tobacconist [te'baekenyst] s.
sprzedawca wyrobów
tytoniowych

toboggan [te'bogen] s. saneczki;
v. sankować się; spadać
(ceny)

today [te'dej] adv. dzisiaj; dziś;
s. dzień dzisiejszy

toddle ['todl] v. dreptać; drobić
nóżkami; s. drobienie
nóżkami; dreptanie; pędrak

toddler ['todler] s. pędrak;

berbeć

to-do [te'du:] s. zamieszanie;
rwetes

toe [tou] s. palec u nogi; nosek;
szpic; stopa wału (tamy);
występ z przodu; przednia
część kopyta; hacel; dno
odwiertu; v. kopnąć;
cerować palec u pończochy;
podporządkować się;
stawać na starcie; stosować
się do linii (też partyjnej);
ukośnie wbijać gwoździe;
krzywo chodzić (palcami zbyt
do wewnątrz lub na zewnątrz)

toffee ['tofi] s. karmelek

together [te'gedzer] adv. razem;
wspólnie; naraz;
równocześnie

toil [tojl] s. znój; mozół; trud; v.
mozolić się; trudzić się;
harować

toilet ['tojlyt] s. ustęp; toaleta;
ubranie; adj. toaletowy

toilet paper ['tojlyt,pejper] s.
papier toaletowy

toils [tojlz] s. sidła; matnia

token ['toukn] s. znak; dowód
autentyczności; symbol;
pamiątka; żeton; bon; adj.
symboliczny; niewiążący

told [tould] v. zob. tell

tolerable ['tolerebl] adj. znośny;
nienajgorszy; dosyć zdrowy

tolerance ['tolerens] s.
tolerancja; luz;
wyrozumiałość

tolerant ['tolerent] adj.
tolerancyjny; wyrozumiały

tolerate ['tolerejt] v. znosić;
tolerować; cierpieć

toleration [,tole'rejszyn] s.
znoszenie; tolerancja;
tolerowanie

toll [toul] s. opłata (np.
telefoniczna); myto: mostowe,
drogowe; miejski podatek;
trybut; danina; dzwonienie; v.
uiszczać opłatę;
wydzwaniać; dzwonić
jednostajnie; wabić
(zwierzyną)

toll bar ['toulba:r] s. szlaban

tollgate ['toulgejt] s. rogatka
wjazdowa na płatny most lub
autostradę
tomato [te'mejtou] s. pomidor
tomatoes [te'mejtouz] pl.
pomidory
tomb [tu:m] s. grób; grobowiec;
pochowanie
tombstone ['tu:m,stoun] s.
kamień nagrobny; nagrobek
tomcat ['tom'kaet] s. kocur
tomorrow [te'mo:rou] s. & adv.
jutro
ton [tan] s. tona (2000 funtów);
(slang): mnóstwo
tone [toun] s. ton; normalny stan
(np. ciała, organizmu);
brzmienie; v. stonować się;
stroić; harmonizować
tone down ['toun,dałn] v.
złagodzić; stonować
tongs [tonz] s. szczypce;
kleszcze; obcęgi
tongue [tan] s. język; mowa;
ozór; v. dotykać językiem;
łajać; mleć językiem
tonic ['tonyk] adj. wzmacniający;
elastyczny; krzepiący; s.
środek tonizujący
tonight [te'najt] s. dziś wieczór;
dzisiejsza noc; adv. dziś
wieczorem; gwara; ubiegłej
nocy; wczoraj wieczór
tonnage ['tanydż] s. tonaż;
opłata od tony ładunku
tonsil ['tonsel] s. migdałek
tonsillitis [,tonsy'lajtys] s.
zapalanie migdałków
too [tu:] adv. tak; także;
ponadto; do tego; zbytnio;
zanadto; zbyt; za; na dodatek;
też
took [tuk] v. zob. take
tool [tu:l] s. narzędzie;
obrabiarka; v. obrabiać;
oporządzać
tool up ['tu:l,ap] v.
oprzyrządzać
tools [tu:ls] pl. przybory; sprzęt
tooth [tu:ʃ] s. ząb; pl. teeth [ti:ʃ]
v. uzębiać; wcinać zęby;
ząbkować; sczepiać zębami
trybów

toothache ['tu:ʃejk] s. ból zęba
toothbrush ['tu:ʃ,brasz] s.
szczotka do zębów
toothless ['tu:ʃlys] adj. bezzębny
toothpaste ['tu:ʃpejst] s. pasta
do zębów
toothpick ['tu:ʃpyk] s.
wykałaczka
top [top] s. wierzchołek; czubek;
szczyt; wierzch; powierzchnia;
góra; bocianie gniazdo;
przykrywka; bąk; fryga; adj.
wierzchni; zewnątrzny; górny;
wyższy; najwyższy;
szczytowy; maksymalny; v.
nakrywać; wieńczyć;
uwieńczać; przewyższać;
stanowić wierzch; osiągnąć
szczyt; ścinać szczyt;
przeskoczyć (przez coś);
położyć kres; mierzyć
wysokość; wznosić się
topaz ['toupez] s. topaz
topic ['topyk] s. temat
(rozmowy)
topple ['topl] v. przechylać;
wywracać
topple down ['topldałn] v.
przewrócić
top-secret ['top'si:kryt] adj.
ściśle tajny
topsy-turvy ['topsy'te:rwy] adj.
do góry nogami; v.
przewracać do góry nogami;
s. rozgardiasz; bałagan;
galimatias
torch [to:rcz] s. pochodnia;
znicz; kaganek; palnik (do
lutowania etc.)
tore [to:r] v. zob. tear
torment ['to:rment] s. męka;
udręka; [to:r'ment] v.
męczyć;
dręczyć
torn [to:rn] v. zob. tear
tornado [,to:r'nejdou] s. trąba
powietrzna; tornado
torrent ['to:rent] s. potok
(rwący); ulewny deszcz; burza
torsion ['to:rszyn] s. skręt;
skręcanie
tortoise ['to:rtes] s. żółw
(słodkowodny)

torture ['to:rczer] s. tortura;
męka; v. torturować;
męczyć; dręczyć;
wykręcać; przekręcać

toch [tosz] s. bzdury; brednie;
banialuki (Brit.)

toss [to:s] v. rzucać się;
podrzucać; zarzucać;
podnosić; niepokoić;
kłopotać; przewracać się (w
łóżku); podbijać (piłką);
wypaść z pokoju; kołysać
się na boki; s. rzut; losowanie;
upadek (z konia)

toss about [,to:s e'baut] v.
przewracać się (po czymś)

toss up ['to:s,ap] v.
przewracać; grać w orła i
reszkę

toss-up ['to:sap] s. 50%
prawdopodobieństwa; orzeł
czy reszka?; rzecz wątpliwa

total ['toutel] adj. ogólny;
zupełny; całkowity; totalny;
kompletny; v. zliczać;
wynosić ogółem; (slang):
niszczyć całkowicie (np.
samochód w wypadku)

totalitarian [tou,taely'teerjen] adj.
totalitarny; totalistyczny; s.
totalista

totter ['toter] v. chwiać się;
zataczać się; s. chwianie się;
zataczanie się (dziecka)

touch [tacz] v. dotykać; stykać
(się); wzruszać (się);
poruszać (coś); brać;
wydobywać; zabarwiać;
lekko uszkadzać; cechować;
mierzyć; retuszować;
rąbnąć kogoś na pieniądze
(slang); s. dotyk; dotknięcie;
pociągnięcie; odrobina;
kontakt; lekka choroba; rys;
nuta (np. złości);
obmacywanie; cecha; probierz;
naciąganie na pieniądze
(slang)

touch down ['tacz,dałn] v.
lądować; uzyskiwać 6
punktów

touchdown [taczdałn] s.
lądowanie; gol w futbolu (6

punktów)

touching ['taczyng] adj.
wzruszający; rozrzewniający;
adv. odnośnie (do czegoś)

touchy ['taczy] adj. drażliwy;
obraźliwy; przewrażliwiony

tough [taf] adj. twardy; trudny;
ciężki; łobuzerski; adv. trudno;
s. człowiek: trudny, twardy;
łobuz; chuligan

tour [tuer] s. objazd; wycieczka;
tura; przechadzka; służba
(wojskowa); v. objeżdżać;
obwozić

tourist ['tueryst] s. turysta; klasa
turystyczna

tourist-agency
['tueryst'ejdżensy] s. biuro
podróży

tournament ['tuernement] s.
turniej

tousle ['tauzl] v. szarpać;
mierzwić; czochrać; targać;
s. rozczochrane włosy;
rozczochranie

tout [taut] v. kaptować;
nagabywać; narzucać się; s.
naganiacz; naganianie (np.
klientów)

tow [tou] v. holować; ciągnąć;
s. holowanie; lina holownicza;
przedmiot holowany; włókna
lniane; paździory

towards [to:rdz; 'tolerdz] prep.
ku; w kierunku; dla; w celu;
na (coś)

tow-boat ['toubout] s. holownik

towel ['tauel] s. ręcznik; v.
wycierać ręcznikiem

tower ['tauer] s. wieża; v.
wznosić (się); sterczeć;
wzbijać się

town [tałn] s. miasto

town councilor [,tałn'kaunsyler]
s. radny miejski

town hall ['tałn,ho:l] s. ratusz

tow-rope ['touroup] s. lina
holownicza

toy [toj] s. zabawka; cacko; v.
bawić się; cackać się; robić
niedbale; flirtować (też np. z
pomysłem)

toxic ['toksyk] adj. trujący;

jadowity

trace [trejs] s. ślad; postronek; drążek przekaźnikowy; v. iść śladami; kopiować rysunek; przypisywać czemuś; wytyczać; nakreślać; kreślić

track [traek] s. tor; koleina; ślad; trop; bieżnia; rozstaw kół; v. śledzić; tropić; zostawiać ślady; zabłocić; zawalać; zakładać tor; mieć rozstęp kół; ciągnąć liną z brzegu

track down ['traek,dałn] v. wytropić; wyśledzić; schwytać

track-and-field events ['traekend -'fi:ldy'wents] s. lekkoatletyka

track events [traek y'wents] s. biegi; zawody na bieżni

traction engine ['traekszyn,endżyn] s. lokomotywa; pociągowy motor; traktor

tractor ['traekter] s. ciągnik; traktor

trade [trejd] s. zawód; zajęcie; rzemiosło; handel; wymiana; klientela; branża; kupiectwo; v. handlować; wymieniać; frymarczyć; przewozić towary; kupczyć; przehandlować

trademark ['trejd,ma:rk] s. znak ochronny; v. przybijać znak ochronny; rejestrować znak ochronny

trader ['trejder] s. handlowiec; statek handlowy; spekulator giełdowy

trade-union ['trejd'ju:njen] s. związek zawodowy

trade unionist ['trejd'ju:njenyst] s. działacz związku zawodowego

tradition [tre'dyszyn] s. tradycja

traditional [tre'dyszynel] adj. tradycyjny

traffic ['traefyk] s. ruch (kołowy, pasażerski, towarowy, telegraficzny, telefoniczny, drogowy etc.); handel czymś;

v. frymarczyć; kupczyć

traffic island ['traefyk-ajlend] s. wysepka na jezdni

traffic jam ['traefyk-dżaem] s. zator ruchu

traffic lights ['traefyk-lajts] pl. semafory uliczne

traffic regulation ['traefyk,regju'lejszyn] s. przepisy ruchu

traffic sign ['traefyk,sajn] s. znak drogowy

traffic-cop ['traefyk,kop] s. policjant ruchu (drogowego)

tragedy ['traedżydy] s. tragedia

tragic ['traedżyk] adj. tragiczny

tragical ['traedżykel] = tragic

trail [trejl] v. pociągnąć (się); powlec (się); holować; wlec (się); pozostawać w tyle; iść za tropem; ścigać; wydeptywać (ścieżkę); nosić (karabin poziomo przy boku); s. szlak; ścieżka; trop; ogon; smuga; struga; bruzda; koleina

trailer ['trejler] s. przyczepa (do samochodu); przyczepa towarowa, mieszkalna, turystyczna etc.; maruder; pnąca (się) roślina

train [trejn] v. szkolić; kształcić; przyuczać; wytresować; ćwiczyć (się); trenować (się); kierować na kogoś (np. wzrok); wlec; s. pociąg; tren; ogon; sznur; szereg; następstwo; orszak; świta; porządek; wątek; łańcuch

trainer ['trejner] s. trener; instruktor; samolot szkolny

training ['trejnyng] s. zaprawa; trening; ćwiczenie; szkolenie

trait [trejt] s. cecha

traitor ['trejtor] s. zdrajca

tram [traem] s. tramwaj

tramp [traemp] v. stąpać; włóczyć się; wędrować pieszo; iść pieszo; s. włóczęga; tramp; wędrowiec; statek (nieregularnej żeglugi)

trample ['traempl] v. deptać

trance [tra:ns] s. trans;
uniesienie; ekstaza
tranquil ['traenkłyl] adj. spokojny
tranquility [traen'kłylyty] s.
spokój
tranquilize ['traenkłylajz] v.
uspokajać
tranquilizer ['traenkłylajzer] s.
środek uspokajający
transact [traen'saekt] v.
załatwiać; pertraktować;
przeprowadzać
transaction [traen'saekszyn] s.
transakcja; przeprowadzenie
sprawy; pl. sprawozdania
naukowe; rozprawy
transalpine [traens'aelpajn] adj.
transalpejski
transatlantic [traenzet'laentyk]
adj. transatlantycki
transcend [traen'send] v.
przewyższać; prześcignąć;
górować
transcribe [traens'krajb] v.
nagrywać na taśmie;
przepisywać
transcript ['traenskrypt] s. kopia;
transkrypcja
transfer [traens'fe:r] v.
przemieścić; przenieść
(się); przewozić; przekazać;
s. ['traensfe:r] przeniesienie;
przewóz; przedruk; przekaz;
przelew; odstąpienie
transferable [traens'fe:rebl] adj.
przenośny
transform [traens'fo:rm] v.
przekształcić; zmienić
postać
transformation
[,traensfer'mejszyn] s.
przekształcenie; przeobrażenie
transfuse [traens'fjuz] v.
przelać; przetoczyć (krew)
transfusion [traens'fjużyn] s.
transfuzja
transgress [traens'gres] v.
naruszyć; zgrzeszyć
transgression [traens'greszyn] s.
naruszenie; grzech;
wykroczenie
transgressor [traens'greser] s.
grzesznik

transient ['traenżent] adj.
przechodni; przejeżdżający;
przelotny
transistor [traen'zyster] s.
tranzystor
transit ['traensyt] s. przejazd;
przelot; przewóz; tranzyt;
teodolit
transition [traen'syszyn] s.
przejście; zmiana
transitive ['traensytyw] adj.
przechodni
translate [traens'lejt] v.
przetłumaczyć; przełożyć
translation [traens'lejszyn] s.
tłumaczenie; przekład
translator [traens'lejter] s.
tłumacz
translucent [traenz'lu:sent] adj.
przeświecający;
półprzeźroczysty
transmission [traenz'myszyn] s.
przekładnia; transmisja
transmit [traenz'myt] v.
przekazywać; nadawać;
transmitować
transmitter [traenz'myter] s.
nadajnik; przekaźnik
transparent [traens'peerent] adj.
przeźroczysty
transpire [traens'pajer] v. pocić
się; wyparować; okazywać
się; zdarzyć się
transplant [traens'pla:nt] v.
przeszczepiać; przesadzać; s.
['traenspla:nt] przesadzanie;
przeszczep
transport [traens'po:rt] v.
przewozić; zachwycać; s.
['traenspo:rt] przewóz;
zachwyt; uniesienie
transportation
[,traenspo:r'tejszyn] s.
przewóz; transport;
deportacja; zesłanie
trap [traep] s. pułapka; potrzask;
sidła; zasadzka; podstęp;
syfon; skała wylewna; (slang):
jadaczka; pl. manatki; v.
złapać w pułapkę;
zaopatrywać w pułapkę;
zatrzymywać (w czymś);
przykrywać czaprakiem;

puszczać rzutki

trap-door ['traep'do:r] s. drzwi zapadowe; zapadnia

trapeze [tre'pi:z] s. trapez

trapper ['traeper] s. traper; myśliwy; zastawiający pułapki; nadzorca szybów powietrznych w kopalni

trappings ['traepyŋgz] s. ozdoby; strój ozdobny; czaprak

trash [traesz] s. śmieci; rupieci; tandeta; odpadki; bzdury; hołota; v. obdzierać (z liści, gałązek)

travel ['traewl] v. podróżować (też za interesem); poruszać się (części maszyny); przesuwać się; biec (w terenie); przechodzić (oczami po czymś); poruszać się żwawo; błądzić; s. (daleka) podróż; ruch (pojazdów); suw (maszynowy); przesunięcie

travel agency ['traewl'ejdżensy] s. biuro podróży

traveler ['traewler] s. podróżnik; wodzik nitkowy; komiwojażer

traveler's check ['traewlers,czek] s. z góry wykupiony czek do użytku w podróży

traveling bag ['traewlyŋg,baeg] s. torba podróżna

traverse [trae'we:rs] v. przecinać; przesuwać na bok; przechodzić; omawiać; pokrzyżować; zaprzeczyć formalnie; nakierowywać (działo); obracać (się) jak na osi

travesty ['traewysty] s. trawestacja; parodia; v. trawestować; parodiować

trawl [tro:l] s. włok; włók; trał; niewód; sieć-worek do holowania; v. ciągnąć niewód; łowić niewodem, włókiem, wędką ciągnioną za łodzią

trawler ['tro:ler] s. trawler

tray [trej] s. taca; szufladka (też wkładowa)

treacherous ['treczeres] adj. zdradziecki; niebezpieczny; zdradliwy; zawodny; perfidny

treachery ['treczery] s. zdrada; zdradzieckość; zdradliwość; perfidia

treacle ['tri:kl] s. syrop; melasa; sok (drzewny)

tread; trod; trod(den) [tred; trod; 'trodn]

tread [tred] v. deptać; stąpać (po czymś); nadepnąć; tłoczyć; wdeptywać; iść (ścieżką); wydeptać (ścieżką); gnieść; iść. stąpanie; krok; podnóżek; guma opony dotykająca jezdni; szyna; bieżnik; podeszwa (dotykająca ziemi); stopień

treadle ['tredl] s. pedał; v. pedałować

treadmill ['tredmyl] s. kierat (cylindryczny ze stopniami)

treason ['tri:zn] s. zdrada

treasure ['treżer] s. skarb; v. zaskarbiać; cenić; strzec skarbu

treasurer ['treżerer] s. skarbnik

treasury ['treżery] s. urząd skarbowy; skarbnica

Treasury Department ['treżery,dy'pa:rtment] s. ministerstwo skarbu (USA)

treat [tri:t] v. traktować; potraktować; obchodzić się z kimś; uważać kogoś za; brać coś (za żart); leczyć coś; poddawać działaniu; pertraktować; fundować (komuś); s. przyjęcie; uczta; majówka; poczęstunek; zabawa; przyjemność; rozkosz

treatise ['tri:tys] s. traktat; rozprawa

treatment ['tri:tment] s. traktowanie; leczenie

treaty ['tri:ty] s. traktat; układ; umowa

treble ['trebl] adj. potrójny; wysoki; ostry; przenikliwy; sopranowy; s. sopran; wysoki dźwięk; v. potrajać (się)

tree [tri:] s. drzewo; forma;

kopyto; rama siodła; belka;
nadproże; krokiew; szubienica;
v. zapędzić (na drzewo);
wsadzić (na kopyto)

treeless ['tri:lys] adj. bezdrzewny

tree-trunk ['tri:‚traŋk] s. pień

trefoil ['trefojl] s. koniczyna
trójlistna; roślina trójlistna;
adj. trójlistny

trellis ['trelys] s. krata; altana; v.
kratować winorośl;
nadawać formę kraty

tremble ['trembl] v. trząść się;
drżeć; dygotać; s. drżenie;
drżączka

tremendous [try'mendes] adj.
straszny; olbrzymi

tremor ['tremer] s. drżenie;
drganie; trzęsienie (ziemi)

tremulous ['tremjules] adj.
drżący

trench [trencz] s. rów; okop;
bruzda; cięcie; rów strzelecki;
v. kopać rów; okopywać się;
kłaść do rowu; żłobić;
ciąć; przecinać;
podkopywać się; graniczyć

trench up ['trencz‚ap] v.
wdzierać się (bezczelnie) w
cudze (prawa etc.)

trend [trend] s. dążność;
ogólna tendencja; ogólny
kierunek; v. dążyć; mieć
tendencję; kształtować się;
ciągnąć się

trespass ['trespas] v. wdzierać
się w cudze; nadużywać;
naruszać; wykraczać;
grzeszyć; v. przekroczenie;
wykroczenie; grzech; szkoda
wyrządzona na cudzym
terenie

trespasser ['trespaser] s.
człowiek naruszający przepisy,
prawo (czyjeś)

tress [tres] s. warkocz; v.
zaplatać warkocz

trestle ['tresl] s. kozioł; kobylica;
most filarowy

trial ['trajel] s. próba; proces
sądowy; zmartwienie; zawody
eliminacyjne; adj. próbny;
doświadczalny

trial and error ['trajel end'erer]
exp.: chaotyczne próby (w
nieznane)

triangle ['trajaengl] s. trójkąt

triangular [traj'aengjular] adj.
trójkątny

triangulate [traj'aengulejt] v.
mierzyć (trójkątami) przy
pomocy triangulacji

tribe [trajb] s. plemię; szczep

tribunal [traj'bju:nl] s. trybunał;
sąd

tribune ['trybju:n] s. trybuna;
mównica; gazeta; trybun
(ludu)

tributary ['trybjutery] adj.
pomocniczy; płacący daninę,
haracz; s. dopływ; kraj
płacący daninę

tribute ['trybju:t] s. haracz;
danina

trick [tryk] s. podstęp; chwyt;
sztuczka; sposób; nawyk;
maniera; psota; fortel; (slang):
dziecko; dziewczynka; v.
oszukać; okpić; wyłudzić;
płatać figla; zawodzić;
zaskakiwać

trick up ['tryk‚ap] v. wystroić

trickle ['trykl] v. sączyć (się);
przeciekać; przesączyć;
puszczać ciurkiem, kroplami;
s. struga (mała)

tricky ['tryky] adj. podstępny;
chytry; sprytny; trudny;
zawiły; zręczny

tricycle ['trajsykl] s. rower na
trzech kołach

trifle ['trajfl] s. drobiazg;
drobnostka; błahostka;
bagatela; odrobina;
głupstewko; byle co; stop
cyny i ołowiu; biszkopt z
kremem; v. nie brać
poważnie; poflirtować;
baraszkować; paplać;
bagatelizować

trifling ['trajflyŋg] adj. płochy;
błahy; znikomy

trigger ['tryger] s. spust; cyngiel;
zapadka; v. pociągać za
spust; wywoływać; dawać
początek; zaczynać (akcję)

trill [tryl] s. trel; wibrująca
spółgłoska; v. wymawiać z
wibracją; trząść głosem;
trelować; wymawiać
wibrująco

trillion ['tryljen] = USA billion
['byljen] num. trylion

trim [trym] v. oporządzać;
usuwać niepotrzebne
(gałęzie, tłuszcz etc.);
przybierać (listwą, taśmą
etc.); rozkładać poprawnie
ładunek; poprawiać (opinię);
być oportunistą; zmyć
komuś głowę; dać komuś
lanie; wyprowadzić w pole;
besztać; rugać; s. stan;
forma; nastrój; gotowość;
porządek; strój; ozdoby;
listwy; taśmy; wstążki do
poprawienia wyglądu;
dekoracja wystawy;
oporządzenie; obcięcie;
równowaga lotu; wyposażenie
wnętrza (np. samochodu,
domu etc.); adj. schludny;
porządny; uporządkowany;
wysprzątany

trimming ['trymyng] s. ozdoby;
uporządkowanie;
przystrzyżenie; garnirowanie

Trinity ['trynyty] s. Trójca Św.

trinket ['trynkyt] s. ozdóbka (na
suknię); świecidełko;
błahostka

trip [tryp] s. podróż; wycieczka;
jazda; trans narkomana;
potknięcie; podstawienie nogi;
zgrabny krok; wyzwalanie
zapadkowe lub wychwytowe;
błąd; pomyłka; v. potknąć
się; iść lekkim krokiem;
drobić nóżkami; tańczyć
(lekko); pomylić się;
podstawiać nogę; złapać na
błędzie; wyzwalać;
odczepiać kotwicę;
przesuwać wychwytem
kotwicowym; obracać reje;
spuszczać nagle część
maszyny

tripe [trajp] s. flaki (też
potrawa); byle co;

paskudztwo; lichota

triple [trypl] adj. potrójny; s.
potrójna ilość; trójka; v.
potrajać (się)

triplets ['tryplyts] pl. trojaczki

tripod ['trajpod] s. trójnóg;
statyw

triumph ['trajemf] s. triumf; v.
triumfować

triumphal [traj'amfel] adj.
triumfalny

triumphant [traj'amfent] adj.
zwycięski; triumfalny

trivial ['trywiel] adj. trywialny;
błahy; płytki; banalny; znikomy

trod [trod] v. zob. tread

trodden ['trodn] v. zob. tread

trolley car ['troly kar] s. tramwaj;
wywrotka (wóz)

trombone [trom'boun] s. puzon

troop [tru:p] s. grupa; gromada;
trupa teatralna; rota; pół
szwadronu; s. iść gromadą;
gromadzić się; formować w
roty (pułk)

trophy ['troufy] s. trofeum

tropic ['tropyk] adj.
podzwrotnikowy; tropikalny; s.
zwrotnik

tropical ['tropykel] adj.
tropikalny; gorący; namiętny

trot [trot] s. kłus; trucht; bryk
(szkolny); (slang): biegunka

trouble ['trabl] s. kłopot;
zmartwienie; zaburzenie;
niepokój; trud; dolegliwość;
fatyga; bieda; awaria;
uszkodzenie; defekt; v.
martwić (się); dręczyć (się);
dokuczać; niepokoić (się);
kłopotać (się)

troublesome ['trablsem] adj.
kłopotliwy

trough [trof] s. koryto; rynna;
rów (też między falami);
niecka; łęk; synklina

trouser leg ['trauzerleg] s.
nogawka

trousers ['trauzez] pl. spodnie

trousseau ['tru:sou] s. wyprawa
(ślubna)

trout [traut] s. pstrąg; v. łowić
pstrągi

truant ['tru:ent] s. wagarowicz; opuszczający pracę; adj. próżniacki; wałęsający (się); v. chodzić na wagary; opuszczać pracę

truce [tru:s] s. rozejm; zawieszenie broni

truck [trak] s. ciężarówka; taczki; wózek; podwozie na kołach; lora; drobne towary; warzywa; wymiana; interes; śmieci; brednie; stosunki z kimś; v. przewozić wozem; ładować na wóz; wymieniać się z kimś; obnosić towar; utrzymywać stosunki z kimś

truck farm [trak,fa:rm] s. gospodarstwo warzywne

trudge [tradż] s. trudny marsz; v. trudzić się marszem; odbywać z trudem drogę

true [tru:] adj. prawdziwy; wierny; ścisły; dokładny; prawdomówny; czysty; faktyczny; szczery; lojalny; dobrze dopasowany; s. prawda; właściwe położenie; v. regulować; wyregulować; adv. prawdziwie; dokładnie; exp.: to jest prawda!

truly ['tru:ly] adv. prawdziwie; dokładnie

true-blue ['tru:'blu:] adj. bezkompromisowy; prawdziwie oddany

trump [tramp] s. atut; as; zuch; złoty człowiek; trąba; v. bić atutem; roztrąbić

trump up ['tramp,ap] v. wyssać z palca; zmyślać (zarzuty); preparować (zarzuty)

trumpet ['trampyt] s. trąbka; dźwięk; trębacz; v. grać na trąbie; trąbić; roztrąbić

truncheon ['tranczen] s. pałka policjanta; buława marszałka

trunk [trank] s. pień; trzon; tułów; tors; kadłub; główny kanał; główna linia; trąba słoniowa; kufer; bagażnik; pl. spodnie (krótkie)

trunk line ['trank-lajn] s. linia międzymiastowa (też

telefoniczna w Anglii)

trunk road ['trank-roud] s. szosa główna

truss [tras] s. więźba; wspornik; kratownica; wiązanie dachowe; wiązka (siana); pas przepuklinowy; v. związać (np. dach); przywiązać; wieszać (zbrodniarza)

trust [trast] s. pewność; zaufanie; wiara; nadzieja; kredyt; opieka; powiernictwo; trust; v. zaufać; mieć zaufanie; ufać; wierzyć; polegać (na pamięci swojej etc.); powierzać; kredytować

trustful ['trastful] adj. ufny

trusting ['trastyng] adj. ufny; pełen zaufania

trustworthy ['trast,łe:rty] adj. godny zaufania; pewny

truth [tru:s] s. prawda; prawdziwość; rzetelność

truthful ['tru:sful] adj. prawdomówny; prawdziwy (np. opis)

truths [tru:zz] pl. prawdy

try [traj] v. próbować; wypróbować; sądzić; sprawdzić; kosztować; doświadczyć; starać się; męczyć; s. próba; usiłowanie; wysiłek

trying ['trajyng] adj. przykry; męczący; nieznośny; irytujący; ciężki

try on ['traj,on] v. przymierzać

try out ['traj,aut] v. wypróbowywać

T-square ['ti:,skłeer] s. węgielnica

tub [tab] s. balia; ceber; kadź; wanna; kąpiel; łódź treningowa (wiosłowa); oszalowanie; v. wsadzać do wanny; prać; szalować

tube [tju:b] s. rura; wąż; dętka; tubka; tunel (kolei podziemnej); v. zamykać w rurze; zaopatrywać w rury; nadawać kształt rury

tuberculosis [tju,be:rkje:'lousys]

s. gruźlica

tuck [tak] v. wtykać; wsuwać; podwijać; zawijać (rąbek); otulać; zbierać w fałdy; obrębiać; schować; (slang): pałaszować; wcinać; wieszać (skazańca); s. fałd; fałda; obręb; koncha

tuck in ['takyn] v. otulać (w łóżku)

tuck up ['tak,ap] v. podkasać

Tuesday ['tju:zdy] s. wtorek

tuft [taft] s. pęk; pęczek; kiść; kępa; kitka; bródka; pikowanie; v. robić pęki; dawać pęki; róść pękami; pikować

tug [tag] v. ciągnąć (z trudem); holować; wciągać; s. holownik; gwałtowne pociągnięcie

tug-of-war ['tag,ow'łor] s. przeciąganie liny (próba sił, zawody); zażarta walka o przewagę

tuition [tju'yszyn] s. czesne; nauczanie; lekcje (płatne)

tulip ['tju:lyp] s. tulipan

tumble ['tambl] v. upaść; zwalić (się); potknąć się; zataczać się; kołysać się; huśtać się; wywalić się; gramolić się; rzucać się; biegać na oślep; cisnąć; zwichrzyć; (slang): kapować; iść do łóżka; s. zwalenie; pobicie rekordu; upadek; sztuka akrobatyczna; bałagan

tummy ['tamy] s. żołądek; brzuch (dziecka)

tumor ['tu:mer] s. tumor; obrzęk; guz; nowotwór

tumult ['tu:melt] s. zgiełk; wrzawa; tumult; podniecenie; zaburzenie

tumultuous [tu:'malczues] adj. burzliwy; podniecony; hałaśliwy

tun [tan] s. beczka; kadź (252 galony); v. wlewać do beczki; przechowywać w beczce

tuna ['tu:na] s. tuńczyk

tune [tu:n] s. melodia; nastrój;

harmonia; v. stroić; dostroić; harmonizować; nucić

tune in ['tu:n,yn] v. nastawiać (radio etc.)

tune up ['tu:n,ap] v. nastrajać (np. motor)

tunnel ['tanl] s. tunel; nora; v. przekopywać tunel, korytarz, norę; przekopywać się

turbine ['te:rbyn] s. turbina

turbot ['te:rbet] s. skarpturbot (ryba)

turbulent ['te:rbjulent] adj. wzburzony; burzliwy; gwałtowny; buntowniczy

turf [te:rf] s. torf; darń; v. pokrywać darniną; (slang): drałować (piechotą)

Turk [te:rk] s. Turek

turkey ['te:rky] s. indyk; v. mówić bez ogródek

Turkish ['te:rkysz] adj. turecki

Turkish bath ['te:kysz,ba:ş] s. parówka; kąpiel parowa; łaźnia

turmoil ['te:rmojl] s. zamieszanie; zgiełk; niepokój; podniecenie

turn [te:rn] v. odwrócić (się); odkręcić (się); przekręcać (się); skręcać (się); zwracać (się); odwracać (się); odpierać (atak); napadać; zmieniać się; nawracać (się); popełniać (zdradą); stawać się (np. katolikiem); wyświadczać; obracać; kierować; robić skręt; wyprawiać; odprawiać; toczyć (na kole); puścić w ruch; okazać się; zdarzać się; zwolnić; wyganiać; wyrzucać etc.; s. obrót; z kolei; po kolei; tura; zakręt; zwrot; skręt; punkt zwrotny; przełom; kształt; forma; przechadzka; transakcja; wstrząs; atak; przysługa; numer (popisowy); kolejność; postępowanie wobec kogoś

turn away ['te:rn,e'łej] v. odwracać się od; porzucić

turn back ['te:rn,baek] v.

zawrócić (z drogi)
turn down ['te:rn,dałn] v.
odmówić; przyciszać;
odrzucać
turn off ['te:rn,of] v. zakręcić
(kurek); skręcić; wyłączać
(światło); odprawić
turn on ['te:rn,on] v. puszczać
(wodę); włączać (światło);
odkręcać (kurek)
turn out ['te:rn,aut] v. wyrzucać
(za drzwi); wyrabiać;
zwalniać (z pracy)
turn over ['te:rn'ouwer] v.
odwracać; rozważać; mieć
obrót; wydawać (policji);
przekazywać
turn round ['te:rn raund] v.
przekręcać; odwracać;
zmieniać przekonania;
przekabacić
turn to ['te:rn,tu] v. zabrać się
(do czegoś)
turn up ['te:rn,ap] v. odwracać;
zawinąć (rękawy);
podkręcać; przychodzić;
zgłosić się; przytrafić (się)
turncoat ['te:rn,kout] s. zdrajca
turning point ['te:rnyng,point] s.
punkt zwrotny
turnip ['te:rnyp] s. rzepa
turnout ['te:rnaut] s. stawienie
się; ilość obecnych;
ekwipunek
turnover ['te:rn,ouwer] s.
zmiana; kapotaż;
przewrócenie; placek;
przemieszczanie (ludzi, rzeczy)
turnpike ['te:rn,pajk] s. kołowrót;
rogatka; autostrada (płatna)
turnstile ['te:rnstajl] s. kołowrót
(do wchodzenia pojedynczo)
turnup ['te:rnap] s. traf;
zamieszanie; część
wywrócona; coś
podwiniętego; podwinięcie
turpentine ['te:rpentajn] s.
terpentyna; v.
terpentynować; zbierać
terpentynę
turret ['te:ryt] s. wieżyczka;
imak wielonożowy
turtle ['te:rtl] s. żółw (morski)

turtledove ['te:rtl,daw] s.
turkawka
tusk [task] s. kieł; ząb (u brony);
v. bóść; kłuć; rozdzierać
kłami
tutor ['tu:ter] s. nauczyciel
prywatny; korepetytor;
opiekun (studentów); v.
uczyć kogoś; mieć opiekę
nad kimś; powściągać (się);
być korepetytorem; uczyć
się pod nadzorem nauczyciela
tutorial [tu:'torjel] adj.
wychowawczy; opiekuńczy
TV [ti:wi:] s. telewizja
tuxedo [tak'si:dou] s. smoking
(USA)
twang [tłaeng] s. brzęk (struny);
mówienie przez nos; v.
brzęczeć; rzępolić;
brzdąkać; mówić przez nos
tweed [tłi:d] s. materiał wełniany
lub wełniano-bawełniany z
szorstką powierzchnią
tweet [tłi:t] s. ćwierkanie; v.
ćwierkać
tweezers ['tłi:zez] s. szczypczyki
(kosmetyczne itp.)
twelfth [tłelfs] adj. dwunasty
twelve [tłelw] num. dwanaście;
s. dwunastka
twentieth ['tłentyjes] adj.
dwudziesty
twenty ['tłenty] num.
dwadzieścia; s. dwudziestka
twice [tłajs] adv. dwa razy;
podwójnie; dwukrotnie
twiddle ['tłydl] s. obracanie; v.
kręcić; obracać; przebierać
palcami; próżnować
twig [tłyg] v. zrozumieć;
połapać się; spostrzec;
zauważyć; rozpoznawać; s.
gałązka; różdżka
czarodziejska
twilight ['tłajlajt] s. zmrok;
półcień; półmrok; zmierzch
twin [tłyn] s. bliźniak; adj.
bliźniaczy; v. rodzić się jako
bliźnięta; łączyć (się)
ściśle ze sobą
twin-engine ['tłyn'endżyn] adj.
dwumotorowy

twinkle [tłyŋkl] v. migotać;
błyszczeć; mrugać; s.
migotanie; błysk; mrugnięcie

twirl [tłe:rl] v. wirować; kręcić
(się); s. wirowanie; kręcenie
się; zakrętas; piruet

twist [tłyst] v. skręcać (się);
zwijać (się); zwichnąć (się);
zawirować; wykrzywiać
(twarz); przekręcać; pokręcić
(się); wić (się); powikłać
(się); tańczyć (twista);
wykręcać; przewijać się
(przez tłum); s. skręt; szpagat;
przędza; lina (skręcona); splot;
obrót; przekręcenie
(znaczenia); zwichnięcie;
skłonność; strucla

twitch [tłycz] v. szarpać;
wyrwać; wydrzeć;
wykrzywić (się); poruszyć
się gwałtownie; s. skurcz;
szarpnięcie; pociągnięcie (za
rękaw); drgawka; tik; drganie
(powieki); spazm; kurcz

twitter [tłyter] v. ćwierkać;
świergotać; chichotać;
drżeć (ze strachu etc.); s.
świergot; chichot;
podniecenie; zdenerwowanie

two [tu:] num. dwa; s. dwójka

two-bit [ˈtu:byt] adj. tandetny;
marny; (slang): wart 25
centów; rzecz mała; rzecz bez
znaczenia

twofold [ˈtu:fould] adj.
podwójny; adv. podwójnie;
dwojako

two-piece [ˈtu:pi:s] adj.
dwuczęściowy

two-stroke [ˈtu:ˌstrouk] adj.
dwutaktowy; dwusuwowy

two-way [ˈtu:ˌłej] adj.
dwukierunkowy (np. ruch);
dwutorowy; dwuwartościowy

type [tajp] s. typ; wzór;
przykład; symbol; klasa; okaz;
czcionka; kaszta (drukarska);
v. pisać na maszynie;
ustalać typ; symbolizować;
wyznaczać role

typewriter [ˈtajp,rajter] s.
maszyna do pisania

typhoid [ˈtajfojd] adj. tyfusowy;
s. tyfus; dur brzuszny

typhoon [tajˈfu:n] s. tajfun; burza
(morska) w układzie wielkiego
wiru

typhus [ˈtajfes] adj. tyfusowy

typical [ˈtypykel] adj. typowy;
charakterystyczny

typify [ˈtypyfaj] v. uosabiać;
stanowić typ; zapowiadać

typist [ˈtajpyst] s. maszynistka

tyrannical [tyˈraenykel] adj.
tyrański

tyrannize [ˈtyrenajz] v.
tyranizować

tyranny [ˈtyreny] s. tyrania

tyrant [ˈtajrent] s. tyran

U

u [ju:] dwudziesta pierwsza litera
alfabetu angielskiego

ubiquity [juˈbykłyty] s.
wszechobecność

U-boat [ˈju:bout] s. łódź
podwodna (niemiecka)

udder [ˈader] s. wymię

ugly [ˈagly] adj. brzydki;
paskudny

uhlan [ˈu:la:n] s. ułan

ulan [ˈu:la:n] s. ułan

ulcer [ˈalser] s. wrzód

ultimate [ˈaltymyt] adj.
ostateczny; ostatni; końcowy;
podstawowy; s. ostateczny
wynik; podstawowy fakt

ultimatum [altyˈmejtem] s.
ultimatum

umbrella [amˈbrela] s. parasol

umpire [ˈampajer] s. sędzia
sportowy; rozjemca; v.
sędziować; rozstrzygać jako
arbiter

unabashed [ˈaneˈbaeszt] adj.
niespeszony; niezmieszany; nie
zbity z tropu

unabated [ˈan,eˈbejtyd] adj.
niesłabnący; niezmniejszony

unable ['an'ejbl] adj. niezdolny;
nieudolny
unacceptable ['ane'kseptebl] adj.
nie do przyjęcia
unaccountable ['ane'kauntebl]
adj. niewytłumaczony;
niezrozumiały; dziwny; nie
tłumaczący się nikomu
unaccustomed ['ane'kastemd]
adj. niezwykły; nie
przyzwyczajony
unacquainted ['ane'kłejntyd] adj.
nie obznajomiony
unaffected [,ane'fektyd] adj.
niekłamany; naturalny
unanimous [ju'naenymes] adj.
jednogłośny
unapproachable [,ane'prouczebl]
adj. niedostępny; niezrównany
unarmed ['an'a:rmd] adj.
bezbronny; nie uzbrojony
unashamed ['an,e'szejmd] adj.
bezwstydny
unassisted ['an,e'systyd] adj. nie
wspomagany
unassuming ['an,e'sju:myng] adj.
skromny; bezpretensjonalny
unauthorized ['an'o:terajzd] adj.
nieupoważniony
unavoidable ['an,e'wojdebl] adj.
nieunikniony; niechybny
unaware [,ane'łeer] adj.
nieświadomy;
niepoinformowany
unawares [,ane'łeerz] adv.
nieświadomie; znienacka;
niespodziewanie; nic nie
wiedząc
unbalanced ['an'baelensd] adj.
niezrównoważony
unbar ['an'ba:r] v. odryglować
unbearable [an'beerebl] adj.
nieznośny; nie do
wytrzymania
unbecoming ['an,by'kamyng] adj.
niestosowny; niewłaściwy;
nieodpowiedni; nietwarzowy
unbelievable [,anby'li:webl] adj.
niewiarygodny;
nieprawdopodobny
unbelieving [,anby'li:wyng] adj.
niewierzący; niedowierzający
unbending ['an'bendyng] adj.

nieugięty; niezłomny
unbiased ['an'bajest] adj.
bezstronny
unbidden ['an'bydn] adj.
nieproszony
unborn baby ['an'bo:rn'bejby] s.
przyszłe dziecko; nieurodzone
(jeszcze) dziecko
unbounded [an'baundyd] adj. bez
granic; bezgraniczny
unbroken [an'brouken] adj.
nieprzerwany; niezbity; nie
ujeżdżony (koń)
unbutton ['an'batn] v. odpiąć;
rozpiąć (się)
uncalled-for [an'ko:ld,fo:r] adj.
niewłaściwy; niezasłużony;
niczym nie usprawiedliwiony
uncanny [an'kaeny] adj.
niesamowity
uncared-for ['an'keerd,fo:r] adj.
porzucony; zaniedbany
unceasing [an'si:syng] adj.
bezustanny; nieprzerwany
uncertain [an'se:rtn] adj.
niepewny; wątpliwy
unchallenged [an'czaelyndżd]
adj. niekwestionowany
unchangeable [an'czejndżebl]
adj. stały; niezmienny
unchanged [an'czejndżd] adj.
niezmieniony
unchecked [an'czekt] adj.
niepowstrzymany;
niepohamowany;
nieposkromiony
uncivil ['an'sywyl] adj.
niegrzeczny; nieuprzejmy;
nieokrzesany; grubiański
uncivilized ['an'sywylajzd] adj.
dziki; niecywilizowany;
barbarzyński
uncle ['ankl] s. wujek; stryjek
unclean ['an'kli:n] adj. nieczysty;
plugawy; sprośny
uncommon ['an'komen] adj.
niezwykły; rzadki; adv.
niezwykle; nadzwyczaj
uncommunicative ['an
-ke'mju:nyketyw] adj.
małomówny; skryty;

niekomunikatywny
uncomplaining ['an-kem'plejnyng]
adj. cierpliwy; nienarzekający
unconcern ['anken'se:rn] s.
beztroska; niefrasobliwość;
obojętność
unconcerned ['anken'se:rnd] adj.
obojętny; niefrasobliwy;
beztroski
unconditional ['an-ken'dyszynl]
adj. bezwarunkowy
unconfirmed ['an-ken'fe:rmd] adj.
nie potwierdzony
unconscious [an'konszes] adj.
nieprzytomny; zemdlony;
nieświadomy; s.
podświadomość
unconsciousness
[an'konszesnys] s. omdlenie;
nieprzytomność
unconstitutional
['an,konsty'tju:szynl] adj.
niezgodny z konstytucją
uncontrollable ['an,kon'troulebl]
adj. nieposkromiony;
niepohamowany
unconventional ['an
-ken'wenszynl] adj.
niekonwencjonalny; oryginalny
unconvinced ['an-ken'wynst] adj.
nieprzekonany
unconvincing ['an-ken'wynsyng]
adj. nieprzekonywający
uncouth [an'ku:s] adj.
nieokrzesany; niezręczny;
niezgrabny
uncover ['an'kawer] v. odkryć;
demaskować
uncultivated ['an'kaltywejtyd]
adj. nieuprawny; leżący
odłogiem; niekulturalny
uncultured ['an'kalczerd] adj.
niewykształcony; niekulturalny
uncut ['an'kat] daj. nie przecięty;
nie ścinany; nie strzyżony
undamaged ['an'daemydżd] adj.
nieuszkodzony
undated ['an'dejtyd] adj. nie
datowany; bez określonego
terminu
undaunted ['an'do:ntyd] adj.
nieposkromiony; nieustraszony
undecayed ['andy'kejd] adj.

nie
zepsuty; nie zgniły
undecided ['an-dy'sajdyd] adj.
niezdecydowany; niepewny;
nieokreślony;
nierozstrzygnięty
undecisive ['andy'sajsyw] adj.
nieroztrzygnięty; nie
decydujący (Brit.)
undecked ['an'dekt] adj. bez
ozdób; nie ozdobiony (stół,
itd.) (Brit.)
undefeated ['andy'fi:tyd] adj.
niepokonany
undefended ['andy'fendyd] adj.
nie broniony
undefinable ['andy'fajnebl] adj.
nieokreślony
undefined ['andy'fajnd] adj.
nieokreślony; mglisty
undelayed ['andy'lejd] adj.
bezzwłoczny; nie opóźniony;
natychmiastowy (Brit.)
undeniable [,andy'najebl] adj.
niezaprzeczalny
undenominational
['andy,nomy'nejsznl] daj.
bezwyznaniowy, świecki
undependable ['andy'pendebl]
adj. niesolidny; niesłowny;
niewiarogodny
under ['ander] prep. pod;
poniżej; w; w trakcie; zgodnie
z; z; adv. poniżej; pod
spodem; adj. spodni; niższy;
dolny; podrzędni; podwładny
underbid ['ander'byd] v. zob. bid;
składać niższą ofertę w
przetargu
underbrush ['ander,brasz] s.
zarośla; podszycie (lasu)
undercarriage ['ander,kaerydż] s.
podwozie
undercharge ['ander'cza:rdż] v.
za mało policzyć; za słabo
naładować
underclothes ['ander,klouzyz] pl.
bielizna
underclothing ['ander,klouzyng]
s. bielizna
undercooling ['andr,ku:lyng] s.
przechłodzenie; przeziębienie
undercurrent ['ander,karent] s.

prąd pod powierzchnią;
tendencja podstawowa
undercut ['ander'kat] v.
podcinać płace, ceny; s.
polędwica; cios od dołu;
podkop
underdeveloped
[,anderdy'welept] adj.
zacofany; nie wywołany
poprawnie; niedorozwinięty
underdog ['ander'dog] s.
człowiek upośledzony,
przegrywający
underdone ['ander'dan] adj.
półsurowy; niedogotowany
underestimate ['ander'estymejt]
v. niedoceniać; za nisko
oszacować
underfed ['ander'fed] v.
niedożywiony
undergo [,ander'gou] v. zob. go;
doznawać czegoś;
przechodzić coś;
doświadczyć; poddawać się
(operacji)
undergraduate [,ander'graedjuit]
s. student bez stopnia
bachelor
underground ['ander,graund] adj.
podziemny; zaskórny; tajny; s.
kolej podziemna; ruch oporu;
adv. [,ander'graund] pod
ziemią; skrycie; tajnie
undergrowth ['ander-grouš] s.
poszycie (lasu)
underline ['anderlajn] v.
podkreślać; s. podkreślenie;
podpis pod ilustracją;
zawiadomienie (u spodu afisza
teatralnego) o następnej
sztuce
underling ['ander'lyng] s.
podwładny; sługa
undermine [,ander'majn] v.
podkopywać (zdrowie etc.);
podmywać (brzegi etc.)
undermost ['andermoust] adj.
adv. najniższy; najniższej
rangi; najniżej
underneath [,ander'ni:s] adv. pod
spodem; poniżej; na dole; pod
spód
underpants ['ander,paents] s.

kalesony
underpass [,ander'pa:s] s.
przejazd poniżej poziomu;
skrzyżowanie bezkolizyjne;
przejście pod jezdnią
underpay ['ander'pej] v. za mało
płacić
underplay ['ander'plej] v.
pomniejszać; podcinać
underprivileged
['ander'prywylydżd] adj.
upośledzony
underrate ['ander,rejt] v.
niedoceniać
underscore ['ander'skor] v.
podkreślać
undershirt ['andersze:rt] s.
podkoszulek
underside ['ander'sajd] s. spód
undersigned ['ander'sajnd] adj.
(niżej) podpisany
undersized ['ander'sajzd] adj.
zbyt mały; małego wzrostu
undersoil ['ander,sojl] s.
podglebie (Brit.)
understaffed ['ander'sta:ft] adj.
mający zbyt mały personel
understand; understood;
understood [,ander'staend;
,ander'stud; ,ander'stud]
understand [,ander'staend] v.
rozumieć; domyślać się;
orientować się; znać;
wywnioskować; wiedzieć
jak; umieć dobrze
understandable
[,ander'staendebl] adj.
zrozumiały
understanding [,ander'staendyng]
adj. pełen zrozumienia; s.
zrozumienie; warunek;
(wyższa) inteligencja;
porozumienie; rozum
understandingly
[,ander'staendyngly] adv. ze
zrozumieniem;
porozumiewawczo
understate ['ander'stejt] v.
umniejszać; wyrażac się zbyt
słabo
understatement
[,ander'stejtment] s. zbyt
skromne wyrażanie się;

niedomówienie
understood [,ander'stud] adj.
zrozumiały, umówiony;
domyślny; niedopowiedziany
undertake [,ander'tejk] v. zob.
take; przedsiębrać;
podejmować się; ręczyć;
zobowiązywać się do
czegoś; być przedsiębiorcą
pogrzebowym
undertaker [,ander'tejker] s.
przedsiębiorca pogrzebowy
undertaking [,ander'tejkyng] s.
przedsięwzięcie;
zobowiązanie; obietnica;
przyrzeczenie;
przedsiębiorstwo pogrzebowe
undervalue [,ander'waelju] v.
niedoceniać; za nisko
szacować
underwaist ['ander,łejst] s.
kamizelka; bezrękawnik
underwear ['ander,łeer] s.
bielizna
underweight ['ander,łejt] s.
niedowaga; adj. nie
dowążony; za mało ważący
underwood ['ander,łu:d] s.
poszycie (lasu) (Brit.)
underworld ['ander,łe:rld] s.
podziemie; świat podziemny;
pl. antypody
underwrite ['ander-rajt] v. zob.
write; zakontraktować
(ubezpieczenie); podpisać
(się); wydawać (polisę
ubezpieczeniową);
zobowiązywać się
underwriter ['ander-rajter] s.
ajent ubezpieczeniowy
undescribable ['andys'krajbabl]
adj. nie do opisania; nie
dający się opisać
underserved ['andy'ze:rwd] adj.
niezasłużony; niesłuszny (Brit.)
undeserving ['andy'ze:rvyng] adj.
nie zasługujący; bez zasług
undesirable [andy'zajerebl] adj.
niepożądany; niedogodny; s.
człowiek niepożądany
undetected ['andy'tektyd] adj.
niezauważony
undetermined ['andy'te:rmynd]

adj. nieokreślony
undeveloped ['andy'welept] adj.
nierozwinięty; niewywołany
undeviating [an'dy:vj,ejtyng] adj.
nie zbaczający; prosty;
wierny; niezawodny
undies [andyz] pl. bielizna
(damska i dziecięca)
undifferentiated
['an'dyfe:renszi'ejtyd] adj. nie
zróżnicowany; nie
różniczkowany
undigested ['andaj'dżestyd] adj.
nie strawiony; nie
dopracowany; nie przyswojony
undigestible ['andaj'dżestybl]
adj. niestrawny
undignified [an'dygnyfajd] adj.
niegodny; bez godności
undiluted ['andaj'ljutyd] adj. nie
rozpuszczony; nie
rozwodniony; nie rozrzedzony;
nie rozcieńczony
undiminished [an'dymynszt] adj.
niezmniejszony
undisciplined [an'dysyplind] adj.
niezdyscyplinowany; niekarny
undisclosed ['andys'klouzd] adj.
nie wyjawniony; nieujawniony
undiscovered ['andys'kawerd]
adj. nie odkryty; nie zbadany
undisguised ['andys'gajzd] adj.
nie ukryty; nie maskowany;
nieukrywany
undisposed ['andys'pouzd] adj.
nieskłonny
undisputable ['andys'pju:tebl]
adj. bezsporny
undisputed ['andys'pju:tyd] adj.
bezsporny; niezaprzeczony
undistinguishable
['andys'tyngłyszebl] adj. nie
do rozpoznania;
niedostrzegalny
undisturbed ['andys'te:rbd] adj.
niezakłócony
undivided ['andy'wajdyd] adj.
niepodzielny; cały; całkowity;
nierozdzielony; jednomyślny
undo; undid; undone ['an'du:;
'an'dyd; an'dan]
undo ['an'du:] v. robić
niebyłym; unieważniać;

usuwać; niszczyć;
rujnować; rozpakować;
rozwiązać; otwierać;
rozpinać; przekreślać

undreamt-of ['an'dremt,ow] adj.
nieprawdopodobny; nie do
pomyślenia; niesłychany

undock ['an'dok] v.
wyprowadzać z doku

undone ['an'dan] adj.
niedokończony; nie zrobiony;
rozpięty; rozwiązany; spruty

undreamed [an'dri:md] adj. nie
do pomyślenia;
nieprwadopodobny

undress [an'dres] v. rozbierać
(się); odbandażowywać; s.
negliż; zwykłe ubranie

undressed [an'drest] adj. nie
przyrządzony; chropowaty; nie
opatrzona (rana); rozebrany

undue [an'dju:] adj. przesadny;
nadmierny; postronny;
niewłaściwy; jeszcze
niepłatny (np. rachunek)

undrinkable ['an'drynkebl] adj.
nie (nadający się) do picia

undue ['an'dju:] adj. nadmierny;
przesadny; zbytni; nielegalny;
bezprawny; niewłaściwy; nie
przypadający do zapłaty

unduly ['an'dju:ly] adv.
nadmiernie; przesadnie;
zbytnio; bezprawnie

undutiful [an'dju:tyful] adj.
nieobowiązkowy

undying [an'dajyng] adj.
nieśmiertelny; dozgonny

uneasiness [an'i:zynys] s.
niepokój; zażenowanie;
zakłopotanie

uneasy [an'i:zy] adj. niespokojny;
niepokojący; nieswój;
zażenowany; nieprzyjemny;
krępujący; budzący niepokój

uneatable ['an'i:tebl] adj.
niejadalny; nie (nadający się)
do jedzenia

uneducated [an'edjukejtyd] adj.
niewykształcony; bez
wykształcenia

unemployed [,anem'plojd] adj.
bez pracy; bezrobotny;

niewykorzystany; nie
zużytkowany

unemployment [an'emplojment]
s. bezrobocie

unending [an'endyng] adj.
bezustanny; nie kończący
się; wieczny

unendurable ['anyn'djuerbl] adj.
nie do zniesienia

unentitled ['an-yn'tajtld] adj. nie
upoważniony; bez tytułu

unenviable ['an'enwjebl] adj. nie
do pozazdroszczenia

unequal ['an'i:kłol] adj. nierówny;
nie na wysokości (zadania)

unequaled ['an'i:kłold] adj.
niezrównany

unequivocal ['any'kływokel] adj.
niedwuznaczny; wyraźny;
jasny

unerring ['an'e:ryng] adj.
nieomylny; niezawodny

uneven ['an'i:wen] adj.
nieparzysty; niejednolity;
nierówny

uneventful ['an,y'wentful] adj.
nieurozmaicony; spokojny;
jednostajny

unexpected ['anyks'pektyd] adj.
niespodziewany;
nieoczekiwany

unexperienced ['an-yks'pierienst]
adj. nigdy nie zaznany;
niedoświadczony

unfailing [an'fejlyng] adj.
niezawodny; pewny;
niewyczerpany

unfair [an'feer] adj.
niesprawiedliwy; krzywdzący;
nieuczciwy; nieprzepisowy

unfaithful [an'fejsful] adj.
niewierny; wiarołomny;
nieścisły

unfamiliar ['anfe'myljer] adj.
nieznany; nie obznajomiony;
obcy; słabo zorientowany

unfashionable ['an'faeszenebl]
adj. niemodny

unfasten ['an'fa:sn] v. odczepić
(się); odpiąć (się);
odwiązywać (się);
odryglować (się); rozluźnić
(się)

unfavorable [ʼanʼfejwerebl] adj.
niepomyślny; nieżyczliwy;
niesprzyjający; nieprzychylny

unfeasible [anʼfi:sebl] adj.
niewykonalny

unfeeling [anʼfi:lyng] adj. bez
uczucia; bez serca; okrutny

unfertile [ʼanʼfe:rtajl] adj.
nieżyzny; nieurodzajny

unfilled [ʼanʼfyld] adj.
niezapełniony; nienapełniony;
nie zajęty; wakujący

unfinished [ʼanʼfynyszt] adj.
niewykończony;
niedokończony

unfit [ʼanʼfyt] adj. nie nadający
się; niezdatny; niezdolny;
nieodpowiedni; v. czynić
niezdolnym do czegoś

unflagging [ʼanʼflaegyng] adj.
niezmordowany; niesłabnący

unflappable [ʼanʼflaepebl] adj. nie
do wytrącenia z równowagi;
beztroski

unflattering [ʼanʼflaeteryng] adj.
niepochlebny

unfold [ʼanʼfould] v. ujawniać
(się); rozwijać (się);
otwierać; odsłonić

unforeseen [ˌanferʼsi:n] adj.
nieprzewidziany;
niespodziewany

unforgettable [ʼan-ferʼgetebl] adj.
pamiętny; niezapomniany

unforgivable [ʼanfe:rgywebl] adj.
nie do darowania;
niewybaczalny

unforgiving [ʼan-ferʼgywyng] adj.
niewybaczający;
nieprzejednany

unforgotten [ʼan-ferʼgotn] adj.
niezapomniany

unfortunate [anʼfo:rcznyt] adj.
niefortunny; pechowy;
niepomyślny; nieszczęśliwy

unfortunately [anʼfo:rcznytly]
adv. niestety; nieszczęśliwie

unfounded [anʼfaundyd] adj.
bezpodstawny

unfriendly [anʼfrendly] adj.
nieprzyjazny; nieprzychylny

unfulfilled [ʼanfulʼfyld] adj.
niespełniony

unfurl [anʼfe:rl] v. rozwinąć;
rozpościerać

unfurnished [anʼfe:rnyszt] adj.
nieumeblowany

ungainly [anʼgejnly] adj.
niezdarny; niezgrabny

ungenerous [anʼdżeneres] adj.
małostkowy; nie szczodry

ungentle [anʼdżentl] adj.
niełagodny

ungodly [anʼgodly] adj.
bezbożny; grzeszny;
skandaliczny

ungovernable [anʼgawernebl] adj.
dziki; niesforny; krnąbrny;
nieopanowany

ungraceful [anʼgrejsful] adj.
niewdzięczny; nieuprzejmy

ungrateful [anʼgrejtful] adj.
niewdzięczny

unguarded [ʼanʼga:rdyd] adj.
niebaczny; nieopatrzny;
nierozważny; niestrzeżony

unhappy [anʼhaepy] adj.
nieszczęśliwy; pechowy;
zmartwiony; nieudany

unharmed [ʼanʼha:rmd] adj.
nietknięty

unharness [ʼanʼha:rnys] v.
wyprzęgać; zdejmować
zbroję etc.

unhealthy [anʼhelsy] adj.
niezdrowy

unheard-of [anʼhe:rd,ow] adj.
niesłychany; niebywały;
nieprawdopodobny

unheated [anʼhi:tyd] adj.
nieogrzewany

unheeded [anʼhi:dyd] adj.
niezauważony; niedostrzeżony

unheeding [anʼhi:dyng] adj.
nieuważający;
niedostrzegający

unhesitating [anʼhezytejtyng] adj.
nie wahający się

unhinge [anʼhyndż] v. zdjąć z
zawiasów; wytrącić z
równowagi

unhitch [ʼanʼhycz] v. odczepić;
wyprząc

unholy [anʼhouly] adj. bezbożny;
piekielny; niesamowity; nie z
tej ziemi

unhoped-for [an'houpt,fo:r] adj.
niespodziewany;
nieoczekiwany
unhurt [an'he:rt] adj.
nieuszkodzony; bez szwanku
unicorn ['ju:nyko:rn] s.
jednorożec; jednoróg
unidentified ['an-aj'denty,fajd]
adj. niezindentyfikowany;
nieznany
unification [,ju:nyfy'kejszyn] s.
zjednoczenie; scalenie;
ujednolicenie
uniform ['ju:nyfo:rm] adj.
jednolity; równomierny;
jednostajny; s. mundur;
uniform
uniformity ['ju:ny'fo:rmyty] s.
jednolitość; jednostajność;
ujednolicenie; ujednostajnienie
unilateral ['ju:ny'laeterel] adj.
jednostronny
unimaginable [any'maedżynebl]
adj. nie do pomyślenia
unimaginative
[any'maedżynejtyw] adj. bez
wyobraźni; bez polotu
unimportant ['anym'po:rtent] adj.
nieważny; błahy; mało ważny
uninfected ['anyn'fektyd] adj. nie
zarażony
uninformed ['anyn'fo:rmd] adj.
nie poinformowany; nie
powiadomiony
uninhabitable ['anyn'haebytebl]
adj. nie do zamieszkania; nie
do życia
uninhabited ['anyn'haebytyd] adj.
niezamieszkały; pustynny
uninitiated ['any'nyszi,ejtyd] adj.
niewtajemniczony
uninjured ['an'yndżerd] adj. bez
szwanku; nie uszkodzony; bez
obrażeń
uninspired ['anyn'spajerd] adj.
banalny
uninsured ['anyn'szurd] adj.
nieubezpieczony
unintelligible ['anyn'telydżebl]
adj. niezrozumiały
unintentional ['anyn'tenszynl]
adj. mimowolny; nie
zamierzony

uninteresting [an'ynterestyng]
adj. nudny; nieciekawy;
nieinteresujący
uninterrupted [an,ynte'raptyd]
adj. nieprzerwany; ciągły;
bezustanny
uninvited ['anyn'wajtyd] adj.
nieproszony
uninviting ['anyn'wajtyng] adj.
nie zachęcający; odpychający;
nieapetyczny
uninvolved ['an-yn'wolwd] adj.
niezaangażowany
union ['ju:njen] s. połączenie;
złącze; łączność; związek;
zjednoczenie; klub;
małżeństwo; zgoda; łącznik;
złączka; godło
unionist ['ju:njenyst] s.
związkowiec; zwolennik
związku
union Jack ['ju:njen'dżaek] s.
flaga angielska
unique [ju:'ni:k] adj. wyjątkowy;
jedyny; niezrównany; s. unikat
unisex ['ju:ny'seks] adj. styl
(wyrobów) do użytku obu
płci; odzież, przybory
toaletowe, zakład fryzjerski
etc.
unison ['ju:nyzn] adj. zgodnie
(razem)
unit ['ju:nyt] s. jednostka; zespół
unite [ju:'najt] v. łączyć;
jednoczyć; zjednoczyć
united [ju:'najtyd] adj.
połączony; zjednoczony;
łączny
unity ['ju:nyty] s. jedność
(czasu, miejsca, działania
etc.); jednostka; jednolitość;
harmonia; zgoda
universal [ju:ny'we:rsel] adj.
powszechny; ogólny;
uniwersalny
universe ['ju:nywers] s.
wszechświat; świat;
ludzkość; kosmos
university [,ju:ny'wersyty] s.
uniwersytet; wszechnica;
uczelnia
unjust ['an'dżast] adj.
niesprawiedliwy

unjustified ['an'dʒasty,fajd] adj.
nieusprawiedliwiony;
nieuzasadniony
unkempt ['an'kempt] adj.
nieuczesany; rozczochrany;
niechlujny
unkind [an'kajnd] adj. niedobry;
okrutny
unknown ['aṅ'noun] adj.
nieznany; niewiadomy
unlabelled [an'lejld] adj. bez
etykiety; nie naznaczony
unlace ['an'lejs] v.
rozsznurować
unlawful ['an'lo:ful] adj.
bezprawny; nielegalny
unlearn ['an'le:rn] v. oduczać
(się); zob. learn
unleash ['an'li:sz] v. spuszczać
ze smyczy; rozpętać (wojnę)
unless [an'les] conj. jeżeli nie;
chyba że
unlike ['an'lajk] adj. niepodobny;
odmienny; prep. odmiennie;
inaczej; w przeciwieństwie
unlikely [an'lajkly] adj.
nieprawdopodobny;
nieoczekiwany; nie rokujący
unlimited [an'lymytyd] adj.
nieograniczony; bezgraniczny;
dowolny
unload ['an'loud] v.
rozładowywać; zrzucać
ciężar
unlock ['an'lok] v. otwierać
zamek; otworzyć
unlocked ['an'lokt] adj. otwarty;
niezamknięty
unlooked-for [an'lukt,fo:r] adj.
nieoczekiwany;
niespodziewany;
nieprzewidziany
unloosen ['an'lu:sn] v.
rozluźnić; rozwiązać;
rozsznurować
unlucky [an'laky] adj. pechowy;
niefortunny; niepomyślny;
nieszczęśliwy
unmanageable [an'maenydʒebl]
adj. niesforny; krnąbrny
unmanly [an'maenly] adj.
zniechęcający; odbierający
odwagę; adv. zniechęcająco

unmarried [an'maeryd] adj.
nieżonaty; niezamężna
unmask ['an'ma:sk] v.
zdemaskować; ujawnić
unmelted ['an'meltyd] adj. nie
stopiony; nie stajały; nie
przetopiony
unmendable [an'mendebl] adj.
nie do naprawienia; nie
nadający się do naprawy
unmistakable ['anmys'tejkbl] adj.
niewątpliwy; wyraźny;
niedwuznaczny
unmoved ['an'mu:wd] adj.
niewzruszony
unnamed ['an'nejmd] adj.
bezimienny; anonimowy
unnatural [an'naeczrel] adj.
sztuczny; nienaturalny; wbrew
naturze; nienormalny
unnecessary [an'nesysery] adj.
zbędny; zbyteczny;
niepotrzebny
unnerve [an'ne:rw] v. odbierać
odwagę; denerwować
unnoticed ['an'noutyst] adj.
niezauważony; pominięty
unobtainable ['aneb'tejnebl] adj.
nie do nabycia (otrzymania)
unobstructed ['anob'straktyd]
adj. nie napotykający
przeszkód; nie zasłonięty
unobtrusive ['aneb'tru:syw] adj.
skromny; dyskretny; nie
narzucający się
unoccupied ['an'okjupajd] adj.
wolny; nie zajęty
unoffending ['ane'fendyng] adj.
nieszkodliwy; niewinny
unofficial ['ane'fyszel] adj. nie
urzędowy; nieoficjalny
unopened [an'oupend] adj. nie
otwarty
unopposed ['ano'pouzd] adj. bez
sprzeciwu
unorthodox ['an'o:r̲t̲o,doks] adj.
nie prawowierny;
nieszablomowy
unpack ['an'paek] v.
rozpakowywać (się)
unpaid ['an'pejd] adj.
niezapłacony; bezinteresowny
unpalatable [an'paeletebl] adj.

niesmaczny
unparalleled [an'paereleld] **adj.**
niezrównany; niespotykany;
bezprzykładny; niesłychany
unpardonable [an'pa:rdnebl] **adj.**
niewybaczalny; nie do
darowania
unpenetrable [an'penytrebl] **adj.**
nie do przebycia; nie do
zrozumienia (Brit.)
unperceived [,anper'si:wd] **adj.**
niepostrzeżony
unpersuaded [,anper'słejdyd] **adj.**
nie przekonany
unperturbed ['an-per'te:rbd] **adj.**
spokojny; nie zaniepokojony;
nie przejmujący się
unpleasant [an'plezent] **adj.**
nieprzyjemny; przykry; niemiły
unplug [an'plag] **v.**
odczepować; wyciągnąć z
kontaktu
unpolished ['an'polyszt] **adj.**
niewyczyszczony;
niewygładzony
unpolluted ['anpe'lu:tyd] **adj.**
nieskażony; nie
zanieczyszczony
unpopular [an'popjuler] **adj.**
niepopularny; niemile widziany
unpopularity [,anpopju'laeryty] **s.**
niepopularność;
nieprzychylne nastawienie; złe
przyjęcie; utrata popularności
unpractical ['an'praektykel] **adj.**
niepraktyczny; nierealny
unpracticed [an'praektyst] **adj.**
nie wypraktykowany;
niewprawny
unprecedented [an'presydentyd]
adj. bezprzykładny; bez
precedensu; niesłychany
unprecise ['anpry'sajs] **adj.**
nieścisły; nie precyzyjny
unprejudiced [an'predżudyst] **adj.**
bezstronny; nie mający
przesądów
unpremeditated
['anpry:'medytejtyd] **adj.** bez
premedytacji; nienaumyślny
unprepared ['anpry'peerd] **adj.**
nieprzygotowany;
nieprzyrządzony

unprincipled [an'prynsepld] **adj.**
bez skrupułów; niegodziwy
unpreventable ['anpry'wentebl]
adj. nie do uniknięcia;
nieunikniony
unproductive [,anpro'daktyw]
adj. niewydajny; nie
wytwórczy; niepłodny
unprofessional ['anpre'fesznl]
adj. laicki; niezawodowy;
dyletancki; amatorski
unprofitable [an'profytebl] **adj.**
niepopłatny; niekorzystny;
nierentowny; jałowy
unprotected ['anpro'tektyd] **adj.**
nie chroniony; bezbronny; nie
zabezpieczony
unproved ['an'pru:wd] **adj. nie**
udowodniony; nie
wypróbowany
unprovided-for ['an
-pre'wajdyd,fo:r] **adj.**
niezabezpieczony; bez
środków do życia
unqualified ['an'kłolyfajd] **adj.**
niewykwalifikowany; bez
kwalifikacji; niesprecyzowany;
nieograniczony (np. zaufanie)
unquestionable [an'kłesczynebl]
adj. bezsporny; niewątpliwy
unquestioned [an'kłesczynd] **adj.**
niezaprzeczony; niepytany
unravel ['an'raewl] **v.**
wystrząpić; rozwikłać;
rozwiązać; wyjaśnić
unreal ['an'ryel] **adj. nierealny;**
zmyślony; iluzoryczny;
wyimaginowany
unreasonable [an'ri:znebl] **adj.**
nierozsądny; niedorzeczny;
wygórowany (w cenie)
unrefined ['anry'faind] **adj.**
niesubtelny; niewyrafinowany;
niewykształcony
unreceptive ['anry'septyw] **adj.**
nieczuły; niepodatny; nie
chłonny; tępy
unreconciled ['an'reken,sajld] **adj.**
nie pogodzony
unreliable ['anry'lajebl] **adj.**
niepewny; niesolidny
unrepaid ['anry'pejd] **adj. nie**
zapłacony

unreserved ['anry'ze:rwd] adj.
otwarty; szczery; bez
zastrzeżeń; całkowity;
niezarezerwowany
unresisting ['anry'zystyng] adj.
nieodporny; nieopierający się
unrest ['an'rest] s. niepokój;
zamieszki; niepokoje
unrestored ['anry'sto:rd] adj. nie
zwrócony; nie odnowiony; nie
przywrócony
unrestrained ['anrys'trejnd] adj.
niepowstrzymany;
niepohamowany;
nieopanowany
unrestricted ['anrys'tryktyd] adj.
nieograniczony
unrig ['an'ryg] v. zdejmować
(żagle); rozbierać (urządzenie)
unripe ['an'rajp] adj. niedojrzały
unrivalled [an'rajweld] adj.
niezrównany;
bezkonkurencyjny
unrobe ['an'roub] v. rozbierać
(się); zdejmować szaty
unroll ['an'roul] v. rozwinąć
(zwój, rolkę)
unruffled [an'rafld] adj.
niezmącony; niezakłócony;
zachowujący równowagę
unruly [an'ru:ly] adj. niesforny
unsaddle ['an'saedl] v.
rozsiodłać; wysadzić z siodła
unsafe ['an'sejf] adj. niepewny;
ryzykowny; niebezpieczny
unsaid ['an'sed] adj. nie
powiedziany; przemilczany
unsalted ['an'so:ltyd] adj. nie
solony
unsanitary ['an'saenytery] adj.
niehigieniczny; szkodliwy;
niezdrowy
unsatisfactory
['an,saetys'faektery] adj.
niezadowalający;
niedostateczny
unsatisfied [an'saetysfajd] adj.
niezadowolony;
niezaspokojony
unsavory ['an'sejwery] adj.
niesmaczny; przykry
unschooled ['an'sku:ld] adj.
nieuczony; nie szkolony;

niewprawny
unscientific ['an,sajen'tyfyk] adj.
nie naukowy; nie zgodny z
nauką
unscrew ['an'skru:] v.
odśrubować; rozśrubować;
odkręcić (gwint)
unscrupulous ['an'skru:pjules]
adj. bez skrupułów;
niegodziwy; bez sumienia
unseal ['an'si:l] v.
rozpieczętowywać; otwierać
unseen [an'si:n] adj. nie
widziany; niewidoczny
unselfish [an'selfysz] adj.
bezinteresowny
unsettled [an'setld] adj.
zaburzony; zakłócony;
nieustalony; niezapłacony;
rozstrojony
unshaven [an'szejwn] adj.
nieogolony
unshielded ['an'szy:ldyd] adj. nie
chroniony
unshrinkable [an'szrynkebl] adj.
nie kurczący się (w praniu)
unshrinking [an'szrynkyng] adj.
nie wahający się; nie
wzdrygający się
unskillful [an'skylful] adj.
niewprawny; niezręczny
unskilled [an'skyld] adj.
niewprawny;
niewykwalifikowany
unsociable [an'souszebl] adj.
nietowarzyski
unsocial [an'souszel] adj.
niesocjalny; niespołeczny
unsolvable [an'solwebl] adj.
nierozwiązalny;
nierozpuszczalny
unsolved [an'solwd] adj.
nierozwiązany;
nierozpuszczony
unsophisticated
[,anso'fystykejtyd] adj. prosty;
naturalny; prawdziwy
unsound [an'saund] adj.
niezdrowy; spróchniały; słaby;
niepewny; ryzykowny; błędny;
niesolidny
unspeakable [an'spi:kebl] adj.
niewypowiedziany; nie do

opisania

unspoiled [an'spojld] adj.
niezepsuty; nierozpieszczony
(dziecko)

unspoken ['an'spouken] adj. nie
mówiony (np. prawo)

unspoken-for [an'spoukn,fo:r]
adj. niezamówiony

unspoken-of [an'spoukn,ow] adj.
nie omawiany

unstable [an'stejbl] adj.
niepewny; chwiejny;
niezrównoważony

unsteady ['an'stedy] adj.
chwiejny; chwiejący się;
niezdecydowany;
nieustabilizowany; zmienny;
niepewny

unstressed ['an'strest] adj.
nieakcentowany;
niepodkreślony; nieobciążony

unsuccessful ['an-sek'sesful] adj.
nieudany; bez powodzenia;
nieudały; nie mający
powodzenia; bezowocny

unsuitable ['an'sju:tebl] adj.
niewłaściwy; niestosowny;
nieodpowiedni

unsure [an'szuer] adj. niepewny;
zawodny

unsurpassed ['an-ser'pa:st] adj.
nieprześcigniony;
niezrównany

unsuspected ['an-ses'pektyd]
adj. (zupełnie) niepodejrzany

unsuspecting ['an-ses'pektyng]
adj. niczego nie
podejrzewający

unsuspicious ['an-ses'pyszes]
adj. ufny; niepodejrzliwy

unthinkable [an'tynkebl] adj. nie
do pomyślenia;
nieprawdopodobny

unthinking ['an'tynkyng] adj.
bezmyślny

untidy [an'tajdy] adj. niechlujny;
niestaranny; rozczochrany;
zaniedbany; nie posprzątany

untie [an'taj] v. rozwiązywać
(się); rozsupłać; uwalniać
(się) z więzów; usuwać
(trudności)

until [an'tyl] prep. & conj. do;

dotychczas; dopiero; aż

untimely [an'tajmly] adj. nie w
porę; przedwczesny; nie na
czasie; wczesny; adv.
przedwcześnie; w
nieodpowiedniej chwili

untiring [an'tajeryng] adj.
niezmordowany

unto ['antu:] prep. = to; do; ku;
aż do

untold [an'told] adj.
niewypowiedziany;
nieprzeliczony

untouchable [an'taczebl] adj.
niedotykalny

untouched [an'taczt] adj.
nietknięty; nieskazitelny;
nieczuły

untried [an'trajd] adj.
niewypróbowany

untroubled [an'trabld] adj.
spokojny; beztroski

untrue ['an'tru:] adj.
nieprawdziwy; fałszywy;
niewierny; sprzeniewierzający
się

untrustworthy [an'trast,łe:rzy]
adj. niegodny zaufania;
niepewny

untruth ['an'tru:s] s. nieprawda;
kłamstwo

unused ['an'ju:zd] adj. nie
używany; nie przyzwyczajony;
nie stosowany

unusual [an'ju:żuel] adj.
niezwykły; wyjątkowy

unutterable [an'aterebl] adj.
niewysłowiony;
niewypowiedziany

unvarying [an'weery-yng] adj.
jednostajny; nieurozmaicony;
nie zmieniający (się)

unvoiced [an'woist] adj.
bezgłośny; bezdźwięczny

unwanted [an'łontyd] adj.
niepożądany; niepotrzebny;
zbędny; zbyteczny

unwarranted ['an'łorentyd] adj.
nieusprawiedliwiony;
bezpodstawny

unwholesome ['an'houlsem] adj.
niezdrowy; szkodliwy

unwilling ['an'łylyng] adj.

niechętny

unwind ['an'łajnd] v. zob. wind; rozwijać (się); odprężać (się); (slang): odpoczywać sobie

unwise ['an'łajz] adj. niemądry; nieostrożny; nieroztropny

unworthy [an'łe:r<u>zy</u>] adj. niegodny; niegodziwy; niewart; niezasługujący; ujemny

unwrap ['an'raep] v. rozwijać (się); rozpakować; odsłonić (się); odwijać (się)

unyielding ['an'ji:ld<u>yng</u>] adj. nieustępliwy; twardy; nieugięty

up [ap] adv. do góry; w górę; wzwyż; w górze; wyżej; na; tam (gdzie); na górze; wysoko; aż (do); aż (po); na (piętro); pod (górę); v. podnosić; zrywać się; podbijać (cenę); zaczynać

up-and-about ['apend,e'baut] exp.: (znowu) na nogach (po chorobie)

up-and-coming ['ap,end'kamy<u>ng</u>] exp.: (slang): obiecujący; rzutki; przedsiębiorczy (człowiek)

up-and-doing ['ap,end'duy<u>ng</u>] exp.: (slang): czynny; ruchliwy

up-and-up ['ap,end'ap] v. być uczciwym

up to ['ap,tu] adv. aż do

upbeat ['apbi:t] adj. optymistyczny; pogodny

upbringing ['ap,bryng<u>yng</u>] s. wychowanie; wychowywanie

uphill ['ap'hyl] adj. wznoszący (się); stromy; trudny; uciążliwy; adv. stromo; pod górę; w górę

upholster [ap'houlster] v. obijać (meble); wyściełać; pokrywać; urządzać

upholsterer [ap'houlsterer] s. tapicer; dekorator

upholstery [ap'houlstry] s. tapicerstwo; meble wyściełane

upkeep ['apki:p] s. utrzymanie;

koszty utrzymania

upmanship ['apmen,szyp] s. wywyższanie się

upon [e'pon] prep. = on; na; po

upper ['aper] adj. wyższy; górny; wierzchni; s. przyszwa

uppermost ['aper,moust] adj. najwyższy; adv. na górze; na górę

uppish ['apysz] adj. (slang): zadzierający nos do góry

upright ['ap'rajt] adj. wyprostowany; prosty; uczciwy; prawy; adv. pionowo; s. pionowy słup; podpora; pianino; pozycja pionowa

uprising [ap'rajzy<u>ng</u>] s. powstanie; wstawanie

uproar ['ap,ro:] s. zgiełk; wrzawa; harmider; tumult

upset [ap'set] v. zob. set; przewracać (się); pokonywać; wzburzać; rozstrajać; rozkuwać; pogrubiać; skręcać; rozklepywać; s. ['ap,set] wywrócenie (się); porażka; podniecenie; zaburzenie; rozstrój; niepokój; bałagan; sztanca do kucia

upside-down ['apsajd'dałn] adv. do góry nogami; do góry dnem; adj. odwrócony do góry nogami

upstairs ['ap'steerz] adv. na górę; na górze

upstart ['ap-sta:rt] s. parweniusz

upstream ['ap'stri:m] adv. pod prąd; w górę rzeki

uptight ['ap'tajt] adj. (slang): napięty; naprężony (nerwowo)

up-to-date ['ap-tu-'dejt] adj. bieżący; nowoczesny

upwards ['apłerdz] adv. w górę; ku górze; na wierzch; wyżej; powyżej (czegoś)

uranium [ju'rejnjem] s. uran

urbane [e:r'bejn] adj. grzeczny; układny; wytworny

urchin ['e:rczyn] s. ulicznik; urwis; łobuz; smyk; jeżowiec; jeżak; czesak

urge [e:rdż] v. poganiać;
popędzać; ponaglać;
przyśpieszać; nalegać;
pilić; namawiać; s.
pragnienie; impuls; tęsknota;
pociąg; bodziec

urge on ['e:rdż,on] v. namawiać
na coś

urgent ['e:rdżent] adj. pilny;
naglący; gwałtowny;
natarczywy; nalegający

urine ['jueryn] s. mocz; uryna

urn [e:rn] s. urna

usage ['ju:sydż] s. zwyczaj;
praktyka; obchodzenie (się);
używanie (zwrotów, języka
poprawnego)

use [ju:s] s. użytek; używanie;
użycie; posługiwanie;
zastosowanie; pożytek;
korzyść; zwyczaj; praktyka;
obrządek; przyzwyczajenie; v.
używać; korzystać;
wykorzystać; zużywać;
zużyć; wyczerpać;
traktować; obejść się;
mieć zwyczaj

used [ju:zd] adj. przyzwyczajony;
używany; stosowany

useful ['ju:sful] adj. użyteczny;
pożyteczny; dogodny;
wygodny; (slang): doskonały;
sprawny; biegły; zdolny

useless ['ju:zlys] adj.
niepotrzebny; bezużyteczny;
zbyteczny; bezcelowy;
nieużyteczny; do niczego

use up ['ju:z,ap] v. zużyć
(wszystko); wyczerpać (np.
pracą)

usher ['aszer] s. odźwierny;
woźny; bileter;
rozprowadzający na miejsca
(w kinie, w kościele etc.); v.
wprowadzać;
zapoczątkować

usher in ['aszer,yn] v.
wprowadzać do

usherette [,asze'ret] s. bileterka;
rozprowadzająca

usual ['ju:żuel] adj. zwykły;
zwyczajny; normalny;
zwyczajowy; utarty

usually ['ju:żuely] adv. zwykle;
zazwyczaj

usurer ['ju:żerer] s. lichwiarz

usurp [ju:ze:rp] v.
przywłaszczać sobie

usury ['ju:żery] s. lichwa

utensil [ju'tensyl] s. sprzęt;
naczynie; narzędzie

utility [ju'tylyty] s. pożytek;
użyteczność; firma
dostarczająca gaz,
elektryczność lub wodę
ludności w USA

utilize ['ju:tylajz] v. zużytkować;
spożytkować; wykorzystać

utmost ['atmoust] adj.
najwyższy; ostateczny;
skrajny; największy; najdalszy;
ostatni

utter ['ater] adj. całkowity;
zupełny; kompletny;
skończony; skrajny; ostatni;
v. wydawać (głos);
powiedzieć; wypowiedzieć
(hasło itp.); wyrażać;
wystawiać (czeki); podrabiać
(np. dokumenty); puszczać
(w obieg)

utterance ['aterens] s.
wypowiedź; wymowa;
wyrażenie; zeznanie;
oświadczenie

uvula ['ju:wjula] s. języczek
miękkiego podniebienia

V

v [wi:] dwudziesta druga litera
alfabetu angielskiego

vacancy ['wejkensy] s. wolne
mieszkanie; wolne pokoje
motelowe; wakans; próżnia;
pustka; bezczynność

vacant ['wejkent] adj. pusty;
próżny; wolny; wakujący;
bezczynny; bezmyślny;
obojętny

vacate [we'kejt] v. opróżniać;

opuszczać; unieważniać
vacation [we'kejszyn] s. wakacje
; ferie; opróżnienie; zwolnienie
(mieszkania); ewakuacja
vaccinate ['waeksynejt] v.
szczepić
vaccination ['waeksynejszyn] s.
szczepienie
vaccine ['waeksi:n] s.
szczepionka
vacuum ['waekjuem] s. próżnia
vacuum bottle ['waekjuem'botl]
s. termos
vacuum cleaner
['waekjuem'kli:ner] s.
odkurzacz
vacuum flask ['waekjuem,fla:sk]
s. termos
vagabond ['waegebond] adj.
włóczęgowski; wędrowny; s.
włóczęga; nierób; próżniak
vagary ['wejgery] s. kaprys;
chimera; wybryk; dziwactwo
vagina [we'dżajne] s. pochwa
(w anatomii kobiecej)
vague [wejg] adj. niejasny;
niewyraźny; nieokreślony;
nieuchwytny; wymijający;
niezdecydowany
vain [wejn] adj. próżny;
zarozumiały; czczy; pusty;
gołosłowny; daremny;
bezcelowy
valance ['waelens] s. krótka
podłużna zasłona (światła);
rodzaj adamaszku; frędzla;
lamberkin
vale ['wejl] s. dolina;
pożegnanie; excl.: żegnajcie!
valerian [we'lerjen] s. waleriana
valet ['waelyt] s. służący; v.
usługiwać
valiant ['waeljent] adj. dzielny; s.
zuch
valid ['waelyd] adj. słuszny;
ważny; uzasadniony
valley ['waely] s. dolina; koryto
fali; wewnętrzny kąt
płaszczyzn dachu
valor ['waeler] s. dzielność
valuable ['waeljuebl] adj.
wartościowy; cenny;
kosztowny; s. (pl.)

kosztowności; biżuteria
valuables ['waljuebls] pl.
kosztowności
valuation [,walju'ejszyn] s.
oszacowanie; cena
value ['waelju:] s. wartość;
cena; stopień jasności barwy
(w obrazie); v. szacować;
cenić; oceniać
valueless ['waelju:lys] adj.
bezwartościowy
valuer ['waelju:er] s. taksator
valve [waelw] s. zawór; wentyl;
klapa; zastawka
van [waen] s. kryty wóz
(ciężarowy); czoło armii; v.
przewozić krytym wozem;
badać rudę pukaniem
vane [wejn] s. chorągiewka (od
wiatru); łopatka śmigła;
brzechwa bomby; skrzydło
wiatraka
vanguard ['waen,ga:rd] s. straż
przednia; awangarda
vanilla [we'nyle] s. wanilia
vanish ['waenysz] v. znikać;
zanikać
vanity ['waenyty] s. próżność;
pycha; marność; czczość;
toaleta; źródło próżności;
rzecz bez wartości
vanity case ['waenyty,kejs] s.
kosmetyczka
vantage ['waentydż] s.
korzystna pozycja; przewaga
(w tenisie)
vapor ['wejper] s. para; mgła;
opary; v. parować
vaporize ['wejporajz] v.
wyparować; zamieniać się w
parę
vapor [wejpor] s. para; mgła; v.
parować; ględzić
vaporous ['wejperes] adj.
mglisty; zamglony
variable ['weerjebl] adj. zmienny;
niestały; s. zmienny wiatr
variance ['weerjens] s.
rozbieżność; niezgodność
variant ['weerjent] s. odmiana;
wariant; adj. odmienny; różny
variation [,weery'ejszyn] s.
zmiana; odmiana; wariant;

wariacja

varicose vein ['waerykous,wejn]
s. żylak

varied ['waeryd] adj. różnorodny;
różny; urozmaicony

variety [we'rajety] s.
rozmaitość; urozmaicenie;
różnorodność;
wielostronność; teatr
rozmaitości; kabaret; szereg;
odmiana

various ['weerjes] adj. różny;
rozmaity; urozmaicony; wiele;
kilka; kilkakrotnie

varnish ['wa:rnysz] s. pokost;
politura; werniks; polewa; v.
pokostować; werniksować

Varsovian [wa:r'souwjen] adj.
warszawski; s. warszawiak

vary ['weery] v. zmieniać (się);
urozmaicać; różnić się; nie
podzielać zdania

vase [wejz] s. waza; wazon

vat [waet] s. zbiornik; kadź;
cysterna

vault [wo:lt] s. sklepienie;
podziemie; piwnica;
grobowiec; skok o tyczce; v.
przesklepiać; osklepić;
przeskoczyć; skoczyć o
tyczce

vaulting horse ['wo:ltyng,ho:rs]
s. kozioł (przyrząd
gimnastyczny)

veal [wi:l] s. cielęcina

vegetable ['wedżytebl] s. jarzyna

vegetarian [,wedży'teerjen] adj.
jarski; s. jarosz; wegetarianin

vegetate ['wedżytejt] v.
wegetować; rosnąć

vehemence ['wi:ymens] s.
gwałtowność; porywczość;
wybuchowość

vehement ['wi:yment] adj.
gwałtowny; porywczy;
wybuchowy

vehicle ['wi:ykl] s. pojazd;
środek; narzędzie;
przymieszka do farby

veil [wejl] s. welon; woalka;
wstąpienie do klasztoru;
zasłona (maska); chrypka; v.
zasłaniać; ukrywać

vein [wejn] s. żyła (też złota);
usposobienie; natura; nastrój;
wena; v. żyłkować

velocity [wy'losyty] s.
szybkość

velvet ['welwyt] s. aksamit;
delikatna skórka; (slang):
zarobek; forsa; adj. aksamitny

venal ['wi:nl] adj. sprzedajny

vend [wend] v. sprzedawać

vender ['wender] s. (uliczny)
sprzedawca; automat do
sprzedaży

vending machine
['wendyng,me'szi:n] s.
automat do sprzedaży

venerable ['wenerebl] adj.
czcigodny; wielebny

venerate ['wenerejt] v. czcić

venereal [wy'njerjel] adj.
weneryczny; chory
wenerycznie;
przeciwweneryczny; płciowy

Venetian blind
[wy'ni:szyn,blajnd]
s. żaluzja (wenecka)

vengeance ['wendżens] s.
zemsta; pomsta

venison ['wenzn] s. dziczyzna

venom ['wenem] s. jad

venomous ['wenemes] adj.
jadowity

vent [went] s. odwietrznik;
wentyl; otwór wentylacyjny;
rozcięcie w tyle marynarki;
ujście; upust; v. dawać
upust czemuś;
wyładowywać (złość);
rozgłaszać; wietrzyć;
wiercić otwór wentylacyjny

ventilate ['wentylejt] v.
wentylować; wietrzyć;
przedyskutować

ventilator ['wentylejtor] s.
wentylator; wietrznik

ventriloquist [wen'tryloklyst] s.
brzuchomówca

venture ['wenczer] s. ryzyko;
stawka; spekulacja; impreza;
interes; próba; v. odważać
się; ośmielać się;
ryzykować; śmieć; narazić
się

veranda [we'raende] s. weranda
verb [we:rb] s. czasownik; słowo
verbal ['we:rbel] adj. ustny;
słowny; werbalny;
czasownikowy
verbatim [wer'bejtym] adj.
dosłowny; adv. dosłownie
verdict ['we:rdykt] s. wyrok;
werdykt; osąd; orzeczenie
verdure ['we:rdżer] s. zieleń
verge ['we:rdż] s. skraj; brzeg;
krawędź; v. graniczyć;
zbliżać się; chylić się;
skłaniać się
verge on ['we:rdż,on] v.
graniczyć
verification [,weryfy'kejszyn] s.
uwierzytelnienie; sprawdzenie
verify ['weryfaj] v. sprawdzać;
potwierdzać; udowadniać
vermicelli [we:rmy'sely] s. cienki
makaron
vermiform appendix
[we:rmy'fo:rme'pendyks] s.
ślepa kiszka; wyrostek
robaczkowy
vermin ['we:rmyn] s. robactwo;
świat przestępczy
vernacular [we:r'naekjuler] adj.
rodzimy; miejscowy; krajowy;
s. gwara; język rodzinny;
dosadne powiedzenie
versatile ['we:rsetail] adj.
wszechstronny
verse [we:rs] s. wiersz; strofa
versed ['we:rst] adj.
doświadczony; wprawiony (w
czymś)
version ['we:rżyn] s. wersja;
przekład; przekręcenie macicy
vertebra ['we:rtybre] s. krąg
vertebrae ['we:rtybri:] pl. kręgi
vertical ['we:rtykel] adj.
pionowy; szczytowy; s.
pionowa płaszczyzna; linia
very ['wery] adv. bardzo;
absolutnie; zaraz; właśnie;
adj. prawdziwy; sam;
skończony (drań)
vessel [wesl] s. naczynie;
pojemnik; statek; okręt
vest [west] s. kamizelka; v.
nadawać; przekazać;

przysługiwać komuś;
przypadać komuś; odziewać
w szaty; przykrywać ołtarz
vestry ['westry] s. zakrystia
vet ['wet] s. weterynarz
veteran ['weteran] s. weteran
veterinary ['weterynery] s.
weterynarz
veto ['wi:tou] s. weto; v.
zakładać weto
vex [weks] v. złościć;
dręczyć; dokuczać
vexation [wek'sejszyn] s.
dokuczanie; drażnienie;
zniecierpliwienie; irytacja;
udręka; przykrość;
zaniepokojenie
vexatious [wek'sejszes] adj.
dokuczliwy; irytujący; przykry;
nieznośny
via ['waje] prep. przez; via
vibrate [waj'brejt] v. zadrgać;
zadrżeć; oscylować;
wprawiać w drganie lub ruch
wahadłowy
vibration [waj'brejszyn] s.
drganie; drżenie; wibracja;
oscylacja; ruch wahadłowy
vibrator [waj'brejter] s. wibrator;
oscylator
vibratory [waj'bretery] adj.
wibracyjny; drganiowy;
drgający; migocący
vicar ['wyker] s. wikary;
wikariusz; zastępca;
namiestnik
vice [wajs] s. imadło; zacisk;
rozpusta; występek; nałóg;
narów; wada; zastępca; v.
zaciskać w imadle
vice-president ['wajs'prezydent]
s. wiceprzewodniczący;
wiceprezydent
vice versa ['wajsy'we:rsa] adv.
odwrotnie
vicinity [wy'synyty] s.
sąsiedztwo; pobliże
vicious ['wy'szes] adj. błędny;
występny; złośliwy; wadliwy;
zepsuty; dokuczliwy;
narowisty; rozpustny
victim ['wyktym] s. ofiara
victor ['wykter] s. zwycięzca

victorian [wyk'to:rjan] adj.
wiktoriański
victorious [wyk'to:rjes] adj.
zwycięski
victory ['wyktery] s. zwycięstwo
victuals ['wytlz] s. żywność;
jedzenie; prowianty; wiktuały
video ['wydjou] s. telewizja; adj.
telewizyjny
video-tape ['wydi:ou,tejp] s.
taśma magnetowidowa; v.
nagrać (obraz i dźwięk) na
taśmie
vie [waj] v. współzawodniczyć;
rywalizować; współubiegać
się
view [wju:] v. oglądać;
rozpatrywać; zbadać;
zapatrywać się; s. obejrzenie;
spojrzenie; wizja; zasięg
wzroku; widok; przegląd
umysłowy; pogląd;
zapatrywanie; intencja; zamiar;
cel; ocena
viewer ['wju:er] s. widz
(telewizyjny etc.)
view-finder ['wju:,fajnder] s.
wizjer
viewpoint ['wju:,pojnt] s. punkt
widzenia; zapatrywanie
vigil ['wydżyl] s. czuwanie;
wigilia
vigilance ['wydżylens] s.
czujność; bezsenność
vigilant ['wydżylent] adj. czujny
vigor ['wyger] s. krzepkość;
tężyzna; rześkość; energia;
siła; moc
vigorous ['wygeres] adj. krzepki;
mocny; jędrny; energiczny
vile [wajl] adj. podły; nędzny;
marny
vilify ['wyly,faj] v. oczerniać;
obmawiać
village ['wylydż] s. wieś
villager ['wylydżer] s. wieśniak
(raczej nieokrzesany)
villain ['wylen] s. łajdak; łotr;
nikczemnik; łobuziak
villainous ['wylenes] adj. łajdacki;
niegodziwy
villainy ['wyleny] s. łajdactwo
vim [wym] s. tężyzna

vincible ['wynsybl] adj.
przezwyciężalny
vindicate ['wyndykejt] v.
oczyszczać z zarzutu,
oskarżenia, podejrzenia;
rehabilitować;
usprawiedliwiać; bronić;
dochodzić; dowodzić
vindication [,wyndy'kejszyn] s.
obrona; windykacja;
usprawiedliwienie;
oczyszczenie się (z zarzutu);
rehabilitacja
vindictive [wyn'dyktyw] adj.
mściwy; karzący
vine [wajn] s. winna latorośl;
winorośl
vinegar ['wynyger] s. ocet; v.
kwasić
vineyard ['wynjerd] s. winnica
vintage ['wyntydż] s. rocznik
wina; winobranie; robienie
wina; model (roczny)
violate ['wajelejt] v. gwałcić;
zgwałcić (kobietę)
violation [,waje'lejszyn] s.
pogwałcenie; zgwałcenie;
gwałt; zbezczeszczenie;
naruszenie (też praw ruchu)
violence ['wajelens] s.
gwałtowność; gwałt;
przemoc
violent ['wajelent] adj.
gwałtowny; niepohamowany;
wściekły
violet ['wajelyt] s. fiołek; adj.
fioletowy (np. promień)
violin [,waje'lyn] s. skrzypce
violinist [,waje'lynyst] s.
skrzypek
viper ['wajper] s. żmija
virgin ['we:rdżyn] s. dziewica
virginity [we:r'dżynyty] s.
dziewictwo
virile ['wyrajl] adj. męski
virility [wy'rylyty] s. męskość;
wiek męski; cechy męskie
virtual ['we:rczuel] adj.
zasadniczy; właściwy;
faktyczny; prawdziwy;
rzeczywisty
virtually ['we:rczuely] adv.
rzeczywiście; faktycznie;

praktycznie biorąc

virtue ['we:rczju:] s. cnota;
prawość; czystość;
skuteczność; siła; moc

virtuoso [,we:rczju'ouzou] s.
wirtuoz; miłośnik-znawca
sztuki

virtuous [,we:rczjues] adj.
cnotliwy; prawy

virulent ['wyrulent] adj. jadowity;
złośliwy; zjadliwy

virus ['wajeres] s. wirus; jad
(chorobowy)

visa ['wi:za] s. wiza; v.
wizować

viscosity [wys'kosyty] s.
lepkość; kleistość

visibility [wyzy'bylyty] s.
widoczność

visible [wyzybl] adj. widoczny;
wyraźny; widzialny

vision ['wyżyn] s. widzenie;
wzrok; wizja; dar
przewidywania; v. okazywać
wizję; mieć wizję

visit ['wyzyt] v. odwiedzać;
wizytować; zwiedzać;
nawiedzać; karać; udzielać
się; gawędzić; s. wizyta;
odwiedziny; pobyt

visitor ['wyzyter] s. gość;
przyjezdny; zwiedzający;
inspektor

vista ['wysta] s. perspektywa;
wizja; widok

visual ['wyżjuel] adj. wzrokowy;
optyczny

visualize ['wyżjuelajz] v.
wyobrażać sobie;
uwidaczniać; uzmysławiać

vital ['wajtl] adj. witalny;
życiowy; żywotny;
zasadniczy; śmiertelny

vitality [waj'taelyty] s.
żywotność; żywość

vitamin ['wajtemyn] s. witamina

vivacious [wy'wejszes] adj.
żywy

vivacity [wy'waesyty] s.
żywość

vivid ['wywyd] adj. żywy

vivify ['wywyfaj] v. ożywiać

vivisection ['wywysekszyn] s.
wiwisekcja

vixen ['wyksen] s. liszka; lisica;
jędza

vixenish ['wyksenysz] adj.
jędzowaty

vocabulary [wou'kaebjulery] s.
słownik (specjalny);
słownictwo

vocal ['woukel] s. samogłoska;
adj. głosowy; wokalny;
głośny; natarczywy

vocalist ['woukelyst] s.
śpiewak; wokalista

vocation [wou'kejszyn] s.
zawód; zamiłowanie;
powołanie; skłonność

vodka ['wodke] s. wódka

vogue [woug] s. moda;
popularność

voice [wois] s. głos; dźwięk
samogłoskowy; strona
(czasownika); v. wymawiać;
wyrażać; dawać wyraz
czemuś; wymawiać
dźwięcznie; udźwięczniać;
pisać partie głosowe do
muzyki; stroić

void [woid] s. próżnia; pustka;
adj. próżny; pusty;
pozbawiony czegoś; wolny
od czegoś; wakujący;
nieważny; v. unieważniać;
wydalać; wypróżniać (się);
oddawać (mocz)

void of ['woid,ow] exp.: bez

volatile ['woletyl] adj. lotny;
ulatniający się; zmienny

volcano [wol'kejnou] s. wulkan

volley ['woly] s. salwa; potok;
odbicie (piłki); wolej; v. dać
salwą; wypuszczać salwę;
podawać wolejem; miotać
potokiem (przekleństw);
lecieć salwą; odbijać w locie

volleyball ['woly,bo:l] s.
siatkówka

volt [woult] s. wolt (elektr.);
wolta; v. robić woltę

voltage ['woultydż] s. napięcie
prądu; woltaż

voluble ['woljubl] adj. gładki;
potoczysty; ze swadą

volume ['wolju:m] s. tom;

objętość; masa; ilość;
pojemność; rozmiar; siła
voluntary ['wolentery] adj.
ochotniczy; dobrowolny; wolą
kontrolowany; spontaniczny;
samorzutny; s. specjalny
wyczyn z wyboru sportowca;
gra solo na organie
volunteer ['wolentier] s. ochotnik
(bezpłatnie pracujący); v.
robić z własnej ochoty;
zgłaszać się na ochotnika;
podejmować coś
dobrowolnie; być ochotnikiem
voluptuous [we'lapczues] adj.
zmysłowy; lubieżny
vomit ['womyt] v. wymiotować;
wyrzucać; pobudzać do
wymiotów; s. wymioty;
środek wymiotny
voodoo ['wu:du:] s. wiara w
czary; czarownik; v.
zaczarować
voracious [we'rejszes] adj.
żarłoczny
voracity [we'raesyty] s.
żarłoczność
vote [wout] s. głos; głosy;
głosowanie; prawo
głosowania; uchwała; wotum
(zaufania); v. głosować;
uchwalać; orzekać;
uznawać powszechnie za
coś
vote down ['wout,dałn] v.
odrzucać w głosowaniu
voting paper ['woutyng'pejper] s.
kartka wyborcza
vouch [waucz] v. ręczyć;
gwarantować; potwierdzać;
zapewnić
voucher ['wauczer] s. dowód
kasowy
vouch for ['waucz,fo:r] v.
ręczyć za kogoś
vouchsafe [waucz'sejf] v.
(łaskawie) raczyć
vow [wau] s. ślub (też
zakonny); przymierze; v.
przysięgać; ślubować;
składać śluby
vowel ['wałel] s. samogłoska
voyage ['wojydż] s. podróż

(statkiem)
voyager ['wojedżer] s. podróżnik
vulcanize ['walkenajz] s.
wulkanizować
vulgar ['walger] adj. ordynarny;
wulgarny; prostacki; gminny;
pospolity; powszechny
vulgarity [wal'gaeryty] s.
wulgarność; wyrażenie
wulgarne
vulnerability [,walnere'byłyty] s.
podatność na zranienie;
wrażliwość na ciosy;
słabość; słaby punkt
vulnerable ['walnerebl] adj.
czuły; wrażliwy; mający słabe
miejsce; narażony na cios;
podatny na zranienie;
niezabezpieczony
vulpine ['walpajn] adj. lisi;
przebiegły; chytry
vulture ['walczer] s. sęp; (slang):
szakal
vying ['wajyn] s. rywalizacja,
współzawodnictwo adj.
współzawodniczący (od
czasownika vie)

W

w ['dablju:] dwudziesta trzecia
litera alfabetu angielskiego
wack [łaek] s. (slang); oryginał;
dziwak; ekscentryk
wacky ['łaeky] adj. (slang):
zwariowany; zdziwaczały;
nieobliczalny
wad [łod] s. tampon; wałek
(zwinięty); wata (w uszach);
przybitka naboju w strzelbie;
(slang): forsa; plik
(banknotów); v. zatykać
(tamponem); watować;
przybijać (nabój); wypychać;
zwijać w wałek
wade [łejd] v. brodzić, brnąć,
przechodzić w bród, torować
sobie drogę

wadding ['łodyng] s. watowanie; watolina; wata; wełna (do utykania); podkład; przybitka

waddle ['łodl] v. chodzić kołysząc się w biodrze jak kaczka; s. kaczy krok

wade [łejd] v. brodzić; brnąć; przechodzić w bród; s. brodzenie

wafer ['łejfer] s. wafel; opłatek; naklejka urzędowa (pieczątkowa); zapieczętowywać naklejką

waffle ['łofl] s. wafel z ciasta naleśnikowego

waft ['łaeft] v. popychać (lekko); posuwać; posyłać (całusa); przepędzać; unosić (w powietrzu); s. śmignięcie skrzydła; powiew; podmuch; tchnienie; przelotne uczucie; smuga (światła)

wag [łaeg] v. kiwać (ogonem); poruszać się; wahać się; chodzić tam i z powrotem; merdać

wage [łejdż] s. płaca; zarobek; zapłata; v. prowadzić (np. wojnę)

wage earner ['łejdż,e:rner] s. człowiek zarobkujący

wages ['łejdżyz] s. zapłata

wager ['łejdżer] s. zakład; v. zakładać się o coś

wagon ['łaegen] s. ciężki wóz (kryty); lora; wóz policyjny; furgon

wail [łejl] v. zawodzić; lamentować; opłakiwać; v. zawodzenie; lament; płacz

wainscot ['łejnsket] s. boazeria; ozdobne obicie ścian drzewem

waist [łejst] s. talia; stan; pas; kibić; stanik; śródokręcie; zwężenie

waistcoat ['łeistkout] s. kamizelka

waist-deep ['łejst,di:p] adj. adv. po pas

wait [łejt] v. czekać; oczekiwać; czyhać; czatować; czaić się;

obsłużyć; obsługiwać kogoś; s. czekanie; oczekiwanie; zasadzka; czaty

wait on ['łejt,on] v. czekać na; usługiwać komuś

waiter ['łejter] s. kelner

wait on ['łejton] v. obsługiwać

waiting [łejtyng] s. czekanie; oczekiwanie; wyczekiwanie; zasadzka

waiting list [łejtyng,lyst] s. lista kolejności (kandydatów, klientów)

waiting room [łejtynrum] s. poczekalnia

waitings [łejtyns] pl. kolędnicy

waitress [łejtryss] s. kelnerka

wake; woke; woken [łejk; łouk; łoukn]

wake [łejk] v. obudzić (się); nie spać; pobudzić; rozbudzić; wzbudzić; wskrzesić; czuwać przy (zwłokach); s. niespanie; czuwanie przy zwłokach; kilwater; fala w ślad za statkiem (motorówką); ślad (po kimś, po czymś)

wake up ['łejk,ap] v. obudzić (się); ocknąć się; oprzytomnieć; zdawać sobie sprawę; zbudzić

wakeful ['łejkful] adj. czuwający; bezsenny; czujny

waken ['łejkn] = woken [łoukn] v. zob. wake

waken ['łejkn] v. zbudzić; obudzić; ożywiać; wzbudzić; wskrzesić (np. zmarłego)

walk [ło:k] v. iść; przechadzać się; chodzić; kroczyć; iść stępa; jechać stępa; wejść; zejść; s. chód; krok; przechadzka; spacer; marsz; deptak; aleja; odległość przebyta

walk about ['ło:ke,baut] v. włóczyć się; łazić

walk along ['ło:ke,long] v. chodzić sobie

walk away ['ło:ke,łej] v. odchodzić; (w zawodach):

łatwo wygrywać
walk back ['ło:k,baek] v.
wracać
walk down ['ło:k,dałn] v.
schodzić
walk in ['ło:k,yn] v. wchodzić
walk off ['ło:k,of] v. odchodzić;
zniknąć; ulotnić się (z
czymś)
walk out ['ło:k,aut] v. wyjść;
opuścić
walk over ['ło:k,ouwer] v.
wygrywać łatwo; traktować
pogardliwie
walk up ['ło:k,ap] v. podejść;
wejść na górę
walker ['ło:ker] s. piechur
walkie-talkie ['ło:ky-'to:ky] s.
przenośny, mały odbiornik-
nadajnik radiowy
walking [ło:kyng] s. chodzenie;
marsz; wycieczka piesza; adj.
chodzący; wędrowny
walking papers ['ło:kyn'pejpers]
pl. zwolnienie z pracy na
piśmie
walking stick ['ło:kyng,styk] s.
laska
walking-tour ['ło:kyng,tu:r] s.
wycieczka piesza; zwiedzanie
piechotą
walk-out ['ło:kaut] s. strajk
walk-over ['ło:kouwer] s.
walkower (sport)
wall [ło:l] s. ściana; mur;
przepierzenie; wał; v.
obmurować
wall in ['ło:l,yn] v. otaczać
wall up ['ło:l,ap] v. zamurować
wallboard ['ło:l,bo:rd] s. licówka
(ściany)
wallet ['łolyt] s. portfel
wallop ['łolep] v. walić; łoić;
prać; pobić na głowę;
galopować; łazić ciężko i
niezgrabnie; s. wyrżnięcie
(cios); galop; ruch ciężki i
niezgrabny
wallow ['łolou] v. tarzać się;
kłębić się; kołysać się; s.
tarzanie się
wallpaper ['łol,pejper] s. tapety;
v. tapetować

Wall Street ['łolstri:t] s. ośrodek
finansowy (USA)
walnut ['ło:lnat] s. orzech włoski
walrus ['ło:lres] s. mors
waltz ['ło:ls] s. walc; v.
tańczyć walca; (slang):
ruszać się żwawo
wan [łon] adj. blady; wybladły;
blednąć
wand [łond] s. laseczka;
pałeczka; pręt; buława
wander ['łonder] v. wędrować;
błądzić; błąkać się
wanderer ['łonderer] s.
wędrowiec
wane [łejn] v. zanikać; gasnąć;
s. zanik
wangle ['łaengl] v. (slang):
wycyganić; wyłudzić;
sfałszować; s. krętactwo;
kant
want [ło:nt] s. brak; potrzeba;
niedostatek; niedopatrzenie;
bieda; nędza; v. pragnąć;
chcieć; brakować;
potrzebować; pożądać
want ad [ło:nt, aed] s. drobne
ogłoszenie
want of food [ło:nt ow fu:d] s.
niedożywienie
want in ['o:nt,yn] v. chcieć
wejść
want out ['ło:nt,ałt] v. chcieć
wyjść
wanted ['ło:ntyd] adj.
poszukiwany
wanting ['ło:ntyng] adj.
brakujący; kiepski;
niedokładny; pozbawiony; nie
na poziomie; słaby na
umyśle; prep. bez; mniej;
przy braku
wanton ['łonten] adj. złośliwy;
krzywdzący; bez powodu;
bezmyślny; samowolny;
bezczelny; nieokiełznany;
wyuzdany; lubieżny; bujny;
zbytkowny; s. lubieżnik;
lubieżnica; v. oddawać się
rozpuście; używać sobie;
swawolić; róść bujnie;
trwonić; psocić; figlować;
bawić się

war [łor] s. wojna; v. wojować;
zawojować

warble ['łorbl] v. nucić;
jodłować; s. nucący głos;
nucona pieśń; guz od siodła
na grzbiecie konia; guz
wywołany larwą gza
bydlęcego

ward [łoːrd] s. dzielnica; cela;
sala; oddział; podopieczny;
opieka; kuratela; postawa
obronna; parada; straż; v.
odparowywać (cios);
odsuwać
(niebezpieczeństwo);
umieszczać na oddziale

ward off ['łoːrd,of] v.
odparowywać cios; odsuwać
(zagrożenie)

warden ['łoːrdn] s. dyrektor
więzienia; dozorca; nadzorca;
gatunek twardej gruszki

warder ['łoːrder] s. strażnik
więzienny; posterunek;
buława

ward heeler ['łoːrd,hiːler] s.
naganiacz partyjny

wardrobe ['łoːdroub] s.
garderoba; szafa na ubranie

ware [łeer] s. towar; wyrób;
ceramika; v. uwaga na coś;
trzymać się z dala od
czegoś; excl.: strzeż się!

warehouse ['łeerhaus] s.
magazyn; składnica; dom
składowy; v. magazynować;
składować

warlike ['łoː,lajk] adj.
wojowniczy, wojenny

warm [łoːrm] adj. ciepły; świeży
(trop); bliski znalezienia;
zadomowiony (na posadzie);
zamożny

warm up ['łoːrm,ap] v. ożywiać
(się); podgrzewać (się);
ogrzewać (się); rozgrzewać
(się)

warmup ['łoːrmap] ćwiczenia
rozluźniające (przed
zawodami etc.); zagrzanie się

warmth ['łoːrms̲] s. ciepło;
serdeczność; zapał

warn [łoːrn] v. ostrzegać;

przypominać; wzywać;
zapowiadać; uprzedzać

warn against [łoːnegejnst] v.
ostrzegać przed czymś

warning ['łoːrnyn̲g] adj.
ostrzegawczy; s. ostrzeżenie;
przestroga; znak
ostrzegawczy; wypowiedzenie
(posady)

warp ['łoːrp] v. wypaczyć (się);
zwichrować (się); wykrzywić
(się); spaczyć (się);
przyholowywać do miejsca
utwierdzenia liny lub
łańcucha; użyźniać (przez
zalewanie osadem); s.
spaczenie; wypaczenie;
osnowa; szew skośny; lina
holownicza; osad

warrant ['łorent] v.
usprawiedliwiać; uzasadniać;
gwarantować; s.
upoważnienie; gwarancja;
nakaz prawny (aresztu, rewizji
etc.); pełnomocnictwo dla
adwokatów; patent starszego
podoficera (USA)

warranty ['łorenty] s. gwarancja;
poręka; rękojmia; podstawa;
usprawiedliwienie;
upoważnienie; dokument
sądowy

warren ['łoːryn] s. królikarnia

warrior ['łoːrjor] s. wojownik;
żołnierz; adj. wojowniczy

wart [łoːrt] s. brodawka;
kurzawka

wary ['łeery] adj. ostrożny

was [łoz] v. zob. be

wash [łoːsz] v. myć (się); prać
(się); oczyszczać; zraszać;
lekko barwić; lawować;
umyć się; sunąć; płynąć z
pluskiem; płukać (rudę); s.
mycie; pranie; płyn
(czyszczący); fale; plusk;
pomyje; lura; wypłukane
miejsce w ziemi; głędzenie;
zaburzenie wody za statkiem;
zaburzenie powietrza za
samolotem; ziemia na tacy
zawierająca złoto;
podmywanie przez fale;

mielizna; kanał wyżłobiony
przez wodę; mielizna
naniesiona wodą; lawowanie;
cienka warstwa metalu;
kilwater; ślad wodny

wash away [ło:sze,łej] v.
spłukać; zmyć; unosić

wash down ['ło:sz,dałn] v.
zmywać strumieniem wody;
popić jedzenie

wash off [ło:sz,of] v. odeprać;
wymywać

wash out ['ło:sz,aut] v.
wupłukiwać (się) (z pieniędzy
etc.)

wash up ['ło:sz,ap] v. zmywać
naczynia; wymyć się

wash and wear ['ło:sz,end'łeer]
s. bielizna i odzież gotowa do
noszenia po praniu bez
prasowania

washbowl ['ło:sz,boul] s.
miednica; umywalka;
umywalnia

washcloth ['ło:sz,klos] s.
zmywak; szmatka do
zmywania

washer ['ło:szer] s. uszczelka;
podkładka; maszyna do prania

washing ['łoszyng] s. mycie;
pranie; przemywanie; woda z
prania; popłuczyny; wypłukane
złoto; wypłukany żwir; bielizna
do prania

washing machine
['ło:szyng,me'szi:n] s. pralka;
maszyna do prania

washing powder ['ło:szyn'pałder]
s. proszek do prania

washing up ['ło:szyng,ap] v.
obmycie się

wash-leather ['ło:sz,ledzer] s.
ircha; zamsz

washout ['ło:szaut] s.
zapadnięcie się; podmycie;
(slang): klapa; niepowodzenie

washtub ['ło:sztab] s. balia

washy ['ło:szy] adj. wodnisty;
rzadki; blady; cienki;
wypłowiały

wasn't = was not

wasp [łosp] s. osa; (slang): biały
-anglosaksonin-protestant

waspish ['łospysz] adj. zjadliwy;
cienki w pasie (jak osa)

wastage ['łejstydż] s. strata;
zużycie

waste [łejst] adj. pustynny;
pusty; nieużyty (ziemia);
opustoszały; wyludniony;
leżący odłogiem; zużyty;
niepotrzebny; zbyteczny;
odpadowy; v. pustoszyć;
psuć; niszczyć (się); stracić
(też zabić); zmarnować;
ginąć; zużywać (się);
zapuścić; zaniedbać; s.
pustynia; marnowanie;
trwonienie; zniszczenie;
ubytek; zużycie; odpady;
bezmiar (np. wody);
zaniedbanie; marnotrawstwo

waste away ['łejst,e'łej] v.
marnieć

wasteful ['łejstful] adj. rozrzutny;
marnotrawny

wastepaper basket ['łejst-pejper
-ba:skyt] s. kosz na śmieci

waste pipe ['łejstpajp] s. rura
odpływowa; rura ściekowa

watch [ło:cz] s. czuwanie;
pilnowanie; czaty; czujność;
wachta; zegarek; oczekiwanie
na coś; wyglądanie czegoś;
v. czuwać; oczekiwać;
czatować; pilnować;
opiekować się; uważać;
mieć na oku; mieć się na
baczności; wyglądać
czegoś; obserwować;
szpiegować; przyglądać się;
patrzyć; oczekiwać
sposobności; śledzić

watch out ['ło:czaut] v.
uważać; strzec się; uwaga!;
uważaj!

watchdog ['ło:czdog] s. pies
podwórzowy

watchful ['ło:czful] adj. czujny;
baczny

watchmaker ['ło:cz,mejker] s.
zegarmistrz

watchman ['ło:czmen] s. stróż;
dozorca

watchtower ['ło:cz,tauer] s.
stażnica; wieża strażnicza

watchword ['ło:cz‌łe:rd] s. hasło;
slogan
watch your step ['ło:cz,jo:r'step]
exp.: uważaj!; pilnuj się!
water [ło:ter] s. woda; wysięk;
przypływ; odpływ; pl. zdrój;
wody lecznicze; ocean; morze;
jezioro; rzeka; v. polewać;
podlewać; pokropić; poić;
iść do wodopoju;
nawadniać; rozwadniać;
rozcieńczać; skrapiać;
łzawić się; ślinić się
water blister ['ło:ter,blyster] s.
pęcherzyk z wodą
waterborne ['ło:ter,born] adj.
przenoszony lub przekazywany
przez wodę
water anchor [ło:ter'aenker] s.
kotwica dryfująca
water bottle ['ło:ter,botl] s.
karafka; manierka
water brush ['ło:ter,brasz] s.
zgaga
water but ['ło:ter,bat] s. zbiornik
na deszczówkę
water cart ['ło:ter,ka:rt] s.
beczkowóz
water closet ['ło:ter'klozet] s.
ustęp
watercolor ['ło:ter'kaler] s.
akwarela
water cool ['ło:ter,ku:l] v.
chłodzić wodą
watercourse ['ło:ter,ko:rs] s.
strumień; rzeka; kanał
watercress ['ło:ter,kres] s.
rzeżucha wodna
water cure ['ło:ter,kjuer] s.
kuracja wodna
water dog ['ło:ter,dog] s. pies
myśliwski aportujący z wody;
(slang): amator pływania etc.
water down [ło:ter,dałn] v.
rozwadniać
waterfall ['ło:ter,fo:l] s.
wodospad
waterfowl ['ło:ter,faul] s.
ptactwo wodne
waterfront ['ło:ter,frant] s.
wybrzeże; doki; dzielnica
portowa
water-gap ['ło:ter,gaep] s.

przełom rzeki
watergate ['ło:ter,gejt] s. śluza
water-gauge ['ło:ter,gejdż] s.
wodowskaz; licznik wodny
water glass ['ło:ter,gla:s] s.
szklanka; naczynie; kubek;
szklany wodowskaz;
przeziernik podwodny
water hammer ['ło:ter,haemer] s.
silny wstrząs wywołany
nagłym zatrzymaniem wody w
rurze
water hen ['ło:ter,hen] s. kurka
wodna
water hole ['ło:terhol] s. stojąca
woda (w suchym łożysku
rzeki); wodopój
water ice ['ło:ter,ajs] s. sorbet
watering place ['ło:teryngplejs] s.
wodopój; kąpielisko;
zdrojowisko
waterless ['ło:terlys] adj.
bezwodny; pozbawiony wody
water level ['ło:ter'lewl] s.
poziom wody
water lily ['ło:ter,lyly] s.
grzybień biały; lilia wodna
waterline ['ło:terlajn] s. linia
zanurzenia statku
waterlogged ['ło:ter,logd] adj.
przesycony wodą
water main ['ło:ter,mejn] s.
główna rura wodociągów
water-man ['ło:termen] s.
przewoźnik; wioślarz
watermark ['ło:terma:rk] s. znak
wodny; wodowskaz; v. robić
znak wodny
watermelon ['ło:ter,melen] s.
arbuz; kawon
water meter ['ło:ter'mi:ter] s.
wodomierz; licznik wodny
water mill ['ło:ter,myl] s. młyn
water moccasin ['ło:ter,mokesyn]
s. żmija wodna w USA
water motor ['ło:ter'mouter] s.
motor wodny
water plane ['ło:ter'plejn] s.
hydroplan
waterpower ['ło:ter'pałer] s. siła
wodna; prawo do używania
wody
water pot ['ło:ter,pot] s.

konewka; polewaczka

waterproof ['ło:ter,pru:f] adj.
nieprzemakalny; v. robić
nieprzemakalnym

water-rat ['ło:ter,raet] s. szczur
wodny

water rate ['ło:ter,rejt] s. opłata
za wodę; cena wody

water scape ['ło:ter,skejp] s.
krajobraz morski

watershed ['ło:ter,szed] s. dział
wodny; (slang): ważna granica

water-ski ['ło:ter,ski:] s. narta
wodna

water spout ['ło:ter,spaut] s.
trąba wodna; rynna pionowa

water supply ['ło:terse,plaj] s.
zaopatrzenie w wodę; sieć
wodociągowa

water table ['ło:ter,tejbl] s.
poziom (w ziemi) wody
zaskórnej

watertight ['ło:ter,tajt] adj.
wodoszczelny

water tower ['łoter,tauer] s.
wieża ciśnień

water wave ['ło:ter,łejw] s.
ondulacja wodna

waterway ['ło:ter,łej] s. droga
wodna; kanał; rzeka spławna

waterwheel ['ło:ter,hłi:l] s. koło
(młyńskie) wodne

water witch ['ło:ter,łycz] s.
różdżkarz

waterworks ['ło:ter,łe:rks] s.
wodociągi; fontanna

watery ['ło:tery] adj. wodnisty;
załzawiony; śliniący się;
wróżący deszcz

watt [łot] s. (electr.) wat

waul [ło:l] v. miauczeć ostro i
przeciągle (Brit.)

wave [łejw] s. fala; falistość;
ondulacja; pokiwanie ręką;
gest ręką; v. falować;
ondulować; machać do
kogoś

wave away ['łejwe'łej] v.
odprawiać machnięciem ręki

wave back ['łejw,baek] v.
przywoływać (z powrotem)
machnięciem ręki

wavelength ['łejw,le_nks_] s.

długość fali

wave meter ['łejwmi:ter] s.
falomierz

waver ['łejwer] v. zachwiać
(się); zamigotać; być
niezdecydowanym;
załamywać się; drżeć;
zawahać się; kołysać się;
trzepotać się; s. chwianie
(się)

wavy ['łejwy] adj. falisty;
sfalowany; drżący; migocący;
karbowany

wawl ['ło:l] v. wrzeszczeć jak
kot (Brit.)

wax [łaeks] s. wosk; adj.
woskowy; v. woskować;
stawać się

waxen ['łaeksn] adj. woskowy;
miękki jak wosk

wax paper ['łaeks'pejper] s.
papier woskowy

waxwork ['łaeksłe:rk] s. figura
woskowa; v. modelować z
wosku

waxy ['łaeksy] adj. woskowy;
woskowaty; (slang):
wściekły; zły; okrutny

way [łej] s. droga; szlak; trakt;
przejście; wolna droga;
odległość; kierunek; strona;
sposób; zwyczaj; bieg; tok;
sens; stan; położenie

way back [łej baek] adv. dawno
temu; daleko w tyle; dawno

waybill ['łejbył] s. list
przewozowy; fracht

wayfarer ['łej,feerer] s.
podróżnik (pieszy)

waylay [łejlej] v. zob. lay;
zaskoczyć kogoś; czyhać na
kogoś; czatować

way of life ['łej ow,lajf] s. styl
życia; sposób życia

way-out ['łej,aut] s. wyjście;
rozwiązanie; adj. (slang):
nadzwyczajny; nadzwyczaj;
dobrze zrobiony; nadzwyczaj
zdolny; (zob. far-out)

wayside ['łej,sajd] s. skraj drogi;
adj. przydrożny

way station [,łej'stejszyn] s.
przystanek

-ways [łejz] (przyrostek) w taki sposób (np. sideways)
wayward ['łejłerd] adj. przewrotny; uparty; kapryśny; nieobliczalny; chimeryczny
we [łi:] pron. my
weak [łi:k] adj. słaby
weaken ['łi:kn] v. osłabiać; słabnąć; rozcieńczać
weak-kneed ['łi:kni:d] adj. słaby
weakling ['łi:klyng] s. słabeusz; cherlak; człowiek słaby; adj. słaby
weakly ['łi:kly] adj. słabowity; adv. słabo
weak-minded ['łi:k,majndyd] adj. słaby na umyśle; słabego charakteru
weakness [łi:knys] s. słabość; słabostka
wealth [łels] s. bogactwo; dobrobyt
wealthy ['łelsy] adj. bogaty
wean [łi:n] v. odłączać od piersi; oduczać; odrywać
weapon ['łepon] s. broń
weaponless ['łepon,les] adj. bezbronny
wear; wore; worn [łeer; ło:r; ło:rn]
wear [łeer] v. nosić; chodzić w czymś; ścierać się; wycierać się; żłobić; zacierać się; przechodzić; mijać; zdzierać; nużyć; męczyć; wyczerpywać; długo trwać; długo służyć; s. noszenie; rzeczy noszone; moda; zużycie; wytrzymałość
wear away ['łeer,e'łej] v. zużywać; wlec się
wear off ['łeer,of] v. zetrzeć (się); zacierać (się); mijać
wear on ['łeer,on] v. wlec się
wear out ['łeer,aut] v. zdzierać (się); wyczerpywać (się)
wearing ['łieryng] adj. przeznaczony do noszenia na sobie
wearisome ['łierysem] adj. męczący; nużący; nudny
weary ['łiery] adj. zmęczony;

znużony; znudzony; męczący; nużący; nudny; v. męczyć; nudzić; naprzykrzać się; uprzykrzać sobie
weasel ['łi:zl] s. łasica
weather ['łedzer] s. pogoda; adj. atmosferyczny; odwietrzny; pogodny; v. zwietrzać; okrywać się patyną (śniedzią)
weather-beaten ['łedzer,bi:tn] adj. zahartowany; skołatany przez burze
weather-bound ['łedzer,baund] adj. zatrzymany przez pogodę (statek)
weather bureau ['łedzer,bjuerou] s. instytut meteorologiczny
weather chart ['łedzer,cza:rt] s. wykres meteorologiczny
weathercock ['łedzer,kok] s. chorągiewka na dachu; kurek na dachu; człowiek niestały
weather forecast ['łedz,fo:rka:st] s. komunikat meteorologiczny
weather vane ['łedzer,wejn] s. wiatrowskaz; chorągiewka na dachu
weave; wove; woven [łi:w; łouw; łouwn]
weave [łi:w] v. tkać (tkaninę); knuć (spisek); układać (intrygę, opowiadanie); spleść; splatać; zajmować się tkactwem
weaver ['łi:wer] s. tkacz
weaving ['łi:wyng] s. tkactwo
web [łeb] s. tkanina; sztuka (materiału); stek (kłamstw); pajęczyna; błona (nietoperza); tkanka łączna; usztywnienie
wed [łed] v. zaślubiać; łączyć się; pobrać się; adj. zaślubiony
wedded ['łedyd] adj. zaślubiony; ślubny; oddany (sprawie)
wedding ['łedyng] s. ślub; wesele; adj. ślubny; weselny
wedding ring ['łedyng,ryng] s. obrączka ślubna
we'd [łi:d] = we had; we would; we should
wedge [łedż] s. klin; trójkątny

kawałek (tortu); golfowy kijek z klinowym zakończeniem; v. klinować; zaklinować; rozklinować; łupać

wedge in ['łedż,yn] v. wpychać (się); wcisnąć (się)

wedge off ['łedż,of] v. wypychać (się)

wedlock ['łedlok] s. małżeństwo

Wednesday ['łenzdy] s. środa

weed [łi:d] s. chwast; zielsko; cygaro; (slang): chuchro; cherlak; mizerak; szkapa; v. pielić; odchwaszczać

weeder ['łi:der] s. pielnik; wypielacz

weed grown ['łi:dgroun] adj. zachwaszczony

weed out ['łi:d,aut] v. wypielać; usuwać

weeds ['łi:ds] pl. krepa żałobna; strój żałobny

weedy ['łi:dy] adj. zachwaszczony; chudy; wysoki

weed killer ['łi:d,kyler] s. trucizna na chwasty

week [łi:k] s. tydzień

weekday ['łi:kdej] s. dzień powszedni

weekend ['łi:kend] s. niedziela oraz części wolne soboty i poniedziałku; v. spędzać weekend

weekly ['łi:kly] adj. tygodniowy; adv. tygodniowo; s. tygodnik

weep; wept; wept [łi:p; łept; łept]

weep [łi:p] v. płakać; opłakiwać; zapłakać; lamentować; cieknąć; wyciekać; ociekać; s. płacz; cieknięcie

weeper ['łi:per] s. beksa, płaczek; płaczka; welon żałobny; krepa żałobna

weep away ['łi:pe,łej] v. wypłakać się

weeping willow ['łi:pyng,łylou] s. wierzba płacząca

weigh [łej] v. ważyć (się); rozważać; mierzyć; równoważyć; podnosić

(kotwicą); s. ważenie

weigh in ['łej,yn] v. ważyć (boksera; dżokeja przed zawodami)

weigh out ['łej,aut] v. wyważyć człowieka przed zawodami

weigh up ['łej,ap] v. rozważyć

weigh upon ['łej,apon] v. przygniatać; ciążyć na kimś

weight [łejt] s. ciężar; waga; obciążenie; ciężarek; odważnik; przycisk; grubość (odzieży); znaczenie; doniosłość; odpowiedzialność; v. obciążać; pogrubiać sztucznie tkaninę

weight lifting ['łejt lyftyng] s. (sport) podnoszenie ciężarów

weightless ['łejtlys] adj. lekki; bez ciężaru

weighty ['łejty] adj. ciężki; ważki; doniosły; ważny; poważny; przekonywujący; rozważony; przemyślany

weir [łier] s. jaz; grobla

weird [łierd] adj. niesamowity; tajemniczy; nadprzyrodzony; dziwny; dziwaczny; s. los

welcome ['łekem] exp.: witaj! witajciel s. powitanie; adj. mile widziany; mający pozwolenie; mogący korzystać; v. powitać; witać (z radością)

weld [łeld] v. spawać (się); spajać; zespalać; zgrzewać; s. spoina; spawanie; spojenie; miejsce spojenia

welder ['łelder] s. spawacz; spawarka; przyrząd do spawania

welfare ['łelfeer] s. dobro; dobrobyt; powodzenie; pomyślność; szczęście

welfare-state ['łelfeer'stejt] s. państwo o bardzo wysokich świadczeniach społecznych

welfare-work ['łelfeer,łe:rk] s. praca społeczna; społecznictwo; praca dobroczynna

well; better; best [łel; beter;

best] adv. dobrze; lepiej;
najlepiej

well [łel] s. studnia; otwór
wiertniczy; odwiert; źródło;
klatka (schodowa); adv.
dobrze; należycie; porządnie;
mocno; solidnie; szczęśliwie;
całkiem; wyraźnie; łatwo;
lekko; słusznie; adj. dobry;
zdrowy; zadowalający;
pomyślny; w porządku; exp.:
dobrze! a więc?

well-balanced ['łel'baelenst] adj.
zrównoważony

well-behaved ['łelby'hejwd] adj.
dobrze wychowany

well-being ['łel'bi:ynɡ] s.
dobrobyt; powodzenie;
pomyślność

well-born ['łel'bo:rn] adj. dobrze
urodzony

well-bred ['łel'bred] adj. rasowy;
dobrze wychowany

well-connected ['łel'konektyd]
adj. dobrze skoligacony

well-disposed ['łeldys'pouzd] adj.
życzliwie usposobiony

well done ['łeldan] exp.: brawo!
dobrze zrobione!

well-fed ['łelfed] adj. dobrze
odżywiony

well-founded ['łelfaundyd] adj.
uzasadniony

wellhead ['łel'hed] s. źródło

well-heeled ['łel'hi:ld] adj.
(slang): forsiasty (ma forsę)

Wellingtons ['łelyntenz] s. buty z
wysokimi cholewami (też z
gumy) (Brit.)

well-informed ['łel-ynfo:rmd] adj.
dobrze poinformowany;
wykształcony

well-intended ['łel-'yntendyd] adj.
dobrze pomyślany

well-judged ['łel-'dżadżd] adj.
rozsądny; roztropny; dobrze
pomyślany

well-knit ['łel'nyt] adj. zwarty;
dobrze zbudowany; jędrny

well-known ['łel'nołn] adj. dobrze
znany

well-meant ['łel'ment] adj.
zrobiony w najlepszej intencji

well-nigh ['łel'naj] adv. nieledwie;
o mało co; o mało nie

well-off ['łel'o:f] adj. dobrze
sytuowany; zamożny

well point ['łel'point] s. rura do
usuwania wody podskórnej
(przed kopaniem)

well-read ['łel'red] adj. oczytany

well-sinker ['łel'synker] s.
studniarz

well-spoken ['łel'spouken] adj.
uprzejmy; pięknie mówiący;
dobrze powiedziany

wellspring [łel'spryng] s. źródło

well-timed ['łel'tajmd] adj. na
czasie; odpowiedni

well-to-do ['łel-te'du:] adj.
zamożny; dobrze sytuowany

well-wisher ['łel'łyszer] s.
sympatyk

well-worn ['łel'ło:rn] adj.
wytrwały; wyświechtany;
oklepany; dobrze noszony

welsh [łelsz] adj. walijski; s.
wykręcanie się od płacenia; v.
uciekać nie zapłaciwszy

welter ['łelter] v. falować;
tarzać się; s. falowanie;
powódź; zamęt; kolos; silne
uderzenie

wench [łencz] s. dziewucha;
ulicznica; v. latać za
dziewkami

Wendish [łendysz] adj. łużycki

went [łent] v. zob. go

wept [łept] v. zob. weep

were [łe:r] v. zob. be

we're [łier] = we are

werewolf ['łe:rłuf] s. wilkołak

west [łest] s. zachód; adj.
zachodni; adv. na zachód; ku
zachodowi

westerly ['łesterly] adj. zachodni;
adv. na zachód

western ['łestern] adj. zachodni;
pochodzący z zachodu

westward ['łestłerd] adj.
zachodni; ku zachodowi; na
zachód

wet [łet] adj. mokry; wilgotny;
zmoczony; przemoczony;
słotny; deszczowy; dżdżysty;
(slang): w błędzie; s. wilgoć;

wilgotność; trunek; v.
moczyć (się); zwilżać;
zraszać

wet nurse ['łet,ne:rse] s. mamka;
v. karmić

wether ['łedzer] s. skop
(kastrowany baran)

wet through ['łet'tru:] v.
przemoczyć (na wylot)

we've [łi:w] = we have

whack [hłaek] v. walić;
grzmocić; (slang): dzielić się
czymś; s. walnięcie;
trzaśnięcie; (slang): część;
próba; stan (rzeczy)

whacker ['hłaeker] s. kolor

whacking ['hłaekyng] adj.
kolosalny

whale [hłejl] s. wieloryb; rzecz
wspaniała; v. polować na
wieloryby; (slang): bić

whale-boat ['hłejl,bout] s. łódź
do połowu wielorybów; łódź
strażnicza, ratunkowa

whalebone ['hłejlboun] s. fiszbin

whale-fin ['hłejlfyn] s. fiszbin

whale-oil ['hłejl,ojl] s. tran
wielorybi

whaler ['hłejler] s. statek do
połowu wielorybów

whammy ['hłaemy] s. (slang):
urok (rzucony na kogoś)

whang [hłaeng] s. grzmotnięcie;
huczenie; rzemień; v. walić;
grzmocić; huczeć

wharf [hło:rf] s. przystań
(wyładunkowa); nabrzeże; v.
cumować do wyładunku;
wyładowywać w przystani

wharves [hło:rfs] pl. nabrzeża
wyładunkowe

what [hłot] adj. jaki; jaki tylko;
ten; który; ten ... co; taki ...
jaki; tyle ... ile; pron. co; to
co; coś; excl.: co? czego? jak
to!

what about ['hłote,baut] exp.: a
co z ... ?; co powiesz o ... ?

whatever ['hłot'ewer] adj.
jakikolwiek; pron. cokolwiek;
wszystko; co tylko; bez
względu; obojętnie co

what for ['hłotfo:r] s. (slang):

bura; lanie; exp.: za co?

what next ['hłot,nekst] exp.: co
dalej?

whatnot ['hłotnot] s. etażerka;
cacka; (slang): cokolwiek;
obojętnie co; wszystko

what's it ['hłotsyt] s. jak się to
nazywa; ten (przedmiot)

whatsoever ['hłotsou'ewer] adj.
jakikolwiek by; cokolwiek by;
co tylko by; pron. wszystko
co tylko

wheat [hłi:t] s. pszenica

wheaten ['hłi:tn] adj. pszeniczny

wheel ['hłi:l] s. koło; kółko; ster;
kierownica; v. obracać (się);
wrócić (się); prowadzić
taczki (rower); wozić
taczkami etc.

wheelbarrow ['hłi:l,baerou] s.
taczki

wheel chair ['hłi:l,czeer] s. fotel
na kółkach

wheeler-dealer ['hłi:ler,di:ler] s.
cwaniak; politykier

wheelwright ['hłi:lrajt] s.
kołodziej

wheeze ['hłi:z] v. sapać; s.
sapanie; (slang): dowcip;
komunał

wheezy ['hłi:zy] adj. sapiący;
zasapany

when [hłen] adv. kiedy; kiedyż;
wtedy; kiedy to; gdy; przy;
podczas gdy; s. czas
(zdarzenia)

whenas [,hłen'aez] conj. kiedy;
podczas gdy

whence [hłens] adv. & conj.
skąd

whenever ['hłenewer] adv. kiedy
tylko; skoro tylko

whensoever ['hłensou'ewer] adv.
skoro tylko; skądkolwiek

where [hłeer] adv. & conj. gdzie;
dokąd

whereabout ['hłeere'baut] adv.
gdzie?

whereabouts ['hłeere'bauts] adv.
zważywszy; gdzie; mniej
więcej; s. miejsce
zamieszkania (pobytu)

whereas ['hłeer'aez] conj.

podczas gdy
whereat ['hłeer,et] conj. podczas gdy
whereby ['hłeer,baj] adv. po czym? po kim? po którym; za pomocą którego? jak? którym
wherefore ['hłeerfo:r] adj. dlaczego; dlatego; z tego powodu
wherefrom [hłeer'fro:m] adv. skąd; z czego
wherein [hłeer'yn] adv. w czym; w którym
whereof [hłeer'ow] adv. z czego; z którego
whereon [hłeer'on] adv. na czym; na którym
wheresoever [,hłeersou'ewer] adv. wszędzie by; dokądkolwiek by; gdzie tylko by
whereupon [,hłeere'pon] adv. na czym; po czym
wherever [,hłeer'ewer] adv. dokądkolwiek; wszędzie; gdzie tylko
wherewith [,hłeer'łyz] adv. (z) czym?
wherewithal [,hłeerły'go:l] s. potrzebne środki (fundusze, przybory)
whet [hłet] v. naostrzyć; zaostrzyć (też apetyt); s. ostrzenie; zakąska
whether ['hłedzer] conj. czy-czy; czy tak, czy owak
whetstone ['hłet,stoun] s. osełka; kamień szlifierski
whey [hłej] s. serwatka
which [hłycz] pron. który; co; którędy; dokąd; w jaki (sposób)
whichever [hłycz,ewer] adj. którykolwiek; jaki; każdy ... jaki; który tylko; pron. którykolwiek; każdy
whichsoever [,hłyczsou'ewer] adj. pron. = whichever (z naciskiem)
whiff [hłyf] s. powiew; podmuch; tchnienie; zapach; dym; lekki wybuch gniewu; v. dmuchać; dymić; palić;

lekko wiać
while [hłajl] s. chwila; pewien czas; po chwili; niebawem; wkrótce; conj. podczas gdy; jak długo; dopóki; póki; natychmiast; chociaż co prawda
while ago [hłajl,egou] adv. jakiś czas temu
whilst [hłajlst] adv. podczas
whim ['hłym] s. kaprys; zachcianka; fantazja; fanaberia; kołowrót górniczy
whimper ['hłymper] v. piszczeć; kwilić; skomleć; skowyczeć; s. kwilenie; skowyt; skamlanie
whimsical ['hłymzykel] adj. kapryśny; dziwaczny; cudaczny
whimsy ['hłymzy] s. kaprys
whim-wham ['hłymhłaem] s. cacko
whine ['hłajn] v. skomleć; jęczeć; powiedzieć jękliwie; s. skomlenie; jęk
whip [hłyp] s. bat; bicz; pomocnik; woźnica; naganiacz; uderzenie biczem; bita śmietana; v. chłostać; zacinać (batem); ubijać (śmietaną); smagać; przyrządzać naprędce; zwyciężyć; zakasować (kogoś); owijać; windować; śmigać; zbierać; wyjechać (pośpiesznie)
whip in ['hłyp,yn] v. zapędzać batem
whip off ['hłyp'o:f] v. zerwać coś; czmychnąć z czymś
whip on ['hłyp'on] v. popędzać batem
whip out ['hłyp,aut] v. wyciągnąć błyskawicznie
whip round ['hłyp,raund] v. odwrócić się znienacka
whip together ['hłyp te'gedzer] v. zganiać batem; zwalać na kupę; montować na gwałt
whipped cream ['hłypt'kri:m] s. bita śmietana
whipper-snapper ['hłyper'snaeper] s. chłystek;

smarkacz

whipping boy ['hłypyng,boj] s.
kozioł ofiarny (chłopak
chłostany za innego)

whipping top ['hłypyng,top] s.
bąk do podbijania

whippy [,hłypy] adj. giętki;
elastyczny

whipsaw [,hłyp'so] s. wąska
piłeczka; v. ciąć piłką;
wygrać podwójnie; pobić
podwójnie

whip-stock [,hłyp'stok] s.
biczysko

whirl [hłe:rl] v. kręcić (się);
wirować; zawirować;
porywać w wir; s. wirowanie;
ruch wirowy; wir; (slang):
próba (czegoś)

whirlpool ['hłe:rl'pu:l] s. wir

whirlwind ['hłe:rl'łynd] s. trąba
powietrzna; wir powietrzny

whirlybird [hłe:rly'be:rd] s.
helikopter (USA)

whirr [hłe:r] v. furkotać;
warkotać; s. furkot; warkot
(maszyny)

whisk [hłysk] s. wiecheć;
śmignięcie; trzepaczka (do
jajek etc.); miotełka; v.
otrzepać; odpędzać;
porywać; szybko odwozić;
przywozić; czmychać;
wymachiwać; śmigać

whisk away ['hłyske'łej] s.
strzepnąć; przewieźć lotem
strzały; czmychnąć

whiskers [hłyskers] pl. baki;
bokobrody; wąsy

whisky ['hłysky] s. (wódka)
whiskey

whisper ['hłysper] v. szeptać;
mówić cicho; szemrać;
szeleścić; s. szeptanie;
szmer

whistle ['hłysl] v. gwizdać;
świstać; zagwizdać; s.
gwizdanie; gwizd; świst;
gwizdek; gardło

whistle away ['hłysle'łej] v.
pogwizdywać sobie

white [hłajt] adj. biały;
bezbarwny; blady; czysty;

niepokalany; uczciwy;
rzetelny; niewinny; s. biel;
biały (człowiek); białko; białe
wino

white coffee [hłajt'kofi] s. kawa
z mlekiem

white-collar ['hłajt,koler] adj.
zajęci biurowo (urzędnicy etc.)

white elephant [hłajt'elyfent] s.
towary wybrakowane; buble

white collar worker ['hłajt,koler
łerker] s. pracownik umysłowy

white frost ['hłajt'fro:st] s. szron

white-headed ['hłajt'hedyd] adj.
siwowłosy

white heat [hłajt'hi:t] s. biały żar

white lie [hłajt'laj] s. kłamstwo;
wykręt towarzyski

white paper ['hłajt,pejper] s.
oficjalna publikacja
wykazująca, że rząd ma
zawsze rację (USA)

whiten ['hłajtn] v. wybielać;
pobielać; bielić; zbieleć

whiteness ['hłajtness] s. biel

whitewash [,hłajt'łosz] s. wapno;
wybielanie czegoś lub
kogoś; v. wybielać;
wymywać na czysto;
uniewinnić; usprawiedliwić;
pobić na sucho (na zero)

Whitsuntide ['hłajtsntajd] s.
Zielone Świąta (Brit.)

whittle down ['hłytl,dałn] v.
strugać; zestrugać;
wystrugać; obstrugać

whity ['hłajty] adj. białawy

whiz [hłyz] s. świst; (slang):
mistrz; rzecz wspaniała; v.
świstać; suszyć

who [hu:] pron. kto; który

whodunit [hu:danyt] s. (slang):
"kryminał"; powieść
detektywistyczna

whoever [hu:'ewer] pron.
ktokolwiek

whole [houl] adj. cały;
pełnowartościowy; zdrowy; s.
całość

wholehearted ['houl'ha:rtyd] adj.
serdeczny; szczery

whole-hogger ['houl'hoger] s.
człowiek idący na całego

whole length ['houl'le<u>nks</u>] s.
(portret) w całości
wholesale ['houl,sejl] s. hurt;
handel hurtowy; adj. hurtowy;
masowy; adv. hurtem;
masowo
wholesaler ['houl,sejler] s.
hurtownik
wholesale trade ['houlsejl,trejd]
s. handel hurtowy
wholesome ['houlsem] adj.
zdrowy; zdrowotny
whole-time ['houltajm] adj. pełno
-etatowy (czasowy)
whole-wheat ['houl'hłi:t] adj.
pełno-ziarnisty (chleb)
who'll [hu:l] `= who shall; who
will
wholly ['houly] adv. całkowicie
whom [hu:m] pron. kogo? zob.
who
whoop [hu:p] s. okrzyk (wesoły
np.)
whooping cough ['hu:py<u>n</u>,kof] s.
koklusz
whopping ['hłopy<u>ng</u>] adj. (slang):
ogromny
whore [ho:r] s. wulg.: kurwa;
dziwka; v. kurwić się; gonić
za dziwkami
whose [hu:z] pron. & adj. czyj;
czyja; czyje; którego
why [hłaj] adv. dlaczego; czemu;
czemuż; dlatego; właśnie; s.
przyczyna; powód; exp.: jak
to! właśnie! patrzcie; no
wiesz!; no to co!
why so ['hłaj'sou] adv. dlaczego
wick [łyk] s. knot; tampon
wicked ['łykyd] adj. niegodziwy;
niedobry; frywolny; paskudny;
złośliwy; zły; nikczemny
wickedness ['łykydnys] s.
nikczemność;
niegodziwość
wicker basket ['łyker,ba:skyt] s.
pleciony kosz
wicker chair [łyker,czeer] s.
plecione krzesło
wicket [łykyt] s. furka; kołowrót;
okienko kasowe; bramka; cel;
drzwi na pół wysokości
(otworu)

wide [łajd] adj. szeroki; rozległy;
szeroko otwarty; obszerny;
wielki; pokaźny; znaczny;
duży; daleki; adv. szeroko; z
dala (od czegoś)
wide-awake ['łajde,e'łejk] adj.
czujny; rozbudzony; bystry; z
szeroko otwartymi oczami
widen ['łajdn] v. poszerzyć;
rozszerzać
wideness ['łajdnys] s.
szerokość; rozległość;
bezmiar
wide-open [,łajd'oupen] adj.
szeroko otwarty
widespread [,łajd'spred] adj.
rozprzestrzeniony; szeroko
rozpostarty
widow ['łydou] s. wdowa; v.
wdowieć
widower ['łydouer] s. wdowiec
width [łyd<u>s</u>] s. szerokość
wife [łajf] s. żona; pl. wives
[łajwz]
wig [łyg] s. peruka; v.
zaopatrywać w perukę
wild [łajld] adj. dziki; dziko
rosnący; gwałtowny;
wściekły; szalony; burzliwy;
rozwichrzony; pustynny;
zdziczały; rozwydrzony;
fantastyczny; nierealny;
podniecony; s. pustynia; dziki
teren; adv. na chybił trafił
wildcat ['łajld,kaet] adj.
porywczy; awanturniczy;
nadzwyczajny (np. pociąg); s.
żbik; szyb naftowy na nowym
terenie; awanturnicze
przedsiębiorstwo; spekulacja;
samotna lokomotywa;
porywcza osoba; v. szukać
nafty na niesprawdzonych
terenach
wilderness [łajldernys] s.
pustynia; puszcza; odludzie
wildfire [,łajld'fajer] s.
błyskawicznie
rozprzestrzeniający się ogień;
ogień grecki; błędny ognik
willful ['łylful] adj. rozmyślny;
umyślny; zamierzony;
świadomy; samowolny;

uparty
will [łyl] s. wola; testament; siła
woli; v. postanowić;
zarządzać; zapisywać (w
testamencie); zmuszać;
chcieć
willing [,łylyng] adj. skłonny
(coś zrobić); chętny; pełen
dobrej woli
willow ['łylou] s. wierzba
willowy ['łyloły] adj. smukły;
gibki; giętki; obfitujący w
wierzby
will power ['łyl,pałer] s. siła woli
willy-nilly ['łyly'nyly] adv. chcąc
nie chcąc (Brit.)
will you? ['łyl,ju:] exp.: czy
zrobisz?; czy zechcesz?; czy
obiecasz?
wilt [łylt] v. więdnąć; opadać;
oklapnąć; powodować
zwiędnięcie; opadać z sił; s.
więdnięcie; osłabienie;
depresja
wily [łajly] adj. chytry
win; won; won [łyn; łon; łon]
win [łyn] v. wygrywać;
zwyciężać; zdobywać;
zarabiać; osiągać;
pozyskać; przedostać się;
przezwyciężać; s. wygrana;
zwycięstwo
win over [łynouwer] v.
pozyskać sobie; przekonać
wince [łyns] v. skrzywić się (z
bólu); drgać; s. drgnięcie;
skrzywienie
winch [łyncz] s. korba; wyciąg;
kołowrót; v. podnosić;
wyciągać kołowrotem lub
korbą
wind; wound; wound [łajnd;
łaund; łaund]
wind [łajnd] v. nawijać; zwijać;
zwinąć; owinąć (się); wić
(się); zakończyć; [łynd] s.
wiatr; podmuch; oddech;
dech; zapach; puste słowa;
gadanie; v. trąbić; dąć w
róg; przewietrzyć; zwietrzyć;
poczuć; zmęczyć; dać
wytchnąć
windbag ['łyndbaeg] s. czczy

gaduła
windfall ['łynd fo:l] s. gratka;
owoc zrzucony wiatrem
winding ['łajndyng] adj. kręcony;
kręcący się
winding-stairs ['łajndyng,steers]
s. kręcące się schody
wind-instrument
[łynd,ynstrument] s.
instrument dęty
windlass [łyndles] s. wyciąg;
kołowrót
windmill ['łynmyl] s. wiatrak
wind off [łajnd,o:f] v. odwinąć
(się)
wind up [łajnd,ap] v. nakręcać
(zegar); kończyć (mowę);
zamykać (zebranie)
window ['łyndou] s. okno;
okienko
window dressing ['łyndou
,dressyng] s. dekoracja
wystawy sklepowej
windowpane ['łyndou,pejn] s.
szyba okienna
window shade ['łyndou,szejd] s.
żaluzja
window shopping
['łyndouszopyng] v. oglądać
wystawy (a nie kupować)
window-sill ['łyndou,syl] s.
parapet
windpipe ['łynd,pajp] s. tchawica
windshield ['łyndszyld] s. szyba
ochronna (przednia) w
samochodzie
windshield wiper
['łyndszyld'łajper] s.
wycieraczka szyby ochronnej
windy ['łyndy] adj. wystawiony
na wiatr; wietrzny; gadatliwy
wine ['łajn] s. wino
wine-glass ['łajngla:s] s. kieliszek
do wina
wine-press ['łajnpres] s.
wytłaczarka do winogron
wing [łyng] s. skrzydło; ramię;
kulisa; dywizjon; lot; v.
uskrzydlać; przewozić na
skrzydłach; przelecieć (przez
coś); lecieć; szybować
wing commander ['łyng
-ke,ma:nder] s. dowódca

dywizjonu lotnictwa (podpułkownik)

wink ['łynk] v. mrugać (na kogoś); przymykać oczy; s. mrugnięcie

winner ['łyner] s. zdobywca nagrody; człowiek wygrywający; laureat

winning ['łynyng] s. otwór do wydobywania węgla; adj. ujmujący; zwycięski

winning post ['łynyng,poust] s. meta

winnings ['łynyngs] pl. wygrana

winsome ['łynsem] adj. ujmujący; pociągający

winter ['łynter] s. zima; adj. zimowy; v. zimować

winter crop ['łynter,krop] s. ozimina

winterize ['łynterajz] v. dostosowywać, przygotowywać do zimy

wintry ['łyntry] adj. zimowy; chłodny; obojętny

winy ['łajny] adj. podchmielony; winny

wipe [łajp] v. wycierać; ocierać; ścierać; wymazać; zamachnąć się; s. starcie; wytarcie; bicie

wipe away ['łajpe,łej] v. wycierać; wymazać

wipe off ['łajp,o:f] v. zetrzeć (plamę etc.)

wipe out ['łajp,aut] v. wytrzeć; wymazać; wyniszczyć; zgładzać

wipe up ['łajp,ap] v. wytrzeć (podłogę etc.)

wire [łajer] s. drut; przewód; telegram; kabel; struna metalowa; sidła; v. drutować; zadrutować; złapać (w sidła); założyć przewody (w domu); zatelegrafować; ciągnąć za sznurki zakulisowe

wire cutter ['łajer,kater] s. szczypce do cięcia drutu

wire haired ['łajer,heerd] adj. ostrowłosy (pies)

wireless ['łajerlys] adj. radiowy; bez drutu

wiry ['łajery] adj. twardy; żylasty; muskularny; druciany

wisdom ['łyzdem] s. mądrość

wisdom tooth ['łyzdem,tu:s] s. ząb mądrości

wise [łajz] s. sposób; adj. mądry; roztropny

wiseacre ['łajz,ejker] s. mądrala; mędrek

wise after ['łajz,a:fter] adj. mądry po ...

wisecrack ['łajzkra:k] s. dowcipna uwaga; v. robić dowcipy

wise guy ['łajzgaj] s. nadęta wielkość

wise saw ['łajzso:] s. przysłowie

wish [łysz] v. życzyć (sobie); pragnąć; chcieć; s. pragnienie; życzenie; chęć; powinszowanie; ochota; rzecz upragniona

wishbone ['łyszboun] s. kość widełkowa (ptaków)

wish for ['łysz fo:r] v. życzyć sobie (np. pogody)

wishful ['łyszful] adj. pragnący

wishful thinking ['łyszful -tynkyng] s. pobożne życzenie

wish well ['łysz,łel] v. dobrze życzyć

wishy-washy ['łyszy,łoszy] adj. bez treści; wodnisty; lurowaty

wisp [łysp] s. wiązka; garść; pęczek; kosmyk; wstęga (dymu)

wistful ['łystful] adj. smutny; zadumany; pełen tęsknoty

wit [łyt] s. umysł; rozum; dowcip; człowiek dowcipny; inteligencja; olej w głowie

witch [łycz] s. czarownica; czarodziejka; v. zaczarować; oczarować

witchcraft ['łycz,kra:ft] s. czary; czarnoksięstwo

witch doctor ['łycz,dakter] s. czarownik; znachor

witchery ['łyczery] = witchcraft

witch hunt ['łyczhant] s. tropienie czarownic; polityczne głośne śledztwo

(propagandowe) w celu
udowadniania działalności
wywrotowej

with [łys] prep. z (kimś,
czymś); u (kogoś); przy
(kimś); za pomocą;
(stosownie) do; (cierpliwość)
dla

withdraw [łys'dro:] v. zob. draw;
cofać (się); wycofywać
(się); odwołać (coś);
odebrać (ze szkoły);
odsuwać (zasłonę)

withdrawal [łys'dro:el] s.
wycofanie

wither ['łydzer] v. powodować
więdnięcie, usychanie;
zabijać (spojrzeniem);
usychać; usuwać się (w
cień itp.)

withers ['łydzers] pl. kłąby (u
konia między łopatkami)

withhold [łys'hould] v. zob. hold;
wstrzymywać; odmawiać;
wycofać

within [łys'yn] adv. wewnątrz; w
domu; u siebie; w (czymś); w
duchu; do wnętrza; w
obrębie; w odległości (np.
mili); w ciągu (np. dnia); w
zasięgu (wzroku); s. wnętrze

without [łysaut] prep. bez; poza;
na zewnątrz; adv. na
zewnątrz; poza domem; s.
strona zewnętrzna

withstand [łys'staend] v. zob.
stand; opierać się;
przeciwstawiać się; być
wytrzymałym; wytrzymywać

witling ['łytlyng] s. dowcipniś

witness ['łytnys] s. świadek;
widz; świadectwo; v. być
świadkiem; świadczyć (też
podpisem)

witness box ['łytnys,boks] s.
miejsce dla świadka w sądzie
(USA)

witness stand ['łytnys,staend] s.
miejsce dla zeznawania w
sądzie (USA)

witticism ['łytysyzem] s.
złośliwy dowcip;
dowcipkowanie

witty [łyty] adj. dowcipny

wives [łajwz] pl. żony; zob. **wife**

wiz [łyz] s. (slang): znawca;
mistrz; rzecz wspaniała

wizard ['łyzerd] s. czarownik;
czarodziej; adj. czarodziejski;
(slang): wspaniały

wo [ło:u] exp.: prrr (na konia,
żeby stanął)

wobble ['łobl] v. chwiać się;
ruszać się chwiejnie; chodzić
chwiejnie; jechać kołysząc
się; mówić drżąco; grać
drżąco (melodią); drgać;
wahać się; być
niezdecydowanym

wobbler ['łobler] s. człowiek
chwiejny

wobbly [łobly] adj. chwiejący
się; chwiejny

woe [łou] s. nieszczęście

woebegone ['łoubi,go:n] adj.
nieszczęsny

woeful ['łouful] adj. bolesny;
żałosny

woke [łouk] v. zob. wake

woken [łoukn] v. zob. wake

wolf [łulf] s. pl. wolves [łulwz];
wilk; (slang): kobieciarz; v.
żreć; pożerać; połykać jak
wilk; polować na wilki

wolf down ['łulf,dałn] v.
pożerać jak wilk;

wolf-call ['łulf,ko:l] s. (slang):
gwizdanie na kobietę (z
podziwem, zaczepką etc.)

wolf-cub ['łulf,kab] s. wilczek;
wilczę; młodszy harcerz

wolf-dog ['łulfdog] s. wilczur

wolfhound ['łulfhaund] s. wilczur
rosyjski lub alzacki

wolfish ['łulfysz] adj. wilczy

wolf skin ['łulf'skyn] s. wilcza
skóra (na podłogę etc.);
wilczura (okrycie)

wolf whistle ['łulfhłysl] =
wolfcall

wolverine [,łulwe'ri:n] s.
rosomak; mieszkaniec stanu
Michigan

woman ['łumen] s. pl. women
['łymyn]; kobieta; baba; żona;
v. mówić per "kobieta";

umieszczać między kobietami
woman doctor ['łumen'dakter] s.
lekarka
womanhood ['łumenhud] s.
kobiety; kobiecość (dojrzała)
womanish ['łumenysz] adj.
babski; zniewieściały
womanize ['łumenajz] v. babieć;
niewieścieć; gonić za
kobietami
womankind ['łumen,kajnd] s.
kobiety; ród niewieści
womanlike ['łumen,lajk] adj.
kobiecy
womanly ['łumenly] adj. kobiecy
womb [łu:m] s. macica; łono;
żywot
women [łymyn] pl. zob. woman
won [łan] v. zob. win
wonder ['łander] s. zdumienie;
cud; v. dziwić się; być
ciekaw; zastanawiać się
wonderful ['łanderful] adj.
cudowny
wonderland ['łanderlaend] s.
kraina cudów (czarów)
wonderment ['łanderment] s.
zdziwienie; zdumienie
wondering ['łanderyng] adj.
zdumiony; niedowierzający
wonder-work ['łanderłe:rk] s. cud
wonder-worker ['łanderłe:rker] s.
cudotwórca
wonder-working ['łanderłe:rkyng]
adj. sprawiający cuda
wondrous ['łandres] adj.
cudowny; adv. cudownie
wont; wont; wonted [łont; łont;
łantyd]
wont [łant] v. przyzwyczajać;
mieć zwyczaj; s. zwyczaj;
przyzwyczajenie
won't [łount] = will not
wonted ['łantyd] adj. zwykły
woo [łu:] v. zalecać się (do
kobiety); umizgać się;
ubiegać się; namawiać do
czegoś
wood [łud] s. drzewo; drewno;
lasek; pl. lasy; puszcza; v.
obsadzać drzewami;
dostarczać drzewo
woodbine ['łudbajn] s. powój

wonny; wiciokrzew pomorski
woodblock ['łudblok] s.
drzeworyt (do odciskania)
wood carving ['łudka:rwyng] s.
drzeworytnictwo
woodchuck ['łudczak] s.
świstak
wood coal ['łudkoul] s. węgiel
drzewny
woodcock ['łudkok] s. słomka
woodcraft ['łudkra:ft] s.
znajomość lasu
woodcraftsman ['łudkra:ftsmen]
s. myśliwy; traper
woodcut ['łudkat] s. drzeworyt
woodcutter ['łudkater] s. drwal;
drzeworytnik
wooded ['łudyd] adj. lesisty;
zalesiony
wooden ['łudn] adj. drewniany;
tępy
wood engraver [,łudyn'grejwer]
s. drzeworytnik
wood engraving
[,łudyn'grejwyng] s.
drzeworytnictwo
wooden head ['łudn,hed] s.
głupiec
woodland ['łudlaend] s. las;
lesisty okręg; adj. lesisty;
leśny
woodman ['łudmen] s. drwal;
leśnik
wood notes ['łudnouts] s.
dźwięki lasu
woodpecker ['łud,peker] s.
dzięcioł
wood pulp ['łud,palp] s. miazga
drzewna
woodruff ['łudraf] s. marzanna
(wonna)
woodshed ['łud,szed] s.
drwalnia; drewutnia
woodsman ['łudsmen] s.
mieszkaniec lasu; drwal
wood sorrel ['łudserel] s.
szczawik zajęczy
woodsy [łudzy] adj. leśny
wood wind ['łud,łynd] s. (dęty)
instrument drewniany
woodwork [łudłe:rk] s. wyroby
drzewne; części drewniane
(np. ramy okien etc.);

drewniana część budowy;
budowa drewniana; stolarka;
ciesiołka

woody ['łudy] adj. lesisty;
drewniany

wooer ['łu:er] s. zalotnik

woof [łu:f] s. wątek

wool [łul] s. wełna (czesana,
strzyżona, zgrzebna);
czupryna; włosy (wełniste);
owcze runo; wełniane rzeczy

wool-ball ['łulbo:l] s. kłębek
wełny

woolen ['łuln] adj. wełniany; s.
wyrób wełniany

wool fat ['łulfaet] s. lanolina

wool-fell ['łulfel] s. baranica;
skóra owcza

woolgathering ['łul,gaedzeryng]
adj. głupio rozmarzony
(roztargniony); s. głupie
marzycielstwo

woolly ['łuly] adj. wełnisty;
oschły (głos); mętny umysł;
nie soczysty; mączysty;
włóknisty (owoc); zamazany;
(slang): surowy i niekulturalny;
s. wełniana odzież; (slang):
owca

wooly ['łuly] = woolly

woozy ['łu:zy] adj. (slang):
wstawiony; otumaniony;
niezdrów

word [łe:rd] s. słowo; wyraz;
słówko; komplement;
przechwałka; obelga; mowa;
wieść; rozkaz; adv. ustnie;
słownie; adj. słowami
wyrażony; v. wyrazić;
redagować; sformułować;
ubierać w szatę słowną;
przybierać w słowa

wordage ['łe:rdydż] s. ilość
słów

word-blind ['łe:rd,blajnd] adj.
niezdolny do rozumienia pisma

wordbook ['łe:rd,buk] s. słownik

wording ['łe:rdyng] s. ujęcie,
wyrażenie słowami

wordplay ['łe:rd,plej] s. gra słów

word-splitter ['łe:rd,splyter] s.
pedant słowny

word-splitting ['łe:rd,splytyng] s.

sofistyka; dzielenie włosa na
czworo

wordy ['łe:rdy] adj. rozwlekły;
gadatliwy; słowny (wojna
słów)

wore [ło:r] v. zob. wear

work; worked; worked [łe:rk;
łe:rkt; łe:rkt]

work [łe:rk] s. praca; robota;
zajęcie; energia; zadanie;
dzieło; utwór; uczynek; pl.
fabryka; huta; fortyfikacje;
ozdoby; v. pracować;
działać; funkcjonować;
skutkować; oddziaływać;
wywoływać; sprawiać;
wykonywać; kazać robić;
prowadzić; obsługiwać;
poruszać (motor); posuwać
(się); przesuwać (się);
wprawiać w (pasją);
nadawać kształt;
przeprowadzać przez coś;
obrabiać; urabiać (się);
wyszywać; robić robótkę;
(slang): wykorzystywać
(znajomości); drgać; burzyć;
falować; fermentować;
trzeszczeć (statek); źle
działać (maszyna);
wyczerpać się; odrabiać;
wypracować; wytwarzać;
uzyskiwać z trudem;
podniecać (się) stopniowo;
zaznajamiać się z czymś;
mieszać w całość;
dokazywać (cudów);
wywierać (wpływ); urabiać;
fasonować; eksploatować
(kopalnie itp.)

work away ['łe:rke,łej] v.
pracować zawzięcie

work in ['łe:rkyn] v. pasować;
wprowadzać coś

work off ['łe:rko:f] v. pozbywać
się czegoś

work on ['łe:rkon] v. pracować
dalej

work out ['łe:rkaut] v.
przeprowadzać; realizować;
obliczać; rozwiązywać;
wyczerpywać;
wyeksploatować; skończyć;

wynosić (w sumie)
work up ['łe:rkap] v. podniecać
(się); doprowadzać (się);
opracowywać; wyrabiać;
rozwijać; wspinać się;
podnosić (się)
workable ['łe:rkebl] adj. możliwy
(do obróbki, uprawy etc.);
opłacalny; wykonalny; realny;
możliwy do przeprowadzenia;
w stanie używalności
workaday ['łe:rkedej] adj.
codzienny; roboczy;
powszedni
work-basket ['łe:rk,ba:skyt] s.
koszyk z robótką
workbook ['łe:rk,buk] s.
podręcznik ze wskazówkami;
dziennik pracy
workday ['łe:rkdej] s. dzień
roboczy; dzień powszedni
worker ['łe:rker] s. pracownik;
robotnik
workhouse ['łe:rk,haus] s. dom
poprawczy; przytułek
working ['łe:rkyng] adj.
pracujący; pracowniczy;
roboczy; praktyczny;
działający; czynny; ruchomy;
powszedni; s. praca; robota;
działanie; ruch;
roboczodniówka; obróbka
working capital
['łe:rkyng'kaepytl] s. kapitał
obrotowy
working knowledge
['łe:rkyng'nolydż] s. wiedza
praktyczna
working-class ['łe:rkyng'kla:s] s.
klasa robotnicza
working day ['łe:rkyngdej] s.
dzień pracy
working hours ['łe:rkyng,auers]
s. godziny pracy
working load ['łe:rkyng,loud] s.
ciężar użyteczny; nośność
workingman ['łe:rkyng,men] s.
robotnik
working pressure ['łe:rkyng
,preszer] s. ciśnienie robocze
workless ['łe:rklys] adj. & s.
bezrobotny
work-like ['łe:rklajk] adj. dobrze

wykonany; dobrze nastawiony
do pracy
workman ['łe:rkmen] s. pl.
workmen ['łe:rkmen]; robotnik
(fizyczny); fachowiec
workmanship ['łe:rkmanszyp] s.
wykonanie; jakość
wykonania; faktura; twór
work of art ['łe:rk-ow,a:rt] s.
dzieło sztuki
workout ['łe:rkaut] s. trening;
zaprawa; danie komuś szkoły
workroom ['łe:rk'rum] s.
pracownia
works council ['łe:rks'kansl] s.
rada zakładowa
workshop ['łe:rkszop] s.
pracownia; warsztat; zakład;
posiedzenie
worktable ['łe:rktejbl] s. biurko
workup ['łe:rkap] s. podniecenie
(się); powalanie podczas
druku
workwoman ['łe:rkłumen] s. pl.
workwomen ['łe:rkłymyn];
robotnica; pracownica fizyczna
world [łe:rld] s. świat; ziemia;
kula ziemska; sfery; masa;
mnóstwo; zatrzęsienie
czegoś; bezmiar; wielka
ilość; adj. światowy
worldling ['łe:rldlyng] s. człowiek
oddany sprawom doczesnym
worldly ['łe:rldly] adj. światowy;
ziemski; doczesny
world-minded ['łe:rld'majndyd]
adj. oddany sprawom
doczesnym
world old ['łe:rld,old] adj. stary
jak świat
world power ['łe:rld'pałer] s.
potęga światowa; wielkie
mocarstwo
world-series ['łe:rld'sieri:z] s.
mistrzostwa palanta (baseball)
USA
world war ['łe:rld'łor] s. wojna
światowa
world-weary ['łe:rld'łeery] adj.
zmęczony życiem
world-wide ['łe:rld,łajd] adj.
światowy
world wise ['łe:rld,łajz] adj.

obyty; doświadczony
worm [łe:rm] s. robak; robaczek;
glista; dżdżownica; gwint;
zwojnik; śruba (nie ostra);
wężownica; v. wkradać się;
wykradać; czołgać się;
wyciągać (tajemnicę z
kogoś); czyścić (zwierzę) z
robaków; czyścić (grządkę)
z robaków
worm-eaten [łe:rm,i:tn] adj.
robaczywy; stoczony przez
robaki; (slang): przestarzały
worm-fishing [łe:rm,fyszyn] s.
łowienie ryb na robaki
worm gear [łe:rm,gier] s.
przekładnia ślimakowa
wormhole [łe:rm,houl] s. dziura
wygryziona przez robaka
wormseed [łe:rm,si:d] s. rośliny
stosowane przeciw robakom
worm wheel [łe:rm,hłi:l] s. koło
przekładni ślimakowej
wormwood [łe:rm,łud] s. piołun;
(też) przykrość
wormy [łe:rmy] adj. robaczywy
worn [ło:rn] v. zob. wear; adj.
używany; noszony;
pomarszczony
worn-out [ło:rn,aut] adj. zużyty;
zniszczony; wynoszony
worried [łe:ryd] adj. zatroskany;
zaniepokojony
worriment [łe:ryment] s.
zmartwienie
worrisome [łe:rysem] adj.
trapiący; lubiący się martwić
worry [łe:ry] v. dręczyć (się);
martwić (się); trapić (się);
zadręczać; zamartwiać;
naprzykrzać (się); narzucać
(się); napastować; kąsać;
szarpać zębami; s.
zmartwienie; troska; kłopot;
kąsanie (zdobyczy przez psa)
worry along [łe:rye,long] v.
uporać się z trudnościami
worry down [łe:ry,dałn] v.
połykać łapczywie
worry out [łe:ry,aut] v.
rozwiązać z wysiłkiem (np.
problem)
worse [łe:rs] adj. gorszy (niż:

bad; evil; ill); podniszczony;
słabszy; bardziej chory; s.
coś gorszego; to co
najgorsze; najgorszy stan;
najgorszy wypadek; v.
pogarszać się; adv. gorzej;
bardziej
worsen [łe:rsn] v. pogorszyć
(się)
worship [łe:rszyp] s. cześć;
kult; uwielbienie;
nabożeństwo;
bałwochwalstwo; v. czcić;
wielbić; uwielbiać; brać
udział w nabożeństwie
worshipful [łe:rszypful] adj.
pełen czci; czcigodny
worshiper [łe:rszyper] s.
czciciel; wielbiciel
worst [łe:rst] adj. najgorszy; s.
coś najgorszego; najgorszy
wypadek; adv. najgorzej;
najbardziej; (slang): bardzo; v.
pokonać; wziąć nad kimś
górę; zadać klęskę; pobić
worsted [łustyd] adj.
czesankowy; s. kamgarn;
przędza wełniana czesana;
czesanka
worth [łe:rg] s. wartość; cena;
adj. wart; opłacający się
worthless [łe:rglys] adj.
bezwartościowy
worth seeing [łe:rg'si:yng] adj.
wart widzenia
worthwhile [łe:rghłajl] adj. wart
zachodu; opłacający się
worthy [łe:rgy] adj. godny;
wartościowy; poczciwy; s.
godny człowiek; wybitny
człowiek (też żartem)
would [łud] v. zob. will (forma
warunkowa)
would be [łud,bi:] adj. rzekomy;
niedoszły; adv. rzekomo; niby
to
wound [łu:nd] s. rana; v. ranić;
zob. v. wind
wounded [łu:ndyd] adj. ranny;
urażony
wove [łouw] v. zob. weave
woven [łouwn] v. zob. weave
wow [łau] (slang): s. szlagier;

świetna rzecz; v. mieć
powodzenie; wywoływać
zachwyt; excl.: aul; cudownie!

wrack [raek] s. = wreck(age);
chwasty morskie wyrzucone
na brzeg, używane na nawóz

wraith [rejs] s. sobowtór; cień
(duch)

wrangle ['raengl] s. kłótnia;
burda; v. kłócić się; (slang):
pilnować koni

wrangler ['raengler] s. kłótnik;
pastuch koński (kowboj)

wrap; wrapt; wrapt [raep; raept;
raept]

wrap [raep] v. zawijać; owijać;
zapakowywać; spowijać;
otulać się; okrywać (się);
zachodzić na siebie; s. szal;
chusta; okrycie

wrap up ['raepap] v. owijać
(się); pakować

wrapper ['raeper] s. opakowanie;
opaska; obwoluta; banderola;
papierek; bibułka; osłona;
podomka (damska); pakowacz

wrapping ['raepyng] s.
opakowanie

wrapping paper ['raepyng pejper]
s. papier do pakowania

wrapt [raept] v. zob. wrap

wrath [ra:s] s. gniew; oburzenie

wrathful [ra:sful] adj. gniewny

wreak [ri:k] v. wywierać
(zemstę); dawać upust;
wyładować (gniew)

wreath [ri:s] s. wieniec

wreathe [ri:z] v. wieńczyć;
wić się; splatać; spowijać;
pleść się; kłębić się (dym
etc.)

wreck [rek] s. ruina; wrak;
rozbicie się (np. statku);
katastrofa; szczątki (np. na
wodzie); zniszczenie; rozbitek
życiowy; kaleka; wypadek; v.
rozbić (pojazd); zniweczyć
(nadzieje); burzyć; być
rozbitym; spowodować
rozbicie; zrujnować; mieć
wypadek

wreckage ['rekydż] s. rozbicie;
szczątki; gruzy

wrecked ['rekt] adj. rozbity;
zniszczony; zepsuty

wrecking company ['rekyng
'kampeny] s. przedsiębiorstwo
rozbiórki budynków

wrecking service
['rekyng'se:rwys] s. przewóz
zepsutych samochodów

wrecker ['reker] s. sprawca
wypadku; ciężarówka (z
dźwigiem) do przewozu
zepsutych samochodów;
kierowca przewożący zepsute
samochody; przedsiębiorca
rozbiórki budynków;
przedsiębiorca wydobywania
zatopionych statków; człowiek
kradnący szczątki statku;
szkodnik; rozbijacz
małżeństwa

wren [ren] s. strzyżyk

wrench [rencz] s. gwałtowne
skręcenie; ukręcenie;
szarpnięcie; wykręcenie;
zwichnięcie; przekręcenie
(faktów); ból (rozstania); klucz
maszynowy; klucz nasadowy;
klucz nakrętkowy; v.
szarpnąć; skręcić;
wykręcić; zwichnąć (nogę);
przekręcać (fakty); ukręcać

wrench open ['rencz'oupen] v.
odkręcić; otwierać;
odśrubowywać

wrest [rest] v. wykręcać;
wyrywać; przekręcać
(fakty); wydobywać zeznania;
s. wykręcanie; wyrywanie;
klucz do strojenia (harfy)

wrest from ['restfrom] v.
wyrwać komuś

wrestle ['resl] v. mocować się;
zmagać się; borykać się;
walczyć; s. zapasy; walka

wrestler ['resler] s. zapaśnik

wrestling ['reslyng] s.
zapaśnictwo

wrest-pins ['rest,pynz] pl. kołki
na struny fortepianowe

wretch [recz] s. nieszczęśnik;
biedaczysko; biedak; nędzarz;
łajdak; łotr; nikczemnik

wretched ['reczyd] adj.

nieszczęśliwy; pechowy;
biedny; nędzny; marny;
fatalny; ohydny; wstrętny;
nadzwyczajny (łotr)
wrick [ryk] v. lekko zwichnąć;
nadwerążyć; s. zwichnięcie;
lekkie naderwanie
wriggle ['rygl] v. wić się;
wkręcać (się); kręcić;
wywinąć się; s. ruch wijący
się; wicie
wriggle along ['rygle'long] v.
posuwać się wijąc
wriggle in ['rygl,yn] v. wkręcać
się
wriggle out ['ryglaut] v.
wykręcać się
wright [rajt] s. robotnik; twórca
wring; wrung; wrung [ryng;
rang; rang]
wring [ryng] v. wyżymać;
wykręcać; ukręcić (łeb);
przekręcać (słowa); ściskać
(serce); uściskać (ręką);
wymóc (coś na kimś);
zniekształcić; s. wyżymanie;
uścisk; ściskanie; wyżęcie;
wyciśnięcie
wringer [rynger] s. wyżymaczka
wrinkle ['rynkl] s. zmarszczka;
fałda; zmarszczenie; (slang):
ciekawy pomysł; rada; v.
marszczyć (się); być
pomarszczonym; zmiąć (się)
wrinkle up ['rynklap] v.
pomarszczyć
wrinkly [rynkly] adj.
pomarszczony
wrist [ryst] s. przegub; ruch ręki
w przegubie
wristband ['rystbaend] s.
mankiet u koszuli
wristwatch ['ryst,łocz] s. zegarek
na rękę
writ [ryt] s. nakaz pisemny,
prawny
writ for ['ryt,fo:r] s. rozpisanie
(wyborów)
write; wrote; written [rajt; rout;
rytn]
write [rajt] v. pisać; napisać;
zapisać; wypisać;
komponować; wystawiać

(czek); spisywać; sławić
(piórem)
write back ['rajt,baek] v.
odpisywać (komuś)
write down ['rajtdałn] v.
spisywać; notować;
określać (ujemnie)
write home ['rajt,houm] v. pisać
do domu
write-in ['rajt,yn] v. wpisywać;
dopisywać
write-off ['rajt,of] v. odpisywać
(na straty); pisać naprędce
write out ['rajt,aut] v.
wypisywać; sporządzać
write-up ['rajt,ap] v. zapisywać;
opisywać; przesadnie
szacować; pochwalić
writer ['rajter] s. pisarz; niżej
podpisany; powieściopisarz
writhe [rajs] v. wić się (z bólu);
cierpieć (zniewagą); skręcać
się (ze wstydu)
writing ['rajtyng] s. pismo;
utwór; artykuł; pisanie;
piśmiennictwo; sztuka
pisania; praca literacka;
napisana rzecz
writing desk ['rajtyng,desk] s.
biurko; pulpit
writing ink ['rajtyng,ynk] s.
atrament
writing paper ['rajtyng,pejper] s.
papier listowy; papier do
pisania
writing table ['rajtyng,tejbl] s.
biurko
written ['rytn] v. zob. write; adj.
pisany
wrong [ro:ng] adj. zły;
niewłaściwy; błędny; nie w
porządku; mylny;
niekorzystny; niesprawiedliwy;
s. zło; wykroczenie; krzywda;
wina; pomyłka; grzech; strata;
niesprawiedliwość; v.
skrzywdzić; niesłusznie
posądzać; być
niesprawiedliwym; adv.
mylnie; niewłaściwie; błędnie;
źle; zdrożnie; niekorzystnie
wrongdoer ['ro:ng'du:er] s.
krzywdziciel; grzesznik;

winowajca
wrongdoing ['ro:ng'duyng] s.
nadużycia; wykroczenia;
grzechy; przestępstwa
wrongful ['ro:ngful] adj. zły;
krzywdzący; niesprawiedliwy;
bezprawny
wronghead ['ro:ng'hed] v.
przekręcać (słowa etc.)
wrongheaded ['ro:ng'hedyd] adj.
uparty; przewrotny
wrote [rout] v. zob. write
wroth [ro:s] adj. gniewny
wrought [ro:t] v. zob. work
wrought iron ['ro:t'ajern] s. kute
żelazo
wrought-up ['ro:t,ap] adj.
napięty; zdenerwowany
wrung ['rang] v. zob. wring
wry [raj] adj. krzywy; skrzywiony
wryneck ['rajnek] s. zastrzał szyi;
kręcz karku

X

x [eks] dwudziesta czwarta litera
alfabetu angielskiego; rzymska
cyfra 10; niewiadoma
x-bit ['eks,byt] s. krzyżowe
ostrze świdra
x-bracing ['eks,brejsyn] s.
wiązanie krzyżowe
xenon ['zenon] s. ksenon
xenophobia [,zene'foubje] s.
ksenofobia
Xmas ['krysmes] = Christmas
x-ray ['eks'rej] adj.
rentgenowski; v.
prześwietlać; robić zdjęcie
rentgenowskie
x-ray diagnosis
['eks'rej,dajeg'nouzys] s.
rozpoznanie rentgenowskie
x-ray examination
['eks'rej,yg'zaemynejszyn] s.
badanie rentgenowskie
x-ray picture ['eks'rej'pykczer] s.
zdjęcie rentgenowskie

x-ray spectrum ['eks
'rej'spektrem] s. widmo
promieniowania
rentgenowskiego
x-rays ['eks'rejs] pl. promienie
rentgenowskie
xylem ['zajlem] s. drewno
xylograph ['zajlou'graph] s.
drzeworyt
xylophagous [zaj'lofeges] adj.
drewnożerny
xylophone ['zylefoun] s. ksylofon

Y

y [łaj] dwudziesta piąta litera
alfabetu angielskiego
yabber ['jaeber] v. gadać
yacht [jot] s. jacht; v. płynąć
jachtem; urządzać wyścigi
jachtowe
yachting ['jotyng] s. sport
żeglarski
yak [jaek] s. jak; (slang):
gadanie; śmiech; v. gadać;
śmiać się
yam [jaem] s. słodki ziemniak
(amerykański)
yap [jaep] v. ujadać; (slang):
paplać; s. ujadanie;
paplanina; krzykacz; jadaczka
yard [ja:rd] s. jard (91.44 cm);
podwórze; dziedziniec; v.
umieszczać w ogrodzeniu
yardage ['jarrdydż] s. metraż
yard-stick ['jard,styk] s. listewka
do mierzenia, kryterium
yarn [ja:rn] s. włókno; przędza;
historyjka; v. opowiadać
historyjki
yawl [jo:l] s. jolka (łódź); v.
zawyć; s. wycie
yawn [jo:n] v. ziewać; ziąć;
zionąć; s. ziewnięcie;
ziewanie
yawningly [jo:niynly] adv.
ziewając
Y-axis ['łaj'aeksys] s. oś Y; oś

rządnych
ye [ji:] pron. wy (biblijne)
yea [jej] adv. tak, zaiste, zaprawdę, ba, nawet; s. głosowanie "tak"
yeah [jej] (slang): tak; excl.: tak!; nie wierzę! ale! czyżby?
year [je:r] s. rok
year-book ['jer:,buk] s. rocznik (statystyczny idt.)
year-long ['jer,loŋ] adj. trwający od roku
yearly [je:rly] adj. roczny; coroczny; adv. corocznie; s. rocznik; adv. raz na rok
yearn [je:rn] v. tęsknić, zatęsknić
yearning ['jer:nyŋ] adj. tęskny; s. tęsknota
yearningly ['je:rnyŋly] adv. tęsknie; z tęsknotą
yeast [ji:st] s. drożdże; ferment; piana; v. fermentować; pienić (się)
yell [jel] v. wrzeszczeć; s. wrzask; dopingowanie
yellow ['jelou] adj. żółty; (slang): tchórzliwy; zawistny; żółty z zazdrości; n. żółty kolor; żółtko; v. żółknąć; powodować żółknięcie
yelp [jelp] s. skowyt; v. skowyczeć
yeoman ['joumen] s. podoficer marynarki; (dawniej) wolny chłop
yep [jep] adv. (slang): tak
yes [jes] adv. tak; v. potakiwać
yes-man [jes'men] s. człowiek potakujący, bez własnego zdania
yesterday ['jesterdy] adv. & s. wczoraj
yet [jet] adv. & conj. dotąd; jeszcze do tej pory; na razie; jak dotąd; jednak; ani też; mimo to
yew [ju:] s. cis
Yiddish [jydysz] s. język żydowski
yield [ji:ld] v. wydawać; dawać; rodzić; przynosić; oddawać (się); porzucać;

ustępować; s. plon; zysk; wydajność
yielding [ji:ldyŋg] s. wydajność; adj. ustąpliwy
yogurt ['jouguert] s. jogurt
yoke [jouk] s. jarzmo; v. zaprzęgać; nakładać jarzmo; (slang): zaskakiwać (przechodnia) w celu rabunku
yolk [jouk] s. żółtko; rodzaj łoju
yonder ['jonder] adj. & adv. tam dalej; tamten
you [ju:] pron. ty; wy; pan; pani; panowie; panie
you'd [ju:d] = you would; you had
you'll [ju:l] = you shall; you will
young [jang] adj. młody; młodzieńczy; młodociany
youngish ['jangysz] adj. młodawy, dość młody
youngster ['jangster] s. dziecko; młodzik
your [ju:r] adj. twój; wasz; pański
you're [jo:r] = you are
yours [juers] pron. twój; wasz; pański (z poważaniem)
yourself [,juer'self] pron. ty sam
yourselves [,juer'selwz] pron. wy sami
youth [ju:s] s. młodość, młodzieniec
youths [ju:dż] pl. młodzież; młodzieniec
youthful ['ju:sful] adj. młody; młodzieńczy
youthfulness ['ju:sfulnys] s. młodość, młodzieńczość
youth-hostel ['ju:s'hostl] s. schronisko młodzieżowe
you've ['ju:w] = you have
Y-shaped ['łaj,szejpt] adj. kształtu litery Y
Yugoslav ['ju:gou'sla:w] adj. jugosłowiański
Yule [ju:l] s. święta Bożego Narodzenia
Yuletide ['ju:l,tajd] s. okres świąt Bożego Narodzenia

Z

soczewka zbliżająca w
kamerze filmowej oraz w
aparacie fotograficznym

z [i:] dwudziesta szósta litera
alfabetu angielskiego
zany ['zejny] adj. pocieszny;
błazeński; s. błazen; głupek
zeal [i:l] s. gorliwość
zealous ['zeles] adj. gorliwy
zebra ['zi:bre] s. zebra; (slang):
mulat; adj. pręgowany
zenith ['senit] s. zenit; szczyt
(sławy)
zero ['zierou] s. zero; v.
ustawiać na zero; brać na
cel
zest [zest] s. smak; pikanteria;
rozkosz; zamiłowanie; v.
dodawać pikanterii
zigzag ['zygzaeg] s. zygzak; adj.
zygzakowaty; adv. zygzakiem
zigzaggy ['zygzagy] adj.
zygzagowaty
zinc [zynk] s. cynk; v.
cynkować
zip [zyp] s. świst; wigor; v.
śmigać; gnać; zapinać
zamek błyskawiczny
zip code ['zyp,koud] s.
numeracja pocztowa
miejscowości
zipper ['zyper] s. zamek
błyskawiczny
zippy ['zypy] adj. żywy; zgrabny;
pełen werwy
zloty ['zlouty] s. złoty (pieniądz
polski)
zodiac ['zoudjaek] s. zodiak
zombie ['zomby] s. bóg-pyton;
(slang): bałwan; tuman
zone [zoun] s. strefa; zona; v.
opasywać; dzielić na zony
zonal ['zounl] adj. strefowy
zoo [zu:] s. ogród zoologiczny
zoology [zou'oledży] s. zoologia
zoom [zu:m] v. buczeć;
wzlatywać; wzbijać się
szybko; śmigać; s.
poderwanie (samolotu);

How to Use This Dictionary

The Polish-English part of this dictionary contains about 16,000 entries. The large Polish-English dictionaries usually contain some 180,000 entries, which give basic forms only and do not include ending changes, etc. discussed below. The term dictionary entry is used here as defined by the U.S. Bureau of Federal Supply, which indicates that each word variant explained constitutes an entry.

The word choice and translation are updated for current usage in America and Poland. Characteristic idiomatic usages are included. Each entry includes a pronunciation guide for sound and stress. A stress mark is placed over the stressed vowel.

The pronunciation guide, following the listing of all entries in this dictionary, gives also an illustrated discussion of Polish and English sounds and an explanation of the phonetic symbols. For practical reasons, the number of phonetic symbols are expressed in Latin letters only. Special care is given to explain and illustrate the pronunciation of Polish consonants and vowels which do not occur in the English language and vice versa. The information presented stresses whenever possible the familiar pronunciation and meaning in common usage in both languages.

Linguists define the language as a raw material for the creative activity of speaking. It is a rule-governed creativity in which we are creating and understanding sentences within rules of grammar. A grammatical rule is a description of a pattern habitually followed in a given language; changes in pattern render changes in meaning. This is true, of course, in both Polish and English languages.

An active language changes at varying rates but always at a rate faster than its changes in rules of grammar. Grammar has greater stability than syntax and vocabulary. Every language offers a special way of seeing and interpreting. Languages within the same Indo-European group are not simply equivalent.

The abundance of Polish grammatical forms that do not occur in English should be noticed. A multitude of inflectional forms of Polish nouns and adjectives is reflected in their structure and spelling. Changes in endings of nouns and adjectives correspond to their function in a sentence, their gender and number. Thus, Polish declension requires seven ending changes in nouns and adjectives for both singular and plural, in each gender. Polish personal verb forms correspond by gender and number to the subject of the sentence; thus, nine verb endings occur in the present tense alone. Impersonal forms and various moods expand this number. Both the perfect and imperfect of Polish verbs are indicated by structural variation (In informal Polish, the distinction between perfect and imperfect forms is not always carefully observed.). Verbs "dać" and "dawać" and "zabrać" and "zabierać" illustrate the structural difference between perfect and imperfect forms characteristic of the Polish language.

If every possible structural form of every Polish noun, adjective, verb, adverb, etc. inclusive of all ending changes was a dictionary entry, the number of Polish words listed would be in millions. The number of Polish words is further increased by multitudes of augmentative and diminutive forms which give expression to emotional values by word structure. These augmentative and diminutive forms serve to make the meaning of nouns and adjectives precise by often achieving broadening and clarifying. Augmentative and diminutive forms in Polish are often used to express feelings and attitudes both positive and negative. A comparison of a Polish, German and English word may be useful in order to illustrate the relative usage of augmentatives and diminutives. The use of the German word offers a chance to see the transition between Slavic and Germanic languages. In German diminutives and augmentatives we see the influence of the languages of the Elbe River Slavs, the Polabians, the Lusatians and the Czechs as well as the influence of the Polish language./Also see page VII/.

Language:	Basic word:	Augmentative Form:	Diminutive Form:
ENGLISH	BOY	BIG BOY	LITTLE BOY
GERMAN	KNABE	KNAB	KNABCHEN, KNABLEIN
POLISH	CHŁOPIEC	CHŁOPAK CHŁOPACZYSKO CHŁOPCZYSKO ETC.	CHŁOPCZYK CHŁOPACZEK CHLOPTAS CHLOPACZYNA ETC.

It should be noticed that in this example the Polish word "chlopiec" is a diminutive form derived from the Polish word "chlop" which among other meanings stands for a grown man. In the Polish language there is a middle voice of verb inflection not used in English. The middle voice represents the subject as acting on and for itself in a way different than the usual active and passive form common to both the Polish and English languages. The middle voice in Polish describes self-reflectiveness not directly describable in English. The Polish middle voice occurs within the reflexive form of verb followed by "się." The gender of nouns in Polish is structurally indicated in conjugation of verbs (See p.VIII). The designation of gender of the Polish nouns is influenced by the sound of the ending. Thus, inanimate things in the Polish, as in most Indo-European languages, often are of masculine or feminine grammatically designated gender. The Polish word "robota," for example, meaning "work," is of feminine gender because of the ending "a"; a derivative noun "robot" which means a mechanical man or brain is of masculine gender indicated by ending sound of the letter "t." The profound differences between the Polish and English language make literal translation of common expressions usually impossible which is the main cause of the difficulty of learning Polish by English speakers and vice versa. The relative difficulty of learning a foreign language depends on the characteristics of one's own language as illustrated on Table 1, (page VI) showing the relative difficulty of languages for English speakers based on the experience of the Foreign Service Institute (1973).

The Slavic languages, including Polish, are a family of languages evolved directly from the original Indo-European language by relatively undisturbed evolution. Any two of the fourteen Slavic languages are sufficiently similar to allow their speakers to communicate quite effectively if each speaks his own language slowly and explains to the other the words that are not common to both languages. All the Slavic languages have almost the same flexional characteristics with the exception of Bulgarian, which like English lost the declesions. It happened in Bulgaria after the imposition of Greek in place of the Old Slavic liturgical language and during the lengthy Turkish occupation. Polish speakers have to learn to express meaning by word structure within the grammatical rules of flexional changes. The English and Bulgarian speakers achieve logical clarity of meaning by order or position of words. Thus, English and Bulgarian are defined as isolating or position languages. Polish speaker learning English encounters much simpler grammatical forms and basic concepts in the English language than does his English counterpart in Polish. Assuming the same intensity of foreign language teaching program Polish speakers learn English about 20 to 30% faster than vice versa. The English language is mixed so much that it does not have a close sister language. However, what remained in English of the Old Anglo-Saxon grammar, is of Germanic character, even though, to the English speakers today, the Old Anglo-Saxon is a foreign language. Also Germanic is the majority of the high-frequency vocabulary in the modern English. Thus, English is usually classified by the linguists as a Germanic language, even though, the Romance languages, including Latin, contribute to English about half of its vocabulary. Both, Romance and Germanic languages have much simpler grammar than do the Slavic languages with exception of Bulgarian. The Polish language belongs to the inflective group of languages and it utilizes the active voice to a greater extent than does the English language. Numerous diacritical markings in Polish give good correlation of sound to spelling. The difficulties of correlating sound to spelling in English result mainly from the fact that two different sound correlations to the Latin alphabet occurred in Britain, first to the Anglo-Saxon and then to the French (brought with the Norman invasion). Polish pronunciation is rather stable and clear. English vowels are relatively less stable and undergo variations under stress. On the other hand, the voiced consonants that occur at the end of an English word are often pronounced clearly. The word "love," for example, has a clear "v" at the end and not an "f" as it would be pronounced in Polish. In Polish, all consonants that occur at the end of a Polish word are voiceless. The word "woz," for example, is pronounced with an "s" at the end: "voos." Typically, rules of grammar and phonetics in English start with words "often," "sometimes," etc. while in Polish similar rules are stated: "always, with very few exceptions." The foreign words enrich English vocabulary and remain relatively unchanged. In Polish the foreign borrowings are assimilated into declension of nouns (single and plural) and adjectives (both subject to expansion in to augmentative and diminutive forms) and conjugation of verbs (each in perfect and imperfect form) and grammatical forms derived from verbs. The English language is much simpler in this respect because each noun without any change in spelling potentially may be used as a verb and sometimes as an adjective. In Polish the vigorous growth of abstract and scientific terms was based mainly on the indigenous words with parallel foreign borrowings. The Polish language achieves the size of its vocabulary by use of prefixes and suffixes to a much greater extent than does the English language. For example the mystical ancient Indo-European root-word "god," common to both Polish and English is expanded in Polish to over 3,000 structurally different words. Meanings of these words include weather, agreements, disagreements, harmony, adventure, comfort, discomfort, toilet (wy-god-ka), injury, dignity, decency, indecency, mystical union, time measurement, reconciliation, hiring etc.(VII).Total vocabulary in English and Polish is about one half a million words. However the make up of each vocabulary is different. English has some 120,000 root-words or about double the 60,000 root-words that are characteristic of an inflective language such as Polish. A practical dictionary is based on the frequency of use of words. Table II (p. VI) includes the plot of high frequency words as a percent of the words printed on an average English page. Thus knowing 1,000 most frequently used words one would know about 70% of words on an average page; and knowing 5,000 would give 86% and knowing 10,000 would give one about 92% of words on an average English page. The size of a person's vocabulary and the degree of comprehension of a native language learned with age and education is shown approximately on Table III (p. VI).

It is interesting to note that throughout Europe, including Poland, many professional and business people with rudimentary knowledge of English prefer to read factual reports in English, rather than in their native language. English is recognized by them as a methodical, energetic, businesslike and sober language, that is somewhat short on finery and elegance, but flexible and unrestrained by strict rules of grammar and lexicion. Centuries of colonial expansion brought English to all corners of the world where hundreds of millions use it.

English today is a dominant world language, while less than sixty million people know the Polish language. However, the Polish language with its logic, finery and elegance will continue to give a good start to abstract thinkers such as mathematicians, logicians, philosophers, anthropologists, novelists and poets and thus contribute to the pluralistic culture of the world.

TABLE I   RELATIVE DIFFICULTY OF LANGUAGES FOR ENGLISH SPEAKERS
Class time for average student to reach between minimal and working professional proficiency according to Foreign Service Institute (1973).
24 weeks=720 hours: Afrikaans;Danish;Dutch;French;German;Haitian;
Creole;Italian;Norwegian;Spanish;Swedish;Swahili.
38 weeks=1140hours: Bulgarian;Dari:Farsi:Greek:Hindi:Indonesian;
Malay;Urdu.
44 weeks=1320hours: Amharic;Bengali;Burmese;Czech;Finnish;Hebrew;
Hungarian;Cambodian-Khmer;Lao;Nepali:Philipino;Polish;Russian;Ser-
bo-Croatian;Sinhala;Thai;Tamil;Turkish;Vietnamese.
65 weeks=1950hours: Arabic;Chinese;Japanese;Korean.

TABLE II   HIGH FREQUENCY ENGLISH WORDS VS. PERCENTAGE OF WORDS ON
            AN AVERAGE PRINTED PAGE according to H.Kučera and W.N.
Francis"Computational Analysis of Present-day American English"1967.

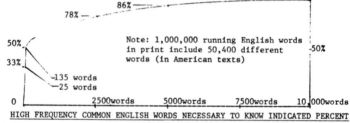

PERCENTAGE OF WORDS UNDERSTOOD ON AN AVERAGE PRINTED PAGE :   100%

Note: 1,000,000 running English words
in print include 50,400 different
words (in American texts)

HIGH FREQUENCY COMMON ENGLISH WORDS NECESSARY TO KNOW INDICATED PERCENT

TABLE III APPROXIMATE GROWTH OF VOCABULARY AND UNDERSTANDING OF
          WORDS WITH AGE AND EDUCATION IN A NATIVE LANGUAGE
Compare with estimated median vocabulary size for each age group by
K.C.Diller "The Language Teaching Controversy" 1978.

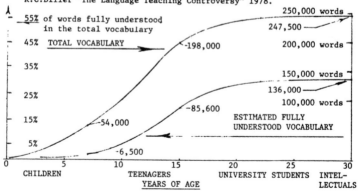

EXAMPLE OF NOUN AND ADJECTIVE DECLENSION IN POLISH LANGUAGE

DOBRY DOM = GOOD HOME, GOOD HOUSE

SINGULAR:

NOMINATIVUS	= MIANOWNIK	DOBRY DOM	GOOD HOME
GENETIVUS	= DOPEŁNIACZ	DOBREGO DOMU	OF A GOOD HOME
DATIVUS	= CELOWNIK	DOBREMU DOMOWI	FOR A GOOD HOME
ACCUSATIVUS	= BIERNIK	DOBRY DOM	A GOOD HOME
INSTRUMENTALIS	=NARZĘDNIK	DOBRYM DOMEM	BY A GOOD HOME
LOCATIVUS	= MIEJSCOWNIK	W DOBRYM DOMU	IN A GOOD HOME
VOCATIVUS	= WOŁACZ	O DOBRY DOMU!	OH! GOOD HOME

PLURAL:

NOMINATIVUS	= MIANOWNIK	DOBRE DOMY (2,3,4)	GOOD HOMES
		DOBRYCH DOMOW (5...)	GOOD HOMES
GENETIVUS	= DOPEŁNIACZ	DOBRYCH DOMOW	OF GOOD HOMES
DATIVUS	= CELOWNIK	DOBRYM DOMOM	FOR GOOD HOMES
ACCUSATIVUS	= BIERNIK	DOBRE DOMY (2,3,4)	GOOD HOMES
		DOBRYCH DOMOW (5...)	GOOD HOMES
INSTRUMENTALIS	=NARZĘDNIK	DOBRYMI DOMAMI	BY GOOD HOMES
LOCATIVUS	= MIEJSCOWNIK	W DOBRYCH DOMACH	IN GOOD HOMES
VOCATIVUS	= WOŁACZ	O DOBRE DOMY!(2,3,4)	OH!GOOD HOMES
		O (PIĘC) DOBRYCH	OH! (FIVE)
		DOMOW! (5...)	GOOD HOMES

NOTE: (2,3,4) = Small Polish plural of two, three and four.
(5...) = Large Polish plural of five and more.

DIMINUTIVES: SING.: DOBRY DOMEK - PLUR.: DOBRE DOMKI (2,3,4)
                                               DOBRYCH DOMKOW (5...)
                    DOBRY DOMECZEK   DOBRE DOMECZKI (2,3,4)
                                       DOBRYCH DOMECZKOW (5...)
AUGMENTATIVES: SING.:DOBRE DOMISKO PLUR.:DOBRE DOMISKA(2,3,4)
                                             DOBRYCH DOMISK (5...)

EXAMPLE OF CONJUGATION OF A VERB IN THE POLISH LANGUAGE

CZYTAC (chi-tach) = TO READ

- PAST TENSE -

PERFECT FORM = SINGLE TIME COMPLETED OCCURENCE

MASCULINE	"I"	(JA)	CZYTAŁEM	I READ
FEMININE	"I"	(JA)	CZYTAŁAM	
MASCULINE	"YOU"	(TY)	CZYTAŁES	YOU READ
FEMININE	"YOU"	(TY)	CZYTAŁAS	
		(ON)	CZYTAŁ	HE READ
		(ONA)	CZYTAŁA	SHE READ
		(ONO)	CZYTAŁO	IT READ
MASCULINE	"WE"	(MY)	CZYTALISMY	WE READ
FEMININE	"WE"	(MY)	CZYTAŁYSMY	
MASC.PLUR.	"YOU"	(WY)	CZYTALISCIE	YOU READ
FEM. PLUR.	"YOU"	(WY)	CZYTAŁYSCIE	
		(ONI)	CZYTALI	THEY READ
FEM.& NEUTER		(ONE)	CZYTAŁY	

CZYTYWAC (chi-ti-vach)=TO READ (OFTEN)

IMPERFECT FORM = MULTIPLE INCOMPLETE OCCURENCE IN THE PAST

MASCULINE	"I"	(JA)	CZYTYWAŁEM	I USED TO READ
FEMININE	"I"	(JA)	CZYTYWAŁAM	
MASCULINE	"YOU"	(TY)	CZYTYWAŁES	YOU USED TO READ
FEMININE	"YOU"	(TY)	CZYTYWAŁAS	
		(ON)	CZYTYWAŁ	HE USED TO READ
		(ONA)	CZYTYWAŁA	SHE USED TO READ
		(ONO)	CZYTYWAŁO	IT USED TO READ
MASCULINE	"WE"	(MY)	CZYTYWALISMY	WE USED TO READ
FEMININE	"WE"	(MY)	CZYTYWAŁYSMY	
MASC.PLUR.	"YOU"	(WY)	CZYTYWALISCIE	YOU USED TO READ
FEM. PLUR.	"YOU"	(WY)	CZYTYWAŁYSCIE	
		(ONI)	CZYTYWALI	THEY USED TO READ
FEM.& NEUTER		(ONE)	CZYTYWAŁY	

EXAMPLES OF WORDS DERIVED FROM THE VERB "CZYTAC"= TO READ

DOCZYTAC, DOCZYTAC SIE, DOCZYTYWAC, DOCZYTYWAC SIE,
NACZYTAC SIE, NACZYTYWAC SIE, OCZYTAC SIE, ODCZYTAC,
ODCZYTYWAC, POCZYTAC, POCZYTAC SOBIE, POCZYTYWAC, POCZY-
TYWAC SOBIE, PRZECZYTAC, ROZCZYTAC SIE, ROZCZYTYWAC SIE,
WCZYTAC SIE, WCZYTYWAC SIE, WYCZYTAC, WYCZYTYWAC, ZACZY-
TYWAC, SIE, ZACZYTAC SIE describe all the possible ways
and conditions of reading with the exception of "reread-
ing" which can not be translated into Polish in one word.
Besides the twenty three verbs are nouns: CZYTANKA, CZY-
TELNICTWO, CZYTELNIK, CZYTELNIA, CZYTELNOSC, ODCZYT, POCZY-
TALNOSC, NIEPOCZYTALNOSC, POCZYTNOSC, and adjectives as:
CZYTELNY, NIECZYTELNY, OCZYTANY, NIEOCZYTANY, POCZYTALNY,
NIEPOCZYTALNY, POCZYTNY etc.

Angielsko-polska część słownika zawiera około 15,000 haseł.

Jak wiadomo pojęcia i myśli formuje się w poszczególnych ję-
zykach w różny sposób. Nawet języki należące do tej samej grupy / jak np polski i angielski do grupy indoeuropejskiej/ nie
są równoznaczne.

Bogactwo polskich form gramatycznych nie ma odpowiednika w
angielskim. Odmiana rzeczowników i przymiotników przez siedem
przypadków oraz czasowników przez wszystkie możliwe osoby z od-
powiednimi zmianami końcówek, typowymi dla języka polskiego,
nie istnieje w angielskim. Język angielski bogatszy jest w wyrażenia zwyczajowo-idiomatyczne; więcej też jest w nim przyim-
ków i zaimków.

Język polski zawiera liczne formy gramatyczne poszczególnych
słów i gdyby wprowadzić każdą z nich jako odrębne hasło słownika to takich haseł byłoby kilka milionów.

Polska forma zwrotna zawiera określenia pośrednie między for-
mami czynną i bierną charakterystycznymi dla obu języków. Tej
formy nie można dosłownie przetłumaczyć na angielski. Na przykład powiedzenie "wzruszyłem się" nie znaczy dokładnie "I am
touched", co równa się polskiemu "jestem wzruszony". "I touched
myself" natomiast wcale nie znaczy "wzruszyłem się".

Inną cechą charakterystyczną języka polskiego jest odróżnienie
małej liczby mnogiej /2,3 i 4/ od dużej /5 i więcej/: tego roz-
różnienia nie ma w języku angielskim.

Ogólnie biorąc język polski ma więcej form rzeczownikowych,
przymiotnikowych oraz czasownikowych. W angielskim natomiast
prawie każdy rzeczownik bez zmiany pisowni może być użyty jako
czasownik a nieraz także jako przymiotnik. Polskie zasady gramatyczne można wyrazić słowami "zawsze z kilkoma wyjątkami", an-
gieskie zasady gramatyczne i fonetyczne są bardziej płynne - mó-
wi się w nich: "często", "czasem" i "nieraz". W angielskim prze-
ważają wyrażenia i fonetyka zwyczajowe.

W części angielsko-polskiej słownika oznaczono formy gramatyczne poszczególnych haseł: rzeczowniki, przymiotniki, czasowniki,
przysłówki, zaimki, przyimki i częste zwroty.

Angielskie czasowniki nieregularne podano w trzech podstawo-

wych formach /infinitive, past and past participle = bezokolicznik, czas przeszły i imiesłów czasu przeszłego/.

Hasła wybrano z uwzględnieniem słownictwa używanego obecnie
w Polsce i w Ameryce; są wśród nich ważniejsze wyrażenia poto-
czne.

Podano wymowę i akcent.

BIBLIOGRAPHICAL NOTE

The spelling used in this dictionary was checked against standard current dictionaries.

The semantic aspects of phrases was analysed in accordance
with Korzybski's General Semantics. Alfred Korzybski, Polish
philosopher, mathematician and engineer founded in 1938 the
Institute of General Semantics in Lakeland, Connecticut. The
works of Jens Otto Jespersen were used as references for ling-
uistic comments.

Glossary of Menu Terms

Polish cuisine is made for hospitality. It abounds in wonderful hors d'oeuvres, fragrant soups, delightful dishes produced with subtle skill and care integrating native traditions and adaptations from other lands. Polish desserts and sweets are unusually good. They never fail to delight Poles and tourists. There is an abundant variety of very tasty Polish bakery products. Polish cuisine includes distinctive seasonal menus for spring, summer, autumn and winter. Examples of Polish food served in quality restaurants are listed in this glossary of menu terms.

A unique item of daily diet is the Polish bread or "chleb." It is always sold in loaves, has a substantial body and a delicious crust. Fresh Polish bread is bought and consumed daily.

Breakfast or "sniadanie" is served from 6:30 until 10 A.M.; dinner or "objad" is served from 1 until 3:30 P.M.; supper or "kolacja" is served from 6 until 9 P.M. Cafes serve good coffee topped with whipped cream during the day and late into the evening. A small serving of strong coffee is called "pol-czarnej" (half-cup of black).

A variety of excellent pastries are served in the "kawiarnia" (cafe) or "cukiernia" (pastry shop). Food is served in the "restauracja" (restaurant).

"Jadłospis" (menu) will list:
"przystawki" (apetizers);
"zupy" (soups);
"dania" (main courses) including:
"dania miesne" (meats),
"dania jarskie" (vegetarian courses),
"ryby" (fish),
"drób" (poultry or other birds),
"wedliny" (smoked meats and fish, also pates),
"jarzyny" (vegetables),
"sałatki" (salads)
"desery" (desserts) which may include:
"owoce" (fruits),
"kompoty" (compotes),
"ciastka" (cakes),
"torty" (multi-layer torts)
"lody" (ice cream).
Menus will also list:
"napoje" (beverages)
"zakaski" (snacks, usually served with vodka).

"Przystawki" (Appetizers)

"grzyby marynowane" (marinated mushrooms)
"jajka faszerowane po polsku" (stuffed eggs Polish style)
"jajka faszerowane z sosem" (stuffed eggs with sauce)
"jajka faszerowane szynka" (eggs stuffed with ham)
"jajka w sosie chrzanowym" (eggs in horseradiash sauce)
"jajka w sosie musztardowym" (eggs in mustard sauce)
"krokiety z jajka" (egg balls with grated cheese)
"pierozki" (browned onion and mushroom ravioli)
"pierozki z miesem" (dumplings with meat)
"sledzie marynowane" (marinated herring)
"sledzie w smietanie" (herring in sour cream)

"Zakaski" (Snacks, Usually With Vodka)

"wybór kanapek" (canapes Polish style many different snacks)

"Sniadanie" (Breakfast)

"boczek" (bacon)
"bułka" (white bread or roll)
"chleb" (bread made in loafs)
"masło" (butter)
"ser biały" (farmer's cheese)
"ser żółty" (cheese, melted)
"jajka na mieko" (soft boiled eggs)
"jajka po wiedeńsku" (soft boiled eggs with butter)
"jajka sadzone" (fried eggs, sunny side up)
"jajecznica" (scrambled eggs)
"szynka" (ham)
"konfitury" (preserves)
"mleko" (milk)
"dżem" (jam)
"miód" (honey)
"naleśniki z dżemem" (pancakes with jam)
"omlet" (omlette)
"sok z czarnej porzeczki" (black currant juice)
"sok jabłkowy" (apple cider)
"sok pomarańczowy" (orange juice)

"Objad" (Dinner, 1.00-3.30 P.M.)
"Kolacja" (Supper, 6.00-9.00 P.M. lighter meal served with the same manu as dinner)

"Zupy Gorace" (Soups Served Hot)

"rosół" (comsomes or broth of traditionally seasoned beef or chicken)
"rosół z zoltkiem" (consome with a raw egg yolk)
"rosół z diablotka" (consome with salty biscuit)
"barszcz z pasztecikiem" (beet-root soup)
"barszcz ukraiński z polska kiełbasa" (Ukrainian barshch with Polish sausage)
"barszcz zabielany" (barshch with sour cream)
"kapuśniak" (sour cabbage soup)
"krupnik" (barley kasha soup)
"zupa grzybowa" (mushroom soup)
"zupa pomidorowa z ryzem" (tomato soup with rice)
"zupa jarzynowa" (vegetable soup)
"zupa grochowa na wędzonce" (pea and smoked ham soup)
"zupa ziemniaczana" (potato soup)
"zupa chlebowa" (bread soup with egg)
"zupa cytrynowa z ryzem" (lemon soup with rice)
"zupa kminkowa" (caraway seed soup)
"zupa szczawiowa z jajkami" (tart sorrel soup with eggs)
"zupa ogórkowa z koperkiem" (dill picle soup)
"żurek" (sour soup)

"Zupy Zimne" (Cold Soups)

"chłodnik" (cold barshch with cream)
"zupa jabłkowa" (apple soup)
"zupa ogórkowa na barszczu" (barszcz and cucumber soup)
"zupa owocowa" (fruit soup)

"Dania Miesne" (Main Meat Courses)

"baranina" (lamb)
"befsztyk po tatarsku" (Tartar steak)
"bigos" sour cabbage with diced pork, veal, beef, ham, sausage and mushrooms; stewed, then fried
"bite kotlety" (pounded cutlets)
"bite zrazy cielęce" (pounded veal chops)
"boczek pieczony" (baked bacon)
"chuda szynka" (lean ham)
"chude mieso" (lean meat)
"cielecina z papryka" (veal with paprica)
"duszona wołowina z grzybami" (simmered beef with mushrooms)
"flaki" (tripe)
"golonka gotowana" (pig's foot jelly)
"gulasz" (goulash, meat stew)
"gulasz wieprzowy" (pork goulash)
"kiełbasa" (sausage)
"kiełbasa wedzona" (smoked sausage)
"kiszka" (sausage of chopped liver and pork with groats)

"klops" (meat loaf)
"kloduny) (meat balls in dough)
"kotlet" (cutlet)
"krokiety" (meat balls)
"królik marynowany" (marinated rabbit)
"krwawa kiszka" (black pudding)
"łopatka barania" (lamb shoulder)
"marynowana baranina" (marinated lamb)
"mielone mięso" (ground meat"
"mózg wieprzowy" (pork brain)
"ozór wołowy" (beef tongue)
"parówki na gorąco" (franks served hot)
"pasztet" (calf's liver, veal and pork meat loaf with bacon, eggs and mushrooms)
"pasztet z watroby" (liver pudding)
"pieczeń barania" (lamb roast)
"pieczeń wołowa duszona" (pot roast of beef)
"potrawka z baraniny" (fricassee of lamb)
"prosię nadziewane" (stuffed piglet)
"rolada mięsna" (meat loaf)
"schab" (loin)
"schabowa pieczeń" (roast loin)
"siekane zrazy" (minced chops)
"smazone mięso" (fried meat)
"szaszłyk" shish kebab
"szynka" (ham)
"szynka gotowana" (cooked ham)
"szynka gotowana, na zimno" (cold cooked ham)
"sztuka miesa" (cooked beef)
"wątróbka" (liver)
"wedzone mięso" (smoked meat)
"żeberka" (ribs)
"zrazy baranie" (lamb chops)
"zrazy wieprzowe" (pork chops)

"Drób" (Poultry, Ducks and Geese)

"kura" (hen or chicken)
"kurczak" (spring chiken)
"kurcze pieczone" (baked chicken)
"kaczka" (duck)
"gęs" (goose)
"gołąb" (pigeon)
"indyk" (turkey)
"bazant" (pheasant)
"nadziewany indyk" (stuffed turkey)
"paprykarz z kurcząt" (chicken stewed with pepers)
"potrawka z kury" (chiken fricassee)
"smazone kotlety z piersi kury" (chicken brest cutlets)

"Dziczyzna" (Venison)

"dzika gęs" (wild goose)
"dzika kaczka" (wild duck)
"kuropatwa" (partridge)
"pasztet z dziczyzny" (venison meat loaf)
"pieczona dziczyzna" (roast venison)
"potrawka z zająca" (fricassee of hare)
"sarnina" (deer meat)
"udziec sarni" (deer haunch)
"zając" (hare)

"Dania Jarskie" (Vegetarian courses)

"Dania Rybne" (Fishes)

"dorsz w sosie chrzanowym" (cod with horseradish sause)
"gotowany szczupak z sosem chrzanowym" (boiled pike with horseradish sause)
"jesiotr z kwaśna śmietana" (sturgeon with sour cream)
"filet z soli z tartym serem" (fillet of sole with grated cheese)
"karp" (grain fed carp)
"karp w galarecie" (carp in jelly)
"losos w galarecie" (salmon in jelly)
"okon na bialym winie" (perch on white wine)
"okoń z rozna z grzybami" (perch broiled with mushrooms)
"potrawka z ryby z tartym serem" (fricassee of fish with grated cheese)
"pstrąg z pietruszka" (trout with parsley)
"szczupak pieczony z sardelami" (baked pike with anchovies)
"szczupak po zydowsku" pike Jewish style
"wegorz duszony w winie" (eel stewed in wine)

"Jarzyny" (Vegetables)

"brokuly" (broccoli)
"brukiew" (turnips)
"buraczki" (beat dish)
"buraki z rabarbarem" (beets with rhubarb)
"brukselka" (Brussels sprouts)
"chrzan" (horseradish)
"cebula" (onion)
"dania ziemniaczane" (potato dishes)
"dynia" (pumpkin)
"fasola" (beans)
"groszek" (green peas)
"kalafior" (cauliflower)
"kalarepa" (kohlrabi)
"kapusta" (cabbage)
"karczochy" (artichokes)
"kiszona kapusta" (sour cabbage)
"marchewka z groszkiem" (carrots with peas)
"młode ziemniaki" (early potatoes)
"placki zemniaczane" (potato pies or pancakes)
"pomidory" (tomatoes)
"szparagi" (asparagus)
"szparagowa fasola" (string beans)
"szpinak" (spinach)
"ziemniaki smazone" (fried potatoes)
"ziemniaki tłuczone" (mashed potatoes)

"Salatki" (Salads)

"cwikla" (red beet salad with horseradish)
"mieszana sałatka" (mixed salad)
"salatka jarzynowa" (vegetable salad)
"sałatka owocowa" (fruit salad)
"salatka pomidorowa" (tomato salad)
"sałatka sledziowa" (herring salad)
"sałatka w galarecie" (jellied salad)
"sałatka z cebuli" (onion salad)
"sałatka z ziemniakow" (potato salad)

"Deser" (dessert)

"babka" (round cofee cake)
"budyń" (pudding)
"budyń czekoladowy" (chocolate pudding)
"chrust" (Polish fried cookies)
"galaretka porzeczkowa" (currant jelly)
"gruszki w rumie" (pears in rum)
"kompot" (compote)
"kompot morelowy" (apricote compote)
"kutia" (wheat grain and honey dessert)
"lody" (ice cream)
"lody waniliowe" (vanilla ice cream)
"lody czekoladowe" (chocolate ice cream)
"makownik" (poppy seed cake)
"mus jablkowy" (creamed apples)
"paczki" (cherry stuffed batter balls)

"suflet kawowy" (cofee souffle)

"Napoje Orzezwiajace" (Refreashments)

"Napoje gorace" (Hot drinks)

"biała kawa" (coffee with cream)
"czarna kawa" (black coffee)
"herbata" (tea)
"kakao" (cocoa)
"mleko" (milk)
"surówka owocowa" (fresh fruit salad)
"truskawki" (strawberries)

"Napoje Alkocholowe" (Alcoholic Drinks)

"ajerkoniak" (eggnog vodka)
"ajerowka" (sweet sedge vodka)
"ciemne piwo" (dark beer)
"cytrynowka" (lemon vodka)
"jarzębiak" (rowanberry vodka)
"jasne piwo" (light beer)
"kminkowka" (caraway seed vodka)
"krupnik" (peppercorns, vanilla, honey vodka)
"miód pitny" (mead, honey wine)
"morelowka" (apricot vodka)
"piwo" (beer)
"piwo słodowe" (malt liquor)
"pomarańczówka" (orange vodka)
"śliwowica" (plum brandy)
"winiak" (wine brandy)
"wiśniówka" (cherry cordial)
"wódka" (vodka)
"wódka wyborowa" (choice grain vodka)
"wyszynk" (retail of alcoholic drinks)
"złota woda" (golden vodka)
"żubrowka" (bison grass wodka)
"żytnia wódka" (rye vodka)

	CARDINAL NUMBERS	-	LICZEBNIKI GŁÓWNE
0	nought, zero, cipher	-	zero
1	one	-	jeden, raz
2	two	-	dwa
3	three	-	trzy
4	four	-	cztery
5	five	-	pięć
6	six	-	sześć
7	seven	-	siedem
8	eight	-	osiem
9	nine	-	dziewięc
10	ten	-	dziesięc
11	eleven	-	jedenaście
12	twelve	-	dwanaście
13	thirteen	-	trzynaście
14	fourteen	-	czternaście
15	fifteen	-	piętnaście
16	sixteen	-	szesnaście
17	seventeen	-	siedemnaście
18	eighteen	-	osiemnaście
19	nineteen	-	dziewiętnaście
20	twenty	-	dwadzieścia
21	twenty-one	-	dwadzieścia jeden
22	twenty-two	-	dwadzieścia dwa
23	twenty-three	-	dwadzieścia trzy
24	twenty-four	-	dwadzieścia cztery
30	thirty	-	trzydzieści
40	forty	-	czterdzieści
50	fifty	-	pięćdziesiąt
60	sixty	-	sześćdziesiąt
70	seventy	-	siedemdziesiąt
80	eighty	-	osiemdziesiąt
90	ninety	-	dziewięćdziesiąt
100	one hundred	-	sto
101	one hundred and one	-	sto jeden
110	one hundred and ten	-	sto dziesięc
200	two hundred	-	dwieście
777	seven hundred seventy seven	-	siedemset siedemdziesiąt siedem
1,000.	one thousand	-	tysiąc
1,500.	fifteen hundred	-	tysiąc pięćset
1978	nineteen hundred and seventy eight	-	tysiąc dziewięćset siedemdziesiąt osiem
500,000.	five hundred thousand	-	pięćset tysięcy
1,000,000.	one million	-	milion
3,000,000.	three million	-	trzy miliony
1,000,000,000.	one billion	-	miliard

	ORDINAL NUMBERS	-	LICZEBNIKI PORZĄDKOWE
1st	first	-	pierwszy
2nd	second	-	drugi
3rd	third	-	trzeci
4th	fourth	-	czwarty
5th	fifth	-	piąty
6th	sixth	-	szósty
7th	seventh	-	siódmy
8th	eighth	-	ósmy
9th	ninth	-	dziewiąty
10th	tenth	-	dziesiąty
11th	eleventh	-	jedenasty
12th	twelfth	-	dwunasty
13th	thirteenth	-	trzynasty
14th	fourteenth	-	czternasty
15th	fifteenth	-	piętnasty
16th	sixteenth	-	szesnasty
17th	seventeenth	-	siedemnasty
18th	eighteenth	-	osiemnasty
19th	nineteenth	-	dziewiętnasty
20th	twentieth	-	dwudziesty
21st	twenty-first	-	dwudziesty pierwszy
22nd	twenty-second	-	dwudziesty drugi
23rd	twenty-third	-	dwudziesty trzeci
24th	twenty-fourth	-	dwudziesty czwarty
30th	thirtieth	-	trzydziesty
40th	fortieth	-	czterdziesty
50th	fiftieth	-	pięćdziesiąty
60th	sixtieth	-	sześćdziesiąty
70th	seventieth	-	siedemdziesiąty
80th	eightieth	-	osiemdziesiąty
90th	ninetieth	-	dziewięćdziesiąty
100th	(one) hundredth	-	setny
101st	(one) hundred and first	-	sto pierwszy
102nd	(one) hundred and second	-	sto drugi
103rd	(one) hundred and third	-	sto trzeci
104th	(one) hundred and fourth	-	sto czwarty
200th	two hundredth	-	dwusetny
500th	five hundredth	-	pięćsetny
1,000th	(one) thousandth	-	tysięczny
3,000th	three thousandth	-	trzytysięczny
1978th	nineteen hundred and seventy eighth	-	tysiąc dziewięćset siedemdziesiąty ósmy
500,000th	five hundred thousandth	-	pięćsettysięczny
1,000,000th	millionth	-	milionowy
3,000,000th	three millionth	-	trzy milionowy